area A width w base b

perimeter P surface area S circumference C volume V

length l altitude (height) h radius r area of base B

                                                                          slant height s

Rectangle

$$A = lw \qquad P = 2l + 2w$$

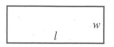

Triangle

$$A = \frac{1}{2}bh$$

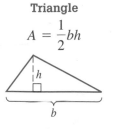

Square

$$A = s^2 \qquad P = 4s$$

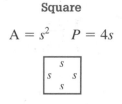

Parallelogram

$$A = bh$$

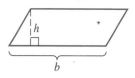

Trapezoid

$$A = \frac{1}{2}h(b_1 + b_2)$$

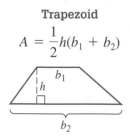

Circle

$$A = \pi r^2 \qquad C = 2\pi r$$

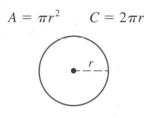

30°–60° Right Triangle

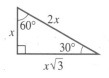

Right Triangle

$$a^2 + b^2 = c^2$$

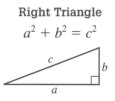

Isosceles Right Triangle

Right Circular Cylinder

$$V = \pi r^2 h \qquad S = 2\pi r^2 + 2\pi rh$$

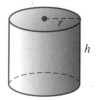

Sphere

$$S = 4\pi r^2 \qquad V = \frac{4}{3}\pi r^3$$

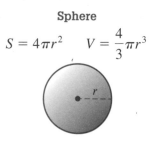

Right Circular Cone

$$V = \frac{1}{3}\pi r^2 h \qquad S = \pi r^2 + \pi rs$$

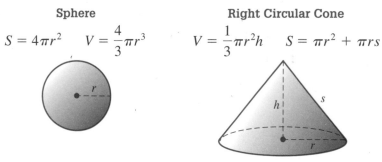

Pyramid

$$V = \frac{1}{3}Bh$$

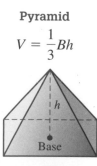

Base

Prism

$$V = Bh$$

Base

College Algebra

8th Edition

Jerome E. Kaufmann | Karen L. Schwitters

CENGAGE
Learning·

Australia • Brazil • Japan • Korea • Mexico • Singapore • Spain • United Kingdom • United States

CENGAGE
Learning·

College Algebra: 8th Edition

College Algebra, 8th Edition
Jerome E. Kaufmann | Karen L. Schwitters

© 2013 Cengage Learning. All rights reserved.

Executive Editors:
Maureen Staudt
Michael Stranz

Senior Project Development Manager:
Linda deStefano

Marketing Specialist:
Courtney Sheldon

Senior Production/Manufacturing Manager:
Donna M. Brown

Production Editorial Manager:
Kim Fry

Sr. Rights Acquisition Account Manager:
Todd Osborne

For product information and technology assistance, contact us at
Cengage Learning Customer & Sales Support, 1-800-354-9706

For permission to use material from this text or product,
submit all requests online at **cengage.com/permissions**
Further permissions questions can be emailed to
permissionrequest@cengage.com

This book contains select works from existing Cengage Learning resources and was produced by Cengage Learning Custom Solutions for collegiate use. As such, those adopting and/or contributing to this work are responsible for editorial content accuracy, continuity and completeness.

Compilation © 2012 Cengage Learning

ISBN-13: 978-1-285-14189-3

ISBN-10: 1-285-14189-X

Cengage Learning
5191 Natorp Boulevard
Mason, Ohio 45040
USA
Cengage Learning is a leading provider of customized learning solutions with office locations around the globe, including Singapore, the United Kingdom, Australia, Mexico, Brazil, and Japan. Locate your local office at:
international.cengage.com/region.

Cengage Learning products are represented in Canada by Nelson Education, Ltd.
For your lifelong learning solutions, visit **www.cengage.com/custom.**
Visit our corporate website at **www.cengage.com.**

Printed in the United States of America

Brief Contents

Excerpted from:
College Algebra
Eighth Edition
Kaufmann and Schwitters

Chapter 0	SOME BASIC CONCEPTS OF ALGEBRA: A REVIEW	1
Chapter 1	EQUATIONS, INEQUALITIES, AND PROBLEM SOLVING	103
Chapter 2	COORDINATE GEOMETRY AND GRAPHING TECHNIQUES	203
Chapter 3	FUNCTIONS	277
Chapter 4	POLYNOMIAL AND RATIONAL FUNCTIONS	365
Chapter 5	EXPONENTIAL AND LOGARITHMIC FUNCTIONS	433
Chapter 6	SYSTEMS OF EQUATIONS	513
Chapter 9	SEQUENCES AND MATHEMATICAL INDUCTION	681
	Appendices	719
	Answers	A-1
	Index	I-1

Excerpted from:
Algebra for College Students
Eighth Edition
Kaufmann and Schwitters

Chapter 15	COUNTING TECHNIQUES, PROBABILITY, AND THE BINOMIAL THEOREM	768

Excerpted from:
Elementary Statistics
Eleventh Edition
Johnson and Kuby

Chapter 5	Probability Distributions (Discrete Variables).	230

CONTENTS

0   Some Basic Concepts of Algebra: A Review   1

0.1   Some Basic Ideas   2

0.2   Exponents   19

0.3   Polynomials   31

0.4   Factoring Polynomials   41

0.5   Rational Expressions   51

0.6   Radicals   64

0.7   Relationship Between Exponents and Roots   75

0.8   Complex Numbers   82

Chapter 0 Summary   91

Chapter 0 Review Problem Set   100

Chapter 0 Test   102

1   Equations, Inequalities, and Problem Solving   103

1.1   Linear Equations and Problem Solving   104

1.2   More Equations and Applications   114

1.3   Quadratic Equations   128

1.4   Applications of Linear and Quadratic Equations   141

1.5   Miscellaneous Equations   155

1.6   Inequalities   164

1.7   Quadratic Inequalities and Inequalities Involving Quotients   174

1.8   Absolute Value Equations and Inequalities   180

Chapter 1 Summary   188

Chapter 1 Review Problem Set   199

Chapter 1 Test   201

2   Coordinate Geometry and Graphing Techniques   203

2.1   Coordinate Geometry   204
2.2   Graphing Techniques: Linear Equations and Inequalities   215
2.3   Determining the Equation of a Line   225
2.4   More on Graphing   242
2.5   Circles, Ellipses, and Hyperbolas   252
Chapter 2 Summary   266
Chapter 2 Review Problem Set   273
Chapter 2 Test   274
Chapters 0–2 Cumulative Review Problem Set   275

3   Functions   277

3.1   Concept of a Function   278
3.2   Linear Functions and Applications   288
3.3   Quadratic Functions and Applications   298
3.4   Transformations of Some Basic Curves   316
3.5   Combining Functions   329
3.6   Direct and Inverse Variation   340
Chapter 3 Summary   349
Chapter 3 Review Problem Set   358
Chapter 3 Test   360
Chapters 0–3 Cumulative Review Problem Set   361

4   Polynomial and Rational Functions   365

4.1   Dividing Polynomials and Synthetic Division   366
4.2   Remainder and Factor Theorems   373
4.3   Polynomial Equations   379
4.4   Graphing Polynomial Functions   392
4.5   Graphing Rational Functions   404
4.6   More on Graphing Rational Functions   415
Chapter 4 Summary   423
Chapter 4 Review Problem Set   428
Chapter 4 Test   429
Chapters 0–4 Cumulative Review Problem Set   430

5 Exponential and Logarithmic Functions 433

5.1 Exponents and Exponential Functions 434

5.2 Applications of Exponential Functions 442

5.3 Inverse Functions 455

5.4 Logarithms 467

5.5 Logarithmic Functions 478

5.6 Exponential Equations, Logarithmic Equations, and Problem Solving 486

Chapter 5 Summary 497

Chapter 5 Review Problem Set 505

Chapter 5 Test 508

Chapters 0–5 Cumulative Review Problem Set 509

6 Systems of Equations 513

6.1 Systems of Two Linear Equations in Two Variables 514

6.2 Systems of Three Linear Equations in Three Variables 526

6.3 Matrix Approach to Solving Linear Systems 534

6.4 Determinants 545

6.5 Cramer's Rule 556

6.6 Partial Fractions (Optional) 563

Chapter 6 Summary 570

Chapter 6 Review Problem Set 576

Chapter 6 Test 578

Chapters 0–6 Cumulative Review Problem Set 580

9   Sequences and Mathematical Induction   681

9.1   Arithmetic Sequences   682

9.2   Geometric Sequences   691

9.3   Another Look at Problem Solving   700

9.4   Mathematical Induction   706

Chapter 9 Summary   712

Chapter 9 Review Problem Set   716

Chapter 9 Test   718

Appendix A   Binomial Theorem   719

Answers to Odd-Numbered Problems and All Chapter Review, Chapter Test, and Cumulative Review Problems   A-1

Index   I-1

PREFACE

College Algebra, Eighth Edition, was written for students who need a college algebra course that serves as a prerequisite for the calculus sequence or that satisfies a liberal arts requirement. Four major ideas unify this text: solving equations and inequalities, solving problems, developing graphing techniques, and developing and using the concept of a function.

College Algebra, Eighth Edition, presents basic concepts of algebra in a simple, straightforward way. Examples motivate students and reinforce algebraic concepts by the application of real-world situations. These examples also guide students to organize their work in a logical fashion and to use meaningful shortcuts whenever appropriate.

In the preparation of this eighth edition, we made a special effort to incorporate improvements suggested by reviewers and users of previous editions without sacrificing the book's many successful features.

New in This Edition

■ *Objectives.* Each section begins with a numbered list of objectives for that section. Then in the Problem Set following that section, groups of problems are identified by section objectives.

■ *Classroom Examples.* For every example in the text there is an associated classroom example problem similar to the example problem. Answers to the classroom example problems are furnished in the Annotated Instructor's Edition but not in the Student's Edition. These classroom examples provide an excellent source of an additional problem to further the understanding of the example presented.

■ *Chapter Summaries.* Chapter Summaries have taken on an entirely new look. The summaries are presented in a grid fashion by objectives. Each row contains the objective, pertinent information summarizing that objective, and an example problem with solution for that objective.

Based on suggestions offered by reviewers of the previous edition, the following content changes have been made to the text:

■ Section 1.6 is now confined to solving linear inequalities and their applications.

■ Quadratic inequalities and rational inequalities are now covered in Section 1.7.

■ Section 1.8 covers absolute value equations and inequalities.

■ In Chapter 3, "Functions," the previous Sections 3.3 and 3.4 have been combined into one section. This allows all the pertinent material for quadratic functions to be presented together in one section.

■ In keeping with the concept of a function, previous Section 4.7, "Direct and Inverse Variation," has been moved to Chapter 3 to become Section 3.6.

- The section on inverse functions has been moved from the chapter on functions, Chapter 3, to the chapter on exponential and logarithmic functions. We are aware that there are different views on the placement of inverse functions in a College Algebra text. In this instance we have decided to place inverse functions in Chapter 5, "Exponential and Logarithmic Functions." Placing inverse functions later allows the students to gain more understanding of the function concept, and hence the students should be better prepared for the topic of inverse functions. Also, with the placement of inverse functions with logarithms, the students apply the concept of inverse function immediately.

Other Special Features

- Photos and applications are used in the chapter openers to introduce some concepts presented in the chapter.

- A **Chapter Test** appears at the end of each chapter. Along with the Chapter Review Problem Sets, these practice tests should provide the students with ample opportunity to prepare for the "real" examinations.

- **Cumulative Review Problem Sets** appear at the ends of Chapter 2 through Chapter 8. *All* answers for Chapter Review Problem Sets, Chapter Tests, and Cumulative Review Problem Sets are included in the back of the text.

- Problems called **Thoughts Into Words** are included in every problem set except the review exercises. These problems are designed to encourage students to express, in written form, their thoughts about various mathematical ideas. For example, see Problem Sets 0.5, 1.2, 1.3, and 4.6.

- Many problem sets contain a special group of problems called **Further Investigations,** which lend themselves to small-group work. These problems encompass a variety of ideas: some are proofs, some exhibit different approaches to topics covered in the text, some bring in supplementary topics and relationships, and some are more challenging problems. Although these problems add variety and flexibility to the problem sets, they can also be omitted entirely without disrupting the continuity of the text. For examples, see Problem Sets 0.6, 1.1, 1.2, 2.1, and 2.3.

- As recommended in the standards produced by NCTM and AMATYC, **problem solving** is an integral part of this text. With problem solving as its focus, Chapter 1 pulls together and expands on a variety of approaches to solving equations and inequalities. Polya's four-phase plan is used as a basis for developing various problem-solving strategies. Applications of radical equations are a part of Section 1.5, and applications of slope are in Section 2.3. Functions are introduced in Chapter 3 and are immediately used to solve problems. Exponential and logarithmic functions become problem-solving tools in Chapter 5. Systems of equations provide more problem-solving power in Chapter 6. Problem solving is the unifying theme of Chapter 9.

   Problems have been chosen so that a variety of problem-solving strategies can be introduced. Sometimes alternate solutions are shown for the same problem (see Example 6 of Section 1.4), while at other times different problems of the same type are used to illustrate different approaches (see Examples 8, 9, and 10 of

Section 1.4). *No attempt is made to dictate a specific problem technique; instead our goal is to introduce the students to a large variety of techniques.*

■ Chapter 0, a review of intermediate algebra concepts, was written so that students can work through this material with a minimum of assistance from the instructor. The concepts are reviewed in enough detail to provide a good basis for understanding the many worked-out examples. The problem sets also provide ample practice material. The chapter test and/or the chapter review problem set could be used to determine problem areas.

■ Chapter 9, if not covered as part of the regular course, could be used as enrichment material. The easy-to-read explanations along with carefully chosen examples make this chapter accessible to students with minimal help from the instructor.

■ The Cartesian coordinate system and the use of graphing utilities are briefly introduced in Section 0.1. This allows instructors (and the authors) *to use the graphing calculator as a teaching tool early in the text.* For example, visual support can be given for the manipulation of algebraic expressions. Students do not need a graphing calculator to benefit from the graphs.

■ A graphical analysis of approximating solution sets is introduced in Chapter 1. Then a graphical approach is used to lend visual support to an algebraic approach and sometimes to *predict approximate solutions before an algebraic approach is shown.*

■ Beginning with Problem Set 0.1, a group of problems called **Graphing Calculator Activities** is included in many of the problem sets. These activities, which are good for either individual or small-group work, have been designed to reinforce concepts (see, for example, Problem Set 5.5) as well as to lay groundwork for concepts about to be discussed (see, for example, Problem Set 2.2). Some of these activities ask students to predict shapes and locations of graphs based on previous graphing experiences, and then to use a graphing utility to check their predictions (see, for example, Problem Set 3.4). The graphing calculator is also used as a problem-solving tool (see, for example, Problem Set 4.5); when students do these activities, they should become familiar with the capabilities and limitations of a graphing utility.

■ Specific graphing ideas (intercepts, symmetry, restrictions, asymptotes, and transformations) are introduced and used throughout Chapters 2, 3, 4, 5, and 8. In Section 3.3 the extensive work with graphing parabolas is used to motivate definitions for translations, reflections, stretchings, and shrinkings. These transformations are then applied to the graphs of $f(x) = x^3, f(x) = x^4, f(x) = \sqrt{x}$, and $f(x) = |x|$. Furthermore, in later chapters the transformations are applied to graphs of exponential, logarithmic, polynomial, and rational functions.

■ Reviewers suggested several places where a page, a paragraph, a sentence, an example, or a solution to a problem could be rewritten to further clarify the intended meaning. Sometimes we included a *Remark* to add a little flavor to the discussion.

■ Please note the exceptionally pleasing design features of this text, including the functional use of color. The open format makes for a continuous and easy flow of material instead of working through a maze of flags, caution symbols, reminder symbols, and so forth.

Ancillaries for the Instructor

Annotated Instructor's Edition (ISBN-10: 1-111-99051-4;
ISBN-13: 978-1-111-99051-0)
Answers are printed next to all respective exercises. Graphs, tables, and other answers appear in a special answer section in the back of the text.

Test Bank (ISBN-10: 1-111-99042-5; ISBN-13: 978-1-111-99042-8)
The Test Bank includes multiple tests per chapter as well as final exams. The tests are made up of a combination of multiple-choice, free-response, true/false, and fill-in-the-blank questions.

ExamView® Computerized Testing
ExamView testing software allows instructors to quickly create, deliver, and customize tests for class in both print and online formats, and features automatic grading. The software includes a test bank with hundreds of questions customized directly to the text. ExamView is available within the PowerLecture CD-ROM.

Solution Builder www.cengage.com/solutionbuilder
This online instructor database offers complete worked solutions to all exercises in the text, allowing instructors to create customized, secure solutions printouts (in PDF format) matched exactly to the problems assigned in class.

Complete Solutions Manual (ISBN-10: 1-111-99043-3; ISBN-13: 978-1-111-99043-5)
The Complete Solutions Manual provides worked-out solutions to all of the problems in the text.

PowerLecture with ExamView (ISBN-10: 1-111-98986-9;
ISBN-13: 978-1-111-98986-6)
This CD-ROM provides instructors with dynamic media tools for teaching. Instructors can create, deliver, and customize tests (both print and online) in minutes with ExamView Computerized Testing Featuring Algorithmic Equations. Instructors can also easily build solution sets for homework or exams using Solution Builder's online solutions manual. Microsoft® PowerPoint® lecture slides and figures from the book are also included on this CD-ROM.

Enhanced WebAssign® (ISBN-10: 0-538-73810-3; ISBN-13: 978-0-538-73810-1)
Exclusively from Cengage Learning, Enhanced WebAssign offers an extensive online program for College Algebra to encourage the practice that is so critical for concept mastery. The meticulously crafted pedagogy and exercises in this text become even more effective in Enhanced WebAssign, supplemented by multimedia tutorial support and immediate feedback as students complete their assignments. Algorithmic problems allow instructors to assign unique versions to each student. The Practice Another Version feature (activated at the instructor's discretion) allows students to attempt the questions with new sets of values until they feel confident enough to work the original problem. Students benefit from a new YouBook with highlighting and search features; Personal Study Plans (based on diagnostic quizzing) that identify chapter topics they still need to master; and links to video solutions, interactive tutorials, and even live online help.

Text-Specific DVDs (ISBN-10: 1-111-99052-2; ISBN-13: 978-1-111-99052-7)
These text-specific DVDs, available at no charge to qualified adopters of the text, feature 10- to 20-minute problem-solving lessons that cover each section of every chapter.

Ancillaries for the Student

Student Solutions Manual (ISBN-10: 1-111-99045-X; ISBN-13: 978-1-111-99045-9)
The Student Solutions Manual provides worked-out solutions to the odd-numbered problems in the text and all chapter review, chapter tests, and cumulative reviews.

CengageBrain.com
Visit **www.CengageBrain.com** to access additional course materials and companion resources. At the CengageBrain.com home page, search for the ISBN of your title (from the back cover of your book) using the search box at the top of the page. This will take you to the product page where free companion resources can be found.

Enhanced WebAssign (ISBN-10: 0-538-73810-3; ISBN-13: 978-0-538-73810-1)
Exclusively from Cengage Learning, Enhanced WebAssign offers an extensive online program for College Algebra to encourage the practice that is so critical for concept mastery. You'll receive multimedia tutorial support as you complete your assignments. You'll also benefit from a new YouBook with highlighting and search features; Personal Study Plans (based on diagnostic quizzing) that identify chapter topics you still need to master; and links to video solutions, interactive tutorials, and even live online help.

Acknowledgments

We would like to take this opportunity to thank the following people who served as reviewers for the eighth edition of *College Algebra:*

Kevin Bolan
Everet Community College

Ramendra Bose
University of Texas–Pan American

John Drake
Cochise College

Rahim Faradineh
East Los Angeles College

Glenn Hunt
Riverside City College

Nam Nguyen
University of Texas–Pan American

Mari Peddycoart
Kingwood College

Ken Reeves
San Antonio College

Lynn Salyer
McCook Community College

Ron Sperber
Keuka College

Alain Togbe
Purdue University

Lynn White
Jones County Junior College

Loris Zucca
Kingwood College

We would like to express our sincere gratitude to the staff of Brooks/Cole, especially Gary Whalen, Cynthia Ashton, and Lynh Pham, for their continuous cooperation and assistance throughout this project; and to Dan Fitzgerald and Jennifer Risden, who carry out the many details of production.

Jerome E. Kaufmann
Karen L. Schwitters

0 Some Basic Concepts of Algebra: A Review

0.1 Some Basic Ideas

0.2 Exponents

0.3 Polynomials

0.4 Factoring Polynomials

0.5 Rational Expressions

0.6 Radicals

0.7 Relationship Between Exponents and Roots

0.8 Complex Numbers

This statue of Fibonacci was constructed and erected in Pisa, Italy. Leonardo Fibonacci was a famous Italian middle-ages mathematician. He is known for spreading the Hindu-Arabic number system in the western world and the Fibonacci sequence of numbers.

© David Lyons/Alamy

The temperature in Big Lake, Alaska at 3 P.M. was $-4°$F. By 11 P.M. the temperature had dropped another $20°$. We can use the *numerical expression* $-4 - 20$ to determine the temperature at 11 P.M.

Megan has p pennies, n nickels, d dimes, and q quarters. The *algebraic expression* $p + 5n + 10d + 25q$ can be used to represent the total amount of money in cents.

Algebra is often described as a generalized arithmetic. That description does not tell the whole story, but it does convey an important idea: A good understanding of arithmetic provides a sound basis for the study of algebra. In this chapter we will often use arithmetic examples to lead into a review of basic algebraic concepts. Then we will use the algebraic concepts in a wide variety of problem-solving situations. Your study of algebra should make you a better problem solver. Be sure that you can work effectively with the algebraic concepts reviewed in this first chapter.

1

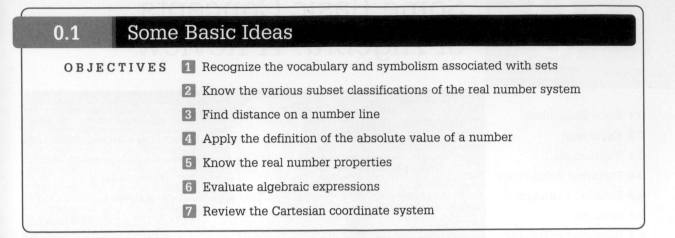

0.1 Some Basic Ideas

OBJECTIVES

1. Recognize the vocabulary and symbolism associated with sets
2. Know the various subset classifications of the real number system
3. Find distance on a number line
4. Apply the definition of the absolute value of a number
5. Know the real number properties
6. Evaluate algebraic expressions
7. Review the Cartesian coordinate system

Let's begin by pulling together the basic tools we need for the study of algebra. In arithmetic, symbols such as 6, $\frac{2}{3}$, 0.27, and π are used to represent numbers. The operations of addition, subtraction, multiplication, and division are commonly indicated by the symbols $+$, $-$, $\times$, and $\div$, respectively. These symbols enable us to form specific **numerical expressions.** For example, the indicated sum of 6 and 8 can be written $6 + 8$.

In algebra, we use variables to generalize arithmetic ideas. For example, by using x and y to represent *any* two numbers, we can use the expression $x + y$ to represent the indicated sum of *any* two numbers. The x and y in such an expression are called **variables,** and the phrase $x + y$ is called an **algebraic expression.**

Many of the notational agreements we make in arithmetic can be extended to algebra, with a few modifications. The following chart summarizes those notational agreements regarding the four basic operations.

Operation	Arithmetic	Algebra	Vocabulary
Addition	$4 + 6$	$x + y$	The sum of x and y
Subtraction	$14 - 10$	$a - b$	The difference of a and b
Multiplication	7×5 or $7 \cdot 5$	$a \cdot b$, $a(b)$, $(a)b$, $(a)(b)$, or ab	The product of a and b
Division	$8 \div 4$, $\frac{8}{4}$, $8/4$ or $4\overline{)8}$	$x \div y$, $\frac{x}{y}$, x/y, or $y\overline{)x}$ $(y \neq 0)$	The quotient of x divided by y

Note the different ways of indicating a product, including the use of parentheses. The *ab* form is the simplest and probably the most widely used form. Expressions such as *abc*, 6*xy*, and 14*xyz* all indicate multiplication. Notice the various forms used to indicate division. In algebra, the fraction forms $\dfrac{x}{y}$ and x/y are generally used, although the other forms do serve a purpose at times.

The Use of Sets

Some of the vocabulary and symbolism associated with the concept of sets can be effectively used in the study of algebra. A **set** is a collection of objects; the objects are called **elements** or **members of the set.** The use of capital letters to name sets and the use of set braces, { }, to enclose the elements or a description of the elements provide a convenient way to communicate about sets. For example, a set A that consists of the vowels of the English alphabet can be represented as follows:

	$A = \{\text{vowels of the English alphabet}\}$	Word description
or	$A = \{\text{a, e, i, o, u}\}$	List or roster description
or	$A = \{x \mid x \text{ is a vowel}\}$	Set-builder notation

A set consisting of no elements is called the **null set** or **empty set** and is written $\varnothing$.

Set-builder notation combines the use of braces and the concept of a variable. For example, $\{x \mid x \text{ is a vowel}\}$ is read "the set of all x such that x is a vowel." Note that the vertical line is read "such that."

Two sets are said to be **equal** if they contain exactly the same elements. For example, $\{1, 2, 3\} = \{2, 1, 3\}$ because both sets contain exactly the same elements; the order in which the elements are listed does not matter. A slash mark through an equality symbol denotes *not equal to*. Thus if $A = \{1, 2, 3\}$ and $B = \{3, 6\}$, we can write $A \neq B$, which is read "set A is not equal to set B."

Real Numbers

The following terminology is commonly used to classify different types of numbers:

$\{1, 2, 3, 4, \ldots\}$	Natural numbers, counting numbers, positive integers
$\{0, 1, 2, 3, \ldots\}$	Whole numbers, nonnegative integers
$\{\ldots, -3, -2, -1\}$	Negative integers
$\{\ldots, -3, -2, -1, 0\}$	Nonpositive integers
$\{\ldots, -2, -1, 0, 1, 2, \ldots\}$	Integers

A **rational number** is defined as any number that can be expressed in the form a/b, where a and b are integers and b is not zero. The following are examples of rational numbers:

$$\frac{2}{3} \qquad -\frac{3}{4} \qquad \frac{-1}{7} \qquad \frac{9}{2}$$

$$6\frac{1}{2} \text{ because } 6\frac{1}{2} = \frac{13}{2} \qquad\qquad -4 \text{ because } -4 = \frac{-4}{1} = \frac{4}{-1}$$

$$0 \text{ because } 0 = \frac{0}{1} = \frac{0}{2} = \frac{0}{3}, \text{ etc.} \qquad 0.3 \text{ because } 0.3 = \frac{3}{10}$$

A rational number can also be defined in terms of a decimal representation. Before doing so, let's briefly review the different possibilities for decimal representations. Decimals can be classified as **terminating, repeating,** or **nonrepeating.** Here are some examples of each:

$$\begin{bmatrix} 0.3 \\ 0.46 \\ 0.789 \\ 0.2143 \end{bmatrix} \quad \text{Terminating decimals}$$

$$\begin{bmatrix} 0.333\ldots \\ 0.1414\ldots \\ 0.7127127\ldots \\ 0.241717\ldots \end{bmatrix} \quad \text{Repeating decimals}$$

$$\begin{bmatrix} 0.472195631\ldots \\ 0.21411711191111\ldots \\ 3.141592654\ldots \\ 1.414213562\ldots \end{bmatrix} \quad \text{Nonrepeating decimals}$$

A **repeating decimal** has a block of digits that repeats indefinitely. This repeating block of digits may be of any size and may or may not begin immediately after the decimal point. A small horizontal bar is commonly used to indicate the repeating block. Thus $0.3333\ldots$ can be expressed as $0.\overline{3}$ and $0.24171717\ldots$ as $0.24\overline{17}$.

In terms of decimals, a rational number is defined as a number with either a terminating or a repeating decimal representation. The following examples illustrate some rational numbers written in $\dfrac{a}{b}$ form and in the equivalent decimal form:

$$\frac{3}{4} = 0.75 \quad \frac{3}{11} = 0.\overline{27} \quad \frac{1}{8} = 0.125 \quad \frac{1}{7} = 0.\overline{142857} \quad \frac{1}{3} = 0.\overline{3}$$

We define an **irrational number** as a number that cannot be expressed in $\dfrac{a}{b}$ form, form, where a and b are integers and b is not zero. Furthermore, an irrational number has a nonrepeating, nonterminating decimal representation. Following are some examples of irrational numbers and a partial decimal representation for each number. Note that the decimals do not terminate and do not repeat.

$$\sqrt{2} = 1.414213562373095\ldots$$
$$\sqrt{3} = 1.73205080756887\ldots$$
$$\pi = 3.14159265358979\ldots$$

The entire set of **real numbers** is composed of the rational numbers along with the irrationals. The following tree diagram can be used to summarize the various classifications of the real number system.

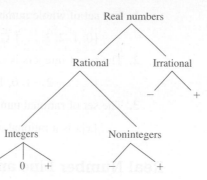

Any real number can be traced down through the tree. Here are some examples:

7 is real, rational, an integer, and positive.

$-\dfrac{2}{3}$ is real, rational, a noninteger, and negative.

$\sqrt{7}$ is real, irrational, and positive.

0.59 is real, rational, a noninteger, and positive.

The concept of a subset is convenient to use at this time. A set A is a **subset** of another set B if and only if every element of A is also an element of B. For example, if $A = \{1, 2\}$ and $B = \{1, 2, 3\}$, then A is a subset of B. This is written $A \subseteq B$ and is read "A is a subset of B." The slash mark can also be used here to denote negation. If $A = \{1, 2, 4, 6\}$ and $B = \{2, 3, 7\}$, we can say A *is not a subset of* B by writing $A \nsubseteq B$. The following statements use the subset vocabulary and symbolism; they are represented in Figure 0.1.

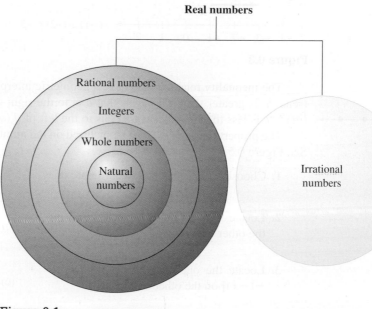

Figure 0.1

1. The set of whole numbers is a subset of the set of integers:

$$\{0, 1, 2, 3, \ldots\} \subseteq \{\ldots, -2, -1, 0, 1, 2, \ldots\}$$

2. The set of integers is a subset of the set of rational numbers:

$$\{\ldots, -2, -1, 0, 1, 2, \ldots\} \subseteq \{x \mid x \text{ is a rational number}\}$$

3. The set of rational numbers is a subset of the set of real numbers:

$$\{x \mid x \text{ is a rational number}\} \subseteq \{y \mid y \text{ is a real number}\}$$

Real Number Line and Absolute Value

It is often helpful to have a geometric representation of the set of real numbers in front of us, as indicated in Figure 0.2. Such a representation, called the **real number line,** indicates a one-to-one correspondence between the set of real numbers and the points on a line. In other words, to each real number there corresponds one and only one point on the line, and to each point on the line there corresponds one and only one real number. The number that corresponds to a particular point on the line is called the **coordinate** of that point.

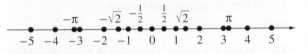

Figure 0.2

Many operations, relations, properties, and concepts pertaining to real numbers can be given a geometric interpretation on the number line. For example, the addition problem $(-1) + (-2)$ can be interpreted on the number line as shown in Figure 0.3.

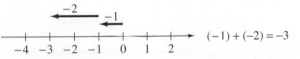

Figure 0.3

The inequality relations also have a geometric interpretation. The statement $a > b$ (read "a is greater than b") means that a is to the right of b, and the statement $c < d$ (read "c is less than d") means that c is to the left of d (see Figure 0.4).

The property $-(-x) = x$ can be pictured on the number line in a sequence of steps. See Figure 0.5.

$$\xrightarrow{\quad \overset{b}{\bullet}\ \overset{a}{\bullet} \qquad \overset{c}{\bullet}\ \overset{d}{\bullet} \quad}$$

Figure 0.4

1. Choose a point that has a coordinate of x.

2. Locate its opposite (written as $-x$) on the other side of zero.

3. Locate the opposite of $-x$ [written as $-(-x)$] on the other side of zero.

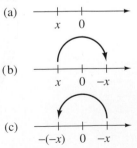

Figure 0.5

Therefore, we conclude that **the opposite of the opposite of any real number is the number itself,** and we express this symbolically by $-(-x) = x$.

Remark: The symbol -1 can be read "negative one," the "negative of one," the "opposite of one," or the "additive inverse of one." The opposite-of and additive-inverse-of terminology is especially meaningful when working with variables. For example, the symbol $-x$, read "the opposite of x or the additive inverse of x," emphasizes an important issue. Because x can be any real number, $-x$ (opposite of x) can be zero, positive, or negative. If x is positive, then $-x$ is negative. If x is negative, then $-x$ is positive. If x is zero, then $-x$ is zero. For example,

If $x = 4$, then $-x = -(4) = -4$.

If $x = -2$, then $-x = -(-2) = 2$.

If $x = 0$, then $-x = -(0) = 0$.

The concept of absolute value can be interpreted on the number line. Geometrically, the **absolute value** of any real number is the distance between that number and zero on the number line. For example, the absolute value of 2 is 2, the absolute value of -3 is 3, and the absolute value of zero is zero (see Figure 0.6).

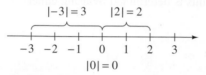

Figure 0.6

Symbolically, absolute value is denoted with vertical bars. Thus we write $|2| = 2$, $|-3| = 3$, and $|0| = 0$. More formally, the concept of absolute value is defined as follows.

Definition 0.1

For all real numbers a,

1. If $a \geq 0$, then $|a| = a$.

2. If $a < 0$, then $|a| = -a$.

According to Definition 0.1, we obtain

$|6| = 6$ by applying part 1

$|0| = 0$ by applying part 1

$|-7| = -(-7) = 7$ by applying part 2

Notice that the absolute value of a positive number is the number itself, but the absolute value of a negative number is its opposite. Thus the absolute value of any number except zero is positive, and the absolute value of zero is zero. Together, these facts indicate that the absolute value of any real number is equal to the absolute value of its opposite. All of these ideas are summarized in the following properties.

Properties of Absolute Value

The variables a and b represent any real number.

1. $|a| \geq 0$ The absolute value of a real number is positive or zero.

2. $|a| = |-a|$ The absolute value of a real number is equal to the absolute value of its opposite

3. $|a - b| = |b - a|$ The expressions $a - b$ and $b - a$ are opposites of each other, hence their absolute values are equal.

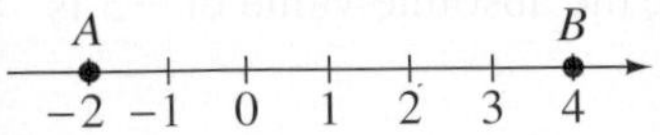

In Figure 0.7 the points A and B are located at -2 and 4, respectively. The distance *between A and B* is 6 units and can be calculated by using either $|-2 - 4|$ or $|4 - (-2)|$. In general, if two points on a number line have coordinates x_1 and x_2, then the distance between the two points is determined by using either

Figure 0.7

$$|x_2 - x_1| \quad \text{or} \quad |x_1 - x_2|$$

because, by property 3 above, they are the same quantity.

Properties of Real Numbers

As you work with the set of real numbers, the basic operations, and the relations of equality and inequality, the following properties will guide your study. Be sure that you understand these properties because they not only facilitate manipulations with real numbers but also serve as a basis for many algebraic computations. The variables a, b, and c represent real numbers.

Properties of Real Numbers

Closure properties	$a + b$ is a unique real number.
	ab is a unique real number.
Commutative properties	$a + b = b + a$
	$ab = ba$
Associative properties	$(a + b) + c = a + (b + c)$
	$(ab)c = a(bc)$

Identity properties	There exists a real number 0 such that $a + 0 = 0 + a = a.$
	There exists a real number 1 such that $a(1) = 1(a) = a.$
Inverse properties	For every real number a, there exists a unique real number $-a$ such that $a + (-a) = (-a) + a = 0.$
	For every nonzero real number a, there exists a unique real number $\dfrac{1}{a}$ such that $a\left(\dfrac{1}{a}\right) = \dfrac{1}{a}(a) = 1.$
Multiplication property of zero	$a(0) = (0)(a) = 0$
Multiplication property of negative one	$a(-1) = -1(a) = -a$
Distributive property	$a(b + c) = ab + ac$

Let's make a few comments about the properties of real numbers. The set of real numbers is said to be **closed** with respect to addition and multiplication. That is, the sum of two real numbers is a real number, and the product of two real numbers is a real number. **Closure** plays an important role when we are proving additional properties that pertain to real numbers.

Addition and multiplication are said to be **commutative operations.** This means that the order in which you add or multiply two real numbers does not affect the result. For example, $6 + (-8) = -8 + 6$ and $(-4)(-3) = (-3)(-4)$. It is important to realize that subtraction and division are *not* commutative operations; order does make a difference. For example, $3 - 4 = -1$, but $4 - 3 = 1$. Likewise, $2 \div 1 = 2$, but $1 \div 2 = \dfrac{1}{2}$.

Addition and multiplication are **associative operations.** The associative properties are grouping properties. For example, $(-8 + 9) + 6 = -8 + (9 + 6)$; changing the grouping of the numbers does not affect the final sum. Likewise, for multiplication, $[(-4)(-3)](2) = (-4)[(-3)(2)]$. Subtraction and division are *not* associative operations. For example, $(8 - 6) - 10 = -8$, but $8 - (6 - 10) = 12$. An example showing that division is not associative is $(8 \div 4) \div 2 = 1$, but $8 \div (4 \div 2) = 4$.

Zero is the **identity element for addition.** This means that the sum of any real number and zero is identically the same real number. For example, $-87 + 0 = 0 + (-87) = -87$. One is the **identity element for multiplication.** The product of any real number and 1 is identically the same real number. For example, $(-119)(1) = (1)(-119) = -119$.

The real number $-a$ is called the **additive inverse of a** or the **opposite of a.** The sum of a number and its additive inverse is the identity element for addition. For example, 16 and -16 are additive inverses, and their sum is zero. The additive inverse of zero is zero.

The real number $1/a$ is called the **multiplicative inverse** or **reciprocal of a.** The product of a number and its multiplicative inverse is the identity element for multiplication. For example, the reciprocal of 2 is $\dfrac{1}{2}$, and $2\left(\dfrac{1}{2}\right) = \dfrac{1}{2}(2) = 1$.

The product of any real number and zero is zero. For example, $(-17)(0) = (0)(-17) = 0$. The product of any real number and -1 is the opposite of the real number. For example, $(-1)(52) = (52)(-1) = -52$.

The **distributive property** ties together the operations of addition and multiplication. We say that *multiplication distributes over addition.* For example, $7(3 + 8) = 7(3) + 7(8)$. Furthermore, because $b - c = b + (-c)$, it follows that *multiplication also distributes over subtraction.* This can be expressed symbolically as $a(b - c) = ab - ac$. For example, $6(8 - 10) = 6(8) - 6(10)$.

Algebraic Expressions

Algebraic expressions such as

$$2x \qquad 8xy \qquad -3xy \qquad -4abc \qquad z$$

are called "terms." A **term** is an indicated product and may have any number of factors. The variables of a term are called "literal factors," and the numerical factor is called the "numerical coefficient." Thus in $8xy$, the x and y are **literal factors,** and 8 is the **numerical coefficient.** Because $1(z) = z$, the numerical coefficient of the term z is understood to be 1. Terms that have the same literal factors are called "similar terms" or "like terms." The distributive property in the form $ba + ca = (b + c)a$ provides the basis for simplifying algebraic expressions by *combining similar terms,* as illustrated in the following examples:

$$3x + 5x = (3 + 5)x = 8x$$
$$-6xy + 4xy = (-6 + 4)xy = -2xy$$
$$4x - x = 4x - 1x = (4 - 1)x = 3x$$

Sometimes we can simplify an algebraic expression by applying the distributive property to remove parentheses and combine similar terms, as the next examples illustrate:

$$4(x + 2) + 3(x + 6) = 4(x) + 4(2) + 3(x) + 3(6)$$
$$= 4x + 8 + 3x + 18$$
$$= 7x + 26$$

$$-5(y + 3) - 2(y - 8) = -5(y) - 5(3) - 2(y) - 2(-8)$$
$$= -5y - 15 - 2y + 16$$
$$= -7y + 1$$

An algebraic expression takes on a numerical value whenever each variable in the expression is replaced by a real number. For example, when x is replaced by 5 and y by 9, the algebraic expression $x + y$ becomes the numerical expression $5 + 9$, which is equal to 14. We say that $x + y$ has a value of 14 when $x = 5$ and $y = 9$.

Consider the following examples, which illustrate the process of finding a value of an algebraic expression. The process is commonly referred to as **evaluating an algebraic expression.**

Classroom Example
Find the value of $-2a + 4bc$ when $a = -3$, $b = 5$, and $c = -1$.

EXAMPLE 1   Find the value of $3xy - 4z$ when $x = 2$, $y = -4$, and $z = -5$.

Solution

$$3xy - 4z = 3(2)(-4) - 4(-5) \quad \text{when } x = 2, y = -4, \text{ and } z = -5$$
$$= -24 + 20$$
$$= -4$$

Classroom Example
Find the value of
$3[2x - (5y - 4)]$ when $x = -1$ and $y = -6$.

EXAMPLE 2

Find the value of $a - [4b - (2c + 1)]$ when $a = -8$, $b = -7$, and $c = 14$.

Solution

$$a - [4b - (2c + 1)] = -8 - [4(-7) - (2(14) + 1)]$$
$$= -8 - [-28 - 29]$$
$$= -8 - [-57]$$
$$= 49$$

Classroom Example
Evaluate $\dfrac{-x - 3y}{x - y}$ when $x = -4$ and $y = 2$.

EXAMPLE 3

Evaluate $\dfrac{a - 2b}{3c + 5d}$ when $a = 14$, $b = -12$, $c = -3$, and $d = -2$.

Solution

$$\frac{a - 2b}{3c + 5d} = \frac{14 - 2(-12)}{3(-3) + 5(-2)}$$
$$= \frac{14 + 24}{-9 - 10}$$
$$= \frac{38}{-19} = -2$$

Look back at Examples 1–3, and note that we use the following **order of operations** when simplifying numerical expressions.

1. Perform the operations inside the symbols of inclusion (parentheses, brackets, and braces) and above and below each fraction bar. Start with the innermost inclusion symbol.

2. Perform all multiplications and divisions in the order in which they appear, from left to right.

3. Perform all additions and subtractions in the order in which they appear, from left to right.

You should also realize that first simplifying by combining similar terms can sometimes aid in the process of evaluating algebraic expressions. The last example of this section illustrates this idea.

Classroom Example
Evaluate $2(-2y - 1) - 2(y + 4)$ when $y = -2$.

EXAMPLE 4   Evaluate $2(3x + 1) - 3(4x - 3)$ when $x = -5$.

Solution

$$2(3x + 1) - 3(4x - 3) = 2(3x) + 2(1) - 3(4x) - 3(-3)$$
$$= 6x + 2 - 12x + 9$$
$$= -6x + 11$$

Now substituting -5 for x, we obtain

$$-6x + 11 = -6(-5) + 11$$
$$= 30 + 11$$
$$= 41$$

Cartesian Coordinate System

Just as real numbers can be associated with points on a line, pairs of real numbers can be associated with points in a plane. To do this, we set up two number lines, one vertical and one horizontal, perpendicular to each other at the point associated with zero on both lines, as shown in Figure 0.8. We refer to these number lines as the **horizontal axis** and the **vertical axis** or together as the **coordinate axes.** They partition a plane into four regions called **quadrants.** The quadrants are numbered counterclockwise from I through IV as indicated in Figure 0.8. The point of intersection of the two axes is called the **origin.**

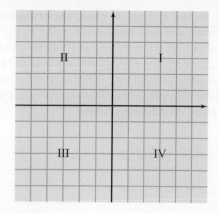

Figure 0.8

The positive direction on the horizontal axis is to the right, and the positive direction on the vertical axis is up. It is now possible to set up a one-to-one correspondence between **ordered pairs** of real numbers and the points in a plane. To each ordered pair of real numbers there corresponds a unique point in the plane, and to each point in the plane there corresponds a unique ordered pair of real numbers. A part of this correspondence is illustrated in Figure 0.9. For example, the ordered pair (3, 2) means that the point A is located 3 units to the right of and 2 units up from the origin. Likewise, the ordered pair $(-3, -5)$ means that the point D is located 3 units to the left of and 5 units down from the origin. The ordered pair (0, 0) is associated with the origin O.

Figure 0.9

In general we refer to the real numbers a and b in an ordered pair (a, b) associated with a point as the **coordinates of the point.** The first number, a, called the **abscissa,** is the directed distance of the point from the vertical axis measured parallel to the horizontal axis. The second number, *b*, called the **ordinate,** is the directed distance of the point from the horizontal axis measured parallel to the vertical axis (Figure 0.10). Thus in the first quadrant, all points have a positive abscissa and a positive ordinate. In the second quadrant all points have a negative abscissa and a positive ordinate. We have indicated the sign situations for all four quadrants in Figure 0.11. This system of associating points in a plane with pairs of real numbers is called the **rectangular coordinate system** or the **Cartesian coordinate system.**

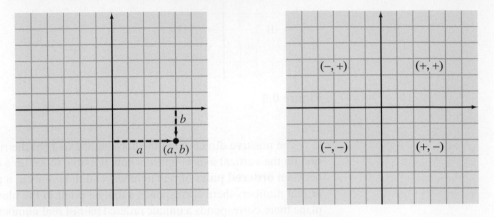

Figure 0.10   **Figure 0.11**

Historically, the rectangular coordinate system provided the basis for the development of the branch of mathematics called **analytic geometry,** or what we presently refer to as **coordinate geometry.** In this discipline, René Descartes, a French 17th-century mathematician, was able to transform geometric problems into an algebraic setting and then use the tools of algebra to solve the problems.

Basically, there are two kinds of problems to solve in coordinate geometry:

1. Given an algebraic equation, find its geometric graph.
2. Given a set of conditions pertaining to a geometric figure, find its algebraic equation.

Throughout this text we will consider a wide variety of situations dealing with both kinds of problems.

For most purposes in coordinate geometry, it is customary to label the horizontal axis the **x-axis** and the vertical axis the **y-axis.** Then ordered pairs of real numbers associated with points in the *xy* plane are of the form (*x, y*); that is, *x* is the first coordinate and *y* is the second coordinate.

Graphing Utilities

The term **graphing utility** is used in current literature to refer to either a graphing calculator (see Figure 0.12) or a computer with a graphing software package. (We will frequently use the phrase "use a graphing calculator" to mean either a graphing calculator or a computer with an appropriate software package.) We will introduce various features of graphing calculators as we need them in the text. Because so many different types of graphing utilities are available, we will use mostly generic terminology and let you consult a user's manual for specific key-punching instructions. We urge you to study the graphing calculator examples in this text even if you do not have access to a graphing utility. The examples are chosen to reinforce concepts under discussion. Furthermore, for those who do have access to a graphing utility, we provide "Graphing Calculator Activities" in many of the problem sets.

Courtesy of Texas Instruments

Figure 0.12

Graphing calculators have display windows large enough to show graphs. This window feature is also helpful when you're using a graphing calculator for computational purposes because it allows you to see the entries of the problem. Figure 0.13 shows a display window for an example of the distributive property. Note that we can check to see that the correct numbers and operational symbols have been entered. Also note that the answer is given below and to the right of the problem.

Figure 0.13

Most calculators, including graphing calculators, can be used to evaluate algebraic expressions. One calculator method for evaluating the algebraic expression in Example 1, $3xy - 4z$ for $x = 2$, $y = -4$, and $z = -5$, is to replace x with 2, y with -4, and z with -5, and then calculate the resulting numerical expression.

Another method is shown in Figure 0.14, in which the values for x, y, and z are stored and then the algebraic expression $3xy - 4z$ is evaluated.

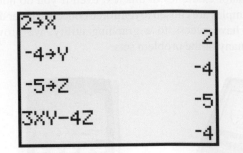

Figure 0.14

Concept Quiz 0.1

For Problems 1–10, answer true or false.

1. The null set is written as $\{\varnothing\}$.
2. The sets $\{a, b, c, d\}$ and $\{a, d, c, b\}$ are equal sets.
3. Decimal numbers that are classified as repeating or terminating decimals represent rational numbers.
4. The absolute value of x is equal to x.
5. The axes of the rectangular coordinate system intersect in a point called the center.
6. Subtraction is a commutative operation.
7. Every real number has a multiplicative inverse.
8. The associative properties are grouping properties.
9. On the rectangular coordinate system, the point of intersection of the two axes is called the origin.
10. The horizontal axis is customarily referred to as the y-axis.

Remark: You can find answers to the Concept Quiz questions at the end of the next Problem Set.

Problem Set 0.1

For Problems 1–10, identify each statement as *true* or *false*. **(Objective 2)**

1. Every rational number is a real number.

2. Every irrational number is a real number.

3. Every real number is a rational number.

4. If a number is real, then it is irrational.

5. Some irrational numbers are also rational numbers.

6. All integers are rational numbers.

7. The number zero is a rational number.

8. Zero is a positive integer.

9. Zero is a negative number.

10. All whole numbers are integers.

For Problems 11–18, list those elements of the set of numbers

$$\left\{0, \sqrt{5}, -\sqrt{2}, \frac{7}{8}, -\frac{10}{13}, 7\frac{1}{8}, 0.279, 0.4\overline{67}, -\pi, -14, 46, 6.75\right\}$$

that belong to each of the following sets. **(Objective 2)**

11. The natural numbers

12. The whole numbers

13. The integers

14. The rational numbers

15. The irrational numbers

16. The nonnegative integers

17. The nonpositive integers

18. The real numbers

For Problems 19–32, use the following set designations:

$N = \{x|x \text{ is a natural number}\}$

$W = \{x|x \text{ is a whole number}\}$

$I = \{x|x \text{ is an integer}\}$

$Q = \{x|x \text{ is a rational number}\}$

$H = \{x|x \text{ is an irrational number}\}$

$R = \{x|x \text{ is a real number}\}$

Place $\subseteq$ or $\not\subseteq$ in each blank to make a true statement. **(Objectives 1 and 2)**

19. N _____ R **20.** R _____ N

21. N _____ I **22.** I _____ Q

23. H _____ Q **24.** Q _____ H

25. W _____ I **26.** N _____ W

27. I _____ W **28.** I _____ N

29. $\{0, 2, 4, \ldots\}$ _____ W

30. $\{1, 3, 5, 7, \ldots\}$ _____ I

31. $\{-2, -1, 0, 1, 2\}$ _____ W

32. $\{0, 3, 6, 9, \ldots\}$ _____ N

For Problems 33–42, list the elements of each set. For example, the elements of $\{x|x \text{ is a natural number less than 4}\}$ can be listed $\{1, 2, 3\}$. **(Objectives 1 and 2)**

33. $\{x|x \text{ is a natural number less than 2}\}$

34. $\{x|x \text{ is a natural number greater than 5}\}$

35. $\{n|n \text{ is a whole number less than 4}\}$

36. $\{y|y \text{ is an integer greater than } -3\}$

37. $\{y|y \text{ is an integer less than 2}\}$

38. $\{n|n \text{ is a positive integer greater than } -4\}$

39. $\{x|x \text{ is a whole number less than 0}\}$

40. $\{x|x \text{ is a negative integer greater than } -5\}$

41. $\{n|n \text{ is a nonnegative integer less than 3}\}$

42. $\{n|n \text{ is a nonpositive integer greater than 1}\}$

43. Find the distance on the real number line between two points whose coordinates are the following. **(Objective 3)**

(a) 17 and 35   **(b)** -14 and 12

(c) 18 and -21 **(d)** -17 and -42

(e) -56 and -21 **(f)** 0 and -37

44. Evaluate each of the following if x is a nonzero real number. **(Objective 4)**

(a) $\dfrac{|x|}{x}$ **(b)** $\dfrac{x}{|x|}$

(c) $\dfrac{|-x|}{-x}$ **(d)** $|x| - |-x|$

In Problems 45–58, state the property that justifies each of the statements. For example, $3 + (-4) = (-4) + 3$ because of the commutative property of addition. **(Objective 5)**

45. $x(2) = 2(x)$

46. $(7 + 4) + 6 = 7 + (4 + 6)$

47. $1(x) = x$

48. $43 + (-18) = (-18) + 43$

49. $(-1)(93) = -93$

50. $109 + (-109) = 0$

51. $5(4 + 7) = 5(4) + 5(7)$

52. $-1(x + y) = -(x + y)$

53. $7yx = 7xy$

54. $(x + 2) + (-2) = x + [2 + (-2)]$

55. $6(4) + 7(4) = (6 + 7)(4)$

56. $\left(\dfrac{2}{3}\right)\left(\dfrac{3}{2}\right) = 1$

57. $4(5x) = (4 \cdot 5)x$

58. $[(17)(8)](25) = (17)[(8)(25)]$

For Problems 59–80, evaluate each of the algebraic expressions for the given values of the variables. (Objective 6)

59. $5x + 3y$; $x = -2$ and $y = -4$

60. $7x - 4y$; $x = -1$ and $y = 6$

61. $-3ab - 2c$; $a = -4$, $b = 7$, and $c = -8$

62. $x - (2y + 3z)$; $x = -3$, $y = -4$, and $z = 9$

63. $(a - 2b) + (3c - 4)$; $a = 6$, $b = -5$, and $c = -11$

64. $3a - [2b - (4c + 1)]$; $a = 4$, $b = 6$, and $c = -8$

65. $\dfrac{-2x + 7y}{x - y}$; $x = -3$ and $y = -2$

66. $\dfrac{x - 3y + 2z}{2x - y}$; $x = 4$, $y = 9$, $z = -12$

67. $(5x - 2y)(-3x + 4y)$; $x = -3$ and $y = -7$

68. $(2a - 7b)(4a + 3b)$; $a = 6$ and $b = -3$

69. $5x + 4y - 9y - 2y$; $x = 2$ and $y = -8$

70. $5a + 7b - 9a - 6b$; $a = -7$ and $b = 8$

71. $-5x + 8y + 7y + 8x$; $x = 5$ and $y = -6$

72. $|x - y| - |x + y|$; $x = -4$ and $y = -7$

73. $|3x + y| + |2x - 4y|$; $x = 5$ and $y = -3$

74. $\left|\dfrac{x - y}{y - x}\right|$; $x = -6$ and $y = 13$

75. $\left|\dfrac{2a - 3b}{3b - 2a}\right|$; $a = -4$ and $b = -8$

76. $5(x - 1) + 7(x + 4)$; $x = 3$

77. $2(3x + 4) - 3(2x - 1)$; $x = -2$

78. $-4(2x - 1) - 5(3x + 7)$; $x = -1$

79. $5(a - 3) - 4(2a + 1) - 2(a - 4)$; $a = -3$

80. $-3(2y - 7) - (y + 10) + 8y + 5$; $y = 10$

For Problems 81–86, plot the following points on a rectangular coordinate system. (Objective 7)

81. $(-4, 1)$ **82.** $(3, -2)$

83. $(0, -3)$ **84.** $(-2, -2)$

85. $(5, -1)$ **86.** $(1, 4)$

For Problems 87–92, state the quadrant that contains the point. (Objective 7)

87. $(4, -2)$ **88.** $(-3, 1)$

89. $(-6, -2)$ **90.** $(5, 2)$

91. $(1, 8)$ **92.** $(-7, -7)$

Thoughts Into Words

93. Do you think $3\sqrt{2}$ is a rational or an irrational number? Defend your answer.

94. Explain why $\dfrac{0}{8} = 0$ but $\dfrac{8}{0}$ is undefined.

95. The solution of the following simplification problem is incorrect. The answer should be -11. Find and correct the error.

$$8 \div (-4)(2) - 3(4) \div 2 + (-1) = (-2)(2) - 12 \div 1$$
$$= -4 - 12$$
$$= -16$$

96. Explain the difference between "simplifying a numerical expression" and "evaluating an algebraic expression."

Graphing Calculator Activities

97. Different graphing calculators use different sequences of key strokes to evaluate algebraic expressions. Be sure that you can do Problems 59–80 with your calculator.

0.2   Exponents

OBJECTIVES

1. Evaluate numerical expressions that have integer exponents

2. Apply the properties of exponents to simplify algebraic expressions

3. Write numbers in scientific notation

4. Convert numbers from scientific notation to ordinary decimal notation

5. Perform calculations with numbers in scientific form

Positive integers are used as *exponents* to indicate repeated multiplication. For example, $4 \cdot 4 \cdot 4$ can be written 4^3, where the raised 3 indicates that 4 is to be used as a factor three times. The following general definition is helpful.

> **Definition 0.2**
>
> If n is a positive integer, and b is any real number, then
>
> $$b^n = \underbrace{bbb \cdots b}_{n \text{ factors of } b}$$

The number b is referred to as the **base**, and n is called the **exponent**. The expression b^n can be read "b to the nth power." The terms **squared** and **cubed** are commonly associated with exponents of 2 and 3, respectively. For example, b^2 is read "b squared" and b^3 as "b cubed." An exponent of 1 is usually not written, so b^1 is simply written b. The following examples illustrate Definition 0.2:

$$2^3 = 2 \cdot 2 \cdot 2 = 8 \qquad \left(\frac{1}{2}\right)^5 = \frac{1}{2} \cdot \frac{1}{2} \cdot \frac{1}{2} \cdot \frac{1}{2} \cdot \frac{1}{2} = \frac{1}{32}$$

$$3^4 = 3 \cdot 3 \cdot 3 \cdot 3 = 81 \qquad (0.7)^2 = (0.7)(0.7) = 0.49$$

$$(-5)^2 = (-5)(-5) = 25 \qquad -5^2 = -(5 \cdot 5) = -25$$

We especially want to call your attention to the last example in each column. Note that $(-5)^2$ means that -5 is the base used as a factor twice. However, -5^2 means that 5 is the base, and after it is squared, we take the opposite of the result.

Properties of Exponents

In a previous algebra course, you may have seen some properties pertaining to the use of positive integers as exponents. Those properties can be summarized as follows.

Property 0.1   Properties of Exponents

If a and b are real numbers, and m and n are positive integers, then

1. $b^n \cdot b^m = b^{n+m}$

2. $(b^n)^m = b^{mn}$

3. $(ab)^n = a^n b^n$

4. $\left(\dfrac{a}{b}\right)^n = \dfrac{a^n}{b^n}$ $b \neq 0$

5. $\dfrac{b^n}{b^m} = b^{n-m}$ when $n > m, b \neq 0$

$\dfrac{b^n}{b^m} = 1$ when $n = m, b \neq 0$

$\dfrac{b^n}{b^m} = \dfrac{1}{b^{m-n}}$ when $n < m, b \neq 0$

Each part of Property 0.1 can be justified by using Definition 0.2. For example, to justify part 1, we can reason as follows:

$$b^n \cdot b^m = \underbrace{(bbb \cdots b)}_{\substack{n \text{ factors} \\ \text{of } b}} \cdot \underbrace{(bbb \cdots b)}_{\substack{m \text{ factors} \\ \text{of } b}}$$

$$= \underbrace{bbb \cdots b}_{(n+m) \text{ factors of } b}$$

$$= b^{n+m}$$

Similar reasoning can be used to verify the other parts of Property 0.1. The following examples illustrate the use of Property 0.1 along with the commutative and associative properties of the real numbers. We have chosen to show all of the steps; however many of the steps can be performed mentally.

Classroom Example
Find the indicated product,
$(5a^3b^2)(-2ab^4)$.

EXAMPLE 1   Find the indicated product, $(3x^2y)(4x^3y^2)$.

Solution

$$(3x^2y)(4x^3y^2) = 3 \cdot 4 \cdot x^2 \cdot x^3 \cdot y \cdot y^2$$
$$= 12x^{2+3}y^{1+2} \qquad\qquad b^n \cdot b^m = b^{n+m}$$
$$= 12x^5y^3$$

Classroom Example
Find the indicated product,
$(-3x^2)^4$.

EXAMPLE 2   Find the indicated product, $(-2y^3)^5$.

Solution

$$(-2y^3)^5 = (-2)^5(y^3)^5 \qquad\qquad (ab)^n = a^n b^n$$
$$= -32y^{15} \qquad\qquad (b^n)^m = b^{mn}$$

Classroom Example
Find the indicated quotient,
$\left(\dfrac{x^5}{y}\right)^3$.

EXAMPLE 3   Find the indicated quotient, $\left(\dfrac{a^2}{b^4}\right)^7$.

Solution

$$\left(\frac{a^2}{b^4}\right)^7 = \frac{(a^2)^7}{(b^4)^7} \qquad\qquad \left(\frac{a}{b}\right)^n = \frac{a^n}{b^n}$$
$$= \frac{a^{14}}{b^{28}} \qquad\qquad (b^n)^m = b^{mn}$$

Classroom Example
Find the indicated quotient,
$\dfrac{21a^8}{-3a^3}$.

EXAMPLE 4   Find the indicated quotient, $\dfrac{-56x^9}{7x^4}$.

Solution

$$\frac{-56x^9}{7x^4} = -8x^{9-4} \qquad\qquad \frac{b^n}{b^m} = b^{n-m} \qquad \text{when } n > m$$
$$= -8x^5$$

Zero and Negative Integers As Exponents

Now we can extend the concept of an exponent to include the use of zero and negative integers. First, let's consider the use of zero as an exponent. We want to use zero in a way that Property 0.1 will continue to hold. For example, if $b^n \cdot b^m = b^{n+m}$ is to hold, then

$x^4 \cdot x^0$ should equal x^{4+0}, which equals x^4. In other words, x^0 *acts like* 1 because $x^4 \cdot x^0 = x^4$. Look at the following definition.

Definition 0.3

If b is a nonzero real number, then

$$b^0 = 1$$

Therefore, according to Definition 0.3, the following statements are all true:

$$5^0 = 1 \qquad (-413)^0 = 1$$

$$\left(\frac{3}{11}\right)^0 = 1 \quad (x^3 y^4)^0 = 1 \ \text{ if } x \neq 0 \text{ and } y \neq 0$$

A similar line of reasoning can be used to motivate a definition for the use of negative integers as exponents. Consider the example $x^4 \cdot x^{-4}$. If $b^n \cdot b^m = b^{n+m}$ is to hold, then $x^4 \cdot x^{-4}$ should equal $x^{4+(-4)}$, which equals $x^0 = 1$. Therefore, x^{-4} must be the reciprocal of x^4 because their product is 1. That is, $x^{-4} = 1/x^4$. This suggests the following definition.

Definition 0.4

If n is a positive integer, and b is a nonzero real number, then

$$b^{-n} = \frac{1}{b^n}$$

According to Definition 0.4, the following statements are true:

$$x^{-5} = \frac{1}{x^5} \qquad\qquad 2^{-4} = \frac{1}{2^4} = \frac{1}{16}$$

$$\left(\frac{3}{4}\right)^{-2} = \frac{1}{\left(\frac{3}{4}\right)^2} = \frac{1}{\frac{9}{16}} = \frac{16}{9} \quad \frac{2}{x^{-3}} = \frac{2}{\frac{1}{x^3}} = 2x^3$$

The first four parts of Property 0.1 hold true *for all integers*. Furthermore, we do not need all three equations in part 5 of Property 0.1. The first equation,

$$\frac{b^n}{b^m} = b^{n-m}$$

can be used for *all integral exponents*. Let's restate Property 0.1 as it pertains to integers. We will include name tags for easy reference.

Property 0.2

If m and n are integers, and a and b are real numbers, with $b \neq 0$ whenever it appears in a denominator, then

1. $b^n \cdot b^m = b^{n+m}$ Product of two powers

2. $(b^n)^m = b^{mn}$ Power of a power

3. $(ab)^n = a^n b^n$ Power of a product

4. $\left(\dfrac{a}{b}\right)^n = \dfrac{a^n}{b^n}$ Power of a quotient

5. $\dfrac{b^n}{b^m} = b^{n-m}$ Quotient of two powers

Having the use of all integers as exponents allows us to work with a large variety of numerical and algebraic expressions. Let's consider some examples that illustrate the various parts of Property 0.2.

Classroom Example
Evaluate each of the numerical expressions.

(a) $(3^{-2} \cdot 4)^{-1}$ **(b)** $\left(\dfrac{5^{-2}}{2^{-3}}\right)^{-2}$

EXAMPLE 5   Evaluate each of the following numerical expressions.

(a) $(2^{-1} \cdot 3^2)^{-1}$ **(b)** $\left(\dfrac{2^{-3}}{3^{-2}}\right)^{-2}$

Solution

(a)
$$(2^{-1} \cdot 3^2)^{-1} = (2^{-1})^{-1}(3^2)^{-1} \quad \text{Power of a product}$$
$$= (2^1)(3^{-2}) \quad \text{Power of a power}$$
$$= (2)\left(\frac{1}{3^2}\right)$$
$$= 2\left(\frac{1}{9}\right) = \frac{2}{9}$$

(b)
$$\left(\frac{2^{-3}}{3^{-2}}\right)^{-2} = \frac{(2^{-3})^{-2}}{(3^{-2})^{-2}} \quad \text{Power of a quotient}$$
$$= \frac{2^6}{3^4} \quad \text{Power of a power}$$
$$= \frac{64}{81}$$

Classroom Example

Find the indicated products and
quotients, and express the final
results with positive integral
exponents only.

(a) $(5a^{-3}b^{-1}c^{-3})(3a^{-2}bc^7)$

(b) $\dfrac{-28x^2y^3}{7x^4y^{-2}}$

(c) $\left(\dfrac{12a^3b^{-2}}{3a^4b^{-3}}\right)^{-1}$

EXAMPLE 6

Find the indicated products and quotients, and express the final results with positive integral exponents only.

(a) $(3x^2y^{-4})(4x^{-3}y)$ **(b)** $\dfrac{12a^3b^2}{-3a^{-1}b^5}$ **(c)** $\left(\dfrac{15x^{-1}y^2}{5xy^{-4}}\right)^{-1}$

Solution

$$\textbf{(a)}\ (3x^2y^{-4})(4x^{-3}y) = 12x^{2+(-3)}y^{-4+1} \qquad \text{Product of powers}$$

$$= 12x^{-1}y^{-3}$$

$$= \frac{12}{xy^3}$$

$$\textbf{(b)}\ \frac{12a^3b^2}{-3a^{-1}b^5} = -4a^{3-(-1)}b^{2-5} \qquad \text{Quotient of powers}$$

$$= -4a^4b^{-3}$$

$$= -\frac{4a^4}{b^3}$$

$$\textbf{(c)}\ \left(\frac{15x^{-1}y^2}{5xy^{-4}}\right)^{-1} = (3x^{-1-1}y^{2-(-4)})^{-1} \qquad \text{First simplify inside parentheses}$$

$$= (3x^{-2}y^6)^{-1}$$

$$= 3^{-1}x^2y^{-6} \qquad \text{Power of a product}$$

$$= \frac{x^2}{3y^6}$$

The next two examples illustrate the simplification of numerical and algebraic expressions involving sums and differences. In such cases, Definition 0.4 can be used to change from negative to positive exponents so that we can proceed in the usual ways.

Classroom Example

Simplify $4^{-1} + 2^{-1}$.

EXAMPLE 7   Simplify $2^{-3} + 3^{-1}$.

Solution

$$2^{-3} + 3^{-1} = \frac{1}{2^3} + \frac{1}{3^1}$$

$$= \frac{1}{8} + \frac{1}{3}$$

$$= \frac{3}{24} + \frac{8}{24}$$

$$= \frac{11}{24}$$

EXAMPLE 8   Simplify $(4^{-1} - 3^{-2})^{-1}$.

Solution

$$
\begin{aligned}
(4^{-1} - 3^{-2})^{-1} &= \left(\frac{1}{4^1} - \frac{1}{3^2}\right)^{-1} \\
&= \left(\frac{1}{4} - \frac{1}{9}\right)^{-1} \\
&= \left(\frac{9}{36} - \frac{4}{36}\right)^{-1} \\
&= \left(\frac{5}{36}\right)^{-1} \\
&= \frac{1}{\left(\frac{5}{36}\right)^1} = \frac{36}{5}
\end{aligned}
$$

Figure 0.15 shows calculator windows for Examples 7 and 8. Note that the answers are given in decimal form. If your calculator also handles common fractions, then the display window may appear as in Figure 0.16.

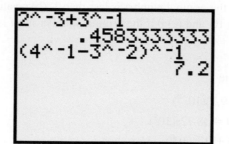

Figure 0.15

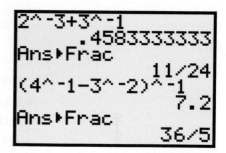

Figure 0.16

EXAMPLE 9

Express $a^{-1} + b^{-2}$ as a single fraction involving positive exponents only.

Solution

$$
\begin{aligned}
a^{-1} + b^{-2} &= \frac{1}{a^1} + \frac{1}{b^2} \\
&= \left(\frac{1}{a}\right)\left(\frac{b^2}{b^2}\right) + \left(\frac{1}{b^2}\right)\left(\frac{a}{a}\right) \\
&= \frac{b^2}{ab^2} + \frac{a}{ab^2} \\
&= \frac{b^2 + a}{ab^2}
\end{aligned}
$$

Scientific Notation

The expression $(n)(10^k)$ (where n is a number greater than or equal to 1 and less than 10, written in decimal form, and k is any integer) is commonly called **scientific notation** or the **scientific form** of a number. The following are examples of numbers expressed in scientific form:

$$(4.23)(10^4) \qquad (8.176)(10^{12}) \qquad (5.02)(10^{-3}) \qquad (1)(10^{-5})$$

Very large and very small numbers can be conveniently expressed in scientific notation. For example, a light year (the distance that a ray of light travels in one year) is approximately 5,900,000,000,000 miles, and this can be written as $(5.9)(10^{12})$. The weight of an oxygen molecule is approximately 0.000000000000000000000053 of a gram, and this can be expressed as $(5.3)(10^{-23})$.

To change from ordinary decimal notation to scientific notation, the following procedure can be used.

Write the given number as the product of a number greater than or equal to 1 and less than 10, and a power of 10. The exponent of 10 is determined by counting the number of places that the decimal point was moved when going from the original number to the number greater than or equal to 1 and less than 10. This exponent is (a) negative if the original number is less than 1, (b) positive if the original number is greater than 10, and (c) 0 if the original number itself is between 1 and 10.

Thus we can write

$$0.00092 = (9.2)(10^{-4})$$
$$872,000,000 = (8.72)(10^8)$$
$$5.1217 = (5.1217)(10^0)$$

To change from scientific notation to ordinary decimal notation, the following procedure can be used.

Move the decimal point the number of places indicated by the exponent of 10. Move the decimal point to the right if the exponent is positive. Move it to the left if the exponent is negative.

Thus we can write

$$(3.14)(10^7) = 31,400,000$$
$$(7.8)(10^{-6}) = 0.0000078$$

Scientific notation can be used to simplify numerical calculations. We merely change the numbers to scientific notation and use the appropriate properties of exponents. Consider the following examples.

Classroom Example
Use scientific notation to
perform the indicated operations.

(a) $\dfrac{(0.0048)(20,000)}{(0.0000016)(400)}$

(b) $\sqrt{4,000,000}$

EXAMPLE 10 Use scientific notation to perform the indicated operations.

(a) $\dfrac{(0.00063)(960,000)}{(3200)(0.0000021)}$ (b) $\sqrt{90,000}$

Solution

(a) $\dfrac{(0.00063)(960,000)}{(3200)(0.0000021)} = \dfrac{(6.3)(10^{-4})(9.6)(10^5)}{(3.2)(10^3)(2.1)(10^{-6})}$

$$= \dfrac{(6.3)(9.6)(10^1)}{(3.2)(2.1)(10^{-3})}$$

$$= (9)(10^4)$$

$$= 90,000$$

(b) $\sqrt{90,000} = \sqrt{(9)(10^4)}$

$$= \sqrt{9}\sqrt{10^4}$$

$$= (3)(10^2)$$

$$= 3(100)$$

$$= 300$$

Many calculators are equipped to display numbers in scientific notation. The display panel shows the number between 1 and 10 and the appropriate exponent of 10. For example, evaluating $(3,800,000)^2$ yields

$$\boxed{1.444\text{E}13}$$

Thus $(3,800,000)^2 = (1.444)(10^{13}) = 14,440,000,000,000$. Similarly, the answer for $(0.000168)^2$ is displayed as

$$\boxed{2.8224\text{E}-8}$$

Thus $(0.000168)^2 = (2.8224)(10^{-8}) = 0.000000028224$.

Calculators vary in the number of digits they display between 1 and 10 when they represent a number in scientific notation. For example, we used two different calculators to estimate $(6729)^6$ and obtained the following results:

$$\boxed{9.283316768\text{E}22}$$

$$\boxed{9.28331676776\text{E}22}$$

Obviously, you need to know the capabilities of your calculator when working with problems in scientific notation.

Many calculators also allow you to enter a number in scientific notation. Such calculators are equipped with an enter-the-exponent key often labeled $\boxed{\text{EE}}$. Thus a number such as $(3.14)(10^8)$ might be entered as follows:

Enter	Press	Display
3.14	$\boxed{\text{EE}}$	3.14E
8		3.14E8

A $\boxed{\text{MODE}}$ key is often used on calculators to let you choose normal decimal notation, scientific notation, or engineering notation. (The abbreviations Norm, Sci, and Eng are commonly used.) If the calculator is in scientific mode, then a number can be entered and changed to scientific form with the $\boxed{\text{ENTER}}$ key. For example, when we enter 589 and press the $\boxed{\text{ENTER}}$ key, the display will show 5.89E2. Likewise, when the calculator is in scientific mode, the answers to computational problems are given in scientific form. For example, the answer for (76)(533) is given as 4.0508E4.

It should be evident from this brief discussion that even when you are using a calculator, you need to have a thorough understanding of scientific notation.

Concept Quiz 0.2

For Problems 1–10, answer true or false.

1. Exponents are used to indicate repeated multiplications.
2. An exponent cannot be zero.
3. $2^{-2} = -4$
4. $(-1)^{-2} = 2$
5. In the expression 6^3, the number 6 is referred to as the baseline number.
6. $(2 + 5)^2 = 4 + 25$
7. $(3^{-2} + 3^{-4}) = 3^{-6}$
8. When writing a number in scientific notation, $(n)(10^k)$, the number n must be greater than 1 and less than or equal to 10.
9. Single-digit numbers can be expressed in scientific notation.
10. The number 357,000 is written as $(35.7)(10^4)$ in scientific notation.

Problem Set 0.2

For Problems 1–42, evaluate each numerical expression. (Objective 1)

1. 2^{-3}

2. 3^{-2}

3. -10^{-3}

4. 10^{-4}

5. $\dfrac{1}{3^{-3}}$

6. $\dfrac{1}{2^{-5}}$

7. $\left(\dfrac{1}{2}\right)^{-2}$

8. $-\left(\dfrac{1}{3}\right)^{-2}$

9. $\left(-\dfrac{2}{3}\right)^{-3}$

10. $\left(\dfrac{5}{6}\right)^{-2}$

11. $\left(-\dfrac{1}{5}\right)^{0}$

12. $\dfrac{1}{\left(\dfrac{3}{5}\right)^{-2}}$

13. $\dfrac{1}{\left(\dfrac{4}{5}\right)^{-2}}$

14. $\left(\dfrac{4}{5}\right)^{0}$

15. $2^5 \cdot 2^{-3}$

16. $3^{-2} \cdot 3^5$

17. $10^{-6} \cdot 10^4$

18. $10^6 \cdot 10^{-9}$

19. $10^{-2} \cdot 10^{-3}$

20. $10^{-1} \cdot 10^{-5}$

21. $(3^{-2})^{-2}$

22. $((-2)^{-1})^{-3}$

23. $(4^2)^{-1}$

24. $(3^{-1})^3$

25. $(3^{-1} \cdot 2^2)^{-1}$

26. $(2^3 \cdot 3^{-2})^{-2}$

27. $(4^2 \cdot 5^{-1})^2$

28. $(2^{-2} \cdot 4^{-1})^3$

29. $\left(\dfrac{2^{-2}}{5^{-1}}\right)^{-2}$

30. $\left(\dfrac{3^{-1}}{2^{-3}}\right)^{-2}$

31. $\left(\dfrac{3^{-2}}{8^{-1}}\right)^2$

32. $\left(\dfrac{4^2}{5^{-1}}\right)^{-1}$

33. $\dfrac{2^3}{2^{-3}}$

34. $\dfrac{2^{-3}}{2^3}$

35. $\dfrac{10^{-1}}{10^4}$

36. $\dfrac{10^{-3}}{10^{-7}}$

37. $3^{-2} + 2^{-3}$

38. $2^{-3} + 5^{-1}$

39. $\left(\dfrac{2}{3}\right)^{-1} - \left(\dfrac{3}{4}\right)^{-1}$

40. $3^{-2} - 2^3$

41. $(2^{-4} + 3^{-1})^{-1}$

42. $(3^{-2} - 5^{-1})^{-1}$

Simplify Problems 43–62; express final results without using zero or negative integers as exponents. **(Objective 2)**

43. $x^3 \cdot x^{-7}$

44. $x^{-2} \cdot x^{-3}$

45. $a^2 \cdot a^{-3} \cdot a^{-1}$

46. $b^{-3} \cdot b^5 \cdot b^{-4}$

47. $(a^{-3})^2$

48. $(b^5)^{-2}$

49. $(x^3y^{-4})^{-1}$

50. $(x^4y^{-2})^{-2}$

51. $(ab^2c^{-1})^{-3}$

52. $(a^2b^{-1}c^{-2})^{-4}$

53. $(2x^2y^{-1})^{-2}$

54. $(3x^4y^{-2})^{-1}$

55. $\left(\dfrac{x^{-2}}{y^{-3}}\right)^{-2}$

56. $\left(\dfrac{y^4}{x^{-1}}\right)^{-3}$

57. $\left(\dfrac{2a^{-1}}{3b^{-2}}\right)^{-2}$

58. $\left(\dfrac{3x^2y}{4a^{-1}b^{-3}}\right)^{-1}$

59. $\dfrac{x^{-5}}{x^{-2}}$

60. $\dfrac{a^{-3}}{a^5}$

61. $\dfrac{a^2b^{-3}}{a^{-1}b^{-2}}$

62. $\dfrac{x^{-1}y^{-2}}{x^3y^{-1}}$

For Problems 63–70, find the indicated products, quotients, and powers; express answers without using zero or negative integers as exponents. **(Objective 2)**

63. $(4x^3y^2)(-5xy^3)$

64. $(-6xy)(3x^2y^4)$

65. $(-3xy^3)^3$

66. $(-2x^2y^4)^4$

67. $\left(\dfrac{2x^2}{3y^3}\right)^3$

68. $\left(\dfrac{4x}{5y^2}\right)^3$

69. $\dfrac{72x^8}{-9x^2}$

70. $\dfrac{108x^6}{-12x^2}$

For Problems 71–80, find the indicated products and quotients; express results using positive integral exponents only. **(Objective 2)**

71. $(2x^{-1}y^2)(3x^{-2}y^{-3})$

72. $(4x^{-2}y^3)(-5x^3y^{-4})$

73. $(-6a^5y^{-4})(-a^{-7}y)$

74. $(-8a^{-4}b^{-5})(-6a^{-1}b^8)$

75. $\dfrac{24x^{-1}y^{-2}}{6x^{-4}y^3}$

76. $\dfrac{56xy^{-3}}{8x^2y^2}$

77. $\dfrac{-35a^3b^{-2}}{7a^5b^{-1}}$

78. $\dfrac{27a^{-4}b^{-5}}{-3a^{-2}b^{-4}}$

79. $\left(\dfrac{14x^{-2}y^{-4}}{7x^{-3}y^{-6}}\right)^{-2}$

80. $\left(\dfrac{24x^5y^{-3}}{-8x^6y^{-1}}\right)^{-3}$

For Problems 81–88, express each as a single fraction involving positive exponents only. **(Objective 2)**

81. $x^{-1} + x^{-2}$

82. $x^{-2} + x^{-4}$

83. $x^{-2} - y^{-1}$

84. $2x^{-1} - 3y^{-3}$

85. $3a^{-2} + 2b^{-3}$

86. $a^{-2} + a^{-1}b^{-2}$

87. $x^{-1}y - xy^{-1}$

88. $x^2y^{-1} - x^{-3}y^2$

For Problems 89–98, find the following products and quotients. Assume that all variables appearing as exponents represent integers. **(Objective 2)** For example,

$$(x^{2b})(x^{-b+1}) = x^{2b+(-b+1)} = x^{b+1}$$

89. $(3x^a)(4x^{2a+1})$

90. $(5x^{-a})(-6x^{3a-1})$

91. $(x^a)(x^{-a})$

92. $(-2y^{3b})(-4y^{b+1})$

93. $\dfrac{x^{3a}}{x^a}$

94. $\dfrac{4x^{2a+1}}{2x^{a-2}}$

95. $\dfrac{-24y^{5b+1}}{6y^{-b-1}}$

96. $(x^a)^{2b}(x^b)^a$

97. $\dfrac{(xy)^b}{y^b}$

98. $\dfrac{(2x^{2b})(-4x^{b+1})}{8x^{-b+2}}$

For Problems 99–102, express each number in scientific notation. **(Objective 3)**

99. 62,000,000

100. 17,000,000,000

101. 0.000412

102. 0.000000078

For Problems 103–106, change each number from scientific notation to ordinary decimal form. **(Objective 4)**

103. $(1.8)(10^5)$

104. $(5.41)(10^7)$

105. $(2.3)(10^{-6})$

106. $(4.13)(10^{-9})$

For Problems 107–112, use scientific notation and the properties of exponents to help perform the indicated operations. **(Objective 5)**

107. $\dfrac{0.00052}{0.013}$

108. $\dfrac{(0.000075)(4,800,000)}{(15,000)(0.0012)}$

109. $\sqrt{900,000,000}$

110. $\sqrt{0.000004}$

111. $\sqrt{0.0009}$

112. $\dfrac{(0.00069)(0.0034)}{(0.0000017)(0.023)}$

Thoughts Into Words

113. Explain how you would simplify $(3^{-1} \cdot 2^{-2})^{-1}$ and also how you would simplify $(3^{-1} + 2^{-2})^{-1}$.

114. How would you explain why the product of x^2 and x^4 is x^6 and not x^8?

Graphing Calculator Activities

115. Use your calculator to check your answers for Problems 107–112.

116. Use your calculator to evaluate each of the following. Express final answers in ordinary notation.

(a) $(27,000)^2$

(b) $(450,000)^2$

(c) $(14,800)^2$

(d) $(1700)^3$

(e) $(900)^4$

(f) $(60)^5$

(g) $(0.0213)^2$

(h) $(0.000213)^2$

(i) $(0.000198)^2$

(j) $(0.000009)^3$

117. Use your calculator to estimate each of the following. Express final answers in scientific notation with the number between 1 and 10 rounded to the nearest one-thousandth.

(a) $(4576)^4$

(b) $(719)^{10}$

(c) $(28)^{12}$

(d) $(8619)^6$

(e) $(314)^5$

(f) $(145,723)^2$

118. Use your calculator to estimate each of the following. Express final answers in ordinary notation rounded to the nearest one-thousandth.

(a) $(1.09)^5$ **(b)** $(1.08)^{10}$

(c) $(1.14)^7$ **(d)** $(1.12)^{20}$

(e) $(0.785)^4$ **(f)** $(0.492)^5$

Answers to the Concept Quiz

1. True **2.** False **3.** False **4.** False **5.** False **6.** False **7.** False **8.** False **9.** True **10.** False

0.3 Polynomials

OBJECTIVES

1 Add and subtract polynomials

2 Multiply polynomials

3 Perform binomial expansions

4 Divide a polynomial by a monomial

Recall that algebraic expressions such as $5x$, $-6y^2$, $2x^{-1}y^{-2}$, $14a^2b$, $5x^{-4}$, and $-17ab^2c^3$ are called **terms**. Terms that contain variables with only nonnegative integers as exponents are called **monomials**. Of the previously listed terms, $5x$, $-6y^2$, $14a^2b$, and $-17ab^2c^3$ are monomials. The **degree** of a monomial is the sum of the exponents of the literal factors. For example, $7xy$ is of degree 2, whereas $14a^2b$ is of degree 3, and $-17ab^2c^3$ is of degree 6. If the monomial contains only one variable, then the exponent of that variable is the degree of the monomial. For example, $5x^3$ is of degree 3, and $-8y^4$ is of degree 4. Any nonzero constant term, such as 8, is of degree zero.

A **polynomial** is a monomial or a finite sum of monomials. Thus all of the following are examples of polynomials:

$$4x^2 \qquad\qquad 3x^2 - 2x - 4 \qquad 7x^4 - 6x^3 + 5x^2 - 2x - 1$$

$$3x^2y + 2y \qquad \frac{1}{5}a^2 - \frac{2}{3}b^2 \qquad 14$$

In addition to calling a polynomial with one term a monomial, we classify polynomials with two terms as **binomials** and those with three terms as **trinomials**. The **degree of a polynomial** is the degree of the term with the highest degree in the polynomial. The following examples illustrate some of this terminology:

The polynomial $4x^3y^4$ is a monomial in two variables of degree 7.

The polynomial $4x^2y - 2xy$ is a binomial in two variables of degree 3.

The polynomial $9x^2 - 7x - 1$ is a trinomial in one variable of degree 2.

Addition and Subtraction of Polynomials

Both adding polynomials and subtracting them rely on the same basic ideas. The commutative, associative, and distributive properties provide the basis for rearranging, regrouping, and combining similar terms. Consider the following addition problems:

$$(4x^2 + 5x + 1) + (7x^2 - 9x + 4) = (4x^2 + 7x^2) + (5x - 9x) + (1 + 4)$$
$$= 11x^2 - 4x + 5$$

$$(5x - 3) + (3x + 2) + (8x + 6) = (5x + 3x + 8x) + (-3 + 2 + 6)$$
$$= 16x + 5$$

The definition of subtraction as *adding the opposite* $[a - b = a + (-b)]$ extends to polynomials in general. The opposite of a polynomial can be formed by taking the opposite of each term. For example, the opposite of $3x^2 - 7x + 1$ is $-3x^2 + 7x - 1$. Symbolically, this is expressed as

$$-(3x^2 - 7x + 1) = -3x^2 + 7x - 1$$

You can also think in terms of the property $-x = -1(x)$ and the distributive property. Therefore,

$$-(3x^2 - 7x + 1) = -1(3x^2 - 7x + 1) = -3x^2 + 7x - 1$$

Now consider the following subtraction problems:

$$(7x^2 - 2x - 4) - (3x^2 + 7x - 1) = (7x^2 - 2x - 4) + (-3x^2 - 7x + 1)$$
$$= (7x^2 - 3x^2) + (-2x - 7x) + (-4 + 1)$$
$$= 4x^2 - 9x - 3$$

$$(4y^2 + 7) - (-3y^2 + y - 2) = (4y^2 + 7) + (3y^2 - y + 2)$$
$$= (4y^2 + 3y^2) + (-y) + (7 + 2)$$
$$= 7y^2 - y + 9$$

Multiplying Polynomials

The distributive property is usually stated as $a(b+c) = ab+ac$, but it can be extended as follows:

$$a(b + c + d) = ab + ac + ad$$
$$a(b + c + d + e) = ab + ac + ad + ae \qquad \text{etc.}$$

The commutative and associative properties, the properties of exponents, and the distributive property work together to form the basis for finding the product of a monomial and a polynomial with more than one term. The following example illustrates this idea:

$$3x^2(2x^2 + 5x + 3) = 3x^2(2x^2) + 3x^2(5x) + 3x^2(3)$$
$$= 6x^4 + 15x^3 + 9x^2$$

Extending the method of finding the product of a monomial and a polynomial to finding the product of two polynomials, each of which has more than one term, is again based on the distributive property:

$$\begin{aligned}(x + 2)(y + 5) &= x(y + 5) + 2(y + 5)\\ &= x(y) + x(5) + 2(y) + 2(5)\\ &= xy + 5x + 2y + 10\end{aligned}$$

In the next example, notice that each term of the first polynomial multiplies each term of the second polynomial:

$$\begin{aligned}(x - 3)(y + z + 3) &= x(y + z + 3) - 3(y + z + 3)\\ &= xy + xz + 3x - 3y - 3z - 9\end{aligned}$$

Frequently, multiplying polynomials produces similar terms that can be combined, which simplifies the resulting polynomial:

$$\begin{aligned}(x + 5)(x + 7) &= x(x + 7) + 5(x + 7)\\ &= x^2 + 7x + 5x + 35\\ &= x^2 + 12x + 35\end{aligned}$$

In a previous algebra course, you may have developed a shortcut for multiplying binomials, as illustrated by Figure 0.17.

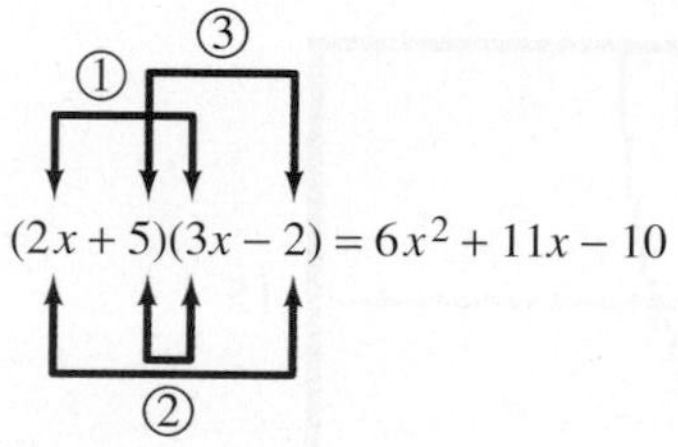
③
①
(2x + 5)(3x − 2) = 6x² + 11x − 10
②

Figure 0.17

STEP 1 Multiply $(2x)(3x)$.

STEP 2 Multiply $(5)(3x)$ and $(2x)(-2)$ and combine.

STEP 3 Multiply $(5)(-2)$.

Remark: Shortcuts can be very helpful for certain manipulations in mathematics. But a word of caution: Do not lose the understanding of what you are doing. Make sure that you are able to do the manipulation without the shortcut.

Keep in mind that the shortcut illustrated in Figure 0.17 applies only to multiplying two binomials. The next example applies the distributive property to find the product of a binomial and a trinomial:

$$\begin{aligned}(x - 2)(x^2 - 3x + 4) &= x(x^2 - 3x + 4) - 2(x^2 - 3x + 4)\\ &= x^3 - 3x^2 + 4x - 2x^2 + 6x - 8\\ &= x^3 - 5x^2 + 10x - 8\end{aligned}$$

In this example we are claiming that

$$(x - 2)(x^2 - 3x + 4) = x^3 - 5x^2 + 10x - 8$$

for all real numbers. In addition to going back over our work, how can we verify such a claim? Obviously, we cannot try all real numbers, but trying at least one number gives us a partial check. Let's try the number 4:

$$(x - 2)(x^2 - 3x + 4) = (4 - 2)(4^2 - 3(4) + 4)$$
$$= 2(16 - 12 + 4)$$
$$= 2(8)$$
$$= 16$$

$$x^3 - 5x^2 + 10x - 8 = 4^3 - 5(4)^2 + 10(4) - 8$$
$$= 64 - 80 + 40 - 8$$
$$= 16$$

We can also use a graphical approach as a partial check for such a problem. In Figure 0.18, we let $Y_1 = (x - 2)(x^2 - 3x + 4)$ and $Y_2 = x^3 - 5x^2 + 10x - 8$ and graphed them on the same set of axes. Note that the graphs appear to be identical.

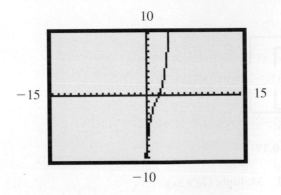

Figure 0.18

Remark: Graphing on the Cartesian coordinate system is not formally reviewed in this text until Chapter 2. However, we feel confident that your knowledge of this topic from previous mathematics courses is sufficient for what we are doing at this time.

Exponents can also be used to indicate repeated multiplication of polynomials. For example, $(3x - 4y)^2$ means $(3x - 4y)(3x - 4y)$, and $(x + 4)^3$ means $(x + 4)(x + 4)(x + 4)$. Therefore, raising a polynomial to a power is merely another multiplication problem.

$$(3x - 4y)^2 = (3x - 4y)(3x - 4y)$$
$$= 9x^2 - 24xy + 16y^2$$

[*Hint*: When squaring a binomial, be careful not to forget the middle term. That is, $(x + 5)^2 \neq x^2 + 25$; instead, $(x + 5)^2 = x^2 + 10x + 25$.]

$$(x + 4)^3 = (x + 4)(x + 4)(x + 4)$$
$$= (x + 4)(x^2 + 8x + 16)$$
$$= x(x^2 + 8x + 16) + 4(x^2 + 8x + 16)$$
$$= x^3 + 8x^2 + 16x + 4x^2 + 32x + 64$$
$$= x^3 + 12x^2 + 48x + 64$$

Special Patterns

In multiplying binomials, you should learn to recognize some special patterns. These patterns can be used to find products, and some of them will be helpful later when you are factoring polynomials.

$$(a + b)^2 = a^2 + 2ab + b^2$$
$$(a - b)^2 = a^2 - 2ab + b^2$$
$$(a + b)(a - b) = a^2 - b^2$$
$$(a + b)^3 = a^3 + 3a^2b + 3ab^2 + b^3$$
$$(a - b)^3 = a^3 - 3a^2b + 3ab^2 - b^3$$

The three following examples illustrate the first three patterns, respectively:

$$(2x + 3)^2 = (2x)^2 + 2(2x)(3) + (3)^2$$
$$= 4x^2 + 12x + 9$$
$$(5x - 2)^2 = (5x)^2 - 2(5x)(2) + (2)^2$$
$$= 25x^2 - 20x + 4$$
$$(3x + 2y)(3x - 2y) = (3x)^2 - (2y)^2 = 9x^2 - 4y^2$$

In the first two examples, the resulting trinomial is called a **perfect-square trinomial**; it is the result of squaring a binomial. In the third example, the resulting binomial is called the **difference of two squares**. Later, we will use both of these patterns extensively when factoring polynomials.

The cubing-of-a-binomial patterns are helpful primarily when you are multiplying. These patterns can shorten the work of cubing a binomial, as the next two examples illustrate:

$$(3x + 2)^3 = (3x)^3 + 3(3x)^2(2) + 3(3x)(2)^2 + (2)^3$$
$$= 27x^3 + 54x^2 + 36x + 8$$
$$(5x - 2y)^3 = (5x)^3 - 3(5x)^2(2y) + 3(5x)(2y)^2 - (2y)^3$$
$$= 125x^3 - 150x^2y + 60xy^2 - 8y^3$$

Keep in mind that these multiplying patterns are useful shortcuts, but if you forget them, simply revert to applying the distributive property.

Binomial Expansion Pattern

It is possible to write the expansion of $(a + b)^n$, where n is *any* positive integer, without showing all of the intermediate steps of multiplying and combining similar terms. To do this, let's observe some patterns in the following examples; each one can be verified by direct multiplication:

$$(a + b)^1 = a + b$$
$$(a + b)^2 = a^2 + 2ab + b^2$$
$$(a + b)^3 = a^3 + 3a^2b + 3ab^2 + b^3$$
$$(a + b)^4 = a^4 + 4a^3b + 6a^2b^2 + 4ab^3 + b^4$$
$$(a + b)^5 = a^5 + 5a^4b + 10a^3b^2 + 10a^2b^3 + 5ab^4 + b^5$$

First, note the patterns of the exponents for a and b on a term-by-term basis. The exponents of a begin with the exponent of the binomial and decrease by 1, term by term, until the last term, which has $a^0 = 1$. The exponents of b begin with zero ($b^0 = 1$) and increase by 1, term by term, until the last term, which contains b to the power of the original binomial. In other words, the variables in the expansion of $(a + b)^n$ have the pattern

$$a^n, \qquad a^{n-1}b, \qquad a^{n-2}b^2, \qquad \ldots, \qquad ab^{n-1}, \qquad b^n$$

where, for each term, the *sum* of the exponents of a and b is n.

Next, let's arrange the *coefficients* in a triangular formation; this yields an easy-to-remember pattern.

Row number n in the formation contains the coefficients of the expansion of $(a + b)^n$. For example, the fifth row contains 1   5   10   10   5   1, and these numbers are the coefficients of the terms in the expansion of $(a + b)^5$. Furthermore, each can be formed from the previous row as follows:

1. Start and end each row with 1.

2. All other entries result from adding the two numbers in the row immediately above, one number to the left and one number to the right.

Thus from row 5, we can form row 6.

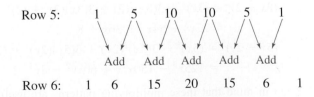

Now we can use these seven coefficients and our discussion about the exponents to write out the expansion for $(a + b)^6$.

$$(a + b)^6 = a^6 + 6a^5b + 15a^4b^2 + 20a^3b^3 + 15a^2b^4 + 6ab^5 + b^6$$

Remark: The triangular formation of numbers that we have been discussing is often referred to as *Pascal's triangle*. This is in honor of Blaise Pascal, a 17th-century mathematician, to whom the discovery of this pattern is attributed.

Let's consider two more examples using Pascal's triangle and the exponent relationships.

Classroom Example
Expand $(x - y)^5$.

EXAMPLE 1   Expand $(a - b)^4$.

Solution

We can treat $a - b$ as $a + (-b)$ and use the fourth row of Pascal's triangle (1, 4, 6, 4, 1) to obtain the coefficients:

$$[a + (-b)]^4 = a^4 + 4a^3(-b) + 6a^2(-b)^2 + 4a(-b)^3 + (-b)^4$$
$$= a^4 - 4a^3b + 6a^2b^2 - 4ab^3 + b^4$$

Classroom Example
Expand $(3a + 2b)^4$.

EXAMPLE 2   Expand $(2x + 3y)^5$.

Solution

Let $2x = a$ and $3y = b$. The coefficients (1, 5, 10, 10, 5, 1) come from the fifth row of Pascal's triangle:

$$(2x + 3y)^5 = (2x)^5 + 5(2x)^4(3y) + 10(2x)^3(3y)^2 + 10(2x)^2(3y)^3 + 5(2x)(3y)^4 + (3y)^5$$
$$= 32x^5 + 240x^4y + 720x^3y^2 + 1080x^2y^3 + 810xy^4 + 243y^5$$

Dividing Polynomials by Monomials

In Section 0.5 we will review the addition and subtraction of rational expressions using the properties

$$\frac{a}{b} + \frac{c}{b} = \frac{a + c}{b} \quad \text{and} \quad \frac{a}{b} - \frac{c}{b} = \frac{a - c}{b}$$

These properties can also be viewed as

$$\frac{a + c}{b} = \frac{a}{b} + \frac{c}{b} \quad \text{and} \quad \frac{a - c}{b} = \frac{a}{b} - \frac{c}{b}$$

Together with our knowledge of dividing monomials, these properties provide the basis for dividing polynomials by monomials. Consider the following examples:

$$\frac{18x^3 + 24x^2}{6x} = \frac{18x^3}{6x} + \frac{24x^2}{6x} = 3x^2 + 4x$$

$$\frac{35x^2y^3 - 55x^3y^4}{5xy^2} = \frac{35x^2y^3}{5xy^2} - \frac{55x^3y^4}{5xy^2} = 7xy - 11x^2y^2$$

Therefore, to divide a polynomial by a monomial, we divide each term of the polynomial by the monomial. As with many skills, once you feel comfortable with the process, you may then choose to perform some of the steps mentally. Your work could take the following format:

$$\frac{40x^4y^5 + 72x^5y^7}{8x^2y} = 5x^2y^4 + 9x^3y^6$$

$$\frac{36a^3b^4 - 48a^3b^3 + 64a^2b^5}{-4a^2b^2} = -9ab^2 + 12ab - 16b^3$$

Concept Quiz 0.3

For Problems 1–8, answer true or false.

1. The variables of a monomial term have exponents that are either positive integers or zero.
2. The term, 3^2xy^2, is of degree 5.
3. Any nonzero constant term is of degree zero.
4. A polynomial is a monomial or a finite sum of monomials.
5. A polynomial with three terms is classified as a binomial.
6. $(x - 6)^2 = x^2 + 36$
7. A perfect-square trinomial is the result when a trinomial is squared.
8. Row number 4 in Pascal's triangle contains the coefficients of the expansion of $(a + b)^3$.

Problem Set 0.3

For Problems 1–10, perform the indicated operations. (Objective 1)

1. $(5x^2 - 7x - 2) + (9x^2 + 8x - 4)$

2. $(-9x^2 + 8x + 4) + (7x^2 - 5x - 3)$

3. $(14x^2 - x - 1) - (15x^2 + 3x + 8)$

4. $(-3x^2 + 2x + 4) - (4x^2 + 6x - 5)$

5. $(3x - 4) - (6x + 3) + (9x - 4)$

6. $(7a - 2) - (8a - 1) - (10a - 2)$

7. $(8x^2 - 6x - 2) + (x^2 - x - 1) - (3x^2 - 2x + 4)$

8. $(12x^2 + 7x - 2) - (3x^2 + 4x + 5) + (-4x^2 - 7x - 2)$

9. $5(x - 2) - 4(x + 3) - 2(x + 6)$

10. $3(2x - 1) - 2(3x + 4) - 4(5x - 1)$

For Problems 11–54, find the indicated products. Remember the special patterns that we discussed in this section. **(Objective 2)**

11. $3xy(4x^2y + 5xy^2)$

12. $-2ab^2(3a^2b - 4ab^3)$

13. $6a^3b^2(5ab - 4a^2b + 3ab^2)$

14. $-xy^4(5x^2y - 4xy^2 + 3x^2y^2)$

15. $(x + 8)(x + 12)$ **16.** $(x - 9)(x + 6)$

17. $(n - 4)(n - 12)$ **18.** $(n + 6)(n - 10)$

19. $(s - t)(x + y)$ **20.** $(a + b)(c + d)$

21. $(3x - 1)(2x + 3)$ **22.** $(5x + 2)(3x + 4)$

23. $(4x - 3)(3x - 7)$ **24.** $(4n + 3)(6n - 1)$

25. $(x + 4)^2$ **26.** $(x - 6)^2$

27. $(2n + 3)^2$ **28.** $(3n - 5)^2$

29. $(x + 2)(x - 4)(x + 3)$

30. $(x - 1)(x + 6)(x - 5)$

31. $(x - 1)(2x + 3)(3x - 2)$

32. $(2x + 5)(x - 4)(3x + 1)$

33. $(x - 1)(x^2 + 3x - 4)$

34. $(t + 1)(t^2 - 2t - 4)$

35. $(t - 1)(t^2 + t + 1)$

36. $(2x - 1)(x^2 + 4x + 3)$

37. $(3x + 2)(2x^2 - x - 1)$

38. $(3x - 2)(2x^2 + 3x + 4)$

39. $(x^2 + 2x - 1)(x^2 + 6x + 4)$

40. $(x^2 - x + 4)(2x^2 - 3x - 1)$

41. $(5x - 2)(5x + 2)$ **42.** $(3x - 4)(3x + 4)$

43. $(x^2 - 5x - 2)^2$ **44.** $(-x^2 + x - 1)^2$

45. $(2x + 3y)(2x - 3y)$ **46.** $(9x + y)(9x - y)$

47. $(x + 5)^3$ **48.** $(x - 6)^3$

49. $(2x + 1)^3$ **50.** $(3x + 4)^3$

51. $(4x - 3)^3$ **52.** $(2x - 5)^3$

53. $(5x - 2y)^3$ **54.** $(x + 3y)^3$

For Problems 55–66, use Pascal's triangle to help expand each expression. **(Objective 3)**

55. $(a + b)^7$

56. $(a + b)^8$

57. $(x - y)^5$

58. $(x - y)^6$

59. $(x + 2y)^4$

60. $(2x + y)^5$

61. $(2a - b)^6$

62. $(3a - b)^4$

63. $(x^2 + y)^7$

64. $(x + 2y^2)^7$

65. $(2a - 3b)^5$

66. $(4a - 3b)^3$

For Problems 67–72, perform the indicated divisions.

67. $\dfrac{15x^4 - 25x^3}{5x^2}$ **68.** $\dfrac{-48x^8 - 72x^6}{-8x^4}$

69. $\dfrac{30a^5 - 24a^3 + 54a^2}{-6a}$ **70.** $\dfrac{18x^3y^2 + 27x^2y^3}{3xy}$

71. $\dfrac{-20a^3b^2 - 44a^4b^5}{-4a^2b}$

72. $\dfrac{21x^5y^6 + 28x^4y^3 - 35x^5y^4}{7x^2y^3}$

For Problems 73–82, find the indicated products. Assume all variables that appear as exponents represent integers. **(Objectives 2 and 3)**

73. $(x^a + y^b)(x^a - y^b)$ **74.** $(x^{2a} + 1)(x^{2a} - 3)$

75. $(x^b + 4)(x^b - 7)$ **76.** $(3x^a - 2)(x^a + 5)$

77. $(2x^b - 1)(3x^b + 2)$ **78.** $(2x^a - 3)(2x^a + 3)$

79. $(x^{2a} - 1)^2$ **80.** $(x^{3b} + 2)^2$

81. $(x^a - 2)^3$ **82.** $(x^b + 3)^3$

Thoughts Into Words

83. Describe how to multiply two binomials.

84. Describe how to multiply a binomial and a trinomial.

85. Determine the number of terms in the product of $(x + y)$ and $(a + b + c + d)$ without doing the multiplication. Explain how you arrived at your answer.

Graphing Calculator Activities

86. Use the computing feature of your graphing calculator to check at least one real number for your answers for Problems 29–40.

87. Use the graphing feature of your graphing calculator to give visual support for your answers for Problems 47–52.

88. Some of the product patterns can be used to do arithmetic computations mentally. For example, let's use the pattern $(a + b)^2 = a^2 + 2ab + b^2$ to compute 31^2 mentally. Your thought process should be "$31^2 = (30 + 1)^2 = 30^2 + 2(30)(1) + 1^2 = 961$." Compute each of the following numbers mentally, and then check your answers with your calculator.

(a) 21^2 **(b)** 41^2

(c) 71^2 **(d)** 32^2

(e) 52^2 **(f)** 82^2

89. Use the pattern $(a - b)^2 = a^2 - 2ab + b^2$ to compute each of the following numbers mentally, and then check your answers with your calculator.

(a) 19^2 **(b)** 29^2

(c) 49^2 **(d)** 79^2

(e) 38^2 **(f)** 58^2

90. Every whole number with a units digit of 5 can be represented by the expression $10x + 5$, where x is a whole number. For example, $35 = 10(3) + 5$ and $145 = 10(14) + 5$. Now let's observe the following pattern when squaring such a number:

$$(10x + 5)^2 = 100x^2 + 100x + 25$$
$$= 100x(x + 1) + 25$$

The pattern inside the dashed box can be stated as "add 25 to the product of x, $x + 1$, and 100." Thus to compute 35^2 mentally, we can think "$35^2 = 3(4)(100) + 25 = 1225$." Compute each of the following numbers mentally, and then check your answers with your calculator.

(a) 15^2 **(b)** 25^2

(c) 45^2 **(d)** 55^2

(e) 65^2 **(f)** 75^2

(g) 85^2 **(h)** 95^2

(i) 105^2

Answers to the Concept Quiz

1. True   **2.** False   **3.** True   **4.** True   **5.** False   **6.** False   **7.** False   **8.** False

0.4   Factoring Polynomials

OBJECTIVES

1 Factor out a common factor

2 Factor by grouping

3 Factor the difference of two squares

4 Factor trinomials

5 Factor the sum or difference of two cubes

6 Apply more than one factoring technique

If a polynomial is equal to the product of other polynomials, then each polynomial in the product is called a **factor** of the original polynomial. For example, because $x^2 - 4$ can be expressed as $(x + 2)(x - 2)$, we say that $x + 2$ and $x - 2$ are factors of $x^2 - 4$. The process of expressing a polynomial as a product of polynomials is called **factoring.** In this section we will consider methods of factoring polynomials with integer coefficients.

In general, factoring is the reverse of multiplication, so we can use our knowledge of multiplication to help develop factoring techniques. For example, we previously used the distributive property to find the product of a monomial and a polynomial, as the next examples illustrate.

$$3(x + 2) = 3(x) + 3(2) = 3x + 6$$
$$3x(x + 4) = 3x(x) + 3x(4) = 3x^2 + 12x$$

For factoring purposes, the distributive property [now in the form $ab + ac = a(b + c)$] can be used to reverse the process.

$$3x + 6 = 3(x) + 3(2) = 3(x + 2)$$
$$3x^2 + 12x = 3x(x) + 3x(4) = 3x(x + 4)$$

Polynomials can be factored in a variety of ways. Consider some factorizations of $3x^2 + 12x$:

$$3x^2 + 12x = 3x(x + 4) \quad \text{or} \quad 3x^2 + 12x = 3(x^2 + 4x) \quad \text{or}$$

$$3x^2 + 12x = x(3x + 12) \quad \text{or} \quad 3x^2 + 12x = \frac{1}{2}(6x^2 + 24x)$$

We are, however, primarily interested in the first of these factorization forms; we refer to it as the **completely factored form.** A polynomial with integral coefficients is in completely factored form if:

1. it is expressed as a product of polynomials with *integral coefficients,* and

2. no polynomial, other than a monomial, within the factored form can be further factored into polynomials with integral coefficients.

Do you see why only the first of the factored forms of $3x^2 + 12x$ is said to be in completely factored form? In each of the other three forms, the polynomial inside the parentheses can be factored further. Moreover, in the last form, $\frac{1}{2}(6x^2 + 24x)$, the condition of using only integers is violated.

This application of the distributive property is often referred to as **factoring out the highest common monomial factor.** The following examples illustrate the process:

$$12x^3 + 16x^2 = 4x^2(3x + 4)$$
$$8ab - 18b = 2b(4a - 9)$$
$$6x^2y^3 + 27xy^4 = 3xy^3(2x + 9y)$$
$$30x^3 + 42x^4 - 24x^5 = 6x^3(5 + 7x - 4x^2)$$

Sometimes there may be a common *binomial* factor rather than a common monomial factor. For example, each of the two terms in the expression $x(y + 2) + z(y + 2)$ has a binomial factor of $y + 2$. Thus we can factor $y + 2$ from each term and obtain the following result:

$$x(y + 2) + z(y + 2) = (y + 2)(x + z)$$

Consider a few more examples involving a common binomial factor:

$$a^2(b + 1) + 2(b + 1) = (b + 1)(a^2 + 2)$$
$$x(2y - 1) - y(2y - 1) = (2y - 1)(x - y)$$
$$x(x + 2) + 3(x + 2) = (x + 2)(x + 3)$$

Factoring by Grouping

It may seem that a given polynomial exhibits no apparent common monomial or binomial factor. Such is the case with $ab + 3c + bc + 3a$. However, by using the commutative property to rearrange the terms, we can factor it as follows.

$$ab + 3c + bc + 3a = ab + 3a + bc + 3c$$

$= a(b + 3) + c(b + 3)$	Factor a from the first two terms and c from the last two terms
$= (b + 3)(a + c)$	Factor $b + 3$ from both terms

This factoring process is referred to as **factoring by grouping.** Let's consider another example of this type.

$ab^2 - 4b^2 + 3a - 12 = b^2(a - 4) + 3(a - 4)$	Factor b^2 from the first two terms, 3 from the last two
$= (a - 4)(b^2 + 3)$	Factor the common binomial from both terms

Difference of Two Squares

In Section 0.3 we called your attention to some special multiplication patterns. One of these patterns was

$$(a + b)(a - b) = a^2 - b^2$$

This same pattern, viewed as a factoring pattern,

$$a^2 - b^2 = (a + b)(a - b)$$

is referred to as the **difference of two squares.** Applying the pattern is a fairly simple process, as these next examples illustrate.

$$x^2 - 16 = (x)^2 - (4)^2 = (x + 4)(x - 4)$$
$$4x^2 - 25 = (2x)^2 - (5)^2 = (2x + 5)(2x - 5)$$

Because multiplication is commutative, the order in which we write the factors is not important. For example, $(x + 4)(x - 4)$ can also be written $(x - 4)(x + 4)$.

You must be careful not to assume an analogous factoring pattern for the *sum* of two squares; *it does not exist.* For example, $x^2 + 4 \neq (x + 2)(x + 2)$ because $(x + 2)(x + 2) = x^2 + 4x + 4$. We say that a polynomial such as $x^2 + 4$ is **not factorable using integers.**

Sometimes the difference-of-two-squares pattern can be applied more than once, as the next example illustrates:

$$16x^4 - 81y^4 = (4x^2 + 9y^2)(4x^2 - 9y^2) = (4x^2 + 9y^2)(2x + 3y)(2x - 3y)$$

It may also happen that the squares are not just simple monomial squares. These next three examples illustrate such polynomials.

$$(x + 3)^2 - y^2 = [(x + 3) + y][(x + 3) - y] = (x + 3 + y)(x + 3 - y)$$
$$4x^2 - (2y + 1)^2 = [2x + (2y + 1)][2x - (2y + 1)]$$
$$= (2x + 2y + 1)(2x - 2y - 1)$$
$$(x - 1)^2 - (x + 4)^2 = [(x - 1) + (x + 4)][(x - 1) - (x + 4)]$$
$$= (x - 1 + x + 4)(x - 1 - x - 4)$$
$$= (2x + 3)(-5)$$

It is possible that both the technique of factoring out a common monomial factor and the pattern of the difference of two squares can be applied to the same problem. *In general, it is best to look first for a common monomial factor.* Consider the following examples.

$$2x^2 - 50 = 2(x^2 - 25)$$
$$= 2(x + 5)(x - 5)$$
$$48y^3 - 27y = 3y(16y^2 - 9)$$
$$= 3y(4y + 3)(4y - 3)$$
$$9x^2 - 36 = 9(x^2 - 4)$$
$$= 9(x + 2)(x - 2)$$

Factoring Trinomials

Expressing a trinomial as the product of two binomials is one of the most common factoring techniques used in algebra. As before, to develop a factoring technique we first look at some multiplication ideas. Let's consider the product $(x + a)(x + b)$, using the distributive property to show how each term of the resulting trinomial is formed:

$$(x + a)(x + b) = x(x + b) + a(x + b)$$
$$= x(x) + x(b) + a(x) + a(b)$$
$$= x^2 + (a + b)x + ab$$

Notice that the coefficient of the middle term is the *sum* of a and b and that the last term is the *product* of a and b. These two relationships can be used to factor trinomials. Let's consider some examples.

Classroom Example
Factor $a^2 + 12a + 32$.

EXAMPLE 1   Factor $x^2 + 12x + 20$.

Solution

We need two integers whose sum is 12 and whose product is 20. The numbers are 2 and 10, and we can complete the factoring as follows:

$$x^2 + 12x + 20 = (x + 2)(x + 10)$$

Classroom Example
Factor $y^2 - 10y - 24$.

EXAMPLE 2   Factor $x^2 - 3x - 54$.

Solution

We need two integers whose sum is -3 and whose product is -54. The integers are -9 and 6, and we can factor as follows:

$$x^2 - 3x - 54 = (x - 9)(x + 6)$$

Classroom Example
Factor $x^2 + 2x + 12$.

EXAMPLE 3   Factor $x^2 + 7x + 16$.

Solution

We need two integers whose sum is 7 and whose product is 16. The only possible pairs of factors of 16 are $1 \cdot 16$, $2 \cdot 8$, and $4 \cdot 4$. A sum of 7 is not produced by any of these pairs, so the polynomial $x^2 + 7x + 16$ is *not factorable using integers*.

Trinomials of the Form $ax^2 + bx + c$

Now let's consider factoring trinomials where the coefficient of the squared term is not one. First, let's illustrate an informal trial-and-error technique that works well for certain types of trinomials. This technique is based on our knowledge of multiplication of binomials.

EXAMPLE 4   Factor $3x^2 + 5x + 2$.

Solution

By looking at the first term, $3x^2$, and the positive signs of the other two terms, we know that the binomials are of the form

$(x +$ __$)(3x +$ __$)$

Because the factors of the last term, 2, are 1 and 2, we have only the following two possibilities to try.

$(x + 2)(3x + 1)$ or $(x + 1)(3x + 2)$

By checking the middle term formed in each of these products, we find that the second possibility yields the desired middle term of $5x$. Therefore

$3x^2 + 5x + 2 = (x + 1)(3x + 2)$ ■

EXAMPLE 5   Factor $8x^2 - 30xy + 7y^2$.

Solution

First, observe that the first term, $8x^2$, can be written as $2x \cdot 4x$ or $x \cdot 8x$. Second, because the middle term is negative and the last term is positive, we know that the binomials are of the form

$(2x -$ __$)(4x -$ __$)$ or $(x -$ __$)(8x -$ __$)$

Third, because the factors of the last term, $7y^2$, are $1y$ and $7y$, the following possibilities exist.

$(2x - 1y)(4x - 7y)$ $(2x - 7y)(4x - 1y)$
$(x - 1y)(8x - 7y)$ $(x - 7y)(8x - 1y)$

By checking the middle term formed in each of these products, we find that $(2x - 7y)(4x - 1y)$ produces the desired middle term of $-30xy$. Therefore

$8x^2 - 30xy + 7y^2 = (2x - 7y)(4x - y)$ ■

EXAMPLE 6   Factor $10x^2 - 36x - 16$.

Solution

First, note that there is a common factor of 2. By using the distributive property we obtain $10x^2 - 36x - 16 = 2(5x^2 - 18x - 8)$. Now, let's determine if $5x^2 - 18x - 8$ can be factored. The first term, $5x^2$, can be written as $x \cdot 5x$. The last term, -8, can be written as $(-2)(4)$, $(2)(-4)$, $(-1)(8)$, or $(1)(-8)$. Therefore we have the following possibilities to try:

$(x - 2)(5x + 4)$ $(x + 4)(5x - 2)$ $(x - 1)(5x + 8)$ $(x + 8)(5x - 1)$
$(x + 2)(5x - 4)$ $(x - 4)(5x + 2)$ $(x + 1)(5x - 8)$ $(x - 8)(5x + 1)$

By checking the middle terms, we find that $(x - 4)(5x + 2)$ yields the desired middle term of $-18x$. Thus

$10x^2 - 36x - 16 = 2(5x^2 - 18x - 8) = 2(x - 4)(5x + 2)$ ■

EXAMPLE 7   Factor $4x^2 + 6x + 9$.

Solution

The first term, $4x^2$, and the positive signs of the middle and last terms indicate that the binomials are of the form

$$(x + \underline{})(4x + \underline{}) \quad \text{or} \quad (2x + \underline{})(2x + \underline{})$$

Because the factors of the last term, 9, are 1 and 9 or 3 and 3, we have the following possibilities to try:

$$(x + 1)(4x + 9)$$
$$(x + 9)(4x + 1)$$
$$(x + 3)(4x + 3)$$
$$(2x + 1)(2x + 9)$$
$$(2x + 3)(2x + 3)$$

None of these possibilities yields a middle term of $6x$. Therefore $4x^2 + 6x + 9$ is *not factorable using integers.* _____ ■

Certainly, as the number of possibilities increases, this trial-and-error technique for factoring becomes more tedious. The key idea is to organize your work so that all possibilities are considered. We have suggested one possible format in the previous examples. However, as you practice such problems, you may devise a format that works better for you. Whatever works best for you is the right approach.

There is another, more systematic technique that you may wish to use with some trinomials. It is an extension of the technique we used earlier with trinomials where the coefficient of the squared term was one. To see the basis of this technique, consider the following general product:

$$(px + r)(qx + s) = px(qx) + px(s) + r(qx) + r(s)$$
$$= (pq)x^2 + ps(x) + rq(x) + rs$$
$$= (pq)x^2 + (ps + rq)x + rs$$

Notice that the product of the coefficient of x^2 and the constant term is $pqrs$. Likewise, the product of the two coefficients of x (ps and rq) is also $pqrs$. Therefore, the coefficient of x must be a sum of the form $ps + rq$, such that the product of the coefficient of x^2 and the constant term is $pqrs$. Now let's see how this works in some specific examples.

EXAMPLE 8   Factor $6x^2 + 17x + 5$.

Solution

$$6x^2 + 17x + 5 \quad \text{Sum of 17}$$

Product of $6 \cdot 5 = 30$

We need two integers whose sum is 17 and whose product is 30. The integers 2 and 15 satisfy these conditions. Therefore the middle term, $17x$, of the given trinomial can be expressed as $2x + 15x$, and we can proceed as follows:

$$6x^2 + 17x + 5 = 6x^2 + 2x + 15x + 5$$
$$= 2x(3x + 1) + 5(3x + 1) \qquad \text{Factor by grouping}$$
$$= (3x + 1)(2x + 5)$$

Classroom Example
Factor $3y^2 + 16y - 12$.

EXAMPLE 9   Factor $5x^2 - 18x - 8$.

Solution

$$5x^2 - 18x - 8 \qquad \text{Sum of } -18$$

Product of $5(-8) = -40$

We need two integers whose sum is -18 and whose product is -40. The integers -20 and 2 satisfy these conditions. Therefore the middle term, $-18x$, of the trinomial can be written $-20x + 2x$, and we can factor as follows:

$$5x^2 - 18x - 8 = 5x^2 - 20x + 2x - 8$$
$$= 5x(x - 4) + 2(x - 4)$$
$$= (x - 4)(5x + 2)$$

Classroom Example
Factor $8a^2 + 22a - 21$.

EXAMPLE 10   Factor $24x^2 + 2x - 15$.

Solution

$$24x^2 + 2x - 15 \qquad \text{Sum of } 2$$

Product of $24(-15) = -360$

We need two integers whose sum is 2 and whose product is -360. To help find these integers, let's factor 360 into primes:

$$360 = 2 \cdot 2 \cdot 2 \cdot 3 \cdot 3 \cdot 5$$

Now by grouping these factors in various ways, we find that $2 \cdot 2 \cdot 5 = 20$ and $2 \cdot 3 \cdot 3 = 18$, so we can use the integers 20 and -18 to produce a sum of 2 and a product of -360. Therefore, the middle term, $2x$, of the trinomial can be expressed as $20x - 18x$, and we can proceed as follows:

$$24x^2 + 2x - 15 = 24x^2 + 20x - 18x - 15$$
$$= 4x(6x + 5) - 3(6x + 5)$$
$$= (6x + 5)(4x - 3)$$

Probably the best way to check a factoring problem is to make sure the conditions for a polynomial to be completely factored are satisfied, and the product of the factors equals the given polynomial. We can also give some visual support to a factoring problem by graphing the given polynomial and its completely factored form on the same set of axes, as shown for Example 10 in Figure 0.19. Note that the graphs for $Y_1 = 24x^2 + 2x - 15$ and $Y_2 = (6x + 5)(4x - 3)$ appear to be identical.

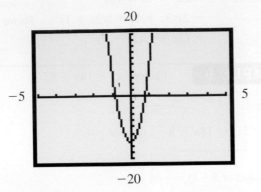

Figure 0.19

Sum and Difference of Two Cubes

Earlier in this section we discussed the difference-of-squares factoring pattern. We pointed out that no analogous sum-of-squares pattern exists; that is, a polynomial such as $x^2 + 9$ is not factorable using integers. However, there do exist patterns for both the *sum* and the *difference of two cubes*. These patterns come from the following special products:

$$(x + y)(x^2 - xy + y^2) = x(x^2 - xy + y^2) + y(x^2 - xy + y^2)$$
$$= x^3 - x^2y + xy^2 + x^2y - xy^2 + y^3$$
$$= x^3 + y^3$$
$$(x - y)(x^2 + xy + y^2) = x(x^2 + xy + y^2) - y(x^2 + xy + y^2)$$
$$= x^3 + x^2y + xy^2 - x^2y - xy^2 - y^3$$
$$= x^3 - y^3$$

Thus we can state the following factoring patterns:

$$x^3 + y^3 = (x + y)(x^2 - xy + y^2)$$
$$x^3 - y^3 = (x - y)(x^2 + xy + y^2)$$

Note how these patterns are used in the next three examples:

$$x^3 + 8 = x^3 + 2^3 = (x + 2)(x^2 - 2x + 4)$$
$$8x^3 - 27y^3 = (2x)^3 - (3y)^3 = (2x - 3y)(4x^2 + 6xy + 9y^2)$$
$$8a^6 + 125b^3 = (2a^2)^3 + (5b)^3 = (2a^2 + 5b)(4a^4 - 10a^2b + 25b^2)$$

Applying More Than One Factoring Technique

We do want to leave you with one final word of caution. **Be sure to factor completely.** Sometimes more than one technique needs to be applied, or perhaps the same technique can be applied more than once. Study the following examples very carefully:

$$2x^2 - 8 = 2(x^2 - 4) = 2(x + 2)(x - 2)$$
$$3x^2 + 18x + 24 = 3(x^2 + 6x + 8) = 3(x + 4)(x + 2)$$
$$3x^3 - 3y^3 = 3(x^3 - y^3) = 3(x - y)(x^2 + xy + y^2)$$
$$a^4 - b^4 = (a^2 + b^2)(a^2 - b^2) = (a^2 + b^2)(a + b)(a - b)$$
$$x^4 - 6x^2 - 27 = (x^2 - 9)(x^2 + 3) = (x + 3)(x - 3)(x^2 + 3)$$
$$3x^4y + 9x^2y - 84y = 3y(x^4 + 3x^2 - 28)$$
$$= 3y(x^2 + 7)(x^2 - 4)$$
$$= 3y(x^2 + 7)(x + 2)(x - 2)$$
$$x^2 - y^2 + 8y - 16 = x^2 - (y^2 - 8y + 16)$$
$$= x^2 - (y - 4)^2$$
$$= (x - (y - 4))(x + (y - 4))$$
$$= (x - y + 4)(x + y - 4)$$

Concept Quiz 0.4

For Problems 1–8, answer true or false.

1. The process of expressing a polynomial as a product of polynomials is called factoring.
2. $x^2(5x - 10)$ is the completely factored form of $5x^2 - 10x^2$.
3. The polynomial, $3a^3b - 4c^2d + 5bd$, does not have a common factor.
4. The sum of two squares is not factorable using integers.
5. The sum of two cubes is not factorable using integers.
6. A factoring problem can be partially checked by making sure the product of the factors equals the polynomial.
7. All trinomials are factorable using integers.
8. All common factors are monomial factors.

Problem Set 0.4

For Problems 1–6, factor completely by factoring out the common factor. (Objective 1)

1. $6xy - 8xy^2$

2. $4a^2b^2 + 12ab^3$

3. $12x^2y^3z^4 - 6x^4y^3z^3 + 6x^2y^3z^2$

4. $3m^2n - 6m^4n^3 - 9m^5n^4$

5. $x(z + 3) + y(z + 3)$

6. $5(x + y) + a(x + y)$

For Problems 7–10, factor completely by using grouping. (Objective 2)

7. $3x + 3y + ax + ay$ 8. $ac + bc + a + b$

9. $ax - ay - bx + by$ 10. $2a^2 - 3bc - 2ab + 3ac$

For Problems 11–18, factor by applying the difference-of-squares pattern. (Objective 3)

11. $9x^2 - 25$ 12. $36x^2 - 121$

13. $1 - 81n^2$ 14. $9x^2y^2 - 64$

15. $(x + 4)^2 - y^2$ 16. $x^2 - (y - 1)^2$

17. $9s^2 - (2t - 1)^2$ 18. $4a^2 - (3b + 1)^2$

For Problems 19–36, factor each trinomial. Indicate any that are not factorable using integers. (Objective 4)

19. $x^2 - 5x - 14$

20. $a^2 + 5a - 24$

21. $15 - 2x - x^2$

22. $40 - 6x - x^2$

23. $x^2 + 7x - 36$

24. $x^2 - 4xy - 5y^2$

25. $3x^2 - 11x + 10$

26. $2x^2 - 7x - 30$

27. $10x^2 + 17x + 7$

28. $8y^2 + 22y - 21$

29. $10x^2 + 39x - 27$

30. $3x^2 + x - 5$

31. $36a^2 - 12a + 1$

32. $18n^3 + 39n^2 - 15n$

33. $8x^2 + 2xy - y^2$

34. $12x^2 + 7xy - 10y^2$

35. $2n^2 - n - 5$

36. $6x^2 - x - 12$

For Problems 37–40, factor the sum or difference of two cubes. (Objective 5)

37. $x^3 - 8$

38. $x^3 + 64$

39. $64x^3 + 27y^3$

40. $27x^3 - 8y^3$

For Problems 41–66, factor each polynomial completely. Indicate any that are not factorable using integers. (Objective 6)

41. $4x^4 + 16$

42. $n^3 - 49n$

43. $x^3 - 9x$

44. $12n^2 + 59n + 72$

45. $9a^2 - 42a + 49$

46. $1 - 16x^4$

47. $2n^3 + 6n^2 + 10n$

48. $25t^2 - 100$

49. $2n^3 + 14n^2 - 20n$

50. $25n^2 + 64$

51. $4x^3 + 32$

52. $2x^3 - 54$

53. $x^4 - 4x^2 - 45$

54. $x^4 - x^2 - 12$

55. $2x^4y - 26x^2y - 96y$

56. $3x^4y - 15x^2y - 108y$

57. $(a + b)^2 - (c + d)^2$

58. $(a - b)^2 - (c - d)^2$

59. $x^2 + 8x + 16 - y^2$

60. $4x^2 + 12x + 9 - y^2$

61. $x^2 - y^2 - 10y - 25z$

62. $y^2 - x^2 + 16x - 64$

63. $60x^2 - 32x - 15$

64. $40x^2 + 37x - 63$

65. $84x^3 + 57x^2 - 60x$

66. $210x^3 - 102x^2 - 180x$

For Problems 67–76, factor each of the following, and assume that all variables appearing as exponents represent integers.

67. $x^{2a} - 16$

68. $x^{4n} - 9$

69. $x^{3n} - y^{3n}$

70. $x^{3a} + y^{6a}$

71. $x^{2a} - 3x^a - 28$

72. $x^{2a} + 10x^a + 21$

73. $2x^{2n} + 7x^n - 30$

74. $3x^{2n} - 16x^n - 12$

75. $x^{4n} - y^{4n}$

76. $16x^{2a} + 24x^a + 9$

77. Suppose that we want to factor $x^2 + 34x + 288$. We need to complete the following with two numbers whose sum is 34 and whose product is 288.

$$x^2 + 34x + 288 = (x + \_\_)(x + \_\_)$$

These numbers can be found as follows: Because we need a product of 288, let's consider the prime factorization of 288.

$$288 = 2^5 \cdot 3^2$$

Now we need to use five 2s and two 3s in the statement

$$(\ \ ) + (\ \ ) = 34$$

Because 34 is divisible by 2 but not by 4, four factors of 2 must be in one number and one factor of 2 in the other number. Also, because 34 is not divisible by 3, both factors of 3 must be in the same number. These facts aid us in determining that

$$(2 \cdot 2 \cdot 2 \cdot 2) + (2 \cdot 3 \cdot 3) = 34$$

or

$$16 \ + \ 18 \ = 34$$

Thus we can complete the original factoring problem:

$$x^2 + 34x + 288 = (x + 16)(x + 18)$$

Use this approach to factor each of the following expressions.

a. $x^2 + 35x + 96$

b. $x^2 + 27x + 176$

c. $x^2 - 45x + 504$

d. $x^2 - 26x + 168$

e. $x^2 + 60x + 896$

f. $x^2 - 84x + 1728$

Thoughts Into Words

78. Describe, in words, the pattern for factoring the sum of two cubes.

79. What does it mean to say that the polynomial $x^2 + 5x + 7$ is not factorable using integers?

80. What role does the distributive property play in the factoring of polynomials?

81. Explain your thought process when factoring $30x^2 + 13x - 56$.

82. Consider the following approach to factoring $12x^2 + 54x + 60$:

$$12x^2 + 54x + 60 = (3x + 6)(4x + 10)$$
$$= 3(x + 2)(2)(2x + 5)$$
$$= 6(x + 2)(2x + 5)$$

Is this factoring process correct? What can you suggest to the person who used this approach?

Answers to the Concept Quiz
1. True   **2.** False   **3.** True   **4.** True   **5.** False   **6.** True   **7.** False   **8.** False

0.5   Rational Expressions

OBJECTIVES

1 Simplify rational expressions

2 Multiply and divide rational expressions

3 Add and subtract rational expressions

4 Simplify complex fractions

Indicated quotients of algebraic expressions are called **algebraic fractions** or **fractional expressions**. The indicated quotient of two polynomials is called a **rational expression**. (This is analogous to defining a rational number as the indicated quotient of two integers.) The following are examples of rational expressions:

$$\frac{3x^2}{5} \quad \frac{x - 2}{x + 3} \quad \frac{x^2 + 5x - 1}{x^2 - 9} \quad \frac{xy^2 + x^2y}{xy} \quad \frac{a^3 - 3a^2 - 5a - 1}{a^4 + a^3 + 6}$$

Because division by zero must be avoided, no values can be assigned to variables that will create a denominator of zero. Thus the rational expression $\dfrac{x - 2}{x + 3}$ is meaningful for all real number values of x except $x = -3$. Rather than making restrictions for each individual expression, we will merely assume that **all denominators represent nonzero real numbers**.

The basic properties of the real numbers can be used for working with rational expressions. For example, the property

$$\frac{a \cdot k}{b \cdot k} = \frac{a}{b}$$

which is used to reduce rational numbers, is also used to *simplify* rational expressions. Consider the following examples:

$$\frac{15xy}{25y} = \frac{3 \cdot \cancel{5} \cdot x \cdot \cancel{y}}{\cancel{5} \cdot 5 \cdot \cancel{y}} = \frac{3x}{5}$$

$$\frac{-9}{18x^2y} = -\frac{\overset{1}{\cancel{9}}}{\underset{2}{\cancel{18}}x^2y} = -\frac{1}{2x^2y}$$

Note that slightly different formats were used in these two examples. In the first one, we factored the coefficients into primes and then proceeded to simplify; however, in the second problem we simply divided a common factor of 9 out of both the numerator and denominator. This is basically a format issue and depends on your personal preference. Also notice that in the second example, we applied the property $\dfrac{-a}{b} = -\dfrac{a}{b}$. This is part of the general property that states

$$\frac{-a}{b} = \frac{a}{-b} = -\frac{a}{b}$$

The properties $(b^n)^m = b^{mn}$ and $(ab)^n = a^n b^n$ may also play a role when simplifying a rational expression, as the next example demonstrates.

$$\frac{(4x^3y)^2}{6x(y^2)^2} = \frac{4^2 \cdot (x^3)^2 \cdot y^2}{6 \cdot x \cdot y^4} = \frac{\overset{8}{\cancel{16}} \overset{x^5}{\cancel{x^6}} y^2}{\underset{3}{\cancel{6}} x \underset{y^2}{\cancel{y^4}}} = \frac{8x^5}{3y^2}$$

The factoring techniques discussed in the previous section can be used to factor numerators and denominators so that the property $(a \cdot k)/(b \cdot k) = a/b$ can be applied. Consider the following examples:

$$\frac{x^2 + 4x}{x^2 - 16} = \frac{x(x + 4)}{(x - 4)(x + 4)} = \frac{x}{x - 4}$$

$$\frac{5n^2 + 6n - 8}{10n^2 - 3n - 4} = \frac{(5n - 4)(n + 2)}{(5n - 4)(2n + 1)} = \frac{n + 2}{2n + 1}$$

$$\frac{x^3 + y^3}{x^2 + xy + 2x + 2y} = \frac{(x + y)(x^2 - xy + y^2)}{x(x + y) + 2(x + y)}$$

$$= \frac{(x + y)(x^2 - xy + y^2)}{(x + y)(x + 2)} = \frac{x^2 - xy + y^2}{x + 2}$$

$$\frac{6x^3y - 6xy}{x^3 + 5x^2 + 4x} = \frac{6xy(x^2 - 1)}{x(x^2 + 5x + 4)} = \frac{6xy(x + 1)(x - 1)}{x(x + 1)(x + 4)} = \frac{6y(x - 1)}{x + 4}$$

Note that in the last example we left the numerator of the final fraction in factored form. This is often done if expressions other than monomials are involved. Either

$$\frac{6y(x-1)}{x+4} \quad \text{or} \quad \frac{6xy-6y}{x+4}$$

is an acceptable answer.

Remember that the quotient of any nonzero real number and its opposite is -1. For example, $6/-6 = -1$ and $-8/8 = -1$. Likewise, the indicated quotient of any polynomial and its opposite is equal to -1. For example,

$$\frac{a}{-a} = -1 \qquad \text{because } a \text{ and } -a \text{ are opposites}$$

$$\frac{a-b}{b-a} = -1 \qquad \text{because } a-b \text{ and } b-a \text{ are opposites}$$

$$\frac{x^2-4}{4-x^2} = -1 \qquad \text{because } x^2-4 \text{ and } 4-x^2 \text{ are opposites}$$

The next example illustrates how we use this idea when simplifying rational expressions.

$$\frac{4-x^2}{x^2+x-6} = \frac{(2+x)(2-x)}{(x+3)(x-2)}$$

$$= (-1)\left(\frac{x+2}{x+3}\right) \qquad \frac{2-x}{x-2} = -1$$

$$= -\frac{x+2}{x+3} \quad \text{or} \quad \frac{-x-2}{x+3}$$

Multiplying and Dividing Rational Expressions

Multiplication of rational expressions is based on the following property:

$$\frac{a}{b} \cdot \frac{c}{d} = \frac{ac}{bd}$$

In other words, we multiply numerators and we multiply denominators and express the final product in simplified form. Study the following examples carefully and pay special attention to the formats used to organize the computational work.

$$\frac{3x}{4y} \cdot \frac{8y^2}{9x} = \frac{3 \cdot \overset{2}{8} \cdot x \cdot \overset{y}{y^2}}{\underset{3}{4} \cdot 9 \cdot x \cdot y} = \frac{2y}{3}$$

$$\frac{12x^2y}{-18xy} \cdot \frac{-24xy^2}{56y^3} = \frac{\overset{2}{12} \cdot \overset{3}{24} \cdot \overset{x^2}{x^3} \cdot y^3}{\underset{3}{18} \cdot \underset{7}{56} \cdot x \cdot \underset{y}{y^4}} = \frac{2x^2}{7y} \qquad \frac{12x^2y}{-18xy} = -\frac{12x^2y}{18xy} \quad \text{and} \quad \frac{-24xy^2}{56y^3} = -\frac{24xy^2}{56y^3}$$

so the product is positive.

$$\frac{y}{x^2-4} \cdot \frac{x+2}{y^2} = \frac{y(x+2)}{y^2(x+2)(x-2)} = \frac{1}{y(x-2)}$$

$$\frac{x^2-x}{x+5} \cdot \frac{x^2+5x+4}{x^4-x^2} = \frac{x(x-1)(x+1)(x+4)}{(x+5)(x^2)(x+1)(x-1)} = \frac{x+4}{x(x+5)}$$

To divide rational expressions, we merely apply the following property:

$$\frac{a}{b} \div \frac{c}{d} = \frac{a}{b} \cdot \frac{d}{c} = \frac{ad}{bc}$$

That is, the quotient of two rational expressions is the product of the first expression times the reciprocal of the second. Consider the following examples:

$$\frac{16x^2y}{24xy^3} \div \frac{9xy}{8x^2y^2} = \frac{16x^2y}{24xy^3} \cdot \frac{8x^2y^2}{9xy} = \frac{16 \cdot 8 \cdot \overset{x^2}{\cancel{x^4}} \cdot y^3}{\underset{3}{24} \cdot 9 \cdot x^2 \cdot \underset{y}{\cancel{y^4}}} = \frac{16x^2}{27y}$$

$$\frac{3a^2 + 12}{3a^2 - 15a} \div \frac{a^4 - 16}{a^2 - 3a - 10} = \frac{3a^2 + 12}{3a^2 - 15a} \cdot \frac{a^2 - 3a - 10}{a^4 - 16}$$

$$= \frac{\cancel{3}(\cancel{a^2 + 4})(\cancel{a - 5})(\cancel{a + 2})}{\cancel{3}a(\cancel{a - 5})(\cancel{a^2 + 4})(\cancel{a + 2})(a - 2)}$$

$$= \frac{1}{a(a - 2)}$$

Adding and Subtracting Rational Expressions

The following two properties provide the basis for adding and subtracting rational expressions:

$$\frac{a}{b} + \frac{c}{b} = \frac{a + c}{b}$$

$$\frac{a}{b} - \frac{c}{b} = \frac{a - c}{b}$$

These properties state that rational expressions with a common denominator can be added (or subtracted) by adding (or subtracting) the numerators and placing the result over the common denominator. Let's illustrate this idea.

$$\frac{8}{x - 2} + \frac{3}{x - 2} = \frac{8 + 3}{x - 2} = \frac{11}{x - 2}$$

$$\frac{9}{4y} - \frac{7}{4y} = \frac{9 - 7}{4y} = \frac{2}{4y} = \frac{1}{2y}$$

Don't forget to simplify the final result.

$$\frac{n^2}{n - 1} - \frac{1}{n - 1} = \frac{n^2 - 1}{n - 1} = \frac{(n + 1)(\cancel{n - 1})}{\cancel{n - 1}} = n + 1$$

If we need to add or subtract rational expressions that do not have a common denominator, then we apply the property $a/b = (a \cdot k)/(b \cdot k)$ to obtain equivalent fractions with a common denominator. Study the next examples and again pay special attention to the format we used to organize our work.

Remark: Remember that the **least common multiple** of a set of whole numbers is the smallest nonzero whole number divisible by each of the numbers in the set. When we add or subtract rational numbers, the least common multiple of the denominators of those numbers is the **least common denominator (LCD).** This concept of a least common denominator can be extended to include polynomials.

Classroom Example
Add $\dfrac{3x + 2}{5} + \dfrac{x + 6}{4}$.

EXAMPLE 1

Add $\dfrac{x + 2}{4} + \dfrac{3x + 1}{3}$.

Solution

By inspection we see that the LCD is 12.

$$\frac{x + 2}{4} + \frac{3x + 1}{3} = \left(\frac{x + 2}{4}\right)\left(\frac{3}{3}\right) + \left(\frac{3x + 1}{3}\right)\left(\frac{4}{4}\right)$$

$$= \frac{3(x + 2)}{12} + \frac{4(3x + 1)}{12}$$

$$= \frac{3x + 6 + 12x + 4}{12}$$

$$= \frac{15x + 10}{12}$$

Classroom Example

Perform the indicated operations.
$\dfrac{x + 7}{20} + \dfrac{3x - 4}{12} - \dfrac{x - 3}{18}$.

EXAMPLE 2

Perform the indicated operations.

$$\frac{x + 3}{10} + \frac{2x + 1}{15} - \frac{x - 2}{18}$$

Solution

If you cannot determine the LCD by inspection, then use the prime-factored forms of the denominators:

$$10 = 2 \cdot 5 \qquad 15 = 3 \cdot 5 \qquad 18 = 2 \cdot 3 \cdot 3$$

The LCD must contain one factor of 2, two factors of 3, and one factor of 5. Thus the LCD is $2 \cdot 3 \cdot 3 \cdot 5 = 90$.

$$\frac{x + 3}{10} + \frac{2x + 1}{15} - \frac{x - 2}{18} = \left(\frac{x + 3}{10}\right)\left(\frac{9}{9}\right) + \left(\frac{2x + 1}{15}\right)\left(\frac{6}{6}\right) - \left(\frac{x - 2}{18}\right)\left(\frac{5}{5}\right)$$

$$= \frac{9(x + 3)}{90} + \frac{6(2x + 1)}{90} - \frac{5(x - 2)}{90}$$

$$= \frac{9x + 27 + 12x + 6 - 5x + 10}{90}$$

$$= \frac{16x + 43}{90}$$

The presence of variables in the denominators does not create any serious difficulty; our approach remains the same. Study the following examples very carefully. For each problem we use the same basic procedure: (1) Find the LCD. (2) Change each fraction to an equivalent fraction having the LCD as its denominator. (3) Add or subtract numerators and place this result over the LCD. (4) Look for possibilities to simplify the resulting fraction.

EXAMPLE 3   Add $\dfrac{3}{2x} + \dfrac{5}{3y}$.

Solution

Using an LCD of $6xy$, we can proceed as follows:

$$\frac{3}{2x} + \frac{5}{3y} = \left(\frac{3}{2x}\right)\left(\frac{3y}{3y}\right) + \left(\frac{5}{3y}\right)\left(\frac{2x}{2x}\right)$$

$$= \frac{9y}{6xy} + \frac{10x}{6xy}$$

$$= \frac{9y + 10x}{6xy}$$

EXAMPLE 4   Subtract $\dfrac{7}{12ab} - \dfrac{11}{15a^2}$.

Solution

We can factor the numerical coefficients of the denominators into primes to help find the LCD.

$$\left.\begin{array}{l} 12ab = 2 \cdot 2 \cdot 3 \cdot a \cdot b \\ 15a^2 = 3 \cdot 5 \cdot a^2 \end{array}\right\} \quad LCD = 2 \cdot 2 \cdot 3 \cdot 5 \cdot a^2 \cdot b = 60a^2b$$

$$\frac{7}{12ab} - \frac{11}{15a^2} = \left(\frac{7}{12ab}\right)\left(\frac{5a}{5a}\right) - \left(\frac{11}{15a^2}\right)\left(\frac{4b}{4b}\right)$$

$$= \frac{35a}{60a^2b} - \frac{44b}{60a^2b}$$

$$= \frac{35a - 44b}{60a^2b}$$

EXAMPLE 5   Add $\dfrac{8}{x^2 - 4x} + \dfrac{2}{x}$.

Solution

$$\left.\begin{array}{l} x^2 - 4x = x(x - 4) \\ x = x \end{array}\right\} \quad LCD = x(x - 4)$$

$$\frac{8}{x(x-4)} + \frac{2}{x} = \frac{8}{x(x-4)} + \left(\frac{2}{x}\right)\left(\frac{x-4}{x-4}\right)$$

$$= \frac{8}{x(x-4)} + \frac{2(x-4)}{x(x-4)}$$

$$= \frac{8+2x-8}{x(x-4)}$$

$$= \frac{2x}{x(x-4)}$$

$$= \frac{2}{x-4}$$

In Figure 0.20 we give some visual support for our answer in Example 5 by graphing $Y_1 = \frac{8}{x^2-4x} + \frac{2}{x}$ and $Y_2 = \frac{2}{x-4}$. Certainly their graphs appear to be identical, but a word of caution is needed here. Actually, the graph of $Y_1 = \frac{8}{x^2-4x} + \frac{2}{x}$ has a hole at $\left(0, -\frac{1}{2}\right)$ because x cannot equal zero. When you use a graphing calculator, this hole may not be detected. Except for the hole, the graphs are identical, and we are claiming that $\frac{8}{x^2-4x} + \frac{2}{x} = \frac{2}{x-4}$ for all values of x except 0 and 4.

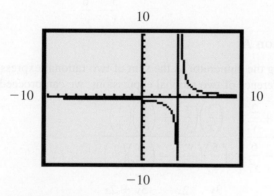

Figure 0.20

EXAMPLE 6   Add $\dfrac{3n}{n^2+6n+5} + \dfrac{4}{n^2-7n-8}$.

Solution

$$\left.\begin{array}{l} n^2 + 6n + 5 = (n+5)(n+1) \\ n^2 - 7n - 8 = (n-8)(n+1) \end{array}\right\} \quad \text{LCD} = (n+1)(n+5)(n-8)$$

$$\frac{3n}{n^2 + 6n + 5} + \frac{4}{n^2 - 7n - 8} = \left[\frac{3n}{(n + 5)(n + 1)}\right]\left(\frac{n - 8}{n - 8}\right) + \left[\frac{4}{(n - 8)(n + 1)}\right]\left(\frac{n + 5}{n + 5}\right)$$

$$= \frac{3n(n - 8)}{(n + 5)(n + 1)(n - 8)} + \frac{4(n + 5)}{(n + 5)(n + 1)(n - 8)}$$

$$= \frac{3n^2 - 24n + 4n + 20}{(n + 5)(n + 1)(n - 8)}$$

$$= \frac{3n^2 - 20n + 20}{(n + 5)(n + 1)(n - 8)}$$ ▬

Simplifying Complex Fractions

Fractional forms that contain rational expressions in the numerator and/or the denominator are called **complex fractions.** The following examples illustrate some approaches to simplifying complex fractions.

Classroom Example

Simplify $\dfrac{\dfrac{4}{a} - \dfrac{5}{b}}{\dfrac{3}{a} + \dfrac{6}{b^2}}$.

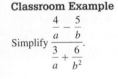

EXAMPLE 7

Simplify $\dfrac{\dfrac{3}{x} + \dfrac{2}{y}}{\dfrac{5}{x} - \dfrac{6}{y^2}}$.

Solution A

Treating the numerator as the sum of two rational expressions and the denominator as the difference of two rational expressions, we can proceed as follows.

$$\frac{\dfrac{3}{x} + \dfrac{2}{y}}{\dfrac{5}{x} - \dfrac{6}{y^2}} = \frac{\left(\dfrac{3}{x}\right)\left(\dfrac{y}{y}\right) + \left(\dfrac{2}{y}\right)\left(\dfrac{x}{x}\right)}{\left(\dfrac{5}{x}\right)\left(\dfrac{y^2}{y^2}\right) - \left(\dfrac{6}{y^2}\right)\left(\dfrac{x}{x}\right)}$$

$$= \frac{\dfrac{3y}{xy} + \dfrac{2x}{xy}}{\dfrac{5y^2}{xy^2} - \dfrac{6x}{xy^2}} = \frac{\dfrac{3y + 2x}{xy}}{\dfrac{5y^2 - 6x}{xy^2}}$$

$$= \frac{3y + 2x}{\cancel{xy}} \cdot \frac{\overset{y}{\cancel{xy^2}}}{5y^2 - 6x}$$

$$= \frac{y(3y + 2x)}{5y^2 - 6x}$$

Solution B

The LCD of all four denominators (x, y, x, and y^2) is xy^2. Let's multiply the entire complex fraction by a form of 1—namely, $(xy^2)/(xy^2)$:

$$\frac{\dfrac{3}{x} + \dfrac{2}{y}}{\dfrac{5}{x} - \dfrac{6}{y^2}} = \left(\frac{\dfrac{3}{x} + \dfrac{2}{y}}{\dfrac{5}{x} - \dfrac{6}{y^2}}\right)\left(\frac{xy^2}{xy^2}\right)$$

$$= \frac{(xy^2)\left(\dfrac{3}{x}\right) + (xy^2)\left(\dfrac{2}{y}\right)}{(xy^2)\left(\dfrac{5}{x}\right) - (xy^2)\left(\dfrac{6}{y^2}\right)}$$

$$= \frac{3y^2 + 2xy}{5y^2 - 6x} \quad \text{or} \quad \frac{y(3y + 2x)}{5y^2 - 6x}$$

Certainly either approach (Solution A or Solution B) will work with a problem such as Example 7. We suggest that you study Solution B very carefully. This approach works effectively with complex fractions when the LCD of all the denominators is easy to find. Let's look at a type of complex fraction used in certain calculus problems.

EXAMPLE 8

Simplify $\dfrac{\dfrac{1}{x+h} - \dfrac{1}{x}}{h}$.

Solution

$$\frac{\dfrac{1}{x+h} - \dfrac{1}{x}}{\dfrac{h}{1}} = \left[\frac{x(x+h)}{x(x+h)}\right]\left[\frac{\dfrac{1}{x+h} - \dfrac{1}{x}}{\dfrac{h}{1}}\right]$$

$$= \frac{x(x+h)\left(\dfrac{1}{x+h}\right) - x(x+h)\left(\dfrac{1}{x}\right)}{x(x+h)(h)}$$

$$= \frac{x - (x+h)}{hx(x+h)} = \frac{x - x - h}{hx(x+h)}$$

$$= \frac{-h}{hx(x+h)} = -\frac{1}{x(x+h)}$$

Example 9 illustrates another way to simplify complex fractions.

Classroom Example

Simplify $4 - \dfrac{y}{1 - \dfrac{4}{y}}$.

EXAMPLE 9 Simplify $1 - \dfrac{n}{1 - \dfrac{1}{n}}$.

Solution

We first simplify the complex fraction by multiplying by n/n:

$$\left(\frac{n}{1 - \frac{1}{n}}\right)\left(\frac{n}{n}\right) = \frac{n^2}{n - 1}$$

Now we can perform the subtraction:

$$1 - \frac{n^2}{n - 1} = \left(\frac{n - 1}{n - 1}\right)\left(\frac{1}{1}\right) - \frac{n^2}{n - 1}$$

$$= \frac{n - 1}{n - 1} - \frac{n^2}{n - 1}$$

$$= \frac{n - 1 - n^2}{n - 1} \quad \text{or} \quad \frac{-n^2 + n - 1}{n - 1}$$

Finally, we need to recognize that complex fractions are sometimes the result of applying the definition $b^{-n} = \dfrac{1}{b^n}$. Our final example illustrates this idea.

Classroom Example

Simplify $\dfrac{5a^{-2} + b^{-1}}{a + 2b^{-1}}$.

EXAMPLE 10 Simplify $\dfrac{2x^{-1} + y^{-1}}{x - 3y^{-2}}$.

Solution

First, let's apply $b^{-n} = \dfrac{1}{b^n}$:

$$\frac{2x^{-1} + y^{-1}}{x - 3y^{-2}} = \frac{\dfrac{2}{x} + \dfrac{1}{y}}{x - \dfrac{3}{y^2}}$$

Now we can proceed as in the previous examples:

$$\left(\frac{\dfrac{2}{x} + \dfrac{1}{y}}{x - \dfrac{3}{y^2}}\right)\left(\frac{xy^2}{xy^2}\right) = \frac{\dfrac{2}{x}(xy^2) + \dfrac{1}{y}(xy^2)}{x(xy^2) - \dfrac{3}{y^2}(xy^2)}$$

$$= \frac{2y^2 + xy}{x^2y^2 - 3x}$$

Concept Quiz 0.5

For Problems 1–7, answer true or false.

1. The indicated quotient of two polynomials is called a rational expression.

2. The rational expression $\dfrac{3x - 4}{x + 2}$ is defined for all values of x.

3. The rational expressions $\dfrac{a^2 - 4}{b - 2}$ and $-\dfrac{4 - a^2}{2 - b}$ are equivalent.

4. The quotient of any nonzero polynomial and its opposite is -1.

5. To multiply rational expressions that do not have a common denominator, we need to obtain equivalent fractions with a common denominator.

6. Complex fractions are fractional forms that contain rational expressions in the numerator and/or the denominator.

7. The difference of $\dfrac{3x - 4}{7x + 8}$ and $\dfrac{5x - 1}{7x + 8}$ would equal zero if $3x - 4 = 5x - 1$.

8. Under what conditions would the product of $\dfrac{x + 2}{x}$ and $\dfrac{x - 2}{x}$ be equal to zero?

Problem Set 0.5

For Problems 1–18, simplify each rational expression. **(Objective 1)**

1. $\dfrac{14x^2y}{21xy}$

2. $\dfrac{-26xy^2}{65y}$

3. $\dfrac{-63xy^4}{-81x^2y}$

4. $\dfrac{x^2 - y^2}{x^2 + xy}$

5. $\dfrac{(2x^2y^2)^3}{(3xy)^2}$

6. $\dfrac{(3a^3b)^2}{6a^2(b^2)^2}$

7. $\dfrac{a^2 + 7a + 12}{a^2 - 6a - 27}$

8. $\dfrac{6x^2 + x - 15}{8x^2 - 10x - 3}$

9. $\dfrac{2x^3 + 3x^2 - 14x}{x^2y + 7xy - 18y}$

10. $\dfrac{3x - x^2}{x^2 - 9}$

11. $\dfrac{x^3 - y^3}{x^2 + xy - 2y^2}$

12. $\dfrac{ax - 3x + 2ay - 6y}{2ax - 6x + ay - 3y}$

13. $\dfrac{2y - 2xy}{x^2y - y}$

14. $\dfrac{16x^3y + 24x^2y^2 - 16xy^3}{24x^2y + 12xy^2 - 12y^3}$

15. $\dfrac{8x^2 + 4xy - 2x - y}{4x^2 - 4xy - x + y}$

16. $\dfrac{2x^3 + 2y^3}{2x^2 + 6x + 2xy + 6y}$

17. $\dfrac{27x^3 + 8y^3}{3x^2 - 15x + 2xy - 10y}$

18. $\dfrac{x^3 + 64}{3x^2 + 11x - 4}$

For Problems 19–68, perform the indicated operations involving rational expressions. Express final answers in simplest form. **(Objectives 2 and 3)**

19. $\dfrac{4x^2}{5y^2} \cdot \dfrac{15xy}{24x^2y^2}$

20. $\dfrac{5xy}{8y^2} \cdot \dfrac{18x^2y}{15}$

21. $\dfrac{-14xy^4}{18y^2} \cdot \dfrac{24x^2y^3}{35y^2}$

22. $\dfrac{6xy}{9y^4} \cdot \dfrac{30x^3y}{-48x}$

23. $\dfrac{7a^2b}{9ab^3} \div \dfrac{3a^4}{2a^2b^2}$

24. $\dfrac{9a^2c}{12bc^2} \div \dfrac{21ab}{14c^3}$

25. $\dfrac{5xy}{x+6} \cdot \dfrac{x^2 - 36}{x^2 - 6x}$

26. $\dfrac{2a^2 + 6}{a^2 - a} \cdot \dfrac{a^3 - a^2}{8a - 4}$

27. $\dfrac{5a^2 + 20a}{a^3 - 2a^2} \cdot \dfrac{a^2 - a - 12}{a^2 - 16}$

28. $\dfrac{t^4 - 81}{t^2 - 6t + 9} \cdot \dfrac{6t^2 - 11t - 21}{5t^2 + 8t - 21}$

29. $\dfrac{x^2 + 5xy - 6y^2}{xy^2 - y^3} \cdot \dfrac{2x^2 + 15xy + 18y^2}{xy + 4y^2}$

30. $\dfrac{10n^2 + 21n - 10}{5n^2 + 33n - 14} \cdot \dfrac{2n^2 + 6n - 56}{2n^2 - 3n - 20}$

31. $\dfrac{9y^2}{x^2 + 12x + 36} \div \dfrac{12y}{x^2 + 6x}$

32. $\dfrac{x^2 - 4xy + 4y^2}{7xy^2} \div \dfrac{4x^2 - 3xy - 10y^2}{20x^2y + 25xy^2}$

33. $\dfrac{2x^2 + 3x}{2x^3 - 10x^2} \cdot \dfrac{x^2 - 8x + 15}{3x^3 - 27x} \div \dfrac{14x + 21}{x^2 - 6x - 27}$

34. $\dfrac{a^2 - 4ab + 4b^2}{6a^2 - 4ab} \cdot \dfrac{3a^2 + 5ab - 2b^2}{6a^2 + ab - b^2} \div \dfrac{a^2 - 4b^2}{8a + 4b}$

35. $\dfrac{x+4}{6} + \dfrac{2x-1}{4}$

36. $\dfrac{3n-1}{9} - \dfrac{n+2}{12}$

37. $\dfrac{x+1}{4} + \dfrac{x-3}{6} - \dfrac{x-2}{8}$

38. $\dfrac{x-2}{5} - \dfrac{x+3}{6} + \dfrac{x+1}{15}$

39. $\dfrac{7}{16a^2b} + \dfrac{3a}{20b^2}$

40. $\dfrac{5b}{24a^2} - \dfrac{11a}{32b}$

41. $\dfrac{1}{n^2} + \dfrac{3}{4n} - \dfrac{5}{6}$

42. $\dfrac{3}{n^2} - \dfrac{2}{5n} + \dfrac{4}{3}$

43. $\dfrac{3}{4x} + \dfrac{2}{3y} - 1$

44. $\dfrac{5}{6x} - \dfrac{3}{4y} + 2$

45. $\dfrac{3}{2x+1} + \dfrac{2}{3x+4}$

46. $\dfrac{5}{x-1} - \dfrac{3}{2x-3}$

47. $\dfrac{4x}{x^2 + 7x} + \dfrac{3}{x}$

48. $\dfrac{6}{x^2 + 8x} - \dfrac{3}{x}$

49. $\dfrac{4a-4}{a^2 - 4} - \dfrac{3}{a+2}$

50. $\dfrac{6a+4}{a^2 - 1} - \dfrac{5}{a-1}$

51. $\dfrac{3}{x-1} - \dfrac{2}{4x-4}$

52. $\dfrac{3x+2}{4x-12} + \dfrac{2x}{6x-18}$

53. $\dfrac{4}{n^2 - 1} + \dfrac{2}{3n+3}$

54. $\dfrac{5}{n^2 - 4} - \dfrac{7}{3n-6}$

55. $\dfrac{3}{x+1} + \dfrac{x+5}{x^2 - 1} - \dfrac{3}{x-1}$

56. $\dfrac{5}{x} - \dfrac{5x-30}{x^2 + 6x} + \dfrac{x}{x+6}$

57. $\dfrac{5}{x^2 + 10x + 21} + \dfrac{4}{x^2 + 12x + 27}$

58. $\dfrac{8}{a^2 - 3a - 18} - \dfrac{10}{a^2 - 7a - 30}$

59. $\dfrac{5}{x^2 - 1} - \dfrac{2}{x^2 + 6x - 16}$

60. $\dfrac{4}{x^2 + 2} - \dfrac{7}{x^2 + x - 12}$

61. $\dfrac{3x}{x^2 - 6x + 9} - \dfrac{2}{x-3}$

62. $\dfrac{6}{x^2 - 9} - \dfrac{9}{x^2 - 6x + 9}$

63. $x - \dfrac{x^2}{x-1} + \dfrac{1}{x^2 - 1}$

64. $x - \dfrac{x^2}{x+7} - \dfrac{x}{x^2 - 49}$

65. $\dfrac{2n^2}{n^4 - 16} - \dfrac{n}{n^2 - 4} + \dfrac{1}{n+2}$

66. $\dfrac{n}{n^2 + 1} + \dfrac{n^2 + 3n}{n^4 - 1} - \dfrac{1}{n-1}$

67. $\dfrac{2x+1}{x^2 - 3x - 4} + \dfrac{3x-2}{x^2 + 3x - 28}$

68. $\dfrac{3x-4}{2x^2 - 9x - 5} - \dfrac{2x-1}{3x^2 - 11x - 20}$

69. Consider the addition problem $\dfrac{8}{x-2}+\dfrac{5}{2-x}$. Note that the denominators are opposites of each other. If the property $\dfrac{a}{-b}=-\dfrac{a}{b}$ is applied to the second fraction, we obtain $\dfrac{5}{2-x}=-\dfrac{5}{x-2}$. Thus we can proceed as follows:

$$\frac{8}{x-2}+\frac{5}{2-x}=\frac{8}{x-2}-\frac{5}{x-2}$$

$$=\frac{8-5}{x-2}=\frac{3}{x-2}$$

Use this approach to do the following problems.

a. $\dfrac{7}{x-1}+\dfrac{2}{1-x}$

b. $\dfrac{5}{2x-1}+\dfrac{8}{1-2x}$

c. $\dfrac{4}{a-3}-\dfrac{1}{3-a}$

d. $\dfrac{10}{a-9}-\dfrac{5}{9-a}$

e. $\dfrac{x^2}{x-1}-\dfrac{2x-3}{1-x}$

f. $\dfrac{x^2}{x-4}-\dfrac{3x-28}{4-x}$

For Problems 70–92, simplify each complex fraction.
(Objective 4)

70. $\dfrac{\dfrac{2}{x}+\dfrac{7}{y}}{\dfrac{3}{x}-\dfrac{10}{y}}$

71. $\dfrac{\dfrac{5}{x^2}-\dfrac{3}{x}}{\dfrac{1}{y}+\dfrac{2}{y^2}}$

72. $\dfrac{\dfrac{1}{x}+3}{\dfrac{2}{y}+4}$

73. $\dfrac{1+\dfrac{1}{x}}{1-\dfrac{1}{x}}$

74. $\dfrac{3-\dfrac{2}{n-4}}{5+\dfrac{4}{n-4}}$

75. $\dfrac{1-\dfrac{1}{n+1}}{1+\dfrac{1}{n-1}}$

76. $\dfrac{\dfrac{2}{x-3}-\dfrac{3}{x+3}}{\dfrac{5}{x^2-9}-\dfrac{2}{x-3}}$

77. $\dfrac{\dfrac{-2}{x}-\dfrac{4}{x+2}}{\dfrac{3}{x^2+2x}+\dfrac{3}{x}}$

78. $\dfrac{\dfrac{-1}{y-2}+\dfrac{5}{x}}{\dfrac{3}{x}-\dfrac{4}{xy-2x}}$

79. $1+\dfrac{x}{1+\dfrac{1}{x}}$

80. $2-\dfrac{x}{3-\dfrac{2}{x}}$

81. $\dfrac{\dfrac{a}{1}+1}{\dfrac{1}{a}+4}$

82. $\dfrac{\dfrac{3a}{1}-1}{2-\dfrac{1}{a}}$

83. $\dfrac{\dfrac{1}{(x+h)^2}-\dfrac{1}{x^2}}{h}$

84. $\dfrac{\dfrac{1}{(x+h)^3}-\dfrac{1}{x^3}}{h}$

85. $\dfrac{\dfrac{1}{x+h+1}-\dfrac{1}{x+1}}{h}$

86. $\dfrac{\dfrac{3}{x+h}-\dfrac{3}{x}}{h}$

87. $\dfrac{\dfrac{2}{2x+2h-1}-\dfrac{2}{2x-1}}{h}$

88. $\dfrac{\dfrac{3}{4x+4h+5}-\dfrac{3}{4x+5}}{h}$

89. $\dfrac{x^{-1}+2y^{-1}}{x-y}$

90. $\dfrac{x+y}{x^{-1}+y^{-1}}$

91. $\dfrac{x+2x^{-1}y^{-2}}{4x^{-1}-3y^{-2}}$

92. $\dfrac{x^{-2}-2y^{-1}}{3x^{-1}+y^{-2}}$

Thoughts Into Words

93. What role does factoring play in the simplifying of rational expressions?

94. Explain in your own words how to multiply two rational expressions.

95. Give a step-by-step description of how to add
$\dfrac{2x-1}{4}+\dfrac{3x+5}{14}$.

96. Look back at the two approaches shown in Example 7. Which approach would you use to simplify
$\dfrac{\dfrac{1}{4}+\dfrac{1}{6}}{\dfrac{1}{2}-\dfrac{3}{4}}$? Which approach would you use to simplify

$\dfrac{\dfrac{5}{8}+\dfrac{4}{9}}{\dfrac{5}{14}-\dfrac{2}{21}}$? Explain the reason for your choice of approach for each problem.

Graphing Calculator Activities

97. Use the graphing feature of your graphing calculator to give visual support for your answers for Problems 60–68.

98. For each of the following, use your graphing calculator to help you decide whether the two given expressions are equivalent for all defined values of x.

(a) $\dfrac{6x^2-7x+2}{8x^2+6x-5}$ and $\dfrac{3x-2}{4x+5}$

(b) $\dfrac{4x^2-15x-54}{4x^2+13x+9}$ and $\dfrac{x-6}{x+1}$

(c) $\dfrac{2x^2+3x-2}{12x^2+19x+5}$ and $\dfrac{2x-1}{4x+5}$

(d) $\dfrac{x^3+2x^2-3x}{x^3+6x^2+5x-12}$ and $\dfrac{x}{x+4}$

(e) $\dfrac{-5x^2-11x+2}{3x^2-13x+14}$ and $\dfrac{-5x-1}{3x-7}$

Answers to the Concept Quiz
1. True **2.** False **3.** False **4.** True **5.** False **6.** True **7.** True **8.** If $x=2$ or $x=-2$

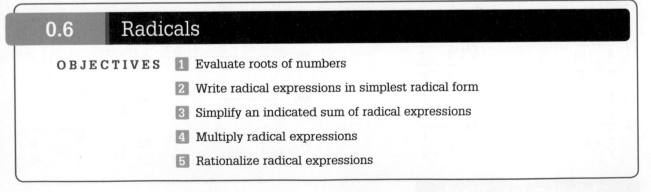

0.6   Radicals

OBJECTIVES

1 Evaluate roots of numbers

2 Write radical expressions in simplest radical form

3 Simplify an indicated sum of radical expressions

4 Multiply radical expressions

5 Rationalize radical expressions

Recall from our work with exponents that to **square a number** means to raise it to the second power—that is, to use the number as a factor twice. For example, $4^2=4\cdot4=16$, and $(-4)^2=(-4)(-4)=16$. A **square root of a number** is one of its two equal factors.

Thus 4 and −4 are both square roots of 16. In general, a is a square root of b if $a^2 = b$. The following statements generalize these ideas:

1. Every positive real number has two square roots; one is positive and the other is negative. They are opposites of each other.

2. Negative real numbers have no real-number square roots because the square of any nonzero real number is positive.

3. The square root of zero is zero.

The symbol $\sqrt{}$, called a **radical sign,** is used to designate the *nonnegative* square root, which is called the **principal square root.** The number under the radical sign is called the **radicand,** and the entire expression, such as $\sqrt{16}$, is referred to as a **radical.**

The following examples demonstrate the use of the square root notation:

$\sqrt{16} = 4$ $\sqrt{16}$ indicates the *nonnegative* or *principal square root* of 16.

$-\sqrt{16} = -4$ $-\sqrt{16}$ indicates the negative square root of 16.

$\sqrt{0} = 0$ Zero has only one square root. Technically, we could also write $-\sqrt{0} = -0 = 0$.

$\sqrt{-4}$ Not a real number

$-\sqrt{-4}$ Not a real number

To **cube a number** means to raise it to the third power—that is, to use the number as a factor three times. For example, $2^3 = 2 \cdot 2 \cdot 2 = 8$ and $(-2)^3 = (-2)(-2)(-2) = -8$. A **cube root of a number** is one of its three equal factors. Thus 2 is a cube root of 8, and as we will discuss later, it is the only real number that is a cube root of 8. Furthermore, -2 is the only real number that is a cube root of -8. In general, a is a cube root of b if $a^3 = b$. The following statements generalize these ideas:

1. Every positive real number has one positive real-number cube root.

2. Every negative real number has one negative real-number cube root.

3. The cube root of zero is zero.

Remark: Every nonzero real number has three cube roots, but only one of them is a real number. The other roots are complex numbers, which we will discuss in Section 0.8.

The symbol $\sqrt[3]{}$ is used to designate the cube root of a number. Thus we can write

$$\sqrt[3]{8} = 2 \qquad \sqrt[3]{-8} = -2 \qquad \sqrt[3]{\frac{1}{27}} = \frac{1}{3} \qquad \sqrt[3]{-\frac{1}{27}} = -\frac{1}{3}$$

The concept of root can be extended to fourth roots, fifth roots, sixth roots, and, in general, *n*th roots. If n is an *even positive integer,* then the following statements are true:

1. Every positive real number has exactly two real *n*th roots, one positive and one negative. For example, the real fourth roots of 16 are 2 and -2.

2. Negative real numbers do not have real *n*th roots. For example, there are no real fourth roots of -16.

If n is an *odd positive integer* greater than 1, then the following statements are true.

1. Every real number has exactly one real nth root.

2. The real nth root of a positive number is positive. For example, the fifth root of 32 is 2.

3. The real nth root of a negative number is negative. For example, the fifth root of -32 is -2.

In general, the following definition is useful.

Definition 0.5

$\sqrt[n]{b} = a$ if and only if $a^n = b$

In Definition 0.5, if n is an even positive integer, then a and b are both nonnegative. If n is an odd positive integer greater than 1, then a and b are both nonnegative or both negative. The symbol $\sqrt[n]{}$ designates the principal root.

The following examples are applications of Definition 0.5:

$$\sqrt[4]{81} = 3 \qquad \text{because } 3^4 = 81$$
$$\sqrt[5]{32} = 2 \qquad \text{because } 2^5 = 32$$
$$\sqrt[5]{-32} = -2 \qquad \text{because } (-2)^5 = -32$$

To complete our terminology, the n in the radical $\sqrt[n]{b}$ is called the **index** of the radical. If $n = 2$, we commonly write $\sqrt{b}$ instead of $\sqrt[2]{b}$. In this text, when we use symbols such as $\sqrt[n]{b}$, $\sqrt[m]{y}$, and $\sqrt[r]{x}$, we will assume the previous agreements relative to the existence of real roots without listing the various restrictions, unless a special restriction is needed.

From Definition 0.5 we see that if n is any positive integer greater than 1 and $\sqrt[n]{b}$ exists, then

$$\left(\sqrt[n]{b}\right)^n = b$$

For example, $\left(\sqrt{4}\right)^2 = 4$, $\left(\sqrt[3]{-8}\right)^3 = -8$, and $\left(\sqrt[4]{81}\right)^4 = 81$. Furthermore, if $b \geq 0$ and n is any positive integer greater than 1, or if $b < 0$ and n is an odd positive integer greater than 1, then

$$\sqrt[n]{b^n} = b$$

For example, $\sqrt{4^2} = 4$, $\sqrt[3]{(-2)^3} = -2$, and $\sqrt[5]{6^5} = 6$. But we must be careful because

$$\sqrt{(-2)^2} \neq -2 \qquad \text{and} \qquad \sqrt[4]{(-2)^4} \neq -2$$

Simplest Radical Form

Let's use some examples to motivate another useful property of radicals.

$$\sqrt{16 \cdot 25} = \sqrt{400} = 20 \quad \text{and} \quad \sqrt{16} \cdot \sqrt{25} = 4 \cdot 5 = 20$$
$$\sqrt[3]{8 \cdot 27} = \sqrt[3]{216} = 6 \quad \text{and} \quad \sqrt[3]{8} \cdot \sqrt[3]{27} = 2 \cdot 3 = 6$$
$$\sqrt[3]{-8 \cdot 64} = \sqrt[3]{-512} = -8 \quad \text{and} \quad \sqrt[3]{-8} \cdot \sqrt[3]{64} = -2 \cdot 4 = -8$$

In general, the following property can be stated.

> **Property 0.3**
>
> $\sqrt[n]{bc} = \sqrt[n]{b}\sqrt[n]{c}$ if $\sqrt[n]{b}$ and $\sqrt[n]{c}$ are real numbers.

Property 0.3 states that **the nth root of a product is equal to the product of the nth roots.**

The definition of nth root, along with Property 0.3, provides the basis for changing radicals to simplest radical form. The concept of **simplest radical form** takes on additional meaning as we encounter more complicated expressions, but for now it simply means that the radicand does not contain any perfect powers of the index. Consider the following examples of reductions to simplest radical form:

$$\sqrt{45} = \sqrt{9 \cdot 5} = \sqrt{9}\sqrt{5} = 3\sqrt{5}$$
$$\sqrt{52} = \sqrt{4 \cdot 13} = \sqrt{4}\sqrt{13} = 2\sqrt{13}$$
$$\sqrt[3]{24} = \sqrt[3]{8 \cdot 3} = \sqrt[3]{8}\sqrt[3]{3} = 2\sqrt[3]{3}$$

A variation of the technique for changing radicals with index n to simplest form is to factor the radicand into primes and then to look for the perfect nth powers in exponential form, as in the following examples:

$$\sqrt{80} = \sqrt{2^4 \cdot 5} = \sqrt{2^4}\sqrt{5} = 2^2\sqrt{5} = 4\sqrt{5}$$
$$\sqrt[3]{108} = \sqrt[3]{2^2 \cdot 3^3} = \sqrt[3]{3^3}\sqrt[3]{2^2} = 3\sqrt[3]{4}$$

The distributive property can be used to combine radicals that have the same index and the same radicand:

$$3\sqrt{2} + 5\sqrt{2} = (3 + 5)\sqrt{2} = 8\sqrt{2}$$
$$7\sqrt[3]{5} - 3\sqrt[3]{5} = (7 - 3)\sqrt[3]{5} = 4\sqrt[3]{5}$$

Sometimes it is necessary to simplify the radicals first and then to combine them by applying the distributive property:

$$3\sqrt{8} + 2\sqrt{18} - 4\sqrt{2} = 3\sqrt{4}\sqrt{2} + 2\sqrt{9}\sqrt{2} - 4\sqrt{2}$$
$$= 6\sqrt{2} + 6\sqrt{2} - 4\sqrt{2}$$
$$= (6 + 6 - 4)\sqrt{2}$$
$$= 8\sqrt{2}$$

Multiplying Radicals

Property 0.3 can also be viewed as $\sqrt[n]{b}\sqrt[n]{c} = \sqrt[n]{bc}$. Then, along with the commutative and associative properties of the real numbers, it provides the basis for multiplying radicals that have the same index. Consider the following two examples:

$$(7\sqrt{6})(3\sqrt{8}) = 7 \cdot 3 \cdot \sqrt{6} \cdot \sqrt{8}$$
$$= 21\sqrt{48}$$
$$= 21\sqrt{16}\sqrt{3}$$

$$= 21 \cdot 4 \cdot \sqrt{3}$$
$$= 84\sqrt{3}$$

$$(2\sqrt[3]{6})(5\sqrt[3]{4}) = 2 \cdot 5 \cdot \sqrt[3]{6} \cdot \sqrt[3]{4}$$
$$= 10\sqrt[3]{24}$$
$$= 10\sqrt[3]{8}\sqrt[3]{3}$$
$$= 10 \cdot 2 \cdot \sqrt[3]{3}$$
$$= 20\sqrt[3]{3}$$

The distributive property, along with Property 0.3, provides a way of handling special products involving radicals, as the next examples illustrate:

$$2\sqrt{2}\,(4\sqrt{3} - 5\sqrt{6}) = (2\sqrt{2})(4\sqrt{3}) - (2\sqrt{2})(5\sqrt{6})$$
$$= 8\sqrt{6} - 10\sqrt{12}$$
$$= 8\sqrt{6} - 10\sqrt{4}\sqrt{3}$$
$$= 8\sqrt{6} - 20\sqrt{3}$$

$$(2\sqrt{2} - \sqrt{7})(3\sqrt{2} + 5\sqrt{7}) = 2\sqrt{2}(3\sqrt{2} + 5\sqrt{7}) - \sqrt{7}(3\sqrt{2} + 5\sqrt{7})$$
$$= (2\sqrt{2})(3\sqrt{2}) + (2\sqrt{2})(5\sqrt{7}) - (\sqrt{7})(3\sqrt{2}) - (\sqrt{7})(5\sqrt{7})$$
$$= 6 \cdot 2 + 10\sqrt{14} - 3\sqrt{14} - 5 \cdot 7$$
$$= -23 + 7\sqrt{14}$$

$$(\sqrt{5} + \sqrt{2})(\sqrt{5} - \sqrt{2}) = \sqrt{5}(\sqrt{5} - \sqrt{2}) + \sqrt{2}(\sqrt{5} - \sqrt{2})$$
$$= (\sqrt{5})(\sqrt{5}) - (\sqrt{5})(\sqrt{2}) + (\sqrt{2})(\sqrt{5}) - (\sqrt{2})(\sqrt{2})$$
$$= 5 - \sqrt{10} + \sqrt{10} - 2$$
$$= 3$$

Pay special attention to the last example. It fits the special-product pattern $(a + b)(a - b) = a^2 - b^2$. We will use that idea in a moment.

More About Simplest Radical Form

Another property of nth roots is motivated by the following examples:

$$\sqrt{\frac{36}{9}} = \sqrt{4} = 2 \quad \text{and} \quad \frac{\sqrt{36}}{\sqrt{9}} = \frac{6}{3} = 2$$

$$\sqrt[3]{\frac{64}{8}} = \sqrt[3]{8} = 2 \quad \text{and} \quad \frac{\sqrt[3]{64}}{\sqrt[3]{8}} = \frac{4}{2} = 2$$

In general, the following property can be stated.

Property 0.4

$$\sqrt[n]{\frac{b}{c}} = \frac{\sqrt[n]{b}}{\sqrt[n]{c}} \quad \text{if } \sqrt[n]{b} \text{ and } \sqrt[n]{c} \text{ are real numbers, and } c \neq 0$$

Property 0.4 states that **the nth root of a quotient is equal to the quotient of the nth roots.**

To evaluate radicals such as $\sqrt{\dfrac{4}{25}}$ and $\sqrt[3]{\dfrac{27}{8}}$, where the numerator and the denominator of the fractional radicands are perfect nth powers, we can either use Property 0.4 or rely on the definition of nth root.

$$\sqrt{\frac{4}{25}} = \frac{\sqrt{4}}{\sqrt{25}} = \frac{2}{5} \quad \text{or} \quad \sqrt{\frac{4}{25}} = \frac{2}{5} \quad \text{because } \frac{2}{5} \cdot \frac{2}{5} = \frac{4}{25}$$

$$\sqrt[3]{\frac{27}{8}} = \frac{\sqrt[3]{27}}{\sqrt[3]{8}} = \frac{3}{2} \quad \text{or} \quad \sqrt[3]{\frac{27}{8}} = \frac{3}{2} \quad \text{because } \frac{3}{2} \cdot \frac{3}{2} \cdot \frac{3}{2} = \frac{27}{8}$$

Radicals such as $\sqrt{\dfrac{28}{9}}$ and $\sqrt[3]{\dfrac{24}{27}}$, where only the denominators of the radicand are perfect nth powers, can be simplified as follows:

$$\sqrt{\frac{28}{9}} = \frac{\sqrt{28}}{\sqrt{9}} = \frac{\sqrt{4}\sqrt{7}}{3} = \frac{2\sqrt{7}}{3}$$

$$\sqrt[3]{\frac{24}{27}} = \frac{\sqrt[3]{24}}{\sqrt[3]{27}} = \frac{\sqrt[3]{8}\sqrt[3]{3}}{3} = \frac{2\sqrt[3]{3}}{3}$$

Before we consider more examples, let's summarize some ideas about simplifying radicals. A radical is said to be in **simplest radical form** if the following conditions are satisfied.

1. No fraction appears within a radical sign.

   Thus $\sqrt{\dfrac{3}{4}}$ violates this condition.

2. No radical appears in the denominator.

   Thus $\dfrac{\sqrt{2}}{\sqrt{3}}$ violates this condition.

3. No radicand contains a perfect power of the index.

   Thus $\sqrt{7^2 \cdot 5}$ violates this condition.

Rationalizing Radical Expressions

Now let's consider an example in which neither the numerator nor the denominator of the radicand is a perfect nth power:

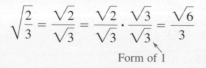

$$\sqrt{\frac{2}{3}} = \frac{\sqrt{2}}{\sqrt{3}} = \frac{\sqrt{2}}{\sqrt{3}} \cdot \frac{\sqrt{3}}{\sqrt{3}} = \frac{\sqrt{6}}{3}$$

Form of 1

The process used to simplify the radical in this example is referred to as **rationalizing the denominator.** There is more than one way to rationalize the denominator, as illustrated by the next example.

Classroom Example

Simplify $\dfrac{\sqrt{7}}{\sqrt{18}}$.

EXAMPLE 1   Simplify $\dfrac{\sqrt{5}}{\sqrt{8}}$.

Solution A

$$\frac{\sqrt{5}}{\sqrt{8}} = \frac{\sqrt{5}}{\sqrt{8}} \cdot \frac{\sqrt{8}}{\sqrt{8}} = \frac{\sqrt{40}}{8} = \frac{\sqrt{4}\sqrt{10}}{8} = \frac{2\sqrt{10}}{8} = \frac{\sqrt{10}}{4}$$

Solution B

$$\frac{\sqrt{5}}{\sqrt{8}} = \frac{\sqrt{5}}{\sqrt{8}} \cdot \frac{\sqrt{2}}{\sqrt{2}} = \frac{\sqrt{10}}{\sqrt{16}} = \frac{\sqrt{10}}{4}$$

Solution C

$$\frac{\sqrt{5}}{\sqrt{8}} = \frac{\sqrt{5}}{\sqrt{4}\sqrt{2}} = \frac{\sqrt{5}}{2\sqrt{2}} = \frac{\sqrt{5}}{2\sqrt{2}} \cdot \frac{\sqrt{2}}{\sqrt{2}} = \frac{\sqrt{10}}{4}$$

The three approaches in Example 1 again illustrate the need to think first and then push the pencil. You may find one approach easier than another.

Classroom Example

Simplify $\dfrac{\sqrt{6}}{\sqrt{27}}$.

EXAMPLE 2   Simplify $\dfrac{\sqrt{6}}{\sqrt{8}}$.

Solution

$$\frac{\sqrt{6}}{\sqrt{8}} = \sqrt{\frac{6}{8}} \qquad \text{Remember that } \frac{\sqrt{a}}{\sqrt{b}} = \sqrt{\frac{a}{b}}$$

$$= \sqrt{\frac{3}{4}} \qquad \text{Reduce the fraction}$$

$$= \frac{\sqrt{3}}{\sqrt{4}}$$

$$= \frac{\sqrt{3}}{2}$$

Classroom Example

Simplify $\dfrac{\sqrt[3]{7}}{\sqrt[3]{2}}$.

EXAMPLE 3   Simplify $\dfrac{\sqrt[3]{5}}{\sqrt[3]{9}}$.

Solution

$$\frac{\sqrt[3]{5}}{\sqrt[3]{9}} = \frac{\sqrt[3]{5}}{\sqrt[3]{9}} \cdot \frac{\sqrt[3]{3}}{\sqrt[3]{3}}$$

$$= \frac{\sqrt[3]{15}}{\sqrt[3]{27}}$$

$$= \frac{\sqrt[3]{15}}{3}$$

Now let's consider an example in which the denominator is of binomial form.

Classroom Example

Simplify $\dfrac{7}{\sqrt{5} - \sqrt{3}}$ by rationalizing the denominator.

EXAMPLE 4 Simplify $\dfrac{4}{\sqrt{5} + \sqrt{2}}$ by rationalizing the denominator.

Solution

Remember that a moment ago we found that $(\sqrt{5} + \sqrt{2})(\sqrt{5} - \sqrt{2}) = 3$. Let's use that idea here:

$$\frac{4}{\sqrt{5} + \sqrt{2}} = \left(\frac{4}{\sqrt{5} + \sqrt{2}}\right)\left(\frac{\sqrt{5} - \sqrt{2}}{\sqrt{5} - \sqrt{2}}\right)$$

$$= \frac{4(\sqrt{5} - \sqrt{2})}{(\sqrt{5} + \sqrt{2})(\sqrt{5} - \sqrt{2})} = \frac{4(\sqrt{5} - \sqrt{2})}{3}$$

The process of rationalizing the denominator does agree with the previously listed conditions. However, for certain problems in calculus, it is necessary to **rationalize the numerator.** Again, the fact that $(\sqrt{a} + \sqrt{b})(\sqrt{a} - \sqrt{b}) = a - b$ can be used.

Classroom Example

Change the form of $\dfrac{\sqrt{3x + 3h} - \sqrt{3x}}{h}$ by rationalizing the numerator.

EXAMPLE 5

Change the form of $\dfrac{\sqrt{x + h} - \sqrt{x}}{h}$ by rationalizing the *numerator*.

Solution

$$\frac{\sqrt{x + h} - \sqrt{x}}{h} = \left(\frac{\sqrt{x + h} - \sqrt{x}}{h}\right)\left(\frac{\sqrt{x + h} + \sqrt{x}}{\sqrt{x + h} + \sqrt{x}}\right)$$

$$= \frac{(x + h) - x}{h(\sqrt{x + h} + \sqrt{x})}$$

$$= \frac{\cancel{h}}{\cancel{h}(\sqrt{x + h} + \sqrt{x})}$$

$$= \frac{1}{\sqrt{x + h} + \sqrt{x}}$$

Radicals Containing Variables

Before we illustrate how to simplify radicals that contain variables, there is one important point we should call to your attention. Let's look at some examples to illustrate the idea.

Consider the radical $\sqrt{x^2}$ for different values of x.

Let $x = 3$; then $\sqrt{x^2} = \sqrt{3^2} = \sqrt{9} = 3$.

Let $x = -3$; then $\sqrt{x^2} = \sqrt{(-3)^2} = \sqrt{9} = 3$.

Thus if $x \geq 0$, then $\sqrt{x^2} = x$, but if $x < 0$, then $\sqrt{x^2} = -x$. Using the concept of absolute value, we can state that **for all real numbers, $\sqrt{x^2} = |x|$.**

Now consider the radical $\sqrt{x^3}$. Because x^3 is negative when x is negative, we need to restrict x to the nonnegative real numbers when working with $\sqrt{x^3}$. Thus we can write

if $x \geq 0$, then $\sqrt{x^3} = \sqrt{x^2}\sqrt{x} = x\sqrt{x}$

and no absolute value sign is needed.

Finally, let's consider the radical $\sqrt[3]{x^3}$.

Let $x = 2$; then $\sqrt[3]{x^3} = \sqrt[3]{2^3} = \sqrt[3]{8} = 2$.

Let $x = -2$; then $\sqrt[3]{x^3} = \sqrt[3]{(-2)^3} = \sqrt[3]{-8} = -2$.

Thus it is correct to write

$\sqrt[3]{x^3} = x$ for all real numbers

and again, no absolute value sign is needed.

The previous discussion indicates that, technically, every radical expression with variables in the radicand needs to be analyzed individually to determine the necessary restrictions on the variables. However, to avoid having to do this on a problem-by-problem basis, we shall merely **assume that all variables represent positive real numbers.**

Let's conclude this section by simplifying some radical expressions that contain variables.

$$\sqrt{72x^2y^7} = \sqrt{36x^2y^6}\sqrt{2xy} = 6xy^3\sqrt{2xy}$$

$$\sqrt[3]{40x^4y^8} = \sqrt[3]{8x^3y^6}\,\sqrt[3]{5xy^2} = 2xy^2\,\sqrt[3]{5xy^2}$$

$$\frac{\sqrt{5}}{\sqrt{12a^3}} = \frac{\sqrt{5}}{\sqrt{12a^3}} \cdot \frac{\sqrt{3a}}{\sqrt{3a}} = \frac{\sqrt{15a}}{\sqrt{36a^4}} = \frac{\sqrt{15a}}{6a^2}$$

$$\frac{3}{\sqrt[3]{4x}} = \frac{3}{\sqrt[3]{4x}} \cdot \frac{\sqrt[3]{2x^2}}{\sqrt[3]{2x^2}} = \frac{3\sqrt[3]{2x^2}}{\sqrt[3]{8x^3}} = \frac{3\sqrt[3]{2x^2}}{2x}$$

Concept Quiz 0.6

For Problems 1–8, answer true or false.

1. The symbol $\sqrt{}$ is used to designate the principal square root.
2. Every positive real number has two principal square roots.
3. The square root of zero does not exist in the real number system.
4. Every real number has one real number cube root.
5. The $\sqrt{25}$ could be 5 or -5.

6. $\sqrt{(-3)^2} = -3$
7. If $x < 0$, then $\sqrt{x^2} = -x$.
8. For real numbers, the process of rationalizing the denominator changes the denominator from an irrational number to a rational number.

Problem Set 0.6

For Problems 1–8, evaluate. (Objective 1)

1. $\sqrt{81}$

2. $-\sqrt{49}$

3. $\sqrt[3]{125}$

4. $\sqrt[4]{81}$

5. $\sqrt{\dfrac{36}{49}}$

6. $\sqrt{\dfrac{256}{64}}$

7. $\sqrt[3]{-\dfrac{27}{8}}$

8. $\sqrt[3]{\dfrac{64}{27}}$

For Problems 9–30, express each in simplest radical form. All variables represent positive real numbers. (Objective 2)

9. $\sqrt{24}$

10. $\sqrt{54}$

11. $\sqrt{112}$

12. $6\sqrt{28}$

13. $-3\sqrt{44}$

14. $-5\sqrt{68}$

15. $\dfrac{3}{4}\sqrt{20}$

16. $\dfrac{3}{8}\sqrt{72}$

17. $\sqrt{12x^2}$

18. $\sqrt{45xy^2}$

19. $\sqrt{64x^4y^7}$

20. $3\sqrt{32a^3}$

21. $\dfrac{3}{7}\sqrt{45xy^6}$

22. $\sqrt[3]{32}$

23. $\sqrt[3]{128}$

24. $\sqrt[3]{54x^3}$

25. $\sqrt[3]{16x^4}$

26. $\sqrt[3]{81x^5y^6}$

27. $\sqrt[4]{48x^5}$

28. $\sqrt[4]{162x^6y^7}$

29. $\sqrt{\dfrac{12}{25}}$

30. $\sqrt{\dfrac{75}{81}}$

For Problems 31–44, rationalize the denominator and express the result in simplest radical form. (Objective 5)

31. $\sqrt{\dfrac{7}{8}}$

32. $\dfrac{\sqrt{35}}{\sqrt{7}}$

33. $\dfrac{4\sqrt{6}}{\sqrt{10}}$

34. $\dfrac{\sqrt{27}}{\sqrt{18}}$

35. $\dfrac{6\sqrt{3}}{7\sqrt{6}}$

36. $\sqrt{\dfrac{3x}{2y}}$

37. $\dfrac{\sqrt{5}}{\sqrt{12x^4}}$

38. $\dfrac{\sqrt{5y}}{\sqrt{18x^3}}$

39. $\dfrac{\sqrt{12a^2b}}{\sqrt{5a^3b^3}}$

40. $\dfrac{5}{\sqrt[3]{3}}$

41. $\dfrac{\sqrt[3]{27}}{\sqrt[3]{4}}$

42. $\sqrt[3]{\dfrac{5}{2x}}$

43. $\dfrac{\sqrt[3]{2y}}{\sqrt[3]{3x}}$

44. $\dfrac{\sqrt[3]{12xy}}{\sqrt[3]{3x^2y^5}}$

For Problems 45–52, use the distributive property to help simplify each. (Objective 3) For example,

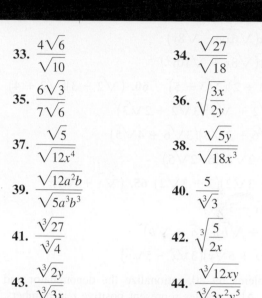

$$3\sqrt{8} + 5\sqrt{2} = 3\sqrt{4}\sqrt{2} + 5\sqrt{2}$$
$$= 6\sqrt{2} + 5\sqrt{2}$$
$$= (6 + 5)\sqrt{2}$$
$$= 11\sqrt{2}$$

45. $5\sqrt{12} + 2\sqrt{3}$

46. $4\sqrt{50} - 9\sqrt{32}$

47. $2\sqrt{28} - 3\sqrt{63} + 8\sqrt{7}$

48. $4\sqrt[3]{2} + 2\sqrt[3]{16} - \sqrt[3]{54}$

49. $\dfrac{5}{6}\sqrt{48} - \dfrac{3}{4}\sqrt{12}$

50. $\dfrac{2}{5}\sqrt{40} + \dfrac{1}{6}\sqrt{90}$

51. $\dfrac{2\sqrt{8}}{3} - \dfrac{3\sqrt{18}}{5} - \dfrac{\sqrt{50}}{2}$

52. $\dfrac{3\sqrt[3]{54}}{2} + \dfrac{5\sqrt[3]{16}}{3}$

For Problems 53–68, multiply and express the results in simplest radical form. All variables represent non-negative real numbers. (Objective 4)

53. $(4\sqrt{3})(6\sqrt{8})$ 54. $(5\sqrt{8})(3\sqrt{7})$

55. $2\sqrt{3}(5\sqrt{2} + 4\sqrt{10})$

56. $3\sqrt{6}(2\sqrt{8} - 3\sqrt{12})$

57. $3\sqrt{x}(\sqrt{6xy} - \sqrt{8y})$

58. $\sqrt{6y}(\sqrt{8x} + \sqrt{10y^2})$

59. $(\sqrt{3} + 2)(\sqrt{3} + 5)$ 60. $(\sqrt{2} - 3)(\sqrt{2} + 4)$

61. $(4\sqrt{2} + \sqrt{3})(3\sqrt{2} + 2\sqrt{3})$

62. $(2\sqrt{6} + 3\sqrt{5})(3\sqrt{6} + 4\sqrt{5})$

63. $(6 + 2\sqrt{5})(6 - 2\sqrt{5})$

64. $(7 - 3\sqrt{2})(7 + 3\sqrt{2})$ 65. $(\sqrt{x} + \sqrt{y})^2$

66. $(2\sqrt{x} - 3\sqrt{y})^2$

67. $(\sqrt{a} + \sqrt{b})(\sqrt{a} - \sqrt{b})$

68. $(3\sqrt{x} + 5\sqrt{y})(3\sqrt{x} - 5\sqrt{y})$

For Problems 69–80, rationalize the denominator and simplify. All variables represent positive real numbers. (Objective 5)

69. $\dfrac{3}{\sqrt{5} + 2}$ 70. $\dfrac{7}{\sqrt{10} - 3}$

71. $\dfrac{4}{\sqrt{7} - \sqrt{3}}$ 72. $\dfrac{2}{\sqrt{5} + \sqrt{3}}$

73. $\dfrac{\sqrt{2}}{2\sqrt{5} + 3\sqrt{7}}$ 74. $\dfrac{5}{5\sqrt{2} - 3\sqrt{5}}$

75. $\dfrac{\sqrt{x}}{\sqrt{x} - 1}$ 76. $\dfrac{\sqrt{x}}{\sqrt{x} + 2}$

77. $\dfrac{\sqrt{x}}{\sqrt{x} + \sqrt{y}}$ 78. $\dfrac{2\sqrt{x}}{\sqrt{x} - \sqrt{y}}$

79. $\dfrac{2\sqrt{x} + \sqrt{y}}{3\sqrt{x} - 2\sqrt{y}}$ 80. $\dfrac{3\sqrt{x} - 2\sqrt{y}}{2\sqrt{x} + 5\sqrt{y}}$

For Problems 81–84, *rationalize the numerator*. All variables represent positive real numbers. (Objective 5)

81. $\dfrac{\sqrt{2x + 2h} - \sqrt{2x}}{h}$

82. $\dfrac{\sqrt{x + h + 1} - \sqrt{x + 1}}{h}$

83. $\dfrac{\sqrt{x + h - 3} - \sqrt{x - 3}}{h}$

84. $\dfrac{2\sqrt{x + h} - 2\sqrt{x}}{h}$

Thoughts Into Words

85. Is the equation $\sqrt{x^2 y} = x\sqrt{y}$ true for all real-number values for x and y? Defend your answer.

86. Is the equation $\sqrt{x^2 y^2} = xy$ true for all real-number values for x and y? Defend your answer.

87. Give a step-by-step description of how you would change $\sqrt{252}$ to simplest radical form.

88. Why is $\sqrt{-9}$ not a real number?

89. How could you find a whole-number approximation for $\sqrt{2750}$ if you did not have a calculator or table available?

Further Investigations

Do the following problems, where the variable could be any real number as long as the radical represents a real number. Use absolute-value signs in the answers as necessary.

90. $\sqrt{125x^2}$ 91. $\sqrt{16x^4}$

92. $\sqrt{8b^3}$ 93. $\sqrt{3y^5}$

94. $\sqrt{288x^6}$ 95. $\sqrt{28m^8}$

96. $\sqrt{128c^{10}}$ 97. $\sqrt{18d^7}$

98. $\sqrt{49x^2}$ 99. $\sqrt{80n^{20}}$

100. $\sqrt{81h^3}$

Graphing Calculator Activities

101. Sometimes it is more convenient to express a large or very small number as a product of a power of 10 and a number that is not between 1 and 10. For example, suppose that we want to calculate $\sqrt{640,000}$. We can proceed as follows:

$$\sqrt{640,000} = \sqrt{(64)(10)^4}$$
$$= ((64)(10)^4)^{1/2}$$
$$= (64)^{1/2}(10^4)^{1/2}$$
$$= (8)(10)^2$$
$$= 8(100) = 800$$

Compute each of the following without a calculator, and then use a calculator to check your answers.

(a) $\sqrt{49,000,000}$ (b) $\sqrt{0.0025}$

(c) $\sqrt{14,400}$ (d) $\sqrt{0.000121}$

(e) $\sqrt[3]{27,000}$ (f) $\sqrt[3]{0.000064}$

102. There are several methods of approximating square roots without using a calculator. One such method works on a "clamping between values" principle. For example, to find a whole-number approximation for $\sqrt{128}$, we can proceed as follows: $11^2 = 121$ and $12^2 = 144$. Therefore $11 < \sqrt{128} < 12$. Because 128 is closer to 121 than to 144, we say that 11 is a whole-number approximation for $\sqrt{128}$. If a more precise approximation is needed, we can do more clamping. We would find that $(11.3)^2 = 127.69$ and $(11.4)^2 = 129.96$. Because 128 is closer to 127.69 than to 129.96, we conclude that $\sqrt{128} = 11.3$, to the nearest tenth.

For each of the following, use the clamping idea to find a whole-number approximation. Then check your answers using a calculator and the square root key.

(a) $\sqrt{52}$ (b) $\sqrt{93}$ (c) $\sqrt{174}$

(d) $\sqrt{200}$ (e) $\sqrt{275}$ (f) $\sqrt{350}$

103. The clamping process discussed in Problem 102 works for any whole-number root greater than or equal to 2. For example, a whole-number approximation for $\sqrt[3]{80}$ is 4 because $4^3 = 64$ and $5^3 = 125$, and 80 is closer to 64 than to 125.

For each of the following, use the clamping idea to find a whole-number approximation. Then use your calculator and the appropriate root keys to check your answers.

(a) $\sqrt[3]{24}$ (b) $\sqrt[3]{32}$ (c) $\sqrt[3]{150}$

(d) $\sqrt[3]{200}$ (e) $\sqrt[4]{50}$ (f) $\sqrt[4]{250}$

Answers to the Concept Quiz

1. True   **2.** False   **3.** False   **4.** True   **5.** False   **6.** False   **7.** True   **8.** True

0.7   Relationship Between Exponents and Roots

OBJECTIVES

1 Evaluate a number raised to a rational exponent

2 Simplify expressions with rational exponents

3 Apply rational exponents to simplify radical expressions

Recall that we used the basic properties of positive integral exponents to motivate a definition of negative integers as exponents. In this section, we shall use the properties of integral exponents to motivate definitions for rational numbers as exponents. These definitions will tie together the concepts of *exponent* and *root*. Let's consider the following comparisons:

From our study of radicals we know that	If $(b^m)^n = b^{nm}$ is to hold when m is a rational number of the form $1/p$, where p is a positive integer greater than 1 and $n = p$, then
$(\sqrt{5})^2 = 5$	$(5^{1/2})^2 = 5^{2(1/2)} = 5^1 = 5$
$(\sqrt[3]{8})^3 = 8$	$(8^{1/3})^3 = 8^{3(1/3)} = 8^1 = 8$
$(\sqrt[4]{21})^4 = 21$	$(21^{1/4})^4 = 21^{4(1/4)} = 21^1 = 21$

Such examples motivate the following definition.

Definition 0.6

If b is a real number, n is a positive integer greater than 1, and $\sqrt[n]{b}$ exists, then

$$b^{1/n} = \sqrt[n]{b}$$

Definition 0.6 states that $b^{1/n}$ means the nth root of b. We shall assume that b and n are chosen so that $\sqrt[n]{b}$ exists in the real number system. For example, $(-25)^{1/2}$ is not meaningful at this time because $\sqrt{-25}$ is not a real number. The following examples illustrate the use of Definition 0.6:

$$25^{1/2} = \sqrt{25} = 5 \qquad 16^{1/4} = \sqrt[4]{16} = 2$$
$$8^{1/3} = \sqrt[3]{8} = 2 \qquad (-27)^{1/3} = \sqrt[3]{-27} = -3$$

Now the following definition provides the basis for the use of *all* rational numbers as exponents.

Definition 0.7

If m/n is a rational number expressed in lowest terms, where n is a positive integer greater than 1, and m is any integer, and if b is a real number such that $\sqrt[n]{b}$ exists, then

$$b^{m/n} = \sqrt[n]{b^m} = (\sqrt[n]{b})^m$$

In Definition 0.7, whether we use the form $\sqrt[n]{b^m}$ or $(\sqrt[n]{b})^m$ for computational purposes depends somewhat on the magnitude of the problem. Let's use both forms on the following two problems:

$$8^{2/3} = \sqrt[3]{8^2} = \sqrt[3]{64} = 4 \quad \text{or} \quad 8^{2/3} = (\sqrt[3]{8})^2 = (2)^2 = 4$$
$$27^{2/3} = \sqrt[3]{27^2} = \sqrt[3]{729} = 9 \quad \text{or} \quad 27^{2/3} = (\sqrt[3]{27})^2 = (3)^2 = 9$$

To compute $8^{2/3}$, both forms work equally well. However, to compute $27^{2/3}$, the form $(\sqrt[3]{27})^2$ is much easier to handle. The following examples further illustrate Definition 0.7:

$$25^{3/2} = (\sqrt{25})^3 = 5^3 = 125$$

$$(32)^{-2/5} = \frac{1}{(32)^{2/5}} = \frac{1}{(\sqrt[5]{32})^2} = \frac{1}{2^2} = \frac{1}{4}$$

$$(-64)^{2/3} = (\sqrt[3]{-64})^2 = (-4)^2 = 16$$

$$-8^{4/3} = -(\sqrt[3]{8})^4 = -(2)^4 = -16$$

It can be shown that all of the results pertaining to integral exponents listed in Property 0.2 (on page 23) also hold for all rational exponents. Let's consider some examples to illustrate each of those results.

$$x^{1/2} \cdot x^{2/3} = x^{1/2+2/3} \qquad\qquad b^n \cdot b^m = b^{n+m}$$
$$= x^{3/6+4/6}$$
$$= x^{7/6}$$

$$(a^{2/3})^{3/2} = a^{(3/2)(2/3)} \qquad\qquad (b^n)^m = b^{nm}$$
$$= a^1 = a$$

$$(16y^{2/3})^{1/2} = (16)^{1/2}(y^{2/3})^{1/2} \qquad\qquad (ab)^n = a^n b^n$$
$$= 4y^{1/3}$$

$$\frac{y^{3/4}}{y^{1/2}} = y^{3/4-1/2} \qquad\qquad \frac{b^n}{b^m} = b^{n-m}$$
$$= y^{3/4-2/4}$$
$$= y^{1/4}$$

$$\left(\frac{x^{1/2}}{y^{1/3}}\right)^6 = \frac{(x^{1/2})^6}{(y^{1/3})^6} \qquad\qquad \left(\frac{a}{b}\right)^n = \frac{a^n}{b^n}$$
$$= \frac{x^3}{y^2}$$

The link between exponents and roots provides a basis for multiplying and dividing some radicals even if they have different indexes. The general procedure is to change from radical to exponential form, apply the properties of exponents, and then change back to radical form. Let's apply these procedures in the next three examples:

$$\sqrt{2}\sqrt[3]{2} = 2^{1/2} \cdot 2^{1/3} = 2^{1/2+1/3} = 2^{5/6} = \sqrt[6]{2^5} = \sqrt[6]{32}$$

$$\sqrt{xy}\sqrt[5]{x^2y} = (xy)^{1/2}(x^2y)^{1/5}$$
$$= x^{1/2}y^{1/2}x^{2/5}y^{1/5}$$
$$= x^{1/2+2/5}y^{1/2+1/5}$$
$$= x^{9/10}y^{7/10}$$
$$= (x^9y^7)^{1/10} = \sqrt[10]{x^9y^7}$$

$$\frac{\sqrt{5}}{\sqrt[3]{5}} = \frac{5^{1/2}}{5^{1/3}} = 5^{1/2-1/3} = 5^{1/6} = \sqrt[6]{5}$$

Earlier we agreed that a radical such as $\sqrt[3]{x^4}$ is not in simplest form because the radicand contains a perfect power of the index. Thus we simplified $\sqrt[3]{x^4}$ by expressing it as $\sqrt[3]{x^3}\sqrt[3]{x}$, which in turn can be written $x\sqrt[3]{x}$. Such simplification can also be done in exponential form, as follows:

$$\sqrt[3]{x^4} = x^{4/3} = x^{3/3} \cdot x^{1/3} = x \cdot x^{1/3} = x\sqrt[3]{x}$$

Note the use of this type of simplification in the following examples.

Classroom Example
Perform the indicated operations and express the answers in simplest radical form.

(a) $\sqrt[3]{x^2}\sqrt[4]{x}$

(b) $\sqrt[4]{3}\sqrt[3]{9}$

(c) $\dfrac{\sqrt[3]{4}}{\sqrt[3]{2}}$

EXAMPLE 1

Perform the indicated operations and express the answers in simplest radical form.

(a) $\sqrt[3]{x^2}\sqrt[4]{x^3}$ (b) $\sqrt{2}\sqrt[3]{4}$ (c) $\dfrac{\sqrt{27}}{\sqrt[3]{3}}$

Solutions

(a) $\sqrt[3]{x^2}\sqrt[4]{x^3} = x^{2/3} \cdot x^{3/4} = x^{2/3+3/4} = x^{17/12} = x^{12/12} \cdot x^{5/12} = x\sqrt[12]{x^5}$

(b) $\sqrt{2}\sqrt[3]{4} = 2^{1/2} \cdot 4^{1/3} = 2^{1/2}(2^2)^{1/3} = 2^{1/2} \cdot 2^{2/3}$

$= 2^{1/2+2/3} = 2^{7/6} = 2^{6/6} \cdot 2^{1/6} = 2\sqrt[6]{2}$

(c) $\dfrac{\sqrt{27}}{\sqrt[3]{3}} = \dfrac{27^{1/2}}{3^{1/3}} = \dfrac{(3^3)^{1/2}}{3^{1/3}} = \dfrac{3^{3/2}}{3^{1/3}} = 3^{3/2-1/3} = 3^{7/6}$

$= 3^{6/6} \cdot 3^{1/6} = 3\sqrt[6]{3}$ ◼

The process of rationalizing the denominator can sometimes be handled more easily in exponential form. Consider the following examples, which illustrate this procedure.

Classroom Example
Rationalize the denominator and express the answer in simplest radical form.

(a) $\dfrac{3}{\sqrt[3]{y^2}}$ (b) $\dfrac{\sqrt{m}}{\sqrt[5]{n^2}}$

EXAMPLE 2

Rationalize the denominator and express the answer in simplest radical form.

(a) $\dfrac{2}{\sqrt[3]{x}}$ (b) $\dfrac{\sqrt[3]{x}}{\sqrt{y}}$

Solutions

(a) $\dfrac{2}{\sqrt[3]{x}} = \dfrac{2}{x^{1/3}} = \dfrac{2}{x^{1/3}} \cdot \dfrac{x^{2/3}}{x^{2/3}} = \dfrac{2x^{2/3}}{x} = \dfrac{2\sqrt[3]{x^2}}{x}$

(b) $\dfrac{\sqrt[3]{x}}{\sqrt{y}} = \dfrac{x^{1/3}}{y^{1/2}} = \dfrac{x^{1/3}}{y^{1/2}} \cdot \dfrac{y^{1/2}}{y^{1/2}} = \dfrac{x^{1/3} \cdot y^{1/2}}{y} = \dfrac{x^{2/6} \cdot y^{3/6}}{y} = \dfrac{\sqrt[6]{x^2y^3}}{y}$ ◼

Note in part b that if we had changed back to radical form at the step $\dfrac{x^{1/3}y^{1/2}}{y}$, we would have obtained the product of two radicals, $\sqrt[3]{x}\sqrt{y}$, in the numerator. Instead we used the exponential form to find this product and express the final result with a single radical in the numerator. Finally, let's consider an example involving *the root of a root*.

Classroom Example
Simplify $\sqrt[4]{\sqrt[3]{5}}$.

EXAMPLE 3   Simplify $\sqrt[3]{\sqrt{2}}$.

Solution

$$\sqrt[3]{\sqrt{2}} = \left(2^{1/2}\right)^{1/3} = 2^{1/6} = \sqrt[6]{2}$$

Concept Quiz 0.7

For Problems 1–4, select the equivalent radical form.

1. $x^{\frac{3}{5}}$ **A.** $\sqrt[3]{x^5}$ **B.** $x\sqrt[3]{x^2}$ **C.** $\sqrt[5]{x^3}$

2. $y^{-\frac{1}{3}}$ **A.** $\dfrac{1}{\sqrt[3]{y}}$ **B.** $\dfrac{\sqrt[3]{y^2}}{y}$ **C.** $-\sqrt[3]{y}$

3. $-w^{-\frac{1}{2}}$ **A.** $-\dfrac{\sqrt{w}}{w}$ **B.** $\sqrt{w}$ **C.** $-\sqrt{w}$

4. $\sqrt[n]{x}\sqrt[m]{x}$ **A.** $\sqrt[mn]{x}$ **B.** $x^{\frac{m+n}{mn}}$ **C.** $x^{\frac{1}{m+n}}$

For Problems 5–8, answer true or false.

5. Assuming the nth root of x exists, $\sqrt[n]{x}$ can be expressed as $x^{\frac{1}{n}}$.
6. The expression $\sqrt[n]{x^m}$ is $\left(\sqrt[n]{x}\right)^m$.
7. The process of rationalizing the denominator can be done with rational exponents.
8. An exponent of $\dfrac{1}{3}$ indicates the cube root.

Problem Set 0.7

For Problems 1–16, evaluate. **(Objective 1)**

1. $49^{1/2}$

2. $64^{1/3}$

3. $32^{3/5}$

4. $(-8)^{1/3}$

5. $-8^{2/3}$

6. $64^{-1/2}$

7. $\left(\dfrac{1}{4}\right)^{-1/2}$

8. $\left(-\dfrac{27}{8}\right)^{-1/3}$

9. $16^{3/2}$

10. $(0.008)^{1/3}$

11. $(0.01)^{3/2}$

12. $\left(\dfrac{1}{27}\right)^{-2/3}$

13. $64^{-5/6}$

14. $-16^{5/4}$

15. $\left(\dfrac{1}{8}\right)^{-1/3}$

16. $\left(-\dfrac{1}{8}\right)^{2/3}$

For Problems 17–32, perform the indicated operations and simplify. Express final answers using positive exponents only. (Objective 2)

17. $(3x^{1/4})(5x^{1/3})$

18. $(2x^{2/5})(6x^{1/4})$

19. $(y^{2/3})(y^{-1/4})$

20. $(2x^{1/3})(x^{-1/2})$

21. $(4x^{1/4}y^{1/2})^3$

22. $(5x^{1/2}y)^2$

23. $\dfrac{24x^{3/5}}{6x^{1/3}}$

24. $\dfrac{18x^{1/2}}{9x^{1/3}}$

25. $\dfrac{56a^{1/6}}{8a^{1/4}}$

26. $\dfrac{48b^{1/3}}{12b^{3/4}}$

27. $\left(\dfrac{2x^{1/3}}{3y^{1/4}}\right)^4$

28. $\left(\dfrac{6x^{2/5}}{7y^{2/3}}\right)^2$

29. $\left(\dfrac{x^2}{y^3}\right)^{-1/2}$

30. $\left(\dfrac{a^3}{b^{-2}}\right)^{-1/3}$

31. $\left(\dfrac{4a^2x}{2a^{1/2}x^{1/3}}\right)^3$

32. $\left(\dfrac{3ax^{-1}}{a^{1/2}x^{-2}}\right)^2$

For Problems 33–48, perform the indicated operations and express the answer in simplest radical form. (Objective 3)

33. $\sqrt{2}\sqrt[4]{2}$

34. $\sqrt[3]{3}\sqrt{3}$

35. $\sqrt[3]{x}\sqrt[4]{x}$

36. $\sqrt[3]{x^2}\sqrt[5]{x^3}$

37. $\sqrt{xy}\sqrt[4]{x^3y^5}$

38. $\sqrt[3]{x^2y^4}\sqrt[4]{x^3y}$

39. $\sqrt[3]{a^2b^2}\sqrt[4]{a^3b}$

40. $\sqrt{ab}\sqrt[3]{a^4b^5}$

41. $\sqrt[3]{4}\sqrt{8}$

42. $\sqrt[3]{9}\sqrt{27}$

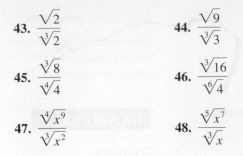

43. $\dfrac{\sqrt{2}}{\sqrt[3]{2}}$

44. $\dfrac{\sqrt{9}}{\sqrt[3]{3}}$

45. $\dfrac{\sqrt[3]{8}}{\sqrt[4]{4}}$

46. $\dfrac{\sqrt[3]{16}}{\sqrt[6]{4}}$

47. $\dfrac{\sqrt[4]{x^9}}{\sqrt[3]{x^2}}$

48. $\dfrac{\sqrt[5]{x^7}}{\sqrt[3]{x}}$

For Problems 49–56, rationalize the denominator and express the final answer in simplest radical form. (Objective 3)

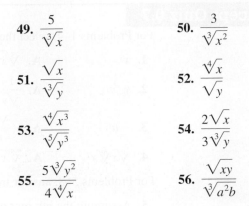

49. $\dfrac{5}{\sqrt[3]{x}}$

50. $\dfrac{3}{\sqrt[3]{x^2}}$

51. $\dfrac{\sqrt{x}}{\sqrt[3]{y}}$

52. $\dfrac{\sqrt[4]{x}}{\sqrt{y}}$

53. $\dfrac{\sqrt[4]{x^3}}{\sqrt[5]{y^3}}$

54. $\dfrac{2\sqrt{x}}{3\sqrt[3]{y}}$

55. $\dfrac{5\sqrt[3]{y^2}}{4\sqrt[4]{x}}$

56. $\dfrac{\sqrt{xy}}{\sqrt[3]{a^2b}}$

57. Simplify each of the following, expressing the final result as one radical. For example,

$$\sqrt{\sqrt{3}} = (3^{1/2})^{1/2} = 3^{1/4} = \sqrt[4]{3}$$

(a) $\sqrt[3]{\sqrt{2}}$

(b) $\sqrt[3]{\sqrt[4]{3}}$

(c) $\sqrt[3]{\sqrt{x^3}}$

(d) $\sqrt{\sqrt[3]{x^4}}$

Thoughts Into Words

58. Your friend keeps getting an error message when evaluating $-4^{5/2}$ on his calculator. What error is he probably making?

59. Explain how you would evaluate $27^{2/3}$ without a calculator.

Further Investigations

Sometimes we meet the following type of simplification problem in calculus:

$$\frac{(x-1)^{1/2} - x(x-1)^{-(1/2)}}{[(x-1)^{1/2}]^2}$$

$$= \left(\frac{(x-1)^{1/2} - x(x-1)^{-(1/2)}}{(x-1)^{2/2}}\right) \cdot \left(\frac{(x-1)^{1/2}}{(x-1)^{1/2}}\right)$$

$$= \frac{x - 1 - x(x-1)^0}{(x-1)^{3/2}}$$

$$= \frac{x - 1 - x}{(x-1)^{3/2}}$$

$$= \frac{-1}{(x-1)^{3/2}} \quad \text{or} \quad -\frac{1}{(x-1)^{3/2}}$$

For Problems 60–65, simplify each expression as we did in the previous example.

60. $\dfrac{2(x+1)^{1/2} - x(x+1)^{-(1/2)}}{[(x+1)^{1/2}]^2}$

61. $\dfrac{2(2x-1)^{1/2} - 2x(2x-1)^{-(1/2)}}{[(2x-1)^{1/2}]^2}$

62. $\dfrac{2x(4x+1)^{1/2} - 2x^2(4x+1)^{-(1/2)}}{[(4x+1)^{1/2}]^2}$

63. $\dfrac{(x^2+2x)^{1/2} - x(x+1)(x^2+2x)^{-(1/2)}}{[(x^2+2x)^{1/2}]^2}$

64. $\dfrac{(3x)^{1/3} - x(3x)^{-(2/3)}}{[(3x)^{1/3}]^2}$

65. $\dfrac{3(2x)^{1/3} - 2x(2x)^{-(2/3)}}{[(2x)^{1/3}]^2}$

Graphing Calculator Activities

66. Use your calculator to evaluate each of the following.

(a) $\sqrt[3]{1728}$ (b) $\sqrt[3]{5832}$

(c) $\sqrt[4]{2401}$ (d) $\sqrt[4]{65,536}$

(e) $\sqrt[5]{161,051}$ (f) $\sqrt[5]{6,436,343}$

67. In Definition 0.7 we stated that $b^{m/n} = \sqrt[n]{b^m} = (\sqrt[n]{b})^m$. Use your calculator to verify each of the following.

(a) $\sqrt[3]{27^2} = (\sqrt[3]{27})^2$ (b) $\sqrt[3]{8^5} = (\sqrt[3]{8})^5$

(c) $\sqrt[4]{16^3} = (\sqrt[4]{16})^3$ (d) $\sqrt[3]{16^2} = (\sqrt[3]{16})^2$

(e) $\sqrt[5]{9^4} = (\sqrt[5]{9})^4$ (f) $\sqrt[3]{12^4} = (\sqrt[3]{12})^4$

68. Use your calculator to evaluate each of the following.

(a) $16^{5/2}$ (b) $25^{7/2}$

(c) $16^{9/4}$ (d) $27^{5/3}$

(e) $343^{2/3}$ (f) $512^{4/3}$

69. Use your calculator to estimate each of the following to the nearest thousandth.

(a) $7^{4/3}$ (b) $10^{4/5}$

(c) $12^{2/5}$ (d) $19^{2/5}$

(e) $7^{3/4}$ (f) $10^{5/4}$

Answers to the Concept Quiz

1. C **2.** B **3.** A **4.** B **5.** True **6.** True **7.** True **8.** True

0.8 Complex Numbers

OBJECTIVES
1. Express the square root of a negative number in terms of i
2. Add and subtract complex numbers
3. Multiply and divide complex numbers

So far we have dealt only with real numbers. However, as we get ready to solve equations in the next chapter, there is a need for *more numbers*. There are some very simple equations that do not have solutions if we restrict ourselves to the set of real numbers. For example, the equation $x^2 + 1 = 0$ has no solutions among the real numbers. To solve such equations, we need to extend the real number system. In this section we will introduce a set of numbers that contains some numbers with squares that are negative real numbers. Then in the next chapter and in Chapter 4 we will see that this set of numbers, called the **complex numbers,** provides solutions not only for equations such as $x^2 + 1 = 0$ but also for *any* polynomial equation in general.

Let's begin by defining a number i such that

$$i^2 = -1$$

The number i is not a real number and is often called the **imaginary unit,** but the number i^2 is the real number -1. The imaginary unit i is used to define a complex number as follows.

> ### Definition 0.8
>
> A **complex number** is any number that can be expressed in the form
>
> $$a + bi$$
>
> where a and b are real numbers, and i is the imaginary unit.

The form $a + bi$ is called the **standard form** of a complex number. The real number a is called the **real part** of the complex number, and b is called the **imaginary part.** (Note that b is a real number even though it is called the imaginary part.) Each of the following represents a complex number:

$6 + 2i$ is already expressed in the form $a + bi$. Traditionally, complex numbers for which $a \neq 0$ and $b \neq 0$ have been called imaginary numbers.

$5 - 3i$ can be written $5 + (-3i)$ even though the form $5 - 3i$ is often used.

$-8 + i\sqrt{2}$ can be written $-8 + \sqrt{2}i$. It is easy to mistake $\sqrt{2}i$ for $\sqrt{2i}$. Thus we commonly write $i\sqrt{2}$ instead of $\sqrt{2}i$ to avoid any difficulties with the radical sign.

$-9i$ can be written $0 + (-9i)$. Complex numbers such as $-9i$, for which $a = 0$ and $b \neq 0$, traditionally have been called **pure imaginary numbers.**

5 can be written $5 + 0i$.

The set of real numbers is a subset of the set of complex numbers. The following diagram indicates the organizational format of the complex number system:

Complex numbers

$a + bi$, where a and b
are real numbers

Real numbers

$a + bi$, where $b = 0$

Imaginary numbers

$a + bi$, where $b \neq 0$

Pure imaginary numbers

$a + bi$, where $a = 0$ and $b \neq 0$

Two complex numbers $a + bi$ and $c + di$ are said to be *equal* if and only if $a = c$ and $b = d$. In other words, two complex numbers are equal if and only if their real parts are equal and their imaginary parts are equal.

Adding and Subtracting Complex Numbers

The following definition provides the basis for adding complex numbers:

$$(a + bi) + (c + di) = (a + c) + (b + d)i$$

We can use this definition to find the sum of two complex numbers.

$$(4 + 3i) + (5 + 9i) = (4 + 5) + (3 + 9)i = 9 + 12i$$

$$(-6 + 4i) + (8 - 7i) = (-6 + 8) + (4 - 7)i = 2 - 3i$$

$$\left(\frac{1}{2} + \frac{3}{4}i\right) + \left(\frac{2}{3} + \frac{1}{5}i\right) = \left(\frac{1}{2} + \frac{2}{3}\right) + \left(\frac{3}{4} + \frac{1}{5}\right)i$$

$$= \left(\frac{3}{6} + \frac{4}{6}\right) + \left(\frac{15}{20} + \frac{4}{20}\right)i = \frac{7}{6} + \frac{19}{20}i$$

$$\left(3 + i\sqrt{2}\right) + \left(-4 + i\sqrt{2}\right) = [3 + (-4)] + \left(\sqrt{2} + \sqrt{2}\right)i = -1 + 2i\sqrt{2}$$

Note the form for writing $2\sqrt{2}i$.

The set of complex numbers is **closed with respect to addition**; that is, the sum of two complex numbers is a complex number. Furthermore, the commutative and associative properties of addition hold for all complex numbers. The additive identity element is $0 + 0i$, or simply the real number 0. The additive inverse of $a + bi$ is $-a - bi$ because

$$(a + bi) + (-a - bi) = [a + (-a)] + [b + (-b)]i = 0$$

Therefore, to *subtract* $c + di$ from $a + bi$, we add the additive inverse of $c + di$:

$$(a + bi) - (c + di) = (a + bi) + (-c - di)$$
$$= (a - c) + (b - d)i$$

The following examples illustrate the subtraction of complex numbers:

$$(9 + 8i) - (5 + 3i) = (9 - 5) + (8 - 3)i = 4 + 5i$$
$$(3 - 2i) - (4 - 10i) = (3 - 4) + [-2 - (-10)]i = -1 + 8i$$
$$\left(-\frac{1}{2} + \frac{1}{3}i\right) - \left(\frac{3}{4} + \frac{1}{2}i\right) = \left(-\frac{1}{2} - \frac{3}{4}\right) + \left(\frac{1}{3} - \frac{1}{2}\right)i = -\frac{5}{4} - \frac{1}{6}i$$

Multiplying and Dividing Complex Numbers

Because $i^2 = -1$, the number i is a square root of -1, so we write $i = \sqrt{-1}$. It should also be evident that $-i$ is a square root of -1 because

$$(-i)^2 = (-i)(-i) = i^2 = -1$$

Therefore, in the set of complex numbers, -1 has two square roots—namely, i and $-i$. This is expressed symbolically as

$$i = \sqrt{-1} \quad \text{and} \quad -i = -\sqrt{-1}$$

Let's extend the definition so that in the set of complex numbers, every negative real number has two square roots. For any positive real number b,

$$\left(i\sqrt{b}\right)^2 = i^2(b) = -1(b) = -b$$

Therefore, let's denote the **principal square root of $-b$** by $\sqrt{-b}$ and define it to be

$$\sqrt{-b} = i\sqrt{b}$$

where b is any positive real number. In other words, the principal square root of any negative real number can be represented as the product of a real number and the imaginary unit i. Consider the following examples:

$$\sqrt{-4} = i\sqrt{4} = 2i$$
$$\sqrt{-17} = i\sqrt{17}$$
$$\sqrt{-24} = i\sqrt{24} = i\sqrt{4}\sqrt{6} = 2i\sqrt{6} \quad \text{Note that we simplified the}$$
$$\text{radical } \sqrt{24} \text{ to } 2\sqrt{6}$$

We should also observe that $-\sqrt{-b}$, where $b > 0$, is a square root of $-b$ because

$$\left(-\sqrt{-b}\right)^2 = \left(-i\sqrt{b}\right)^2 = i^2(b) = (-1)b = -b$$

Thus in the set of complex numbers, $-b$ (where $b > 0$) has two square roots: $i\sqrt{b}$ and $-i\sqrt{b}$. These are expressed as

$$\sqrt{-b} = i\sqrt{b} \quad \text{and} \quad -\sqrt{-b} = -i\sqrt{b}$$

We must be careful with the use of the symbol $\sqrt{-b}$, where $b > 0$. Some properties that are true in the set of real numbers involving the square root symbol do not hold if the square root symbol does not represent a real number. For example, $\sqrt{a}\sqrt{b} = \sqrt{ab}$ *does not hold if a and b are both negative numbers.*

Correct $\qquad \sqrt{-4}\sqrt{-9} = (2i)(3i) = 6i^2 = 6(-1) = -6$

Incorrect $\qquad \sqrt{-4}\sqrt{-9} = \sqrt{(-4)(-9)} = \sqrt{36} = 6$

To avoid difficulty with this idea, you should rewrite all expressions of the form $\sqrt{-b}$, where $b > 0$, in the form $i\sqrt{b}$ *before* doing any computations. The following examples further illustrate this point:

$$\sqrt{-5}\sqrt{-7} = (i\sqrt{5})(i\sqrt{7}) = i^2\sqrt{35} = (-1)\sqrt{35} = -\sqrt{35}$$

$$\sqrt{-2}\sqrt{-8} = (i\sqrt{2})(i\sqrt{8}) = i^2\sqrt{16} = (-1)(4) = -4$$

$$\sqrt{-2}\sqrt{8} = (i\sqrt{2})(\sqrt{8}) = i\sqrt{16} = 4i$$

$$\sqrt{-6}\sqrt{-8} = (i\sqrt{6})(i\sqrt{8}) = i^2\sqrt{48} = i^2\sqrt{16}\sqrt{3} = 4i^2\sqrt{3} = -4\sqrt{3}$$

$$\frac{\sqrt{-2}}{\sqrt{3}} = \frac{i\sqrt{2}}{\sqrt{3}} = \frac{i\sqrt{2}}{\sqrt{3}} \cdot \frac{\sqrt{3}}{\sqrt{3}} = \frac{i\sqrt{6}}{3}$$

$$\frac{\sqrt{-48}}{\sqrt{12}} = \frac{i\sqrt{48}}{\sqrt{12}} = i\sqrt{\frac{48}{12}} = i\sqrt{4} = 2i$$

Because complex numbers have a *binomial form,* we can find the product of two complex numbers in the same way that we find the product of two binomials. Then, by replacing i^2 with -1 we can simplify and express the final product in the standard form of a complex number. Consider the following examples:

$$(2 + 3i)(4 + 5i) = 2(4 + 5i) + 3i(4 + 5i)$$
$$= 8 + 10i + 12i + 15i^2$$
$$= 8 + 22i + 15(-1)$$
$$= 8 + 22i - 15$$
$$= -7 + 22i$$

$$(1 - 7i)^2 = (1 - 7i)(1 - 7i)$$
$$= 1(1 - 7i) - 7i(1 - 7i)$$
$$= 1 - 7i - 7i + 49i^2$$
$$= 1 - 14i + 49(-1)$$
$$= 1 - 14i - 49$$
$$= -48 - 14i$$

$$(2 + 3i)(2 - 3i) = 2(2 - 3i) + 3i(2 - 3i)$$
$$= 4 - 6i + 6i - 9i^2$$
$$= 4 - 9(-1)$$
$$= 4 + 9$$
$$= 13$$

Remark: Don't forget that when multiplying complex numbers, we can also use the multiplication patterns

$$(a + b)^2 = a^2 + 2ab + b^2$$
$$(a - b)^2 = a^2 - 2ab + b^2$$
$$(a + b)(a - b) = a^2 - b^2$$

The last example illustrates an important idea. The complex numbers $2 + 3i$ and $2 - 3i$ are called *conjugates* of each other. In general, the two complex numbers $a + bi$ and $a - bi$ are called **conjugates** of each other, and **the product of a complex number and its conjugate is a real number.** This can be shown as follows:

$$(a + bi)(a - bi) = a(a - bi) + bi(a - bi)$$
$$= a^2 - abi + abi - b^2i^2$$
$$= a^2 - b^2(-1)$$
$$= a^2 + b^2$$

Conjugates are used to simplify an expression such as $3i/(5 + 2i)$, which *indicates the quotient of two complex numbers*. To eliminate i in the denominator and to change the indicated quotient to the standard form of a complex number, we can multiply both the numerator and denominator by the conjugate of the denominator.

$$\frac{3i}{5 + 2i} = \frac{3i}{5 + 2i} \cdot \frac{5 - 2i}{5 - 2i}$$
$$= \frac{3i(5 - 2i)}{(5 + 2i)(5 - 2i)}$$
$$= \frac{15i - 6i^2}{25 - 4i^2}$$
$$= \frac{15i - 6(-1)}{25 - 4(-1)}$$
$$= \frac{6 + 15i}{29}$$
$$= \frac{6}{29} + \frac{15}{29}i$$

The following examples further illustrate the process of dividing complex numbers:

$$\frac{2 - 3i}{4 - 7i} = \frac{2 - 3i}{4 - 7i} \cdot \frac{4 + 7i}{4 + 7i}$$
$$= \frac{(2 - 3i)(4 + 7i)}{(4 - 7i)(4 + 7i)}$$
$$= \frac{8 + 14i - 12i - 21i^2}{16 - 49i^2}$$
$$= \frac{8 + 2i - 21(-1)}{16 - 49(-1)}$$
$$= \frac{29 + 2i}{65} = \frac{29}{65} + \frac{2}{65}i$$

$$\frac{4 - 5i}{2i} = \frac{4 - 5i}{2i} \cdot \frac{-2i}{-2i}$$

$$= \frac{(4 - 5i)(-2i)}{(2i)(-2i)}$$

$$= \frac{-8i + 10i^2}{-4i^2}$$

$$= \frac{-8i + 10(-1)}{-4(-1)}$$

$$= \frac{-10 - 8i}{4} = -\frac{5}{2} - 2i$$

For a problem such as the last one, in which the denominator is a pure imaginary number, we can change to standard form by choosing a multiplier other than the conjugate of the denominator. Consider the following alternative approach:

$$\frac{4 - 5i}{2i} = \frac{4 - 5i}{2i} \cdot \frac{i}{i}$$

$$= \frac{(4 - 5i)(i)}{(2i)(i)}$$

$$= \frac{4i - 5i^2}{2i^2}$$

$$= \frac{4i - 5(-1)}{2(-1)}$$

$$= \frac{5 + 4i}{-2}$$

$$= -\frac{5}{2} - 2i$$

Concept Quiz 0.8

For Problems 1–8, answer true or false.

1. The number i is not a real number.
2. The number i^2 is a real number.
3. The form $ai + b$ is called the standard form of a complex number.
4. Every real number is a member of the set of complex numbers.
5. The principal square root of any negative real number can be represented as the product of a real number and the imaginary unit i.
6. $6 - 4i$ and $-6 + 4i$ are additive inverses.
7. The conjugate of the number $-2 - 3i$ is $2 + 3i$.
8. The product of a complex number and its conjugate is a real number.

Problem Set 0.8

For Problems 1–14, add or subtract as indicated. (Objective 2)

1. $(5 + 2i) + (8 + 6i)$

2. $(-9 + 3i) + (4 + 5i)$

3. $(8 + 6i) - (5 + 2i)$

4. $(-6 + 4i) - (4 + 6i)$

5. $(-7 - 3i) + (-4 + 4i)$ **6.** $(6 - 7i) - (7 - 6i)$

7. $(-2 - 3i) - (-1 - i)$

8. $\left(\dfrac{1}{3} + \dfrac{2}{5}i\right) + \left(\dfrac{1}{2} + \dfrac{1}{4}i\right)$

9. $\left(-\dfrac{3}{4} - \dfrac{1}{4}i\right) + \left(\dfrac{3}{5} + \dfrac{2}{3}i\right)$

10. $\left(\dfrac{5}{8} + \dfrac{1}{2}i\right) - \left(\dfrac{7}{8} + \dfrac{1}{5}i\right)$

11. $\left(\dfrac{3}{10} - \dfrac{3}{4}i\right) - \left(-\dfrac{2}{5} + \dfrac{1}{6}i\right)$

12. $\left(4 + i\sqrt{3}\right) + \left(-6 - 2i\sqrt{3}\right)$

13. $(5 + 3i) + (7 - 2i) + (-8 - i)$

14. $(5 - 7i) - (6 - 2i) - (-1 - 2i)$

For Problems 15–30, write each in terms of i and simplify. (Objective 1) For example,
$$\sqrt{-20} = i\sqrt{20} = i\sqrt{4}\sqrt{5} = 2i\sqrt{5}$$

15. $\sqrt{-9}$ **16.** $\sqrt{-49}$

17. $\sqrt{-19}$ **18.** $\sqrt{-31}$

19. $\sqrt{-\dfrac{4}{9}}$ **20.** $\sqrt{-\dfrac{25}{36}}$

21. $\sqrt{-8}$ **22.** $\sqrt{-18}$

23. $\sqrt{-27}$ **24.** $\sqrt{-32}$

25. $\sqrt{-54}$ **26.** $\sqrt{-40}$

27. $3\sqrt{-36}$ **28.** $5\sqrt{-64}$

29. $4\sqrt{-18}$ **30.** $6\sqrt{-8}$

Some of the solution sets for quadratic equations in the next chapter will contain complex numbers such as $\dfrac{-4 + \sqrt{-12}}{2}$ and $\dfrac{-4 - \sqrt{-12}}{2}$. We can simplify the first number as follows.

$$\dfrac{-4 + \sqrt{-12}}{2} = \dfrac{-4 + i\sqrt{12}}{2} =$$

$$\dfrac{-4 + 2i\sqrt{3}}{2} = \dfrac{2(-2 + i\sqrt{3})}{2} = -2 + i\sqrt{3}$$

For Problems 31–36, simplify each of the following complex numbers.

31. $\dfrac{-4 - \sqrt{-12}}{2}$ **32.** $\dfrac{6 + \sqrt{-24}}{4}$

33. $\dfrac{-3 - \sqrt{-18}}{3}$ **34.** $\dfrac{-6 + \sqrt{-27}}{3}$

35. $\dfrac{12 + \sqrt{-45}}{6}$ **36.** $\dfrac{4 - \sqrt{-48}}{2}$

For Problems 37–50, write each in terms of i, perform the indicated operations, and simplify. (Objective 1) For example,

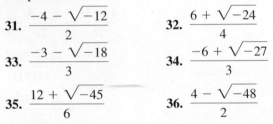

$$\sqrt{-9}\sqrt{-16} = \left(i\sqrt{9}\right)\left(i\sqrt{16}\right) = (3i)(4i)$$
$$= 12i^2 = 12(-1) = -12$$

37. $\sqrt{-4}\sqrt{-16}$ **38.** $\sqrt{-25}\sqrt{-9}$

39. $\sqrt{-2}\sqrt{-3}$ **40.** $\sqrt{-3}\sqrt{-7}$

41. $\sqrt{-5}\sqrt{-4}$ **42.** $\sqrt{-7}\sqrt{-9}$

43. $\sqrt{-6}\sqrt{-10}$ **44.** $\sqrt{-2}\sqrt{-12}$

45. $\sqrt{-8}\sqrt{-7}$ **46.** $\sqrt{-12}\sqrt{-5}$

47. $\dfrac{\sqrt{-36}}{\sqrt{-4}}$ **48.** $\dfrac{\sqrt{-64}}{\sqrt{-16}}$

49. $\dfrac{\sqrt{-54}}{\sqrt{-9}}$ **50.** $\dfrac{\sqrt{-18}}{\sqrt{-3}}$

For Problems 51–70, find each product and express the answers in standard form. (Objective 3)

51. $(3i)(7i)$

52. $(-5i)(8i)$

53. $(4i)(3 - 2i)$

54. $(5i)(2 + 6i)$

55. $(3 + 2i)(4 + 6i)$

56. $(7 + 3i)(8 + 4i)$

57. $(4 + 5i)(2 - 9i)$

58. $(1 + i)(2 - i)$

59. $(-2 - 3i)(4 + 6i)$

60. $(-3 - 7i)(2 + 10i)$

61. $(6 - 4i)(-1 - 2i)$

62. $(7 - 3i)(-2 - 8i)$

63. $(3 + 4i)^2$

64. $(4 - 2i)^2$

65. $(-1 - 2i)^2$

66. $(-2 + 5i)^2$

67. $(8 - 7i)(8 + 7i)$

68. $(5 + 3i)(5 - 3i)$

69. $(-2 + 3i)(-2 - 3i)$

70. $(-6 - 7i)(-6 + 7i)$

For Problems 71–84, find each quotient and express the answers in standard form. (Objective 3)

71. $\dfrac{4i}{3 - 2i}$

72. $\dfrac{3i}{6 + 2i}$

73. $\dfrac{2 + 3i}{3i}$

74. $\dfrac{3 - 5i}{4i}$

75. $\dfrac{3}{2i}$

76. $\dfrac{7}{4i}$

77. $\dfrac{3 + 2i}{4 + 5i}$

78. $\dfrac{2 + 5i}{3 + 7i}$

79. $\dfrac{4 + 7i}{2 - 3i}$

80. $\dfrac{3 + 9i}{4 - i}$

81. $\dfrac{3 - 7i}{-2 + 4i}$

82. $\dfrac{4 - 10i}{-3 + 7i}$

83. $\dfrac{-1 - i}{-2 - 3i}$

84. $\dfrac{-4 + 9i}{-3 - 6i}$

85. Using $a + bi$ and $c + di$ to represent two complex numbers, verify the following properties.

(a) The conjugate of the sum of two complex numbers is equal to the sum of the conjugates of the two numbers.

(b) The conjugate of the product of two complex numbers is equal to the product of the conjugates of the numbers.

Thoughts Into Words

86. Is every real number also a complex number? Explain your answer.

87. Can the product of two nonreal complex numbers be a real number? Explain your answer.

Further Investigations

88. Observe the following powers of i:

$$i = \sqrt{-1}$$
$$i^2 = -1$$
$$i^3 = i^2 \cdot i = -1(i) = -i$$
$$i^4 = i^2 \cdot i^2 = (-1)(-1) = 1$$

Any power of i greater than 4 can be simplified to $i, -1, -i$, or 1 as follows:

$$i^9 = (i^4)^2(i) = (1)(i) = i$$
$$i^{14} = (i^4)^3(i^2) = (1)(-1) = -1$$
$$i^{19} = (i^4)^4(i^3) = (1)(-i) = -i$$
$$i^{28} = (i^4)^7 = (1)^7 = 1$$

Express each of the following as $i, -1, -i$, or 1.

(a) i^5

(b) i^6

(c) i^{11}

(d) i^{12}

(e) i^{16}

(f) i^{22}

(g) i^{33}

(h) i^{63}

89. We can use the information from Problem 88 and the binomial expansion patterns to find powers of complex numbers as follows:

$$(3 + 2i)^3 = (3)^3 + 3(3)^2(2i) + 3(3)(2i)^2 + (2i)^3$$
$$= 27 + 54i + 36i^2 + 8i^3$$
$$= 27 + 54i + 36(-1) + 8(-i)$$
$$= -9 + 46i$$

Find the indicated power of each expression:

(a) $(2 + i)^3$ **(b)** $(1 - i)^3$

(c) $(1 - 2i)^3$ **(d)** $(1 + i)^4$

(e) $(2 - i)^4$ **(f)** $(-1 + i)^5$

Answers to the Concept Quiz

1. True **2.** True **3.** False **4.** True **5.** True **6.** True **7.** False **8.** True

OBJECTIVE	SUMMARY	EXAMPLE
Recognize the vocabulary and symbolism associated with sets. (Section 0.1/Objective 1)	Be sure of the following key concepts about sets: Elements, null set, equal sets, subsets, and set builder notation.	Answer True or False. **(a)** $\{a, b, c\} = \{b, a, c\}$ **(b)** $\{1, 3, 5\} \subset \{0, 1, 2, 3, 4, 5\}$ **Solution** **(a)** True **(b)** True
Know the various subset classifications of the real number system. (Section 0.1/Objective 2)	The sets of natural numbers, whole numbers, integers, rational numbers, and irrational numbers are all subsets of the real number system.	Name each of the following sets. **(a)** $\{0, 1, 2, 3, \ldots\}$ **(b)** $\{\ldots -3, -2, -1, 0\}$ **(c)** $\{1, 2, 3, \ldots\}$ **Solution** **(a)** Whole numbers **(b)** Nonpositive integers **(c)** Natural numbers
Apply the definition of the absolute value of a number. (Section 0.1/Objective 4)	For all real numbers a, If $a \geq 0$, then $|a| = a$. If $a < 0$, then $|a| = -a$. The following properties of absolute value are useful: **1.** $|a| \geq 0$ **2.** $|a| = |-a|$ **3.** $|a - b| = |b - a|$	Evaluate $\dfrac{2|x - y|}{|y - x|}$. **Solution** By the absolute value properties, $|x - y| = |y - x|$. Therefore $\dfrac{2|x - y|}{|y - x|} = 2(1) = 2$.
Know the real number properties. (Section 0.1/Objective 5)	As you study the operations on the set of real numbers, the following properties will serve as the bases for many algebraic operations. • Commutative properties for addition and multiplication • Associative properties for addition and multiplication • Identity properties for addition and multiplication • Inverse properties for addition and multiplication • Distributive property	State the property that justifies the statement. **(a)** $(a + b) + c = (b + a) + c$ **(b)** $(x + y) + z = x + (y + z)$ **(c)** $4m + 4n = 4(m + n)$ **Solution** **(a)** Commutative property of addition **(b)** Associative property of addition **(c)** Distributive property

(continued)

OBJECTIVE	SUMMARY	EXAMPLE
Evaluate algebraic expressions. (Section 0.1/Objective 6)	An algebraic expression takes on a numerical value whenever each variable in the expression is replaced by a real number. It is good practice to use parentheses when replacing the variable with a number.	Evaluate $\dfrac{a - 4b}{(a - b)^2}$ when $a = 4$ and $b = -1$. **Solution** $\dfrac{a - 4b}{(a - b)^2} = \dfrac{4 - 4(-1)}{(4 - (-1))^2} = $ $\dfrac{4 + 4}{(5)^2} = \dfrac{8}{25}$ when $a = 4$ and $b = -1$.
Apply the properties of exponents to simplify algebraic expressions. (Section 0.2/Objective 2)	Read Property 0.2 on page 23. A quick summary of some of that information is as follows: 1. When multiplying like bases, add the exponents. 2. When dividing like bases, subtract the exponents. 3. When a power is raised to another power, multiply the exponents.	Simplify $\left(\dfrac{6x^3 y^{-4}}{3x^{-2} y^{-1}}\right)^2$. **Solution** $\left(\dfrac{6x^3 y^{-4}}{3x^{-2} y^{-1}}\right)^2 = (2x^{3-(-2)} y^{-4-(-1)})^2$ $= (2x^5 y^{-3})^2$ $= 2^2 x^{10} y^{-6}$ $= \dfrac{4x^{10}}{y^6}$
Write numbers in scientific notation. (Section 0.2/Objective 3)	Scientific notation is often used to write numbers that are very small or very large in magnitude. The scientific form of a number is expressed as $(N)(10^k)$, where N is a number greater than or equal to 1 and less than 10, written in decimal form, and k is an integer.	Write each of the following in scientific notation. (a) 0.00000342 (b) 678,000,000,000 **Solution** (a) $0.00000342 = 3.42(10^{-6})$ (b) $678,000,000,000 = 6.78(10^{11})$
Convert numbers from scientific notation to ordinary decimal notation. (Section 0.2/Objective 4)	To switch from scientific notation to ordinary decimal notation, move the decimal point the number of places indicated by the exponent of the 10. The decimal point is moved to the right if the exponent is positive and to the left if the exponent is negative.	Write each of the following in ordinary decimal notation. (a) $(8.5)(10^{-5})$ (b) $(3.4)(10^6)$ **Solution** (a) $(8.5)(10^{-5}) = 0.000085$ (b) $(3.4)(10^6) = 3,400,000$

OBJECTIVE	SUMMARY	EXAMPLE
Perform calculations with numbers in scientific form. (Section 0.2/Objective 5)	Scientific notation can be used to simplify numerical operations by changing the numbers to scientific notation and using the appropriate properties of exponents.	Simplify $\dfrac{0.0000068}{0.04}$. **Solution** $\dfrac{0.0000068}{0.04} = \dfrac{(6.8)(10^{-6})}{(4)(10^{-2})}$ $= (1.7)(10^{-4}) = 0.00017$
Add and subtract polynomials. (Section 0.3/Objective 1)	Similar or like terms have the same literal factors. The commutative, associative, and distributive properties provide the basis for rearranging, regrouping, and combining similar terms.	Simplify $5x - \left[3x^2 - 4(6x - 2x^2)\right]$. **Solution** $5x - \left[3x^2 - 4(6x - 2x^2)\right]$ $= 5x - \left[3x^2 - 24x + 8x^2\right]$ $= 5x - \left[11x^2 - 24x\right]$ $= 5x - 11x^2 + 24x$ $= -11x^2 + 29x$
Multiply polynomials. (Section 0.3/Objective 2)	To multiply two polynomials, every term of the first polynomial is multiplied by each term of the second polynomial. Multiplying polynomials often produces similar terms that can be combined to simplify the resulting polynomial.	Find the indicated product. $(3x + 5)(x^2 - 2x + 7)$ **Solution** $(3x + 5)(x^2 - 2x + 7)$ $= 3x(x^2 - 2x + 7) + 5(x^2 - 2x + 7)$ $= 3x^3 - 6x^2 + 21x + 5x^2 - 10x + 35$ $= 3x^3 - x^2 + 11x + 35$
Perform binomial expansions. (Section 0.3/Objective 3)	It is possible to write the expansion of $(a + b)^n$, where n is a natural number, without doing all the intermediate steps. This can be done by realizing the pattern of the exponents for each term of the expansion and using Pascal's triangle to determine the coefficient for each term.	Expand $(2x + y)^4$. **Solution** $(2x + y)^4$ $= (2x)^4 + 4(2x)^3 y + 6(2x)^2 y^2 + 4(2x)y^3 + y^4$ $= 16x^4 + 32x^3 y + 24x^2 y^2 + 8xy^3 + y^4$

(continued)

OBJECTIVE	SUMMARY	EXAMPLE
Divide a polynomial by a monomial. (Section 0.3/Objective 4)	To divide a polynomial by a monomial, divide each term of the polynomial by the monomial.	Perform the indicated division. $$\frac{15a^3b^4 - 30a^5b^7 + 5a^2b^3}{5a^2b^3}$$ **Solution** Rewrite the problem as separate fractions obtained by each term in the numerator divided by the denominator. Then simplify each fraction. $$\frac{15a^3b^4 - 30a^5b^7 + 5a^2b^3}{5a^2b^3}$$ $$= \frac{15a^3b^4}{5a^2b^3} - \frac{30a^5b^7}{5a^2b^3} + \frac{5a^2b^3}{5a^2b^3}$$ $$= 3ab - 6a^3b^4 + 1$$
Factor out a common factor. (Section 0.4/Objective 1)	The distributive property in the form $ab + ac = a(b + c)$ is the basis for factoring out a common factor. The common factor can be a binomial factor, as when performing factoring by grouping.	Factor $-6x^5y^4 - 3x^6y^3 - 24x^7y^2$. **Solution** The common factor is $-3x^5y^2$. $$-6x^5y^4 - 3x^6y^3 - 24x^7y^2$$ $$= -3x^5y^2(2y^2 + xy + 8x^2)$$
Factor by grouping. (Section 0.4/Objective 2)	It may be that the polynomial exhibits no common monomial or binomial factor. However, by factoring common factors from groups of terms, a common factor may be evident.	Factor $2xz + 6x + yz + 3y$. **Solution** $$2xz + 6x + yz + 3y$$ $$= 2x(z + 3) + y(z + 3)$$ $$= (z + 3)(2x + y)$$
Factor the difference of two squares. (Section 0.4/Objective 3)	The factoring pattern $a^2 - b^2 = (a + b)(a - b)$ is called the difference of two squares.	Factor $36a^2 - 25b^2$. **Solution** $$36a^2 - 25b^2 = (6a - 5b)(6a + 5b)$$

OBJECTIVE	SUMMARY	EXAMPLE
Factor trinomials of the form $x^2 + bx + c$ and trinomials of the form $ax^2 + bx + c$. (Section 0.4/Objective 4)	Expressing a trinomial (for which the coefficient of the squared term is 1) as a product of two binomials is based on the relationship $$(x + a)(x + b) =$$ $$x^2 + (a + b)x + ab$$ The coefficient of the middle term is the sum of a and b, and the last term is the product of a and b. Two methods were presented for factoring trinomials of the form $ax^2 + bx + c$. One technique is to try the various possibilities of factors and check by multiplying. This method is referred to as trial-and-error. The other method is structured technique and is shown in Section 0.4 Examples 8 and 9.	Factor $x^2 - 2x - 35$. **Solution** $$x^2 - 2x - 35 = (x - 7)(x + 5)$$ Factor $4x^2 + 16x + 15$. **Solution** Multiply 4 times 15 to get 60. The factors of 60 that add to 16 are 6 and 10. Rewrite the problem and factor by grouping. $$4x^2 + 16x + 15$$ $$= 4x^2 + 10x + 6x + 15$$ $$= 2x(2x + 5) + 3(2x + 5)$$ $$= (2x + 5)(2x + 3)$$
Factor the sum or difference of two cubes. (Section 0.4/Objective 5)	The factoring patterns $a^3 + b^3 =$ $(a + b)(a^2 - ab + b^2)$ and $a^3 - b^3 =$ $(a - b)(a^2 + ab + b^2)$ are called the sum of two cubes or the difference of two cubes.	Factor $8x^3 + 27y^3$. **Solution** $8x^3 + 27y^3 = (2x + 3y)(4x^2 - 6xy + 9y^2)$
Apply more than one factoring technique. (Section 0.4/Objective 6)	Be sure to factor completely. Some problems require that more than one factoring technique may be necessary or perhaps the same technique used twice.	Factor $81a^4 - 16b^4$. **Solution** $81a^4 - 16b^4$ $= (9a^2 + 4b^2)(9a^2 - 4b^2)$ $= (9a^2 + 4b^2)(3a + 2b)(3a - 2b)$
Simplify rational expressions. (Section 0.5/Objective 1)	A rational expression is defined as the indicated quotient of two polynomials. The Fundamental Principle of Fractions, $\dfrac{a \cdot k}{b \cdot k} = \dfrac{a}{b}$, is used when reducing rational numbers or rational expressions.	Simplify $\dfrac{x^2 - 2x - 15}{x^2 + x - 6}$. **Solution** $\dfrac{x^2 - 2x - 15}{x^2 + x - 6}$ $= \dfrac{(x + 3)(x - 5)}{(x + 3)(x - 2)} = \dfrac{x - 5}{x - 2}$

(continued)

OBJECTIVE	SUMMARY	EXAMPLE
Multiply and divide rational expressions. (Section 0.5/Objective 2)	Multiplication of rational expressions is based on the following definition: $$\frac{a}{b} \cdot \frac{c}{d} = \frac{ac}{bd}$$ Division of rational expressions is based on the following definition: $$\frac{a}{b} \div \frac{c}{d} = \frac{a}{b} \cdot \frac{d}{c} = \frac{ad}{bc}$$	Find the quotient $\dfrac{6xy}{x^2 - 6x + 9} \div \dfrac{18x}{x^2 - 9}$. **Solution** $$\frac{6xy}{x^2 - 6x + 9} \div \frac{18x}{x^2 - 9}$$ $$= \frac{6xy}{x^2 - 6x + 9} \cdot \frac{x^2 - 9}{18x}$$ $$= \frac{6xy}{(x - 3)(x - 3)} \cdot \frac{(x + 3)(x - 3)}{18x}$$ $$= \frac{\cancel{6}xy}{(x - 3)\cancel{(x - 3)}} \cdot \frac{(x + 3)\cancel{(x - 3)}}{\underset{3}{\cancel{18}x}}$$ $$= \frac{y(x + 3)}{3(x - 3)}$$
Add and subtract rational expressions. (Section 0.5/Objective 3)	Addition and subtraction of rational expressions are based on the following definitions: $$\frac{a}{b} + \frac{c}{b} = \frac{a + c}{b} \quad \text{Addition}$$ $$\frac{a}{b} - \frac{c}{b} = \frac{a - c}{b} \quad \text{Subtraction}$$ The following basic procedure is used to add or subtract rational expressions: **1.** Factor the denominators. **2.** Find the LCD. **3.** Change each fraction to an equivalent fraction that has the LCD as the denominator. **4.** Combine the numerators and place over the LCD. **5.** Simplify by performing the addition or subtraction in the numerator. **6.** If possible, reduce the resulting fraction.	Subtract $\dfrac{2}{x^2 - 2x - 3} - \dfrac{5}{x^2 + 5x + 4}$. **Solution** $$\frac{2}{x^2 - 2x - 3} - \frac{5}{x^2 + 5x + 4}$$ $$= \frac{2}{(x - 3)(x + 1)} - \frac{5}{(x + 1)(x + 4)}$$ The LCD is $(x - 3)(x + 1)(x + 4)$. $$= \frac{2(x + 4)}{(x - 3)(x + 1)(x + 4)} - $$ $$\frac{5(x - 3)}{(x + 1)(x + 4)(x - 3)}$$ $$= \frac{2(x + 4) - 5(x - 3)}{(x - 3)(x + 1)(x + 4)}$$ $$= \frac{2x + 8 - 5x + 15}{(x - 3)(x + 1)(x + 4)}$$ $$= \frac{-3x + 23}{(x - 3)(x + 1)(x + 4)}$$

OBJECTIVE	SUMMARY	EXAMPLE
Simplify complex fractions. (Section 0.5/Objective 4)	Fractions that contain rational expressions in the numerators or denominators are called complex fractions. In Section 0.5 two methods were shown for simplifying complex fractions.	Simplify $\dfrac{\dfrac{2}{x}-\dfrac{3}{y}}{\dfrac{4}{x^2}+\dfrac{5}{y}}$. **Solution** $\dfrac{\dfrac{2}{x}-\dfrac{3}{y}}{\dfrac{4}{x^2}+\dfrac{5}{y}}$ Multiply the numerator and denominator by x^2y. $\dfrac{x^2y\left(\dfrac{2}{x}-\dfrac{3}{y}\right)}{x^2y\left(\dfrac{4}{x^2}+\dfrac{5}{y}\right)}=\dfrac{x^2y\left(\dfrac{2}{x}\right)+x^2y\left(-\dfrac{3}{y}\right)}{x^2y\left(\dfrac{4}{x^2}\right)+x^2y\left(\dfrac{5}{y}\right)}$ $=\dfrac{2xy-3x^2}{4y+5x^2}$
Write radical expressions in simplest radical form. (Section 0.6/Objective 2)	A radical expression is in simplest form if **1.** No fraction appears within a radical sign. **2.** No radical appears in the denominator. **3.** No radicand contains a perfect power of the index. The following properties are used to express radicals in simplest form: $\sqrt[n]{bc}=\sqrt[n]{b}\sqrt[n]{c}$ $\sqrt[n]{\dfrac{b}{c}}=\dfrac{\sqrt[n]{b}}{\sqrt[n]{c}}$	Simplify $\sqrt{150a^3b^2}$. Assume all variables represent nonnegative values. **Solution** $\sqrt{150a^3b^2}=\sqrt{25a^2b^2}\sqrt{6a}$ $\qquad\qquad=5ab\sqrt{6a}$
Simplify an indicated sum of radical expressions. (Section 0.6/Objective 3)	The distributive property can be used to combine radicals that have the same index and the same radicand. Sometimes the problem requires that the given radicals be expressed in simplest form.	Simplify $\sqrt{24}-\sqrt{54}+8\sqrt{6}$. **Solution** $\sqrt{24}-\sqrt{54}+8\sqrt{6}$ $=\sqrt{4}\sqrt{6}-\sqrt{9}\sqrt{6}+8\sqrt{6}$ $=2\sqrt{6}-3\sqrt{6}+8\sqrt{6}$ $=7\sqrt{6}$

(continued)

OBJECTIVE	SUMMARY	EXAMPLE
Multiply radical expressions. (Section 0.6/Objective 4)	Property 0.3 can be viewed as $\sqrt[n]{b}\sqrt[n]{c} = \sqrt[n]{bc}$. This property, along with commutative, associative, and distributive properties of real numbers, provides a basis for multiplying radicals that have the same index.	Multiply $\sqrt{2x}(\sqrt{6x} + \sqrt{18xy})$ and simplify where possible. **Solution** $\sqrt{2x}(\sqrt{6x} + \sqrt{18xy})$ $= \sqrt{12x^2} + \sqrt{36x^2y}$ $= \sqrt{4x^2}\sqrt{3} + \sqrt{36x^2}\sqrt{y}$ $= 2x\sqrt{3} + 6x\sqrt{y}$
Rationalize radical expressions. (Section 0.6/Objective 5)	If a radical appears in the denominator, then it will be necessary to rationalize the denominator for the expression to be in simplest form. To rationalize a binomial denominator, multiply the numerator and denominator by the conjugate of the denominator. The factors $a - b$ and $a + b$ are called conjugates.	Simplify $\dfrac{3}{\sqrt{7} - \sqrt{5}}$. **Solution** $\dfrac{3}{\sqrt{7} - \sqrt{5}}$ $= \dfrac{3}{(\sqrt{7} - \sqrt{5})} \cdot \dfrac{(\sqrt{7} + \sqrt{5})}{(\sqrt{7} + \sqrt{5})}$ $= \dfrac{3(\sqrt{7} + \sqrt{5})}{\sqrt{49} - \sqrt{25}} = \dfrac{3(\sqrt{7} + \sqrt{5})}{7 - 5}$ $= \dfrac{3(\sqrt{7} + \sqrt{5})}{2}$
Evaluate a number raised to a rational exponent. (Section 0.7/Objective 1)	If b is a real number, n is a positive integer greater than 1, and $\sqrt[n]{b}$ exists, then $b^{1/n} = \sqrt[n]{b}$. Thus $b^{1/n}$ means the nth root of b.	Simplify $16^{3/2}$. **Solution** $16^{3/2} = (16^{1/2})^3 = 4^3 = 64$
Simplify expressions with rational exponents. (Section 0.7/Objective 2)	Properties of exponents are used to simplify products and quotients involving rational exponents.	Simplify $(4x^{1/3})(-3x^{3/4})$ and express the result with positive exponents only. **Solution** $(4x^{1/3})(-3x^{-3/4}) = -12x^{1/3-3/4}$ $\qquad\qquad\qquad = -12x^{-5/12}$ $\qquad\qquad\qquad = \dfrac{-12}{x^{5/12}}$

OBJECTIVE	SUMMARY	EXAMPLE
Apply rational exponents to simplify radical expressions. (Section 0.7/Objective 3)	To multiply or divide radical expressions with different indexes, change from radical to exponential form. Then apply the properties of exponents. Finally change back to radical form.	Perform the indicated operation and express the answers in simplest radical form. $$\sqrt[4]{xy^3}\sqrt[5]{x^2y}$$ **Solution** $$\sqrt[4]{xy^3}\sqrt[5]{x^2y} = (x^{1/4}y^{3/4})(x^{2/5}y^{1/5})$$ $$= x^{1/4+2/5}y^{3/4+1/5}$$ $$= x^{13/20}y^{19/20} = \sqrt[20]{x^{13}y^{19}}$$
Express the square root of a negative number in terms of i. (Section 0.8/Objective 1)	We can represent a square root of any negative real number as the product of a real number and the imaginary unit i. That is, $\sqrt{-b} = i\sqrt{b}$, where b is a positive real number.	Write $\sqrt{-48}$ in terms of i and simplify. **Solution** $$\sqrt{-48} = \sqrt{-1}\sqrt{48}$$ $$= i\sqrt{16}\sqrt{3}$$ $$= 4i\sqrt{3}$$
Add and subtract complex numbers. (Section 0.8/Objective 2)	We describe the addition and subtraction of complex numbers as follows: $$(a + bi) + (c + di)$$ $$= (a + c) + (b + d)i$$ $$(a + bi) - (c + di)$$ $$= (a - c) + (b - d)i$$	Add the complex numbers $(3 - 6i) + (-7 - 3i)$. **Solution** $$(3 - 6i) + (-7 - 3i)$$ $$= (3 - 7) + (-6 - 3)i$$ $$= -4 - 9i$$
Multiply and divide complex numbers. (Section 0.8/Objective 3)	The product of two complex numbers follows the same pattern as the product of two binomials. When simplifying replace any i^2 with -1. To simplify expressions that indicate the quotient of complex numbers, like $\dfrac{4 + 3i}{5 - 2i}$, multiply the numerator and denominator by the conjugate of the denominator. The **conjugate** of $a + bi$ is $a - bi$. The product of a complex number and its conjugate is a real number.	Find the quotient $\dfrac{2 + 3i}{4 - i}$ and express the answer in standard form of a complex number. **Solution** Multiply the numerator and denominator by $4 + i$, the conjugate of the denominator. $$\frac{2 + 3i}{4 - i} = \frac{(2 + 3i)}{(4 - i)} \cdot \frac{(4 + i)}{(4 + i)}$$ $$= \frac{8 + 14i + 3i^2}{16 - i^2}$$ $$= \frac{8 + 14i + 3(-1)}{16 - (-1)}$$ $$= \frac{5 + 14i}{17} = \frac{5}{17} + \frac{14}{17}i$$

Chapter 0   Review Problem Set

For Problems 1–10, evaluate.

1. 5^{-3}

2. -3^{-4}

3. $\left(\dfrac{3}{4}\right)^{-2}$

4. $\dfrac{1}{\left(\dfrac{1}{3}\right)^{-2}}$

5. $-\sqrt{64}$

6. $\sqrt[3]{\dfrac{27}{8}}$

7. $\sqrt[5]{-\dfrac{1}{32}}$

8. $36^{-1/2}$

9. $\left(\dfrac{1}{8}\right)^{-2/3}$

10. $-32^{3/5}$

For Problems 11–18, perform the indicated operations and simplify. Express the final answers using positive exponents only.

11. $(3x^{-2}y^{-1})(4x^4y^2)$

12. $(5x^{2/3})(-6x^{1/2})$

13. $(-8a^{-1/2})(-6a^{1/3})$

14. $(3x^{-2/3}y^{1/5})^3$

15. $\dfrac{64x^{-2}y^3}{16x^3y^{-2}}$

16. $\dfrac{56x^{-1/3}y^{2/5}}{7x^{1/4}y^{-3/5}}$

17. $\left(\dfrac{-8x^2y^{-1}}{2x^{-1}y^2}\right)^2$

18. $\left(\dfrac{36a^{-1}b^4}{-12a^2b^5}\right)^{-1}$

For Problems 19–34, perform the indicated operations.

19. $(-7x - 3) + (5x - 2) + (6x + 4)$

20. $(12x + 5) - (7x - 4) - (8x + 1)$

21. $3(a - 2) - 2(3a + 5) + 3(5a - 1)$

22. $(4x - 7)(5x + 6)$

23. $(-3x + 2)(4x - 3)$

24. $(7x - 3)(-5x + 1)$

25. $(x + 4)(x^2 - 3x - 7)$

26. $(2x + 1)(3x^2 - 2x + 6)$

27. $(5x - 3)^2$

28. $(3x + 7)^2$

29. $(2x - 1)^3$

30. $(3x + 5)^3$

31. $(x^2 - 2x - 3)(x^2 + 4x + 5)$

32. $(2x^2 - x - 2)(x^2 + 6x - 4)$

33. $\dfrac{24x^3y^4 - 48x^2y^3}{-6xy}$

34. $\dfrac{-56x^2y + 72x^3y^2}{8x^2}$

For Problems 35–46, factor each polynomial completely. Indicate any that are not factorable using integers.

35. $9x^2 - 4y^2$

36. $3x^3 - 9x^2 - 120x$

37. $4x^2 + 20x + 25$

38. $(x - y)^2 - 9$

39. $x^2 - 2x - xy + 2y$

40. $64x^3 - 27y^3$

41. $15x^2 - 14x - 8$

42. $3x^3 + 36$

43. $2x^2 - x - 8$

44. $3x^3 + 24$

45. $x^4 - 13x^2 + 36$

46. $4x^2 - 4x + 1 - y^2$

For Problems 47–56, perform the indicated operations involving rational expressions. Express final answers in simplest form.

47. $\dfrac{8xy}{18x^2y} \cdot \dfrac{24xy^2}{16y^3}$

48. $\dfrac{-14a^2b^2}{6b^3} \div \dfrac{21a}{15ab}$

49. $\dfrac{x^2 + 3x - 4}{x^2 - 1} \cdot \dfrac{3x^2 + 8x + 5}{x^2 + 4x}$

50. $\dfrac{9x^2 - 6x + 1}{2x^2 + 8} \cdot \dfrac{8x + 20}{6x^2 + 13x - 5}$

51. $\dfrac{3x - 2}{4} + \dfrac{5x - 1}{3}$

52. $\dfrac{2x - 6}{5} - \dfrac{x + 4}{3}$

53. $\dfrac{3}{n^2} + \dfrac{4}{5n} - \dfrac{2}{n}$

54. $\dfrac{5}{x^2 + 7x} - \dfrac{3}{x}$

55. $\dfrac{3x}{x^2 - 6x - 40} + \dfrac{4}{x^2 - 16}$

56. $\dfrac{2}{x-2} - \dfrac{2}{x+2} - \dfrac{4}{x^3-4x}$

For Problems 57–59, simplify each complex fraction.

57. $\dfrac{\dfrac{3}{x} - \dfrac{2}{y}}{\dfrac{5}{x^2} + \dfrac{7}{y}}$

58. $\dfrac{3 - \dfrac{2}{x}}{4 + \dfrac{3}{x}}$

59. $\dfrac{\dfrac{3}{(x+h)^2} - \dfrac{3}{x^2}}{h}$

60. Simplify the expression

$$\dfrac{6(x^2+2)^{1/2} - 6x^2(x^2+2)^{-1/2}}{[(x^2+2)^{1/2}]^2}$$

For Problems 61–68, express each in simplest radical form. All variables represent positive real numbers.

61. $5\sqrt{48}$

62. $3\sqrt{24x^3}$

63. $\sqrt[3]{32x^4y^5}$

64. $\dfrac{3\sqrt{8}}{2\sqrt{6}}$

65. $\sqrt{\dfrac{5x}{2y^2}}$

66. $\dfrac{3}{\sqrt{2}+5}$

67. $\dfrac{4\sqrt{2}}{3\sqrt{2}+\sqrt{3}}$

68. $\dfrac{3\sqrt{x}}{\sqrt{x}-2\sqrt{y}}$

For Problems 69–74, perform the indicated operations and express the answers in simplest radical form.

69. $\sqrt{5}\sqrt[3]{5}$

70. $\sqrt[3]{x^2}\sqrt[4]{x}$

71. $\sqrt{x^3}\sqrt[3]{x^4}$

72. $\sqrt{xy}\sqrt[5]{x^3y^2}$

73. $\dfrac{\sqrt{5}}{\sqrt[3]{5}}$

74. $\dfrac{\sqrt[3]{x^2}}{\sqrt[4]{x^3}}$

For Problems 75–86, perform the indicated operations and express the resulting complex number in standard form.

75. $(-7+3i) + (-4-9i)$

76. $(2-10i) - (3-8i)$ **77.** $(-1+4i) - (-2+6i)$

78. $(3i)(-7i)$

79. $(2-5i)(3+4i)$

80. $(-3-i)(6-7i)$

81. $(4+2i)(-4-i)$

82. $(5-2i)(5+2i)$

83. $\dfrac{5}{3i}$

84. $\dfrac{2+3i}{3-4i}$

85. $\dfrac{-1-2i}{-2+i}$

86. $\dfrac{-6i}{5+2i}$

For Problems 87–92, write each in terms of i and simplify.

87. $\sqrt{-100}$

88. $\sqrt{-40}$

89. $4\sqrt{-80}$

90. $(\sqrt{-9})(\sqrt{-16})$

91. $(\sqrt{-6})(\sqrt{-8})$

92. $\dfrac{\sqrt{-24}}{\sqrt{-3}}$

For Problems 93 and 94, use scientific notation and the properties of exponents to help with the computations.

93. $\dfrac{(0.0064)(420,000)}{(0.00014)(0.032)}$

94. $\dfrac{(8600)(0.0000064)}{(0.0016)(0.000043)}$

Chapter 0 Test

1. Evaluate each of the following.

   a. -7^{-2} b. $\left(\dfrac{3}{2}\right)^{-3}$

   c. $\left(\dfrac{4}{9}\right)^{3/2}$ d. $\sqrt[3]{\dfrac{27}{64}}$

2. Find the product $(-3x^{-1}y^2)(5x^{-3}y^{-4})$ and express the result using positive exponents only.

For Problems 3–7, perform the indicated operations.

3. $(-3x - 4) - (7x - 5) + (-2x - 9)$

4. $(5x - 2)(-6x + 4)$

5. $(x + 2)(3x^2 - 2x - 7)$

6. $(4x - 1)^3$

7. $\dfrac{-18x^4y^3 - 24x^5y^4}{-2xy^2}$

For Problems 8–11, factor each polynomial completely.

8. $18x^3 - 15x^2 - 12x$

9. $30x^2 - 13x - 10$

10. $8x^3 + 64$

11. $x^2 + xy - 2y - 2x$

For Problems 12–16, perform the indicated operations involving rational expressions. Express final answers in simplest form.

12. $\dfrac{6x^3y^2}{5xy} \div \dfrac{8y}{7x^3}$

13. $\dfrac{x^2 - 4}{2x^2 + 5x + 2} \cdot \dfrac{2x^2 + 7x + 3}{x^3 - 8}$

14. $\dfrac{3n - 2}{4} - \dfrac{4n + 1}{6}$

15. $\dfrac{5}{2x^2 - 6x} + \dfrac{4}{3x^2 + 6x}$

16. $\dfrac{4}{n^2} - \dfrac{3}{2n} - \dfrac{5}{n}$

17. Simplify the complex fraction $\dfrac{\dfrac{2}{x} - \dfrac{5}{y}}{\dfrac{3}{x} + \dfrac{4}{y^2}}$.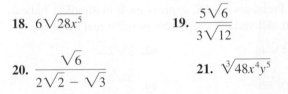

For Problems 18–21, express each radical expression in simplest radical form. All variables represent positive real numbers.

18. $6\sqrt{28x^5}$ 19. $\dfrac{5\sqrt{6}}{3\sqrt{12}}$

20. $\dfrac{\sqrt{6}}{2\sqrt{2} - \sqrt{3}}$ 21. $\sqrt[3]{48x^4y^5}$

For Problems 22–25, perform the indicated operations and express the resulting complex numbers in standard form.

22. $(-2 - 4i) - (-1 + 6i) + (-3 + 7i)$

23. $(5 - 7i)(4 + 2i)$

24. $(7 - 6i)(7 + 6i)$

25. $\dfrac{1 + 2i}{3 - i}$

1

Equations, Inequalities, and Problem Solving

1.1 Linear Equations and Problem Solving

1.2 More Equations and Applications

1.3 Quadratic Equations

1.4 Applications of Linear and Quadratic Equations

1.5 Miscellaneous Equations

1.6 Inequalities

1.7 Quadratic Inequalities and Inequalities Involving Quotients

1.8 Absolute Value Equations and Inequalities

Shown here is a partial view of the quadratic formula. In this chapter you will gain the ability to solve equations and inequalities. That enables you to develop formulas, such as the quadratic formula, and solve application problems.

© Corbis Premium RF/Alamy

A precinct reported that 316 people voted in an election. The number of Republican voters was 6 more than two-thirds the number of Democrat voters. The equation $d + \left(\dfrac{2}{3}d + 6\right) = 316$ can be used to determine the number of voters from each of the two parties.

If a ring costs a jeweler $250, at what price should it be sold to make a profit of 60% based on the selling price? The equation $s = 250 + 0.6s$ can be used to determine the selling price.

How much water must be evaporated from 20 gallons of a 10% salt solution in order to obtain a 20% salt solution? The guideline *water in original solution minus water evaporated equals water in final solution* can be used to set up the equation $18 - x = 0.8(20 - x)$. Solving this equation produces the amount of water, x, to be evaporated.

A common sequence in precalculus algebra courses is to develop algebraic skills, then use the skills to solve equations and inequalities, and finally use equations and inequalities to solve applied problems. In this chapter we shall review and extend a variety of concepts related to that process.

| **1.1** | **Linear Equations and Problem Solving** |

OBJECTIVES

1 Solve linear equations

2 Solve application problems involving linear equations

An algebraic equation such as $5x + 2 = 12$ is neither true nor false as it stands; it is sometimes referred to as an **open sentence.** Each time that a number is substituted for x, the algebraic equation $5x + 2 = 12$ becomes a **numerical statement,** which is either true or false. For example, if $x = 5$, then $5x + 2 = 12$ becomes $5(5) + 2 = 12$, which is a false statement. If $x = 2$, then $5x + 2 = 12$ becomes $5(2) + 2 = 12$, which is a true statement. "Solving an equation" refers to the process of finding the number (or numbers) that make(s) an algebraic equation a true numerical statement. Such numbers are called the **solutions** or **roots** of the equation and are said to *satisfy the equation.* The set of all solutions of an equation is called its **solution set.** Thus $\{2\}$ is the solution set of $5x + 2 = 12$.

An equation that is satisfied by all numbers that can meaningfully replace the variable is called an **identity.** For example,

$$3(x + 2) = 3x + 6 \qquad x^2 - 4 = (x + 2)(x - 2) \qquad \text{and}$$
$$\frac{1}{x} + \frac{1}{2} = \frac{2 + x}{2x}$$

are all identities. In the last identity, x cannot equal zero; thus the statement

$$\frac{1}{x} + \frac{1}{2} = \frac{2 + x}{2x}$$

is true for all real numbers except zero. An equation that is true for some but not all permissible values of the variable is called a **conditional equation.** Thus the equation $5x + 2 = 12$ is a conditional equation.

Equivalent equations are equations that have the same solution set. For example,

$$7x - 1 = 20 \qquad 7x = 21 \qquad \text{and} \qquad x = 3$$

are all equivalent equations because $\{3\}$ is the solution set of each. The general procedure for solving an equation is to continue replacing the given equation with equivalent but simpler equations until an equation of the form *variable* = *constant* or *constant* = *variable* is obtained. Thus in the example above, $7x - 1 = 20$ was simplified to $7x = 21$, which was further simplified to $x = 3$, which gives us the solution set, $\{3\}$.

Techniques for solving equations revolve around properties of equality. The following list summarizes some basic properties of equality.

Property 1.1   Properties of Equality

For all real numbers, a, b, and c,

1. $a = a$ Reflexive property
2. If $a = b$, then $b = a$ Symmetric property
3. If $a = b$ and $b = c$, then $a = c$ Transitive property
4. If $a = b$, then a may be replaced by b, or b may be replaced by a, in any statement without changing the meaning of the statement.   Substitution property
5. $a = b$ if and only if $a + c = b + c$ Addition property
6. $a = b$ if and only if $ac = bc$, where $c \neq 0$ Multiplication property

---

The addition property of equality states that any number can be added to both sides of an equation to produce an equivalent equation. The multiplication property of equality states that an equivalent equation is produced whenever both sides of an equation are multiplied by the same nonzero real number.

Linear Equations

Now let's consider how these properties of equality can be used to solve a variety of linear equations. A **linear equation** in the variable x is one that can be written in the form

$$ax + b = 0$$

where a and b are real numbers and $a \neq 0$.

Classroom Example
Solve the equation
$-6x - 4 = 5x + 7$.

EXAMPLE 1   Solve the equation $-4x - 3 = 2x + 9$.

Solution

$$-4x - 3 = 2x + 9$$
$$-4x - 3 + (-2x) = 2x + 9 + (-2x) \qquad \text{Add } -2x \text{ to both sides}$$
$$-6x - 3 = 9$$
$$-6x - 3 + 3 = 9 + 3 \qquad \text{Add 3 to both sides}$$
$$-6x = 12$$
$$-\frac{1}{6}(-6x) = -\frac{1}{6}(12) \qquad \text{Multiply both sides by } -\frac{1}{6}$$
$$x = -2$$

✔ **Check**

To check an apparent solution, we can substitute it into the original equation to see whether we obtain a true numerical statement.

$$-4x - 3 = 2x + 9$$
$$-4(-2) - 3 \stackrel{?}{=} 2(-2) + 9$$
$$8 - 3 \stackrel{?}{=} -4 + 9$$
$$5 = 5$$

Now we know that the solution set is $\{-2\}$.

Classroom Example
Solve the equation
$-3(x + 4) - 2(x - 1) = 5(x + 8)$.

EXAMPLE 2   Solve $4(n - 2) - 3(n - 1) = 2(n + 6)$.

Solution

First let's use the distributive property to remove parentheses and combine similar terms:

$$4(n - 2) - 3(n - 1) = 2(n + 6)$$
$$4n - 8 - 3n + 3 = 2n + 12$$
$$n - 5 = 2n + 12$$

Now we can apply the addition property of equality:

$$n - 5 + (-n) = 2n + 12 + (-n)$$
$$-5 = n + 12$$
$$-5 + (-12) = n + 12 + (-12)$$
$$-17 = n$$

✔ **Check**

$$4(n - 2) - 3(n - 1) = 2(n + 6)$$
$$4(-17 - 2) - 3(-17 - 1) \stackrel{?}{=} 2(-17 + 6)$$
$$4(-19) - 3(-18) \stackrel{?}{=} 2(-11)$$
$$-76 + 54 \stackrel{?}{=} -22$$
$$-22 = -22$$

The solution set is $\{-17\}$.

As you study these examples, pay special attention to the steps shown in the solutions. Certainly there are no rules about which steps should be performed mentally; this is an individual decision. We suggest that you show enough steps so that the flow of the process is understood and so that the chances of making careless computational errors are minimized. We shall discontinue showing the check for each problem, but remember that checking an answer is the only way to be sure of your result.

Classroom Example
Solve $\frac{4}{5}m - \frac{1}{2}m = \frac{9}{10}$.

EXAMPLE 3   Solve $\frac{1}{4}x - \frac{2}{3}x = \frac{5}{6}$.

Solution

$$\frac{1}{4}x - \frac{2}{3}x = \frac{5}{6}$$

$$12\left(\frac{1}{4}x - \frac{2}{3}x\right) = 12\left(\frac{5}{6}\right) \qquad \text{Multiply both sides by 12, the LCD}$$

$$12\left(\frac{1}{4}x\right) - 12\left(\frac{2}{3}x\right) = 12\left(\frac{5}{6}\right) \qquad \text{Apply the distributive property on the left side}$$

$$3x - 8x = 10$$

$$-5x = 10$$

$$x = -2$$

The solution set is $\{-2\}$.

Classroom Example
Solve $\frac{4n - 5}{3} + \frac{n + 2}{4} = 2$.

EXAMPLE 4   Solve $\frac{2y - 3}{3} + \frac{y + 1}{2} = 3$.

Solution

$$\frac{2y - 3}{3} + \frac{y + 1}{2} = 3$$

$$6\left(\frac{2y - 3}{3} + \frac{y + 1}{2}\right) = 6(3) \qquad \text{Multiply both sides by 6, the LCD}$$

$$6\left(\frac{2y - 3}{3}\right) + 6\left(\frac{y + 1}{2}\right) = 6(3) \qquad \text{Apply the distributive property on the left side}$$

$$2(2y - 3) + 3(y + 1) = 18$$

$$4y - 6 + 3y + 3 = 18$$

$$7y - 3 = 18$$

$$7y = 21$$

$$y = 3$$

The solution set is $\{3\}$. (Check it!)

Classroom Example
Solve $\frac{3y - 2}{8} - \frac{4y + 1}{6} + 2 = 0$.

EXAMPLE 5   Solve $\frac{4x - 1}{10} - \frac{5x + 2}{4} + 3 = 0$.

Solution

$$\frac{4x - 1}{10} - \frac{5x + 2}{4} + 3 = 0$$

$$20\left(\frac{4x - 1}{10} - \frac{5x + 2}{4} + 3\right) = 20(0)$$

$$20\left(\frac{4x-1}{10}\right) - 20\left(\frac{5x+2}{4}\right) + 20(3) = 20(0)$$

$$2(4x - 1) - 5(5x + 2) + 60 = 0$$

$$8x - 2 - 25x - 10 + 60 = 0$$

$$-17x + 48 = 0$$

$$-17x = -48$$

$$x = \frac{48}{17}$$

The solution set is $\left\{\dfrac{48}{17}\right\}$.

In Example 5 checking $\dfrac{48}{17}$ in the original equation is a bit messy. So let's give ourselves a partial check by looking at a picture of this situation. Figure 1.1 shows a graph of the equation $y = \dfrac{4x-1}{10} - \dfrac{5x+2}{4} + 3$. If we let $y = 0$, then the equation $y = \dfrac{4x-1}{10} - \dfrac{5x+2}{4} + 3$ is the given equation in Example 5. Graphically speaking, we see that y equals zero at the point where the line crosses the x axis, which is between 2 and 3. Our solution of $\dfrac{48}{17}$ is also between 2 and 3, so at least we have a partial check.

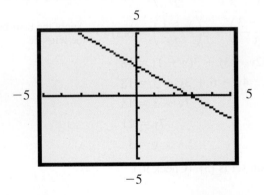

Figure 1.1

We need to emphasize two points pertaining to the previous discussion. First, it is possible to use some features of a graphing calculator to obtain a much better approximation than simply *between 2 and 3*. We will use some of these features later in the text, but for now our focus is on the relationship between the solutions of an algebraic equation and the x intercepts of a geometric graph. Second, we give the following precise definition of an x intercept: The x coordinates of the points that a graph has in common with the x axis are called the **x intercepts** of the graph. (To compute the x intercepts, let $y = 0$ and solve for x.)

Problem Solving

The ability to use the tools of algebra to solve problems requires that we be able to translate the English language into the language of algebra. More specifically, at this time we need to translate *English sentences* into *algebraic equations* so that we can use our equation-solving skills. Let's work through an example and then comment on some of the problem-solving aspects of it.

Classroom Example
During a midnight-madness sale, a store sold two models of plasma televisions. Within 2 hours, 89 televisions were sold. The number of 1080p-models sold was 15 less than three times the number of 720p-models sold. Find the number of 720 p-models sold.

EXAMPLE 6

During an early-bird promotion to sell two models of digital televisions, a store sold 765 televisions in 6 hours. The number of WiFi-capable models sold was 30 less than twice the number of non–WiFi-capable models sold. Find the number of non–WiFi-capable models sold.

Solution

Let n represent the number of non–WiFi-capable models sold. The statement, "The number of WiFi-capable models sold was 30 less than twice the number of non–WiFi-capable models sold" tells us that the expression $2n - 30$ represents the number of WiFi-capable models sold. Then we can form an equation knowing that the sum of the number of non–WiFi-capable models sold plus the number of WiFi-capable models sold equals 765. Solving this equation, we obtain

$$n + 2n - 30 = 765$$
$$3n - 30 = 765$$
$$3n = 795$$
$$n = 265$$

There were 265 of the non–WiFi-capable models sold.

Now let's make a few comments about our approach to Example 6. Making a statement such as *Let n represent the number to be found* is often referred to as **declaring the variable.** It amounts to choosing a letter to use as a variable and indicating what the variable represents for a specific problem. This may seem like an insignificant idea, but as the problems become more complex, the process of declaring the variable becomes more important. It is also a good idea to choose a *meaningful* variable. For example, if the problem involves finding the width of a rectangle, then a choice of w for the variable is reasonable. Furthermore, it is true that some people can solve a problem such as Example 6 without setting up an algebraic equation. However, as problems increase in difficulty, the translation from English to algebra becomes a key issue. Therefore, even with these relatively easy problems, we suggest that you concentrate on the translation process.

To check our answer for Example 6, we must determine whether it satisfies the conditions stated in the original problem. Because the number of WiFi-capable models is $2n - 30 = 2(265) - 30 = 500$ and $265 + 500 = 765$, we know our answer of 265 is correct. Remember, when you are checking a potential answer for a word problem, it is *not* sufficient to check the result in the equation used to solve the problem because the equation itself may be in error.

Sometimes it is necessary not only to declare the variable but also to represent other unknown quantities in terms of that variable. Let's consider a problem that illustrates this idea.

EXAMPLE 7   Find three consecutive integers whose sum is -45.

Solution

Let n represent the smallest integer; then $n + 1$ is the next integer, and $n + 2$ is the largest of the three integers. Because the sum of the three consecutive integers is to be -45, we have the following equation.

$$n + (n + 1) + (n + 2) = -45$$
$$3n + 3 = -45$$
$$3n = -48$$
$$n = -16$$

If $n = -16$, then $n + 1$ is -15 and $n + 2$ is -14. Thus the three consecutive integers are -16, -15, and -14.   ∎

Frequently, the translation from English to algebra can be made easier by recognizing a guideline that can be used to set up an appropriate equation. Pay special attention to the guidelines used in the solutions of the next two problems.

EXAMPLE 8

Tina is paid time-and-a-half for each hour worked over 40 hours in a week. Last week she worked 45 hours and earned $380. What is her normal hourly rate?

Solution

Let r represent Tina's normal hourly rate. Then $\frac{3}{2}r$ represents $1\frac{1}{2}$ times her normal hourly rate (time-and-a-half). The following guideline can be used to help set up the equation:

Regular wages for first 40 hours	+	Wages for 5 hours of overtime	=	Total wages
$40r$	+	$5\left(\dfrac{3}{2}r\right)$	=	$380

Solving this equation, we obtain

$$2\left[40r + 5\left(\frac{3}{2}r\right)\right] = 2(380)$$
$$2(40r) + 2\left[5\left(\frac{3}{2}r\right)\right] = 760$$

$$80r + 15r = 760$$
$$95r = 760$$
$$r = 8$$

Her normal hourly rate is thus $8 per hour. (Check the answer in the original statement of the problem!)

Classroom Example
Christopher's present age is 10 years older than Erin's age. Five years ago Christopher's age was two times Erin's age at that time. Find the present ages of Christopher and Erin.

EXAMPLE 9

Rafael's present age is 12 years older than Rosa's present age. Ten years ago Rafael's age was three times Rosa's age at that time. Find the present ages of Rafael and Rosa.

Solution

Let x represent Rosa's present age; then $x + 12$ represents Rafael's present age. Ten years ago Rosa and Rafael were 10 years younger. To represent their ages 10 years ago, subtract 10 from their present age. Therefore, $x - 10$ represents Rosa's age 10 years ago, and $x + 12 - 10 = x + 2$ represents Rafael's age 10 years ago. The statement, "ten years ago Rafael's age was three times Rosa's age at that time" translates into the equation $x + 2 = 3(x - 10)$. Solving the equation, we obtain

$$x + 2 = 3(x - 10)$$
$$x + 2 = 3x - 30$$
$$-2x = -32$$
$$x = 16$$

So Rosa's present age is 16 years and Rafael's present age is $x + 12 = 16 + 12 = 28$ years.

Concept Quiz 1.1

For Problems 1–7, answer true or false.

1. An algebraic equation is called an open sentence because it is neither a true nor a false statement.
2. Equivalent equations have the same solution set.
3. An equation that is true for all meaningful values of x is called an identity.
4. The addition property of equality states that if the same number is added to both sides of an equation, the result is an equivalent equation.
5. The equation $8x = 0$ does not have a solution.
6. Changing an equation from $3 = x$ to $x = 3$ is the application of the symmetric property.
7. If $x = b$ and $b = 6$, then by the reflexive property we know $x = 6$.
8. If the equation $2(x + 4) = 2x + 5$ is simplified, does the equivalent equation fit the definition of a linear equation?

Problem Set 1.1

For Problems 1–42, solve each equation. **(Objective 1)**

1. $9x - 3 = -21$

2. $-5x + 4 = -11$

3. $13 - 2x = 14$

4. $17 = 6a + 5$

5. $3n - 2 = 2n + 5$

6. $4n + 3 = 5n - 9$

7. $-5a + 3 = -3a + 6$

8. $4x - 3 + 2x = 8x - 3 - x$

9. $-3(x + 1) = 7$

10. $5(2x - 1) = 13$

11. $4(2x - 1) = 3(3x + 2)$

12. $5x - 4(x - 6) = -11$

13. $3(n - 1) = -2(n + 4) + 6(n - 3)$

14. $-3(2t - 5) = 2(4t + 7)$

15. $3(2t - 1) - 2(5t + 1) = 4(3t + 4)$

16. $-(3x - 1) + (2x + 3) = -4 + 3(x - 1)$

17. $-2(y - 4) - (3y - 1) = -2 + 5(y + 1)$

18. $\dfrac{-3x}{4} = \dfrac{9}{2}$

19. $-\dfrac{6x}{7} = 12$

20. $\dfrac{n}{2} - \dfrac{1}{3} = \dfrac{13}{6}$

21. $\dfrac{3}{4}n - \dfrac{1}{12}n = 6$

22. $\dfrac{2}{3}x - \dfrac{1}{5}x = 7$

23. $\dfrac{h}{2} + \dfrac{h}{5} = 1$

24. $\dfrac{4y}{5} - 7 = \dfrac{y}{10}$

25. $\dfrac{y}{5} - 2 = \dfrac{y}{2} + 1$

26. $\dfrac{x + 2}{3} + \dfrac{x - 1}{4} = \dfrac{9}{2}$

27. $\dfrac{c + 5}{7} + \dfrac{c - 3}{4} = \dfrac{5}{14}$

28. $\dfrac{2x - 5}{6} - \dfrac{3x - 4}{8} = 0$

29. $\dfrac{n - 3}{2} - \dfrac{4n - 1}{6} = \dfrac{2}{3}$

30. $\dfrac{3x - 1}{2} + \dfrac{x - 3}{4} = \dfrac{1}{2}$

31. $\dfrac{2t + 3}{6} - \dfrac{t - 9}{4} = 5$

32. $\dfrac{2x + 7}{9} - 4 = \dfrac{x - 7}{12}$

33. $\dfrac{3n - 1}{8} - 2 = \dfrac{2n + 5}{7}$

34. $\dfrac{x + 2}{3} + \dfrac{3x + 1}{4} + \dfrac{2x - 1}{6} = 2$

35. $\dfrac{2t - 3}{6} + \dfrac{3t - 2}{4} + \dfrac{5t + 6}{12} = 4$

36. $\dfrac{3y - 1}{8} + y - 2 = \dfrac{y + 4}{4}$

37. $\dfrac{2x + 1}{14} - \dfrac{3x + 4}{7} = \dfrac{x - 1}{2}$

38. $n + \dfrac{2n - 3}{9} - 2 = \dfrac{2n + 1}{3}$

39. $(x - 3)(x - 1) - x(x + 2) = 7$

40. $(3n + 4)(n - 2) - 3n(n + 3) = 3$

41. $(2y + 1)(3y - 2) - (6y - 1)(y + 4) = -20y$

42. $(4t - 3)(t + 2) - (2t + 3)^2 = -1$

Solve each of Problems 43–62 by setting up and solving an algebraic equation. **(Objective 2)**

43. A meal of a chicken sandwich and some pasta salad had 100 grams of carbohydrates. The pasta salad had 10 grams more than twice the grams of carbohydrates in the chicken sandwich. Find the number of grams of carbohydrates for both.

44. The sum of three consecutive integers is 21 larger than twice the smallest integer. Find the integers.

45. Find three consecutive even integers such that if the largest integer is subtracted from four times the smallest, the result is 6 more than twice the middle integer.

46. Find three consecutive odd integers such that three times the largest is 23 less than twice the sum of the two smallest integers.

47. Find two consecutive positive integers such that the difference of their squares is 37.

48. Find three consecutive integers such that the product of the two largest is 20 more than the square of the smallest integer.

49. Find four consecutive integers such that the product of the two largest is 46 more than the product of the two smallest integers.

50. Over the weekend, Mario bicycled 69 miles. On Sunday he rode 9 miles more than two-thirds of his distance on Saturday. Find the number of miles he rode each day.

51. For a given triangle, the measure of angle A is $10°$ less than three times the measure of angle B. The measure of angle C is one-fifth the sum of the measures of angles A and B. Knowing that the sum of the measures of the angles of a triangle equals $180°$, find the measure of each angle.

52. Jennifer went on a shopping spree, spending a total of \$150 on a skirt, a sweater, and a pair of shoes. The cost of the sweater was $\frac{8}{7}$ of the cost of the skirt. The shoes cost \$18 more than the skirt. Find the cost of each item.

53. Barry is paid double-time for each hour worked over 40 hours in a week. Last week he worked 47 hours and earned \$648. What is his normal hourly rate?

54. The average of the salaries of Kelly, Renee, and Nina is \$40,000 a year. If Kelly earns \$8000 less than Renee, and Nina's salary is two-thirds of Renee's salary, find the salary of each person.

55. Greg had 80 coins consisting of pennies, nickels, and dimes. The number of nickels was 5 more than one-third the number of pennies, and the number of dimes was 1 less than one-fourth the number of pennies. How many coins of each kind did he have?

56. Rita has a collection of 105 coins consisting of nickels, dimes, and quarters. The number of dimes is 5 more than one-third the number of nickels, and the number of quarters is twice the number of dimes. How many coins of each kind does she have?

57. In a class of 43 students, the number of males is 8 less than twice the number of females. How many females and how many males are there in the class?

58. A precinct reported that 316 people had voted in an election. The number of Republican voters was 6 more than two-thirds the number of Democrats. How many Republicans and how many Democrats voted in that precinct?

59. Two years ago Janie was half as old as she will be 9 years from now. How old is she now?

60. The sum of the present ages of Eric and his father is 58 years. In 10 years, his father will be twice as old as Eric will be at that time. Find their present ages.

61. Brad is 6 years older than Pedro. Five years ago Pedro's age was three-fourths of Brad's age at that time. Find the present ages of Brad and Pedro.

62. Tina is 4 years older than Sherry. In 5 years the sum of their ages will be 48. Find their present ages.

Thoughts Into Words

63. Explain the difference between a numerical statement and an algebraic equation.

64. Are the equations $9 = 3x - 2$ and $3x - 2 = 9$ equivalent equations? Defend your answer.

65. How do you defend the statement that the equation $x + 3 = x + 2$ has no real number solutions?

66. How do you defend the statement that the solution set of the equation $3(x - 4) = 3x - 12$ is the entire set of real numbers?

Further Investigations

67. Verify that for any three consecutive integers, the sum of the smallest and the largest is equal to twice the middle integer.

68. Verify that no four consecutive integers can be found such that the product of the smallest and the largest is equal to the product of the other two integers.

69. Some algebraic identities provide a basis for shortcuts to do mental arithmetic. For example, the identity $(x + y)(x - y) = x^2 - y^2$ indicates that a multiplication problem such as $(31)(29)$ can be treated as $(30 + 1)(30 - 1) = 30^2 - 1^2 = 900 - 1 = 899$.

For each of the following, use the given identity to provide a way of mentally performing the indicated computations. Check your answers with a calculator.

(a) $(x + y)(x - y) = x^2 - y^2$: $(21)(19)$; $(39)(41)$; $(22)(18)$; $(42)(38)$; $(47)(53)$

(b) $(x + y)^2 = x^2 + 2xy + y^2$: $(21)^2$; $(32)^2$; $(51)^2$; $(62)^2$; $(43)^2$

(c) $(x - y)^2 = x^2 - 2xy + y^2$: $(29)^2$; $(49)^2$; $(18)^2$; $(38)^2$; $(67)^2$

(d) $(10t + 5)^2 = 100t^2 + 100t + 25 = 100t(t + 1) + 25$: $(15)^2$; $(35)^2$; $(45)^2$; $(65)^2$; $(85)^2$

Graphing Calculator Activities

70. Graph the appropriate equations to give visual support for your solutions for Problems 38–42.

71. For each of the following, first graph the appropriate equation and use your graph to predict an approximate solution for the given equation. Then solve the equation algebraically to see how close your prediction came.

(a) $5(x - 2) - (2x + 3) = 4$

(b) $\dfrac{2x - 1}{4} - \dfrac{3x + 1}{5} = 0$

(c) $\dfrac{4x + 1}{3} = \dfrac{x - 3}{2}$

(d) $(x - 2)(x + 3) - (x - 2)(x + 1) = 0$

(e) $(x + 1)(x - 1) - (x + 6)(x - 2) = 0$

(f) $(x + 3)(x + 2) - (x + 4)(x + 1) = 0$

Answers to the Concept Quiz

1. True **2.** True **3.** True **4.** True **5.** False **6.** True **7.** False **8.** No

---

1.2 More Equations and Applications

OBJECTIVES

1 Solve linear equations involving fractions

2 Solve proportions

3 Solve linear equations involving decimals

4 Solve formulas for a specified variable

5 Solve application problems

In the previous section we considered linear equations, such as

$$\frac{x-1}{3} + \frac{x+2}{4} = \frac{1}{6}$$

that have fractional coefficients with constants as denominators. Now let's consider equations that contain the variable in one or more of the denominators. Our approach to solving such equations remains essentially the same except **we must avoid any values of the variable that make a denominator zero.** Consider the following examples.

Classroom Example
Solve $\dfrac{6}{7m} - \dfrac{1}{21} = \dfrac{1}{m}$.

EXAMPLE 1   Solve $\dfrac{5}{3x} - \dfrac{1}{9} = \dfrac{1}{x}$.

Solution

First we need to realize that *x cannot equal zero.* Let's indicate this restriction so that it is not forgotten; then we can proceed as follows.

$$\frac{5}{3x} - \frac{1}{9} = \frac{1}{x}, \quad x \neq 0$$

$$9x\left(\frac{5}{3x} - \frac{1}{9}\right) = 9x\left(\frac{1}{x}\right) \qquad \text{Multiply both sides by the LCD}$$

$$9x\left(\frac{5}{3x}\right) - 9x\left(\frac{1}{9}\right) = 9x\left(\frac{1}{x}\right)$$

$$15 - x = 9$$

$$-x = -6$$

$$x = 6$$

The solution set is {6}. (Check it!)

Classroom Example
Solve $\dfrac{48 - x}{x} = 3 + \dfrac{8}{x}$.

EXAMPLE 2   Solve $\dfrac{65 - n}{n} = 4 + \dfrac{5}{n}$.

Solution

$$\frac{65 - n}{n} = 4 + \frac{5}{n}, \quad n \neq 0$$

$$n\left(\frac{65 - n}{n}\right) = n\left(4 + \frac{5}{n}\right)$$

$$65 - n = 4n + 5$$

$$60 = 5n$$

$$12 = n$$

The solution set is {12}.

Classroom Example

Solve $\dfrac{1}{5} - \dfrac{x}{x+4} = \dfrac{4}{x+4}$.

EXAMPLE 3 Solve $\dfrac{a}{a-2} + \dfrac{2}{3} = \dfrac{2}{a-2}$.

Solution

$$\frac{a}{a-2} + \frac{2}{3} = \frac{2}{a-2}, \quad a \neq 2$$

$$3(a-2)\left(\frac{a}{a-2} + \frac{2}{3}\right) = 3(a-2)\left(\frac{2}{a-2}\right)$$

$$3a + 2(a-2) = 6$$

$$3a + 2a - 4 = 6$$

$$5a = 10$$

$$a = 2$$

Because our initial restriction was $a \neq 2$, we conclude that this equation *has no solution*. The solution set is $\varnothing$.

Example 3 illustrates the importance of recognizing the restrictions that must be made to exclude division by zero. By the way, what should happen if we graph $y = \dfrac{x}{x-2} + \dfrac{2}{3} - \dfrac{2}{x-2}$? (We had to change the variable a to x for graphing purposes.) Do you agree that the graph must not have any x intercept? Figure 1.2 shows the graph; we should feel good that our answer was an empty solution set.

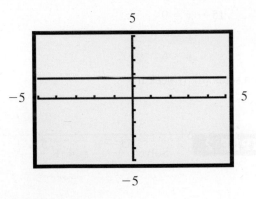

Figure 1.2

Ratio and Proportion

A **ratio** is the comparison of two numbers by division. The fractional form is frequently used to express ratios. For example, the ratio of a to b can be written a/b. A statement of equality between two ratios is called a **proportion.** Thus if a/b and c/d are equal ratios, then the proportion $a/b = c/d$ ($b \neq 0$ and $d \neq 0$) can be formed. There is a useful property of proportions:

$$\text{If } \frac{a}{b} = \frac{c}{d}, \text{ then } ad = bc.$$

This property can be deduced as follows:

$$\frac{a}{b} = \frac{c}{d}, \quad b \neq 0 \text{ and } d \neq 0$$

$$bd\left(\frac{a}{b}\right) = bd\left(\frac{c}{d}\right) \qquad \text{Multiply both sides by } bd$$

$$ad = bc$$

This is sometimes referred to as the **cross-multiplication property of proportions.**

Some equations can be treated as proportions and solved by using the cross-multiplication idea, as the next example illustrates.

Classroom Example

Solve $\dfrac{6}{4n + 1} = \dfrac{2}{3n - 4}$.

EXAMPLE 4   Solve $\dfrac{3}{3x - 2} = \dfrac{4}{2x + 1}$.

Solution

$$\frac{3}{3x - 2} = \frac{4}{2x + 1}, \quad x \neq \frac{2}{3}, x \neq -\frac{1}{2}$$

$$3(2x + 1) = 4(3x - 2) \qquad \text{Apply the cross-multiplication property}$$

$$6x + 3 = 12x - 8$$

$$11 = 6x$$

$$\frac{11}{6} = x$$

The solution set is $\left\{\dfrac{11}{6}\right\}$.

Linear Equations Involving Decimals

To solve an equation such as $x + 2.4 = 0.36$, we can add -2.4 to both sides. However, as equations containing decimals become more complex, it is often easier to begin by *clearing the equation of all decimals,* which we accomplish by multiplying both sides by an appropriate power of 10. Let's consider two examples.

Classroom Example

Solve $0.23r - 4.3 = 0.05r + 0.2$.

EXAMPLE 5   Solve $0.12t - 2.1 = 0.07t - 0.2$.

Solution

$$0.12t - 2.1 = 0.07t - 0.2$$

$$100(0.12t - 2.1) = 100(0.07t - 0.2) \qquad \text{Multiply both sides by 100}$$

$$12t - 210 = 7t - 20$$

$$5t = 190$$
$$t = 38$$

The solution set is $\{38\}$.

Classroom Example
Solve $0.7m + 0.5(484 - m) = 310$.

EXAMPLE 6   Solve $0.8x + 0.9(850 - x) = 715$.

Solution

$$0.8x + 0.9(850 - x) = 715$$
$$10[0.8x + 0.9(850 - x)] = 10(715) \qquad \text{Multiply both sides by 10}$$
$$10(0.8x) + 10[0.9(850 - x)] = 10(715)$$
$$8x + 9(850 - x) = 7150$$
$$8x + 7650 - 9x = 7150$$
$$-x = -500$$
$$x = 500$$

The solution set is $\{500\}$.

Changing Forms of Formulas

Many practical applications of mathematics involve the use of formulas. For example, to find the distance traveled in 4 hours at a rate of 55 miles per hour, we multiply the rate times the time; thus the distance is $55(4) = 220$ miles. The rule *distance equals rate times time* is commonly stated as a formula: $d = rt$. When we use a formula, it is sometimes convenient first to change its form. For example, multiplying both sides of $d = rt$ by $1/t$ produces the equivalent form $r = d/t$. Multiplying both sides of $d = rt$ by $1/r$ produces another equivalent form, $t = d/r$. The following two examples further illustrate the process of obtaining equivalent forms of certain formulas.

Classroom Example
The sum of n terms of a geometric sequence is given by the formula $S_n = \dfrac{a_1 r^n - a_1}{r - 1}$, where a_1 is the first term in the sequence, n is the number of terms, and r is the common ratio of the sequence. Solve $S_n = \dfrac{a_1 r^n - a_1}{r - 1}$ for a_1.

EXAMPLE 7

If P dollars are invested at a simple rate of r percent, then the amount, A, accumulated after t years is given by the formula $A = P + Prt$. Solve this formula for P.

Solution

$$A = P + Prt$$
$$A = P(1 + rt) \qquad \text{Apply the distributive property to factor the right side}$$
$$\frac{A}{1 + rt} = P \qquad \text{Multiply both sides by } \frac{1}{1 + rt}$$
$$P = \frac{A}{1 + rt} \qquad \text{Apply the symmetric property of equality}$$

Classroom Example
The sum of n terms of an arithmetic sequence is given by the formula $S_n = \dfrac{n(a_1 + a_n)}{2}$, where a_1 is the first term in the sequence, n is the number of terms, and a_n is the nth term in the sequence. Solve

$$S_n = \frac{n(a_1 + a_n)}{2} \text{ for } a_1.$$

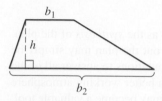

Figure 1.3

EXAMPLE 8

The area, A, of a trapezoid (see Figure 1.3) is given by the formula $A = \dfrac{1}{2}h(b_1 + b_2)$. Solve this equation for b_1.

Solution

$$A = \frac{1}{2}h(b_1 + b_2)$$

$$2A = h(b_1 + b_2)$$ Multiply both sides by 2

$$2A = hb_1 + hb_2$$ Apply the distributive property to the right side

$$2A - hb_2 = hb_1$$ Add $-hb_2$ to both sides

$$\frac{2A - hb_2}{h} = b_1$$ Multiply both sides by $\dfrac{1}{h}$

Notice that in Example 7 the distributive property was used to change from the form $P + Prt$ to $P(1 + rt)$. However, in Example 8 the distributive property was used to change $h(b_1 + b_2)$ to $hb_1 + hb_2$. In both examples the goal is to *isolate the term* containing the variable being solved for so that an appropriate application of the multiplication property will produce the desired result. Also note the use of *subscripts* to identify the two bases of the trapezoid. Subscripts allow us to use the same letter b to identify the bases, but b_1 represents one base and b_2 the other.

More on Problem Solving

Volumes have been written on the topic of problem solving, but certainly one of the best-known sources is George Polya's book *How to Solve It.** In this book, Polya suggests the following four-phase plan for solving problems.

1. *Understand the problem.*
2. *Devise a plan* to solve the problem.
3. *Carry out the plan* to solve the problem.
4. *Look back* at the completed solution to review and discuss it.

We will comment briefly on each of the phases and offer some suggestions for using an algebraic approach to solve problems.

Understand the Problem   Read the problem carefully, making certain that you understand the meanings of all the words. Be especially alert for any technical terms used in the statement of the problem. Often it is helpful to sketch a figure, diagram, or chart to visualize and organize the conditions of the problem. Determine the known and unknown facts, and if one of the previously mentioned pictorial devices is used, record these facts in the appropriate places on the diagram or chart.

Devise a Plan   This is the key part of the four-phase plan. It is sometimes referred to as the *analysis* of the problem. There are numerous strategies and techniques used to solve

*Polya, George. 1945. *How to Solve It.* Princeton, NJ: Princeton University Press.

problems. We shall discuss some of these strategies at various places throughout this text; however, at this time we offer the following general suggestions.

1. Choose a meaningful *variable* to represent an unknown quantity in the problem (perhaps t if time is an unknown quantity), and represent any other unknowns in terms of that variable.

2. Look for a *guideline* that can be used to set up an equation. A guideline might be a formula, such as $A = P + Prt$ from Example 7, or a statement of a relationship, such as *the sum of the two numbers is 28*. Sometimes a relationship suggested by a pictorial device can be used as a guideline for setting up the equation. Also, be alert to the possibility that this *new* problem might really be an *old* problem in a new setting, perhaps even stated with different vocabulary.

3. Form an *equation* containing the variable so that the conditions of the guideline are translated from English into algebra.

Carry out the Plan   This phase is sometimes referred to as the *synthesis* of the plan. If phase 2 has been successfully completed, then carrying out the plan may simply be a matter of solving the equation and doing any further computations to answer all of the questions in the problem. Confidence in your plan creates a better working atmosphere for carrying it out. It is also in this phase that the calculator may become a valuable tool. The type of data and the amount of complexity involved in the computations are two factors that can influence your decision whether to use one.

Look Back   This is an important but often overlooked part of problem solving. The following list of questions suggests some things for you to consider in this phase.

1. Is your answer to the problem a *reasonable* answer?

2. Have you *checked* your answer by substituting it back into the conditions stated in the problem?

3. Looking back over your solution, do you now see another plan that could be used to solve the problem?

4. Do you see a way of generalizing your procedure for this problem that could be used to solve other problems of this type?

5. Do you now see that this problem is closely related to another problem that you have previously solved?

6. Have you tucked away for future reference the technique used to solve this problem?

Looking back over the solution of a newly solved problem can lay important groundwork for solving problems in the future.

Remark: If you are interested in finding out more about George Polya and his insights into problem solving, check the Internet. For example, Google has some interesting information about his problem-solving techniques.

Keep Polya's suggestions in mind as we tackle some more word problems. Perhaps it would also be helpful for you to attempt to solve these problems on your own before looking at our approach.

Sometimes we can use the concepts of ratio and proportion to set up an equation and solve a problem, as the next problem illustrates.

Classroom Example
At a career university, the ratio of physical therapy students to nursing students is 2 to 11. If there is a total of 260 students enrolled in the two programs, find the number of nursing students.

EXAMPLE 9

At a community college, the ratio of transfer students to career education students is 12 to 5. If there is a total of 18,360 students enrolled in the two areas, find the number of transfer students and the number of career students.

Solution

Let x represent the number of transfer students; then $18,360 - x$ represents the number of career students. The following proportion can be set up and solved:

$$\frac{x}{18,360 - x} = \frac{12}{5}$$

$$5x = 12(18,360 - x)$$
$$5x = 220,320 - 12x$$
$$17x = 220,320$$
$$x = 12,960$$

Therefore, there are 12,960 transfer students and $18,360 - 12,960 = 5400$ career education students.

The next problem has a geometric setting. In such cases, the use of figures is very helpful.

Classroom Example
Since 1955, a pizza company has made a rectangular medium pizza with a length 4 inches more than the width. If the width is decreased by 1 inch and the length is decreased by 5 inches, the pizza would be the same size as the company's small pizza. Given that the area of the small pizza is 59 square inches smaller than the medium pizza, find the dimensions of the small and medium pizzas.

EXAMPLE 10

The length of a residential bathroom is 3 feet longer than the width. In order to make the bathroom handicapped accessible, the length of the bathroom is increased by 3 feet, and the width is increased by 2 feet. The area of the handicapped-accessible bathroom is 37 square feet larger than the area of the residential bathroom. Find the dimensions of the residential bathroom and the handicapped-accessible bathroom.

Solution

Let x represent the width of the residential bathroom. Then $x + 3$ represents the length of the residential bathroom. For the handicapped-accessible bathroom, $x + 2$ represents the width, and $x + 3 + 3 = x + 6$ represents the length. Because the area of the handicapped-accessible bathroom is 37 square feet larger than the residential bathroom (see Figure 1.4), the following equation can be set up and solved:

$$
\begin{array}{c}
\text{Area of residential} + 37 = \text{Area of handicapped-} \\
\text{bathroom} \qquad\qquad \text{accessible bathroom}
\end{array}
$$

$$x(x + 3) + 37 = (x + 2)(x + 6)$$
$$x^2 + 3x + 37 = x^2 + 8x + 12$$
$$3x + 37 = 8x + 12$$
$$25 = 5x$$
$$x = 5$$

For the residential bathroom:

Width = x = 5 feet

Length = $x + 3 = 5 + 3$
  = 8 feet

For the handicapped-accessible bathroom:

Width = $x + 2 = 5 + 2$
  = 7 feet

Length = $x + 6 = 5 + 6$
  = 11 feet

Thus the dimensions for the residential bathroom are 5 feet by 8 feet, and the dimensions for the handicapped-accessible bathroom are 7 feet by 11 feet.

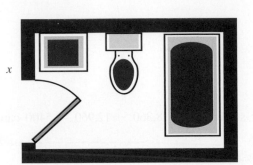

x

$x + 3$

Residential bathroom

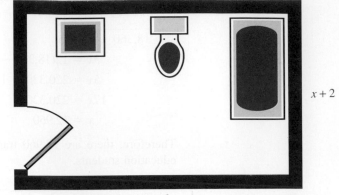

$x + 2$

$x + 6$

Handicapped-accessible bathroom

Figure 1.4

Many consumer problems can be solved by using an algebraic approach. For example, let's consider a discount sale problem involving the relationship *original selling price minus discount equals discount sale price*.

Classroom Example
Tasha bought a dress at a 60% discount sale for $132. What was the original price of the dress?

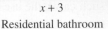

EXAMPLE 11

Jim bought a pair of jeans at a 30% discount sale for $28. What was the original price of the jeans?

Solution

Let p represent the original price of the jeans.

Original price − Discount = Discount sale price

$$(100\%)(p) \quad - \quad (30\%)(p) \quad = \quad \$28$$

We switch this equation to decimal form to solve it.

$$p - 0.3p = 28$$
$$0.7p = 28$$
$$p = 40$$

The original price of the jeans was $40.

Another basic relationship pertaining to consumer problems is *selling price equals cost plus profit*. Profit (also called markup, markon, and margin of profit) may be stated in different ways. It can be expressed as a percent of the cost, as a percent of the selling price, or simply in terms of dollars and cents. Let's consider a problem where the profit is stated as a percent of the selling price.

EXAMPLE 12

A retailer of sporting goods bought a putter for $25. He wants to price the putter to make a profit of 20% of the selling price. What price should he mark on the putter?

Solution

Let s represent the selling price.

Solving this equation involves using the methods we developed earlier for working with decimals:

$$s = 25 + (20\%)(s)$$
$$s = 25 + 0.2s$$
$$10s = 250 + 2s$$
$$8s = 250$$
$$s = 31.25$$

The selling price should be $31.25.

Certain types of investment problems can be solved by using an algebraic approach. As our final example of this section, let's consider one such problem.

EXAMPLE 13

Cindy invested a certain amount of money at 2% interest and $1500 more than that amount at 5% interest. Her total yearly interest was $285. How much did she invest at each rate?

Solution

Let d represent the amount invested at 2%; then $d + 1500$ represents the amount invested at 5%. The following guideline can be used to set up an equation:

Interest earned at 2% + Interest earned at 5% = Total interest

$$(2\%)(d) \quad + \quad (5\%)(d + 1500) = \quad \$285$$

We can solve this equation by multiplying both sides by 100:

$$0.02d + 0.05(d + 1500) = 285$$
$$2d + 5(d + 1500) = 28{,}500$$
$$2d + 5d + 7500 = 28{,}500$$
$$7d = 21{,}000$$
$$d = 3000$$

Cindy invested $3000 at 2% and $3000 + $1500 = $4500 at 5%. ∎

Don't forget phase 4 of Polya's problem-solving plan. We have not taken the space to look back over and discuss each of our examples. However, it would be beneficial for you to do so, keeping in mind the questions posed earlier regarding this phase.

Concept Quiz 1.2

For Problems 1–6, answer true or false.

1. When solving equations, restricted values are any values of the variable that make the numerator or the denominator zero.
2. A statement of equality between two ratios is called a proportion.
3. The equation $4 + \dfrac{3}{x - 2} = \dfrac{5}{3x + 1}$ is an example of a proportion.
4. Profit is always expressed as a percent of the cost.
5. The goal in solving a formula for a specified variable is to isolate that variable in a single term and then apply the multiplication property to produce the result.
6. The formulas $d = rt$, $r = \dfrac{d}{t}$, and $t = \dfrac{d}{r}$ are equivalent.

Problem Set 1.2

For Problems 1–32, solve each equation. (Objectives 1, 2, and 3)

1. $\dfrac{x - 2}{3} + \dfrac{x + 1}{4} = \dfrac{1}{6}$

2. $\dfrac{5n - 1}{4} - \dfrac{2n - 3}{10} = \dfrac{3}{5}$

3. $\dfrac{5}{x} + \dfrac{1}{3} = \dfrac{8}{x}$

4. $\dfrac{5}{3n} - \dfrac{1}{9} = \dfrac{1}{n}$

5. $\dfrac{1}{3n} + \dfrac{1}{2n} = \dfrac{1}{4}$

6. $\dfrac{1}{x} - \dfrac{3}{2x} = \dfrac{1}{5}$

7. $\dfrac{35 - x}{x} = 7 + \dfrac{3}{x}$

8. $\dfrac{n}{46 - n} = 5 + \dfrac{4}{46 - n}$

9. $\dfrac{n + 67}{n} = 5 + \dfrac{11}{n}$

10. $\dfrac{n + 52}{n} = 4 + \dfrac{1}{n}$

11. $\dfrac{5}{3x - 2} = \dfrac{1}{x - 4}$

12. $\dfrac{-2}{5x - 3} = \dfrac{4}{4x - 1}$

13. $\dfrac{4}{2y - 3} - \dfrac{7}{3y - 5} = 0$

14. $\dfrac{3}{2n + 1} + \dfrac{5}{3n - 4} = 0$

15. $\dfrac{n}{n + 1} + 3 = \dfrac{4}{n + 1}$ **16.** $\dfrac{a}{a + 5} - 2 = \dfrac{3a}{a + 5}$

17. $\dfrac{3x}{2x - 1} - 4 = \dfrac{x}{2x - 1}$

18. $\dfrac{x}{x - 8} - 4 = \dfrac{8}{x - 8}$

19. $\dfrac{3}{x + 3} - \dfrac{1}{x - 2} = \dfrac{5}{2x + 6}$

20. $\dfrac{6}{x + 3} + \dfrac{20}{x^2 + x - 6} = \dfrac{5}{x - 2}$

21. $\dfrac{n}{n - 3} - \dfrac{3}{2} = \dfrac{3}{n - 3}$

22. $\dfrac{4}{x - 2} + \dfrac{x}{x + 1} = \dfrac{x^2 - 2}{x^2 - x - 2}$

23. $s = 9 + 0.25s$

24. $s = 1.95 + 0.35s$

25. $0.09x + 0.1(700 - x) = 67$

26. $0.08x + 0.09(950 - x) = 81$

27. $0.09x + 0.11(x + 125) = 68.75$

28. $0.08(x + 200) = 0.07x + 20$

29. $0.8(t - 2) = 0.5(9t + 10)$

30. $0.3(2n - 5) = 11 - 0.65n$

31. $0.92 + 0.9(x - 0.3) = 2x - 5.95$

32. $0.5(3x + 0.7) = 20.6$

For Problems 33–46, solve each formula for the indicated variable. (Objective 4)

33. $P = 2l + 2w$ for w (Perimeter of a rectangle)

34. $V = \dfrac{1}{3}Bh$ for B (Volume of a pyramid)

35. $A = 2lw + 2lh + 2wh$ for h (Surface area of rectangular box)

36. $z = \dfrac{x - \mu}{\sigma}$ for x (z-score in statistics)

37. $A = 2\pi r^2 + 2\pi rh$ for h (Surface area of a right circular cylinder)

38. $A = \dfrac{1}{2}h(b_1 + b_2)$ for h (Area of a trapezoid)

39. $C = \dfrac{5}{9}(F - 32)$ for F (Fahrenheit to Celsius)

40. $F = \dfrac{9}{5}C + 32$ for C (Celsius to Fahrenheit)

41. $V = C\left(1 - \dfrac{T}{N}\right)$ for T (Linear depreciation)

42. $V = C\left(1 - \dfrac{T}{N}\right)$ for N (Linear depreciation)

43. $I = kl(T - t)$ for T (Expansion allowance in highway construction)

44. $S = \dfrac{CRD}{12d}$ for d (Cutting speed of a circular saw)

45. $\dfrac{1}{R_n} = \dfrac{1}{R_1} + \dfrac{1}{R_2}$ for R_n (Resistance in parallel circuit design)

46. $f = \dfrac{1}{\dfrac{1}{a} + \dfrac{1}{b}}$ for b (Focal length of a camera lens)

For Problems 47–73, set up an equation and solve each problem. (Objective 5)

47. Working as a waiter, Tom made $157.50 in tips. Assuming that every customer tipped 15% of the cost of the meal, find the cost of all the meals Tom served.

48. A realtor who is paid 7% of the selling price in commission recently received $10,794 in commission on the sale of a property. What was the selling price of the property?

49. A total of $2250 for a house painting job is to be divided between two painters in the ratio of 2 to 3. How much does each painter receive?

50. One type of motor requires a mixture of oil and gasoline in a ratio of 1 to 15 (that is, 1 part of oil to 15 parts of gasoline). How many liters of each are contained in a 20-liter mixture?

51. The ratio of 2-wheel-drive trucks to 4-wheel-drive trucks at an auto dealership is 8 to 1. If the total number of trucks at the dealership is 189, find the number of each.

52. The ratio of the weight of sodium to that of chlorine in common table salt is 5 to 3. Find the amount of each element in a salt compound weighing 200 pounds.

53. Gary bought an MP3 player at a 20% discount sale for $52. What was the original price of the MP3 player?

54. Roya bought a pair of jeans at a 30% discount sale for $33.60. What was the original price of the jeans?

55. After a 7% increase in salary, Laurie makes $1647.80 per month. How much did she earn per month before the increase?

56. Russ bought a used car for $11,025, including 5% sales tax. What was the selling price of the used car without the tax?

57. A retailer has some shoes that cost $28 per pair. At what price should they be sold to obtain a profit of 75% of the cost?

58. If a head of lettuce costs a retailer $1.10, at what price should it be sold to make a profit of 45% of the cost?

59. Karla sold a bicycle on e-store for $97.50. This selling price represented a 30% profit for her, based on what she had originally paid for the bike. Find Karla's original cost for the bicycle.

60. If a ring costs a jeweler $250, at what price should it be sold to make a profit of 60% of the selling price?

61. A retailer has some skirts that cost $18 each. She wants to sell them at a profit of 40% of the selling price. What price should she charge for the skirts?

62. Suppose that an item costs a retailer $50. How much more profit could be gained by fixing a 50% profit based on selling price rather than a 50% profit based on cost?

63. Derek has some nickels and dimes worth $3.60. The number of dimes is one more than twice the number of nickels. How many nickels and dimes does he have?

64. Robin has a collection of nickels, dimes, and quarters worth $38.50. She has 10 more dimes than nickels and twice as many quarters as dimes. How many coins of each kind does she have?

65. A collection of 70 coins consisting of dimes, quarters, and half-dollars has a value of $17.75. There are three times as many quarters as dimes. Find the number of each kind of coin.

66. A certain amount of money is invested at 3% per year, and $1500 more than that amount is invested at 5% per year. The annual interest from the 5% investment exceeds the annual interest from the 3% investment by $125. How much is invested at each rate?

67. A total of $5500 was invested, part of it at 4% per year and the remainder at 6% per year. If the total yearly interest amounted to $290, how much was invested at each rate?

68. A sum of $3500 is split between two investments, one paying 5% yearly interest and the other 7%. If the return on the 7% investment exceeds that on the 5% investment by $65 the first year, how much is invested at each rate?

69. Celia has invested $2500 at 2% yearly interest. How much must she invest at 5% so that the interest from both investments totals $250 after a year?

70. The length of a rectangle is 2 inches less than three times its width. If the perimeter of the rectangle is 108 inches, find its length and width.

71. The length of a rectangle is 4 centimeters more than its width. If the width is increased by 2 centimeters and the length is increased by 3 centimeters, a new rectangle is formed that has an area of 44 square centimeters more than the area of the original rectangle. Find the dimensions of the original rectangle.

72. The length of a picture without its border is 7 inches less than twice its width. If the border is 1 inch wide,

and its area is 62 square inches, what are the dimensions of the picture alone?

73. If two opposite sides of a square are each increased by 3 centimeters, and the other two sides are each decreased by 2 centimeters, the area is increased by 8 square centimeters. Find the length of a side of the square.

Thoughts Into Words

74. Give a step-by-step description of how you would solve the formula $F = \frac{9}{5}C + 32$ for C.

75. What does the phrase "declare a variable" mean when following the steps to solve a word problem?

76. Why must potential answers to word problems be checked against the original statement of the problem?

77. From a consumer's viewpoint, would you prefer that retailers figure their profit on the basis of the cost or the selling price? Explain your answer.

78. Some people multiply by 2 and add 30 to estimate the change from a Celsius reading to a Fahrenheit reading. Why does this give an estimate? How good is the estimate?

Further Investigations

79. Is a 10% discount followed by a 20% discount equal to a 30% discount? Defend your answer.

80. Is a 10% discount followed by a 30% discount the same as a 30% discount followed by a 10% discount? Justify your answer.

81. A retailer buys an item for $90, resells it for $100, and claims that he is making only a 10% profit. Is his claim correct?

82. The following formula can be used to determine the selling price of an item when the profit is based on a percent of the selling price.

$$\text{Selling price} = \frac{\text{Cost}}{100\% - \text{Percent of profit}}$$

Show how this formula is developed.

83. Use the formula from Problem 82 to determine the selling price of each of the following items. The given percent of profit is based on the selling price. Be sure to check each answer.

(a) $0.80 bottle of water;   20% profit
(b) $8.50 music CD;   25% profit
(c) $50 pair of athletic shoes;   40% profit
(d) $200 digital camera;   50% profit
(e) $18,000 car;   15% profit

Graphing Calculator Activities

84. Graph the appropriate equations to give visual support for your solutions for Problems 15–21.

Answers to the Concept Quiz
1. False   **2.** True   **3.** False   **4.** False   **5.** True   **6.** True

1.3   Quadratic Equations

OBJECTIVES

1 Solve quadratic equations by factoring

2 Solve quadratic equations by applying the square root property

3 Solve quadratic equations by completing the square

4 Solve quadratic equations by using the quadratic formula

5 Use the discriminant to determine the nature of the solutions of a quadratic equation

6 Solve application problems involving quadratic equations

A **quadratic equation** in the variable x is defined as any equation that can be written in the form

$$ax^2 + bx + c = 0$$

where a, b, and c are real numbers and $a \neq 0$. The form $ax^2 + bx + c = 0$ is called the **standard form** of a quadratic equation. The choice of x for the variable is arbitrary. An equation such as $3t^2 + 5t - 4 = 0$ is a quadratic equation in the variable t.

Quadratic equations such as $x^2 + 2x - 15 = 0$, where the polynomial is factorable, can be solved by applying the following property: **$ab = 0$ if and only if $a = 0$ or $b = 0$.** Our work might take on the following format.

$$x^2 + 2x - 15 = 0$$
$$(x + 5)(x - 3) = 0$$
$$x + 5 = 0 \quad \text{or} \quad x - 3 = 0$$
$$x = -5 \quad \text{or} \quad x = 3$$

The solution set for this equation is $\{-5, 3\}$.

Let's consider another example of this type.

EXAMPLE 1   Solve the equation $n = -6n^2 + 12$.

Solution

$$n = -6n^2 + 12$$
$$6n^2 + n - 12 = 0$$
$$(3n - 4)(2n + 3) = 0$$
$$3n - 4 = 0 \quad \text{or} \quad 2n + 3 = 0$$
$$3n = 4 \quad \text{or} \quad 2n = -3$$
$$n = \frac{4}{3} \quad \text{or} \quad n = -\frac{3}{2}$$

The solution set is $\left\{ -\dfrac{3}{2}, \dfrac{4}{3} \right\}$.

Now suppose that we want to solve $x^2 = k$, where k is any real number. We can proceed as follows:

$$x^2 = k$$
$$x^2 - k = 0$$
$$\left(x + \sqrt{k}\right)\left(x - \sqrt{k}\right) = 0$$
$$x + \sqrt{k} = 0 \quad \text{or} \quad x - \sqrt{k} = 0$$
$$x = -\sqrt{k} \quad \text{or} \quad x = \sqrt{k}$$

Thus we can state the following property for any real number k.

> **Property 1.2**
>
> The solution set of $x^2 = k$ is $\{-\sqrt{k}, \sqrt{k}\}$, which can also be written $\{\pm\sqrt{k}\}$.

Property 1.2, along with our knowledge of square root, makes it very easy to solve quadratic equations of the form $x^2 = k$.

EXAMPLE 2   Solve each of the following.

(a) $x^2 = 72$ **(b)** $(3n - 1)^2 = 26$ **(c)** $(y + 2)^2 = -24$

Solutions

(a) $x^2 = 72$
$$x = \pm\sqrt{72}$$
$$x = \pm 6\sqrt{2}$$

The solution set is $\{\pm 6\sqrt{2}\}$.

(b) $(3n - 1)^2 = 26$

$$3n - 1 = \pm\sqrt{26}$$

$3n - 1 = \sqrt{26}$ or $3n - 1 = -\sqrt{26}$

$3n = 1 + \sqrt{26}$ or $3n = 1 - \sqrt{26}$

$n = \dfrac{1 + \sqrt{26}}{3}$ or $n = \dfrac{1 - \sqrt{26}}{3}$

The solution set is $\left\{\dfrac{1 \pm \sqrt{26}}{3}\right\}$.

c. $(y + 2)^2 = -24$

$$y + 2 = \pm\sqrt{-24}$$

$y + 2 = \pm 2i\sqrt{6}$ Remember that $\sqrt{-24} = i\sqrt{24} = i\sqrt{4}\sqrt{6} = 2i\sqrt{6}$

$y + 2 = 2i\sqrt{6}$ or $y + 2 = -2i\sqrt{6}$

$y = -2 + 2i\sqrt{6}$ or $y = -2 - 2i\sqrt{6}$

The solution set is $\{-2 \pm 2i\sqrt{6}\}$. ▬▬▬▬▬▬▬▬▬▬ ∎

Completing the Square

A factoring technique we reviewed in Chapter 0 relied on recognizing *perfect-square trinomials*. In each of the following examples, the perfect-square trinomial on the right side of the identity is the result of squaring the binomial on the left side.

$$(x + 5)^2 = x^2 + 10x + 25 \qquad (x - 7)^2 = x^2 - 14x + 49$$
$$(x + 9)^2 = x^2 + 18x + 81 \qquad (x - 12)^2 = x^2 - 24x + 144$$

Note that in each of the square trinomials, the constant term is equal to the square of one-half of the coefficient of the x term. This relationship allows us to *form* a perfect-square trinomial by adding a proper constant term. For example, suppose that we want to form a perfect-square trinomial from $x^2 + 8x$. Because $\dfrac{1}{2}(8) = 4$ and $4^2 = 16$, the perfect-square trinomial is $x^2 + 8x + 16$. Now let's use this idea to solve a quadratic equation.

Classroom Example
Solve $n^2 + 6n - 3 = 0$.

EXAMPLE 3   Solve $x^2 + 8x - 2 = 0$.

To solve the equation, $x^2 + 8x - 2 = 0$, by completing the square, employ the following steps:

1. The coefficient of the squared term is 1 so nothing needs to be done to achieve that.

2. Rewrite the equation with the constant term alone on one side of the equation.

$$x^2 + 8x = 2$$

3. Take one-half of the coefficient of the *x* term and square the result.

$$\frac{1}{2}(8) = 4 \quad \text{and} \quad 4^2 = 16$$

4. Add the result in step 3 to both sides of the equation.

$$x^2 + 8x + 16 = 2 + 16$$

5. Now factor the left-hand side of the equation.

$$(x + 4)^2 = 18$$

6. Now apply Property 1.2 to finish solving the equation.

$$(x + 4)^2 = 18$$
$$x + 4 = \pm\sqrt{18}$$
$$x + 4 = \pm 3\sqrt{2}$$
$$x = -4 \pm 3\sqrt{2}$$

The solution set is $\{-4 \pm 3\sqrt{2}\}$.   ■

We have been using a relationship for a perfect-square trinomial that states *the constant term is equal to the square of one-half of the coefficient of the x term.* This relationship holds only if the coefficient of x^2 is 1. Thus we need to make a slight adjustment when we are solving quadratic equations that have a coefficient of x^2 other than 1. The next example shows how to make this adjustment.

Classroom Example
Solve $4m^2 + 12m - 1 = 0$.

EXAMPLE 4   Solve $2x^2 + 6x - 3 = 0$.

Solution

To solve the equation, $2x^2 - 6x - 3 = 0$, by completing the square, employ the following steps:

1. The coefficient of the squared term is 2, so multiply both sides by $\frac{1}{2}$.

$$\frac{1}{2}(2x^2 - 6x - 3) = \frac{1}{2}(0)$$

$$x^2 - 3x - \frac{3}{2} = 0$$

2. Rewrite the equation with the constant term alone on one side of the equation.

$$x^2 - 3x = \frac{3}{2}$$

3. Take one-half of the coefficient of the *x* term and square the result.

$$\frac{1}{2}(3) = \frac{3}{2} \quad \text{and} \quad \left(\frac{3}{2}\right)^2 = \frac{9}{4}$$

4. Add the result in step 3 to both sides of the equation.

$$x^2 + 3x + \frac{9}{4} = \frac{3}{2} + \frac{9}{4}$$

5. Now factor the left-hand side of the equation.

$$\left(x + \frac{3}{2}\right)^2 = \frac{15}{4}$$

6. Now apply Property 1.2 to finish solving the equation.

$$\left(x + \frac{3}{2}\right)^2 = \frac{15}{4}$$

$$x + \frac{3}{2} = \pm\sqrt{\frac{15}{4}}$$

$$x + \frac{3}{2} = \pm\frac{\sqrt{15}}{2}$$

$$x = -\frac{3}{2} \pm \frac{\sqrt{15}}{2} = \frac{3 \pm \sqrt{15}}{2}$$

The solution set is $\left\{\dfrac{-3 \pm \sqrt{15}}{2}\right\}$.

Again let's pause for a moment and take another look at the relationship between the solutions of an algebraic equation and the x intercepts of a geometric graph. Figure 1.5 shows a graph of $y = 2x^2 + 6x - 3$. Note that one x intercept is between -4 and -3, and the other x intercept is between 0 and 1. The solutions are $\dfrac{-3 - \sqrt{15}}{2} \approx -3.4$ and $\dfrac{-3 + \sqrt{15}}{2} \approx 0.4$. So our geometric analysis appears to agree with our algebraic solutions.

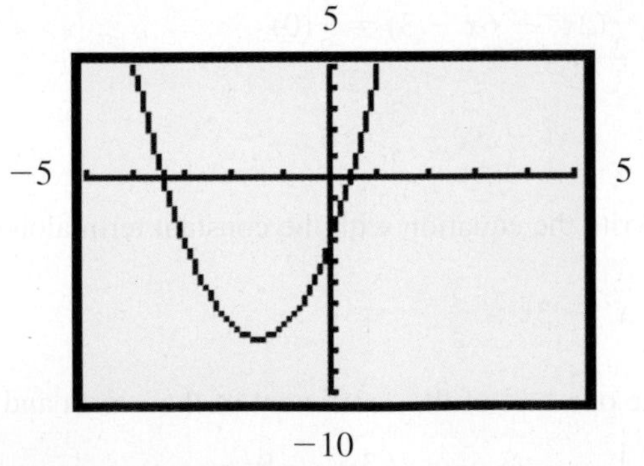

Figure 1.5

Quadratic Formula

The process used in Examples 3 and 4 is called **completing the square.** It can be used to solve *any* quadratic equation. If we use this process of completing the square to solve the general quadratic equation, $ax^2 + bx + c = 0$, we obtain a formula known as the **quadratic formula.** The details are as follows:

$$ax^2 + bx + c = 0 \qquad a \neq 0$$

$$ax^2 + bx = -c$$

$$x^2 + \frac{b}{a}x = -\frac{c}{a} \qquad\qquad \text{Multiply both sides by } \frac{1}{a}$$

$$x^2 + \frac{b}{a}x + \frac{b^2}{4a^2} = -\frac{c}{a} + \frac{b^2}{4a^2} \qquad \text{Complete the square by adding } \frac{b^2}{4a^2} \text{ to both sides}$$

$$\left(x + \frac{b}{2a}\right)^2 = \frac{b^2 - 4ac}{4a^2} \qquad \begin{array}{l}\text{Combine the right side into a} \\ \text{single fraction}\end{array}$$

$$x + \frac{b}{2a} = \pm\sqrt{\frac{b^2 - 4ac}{4a^2}}$$

$$x + \frac{b}{2a} = \pm\frac{\sqrt{b^2 - 4ac}}{\sqrt{4a^2}}$$

$$x + \frac{b}{2a} = \pm\frac{\sqrt{b^2 - 4ac}}{2a} \qquad \begin{array}{l}\sqrt{4a^2} = |2a| \text{ but } 2a \text{ can be used} \\ \text{because of the use of } \pm\end{array}$$

$$x + \frac{b}{2a} = \frac{\sqrt{b^2 - 4ac}}{2a} \qquad \text{or} \qquad x + \frac{b}{2a} = -\frac{\sqrt{b^2 - 4ac}}{2a}$$

$$x = -\frac{b}{2a} + \frac{\sqrt{b^2 - 4ac}}{2a} \qquad \text{or} \qquad x = -\frac{b}{2a} - \frac{\sqrt{b^2 - 4ac}}{2a}$$

$$x = \frac{-b + \sqrt{b^2 - 4ac}}{2a} \qquad \text{or} \qquad x = \frac{-b - \sqrt{b^2 - 4ac}}{2a}$$

The quadratic formula can be stated as follows.

> ### Quadratic Formula
>
> If $a \neq 0$, then the solutions (roots) of the equation $ax^2 + bx + c = 0$ are given by
>
> $$x = \frac{-b \pm \sqrt{b^2 - 4ac}}{2a}$$

We can use the quadratic formula to solve *any* quadratic equation by expressing the equation in the standard form $ax^2 + bx + c = 0$ and then substituting the values for a, b, and c into the formula. Let's consider some examples and use a graphical approach to predict approximate solutions whenever possible.

Classroom Example
Solve each of the following by using the quadratic formula.
(a) $2x^2 + x - 5 = 0$
(b) $36x^2 - 60x = -25$
(c) $x^2 - 4x + 8 = 0$

EXAMPLE 5

Solve each of the following by using the quadratic formula.

(a) $3x^2 - x - 5 = 0$ **(b)** $25n^2 - 30n = -9$ **(c)** $t^2 - 2t + 4 = 0$

Solutions

(a) Graph $y = 3x^2 - x - 5$. (See Figure 1.6.)

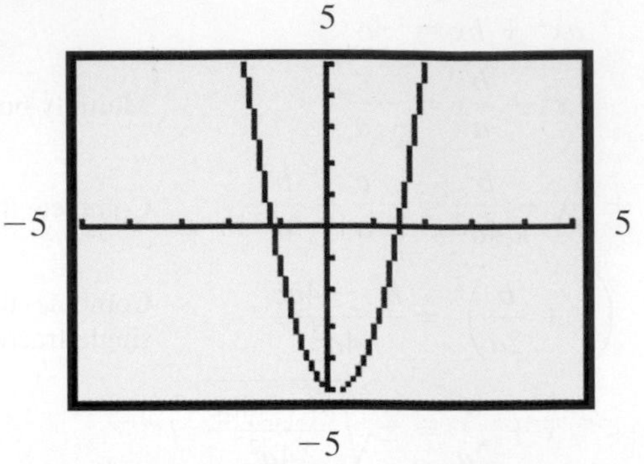

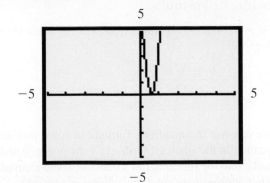

One intercept is between −2 and −1, and the other is between 1 and 2

Figure 1.6

We need to think of $3x^2 - x - 5 = 0$ as $3x^2 + (-x) + (-5) = 0$; thus $a = 3$, $b = -1$, and $c = -5$. We then substitute these values into the quadratic formula and simplify:

$$x = \frac{-b \pm \sqrt{b^2 - 4ac}}{2a}$$

$$x = \frac{-(-1) \pm \sqrt{(-1)^2 - 4(3)(-5)}}{2(3)}$$

$$= \frac{1 \pm \sqrt{61}}{6}$$

The solution set is $\left\{\frac{1 \pm \sqrt{61}}{6}\right\}$. (You should evaluate these solutions to be sure they agree with the intercepts.)

(b) Graph $y = 25x^2 - 30x + 9$. (See Figure 1.7.)

There appears to be one intercept between 0 and 1

Figure 1.7

The quadratic formula is usually stated in terms of the variable x, but again the choice of variable is arbitrary. The given equation, $25n^2 - 30n = -9$, needs to be changed to standard form: $25n^2 - 30n + 9 = 0$. From this we obtain $a = 25$, $b = -30$, and $c = 9$. Now we use the formula:

$$n = \frac{-(-30) \pm \sqrt{(-30)^2 - 4(25)(9)}}{2(25)}$$

$$= \frac{30 \pm \sqrt{0}}{50}$$

$$= \frac{3}{5}$$

The solution set is $\left\{ \dfrac{3}{5} \right\}$.

(c) Graph $y = x^2 - 2x + 4$. (See Figure 1.8.)

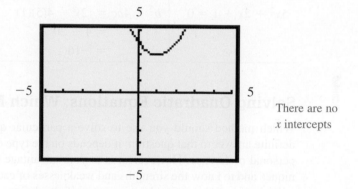

There are no x intercepts

Figure 1.8

To solve $t^2 - 2t + 4 = 0$, we substitute $a = 1$, $b = -2$, and $c = 4$ into the quadratic formula:

$$t = \frac{-(-2) \pm \sqrt{(-2)^2 - 4(1)(4)}}{2(1)}$$

$$= \frac{2 \pm \sqrt{-12}}{2}$$

$$= \frac{2 \pm 2i\sqrt{3}}{2}$$

$$= \frac{2(1 \pm i\sqrt{3})}{2}$$

The solution set is $\{1 \pm i\sqrt{3}\}$.

From Example 5 we see that different kinds of solutions are obtained depending upon the radicand $(b^2 - 4ac)$ inside the radical in the quadratic formula. For this reason, the number $b^2 - 4ac$ is called the **discriminant** of the quadratic equation. It can be used to determine the nature of the solutions as follows.

1. If $b^2 - 4ac > 0$, the equation has two unequal real solutions.

2. If $b^2 - 4ac = 0$, the equation has two equal real solutions.

3. If $b^2 - 4ac < 0$, the equation has two complex but nonreal solutions.

The following examples illustrate each of these situations. (You may want to solve the equations completely to verify our conclusions.)

Equation	Discriminant	Nature of Solutions
$4x^2 - 7x - 1 = 0$	$b^2 - 4ac = (-7)^2 - 4(4)(-1)$ $= 49 + 16$ $= 65$	Two real solutions
$4x^2 + 12x + 9 = 0$	$b^2 - 4ac = (12)^2 - 4(4)(9)$ $= 144 - 144$ $= 0$	Two equal real solutions
$5x^2 + 2x + 1 = 0$	$b^2 - 4ac = (2)^2 - 4(5)(1)$ $= 4 - 20$ $= -16$	Two complex solutions

Solving Quadratic Equations: Which Method?

Which method should you use to solve a particular quadratic equation? There is no definite answer to that question; it depends on the type of equation and perhaps on your personal preference. However, it is to your advantage to be able to use all three techniques and to know the strengths and weaknesses of each. In the next two examples we will give our reasons for choosing a specific technique.

Classroom Example
Solve $x^2 - 6x - 216 = 0$.

EXAMPLE 6   Solve $x^2 - 4x - 192 = 0$.

Solution

The size of the constant term makes the factoring approach a little cumbersome for this problem. However, because the coefficient of the x^2 term is 1, and the coefficient of the x term is even, the method for completing the square should work effectively.

$$x^2 - 4x - 192 = 0$$
$$x^2 - 4x = 192$$
$$x^2 - 4x + 4 = 192 + 4$$
$$(x - 2)^2 = 196$$
$$x - 2 = \pm\sqrt{196}$$
$$x - 2 = \pm 14$$
$$x - 2 = 14 \quad \text{or} \quad x - 2 = -14$$
$$x = 16 \quad \text{or} \quad x = -12$$

Classroom Example
Solve $5m^2 - 2m + 3 = 0$.

EXAMPLE 7   Solve $2x^2 - x + 3 = 0$.

Solution

It would be reasonable first to try factoring the polynomial $2x^2 - x + 3$. Unfortunately, it is not factorable using integers; thus we must solve the equation by completing the square or by using the quadratic formula. The coefficient of the x^2 term is not 1, so let's avoid completing the square and use the formula instead.

$$x = \frac{-b \pm \sqrt{b^2 - 4ac}}{2a}$$

$$= \frac{-(-1) \pm \sqrt{(-1)^2 - 4(2)(3)}}{2(2)}$$

$$= \frac{1 \pm \sqrt{-23}}{4}$$

$$= \frac{1 \pm i\sqrt{23}}{4}$$

The ability to solve quadratic equations enables us to solve more word problems. Some of these problems involve geometric formulas and relationships. We have included a brief summary of some basic geometric formulas in the back sheets of this text.

Classroom Example
One leg of a right triangle is 17 yards longer than the other leg. If the length of the hypotenuse is 25 yards, find the length of each leg.

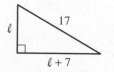

Figure 1.9

EXAMPLE 8

One leg of a right triangle is 7 meters longer than the other leg. If the length of the hypotenuse is 17 meters, find the length of each leg.

Solution

Look at Figure 1.9. Let l represent the length of one leg; then $l + 7$ represents the length of the other leg. Using the Pythagorean theorem as a guideline, we can set up and solve a quadratic equation:

$$l^2 + (l + 7)^2 = 17^2$$
$$l^2 + l^2 + 14l + 49 = 289$$
$$2l^2 + 14l - 240 = 0$$
$$l^2 + 7l - 120 = 0$$
$$(l + 15)(l - 8) = 0$$
$$l + 15 = 0 \quad \text{or} \quad l - 8 = 0$$
$$l = -15 \quad \text{or} \quad l = 8$$

The negative solution must be disregarded (because l is a length), so the length of one leg is 8 meters. The other leg, represented by $l + 7$, is $8 + 7 = 15$ meters long.

Concept Quiz 1.3

For Problems 1–8, answer true or false.
1. The product of two factors is equal to zero if either of the factors equals zero.
2. Solving a quadratic equation by factoring gives the same result as solving the equation by completing the square.
3. For the perfect-square trinomial $x^2 + bx + c$, the constant term is equal to one-half the square of the coefficient of the x term.
4. Any quadratic equation can be solved by completing the square.
5. To use the quadratic formula to solve quadratic equations, the equation needs to be in the standard form, $ax^2 + bx + c = 0$.
6. Every quadratic equation has two real number solutions.
7. The discriminant is $\sqrt{b^2 - 4ac}$.
8. The equation $ax^2 + bx + c = 0$ has two complex nonreal number solutions if $b^2 - 4ac < 0$.

Problem Set 1.3

For Problems 1–16, solve each equation by factoring or by using the property *If* $x^2 = k$, *then* $x = \pm\sqrt{k}$. **(Objectives 1 and 2)**

1. $x^2 - 3x - 28 = 0$ **2.** $x^2 - 4x - 12 = 0$

3. $3x^2 + 5x - 12 = 0$ **4.** $2x^2 - 13x + 6 = 0$

5. $2x^2 - 3x = 0$ **6.** $3n^2 = 3n$

7. $9y^2 = 12$ **8.** $(4n - 1)^2 = 16$

9. $(2n + 1)^2 = 20$ **10.** $3(4x - 1)^2 + 1 = 16$

11. $15n^2 + 19n - 10 = 0$ **12.** $6t^2 + 23t - 4 = 0$

13. $(x - 2)^2 = -4$ **14.** $24x^2 + 23x - 12 = 0$

15. $10y^2 + 33y - 7 = 0$ **16.** $(x - 3)^2 = -9$

17. $2(x + 3)^2 + 8 = -2$ **18.** $6(3x + 1)^2 - 5 = 7$

For Problems 19–32, use the method of completing the square to solve each equation. **(Objective 3)**

19. $x^2 - 10x + 24 = 0$ **20.** $x^2 + x - 20 = 0$

21. $n^2 + 10n - 2 = 0$ **22.** $n^2 + 6n - 1 = 0$

23. $y^2 - 3y = -1$ **24.** $y^2 + 5y = -2$

25. $x^2 + 4x + 6 = 0$ **26.** $x^2 - 6x + 21 = 0$

27. $2t^2 + 12t - 5 = 0$ **28.** $3p^2 + 12p - 2 = 0$

29. $x(x - 2) = 288$ **30.** $x(x + 4) = 221$

31. $3n^2 + 5n - 1 = 0$ **32.** $2n^2 + n - 4 = 0$

For Problems 33–46, use the quadratic formula to solve each equation. **(Objective 4)**

33. $n^2 - 3n - 54 = 0$ **34.** $y^2 + 13y + 22 = 0$

35. $3x^2 + 16x = -5$ **36.** $10x^2 - 29x - 21 = 0$

37. $y^2 - 2y - 4 = 0$ **38.** $n^2 - 6n - 3 = 0$

39. $2a(a - 3) = -1$ **40.** $x(2x + 3) - 1 = 0$

41. $n^2 - 3n = -7$ **42.** $n^2 - 5n = -8$

43. $x^2 + 4 = 8x$ **44.** $x^2 + 31 = -14x$

45. $4x^2 - 4x + 1 = 0$ **46.** $x^2 + 24 = 0$

For Problems 47–62, solve each quadratic equation by using the method that seems most appropriate to you.

47. $8x^2 + 10x - 3 = 0$ **48.** $18x^2 - 39x + 20 = 0$

49. $x^2 + 2x = 168$ **50.** $x^2 + 28x = -187$

51. $2t^2 - 3t + 7 = 0$ **52.** $3n^2 - 2n + 5 = 0$

53. $(3n - 1)^2 + 2 = 18$ **54.** $20y^2 + 17y - 10 = 0$

55. $4y(y + 1) = 1$ **56.** $(5n + 2)^2 + 1 = -27$

57. $x^2 - 16x + 14 = 0$ **58.** $x^2 - 18x + 15 = 0$

59. $t^2 + 20t = 25$ **60.** $n(n - 18) = 9$

61. $5x^2 - 2x - 1 = 0$ **62.** $-x^2 + 11x - 18 = 0$

63. Find the discriminant of each of the following quadratic equations, and determine whether the equation has (1) two complex but nonreal solutions, (2) two equal real solutions, or (3) two unequal real solutions. (Objective 5)
(a) $4x^2 + 20x + 25 = 0$
(b) $x^2 + 4x + 7 = 0$
(c) $x^2 - 18x + 81 = 0$
(d) $36x^2 - 31x + 3 = 0$
(e) $2x^2 + 5x + 7 = 0$
(f) $16x^2 = 40x - 25$
(g) $6x^2 - 4x - 7 = 0$
(h) $5x^2 - 2x - 4 = 0$

For Problems 64–79, set up a quadratic equation and solve each problem. (Objective 6)

64. Find two consecutive positive even integers whose product is 528.

65. Find two consecutive whole numbers such that the sum of their squares is 265.

66. For a remodeling job, an architect suggested increasing the sides of a square patio by 3 feet per side. This made the area of the new patio 49 square feet. What was the area of the original patio?

67. A sailboat has a triangular sail with an area of 30 square feet. The height of the sail is 7 feet more than the length of the base of the sail. Find the height of the sail.

68. One leg of a right triangle is 4 inches longer than the other leg. If the length of the hypotenuse is 20 inches, find the length of each leg.

69. The sum of the lengths of the two legs of a right triangle is 34 meters. If the length of the hypotenuse is 26 meters, find the length of each leg.

70. The lengths of the three sides of a right triangle are consecutive even integers. Find the length of each side.

71. The perimeter of a rectangle is 44 inches and its area is 112 square inches. Find the length and width of the rectangle.

72. A page of a magazine contains 70 square inches of type. The height of the page is twice the width. If the margin around the type is 2 inches uniformly, what are the dimensions of the page?

73. The length of a rectangle is 4 meters more than twice its width. If the area of the rectangle is 126 square meters, find its length and width.

74. The length of one side of a triangle is 3 centimeters less than twice the length of the altitude to that side. If the area of the triangle is 52 square centimeters, find the length of the side and the length of the altitude to that side.

75. A rectangular plot of ground measuring 12 meters by 20 meters is surrounded by a sidewalk of uniform width. The area of the sidewalk is 68 square meters. Find the width of the sidewalk.

76. A piece of wire 60 inches long is cut into two pieces and then each piece is bent into the shape of a square. If the sum of the areas of the two squares is 117 square inches, find the length of each piece of wire.

77. A rectangular piece of cardboard is 4 inches longer than it is wide. From each of its corners, a square piece 2 inches on a side is cut out. The flaps are then turned up to form an open box, which has a volume of 42 cubic inches. Find the length and width of the original piece of cardboard. See Figure 1.10.

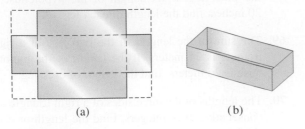

(a)   (b)

Figure 1.10

78. The area of a rectangular region is 52 square feet. If the length of the rectangle is increased by 4 feet and the width by 2 feet, then the area is increased by 50 square feet. Find the length and width of the original rectangular region.

79. The area of a circular region is numerically equal to four times the circumference of the circle. Find the length of a radius of the circle.

Thoughts Into Words

80. Explain how you would solve $(x - 3)(x + 4) = 0$ and also how you would solve $(x - 3)(x + 4) = 8$.

81. Explain the process of completing the square to solve a quadratic equation.

82. Explain how to use the quadratic formula to solve $3x = x^2 - 2$.

83. Your friend states that the equation $-2x^2 + 4x - 1 = 0$ must be changed to $2x^2 - 4x + 1 = 0$ (by multiplying both sides by -1) before the quadratic formula can be applied. Is she right about this, and if not, how would you convince her?

Further Investigations

84. Solve each of the following equations for x.

(a) $x^2 - 7kx = 0$ (b) $x^2 = 25kx$

(c) $x^2 - 3kx - 10k^2 = 0$ (d) $6x^2 + kx - 2k^2 = 0$

(e) $9x^2 - 6kx + k^2 = 0$ (f) $k^2x^2 - kx - 6 = 0$

(g) $x^2 + \sqrt{2}x - 3 = 0$ (h) $x^2 - \sqrt{3}x + 5 = 0$

85. Solve each of the following for the indicated variable. (Assume that all letters represent positive numbers.)

(a) $A = \pi r^2$ for r

(b) $E = c^2m - c^2m_0$ for c

(c) $s = \dfrac{1}{2}gt^2$ for t (d) $\dfrac{x^2}{a^2} + \dfrac{y^2}{b^2} = 1$ for x

(e) $\dfrac{x^2}{a^2} - \dfrac{y^2}{b^2} = 1$ for y (f) $s = \dfrac{1}{2}gt^2 + V_0t$ for t

For Problems 86–88, use the discriminant to help solve each problem.

86. Determine k so that the solutions of $x^2 - 2x + k = 0$ are complex but nonreal.

87. Determine k so that $4x^2 - kx + 1 = 0$ has two equal real solutions.

88. Determine k so that $3x^2 - kx - 2 = 0$ has real solutions.

Graphing Calculator Activities

89. The solution set for $x^2 - 4x - 37 = 0$ is $\{2 \pm \sqrt{41}\}$. With a calculator, we found a rational approximation, to the nearest one-thousandth, for each of these solutions.

$2 - \sqrt{41} = -4.403$

$2 + \sqrt{41} = 8.403$

Thus the solution set is $\{-4.403, 8.403\}$, with answers rounded to the nearest one-thousandth.
    Solve each of the following equations and express the solutions to the nearest one-thousandth.

(a) $x^2 - 6x - 10 = 0$ **(b)** $x^2 - 16x - 24 = 0$

(c) $x^2 + 6x - 44 = 0$ **(d)** $x^2 + 10x - 46 = 0$

(e) $x^2 + 8x + 2 = 0$ **(f)** $x^2 + 9x + 3 = 0$

(g) $4x^2 - 6x + 1 = 0$ **(h)** $5x^2 - 9x + 1 = 0$

(i) $2x^2 - 11x - 5 = 0$ **(j)** $3x^2 - 12x - 10 = 0$

90. Graph the appropriate equations to give visual support for your solutions for Problems 45–60.

91. For each of the following, first graph the appropriate equation and use your graph to predict approximate solutions for the given equation. Then solve the equation to see how well you predicted.

(a) $4x^2 - 12x + 9 = 0$

(b) $2x^2 - x + 2 = 0$

(c) $-3x^2 + 2x - 4 = 0$

(d) $2x^2 - 23x - 12 = 0$

(e) $x^2 + 2\sqrt{5}x + 5 = 0$

(f) $-x^2 + 2\sqrt{3}x - 3 = 0$

Answers to the Concept Quiz
1. True   **2.** True   **3.** False   **4.** True   **5.** True   **6.** False   **7.** False   **8.** True

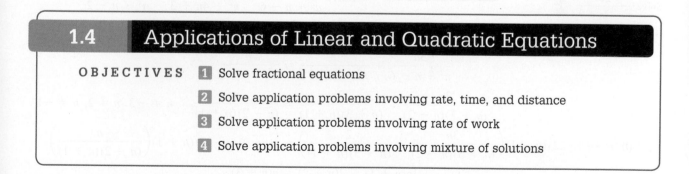

| 1.4 | Applications of Linear and Quadratic Equations |

OBJECTIVES

1 Solve fractional equations

2 Solve application problems involving rate, time, and distance

3 Solve application problems involving rate of work

4 Solve application problems involving mixture of solutions

Let's begin this section by considering three fractional equations, one that is equivalent to a linear equation and two that are equivalent to quadratic equations.

EXAMPLE 1

Solve $\dfrac{3}{2x-8} - \dfrac{x-5}{x^2-2x-8} = \dfrac{7}{x+2}$.

Solution

$$\frac{3}{2x-8} - \frac{x-5}{x^2-2x-8} = \frac{7}{x+2}$$

$$\frac{3}{2(x-4)} - \frac{x-5}{(x-4)(x+2)} = \frac{7}{x+2}, \quad x \neq 4,\ x \neq -2$$

$$2(x-4)(x+2)\left(\frac{3}{2(x-4)} - \frac{x-5}{(x-4)(x+2)}\right) = 2(x-4)(x+2)\left(\frac{7}{x+2}\right)$$

$$3(x+2) - 2(x-5) = 14(x-4)$$

$$3x + 6 - 2x + 10 = 14x - 56$$

$$x + 16 = 14x - 56$$

$$72 = 13x$$

$$\frac{72}{13} = x$$

The solution set is $\left\{\dfrac{72}{13}\right\}$.

In Example 1, notice that we did not indicate the restrictions until the denominators were expressed in factored form. It is usually easier to determine the necessary restrictions at that step.

EXAMPLE 2

Solve $\dfrac{3n}{n^2+n-6} + \dfrac{2}{n^2+4n+3} = \dfrac{n}{n^2-n-2}$.

Solution

$$\frac{3n}{n^2+n-6} + \frac{2}{n^2+4n+3} = \frac{n}{n^2-n-2}$$

$$\frac{3n}{(n+3)(n-2)} + \frac{2}{(n+3)(n+1)} = \frac{n}{(n-2)(n+1)}, \quad n \neq -3,\ n \neq 2,\ n \neq -1$$

$$(n+3)(n-2)(n+1)\left(\frac{3n}{(n+3)(n-2)} + \frac{2}{(n+3)(n+1)}\right) = (n+3)(n-2)(n+1)\left(\frac{n}{(n-2)(n+1)}\right)$$

$$3n(n+1) + 2(n-2) = n(n+3)$$

$$3n^2 + 3n + 2n - 4 = n^2 + 3n$$

$$3n^2 + 5n - 4 = n^2 + 3n$$

$$2n^2 + 2n - 4 = 0$$

$$n^2 + n - 2 = 0$$
$$(n + 2)(n - 1) = 0$$
$$n + 2 = 0 \quad \text{or} \quad n - 1 = 0$$
$$n = -2 \quad \text{or} \quad n = 1$$

The solution set is $\{-2, 1\}$.

Classroom Example
Solve $\dfrac{m}{m + 2} -$
$\dfrac{3}{m + 5} = \dfrac{9}{m^2 + 7m + 10}$.

EXAMPLE 3 Solve $\dfrac{x}{x + 1} - \dfrac{2}{x + 3} = \dfrac{4}{x^2 + 4x + 3}$

Solution

$$\frac{x}{x + 1} - \frac{2}{x + 3} = \frac{4}{x^2 + 4x + 3}$$

$$\frac{x}{x + 1} - \frac{2}{x + 3} = \frac{4}{(x + 1)(x + 3)}, \qquad x \neq -1, x \neq -3$$

$$(x + 1)(x + 3)\left(\frac{x}{x + 1} - \frac{2}{x + 3}\right) = \left(\frac{4}{(x + 1)(x + 3)}\right)(x + 1)(x + 3)$$

$$x(x + 3) - 2(x + 1) = 4$$

$$x^2 + 3x - 2x - 2 = 4$$

$$x^2 + x - 6 = 0$$

$$(x + 3)(x - 2) = 0$$

$$x + 3 = 0 \quad \text{or} \quad x - 2 = 0$$

$$x = -3 \quad \text{or} \quad x = 2$$

Because -3 produces a denominator of zero in the original equation, it must be discarded. Thus the solution set is $\{2\}$.

Example 3 reinforces the importance of recognizing the restrictions that must be made to exclude division by zero. Even though the original equation was transformed into a quadratic equation with two roots, one of them had to be discarded because of the restrictions.

More on Problem Solving

Before tackling a variety of applications of linear and quadratic equations, let's restate some suggestions made earlier in this chapter for solving word problems.

Suggestions for Solving Word Problems

1. Read the problem carefully, making certain that you understand the meanings of all the words. Be especially alert for any technical terms used in the statement of the problem.

2. Read the problem a second time (perhaps even a third time) to get an overview of the situation being described and to determine the known facts as well as what is to be found.

3. Sketch any figure, diagram, or chart that might be helpful in analyzing the problem.

4. Choose a meaningful variable to represent an unknown quantity in the problem (for example, l for the length of a rectangle), and represent any other unknowns in terms of that variable.

5. Look for a *guideline* that can be used in setting up an equation. A guideline might be a formula, such as $A = lw$, or a relationship, such as *the fractional part of the job done by Bill plus the fractional part of the job done by Mary equals the total job.*

6. Form an equation containing the variable to translate the conditions of the guideline from English to algebra.

7. Solve the equation and use the solution to determine all the facts requested in the problem.

8. Check all answers against the *original statement of the problem.*

Suggestion 5 is a key part of the analysis of a problem. A formula to be used as a guideline may or may not be explicitly stated in the problem. Likewise, a relationship to be used as a guideline may not be actually stated in the problem but must be determined from what is stated. Let's consider some examples.

Classroom Example
An orchard contains 60 trees planted in rows. The number of trees per row is eight less than three times the number of rows. Find the number of rows and the number of trees per row.

EXAMPLE 4

A theater contains 120 chairs. The number of chairs per row is one less than twice the number of rows. Find the number of rows and the number of chairs per row.

Solution

Let r represent the number of rows. Then $2r - 1$ represents the number of chairs per row. The statement of the problem implies a formation of chairs such that the total number of chairs is equal to the number of rows times the number of chairs per row. This gives us an equation:

Number of rows × Number of chairs per row = Total number of chairs

$$r \times (2r - 1) = 120$$

We solve this equation by the factorization method:

$$2r^2 - r = 120$$
$$2r^2 - r - 120 = 0$$
$$(2r + 15)(r - 8) = 0$$

$$2r + 15 = 0 \quad \text{or} \quad r - 8 = 0$$
$$2r = -15 \quad \text{or} \quad r = 8$$
$$r = -\frac{15}{2} \quad \text{or} \quad r = 8$$

The solution $-\dfrac{15}{2}$ must be disregarded, so there are 8 rows and $2(8) - 1 = 15$ chairs per row.

The basic relationship *distance equals rate times time* is used to help solve a variety of *uniform-motion problems*. This relationship may be expressed by any one of the following equations.

$$d = rt \quad r = \frac{d}{t} \quad t = \frac{d}{r}$$

EXAMPLE 5

Domenica and Javier start from the same location at the same time and ride their bicycles in opposite directions for 4 hours, at which time they are 140 miles apart. If Domenica rides 3 miles per hour faster than Javier, find the rate of each rider.

Solution

Let r represent Javier's rate; then $r + 3$ represents Domenica's rate. A sketch such as Figure 1.11 may help in our analysis. The fact that the total distance is 140 miles can be used as a guideline. We use the $d = rt$ equation.

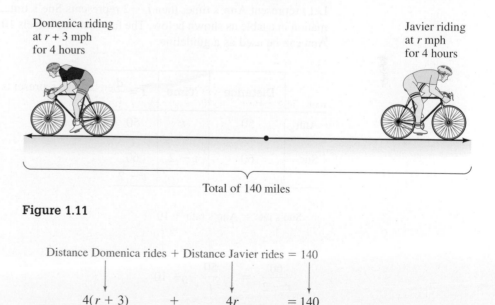

Domenica riding at $r + 3$ mph for 4 hours

Javier riding at r mph for 4 hours

Total of 140 miles

Figure 1.11

Distance Domenica rides + Distance Javier rides = 140

$$4(r + 3) \quad + \quad 4r \quad = 140$$

Solving this equation yields Javier's speed.

$$4r + 12 + 4r = 140$$
$$8r = 128$$
$$r = 16$$

Thus Javier rides at 16 miles per hour and Domenica at $16 + 3 = 19$ miles per hour. ■

Remark: An important part of problem solving is the ability to sketch a meaningful figure that can be used to record the given information and help in the analysis of the problem. Our sketches were done by professional artists for aesthetic purposes. Your sketches can be drawn very roughly as long as they depict the situation in a way that helps you analyze the problem.

Note that in the solution of Example 5 we used a figure and a simple arrow diagram to record and organize the information pertinent to the problem. Some people find it helpful to use a chart for that purpose. We shall use a chart in Example 6 and show alternative solutions. Keep in mind that we are not trying to dictate a particular approach; you decide what works best for you.

Classroom Example
Riding on a motorcycle, Zach takes 3 hours less time to travel 120 miles than Josh takes to travel 270 miles on a motorcycle. Zach travels 6 miles per hour faster than Josh. Find the time and rates of both boys.

EXAMPLE 6

Riding on a moped, Sue takes 2 hours less time to travel 60 miles than Ann takes to travel 50 miles on a bicycle. Sue travels 10 miles per hour faster than Ann. Find the times and rates of both girls.

Solution A

Let t represent Ann's time; then $t - 2$ represents Sue's time. We can record the information in a table as shown below. The fact that Sue travels 10 miles per hour faster than Ann can be used as a guideline.

	Distance	Time	$r = \dfrac{d}{t}$
Ann	50	t	$\dfrac{50}{t}$
Sue	60	$t - 2$	$\dfrac{60}{t - 2}$

Sue's rate = Ann's rate + 10

$$\frac{60}{t - 2} = \frac{50}{t} + 10$$

Solving this equation yields Ann's time.

$$t(t-2)\left(\frac{60}{t-2}\right) = t(t-2)\left(\frac{50}{t}+10\right), \quad t \neq 0, t \neq 2$$

$$60t = 50(t-2) + 10t(t-2)$$

$$60t = 50t - 100 + 10t^2 - 20t$$

$$0 = 10t^2 - 30t - 100$$

$$0 = t^2 - 3t - 10$$

$$0 = (t-5)(t+2)$$

$$t - 5 = 0 \quad \text{or} \quad t + 2 = 0$$

$$t = 5 \quad \text{or} \quad t = -2$$

The solution -2 must be disregarded because we're solving for time. Therefore Ann rides for 5 hours at $\frac{50}{5} = 10$ miles per hour, and Sue rides for $5 - 2 = 3$ hours at $\frac{60}{3} = 20$ miles per hour.

Solution B

Let r represent Ann's rate; then $r + 10$ represents Sue's rate. Again, let's record the information in a table.

	Distance	Rate	$t = \dfrac{d}{r}$
Ann	50	r	$\dfrac{50}{r}$
Sue	60	$r+10$	$\dfrac{60}{r+10}$

This time, let's use as a guideline the fact that Sue's time is 2 hours less than Ann's time.

Sue's time = Ann's time − 2

$$\frac{60}{r+10} = \frac{50}{r} - 2$$

Solving this equation yields Ann's rate.

$$r(r+10)\left(\frac{60}{r+10}\right) = r(r+10)\left(\frac{50}{r}-2\right), \quad r \neq -10, r \neq 0$$

$$60r = (r+10)(50) - 2r(r+10)$$

$$60r = 50r + 500 - 2r^2 - 20r$$

$$2r^2 + 30r - 500 = 0$$

$$r^2 + 15r - 250 = 0$$
$$(r + 25)(r - 10) = 0$$
$$r + 25 = 0 \quad \text{or} \quad r - 10 = 0$$
$$r = -25 \quad \text{or} \quad r = 10$$

The solution -25 must be disregarded because we are solving for a rate. Therefore Ann rides at 10 miles per hour for $\dfrac{50}{10} = 5$ hours, and Sue rides at $10 + 10 = 20$ miles per hour for $\dfrac{60}{20} = 3$ hours.   ◼

Take a good look at both Solution A and Solution B for Example 6. Both are reasonable approaches, but note that the approach in Solution A generates a quadratic equation that is a little easier to solve than the one generated in Solution B. We might have expected this to happen because the *times* in a motion problem are frequently smaller numbers than the *rates*. Thus thinking first before pushing the pencil can make things a bit easier.

Now let's consider a problem that is often referred to as a *mixture problem*. There is no basic formula that applies to all of these problems, but we suggest that you think in terms of a pure substance, which is often helpful in setting up a guideline. Also keep in mind that the phrase "a 40% solution of some substance" means that the solution contains 40% of that particular substance and 60% of something else mixed with it. For example, a 40% salt solution contains 40% salt, and the other 60% is something else, probably water. Now let's illustrate what we mean by the suggestion *think in terms of a pure substance*.

Classroom Example
How many milliliters of pure acid must be added to 30 milliliters of a 30% solution to obtain a 60% acid solution?

EXAMPLE 7

How many milliliters of pure acid must be added to 50 milliliters of a 40% acid solution to obtain a 50% acid solution?

Solution

Let a represent the number of milliliters of pure acid to be added. Thinking in terms of pure acid, we know that *the amount of pure acid to start with, plus the amount of pure acid added, equals the amount of pure acid in the final solution*. Let's use that as a guideline and set up an equation.

Pure acid to start with + Pure acid added = Pure acid in final solution

$$40\%(50) \quad + \quad a \quad = \quad 50\%(50 + a)$$

Solving this equation, we obtain the amount of acid we must add.

$$0.4(50) + a = 0.5(50 + a)$$
$$4(50) + 10a = 5(50 + a)$$
$$200 + 10a = 250 + 5a$$
$$5a = 50$$
$$a = 10$$

We need to add 10 milliliters of pure acid.   ◼

There is another class of problems commonly referred to as *work problems*, or sometimes as *rate-time problems*. For example, if a certain machine produces 120 items in 10 minutes, then we say that it is working at a rate of $\frac{120}{10} = 12$ items per minute. Likewise, a person who can do a certain job in 5 hours is working at a rate of $\frac{1}{5}$ of the job per hour. In general, if Q is the quantity of something done in t units of time, then the rate, r, is given by $r = Q/t$. The rate is stated in terms of *so much quantity per unit of time*. The uniform-motion problems discussed earlier are a special kind of rate-time problem in which the quantity is distance. Using tables to organize information (as we illustrated with the motion problems) is a convenient aid for rate-time problems in general. Let's consider some problems.

Classroom Example
It takes Jacob three times as long to paint a room as it does Sanjay. How long does it take each person by himself if they can paint the room together in 30 minutes?

EXAMPLE 8

It takes Amy twice as long to deliver newspapers as it does Nancy. How long does it take each girl by herself if they can deliver the papers together in 40 minutes?

Solution

Let m represent the number of minutes that it takes Nancy by herself. Then $2m$ represents Amy's time by herself. Thus the information can be organized as shown below. (Note that the *quantity* is 1; there is one job to be done.)

	Quantity	Time	Rate
Nancy	1	m	$\frac{1}{m}$
Amy	1	$2m$	$\frac{1}{2m}$

Because their combined rate is $\frac{1}{40}$, we can solve the following equation:

$$\frac{1}{m} + \frac{1}{2m} = \frac{1}{40}, \quad m \neq 0$$

$$40m\left(\frac{1}{m} + \frac{1}{2m}\right) = 40m\left(\frac{1}{40}\right)$$

$$40 + 20 = m$$

$$60 = m$$

Therefore, Nancy can deliver the papers by herself in 60 minutes, and Amy can deliver them by herself in $2(60) = 120$ minutes.

The next problem illustrates another approach that some people find works well for rate-time problems. The basic idea used in this approach involves representing the fractional parts of a job. For example, if a man can do a certain job in 7 hours, then at the end of 3 hours he has finished $\frac{3}{7}$ of the job. (Again, a constant rate of work is assumed.) At the end of 5 hours he has finished $\frac{5}{7}$ of the job, and, in general, at the end of h hours he has finished $\frac{h}{7}$ of the job.

EXAMPLE 9

Carlos can mow a lawn in 45 minutes, and Felipe can mow the same lawn in 30 minutes. How long would it take the two of them working together to mow the lawn?

Solution

(Before you read any further, *estimate* an answer for this problem. Remember that Felipe can mow the lawn by himself in 30 minutes.) Let m represent the number of minutes that it takes them working together. Then we can set up the following equation.

$$\underset{\begin{array}{c}\text{Fractional part}\\\text{of the lawn that}\\\text{Carlos will mow}\end{array}}{\dfrac{m}{45}} + \underset{\begin{array}{c}\text{Fractional part}\\\text{of the lawn that}\\\text{Felipe will mow}\end{array}}{\dfrac{m}{30}} = \underset{\begin{array}{c}\text{The whole}\\\text{lawn}\end{array}}{1}$$

Solving this equation yields the time that it will take when they work together.

$$90\left(\frac{m}{45} + \frac{m}{30}\right) = 90(1)$$

$$2m + 3m = 90$$

$$5m = 90$$

$$m = 18$$

It should take them 18 minutes to mow the lawn when they work together. ◼

EXAMPLE 10

Walt can mow a lawn in 50 minutes, and his son Mike can mow the same lawn in 40 minutes. One day Mike started to mow the lawn by himself and worked for 10 minutes. Then Walt joined him with another mower and they finished the lawn. How long did it take them to finish mowing the lawn after Walt started to help?

Solution

Let m represent the number of minutes that it takes for them to finish the mowing after Walt starts to help. Because Mike has been mowing for 10 minutes, he has done $\frac{10}{40}$, or $\frac{1}{4}$, of the lawn when Walt starts. Thus there is $\frac{3}{4}$ of the lawn yet to mow. The following guideline can be used to set up an equation:

Fractional part of the remaining 3/4 of the lawn that Mike will mow in m minutes $+$ Fractional part of the remaining 3/4 of the lawn that Walt will mow in m minutes $= \dfrac{3}{4}$

$$\frac{m}{40} + \frac{m}{50} = \frac{3}{4}$$

Solving this equation yields the time they mow the lawn together.

$$200\left(\frac{m}{40} + \frac{m}{50}\right) = 200\left(\frac{3}{4}\right)$$

$$5m + 4m = 150$$

$$9m = 150$$

$$m = \frac{150}{9} = \frac{50}{3}$$

They should finish mowing the lawn in $16\frac{2}{3}$ minutes.

Classroom Example
Joanne is being paid $792 to provide nutrition counseling. It took her 8 hours more than she expected, so she earned $4 per hour less than she originally calculated. How long had she anticipated it would take to do the counseling?

EXAMPLE 11

John is being paid $864 to do a landscape job. It took him 6 hours less than he expected, so he earned $2 per hour more than he originally calculated. How long had he anticipated it would take to do the landscaping?

Solution

Let x represent the number of hours he anticipated the landscaping would take. Then the hourly rate of pay he expected was $\dfrac{864}{x}$. Because he worked 6 hours less than expected, his actual rate of pay was $\dfrac{864}{x-6}$. Now we can form an equation knowing that his actual rate of pay was $2 more than his expected rate of pay.

$$\frac{864}{x} + 2 = \frac{864}{x-6}$$

Solving this equation gives the number of hours he anticipated for the landscaping.

$$x(x-6)\left(\frac{864}{x} + 2\right) = x(x-6)\left(\frac{864}{x-6}\right)$$

$$864(x-6) + 2x(x-6) = 864x$$

$$864x - 5184 + 2x^2 - 12x = 864x$$

$$2x^2 + 852x - 5184 = 864x$$

$$2x^2 - 12x - 5184 = 0$$

$$2(x^2 - 6x - 2592) = 0$$

$$2(x-54)(x+48) = 0$$

$$x = 54 \quad \text{or} \quad x = -48$$

The solution -48 must be disregarded because we are solving for the number of hours. Therefore John anticipated the landscaping would take 54 hours. ∎

As you tackle word problems throughout this text, keep in mind that our primary objective is to expand your repertoire of problem-solving techniques. We have chosen problems that provide you with the opportunity to use a variety of approaches to solving problems. Don't fall into the trap of thinking, "I will never be faced with this kind of problem." That is not the issue; the development of problem-solving techniques is the goal. In the examples we are sharing some of our ideas for solving problems, but don't hesitate to use your own ingenuity. Furthermore, don't become discouraged—all of us have difficulty with some problems. Give each your best shot!

Concept Quiz 1.4

For Problems 1–5, answer true or false.

1. The only restrictions for the equation $\dfrac{5}{x-3} + \dfrac{7}{2x-1} = \dfrac{x}{x^2-3x}$ are that x can not equal $\dfrac{1}{2}$ or 3.

2. In general, if x is the quantity of something done in y units of time, then the rate is given by $r = \dfrac{x}{y}$.

3. Five hundred milliliters of a 30% alcohol solution would contain 150 milliliters of pure alcohol.

4. Kay works at a rate of solving 18 math problems in an hour. She has worked for one hour. She will need to work another three hours to solve 54 problems.

5. Lawton travels 359 miles on 11.5 gallons of gasoline. The proportion $\dfrac{11.5}{359} = \dfrac{x}{35}$ when solved for x would determine how many miles Lawton can travel on 35 gallons of gasoline.

6. John can mow a lawn in 30 minutes, and Marcos can mow the same lawn in 20 minutes. Would a time of 40 minutes for mowing the lawn together be reasonable?

Problem Set 1.4

For Problems 1–20, solve each equation. (Objective 1)

1. $\dfrac{x}{2x-8} + \dfrac{16}{x^2-16} = \dfrac{1}{2}$

2. $\dfrac{3}{n-5} - \dfrac{2}{2n+1} = \dfrac{n+3}{2n^2-9n-5}$

3. $\dfrac{5t}{2t+6} - \dfrac{4}{t^2-9} = \dfrac{5}{2}$

4. $\dfrac{x}{4x-4} + \dfrac{5}{x^2-1} = \dfrac{1}{4}$

5. $2 + \dfrac{4}{n-2} = \dfrac{8}{n^2-2n}$

6. $3 + \dfrac{6}{t - 3} = \dfrac{6}{t^2 - 3t}$

7. $\dfrac{a}{a + 2} + \dfrac{3}{a + 4} = \dfrac{14}{a^2 + 6a + 8}$

8. $\dfrac{3}{x + 1} + \dfrac{2}{x + 3} = 2$

9. $\dfrac{-2}{3x + 2} + \dfrac{x - 1}{9x^2 - 4} = \dfrac{3}{12x - 8}$

10. $\dfrac{-1}{2x - 5} + \dfrac{2x - 4}{4x^2 - 25} = \dfrac{5}{6x + 15}$

11. $\dfrac{n}{2n - 3} + \dfrac{1}{n - 3} = \dfrac{n^2 - n - 3}{2n^2 - 9n + 9}$

12. $\dfrac{3y}{y^2 + y - 6} + \dfrac{2}{y^2 + 4y + 3} = \dfrac{y}{y^2 - y - 2}$

13. $\dfrac{3y + 1}{3y^2 - 4y - 4} + \dfrac{9}{9y^2 - 4} = \dfrac{2y - 2}{3y^2 - 8y + 4}$

14. $\dfrac{4n + 10}{2n^2 - n - 6} - \dfrac{3n + 1}{2n^2 - 5n + 2} = \dfrac{2}{4n^2 + 4n - 3}$

15. $\dfrac{x + 1}{2x^2 + 7x - 4} - \dfrac{x}{2x^2 - 7x + 3} = \dfrac{1}{x^2 + x - 12}$

16. $\dfrac{3}{x - 2} + \dfrac{5}{x + 3} = \dfrac{8x - 1}{x^2 + x - 6}$

17. $\dfrac{7x + 2}{12x^2 + 11x - 15} - \dfrac{1}{3x + 5} = \dfrac{2}{4x - 3}$

18. $\dfrac{2n}{6n^2 + 7n - 3} - \dfrac{n - 3}{3n^2 + 11n - 4} = \dfrac{5}{2n^2 + 11n + 12}$

19. $\dfrac{x}{x + 2} - \dfrac{3}{x + 4} = \dfrac{6}{x^2 + 6x + 8}$

20. $\dfrac{x}{x - 1} + \dfrac{3}{x - 2} = \dfrac{-1}{x^2 - 3x + 2}$

For Problems 21–45, solve each problem. (Objectives 2, 3, and 4)

21. An apple orchard contains 126 trees. The number of trees in each row is 4 less than twice the number of rows. Find the number of rows and the number of trees per row.

22. The sum of a number and its reciprocal is $\dfrac{10}{3}$. Find the number.

23. Jill starts at city A and travels toward city B at 50 miles per hour. At the same time, Russ starts at city B and travels on the same highway toward city A at 52 miles per hour. How long will it take before they meet if the two cities are 459 miles apart?

24. Two cars, which are 510 miles apart and whose speeds differ by 6 miles per hour, are moving toward each other. If they meet in 5 hours, find the speed of each car.

25. Rita rode her bicycle out into the country at a speed of 20 miles per hour and returned along the same route at 15 miles per hour. If the round trip took 5 hours and 50 minutes, how far out did she ride?

26. A jogger who can run an 8-minute mile starts a half-mile ahead of a jogger who can run a 6-minute mile. How long will it take the faster jogger to catch the slower jogger?

27. It takes a freight train 2 hours more to travel 300 miles than it takes an express train to travel 280 miles. The rate of the express train is 20 miles per hour faster than the rate of the freight train. Find the rates of both trains.

28. An airplane travels 2050 miles in the same time that a car travels 260 miles. If the rate of the plane is 358 miles per hour faster than the rate of the car, find the rate of the plane.

29. A container has 6 liters of a 40% alcohol solution in it. How much pure alcohol should be added to raise it to a 60% solution?

30. How many liters of a 60% acid solution must be added to 14 liters of a 10% acid solution to produce a 25% acid solution?

31. One solution contains 50% alcohol and another solution contains 80% alcohol. How many liters of each solution should be mixed to produce 10.5 liters of a 70% alcohol solution?

32. A contractor has a 24-pound mixture that is one-fourth cement and three-fourths sand. How much of a mixture that is half cement and half sand needs to be added to produce a mixture that is one-third cement?

33. A 10-quart radiator contains a 40% antifreeze solution. How much of the solution needs to be drained out and replaced with pure antifreeze in order to raise the solution to 70% antifreeze?

34. How much water must be evaporated from 20 gallons of a 10% salt solution in order to obtain a 20% salt solution?

35. One pipe can fill a tank in 4 hours, and another pipe can fill the tank in 6 hours. How long will it take to fill the tank if both pipes are used?

36. Lolita and Doug working together can paint a shed in 3 hours and 20 minutes. If Doug can paint the shed by himself in 10 hours, how long would it take Lolita to paint the shed by herself?

37. An inlet pipe can fill a tank in 10 minutes. A drain can empty the tank in 12 minutes. If the tank is empty and both the pipe and drain are open, how long will it be before the tank overflows?

38. Pat and Mike working together can assemble a bookcase in 6 minutes. It takes Mike, working by himself, 9 minutes longer than it takes Pat working by himself to assemble the bookcase. How long does it take each, working alone, to do the job?

39. Mark can overhaul an engine in 20 hours, and Phil can do the same job by himself in 30 hours. If they both work together for a time and then Mark finishes the job by himself in 5 hours, how long did they work together?

40. A printing company purchased a new copier that is twice as fast as the old copier. With both copiers working at the same time, it takes 5 hours to do a job. How long would it take the new copier working alone?

41. A professor can grade three tests in the time it takes a student assistant to grade one test. Working together, they can grade the tests for a class in 2 hours. How long would it take the student assistant working alone?

42. A car that averages 16 miles per gallon of gasoline for city driving and 22 miles per gallon for highway driving uses 14 gallons in 296 miles of driving. How much of the driving was city driving?

43. Angie bought some candy bars for $14. If each candy bar had cost $0.25 less, she could have purchased one more bar for the same amount of money. How many candy bars did Angie buy?

44. A new labor contract provides for a wage increase of $1 per hour and a reduction of 5 hours in the workweek. A worker who received $320 per week under the old contract will receive $315 per week under the new contract. How long was the workweek under the old contract?

45. Todd contracted to paint a house for $480. It took him 4 hours longer than he had anticipated, so he earned $0.50 per hour less than he originally calculated. How long had he anticipated it would take him to paint the house?

Thoughts Into Words

46. One of our problem-solving suggestions is to *look for a guideline that can be used to help determine an equation.* What does this suggestion mean to you?

47. Write a paragraph or two summarizing the various problem-solving ideas presented in this chapter.

1.5 Miscellaneous Equations

OBJECTIVES

1 Solve polynomial equations by factoring

2 Solve radical equations

3 Solve equations that are quadratic in form

Our previous work with solving linear and quadratic equations provides us with a basis for solving a variety of other types of equations. For example, the technique of factoring and applying the property

$$ab = 0 \quad \text{if and only if } a = 0 \text{ or } b = 0$$

can sometimes be used for solving equations other than quadratic equations.

Classroom Example
Solve $x^3 - 64 = 0$.

EXAMPLE 1   Solve $x^3 - 8 = 0$.

Solution

$$x^3 - 8 = 0$$
$$(x - 2)(x^2 + 2x + 4) = 0$$
$$x - 2 = 0 \quad \text{or} \quad x^2 + 2x + 4 = 0$$
$$x = 2 \quad \text{or} \quad x = \frac{-2 \pm \sqrt{4 - 16}}{2}$$
$$= \frac{-2 \pm \sqrt{-12}}{2}$$
$$= \frac{-2 \pm 2i\sqrt{3}}{2}$$
$$= -1 \pm i\sqrt{3}$$

The solution set is $\{2, -1 \pm i\sqrt{3}\}$.

Classroom Example
Solve $x^3 - 3x^2 - 4x + 12 = 0$.

EXAMPLE 2   Solve $x^3 + 2x^2 - 9x - 18 = 0$.

Solution

$$x^3 + 2x^2 - 9x - 18 = 0$$
$$x^2(x + 2) - 9(x + 2) = 0$$

$$(x + 2)(x^2 - 9) = 0$$
$$(x + 2)(x + 3)(x - 3) = 0$$

$$x + 2 = 0 \quad \text{or} \quad x + 3 = 0 \quad \text{or} \quad x - 3 = 0$$
$$x = -2 \quad \text{or} \quad x = -3 \quad \text{or} \quad x = 3$$

The solution set is $\{-3, -2, 3\}$.

Classroom Example
Solve $2x^5 + 3x^4 = 2x^3 + 3x^2$.

EXAMPLE 3   Solve $3x^5 + 5x^4 = 3x^3 + 5x^2$.

Solution

$$3x^5 + 5x^4 = 3x^3 + 5x^2$$
$$3x^5 + 5x^4 - 3x^3 - 5x^2 = 0$$
$$x^4(3x + 5) - x^2(3x + 5) = 0$$
$$(3x + 5)(x^4 - x^2) = 0$$
$$(3x + 5)(x^2)(x^2 - 1) = 0$$
$$(3x + 5)(x^2)(x + 1)(x - 1) = 0$$

$$3x + 5 = 0 \quad \text{or} \quad x^2 = 0 \quad \text{or} \quad x + 1 = 0 \quad \text{or} \quad x - 1 = 0$$
$$3x = -5$$
$$x = -\frac{5}{3} \quad \text{or} \quad x = 0 \quad \text{or} \quad x = -1 \quad \text{or} \quad x = 1$$

The solution set is $\left\{ -\dfrac{5}{3}, 0, -1, 1 \right\}$.

Be careful with an equation like the one in Example 3. Don't be tempted to divide both sides of the equation by x^2. In so doing, you will lose the solution of zero. *In general, don't divide both sides of an equation by an expression that contains the variable.*

Figure 1.12 shows the graph of $y = 3x^5 + 5x^4 - 3x^3 - 5x^2$. Note that the x intercepts appear to agree with our solution set for Example 3. Again it's good to have a visual confirmation of what we did algebraically.

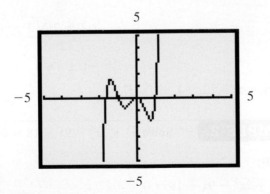

Figure 1.12

Radical Equations

An equation such as

$$\sqrt{2x - 4} = x - 2$$

which contains a radical with the variable in the radicand, is often referred to as a **radical equation.** To solve radical equations, we need the following additional property of equality.

Property 1.3

Let a and b be real numbers and n a positive integer.

If $a = b$, then $a^n = b^n$.

Property 1.3 states that *we can raise both sides of an equation to a positive integral power*. However, we must be very careful when applying Property 1.3. Raising both sides of an equation to a positive integral power sometimes produces results that do not satisfy the original equation. Consider the following examples.

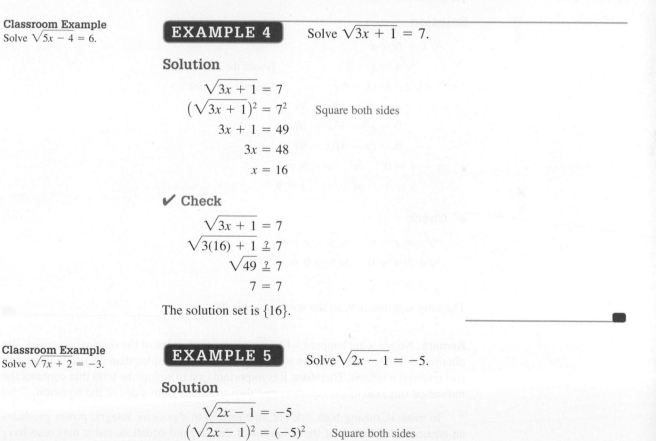

Classroom Example
Solve $\sqrt{5x - 4} = 6$.

EXAMPLE 4   Solve $\sqrt{3x + 1} = 7$.

Solution

$$\sqrt{3x + 1} = 7$$
$$(\sqrt{3x + 1})^2 = 7^2 \qquad \text{Square both sides}$$
$$3x + 1 = 49$$
$$3x = 48$$
$$x = 16$$

✔ **Check**

$$\sqrt{3x + 1} = 7$$
$$\sqrt{3(16) + 1} \overset{?}{=} 7$$
$$\sqrt{49} \overset{?}{=} 7$$
$$7 = 7$$

The solution set is $\{16\}$.

Classroom Example
Solve $\sqrt{7x + 2} = -3$.

EXAMPLE 5   Solve $\sqrt{2x - 1} = -5$.

Solution

$$\sqrt{2x - 1} = -5$$
$$(\sqrt{2x - 1})^2 = (-5)^2 \qquad \text{Square both sides}$$

$$2x - 1 = 25$$
$$2x = 26$$
$$x = 13$$

✔ **Check**

$$\sqrt{2x - 1} = -5$$
$$\sqrt{2(13) - 1} \overset{?}{=} -5$$
$$\sqrt{25} \overset{?}{=} -5$$
$$5 \neq -5$$

Because 13 does not check, the equation has no solutions; the solution set is $\varnothing$. ∎

Remark: It is true that the equation in Example 5 could be solved by inspection because the symbol $\sqrt{}$ refers to nonnegative numbers. However, we did want to demonstrate what happens if Property 1.3 is used.

Classroom Example
Solve $x = 2\sqrt{x} + 3$.

EXAMPLE 6   Solve $\sqrt{x} + 6 = x$.

Solution

$$\sqrt{x} + 6 = x$$
$$\sqrt{x} = x - 6 \qquad \text{Isolate the radical term}$$
$$(\sqrt{x})^2 = (x - 6)^2 \qquad \text{Square both sides}$$
$$x = x^2 - 12x + 36$$
$$0 = x^2 - 13x + 36$$
$$0 = (x - 4)(x - 9)$$
$$x - 4 = 0 \quad \text{or} \quad x - 9 = 0$$
$$x = 4 \quad \text{or} \quad x = 9$$

✔ **Check**

$$\sqrt{x} = x - 6 \qquad \sqrt{x} = x - 6$$
$$\sqrt{4} \overset{?}{=} 4 - 6 \qquad \sqrt{9} \overset{?}{=} 9 - 6$$
$$2 \neq -2 \qquad 3 = 3$$

The only solution is 9, so the solution set is $\{9\}$. ∎

Remark: Notice what happens when we square both sides of the original equation. We obtain $x + 12\sqrt{x} + 36 = x^2$, an equation that is more complex than the original one and still contains a radical. Therefore, it is important first to isolate the term that contains the radical on one side of the equation and then to square both sides of the equation.

In general, raising both sides of an equation to a positive integral power produces an equation that has all of the solutions of the original equation, *but* it may also have some extra solutions that will not satisfy the original equation. Such extra solutions are called **extraneous solutions.** Therefore, when using Property 1.3, you *must* check each potential solution in the original equation.

Classroom Example
Solve $\sqrt[3]{7x + 6} = -2$.

EXAMPLE 7   Solve $\sqrt[3]{2x + 3} = -3$.

Solution

$$\sqrt[3]{2x + 3} = -3$$
$$(\sqrt[3]{2x + 3})^3 = (-3)^3 \qquad \text{Cube both sides}$$
$$2x + 3 = -27$$
$$2x = -30$$
$$x = -15$$

✔ **Check**

$$\sqrt[3]{2x + 3} = -3$$
$$\sqrt[3]{2(-15) + 3} \overset{?}{=} -3$$
$$\sqrt[3]{-27} \overset{?}{=} -3$$
$$-3 = -3$$

The solution set is $\{-15\}$.

Classroom Example
Solve $\sqrt{x + 25} = \sqrt{x - 2} + 3$.

EXAMPLE 8   Solve $\sqrt{x + 4} = \sqrt{x - 1} + 1$.

Solution

$$\sqrt{x + 4} = \sqrt{x - 1} + 1$$
$$(\sqrt{x + 4})^2 = (\sqrt{x - 1} + 1)^2 \qquad \text{Square both sides}$$
$$x + 4 = x - 1 + 2\sqrt{x - 1} + 1 \qquad \begin{array}{l}\text{Remember the middle term when}\\ \text{squaring the binomial}\end{array}$$
$$4 = 2\sqrt{x - 1}$$
$$2 = \sqrt{x - 1}$$
$$2^2 = (\sqrt{x - 1})^2 \qquad \text{Square both sides}$$
$$4 = x - 1$$
$$5 = x$$

✔ **Check**

$$\sqrt{x + 4} = \sqrt{x - 1} + 1$$
$$\sqrt{5 + 4} \overset{?}{=} \sqrt{5 - 1} + 1$$
$$\sqrt{9} \overset{?}{=} \sqrt{4} + 1$$
$$3 = 3$$

The solution set is $\{5\}$.

Equations of Quadratic Form

An equation such as $x^4 + 5x^2 - 36 = 0$ is not a quadratic equation. However, if we let $u = x^2$, then we get $u^2 = x^4$. Substituting u for x^2 and u^2 for x^4 in $x^4 + 5x^2 - 36 = 0$ produces

$$u^2 + 5u - 36 = 0$$

which is a quadratic equation. In general, an equation in the variable x is said to be of **quadratic form** if it can be written in the form

$$au^2 + bu + c = 0$$

where $a \neq 0$ and u is some algebraic expression in x. We have two basic approaches to solving equations of quadratic form, as illustrated by the next two examples.

Classroom Example
Solve $x^{2/3} - 3x^{1/3} - 4 = 0$.

EXAMPLE 9   Solve $x^{2/3} + x^{1/3} - 6 = 0$.

Solution

Let $u = x^{1/3}$; then $u^2 = x^{2/3}$ and the given equation can be rewritten $u^2 + u - 6 = 0$. Solving this equation yields two solutions.

$$u^2 + u - 6 = 0$$
$$(u + 3)(u - 2) = 0$$
$$u + 3 = 0 \quad \text{or} \quad u - 2 = 0$$
$$u = -3 \quad \text{or} \quad u = 2$$

Now, substituting $x^{1/3}$ for u, we have

$$x^{1/3} = -3 \quad \text{or} \quad x^{1/3} = 2$$

from which we obtain

$$(x^{1/3})^3 = (-3)^3 \quad \text{or} \quad (x^{1/3})^3 = 2^3$$
$$x = -27 \quad \text{or} \quad x = 8$$

✔ Check

$$x^{2/3} + x^{1/3} - 6 = 0 \qquad x^{2/3} + x^{1/3} - 6 = 0$$
$$(-27)^{2/3} + (-27)^{1/3} - 6 \stackrel{?}{=} 0 \qquad (8)^{2/3} + (8)^{1/3} - 6 \stackrel{?}{=} 0$$
$$9 + (-3) - 6 \stackrel{?}{=} 0 \qquad 4 + 2 - 6 \stackrel{?}{=} 0$$
$$0 = 0 \qquad 0 = 0$$

The solution set is $\{-27, 8\}$.

Classroom Example
Solve $x^4 - 12x^2 - 64 = 0$.

EXAMPLE 10   Solve $x^4 + 5x^2 - 36 = 0$.

Solution

$$x^4 + 5x^2 - 36 = 0$$
$$(x^2 + 9)(x^2 - 4) = 0$$

$$x^2 + 9 = 0 \qquad \text{or} \qquad x^2 - 4 = 0$$
$$x^2 = -9 \qquad \text{or} \qquad x^2 = 4$$
$$x = \pm 3i \qquad \text{or} \qquad x = \pm 2$$

The solution set is $\{\pm 3i, \ \pm 2\}$.

Notice in Example 9 that we made a substitution (u for $x^{1/3}$) to change the original equation to a quadratic equation in terms of the variable u. Then, after solving for u, we substituted $x^{1/3}$ for u to obtain the solutions of the original equation. However, in Example 10 we factored the given polynomial and proceeded without changing to a quadratic equation. Which approach you use may depend on the complexity of the given equation and your own personal preference.

Classroom Example
Solve $14x^{-2} + 17x^{-1} - 45 = 0$.

EXAMPLE 11   Solve $15x^{-2} - 11x^{-1} - 12 = 0$.

Solution

Let $u = x^{-1}$; then $u^2 = x^{-2}$ and the given equation can be written and solved as follows:

$$15u^2 - 11u - 12 = 0$$
$$(5u + 3)(3u - 4) = 0$$
$$5u + 3 = 0 \qquad \text{or} \qquad 3u - 4 = 0$$
$$5u = -3 \qquad \text{or} \qquad 3u = 4$$
$$u = -\frac{3}{5} \qquad \text{or} \qquad u = \frac{4}{3}$$

Now, substituting x^{-1} back for u, we have

$$x^{-1} = -\frac{3}{5} \qquad \text{or} \qquad x^{-1} = \frac{4}{3}$$

from which we obtain

$$\frac{1}{x} = \frac{-3}{5} \qquad \text{or} \qquad \frac{1}{x} = \frac{4}{3}$$
$$-3x = 5 \qquad \text{or} \qquad 4x = 3$$
$$x = -\frac{5}{3} \qquad \text{or} \qquad x = \frac{3}{4}$$

The solution set is $\left\{-\frac{5}{3}, \frac{3}{4}\right\}$.

Concept Quiz 1.5

For Problems 1–5, answer true or false.

1. To solve the equation $2x^3 - 5x^2 = 4x$, both sides of the equation can be divided by x.

2. The equations $\sqrt{3x + 2} = -4$ and $(\sqrt{3x + 2})^2 = (-4)^2$ are equivalent equations.

3. The equation produced from raising both sides of an equation to a positive integral power may have solutions that the original equation does not have.

4. An equation in the variable x is quadratic in form if the equation can be written in the form $au^2 + bu + c = 0$ where u is an algebraic expression for x and $a \neq 0$.

5. An equation such as $\sqrt{2x - 1} = 9$ is referred to as a rational equation.

Problem Set 1.5

For Problems 1–14, solve each equation. **(Objective 1)**

1. $x^3 + 8 = 0$

2. $x^3 - 27 = 0$

3. $x^3 = 1$

4. $x^4 - 9 = 0$

5. $x^3 + x^2 - 4x - 4 = 0$ **6.** $x^3 - 5x^2 - x + 5 = 0$

7. $2x^3 - 3x^2 + 2x - 3 = 0$

8. $3x^3 + 5x^2 + 12x + 20 = 0$

9. $8x^5 + 10x^4 = 4x^3 + 5x^2$

10. $10x^5 + 15x^4 = 2x^3 + 3x^2$

11. $x^{3/2} = 4x$

12. $5x^4 = 6x^3$

13. $n^{-2} = n^{-3}$

14. $n^{4/3} = 4n$

For Problems 15–42, solve each radical equation. Don't forget that you *must* check potential solutions whenever Property 1.3 is applied. **(Objective 2)**

15. $\sqrt{3x - 2} = 4$

16. $\sqrt{5x - 1} = -4$

17. $\sqrt{3x - 8} - \sqrt{x - 2} = 0$

18. $\sqrt{2x - 3} = 1$

19. $\sqrt{4x - 3} = -2$

20. $\sqrt{3x - 1} + 1 = 4$

21. $\sqrt{2n + 3} - 2 = -1$

22. $\sqrt{5n + 1} - 6 = -4$

23. $\sqrt{4x - 1} - 3 = 2$

24. $\sqrt{2x - 1} - \sqrt{x + 2} = 0$

25. $\sqrt[3]{2x + 3} + 5 = 2$

26. $\sqrt[3]{n^2 - 1} + 4 = 3$

27. $2\sqrt{n} + 3 = n$

28. $\sqrt{3t} - t = -6$

29. $\sqrt{3x - 2} = 3x - 2$

30. $5x - 4 = \sqrt{5x - 4}$

31. $\sqrt{2t - 1} + 2 = t$

32. $p = \sqrt{-4p + 17} + 3$

33. $\sqrt{x + 2} - 1 = \sqrt{x - 3}$

34. $\sqrt{x + 5} - 2 = \sqrt{x - 7}$

35. $\sqrt{7n + 23} - \sqrt{3n + 7} = 2$

36. $\sqrt{5t + 31} - \sqrt{t + 3} = 4$

37. $\sqrt{3x + 1} + \sqrt{2x + 4} = 3$

38. $\sqrt{2x - 1} - \sqrt{x + 3} = 1$

39. $\sqrt{x - 2} - \sqrt{2x - 11} = \sqrt{x - 5}$

40. $\sqrt{-2x - 7} + \sqrt{x + 9} = \sqrt{8 - x}$

41. $\sqrt{1 + 2\sqrt{x}} = \sqrt{x + 1}$

42. $\sqrt{7 + 3\sqrt{x}} = \sqrt{x + 1}$

For Problems 43–66, solve each quadratic-in-form equation. **(Objective 3)**

43. $x^4 - 5x^2 + 4 = 0$

44. $x^4 - 25x^2 + 144 = 0$

45. $2n^4 - 9n^2 + 4 = 0$ **46.** $3n^4 - 4n^2 + 1 = 0$

47. $x^4 - 2x^2 - 35 = 0$ **48.** $2x^4 + 5x^2 - 12 = 0$

49. $x^4 - 4x^2 + 1 = 0$ **50.** $x^4 - 8x^2 + 11 = 0$

51. $x^{2/3} + 3x^{1/3} - 10 = 0$

52. $x^{2/3} + x^{1/3} - 2 = 0$

53. $6x^{2/3} - 5x^{1/3} - 6 = 0$

54. $3x^{2/3} - 11x^{1/3} - 4 = 0$

55. $x^{-2} + 4x^{-1} - 12 = 0$

56. $12t^{-2} - 17t^{-1} - 5 = 0$

57. $x - 11\sqrt{x} + 30 = 0$ **58.** $2x - 11\sqrt{x} + 12 = 0$

59. $x + 3\sqrt{x} - 10 = 0$ **60.** $6x - 19\sqrt{x} - 7 = 0$

61. $4x^{-4} - 17x^{-2} + 4 = 0$

62. $x^3 - 7x^{3/2} - 8 = 0$

63. $x^{-4/3} - 5x^{-2/3} + 4 = 0$

64. $3x^{-2} + 2x^{-1} - 8 = 0$

65. $10x^{-2} + 13x^{-1} - 3 = 0$

66. $7x^{-2} - 26x^{-1} - 8 = 0$

For Problems 67–70, solve each problem.

67. The formula for the slant height of a right circular cone is $s = \sqrt{r^2 + h^2}$, where r is the length of a radius of the base, and h is the altitude of the cone. Find the altitude of a cone whose slant height is 13 inches and whose radius is 5 inches.

68. A clockmaker wants to build a grandfather clock with a pendulum whose period will be 1.5 seconds. He knows the formula for the period is $T = 2\pi\sqrt{\dfrac{L}{32.144}}$, where T represents the period in seconds, and L represents the length of the pendulum in feet. What length should the clockmaker use for the pendulum? Express your answer to the nearest hundredth of a foot.

69. Police sometimes use the formula $S = \sqrt{30Df}$ to correlate the speed of a car and the length of skid marks when the brakes have been applied. In this formula, S represents the speed of the car in miles per hour, D represents the length of skid marks measured in feet, and f represents a coefficient of friction. For a particular situation, the coefficient of friction is a constant that depends on the type and condition of the road surface. Using 0.35 as a coefficient of friction, determine, to the nearest foot, how far a car will skid if the brakes are applied when the car is traveling at a speed of 58 miles per hour.

70. Using the formula given in Problem 69 and a coefficient of friction of 0.95, determine, to the nearest foot, how far a car will skid if the brakes are applied when the car is traveling at a speed of 65 miles per hour.

Thoughts Into Words

71. Explain the concept of extraneous solutions.

72. What does it mean to say that an equation is of quadratic form?

73. Your friend attempts to solve the equation $3 + 2\sqrt{x} = x$ as follows:

$$(3 + 2\sqrt{x})^2 = x^2$$
$$9 + 12\sqrt{x} + 4x = x^2$$

At this step, he stops and doesn't know how to proceed. What help would you give him?

Further Investigations

74. Verify that $x = a$ and $x^2 = a^2$ are *not* equivalent equations.

75. Solve the following equations, and express the solutions to the nearest hundredth.

(a) $x^4 - 3x^2 + 1 = 0$ (b) $x^4 - 5x^2 + 2 = 0$

(c) $2x^4 - 7x^2 + 2 = 0$ (d) $3x^4 - 9x^2 + 1 = 0$

(e) $x^4 - 100x^2 + 2304 = 0$

(f) $4x^4 - 373x^2 + 3969 = 0$

Graphing Calculator Activities

76. Graph the appropriate equations to give visual support for your solutions for Examples 1, 2, 4, and 6–11.

77. Graph the appropriate equations to give visual support for your solutions for the odd-numbered Problems 1–65.

Answers to the Concept Quiz

1. False **2.** False **3.** True **4.** True **5.** False

1.6 Inequalities

OBJECTIVES

1. Solve inequalities
2. Express intervals in interval notation
3. Solve compound inequalities
4. Solve application problems involving inequalities

Just as we use the symbol = to represent "is equal to," we also use the symbols < and > to represent "is less than" and "is greater than," respectively. Thus various **statements of inequality** can be made:

$a < b$ means a is less than b.

$a \leq b$ means a is less than or equal to b.

$a > b$ means a is greater than b.

$a \geq b$ means a is greater than or equal to b.

The following are examples of **numerical statements of inequality:**

$7 + 8 > 10$ $-4 + (-6) \geq -10$

$-4 > -6$ $7 - 9 \leq -2$

$7 - 1 < 20$ $3 + 4 > 12$

$8(-3) < 5(-3)$ $7 - 1 < 0$

Notice that only $3 + 4 > 12$ and $7 - 1 < 0$ are *false;* the other six are *true* numerical statements.

Algebraic inequalities contain one or more variables. The following are examples of algebraic inequalities:

$$x + 4 > 8 \qquad 3x + 2y \leq 4$$
$$(x - 2)(x + 4) \geq 0 \qquad x^2 + y^2 + z^2 \leq 16$$

An algebraic inequality such as $x + 4 > 8$ is neither true nor false as it stands and is called an **open sentence.** For each numerical value substituted for x, the algebraic inequality $x + 4 > 8$ becomes a numerical statement of inequality that is true or false. For example, if $x = -3$, then $x + 4 > 8$ becomes $-3 + 4 > 8$, which is false. If $x = 5$, then $x + 4 > 8$ becomes $5 + 4 > 8$, which is true. **Solving an algebraic inequality** refers to the process of finding the numbers that make it a true numerical statement. Such numbers are called the **solutions** of the inequality and are said to **satisfy** it.

The general process for solving inequalities closely parallels that for solving equations. We repeatedly replace the given inequality with equivalent but simpler inequalities until the solution set is obvious. The following property provides the basis for producing equivalent inequalities.

> **Property 1.4**
>
> **1.** For all real numbers a, b, and c,
>
> $\qquad a > b$ if and only if $a + c > b + c$
>
> **2.** For all real numbers a, b, and c, **with $c > 0$,**
>
> $\qquad a > b$ if and only if $ac > bc$
>
> **3.** For all real numbers a, b, and c, **with $c < 0$,**
>
> $\qquad a > b$ if and only if $ac < bc$

Similar properties exist if $>$ is replaced by $<$, $\leq$, or $\geq$. Part 1 of Property 1.4 is commonly called the **addition property of inequality.** Parts 2 and 3 together make up the **multiplication property of inequality.** Pay special attention to part 3. **If both sides of an inequality are multiplied by a negative number, the inequality symbol must be reversed.** For example, if both sides of $-3 < 5$ are multiplied by -2, the equivalent inequality $6 > -10$ is produced. Now let's consider using the addition and multiplication properties of inequality to help solve some inequalities.

Classroom Example
Solve $4(3x + 2) < 9x + 5$.

EXAMPLE 1   Solve $3(2x - 1) < 8x - 7$.

Solution

$$3(2x - 1) < 8x - 7$$
$$6x - 3 < 8x - 7 \qquad \text{Apply distributive property to left side}$$
$$-2x - 3 < -7 \qquad \text{Add } -8x \text{ to both sides}$$

$$-2x < -4 \qquad \text{Add 3 to both sides}$$

$$-\frac{1}{2}(-2x) > -\frac{1}{2}(-4) \qquad \text{Multiply both sides by } -\frac{1}{2}, \text{ which reverses the inequality}$$

$$x > 2$$

The solution set is $\{x | x > 2\}$.

A graph of the solution set $\{x | x > 2\}$ in Example 1 is shown in Figure 1.13. The parenthesis indicates that 2 does not belong to the solution set.

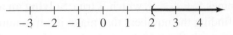

Figure 1.13

Checking the solutions of an inequality presents a problem. Obviously, we cannot check all of the infinitely many solutions for a particular inequality. However, by checking at least one solution, especially when the multiplication property has been used, we might catch a mistake of forgetting to reverse the inequality. In Example 1 we are claiming that all numbers greater than 2 will satisfy the original inequality. Let's check the number 3.

$$3(2x - 1) < 8x - 7$$

$$3[2(3) - 1] \overset{?}{<} 8(3) - 7$$

$$3(5) \overset{?}{<} 17$$

$$15 < 17 \qquad \text{It checks!}$$

We also can get some visual support from a graphical analysis of the inequality. Figure 1.14 shows a graph of the equation $y = 3(2x - 1) - 8x + 7$. To satisfy the inequality $3(2x - 1) - 8x + 7 < 0$, which is equivalent to the given inequality in Example 1, y has to be less than zero. As we see in Figure 1.14, $y < 0$ when $x > 2$. This agrees with our solution set.

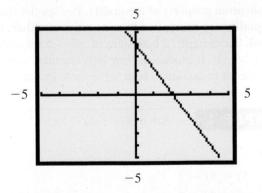

Figure 1.14

Interval Notation

It is also convenient to express solution sets of inequalities by using **interval notation.** For example, the symbol $(2, \infty)$ refers to the interval of all real numbers greater than 2. As on the graph in Figure 1.13, the left-hand parenthesis indicates that 2 is not to be included. The infinity symbol, ∞, along with the right-hand parenthesis, indicates that there is no right-hand endpoint. Following is a partial list of interval notations, along with the sets and graphs that they represent. Note the use of square brackets to *include* endpoints.

Set	Graph	Interval Notation
$\{x \mid x > a\}$		(a, ∞)
$\{x \mid x \geq a\}$		$[a, \infty)$
$\{x \mid x < b\}$		$(-\infty, b)$
$\{x \mid x \leq b\}$		$(-\infty, b]$

Classroom Example
Solve $\dfrac{-7x + 4}{3} > 6$.

EXAMPLE 2   Solve $\dfrac{-3x + 1}{2} > 4$.

Solution

$$\frac{-3x + 1}{2} > 4$$

$$2\left(\frac{-3x + 1}{2}\right) > 2(4) \qquad \text{Multiply both sides by 2}$$

$$-3x + 1 > 8$$

$$-3x > 7$$

$$-\frac{1}{3}(-3x) < -\frac{1}{3}(7) \qquad \text{Multiply both sides by } -\frac{1}{3}, \text{ which reverses the inequality}$$

$$x < -\frac{7}{3}$$

The solution set is $\left(-\infty, -\dfrac{7}{3}\right)$.

Classroom Example
Solve $\dfrac{x + 3}{12} - \dfrac{x - 4}{8} \leq \dfrac{7}{24}$.

EXAMPLE 3   Solve $\dfrac{x - 4}{6} - \dfrac{x - 2}{9} \leq \dfrac{5}{18}$.

Solution

$$\frac{x - 4}{6} - \frac{x - 2}{9} \leq \frac{5}{18}$$

$$18\left(\frac{x-4}{6} - \frac{x-2}{9}\right) \le 18\left(\frac{5}{18}\right) \qquad \text{Multiply both sides by the LCD}$$

$$18\left(\frac{x-4}{6}\right) - 18\left(\frac{x-2}{9}\right) \le 18\left(\frac{5}{18}\right)$$

$$3(x-4) - 2(x-2) \le 5$$

$$3x - 12 - 2x + 4 \le 5$$

$$x - 8 \le 5$$

$$x \le 13$$

The solution set is $(-\infty, 13]$. ▬▬▬▬▬▬▬▬▬▬ ■

Compound Statements

We use the words "and" and "or" in mathematics to form **compound statements.** The following are examples of some compound numerical statements that use "and." We call such statements **conjunctions.** We agree to call a conjunction true only if all of its component parts are true. Statements 1 and 2 below are true, but statements 3, 4, and 5 are false.

1. $3 + 4 = 7$ and $-4 < -3$	True	
2. $-3 < -2$ and $-6 > -10$	True	
3. $6 > 5$ and $-4 < -8$	False	
4. $4 < 2$ and $0 < 10$	False	
5. $-3 + 2 = 1$ and $5 + 4 = 8$	False	

We call compound statements that use "or" **disjunctions.** The following are some examples of disjunctions that involve numerical statements:

6. $0.14 > 0.13$ or $0.235 < 0.237$	True	
7. $\frac{3}{4} > \frac{1}{2}$ or $-4 + (-3) = 10$	True	
8. $-\frac{2}{3} > \frac{1}{3}$ or $(0.4)(0.3) = 0.12$	True	
9. $\frac{2}{5} < -\frac{2}{5}$ or $7 + (-9) = 16$	False	

A disjunction is true if at least one of its component parts is true. In other words, disjunctions are false only if all of the component parts are false. In the statements above, 6, 7, and 8 are true, but 9 is false.

Now let's consider finding solutions for some compound statements that involve algebraic inequalities. Keep in mind that our previous agreements for labeling conjunctions and disjunctions true or false form the basis for our reasoning.

Classroom Example
Graph the solution set for the conjunction $x > -2$ and $x < 1$.

EXAMPLE 4

Graph the solution set for the conjunction $x > -1$ *and* $x < 3$.

Solution

The key word is *and*, so we need to satisfy both inequalities. Thus all numbers between -1 and 3 are solutions, and we can indicate this on a number line as in Figure 1.15.

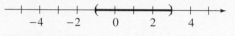

Figure 1.15

Using interval notation, we can represent the interval enclosed in parentheses in Figure 1.15 by $(-1, 3)$. Using set-builder notation, we can express the same interval as $\{x| -1 < x < 3\}$, where the statement $-1 < x < 3$ is read "negative one is less than x and x is less than three." In other words, x is between -1 and 3.

Example 4 represents another concept that pertains to sets. The set of all elements common to two sets is called the **intersection** of the two sets. Thus in Example 4 we found the intersection of the two sets $\{x|x > -1\}$ and $\{x|x < 3\}$ to be the set $\{x|-1 < x < 3\}$. In general, we define the intersection of two sets as follows.

Definition 1.1

The **intersection** of two sets A and B (written $A \cap B$) is the set of all elements that are in both A and B. Using set-builder notation, we can write

$$A \cap B = \{x|x \in A \ \ and \ \ x \in B\}$$

We can solve a conjunction such as $\dfrac{3x + 2}{2} > -2$ and $\dfrac{3x + 2}{2} < 7$, in which the same algebraic expression is contained in both inequalities, by using the compact form $-2 < \dfrac{3x + 2}{2} < 7$ as follows.

Classroom Example
Solve $-6 < \dfrac{9x - 3}{5} < 3$.

EXAMPLE 5   Solve $-2 < \dfrac{3x + 2}{2} < 7$.

Solution

$$-2 < \frac{3x + 2}{2} < 7$$

$$2(-2) < 2\left(\frac{3x + 2}{2}\right) < 2(7) \qquad \text{Multiply through by 2}$$

$$-4 < 3x + 2 < 14$$

$$-6 < 3x < 12 \qquad \text{Add } -2 \text{ to all three quantities}$$

$$2 < x < 4 \qquad \text{Multiply through by } \frac{1}{3}$$

The solution set is the interval $(-2, 4)$.

The word "and" ties the concept of a conjunction to the set concept of intersection. In a like manner, the word "or" links the idea of a disjunction to the set concept of **union.** We define the union of two sets as follows.

> **Definition 1.2**
>
> The **union** of two sets A and B (written $A \cup B$) is the set of all elements that are in A or in B or in both. Using set-builder notation, we can write
>
> $$A \cup B = \{x | x \in A \quad or \quad x \in B\}$$

Classroom Example
Graph the solution set for the disjunction $x < -2$ or $x > 1$, and express it using interval notation.

EXAMPLE 6

Graph the solution set for the disjunction $x < -1$ or $x > 2$, and express it using interval notation.

Solution

The key word is "or," so all numbers that satisfy either inequality (or both) are solutions. Thus all numbers less than -1, along with all numbers greater than 2, are the solutions. The graph of the solution set is shown in Figure 1.16. Using interval notation and the set concept of union, we can express the solution set as $(-\infty, -1) \cup (2, \infty)$.

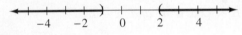

Figure 1.16

Example 6 illustrates that in terms of set vocabulary, the solution set of a disjunction is the union of the solution sets of the component parts of the disjunction. Note that there is *no compact form* for writing $x < -1$ or $x > 2$ *or for any disjunction.*

The following agreements on the use of interval notation should be added to the list on page 167.

Set	Graph	Interval Notation
$\{x | a < x < b\}$	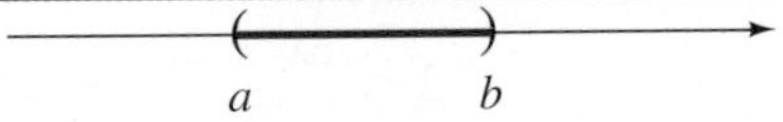	(a, b)
$\{x | a \leq x < b\}$	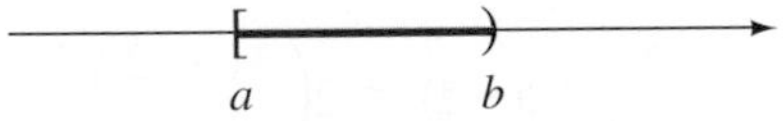	$[a, b)$
$\{x | a < x \leq b\}$	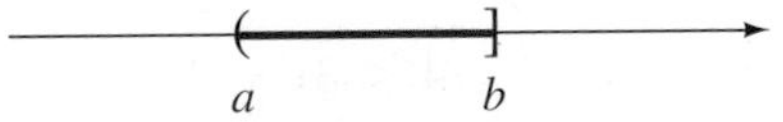	$(a, b]$
$\{x | a \leq x \leq b\}$	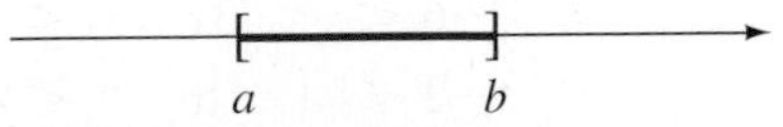	$[a, b]$
$\{x | x$ is a real number$\}$		$(-\infty, \infty)$

Let's conclude this section by considering a word problem that involves an inequality. All of the problem-solving techniques offered earlier continue to apply except that now we look for a guideline that can be used to generate an inequality rather than an equation.

Classroom Example
Honoree has $9000 to invest. If she invests $4800 at 4%, at what rate must she invest the remaining $4200 so that the total yearly interest from the two investments exceeds $465?

EXAMPLE 7

Lance has $5000 to invest. If he invests $3000 at 3%, at what rate must he invest the remaining $2000 so that the total yearly interest from the two investments exceeds $180?

Solution

Let r represent the unknown rate of interest. The following guideline can be used to set up an inequality:

Interest from 3% investment + Interest from r% investment > $180

$$(3\%)(\$3000) \quad + \quad r(\$2000) \quad > \$180$$

We solve this inequality using methods we have already acquired:

$$(0.03)(3000) + 2000r > 180$$
$$90 + 2000r > 180$$
$$2000r > 90$$
$$r > 0.045$$

The remaining $2000 must be invested at a rate higher than 4.5%.

Concept Quiz 1.6

For Problems 1–7, answer true or false.

1. The inequality $3x - 4 \geq -2x - 3$ is a true statement if $x = 1$.
2. If both sides of an inequality are divided by a negative number, the inequality symbol must be reversed.
3. The solution set $\{x|x \leq -3\}$ is written as $[-3, -\infty)$.
4. The solution set for the conjunction $x > -3$ and $x < 7$ is the set of all real numbers.
5. The solution set for the disjunction $x < 5$ or $x > 1$ is the set of all real numbers.
6. The compound statement $2x + 5 > -3$ and $2x + 5 < 13$ can be rewritten using the compact form $-3 < 2x + 5 < 13$.
7. The compound statement $3x - 4 > 12$ or $3x - 4 < -8$ can be rewritten using the compact form $-8 < 3x - 4 > 12$.

Problem Set 1.6

For Problems 1–18, express each solution set in interval notation and graph each solution set. (Objectives 2 and 3)

1. $x \leq -2$

2. $x > -1$

3. $1 < x < 4$

4. $-1 < x \leq 2$

5. $2 > x > 0$

6. $-3 \geq x$

7. $-2 \leq x \leq -1$

8. $1 \leq x$

9. $x < 1$ or $x > 3$

10. $x > 2$ or $x < -1$

11. $x > -2$ or $x > 2$

12. $x > 2$ or $x < 4$

13. $x \leq 4$ or $x \geq 0$

14. $x < -4$ or $x \leq 0$

15. $x > 4$ and $x > -2$

16. $x < 3$ and $x < 6$

17. $x \geq -3$ and $x < 2$

18. $x > 0$ and $x \geq 3$

For Problems 19–26, solve each conjunction by using the compact form and express the solution sets in interval notation. (Objective 3)

19. $-17 \leq 3x - 2 \leq 10$

20. $-25 \leq 4x + 3 \leq 19$

21. $2 > 2x - 1 > -3$

22. $4 > 3x + 1 > 1$

23. $-4 < \dfrac{x - 1}{3} < 4$

24. $-1 \leq \dfrac{x + 2}{4} \leq 1$

25. $-3 < 2 - x < 3$

26. $-4 < 3 - x < 4$

For Problems 27–44, solve each inequality and express the solution sets in interval notation. (Objective 1)

27. $-2x + 1 > 5$

28. $6 - 3x < 12$

29. $-3n + 5n - 2 \geq 8n - 7 - 9n$

30. $3n - 5 > 8n + 5$

31. $6(2t - 5) - 2(4t - 1) \geq 0$

32. $3(2x + 1) - 2(2x + 5) < 5(3x - 2)$

33. $\dfrac{2}{3}x - \dfrac{3}{4} \leq \dfrac{1}{4}x + \dfrac{2}{3}$

34. $\dfrac{3}{5} - \dfrac{x}{2} \geq \dfrac{1}{2} + \dfrac{x}{5}$

35. $\dfrac{n + 2}{4} + \dfrac{n - 3}{8} < 1$

36. $\dfrac{2n + 1}{6} + \dfrac{3n - 1}{5} > \dfrac{2}{15}$

37. $\dfrac{x}{2} - \dfrac{x - 1}{5} \geq \dfrac{x + 2}{10} - 4$

38. $\dfrac{4x - 3}{6} - \dfrac{2x - 1}{12} < -2$

39. $0.09x + 0.1(x + 200) > 77$

40. $0.06x + 0.08(250 - x) \geq 19$

41. $0 < \dfrac{5x - 1}{3} < 2$

42. $-3 \leq \dfrac{4x + 3}{2} \leq 1$

43. $1 \leq \dfrac{7 - x}{2} \leq 3$

44. $-2 \leq \dfrac{5 - 3x}{4} \leq \dfrac{1}{2}$

For Problems 45–53, use inequalities to help solve each problem. (Objective 5)

45. Felix has \$10,000 to invest. Suppose he invests \$5000 at 4% interest. At what rate must he invest the other \$5000 so that the two investments yield more than \$500 of yearly interest?

46. Suppose that Annette invests \$7000 at 7%. How much must she invest at 11% so that the total yearly interest from the two investments exceeds \$974?

47. Rhonda had scores of 94, 84, 86, and 88 on her first four history exams of the semester. What score must she obtain on the fifth exam to have an average of 90 or higher for the five exams?

48. The average height of the two forwards and the center of a basketball team is 6 feet 8 inches. What must the average height of the two guards be so that the team average is at least 6 feet 4 inches?

49. If the temperature for a 24-hour period ranged between 41°F and 59°F, inclusive, what was the range in Celsius degrees? $\left(F = \dfrac{9}{5}C + 32\right)$

50. If the temperature for a 24-hour period ranged between −20°C and −5°C, inclusive, what was the range in Fahrenheit degrees? $\left(C = \dfrac{5}{9}(F - 32)\right)$

51. A person's intelligence quotient (IQ) is found by dividing mental age (M), as indicated by standard tests, by chronological age (C), and then multiplying this ratio by 100. The formula IQ = 100M/C can be used. If the IQ range of a group of 11-year-olds is given by $80 \le IQ \le 140$, find the mental-age range of this group.

52. A car can be rented from agency A at $75 per day plus $0.10 a mile or from agency B at $50 a day plus $0.20 a mile. If the car is driven m miles, for what values of m does it cost less to rent from agency A?

53. In statistics the formula for a z-score is $z = \dfrac{x - \bar{x}}{s}$, where x is a score, $\bar{x}$ is the mean, and s is the standard deviation. To give credibility to our results in a statistical claim, we want to determine the values of x that will produce a z-score greater than 2.5 when $\bar{x} = 8.7$ and $s = 1.2$. Find such values of x.

Thoughts Into Words

54. Explain the difference between a conjunction and a disjunction. Give an example of each (outside the field of mathematics).

55. How do you know by inspection that the solution set of the inequality $x + 3 > x + 2$ is the entire set of real numbers?

56. Give a step-by-step description of how you would solve the inequality $-4 < 2(x - 1) - 3(x + 2)$.

57. Find the solution set for each of the following compound statements and explain your reasoning in each case.

(a) $x < 3$ and $5 > 2$
(b) $x < 3$ or $5 > 2$
(c) $x < 3$ and $6 < 4$
(d) $x < 3$ or $6 < 4$

Further Investigations

58. If $a > b > 0$, verify that $1/a < 1/b$.

59. If $a > b$, is it always true that $1/a < 1/b$? Defend your answer.

Answers to the Concept Quiz

1. True **2.** True **3.** False **4.** False **5.** True **6.** True **7.** False

1.7   Quadratic Inequalities and Inequalities Involving Quotients

OBJECTIVES
1. Solve quadratic inequalities
2. Solve inequalities involving quotients

The equation $ax^2 + bx + c = 0$ has been referred to as the standard form of a quadratic equation in one variable. Similarly, the form $ax^2 + bx + c < 0$ is used to represent a **quadratic inequality**. (The symbol $<$ can be replaced by $>$, $\leq$, or $\geq$ to produce other forms of quadratic inequalities.)

The number line can be used to help solve quadratic inequalities where the quadratic polynomial is factorable. Let's consider two examples to illustrate this procedure.

Classroom Example
Solve $x^2 - 7x - 18 < 0$.

EXAMPLE 1   Solve $x^2 + x - 6 < 0$.

Solution

First, let's factor the polynomial.

$$x^2 + x - 6 < 0$$
$$(x + 3)(x - 2) < 0$$

Second, let's locate the values for which the product $(x + 3)(x - 2)$ is equal to zero. The numbers -3 and 2 divide the number line into three intervals (see Figure 1.17):

the numbers less than -3

the numbers between -3 and 2

the numbers greater than 2

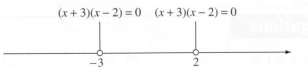

Figure 1.17

We can choose a **test number** from each of these intervals and see how it affects the signs of the factors $x + 3$ and $x - 2$ and, consequently, the sign of the product of these factors. For example, if $x < -3$ (try $x = -4$), then $x + 3$ is negative and $x - 2$ is negative; thus their product is positive. If $-3 < x < 2$ (try $x = 0$), then $x + 3$ is positive and $x - 2$ is negative; thus their product is negative. If $x > 2$ (try $x = 3$), then $x + 3$ is positive and $x - 2$ is positive; thus their product is positive. This information can be conveniently arranged by using a number line, as in Figure 1.18.

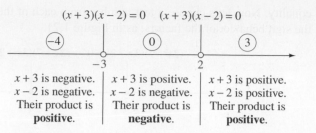

$$(x+3)(x-2)=0 \quad (x+3)(x-2)=0$$

$x+3$ is negative.	$x+3$ is positive.	$x+3$ is positive.
$x-2$ is negative.	$x-2$ is negative.	$x-2$ is positive.
Their product is **positive**.	Their product is **negative**.	Their product is **positive**.

Figure 1.18

Therefore, the given inequality, $x^2 + x - 6 < 0$, is satisfied by the numbers between -3 and 2. That is, the solution set is the open interval $(-3, 2)$.

A graphical analysis of a quadratic inequality like the one in Example 1 can also be very helpful. In Figure 1.19 we show the graph of $y = x^2 + x - 6$. It certainly appears that $y < 0$ in the x interval $(-3, 2)$, which agrees with our solution set in Example 1.

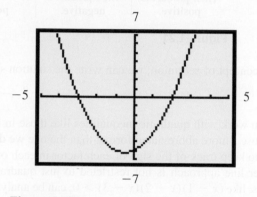

Figure 1.19

Numbers such as -3 and 2 in the preceding example, where the given polynomial or algebraic expression equals zero or is undefined, are referred to as **critical numbers.** Let's consider another example where we make use of critical numbers and test numbers.

Classroom Example
Solve $10x^2 + x - 2 \geq 0$.

EXAMPLE 2   Solve $6x^2 + 17x - 14 \geq 0$.

Solution

First, we factor the polynomial.

$$6x^2 + 17x - 14 \geq 0$$
$$(2x + 7)(3x - 2) \geq 0$$

Second, we locate the values where the product $(2x + 7)(3x - 2)$ equals zero. We suggest putting dots at $-\dfrac{7}{2}$ and $\dfrac{2}{3}$ (see Figure 1.20) to remind ourselves that these two numbers must be included in the solution set because the given statement includes equality. Now let's choose a test number from each of the three intervals and observe the sign behavior of the factors, as in Figure 1.21.

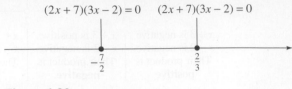

Figure 1.20

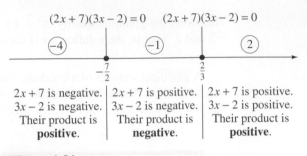

Figure 1.21

Using the concept of set union, we can write the solution set $\left(-\infty, -\frac{7}{2}\right] \cup \left[\frac{2}{3}, \infty\right)$.

As you work with quadratic inequalities like those in Examples 1 and 2, you may be able to use a more abbreviated format than the one we demonstrated. Basically, it is necessary to keep track of the sign of each factor in each of the intervals. Furthermore, this number line approach is not restricted to just quadratic inequalities. Polynomial inequalities, like $(x - 1)(x + 2)(x - 3) > 0$, can be analyzed nicely on a number line. We will have you do this in the next problem set.

Inequalities Involving Quotients

The same type of number-line analysis for indicated products can be used for indicated quotients as well. In other words, inequalities such as

$$\frac{x - 2}{x + 3} > 0$$

can be solved very efficiently using the same basic approach that we used with quadratic inequalities. Let's illustrate this procedure.

Classroom Example
Solve $\dfrac{x + 7}{x - 8} > 0$.

> **EXAMPLE 3**   Solve $\dfrac{x - 2}{x + 3} > 0$.

Solution
First we find that at $x = 2$ the quotient $\dfrac{x - 2}{x + 3}$ equals zero, and that at $x = -3$ the quotient is undefined. The critical numbers -3 and 2 divide the number line into three intervals. Then, using a test number from each interval (such as -4, 1, and 3), we can

observe the sign behavior of the quotient, as in Figure 1.22. Therefore, the solution set for $\dfrac{x-2}{x+3} > 0$ is $(-\infty, -3) \cup (2, \infty)$.

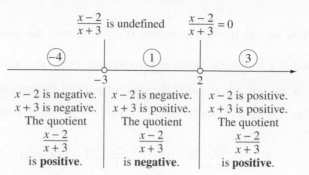

Figure 1.22

In Figure 1.23 we show the graph of $y = \dfrac{x-2}{x+3}$. Notice that y is greater than zero when x is less than -3 and when x is greater than 2. Again this agrees with our solution set in Example 3.

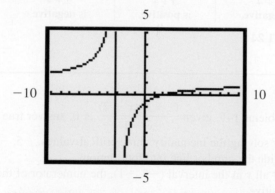

Figure 1.23

Classroom Example
Solve $\dfrac{x+8}{x+3} \le 6$.

EXAMPLE 4   Solve $\dfrac{x+2}{x+4} \le 3$.

Solution

First, let's change the form of the given inequality:

$$\frac{x+2}{x+4} \le 3$$

$$\frac{x+2}{x+4} - 3 \le 0$$

$$\frac{x + 2 - 3(x+4)}{x+4} \le 0$$

$$\frac{x + 2 - 3x - 12}{x + 4} \leq 0$$

$$\frac{-2x - 10}{x + 4} \leq 0$$

Now we can proceed as before. If $x = -5$, then the quotient $\dfrac{-2x - 10}{x + 4}$ equals zero, and if $x = -4$, the quotient is undefined. Using test numbers such as -6, $-4\dfrac{1}{2}$, and -3, we are able to study the sign behavior of the quotient, as in Figure 1.24. Therefore, the solution set for $\dfrac{x + 2}{x + 4} \leq 3$ is $(-\infty, -5] \cup (-4, \infty)$.

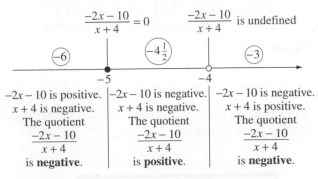

Figure 1.24

Concept Quiz 1.7

For Problems 1–5, given $\dfrac{(x + 5)(x - 2)}{x + 1} \geq 0$, answer true or false.

1. For solving the inequality, three critical values, -5, -1, and 2 would be used to divide the number line into four regions.
2. For all x in the interval $(-5, -1)$, the numerator of the quotient $(x + 5)(x - 2)$ is positive.
3. The quotient $\dfrac{(x + 5)(x - 2)}{x + 1}$ would be undefined if $x = 2$.
4. The denominator, $x + 1$, is positive for all values of x in the interval $(-\infty, -1)$.
5. The quotient $\dfrac{(x + 5)(x - 2)}{x + 1}$ is equal to zero if $x = -1$.

Problem Set 1.7

For Problems 1–34, solve each inequality and express the solution sets in interval notation. **(Objective 1)**

1. $x^2 + 3x - 4 < 0$
2. $x^2 - 4 < 0$
3. $x^2 - 2x - 15 > 0$
4. $x^2 - 12x + 32 \geq 0$

5. $n^2 - n \leq 2$
6. $n^2 + 5n \leq 6$
7. $3t^2 + 11t - 4 > 0$
8. $2t^2 - 9t - 5 > 0$
9. $15x^2 - 26x + 8 \leq 0$
10. $6x^2 + 25x + 14 \leq 0$

11. $4x^2 - 4x + 1 > 0$

12. $9x^2 + 6x + 1 \leq 0$

13. $4 - x^2 < 0$

14. $2x^2 - 18 \geq 0$

15. $4(x^2 - 36) < 0$

16. $-4(x^2 - 36) \geq 0$

17. $5x^2 + 20 > 0$

18. $-3x^2 - 27 \geq 0$

19. $x^2 - 2x \geq 0$

20. $2x^2 + 6x < 0$

21. $3x^3 + 12x^2 > 0$

22. $2x^3 + 4x^2 \leq 0$

23. $(x + 1)(x - 3) > (x + 1)(2x - 1)$

24. $(x - 2)(2x + 5) > (x - 2)(x - 3)$

25. $(x + 1)(x - 2) \geq (x - 4)(x + 6)$

26. $(2x - 1)(x + 4) \geq (2x + 1)(x - 3)$

27. $(x - 1)(x - 2)(x + 4) > 0$

28. $(x + 1)(x - 3)(x + 7) \geq 0$

29. $(x + 2)(2x - 1)(x - 5) \leq 0$

30. $(x - 3)(3x + 2)(x + 4) < 0$

31. $x^3 - 2x^2 - 24x \geq 0$ **32.** $x^3 + 2x^2 - 3x > 0$

33. $(x - 2)^2(x + 3) > 0$ **34.** $(x + 4)^2(x + 5) > 0$

For Problems 35–48, solve each inequality and express the solution set in interval notation. **(Objective 2)**

35. $\dfrac{x + 1}{x - 5} > 0$

36. $\dfrac{x + 2}{x + 4} \leq 0$

37. $\dfrac{2x - 1}{x + 2} < 0$

38. $\dfrac{3x + 2}{x - 1} > 0$

39. $\dfrac{-x + 3}{3x - 1} \geq 0$

40. $\dfrac{-n - 2}{n + 4} < 0$

41. $\dfrac{n}{n + 2} \geq 3$

42. $\dfrac{x}{x - 1} > 2$

43. $\dfrac{x - 1}{x + 2} < 2$

44. $\dfrac{t - 1}{t - 5} \leq 2$

45. $\dfrac{t - 3}{t + 5} > 1$

46. $\dfrac{x + 2}{x + 7} < 1$

47. $\dfrac{1}{x - 2} < \dfrac{1}{x + 3}$

48. $\dfrac{2}{x + 1} > \dfrac{3}{x - 4}$

Thoughts Into Words

49. Explain how you would solve the inequality
$$\frac{x - 2}{(x + 1)^2} > 0.$$

50. Explain how you would solve the inequality $(x - 1)^2(x + 2)^2 > 0$.

51. Consider the following approach for solving the inequality in Example 4 of this section.

$$\frac{x + 2}{x + 4} \leq 3$$

$$(x + 4)\left(\frac{x + 2}{x + 4}\right) \leq 3(x + 4) \quad \text{Multiply both sides by } x + 4.$$

$$x + 2 \leq 3x + 12$$
$$-2x \leq 10$$
$$x \geq -5$$

Obviously, the solution set that we obtain using this approach differs from what we obtained in the text. What is wrong with this approach? Can we make any adjustments so that this basic approach works?

52. The product $(x - 2)(x + 3)$ is positive if both factors are negative *or* if both factors are positive. Therefore, we can solve $(x - 2)(x + 3) > 0$ as follows.

$(x - 2 < 0 \text{ and } x + 3 < 0)$ or $(x - 2 > 0 \text{ and } x + 3 > 0)$

$(x < 2 \text{ and } x < -3)$ or $(x > 2 \text{ and } x > -3)$

$x < -3$ or $x > 2$

The solution set is $(-\infty, -3) \cup (2, \infty)$. Use this type of analysis to solve each inequality.

(a) $(x - 1)(x + 5) > 0$

(b) $(x + 2)(x - 4) \geq 0$

(c) $(x + 4)(x - 3) < 0$

(d) $(2x - 1)(x + 5) \leq 0$

(e) $(x + 4)(x + 1)(x - 2) > 0$

(f) $(x + 2)(x - 1)(x - 3) < 0$

Answers to the Concept Quiz

1. True   **2.** False   **3.** False   **4.** False   **5.** False

---

1.8   Absolute Value Equations and Inequalities

OBJECTIVES   **1** Solve absolute value equations

2 Solve absolute value inequalities

In Section 0.1 we defined the **absolute value** of a real number by

$$|a| = \begin{cases} a & \text{if } a \geq 0 \\ -a & \text{if } a < 0 \end{cases}$$

We also interpreted the absolute value of any real number to be the distance between the number and zero on the real number line. For example, $|6| = 6$ because the distance between 6 and 0 is six units. Likewise, $|-8| = 8$ because the distance between -8 and 0 is eight units.

Both the definition and the number-line interpretation of absolute value provide ways of analyzing a variety of equations and inequalities involving absolute value. For example, suppose that we need to solve the equation $|x| = 4$. If we think in terms of distance on the number line, the equation $|x| = 4$ means that we are looking for numbers that are four units from zero. Thus x must be 4 or -4. From the definition viewpoint, we could proceed as follows.

If $x \geq 0$, then $|x| = x$, and the equation $|x| = 4$ becomes $x = 4$.

If $x < 0$, then $|x| = -x$, and the equation $|x| = 4$ becomes $-x = 4$, which is equivalent to $x = -4$.

Using either approach, we see that the solution set for $|x| = 4$ is $\{-4, 4\}$.

The following property should seem reasonable from the distance interpretation and can be verified using the definition of absolute value.

> **Property 1.5**
>
> For any real number $k > 0$,
>
> $$|x| = k \quad \text{if and only if } x = k \text{ or } x = -k$$

Classroom Example
Solve $|6x - 7| = 5$.

EXAMPLE 1   Solve $|3x - 2| = 7$.

Solution

$$|3x - 2| = 7$$
$$3x - 2 = 7 \quad \text{or} \quad 3x - 2 = -7$$
$$3x = 9 \quad \text{or} \quad 3x = -5$$
$$x = 3 \quad \text{or} \quad x = -\frac{5}{3}$$

The solution set is $\left\{-\frac{5}{3}, 3\right\}$.

Classroom Example
Solve $|2x - 7| = |x + 6|$

EXAMPLE 2   Solve the equation $|3x - 1| = |x + 4|$.

Solution

We could solve this equation by applying the definition of absolute value to both expressions; however, let's approach it in a less formal way. For the two numbers, $3x - 1$ and $x + 4$, to have the same absolute value, they must either be equal or be opposites of each other. Therefore the equation $|3x - 1| = |x + 4|$ is equivalent to $3x - 1 = x + 4$ or $3x - 1 = -(x + 4)$, which can be solved as follows:

$$3x - 1 = x + 4 \quad \text{or} \quad 3x - 1 = -(x + 4)$$
$$2x = 5 \quad \text{or} \quad 3x - 1 = -x - 4$$
$$x = \frac{5}{2} \quad \text{or} \quad 4x = -3$$
$$x = \frac{5}{2} \quad \text{or} \quad x = -\frac{3}{4}$$

The solution set is $\left\{-\frac{3}{4}, \frac{5}{2}\right\}$.

The distance interpretation for absolute value also provides a good basis for solving some inequalities. For example, to solve $|x| < 4$, we know that the distance between x and 0 must be less than four units. In other words, x is to be less than four units away from zero. Thus $|x| < 4$ is equivalent to $-4 < x < 4$, and the solution set is the interval

$(-4, 4)$. We will have you use the definition of absolute value and verify the following general property in the next set of exercises.

> ### Property 1.6
>
> For any real number $k > 0$,
>
> $$|x| < k \quad \text{if and only if} \quad -k < x < k$$

Example 3 illustrates the use of Property 1.6.

Classroom Example
Solve $|3x + 12| < 3$.

EXAMPLE 3   Solve $|2x + 1| < 5$.

Solution

$$|2x + 1| < 5$$
$$-5 < 2x + 1 < 5$$
$$-6 < 2x < 4$$
$$-3 < x < 2$$

The solution set is the interval $(-3, 2)$.

Property 1.6 can also be expanded to include the $\leq$ situation; that is, $|x| \leq k$ if and only if $-k \leq x \leq k$.

Classroom Example
Solve $|-2x - 8| \leq 10$.

EXAMPLE 4   Solve $|-3x - 2| \leq 6$.

Solution

$$|-3x - 2| \leq 6$$
$$-6 \leq -3x - 2 \leq 6$$
$$-4 \leq -3x \leq 8$$
$$\frac{4}{3} \geq x \geq -\frac{8}{3} \qquad \text{Note that multiplying through by } -\frac{1}{3}$$
$$\text{reverses the inequalities.}$$

The statement $\dfrac{4}{3} \geq x \geq -\dfrac{8}{3}$ is equivalent to $-\dfrac{8}{3} \leq x \leq \dfrac{4}{3}$. Therefore, the solution set is $\left[-\dfrac{8}{3}, \dfrac{4}{3} \right]$.

Now suppose that we want to solve $|x| > 4$. The distance between x and zero must be more than four units; in other words, x is to be more than four units away from zero. Therefore $|x| > 4$ is equivalent to $x < -4$ or $x > 4$, and the solution set is $(-\infty, -4) \cup (4, \infty)$. The following general property can be verified by using the definition of absolute value.

> **Property 1.7**
>
> For any real number $k > 0$,
>
> $$|x| > k \quad \text{if and only if } x < -k \text{ or } x > k$$

Classroom Example
Solve $|3x - 10| > 8$.

EXAMPLE 5   Solve $|4x - 3| > 9$.

Solution

$$|4x - 3| > 9$$
$$4x - 3 < -9 \quad \text{or} \quad 4x - 3 > 9$$
$$4x < -6 \quad \text{or} \quad 4x > 12$$
$$x < -\frac{6}{4} \quad \text{or} \quad x > 3$$
$$x < -\frac{3}{2} \quad \text{or} \quad x > 3$$

The solution set is $\left(-\infty, -\dfrac{3}{2}\right) \cup (3, \infty)$.

Property 1.7 can also be expanded to include the $\geq$ situation; that is, $|x| \geq k$ if and only if $x \leq -k$ or $x \geq k$.

Classroom Example
Solve $|-3 - x| \geq 7$.

EXAMPLE 6   Solve $|-2 - x| \geq 9$.

Solution

$$|-2 - x| \geq 9$$
$$-2 - x \leq -9 \quad \text{or} \quad -2 - x \geq 9$$
$$-x \leq -7 \quad \text{or} \quad -x \geq 11$$
$$x \geq 7 \quad \text{or} \quad x \leq -11$$

The solution set is $(-\infty, -11] \cup [7, \infty)$.

Properties 1.5, 1.6, and 1.7 provide a sound basis for solving many equations and inequalities involving absolute value. However, if at any time you become doubtful about which property applies, don't forget the definition and the distance interpretation for absolute value.

We should also note that in Properties 1.5, 1.6, and 1.7, k is a positive number. This is not a serious restriction because problems where k is nonpositive are easily solved as follows:

$|x - 2| = 0$ The solution set is $\{2\}$ because $x - 2$ has to equal zero

$|3x - 7| = -4$ The solution set is $\varnothing$; for any real number, the absolute value of $3x - 7$ will always be nonnegative

$$|2x - 1| < -3$$

The solution set is $\varnothing$; for any real number, the absolute value of $2x - 1$ will always be nonnegative

$$|5x + 2| > -4$$

The solution set is $(-\infty, \infty)$; the absolute value of $5x + 2$, regardless of which real number is substituted for x, will always be greater than -4

The number-line approach used in Examples 3 and 4 of this section, along with Properties 1.6 and 1.7, provides a systematic way of solving absolute value inequalities that have the variable in the denominator of a fraction. Let's analyze one such problem.

Classroom Example

Solve $\left|\dfrac{x + 8}{x - 4}\right| < 3$.

EXAMPLE 7   Solve $\left|\dfrac{x - 2}{x + 3}\right| < 4$.

Solution

By Property 1.6, $\left|\dfrac{x - 2}{x + 3}\right| < 4$ becomes $-4 < \dfrac{x - 2}{x + 3} < 4$, which can be written

$$\frac{x - 2}{x + 3} > -4 \quad \text{and} \quad \frac{x - 2}{x + 3} < 4$$

Each part of this *and* statement can be solved as we handled Example 2 earlier.

(a)

$$\frac{x - 2}{x + 3} > -4 \quad \text{and}$$

$$\frac{x - 2}{x + 3} + 4 > 0 \quad \text{and}$$

$$\frac{x - 2 + 4(x + 3)}{x + 3} > 0 \quad \text{and}$$

$$\frac{x - 2 + 4x + 12}{x + 3} > 0 \quad \text{and}$$

$$\frac{5x + 10}{x + 3} > 0 \quad \text{and}$$

This solution set is shown in Figure 1.25(a).

(b)

$$\frac{x - 2}{x + 3} < 4$$

$$\frac{x - 2}{x + 3} - 4 < 0$$

$$\frac{x - 2 - 4(x + 3)}{x + 3} < 0$$

$$\frac{x - 2 - 4x - 12}{x + 3} < 0$$

$$\frac{-3x - 14}{x + 3} < 0$$

This solution set is shown in Figure 1.25(b).

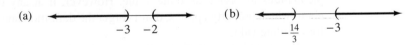

Figure 1.25

The intersection of the two solution sets pictured is the set shown in Figure 1.26.

Therefore, the solution set of $\left|\dfrac{x - 2}{x + 3}\right| < 4$ is $\left(-\infty, -\dfrac{14}{3}\right) \cup (-2, \infty)$.

Figure 1.26

Yes, Example 7 is a little messy, but it does illustrate the weaving together of previously used techniques to solve a more complicated problem. Don't be in a hurry when doing such problems. First analyze the general approach to be taken and then carry out the details in a neatly organized format to minimize your chances of making careless errors.

Finally, let's show a graphical analysis of Example 7. Figure 1.27 shows the graph of $y = \left| \dfrac{x - 2}{x + 3} \right| - 4$. Notice that one x intercept is between -5 and -4, and the other intercept appears to be at -2. Furthermore, y is less than zero when x is less than that intercept between -5 and -4, and y is less than zero when x is greater than -2. So our solution set for Example 7 looks good.

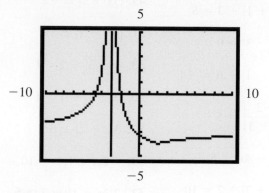

Figure 1.27

Concept Quiz 1.8

For Problems 1–7, answer true or false.

1. The absolute value of any real number can be interpreted as the distance between the number and zero on the real number line.
2. For any real number a, $|a| = |-a|$.
3. Every absolute value equation has at least one solution.
4. The absolute value equation $|2x - 6| = 0$ has two solutions.
5. When solving the absolute value inequality, $|ax + b| > c$, we solve the disjunction $ax + b < -c$ or $ax + b > c$.
6. The solution set for the absolute value inequality $|x - 4| > 0$ is all real numbers.
7. The solution set for the absolute value inequality $|3x - 5| > -2$ is all real numbers.

Problem Set 1.8

For Problems 1–32, solve each equation. (Objective 1)

1. $|x - 2| = 6$

2. $|x + 3| = 4$

3. $\left|x + \dfrac{1}{4}\right| = \dfrac{2}{5}$

4. $\left|x - \dfrac{2}{3}\right| = \dfrac{3}{4}$

5. $|2n - 1| = 7$

6. $|2n + 1| = 11$

7. $|3x + 4| = 5$

8. $|5x - 3| = 10$

9. $|7x - 1| = -4$

10. $|-2x - 1| = 6$

11. $|-3x - 2| = 8$

12. $|5x - 4| = -3$

13. $|x - 3| - 2 = 4$

14. $|2x + 1| + 3 = 8$

15. $|5x + 1| = 0$

16. $|4x - 3| = 0$

17. $|2n + 3| - 7 = -2$

18. $|3n - 1| - 6 = -4$

19. $\left|\dfrac{3}{k - 1}\right| = 4$

20. $\left|\dfrac{-2}{n + 3}\right| = 5$

21. $|3 - 2x| = 7$

22. $|13 - 4x| = 5$

23. $3|x - 4| - 2 = 7$

24. $2|x + 7| + 2 = 10$

25. $2|3x + 1| - 12 = -4$

26. $2|3 - x| - 20 = -6$

27. $|3x - 1| = |2x + 3|$ **28.** $|2x + 1| = |4x - 3|$

29. $|-2n + 1| = |-3n - 1|$

30. $|-4n + 5| = |-3n - 5|$

31. $|x - 2| = |x + 4|$ **32.** $|2x - 3| = |2x + 5|$

For Problems 33–72, solve each inequality and express the solution set in interval notation. (Objective 2)

33. $|x| < 6$

34. $|x| \geq 4$

35. $|x| > 8$

36. $|x| \leq 1$

37. $|x| \geq -4$

38. $|x| < -5$

39. $|t - 3| > 5$

40. $|n + 2| < 1$

41. $|2x - 1| \leq 7$

42. $|2x + 1| \geq 3$

43. $|3n + 2| > 9$

44. $|5n - 2| < 2$

45. $|4x - 3| < -5$

46. $|2 - x| > 1$

47. $|3 - 2x| < 4$

48. $|4x + 5| > -3$

49. $|7x + 2| \geq -2$

50. $|-2 - x| \leq 5$

51. $|-1 - x| \geq 8$

52. $|x - 1| + 2 < 4$

53. $|x + 3| - 2 < 1$

54. $|x - 5| + 4 \leq 2$

55. $|x + 4| - 1 > 1$

56. $|x - 2| + 3 > 6$

57. $3|x - 2| \geq 6$

58. $2|x + 1| < 8$

59. $-2|x + 1| > -10$

60. $-|x - 4| \leq -4$

61. $2|3x - 1| - 3 \geq 5$

62. $3|2x + 1| + 1 < 7$

63. $-2|x + 3| - 1 > 4$

64. $-2|x - 1| - 3 > -5$

65. $\left|\dfrac{x + 1}{x - 2}\right| < 3$

66. $\left|\dfrac{x - 1}{x - 4}\right| < 2$

67. $\left|\dfrac{x - 1}{x + 3}\right| > 1$

68. $\left|\dfrac{x + 4}{x - 5}\right| \geq 3$

69. $\left|\dfrac{n + 2}{n}\right| \geq 4$

70. $\left|\dfrac{t + 6}{t - 2}\right| < 1$

71. $\left|\dfrac{k}{2k - 1}\right| \leq 2$

72. $\left|\dfrac{k}{k + 2}\right| > 4$

Thoughts Into Words

73. Explain how you would solve the inequality $|3x - 7| > -2$.

74. Why is $\left\{\dfrac{3}{2}\right\}$ the solution set for $|2x - 3| \leq 0$?

Further Investigations

75. Use the definition of absolute value and prove Property 1.5.

76. Use the definition of absolute value and prove Property 1.6.

77. Use the definition of absolute value and prove Property 1.7.

78. Solve each of the following inequalities by using the definition of absolute value. Do not use Properties 1.6 and 1.7.

(a) $|x + 5| < 11$ (b) $|x - 4| \leq 10$

(c) $|2x - 1| > 7$ (d) $|3x + 2| \geq 1$

(e) $|2 - x| < 5$ (f) $|3 - x| > 6$

Answers to the Concept Quiz

1. True   **2.** True   **3.** False   **4.** False   **5.** True   **6.** False   **7.** True

OBJECTIVE	SUMMARY	EXAMPLE
Solve linear equations. (Section 1.1/Objective 1)	Solving an algebraic equation refers to the process of finding the number (or numbers) that make(s) the algebraic equation a true numerical statement. Two properties of equality play an important role in solving equations. **Addition Property of Equality** $a = b$ if and only if $a + c = b + c$. **Multiplication Property of Equality** For $c \neq 0$, $a = b$ if and only if $ac = bc$.	Solve $3(2x - 1) = 2x + 6 - 5x$. **Solution** $$3(2x - 1) = 2x + 6 - 5x$$ $$6x - 3 = -3x + 6$$ $$9x - 3 = 6$$ $$9x = 9$$ $$x = 1$$ The solution set is $\{1\}$.
Solve linear equations involving fractions. (Section 1.2/Objective 1)	Linear equations involving fractions can have denominators that are constants, such as $\dfrac{x}{2} - \dfrac{x}{5} = \dfrac{7}{10}$, or denominators that contain the variable in one or more terms, such as $\dfrac{4}{x} - \dfrac{6}{5} = \dfrac{3}{2x - 1}$. The approach to solving either type is to begin by multiplying both sides of the equation by the least common multiple of all the denominators in the equation. This process clears the equation of the fractions. However, when there are variables in the denominator we must discard any potential solutions that make a denominator equal to zero.	Solve $\dfrac{6}{x + 4} - \dfrac{3}{x - 1} = \dfrac{-2}{x - 1}$. **Solution** $$\dfrac{6}{x + 4} - \dfrac{3}{x - 1} = \dfrac{-2}{x - 1}$$ $$(x + 4)(x - 1)\left(\dfrac{6}{x + 4} - \dfrac{3}{x - 1}\right)$$ $$= (x + 4)(x - 1)\left(\dfrac{-2}{x - 1}\right)$$ $$6(x - 1) - 3(x + 4) = -2(x + 4)$$ $$6x - 6 - 3x - 12 = -2x - 8$$ $$3x - 18 = -2x - 8$$ $$5x = 10$$ $$x = 2$$ Because 2 does not make any denominator equal to zero, it is a solution. The solution set is $\{2\}$.

OBJECTIVE	SUMMARY	EXAMPLE
Solve proportions. (Section 1.2/Objective 2)	A ratio is the comparison of two numbers by division. A statement of equality between two ratios is called a proportion. Thus $\dfrac{a}{b} = \dfrac{c}{d}$ ($b \neq 0$, $d \neq 0$) is a proportion. The cross-multiplication property of proportions, if $\dfrac{a}{b} = \dfrac{c}{d}$, then $ad = bc$ is used to solve proportions.	Solve $\dfrac{5}{2x - 1} = \dfrac{3}{x + 4}$. **Solution** $$\dfrac{5}{2x - 1} = \dfrac{3}{x + 4}, x \neq \dfrac{1}{2}, x \neq -4$$ $$3(2x - 1) = 5(x + 4)$$ $$6x - 3 = 5x + 20$$ $$x = 23$$ The solution set is $\{23\}$.
Solve linear equations involving decimals. (Section 1.2/Objective 3)	To solve equations that contain decimals, you can clear the equation of the decimals by multiplying both sides by an appropriate power of 10, or you can keep the problem in decimal form and perform the calculations with decimals.	Solve $0.04x + 0.07(2x) = 90$. **Solution** $$0.04x + 0.07(2x) = 90$$ $$100[0.04x + 0.07(2x)] = 100(90)$$ $$4x + 7(2x) = 9000$$ $$4x + 14x = 9000$$ $$18x = 9000$$ $$x = 500$$ The solution set is $\{500\}$.
Solve formulas for a specified variable. (Section 1.2/Objective 4)	The form of a formula can be changed by applying the Addition Property of Equality and/or the Multiplication Property of Equality. These properties are applied until we reach the goal of isolating the variable on one side of the equation, and all the other terms are on the other side of the equation. There are often several forms of the result, which can all be equivalent formulas.	Solve $A = \dfrac{1}{2}bh$ for b. **Solution** $$A = \dfrac{1}{2}bh$$ $$2A = 2\left(\dfrac{1}{2}bh\right)$$ $$2A = bh$$ $$\dfrac{2A}{h} = b$$

(continued)

OBJECTIVE	SUMMARY	EXAMPLE
Solve application problems. (Section 1.1/Objective 2) (Section 1.2/Objective 5)	Keep the following suggestions in mind as you solve word problems. 1. Read the problem carefully. 2. Sketch any figure, diagram, or chart that might be helpful. 3. Choose a meaningful variable. 4. Look for a guideline. 5. Form an equation. 6. Solve the equation. 7. Check your answers.	Marcos bought a 3-D television for \$2343, including 6.5% sales tax. What was the selling price of the television without the tax? **Solution** Let x represent the selling price of the television. The guideline is: Selling price plus tax equals the cost $x + 0.065x = 2343$ $1.065x = 2343$ $x = 2200$ The selling price of the television is \$2200.
Solve quadratic equations by factoring. (Section 1.3/Objective 1)	The standard form for a quadratic equation in one variable is $ax^2 + bx + c = 0$, where a, b, and c are real numbers and $a \neq 0$. Some quadratic equations can be solved by factoring and applying the property, $ab = 0$ if and only if $a = 0$ or $b = 0$.	Solve $5x^2 + 2x = 3$. **Solution** $5x^2 + 2x = 3$ $5x^2 + 2x - 3 = 0$ $(5x - 3)(x + 1) = 0$ $5x - 3 = 0$ or $x + 1 = 0$ $x = \dfrac{3}{5}$ or $x = -1$ The solution set is $\left\{-1, \dfrac{3}{5}\right\}$.
Solve quadratic equations by applying the square root property. (Section 1.3/Objective 2)	We can solve some quadratic equations by applying the property, $x^2 = a$ if and only if $x = \pm\sqrt{a}$.	Solve $2(x + 5)^2 = -16$. **Solution** $2(x + 5)^2 = -16$ First divide both sides of the equation by 2. $(x + 5)^2 = -8$ $x + 5 = \pm\sqrt{-8}$ $x + 5 = \pm 2i\sqrt{2}$ $x = -5 \pm 2i\sqrt{2}$ The solution set is $\{-5 \pm 2i\sqrt{2}\}$.

OBJECTIVE	SUMMARY	EXAMPLE
Solve quadratic equations by completing the square. (Section 1.3/Objective 3)	To solve a quadratic equation by completing the square, first put the equation in the form $x^2 + bx = k$. Then perform the following steps. **1.** Take one-half of b, square that result, and add to each side of the equation. **2.** Factor the left side. **3.** Apply the property, $x^2 = a$ if and only if $x = \pm\sqrt{a}$.	Solve $2x^2 + 24x - 8 = 0$. **Solution** $$2x^2 + 24x - 8 = 0$$ $$2x^2 + 24x = 8$$ Multiply both sides of the equation by $\frac{1}{2}$. $$x^2 + 12x = 4$$ $$x^2 + 12x + 36 = 4 + 36$$ $$(x + 6)^2 = 40$$ $$x + 6 = \pm\sqrt{40}$$ $$x = -6 \pm 2\sqrt{10}$$ The solution set is $\{-6 \pm 2\sqrt{10}\}$.
Solve quadratic equations by using the quadratic formula. (Section 1.3/Objective 4)	Any quadratic equation of the form $ax^2 + bx + c = 0$ can be solved by the quadratic formula, which is usually stated as $$x = \frac{-b \pm \sqrt{b^2 - 4ac}}{2a}$$	Solve $x(3x - 2) = 6$. **Solution** $$x(3x - 2) = 6$$ $$3x^2 - 2x - 6 = 0$$ $$a = 3, b = -2, \text{ and } c = -6$$ $$x = \frac{-(-2) \pm \sqrt{(-2)^2 - 4(3)(-6)}}{2(3)}$$ $$x = \frac{2 \pm \sqrt{76}}{6}$$ $$x = \frac{2 \pm 2\sqrt{19}}{6} = \frac{2(1 \pm \sqrt{19})}{6}$$ $$x = \frac{1 \pm \sqrt{19}}{3}$$ The solution set is $\left\{\frac{1 \pm \sqrt{19}}{3}\right\}$.

(continued)

OBJECTIVE	SUMMARY	EXAMPLE
Use the discriminant to determine the nature of the solutions of a quadratic equation. (Section 1.3/Objective 5)	The discriminant, $b^2 - 4ac$, can be used to determine the nature of the roots of a quadratic equation. **1.** If $b^2 - 4ac < 0$, then the equation has two nonreal complex solutions. **2.** If $b^2 - 4ac = 0$, then the equation has two equal real solutions. **3.** If $b^2 - 4ac > 0$, then the equation has two unequal real solutions.	Use the discriminant to determine the nature of the solutions for the equation $3x^2 + -7x + 5 = 0$. **Solution** $3x^2 - 7x + 5 = 0$ $a = 3, b = -7,$ and $c = 5$ $b^2 - 4ac$ $(-7)^2 - 4(3)(5) = -11$ Because the discriminant is less than zero, the equation has two nonreal complex solutions.
Solve application problems involving quadratic equations. (Section 1.3/Objective 6)	Some of the application problems that result in quadratic equations involve geometry formulas such as the Pythagorean theorem. For a right triangle with legs of lengths a and b and hypotenuse of length c the following formula holds true, $a^2 + b^2 = c^2$.	The sum of the lengths of the two legs of a right triangle is 17 feet. If the length of the hypotenuse is 13 feet, find the length of each leg. **Solution** Let $x =$ length of one leg. Then $17 - x =$ length of the other leg. By Pythagorean theorem, $$x^2 + (17 - x)^2 = 13^2$$ $$x^2 + 289 - 34x + x^2 = 169$$ $$2x^2 - 34x + 120 = 0$$ $$2(x^2 - 17x + 60) = 0$$ $$2(x - 5)(x - 12) = 0$$ $$x = 5 \text{ or } x = 12$$ The lengths of the legs are 5 feet and 12 feet.

OBJECTIVE	SUMMARY	EXAMPLE
Solve radical equations. (Section 1.5/Objective 2)	Equations with variables in a radicand are called radical equations. Radical equations are solved by raising each side of the equation to the appropriate power. However raising both sides of the equation to a power may produce **extraneous roots.** Therefore you must check each potential solution.	Solve $3\sqrt{y} + 4 = y$. **Solution** $3\sqrt{y} + 4 = y$ $3\sqrt{y} = y - 4$ Isolate the radical term $(3\sqrt{y})^2 = (y - 4)^2$ $9y = y^2 - 8y + 16$ $0 = y^2 - 17y + 16$ $0 = (y - 16)(y - 1)$ $y = 16$ or $y = 1$ **✔ Check** $3\sqrt{y} + 4 = y$ If $y = 16$ $\qquad$ If $y = 1$ $3\sqrt{16} + 4 \overset{?}{=} 16$ $\quad$ $\sqrt{1} + 4 \overset{?}{=} 16$ $16 = 16$ $\qquad$ $5 \neq 16$ The solution set is $\{16\}$.
Solve equations that are quadratic in form. (Section 1.5/Objective 3)	Equations such as $x^4 + x^2 - 6 = 0$ that can be represented as $u^2 + u - 6 = 0$ by an appropriate substitution are said to be of quadratic form.	Solve $12x^{-2} - 17x^{-1} - 5 = 0$. **Solution** $12x^{-2} - 17x^{-1} - 5 = 0$ Let $u = x^{-1}$, then $u^2 = x^{-2}$ and substitute. $12u^2 - 17u - 5 = 0$ $(3u - 5)(4u + 1) = 0$ $u = \dfrac{5}{3}$ or $u = -\dfrac{1}{4}$ Now substitute to find x. $x^{-1} = \dfrac{5}{3}$ or $x^{-1} = -\dfrac{1}{4}$ $x = \dfrac{3}{5}$ or $\quad x = -4$ The solution set is $\left\{-4, \dfrac{3}{5}\right\}$.

(continued)

OBJECTIVE	SUMMARY	EXAMPLE
Solve inequalities. (Section 1.6/Objective 1)	For all real numbers a, b, and c **1.** $a > b$ if and only if $a + c > b + c$ **2.** With $c > 0$ $a > b$ if and only if $ac > bc$ **3.** With $c < 0$ $a > b$ if and only if $ac < bc$ If both sides of an inequality are multiplied or divided by a negative number, the inequality symbol must be reversed.	Solve $10 - 2x \geq -30$. **Solution** $10 - 2x \geq -30$ $-2x \geq -30$ $x \leq 15$ The solution set is $\{x \mid x \leq 15\}$.
Express intervals in interval notation. (Section 1.6/Objective 2)	The solution set for an algebraic inequality can be displayed on a number line graph, written as an inequality, or written in interval notation. See the table on page 167 for examples of various algebraic inequalities and how their solution sets would be written in interval notation.	Express the solution set for $x \leq -3$ in interval notation. **Solution** For the solution set we want all numbers less than or equal to -3. In interval notation the solution set is written as $(-\infty, -3]$.
Solve compound inequalities. (Section 1.6/Objective 3)	Inequalities connected with the word "and" form a compound statement called a **conjunction.** A conjunction is true only if all of its component parts are true. The solution set of a conjunction is the *intersection* of the solution sets of each inequality. Inequalities connected with the word "or" form a compound statement called a **disjunction.** A disjunction is true if at least one of its component parts is true. The solution set of a disjunction is the *union* of the solution sets of each inequality.	Solve $11 > 3 - 2x \geq 2$. **Solution** $11 > 3 - 2x \geq 2$ $8 > -2x \geq 2$ $\dfrac{8}{-2} < \dfrac{-2x}{-2} \leq \dfrac{2}{-2}$ $-4 < x \leq -1$ The solution set is $(-4, -1]$.

OBJECTIVE	SUMMARY	EXAMPLE
Solve application problems involving inequalities. (Section 1.6/Objective 4)	Use the same suggestions as for solving word problems. However the guideline will translate into an inequality rather than an equation.	Cheryl scored 92 and 86 on her first two algebra tests. What must she score on the third test to have an average of at least 90 for the three tests? **Solution** Let s represent the score on the third test. $$\frac{92 + 86 + s}{3} \geq 90$$ $$92 + 86 + s \geq 270$$ $$178 + s \geq 270$$ $$s \geq 92$$ She must score 92 or more.
Solve quadratic inequalities. (Section 1.7/Objective 1)	To solve quadratic inequalities that are factorable polynomials, the critical numbers are found by factoring the polynomial. The critical numbers partition the number line into regions. A test point from each region is used to determine whether the values in that region make the inequality a true statement. The answer is usually expressed in interval notation.	Solve $x^2 - 3x - 4 > 0$. **Solution** Solve the equation $x^2 - 3x - 4 = 0$ to find the critical numbers. $$x^2 - 3x - 4 = 0$$ $$(x + 1)(x - 4) = 0$$ $$x = -1 \text{ or } x = 4$$ The critical numbers are -1 and 4. Choose a test point from each of the following intervals, $(-\infty, -1), (-1, 4), \text{ and } (4, \infty)$. Evaluating the inequality $x^2 - 3x - 4 > 0$ for each of the test points shows that the numbers in the intervals $(-\infty, -1)$ and $(4, \infty)$ make the inequality a true statement. The solution is $(-\infty, -1) \cup (4, \infty)$.

(continued)

OBJECTIVE	SUMMARY	EXAMPLE
Solve inequalities involving quotients. (Section 1.7/Objective 2)	To solve inequalities involving quotients, use the same basic approach as solving quadratic inequalities. Be careful to avoid any values that make the denominator zero.	Solve $\dfrac{x + 6}{x - 3} \geq 0$. **Solution** Set the numerator equal to zero and set the denominator equal to zero to find the critical numbers. $x + 6 = 0$ and $x - 3 = 0$ $x = -6$ and $x = 3$ The critical numbers are -6 and 3. Evaluating the inequality with a test point from each of the intervals $(-\infty, -6)$, $(-6, 3)$, and $(3, \infty)$ shows that the values in the intervals $(-\infty, -6)$ and $(3, \infty)$ make the inequality a true statement. Because the inequality is a greater than or equal to statement the solution set should include -6. However, 3 should not be included in the solution set because 3 would make the denominator equal to zero and the quotient would be undefined. The solution set is $(-\infty, -6] \cup (3, \infty)$.
Solve absolute value equations. (Section 1.8/Objective 1)	Property 1.5 states that $\lvert x \rvert = k$ is equivalent to $x = k$ or $x = -k$, where k is a positive number. This property is applied to solve absolute value equations.	Solve $\lvert x - 5 \rvert + 3 = 9$. **Solution** $\lvert x - 5 \rvert + 3 = 9$ $\lvert x - 5 \rvert = 6$ $x - 5 = 6$ or $x - 5 = -6$ $x = 11$ or $x = -1$ The solution set is $\{-1, 11\}$.
Solve absolute value inequalities. (Section 1.8/Objective 2)	Property 1.6 states that $\lvert x \rvert < k$ is equivalent to $x > -k$ or $x < k$, where k is a positive number. This conjunction can be written in compact form as $-k < x < k$. For example $\lvert x + 3 \rvert < 7$ can be written as $-7 < x + 3 < 7$ to begin the process of solving the inequality. Property 1.7 states that $\lvert x \rvert > k$ is equivalent to $x < -k$ or $x > k$, where k is a positive number. This disjunction cannot be written in a compact form.	Solve $\left\lvert \dfrac{x + 5}{3} \right\rvert \leq 4$. **Solution** $\left\lvert \dfrac{x + 5}{3} \right\rvert \leq 4$ $-4 \leq \dfrac{x + 5}{3} \leq 4$ $-12 \leq x + 5 \leq 12$ $-17 \leq x \leq 7$ The solution set is $[-17, 7]$.

Chapter 1 Review Problem Set

For Problems 1–22, solve each equation.

1. $2(3x - 1) - 3(x - 2) = 2(x - 5)$

2. $\dfrac{n - 1}{4} - \dfrac{2n + 3}{5} = 2$

3. $\dfrac{2}{x + 2} + \dfrac{5}{x - 4} = \dfrac{7}{2x - 8}$

4. $0.07x + 0.12(550 - x) = 56$

5. $(3x - 1)^2 = 16$ **6.** $4x^2 - 29x + 30 = 0$

7. $x^2 - 6x + 10 = 0$ **8.** $n^2 + 4n = 396$

9. $15x^3 + x^2 - 2x = 0$

10. $\dfrac{t + 3}{t - 1} - \dfrac{2t + 3}{t - 5} = \dfrac{3 - t^2}{t^2 - 6t + 5}$

11. $\dfrac{5 - x}{2 - x} - \dfrac{3 - 2x}{2x} = 1$ **12.** $x^4 + 4x^2 - 45 = 0$

13. $2n^{-4} - 11n^{-2} + 5 = 0$

14. $\left(x - \dfrac{2}{x}\right)^2 + 4\left(x - \dfrac{2}{x}\right) = 5$

15. $\sqrt{5 + 2x} = 1 + \sqrt{2x}$

16. $\sqrt{3 + 2n} + \sqrt{2 - 2n} = 3$

17. $\sqrt{3 - t} - \sqrt{3 + t} = \sqrt{t}$

18. $|5x - 1| = 7$ **19.** $|2x + 5| = |3x - 7|$

20. $\left|\dfrac{-3}{n - 1}\right| = 4$

21. $x^3 + x^2 - 2x - 2 = 0$

22. $2x^{2/3} + 5x^{1/3} - 12 = 0$

For Problems 23–40, solve each inequality. Express the solution sets using interval notation.

23. $3(2 - x) + 2(x - 4) > -2(x + 5)$

24. $\dfrac{3}{5}x - \dfrac{1}{3} \leq \dfrac{2}{3}x + \dfrac{3}{4}$

25. $\dfrac{n - 1}{3} - \dfrac{2n + 1}{4} > \dfrac{1}{6}$

26. $0.08x + 0.09(700 - x) \geq 59$

27. $-16 \leq 7x - 2 \leq 5$ **28.** $5 > \dfrac{3y + 4}{2} > 1$

29. $x^2 - 3x - 18 < 0$ **30.** $n^2 - 5n \geq 14$

31. $(x - 1)(x - 4)(x + 2) < 0$

32. $\dfrac{x + 4}{2x - 3} \leq 0$ **33.** $\dfrac{5n - 1}{n - 2} > 0$

34. $\dfrac{x - 1}{x + 3} \geq 2$ **35.** $\dfrac{t + 5}{t - 4} < 1$

36. $|4x - 3| > 5$ **37.** $|3x + 5| \leq 14$

38. $|-3 - 2x| < 6$ **39.** $\left|\dfrac{x - 1}{x}\right| > 2$

40. $\left|\dfrac{n + 1}{n + 2}\right| < 1$

For Problems 41–56, solve each problem.

41. The sum of three consecutive odd integers is 31 less than four times the largest integer. Find the integers.

42. The ratio of men to women on a crew team is 7 to 2. If there is a total of 63 members on the crew team, find the number of men on the team.

43. The perimeter of a rectangle is 38 centimeters, and its area is 84 square centimeters. Find the dimensions of the rectangle.

44. A sum of money amounting to $13.55 consists of nickels, dimes, and quarters. There are three times as many dimes as nickels and three fewer quarters than dimes. How many coins of each denomination are there?

45. A retailer has some computer flash drives that cost him $14 each. He wants to sell them to make a profit of 30% of the selling price. What price should he charge for the flash drives?

46. How many gallons of a solution of glycerine and water containing 55% glycerine should be added to 15 gallons of a 20% solution to give a 40% solution?

47. The sum of the present ages of Rosie and her mother is 47 years. In 5 years, Rosie will be one-half as old as her mother at that time. Find the present ages of both Rosie and her mother.

48. Kelly invested $8000, part of it at 4% and the remainder at 6.5%. Her total yearly interest from the two investments was $432.50. How much did she invest at each rate?

49. Regina has scores of 93, 88, 89, and 95 on her first four math exams. What score must she get on the fifth exam to have an average of 92 or higher for the five exams?

50. It takes Angie twice as long as Amy to clean a house. How long does it take each girl by herself if they can clean the house together in 3 hours?

51. Russ started to mow the lawn, a task that usually takes him 40 minutes. After he had been working for 15 minutes, his friend Jay came along with his mower and began to help Russ. Working together, they finished the lawn in 10 minutes. How long would it have taken Jay to mow the lawn by himself?

52. Melinda invested a certain amount of money at 5% and also invested $4000 less than that amount at 3%. Her total yearly interest from the investments was $488. How much did she invest at each rate?

53. Larry drove 156 miles in one hour more than it took Mike to drive 108 miles. Mike drove at an average rate of 2 miles per hour faster than Larry. How fast did each one travel?

54. It takes Bill 2 hours longer to do a certain job than it takes Cindy. They worked together for 2 hours; then Cindy left and Bill finished the job in 1 hour. How long would it take each of them to do the job alone?

55. One leg of a right triangle is 5 centimeters longer than the other leg. The hypotenuse is 25 centimeters long. Find the length of each leg.

56. The area of a rectangle is 35 square inches. If both the length and width are increased by 3 inches, the area is increased by 45 square inches. Find the dimensions of the original rectangle.

Chapter 1   Test

For Problems 1–14, solve each equation.

1. $3(2x - 1) - 4(x + 2) = -7$

2. $10x^2 + 13x - 3 = 0$

3. $(5x + 2)^2 = 25$

4. $\dfrac{3n + 4}{4} - \dfrac{2n - 1}{10} = \dfrac{11}{20}$

5. $2x^2 - x + 4 = 0$

6. $(n - 2)(n + 7) = -18$

7. $0.06x + 0.08(1400 - x) = 100$

8. $|3x - 4| = 7$

9. $3x^2 - 2x - 2 = 0$

10. $3x^3 + 21x^2 - 54x = 0$

11. $\dfrac{x}{2x + 1} - 1 = \dfrac{-4}{7(x - 2)}$

12. $\sqrt{2x} = x - 4$

13. $\sqrt{x + 1} + 2 = \sqrt{x}$

14. $2n^{-2} + 5n^{-1} - 12 = 0$

For Problems 15–21, solve each inequality and express the solution set using interval notation.

15. $2(x - 1) - 3(3x + 1) \geq -6(x - 5)$

16. $\dfrac{x - 2}{6} - \dfrac{x + 3}{9} > -\dfrac{1}{2}$

17. $|6x - 4| < 10$

18. $|4x + 5| \geq 6$

19. $2x^2 - 9x - 5 \leq 0$

20. $\dfrac{3x - 1}{x + 2} > 0$

21. $\dfrac{x - 2}{x + 6} \geq 3$

For Problems 22–25, solve each problem.

22. How many cups of grapefruit juice must be added to 30 cups of a punch that contains 8% grapefruit juice to obtain a punch that is 10% grapefruit juice?

23. Lian can ride her bike 60 miles in one hour less time than it takes Tasya to ride 60 miles. Lian's rate is 3 miles per hour faster than Tasya's rate. Find Lian's rate.

24. Alexander invested a certain amount of money at 4.5% and also invested $2000 more than that amount at 5%. His total yearly interest from the investments was $860. How much did he invest at each rate?

25. The perimeter of a rectangle is 46 centimeters and its area is 126 square centimeters. Find the dimensions of the rectangle.

2

Coordinate Geometry and Graphing Techniques

2.1 Coordinate Geometry

2.2 Graphing Techniques: Linear Equations and Inequalities

2.3 Determining the Equation of a Line

2.4 More on Graphing

2.5 Circles, Ellipses, and Hyperbolas

René Descartes, a French philosopher and mathematician, developed a system to locate a point on a plane. That system is our current rectangular coordinate grid, called the Cartesian coordinate system, that we use for graphing.

© The Print Collector/Alamy

A section of a certain highway has a 2% grade. How many feet does it rise in a horizontal distance of 1 mile? The equation $\dfrac{2}{100} = \dfrac{Y}{5280}$ can be used to determine that the amount of rise in a horizontal distance of 1 mile is 105.6 feet. This equation is based on the concept of slope.

René Descartes, a French mathematician of the 17th century, was able to transform geometric problems into an algebraic setting so that he could use the tools of algebra to solve the problems. This merging of algebraic and geometric ideas is the foundation of a branch of mathematics called **analytic geometry,** now more commonly called **coordinate geometry.** Basically, there are two kinds of problems in coordinate geometry: (1) given an algebraic equation, find its geometric graph, and (2) given a set of conditions pertaining to a geometric graph, find its algebraic equation. We will discuss problems of both types in this chapter.

René Descartes lived only to the age of 54, but in his short life he made some great contributions to both mathematics and philosophy. You may find it interesting to browse through some of his contributions on the Internet.

2.1   Coordinate Geometry

OBJECTIVES   **1** Find the distance between two points on a number line

2 Find the distance between two points in the rectangular coordinate system

Recall from Section 0.1 that the real number line exhibits a one-to-one correspondence between the set of real numbers and the points on a line (see Figure 2.1). That is, to each real number there corresponds one and only one point on the line, and to each point on the line there corresponds one and only one real number. The number that corresponds to a particular point on the line is called the **coordinate** of that point. Also recall that the distance *between* any two points with coordinates x_1 and x_2 can be found by using either $|x_2 - x_1|$ or $|x_1 - x_2|$.

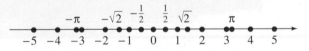

Figure 2.1

Suppose that on the number line we want to know the distance *from −2 to 6*. The *from–to* vocabulary implies a **directed distance,** which is $6 - (-2) = 8$ units. In other words, it is 8 units in a *positive direction* from −2 to 6. Likewise, the distance from 9 to −4 is $-4 - 9 = -13$; it is 13 units in a *negative direction*. In general, if x_1 and x_2 are the coordinates of two points on the number line, then the distance **from** x_1 **to** x_2 is given by $x_2 - x_1$, and the distance **from** x_2 **to** x_1 is given by $x_1 - x_2$.

Sometimes it is necessary to find the coordinate of a point located somewhere between the two given points. For example, in Figure 2.2 suppose that we want to find the coordinate, x, of the point located two-thirds of the distance *from 2 to 8*. Because the total distance from 2 to 8 is $8 - 2 = 6$ units, we can start at 2 and move $\frac{2}{3}(6) = 4$ units toward 8. Thus

$$x = 2 + \frac{2}{3}(6) = 2 + 4 = 6$$

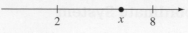

Figure 2.2

The following examples further illustrate the process of finding the coordinate of a point somewhere between two given points (see Figure 2.3).

| Problem | Solution |

(a) Three-fourths of the distance from -2 to 10

$$x = -2 + \frac{3}{4}[10 - (-2)]$$

$$= -2 + \frac{3}{4}(12)$$

$$= 7$$

Figure 2.3(a)

(b) Two-fifths of the distance from -1 to 7

$$x = -1 + \frac{2}{5}[7 - (-1)]$$

$$= -1 + \frac{2}{5}(8)$$

$$= \frac{11}{5}$$

Figure 2.3(b)

(c) One-third of the distance from 9 to 1

$$x = 9 + \frac{1}{3}(1 - 9)$$

$$= 9 + \frac{1}{3}(-8)$$

$$= \frac{19}{3}$$

Figure 2.3(c)

(d) a/b of the distance from x_1 to x_2

$$x = x_1 + \frac{a}{b}(x_2 - x_1)$$

Figure 2.3(d)

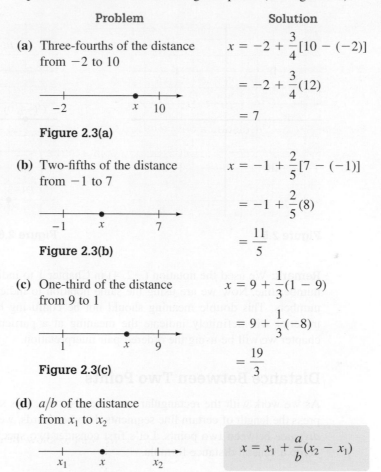

Part d indicates that a general formula can be developed for this type of problem. However, it may be easier to remember the basic approach than it is to memorize the formula.

As we saw in Chapter 1, the real number line provides a geometric model for graphing solutions of algebraic equations and inequalities involving *one variable*. For example, the solutions of $x > 2$ or $x \leq -1$ are graphed in Figure 2.4.

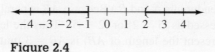

Figure 2.4

Rectangular Coordinate System

Recall from Section 0.1 that a pair of real number lines, perpendicular to each other at the point associated with zero on both lines (see Figure 2.5), can be used to exhibit a one-to-one correspondence between pairs of real numbers and points in a plane. Figure 2.6 shows examples of this correspondence.

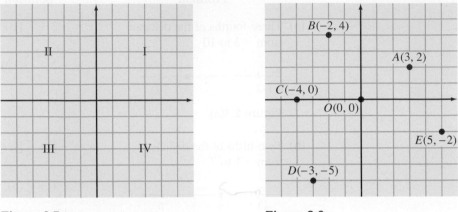

Figure 2.5   **Figure 2.6**

Remark: We used the notation $(-2, 4)$ in Chapter 1 to indicate an interval of the real number line. Now we are using the same notation to indicate an ordered pair of real numbers. This double meaning should not be confusing because the context of the material will definitely indicate the meaning at a particular time. Throughout this chapter we will be using the ordered-pair interpretation.

Distance Between Two Points

As we work with the rectangular coordinate system, it is sometimes necessary to express the length of certain line segments. In other words, we need to be able to find the *distance* between two points. Let's first consider two specific examples and then develop a general distance formula.

EXAMPLE 1

Find the distance between the points $A(2, 2)$ and $B(5, 2)$ and also between the points $C(-2, 5)$ and $D(-2, -4)$.

Solution

Let's plot the points and draw $\overline{AB}$ and $\overline{CD}$ as in Figure 2.7. (The symbol $\overline{AB}$ denotes the line segment with endpoints A and B.) Because $\overline{AB}$ is parallel to the horizontal axis, its length can be expressed as $|5 - 2|$ or $|2 - 5|$. Thus the length of $\overline{AB}$ (we will use the notation AB to represent the length of $\overline{AB}$) is $AB = 3$ units. Likewise, because $\overline{CD}$ is parallel to the vertical axis, we obtain $CD = |5 - (-4)| = 9$ units.

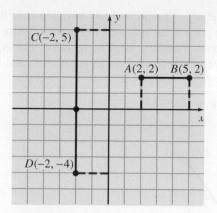

Figure 2.7

 EXAMPLE 2   Find the distance between the points $A(2, 3)$ and $B(5, 7)$.

Solution

Let's plot the points and form a right triangle using point D, as indicated in Figure 2.8. Note that the coordinates of point D are $(5, 3)$. Because $\overline{AD}$ is parallel to the horizontal axis, as in Example 1, we have $AD = |5 - 2| = 3$ units. Likewise, $\overline{DB}$ is parallel to the vertical axis, and therefore $DB = |7 - 3| = 4$ units. Applying the Pythagorean theorem, we obtain

$$(AB)^2 = (AD)^2 + (DB)^2$$
$$= 3^2 + 4^2$$
$$= 9 + 16$$
$$= 25$$

Thus

$$AB = \sqrt{25} = 5 \text{ units}$$

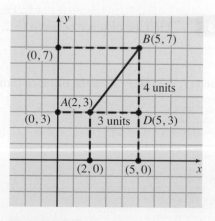

Figure 2.8

Let $P_1(x_1, y_1)$ and $P_2(x_2, y_2)$ represent any two points in the xy plane. We can form a right triangle using point R, as indicated in Figure 2.9. The coordinates of the vertex of the right angle at point R are (x_2, y_1). The length of $\overline{P_1R}$ is $|x_2 - x_1|$, and the length of $\overline{RP_2}$ is $|y_2 - y_1|$. We let d represent the length of $\overline{P_1P_2}$ and apply the Pythagorean theorem to obtain

$$d^2 = |x_2 - x_1|^2 + |y_2 - y_1|^2$$

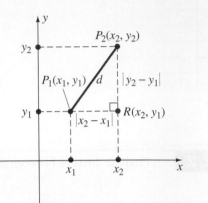

Figure 2.9

Because $|a|^2 = a^2$ for any real number a, the distance formula can be stated

$$d = \sqrt{(x_2 - x_1)^2 + (y_2 - y_1)^2}$$

It makes no difference which point you call P_1 and which you call P_2. Also, remember that if you forget the formula, there is no need to panic: form a right triangle and apply the Pythagorean theorem as we did in Example 2.

Let's consider some examples that illustrate the use of the distance formula.

EXAMPLE 3   Find the distance between $(-2, 5)$ and $(1, -1)$.

Solution

Let $(-2, 5)$ be P_1 and $(1, -1)$ be P_2. Use the distance formula to obtain

$$\begin{aligned}
d &= \sqrt{(x_2 - x_1)^2 + (y_2 - y_1)^2} \\
&= \sqrt{[1 - (-2)]^2 + (-1 - 5)^2} \\
&= \sqrt{3^2 + (-6)^2} \\
&= \sqrt{9 + 36} \\
&= \sqrt{45} = 3\sqrt{5}
\end{aligned}$$

The distance between the two points is $3\sqrt{5}$ units.

In Example 3 note the simplicity of the approach when we use the distance formula. No diagram was needed; we merely plugged in the values and did the computation. However, many times a figure *is* helpful in the analysis of the problem, as we will see in the next example.

EXAMPLE 4

Verify that the points $(-3, 6)$, $(3, 4)$, and $(1, -2)$ are vertices of an isosceles triangle. (An isosceles triangle has two sides of the same length.)

Solution

Let's plot the points and draw the triangle (see Figure 2.10). The lengths d_1, d_2, and d_3 can all be found by using the distance formula.

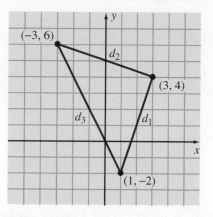

Figure 2.10

$$d_1 = \sqrt{(3 - 1)^2 + [4 - (-2)]^2}$$
$$= \sqrt{4 + 36}$$
$$= \sqrt{40} = 2\sqrt{10}$$
$$d_2 = \sqrt{(-3 - 3)^2 + (6 - 4)^2}$$
$$= \sqrt{36 + 4}$$
$$= \sqrt{40} = 2\sqrt{10}$$
$$d_3 = \sqrt{(-3 - 1)^2 + [6 - (-2)]^2}$$
$$= \sqrt{16 + 64}$$
$$= \sqrt{80} = 4\sqrt{5}$$

Because $d_1 = d_2$, it is an isosceles triangle. ∎

Points of Division of a Line Segment

Earlier in this section we discussed the process of finding the coordinate of a point on a number line, given that it is located somewhere between two other points on the line.

This same type of problem can occur in the xy plane, and the approach we used earlier can be extended to handle it. Let's consider some examples.

Classroom Example
Find the coordinates of the point P, which is three-fourths of the distance from $A(-1, 2)$ to $B(3, 10)$.

EXAMPLE 5

Find the coordinates of the point P, which is two-thirds of the distance from $A(1, 2)$ to $B(7, 5)$.

Solution

In Figure 2.11 we plotted the given points A and B and completed a figure to help us analyze the problem. To find the coordinates of point P, we can proceed as follows. Point D is two-thirds of the distance from A to C because parallel lines cut off proportional segments on every transversal that intersects the lines.

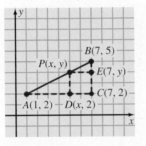

Figure 2.11

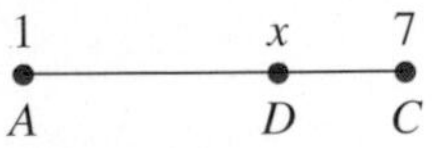

Figure 2.12

Therefore, because $\overline{AC}$ is parallel to the x axis, it can be treated as a segment of the number line (see Figure 2.12). Thus we have

$$x = 1 + \frac{2}{3}(7 - 1) = 1 + \frac{2}{3}(6) = 5$$

Figure 2.13

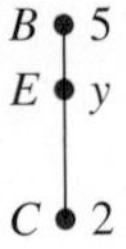

Similarly, $\overline{CB}$ is parallel to the y axis, so it can also be treated as a segment of the number line (see Figure 2.13). Thus we obtain

$$y = 2 + \frac{2}{3}(5 - 2)$$

$$= 2 + \frac{2}{3}(3) = 4$$

The point P has the coordinates $(5, 4)$.

EXAMPLE 6

Find the coordinates of the midpoint of the line segment determined by the points $P_1(x_1, y_1)$ and $P_2(x_2, y_2)$.

Solution

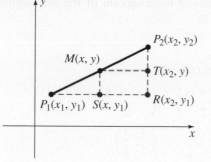

Figure 2.14

Figure 2.15

Figure 2.16

Figure 2.14 helps with the analysis of the problem. The line segment $\overline{P_1R}$ is parallel to the x axis, and $S(x, y_1)$ is the midpoint of $\overline{P_1R}$ (see Figure 2.15). Thus we can determine the x coordinate of S:

$$x = x_1 + \frac{1}{2}(x_2 - x_1)$$

$$= x_1 + \frac{1}{2}x_2 - \frac{1}{2}x_1$$

$$= \frac{1}{2}x_1 + \frac{1}{2}x_2 = \frac{x_1 + x_2}{2}$$

Similarly, $\overline{RP_2}$ is parallel to the y axis, and $T(x_2, y)$ is the midpoint of $\overline{RP_2}$ (see Figure 2.16). Therefore we can calculate the y coordinate of T:

$$y = y_1 + \frac{1}{2}(y_2 - y_1)$$

$$= y_1 + \frac{1}{2}y_2 - \frac{1}{2}y_1$$

$$= \frac{1}{2}y_1 + \frac{1}{2}y_2 = \frac{y_1 + y_2}{2}$$

Thus the coordinates of the midpoint of a line segment determined by $P_1(x_1, y_1)$ and $P_2(x_2, y_2)$ are

$$\left(\frac{x_1 + x_2}{2}, \frac{y_1 + y_2}{2} \right)$$

Classroom Example
Find the coordinates of the
midpoint of the line segment
determined by the points $(3, -2)$
and $(-11, 4)$.

EXAMPLE 7

Find the coordinates of the midpoint of the line segment determined by the points $(-2, 4)$ and $(6, -1)$.

Solution

Using the midpoint formula, we obtain

$$\left(\frac{x_1 + x_2}{2}, \frac{y_1 + y_2}{2}\right) = \left(\frac{-2 + 6}{2}, \frac{4 + (-1)}{2}\right)$$

$$= \left(\frac{4}{2}, \frac{3}{2}\right)$$

$$= \left(2, \frac{3}{2}\right)$$

We want to emphasize two ideas that emerge from Examples 5, 6, and 7. If we want to find a point of division of a line segment, then we use the same approach as in Example 5. However, for the special case of the midpoint, the formula developed in Example 6 is convenient to use.

Concept Quiz 2.1

For Problems 1–8, answer true or false.

1. The statement "the distance from x_1 to x_2" implies a directed distance.
2. For a directed distance, the distance could be negative.
3. The symbol $\overline{EF}$ denotes the line segment with endpoints E and F.
4. When applying the distance formula $\sqrt{(x_2 - x_1)^2 + (y_2 - y_1)^2}$ to find the distance between two points, you can designate either of the points as P_1.
5. The formula $\left(\dfrac{x_1 + x_2}{2}, \dfrac{y_1 + y_2}{2}\right)$ for determining the coordinates of the mid-point between two points can be described as finding the average of the x coordinates and the average of the y coordinates.
6. The distance formula $\sqrt{(x_2 - x_1)^2 + (y_2 - y_1)^2}$ can be derived by applying the Pythagorean theorem to a right triangle formed by the points $P_1(x_1, y_1)$, $P_2(x_2, y_2)$, and $R\,(x_1, y_2)$.
7. The distance between the two points (a, y) and (b, y) is $|b - a|$.
8. An isosceles triangle has three sides of the same length.

Problem Set 2.1

For Problems 1–4, find the indicated distances on a number line. **(Objective 1)**

1. From -4 to 6
2. From 5 to -14
3. From -6 to -11
4. From -7 to 10

For Problems 5–8, find the distance between the points A and B. **(Objective 1)**

5. $A\,(3, -7)$, $B\,(3, -2)$
6. $A\,(-1, 6)$, $B\,(-1, -2)$

7. A $(-4, 8)$, B $(5, 8)$

8. A $(3, -4)$, B $(-1, -4)$

For Problems 9–14, find the coordinate of the indicated point on a number line. (Objective 1)

9. Two-thirds of the distance from 1 to 10

10. Three-fourths of the distance from -2 to 14

11. One-third of the distance from -3 to 7

12. Two-fifths of the distance from -5 to 6

13. Three-fifths of the distance from -1 to -11

14. Five-sixths of the distance from 3 to -7

For Problems 15–20, find the distance between the points A and B. (Objective 2)

15. A $(4, 1)$, B $(7, 5)$ **16.** A $(-7, 5)$, B $(-2, 17)$

17. A $(-1, 4)$, B $(3, -2)$ **18.** A $(3, -5)$, B $(-4, -2)$

19. $A(2, 1)$, $B(10, 7)$ **20.** $A(-2, -1)$, $B(7, 11)$

For Problems 21–26, find the midpoint of the line segment determined by the given points. (Objective 2)

21. $A(1, -1)$, $B(3, -4)$ **22.** $A(-5, 2)$, $B(-1, 6)$

23. $A(6, -4)$, $B(9, -7)$ **24.** $A(-3, 3)$, $B(0, -3)$

25. $A\left(\dfrac{1}{2}, \dfrac{1}{3}\right)$, $B\left(-\dfrac{1}{3}, \dfrac{3}{2}\right)$

26. $A\left(-\dfrac{3}{4}, 2\right)$, $B\left(-1, -\dfrac{5}{4}\right)$

For Problems 27–36, find the coordinates of the indicated point in the xy plane. (Objective 2)

27. One-third of the distance from $(2, 3)$ to $(5, 9)$

28. Two-thirds of the distance from $(1, 4)$ to $(7, 13)$

29. Two-fifths of the distance from $(-2, 1)$ to $(8, 11)$

30. Three-fifths of the distance from $(2, -3)$ to $(-3, 8)$

31. Five-eighths of the distance from $(-1, -2)$ to $(4, -10)$

32. Seven-eighths of the distance from $(-2, 3)$ to $(-1, -9)$

33. Five-sixths of the distance from $(-7, 2)$ to $(-1, -4)$

34. Three-fourths of the distance from $(-1, -6)$ to $(-5, 2)$

35. Three-eighths of the distance from $(6, 8)$ to $(-2, 4)$

36. One-third of the distance from $(4, -1)$ to $(-3, -5)$

For Problems 37–52, solve each of the problems. (Objectives 1 and 2)

37. Find the coordinates of the point that is one-fourth of the distance from $(2, 4)$ to $(10, 13)$ by (a) using the midpoint formula twice and (b) using the same approach as for Problems 27–36.

38. If one endpoint of a line segment is $(-6, 4)$, and the midpoint of the segment is $(-2, 7)$, find the other endpoint.

39. Use the distance formula to verify that the points $(-2, 7)$, $(2, 1)$, and $(4, -2)$ lie on a straight line.

40. Use the distance formula to verify that the points $(-3, 8)$, $(7, 4)$, and $(5, -1)$ are vertices of a right triangle.

41. Verify that the points $(0, 3)$, $(2, -3)$, and $(-4, -5)$ are vertices of an isosceles triangle.

42. Verify that the points $(7, 12)$ and $(11, 18)$ divide the line segment joining $(3, 6)$ and $(15, 24)$ into three segments of equal length.

43. Find the perimeter of the triangle with vertices $(-6, -4)$, $(0, 8)$, and $(6, 5)$.

44. Verify that $(-4, 9)$, $(8, 4)$, $(3, -8)$, and $(-9, -3)$ are vertices of a square.

45. Verify that the points $(4, -5)$, $(6, 7)$, and $(-8, -3)$ lie on a circle that has its center at $(-1, 2)$.

46. Suppose that $(-2, 5)$, $(6, 3)$, and $(-4, -1)$ are three vertices of a parallelogram. How many possibilities are there for the fourth vertex? Find the coordinates of each of these points. [*Hint:* The diagonals of a parallelogram bisect each other.]

47. Find x such that the line segment determined by $(x, -2)$ and $(-2, -14)$ is 13 units long.

48. Consider the triangle with vertices $(4, -6)$, $(2, 8)$, and $(-4, 2)$. Verify that the medians of this triangle intersect at a point that is two-thirds of the distance from a vertex to the midpoint of the opposite side. (A **median** of the triangle is the line segment determined by a vertex and the midpoint of the opposite side. Every triangle has three medians.)

49. Consider the line segment determined by $A(-1, 2)$ and $B(5, 11)$. Find the coordinates of a point P such that $\overline{AP}/\overline{PB} = 2/1$.

50. Verify that the midpoint of the hypotenuse of the right triangle formed by the points $A(4, 0)$, $B(0, 0)$, and $C(0, 6)$ is the same distance from all three vertices.

51. Consider the parallelogram determined by the points $A(1, 1)$, $B(5, 1)$, $C(6, 4)$, and $D(2, 4)$. Verify that the diagonals of this parallelogram bisect each other.

52. Consider the quadrilateral determined by the points $A(5, -3)$, $B(3, 4)$, $C(-2, 1)$, and $D(-1, -2)$. Verify that the line segments joining the midpoints of the opposite sides of this quadrilateral bisect each other.

Thoughts Into Words

53. Consider the line segment determined by the two endpoints $A(2, 1)$ and $B(5, 10)$. Describe how you would find the coordinates of the point that is two-thirds of the distance from A to B. Then describe how you would find the point that is two-thirds of the distance from B to A.

54. How would you define the term "coordinate geometry" to a group of elementary algebra students?

Further Investigations

55. The tools of coordinate geometry can be used to prove various geometric properties. For example, consider the following way of proving that the diagonals of a rectangle are equal in length.

First we draw a rectangle and display it on coordinate axes by using a convenient position for the origin. Now we can use the distance formula to find the lengths of the diagonals $\overline{AC}$ and $\overline{BD}$ (see Figure 2.17):

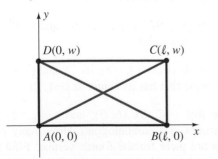

Figure 2.17

$$AC = \sqrt{(l - 0)^2 + (w - 0)^2} = \sqrt{l^2 + w^2}$$
$$BD = \sqrt{(0 - l)^2 + (w - 0)^2} = \sqrt{l^2 + w^2}$$

Thus $AC = BD$, and we have proved that the diagonals are equal in length. Prove each of the following:

(a) The diagonals of an isosceles trapezoid are equal in length.

(b) The line segment joining the midpoints of two sides of a triangle is equal in length to one-half of the third side.

(c) The midpoint of the hypotenuse of a right triangle is equally distant from all three vertices.

(d) The diagonals of a parallelogram bisect each other.

(e) The line segments joining the midpoints of the opposite sides of a quadrilateral bisect each other.

(f) The medians of a triangle intersect at a point that is two-thirds of the distance from a vertex to the midpoint of the opposite side. (See Problem 48.)

2.2	**Graphing Techniques: Linear Equations and Inequalities**

OBJECTIVES   **1** Graph linear equations

2 Find the *x* and *y* intercepts for the graph of a linear equation

3 Graph linear inequalities

We have been showing different graphs throughout the text to emphasize the relationship between geometric graphs and solutions of algebraic equations. You have not been required to actually sketch any graphs. In this chapter we will discuss some specific graphing techniques and get you involved in the graphing process.

First, let's briefly review some basic ideas by considering the solutions for the equation $y = x + 2$. A **solution** of an equation in two variables is an ordered pair of real numbers that satisfy the equation. When the variables are x and y, the ordered pairs are of the form (x, y). We see that $(1, 3)$ is a solution for $y = x + 2$ because replacing x by 1 and y by 3 yields a true numerical statement: $3 = 1 + 2$. Likewise, $(-2, 0)$ is a solution because $0 = -2 + 2$ is a true statement. We can find an infinite number of pairs of real numbers that satisfy $y = x + 2$ by arbitrarily choosing values for x and, for each value of x chosen, determining a corresponding value for y. Let's use a table to record some of the solutions for $y = x + 2$.

Choose *x*	Determine *y* from *y* = *x* + 2	Solutions for *y* = *x* + 2
0	2	(0, 2)
1	3	(1, 3)
3	5	(3, 5)
5	7	(5, 7)
−2	0	(−2, 0)
−4	−2	(−4, −2)
−6	−4	(−6, −4)

Plotting the points associated with the ordered pairs from the table produces Figure 2.18(a). The straight line that contains the points is called the **graph of the equation** $y = x + 2$ [see Figure 2.18(b)].

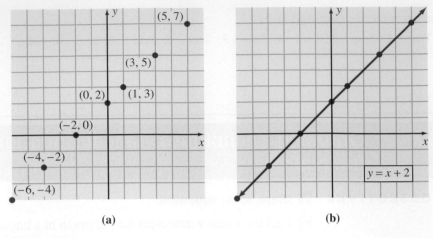

(a) **(b)**

Figure 2.18

Graphing Linear Equations

Probably the most valuable graphing technique is the ability to recognize the kind of graph that is produced by a particular type of equation. For example, from previous mathematics courses you may remember that any equation of the form $Ax + By = C$, where A, B, and C are constants (A and B not both zero) and x and y are variables, is a **linear equation** and that its graph is a **straight line.** Two comments about this description of a linear equation should be made. First, the choice of x and y as variables is arbitrary; any two letters can be used to represent the variables. For example, an equation such as $3r + 2s = 9$ is also a linear equation in two variables. To avoid constantly changing the labeling of the coordinate axes when graphing equations, we will use the same two variables, x and y, in all equations. Second, the statement "any equation of the form $Ax + By = C$" technically means any equation of that form or equivalent to that form. For example, the equation $y = 2x - 1$ is equivalent to $-2x + y = -1$ and therefore is linear and produces a straight-line graph.

Before we graph some linear equations, let's define in general the **intercepts** of a graph.

> The x coordinates of the points that a graph has in common with the x axis are called the **x intercepts** of the graph. (To compute the x intercepts, let $y = 0$ and solve for x.)
>
> The y coordinates of the points that a graph has in common with the y axis are called the **y intercepts** of the graph. (To compute the y intercepts, let $x = 0$ and solve for y.)

Once we know that any equation of the form $Ax + By = C$ produces a straight-line graph, along with the fact that two points determine a straight line, graphing linear equations becomes a simple process. We can find two points on the graph and draw the line determined by those two points. Usually the two points that involve the intercepts are easy to find, and generally it's a good idea to plot a third point to serve as a check.

EXAMPLE 1   Graph $3x - 2y = 6$.

Solution

First let's find the intercepts. If $x = 0$, then

$$3(0) - 2y = 6$$
$$-2y = 6$$
$$y = -3$$

Therefore the point $(0, -3)$ is on the line. If $y = 0$, then

$$3x - 2(0) = 6$$
$$3x = 6$$
$$x = 2$$

Thus the point $(2, 0)$ is also on the line. Now let's find a check point. If $x = -2$, then

$$3(-2) - 2y = 6$$
$$-6 - 2y = 6$$
$$-2y = 12$$
$$y = -6$$

Thus the point $(-2, -6)$ is also on the line. In Figure 2.19 the three points are plotted, and the graph of $3x - 2y = 6$ is drawn.

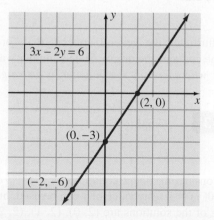

Figure 2.19

Note in Example 1 that we did not solve the given equation for y in terms of x or for x in terms of y. Because we know the graph is a straight line, there is no need for an extensive table of values; thus there is no need to change the form of the original equation. Furthermore, the point $(-2, -6)$ served as a check point. If it had not been on the line determined by the two intercepts, then we would have known that we had made an error in finding the intercepts.

Classroom Example

Graph $y = \dfrac{2}{3}x$.

EXAMPLE 2   Graph $y = -2x$.

Solution

If $x = 0$, then $y = -2(0) = 0$, so the origin $(0, 0)$ is on the line. Because both intercepts are determined by the point $(0, 0)$, another point is necessary to determine the line. Then a third point should be found as a check point. The graph of $y = -2x$ is shown in Figure 2.20.

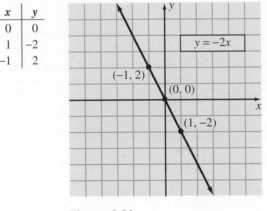

x	y
0	0
1	-2
-1	2

Figure 2.20

Example 2 illustrates the general concept that for the form $Ax + By = C$, if $C = 0$, then the line contains the origin. Stated another way, *the graph of any equation of the form $y = kx$, where k is any real number, is a straight line containing the origin.*

Classroom Example

Graph $y = 4$.

EXAMPLE 3   Graph $x = 2$.

Solution

Because we are considering linear equations *in two variables,* the equation $x = 2$ is equivalent to $x + 0(y) = 2$. Any value of y can be used, but the x value must always be 2. Therefore some of the solutions are $(2, 0)$, $(2, 1)$, $(2, 2)$, $(2, -1)$, and $(2, -2)$. The graph of $x = 2$ is the vertical line shown in Figure 2.21.

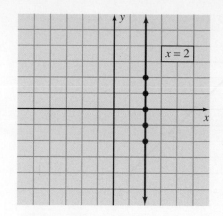

Figure 2.21

Remark: It is important to realize that we are presently graphing **equations in two variables** (graphing in two-dimensional space). Thus as shown in Example 3, the graph of $x = 2$ is a line. If we were graphing **equations in one variable** (graphing on a number line), then the graph of $x = 2$ would be a dot at 2. In subsequent mathematics courses, you may do some graphing of **equations in three variables** (graphing in three-dimensional space). At that time, the graph of $x = 2$ will be a plane.

In general, the graph of any equation of the form $Ax + By = C$, where $A = 0$ or $B = 0$ (not both), is a line parallel to one of the axes. More specifically, **any equation of the form $x = a$,** where a is any nonzero real number, is a *line parallel to the y axis* having an x intercept of a. **Any equation of the form $y = b$,** where b is a nonzero real number, is a *line parallel to the x axis* having a y intercept of b.

Graphing Linear Inequalities

Linear inequalities in two variables are of the form $Ax + By > C$ or $Ax + By < C$, where A, B, and C are real numbers. (*Combined linear equality and inequality statements* are of the form $Ax + By \geq C$ or $Ax + By \leq C$.) Graphing linear inequalities is almost as easy as graphing linear equations. The following discussion will lead us to a simple, step-by-step process.

Let's consider the following equation and related inequalities:

$$x + y = 2 \quad x + y > 2 \quad x + y < 2$$

The straight line in Figure 2.22 is the graph of $x + y = 2$. The line divides the plane into two half-planes, one above the line and one below the line. For each point in the half-plane *above* the line, the ordered pair (x, y) associated with the point satisfies the inequality $x + y > 2$. For example, the ordered pair $(3, 4)$ produces the true statement $3 + 4 > 2$. Likewise, for each point in the half-plane *below* the line, the ordered pair (x, y) associated with the point satisfies the inequality $x + y < 2$. For example, $(-3, 1)$ produces the true statement $-3 + 1 < 2$.

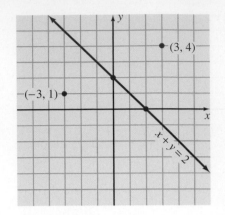

Figure 2.22

Now let's use these ideas to help graph some inequalities.

Classroom Example
Graph $4x + y > -4$.

EXAMPLE 4   Graph $x - 2y > 4$.

Solution

First, we graph $x - 2y = 4$ as a dashed line because equality is not included in $x - 2y > 4$ (see Figure 2.23). Second, because *all* of the points in a specific half-plane satisfy either $x - 2y > 4$ or $x - 2y < 4$, we must try a *test point*. For example, consider the origin:

$$x - 2y > 4 \quad \text{becomes } 0 - 2(0) > 4, \text{ which is a false statement}$$

Because the ordered pairs in the half-plane containing the origin do not satisfy $x - 2y > 4$, the ordered pairs in the other half-plane must satisfy it. Therefore the graph of $x - 2y > 4$ is the half-plane *below* the line, as indicated by the shaded portion in Figure 2.24.

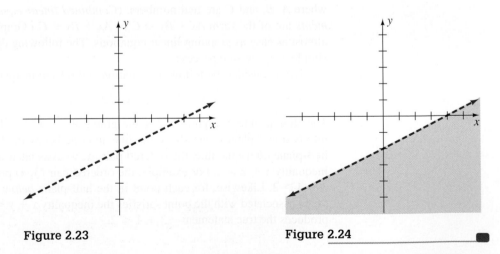

Figure 2.23   **Figure 2.24**

To graph a linear inequality, we suggest the following steps:

1. Graph the corresponding equality. Use a solid line if equality is included in the original statement and a dashed line if equality is not included.

2. Choose a *test point* not on the line and substitute its coordinates into the inequality. (The origin is a convenient point if it is not on the line.)

3. The graph of the original inequality is
   a. the half-plane containing the test point if the inequality is satisfied by that point;
   b. the half-plane not containing the test point if the inequality is not satisfied by the point.

Classroom Example
Graph $3x - y \leq 3$.

EXAMPLE 5   Graph $2x + 3y \geq -6$.

Solution

Step 1   Graph $2x + 3y = -6$ as a solid line (see Figure 2.25).

Step 2   Choose the origin as a test point:

$$2x + 3y \geq -6 \quad \text{becomes} \quad 2(0) + 3(0) \geq -6$$

which is true.

Step 3   The test point satisfies the given inequality, so all points in the same half-plane as the test point satisfy it. The graph of $2x + 3y \geq -6$ is the line and the half-plane above the line (see Figure 2.25).

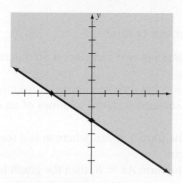

Figure 2.25

Classroom Example
Use a graphing utility to obtain a graph of the line
$3.4x - 4.1y = 10.2$.

EXAMPLE 6

Use a graphing utility to obtain a graph of the line $2.1x + 5.3y = 7.9$.

Solution

First, we need to solve the equation for y in terms of x. (If you are using a computer for this problem, you may not need to change the form of the given equation. Some software packages will allow you to graph two-variable equations without solving for y.)

$$2.1x + 5.3y = 7.9$$
$$5.3y = 7.9 - 2.1x$$
$$y = \frac{7.9 - 2.1x}{5.3}$$

Now we can enter the expression $\dfrac{7.9 - 2.1x}{5.3}$ for Y_1 and obtain the graph as shown in Figure 2.26.

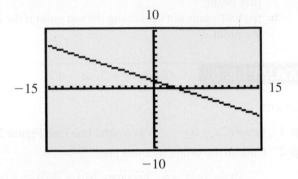

Figure 2.26

Concept Quiz 2.2

For Problems 1–8, answer true or false.

1. A solution of an equation in two variables is an ordered pair of real numbers that satisfies the equation.
2. The equation $y = x + 5$ has a finite number of solutions.
3. The plot of points associated with the solutions of an equation is called a graph of the equation.
4. If an equation is of the form $y = mx$, where m is a real number, its graph will pass through the origin.
5. If an equation is of the form $Ax = B$, then the graph is a line parallel to the x axis.
6. The graph of the solution of $2x - y > 4$ is either all the points in the half plane above the line $2x - y = 4$ or all the points in the half plane below the line $2x - y = 4$.
7. When graphing in two-dimensional space, the graph of the equation $x = 2$ is one point at $(2, 0)$.
8. When graphing in the rectangular coordinate system, the graph of $x > 0$ is all the points in quadrant I and quadrant II.

Problem Set 2.2

For Problems 1–16, find the x and y intercepts and graph each linear equation. **(Objectives 1 and 2)**

1. $x - 2y = 4$

2. $2x + y = -4$

3. $3x + 2y = 6$

4. $2x - 3y = 6$

5. $4x - 5y = 20$

6. $5x + 4y = 20$

7. $x - y = 3$

8. $-x + y = 4$

9. $y = 3x - 1$

10. $y = -2x + 3$

11. $y = -x$

12. $y = 4x$

13. $x = 0$

14. $y = -1$

15. $y = \dfrac{2}{3}x$

16. $y = -\dfrac{1}{2}x$

17. $y = 4$

18. $x = -3$

19. $y = -\dfrac{1}{5}x - 2$

20. $y = \dfrac{1}{3}x + 2$

21. $2x - y = 0$

22. $5x - 2y = 0$

23. $x = -2$

24. $y = 2$

For Problems 25–46, graph each linear inequality. **(Objective 3)**

25. $x + 2y > 4$

26. $2x - y < -4$

27. $3x - 2y < 6$

28. $2x + 3y < 6$

29. $2x + 5y \le 10$

30. $4x + 5y \le 20$

31. $y > -x - 1$

32. $y < 3x - 2$

33. $y \le -x$

34. $y \ge x$

35. $x + 2y < 0$

36. $3x - y > 0$

37. $x > -1$

38. $y < 3$

39. $y < \dfrac{2}{3}x - 4$

40. $y > \dfrac{5}{2}x - 1$

41. $y \ge -\dfrac{1}{2}x + 6$

42. $y \le \dfrac{1}{3}x + 2$

43. $x + 4 > 0$

44. $y \le 1$

45. $3x - y < 0$

46. $x + 3y \ge 0$

Thoughts Into Words

47. Explain how you would graph the inequality $-x + 2y > -4$.

48. What is the graph of the disjunction $x = 0$ *or* $y = 0$? What is the graph of the conjunction $x = 0$ *and* $y = 0$? Explain your answers.

Further Investigations

From our work with absolute value, we know that $|x + y| = 4$ is equivalent to $x + y = 4$ or $x + y = -4$. Therefore the graph of $|x + y| = 4$ is the two lines $x + y = 4$ and $x + y = -4$. For Problems 49–54, graph each equation.

49. $|x - y| = 2$

50. $|2x + y| = 1$

51. $|x - 2y| \le 4$

52. $|3x - 2y| \ge 6$

53. $|2x + 3y| > 6$

54. $|5x + 2y| < 10$

From the definition of absolute value, the equation $y = |x| + 2$ becomes $y = x + 2$ for $x \geq 0$ and $y = -x + 2$ for $x < 0$. Therefore the graph of $y = |x| + 2$ is as shown in Figure 2.27. For Problems 55–60, graph each equation.

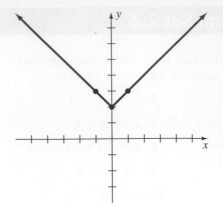

55. $y = |x| - 1$

56. $y = |x| + 1$

57. $y = |x + 2|$

58. $y = |x - 1|$

59. $y = 2|x|$

60. $y = \dfrac{1}{3}|x|$

Figure 2.27

Graphing Calculator Activities

The following problems are designed to lay some groundwork for concepts we will present in the next section. Set your boundaries so that the distance between tick marks is the same on both axes.

61. (a) Graph $y = 4x$, $y = 4x - 3$, $y = 4x + 2$, and $y = 4x + 5$ on the same set of axes. Do they appear to be parallel lines?

(b) Graph $y = -2x + 1$, $y = -2x + 4$, $y = -2x - 2$, and $y = -2x - 5$ on the same set of axes. Do they appear to be parallel lines?

(c) Graph $y = -\dfrac{1}{2}x + 3$, $y = -\dfrac{1}{2}x + 1$, $y = -\dfrac{1}{2}x - 1$ and $y = -\dfrac{1}{2}x - 4$ on the same set of axes. Do they appear to be parallel lines?

(d) Graph $2x + 5y = 1$, $2x + 5y = -3$, $2x + 5y = 4$, and $2x + 5y = -5$ on the same set of axes. Do they appear to be parallel lines?

(e) Graph $3x - 4y = 7$, $-3x + 4y = 8$, $3x - 4y = -2$, and $4x - 3y = 6$ on the same set of axes. Do they appear to be parallel lines?

(f) On the basis of your results in parts a–e, make a statement about how we can recognize parallel lines from their equations.

62. (a) Graph $y = 4x$ and $y = -\dfrac{1}{4}x$ on the same set of axes. Do they appear to be perpendicular lines?

(b) Graph $y = 3x$ and $y = \dfrac{1}{3}x$ on the same set of axes. Do they appear to be perpendicular lines?

(c) Graph $y = \dfrac{2}{5}x - 1$ and $y = -\dfrac{5}{2}x + 2$ on the same set of axes. Do they appear to be perpendicular lines?

(d) Graph $y = \dfrac{3}{4}x - 3$, $y = \dfrac{4}{3}x + 2$, and $y = -\dfrac{4}{3}x + 2$ on the same set of axes. Does there appear to be a pair of perpendicular lines?

(e) On the basis of your results in parts a–d, make a statement about how we can recognize perpendicular lines from their equations.

63. For each of the following pairs of equations, (1) predict whether they represent parallel lines, perpendicular lines, or lines that intersect but are not perpendicular, and (2) graph each pair of lines to check your prediction.

(a) $5.2x + 3.3y = 9.4$ and $5.2x + 3.3y = 12.6$

(b) $1.3x - 4.7y = 3.4$ and $1.3x - 4.7y = 11.6$

(c) $2.7x + 3.9y = 1.4$ and $2.7x - 3.9y = 8.2$

(d) $5x - 7y = 17$ and $7x + 5y = 19$

(e) $9x + 2y = 14$ and $2x + 9y = 17$

(f) $2.1x + 3.4y = 11.7$ and $3.4x - 2.1y = 17.3$

Answers to the Concept Quiz

1. True **2.** False **3.** True **4.** True **5.** False **6.** True **7.** False **8.** False

2.3 Determining the Equation of a Line

OBJECTIVES

1. Find the slope of a line determined by two points
2. Write the equation of a line, given a slope and a point contained in the line
3. Write the equation of a line, given two points contained in the line
4. Write the equation of a line parallel or perpendicular to another line and containing a specified point
5. Solve application problems involving the slope of a line

As we stated earlier, there are basically two types of problems in coordinate geometry: given an algebraic equation, find its geometric graph, and given a set of conditions pertaining to a geometric figure, find its algebraic equation. In the previous section we considered some of the first type of problem; that is, we did some graphing. Now we want to consider some problems of the second type that deal specifically with straight lines; in other words, given certain facts about a line, we need to be able to determine its algebraic equation.

As we work with straight lines, it is often helpful to be able to refer to the *steepness* or *slant* of a particular line. The concept of *slope* is used as a measure of the slant of a line. The **slope** of a line is the ratio of the vertical change of distance to the horizontal change of distance as we move from one point on a line to another. Consider the line in Figure 2.28. From point A to point B there is a vertical change of two units and a horizontal change of three units; therefore the slope of the line is $\frac{2}{3}$.

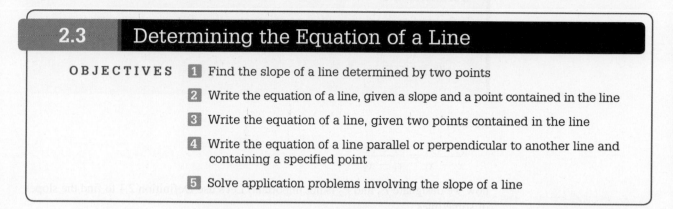

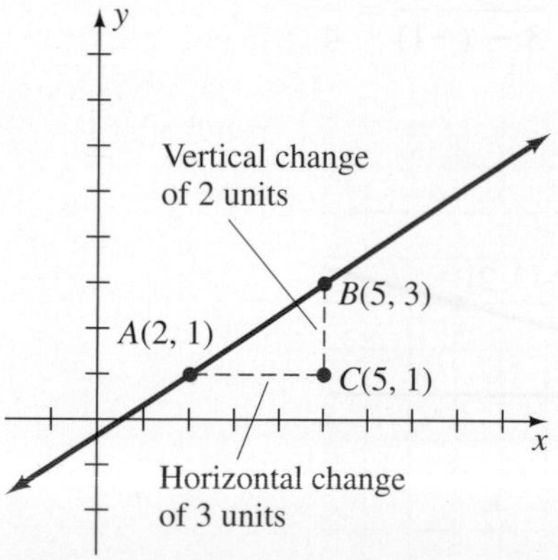

Figure 2.28

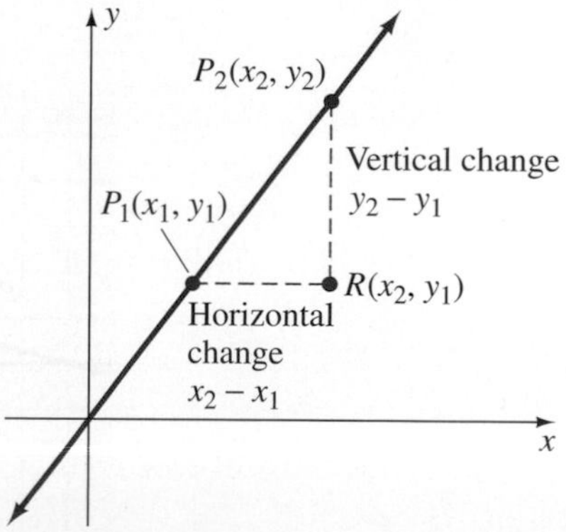

Figure 2.29

A precise definition for slope can be given by considering the coordinates of the points P_1, P_2, and R in Figure 2.29. The horizontal change of distance as we move from P_1 to P_2 is $x_2 - x_1$, and the vertical change is $y_2 - y_1$. Thus we have the following definition.

Definition 2.1

If P_1 and P_2 are any two different points on a line, P_1 with coordinates (x_1, y_1) and P_2 with coordinates (x_2, x_2), then the **slope** of the line (denoted by m) is

$$m = \frac{y_2 - y_1}{x_2 - x_1}, \quad x_2 \neq x_1$$

Because

$$\frac{y_2 - y_1}{x_2 - x_1} = \frac{y_1 - y_2}{x_1 - x_2}$$

how we designate P_1 and P_2 is not important. Let's use Definition 2.1 to find the slopes of some lines.

Classroom Example
Find the slope of the line determined by the points $(-4, 3)$ and $(2, 0)$ and graph the line.

EXAMPLE 1

Find the slope of the line determined by each of the following pairs of points and graph each line.

(a) $(-1, 1)$ and $(3, 2)$
(b) $(4, -2)$ and $(-1, 5)$
(c) $(2, -3)$ and $(-3, -3)$

Solutions

(a) Let $(-1, 1)$ be P_1 and $(3, 2)$ be P_2 (see Figure 2.30):

$$m = \frac{y_2 - y_1}{x_2 - x_1} = \frac{2 - 1}{3 - (-1)} = \frac{1}{4}$$

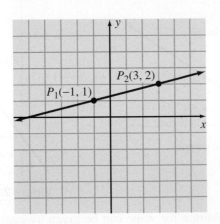

Figure 2.30

(b) Let $(4, -2)$ be P_1 and $(-1, 5)$ be P_2 (see Figure 2.31):

$$m = \frac{5 - (-2)}{-1 - 4} = \frac{7}{-5} = -\frac{7}{5}$$

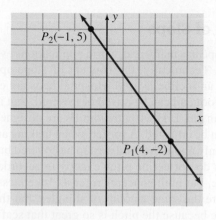

Figure 2.31

(c) Let $(2, -3)$ be P_1 and $(-3, -3)$ be P_2 (see Figure 2.32):

$$m = \frac{-3 - (-3)}{-3 - 2} = \frac{0}{-5} = 0$$

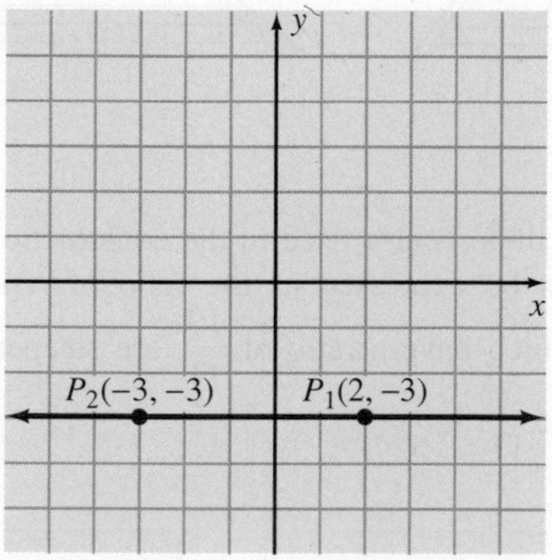

Figure 2.32

The three parts of Example 1 illustrate the three basic possibilities for slope; that is, the slope of a line can be positive, negative, or zero. A line that has a positive slope rises as we move from left to right, as in Figure 2.30. A line that has a negative slope falls as we move from left to right, as in Figure 2.31. A horizontal line, as in Figure 2.32, has a slope of zero. Finally, we need to realize that **the concept of slope is undefined for vertical lines.** This is because, for any vertical line, the horizontal change is zero as we move from one point on the line to another. Thus the ratio $(y_2 - y_1)/(x_2 - x_1)$ will have a denominator of zero and be undefined. Hence the restriction $x_2 \neq x_1$ is included in Definition 2.1.

Don't forget that **the slope of a line is a ratio,** the ratio of vertical change to horizontal change. For example, a slope of $\frac{2}{3}$ means that for every two units of vertical change, there must be a corresponding three units of horizontal change.

Applications of Slope

The concept of slope has many real-world applications even though the word "slope" is often not used. Technically, the concept of slope applies in most situations in which the idea of an incline is used. Hospital beds are constructed so that both the head end and the foot end can be raised or lowered; that is, the slope of either end of the bed can be changed. Likewise, treadmills are designed so that the incline (slope) of the platform can be adjusted. A roofer, when making an estimate to replace a roof, is concerned not only about the total area to be covered but also about the pitch of the roof. (Contractors do not define pitch exactly in accordance with the mathematical definition of slope, but both concepts refer to "steepness.") In Figure 2.33, the two roofs might require the same amount of shingles, but the roof on the left will take longer to complete because the pitch is so great that scaffolding will be required.

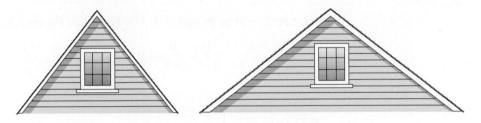

Figure 2.33

The concept of slope is also used in the construction of stairways. The steepness (slope) of stairs can be expressed as the ratio of *rise* to *run*. In Figure 2.34 the stairs on the left, which have a ratio of $\frac{10}{11}$, are steeper than the stairs on the right, which have a ratio of $\frac{7}{11}$.

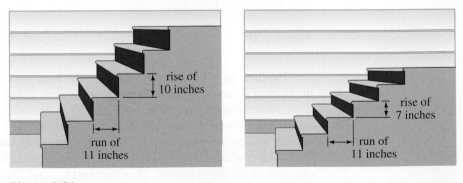

rise of 10 inches

run of 11 inches

rise of 7 inches

run of 11 inches

Figure 2.34

In highway construction, the word *grade* is used to describe the slope. For example, the highway in Figure 2.35 is said to have a grade of 17%. This means that for every horizontal distance of 100 feet, the highway rises or drops 17 feet. In other words, the slope of the highway is $\dfrac{17}{100}$.

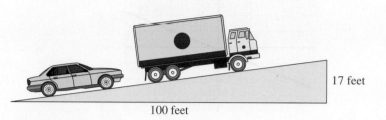

17 feet

100 feet

Figure 2.35

EXAMPLE 2

A certain highway has a 3% grade. How many feet does it rise in a horizontal distance of 1 mile?

Solution

A 3% grade means a slope of $\dfrac{3}{100}$. Therefore if we let y represent the unknown vertical distance and use the fact that 1 mile = 5280 feet, we can set up and solve the following proportion:

$$\frac{3}{100} = \frac{y}{5280}$$
$$100y = 3(5280) = 15{,}840$$
$$y = 158.4$$

The highway rises 158.4 feet in a horizontal distance of 1 mile. ▪

Equations of Lines

Now let's consider some techniques for determining the equation of a line when given certain facts about the line.

EXAMPLE 3

Find the equation of the line that has a slope of $\dfrac{2}{5}$ and contains the point $(3, 1)$.

Solution

First, let's draw the line and record the given information, as in Figure 2.36. Then we choose a point (x, y) that represents any point on the line other than the given point $(3, 1)$. The slope determined by $(3, 1)$ and (x, y) is to be $\dfrac{2}{5}$. Thus

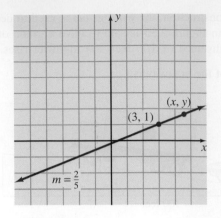

Figure 2.36

$$\frac{y-1}{x-3} = \frac{2}{5}$$

$$2(x-3) = 5(y-1)$$

$$2x - 6 = 5y - 5$$

$$2x - 5y = 1$$

EXAMPLE 4

Find the equation of the line determined by $(1, -2)$ and $(-3, 4)$.

Solution

First, let's draw the line determined by the two given points, as in Figure 2.37. These two points determine the slope of the line.

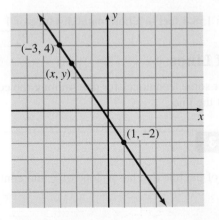

Figure 2.37

$$m = \frac{4 - (-2)}{-3 - 1} = \frac{6}{-4} = -\frac{3}{2}$$

Now we can use the same approach as in Example 3. We form an equation using one of the two given points, a point (x, y), and a slope of $-\dfrac{3}{2}$:

$$\frac{y + 2}{x - 1} = \frac{3}{-2}$$
$$3(x - 1) = -2(y + 2)$$
$$3x - 3 = -2y - 4$$
$$3x + 2y = -1$$

Classroom Example
Find the equation of a line that has a slope of $-\dfrac{2}{3}$ and a y intercept of -1.

EXAMPLE 5

Find the equation of the line that has a slope of $\dfrac{1}{4}$ and a y intercept of 2.

Solution

A y intercept of 2 means that the point $(0, 2)$ is on the line (see Figure 2.38). Choosing a point (x, y), we can proceed as in the previous examples:

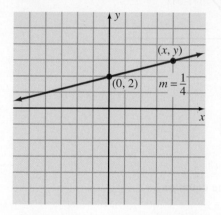

Figure 2.38

$$\frac{y - 2}{x - 0} = \frac{1}{4}$$
$$1(x - 0) = 4(y - 2)$$
$$x = 4y - 8$$
$$x - 4y = -8$$

At this point you might pause for a moment and look back over Examples 3, 4, and 5. Note that we used the same basic approach in all three examples: We chose a point (x, y) and used it to determine the equation that satisfies the conditions stated in the problem. We will use this same approach later with figures other than straight lines. Furthermore, you should realize that this approach can be used to develop some general forms of equations of straight lines.

Point–Slope Form

EXAMPLE 6

Find the equation of the line that has a slope of m and contains the point (x_1, y_1).

Solution

Choosing (x, y) to represent another point on the line (see Figure 2.39), we can give the slope of the line:

$$m = \frac{y - y_1}{x - x_1}, \quad x \neq x_1$$

from which we obtain

$$y - y_1 = m(x - x_1)$$

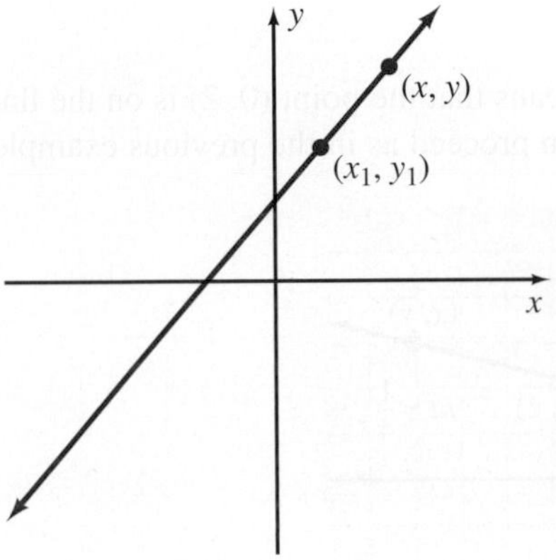

Figure 2.39

We refer to the equation

$$y - y_1 = m(x - x_1)$$

as the **point–slope form** of the equation of a straight line. Therefore, instead of using the approach of Example 3, we can substitute information into the point–slope form to write the equation of a line with a given slope that contains a given point. For example, the equation of the line that has a slope of $\frac{3}{5}$ and contains the point $(2, 4)$ can be determined this way. We substitute $(2, 4)$ for (x_1, y_1) and $\frac{3}{5}$ for m in the point–slope equation:

$$y - 4 = \frac{3}{5}(x - 2)$$

$$5(y - 4) = 3(x - 2)$$

$$5y - 20 = 3x - 6$$

$$-14 = 3x - 5y$$

Slope–Intercept Form

EXAMPLE 7

Find the equation of the line that has a slope of m and a y intercept of b.

Solution

A y intercept of b means that $(0, b)$ is on the line (see Figure 2.40). Therefore, using the point–slope form with $(x_1, y_1) = (0, b)$, we obtain

$$y - y_1 = m(x - x_1)$$
$$y - b = m(x - 0)$$
$$y - b = mx$$
$$y = mx + b$$

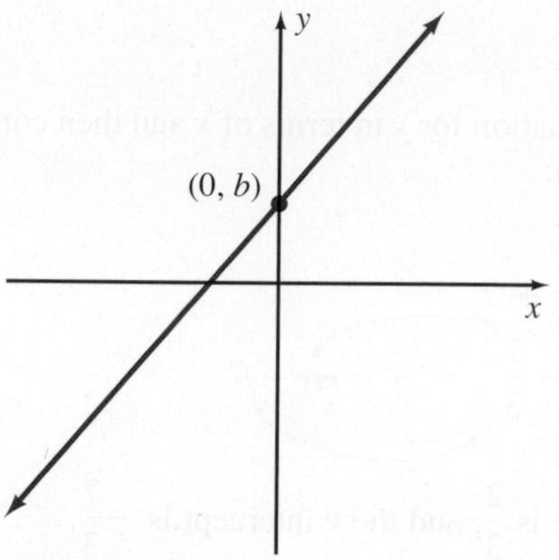

Figure 2.40

We refer to the equation

$$y = mx + b$$

as the **slope–intercept form** of the equation of a straight line. It can be used for two primary purposes, as the next two examples illustrate.

Classroom Example
Find the equation of a line that has a slope of $\dfrac{3}{5}$ and a y intercept of 4.

EXAMPLE 8

Find the equation of the line that has a slope of $\dfrac{1}{4}$ and a y intercept of 2.

Solution

This is a restatement of Example 5, but this time we will use the slope–intercept form $(y = mx + b)$ of the equation of a line to write its equation. Because $m = \dfrac{1}{4}$ and $b = 2$, we obtain

$$y = mx + b$$

$$y = \frac{1}{4}x + 2$$

$$4y = x + 8$$

$$-8 = x - 4y \qquad \text{Same result as in Example 5}$$

Remark: Sometimes we leave linear equations in slope–intercept form. We did not do so in Example 8 because we wanted to show that it was the same result as in Example 5.

Classroom Example
Find the slope and y intercept of
the line that has an equation
$x + 3y = -6$.

EXAMPLE 9

Find the slope and y intercept of the line that has an equation $2x - 3y = 7$.

Solution

We can solve the equation for y in terms of x and then compare the result to the general slope–intercept form.

$$2x - 3y = 7$$

$$-3y = -2x + 7$$

$$y = \frac{2}{3}x - \frac{7}{3} \qquad y = mx + b$$

The slope of the line is $\frac{2}{3}$, and the y intercept is $-\frac{7}{3}$.

In general, **if the equation of a nonvertical line is written in slope–intercept form, the coefficient of x is the slope of the line, and the constant term is the y intercept.**

Parallel and Perpendicular Lines

Because the concept of slope is used to indicate the slant of a line, it seems reasonable to expect slope to be related to the concepts of parallelism and perpendicularity. Such is the case, and the following two properties summarize this link.

> ### Property 2.1
>
> If two nonvertical lines have slopes of m_1 and m_2, then
>
> **1.** The two lines are parallel if and only if $m_1 = m_2$.
> **2.** The two lines are perpendicular if and only if $m_1 m_2 = -1$.

We will test your ingenuity in devising proofs of these properties in the next problem set; here we will illustrate their use.

Classroom Example
(a) Verify that the graphs of
$2x - y = 4$ and
$4x - 2y = -4$ are parallel
lines.
(b) Verify that the graphs of
$x + 2y = 4$ and
$4x - 2y = -6$ are
perpendicular lines.

EXAMPLE 10

(a) Verify that the graphs of $3x + 2y = 9$ and $6x + 4y = 19$ are parallel lines.

(b) Verify that the graphs of $5x - 3y = 12$ and $3x + 5y = 27$ are perpendicular lines.

Solution

(a) Let's change each equation to slope–intercept form.

$$3x + 2y = 9 \longrightarrow 2y = -3x + 9$$

$$y = -\frac{3}{2}x + \frac{9}{2}$$

$$6x + 4y = 19 \longrightarrow 4y = -6x + 19$$

$$y = -\frac{6}{4}x + \frac{19}{4}$$

$$y = -\frac{3}{2}x + \frac{19}{4}$$

The two lines have the same slope but different y intercepts. Therefore they are parallel.

(b) Change each equation to slope–intercept form.

$$5x - 3y = 12 \longrightarrow -3y = -5x + 12$$

$$y = \frac{5}{3}x - 4$$

$$3x + 5y = 27 \longrightarrow 5y = -3x + 27$$

$$y = -\frac{3}{5}x + \frac{27}{5}$$

Because $\left(\dfrac{5}{3}\right)\left(-\dfrac{3}{5}\right) = -1$, the product of the two slopes is -1, and the lines are perpendicular.

Remark: The statement "the product of two slopes is -1" is equivalent to saying that the two slopes are **negative reciprocals** of each other, that is, $m_1 = -1/m_2$.

Classroom Example
Find the equation of the line that
contains the point $(-2, 1)$ and is
parallel to the line with the
equation $3x + y = 1$.

EXAMPLE 11

Find the equation of the line that contains the point $(-1, 2)$ and is parallel to the line with the equation $2x - y = 4$.

Solution

First, we draw Figure 2.41 to help in our analysis of the problem. Because the line through $(-1, 2)$ is to be parallel to the given line, it must have the same slope. Let's find the slope by changing $2x - y = 4$ to slope–intercept form:

$$2x - y = 4$$
$$-y = -2x + 4$$
$$y = 2x - 4$$

The slope of both lines is 2. Now, using the point–slope form with $(x_1, y_1) = (-1, 2)$, we obtain the equation of the line:

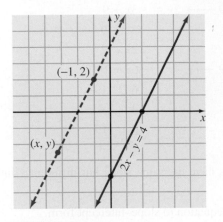

Figure 2.41

$$y - y_1 = m(x - x_1)$$
$$y - 2 = 2[x - (-1)]$$
$$y - 2 = 2(x + 1)$$
$$y - 2 = 2x + 2$$
$$-4 = 2x - y$$

Thus the equation of the line that contains the point $(-1, 2)$ and is parallel to the line with the equation $2x - y = 4$ is $2x - y = -4$. ∎

EXAMPLE 12

Find the equation of the line that contains the point $(-1, -3)$ and is perpendicular to the line determined by $3x + 4y = 12$.

Solution

Again let's start by drawing a figure to help with our analysis (see Figure 2.42). Because the line through $(-1, -3)$ is to be perpendicular to the given line, its slope must be the negative reciprocal of the slope of the line with the equation $3x + 4y = 12$. Let's find the slope of $3x + 4y = 12$ by changing to slope–intercept form:

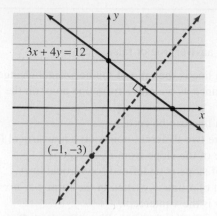

Figure 2.42

$$3x + 4y = 12$$
$$4y = -3x + 12$$
$$y = -\frac{3}{4}x + 3$$

The slope of the desired line is $\frac{4}{3}$ (the negative reciprocal of $-\frac{3}{4}$), and we can proceed as before to obtain its equation:

$$y - y_1 = m(x - x_1)$$
$$y - (-3) = \frac{4}{3}[x - (-1)]$$
$$y + 3 = \frac{4}{3}(x + 1)$$
$$3y + 9 = 4x + 4$$
$$5 = 4x - 3y$$

Thus the equation of the line that contains the point $(-1, -3)$ and is perpendicular to the line with the equation $3x + 4y = 12$ is $4x - 3y = 5$. ▄

Two forms of equations of straight lines are used extensively. They are the *standard form* and the *slope–intercept form*.

Standard Form $Ax + By = C$, where B and C are integers and A is a nonnegative integer (A and B are not both zero).

Slope–Intercept Form $y = mx + b$, where m is a real number representing the slope of the line, and b is a real number representing the y intercept.

Concept Quiz 2.3

For Problems 1–8, answer true or false.

1. The slope of a line is the ratio of the horizontal change in distance to the vertical change in distance as we move from one point on the line to another point on the line.
2. The slope of a line can be zero.
3. If P_1 and P_2 are two different points on a nonvertical line, the slope from P_2 to P_1 is the opposite of the slope from P_1 to P_2.
4. The concept of slope is undefined for vertical lines.
5. If the equation of a line is written in the form $y = mx + b$, then m is the slope of the line, and b is the x intercept.
6. If the equation of a line is $Ax + By = C$, where $B \neq 0$, then the slope of the line is $\dfrac{-A}{B}$.
7. The two lines whose equations are $Ax + By = C$ and $Ax + By = D$ are parallel lines.
8. The two lines whose equations are $Ax + By = C$ and $Bx - Ay = C$ are perpendicular lines.

Problem Set 2.3

For Problems 1–8, find the slope of the line determined by each pair of points. (Objective 1)

1. $(3, 1)$ and $(7, 4)$
2. $(-1, 2)$ and $(5, -3)$
3. $(-2, -1)$ and $(-1, -6)$
4. $(-2, -4)$ and $(3, 7)$
5. $(-4, 2)$ and $(-2, 2)$
6. $(4, -5)$ and $(-1, -5)$
7. $(a, 0)$ and $(0, b)$
8. (a, b) and (c, d)

9. Find x if the line through $(-2, 4)$ and $(x, 7)$ has a slope of $\dfrac{2}{9}$.

10. Find y if the line through $(1, y)$ and $(4, 2)$ has a slope of $\dfrac{5}{3}$.

11. Find x if the line through $(x, 4)$ and $(2, -6)$ has a slope of $-\dfrac{9}{4}$.

12. Find y if the line through $(5, 2)$ and $(-3, y)$ has a slope of $-\dfrac{7}{8}$.

For Problems 13–20, change the equation to slope–intercept form and determine the slope and the y intercept of each line.

13. $2x - 3y = 4$
14. $3x + 4y = 7$
15. $x - 2y = 7$
16. $2x + y = 9$
17. $y = -3x$
18. $x - 5y = 0$
19. $7x - 5y = 12$
20. $-5x + 6y = 13$

The slope-intercept form of a line can also be used for graphing purposes. Suppose that we want to graph $y = \dfrac{2}{3}x + 1$. Because the y intercept is 1, the point $(0, 1)$ is on the line. Furthermore, because the slope is $\dfrac{2}{3}$, another point can be found by moving two units *up* and three units to the *right*. Thus the point $(3, 3)$ is also on the line. The two points $(0, 1)$ and $(3, 3)$ determine the line.

For Problems 21–26, use the slope–intercept form to help graph each of the following lines.

21. $y = \frac{3}{4}x + 2$ **22.** $y = \frac{1}{2}x - 4$

23. $y = -\frac{4}{5}x + 1$ **24.** $y = -\frac{2}{3}x - 6$

25. $y = -2x + \frac{5}{4}$ **26.** $y = x - \frac{3}{2}$

For Problems 27–36, write the equation of the line that has the indicated slope and contains the indicated point. Express final equations in standard form. **(Objective 2)**

27. $m = \frac{1}{3}$; $(2, 4)$ **28.** $m = \frac{3}{5}$; $(-1, 4)$

29. $m = 2$; $(-1, -2)$ **30.** $m = -3$; $(2, 5)$

31. $m = -\frac{2}{3}$; $(4, -3)$ **32.** $m = -\frac{1}{5}$; $(-3, 7)$

33. $m = 0$; $(5, -2)$ **34.** $m = \frac{4}{3}$; $(-4, -5)$

35. m is undefined; $(3, -4)$ **36.** $m = 0$; $(-4, -6)$

For Problems 37–44, write the equation of each line that has the indicated slope, m, and y intercept, b. Express final equations in slope–intercept form. **(Objective 2)**

37. $m = \frac{1}{2}$, $b = 3$ **38.** $m = \frac{5}{3}$, $b = -1$

39. $m = -\frac{3}{7}$, $b = 2$ **40.** $m = -3$, $b = -4$

41. $m = 4$, $b = \frac{3}{2}$ **42.** $m = \frac{2}{3}$, $b = \frac{3}{5}$

43. $m = 0$, $b = \frac{1}{4}$ **44.** $m = -\frac{4}{5}$, $b = 0$

For Problems 45–54, write the equation of each line that contains the indicated pair of points. Express final equations in standard form. **(Objective 3)**

45. $(2, 3)$ and $(9, 8)$ **46.** $(1, -4)$ and $(4, 4)$

47. $(-1, 7)$ and $(5, 2)$ **48.** $(-3, 1)$ and $(6, -2)$

49. $(4, 2)$ and $(-1, 3)$ **50.** $(2, 7)$ and $(2, 5)$

51. $(4, -3)$ and $(-7, -3)$ **52.** $(-4, 2)$ and $(2, -3)$

53. $(-2, 6)$ and $(-2, -7)$ **54.** $(4, 5)$ and $(-1, 5)$

For each pair of lines in Problems 55–62, determine whether they are parallel, perpendicular, or intersecting lines that are not perpendicular.

55. $y = \frac{5}{6}x + 2$ **56.** $y = 5x - 1$

$y = \frac{5}{6}x - 4$ $y = -\frac{1}{5}x + \frac{2}{3}$

57. $5x - 7y = 14$ **58.** $2x - y = 4$

$7x + 5y = 12$ $4x - 2y = 17$

59. $4x + 9y = 13$ **60.** $y = 5x$

$-4x + y = 11$ $y = -5x$

61. $x + y = 0$ **62.** $2x - y = 14$

$x - y = 0$ $3x - y = 17$

For Problems 63–78, write the equation of each line that satisfies the given conditions. Express final equations in standard form. **(Objectives 2 and 4)**

63. The x intercept is 4 and the y intercept is -5.

64. Contains the point $(3, -1)$ and is parallel to the x axis

65. Contains the point $(-4, 3)$ and is parallel to the y axis

66. Contains the point $(1, 2)$ and is parallel to the line $3x - y = 5$

67. Contains the point $(4, -3)$ and is parallel to the line $5x + 2y = 1$

68. Contains the origin and is parallel to the line $5x - 2y = 10$

69. Contains the point $(-2, 6)$ and is perpendicular to the line $x - 4y = 7$

70. Contains the point $(-3, -5)$ and is perpendicular to the line $3x + 7y = 4$

71. Contains the point $(1, -6)$ and is parallel to the line $x = 4$

72. The x intercept is -2, and the y intercept is 5

73. Contains the point $(-3, 5)$ and is perpendicular to the line $y = 3$

74. Contains the point $(-1, -4)$ and is perpendicular to the line $x = 5$

75. Is the perpendicular bisector of the line segment with endpoints at $(2, 6)$ and $(10, -4)$

76. Is the perpendicular bisector of the line segment with endpoints at $(1, 3)$ and $(-7, 5)$

77. Is the perpendicular bisector of the line segment with endpoints at $(-4, 0)$ and $(6, 2)$

78. Is the perpendicular bisector of the line segment with endpoints at $(5, -3)$ and $(-1, 0)$

For Problems 79–85, solve the problem. (Objective 5)

79. A certain highway has a 2% grade. How many feet does it rise in a horizontal distance of 1 mile? (1 mile = 5280 feet)

80. The grade of a highway up a hill is 30%. How much change in horizontal distance is there if the vertical height of the hill is 75 feet?

81. If the ratio of rise to run is to be $\dfrac{3}{5}$ for some stairs and the rise is 19 centimeters, find the measure of the run to the nearest centimeter.

82. If the ratio of rise to run is to be $\dfrac{2}{3}$ for some stairs and the run is 28 centimeters, find the rise to the nearest centimeter.

83. Suppose that a county ordinance requires a $2\dfrac{1}{4}\%$ fall for a sewage pipe from the house to the main pipe at the street. How much vertical drop must there be for a horizontal distance of 45 feet? Express the answer to the nearest tenth of a foot.

84. The vertices of a certain triangle are $(2, 6)$, $(5, 1)$, and $(1, -4)$. Find the equations of the lines that contain the three altitudes of the triangle. (An altitude of a triangle is the perpendicular line segment from a vertex to the opposite side.)

85. The vertices of a certain triangle are $(1, -6)$, $(3, 1)$, and $(-2, 2)$. Find the equations of the lines that contain the three medians of the triangle. (A median of a triangle is the line segment from a vertex to the midpoint of the opposite side.)

86. Use the concept of slope to verify that $(-4, 6)$, $(6, 10)$, $(10, 0)$, and $(0, -4)$ are the vertices of a square.

87. Use the concept of slope to verify that $(6, 6)$, $(2, -2)$, $(-8, -5)$, and $(-4, 3)$ are vertices of a parallelogram.

88. Use the concept of slope to verify that the triangle determined by $(4, 3)$, $(5, 1)$, and $(3, 0)$ is a right triangle.

89. Use the concept of slope to verify that the quadrilateral with vertices $(0, 7)$, $(-2, -1)$, $(2, -2)$, and $(4, 6)$ is a rectangle.

90. Use the concept of slope to verify that the points $(8, -3)$, $(2, 1)$, and $(-4, 5)$ lie on a straight line.

Thoughts Into Words

91. How would you explain the concept of slope to someone who was absent from class the day it was discussed?

92. If one line has a slope of $\dfrac{2}{5}$, and another line has a slope of $\dfrac{3}{7}$, which line is steeper? Explain your answer.

93. What does it mean to say that two points *determine* a line? Do three points *determine* a line? Explain your answers.

94. Explain how you would find the slope of the line $y = 2$.

Further Investigations

95. The form

$$\frac{y - y_1}{x - x_1} = \frac{y_2 - y_1}{x_2 - x_1}$$

is called the **two-point form** of the equation of a straight line. Using points (x_1, y_1) and (x_2, y_2), develop the two-point form for the equation of a line. Then use the two-point form to write the equation of each of the following lines that contain the indicated pair of points. Express the final equations in standard form.

(a) $(4, 3)$ and $(5, 6)$ **(b)** $(-3, 5)$ and $(2, -1)$

(c) $(0, 0)$ and $(-7, 2)$

(d) $(-3, -4)$ and $(5, -1)$

96. The form $(x/a) + (y/b) = 1$ is called the **intercept form** of the equation of a straight line. Using a to represent the x intercept and b to represent the y intercept, develop the intercept form. Then use the intercept form to write the equation of each of the following lines. Express the final equations in standard form.

(a) $a = 2, b = 5$ **(b)** $a = -3, b = 1$

(c) $a = 6, b = -4$ **(d)** $a = -1, b = -2$

97. Prove each of the following statements.

(a) Two nonvertical parallel lines have the same slope.

(b) Two lines with the same slope are parallel.

(c) If two nonvertical lines are perpendicular, then their slopes are negative reciprocals of each other.

(d) If the slopes of two lines are negative reciprocals of each other, then the lines are perpendicular.

98. Let $Ax + By = C$ and $A'x + B'y = C'$ represent two lines. Verify each of the following properties.

(a) If $(A/A') = (B/B') \neq (C/C')$, then the lines are parallel.

(b) If $AA' = -BB'$, then the lines are perpendicular.

99. The properties in Problem 98 give us another way to write the equation of a line parallel or perpendicular to a given line through a point not on the given line. For example, suppose we want the equation of the line perpendicular to $3x + 4y = 6$ that contains the point $(1, 2)$. The form $4x - 3y = k$, where k is a constant, represents a family of lines perpendicular to $3x + 4y = 6$ because we have satisfied the condition $AA' = -BB'$. Therefore, to find the specific line of the family containing $(1, 2)$, we substitute 1 for x and 2 for y to determine k:

$$4x - 3y = k$$
$$4(1) - 3(2) = k$$
$$-2 = k$$

Thus the equation of the desired line is $4x - 3y = -2$. Use the properties from Problem 98 to help write the equation of each of the following lines.

(a) Contains $(5, 6)$ and is parallel to the line $2x - y = 1$

(b) Contains $(-3, 4)$ and is parallel to the line $3x + 7y = 2$

(c) Contains $(2, -4)$ and is perpendicular to the line $2x - 5y = 9$

(d) Contains $(-3, -5)$ and is perpendicular to the line $4x + 6y = 7$

100. The relationships that tie slope to parallelism and perpendicularity are powerful tools for constructing coordinate geometry proofs. Prove each of the following using a coordinate geometry approach.

(a) The diagonals of a square are perpendicular.

(b) The line segment joining the midpoints of two sides of a triangle is parallel to the third side.

(c) The line segments joining successive midpoints of the sides of a quadrilateral form a parallelogram.

(d) The line segments joining successive midpoints of the sides of a rectangle form a rhombus. (A rhombus is a parallelogram with all sides of the same length.)

Graphing Calculator Activities

101. Predict whether each of the following pairs of equations represents parallel lines, perpendicular lines, or lines that intersect but are not perpendicular. Then graph each pair of lines to check your predictions. (The properties presented in Problem 98 should be very helpful.)

(a) $5.2x + 3.3y = 9.4$ and $5.2x + 3.3y = 12.6$

(b) $1.3x - 4.7y = 3.4$ and $1.3x - 4.7y = 11.6$

(c) $2.7x + 3.9y = 1.4$ and $2.7x - 3.9y = 8.2$

(d) $5x - 7y = 17$ and $7x + 5y = 19$

(e) $9x + 2y = 14$ and $2x + 9y = 17$

(f) $2.1x + 3.4y = 11.7$ and $3.4x - 2.1y = 17.3$

(g) $7.1x - 2.3y = 6.2$ and $2.3x + 7.1y = 9.9$

(h) $-3x + 9y = 12$ and $9x - 3y = 14$

(i) $2.6x - 5.3y = 3.4$ and $5.2x - 10.6y = 19.2$

(j) $4.8x - 5.6y = 3.4$ and $6.1x + 7.6y = 12.3$

2.4   More on Graphing

OBJECTIVES   **1** Graph nonlinear equations

2 Determine if the graph of an equation is symmetric to the *x* axis, the *y* axis, or the origin

As we stated earlier, it is very helpful to recognize that a certain type of equation produces a particular kind of graph. In a later chapter, we will pursue that idea in much more detail. However, we also need to develop some general graphing techniques to use with equations when we do not recognize the graph. Let's begin with the following suggestions and then add to the list throughout the remainder of the text. (You may recognize some of the graphs in this section from previous graphing experiences, but keep in mind that the primary objective at this time is to develop some additional graphing techniques.)

1. Find the intercepts.
2. Solve the equation for *y* in terms of *x* or for *x* in terms of *y* if it is not already in such a form.
3. Set up a table of ordered pairs that satisfy the equation.
4. Plot the points associated with the ordered pairs and connect them with a smooth curve.

Classroom Example
Graph $y = x^2 + 2$.

EXAMPLE 1   Graph $y = x^2 - 4$.

Solution

First, let's find the intercepts. If $x = 0$, then

$$y = 0^2 - 4$$
$$y = -4$$

This determines the point $(0, -4)$. If $y = 0$, then

$$0 = x^2 - 4$$
$$4 = x^2$$
$$\pm 2 = x$$

Thus the points $(2, 0)$ and $(-2, 0)$ are determined.

Second, because the given equation expresses y in terms of x, the form is convenient for setting up a table of ordered pairs. Plotting these points, and connecting them with a smooth curve, produces Figure 2.43.

x	y	
0	-4	
2	0	intercepts
-2	0	
1	-3	
-1	-3	other
3	5	points
-3	5	

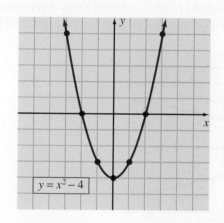

$y = x^2 - 4$

Figure 2.43

The curve in Figure 2.43 is said to be **symmetric with respect to the y axis.** Stated another way, each half of the curve is a mirror image of the other half through the y axis. Note in the table of values that for each ordered pair (x, y), the ordered pair $(-x, y)$ is also a solution. Thus a general test for y-axis symmetry can be stated as follows.

y-Axis Symmetry

The graph of an equation is symmetric with respect to the y axis if replacing x with $-x$ results in an equivalent equation.

Thus the equation $y = x^2 - 4$ exhibits y-axis symmetry because replacing x with $-x$ produces $y = (-x)^2 - 4 = x^2 - 4$. Likewise, the equations $y = x^2 + 6$, $y = x^4$, and $y = x^4 + 2x^2$ exhibit y-axis symmetry.

Classroom Example
Graph $x + 3 = y^2$.

 **EXAMPLE 2**   Graph $x - 1 = y^2$.

Solution

If $x = 0$, then

$$0 - 1 = y^2$$
$$-1 = y^2$$

The equation $y^2 = -1$ has no real number solutions; therefore, this graph has no points on the y axis. If $y = 0$, then

$$x - 1 = 0$$
$$x = 1$$

Thus the point $(1, 0)$ is determined. Solving the original equation for x produces $x = y^2 + 1$, for which the table of values is easily determined. Plotting these points, and connecting them with a smooth curve, produces Figure 2.44.

x	y	
1	0	intercept
2	1	
2	−1	other
5	2	points
5	−2	

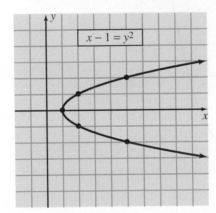

Figure 2.44

The curve in Figure 2.44 is said to be **symmetric with respect to the x axis.** That is to say, each half of the curve is a mirror image of the other half through the x axis. Note in the table of values that for each ordered pair (x, y), the ordered pair $(x, -y)$ is also a solution. The following general test of x-axis symmetry can be stated.

> **x-Axis Symmetry**
>
> The graph of an equation is symmetric with respect to the x axis if replacing y with $-y$ results in an equivalent equation.

Thus the equation $x - 1 = y^2$ exhibits x-axis symmetry because replacing y with $-y$ produces $x - 1 = (-y)^2 = y^2$. Likewise, the equations $x = y^2$, $x = y^4 + 2$, and $x^3 = y^2$ exhibit x-axis symmetry.

EXAMPLE 3   Graph $y = x^3$.

Solution

If $x = 0$, then

$$y = 0^3 = 0$$

Thus the origin $(0, 0)$ is on the graph. The table of values is easily determined from the equation. Plotting these points, and connecting them with a smooth curve, produces Figure 2.45.

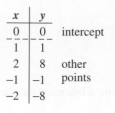

x	y	
0	0	intercept
1	1	
2	8	other
−1	−1	points
−2	−8	

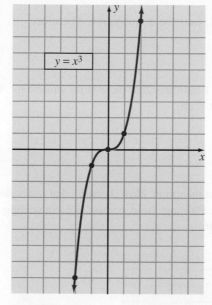

$y = x^3$

Figure 2.45

The curve in Figure 2.45 is said to be **symmetric with respect to the origin.** Each half of the curve is a mirror image of the other half through the origin. In the table of values, we see that for each ordered pair (x, y), the ordered pair $(-x, -y)$ is also a solution. The following general test for origin symmetry can be stated.

Origin Symmetry

The graph of an equation is symmetric with respect to the origin if replacing x with $-x$ and y with $-y$ results in an equivalent equation.

The equation $y = x^3$ exhibits origin symmetry because replacing x with $-x$ and y with $-y$ produces $-y = -x^3$, which is equivalent to $y = x^3$. (Multiplying both sides of $-y = -x^3$ by -1 produces $y = x^3$.) Likewise, the equations $xy = 4$, $x^2 + y^2 = 10$, and $4x^2 - y^2 = 12$ exhibit origin symmetry.

Remark: From the symmetry tests, we observe that if a curve has both x-axis and y-axis symmetry, then it must have origin symmetry. However, it is possible for a curve to have origin symmetry and not be symmetric to either axis. Figure 2.45 is an example of such a curve.

Another graphing consideration is that of **restricting a variable** to ensure real number solutions. The following example illustrates this point.

Classroom Example
Graph $y = \sqrt{x + 3}$.

EXAMPLE 4   Graph $y = \sqrt{x - 1}$.

Solution

The radicand, $x - 1$, must be nonnegative. Therefore,

$$x - 1 \geq 0$$
$$x \geq 1$$

The restriction $x \geq 1$ indicates that there is no y intercept. The x intercept can be found as follows: If $y = 0$, then

$$0 = \sqrt{x - 1}$$
$$0 = x - 1$$
$$1 = x$$

The point $(1, 0)$ is on the graph. Now, keeping that restriction in mind, we can determine the table of values. Plotting these points, and connecting them with a smooth curve, produces Figure 2.46.

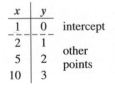

x	y	
1	0	intercept
2	1	other
5	2	points
10	3	

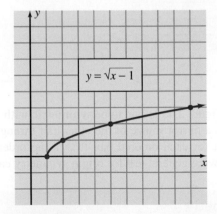

$y = \sqrt{x - 1}$

Figure 2.46

Now let's restate and add the concepts of symmetry and restrictions to the list of graphing suggestions. The order of the suggestions also indicates the order in which we usually attack a graphing problem if it is a new graph, that is, one that we do not recognize from its equation.

1. Determine what type of symmetry the equation exhibits.

2. Find the intercepts.

3. Solve the equation for y in terms of x or for x in terms of y, if it is not already in such a form.

4. Determine the restrictions necessary to ensure real number solutions.

5. Set up a table of ordered pairs that satisfy the equation. The type of symmetry and the restrictions will affect your choice of values in the table.

6. Plot the points associated with the ordered pairs and connect them with a smooth curve. Then, if appropriate, reflect this curve according to the symmetry possessed by the graph.

The final two examples of this section should help you pull these ideas together and demonstrate the power of having these techniques at your fingertips.

Classroom Example
Graph $y = -x^2 + 4$.

EXAMPLE 5   Graph $x = -y^2 - 3$.

Solution

Symmetry   The graph is symmetric with respect to the x axis because replacing y with $-y$ produces $x = -(-y)^2 - 3$, which is equivalent to $x = -y^2 - 3$.

Intercepts   If $x = 0$, then

$$0 = -y^2 - 3$$
$$y^2 = -3$$

Therefore the graph contains no points on the y axis. If $y = 0$, then

$$x = -0^2 - 3$$
$$x = -3$$

Thus the point $(-3, 0)$ is on the graph.

Restrictions   Because $x = -y^2 - 3$, y can take on any real number value, and for every value of y, x will be less than or equal to -3.

Table of Values   Because of the x-axis symmetry, let's choose only nonnegative values for y.

Plotting the Graph   Plotting the points determined by the table, and connecting them with a smooth curve, produces Figure 2.47(a). Then reflecting that portion of the curve across the x axis produces the complete curve in Figure 2.47(b).

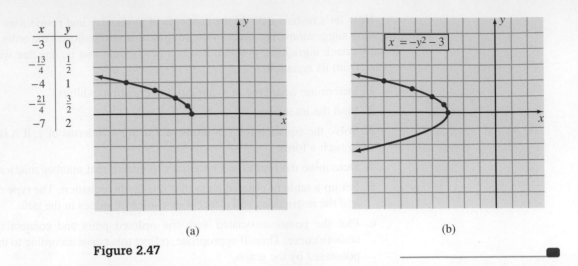

x	y
-3	0
$-\dfrac{13}{4}$	$\dfrac{1}{2}$
-4	1
$-\dfrac{21}{4}$	$\dfrac{3}{2}$
-7	2

(a)

(b)

Figure 2.47

EXAMPLE 6   Graph $x^2 - y^2 = 4$.

Solution

Symmetry   The graph is symmetric with respect to both axes and the origin because replacing x with $-x$ and y with $-y$ produces $(-x)^2 - (-y)^2 = 4$, which is equivalent to $x^2 - y^2 = 4$.

Intercepts   If $x = 0$, then

$$0^2 - y^2 = 4$$
$$-y^2 = 4$$
$$y^2 = -4$$

Therefore the graph contains no points on the y axis. If $y = 0$, then

$$x^2 - 0^2 = 4$$
$$x^2 = 4$$
$$x = \pm 2$$

Thus the points $(2, 0)$ and $(-2, 0)$ are on the graph.

Restrictions   Solving the given equation for y produces

$$x^2 - y^2 = 4$$
$$-y^2 = 4 - x^2$$
$$y^2 = x^2 - 4$$
$$y = \pm\sqrt{x^2 - 4}$$

Therefore $x^2 - 4 \geq 0$, which is equivalent to $x \geq 2$ or $x \leq -2$.

Table of Values Because of the restrictions and symmetries, we need only choose values corresponding to $x \geq 2$.

Plotting the Graph Plotting the points in the table of values, and connecting them with a smooth curve, produces Figure 2.48(a). Because of the symmetry with respect to both axes and the origin, the portion of the curve in Figure 2.48(a) can be reflected across both axes and through the origin to produce the complete curve shown in Figure 2.48(b).

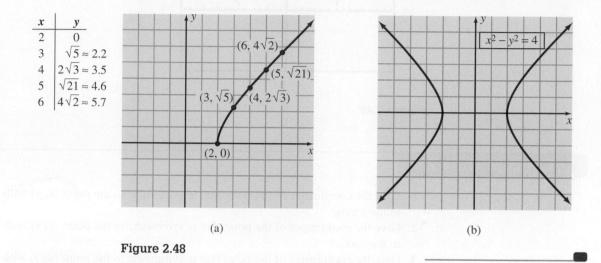

x	y
2	0
3	$\sqrt{5} \approx 2.2$
4	$2\sqrt{3} \approx 3.5$
5	$\sqrt{21} \approx 4.6$
6	$4\sqrt{2} \approx 5.7$

(a)   (b)

Figure 2.48

Even when you are using a graphing utility, it is often helpful to determine symmetry, intercepts, and restrictions before graphing the equations. This can serve as a partial check against using the utility incorrectly.

Classroom Example
Use a graphing utility to obtain the graph of $y = -\sqrt{25 - x^2}$.

EXAMPLE 7

Use a graphing utility to obtain the graph of $y = \sqrt{x^2 - 49}$.

Solution

Symmetry The graph is symmetric with respect to the y axis because replacing x with $-x$ produces the same equation.

Intercepts If $x = 0$, then $y = \sqrt{-49}$; thus the graph has no points on the y axis. If $y = 0$, then $x = \pm 7$; thus the points $(7, 0)$ and $(-7, 0)$ are on the graph.

Restrictions Because $x^2 - 49$ has to be nonnegative, we know that $x \leq -7$ or $x \geq 7$.

Now let's enter the expression $\sqrt{x^2 - 49}$ for Y_1 and obtain the graph in Figure 2.49. Note that the graph does exhibit the symmetry, intercepts, and restrictions that we determined earlier.

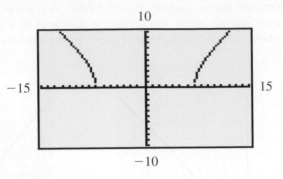

Figure 2.49

Concept Quiz 2.4

1. Give the coordinates of the point that is symmetric to the point (x, y) with respect to the x axis.
2. Give the coordinates of the point that is symmetric to the point (x, y) with respect to the y axis.
3. Give the coordinates of the point that is symmetric to the point (x, y) with respect to the origin.

For Problems 4–8, answer true or false.

4. The graph of the line $y = 3x$ is symmetric to the y axis.
5. If a graph is symmetric to both the x axis and the y axis, the graph is symmetric to the origin.
6. If a graph is symmetric to the origin, then it is symmetric to both the x axis and the y axis.
7. The graph of a straight line is symmetric to the origin only if the graph passes through the origin.
8. Every straight line that passes through the origin is symmetric with respect to the origin.

Problem Set 2.4

For Problems 1–6, determine the points that are symmetric to the given point with respect to the x axis, the y axis, and the origin. (Objective 2)

1. $(4, 3)$

2. $(-2, 5)$

3. $(-6, -1)$

4. $(3, -7)$

5. $(0, 4)$

6. $(-5, 0)$

For Problems 7–30, determine the type of symmetry (x axis, y axis, origin) possessed by each graph. Do not sketch the graph. **(Objective 2)**

7. $y = x^2 - 6$

8. $x = y^2 + 1$

9. $x^3 = y^2$

10. $x^2 y^2 = 4$

11. $x^2 + 2y^2 = 6$

12. $3x^2 - y^2 + 4x = 6$

13. $x^2 - 2x + y^2 - 3y - 4 = 0$

14. $xy = 4$

15. $y = x$

16. $2x - 3y = 15$

17. $y = x^3 + 2$

18. $y = x^4 + x^2$

19. $5x^2 - y^2 + 2y - 1 = 0$

20. $x^2 + y^2 - 2y - 4 = 0$

21. $x^2 - xy = y^2$

22. $x^2 + y^2 = 1$

23. $y^2 = x^2 + 2x - 1$

24. $x^2 + y^2 - 2x - y = 4$

25. $x^2 + y^2 = 49$

26. $y = |x|$

27. $y = \sqrt{x - 2}$

28. $x = 2y^2 + 3y$

29. $y = \dfrac{4}{x}$

30. $2x^2 + 3xy - y^2 = 0$

For Problems 31–58, use symmetry, intercepts, restrictions, and point plotting to help graph each equation. **(Objective 1)**

31. $y = x^2$

32. $y = -x^2$

33. $y = x^2 + 2$

34. $y = -x^2 - 1$

35. $xy = 4$

36. $xy = -2$

37. $y = -x^3$

38. $y = x^3 + 2$

39. $y^2 = x^3$

40. $y^3 = x^2$

41. $y^2 - x^2 = 4$

42. $x^2 - 2y^2 = 8$

43. $y = -\sqrt{x}$

44. $y = \sqrt{x + 1}$

45. $x^2 y = 4$

46. $xy^2 = 4$

47. $x^2 + 2y^2 = 8$

48. $2x^2 + y^2 = 4$

49. $y = \dfrac{4}{x^2 + 1}$

50. $y = \dfrac{-2}{x^2 + 1}$

51. $y = \sqrt{x - 2}$

52. $y = \sqrt{3 - x}$

53. $-xy = 3$

54. $-x^2 y = 4$

55. $x = y^2 + 2$

56. $x = -y^2 + 4$

57. $x = -y^2 - 1$

58. $x = y^2 - 3$

Thoughts Into Words

59. How does the concept of symmetry help when we are graphing equations?

60. Explain how you would go about graphing $x^2 y^2 = 4$.

Graphing Calculator Activities

61. Graph $y = \dfrac{4}{x^2}$, $y = \dfrac{4}{(x - 2)^2}$, $y = \dfrac{4}{(x - 4)^2}$, and $y = \dfrac{4}{(x + 2)^2}$ on the same set of axes. Now predict the graph for $y = \dfrac{1}{(x - 6)^2}$. Check your prediction.

62. Graph $y = \sqrt{x}$, $y = \sqrt{x + 1}$, $y = \sqrt{x - 2}$, and $y = \sqrt{x - 4}$ on the same set of axes. Now predict the graph for $y = \sqrt{x + 3}$. Check your prediction.

63. Graph $y = \sqrt{x}$, $y = 2\sqrt{x}$, $y = 4\sqrt{x}$, and $y = 7\sqrt{x}$ on the same set of axes. How does the constant in front of the radical seem to affect the graph?

64. Graph $y = \dfrac{8}{x^2}$ and $y = -\dfrac{8}{x^2}$ on the same set of axes. How does the negative sign seem to affect the graph?

65. Graph $y = \sqrt{x}$ and $y = -\sqrt{x}$ on the same set of axes. How does the negative sign seem to affect the graph?

66. Graph $y = \sqrt{x}$, $y = \sqrt{x} + 2$, $y = \sqrt{x} + 4$, and $y = \sqrt{x} - 3$ on the same set of axes. How does the constant term seem to affect the graph?

67. Graph $y = \sqrt{x}$, $y = \sqrt{x + 3}$, $y = \sqrt{x - 1}$, and $y = \sqrt{x - 5}$ on the same set of axes. How are the graphs related? Predict the location of $y = \sqrt{x + 5}$. Check your prediction.

68. To graph $x = y^2$ we need first to solve for y in terms of x. This produces $y = \pm\sqrt{x}$. Now we can let $Y_1 = \sqrt{x}$ and $Y_2 = -\sqrt{x}$ and graph the two equations on the same set of axes. Then graph $x = y^2 + 4$ on this same set of axes. How are the graphs related? Predict the location of the graph of $x = y^2 - 4$. Check your prediction.

69. To graph $x = y^2 + 2y$ we need first to solve for y in terms of x. Let's complete the square to do this:

$$y^2 + 2y = x$$
$$y^2 + 2y + 1 = x + 1$$
$$(y + 1)^2 = (\sqrt{x + 1})^2$$
$$y + 1 = \sqrt{x + 1} \quad \text{or} \quad y + 1 = -\sqrt{x + 1}$$
$$y = -1 + \sqrt{x + 1} \quad \text{or} \quad y = -1 - \sqrt{x + 1}$$

Thus let's make the assignments $Y_1 = -1 + \sqrt{x + 1}$ and $Y_2 = -1 - \sqrt{x + 1}$ and graph them on the same set of axes to produce the graph of $x = y^2 + 2y$. Then graph $x = y^2 + 2y - 4$ on this same set of axes. Now predict the location of the graph of $x = y^2 + 2y + 4$. Check your prediction.

Answers to the Concept Quiz

1. $(x, -y)$ **2.** $(-x, y)$ **3.** $(-x, -y)$ **4.** False   **5.** True   **6.** False   **7.** True   **8.** True

---

2.5   Circles, Ellipses, and Hyperbolas

OBJECTIVES   **1** Write the equation of a circle

2 Find the center and length of a radius, given the equation of a circle

3 Draw graphs of circles, ellipses, and hyperbolas

Circles

When we apply the distance formula

$$d = \sqrt{(x_2 - x_1)^2 + (y_2 - y_1)^2}$$

(developed in Section 2.1) to the definition of a circle, we get what is known as the **standard form of the equation of a circle.** We start with a precise definition of a circle.

> **Definition 2.2**
>
> A **circle** is the set of all points in a plane equidistant from a given fixed point called the **center.** A line segment determined by the center and any point on the circle is called a **radius.**

Now let's consider a circle that has a radius of length r and a center at (h, k) on a coordinate system (see Figure 2.50). For any point P on the circle with coordinates (x, y), the length of a radius, denoted by r, can be expressed as

$$r = \sqrt{(x - h)^2 + (y - k)^2}$$

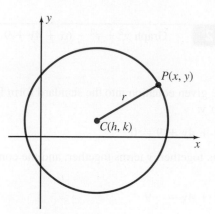

Figure 2.50

Squaring both sides of this equation, we obtain the standard form of the equation of a circle:

$$(x - h)^2 + (y - k)^2 = r^2$$

This form of the equation of a circle can be used to solve the two basic kinds of problems: (1) given the coordinates of the center of a circle and the length of a radius of a circle, find its equation, and (2) given the equation of a circle, determine its graph. Let's illustrate each of these types of problems.

Classroom Example
Find the equation of a circle that has its center at $(2, -1)$ and has a radius of length five units.

EXAMPLE 1

Find the equation of a circle that has its center at $(-3, 5)$ and has a radius of length four units.

Solution

Substitute -3 for h, 5 for k, and 4 for r in the standard equation and simplify to give the equation of the circle.

$$(x - h)^2 + (y - k)^2 = r^2$$
$$[x - (-3)]^2 + (y - 5)^2 = 4^2$$
$$(x + 3)^2 + (y - 5)^2 = 4^2$$
$$x^2 + 6x + 9 + y^2 - 10y + 25 = 16$$
$$x^2 + y^2 + 6x - 10y + 18 = 0$$

Note that in Example 1 we simplified the equation to the form $x^2 + y^2 + Dx + Ey + F = 0$, where D, E, and F are constants. This is another form that we commonly use when working with circles.

Classroom Example
Graph
$x^2 + y^2 - 2x + 6y + 6 = 0.$

EXAMPLE 2   Graph $x^2 + y^2 - 6x + 4y + 9 = 0$.

Solution

We can change the given equation into the standard form for a circle by completing the square on x and on y:

$$x^2 + y^2 - 6x + 4y + 9 = 0$$

Rewrite the x terms together, y terms together, and the constant on the other side of the equation.

$$x^2 - 6x + y^2 + 4y = -9$$

Let's review the steps for completing the square:

1. The coefficient of the squared term must be one. Otherwise, factor out the coefficient so that the coefficient of the squared term is one.
2. Take one-half of the coefficient of the x (or y) term and square the result.

$$\frac{1}{2}(-6) = -3 \text{ and } (-3)^2 = 9 \qquad \frac{1}{2}(4) = 2 \text{ and } (2)^2 = 4$$

3. Add the results in step 2 to both sides of the equation.

$$x^2 - 6x + 9 + y^2 + 4y + 4 = -9 + 9 + 4$$

4. Now factor the perfect square trinomials in x and in y.

$$(x - 3)^2 + (y + 2)^2 = 4$$

5. Now rewrite to match the equation of a circle.

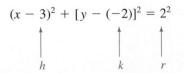

$$(x - 3)^2 + [y - (-2)]^2 = 2^2$$

$$h \qquad\qquad k \qquad r$$

The center is at $(3, -2)$, and the length of a radius is two units. The circle is drawn in Figure 2.51.

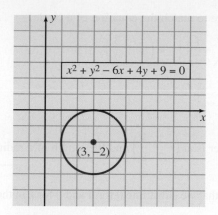

$$x^2 + y^2 - 6x + 4y + 9 = 0$$

Figure 2.51

EXAMPLE 3   Find the center and length of a radius of the circle

$$4x^2 + 4x + 4y^2 - 12y - 26 = 0.$$

Solution

$$4x^2 + 4x + 4y^2 - 12y - 26 = 0$$

The x terms are written together and the y terms are written together, so rewrite with the constant on the other side of the equation.

$$4x^2 + 4x + 4y^2 - 12y = 26$$

1. Because the coefficient of the squared term is not one, factor out the coefficient so that the coefficient of the squared term is one.

$$4(x^2 + x) + 4(y^2 - 3y) = 26$$

2. Take one-half of the coefficient of the x (or y) term and square the result.

$$\frac{1}{2}(1) = \frac{1}{2} \text{ and } \left(\frac{1}{2}\right)^2 = \frac{1}{4} \qquad \frac{1}{2}(-3) = -\frac{3}{2} \text{ and } \left(-\frac{3}{2}\right)^2 = \frac{9}{4}$$

3. When adding the results in step 2 to both sides of the equation, be sure to take into account the factor in front of the parentheses.

$$4\left(x^2 + x + \frac{1}{4}\right) + 4\left(y^2 - 3y + \frac{9}{4}\right) = 26 + 4\left(\frac{1}{4}\right) + 4\left(\frac{9}{4}\right)$$

4. Now factor the perfect square trinomials in x and in y.

$$4\left(x + \frac{1}{2}\right)^2 + 4\left(y - \frac{3}{2}\right)^2 = 26 + 1 + 9$$

$$4\left(x + \frac{1}{2}\right)^2 + 4\left(y - \frac{3}{2}\right)^2 = 36$$

$$\left(x + \frac{1}{2}\right)^2 + \left(y - \frac{3}{2}\right)^2 = 9 \qquad \text{Divided both sides by 4}$$

5. Now rewrite to match the equation of a circle.

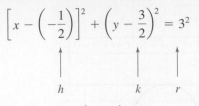

$$\left[x - \left(-\frac{1}{2}\right)\right]^2 + \left(y - \frac{3}{2}\right)^2 = 3^2$$

$$\uparrow \qquad\qquad \uparrow \quad\ \uparrow$$
$$h \qquad\qquad\ k \quad\ r$$

Therefore the center is at $\left(-\dfrac{1}{2}, \dfrac{3}{2}\right)$ and the length of a radius is three units. ∎

Now suppose that we substitute 0 for h and 0 for k in the standard form of the equation of a circle.

$$(x - h)^2 + (y - k)^2 = r^2$$
$$(x - 0)^2 + (y - 0)^2 = r^2$$
$$x^2 + y^2 = r^2$$

The form $x^2 + y^2 = r^2$ is called the **standard form of the equation of a circle that has its center at the origin.** For example, by inspection we can recognize that $x^2 + y^2 = 9$ is a circle with its center at the origin and a radius of length three units. Likewise, the equation $5x^2 + 5y^2 = 10$ is equivalent to $x^2 + y^2 = 2$; therefore its graph is a circle with its center at the origin and a radius of length $\sqrt{2}$ units. Furthermore, we can easily determine that the equation of the circle with its center at the origin and a radius of eight units is $x^2 + y^2 = 64$.

Ellipses

Generally it is true that any equation of the form $Ax^2 + By^2 = F$ (where $A = B$ and A, B, and F are nonzero constants that have the same sign) is a circle with its center at the origin. We can use the general equation $Ax^2 + By^2 = F$ to describe other geometric figures by changing the restrictions on A and B. For example, if A, B, and F are of the same sign but $A \neq B$, then the graph of the equation $Ax^2 + By^2 = F$ is an **ellipse.** Let's consider two examples.

Classroom Example
Graph $16x^2 + 9y^2 = 144$.

EXAMPLE 4   Graph $4x^2 + 9y^2 = 36$.

Solution

Let's find the intercepts. If $x = 0$, then

$$4(0)^2 + 9y^2 = 36$$
$$9y^2 = 36$$
$$y^2 = 4$$
$$y = \pm 2$$

Thus the points (0, 2) and (0, −2) are on the graph. If $y = 0$, then

$$4x^2 + 9(0)^2 = 36$$
$$4x^2 = 36$$
$$x^2 = 9$$
$$x = \pm 3$$

Thus the points (3, 0) and (−3, 0) are on the graph. Because we know that it is an ellipse, plotting the four points that we have gives us a pretty good sketch of the figure (see Figure 2.52).

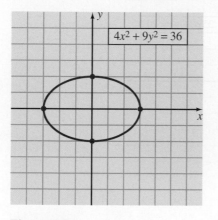

$4x^2 + 9y^2 = 36$

Figure 2.52

In Figure 2.52, the line segment with endpoints at (−3, 0) and (3, 0) is called the **major axis** of the ellipse. The shorter segment with endpoints at (0, −2) and (0, 2) is called the **minor axis.** Establishing the endpoints of the major and minor axes provides a basis for sketching an ellipse. Also note that the equation $4x^2 + 9y^2 = 36$ exhibits symmetry with respect to both axes and the origin, as we see in Figure 2.52.

Classroom Example
Graph $x^2 + 16y^2 = 16$.

 EXAMPLE 5   Graph $25x^2 + y^2 = 25$.

Solution

The endpoints of the major and minor axes can be determined by finding the intercepts. If $x = 0$, then

$$25(0)^2 + y^2 = 25$$
$$y^2 = 25$$
$$y = \pm 5$$

The endpoints of the major axis are therefore at $(0, 5)$ and $(0, -5)$. If $y = 0$, then

$$25x^2 + (0)^2 = 25$$
$$25x^2 = 25$$
$$x^2 = 1$$
$$x = \pm 1$$

The endpoints of the minor axis are at $(1, 0)$ and $(-1, 0)$. The ellipse is sketched in Figure 2.53.

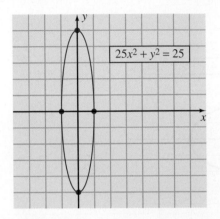

Figure 2.53

Hyperbolas

The graph of an equation of the form $Ax^2 + By^2 = F$, where A and B are of *unlike* signs, is a **hyperbola.** The next two examples illustrate the graphing of hyperbolas.

Classroom Example
Graph $9x^2 - y^2 = 9$.

EXAMPLE 6   Graph $x^2 - 4y^2 = 4$.

Solution

If we let $y = 0$, then

$$x^2 - 4(0)^2 = 4$$
$$x^2 = 4$$
$$x = \pm 2$$

Thus the points $(2, 0)$ and $(-2, 0)$ are on the graph. If we let $x = 0$, then

$$0^2 - 4y^2 = 4$$
$$-4y^2 = 4$$
$$y^2 = -1$$

Because $y^2 = -1$ has no real number solutions, there are no points of the graph on the y axis.

Note that the equation $x^2 - 4y^2 = 4$ exhibits symmetry with respect to both axes and the origin. Now let's solve the given equation for y to get a more convenient form for finding other solutions.

$$x^2 - 4y^2 = 4$$
$$-4y^2 = 4 - x^2$$
$$4y^2 = x^2 - 4$$
$$y^2 = \frac{x^2 - 4}{4}$$
$$y = \frac{\pm\sqrt{x^2 - 4}}{2}$$

Because the radicand, $x^2 - 4$, must be nonnegative, the values chosen for x must be such that $x \geq 2$ or $x \leq -2$. Symmetry and the points determined by the table provide the basis for sketching Figure 2.54.

x	y	
2	0	intercepts
−2	0	
3	$\pm\frac{\sqrt{5}}{2}$	
4	$\pm\sqrt{3}$	other points
5	$\pm\frac{\sqrt{21}}{2}$	

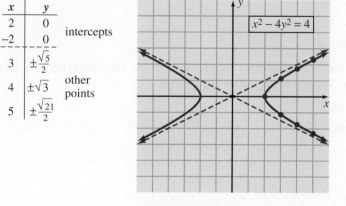

$x^2 - 4y^2 = 4$

Figure 2.54

Note the dashed lines in Figure 2.54; they are called **asymptotes**. Each **branch** of the hyperbola approaches one of these lines but does not intersect it. Therefore, being able to sketch the asymptotes of a hyperbola is very helpful for graphing purposes. Fortunately, the equations of the asymptotes are easy to determine. They can be found by replacing the constant term in the given equation of the hyperbola with zero and then solving for y. (The reason this works will be discussed in a later chapter.) For the hyperbola in Example 6, we obtain

$$x^2 - 4y^2 = 0$$
$$-4y^2 = -x^2$$
$$y^2 = \frac{1}{4}x^2$$
$$y = \pm\frac{1}{2}x$$

Thus the lines $y = \dfrac{1}{2}x$ and $y = -\dfrac{1}{2}x$ are the asymptotes indicated by the dashed lines in Figure 2.54.

Classroom Example
Graph $25x^2 - 4y^2 = 100$.

EXAMPLE 7   Graph $4y^2 - 9x^2 = 36$.

Solution

If $x = 0$, then

$$4y^2 - 9(0)^2 = 36$$
$$4y^2 = 36$$
$$y^2 = 9$$
$$y = \pm 3$$

The points $(0, 3)$ and $(0, -3)$ are on the graph. If $y = 0$, then

$$4(0)^2 - 9x^2 = 36$$
$$-9x^2 = 36$$
$$x^2 = -4$$

Because $x^2 = -4$ has no real number solutions, we know that this hyperbola does not intersect the x axis. Solving the equation for y yields

$$4y^2 - 9x^2 = 36$$
$$4y^2 = 9x^2 + 36$$
$$y^2 = \frac{9x^2 + 36}{4}$$
$$y = \frac{\pm\sqrt{9x^2 + 36}}{2}$$
$$y = \frac{\pm\sqrt{9(x^2 + 4)}}{2}$$
$$y = \pm\frac{3\sqrt{x^2 + 4}}{2}$$

The table shows some additional solutions. The equations of the asymptotes are determined as follows:

$$4y^2 - 9x^2 = 0$$
$$4y^2 = 9x^2$$
$$y^2 = \frac{9}{4}x^2$$
$$y = \pm\frac{3}{2}x$$

Sketching the asymptotes, plotting the points from the table, and using symmetry, we determine the hyperbola in Figure 2.55.

x	y	
0	3	intercepts
0	−3	
1	$\pm\dfrac{3\sqrt{5}}{2}$	
2	$\pm 3\sqrt{2}$	other points
3	$\pm\dfrac{3\sqrt{13}}{2}$	

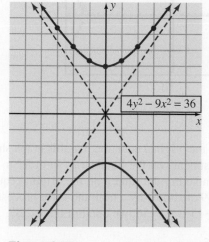

$$4y^2 - 9x^2 = 36$$

Figure 2.55

When using a graphing utility, we may find it necessary to change the boundaries on x or y (or both) to obtain a complete graph. Consider the following example.

EXAMPLE 8

Use a graphing utility to graph $x^2 - 40x + y^2 + 351 = 0$.

Solution

First we need to solve for y in terms of x:

$$x^2 - 40x + y^2 + 351 = 0$$
$$y^2 = -x^2 + 40x - 351$$
$$y = \pm\sqrt{-x^2 + 40x - 351}$$

Now we can make the following assignments:

$$Y_1 = \sqrt{-x^2 + 40x - 351}$$
$$Y_2 = -Y_1$$

(Note that we assigned Y_2 in terms of Y_1. By doing this, we avoid repetitive key strokes and reduce the chance for errors. You may need to consult your user's manual for instructions on how to key stroke $-Y_1$.) Figure 2.56 shows the graph.

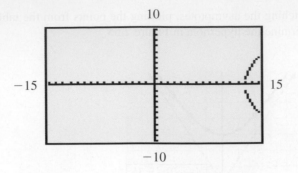

Figure 2.56

We know from the original equation that this graph should be a circle, so we need to make some adjustments on the boundaries in order to get a complete graph. This can be done by completing the square on the original equation to change its form to $(x - 20)^2 + y^2 = 49$ or simply by a trial-and-error process. By changing the boundaries on x such that $-15 \leq x \leq 30$, we obtain Figure 2.57.

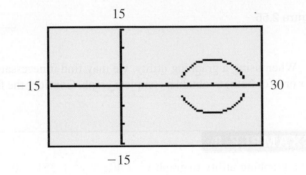

Figure 2.57

In summarizing this section, we do want you to be aware of the continuity pattern used. We started by using the definition of a circle to generate the standard form of the equation of a circle. Then we discussed ellipses and hyperbolas, not from a definition viewpoint, but by considering variations of the general equation of a circle with its center at the origin ($Ax^2 + By^2 = F$, where A, B, and F are of the same sign and $A = B$). In Chapter 8 we will develop parabolas, ellipses, and hyperbolas from a definition viewpoint. In other words, we first define each of the concepts and then use those definitions to generate standard forms for their equations.

Concept Quiz 2.5

For Problems 1–3, match each equation with its name.

1. $x^2 - y^2 = 36$ A. Circle
2. $4x^2 + y^2 = 36$ B. Ellipse
3. $x^2 + y^2 = 36$ C. Hyperbola

For Problems 4–8, answer true or false.

4. A circle is the set of all points in a plane that are equidistant from a fixed point.
5. The circle $(x - 2)^2 + (y + 4)^2 = 20$ has its center at $(2, 4)$.
6. The circle $(x - 2)^2 + (y + 4)^2 = 20$ has a radius of length 20 units.
7. For ellipses, the major axis is always parallel to the x axis.
8. The graph of a hyperbola has two branches.

Problem Set 2.5

For Problems 1–8, write the equation of each circle. Express the final equations in the form $x^2 + y^2 + Dx + Ey + F = 0$. (Objective 1)

1. Center at $(2, 3)$ and $r = 5$

2. Center at $(-3, 4)$ and $r = 2$

3. Center at $(-1, -5)$ and $r = 3$

4. Center at $(4, -2)$ and $r = 1$

5. Center at $(3, 0)$ and $r = 3$

6. Center at $(0, -4)$ and $r = 6$

7. Center at the origin and $r = 7$

8. Center at the origin and $r = 1$

For Problems 9–24, find the center and length of a radius of each circle. (Objective 2)

9. $x^2 + y^2 - 6x - 10y + 30 = 0$

10. $x^2 + y^2 + 8x - 12y + 43 = 0$

11. $x^2 + y^2 + 10x + 1 = 0$

12. $x^2 + y^2 + 6y - 7 = 0$

13. $x^2 + y^2 - 10x = 0$

14. $x^2 + y^2 - 4x + 2y = 0$

15. $x^2 + y^2 - 8$ 16. $4x^2 + 4y^2 = 1$

17. $4x^2 + 4y^2 - 4x - 8y - 11 = 0$

18. $36x^2 + 36y^2 + 48x - 36y - 11 = 0$

19. $x^2 + y^2 - 4y - 2 = 0$

20. $x^2 + y^2 + 8x + 4 = 0$

21. $3x^2 + 3y^2 - 6x + 12y - 1 = 0$

22. $2x^2 + 2y^2 - 10x - 2y + 2 = 0$

23. $2x^2 + 2y^2 + 6x + 14y + 4 = 0$

24. $4x^2 + 4y^2 + 8x - 3 = 0$

25. Find the equation of the circle that passes through the origin and has its center at $(6, -8)$.

26. Find the equation of the circle where the line segment determined by the points $(3, -4)$ and $(-3, 2)$ is a diameter.

27. Find the equation of the circle where the line segment determined by $(-4, 9)$ and $(10, -3)$ is a diameter.

28. Find the equation of the circle that passes through the origin and has its center at $(-3, -4)$.

29. Find the equation of the circle that is tangent to both axes, has a radius of length seven units, and has its center in the fourth quadrant.

30. Find the equation of the circle that passes through the origin, has an x intercept of -6, and has a y intercept of 12. (The perpendicular bisector of a chord contains the center of the circle.)

31. Find the equations of the circles that are tangent to the x axis and have a radius of length five units. In each case, the abscissa of the center is -3. (There is more than one circle that satisfies these conditions.)

For Problems 32–48, graph each equation.
(Objective 3)

32. $4x^2 + 25y^2 = 100$ **33.** $9x^2 + 4y^2 = 36$

34. $x^2 - y^2 = 4$ **35.** $y^2 - x^2 = 9$

36. $x^2 + y^2 - 4x - 2y - 4 = 0$

37. $x^2 + y^2 - 4x = 0$ **38.** $4x^2 + y^2 = 4$

39. $x^2 + 9y^2 = 36$

40. $x^2 + y^2 + 2x - 6y - 6 = 0$

41. $y^2 - 3x^2 = 9$ **42.** $4x^2 - 9y^2 = 16$

43. $x^2 + y^2 + 4x + 6y - 12 = 0$

44. $2x^2 + 5y^2 = 50$ **45.** $4x^2 + 3y^2 = 12$

46. $x^2 + y^2 - 6x + 8y = 0$

47. $3x^2 - 2y^2 = 3$ **48.** $y^2 - 8x^2 = 9$

The graphs of equations of the form $xy = k$, where k is a nonzero constant, are also hyperbolas, sometimes referred to as **rectangular hyperbolas.** For Problems 49–52, graph each rectangular hyperbola.

49. $xy = 2$ **50.** $xy = 4$

51. $xy = -3$ **52.** $xy = -2$

Thoughts Into Words

53. What is the graph of $xy = 0$? Explain your answer.

54. We have graphed various equations of the form $Ax^2 + By^2 = F$, where F is a nonzero constant. Describe the graph of each of the following and explain your answers.

(a) $x^2 + y^2 = 0$ **(b)** $2x^2 + 3y^2 = 0$

(c) $x^2 - y^2 = 0$ **(d)** $4x^2 - 9y^2 = 0$

Further Investigations

55. By expanding $(x - h)^2 + (y - k)^2 = r^2$, we obtain $x^2 - 2hx + h^2 + y^2 - 2ky + k^2 - r^2 = 0$. Comparing this result to the form $x^2 + y^2 + Dx + Ey + F = 0$, we see that $D = -2h$, $E = -2k$, and $F = h^2 + k^2 - r^2$. Therefore the center and the length of a radius of a circle can be found by using $h = D/2$, $k = E/-2$, and $r = \sqrt{h^2 - k^2 - F}$. Use these relationships to find the center and the length of a radius of each of the following circles.

(a) $x^2 + y^2 - 2x - 8y + 8 = 0$

(b) $x^2 + y^2 + 4x - 14y + 49 = 0$

(c) $x^2 + y^2 + 12x + 8y - 12 = 0$

(d) $x^2 + y^2 - 16x + 20y + 115 = 0$

(e) $x^2 + y^2 - 12y - 45 = 0$

(f) $x^2 + y^2 + 14x = 0$

56. Use a coordinate geometry approach to prove that an angle inscribed in a semicircle is a right angle (see Figure 2.58).

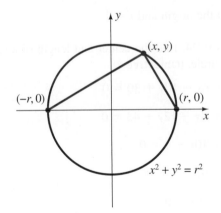

Figure 2.58

57. Use a coordinate geometry approach to prove that a line segment from the center of a circle bisecting a chord is perpendicular to the chord. [*Hint*: Let the ends of the chord be $(r, 0)$ and (a, b).]

Graphing Calculator Activities

58. For each of the following equations, predict the type and location of the graph, and then use your graphing calculator to check your prediction.

(a) $x^2 + y^2 = 9$ **(b)** $2x^2 + y^2 = 4$

(c) $x^2 - y^2 = 9$ **(d)** $4x^2 - y^2 = 16$

(e) $x^2 + 2x + y^2 - 4 = 0$

(f) $x^2 + y^2 - 4y - 2 = 0$

(g) $(x - 2)^2 + (y + 1)^2 = 4$

(h) $(x + 3)^2 - (y - 4)^2 = 9$

(i) $9y^2 - 4x^2 = 36$ **(j)** $9y^2 + 4x^2 = 36$

Answers to the Concept Quiz

1. C **2.** B **3.** A **4.** True **5.** False **6.** False **7.** False **8.** True

OBJECTIVE	SUMMARY	EXAMPLE
Find the distance between two points on a number line. (Section 2.1/Objective 1)	The distance on a number line between any two points with coordinates x_1 and x_2 is determined by $\lvert x_2 - x_1 \rvert$. Use the formula $x = x_1 + \dfrac{a}{b}(x_2 - x_1)$ to find the coordinate of a point that is somewhere between x_1 and x_2.	Find the coordinates of a point on a number line that is three-fourths of the distance from -4 and 12. **Solution** Apply the formula $x = x_1 + \dfrac{a}{b}(x_2 - x_1)$, where $x_1 = -4$, $x_2 = 12$, and $\dfrac{a}{b} = \dfrac{3}{4}$. $x = -4 + \dfrac{3}{4}[12 - (-4)] = -4 + \dfrac{3}{4}(16) = 8$
Find the distance between two points in the rectangular coordinate system. (Section 2.1/Objective 2)	The distance between two points, $P_1(x_1, y_1)$ and $P_2(x_2, y_2)$ is given by the formula $d = \sqrt{(x_2 - x_1)^2 + (y_2 - y_1)^2}$.	Find the distance between $(3, -1)$ and $(-5, 0)$. **Solution** $d = \sqrt{(x_2 - x_1)^2 + (y_2 - y_1)^2}$ $d = \sqrt{(-5 - 3)^2 + (0 - (-1))^2}$ $d = \sqrt{(8)^2 + (1)^2} = \sqrt{64 + 1} = \sqrt{65}$
Graph linear equations. (Section 2.2/Objective 1)	A solution of an equation in two variables is an ordered pair of real numbers that satisfy the equation. The ordered pair solutions can be plotted as points on a rectangular coordinate system. Equations of the form $Ax + By = C$, where A, B, and C are constants (A and B not both zero) are linear equations and have straight line graphs.	Graph $2x - y = 4$. **Solution** Find ordered pairs that satisfy the equation by choosing values of x and determining y. <table><tr><td>x</td><td>-1</td><td>0</td><td>1</td></tr><tr><td>y</td><td>-6</td><td>-4</td><td>-2</td></tr></table> Plot the points.

OBJECTIVE	SUMMARY	EXAMPLE
Find the x and y intercepts for the graph of a linear equation. (Section 2.2/Objective 2)	The x coordinates of the points that a graph has in common with the x axis are called the x intercepts of the graph. The y coordinates of the points that a graph has in common with the y axis are called the y intercepts of the graph. To find the x intercept(s), let $y = 0$ and solve for x. To find the y intercept(s), let $x = 0$ and solve for y.	Find the x and y intercepts and graph the linear equation $3x - 2y = 6$. **Solution** x intercept $\qquad$ y intercept Let $y - 0$ $\qquad$ Let $x = 0$ $3x - 2(0) = 6$ $\qquad$ $0 - 2y = 6$ $x = 2$ $\qquad\quad$ $y = -3$

(continued)

OBJECTIVE	SUMMARY	EXAMPLE
Graph linear inequalities. (Section 2.2/Objective 3)	To graph a linear inequality: 1. Graph the line for the corresponding equality. Use a solid line if the equality is included in the given statement or a dashed line if the equality is not included. 2. Then a test point is used to determine which half-plane is included in the solution set. See page 221 for the detailed steps.	Graph $x - 2y \leq -4$. **Solution** First graph $x - 2y = -4$. Choose $(0, 0)$ as a test point. Substituting $(0, 0)$ into the inequality yields $0 \leq -4$. Because the test point $(0, 0)$ makes the inequality a false statement, the half-plane containing the point $(0, 0)$ is not in the solution.
Find the slope of a line determined by two points. (Section 2.3/Objective 1)	The slope (denoted by m) of a line determined by the points (x_1, y_1) and (x_2, y_2) is given by the slope formula $m = \dfrac{y_2 - y_1}{x_2 - x_1}$, where $x_2 \neq x_1$.	Find the slope of a line that contains the points $(-1, 2)$ and $(7, 8)$. **Solution** Use the slope formula. $$m = \frac{8 - 2}{7 - (-1)} = \frac{6}{8} = \frac{3}{4}$$ Thus the slope of the line is $\dfrac{3}{4}$.

OBJECTIVE	SUMMARY	EXAMPLE
Write the equation of a line, given a slope and a point contained in the line. (Section 2.3/Objective 2)	To determine the equation of a line given a set of conditions, we can use the point–slope form $y - y_1 = m(x - x_1)$, or $m = \dfrac{y - y_1}{x - x_1}$. The result can be expressed in standard form or slope–intercept form.	Find the equation of a line that contains the point $(1, -4)$ and has a slope of $\dfrac{3}{2}$. **Solution** Substitute $\dfrac{3}{2}$ for m and $(1, -4)$ for (x_1, y_1) into the formula $m = \dfrac{y - y_1}{x - x_1}$. $\dfrac{3}{2} = \dfrac{y - (-4)}{x - 1}$ Simplifying this equation yields $3x - 2y = 11$.
Write the equation of a line, given two points contained in the line. (Section 2.3/Objective 3)	First calculate the slope of the line. Substitute the slope and the coordinates of one of the points into $y - y_1 = m(x - x_1)$ or $m = \dfrac{y - y_1}{x - x_1}$.	Find the equation of a line that contains the points $(-3, 4)$ and $(-6, 10)$. **Solution** First calculate the slope. $m = \dfrac{10 - 4}{-6 - (-3)} = \dfrac{6}{-3} = -2$ Now substitute -2 for m and $(-3, 4)$ for (x_1, y_1) in the formula $y - y_1 = m(x - x_1)$. $y - 4 = -2[x - (-3)]$ Simplifying this equation yields $2x + y = -2$.
Write the equation of a line parallel or perpendicular to another line and containing a specified point. (Section 2.3/Objective 4)	If two lines have slopes m_1 and m_2, respectively, then 1. The two lines are parallel if and only if $m_1 = m_2$. 2. The two lines are perpendicular if and only if $(m_1)(m_2) = -1$.	Find the equation of a line that contains the point $(2, 1)$ and is parallel to the line $y = 3x + 4$. **Solution** The slope of the given line is 3. Therefore the slope of the parallel line is 3. Use the slope, 3, and the point $(2, 1)$ to determine the equation. $y - 1 = 3(x - 2)$ Simplifying this equation yields $y = 3x - 5$.

(continued)

OBJECTIVE	SUMMARY	EXAMPLE
Solve application problems involving the slope of a line. (Section 2.3/Objective 5)	The concept of slope is used in most situations in which an incline is involved. In highway construction, the word *grade* is used for slope.	A certain highway has a grade of 2%. How many feet does it rise in a horizontal distance of one-third of a mile, which is 1760 feet. **Solution** A 2% grade is equivalent to a slope of $\dfrac{2}{100}$. We can set up the proportion $\dfrac{2}{100} = \dfrac{y}{1760}$, and solving for y gives us $y = 35.2$. So the highway rises 35.2 feet in one-third of a mile.
Determine if the graph of an equation is symmetric to the x axis, the y axis, or the origin. (Section 2.4/Objective 2)	The graph of an equation is symmetric with respect to the y axis if replacing x with $-x$ results in an equivalent equation. The graph of an equation is symmetric with respect to the x axis if replacing y with $-y$ results in an equivalent equation. The graph of an equation is symmetric with respect to origin if replacing x with $-x$ and y with $-y$ results in an equivalent equation.	Determine the type of symmetry exhibited by the graph of the following equation. $x = y^2 + 4$ **Solution** Replacing x with $-x$ gives $-x = y^2 + 4$. This is not an equivalent equation, so the graph will not exhibit x-axis symmetry. Replacing y with $-y$ gives $x = (-y)^2 + 4 = y^2 + 4$. This is an equivalent equation, so the graph will exhibit y-axis symmetry. Replacing x with $-x$ and y with $-y$ gives $(-x) = (-y)^2 + 4$ $-x = y^2 + 4$ This is not an equivalent equation, so the graph will not exhibit symmetry with respect to the origin.

OBJECTIVE	SUMMARY	EXAMPLE
Graph nonlinear equations. (Section 2.4/Objective 1)	The following suggestions are offered for graphing an equation in two variables. 1. Determine what type of symmetry the equation exhibits. 2. Find the intercepts. 3. Solve the equation for y or x if it is not already in such a form. 4. Set up a table of ordered pairs that satisfy the equation. The type of symmetry will affect your choice of values in the table. 5. Plot the points associated with the ordered pairs and connect them with a smooth curve. Then, if appropriate, reflect this part of the curve according to the symmetry shown by the equation.	Graph $x - y^2 + 4 = 0$. **Solution** Replacing y with $-y$ gives an equivalent equation, so the graph will be symmetric with respect to the x axis. To find the x intercept, let $y = 0$ and solve for x. This gives an x intercept of -4. To find the y intercept, let $x = 0$ and solve for y. This gives y intercepts of 2 and -2. Solving the equation for x gives the equation $x = y^2 - 4$. Choose values for y to obtain the table of points. $$\begin{array}{c\|c c c c} x & -4 & -3 & 0 & 5 \\ \hline y & 0 & 1 & 2 & 3 \end{array}$$
Write the equation of a circle. (Section 2.5/Objective 1)	The standard form of the equation of a circle that has a radius of length r and center at (h, k) is $(x - h)^2 + (y - k)^2 = r^2$.	Write the equation of circle that has its center at $(-7, 3)$ and a radius of length 4 units. **Solution** Substitute -7 for h, 3 for k, and 4 for r in $(x - h)^2 + (y - k)^2 = r^2$. $(x - (-7))^2 + (y - 3)^2 = 4^2$ $(x + 7)^2 + (y - 3)^2 = 16$

(continued)

OBJECTIVE	SUMMARY	EXAMPLE
Find the center and length of a radius, given the equation of a circle. (Section 2.5/Objective 2)	The graph of the equation $x^2 + y^2 + Dx + Ey + F = 0$ is a circle. The center and the length of a radius can be found by completing the square and comparing the result to the standard form of the equation of a circle $(x - h)^2 + (y - k)^2 = r^2$.	Find the center and the length of a radius of the circle $x^2 + y^2 + 4x - 10y + 20 = 0$. **Solution** $x^2 + y^2 + 4x - 10y + 20 = 0$ $x^2 + 4x + y^2 - 10y = -20$ $x^2 + 4x + 4 + y^2 - 10y + 25 =$ $\qquad\qquad\qquad\quad -20 + 4 + 25$ $(x + 2)^2 + (y - 5)^2 = 9$ The center is at $(-2, 5)$ and the length of a radius is $\sqrt{9} = 3$ units.
Draw graphs of circles, ellipses, and hyperbolas. (Section 2.5/Objective 3)	The graph of the equation $Ax^2 + By^2 = F$, where A, B, and F have the same sign and $A = B$ is a circle with the center at $(0, 0)$. The graph of the equation $Ax^2 + By^2 = F$, where A, B, and F have the same sign and $A \neq B$ is an ellipse with the center at $(0, 0)$. The graph of the equation $Ax^2 + By^2 = F$, where A and B are of unlike signs is a hyperbola with the center at $(0, 0)$.	Graph $9x^2 - y^2 = 9$. **Solution** When $y = 0$, then $x = \pm 1$. Hence the points $(1, 0)$ and $(-1, 0)$ are on the graph. To find the asymptotes, replace the constant term with zero and solve for y. $9x^2 - y^2 = 0$ $9x^2 = y^2$ $y = \pm 3x$ So the equations of the asymptotes are $y = 3x$ and $y = -3x$.

Chapter 2   Review Problem Set

1. On a number line, find the coordinate of the point located three-fifths of the distance from -4 to 11.

2. On a number line, find the coordinate of the point located four-ninths of the distance from 3 to -15.

3. In the xy plane, find the coordinates of the point located five-sixths of the distance from $(-1, -3)$ to $(11, 1)$.

4. If one endpoint of a line segment is at $(8, 14)$, and the midpoint of the segment is $(3, 10)$, find the coordinates of the other endpoint.

5. Verify that the points $(2, 2)$, $(6, 4)$, and $(5, 6)$ are vertices of a right triangle.

6. Verify that the points $(-3, 1)$, $(1, 3)$, and $(9, 7)$ lie in a straight line.

For Problems 7–12, identify any symmetries (x axis, y axis, origin) that the equation exhibits.

7. $x = y^2 + 4$ 8. $y = x^2 + 6x - 1$

9. $5x^2 - y^2 = 4$

10. $x^2 + y^2 - 2y - 4 = 0$

11. $y = -x$ 12. $y = \dfrac{6}{x^2 + 4}$

For Problems 13–22, graph each of the following.

13. $x^2 + y^2 - 6x + 4y - 3 = 0$

14. $x^2 + 4y^2 = 16$ 15. $x^2 - 4y^2 = 16$

16. $-2x + 3y = 6$ 17. $2x - y < 4$

18. $x^2 y^2 = 4$ 19. $4y^2 - 3x^2 = 8$

20. $x^2 + y^2 + 10y = 0$ 21. $9x^2 + 2y^2 = 36$

22. $y \le -2x - 3$

23. Find the slope of the line determined by $(-3, -4)$ and $(-5, 6)$.

24. Find the slope of the line with equation $5x - 7y = 12$.

For Problems 25–28, write the equation of the line that satisfies the stated conditions. Express final equations in standard form ($Ax + By = C$).

25. Contains the point $(7, 2)$ and has a slope of $-\dfrac{3}{4}$

26. Contains the points $(-3, -2)$ and $(1, 6)$

27. Contains the point $(2, -4)$ and is parallel to $4x + 3y = 17$

28. Contains the point $(-5, 4)$ and is perpendicular to $2x - y = 7$

For Problems 29–32, write the equation of the circle that satisfies the stated conditions. Express final equations in the form $x^2 + y^2 + Dx + Ey + F = 0$.

29. Center at $(5, -6)$ and $r = 1$

30. The endpoints of a diameter are $(-2, 4)$ and $(6, 2)$.

31. Center at $(-5, 12)$ and passes through the origin

32. Tangent to both axes, $r = 4$, and center in the third quadrant

Chapter 2 Test

1. On a number line, find the coordinate of the point located two-thirds of the distance from -4 to 14.

2. In the xy plane, find the coordinates of the point located three-fourths of the distance from $(2, -3)$ to $(-6, 9)$.

3. If one endpoint of a line segment is at $(-2, -1)$, and the midpoint of the segment is at $\left(2, -\dfrac{5}{2}\right)$, find the coordinates of the other endpoint.

4. Find the slope of the line determined by $(-4, -2)$ and $(5, -6)$.

5. Find the slope of the line determined by the equation $2x - 7y = -9$.

For Problems 6–10, determine the equation of the line that satisfies the stated conditions. Express final equations in standard form.

6. Has a slope of $-\dfrac{3}{4}$ and a y intercept of -3

7. Contains the points $(1, -4)$ and $(4, 7)$

8. Contains the point $(-1, 4)$ and is parallel to $x - 5y = 5$

9. Contains the point $(3, 5)$ and is perpendicular to $4x + 7y = 3$

10. Contains the point $(-2, -4)$ and is perpendicular to the x axis

For Problems 11–13, determine the equation of the circle that satisfies the stated conditions. Express final equations in the form $x^2 + y^2 + Dx + Ey + F = 0$.

11. Center at $(-3, -6)$ and a radius of length four units

12. The endpoints of a diameter are at $(-1, 3)$ and $(5, 5)$.

13. Center at $(4, -3)$ and passes through the origin

14. Find the center and the length of a radius of the circle $x^2 + 16x + y^2 - 10y + 80 = 0$.

15. Find the lengths of the three sides of the triangle determined by $(3, 2)$, $(5, -2)$, and $(-1, -1)$. Express the lengths in simplest radical form.

16. Find the x intercepts of the graph of the equation $x^2 - 6x + y^2 + 2y + 5 = 0$.

17. Find the y intercepts of the graph of the equation $5x^2 + 12y^2 = 36$.

18. Find the length of the major axis of the ellipse $9x^2 + 2y^2 = 18$.

19. Find the equations of the asymptotes for the hyperbola $9x^2 - 16y^2 = 48$.

20. Identify any symmetries (x axis, y axis, origin) that the equation exhibits.

    a. $x^2 + 2x + y^2 - 6 = 0$

    b. $xy = -4$

    c. $y = \dfrac{4}{x^2 + 1}$

    d. $x^2y^2 = 5$

21. Graph the inequality $3x - y \leq 6$.

For Problems 22–25, graph the equation.

22. $y^2 - 2x^2 = 9$

23. $x = y^2 - 4$

24. $3x^2 + 5y^2 = 45$

25. $x^2 + 4x + y^2 - 12 = 0$

Chapters 0–2 Cumulative Review Problem Set

For Problems 1–6, evaluate each expression.

1. 3^{-3}

2. -4^{-2}

3. $\left(\dfrac{2}{3}\right)^{-2}$

4. $-\sqrt[3]{\dfrac{8}{27}}$

5. $\left(\dfrac{1}{27}\right)^{-2/3}$

6. $\dfrac{1}{\left(\dfrac{3}{4}\right)^{-2}}$

For Problems 7–12, perform the indicated operations and simplify. Express final answers using positive exponents only.

7. $(5x^{-3}y^{-2})(4xy^{-1})$

8. $(-7a^{-3}b^2)(8a^4b^{-3})$

9. $\left(\dfrac{1}{2}x^{-2}y^{-1}\right)^{-2}$

10. $\dfrac{80x^{-3}y^{-4}}{16xy^{-6}}$

11. $\left(\dfrac{102x^{2/3}y^{3/4}}{6xy^{-1}}\right)^{-1}$

12. $\left(\dfrac{14a^3b^{-4}}{7a^{-1}b^3}\right)^2$

For Problems 13–20, express each in simplest radical form. All variables represent positive real numbers.

13. $-5\sqrt{72}$

14. $2\sqrt{27x^3y^2}$

15. $\sqrt[3]{56x^4y^7}$

16. $\dfrac{3\sqrt{18}}{5\sqrt{12}}$

17. $\sqrt{\dfrac{3x}{7y}}$

18. $\dfrac{5}{\sqrt{2}-3}$

19. $\dfrac{3\sqrt{7}}{2\sqrt{2}-\sqrt{6}}$

20. $\dfrac{4\sqrt{x}}{\sqrt{x}+3\sqrt{y}}$

For Problems 21–26, perform the indicated operations involving rational expressions. Express final answers in simplest form.

21. $\dfrac{12x^2y}{18x}\cdot\dfrac{9x^3y^3}{16xy^2}$

22. $\dfrac{-15ab^2}{14a^3b}\div\dfrac{20a}{7b^2}$

23. $\dfrac{3x^2+5x-2}{x^2-4}\cdot\dfrac{5x^2-9x-2}{3x^2-x}$

24. $\dfrac{2x-1}{4}+\dfrac{3x+2}{6}-\dfrac{x-1}{8}$

25. $\dfrac{5}{3n^2}-\dfrac{2}{n}+\dfrac{3}{2n}$

26. $\dfrac{5x}{x^2+6x-27}+\dfrac{3}{x^2-9}$

For Problems 27–38, solve each equation.

27. $3(-2x-1)-2(3x+4)=-4(2x-3)$

28. $(2x-1)(3x+4)=(x+2)(6x-5)$

29. $\dfrac{3x-1}{4}-\dfrac{2x-1}{5}=\dfrac{1}{10}$

30. $9x^2-4=0$

31. $5x^3+10x^2-40x=0$

32. $7t^2-31t+12=0$

33. $x^4+15x^2-16=0$

34. $|5x-2|=3$

35. $2x^2-3x-1=0$

36. $(3x-2)(x+4)=(2x-1)(x-1)$

37. $\sqrt{5-t}+1=\sqrt{7+2t}$

38. $(2x-1)^2+4=0$

For Problems 39–48, solve each inequality. Express the solution sets using interval notation.

39. $-2(x-1)+(3-2x)>4(x+1)$

40. $2n+1+\dfrac{3n-1}{4}\geq\dfrac{n-1}{2}$

41. $0.09x+0.12(450-x)\geq46.5$

42. $n^2+5n>24$

43. $6x^2+7x-3<0$

275

44. $(2x - 1)(x + 3)(x - 4) > 0$

45. $\dfrac{3x - 2}{x + 1} \leq 0$ **46.** $\dfrac{x + 5}{x - 1} \geq 2$

47. $|3x - 1| > 5$ **48.** $|5x - 3| < 12$

For Problems 49–54, graph each equation.

49. $x^2 + 4y^2 = 36$ **50.** $4x^2 - y^2 = 4$

51. $y = -x^3 - 1$ **52.** $y = -x + 3$

53. $y^2 - 5x^2 = 9$ **54.** $y = -\dfrac{3}{4}x - 1$

For Problems 55–58, solve each problem.

55. Find the center and the length of a radius of the circle with equation $x^2 + y^2 + 14x - 8y + 56 = 0$.

56. Write the equation of the line that is parallel to $3x - 4y = 17$ and contains the point $(2, 8)$.

57. Find the coordinates of the point located one-fifth of the distance from $(-3, 4)$ to $(2, 14)$.

58. Write the equation of the perpendicular bisector of the line segment determined by $(-3, 4)$ and $(5, 10)$.

For Problems 59–65, set up an equation and solve the problem.

59. A retailer has some shirts that cost $22 per shirt. At what price should they be sold to obtain a profit of 30% of the cost? At what price should they be sold to obtain a profit of 30% of the selling price?

60. A total of $7500 was invested, part of it at 5% yearly interest and the remainder at 6%. The total yearly interest was $420. How much was invested at each rate?

61. The length of a rectangle is 1 inch less than twice the width. The area of the rectangular region is 36 square inches. Find the length and width of the rectangle.

62. The length of one side of a triangle is 4 centimeters less than three times the length of the altitude to that side. The area of the triangle is 80 square centimeters. Find the length of the side and the length of the altitude to that side.

63. How many milliliters of pure acid must be added to 40 milliliters of a 30% acid solution to obtain a 50% acid solution?

64. Amanda rode her bicycle out into the country at a speed of 15 miles per hour and returned along the same route at 10 miles per hour. The round trip took 5 hours. How far out did she ride?

65. If two inlet pipes are both open, they can fill a pool in 1 hour and 12 minutes. One of the pipes can fill the pool by itself in 2 hours. How long would it take the other pipe to fill the pool by itself?

3

Functions

3.1 Concept of a Function

3.2 Linear Functions and Applications

3.3 Quadratic Functions and Applications

3.4 Transformations of Some Basic Curves

3.5 Combining Functions

3.6 Direct and Inverse Variation

The volume of a pyramid is a function of its height and the area of its base.

© sculpies/Shutterstock.com

A golf pro-shop operator finds that she can sell 30 sets of golf clubs in a year at $500 per set. Furthermore, she predicts that for each $25 decrease in price, she could sell three extra sets of golf clubs. At what price should she sell the clubs to maximize gross income? We can use the quadratic function $f(x) = (30 + 3x)(500 - 25x)$ to determine that the clubs should be sold at $375 per set.

One of the fundamental concepts of mathematics is that of a function. Functions unify different areas of mathematics, and they also serve as a meaningful way of applying mathematics to many problems. They provide a means of studying quantities that vary with one another; that is, a change in one produces a corresponding change in another. In this chapter, we will (1) introduce the basic ideas pertaining to functions, (2) use the idea of a function to show how some concepts from previous chapters are related, and (3) discuss some applications in which functions are used.

3.1   Concept of a Function

OBJECTIVES

1 Know the definition of a function

2 Evaluate a function for a given input value

3 Evaluate a piecewise-defined function for a given input value

4 Determine the domain and range of a function

5 Determine if a function is even, odd, or neither

6 Solve application problems involving functions

The notion of correspondence is used in everyday situations and is central to the concept of a function. Consider the following correspondences.

1. To each person in a class, there corresponds an assigned seat.

2. To each day of a year, there corresponds an assigned integer that represents the high temperature for that day in a certain geographic location.

3. To each book in a library, there corresponds a whole number that represents the number of pages in the book.

Such correspondences can be depicted as in Figure 3.1. To each member in set A, there corresponds *one and only one* member in set B. For example, in the first correspondence, set A would consist of the students in a class, and set B would be the assigned seats. In the second example, set A would consist of the days of a year and set B would be a set of integers. Furthermore, the same integer might be assigned to more than one day of the year. (Different days might have the same high temperature.) The key idea is that *one and only one* integer is assigned to *each* day of the year. Likewise, in the third example, more than one book may have the same number of pages, but to each book, there is assigned one and only one number that represents the number of pages.

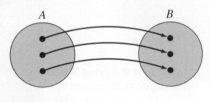

Figure 3.1

Mathematically, the general concept of a function can be defined as follows:

Definition 3.1

A **function** f is a correspondence between two non-empty sets X and Y that assigns to each element x of set X one and only one element y of set Y. The element y being assigned is called the **image** of x. The set X is called the **domain** of the function, and the set of all images is called the **range** of the function.

In Definition 3.1, the image y is usually denoted by $f(x)$. Thus the symbol $f(x)$, which is read "f of x" or "the value of f at x," represents the element in the range associated with the element x from the domain. Figure 3.2 depicts this situation. Again we emphasize that each member of the domain has precisely one image in the range; however, different members in the domain, such as a and b in Figure 3.2, may have the same image.

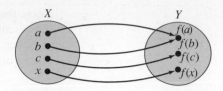

Figure 3.2

In Definition 3.1, we named the function f. It is common to name a function with a single letter, and the letters f, g, and h are often used. We suggest more meaningful choices when functions are used in real-world situations. For example, if a problem involves a profit function, then naming the function p or even P seems natural. Be careful not to confuse f and $f(x)$. Remember that f is used to name a function, whereas $f(x)$ is an element of the range—namely, the element assigned to x by f.

The assignments made by a function are often expressed as ordered pairs. For example, the assignments in Figure 3.2 could be expressed as $(a, f(a))$, $(b, f(b))$, $(c, f(c))$, and $(x, f(x))$, where the first components are from the domain, and the second components are from the range. Thus a function can also be thought of as a set of ordered pairs in which no two of the ordered pairs have the same first component.

Remark: In some texts, the concept of a relation is introduced first, and then functions are defined as special kinds of relations. A **relation** is defined as a set of ordered pairs, and a function is defined as a relation in which no two ordered pairs have the same first element.

The ordered pairs that represent a function can be generated by various means, such as a graph or a chart. However, one of the most common ways of generating ordered pairs is by using equations. For example, the equation $f(x) = 2x + 3$ indicates that to each value of x in the domain, we assign $2x + 3$ from the range. For example,

$f(1) = 2(1) + 3 = 5$ produces the ordered pair $(1, 5)$

$f(4) = 2(4) + 3 = 11$ produces the ordered pair $(4, 11)$

$f(-2) = 2(-2) + 3 = -1$ produces the ordered pair $(-2, -1)$

It may be helpful for you to picture the concept of a function in terms of a function machine, as illustrated in Figure 3.3. Each time a value of x is put into the machine, the equation $f(x) = 2x + 3$ is used to generate one and only one value for $f(x)$.

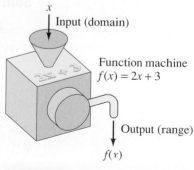

Figure 3.3

Using the ordered-pair interpretation of a function, we can define the **graph** of a function f to be the set of all points in a plane of the form $(x, f(x))$, where x is from the domain of f. In other words, the graph of f is the same as the graph of the equation $y = f(x)$. Furthermore, because $f(x)$, or y, takes on only one value for each value of x, we can easily tell whether a given graph represents a function. For example, in Figure 3.4(a), for any choice of x there is only one value for y. Geometrically this means that no vertical line intersects the curve in more than one point. On the other hand, Figure 3.4(b) does not represent the graph of a function because certain values of x (all positive values) produce more than one value for y. In other words, some vertical lines intersect the curve in more than one point, as illustrated in Figure 3.4(b).

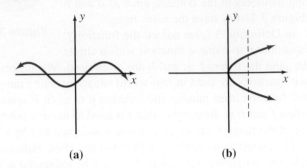

(a)   (b)

Figure 3.4

A vertical-line test for functions can be stated as follows.

Vertical-Line Test

If each vertical line intersects a graph in no more than one point, then the graph represents a function.

Let's consider some examples to illustrate these ideas about functions.

Classroom Example
If $f(x) = x^2 + x - 3$, find $f(2)$, $f(-2), f(a)$, and $f(3a)$.

EXAMPLE 1

If $f(x) = x^2 - x + 4$ and $g(x) = -2x + 7$, find $f(3), g(-5), f(-1), g(a), g(2a)$ and $f(a + 3)$.

Solution

$$f(3) = (3)^2 - (3) + 4 = 9 - 3 + 4 = 10$$
$$g(-5) = -2(-5) + 7 = 10 + 7 = 17$$
$$f(-1) = (-1)^2 - (-1) + 4 = 1 + 1 + 4 = 6$$
$$g(a) = -2a + 7$$
$$g(2a) = -2(2a) + 7 = -4a + 7$$
$$f(a + 3) = (a + 3)^2 - (a + 3) + 4 = a^2 + 6a + 9 - a - 3 + 4 = a^2 + 5a + 10$$

Evaluating Piecewise-Defined Functions

Sometimes the rule of assignment for a function consists of more than one part. Different rules are assigned depending on x, the element in the domain. An everyday example of this concept is that the price of admission to a theme park depends on whether you are a child, an adult, or a senior citizen. In mathematics we often refer to such functions as *piecewise-defined functions*. Let's consider examples of such functions.

Classroom Example
If $f(x) = \begin{cases} 4x - 3 & x \geq 0 \\ 2x + 5 & x < 0 \end{cases}$
find $f(1), f(3), f(-2), f(-5)$.

EXAMPLE 2

If $f(x) = \begin{cases} 2x + 1 & \text{for } x \geq 0 \\ 3x - 1 & \text{for } x < 0 \end{cases}$ find $f(2), f(4), f(-1)$, and $f(-3)$.

Solution

For $x \geq 0$, we use the assignment $f(x) = 2x + 1$.

$$f(2) = 2(2) + 1 = 5$$
$$f(4) = 2(4) + 1 = 9$$

For $x < 0$, we use the assignment $f(x) = 3x - 1$.

$$f(-1) = 3(-1) - 1 = -4$$
$$f(-3) = 3(-3) - 1 = -10$$

Classroom Example
A state government decides to collect taxes based on an individual's income. The following function determines the taxes due; x represents an individual's income in dollars.

$f(x) = \begin{cases} 0.04x & 0 < x \leq 30{,}000 \\ 0.06x & 30{,}000 < x \leq 60{,}000 \\ 0.08x & x > 60{,}000 \end{cases}$

Find the state tax on incomes of $28,000, $74,000, $56,000, and $60,000.

EXAMPLE 3

A county government collects taxes for schools based on the income of its citizens rather than on real estate taxes. The county uses the following function to determine the amount of tax due; x represents a citizen's annual income in dollars.

$$f(x) = \begin{cases} 0.05x & 0 < x \leq 20{,}000 \\ 0.06x & 20{,}000 < x \leq 50{,}000 \\ 0.08x & 50{,}000 < x \end{cases}$$

If Darren, Martha, Tonieka, and Caleb earn annual incomes of $23,000, $18,500, $55,000, and $20,000, respectively, find the amount of tax each of them owes.

Solution

Because Darren has an income of $23,000, the function to be used is $f(x) = 0.06x$. Therefore, the tax is figured as $f(23000) = 0.06(23000) = 1380$. Darren will owe $1,380 in tax.

Because Martha has an income of $18,500, the function to be used is $f(x) = 0.05x$. Therefore, the tax is figured as $f(18500) = 0.05(18500) = 925$. Martha will owe $925 in tax.

Because Tonieka has an income of $55,000, the function to be used is $f(x) = 0.08x$. Therefore, the tax is figured as $f(55000) = 0.08(55000) = 4400$. Tonieka will owe $4,400 in tax.

Because Caleb has an income of $20,000, the function to be used is $f(x) = 0.05x$. Therefore, the tax is figured as $f(20000) = 0.05(20000) = 1000$. Caleb will owe $1000 in tax.

Determining the Domain and Range of a Function

For our purposes in this text, if the domain of a function is not specifically indicated or determined by a real-world application, then we will assume the domain is *all real number* replacements for the variable, provided that they represent elements in the domain and produce real number functional values. We have to be careful with functions that involve fractions and radicals. For functions that involve fractions, the domain cannot include any values that would make the denominator of the fraction equal to zero. For functions that involve radicals, the domain cannot include any values for which the radical would not be a real number, such as taking the square root of a negative number.

Classroom Example
For the function
$f(x) = \sqrt{2x + 6}$, (a) specify the domain, (b) determine the range, and (c) evaluate
$f\left(\dfrac{3}{2}\right)$, $f(29)$, and $f(6)$.

EXAMPLE 4

For the function $f(x) = \sqrt{x - 1}$, (a) specify the domain, (b) determine the range, and (c) evaluate $f(5)$, $f(50)$, and $f(25)$.

Solutions

(a) The radicand must be nonnegative, so $x - 1 \geq 0$ and thus $x \geq 1$. Therefore the domain (D) is

$$D = \{x \mid x \geq 1\}$$

(b) The symbol $\sqrt{}$ indicates the nonnegative square root; thus the range (R) is

$$R = \{f(x) \mid f(x) \geq 0\}$$

(c) $f(5) = \sqrt{5 - 1} = \sqrt{4} = 2$

$f(50) = \sqrt{50 - 1} = \sqrt{49} = 7$

$f(25) = \sqrt{25 - 1} = \sqrt{24} = \sqrt{4}\sqrt{6} = 2\sqrt{6}$ ∎

As we will see later, the range of a function is often easier to determine after we have graphed the function. However, our equation- and inequality-solving processes are frequently sufficient to determine the domain of a function. Let's consider some examples.

Classroom Example
Determine the domain for each of the following functions:

(a) $f(x) = \dfrac{7}{3x + 4}$

(b) $f(x) = \dfrac{1}{x^2 - 16}$

(c) $f(x) = \sqrt{x^2 - 5x - 24}$

EXAMPLE 5   Determine the domain for each of the following functions:

(a) $f(x) = \dfrac{3}{2x - 5}$ **(b)** $g(x) = \dfrac{1}{x^2 - 9}$ **(c)** $f(x) = \sqrt{x^2 + 4x - 12}$

Solutions

(a) We need to eliminate any values of x that will make the denominator zero. Therefore let's solve the equation $2x - 5 = 0$:

$$2x - 5 = 0$$
$$2x = 5$$
$$x = \frac{5}{2}$$

We can replace x with any real number except $\frac{5}{2}$ because $\frac{5}{2}$ makes the denominator zero. Thus the domain is

$$D = \left\{ x \mid x \neq \frac{5}{2} \right\}$$

(b) We need to eliminate any values of x that will make the denominator zero. Let's solve the equation $x^2 - 9 = 0$:

$$x^2 - 9 = 0$$
$$x^2 = 9$$
$$x = \pm 3$$

The domain is thus the set

$$D = \{x \mid x \neq 3 \text{ and } x \neq -3\}$$

(c) The radicand, $x^2 + 4x - 12$, must be nonnegative. Let's use a number line approach, as we did in Chapter 1, to solve the inequality $x^2 + 4x - 12 \geq 0$ (see Figure 3.5):

$$x^2 + 4x - 12 \geq 0$$
$$(x + 6)(x - 2) \geq 0$$

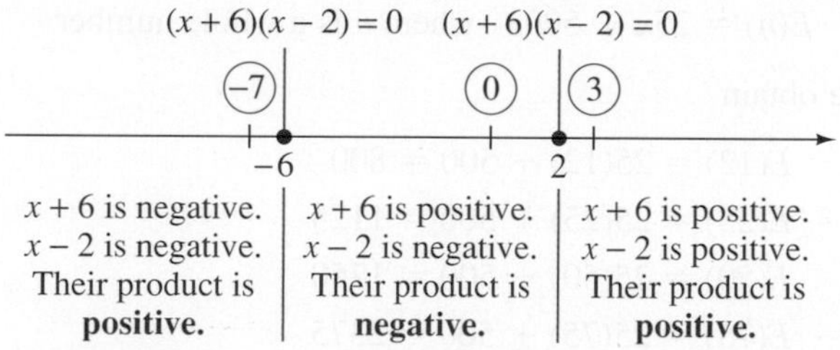
(x + 6)(x – 2) = 0
(x + 6)(x – 2) = 0
–7
0
3
–6
2
x + 6 is negative.
x – 2 is negative.
Their product is
positive.
x + 6 is positive.
x – 2 is negative.
Their product is
negative.
x + 6 is positive.
x – 2 is positive.
Their product is
positive.

Figure 3.5

The product $(x + 6)(x - 2)$ is nonnegative if $x \leq -6$ or $x \geq 2$. Using interval notation, we can express the domain as $(-\infty, -6] \cup [2, \infty)$. ■

Many functions that we will study throughout this text can be classified as even or odd functions. A function f having the property that $f(-x) = f(x)$ for every x in the domain of f is called an **even function.** A function f having the property that $f(-x) = -f(x)$ for every x in the domain of f is called an **odd function.**

Classroom Example
For each of the following, classify the function as even, odd, or neither even nor odd.
(a) $f(x) = 2x^4 - x^2$
(b) $f(x) = 2x^2 - 4x$
(c) $f(x) = 5x^3 - 2x$

EXAMPLE 6

For each of the following, classify the function as even, odd, or neither even nor odd.

(a) $f(x) = 2x^3 - 4x$ **(b)** $f(x) = x^4 - 7x^2$ **(c)** $f(x) = x^2 + 2x - 3$

Solutions

(a) The function $f(x) = 2x^3 - 4x$ is an odd function because $f(-x) = 2(-x)^3 - 4(-x) = -2x^3 + 4x$, which equals $-f(x)$.

(b) The function $f(x) = x^4 - 7x^2$ is an even function because $f(-x) = (-x)^4 - 7(-x)^2 = x^4 - 7x^2$, which equals $f(x)$.

(c) The function $f(x) = x^2 + 2x - 3$ is neither even nor odd because $f(-x) = (-x)^2 + 2(-x) - 3 = x^2 - 2x - 3$, which does not equal either $f(x)$ or $-f(x)$. ∎

Functions and function notation provide the basis for describing many real-world relationships. The next example illustrates this point.

Classroom Example
Suppose a factory determines that the overhead for producing a quantity of a certain item is $1500 and that the cost for producing each item is $95. Express the total expenses as a function of the number of items produced, and compute the expenses for producing 15, 21, 80, and 110 items.

EXAMPLE 7

Suppose a factory determines that the overhead for producing a quantity of a certain item is $500 and that the cost for producing each item is $25. Express the total expenses as a function of the number of items produced, and compute the expenses for producing 12, 25, 50, 75, and 100 items.

Solution

Let n represent the number of items produced. Then $25n + 500$ represents the total expenses. Using E to represent the expense function, we have

$$E(n) = 25n + 500, \quad \text{where } n \text{ is a whole number}$$

We obtain

$$E(12) = 25(12) + 500 = 800$$
$$E(25) = 25(25) + 500 = 1125$$
$$E(50) = 25(50) + 500 = 1750$$
$$E(75) = 25(75) + 500 = 2375$$
$$E(100) = 25(100) + 500 = 3000$$

Thus the total expenses for producing 12, 25, 50, 75, and 100 items are $800, $1125, $1750, $2375, and $3000, respectively. ∎

As we stated before, an equation such as $f(x) = 5x - 7$ that is used to determine a function can also be written $y = 5x - 7$. In either form, we refer to x as the **independent variable** and to y, or $f(x)$, as the **dependent variable**. Many formulas in mathematics and other related areas also determine functions. For example, the area formula for a circular region, $A = \pi r^2$, assigns to each positive real value for r a unique value for A. This formula determines a function f, where $f(r) = \pi r^2$. The variable r is the independent variable, and A, or $f(r)$, is the dependent variable.

Concept Quiz 3.1

For Problems 1–10, answer true or false.

1. For a function, each member of the domain has precisely one image in the range.
2. The set of ordered pairs $\{(1, 2), (2, 2), (3, 2), (4, 2)\}$ is a function.

3. The graph of a function g is the set of all points in a plane of the form $(x, g(x))$, where x is from the domain of g.
4. If a vertical line intersects a graph at more than one point, then the graph does not represent a function.
5. A piecewise-defined function assigns different rules to subsets of the domain.
6. For the function $f(t) = t^2 - 3t + 5$, the independent variable is t.
7. For the function $f(r) = 2\pi r$, r is the dependent variable.
8. The domain of the function $\{(1, 1), (2, 4), (3, 9), (4, 16)\}$ is the set $\{1, 2, 3, 4, 9, 16\}$.
9. The range of the function $\{(-2, 4), (-1, 1), (0, 0), (1, 1), (2, 4)\}$ is the set $\{0, 1, 4\}$.
10. The definition of a relation and the definition of a function are the same.

Problem Set 3.1

For Problems 1–6, state whether or not the set of ordered pairs represents a function. (Objective 1)

1. $\{(1, 5), (2, 8), (3, 11), (4, 14)\}$

2. $\{(0, 0), (2, 10), (4, 20), (6, 30), (8, 40)\}$

3. $\{(0, 5), (0, -5), (1, 2\sqrt{6}), (1, -2\sqrt{6})\}$

4. $\{(1, 1), (1, 2), (1, -1), (1, -2), (1, 3)\}$

5. $\{(1, 2), (2, 5), (3, 10), (4, 17), (5, 26)\}$

6. $\{(-1, 5), (0, 1), (1, -3), (2, -7)\}$

For Problems 7–14, determine whether the indicated graph represents a function of x. (Objective 1)

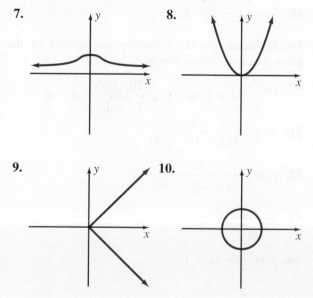

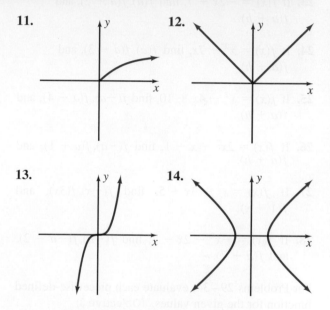

For Problems 15–28, evaluate each function for the given values. (Objective 2)

15. If $f(x) = -2x + 5$, find $f(3), f(5),$ and $f(-2)$.

16. If $f(x) = x^2 - 3x - 4$, find $f(2), f(4),$ and $f(-3)$.

17. If $g(x) = -2x^2 + x - 5$, find $g(3), g(-1),$ and $g(2a)$.

18. If $g(x) = -x^2 - 4x + 6$, find $g(0), g(5),$ and $g(-a)$.

19. If $h(x) = \dfrac{2}{3}x - \dfrac{3}{4}$, find $h(3)$, $h(4)$, and $h\left(-\dfrac{1}{2}\right)$.

20. If $h(x) = -\dfrac{1}{2}x + \dfrac{2}{3}$, find $h(-2)$, $h(6)$, and $h\left(-\dfrac{2}{3}\right)$.

21. If $f(x) = \sqrt{2x - 1}$, find $f(5)$, $f\left(\dfrac{1}{2}\right)$, and $f(23)$.

22. If $f(x) = \sqrt{3x + 2}$, find $f\left(\dfrac{14}{3}\right)$, $f(10)$, and $f\left(-\dfrac{1}{3}\right)$.

23. If $f(x) = -2x + 7$, find $f(a)$, $f(a + 2)$, and $f(a + h)$.

24. If $f(x) = x^2 - 7x$, find $f(a)$, $f(a - 3)$, and $f(a + h)$.

25. If $f(x) = x^2 - 4x + 10$, find $f(-a)$, $f(a - 4)$, and $f(a + h)$.

26. If $f(x) = 2x^2 - x - 1$, find $f(-a)$, $f(a + 1)$, and $f(a + h)$.

27. If $f(x) = x^2 + 3x + 5$, find $f(-x)$, $f(3x)$, and $f(1 - x)$.

28. If $f(x) = -x^2 - 2x - 7$, find $f(-a)$, $f(-a - 2)$, and $f(a + 7)$.

For Problems 29–34, evaluate each piecewise-defined function for the given values. **(Objective 3)**

29. If $f(x) = \begin{cases} x & \text{for } x \geq 0 \\ x^2 & \text{for } x < 0 \end{cases}$, find $f(4)$, $f(10)$, $f(-3)$, and $f(-5)$.

30. If $f(x) = \begin{cases} 3x + 2 & \text{for } x \geq 0 \\ 5x - 1 & \text{for } x < 0 \end{cases}$, find $f(2)$, $f(6)$, $f(-1)$, and $f(-4)$.

31. If $f(x) = \begin{cases} 2x & \text{for } x \geq 0 \\ -2x & \text{for } x < 0 \end{cases}$, find $f(3)$, $f(5)$, $f(-3)$, and $f(-5)$.

32. If $f(x) = \begin{cases} 2 & \text{for } x < 0 \\ x^2 + 1 & \text{for } 0 \leq x \leq 4, \\ -1 & \text{for } x > 4 \end{cases}$, find $f(3)$, $f(6)$, $f(0)$, and $f(-3)$.

33. If $f(x) = \begin{cases} 1 & \text{for } x > 0 \\ 0 & \text{for } -1 < x \leq 0, \\ -1 & \text{for } x \leq -1 \end{cases}$, find $f(2)$, $f(0)$, $f\left(-\dfrac{1}{2}\right)$, and $f(-4)$.

34. If $f(x) = \begin{cases} -x^2 & \text{for } x < 0 \\ x^2 & \text{for } x \geq 0 \end{cases}$, find $f(3)$, $f(-1)$, $f(-2)$, and $f(1)$.

For Problems 35–48, determine the domain and the range of the given function. **(Objective 4)**

35. $f(x) = \sqrt{3x - 4}$

36. $f(x) = \sqrt{x}$

37. $f(x) = x^2 - 2$

38. $f(x) = x^2 + 1$

39. $f(x) = |x|$

40. $f(x) = x^3$

41. $f(x) = -\sqrt{x}$

42. $f(x) = x^4$

43. $f(x) = 6$

44. $f(x) = \sqrt{x - 2} + 3$

45. $f(x) = \sqrt{x + 4} - 2$

46. $f(x) = |x| + 5$

47. $f(x) = -|x| - 6$

48. $f(x) = |x - 1| - 3$

For Problems 49–72, determine the domain of the given function. **(Objective 4)**

49. $f(x) = \dfrac{-4}{x + 2}$

50. $f(x) = \dfrac{3}{x - 4}$

51. $f(x) = \dfrac{5}{(2x - 1)(x + 4)}$

52. $f(x) = \dfrac{2x}{(x - 2)(x + 3)}$

53. $f(x) = \dfrac{1}{x^2 - 4}$

54. $f(x) = \sqrt{5x + 1}$

55. $f(x) = \dfrac{4x}{x^2 - x - 12}$

56. $g(x) = \dfrac{3}{x^2 + 5x + 6}$

57. $g(x) = \dfrac{x}{6x^2 + 13x - 5}$

58. $g(x) = \dfrac{5}{x^2 + 4x}$

59. $f(x) = \dfrac{x + 2}{x^2 + 1}$

60. $f(x) = \sqrt{-3x - 1}$

61. $f(x) = \sqrt{-4x + 3}$

62. $f(x) = \dfrac{2x - 1}{x^2 + 4}$

For Problems 63–72, express the domain of the given function using interval notation. **(Objective 4)**

63. $f(x) = \sqrt{x^2 - 16}$

64. $f(x) = \sqrt{x^2 - 1}$

65. $f(x) = \sqrt{x^2 + 1} - 4$

66. $f(x) = \sqrt{x^2 + 4}$

67. $f(x) = \sqrt{x^2 - 3x - 40}$

68. $f(x) = \sqrt{x^2 - 2x - 24}$

69. $f(x) = -\sqrt{8x^2 + 6x - 35}$

70. $f(x) = \sqrt{12x^2 + x - 6}$

71. $f(x) = \sqrt{1 - x^2}$

72. $f(x) = \sqrt{16 - x^2}$

For Problems 73–82, determine whether f is even, odd, or neither even nor odd. **(Objective 5)**

73. $f(x) = x^2$

74. $f(x) = x^3$

75. $f(x) = x^2 + 1$

76. $f(x) = 3x - 1$

77. $f(x) = x^2 + x$

78. $f(x) = x^3 + 1$

79. $f(x) = x^5$

80. $f(x) = x^4 + x^2 + 1$

81. $f(x) = -x^3$

82. $f(x) = x^5 + x^3 + x$

For Problems 83–92, solve each problem. **(Objective 6)**

83. A copy center charges for copies depending on the number of copies made. The following functions are used to determine the cost in dollars of color or black and white copies, where n is the number of copies.

Color Copies

$$f(n) = \begin{cases} 0.89n & 0 < n \le 20 \\ 0.79n & 20 < n \le 50 \\ 0.69n & 50 < n \end{cases}$$

Black and White Copies

$$f(n) = \begin{cases} 0.09n & 0 < n \le 50 \\ 0.08n & 50 < n \le 200 \\ 0.06n & 200 < n \end{cases}$$

Isaac is producing a cookbook that requires him to make 20 color copies and 210 black and white copies. What will it cost Isaac to make the copies?

84. An equipment rental agency charges rent in dollars for a small backhoe according to the following function, in which h represents the number of hours the backhoe is rented. Find the rent charged when the backhoe is rented for 6.5 hours; 3 hours; and 10 hours.

$$f(h) = \begin{cases} 100 + 50h & 0 < h \le 3 \\ 160 + 30h & 3 < h \le 8 \\ 200 + 25h & 8 < h \end{cases}$$

85. The equation $A(r) = \pi r^2$ expresses the area of a circular region as a function of the length of a radius (r). Compute $A(2)$, $A(3)$, $A(12)$, and $A(17)$ and express your answers to the nearest hundredth.

86. Suppose that the profit function for selling n items is given by

$$P(n) = -n^2 + 500n - 61{,}500$$

Evaluate $P(200)$, $P(230)$, $P(250)$, and $P(260)$.

87. The height of a projectile fired vertically into the air (neglecting air resistance) at an initial velocity of 64 feet per second is a function of the time (t) and is given by the equation $h(t) = 64t - 16t^2$. Compute $h(1)$, $h(2)$, $h(3)$, and $h(4)$.

88. In a physics experiment, it is found that the equation $V(t) = 1667t - 6940t^2$ expresses the velocity of an object as a function of time (t). Compute $V(0.1)$, $V(0.15)$, and $V(0.2)$.

89. The equation $I(r) = 500r$ expresses the amount of simple interest earned by an investment of $500 for 1 year as a function of the rate of interest (r). Compute $I(0.11)$, $I(0.12)$, $I(0.135)$, and $I(0.15)$.

90. A car rental agency charges $50 per day plus $0.32 a mile. Therefore the daily charge for renting a car is a function of the number of miles traveled (m) and can be expressed as $C(m) = 50 + 0.32m$. Compute $C(75)$, $C(150)$, $C(225)$, and $C(650)$.

91. The equation $A(r) = 2\pi r^2 + 16\pi r$ expresses the total surface area of a right circular cylinder of height 8 centimeters as a function of the length of a radius (r). Compute $A(2)$, $A(4)$, and $A(8)$ and express your answers to the nearest hundredth.

92. Suppose the height of a semielliptical archway is given by the function $h(x) = \sqrt{64 - 4x^2}$, where x is the distance from the center line of the arch. Compute $h(0)$, $h(2)$, and $h(4)$.

Thoughts Into Words

93. What does it mean to say that the domain of a function may be restricted if the function represents a real-world situation? Give three examples of such functions.

94. Expand Definition 3.1 to include a definition for the concept of a relation.

95. Are there any functions for which $f(a + b) = f(a) + f(b)$? Defend your answer.

96. Does $f(a + b) = f(a) + f(b)$ for all functions? Defend your answer.

Answers to the Concept Quiz

1. True **2.** True **3.** True **4.** True **5.** True **6.** True **7.** False **8.** False **9.** True **10.** False

3.2   Linear Functions and Applications

OBJECTIVES

1 Graph linear functions

2 Graph piecewise-defined functions

3 Determine a linear function for specified conditions

4 Solve application problems involving linear functions

As we use the function concept in our study of mathematics, it is helpful to classify certain types of functions and become familiar with their equations, characteristics, and graphs. This will enhance our problem-solving capabilities.

Any function that can be written in the form

$$f(x) = ax + b$$

where a and b are real numbers, is called a **linear function**. The following equations are examples of linear functions.

$$f(x) = -2x + 4 \qquad f(x) = 3x - 6 \qquad f(x) = \frac{2}{3}x + \frac{5}{6}$$

The equation $f(x) = ax + b$ can also be written as $y = ax + b$. From our work in Section 2.3, we know that $y = ax + b$ is the equation of a straight line that has a slope of a and a y intercept of b. This information can be used to graph linear functions, as illustrated by the following example.

Classroom Example
Graph $f(x) = -x - 2$.

EXAMPLE 1

Graph $f(x) = -2x + 4$.

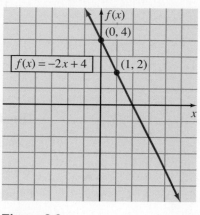

Solution

Because the y intercept is 4, the point $(0, 4)$ is on the line. Furthermore, because the slope is -2, we can move two units down and one unit to the right of $(0, 4)$ to determine the point $(1, 2)$. The line determined by $(0, 4)$ and $(1, 2)$ is drawn in Figure 3.6.

Figure 3.6

Note that in Figure 3.6, we labeled the vertical axis $f(x)$. We could also label it y because $y = f(x)$. We will use the $f(x)$ labeling for most of our work with functions; however, we will continue to refer to y-axis symmetry instead of $f(x)$-axis symmetry.

Recall from Section 2.2 that we can also graph linear equations by finding the two intercepts. This same approach can be used with linear functions, as illustrated by the next two examples.

Classroom Example
Graph $f(x) = 2x + 3$.

EXAMPLE 2   Graph $f(x) = 3x - 6$.

Solution

First, we see that $f(0) = -6$; thus the point $(0, -6)$ is on the graph. Second, by setting $3x - 6$ equal to zero and solving for x, we obtain

$$3x - 6 = 0$$
$$3x = 6$$
$$x = 2$$

Therefore $f(2) = 3(2) - 6 = 0$, and the point $(2, 0)$ is on the graph. The line determined by $(0, -6)$ and $(2, 0)$ is shown in Figure 3.7.

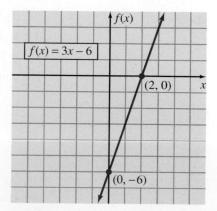

Figure 3.7

Classroom Example

Graph $f(x) = \dfrac{3}{4}x - \dfrac{3}{2}$.

 **EXAMPLE 3**   Graph the function $f(x) = \dfrac{2}{3}x + \dfrac{5}{6}$.

Solution

Because $f(0) = \dfrac{5}{6}$, the point $\left(0, \dfrac{5}{6}\right)$ is on the graph. By setting $\dfrac{2}{3}x + \dfrac{5}{6}$ equal to zero and solving for x, we obtain

$$\frac{2}{3}x + \frac{5}{6} = 0$$

$$\frac{2}{3}x = -\frac{5}{6}$$

$$x = -\frac{5}{4}$$

Therefore $f\left(-\dfrac{5}{4}\right) = 0$, and the point $\left(-\dfrac{5}{4}, 0\right)$ is on the graph. The line determined by the two points $\left(0, \dfrac{5}{6}\right)$ and $\left(-\dfrac{5}{4}, 0\right)$ is shown in Figure 3.8.

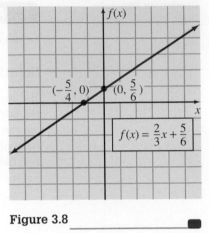

Figure 3.8

Now let's graph a piecewise-defined function that involves linear functions.

Classroom Example

Graph

$f(x) = \begin{cases} x - 2 & \text{for } x \le 0 \\ -x - 2 & \text{for } x > 0 \end{cases}$

EXAMPLE 4   Graph $f(x) = \begin{cases} -2x & \text{for } x < 1 \\ x + 3 & \text{for } x \ge 1 \end{cases}$

Solution

Because this function is defined piecewise, there are different assignments for values in the domain.

If $x < 1$, then $f(x) = -2x$. Thus for values of $x < 1$, we graph the linear function $f(x) = -2x$.

If $x \ge 1$, then $f(x) = x + 3$. Thus for values of $x \ge 1$, we graph the linear function $f(x) = x + 3$.

The complete graph is shown in Figure 3.9.

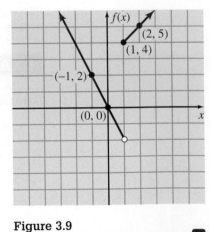

Figure 3.9

As you graph functions using function notation, it is often helpful to think of the ordinate of every point on the graph as the value of the function at a specific value of x. Geometrically the functional value is the directed distance of the point from the x axis.

This idea is illustrated in Figure 3.10 for the function $f(x) = x$ and in Figure 3.11 for the function $f(x) = 2$. The linear function $f(x) = x$ is often called the **identity function**. Any linear function of the form $f(x) = ax + b$, where $a = 0$, is called a **constant function**.

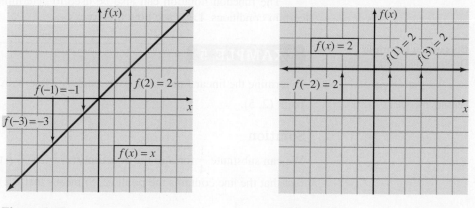

Figure 3.10   **Figure 3.11**

From our previous work with linear equations, we know that parallel lines have equal slopes and that two perpendicular lines have slopes that are negative reciprocals of each other. Thus when we work with linear functions of the form $f(x) = ax + b$, it is easy to recognize parallel and perpendicular lines. For example, the lines determined by $f(x) = 0.21x + 4$ and $g(x) = 0.21x - 3$ are parallel lines because both lines have a slope of 0.21 and different y intercepts. Let's use a graphing calculator to graph these two functions along with $h(x) = 0.21x + 2$ and $p(x) = 0.21x - 7$ (Figure 3.12).

The graphs of the functions $f(x) = \dfrac{2}{5}x + 8$ and $g(x) = -\dfrac{5}{2}x - 4$ are perpendicular lines because the slopes $\left(\dfrac{2}{5} \text{ and } -\dfrac{5}{2}\right)$ of the two lines are negative reciprocals of each other. Again using our graphing calculator, let's graph these two functions along with $h(x) = -\dfrac{5}{2}x + 2$ and $p(x) = -\dfrac{5}{2}x - 6$ (Figure 3.13). If the lines do not appear to be perpendicular, you may want to change the window with a zoom square option.

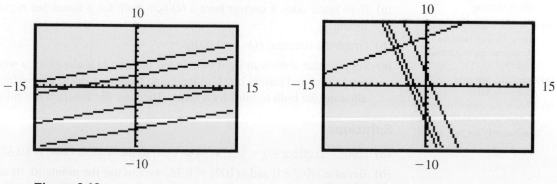

Figure 3.12   **Figure 3.13**

Remark: A property of plane geometry states that if two or more lines are perpendicular to the same line, then they are parallel lines. Figure 3.13 is a good illustration of that property.

The function notation can also be used to determine linear functions that satisfy certain conditions. Let's see how this works.

Classroom Example
Determine the linear function for a line with a slope of $-\dfrac{2}{3}$ that contains the point $(-3, 4)$.

EXAMPLE 5

Determine the linear function whose graph is a line with a slope of $\dfrac{1}{4}$ that contains the point $(2, 5)$.

Solution

We can substitute $\dfrac{1}{4}$ for a in the equation $f(x) = ax + b$ to obtain $f(x) = \dfrac{1}{4}x + b$. The fact that the line contains the point $(2, 5)$ means that $f(2) = 5$. Therefore

$$f(2) = \frac{1}{4}(2) + b = 5$$

$$b = \frac{9}{2}$$

and the function is $f(x) = \dfrac{1}{4}x + \dfrac{9}{2}$.

Applications of Linear Functions

We worked with some applications of linear equations in Section 2.2. Now let's consider some additional applications that use the concept of a linear function to connect mathematics to the real world.

Classroom Example
The cost for burning a 75-watt bulb is given by the function $c(h) = 0.0045h$, and h represents the number of hours that the bulb is burning.

(a) How much does it cost to burn a 75-watt bulb for 4 hours per night for two weeks?

(b) Graph the function $c(h) = 0.0045h$.

(c) What is the approximate cost of allowing the bulb to burn continuously for two weeks?

EXAMPLE 6

The cost for burning a 60-watt light bulb is given by the function $c(h) = 0.0036h$, where h represents the number of hours that the bulb is burning.

(a) How much does it cost to burn a 60-watt bulb for 3 hours per night for a 30-day month?

(b) Graph the function $c(h) = 0.0036h$.

(c) Suppose that a 60-watt light bulb is left burning in a closet for a week before it is discovered and turned off. Use the graph from part (b) to approximate the cost of allowing the bulb to burn for a week. Then use the function to find the exact cost.

Solutions

(a) $c(90) = 0.0036(90) = 0.324$ The cost, to the nearest cent, is $0.32.

(b) Because $c(0) = 0$ and $c(100) = 0.36$, we can use the points $(0, 0)$ and $(100, 0.36)$ to graph the linear function $c(h) = 0.0036h$ (Figure 3.14).

(c) If the bulb burns for 24 hours per day for a week, it burns for 24(7) = 168 hours. Reading from the graph, we can approximate 168 on the horizontal axis, read up to the line, and then read across to the vertical axis. It looks as though it will cost approximately 60 cents. Using $c(h) = 0.0036h$, we obtain exactly $c(168) = 0.0036(168) = 0.6048$.

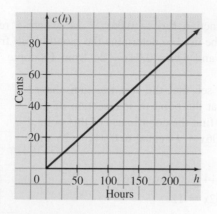

Figure 3.14

EXAMPLE 7

The Clear Call Cellular phone company has a fixed monthly charge plus an amount per minute of airtime. In May, Anna used 720 minutes of airtime and had a bill of $54.80. For the month of June, she used 510 minutes of airtime and had a bill of $46.40. Determine the linear function that Clear Call Cellular uses to determine its monthly bills.

Solution

The linear function $f(x) = ax + b$, where x represents the number of airtime minutes, models this situation. Anna's two monthly bills can be represented by the ordered pairs (720, 54.80) and (510, 46.40). From these two ordered pairs, we can determine a, which is the slope of the line:

$$a = \frac{46.40 - 54.80}{510 - 720} = \frac{-8.4}{-210} = 0.04$$

Thus $f(x) = ax + b$ becomes $f(x) = 0.04x + b$. Now either ordered pair can be used to determine the value of b. Using (510, 46.40), we have $f(510) = 46.40$, so

$$f(510) = 0.04(510) + b = 46.40$$
$$b = 26$$

The linear function is $f(x) = 0.04x + 26$. In other words, Clear Call Cellular charges a monthly fee of $26.00 plus $0.04 per minute of airtime.

EXAMPLE 8

Suppose that Anna (Example 7) is thinking of switching to Simple Cellular phone company, which charges a monthly fee of $14 plus $0.06 per minute of airtime. Should Anna use Clear Cellular from Example 7 or Simple Cellular?

Solution

The linear function $f(x) = 0.06x + 14$, where x represents the number of airtime minutes, can be used to determine the monthly bill from Simple Cellular. Let's graph this function and $f(x) = 0.04x + 26$ from Example 7 on the same set of axes (see Figure 3.15).

Now we see that the two functions have equal values at the point of intersection of the two lines. To find the coordinates of this point, we can set $0.06x + 14$ equal to $0.04x + 26$ and solve for x:

$$0.06x + 14 = 0.04x + 26$$
$$0.02x = 12$$
$$x = 600$$

If $x = 600$, then $0.06(600) + 14 = 50$, and the point of intersection is $(600, 50)$. Again from the lines in Figure 3.15, Anna should switch to Simple Cellular if she uses less than 600 minutes of airtime, but she should stay with Clear Cellular if she plans on using more than 600 minutes of airtime.

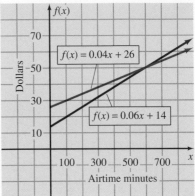

Figure 3.15

Concept Quiz 3.2

For Problems 1–10, answer true or false.

1. Any function of the form $f(x) = ax^n + b$, where a, b, and c are real numbers, is a linear function.
2. Geometrically, the functional value is the directed distance from the y axis.
3. The graph of a horizontal line represents a function.
4. The linear function $f(x) = 1$ is called the identity function.
5. The graphs of $f(x) = mx + b$ and $f(x) = -mx + b$ are perpendicular lines.
6. Every straight line graph represents a function.
7. If a city has a 7% sales tax on the dollars spent for hotel rooms, then the sales tax is a linear function of the dollars spent on hotel rooms.
8. If the amount of a paycheck varies directly as the number of hours worked, then the amount of the paycheck is a linear function of the hours worked.
9. The equation $f(x) = ax + b$ can also be written as $y = ax + b$.
10. The graph of the linear function, $f(x) = -4x + 5$, is a straight line with a slope of -4.

Problem Set 3.2

For Problems 1–16, graph each of the linear functions.
(**Objective 1**)

1. $f(x) = 2x - 4$

2. $f(x) = 3x + 3$

3. $f(x) = -x + 3$

4. $f(x) = -2x + 6$

5. $f(x) = 3x + 9$

6. $f(x) = 2x - 6$

7. $f(x) = -4x - 4$

8. $f(x) = -x - 5$

9. $f(x) = -3x$

10. $f(x) = -4x$

11. $f(x) = -3$

12. $f(x) = -1$

13. $f(x) = \dfrac{1}{2}x + 3$

14. $f(x) = \dfrac{2}{3}x + 4$

15. $f(x) = -\dfrac{3}{4}x$

16. $f(x) = -\dfrac{1}{2}x$

17. $f(x) = -\dfrac{1}{3}x$

18. $f(x) = \dfrac{3}{5}x$

19. $f(x) = \dfrac{1}{4}x + 2$

20. $f(x) = -\dfrac{1}{3}x + 3$

For Problems 21–30, graph the piecewise-defined functions. (**Objective 2**)

21. $f(x) = \begin{cases} -2x & \text{for } x < 0 \\ x & \text{for } x \ge 0 \end{cases}$

22. $f(x) = \begin{cases} -x & \text{for } x < 0 \\ 2x & \text{for } x \ge 0 \end{cases}$

23. $f(x) = \begin{cases} x + 4 & \text{for } x \le 0 \\ -x & \text{for } x > 0 \end{cases}$

24. $f(x) = \begin{cases} x - 2 & \text{for } x \le 0 \\ x + 1 & \text{for } x > 0 \end{cases}$

25. $f(x) = \begin{cases} x + 4 & \text{for } x < -4 \\ x + 1 & \text{for } x \ge -4 \end{cases}$

26. $f(x) = \begin{cases} -x - 2 & \text{for } x < 2 \\ x + 3 & \text{for } x \ge 2 \end{cases}$

27. $f(x) = \begin{cases} -x & \text{for } x < -2 \\ 2 & \text{for } -2 \le x \le 2 \\ -x + 4 & \text{for } x > 2 \end{cases}$

28. $f(x) = \begin{cases} -2x & \text{for } x < -3 \\ 6 & \text{for } -3 \le x \le 0 \\ -x + 4 & \text{for } x > 0 \end{cases}$

29. $f(x) = \begin{cases} 3 & \text{for } x < -1 \\ -3x & \text{for } -1 \le x \le 1 \\ -3 & \text{for } x > 1 \end{cases}$

30. $f(x) = \begin{cases} -4 & \text{for } x < -2 \\ 2x & \text{for } -2 \le x \le 2 \\ 4 & \text{for } x > 2 \end{cases}$

For Problems 31–36, determine the linear equation for the stated conditions. (**Objective 3**)

31. Determine the linear function for a graph that is a line with a slope of $\dfrac{2}{3}$ and contains the point $(-1, 3)$.

32. Determine the linear function for a graph that is a line with a slope of $-\dfrac{3}{5}$ and contains the point $(4, -5)$.

33. Determine the linear function for a graph that is a line containing the points $(-3, -1)$ and $(2, -6)$.

34. If a graph is a line that contains the points $(-2, -3)$ and $(4, 3)$, determine the linear function.

35. If a graph is a line that is perpendicular to the line $g(x) = 5x - 2$ and contains the point $(6, 3)$, determine the linear function.

36. If a graph is a line that is parallel to the line $g(x) = -3x - 4$ and contains the point $(2, 7)$, determine the linear function.

For Problems 37–45, apply the concepts of linear functions to answer the questions. (**Objective 4**)

37. The cost of burning a 75-watt bulb is given by the function $c(h) = 0.0045h$, where h represents the number of hours that the bulb burns.
(**a**) How much does it cost to burn a 75-watt bulb for 3 hours per night for a 31-day month? Express your answer to the nearest cent.

(b) Graph the function $c(h) = 0.0045h$.

(c) Use the graph in part (b) to approximate the cost of burning a 75-watt bulb for 225 hours.

(d) Use $c(h) = 0.0045h$ to find the exact cost, to the nearest cent, of burning a 75-watt bulb for 225 hours.

38. The Rent-Me Car Rental charges $15 per day plus $0.22 per mile to rent a car. Determine a linear function that can be used to calculate the cost of daily car rentals. Then use that function to determine the cost of renting a car for a day and driving 175 miles; 220 miles; 300 miles; 460 miles.

39. Suppose that ABC Car Rental agency charges a fixed amount per day plus an amount per mile for renting a car. Heidi rented a car one day and paid $80 for 200 miles. On another day she rented a car from the same agency and paid $117.50 for 350 miles. Determine the linear function the agency uses to calculate its daily rental charges.

40. Suppose that Heidi (Problem 39) also has access to Speedy Car Rental, which charges a daily fee of $15.00 plus $0.31 per mile. Should Heidi use ABC Car Rental from Problem 39 or Speedy Car Rental?

41. The Hybrid-Only Car Rental agency uses the function $f(x) = 26$ for any daily use of a car up to and including 200 miles. For driving more than 200 miles per day, it uses the function $g(x) = 26 + 0.15(x - 200)$ to determine the charges. How much would the company charge for daily driving of 150 miles? of 230 miles? of 360 miles? of 430 miles?

42. Zack wants to sell five items that cost him $1.20, $2.30, $6.50, $12, and $15.60. He wants to make a profit of 60% of the cost. Create a function that you can use to determine the selling price of each item, and then use the function to calculate each selling price.

43. "All Items 20% Off Marked Price" is a sign at a local golf pro shop. Create a function and then use it to determine how much one has to pay for each of the following marked items: a $9.50 hat, a $15 umbrella, a $75 pair of golf shoes, a $12.50 golf glove, a $750 set of golf clubs.

44. The linear depreciation method assumes that an item depreciates the same amount each year. Suppose a new piece of machinery costs $32,500, and it depreciates $1950 each year for t years.

(a) Set up a linear function that yields the value of the machinery after t years.

(b) Find the value of the machinery after 5 years.

(c) Find the value of the machinery after 8 years.

(d) Graph the function from part (a).

(e) Use the graph from part (d) to approximate how many years it takes for the value of the machinery to become zero.

(f) Use the function to determine how long it takes for the value of the machinery to become zero.

45. Some real-world situations can be described by the use of linear functions. If two pairs of values are known, then by using the point-slope formula the equation of the line that represents the linear function can be determined. For each of the following, assume that the relationship can be expressed as a linear function and use the information given to determine the linear function.

(a) A company produces 10 fiberglass shower stalls for $2015 and 15 stalls for $3015. Let cost be a function of the number of stalls produced.

(b) A company can produce 6 boxes of candy for $8 and 10 boxes of candy for $13. Let the cost be a function of the number of boxes of candy.

(c) Two banks on opposite corners of a town square have signs displaying the current temperature. One bank displays the temperature in degrees Celsius and the other in degrees Fahrenheit. A temperature of 10°C was displayed at the same time as a temperature of 50°F. On another day a temperature of −5°C showed on one sign while the sign across the corner read 23°F. Let the temperature in Fahrenheit be a function of the temperature in Celsius.

Thoughts Into Words

46. Is $f(x) = (3x - 2) - (2x + 1)$ a linear function? Explain your answer.

47. Is $f(x) = (2x + 5) - (2x + 1)$ a linear function? Explain your answer.

48. Suppose that Bianca walks at a constant rate of 3 miles per hour. Explain what it means that the distance Bianca walks is a linear function of the time that she walks.

Graphing Calculator Activities

49. Use a graphing calculator to check your graphs for Problems 1–20.

50. Use a graphing calculator to do parts (b) and (c) of Example 5.

51. Use a graphing calculator to check our solution for Example 8.

52. Use a graphing calculator to do parts (b) and (c) of Problem 37.

53. (a) Graph $f(x) = |x|, f(x) = 2|x|, f(x) = 4|x|$, and $f(x) = \dfrac{1}{2}|x|$ on the same set of axes.

(b) Graph $f(x) = |x|, f(x) = -|x|, f(x) = -3|x|$, and $f(x) = -\dfrac{1}{2}|x|$ on the same set of axes.

(c) Use your results from parts (a) and (b) to make a conjecture about the graphs of $f(x) = a|x|$, where a is a nonzero real number.

(d) Graph $f(x) = |x|, f(x) = |x| + 3, f(x) = |x| - 4$, and $f(x) = |x| + 1$ on the same set of axes. Make a conjecture about the graphs of $f(x) = |x| + k$, where k is a nonzero real number.

(e) Graph $f(x) = |x|, f(x) = |x - 3|$, $f(x) = |x - 1|$, and $f(x) = |x + 4|$ on the same set of axes. Make a conjecture about the graphs of $f(x) = |x - h|$, where h is a nonzero real number.

(f) On the basis of your results from parts (a) through (e), sketch each of the following graphs. Then use a graphing calculator to check your sketches.

(1) $f(x) = |x - 2| + 3$

(2) $f(x) = |x + 1| - 4$

(3) $f(x) = 2|x - 4| - 1$

(4) $f(x) = -3|x + 2| + 4$

(5) $f(x) = -\dfrac{1}{2}|x - 3| - 2$

Answers to the Concept Quiz

1. False   **2.** False   **3.** True   **4.** False   **5.** False   **6.** False   **7.** True   **8.** True   **9.** True   **10.** True

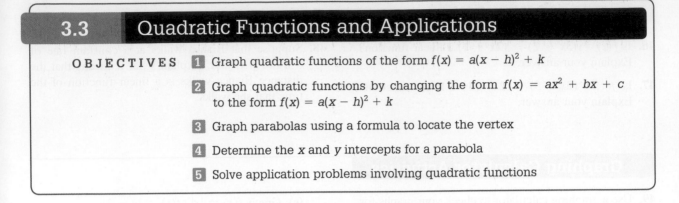

3.3   Quadratic Functions and Applications

OBJECTIVES

1. Graph quadratic functions of the form $f(x) = a(x - h)^2 + k$

2. Graph quadratic functions by changing the form $f(x) = ax^2 + bx + c$ to the form $f(x) = a(x - h)^2 + k$

3. Graph parabolas using a formula to locate the vertex

4. Determine the x and y intercepts for a parabola

5. Solve application problems involving quadratic functions

Any function that can be written in the form

$$f(x) = ax^2 + bx + c$$

where a, b, and c are real numbers and $a \neq 0$, is called a **quadratic function**. The graph of any quadratic function is a **parabola**. As we work with parabolas, we will use the vocabulary indicated in Figure 3.16.

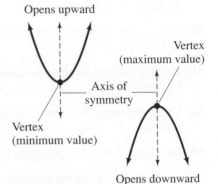

Figure 3.16

Graphing a parabola relies on finding the vertex, determining whether the parabola opens upward or downward, and locating two points on opposite sides of the axis of symmetry. We are also interested in comparing parabolas produced by equations such as $f(x) = x^2 + k$, $f(x) = ax^2$, $f(x) = (x - h)^2$, and $f(x) = a(x - h)^2 + k$ to the basic parabola produced by the equation $f(x) = x^2$. The graph of $f(x) = x^2$ is shown in Figure 3.17. Note that the vertex of the parabola is at the origin, $(0, 0)$, and the graph is symmetric to the y, or $f(x)$, axis. Remember that an equation exhibits y-axis symmetry if replacing x with $-x$ produces an equivalent equation. Therefore, because $f(-x) = (-x)^2 = x^2$, the equation exhibits y-axis symmetry.

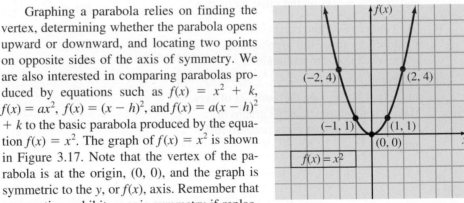

Figure 3.17

Now let's consider an equation of the form $f(x) = x^2 + k$, where k is a constant. (Keep in mind that all such equations exhibit y-axis symmetry.)

EXAMPLE 1   Graph $f(x) = x^2 - 2$.

Solution

Let's set up a table to make some comparisons of function values. Because the graph exhibits y-axis symmetry, we will calculate only positive values and then reflect the points across the y axis.

x	$f(x) = x^2$	$f(x) = x^2 - 2$
0	0	-2
1	1	-1
2	4	2
3	9	7

Notice that the functional values for $f(x) = x^2 - 2$ are 2 less than the corresponding functional values for $f(x) = x^2$. Thus the graph of $f(x) = x^2 - 2$ is the same as the parabola of $f(x) = x^2$ except that it is moved down two units (Figure 3.18).

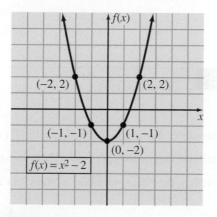

Figure 3.18

In general, the graph of a quadratic function of the form $f(x) = x^2 + k$ is the same as the graph of $f(x) = x^2$, except that it is moved up or down $|k|$ units, depending on whether k is positive or negative. We say that the graph of $f(x) = x^2 + k$ is a **vertical translation** of the graph of $f(x) = x^2$.

Now let's consider some quadratic functions of the form $f(x) = ax^2$, where a is a nonzero constant. (The graphs of these equations also have y-axis symmetry.)

EXAMPLE 2   Graph $f(x) = 2x^2$.

Solution

Let's set up a table to make some comparisons of functional values. Note that in the table, the functional values for $f(x) = 2x^2$ are *twice* the corresponding functional values for $f(x) = x^2$. Thus the parabola associated with $f(x) = 2x^2$ has the same vertex (the origin) as the graph of $f(x) = x^2$, but it is *narrower*, as shown in Figure 3.19.

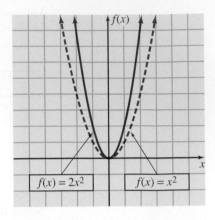

x	$f(x) = x^2$	$f(x) = 2x^2$
0	0	0
1	1	2
2	4	8
3	9	18

Figure 3.19

EXAMPLE 3   Graph $f(x) = \dfrac{1}{2}x^2$.

Solution

As we see from the table, the functional values for $f(x) = \dfrac{1}{2}x^2$ are *one-half* of the corresponding functional values for $f(x) = x^2$. Therefore the parabola associated with $f(x) = \dfrac{1}{2}x^2$ is *wider* than the basic parabola, as shown in Figure 3.20.

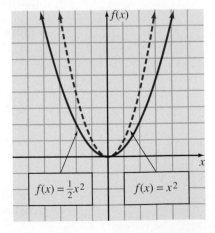

x	$f(x) = x^2$	$f(x) = \frac{1}{2}x^2$
0	0	0
1	1	$\dfrac{1}{2}$
2	4	2
3	9	$\dfrac{9}{2}$
4	16	8

Figure 3.20

EXAMPLE 4   Graph $f(x) = -x^2$.

Solution

It should be evident that the functional values for $f(x) = -x^2$ are the *opposites* of the corresponding functional values for $f(x) = x^2$. Therefore the graph of $f(x) = -x^2$ is a reflection across the x axis of the basic parabola (Figure 3.21).

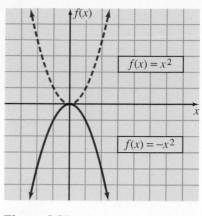

Figure 3.21

In general, the graph of a quadratic function of the form $f(x) = ax^2$ has its vertex at the origin and opens upward if a is positive and downward if a is negative. The parabola is narrower than the basic parabola if $|a| > 1$ and wider if $|a| < 1$.

Let's continue our investigation of quadratic functions by considering those of the form $f(x) = (x - h)^2$, in which h is a nonzero constant.

Classroom Example
Graph $y = (x - 1)^2$.

EXAMPLE 5   Graph $f(x) = (x - 3)^2$.

Solution

A fairly extensive table of values illustrates a pattern. Note that $f(x) = (x - 3)^2$ and $f(x) = x^2$ take on the same functional values but for different values of x. More specifically, if $f(x) = x^2$ achieves a certain functional value at a specific value of x, then $f(x) = (x - 3)^2$ achieves that same functional value at $x + 3$. In other words, the graph of $f(x) = (x - 3)^2$ is the graph of $f(x) = x^2$ *moved three units to the right* (Figure 3.22).

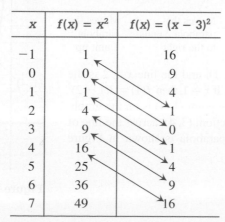

x	$f(x) = x^2$	$f(x) = (x - 3)^2$
-1	1	16
0	0	9
1	1	4
2	4	1
3	9	0
4	16	1
5	25	4
6	36	9
7	49	16

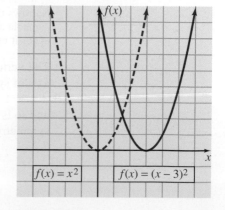

Figure 3.22

In general, the graph of a quadratic function of the form $f(x) = (x - h)^2$ is the same as the graph of $f(x) = x^2$, except that it is moved to the right h units if h is positive or moved to the left $|h|$ units if h is negative. We say that the graph of $f(x) = (x - h)^2$ is a **horizontal translation** of the graph of $f(x) = x^2$.

The following diagram summarizes our work thus far for graphing quadratic functions.

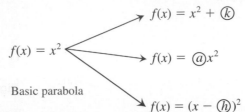

$f(x) = x^2 + \boxed{k}$ Moves the parabola up or down

$f(x) = x^2$

Basic parabola

$f(x) = \boxed{a}x^2$ Affects the width and the way the parabola opens

$f(x) = (x - \boxed{h})^2$ Moves the parabola right or left

We have studied, separately, the effects a, h, and k have on the graph of a quadratic function. However, we need to consider the general form of a quadratic function when all of these effects are present.

In general, the graph of a quadratic function of the form $f(x) = a(x - h)^2 + k$ has its vertex at (h, k) and opens upward if a is positive and downward if a is negative. The parabola is narrower than the basic parabola if $|a| > 1$ and wider if $|a| < 1$.

Classroom Example
Graph $y = 3(x + 2)^2 - 2$.

EXAMPLE 6   Graph $f(x) = 3(x - 2)^2 + 1$.

Solution

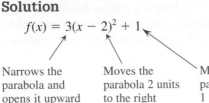

$f(x) = 3(x - 2)^2 + 1$

Narrows the parabola and opens it upward   Moves the parabola 2 units to the right   Moves the parabola 1 unit up

The vertex is $(2, 1)$, and the line $x = 2$ is the axis of symmetry. If $x = 1$, then $f(1) = 3(1 - 2)^2 + 1 = 4$. Thus the point $(1, 4)$ is on the graph, and so is its reflection, $(3, 4)$, across the line of symmetry. The parabola is shown in Figure 3.23.

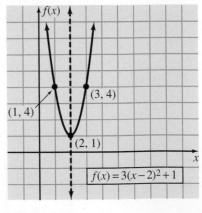

Figure 3.23

EXAMPLE 7   Graph $f(x) = -\dfrac{1}{2}(x + 1)^2 - 3$.

Solution

$$f(x) = -\frac{1}{2}[x - (-1)]^2 - 3$$

Widens the parabola and opens it downward

Moves the parabola 1 unit to the left

Moves the parabola 3 units down

The vertex is at $(-1, -3)$, and the line $x = -1$ is the axis of symmetry. If $x = 0$,

then $f(0) = -\dfrac{1}{2}(0 + 1)^2 - 3 = -\dfrac{7}{2}$. Thus

the point $\left(0, -\dfrac{7}{2}\right)$ is on the graph, and so is

its reflection, $\left(-2, -\dfrac{7}{2}\right)$, across the line of

symmetry. The parabola is shown in Figure 3.24.

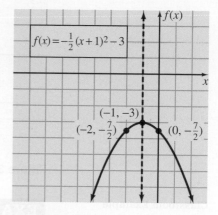

Figure 3.24

Graphing Quadratic Functions of the Form $f(x) = ax^2 + bx + c$

We are now ready to graph quadratic functions of the form $f(x) = ax^2 + bx + c$. The general approach is to change from the form $f(x) = ax^2 + bx + c$ to the form $f(x) = a(x - h)^2 + k$ and then proceed as we did in Examples 6 and 7. The process of *completing the square* serves as the basis for making the change in form. Let's consider two examples to illustrate the details.

EXAMPLE 8   Graph $f(x) = x^2 - 4x + 3$.

Solution

$$f(x) = x^2 - 4x + 3$$
$$= (x^2 - 4x) + 3$$

Add 4, which is the square of one-half of the coefficient of x

$$= (x^2 - 4x + 4) + 3 - 4$$

Subtract 4 to compensate for the 4 that was added

$$= (x - 2)^2 - 1$$

The graph of $f(x) = (x - 2)^2 - 1$ is the basic parabola moved two units to the right and one unit down (Figure 3.25).

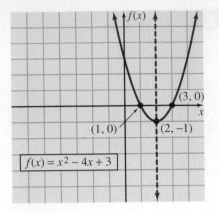

Figure 3.25

EXAMPLE 9   Graph $f(x) = -2x^2 - 4x + 1$.

Solution

$$f(x) = -2x^2 - 4x + 1$$
$$= -2(x^2 + 2x) + 1 \qquad \text{Factor } -2 \text{ from the first two terms}$$
$$= -2(x^2 + 2x + 1) - (-2)(1) + 1 \qquad \text{Add 1 inside the parentheses to complete the square}$$

Subtract 1, but it must also be multiplied by a factor of -2

$$= -2(x^2 + 2x + 1) + 2 + 1$$
$$= -2(x + 1)^2 + 3$$

The graph of $f(x) = -2(x + 1)^2 + 3$ is shown in Figure 3.26.

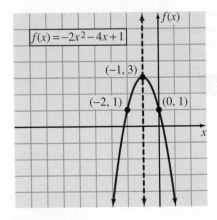

Figure 3.26

What we know about parabolas and the process of completing the square can be helpful when we are using a graphing utility to graph a quadratic function. Consider the following example.

Classroom Example
Use a graphing utility to obtain
the graph of the quadratic function
$f(x) = -x^2 - 13x - 41$.

EXAMPLE 10

Use a graphing utility to obtain the graph of the quadratic function
$f(x) = -x^2 + 37x - 311$.

Solution

First, we know that the parabola opens downward, and its width is the same as that of
the basic parabola $f(x) = x^2$. Then we can start the process of completing the square to
determine an approximate location of the vertex:

$$f(x) = -x^2 + 37x - 311$$
$$= -(x^2 - 37x) - 311$$
$$= -\left(x^2 - 37x + \left(\frac{37}{2}\right)^2\right) - 311 + \left(\frac{37}{2}\right)^2$$
$$= -(x^2 - 37x + (18.5)^2) - 311 + 342.25$$
$$= -(x - 18.5)^2 + 31.25$$

Thus the vertex is near $x = 18$ and
$y = 31$. Setting the boundaries of
the viewing rectangle so that
$-2 \leq x \leq 25$ and $-10 \leq y \leq 35$,
we obtain the graph shown in
Figure 3.27.

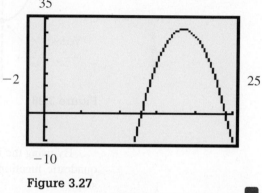

Figure 3.27

Remark: The graph in Figure 3.27 is sufficient for most purposes because it shows the
vertex and the x intercepts of the parabola. Certainly we could use other boundaries that
would also give this information.

So far, we have used the process of completing the square to change a quadratic function such as $f(x) = x^2 - 4x + 3$ to the form $f(x) = (x - 2)^2 - 1$. From the form
$f(x) = (x - 2)^2 - 1$, it is easy to identify the vertex $(2, -1)$ and the axis of symmetry
$x = 2$ of the parabola. In general, if we complete the square on

$$f(x) = ax^2 + bx + c$$

we obtain

$$f(x) = a\left(x^2 + \frac{b}{a}x\right) + c$$
$$= a\left(x^2 + \frac{b}{a}x + \frac{b^2}{4a^2}\right) + c - \frac{b^2}{4a}$$
$$= a\left(x + \frac{b}{2a}\right)^2 + \frac{4ac - b^2}{4a}$$

Therefore the parabola associated with the function $f(x) = ax^2 + bx + c$ has its vertex at

$$\left(-\frac{b}{2a}, \frac{4ac - b^2}{4a}\right)$$

and the equation of its axis of symmetry is $x = -\dfrac{b}{2a}$. These facts are illustrated in Figure 3.28.

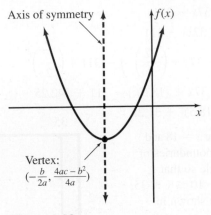

Axis of symmetry

$f(x)$

x

Vertex:
$(-\frac{b}{2a}, \frac{4ac - b^2}{4a})$

Figure 3.28

By using the information from Figure 3.28, we now have another way of graphing quadratic functions of the form $f(x) = ax^2 + bx + c$, as indicated by the following steps:

Step 1 Determine whether the parabola opens upward (if $a > 0$) or downward (if $a < 0$).

Step 2 Find $-\dfrac{b}{2a}$, which is the x coordinate of the vertex.

Step 3 Find $f\left(-\dfrac{b}{2a}\right)$, which is the y coordinate of the vertex, or find the y coordinate by evaluating

$$\frac{4ac - b^2}{4a}$$

Step 4 Locate another point on the parabola, and also locate its image across the axis of symmetry, which is the line with equation $x = -\dfrac{b}{2a}$.

The three points found in steps 2, 3, and 4 should determine the general shape of the parabola. Let's illustrate this procedure with two examples.

EXAMPLE 11   Graph $f(x) = 3x^2 - 6x + 5$.

Solution

Step 1   Because $a > 0$, the parabola opens upward.

Step 2 $-\dfrac{b}{2a} = -\dfrac{(-6)}{2(3)} = -\dfrac{(-6)}{6} = 1$

Step 3 $f\left(-\dfrac{b}{2a}\right) = f(1)$

$= 3(1)^2 - 6(1) + 5 = 2.$

Thus the vertex is at $(1, 2)$.

Step 4   Letting $x = 2$, we obtain $f(2) = 12 - 12 + 5 = 5$. Thus $(2, 5)$ is on the graph, and so is its reflection, $(0, 5)$, across the line of symmetry, $x = 1$.

The three points $(1, 2)$, $(2, 5)$, and $(0, 5)$ are used to graph the parabola in Figure 3.29.

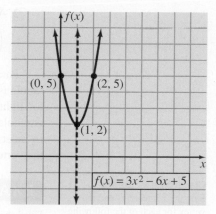

$(0, 5)$ $(2, 5)$

$(1, 2)$

$f(x) = 3x^2 - 6x + 5$

Figure 3.29

EXAMPLE 12   Graph $f(x) = -x^2 - 4x - 7$.

Solution

Step 1   Because $a < 0$, the parabola opens downward.

Step 2 $-\dfrac{b}{2a} = -\dfrac{(-4)}{2(-1)} = -\dfrac{(-4)}{(-2)} = -2$

Step 3 $f\left(-\dfrac{b}{2a}\right) = f(-2)$

$= -(-2)^2 - 4(-2) - 7 = -3$

Thus the vertex is at $(-2, -3)$.

Step 4   Letting $x = 0$, we obtain $f(0) = -7$. Thus $(0, -7)$ is on the graph, and so is its reflection, $(-4, -7)$, across the line of symmetry, $x = -2$.

The three points $(-2, -3)$, $(0, -7)$, and $(-4, -7)$ are used to draw the parabola in Figure 3.30.

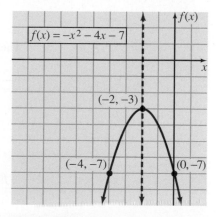

$f(x) = -x^2 - 4x - 7$

$(-2, -3)$

$(-4, -7)$ $(0, -7)$

Figure 3.30

In summary, we have two methods to graph a quadratic function:

1. We can express the function in the form $f(x) = a(x - h)^2 + k$ and use the values of a, h, and k to determine the parabola.

2. We can express the function in the form $f(x) = ax^2 + bx + c$, locate the vertex at $\left(-\dfrac{b}{2a}, f\left(-\dfrac{b}{2a}\right)\right)$, and use the approach demonstrated in Examples 11 and 12.

Parabolas possess various properties that make them useful. For example, if a parabola is rotated about its axis, a parabolic surface is formed, and such surfaces are used for light and sound reflectors. A projectile fired into the air follows the curvature of a parabola. The trend line of profit and cost functions sometimes follows a parabolic curve. In most applications of the parabola, we are primarily interested in the x intercepts and the vertex. Let's consider some examples of finding the x intercepts and the vertex.

Classroom Example
Find the x intercepts and the vertex for each of the following parabolas:

(a) $f(x) = -x^2 + 2x + 15$
(b) $f(x) = x^2 + 6x - 10$
(c) $f(x) = 5x^2 - 2x - 6$

EXAMPLE 13

Find the x intercepts and the vertex for each of the following parabolas:

(a) $f(x) = -x^2 + 11x - 18$ (b) $f(x) = x^2 - 8x - 3$ (c) $f(x) = 2x^2 - 12x + 23$

Solutions

(a) To find the x intercepts for $f(x) = -x^2 + 11x - 18$, let $f(x) = 0$ and solve the resulting equation:

$$-x^2 + 11x - 18 = 0$$
$$x^2 - 11x + 18 = 0$$
$$(x - 2)(x - 9) = 0$$
$$x - 2 = 0 \quad \text{or} \quad x - 9 = 0$$
$$x = 2 \quad\quad\quad\quad x = 9$$

Therefore the x intercepts are 2 and 9. To find the vertex, let's determine the point $\left(-\dfrac{b}{2a}, f\left(-\dfrac{b}{2a}\right)\right)$:

$$f(x) = -x^2 + 11x - 18$$
$$-\frac{b}{2a} = -\frac{11}{2(-1)} = -\frac{11}{-2} = \frac{11}{2}$$
$$f\left(\frac{11}{2}\right) = -\left(\frac{11}{2}\right)^2 + 11\left(\frac{11}{2}\right) - 18$$
$$= -\frac{121}{4} + \frac{121}{2} - 18$$
$$= \frac{-121 + 242 - 72}{4}$$
$$= \frac{49}{4}$$

Therefore the vertex is at $\left(\dfrac{11}{2}, \dfrac{49}{4}\right)$.

(b) To find the x intercepts for $f(x) = x^2 - 8x - 3$, let $f(x) = 0$, and solve the resulting equation:

$$x^2 - 8x - 3 = 0$$

$$x = \frac{-(-8) \pm \sqrt{(-8)^2 - 4(1)(-3)}}{2(1)}$$

$$= \frac{8 \pm \sqrt{76}}{2}$$

$$= \frac{8 \pm 2\sqrt{19}}{2}$$

$$= 4 \pm \sqrt{19}$$

Therefore the x intercepts are $4 + \sqrt{19}$ and $4 - \sqrt{19}$. This time, to find the vertex, let's complete the square on x:

$$f(x) = x^2 - 8x - 3$$

$$= x^2 - 8x + 16 - 3 - 16$$

$$= (x - 4)^2 - 19$$

Therefore the vertex is at $(4, -19)$.

(c) To find the x intercepts for $f(x) = 2x^2 - 12x + 23$, let $f(x) = 0$ and solve the resulting equation:

$$2x^2 - 12x + 23 = 0$$

$$x = \frac{-(-12) \pm \sqrt{(-12)^2 - 4(2)(23)}}{2(2)}$$

$$= \frac{12 \pm \sqrt{-40}}{4}$$

Because these solutions are nonreal complex numbers, there are no x intercepts. To find the vertex, let's determine the point $\left(-\dfrac{b}{2a}, f\left(-\dfrac{b}{2a}\right)\right)$:

$$f(x) = 2x^2 - 12x + 23$$

$$-\frac{b}{2a} = -\frac{-12}{2(2)}$$

$$= 3$$

$$f(3) = 2(3)^2 - 12(3) + 23$$

$$= 18 - 36 + 23$$

$$= 5$$

Therefore the vertex is at $(3, 5)$.

Remark: Note that in parts (a) and (c), we used the general point

$$\left(-\frac{b}{2a}, f\left(-\frac{b}{2a}\right)\right)$$

to find the vertices. In part (b), however, we completed the square and used that form to determine the vertex. Which approach you use is up to you. We chose to complete the square in part (b) because the algebra involved was quite easy.

- In part (a) of Example 13, we solved the equation $-x^2 + 11x - 18 = 0$ to determine that 2 and 9 are the x intercepts of the graph of the function $f(x) = -x^2 + 11x - 18$. The numbers 2 and 9 are also called the **real number zeros** of the function. That is to say, $f(2) = 0$ and $f(9) = 0$.
- In part (b) of Example 13, the real numbers $4 + \sqrt{19}$ and $4 - \sqrt{19}$ are the x intercepts of the graph of the function $f(x) = x^2 - 8x - 3$ and are the real number zeros of the function. Again, this means that $f(4 + \sqrt{19}) = 0$ and $f(4 - \sqrt{19}) = 0$.
- In part (c) of Example 13, the nonreal complex numbers $\dfrac{12 \pm \sqrt{-40}}{4}$, which simplify to $\dfrac{6 \pm i\sqrt{10}}{2}$, indicate that the graph of the function $f(x) = 2x^2 - 12x + 23$ has no points on the x axis. The complex numbers are zeros of the function, but they have no physical significance for the graph other than indicating that the graph has no points on the x axis.

Figure 3.31 shows our result when we used a graphing calculator to graph the three functions of Example 13 on the same set of axes. This gives us a visual interpretation of the conclusions drawn regarding the x intercepts and vertices.

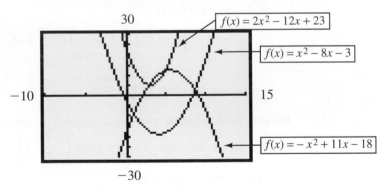

Figure 3.31

Back to Problem Solving

As we have seen, the vertex of the graph of a quadratic function is either the lowest or the highest point on the graph. Thus we often speak of the **minimum value** or **maximum value** of a function when we discuss applications of the parabola. The x value of the vertex indicates where the minimum or maximum occurs, and $f(x)$ yields the minimum or maximum value of the function. Let's consider some examples that illustrate these ideas.

EXAMPLE 14

A farmer has 120 rods of fencing and wants to enclose a rectangular plot of land that requires fencing on only three sides because it is bounded on one side by a river. Find the length and width of the plot that will maximize the area.

Solution

Let x represent the width; then $120 - 2x$ represents the length, as indicated in Figure 3.32.

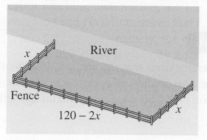

Figure 3.32

The function $A(x) = x(120 - 2x)$ represents the area of the plot in terms of the width x. Because

$$A(x) = x(120 - 2x)$$
$$= 120x - 2x^2$$
$$= -2x^2 + 120x$$

we have a quadratic function with $a = -2$, $b = 120$, and $c = 0$. Therefore the *maximum* value ($a < 0$ so the parabola opens downward) of the function is obtained where the x value is

$$-\frac{b}{2a} = -\frac{120}{2(-2)} = 30$$

If $x = 30$, then $120 - 2x = 120 - 2(30) = 60$. Thus the farmer should make the plot 30 rods wide and 60 rods long to maximize the area at $(30)(60) = 1800$ square rods.

EXAMPLE 15

Find two numbers whose sum is 30, such that the sum of their squares is a minimum.

Solution

Let x represent one of the numbers; then $30 - x$ represents the other number. By expressing the sum of their squares as a function of x, we obtain

$$f(x) = x^2 + (30 - x)^2$$

which can be simplified to

$$f(x) = x^2 + 900 - 60x + x^2$$
$$= 2x^2 - 60x + 900$$

This is a quadratic function with $a = 2$, $b = -60$, and $c = 900$. Therefore the x value where the *minimum* occurs is

$$-\frac{b}{2a} = -\frac{-60}{4} = 15$$

If $x = 15$, then $30 - x = 30 - 15 = 15$. Thus the two numbers should both be 15. ▪

Classroom Example
A travel agent can sell 42 tickets for a 3-day cruise at $450 each. For each $20 decrease in price, the number of tickets sold increases by four. At what price should the tickets be sold to maximize gross income?

EXAMPLE 16

A golf pro-shop operator finds that she can sell 30 sets of golf clubs at $500 per set in a year. Furthermore, she predicts that for each $25 decrease in price, she could sell three extra sets of golf clubs. At what price should she sell the clubs to maximize gross income?

Solution

In analyzing such a problem, it sometimes helps to start by setting up a table. We use the fact that three additional sets can be sold for each $25 decrease in price.

Number of sets	×	Price per set	=	Income
30	×	$500	=	$15,000
33	×	$475	=	$15,675
36	×	$450	=	$16,200

Let x represent the number of $25 decreases in price. Then the income can be expressed as a function of x.

$$f(x) = (30 + 3x)(500 - 25x)$$

Number of sets   Price per set

Simplifying this equation, we obtain

$$f(x) = 15,000 - 750x + 1500x - 75x^2$$
$$= -75x^2 + 750x + 15,000$$

We complete the square in order to analyze the parabola.

$$f(x) = -75x^2 + 750x + 15,000$$
$$= -75(x^2 - 10x) + 15,000$$
$$= -75(x^2 - 10x + 25) + 15,000 + 1875$$
$$= -75(x - 5)^2 + 16,875$$

From this form, we know that the vertex of the parabola is at (5, 16,875), and because $a = -75$, we know that a *maximum* occurs at the vertex. Thus five decreases of $25—that is, a $125 reduction in price—will give a maximum income of $16,875. The golf clubs should be sold at $375 per set.

■

Concept Quiz 3.3

For Problems 1–10, answer true or false.

1. The graph of any quadratic function is a parabola.
2. For the quadratic function $f(x) = ax^2 + bx + c$, the vertex of the parabola is always the minimum value of the function.
3. Every parabola has an axis of symmetry that passes through the vertex.
4. The process of changing the form of $f(x) = ax^2 + bx + c$ to the equivalent form $f(x) = a(x - h)^2 + k$ is called factoring the square.
5. For the parabola associated with $f(x) = ax^2 + bx + c$, the parabola will always open upward if b is a positive number.
6. The y coordinate of the vertex for the parabola associated with $f(x) = ax^2 + bx + c$ is equal to $-\dfrac{b}{2a}$.
7. The minimum value of the function $f(x) = 2x^2 + 5x + 8$ is equal to $f\left(-\dfrac{5}{4}\right)$.
8. The x intercepts for the parabola associated with $f(x) = ax^2 + bx + c$ can be found by using the quadratic formula $x = \dfrac{-b \pm \sqrt{b^2 - 4ac}}{2a}$.
9. Every graph of a quadratic function has x intercepts.
10. Every graph of a quadratic function has a y intercept.

For Problems 11–13, match the quadratic function with its graph.

11. $y = x^2 + 2$ **12.** $y = (x - 2)^2$ **13.** $y = 2x^2$

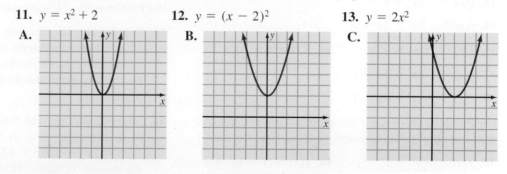

A.   **B.**   **C.**

Problem Set 3.3

For Problems 1–14, graph each quadratic function. (Objective 1)

1. $f(x) = x^2 + 1$

2. $f(x) = x^2 - 3$

3. $f(x) = 3x^2$

4. $f(x) = -2x^2$

5. $f(x) = -x^2 + 2$

6. $f(x) = -3x^2 - 1$

7. $f(x) = (x + 2)^2$

8. $f(x) = (x - 1)^2$

9. $f(x) = -2(x + 1)^2$

10. $f(x) = 3(x - 2)^2$

11. $f(x) = (x - 1)^2 + 2$

12. $f(x) = -(x + 2)^2 + 3$

13. $f(x) = \dfrac{1}{2}(x - 2)^2 - 3$

14. $f(x) = 2(x - 3)^2 - 1$

For Problems 15–26, use completing the square to change the form of the function and then graph each quadratic function. (**Objective 2**)

15. $f(x) = x^2 + 2x + 4$

16. $f(x) = x^2 - 4x + 2$

17. $f(x) = x^2 - 3x + 1$

18. $f(x) = x^2 + 5x + 5$

19. $f(x) = 2x^2 + 4x$

20. $f(x) = 3x^2 - 6x$

21. $f(x) = -x^2 - 2x + 1$

22. $f(x) = -2x^2 + 12x - 16$

23. $f(x) = 2x^2 - 2x + 3$

24. $f(x) = 2x^2 + 3x - 1$

25. $f(x) = -2x^2 - 5x + 1$

26. $f(x) = -3x^2 + x - 2$

For Problems 27–38, locate the vertex of the parabola by using $\left(-\dfrac{b}{2a}, f\left(-\dfrac{b}{2a}\right)\right)$ and graph the quadratic function. (**Objective 3**)

27. $f(x) = x^2 - 8x + 15$

28. $f(x) = x^2 + 6x + 11$

29. $f(x) = 2x^2 + 20x + 52$

30. $f(x) = 3x^2 - 6x - 1$

31. $f(x) = -x^2 + 4x - 7$

32. $f(x) = -x^2 - 6x - 5$

33. $f(x) = -3x^2 + 6x - 5$

34. $f(x) = -2x^2 - 4x + 2$

35. $f(x) = x^2 + 3x - 1$

36. $f(x) = x^2 + 5x + 2$

37. $f(x) = -2x^2 + 5x + 1$

38. $f(x) = -3x^2 + 2x - 1$

For Problems 39–46, use the approach that you think is the most appropriate to graph each quadratic function.

39. $f(x) = -x^2 + 3$

40. $f(x) = (x + 1)^2 + 1$

41. $f(x) = x^2 + x - 1$

42. $f(x) = -x^2 + 3x - 4$

43. $f(x) = -2x^2 + 4x + 1$

44. $f(x) = 4x^2 - 8x + 5$

45. $f(x) = -\left(x + \dfrac{5}{2}\right)^2 + \dfrac{3}{2}$

46. $f(x) = x^2 - 4x$

For Problems 47–58, find the x intercepts and the vertex of each parabola. (**Objective 4**)

47. $f(x) = 3x^2 - 12$

48. $f(x) = 6x^2 - 4$

49. $f(x) = 5x^2 - 10x$

50. $f(x) = 3x^2 + 9x$

51. $f(x) = x^2 - 8x + 15$

52. $f(x) = x^2 - 16x + 63$

53. $f(x) = -x^2 + 10x - 24$

54. $f(x) = -2x^2 + 36x - 160$

55. $f(x) = -x^2 + 9x - 21$

56. $f(x) = 2x^2 + 3x + 3$

57. $f(x) = -4x^2 + 4x + 4$

58. $f(x) = -2x^2 + 3x + 7$

For Problems 59–64, find the zeros of each function.

59. $f(x) = x^2 + 3x - 88$

60. $f(x) = 6x^2 - 5x - 4$

61. $f(x) = 4x^2 - 48x + 108$

62. $f(x) = x^2 - 6x - 6$

63. $f(x) = x^2 - 4x + 11$

64. $f(x) = x^2 - 23x + 126$

For Problems 65–74, solve each problem. (**Objective 5**)

65. Suppose that the equation $p(x) = -2x^2 + 280x - 1000$, where x represents the number of items sold, describes the profit function for a certain business. How many items should be sold to maximize the profit?

66. Suppose that the cost function for the production of a particular item is given by the equation $C(x) = 2x^2 - 320x + 12{,}920$, where x represents the number of items. How many items should be produced to minimize the cost?

67. Neglecting air resistance, the height of a projectile fired vertically into the air at an initial velocity of 96 feet per second is a function of time x and is given by the equation $f(x) = 96x - 16x^2$. Find the highest point reached by the projectile.

68. Find two numbers whose sum is 30, such that the sum of the square of one number plus ten times the other number is a minimum.

69. Find two numbers whose sum is 50 and whose product is a maximum.

70. Find two numbers whose difference is 40 and whose product is a minimum.

71. Two hundred forty meters of fencing is available to enclose a rectangular playground. What should the dimensions of the playground be to maximize the area?

72. An outdoor adventure company advertises that they will provide a guided mountain bike trip and a picnic lunch for $50 per person. They must have a guarantee of 30 people to do the trip. Furthermore, they agree that for each person in excess of 30, they will reduce the price per person for all riders by $0.50. How many people will it take to maximize the company's revenue?

73. A video rental service has 1000 subscribers, each of whom pays $15 per month. On the basis of a survey, the company believes that for each decrease of $0.25 in the monthly rate, it could obtain 20 additional subscribers. At what rate will the maximum revenue be obtained, and how many subscribers will there be at that rate?

74. A manufacturer finds that for the first 500 units of its product that are produced and sold, the profit is $50 per unit. The profit on each of the units beyond 500 is decreased by $0.10 times the number of additional units sold. What level of output will maximize profit?

Thoughts Into Words

75. Suppose your friend was absent the day this section was discussed. How would you explain to her the ideas pertaining to x intercepts of the graph of a function, zeros of the function, and solutions of the equation $f(x) = 0$?

76. Give a step-by-step explanation of how to find the x intercepts of the graph of the function $f(x) = 2x^2 + 7x - 4$.

77. Give a step-by-step explanation of how to find the vertex of the parabola determined by the equation $f(x) = -x^2 - 6x - 5$.

Graphing Calculator Activities

78. This problem is designed to reinforce ideas presented in this section. For each part, first predict the shapes and locations of the parabolas, and then use your graphing calculator to graph them on the same set of axes.

(a) $f(x) = x^2$, $f(x) = x^2 - 4$, $f(x) = x^2 + 1$, $f(x) = x^2 + 5$

(b) $f(x) = x^2$, $f(x) = (x - 5)^2$, $f(x) = (x + 5)^2$, $f(x) = (x - 3)^2$

(c) $f(x) = x^2$, $f(x) = 5x^2$, $f(x) = \dfrac{1}{3}x^2$, $f(x) = -2x^2$

(d) $f(x) = x^2$, $f(x) = (x - 7)^2 - 3$, $f(x) = -(x + 8)^2 + 4$, $f(x) = -3x^2 - 4$

(e) $f(x) = x^2 - 4x - 2$, $f(x) = -x^2 + 4x + 2$, $f(x) = -x^2 - 16x - 58$, $f(x) = x^2 + 16x + 58$

79. (a) Graph both $f(x) = x^2 - 14x + 51$ and $f(x) = x^2 + 14x + 51$ on the same set of axes. What relationship seems to exist between the two graphs?

(b) Graph both $f(x) = x^2 + 12x + 34$ and $f(x) = x^2 - 12x + 34$ on the same set of axes. What relationship seems to exist between the two graphs?

(c) Graph both $f(x) = -x^2 + 8x - 20$ and $f(x) = -x^2 - 8x - 20$ on the same set of axes. What relationship seems to exist between the two graphs?

(d) Make a statement that generalizes your findings in parts (a) through (c).

80. Suppose that the viewing window on your graphing calculator is set so that $-15 \leq x \leq 15$ and $-10 \leq y \leq 10$. Now try to graph the function $f(x) = x^2 - 8x + 28$. Nothing appears on the screen, so the parabola must be outside the viewing window. We could arbitrarily expand the window until the parabola appeared. However, let's be a little more systematic and use $\left(-\dfrac{b}{2a}, f\left(-\dfrac{b}{2a}\right)\right)$ to find the vertex. We find the vertex is at $(4, 12)$, so let's change the y values of the window so that $0 \leq y \leq 25$. Now we get a good picture of the parabola.

Graph each of the following parabolas, and keep in mind that you may need to change the dimensions of the viewing window to obtain a good picture.

(a) $f(x) = x^2 - 2x + 12$
(b) $f(x) = -x^2 - 4x - 16$
(c) $f(x) = x^2 + 12x + 44$
(d) $f(x) = x^2 - 30x + 229$
(e) $f(x) = -2x^2 + 8x - 19$

81. Use a graphing calculator to graph each of the following parabolas, and then use the TRACE function to help estimate the x intercepts and the vertex.

(a) $f(x) = x^2 - 6x + 3$
(b) $f(x) = x^2 - 18x + 66$
(c) $f(x) = -x^2 + 8x - 3$
(d) $f(x) = -x^2 + 24x - 129$
(e) $f(x) = 14x^2 - 7x + 1$
(f) $f(x) = -\dfrac{1}{2}x^2 + 5x - \dfrac{17}{2}$

82. In Problems 47–58, you were asked to find the x intercepts and the vertex of some parabolas. Now use a graphing calculator to graph each parabola and visually justify your answers.

83. For each of the following quadratic functions, use the discriminant to determine the number of real-number zeros, and then graph the function with a graphing calculator to check your answer.

(a) $f(x) = 3x^2 - 15x - 42$
(b) $f(x) = 2x^2 - 36x + 162$
(c) $f(x) = -4x^2 - 48x - 144$
(d) $f(x) = 2x^2 + 2x + 5$
(e) $f(x) = 4x^2 - 4x - 120$
(f) $f(x) = 5x^2 - x + 4$

Answers to the Concept Quiz

1. True **2.** False **3.** True **4.** False **5.** False **6.** False **7.** True **8.** True **9.** False **10.** True
11. B **12.** C **13.** A

3.4   Transformations of Some Basic Curves

OBJECTIVES

1 Graph functions by applying horizontal and vertical translations, vertical stretchings or shrinkings, or reflections to the basic graphs of $f(x) = x^2$, $f(x) = x^3$, $f(x) = x^4$, $f(x) = \sqrt{x}$, and $f(x) = |x|$

2 Graph piecewise-defined functions

From our work in Section 3.3, we know that the graph of $f(x) = (x - 5)^2$ is the basic parabola $f(x) = x^2$ translated five units to the right. Likewise, we know that the graph of $f(x) = -x^2 - 2$ is the basic parabola reflected across the x axis and translated downward two units. Translations and reflections apply not only to parabolas but also to curves in general. Therefore, if we know the shapes of a few basic curves, then it is easy to sketch numerous variations of these curves by using the concepts of translation and reflection.

Let's begin this section by establishing the graphs of four basic curves and then apply some transformations to these curves. First, let's restate, in terms of function vocabulary, the graphing suggestions offered in Chapter 2. Pay special attention to suggestions 2 and 3, in which we restate the concepts of intercepts and symmetry using function notation.

1. Determine the domain of the function.

2. Find the y intercept (we are labeling the y axis with $f(x)$) by evaluating $f(0)$. Find the x intercept by finding the value(s) of x such that $f(x) = 0$.

3. Determine any types of symmetry that the equation possesses. If $f(-x) = f(x)$, then the function exhibits y-axis symmetry. If $f(-x) = -f(x)$, then the function exhibits origin symmetry. (Note that the definition of a function rules out the possibility that the graph of a function has x-axis symmetry.)

4. Set up a table of ordered pairs that satisfy the equation. The type of symmetry and the domain will affect your choice of values of x in the table.

5. Plot the points associated with the ordered pairs and connect them with a smooth curve. Then, if appropriate, reflect this part of the curve according to any symmetries possessed by the graph.

EXAMPLE 1   Graph $f(x) = x^3$.

Solution

The domain is the set of real numbers. Because $f(0) = 0$, the origin is on the graph. Because $f(-x) = (-x)^3 = -x^3 = -f(x)$, the graph is symmetric with respect to the origin. Therefore, we can concentrate on the positive values of x for our table. By connecting the points associated with the ordered pairs in the table with a smooth curve and then reflecting it through the origin, we get the graph in Figure 3.33.

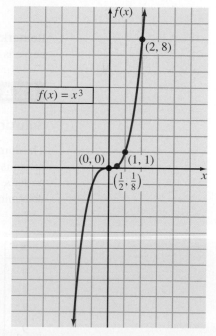

x	$f(x) = x^3$
0	0
1	1
2	8
$\dfrac{1}{2}$	$\dfrac{1}{8}$

Figure 3.33

EXAMPLE 2   Graph $f(x) = x^4$.

Solution

The domain is the set of real numbers. Because $f(0) = 0$, the origin is on the graph. Because $f(-x) = (-x)^4 = x^4 = f(x)$, the graph has y-axis symmetry, and we can concentrate our table of values on the positive values of x. If we connect the points associated with the ordered pairs in the table with a smooth curve and then reflect across the vertical axis, we get the graph in Figure 3.34.

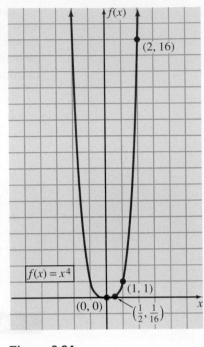

x	$f(x) = x^4$
0	0
1	1
2	16
$\frac{1}{2}$	$\frac{1}{16}$

Figure 3.34

Remark: The curve in Figure 3.34 is not a parabola, even though it resembles one; this curve is flatter at the bottom and steeper than a parabola would be.

EXAMPLE 3   Graph $f(x) = \sqrt{x}$.

Solution

The domain of the function is the set of nonnegative real numbers. Because $f(0) = 0$, the origin is on the graph. Because $f(-x) \neq f(x)$ and $f(-x) \neq -f(x)$, there is no symmetry, so let's set up a table of values using nonnegative values for x. Plotting the points determined by the table and connecting them with a smooth curve produces Figure 3.35.

x	$f(x) = \sqrt{x}$
0	0
1	1
4	2
9	3

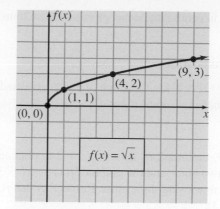

Figure 3.35

Sometimes a new function is defined in terms of old functions. In such cases, the definition plays an important role in the study of the new function. Consider the following example.

EXAMPLE 4   Graph $f(x) = |x|$.

Solution

The concept of absolute value is defined for all real numbers by

$$|x| = x \quad \text{if } x \geq 0$$
$$|x| = -x \quad \text{if } x < 0$$

Therefore the absolute value function can be expressed as

$$f(x) = |x| = \begin{cases} x & \text{if } x \geq 0 \\ -x & \text{if } x < 0 \end{cases}$$

The graph of $f(x) = x$ for $x \geq 0$ is the ray in the first quadrant, and the graph of $f(x) = -x$ for $x < 0$ is the half line (not including the origin) in the second quadrant, as indicated in Figure 3.36. Note that the graph has y-axis symmetry.

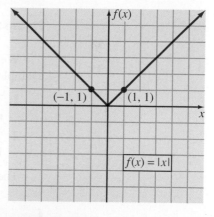

Figure 3.36

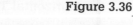

Translations of the Basic Curves

From our work in Section 3.3, we know that

1. The graph of $f(x) = x^2 + 3$ is the graph of $f(x) = x^2$ moved up three units.

2. The graph of $f(x) = x^2 - 2$ is the graph of $f(x) = x^2$ moved down two units.

Now let's describe in general the concept of a vertical translation.

> ### Vertical Translation
>
> The graph of $y = f(x) + k$ is the graph of $y = f(x)$ shifted k units upward if $k > 0$ or shifted $|k|$ units downward if $k < 0$.

In Figure 3.37, the graph of $f(x) = |x| + 2$ is obtained by shifting the graph of $f(x) = |x|$ upward two units, and the graph of $f(x) = |x| - 3$ is obtained by shifting the graph of $f(x) = |x|$ downward three units. Remember that $f(x) = |x| - 3$ can be written as $f(x) = |x| + (-3)$.

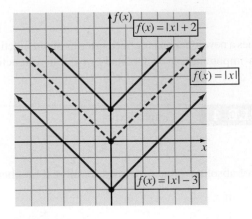

Figure 3.37

We also graphed horizontal translations of the basic parabola in Section 3.3. For example:

1. The graph of $f(x) = (x - 4)^2$ is the graph of $f(x) = x^2$ shifted four units to the right.

2. The graph of $f(x) = (x + 5)^2$ is the graph of $f(x) = x^2$ shifted five units to the left.

The general concept of a horizontal translation can be described as follows.

> ### Horizontal Translation
>
> The graph of $y = f(x - h)$ is the graph of $y = f(x)$ shifted h units to the right if $h > 0$ or shifted $|h|$ units to the left if $h < 0$.

In Figure 3.38, the graph of $f(x) = (x - 3)^3$ is obtained by shifting the graph of $f(x) = x^3$ three units to the right. Likewise, the graph of $f(x) = (x + 2)^3$ is obtained by shifting the graph of $f(x) = x^3$ two units to the left.

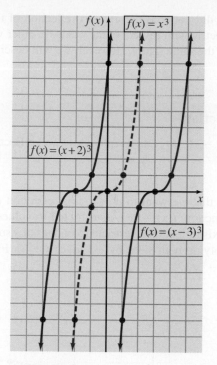

Figure 3.38

Reflections of the Basic Curves

From our work in Section 3.3, we know that the graph of $f(x) = -x^2$ is the graph of $f(x) = x^2$ reflected through the x axis. The general concept of an x-axis reflection can be described as follows:

> ### x-Axis Reflection
>
> The graph of $y = -f(x)$ is the graph of $y = f(x)$ reflected through the x axis.

In Figure 3.39, the graph of $f(x) = -\sqrt{x}$ is obtained by reflecting the graph of $f(x) = \sqrt{x}$ through the x axis. Reflections are sometimes referred to as **mirror images**. Thus if we think of the x axis in Figure 3.39 as a mirror, then the graphs of $f(x) = \sqrt{x}$ and $f(x) = -\sqrt{x}$ are mirror images of each other.

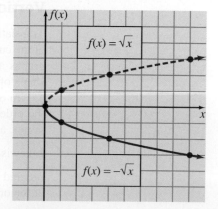

Figure 3.39

In Section 3.3, we did not consider a y-axis reflection of the basic parabola $f(x) = x^2$ because it is symmetric with respect to the y axis. In other words, a y-axis reflection of $f(x) = x^2$ produces the same figure. However, we will describe the general concept of a y-axis reflection.

---

y-Axis Reflection

The graph of $y = f(-x)$ is the graph of $y = f(x)$ reflected through the y axis.

Now suppose that we want to do a y-axis reflection of $f(x) = \sqrt{x}$. Because the domain for the function $f(x) = \sqrt{x}$ is restricted to values of x, such that $x \geq 0$, the domain for the y-axis reflection is restricted to values of x such that $-x \geq 0$. Simplifying $-x \geq 0$ by multiplying both sides by -1 gives $x \leq 0$. Figure 3.40 shows the y-axis reflection of $f(x) = \sqrt{x}$.

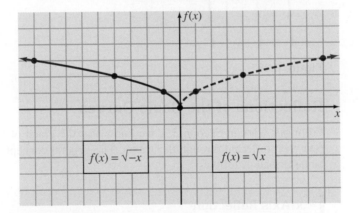

Figure 3.40

Vertical Stretching and Shrinking

Translations and reflections are called **rigid transformations** because the basic shape of the curve being transformed is not changed. In other words, only the positions of the graphs are changed. Now we want to consider some transformations that distort the shape of the original figure somewhat.

In Section 3.3, we graphed the function $f(x) = 2x^2$ by doubling the $f(x)$ values of the ordered pairs that satisfy the function $f(x) = x^2$. We obtained a parabola with its vertex at the origin, symmetric to the y axis, but *narrower* than the basic parabola. Likewise, we graphed the function $f(x) = \dfrac{1}{2}x^2$ by halving the $f(x)$ values of the ordered pairs that satisfy $f(x) = x^2$. In this case, we obtained a parabola with its vertex at the origin, symmetric to the y axis, but *wider* than the basic parabola.

The concepts of *narrower* and *wider* can be used to describe parabolas, but they cannot be used to describe accurately some other curves. Instead, we use the more general concepts of vertical stretching and shrinking.

> **Vertical Stretching and Shrinking**
>
> The graph of $y = cf(x)$ is obtained from the graph of $y = f(x)$ by multiplying the y coordinates for $y = f(x)$ by c. If $|c| > 1$, the graph is said to be *stretched* by a factor of $|c|$, and if $0 < |c| < 1$, the graph is said to be *shrunk* by a factor of $|c|$.

In Figure 3.41, the graph of $f(x) = 2\sqrt{x}$ is obtained by doubling the y coordinates of points on the graph of $f(x) = \sqrt{x}$. Likewise, the graph of $f(x) = \dfrac{1}{2}\sqrt{x}$ is obtained by halving the y coordinates of points on the graph of $f(x) = \sqrt{x}$.

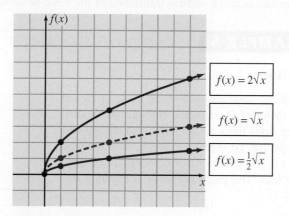

$$f(x) = 2\sqrt{x}$$

$$f(x) = \sqrt{x}$$

$$f(x) = \tfrac{1}{2}\sqrt{x}$$

Figure 3.41

Successive Transformations

Some curves are the result of performing more than one transformation on a basic curve. Before reading the next example, look over the following table that summarizes various transformations of the basic curve $f(x) = x^2$.

Function	Vertical Stretching or Shrinking	Reflection	Vertical Translation	Horizontal Translation
$f(x) = x^2 - 2$	none	none	Down 2 units	none
$f(x) = x^2 + 5$	none	none	Up 5 units	none
$f(x) = (x - 3)^2$	none	none	none	Right 3 units
$f(x) = (x + 4)^2$	none	none	none	Left 4 units

(continued)

Function	Vertical Stretching or Shrinking	Reflection	Vertical Translation	Horizontal Translation
$f(x) = -2x^2$	Stretched by a factor of 2	Reflected through the x axis	none	none
$f(x) = \dfrac{1}{3}x^2$	Shrunk by a factor of 1/3	none	none	none
$f(x) = (x + 1)^2 - 3$	none	none	Down 3 units	Left 1 unit
$f(x) = -(x - 6)^2 + 7$	none	Reflected through the x axis	Up 7 units	Right 6 units
$f(x) = -4(x + 1)^2 - 8$	Stretched by a factor of 4	Reflected through the x axis	Down 8 units	Left 1 unit

Let's consider the graph of a function that involves a stretching, a reflection, a horizontal translation, and a vertical translation of the basic absolute-value function.

Classroom Example

Graph $f(x) = -\dfrac{1}{2}\sqrt{x + 1} + 2$.

EXAMPLE 5   Graph $f(x) = -2|x - 3| + 1$.

Solution

This is the basic absolute-value curve stretched by a factor of 2, reflected through the x axis, shifted three units to the right, and shifted one unit upward. To sketch the graph, we locate the point $(3, 1)$ and then determine a point on each of the rays. The graph is shown in Figure 3.42.

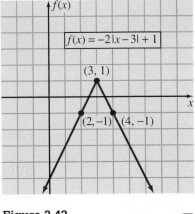

$$f(x) = -2|x - 3| + 1$$

$(3, 1)$

$(2, -1)$ $(4, -1)$

Figure 3.42

Remark: Note that in Example 5 we did not sketch the original basic curve $f(x) = |x|$ or any of the intermediate transformations. However, it is helpful to picture each transformation mentally. This locates the point $(3, 1)$ and establishes the fact that the two rays point downward. Then a point on each ray determines the final graph.

We do need to realize that changing the order of doing the transformations may produce an incorrect graph. In Example 5, performing the translations first, and then performing the stretching and x-axis reflection, would locate the vertex of the graph at $(3, -1)$ instead of $(3, 1)$. *Unless parentheses indicate otherwise, stretchings, shrinkings, and reflections should be performed before translations.*

Classroom Example
Graph $f(x) = \sqrt{-4 - x}$.

EXAMPLE 6   Graph $f(x) = \sqrt{-3 - x}$.

Solution

It appears that this function is a y-axis reflection and a horizontal translation of the basic function $f(x) = \sqrt{x}$. First let's rewrite the expression under the radical.

$$f(x) = \sqrt{-3 - x} = \sqrt{-(3 + x)} = \sqrt{-(x + 3)}$$

Now to graph $f(x) = \sqrt{-(x + 3)}$, we would first reflect the graph of $f(x) = \sqrt{x}$ across the y axis and then shift the graph 3 units to the left. The graph is shown in Figure 3.43. Because it is always a good idea to check your graph by plotting a few points, we have added the points $(-7, 2)$ and $(-4, 1)$ to the graph.

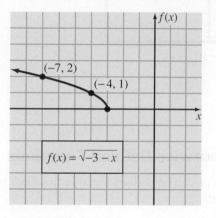

Figure 3.43

Let's use a graphing utility to give another illustration of the concept of stretching and shrinking a curve.

Classroom Example
If $f(x) = \sqrt{36 - x^2}$, sketch a graph of $y = 3f(x)$ and $y = \dfrac{1}{3}f(x)$.

EXAMPLE 7

If $f(x) = \sqrt{25 - x^2}$, use a graphing utility to sketch a graph of $y = 2(f(x))$ and $y = \dfrac{1}{2}(f(x))$.

Solution

If $y = f(x) = \sqrt{25 - x^2}$, then

$$y = 2(f(x)) = 2\sqrt{25 - x^2} \quad \text{and} \quad y = \frac{1}{2}(f(x)) = \frac{1}{2}\sqrt{25 - x^2}$$

Graphing all three of these functions on the same set of axes produces Figure 3.44.

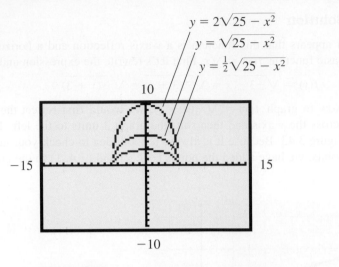

Figure 3.44

Graphing Piecewise-Defined Functions

Now let's graph a piecewise-defined function that involves both linear and quadratic rules of assignment.

Classroom Example
Graph

$$f(x) = \begin{cases} \frac{1}{2}x & \text{for } x \geq 0 \\ x^2 - 2 & \text{for } x < 0 \end{cases}.$$

EXAMPLE 8

Graph $f(x) = \begin{cases} 2x & \text{for } x \geq 0 \\ x^2 + 1 & \text{for } x < 0 \end{cases}$.

Solution

If $x \geq 0$, then $f(x) = 2x$. Thus for nonnegative values of x, we graph the linear function $f(x) = 2x$. If $x < 0$, then $f(x) = x^2 + 1$. Thus for negative values of x, we graph the quadratic function $f(x) = x^2 + 1$. The complete graph is shown in Figure 3.45.

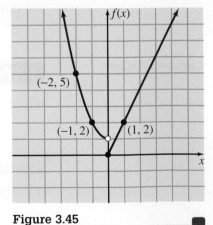

Figure 3.45

Concept Quiz 3.4

1. What is the domain of $f(x) = \sqrt{x}$?
   A. $x > 0$ **B.** $x \geq 0$ **C.** All real numbers

2. What is the domain of $f(x) = |x|$?
   A. $x > 0$ **B.** $x \geq 0$ **C.** All real numbers

3. If a graph is symmetric to the y axis, then which of the following is equal to $f(2)$?
   A. $-f(2)$ **B.** $f(-2)$ **C.** $-f(-2)$

4. Which of the following describes the graph of $f(x) = x^4 + 3$?
   A. The graph of $f(x) = x^4$ shifted up 3 units
   B. The graph of $f(x) = x^4$ shifted to the left 3 units
   C. The graph of $f(x) = x^4$ shifted to the right 3 units

5. For the graph of the function $f(x) = -2|x + 1| - 3$, what are the coordinates of the vertex?
   A. $(-1, 3)$ **B.** $(1, -3)$ **C.** $(-1, -3)$ **D.** $(0, 5)$

For Problems 6–10, answer true or false.

6. When the graph of a parabola is stretched, it is said to be narrower than the basic parabola.

7. A horizontal translation is a rigid transformation, and the shape of the graph does not change.

8. When applying successive transformations to a graph, unless parentheses indicate otherwise, stretchings, shrinkings, or reflections should be performed before translations.

9. The graphs of $f(x) = x^4$ and $f(x) = x^2$ are parabolas.

10. The graph of $y = f(-x)$ is the graph of $y = f(x)$ reflected across the x axis.

Problem Set 3.4

For Problems 1–30, graph each function. **(Objective 1)**

1. $f(x) = x^4 + 2$
2. $f(x) = -x^4 - 1$
3. $f(x) = (x - 2)^4$
4. $f(x) = (x + 3)^4 + 1$
5. $f(x) = -x^3$
6. $f(x) = x^3 - 2$
7. $f(x) = (x + 2)^3$
8. $f(x) = (x - 3)^3 - 1$
9. $f(x) = |x - 1| + 2$
10. $f(x) = -|x + 2|$
11. $f(x) = |x + 1| - 3$
12. $f(x) = 2|x|$
13. $f(x) = -(x + 3)^2 + 4$
14. $f(x) = (x - 2)^2 + 1$
15. $f(x) = -|x - 2| - 1$
16. $f(x) = 2|x + 1| - 4$
17. $f(x) = 2x^2 + 4$
18. $f(x) = -x^2 - 2$
19. $f(x) = -2\sqrt{x}$
20. $f(x) = 2\sqrt{x - 1}$
21. $f(x) = \sqrt{x + 2} - 3$
22. $f(x) = -\sqrt{x + 2} + 2$
23. $f(x) = \sqrt{2 - x}$
24. $f(x) = \sqrt{-1 - x}$
25. $f(x) = -2x^4 + 1$
26. $f(x) = 2(x - 2)^4 - 4$
27. $f(x) = -2x^3$
28. $f(x) = 2x^3 + 3$
29. $f(x) = 3(x - 2)^3 - 1$
30. $f(x) = -2(x + 1)^3 + 2$

31. Suppose that the graph of $y = f(x)$ with a domain of $-2 \leq x \leq 2$ is shown in Figure 3.46.

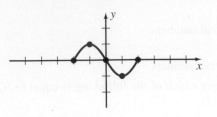

Figure 3.46

Sketch the graph of each of the following transformations of $y = f(x)$.

(a) $y = f(x) + 3$ **(b)** $y = f(x - 2)$
(c) $y = -f(x)$ **(d)** $y = f(x + 3) - 4$

32. Suppose the graph $y = f(x)$ with a domain of $-4 \leq x \leq 4$ is shown in Figure 3.47.

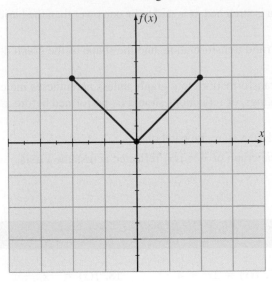

Figure 3.47

Sketch the graph of each of the following transformations of $y = f(x)$.

(a) $y = f(x - 2)$ **(b)** $y = -f(x) + 2$
(c) $y = f(x) - 4$ **(d)** $y = f(x + 2) - 4$

For Problems 33–40, graph the piecewise-defined functions. **(Objective 2)**

33. $f(x) = \begin{cases} -x^2 & \text{for } x < 0 \\ x^2 + 1 & \text{for } x \geq 0 \end{cases}$

34. $f(x) = \begin{cases} -x^2 & \text{for } x < 0 \\ x^2 - 3 & \text{for } x \geq 0 \end{cases}$

35. $f(x) = \begin{cases} -x^2 & \text{for } x < -1 \\ x + 2 & \text{for } -1 \leq x \leq 1 \\ \sqrt{x} & \text{for } x > 1 \end{cases}$

36. $f(x) = \begin{cases} -2x & \text{for } x < 0 \\ x^3 & \text{for } 0 \leq x \leq 2 \\ -x + 10 & \text{for } x > 2 \end{cases}$

37. $f(x) = \begin{cases} 2x^2 & \text{for } x < 0 \\ -x^2 & \text{for } x \geq 0 \end{cases}$

38. $f(x) = \begin{cases} |x| & \text{for } x < 2 \\ -x & \text{for } x \geq 2 \end{cases}$

39. $f(x) = \begin{cases} -1 & \text{for } x \leq 0 \\ 1 & \text{for } 0 < x < 2 \\ 2 & \text{for } x \geq 2 \end{cases}$

40. $f(x) = \begin{cases} 1 & \text{for } 0 \leq x < 1 \\ 2 & \text{for } 1 \leq x < 2 \\ 3 & \text{for } 2 \leq x < 3 \\ 4 & \text{for } 3 \leq x < 4 \end{cases}$

For problems 41–44, graph each of the functions. Although these functions are not written as piecewise-defined functions, they behave similarly because the definition of absolute value is defined by pieces.

41. $f(x) = x + |x|$ **42.** $f(x) = \dfrac{|x|}{x}$

43. $f(x) = x - |x|$ **44.** $f(x) = |x| - x$

Thoughts Into Words

45. Are the graphs of the two functions $f(x) = \sqrt{x - 2}$ and $g(x) = \sqrt{2 - x}$ y-axis reflections of each other? Defend your answer.

46. Are the graphs of $f(x) = 2\sqrt{x}$ and $g(x) = \sqrt{2x}$ identical? Defend your answer.

47. Are the graphs of $f(x) = \sqrt{x + 4}$ and $g(x) = \sqrt{-x + 4}$ y-axis reflections of each other? Defend your answer.

Graphing Calculator Activities

48. Use your graphing calculator to check your graphs for Problems 13–30.

49. Graph $f(x) = \sqrt{x^2 + 8}$, $f(x) = \sqrt{x^2 + 4}$, and $f(x) = \sqrt{x^2 + 1}$ on the same set of axes. Look at these graphs and predict the graph of $f(x) = \sqrt{x^2 - 4}$. Now graph it with the calculator to test your prediction.

50. For each of the following, predict the general shape and location of the graph, and then use your calculator to graph the function to check your prediction.
   (a) $f(x) = \sqrt{x^2}$ **(b)** $f(x) = \sqrt{x^3}$
   (c) $f(x) = |x^2|$ **(d)** $f(x) = |x^3|$

51. Graph $f(x) = x^4 + x^3$. Now predict the graph for each of the following, and check each prediction with your graphing calculator.
   (a) $f(x) = x^4 + x^3 - 4$
   (b) $f(x) = (x - 3)^4 + (x - 3)^3$
   (c) $f(x) = -x^4 - x^3$
   (d) $f(x) = x^4 - x^3$

52. Graph $f(x) = \sqrt[3]{x}$. Now predict the graph for each of the following, and check each prediction with your graphing calculator.
   (a) $f(x) = 5 + \sqrt[3]{x}$ **(b)** $f(x) = \sqrt[3]{x + 4}$
   (c) $f(x) = -\sqrt[3]{x}$ **(d)** $f(x) = \sqrt[3]{x - 3} - 5$
   (e) $f(x) = \sqrt[3]{-x}$

Answers to the Concept Quiz

1. B   **2.** C   **3.** B   **4.** A   **5.** C   **6.** True   **7.** True   **8.** True   **9.** False   **10.** False

---

3.5   Combining Functions

OBJECTIVES

1 Combine functions by finding the sum, difference, product, or quotient

2 Find the composition of two functions

3 Evaluate a composite function for a specified value

4 Find the difference quotient of a function

In subsequent mathematics courses, it is common to encounter functions that are defined in terms of sums, differences, products, and quotients of simpler functions. For example, if $h(x) = x^2 + \sqrt{x - 1}$, then we may consider the function h as the sum of f and g, where $f(x) = x^2$ and $g(x) = \sqrt{x - 1}$. In general, if f and g are functions, and D is the intersection of their domains, then the following definitions can be made:

Sum $(f + g)(x) = f(x) + g(x)$

Difference $(f - g)(x) = f(x) - g(x)$

Product $(f \cdot g)(x) = f(x) \cdot g(x)$

Quotient $\left(\dfrac{f}{g}\right)(x) = \dfrac{f(x)}{g(x)}, \quad g(x) \neq 0$

EXAMPLE 1

If $f(x) = 3x - 1$ and $g(x) = x^2 - x - 2$, find **(a)** $(f + g)(x)$; **(b)** $(f - g)(x)$; **(c)** $(f \cdot g)(x)$; and **(d)** $(f/g)(x)$. Determine the domain of each.

Solutions

(a) $(f + g)(x) = f(x) + g(x) = (3x - 1) + (x^2 - x - 2) = x^2 + 2x - 3$

(b) $(f - g)(x) = f(x) - g(x)$

$$= (3x - 1) - (x^2 - x - 2)$$
$$= 3x - 1 - x^2 + x + 2$$
$$= -x^2 + 4x + 1$$

(c) $(f \cdot g)(x) = f(x) \cdot g(x)$

$$= (3x - 1)(x^2 - x - 2)$$
$$= 3x^3 - 3x^2 - 6x - x^2 + x + 2$$
$$= 3x^3 - 4x^2 - 5x + 2$$

(d) $\left(\dfrac{f}{g}\right)(x) = \dfrac{f(x)}{g(x)} = \dfrac{3x - 1}{x^2 - x - 2}$

The domain of both f and g is the set of all real numbers. Therefore the domain of $f + g$, $f - g$, and $f \cdot g$ is the set of all real numbers. For f/g, the denominator $x^2 - x - 2$ cannot equal zero. Solving $x^2 - x - 2 = 0$ produces

$$(x - 2)(x + 1) = 0$$
$$x - 2 = 0 \quad \text{or} \quad x + 1 = 0$$
$$x = 2 \quad\quad\quad x = -1$$

Therefore the domain for f/g is the set of all real numbers except 2 and -1. ∎

Graphs of functions can help us visually sort out our thought processes. For example, suppose that $f(x) = 0.46x - 4$ and $g(x) = 3$. If we think in terms of ordinate values, it seems reasonable that the graph of $f + g$ is the graph of f moved up three units. Likewise, the graph of $f - g$ should be the graph of f moved down three units. Let's use a graphing calculator to support these conclusions. Letting $Y_1 = 0.46x - 4$, $Y_2 = 3$, $Y_3 = Y_1 + Y_2$, and $Y_4 = Y_1 - Y_2$, we obtain Figure 3.48. Certainly this figure

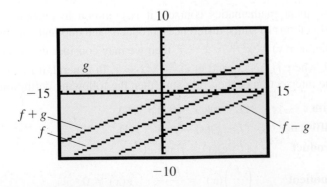

Figure 3.48

supports our conclusions. This type of graphical analysis becomes more important as the functions become more complex.

Composition of Functions

Besides adding, subtracting, multiplying, and dividing functions, there is another important operation called *composition*. The composition of two functions can be defined as follows:

> ### Definition 3.2
>
> The **composition** of functions f and g is defined by
>
> $$(f \circ g)(x) = f(g(x))$$
>
> for all x in the domain of g such that $g(x)$ is in the domain of f.

The left side, $(f \circ g)(x)$, of the equation in Definition 3.2 is read "the composition of f and g," and the right side is read "f of g of x." It may also be helpful for you to have a mental picture of Definition 3.2 as two function machines hooked together to produce another function (called the **composite function**), as illustrated in Figure 3.49. Note that what comes out of the g function is substituted into the f function. Thus composition is sometimes called the **substitution of functions**.

Figure 3.49 also illustrates the fact that $f \circ g$ is defined for all x in the domain of g such that $g(x)$ is in the domain of f. In other words, what comes out of g must be capable of being fed into f. Let's consider some examples.

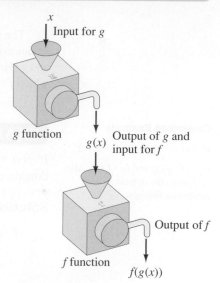

x

Input for g

g function

$g(x)$　Output of g and input for f

f function

$f(g(x))$

Output of f

Figure 3.49

EXAMPLE 2

If $f(x) = x^2$ and $g(x) = 3x - 4$, find $(f \circ g)(x)$ and determine its domain.

Solution

Apply Definition 3.2 to obtain

$$(f \circ g)(x) = f(g(x))$$
$$= f(3x - 4)$$
$$= (3x - 4)^2 = 9x^2 - 24x + 16$$

Because g and f are both defined for all real numbers, so is $f \circ g$. Therefore, the domain of $f \circ g$ is all real numbers.

Definition 3.2, with f and g interchanged, defines the composition of g and f as $(g \circ f)(x) = g(f(x))$.

EXAMPLE 3

If $f(x) = x^2$ and $g(x) = 3x - 4$, find $(g \circ f)(x)$ and determine its domain.

Solution

$$(g \circ f)(x) = g(f(x))$$
$$= g(x^2)$$
$$= 3x^2 - 4$$

Because f and g are defined for all real numbers, so is $g \circ f$. Therefore, the domain of $g \circ f$ is all real numbers. ∎

The results of Examples 2 and 3 demonstrate an important idea: *The composition of functions is not a commutative operation.* In other words, $f \circ g \neq g \circ f$ for all functions f and g. However, as we will see in Section 5.3, there is a special class of functions for which $f \circ g = g \circ f$.

EXAMPLE 4

If $f(x) = \sqrt{x}$ and $g(x) = 2x - 1$, find $(f \circ g)(x)$ and $(g \circ f)(x)$. Also determine the domain of each composite function.

Solution

$$(f \circ g)(x) = f(g(x))$$
$$= f(2x - 1)$$
$$= \sqrt{2x - 1}$$

The domain and range of g are the set of all real numbers, but the domain of f is all *nonnegative* real numbers. Therefore $g(x)$, which is $2x - 1$, must be nonnegative.

$$2x - 1 \geq 0$$
$$2x \geq 1$$
$$x \geq \frac{1}{2}$$

Thus the domain of $f \circ g$ is $D = \left\{ x \mid x \geq \dfrac{1}{2} \right\}$.

$$(g \circ f)(x) = g(f(x))$$
$$= g(\sqrt{x})$$
$$= 2\sqrt{x} - 1$$

The domain and range of f are the set of nonnegative real numbers. The domain of g is the set of all real numbers. Therefore the domain of $g \circ f$ is $D = \{x \mid x \geq 0\}$.

Classroom Example

If $f(x) = \dfrac{3}{x + 2}$ and $g(x) = \dfrac{2}{x}$, find $(f \circ g)(x)$ and $(g \circ f)(x)$. Determine the domain for each composite function.

EXAMPLE 5

If $f(x) = \dfrac{3}{x - 1}$ and $g(x) = \dfrac{1}{2x}$, find $(f \circ g)(x)$ and $(g \circ f)(x)$. Determine the domain for each composite function.

Solution

$$(f \circ g)(x) = f(g(x))$$

$$= f\left(\frac{1}{2x}\right)$$

$$= \frac{3}{\dfrac{1}{2x} - 1} = \frac{3}{\dfrac{1}{2x} - \dfrac{2x}{2x}} = \frac{3}{\dfrac{1 - 2x}{2x}}$$

$$= \frac{6x}{1 - 2x}$$

The domain of g is all real numbers except 0, and the domain of f is all real numbers except 1. Therefore $g(x) \neq 1$. So we need to solve $g(x) = 1$ to find the values of x that will make $g(x) = 1$.

$$g(x) = 1$$

$$\frac{1}{2x} = 1$$

$$1 = 2x$$

$$\frac{1}{2} = x$$

Therefore $x \neq \dfrac{1}{2}$, so the domain of $f \circ g$ is $D = \left\{ x \mid x \neq 0 \text{ and } x \neq \dfrac{1}{2} \right\}$.

$$(g \circ f)(x) = g(f(x))$$

$$= g\left(\frac{3}{x - 1}\right)$$

$$= \frac{1}{2\left(\dfrac{3}{x - 1}\right)} = \frac{1}{\dfrac{6}{x - 1}}$$

$$= \frac{x - 1}{6}$$

The domain of f is all real numbers except 1, and the domain of g is all real numbers except 0. Because $f(x)$, which is $3/(x - 1)$, will never equal 0, the domain of $g \circ f$ is $D = \{x \mid x \neq 1\}$.

EXAMPLE 6   If $f(x) = 5x + 2$ and $g(x) = \dfrac{1}{x + 1}$, find $(g \circ f)(-2)$.

Solution A

First determine $(g \circ f)(x)$.

$$(g \circ f)(x) = g[f(x)]$$
$$= g(5x + 2)$$
$$= \frac{1}{(5x + 2) + 1}$$
$$= \frac{1}{5x + 3}$$

Now substitute -2 for x in $(g \circ f)(x)$.

$$(g \circ f)(-2) = \frac{1}{5(-2) + 3} = -\frac{1}{7}$$

Solution B

The composition $(g \circ f)(-2)$ can be rewritten as $g[f(-2)]$. Let's evaluate $f(-2)$.

$$f(-2) = 5(-2) + 2 = -8$$

Now the value -8 can be substituted for $f(-2)$ and $g[f(-2)]$ can be determined.

$$g[f(-2)] = g(-8) = \frac{1}{-8 + 1} = -\frac{1}{7}$$

Depending on the functions given in the problem, you may find one approach simpler than the other approach.   ■

A graphing utility can be used to find the graph of a composite function without actually forming the function algebraically. Let's see how this works.

EXAMPLE 7

If $f(x) = x^3$ and $g(x) = x - 4$, use a graphing utility to obtain the graphs of $y = (f \circ g)(x)$ and of $y = (g \circ f)(x)$.

Solution

To find the graph of $y = (f \circ g)(x)$, we can make the following assignments:

$$Y_1 = x - 4$$
$$Y_2 = (Y_1)^3$$

(Note that we have substituted Y_1 for x in $f(x)$ and assigned this expression to Y_2, much the same way as we would do it algebraically.) The graph of $y = (f \circ g)(x)$ is shown in Figure 3.50.

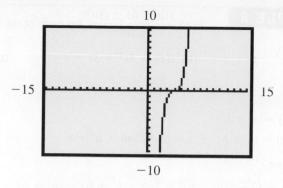

Figure 3.50

To find the graph of $y = (g \circ f)(x)$, we can make the following assignments.

$$Y_1 = x^3$$
$$Y_2 = Y_1 - 4$$

The graph of $y = (g \circ f)(x)$ is shown in Figure 3.51.

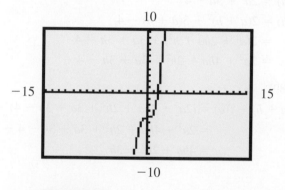

Figure 3.51

Take another look at Figures 3.50 and 3.51. Note that in Figure 3.50, the graph of $y = (f \circ g)(x)$ is the basic cubic curve $f(x) = x^3$ translated four units to the right. Likewise, in Figure 3.51, the graph of $y = (g \circ f)(x)$ is the basic cubic curve translated four units downward. These are examples of a more general concept of using composite functions to represent various geometric transformations.

Finding the Difference Quotient

The quotient $\dfrac{f(a + h) - f(a)}{h}$ is often called a **difference quotient**. We use it extensively with functions when we study the limit concept in calculus. The next examples illustrate finding the difference quotient for specific functions.

Classroom Example

Find $\dfrac{f(a+h)-f(a)}{h}$ for each

of the following functions.

(a) $f(x) = x^2 - 3$

(b) $f(x) = 3x^2 - 2x + 1$

(c) $f(x) = \dfrac{1}{x-1}$

EXAMPLE 8   Find $\dfrac{f(a+h)-f(a)}{h}$ for each of the following functions.

(a) $f(x) = x^2 + 6$ (b) $f(x) = 2x^2 + 3x - 4$ (c) $f(x) = \dfrac{1}{x}$

Solutions

(a) $f(a) = a^2 + 6$

$f(a + h) = (a + h)^2 + 6 = a^2 + 2ah + h^2 + 6$

Therefore

$$f(a + h) - f(a) = (a^2 + 2ah + h^2 + 6) - (a^2 + 6)$$
$$= a^2 + 2ah + h^2 + 6 - a^2 - 6$$
$$= 2ah + h^2$$

and

$$\frac{f(a+h)-f(a)}{h} = \frac{2ah + h^2}{h} = \frac{h(2a + h)}{h} = 2a + h$$

(b) $f(a) = 2a^2 + 3a - 4$

$f(a + h) = 2(a + h)^2 + 3(a + h) - 4$

$\qquad\quad = 2(a^2 + 2ha + h^2) + 3a + 3h - 4$

$\qquad\quad = 2a^2 + 4ha + 2h^2 + 3a + 3h - 4$

Therefore

$$f(a + h) - f(a) = (2a^2 + 4ha + 2h^2 + 3a + 3h - 4) - (2a^2 + 3a - 4)$$
$$= 2a^2 + 4ha + 2h^2 + 3a + 3h - 4 - 2a^2 - 3a + 4$$
$$= 4ha + 2h^2 + 3h$$

and

$$\frac{f(a+h)-f(a)}{h} = \frac{4ha + 2h^2 + 3h}{h}$$
$$= \frac{h(4a + 2h + 3)}{h}$$
$$= 4a + 2h + 3$$

(c) $f(a) = \dfrac{1}{a}$

$f(a + h) = \dfrac{1}{a + h}$

Therefore

$$f(a + h) - f(a) = \frac{1}{a + h} - \frac{1}{a}$$

$$= \frac{a}{a(a + h)} - \frac{a + h}{a(a + h)} \qquad \text{Common denominator of } a(a + h)$$

$$= \frac{a - (a + h)}{a(a + h)}$$

$$= \frac{a - a - h}{a(a + h)}$$

$$= \frac{-h}{a(a + h)} \qquad \text{or} \qquad -\frac{h}{a(a + h)}$$

and

$$\frac{f(a + h) - f(a)}{h} = \frac{-\dfrac{h}{a(a + h)}}{h}$$

$$= -\frac{h}{a(a + h)} \cdot \frac{1}{h}$$

$$= -\frac{1}{a(a + h)}$$

Concept Quiz 3.5

For Problems 1–10, answer true or false.

1. If $f(x) = \sqrt{x}$ and $g(x) = x^2$, then the domain of $f \circ g$ is all real numbers.

2. If $f(x) = 2x + 6$ and $g(x) = x - 7$, then the domain of $\dfrac{f}{g}$ is all real numbers.

3. The composition of functions is a commutative operation.

4. The sum of two functions is a commutative operation.

5. The composition of two functions $f \circ g$ means to multiply the functions.

6. When forming the composition of two functions $f \circ g$, the range elements of g are members of the domain of f.

7. If $f(x) = \dfrac{1}{x - 6}$ and $g(x) = 2x$, then the domain of $f \circ g$ is all real numbers except 3 and 6.

8. If the domain of f is $x > 0$ and the domain of g is $x < 0$, then the sum $(f + g)(x)$ is not defined.

9. If $f(x) = \dfrac{1}{x - 6}$ and $g(x) = \dfrac{6}{x - 3}$, then the domain of $f \circ g$ is
$D = \{x \mid x \neq 3 \text{ and } x \neq 4\}$.

10. If $f(x) = \dfrac{1}{x - 6}$ and $g(x) = \dfrac{6}{x - 3}$, then the domain of $g \circ f$ is
$D = \left\{x \mid x \neq 6 \text{ and } x \neq \dfrac{19}{3}\right\}$.

Problem Set 3.5

For Problems 1–8, find $f + g$, $f - g$, $f \cdot g$, and f/g. Also specify the domain for each. (Objective 1)

1. $f(x) = 3x - 4$, $g(x) = 5x + 2$

2. $f(x) = -6x - 1$, $g(x) = -8x + 7$

3. $f(x) = x^2 - 6x + 4$, $g(x) = -x - 1$

4. $f(x) = 2x^2 - 3x + 5$, $g(x) = x^2 - 4$

5. $f(x) = x^2 - x - 1$, $g(x) = x^2 + 4x - 5$

6. $f(x) = x^2 - 2x - 24$, $g(x) = x^2 - x - 30$

7. $f(x) = \sqrt{x - 1}$, $g(x) = \sqrt{x}$

8. $f(x) = \sqrt{x + 2}$, $g(x) = \sqrt{3x - 1}$

For Problems 9–22, find $\dfrac{f(a + h) - f(a)}{h}$.
(Objective 5)

9. $f(x) = 3x + 8$

10. $f(x) = 4x + 5$

11. $f(x) = -7x - 2$

12. $f(x) = -2x + 3$

13. $f(x) = -x^2 + 4x - 2$

14. $f(x) = x^2 - 3x$

15. $f(x) = 3x^2 - x - 4$

16. $f(x) = 2x^2 + 7x - 4$

17. $f(x) = x^3 - x^2 + 2x - 1$

18. $f(x) = x^3$

19. $f(x) = \dfrac{2}{x - 1}$

20. $f(x) = \dfrac{1}{x + 1}$

21. $f(x) = \dfrac{1}{x^2}$

22. $f(x) = \dfrac{x}{x + 1}$

For Problems 23–40, find $(f \circ g)(x)$ and $(g \circ f)(x)$. Also specify the domain for each. (Objective 2)

23. $f(x) = 2x$, $g(x) = 3x - 1$

24. $f(x) = 4x + 1$, $g(x) = 3x$

25. $f(x) = 5x - 3$, $g(x) = 2x + 1$

26. $f(x) = 3 - 2x$, $g(x) = -4x$

27. $f(x) = 3x + 4$, $g(x) = x^2 + 1$

28. $f(x) = 3$, $g(x) = -3x^2 - 1$

29. $f(x) = 3x - 4$, $g(x) = x^2 + 3x - 4$

30. $f(x) = 2x^2 - x - 1$, $g(x) = x + 4$

31. $f(x) = \dfrac{1}{x}$, $g(x) = 2x + 7$

32. $f(x) = \dfrac{1}{x^2}$, $g(x) = x$

33. $f(x) = \sqrt{x - 2}$, $g(x) = 3x - 1$

34. $f(x) = \dfrac{1}{x}$, $g(x) = \dfrac{1}{x^2}$

35. $f(x) = \dfrac{1}{x - 1}$, $g(x) = \dfrac{2}{x}$

36. $f(x) = \dfrac{4}{x + 2}$, $g(x) = \dfrac{3}{2x}$

37. $f(x) = 2x + 1$, $g(x) = \sqrt{x - 1}$

38. $f(x) = \sqrt{x + 1}$, $g(x) = 5x - 2$

39. $f(x) = \dfrac{1}{x - 1}$, $g(x) = \dfrac{x + 1}{x}$

40. $f(x) = \dfrac{x - 1}{x + 2}$, $g(x) = \dfrac{1}{x}$

For Problems 41–46, solve each problem. (Objective 3)

41. If $f(x) = 3x - 2$ and $g(x) = x^2 + 1$, find $(f \circ g)(-1)$ and $(g \circ f)(3)$.

42. If $f(x) = x^2 - 2$ and $g(x) = x + 4$, find $(f \circ g)(2)$ and $(g \circ f)(-4)$.

43. If $f(x) = 2x - 3$ and $g(x) = x^2 - 3x - 4$, find $(f \circ g)(-2)$ and $(g \circ f)(1)$.

44. If $f(x) = 1/x$ and $g(x) = 2x + 1$, find $(f \circ g)(1)$ and $(g \circ f)(2)$.

45. If $f(x) = \sqrt{x}$ and $g(x) = 3x - 1$, find $(f \circ g)(4)$ and $(g \circ f)(4)$.

46. If $f(x) = x + 5$ and $g(x) = |x|$, find $(f \circ g)(-4)$ and $(g \circ f)(-4)$.

For Problems 47–52, show that $(f \circ g)(x) = x$ and that $(g \circ f)(x) = x$.

47. $f(x) = 2x, \quad g(x) = \dfrac{1}{2}x$

48. $f(x) = \dfrac{3}{4}x, \quad g(x) = \dfrac{4}{3}x$

49. $f(x) = x - 2, \quad g(x) = x + 2$

50. $f(x) = 2x + 1, \quad g(x) = \dfrac{x - 1}{2}$

51. $f(x) = 3x + 4 \quad g(x) = \dfrac{x - 4}{3}$

52. $f(x) = 4x - 3, \quad g(x) = \dfrac{x + 3}{4}$

Thoughts Into Words

53. Discuss whether addition, subtraction, multiplication, and division of functions are commutative operations.

54. Explain why the composition of two functions is not a commutative operation.

55. Explain how to find the domain of

$$\left(\frac{f}{g}\right)(x) \text{ if } f(x) = \frac{x - 1}{x + 2} \text{ and } g(x) = \frac{x + 3}{x - 5}.$$

Further Investigations

56. If $f(x) = 3x - 4$ and $g(x) = ax + b$, find conditions on a and b that will guarantee that $f \circ g = g \circ f$.

57. If $f(x) = x^2$ and $g(x) = \sqrt{x}$, with both having a domain of the set of nonnegative real numbers, then show that $(f \circ g)(x) = x$ and $(g \circ f)(x) = x$.

58. If $f(x) = 3x^2 - 2x - 1$ and $g(x) = x$, find $f \circ g$ and $g \circ f$. (Recall that we have previously named $g(x) = x$ the "identity function.")

Graphing Calculator Activities

59. For each of the following, predict the general shape and location of the graph, and then use your calculator to graph the function to check your prediction. (Your knowledge of the graphs of the basic functions that are being added or subtracted should be helpful when you are making your predictions.)
(a) $f(x) = x^4 + x^2$ **(b)** $f(x) = x^3 + x^2$
(c) $f(x) = x^4 - x^2$ **(d)** $f(x) = x^2 - x^4$
(e) $f(x) = x^2 - x^3$ **(f)** $f(x) = x^3 - x^2$
(g) $f(x) = |x| + \sqrt{x}$ **(h)** $f(x) = |x| - \sqrt{x}$

60. For each of the following, find the graph of $y = (f \circ g)(x)$ and of $y = (g \circ f)(x)$.
(a) $f(x) = x^2$ and $g(x) = x + 5$
(b) $f(x) = x^3$ and $g(x) = x + 3$
(c) $f(x) = x - 6$ and $g(x) = -x^3$
(d) $f(x) = x^2 - 4$ and $g(x) = \sqrt{x}$
(e) $f(x) = \sqrt{x}$ and $g(x) = x^2 + 4$
(f) $f(x) = \sqrt[3]{x}$ and $g(x) = x^3 - 5$

Answers to the Concept Quiz
1. True   **2.** False   **3.** False   **4.** True   **5.** False   **6.** True   **7.** False   **8.** True   **9.** True   **10.** True

3.6 Direct and Inverse Variation

OBJECTIVES

1. Translate statements of variation into equations
2. Find the value for the constant of variation
3. Solve application problems for direct, inverse, or joint variation

The amount of simple interest earned by a fixed amount of money invested at a certain rate *varies directly* as the time.

At a constant temperature, the volume of an enclosed gas *varies inversely* as the pressure.

Such statements illustrate two basic types of functional relationships, **direct variation** and **inverse variation**, that are widely used, especially in the physical sciences. These relationships can be expressed by equations that determine functions. The purpose of this section is to investigate these special functions.

Direct Variation

The statement "*y* varies directly as *x*" means

$$y = kx$$

where k is a nonzero constant called the **constant of variation**. The phrase "*y* is directly proportional to *x*" is also used to indicate direct variation; k is then referred to as the **constant of proportionality**.

Remark: Note that the equation $y = kx$ defines a function and can be written $f(x) = kx$. However, in this section, it is more convenient not to use function notation but instead to use variables that are meaningful in terms of the physical entities involved in the particular problem.

Statements that indicate direct variation may also involve powers of a variable. For example, "*y* varies directly as the square of *x*" can be written $y = kx^2$. In general, *y* varies directly as the *n*th power of *x* $(n > 0)$ means

$$y = kx^n$$

There are three basic types of problems in which we deal with direct variation:

1. Translating an English statement into an equation expressing the direct variation;
2. Finding the constant of variation from the given values of the variables; and
3. Finding additional values of the variables once the constant of variation has been determined.

Let's consider an example of each type of problem.

Classroom Example
Translate the statement "the distance traveled varies directly as the time traveled" into an equation, and use k as the constant of variation.

EXAMPLE 1

Translate the statement "The tension on a spring varies directly as the distance it is stretched" into an equation, using k as the constant of variation.

Solution

Let t represent the tension and d the distance; the equation is

$$t = kd$$

Classroom Example
If A varies directly as the square root of s, and if $A = 28$ when $s = 49$, find the constant of variation.

EXAMPLE 2

If A varies directly as the square of e, and if $A = 96$ when $e = 4$, find the constant of variation.

Solution

Because A varies directly as the square of e, we have

$$A = ke^2$$

Substitute 96 for A and 4 for e to obtain

$$96 = k(4)^2$$
$$96 = 16k$$
$$6 = k$$

The constant of variation is 6.

Classroom Example
If r is directly proportional to t and if $r = 40$ when $t = 48$, find the value of r when $t = 84$.

EXAMPLE 3

If y is directly proportional to x, and if $y = 6$ when $x = 8$, find the value of y when $x = 24$.

Solution

The statement "y is directly proportional to x" translates into

$$y = kx$$

Let $y = 6$ and $x = 8$; the constant of variation becomes

$$6 = k(8)$$
$$\frac{6}{8} = k$$
$$\frac{3}{4} = k$$

Thus the specific equation is

$$y = \frac{3}{4}x$$

Now let $x = 24$ to obtain

$$y = \frac{3}{4}(24) = 18$$

The value of y is 18.

Inverse Variation

The second basic type of variation is *inverse variation*. The statement "y varies inversely as x" means

$$y = \frac{k}{x}$$

where k is a nonzero constant, which is again referred to as the constant of variation. The phrase "y is inversely proportional to x" is also used to express inverse variation. As with direct variation, statements indicating inverse variation may involve powers of x. For example, "y varies inversely as the square of x" can be written $y = k/x^2$. In general, y varies inversely as the nth power of x ($n > 0$) means

$$y = \frac{k}{x^n}$$

The following examples illustrate the three basic kinds of problems that involve inverse variation.

Classroom Example
Translate the statement "the volume of a gas varies inversely as the pressure" into an equation that uses k as the constant of variation.

EXAMPLE 4

Translate the statement "The length of a rectangle of fixed area varies inversely as the width" into an equation, using k as the constant of variation.

Solution

Let l represent the length and w the width; the equation is

$$l = \frac{k}{w}$$

Classroom Example
If m is inversely proportional to n, and if $m = 6$ when $n = 15$, find the constant of variation.

EXAMPLE 5

If y is inversely proportional to x, and if $y = 14$ when $x = 4$, find the constant of variation.

Solution

Because y is inversely proportional to x, we have

$$y = \frac{k}{x}$$

Substitute 4 for x and 14 for y to obtain

$$14 = \frac{k}{4}$$

Solving this equation yields

$$k = 56$$

The constant of variation is 56.

Classroom Example
Suppose that the time traveled
a fixed distance varies inversely
with the speed. If it takes 4 hours
at 70 miles per hour to travel that
distance, how long would it take
at 56 miles per hour?

EXAMPLE 6

The time required for a car to travel a certain distance varies inversely as the rate at which it travels. If it takes 4 hours at 50 miles per hour to travel the distance, how long will it take at 40 miles per hour?

Solution

Let t represent time and r rate. The phrase "time required . . . varies inversely as the rate" translates into

$$t = \frac{k}{r}$$

Substitute 4 for t and 50 for r to find the constant of variation.

$$4 = \frac{k}{50}$$

$$k = 200$$

Thus the specific equation is

$$t = \frac{200}{r}$$

Now substitute 40 for r to produce

$$t = \frac{200}{40}$$

$$= 5$$

It will take 5 hours at 40 miles per hour.

The terms *direct* and *inverse*, as applied to variation, refer to the relative behavior of the variables involved in the equation. That is, in **direct variation** ($y = kx$), an assignment of *increasing absolute values for x* produces *increasing absolute values for y*. However, in **inverse variation** ($y = k/x$), an assignment of *increasing absolute values for x* produces *decreasing absolute values for y*.

Joint Variation

Variation may involve more than two variables. The following table illustrates some different types of variation statements and their equivalent algebraic equations that use k as the constant of variation. Statements 1, 2, and 3 illustrate the concept of **joint variation**. Statements 4 and 5 show that both direct and inverse variation may occur in the same problem. Statement 6 combines joint variation with inverse variation.

Variation Statement	Algebraic Equation
1. y varies jointly as x and z.	$y = kxz$
2. y varies jointly as x, z, and w.	$y = kxzw$
3. V varies jointly as h and the square of r.	$V = khr^2$
4. h varies directly as V and inversely as w.	$h = \dfrac{kV}{w}$
5. y is directly proportional to x and inversely proportional to the square of z.	$y = \dfrac{kx}{z^2}$
6. y varies jointly as w and z and inversely as x.	$y = \dfrac{kwz}{x}$

The final two examples of this section illustrate different kinds of problems involving some of these variation situations.

Classroom Example
The volume of a gas varies directly as the absolute temperature and inversely as the pressure. If the gas occupies 3.75 liters when the temperature is 250 K, and the pressure is 40 pounds, what is the volume of the gas when the temperature is 320 K and the pressurre is 48 pounds?

EXAMPLE 7

The volume of a pyramid varies jointly as its altitude and the area of its base. If a pyramid with an altitude of 9 feet and a base with an area of 17 square feet has a volume of 51 cubic feet, find the volume of a pyramid with an altitude of 14 feet and a base with an area of 45 square feet.

Solution

Let's use the following variables:

V = volume $\qquad h$ = altitude

B = area of base $\qquad k$ = constant of variation

The fact that the volume varies jointly as the altitude and the area of the base can be represented by the equation

$V = kBh$

Substitute 51 for V, 17 for B, and 9 for h to obtain

$$51 = k(17)(9)$$

$$51 = 153k$$

$$\frac{51}{153} = k$$

$$\frac{1}{3} = k$$

Therefore the specific equation is $V = \frac{1}{3}Bh$. Now substitute 45 for B and 14 for h to obtain

$$V = \frac{1}{3}(45)(14) = (15)(14) = 210$$

The volume is 210 cubic feet.

Classroom Example
Suppose that a varies jointly as b and c, and inversely as d. If $a = 2$ when $b = 16$, $c = 7$, and $d = 28$, find a when $b = 10$, $c = 9$, and $d = 45$.

EXAMPLE 8

Suppose that y varies jointly as x and z and inversely as w. If $y = 154$ when $x = 6$, $z = 11$, and $w = 3$, find y when $x = 8$, $z = 9$, and $w = 6$.

Solution

The statement "y varies jointly as x and z and inversely as w" translates into the equation

$$y = \frac{kxz}{w}$$

Substitute 154 for y, 6 for x, 11 for z, and 3 for w to produce

$$154 = \frac{(k)(6)(11)}{3}$$

$$154 = 22k$$

$$7 = k$$

Thus the specific equation is

$$y = \frac{7xz}{w}$$

Now substitute 8 for x, 9 for z, and 6 for w to obtain

$$y = \frac{7(8)(9)}{6}$$

$$= 84$$

The value of y is 84.

Concept Quiz 3.6

For Problems 1–4, match the statement of variation with its equation.

1. y varies inversely as the cube of x.
2. y varies directly as the cube of x.
3. y varies directly as the square of w and inversely as the cube of x.
4. y varies jointly as the square of w and the cube of x.

A. $y = \dfrac{kw^2}{x^3}$ **B.** $y = \dfrac{k}{x^3}$ **C.** $y = kw^2x^3$ **D.** $y = kx^3$

For Problems 5–10, answer true or false.

5. The statement y varies jointly as x and w means that y varies directly as x and inversely as w.
6. The constant of variation is always a positive number.
7. If a worker gets paid \$9.50 for each hour worked, we would say that his pay varies directly with the number of hours worked.
8. If a fast food restaurant loses \$0.25 for each special burger sold, we would say that the amount of money lost varies inversely as the number of special burgers sold.
9. Joint variation means that the variation involves three or more variables.
10. The equation $y = -2x$ is an example of inverse variation because the y values decrease as the x values increase.

Problem Set 3.6

For Problems 1–8, translate each statement of variation into an equation; use k as the constant of variation. (Objective 1)

1. y varies directly as the cube of x.

2. a varies inversely as the square of b.

3. A varies jointly as l and w.

4. s varies jointly as g and the square of t.

5. At a constant temperature, the volume (V) of a gas varies inversely as the pressure (P).

6. y varies directly as the square of x and inversely as the cube of w.

7. The volume (V) of a cone varies jointly as its height (h) and the square of a radius (r).

8. l is directly proportional to r and t.

For Problems 9–18, find the constant of variation for each stated condition. (Objective 2)

9. y varies directly as x, and $y = 72$ when $x = 3$.

10. y varies inversely as the square of x, and $y = 4$ when $x = 2$.

11. A varies directly as the square of r, and $A = 154$ when $r = 7$.

12. V varies jointly as B and h, and $V = 104$ when $B = 24$ and $h = 13$.

13. A varies jointly as b and h, and $A = 81$ when $b = 9$ and $h = 18$.

14. s varies jointly as g and the square of t, and $s = -108$ when $g = 24$ and $t = 3$.

15. y varies jointly as x and z and inversely as w, and $y = 154$ when $x = 6$, $z = 11$, and $w = 3$.

16. V varies jointly as h and the square of r, and $V = 1100$ when $h = 14$ and $r = 5$.

17. y is directly proportional to the square of x and inversely proportional to the cube of w, and $y = 18$ when $x = 9$ and $w = 3$.

18. y is directly proportional to x and inversely proportional to the square root of w, and $y = \dfrac{1}{5}$ when $x = 9$ and $w = 10$.

For Problems 19–32, solve each problem. (Objective 3)

19. If y is directly proportional to x, and $y = 5$ when $x = -15$, find the value of y when $x = -24$.

20. If y is inversely proportional to the square of x, and $y = \dfrac{1}{8}$ when $x = 4$, find y when $x = 8$.

21. If V varies jointly as B and h, and $V = 96$ when $B = 36$ and $h = 8$, find V when $B = 48$ and $h = 6$.

22. If A varies directly as the square of e, and $A = 150$ when $e = 5$, find A when $e = 10$.

23. The time required for a car to travel a certain distance varies inversely as the rate at which it travels. If it takes 3 hours to travel the distance at 50 miles per hour, how long will it take at 30 miles per hour?

24. The distance that a freely falling body falls varies directly as the square of the time it falls. If a body falls 144 feet in 3 seconds, how far will it fall in 5 seconds?

25. The period (the time required for one complete oscillation) of a simple pendulum varies directly as the square root of its length. If a pendulum 12 feet long has a period of 4 seconds, find the period of a pendulum of length 3 feet.

26. Suppose the number of days it takes to complete a construction job varies inversely as the number of people assigned to the job. If it takes 7 people 8 days to do the job, how long will it take 10 people to complete the job?

27. The number of days needed to assemble some machines varies directly as the number of machines and inversely as the number of people working. If it takes 4 people 32 days to assemble 16 machines, how many days will it take 8 people to assemble 24 machines?

28. The volume of a gas at a constant temperature varies inversely as the pressure. What is the volume of a gas under a pressure of 25 pounds if the gas occupies 15 cubic centimeters under a pressure of 20 pounds?

29. The volume (V) of a gas varies directly as the temperature (T) and inversely as the pressure (P). If $V = 48$ when $T = 320$ and $P = 20$, find V when $T = 280$ and $P = 30$.

30. The volume of a cylinder varies jointly as its altitude and the square of the radius of its base. If the volume of a cylinder is 1386 cubic centimeters when the radius of the base is 7 centimeters, and its altitude is 9 centimeters, find the volume of a cylinder that has a base of radius 14 centimeters if the altitude of the cylinder is 5 centimeters.

31. The cost of labor varies jointly as the number of workers and the number of days that they work. If it costs $900 to have 15 people work for 5 days, how much will it cost to have 20 people work for 10 days?

32. The cost of publishing pamphlets varies directly as the number of pamphlets produced. If it costs $96 to publish 600 pamphlets, how much does it cost to publish 800 pamphlets?

Thoughts Into Words

33. How would you explain the difference between direct variation and inverse variation?

34. Suppose that y varies directly as the square of x. Does doubling the value of x also double the value of y? Explain your answer.

35. Suppose that y varies inversely as x. Does doubling the value of x also double the value of y? Explain your answer.

Further Investigations

In the previous problems, we chose numbers to make computations reasonable without the use of a calculator. However, variation-type problems often involve messy computations, and the calculator becomes a very useful tool. Use your calculator to help solve the following problems.

36. The simple interest earned by a certain amount of money varies jointly as the rate of interest and the time (in years) that the money is invested.
    (a) If some money invested at 11% for 2 years earns $385, how much would the same amount earn at 12% for 1 year?
    (b) If some money invested at 12% for 3 years earns $819, how much would the same amount earn at 14% for 2 years?
    (c) If some money invested at 14% for 4 years earns $1960, how much would the same amount earn at 15% for 2 years?

37. The period (the time required for one complete oscillation) of a simple pendulum varies directly as the square root of its length. If a pendulum 9 inches long has a period of 2.4 seconds, find the period of a pendulum of length 12 inches. Express the answer to the nearest tenth of a second.

38. The volume of a cylinder varies jointly as its altitude and the square of the radius of its base. If the volume of a cylinder is 549.5 cubic meters when the radius of the base is 5 meters and its altitude is 7 meters, find the volume of a cylinder that has a base of radius 9 meters and an altitude of 14 meters.

39. If y is directly proportional to x and inversely proportional to the square of z, and if $y = 0.336$ when $x = 6$ and $z = 5$, find the constant of variation.

40. If y is inversely proportional to the square root of x, and $y = 0.08$ when $x = 225$, find y when $x = 625$.

Answers to the Concept Quiz
1. B   **2.** D   **3.** A   **4.** C   **5.** False   **6.** False   **7.** True   **8.** False   **9.** True   **10.** False

OBJECTIVE	SUMMARY	EXAMPLE
Know the definition of a function. (Section 3.1/Objective 1)	A function f is a correspondence between two sets X and Y that assigns to each element x of set X one and only one element y of set Y. The element y being assigned is called the image of x. The set X is called the **domain** of the function, and the set of all the images is called the **range** of the function. A function can be thought of as a set of ordered pairs in which no two ordered pairs have the same first component with different second components. The vertical line test is used to determine if a graph is the graph of a function. If each vertical line intersects a graph in no more than one point, then the graph represents a function.	**A.** Specify the domain and range of the relation, and state whether or not it is a function. $\{(1, 8), (2, 7), (5, 6), (3, 8)\}$ **Solution** $D = \{1, 2, 3, 5\}$ $R = \{6, 7, 8\}$ Because each element in the domain is assigned one and only element in the range, it is a function. **B.** Identify the graph as the graph of a function or the graph of a relation that is not a function. **Solution** It is the graph of a relation that is not a function because a vertical line will intersect the graph in more than one point.
Evaluate a function for a given input value. (Section 3.1/Objective 2)	Single letters such as f, g, and h are commonly used to name functions. The symbol $f(x)$ represents the element in the range associated with x from the domain.	If $f(x) = 2x^2 + 3x - 5$, find $f(4)$. **Solution** Substitute 4 for x in the equation. $f(4) = 2(4)^2 + 3(4) - 5$ $f(4) = 32 + 12 - 5$ $f(4) = 39$

(continued)

OBJECTIVE	SUMMARY	EXAMPLE
Evaluate a piecewise-defined function for a given input value. (Section 3.1/Objective 3)	Sometimes the rule of assignment for a function may consist of more than one part. Such a function is called a piecewise-defined function. An everyday example of this concept is that there is a different formula for the fee for legal aid services depending upon the income group to which a client belongs.	If $f(x) = \begin{cases} 2x + 3 & x \le 4 \\ 5x - 1 & x > 4 \end{cases}$, find $f(8)$. **Solution** Because 8 is greater than 4, we use the function rule $f(x) = 5x - 1$ to find $f(8)$. $f(8) = 5(8) - 1 = 39$
Determine the domain and range of a function. (Section 3.1/Objective 4)	The domain of a function is the set of all real number replacements for the variable that will produce real number functional values. Replacement values that make a denominator zero or a radical expression undefined are excluded from the domain. The range of a function is often easier to determine from the graph of the function.	Specify the domain for $f(x) = \sqrt{2x - 5}$. **Solution** The replacement values for x that make the radicand negative must be excluded from the domain. To find the domain, set the radicand equal to or greater than zero and solve. $2x - 5 \ge 0$ $x \ge \dfrac{5}{2}$ The domain is the set $\left\{ x \mid x \ge \dfrac{5}{2} \right\}$ or stated in interval notation, $\left[\dfrac{5}{2}, \infty \right)$. For any domain value, all the range elements will be positive or zero because the function is the principal square root.
Determine if a function is even, odd, or neither. (Section 3.1/Objective 5)	Many functions can be classified as even or odd functions. If $f(-x) = f(x)$ for every x in the domain of f, then the function is called even. If $f(-x) = -f(x)$ for every x in the domain of f, then the function is called odd.	Classify the functrion $f(x) = 4x^3 - 2x$ as even, odd, or neither even nor odd. **Solution** Replace x with $-x$ and simplify the function. $f(-x) = 4(-x)^3 - 2(-x) = -4x^3 + 2x$ Because $f(-x) = -f(x)$ the function is classified as odd.

OBJECTIVE	SUMMARY	EXAMPLE
Graph linear functions. (Section 3.2/Objective 1)	Any function that can be written in the form $$f(x) = ax + b$$ where a and b are real numbers, is a **linear function**. The graph of a linear function is a straight line.	Graph $f(x) = 3x + 1$. **Solution** Because $f(0) = 1$, the point $(0, 1)$ is on the graph. Also $f(1) = 4$, so the point $(1, 4)$ is on the graph.
Determine a linear function for specified conditions. (Section 3.2/Objective 3)	Knowing two distinct ordered pairs of a linear function makes it possible to determine the equation for the function.	Determine the linear function whose graph is a line that contains the points $(-1, 6)$ and $(1, 12)$. **Solution** The linear function $f(x) = ax + b$ models the situation. From the two ordered pairs we can determine a. $$a = \frac{12 - 6}{1 - (-1)} = 3$$ So $f(x) = ax + b$ becomes $f(x) = 3x + b$. Now substitute either ordered pair into the equation to determine b. $$6 = 3(-1) + b$$ $$b = 9$$ The linear function is $f(x) = 3x + 9$.

(continued)

OBJECTIVE	SUMMARY	EXAMPLE
Solve application problems involving linear functions. (Section 3.2/Objective 4)	Linear functions and their graphs can be useful when problem solving.	The FixItFast computer repair company uses the equation $C(m) = 2m + 15$, where m is the number of minutes for the service call, to determine the charge for a service call. Graph the function and use the graph to approximate the charge for a 25-minute service call. Then use the function to find the exact charge for a 25-minute service call. **Solution** Compare your approximation to the exact charge $C(25) = 2(25) + 15 = 65$.
Graph quadratic functions. (Section 3.3/Objectives 1, 2, 3, and 4)	Any function that can be written in the form $f(x) = ax^2 + bx + c$, where a, b, and c are real numbers and $a \neq 0$ is a **quadratic function**. The graph of any quadratic function is a **parabola**, which can be drawn using either of the following methods. 1. Express the function in the form $f(x) = a(x - h)^2 + k$ and use the values of a, h, and k to determine the parabola. 2. Express the function in the form $f(x) = ax^2 + bx + c$ and use the fact that the vertex is at $\left(-\dfrac{b}{2a}, f\left(-\dfrac{b}{2a}\right)\right)$ and the axis of symmetry is $x = -\dfrac{b}{2a}$. 3. To find the x intercepts set the equation to zero and solve for x. 4. To find the y intercept, evaluate $f(0)$.	Graph $f(x) = 2x^2 + 8x + 7$. **Solution** $$f(x) = 2x^2 + 8x + 7 = 2(x^2 + 4x) + 7$$ $$= 2(x^2 + 4x + 4) - 8 + 7$$ $$= 2(x + 2)^2 - 1$$ $$f(x) = 2(x + 2)^2 - 1$$ Solving $0 = 2x^2 + 8x + 7$, gives x intercepts of -1.3 and -2.7 to one decimal place. Evaluating $f(0)$ gives $f(0) = 2(0)^2 + 8(0) + 7 = 7$. Hence the y intercept is 7.

OBJECTIVE	SUMMARY	EXAMPLE
Solve application problems involving quadratic functions. (Section 3.3/Objective 5)	We can solve some applications that involve maximum and minimum values by using our knowledge of parabolas generated by quadratic functions.	Suppose the cost function for producing a particular item is given by the equation $C(x) = 3x^2 - 270x + 15{,}800$, where x represents the number of items. How many items should be produced to minimize the cost? **Solution** The function represents a parabola. The minimum will occur at the vertex, so we want to find the x coordinate of the vertex. $$x = -\frac{b}{2a}$$ $$x = -\frac{-270}{2(3)} = 45$$ Therefore 45 items should be produced to minimize the cost.

Graph functions by applying translations, stretchings or shrinkings, and reflections to the basic graphs shown here. (Section 3.4/Objective 1)

$f(x) = x^2$ $f(x) = x^3$ $f(x) = x^4$

$f(x) = \sqrt{x}$ $f(x) = |x|$

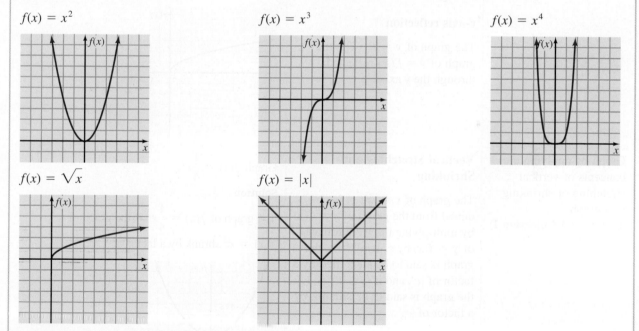

(continued)

OBJECTIVE	SUMMARY	EXAMPLE
Graph by applying horizontal and vertical translations. (Section 3.4/Objective 1)	**Vertical Translation** The graph of $y = f(x) + k$ is the graph of $y = f(x)$ shifted k units upward if k is positive and $\|k\|$ units downward if k is negative. **Horizontal Translation** The graph of $y = f(x - h)$ is the graph of $y = f(x)$ shifted h units to the right if h is positive and $\|h\|$ units to the left if h is negative.	Graph $f(x) = \|x + 4\|$. **Solution** To fit the form, change the equation to the equivalent form $f(x) = \|x - (-4)\|$. Because h is negative, the graph of $f(x) = \|x\|$ is shifted 4 units to the left. $f(x) = \|x + 4\|$
Graph by applying reflections. (Section 3.4/Objective 1)	**x-axis reflection** The graph of $y = -f(x)$ is the graph of $y = f(x)$ reflected through the x axis. **y-axis reflection** The graph of $y = f(-x)$ is the graph of $y = f(x)$ reflected through the y axis.	Graph $f(x) = \sqrt{-x}$. **Solution** The graph of $f(x) = \sqrt{-x}$ is the graph of $f(x) = \sqrt{x}$ reflected through the y axis. $f(x) = \sqrt{-x}$
Graph by applying the concepts of vertical stretching or shrinking of a graph. (Section 3.4/Objective 1)	**Vertical Stretching and Shrinking** The graph of $y = cf(x)$ is obtained from the graph of $y = f(x)$ by multiplying the y coordinates of $y = f(x)$ by c. If $\|c\| > 1$, the graph is said to be **stretched** by a factor of $\|c\|$, and if $0 < \|c\| < 1$, the graph is said to be **shrunk** by a factor of $\|c\|$.	Graph $f(x) = \frac{1}{4}x^2$. **Solution** The graph of $f(x) = \frac{1}{4}x^2$ is the graph of $f(x) = x^2$ shrunk by a factor of $\frac{1}{4}$. $f(x) = \frac{1}{4}x^2$

OBJECTIVE	SUMMARY	EXAMPLE
Graph functions by using successive transformations (Section 3.4/Objective 1)	Some curves result from performing more than one transformation on a basic curve. Unless parentheses indicate otherwise, stretchings, shrinkings, and reflections should be performed before translations.	Graph $f(x) = -2(x + 1)^2 + 3$. **Solution** $f(x) = -2(x + 1)^2 + 3$ Narrows the parabola and opens it downward / Moves the parabola 1 unit to the left / Moves the parabola 3 units up $f(x) = -2(x + 1)^2 + 3$
Graph piecewise-defined functions. (Section 3.4/Objective 2)	Piecewise-defined functions have different rules of assignment for intervals of the domain. Graph the function for each specified interval of the domain on the same coordinate system.	Graph $f(x) = \begin{cases} -2x & x < -1 \\ 2 & -1 \leq x \leq 1 \\ 2x & x > 1 \end{cases}$ **Solution**

(continued)

OBJECTIVE	SUMMARY	EXAMPLE
Combine functions by finding the sum, difference, product, or quotient. (Section 3.5/Objective 1)	In general, if f and g are functions, and D is the intersection of their domain, then the following definitions can be stated: **Sum of two functions** $$(f + g)(x) = f(x) + g(x)$$ **Difference of two functions** $$(f - g)(x) = f(x) - g(x)$$ **Product of two functions** $$(f \cdot g)(x) = f(x) \cdot g(x)$$ **Quotient of two functions** $$\left(\frac{f}{g}\right)(x) = \frac{f(x)}{g(x)}, \quad g(x) \neq 0$$	If $f(x) = -x^3 + 10$ and $g(x) = x - 4$, find $\left(\dfrac{f}{g}\right)(x)$ and determine its domain. **Solution** $$\left(\frac{f}{g}\right)(x) = \frac{-x^3 + 10}{x - 4}$$ The domain of f is all real numbers, and the domain of g is all real numbers except 4. Therefore the domain of $\dfrac{f}{g}$ is all real numbers except 4.
Find the composition of two functions. (Section 3.5/Objective 2)	The **composition** of two functions f and g is defined by $(f \circ g)(x) = f(g(x))$ for all x in the domain of g such that $g(x)$ is in the domain of f. Remember that the composition of functions is not a commutative operation.	If $f(x) = x + 5$ and $g(x) = x^2 + 4x - 6$ find $(g \circ f)(x)$. **Solution** In the function g, substitute $f(x)$ for x. $(g \circ f)(x) = g(f(x))$ $(g \circ f)(x) = (x + 5)^2 + 4(x + 5) - 6$ $\qquad = x^2 + 10x + 25 + 4x + 20 - 6$ $\qquad = x^2 + 14x + 39$
Evaluate a composite function for a specified value. (Section 3.5/Objective 3)	Evaluating the composition of functions can be done with two different methods. 1. Given two functions, the composite function could be formed and then evaluated by substituting directly into the composite function. 2. To find $(f \circ g)(a)$, first evaluate $g(a)$ and then substitute the value of $g(a)$ into f. Depending on the functions given in the problem, one method might be simpler than the other method.	If $f(x) = \sqrt{2x + 1}$ and $g(x) = x^2 + 3$, find $(f \circ g)(5)$. **Solution A** The composite function is $(f \circ g)(x) = \sqrt{2x^2 + 7}$ Therefore, $(f \circ g)(5) = \sqrt{2(5)^2 + 7} = \sqrt{57}$ **Solution B** $(f \circ g)(5) = f(g(5))$ $g(5) = (5)^2 + 3 = 28$ Substituting 28 for $g(5)$ gives $f(g(5)) = f(28) = \sqrt{2(28) + 1} = \sqrt{57}$

OBJECTIVE	SUMMARY	EXAMPLE
Find the difference quotient of a function. (Section 3.5/Objective 4)	The quotient $\dfrac{f(a+h) - f(a)}{h}$ is called the difference quotient. Being able to determine the difference quotient is an essential skill when studying limits in a calculus course.	If $f(x) = 5x + 7$, find the difference quotient. **Solution** $$\dfrac{f(a+h) - f(a)}{h} = \dfrac{5(a+h) + 7 - (5a+7)}{h}$$ $$= \dfrac{5a + 5h + 7 - 5a - 7}{h}$$ $$= \dfrac{5h}{h}$$ $$= 5$$
Translate statements of variation into equations. (Section 3.6/Objective 1)	Relationships that involve direct and inverse variation can be expressed by equations that determine functions. The statement y *varies directly as x* means $y = kx$ where k is the constant of variation. The statement y *varies directly as the nth power of $x(n > 0)$* means $y = kx^n$. The statement y *varies inversely as x* means $y = \dfrac{k}{x}$. The statement y *varies inversely as the nth power of $x(n > 0)$* means $y = \dfrac{k}{x^n}$. The statement y *varies jointly as x and w* means $y = kxw$.	Translate the statement "w varies inversely as the square of y" into an equation using k as the constant of variation. **Solution** $$w = \dfrac{k}{y^2}$$
Solve application problems for direct, inverse, or joint variation. (Section 3.6/ Objectives 2, 3)	There are basically three steps for solving variation problems. 1. Translate the English statement into an equation of variation. 2. Determine the value for the constant of variation. 3. Substitute k and the given values for the variables into the equation of variation to produce the desired answer.	Andrew's paycheck varies directly with the number of hours he works. If he earned $400 for working 32 hours, how much will he earn if he works 40 hours? **Solution** Let p represent the pay and h represent the number of hours worked. The equation of variation will be $p = kh$. Substitute $400 for p and 32 for h to determine k. $$400 = 32k$$ $$k = 12.5$$ The equation of variation is $p = 12.5h$. For 40 hours of work, $$p = 12.5(40) = 500.$$ So Andrew will earn $500 for 40 hours of work.

Chapter 3   Review Problem Set

1. If $f(x) = 3x^2 - 2x - 1$, find $f(2)$, $f(-1)$, and $f(-3)$.

2. For each of the following functions, find

$$\frac{f(a + h) - f(a)}{h}$$

(a) $f(x) = -5x + 4$ (b) $f(x) = 2x^2 - x + 4$
(c) $f(x) = -3x^2 + 2x - 5$

3. Determine the domain and range of the function $f(x) = x^2 + 5$.

4. Determine the domain of the function

$$f(x) = \frac{2}{2x^2 + 7x - 4}$$

5. Express the domain of $f(x) = \sqrt{x^2 - 7x + 10}$ using interval notation.

For Problems 6–23, graph each function.

6. $f(x) = -2x + 2$ **7.** $f(x) = 2x^2 - 1$

8. $f(x) = -\sqrt{x - 2} + 1$ **9.** $f(x) = x^2 - 8x + 17$

10. $f(x) = -x^3 + 2$ **11.** $f(x) = 2|x - 1| + 3$

12. $f(x) = -2x^2 - 12x - 19$ **13.** $f(x) = -\frac{1}{3}x + 1$

14. $f(x) = -\frac{2}{x^2}$ **15.** $f(x) = 2|x| - x$

16. $f(x) = (x - 2)^2$ **17.** $f(x) = \sqrt{-x + 4}$

18. $f(x) = -(x + 1)^2 - 3$ **19.** $f(x) = \sqrt{x + 3} - 2$

20. $f(x) = -|x| + 4$ **21.** $f(x) = (x - 2)^3$

22. $f(x) = \begin{cases} x^2 - 1 & \text{for } x < 0 \\ 3x - 1 & \text{for } x \geq 0 \end{cases}$

23. $f(x) = \begin{cases} 3 & \text{for } x \leq -3 \\ |x| & \text{for } -3 < x < 3 \\ 2x - 3 & \text{for } x \geq 3 \end{cases}$

24. If $f(x) = 2x + 3$ and $g(x) = x^2 - 4x - 3$, find $f + g$, $f - g$, $f \cdot g$, and f/g.

For Problems 25–30, find $(f \circ g)(x)$ and $(g \circ f)(x)$. Also specify the domain for each.

25. $f(x) = 3x - 9$ and $g(x) = -2x + 7$

26. $f(x) = x^2 - 5$ and $g(x) = 5x - 4$

27. $f(x) = \sqrt{x - 5}$ and $g(x) = x + 2$

28. $f(x) = \frac{1}{x}$ and $g(x) = x^2 - x - 6$

29. $f(x) = x^2$ and $g(x) = \sqrt{x - 1}$

30. $f(x) = \frac{1}{x - 3}$ and $g(x) = \frac{1}{x + 2}$

31. If $f(x) = \begin{cases} x^2 - 2 & \text{for } x \geq 0 \\ -3x + 4 & \text{for } x < 0 \end{cases}$

find $f(5)$, $f(0)$, and $f(-3)$.

32. If $f(x) = -x^2 - x + 4$ and $g(x) = \sqrt{x - 2}$, find $f(g(6))$ and $g(f(-2))$.

33. If $f(x) = |x|$ and $g(x) = x^2 - x - 1$, find $(f \circ g)(1)$ and $(g \circ f)(-3)$.

34. Determine the linear function whose graph is a line that is parallel to the line determined by

$$g(x) = \frac{2}{3}x + 4$$

and contains the point $(5, -2)$.

35. Determine the linear function whose graph is a line that is perpendicular to the line determined by

$$g(x) = -\frac{1}{2}x - 6$$

and contains the point $(-6, 3)$.

36. The cost for burning a 100-watt light bulb is given by the function $c(h) = 0.006h$, where h represents the number of hours that the bulb burns. How much, to the nearest cent, does it cost to burn a 100-watt bulb for 4 hours per night for a 30-day month?

37. "All Items 30% Off Marked Price" is a sign in a local department store. Form a function and then use it to determine how much one has to pay for each of the following marked items: a $65 pair of shoes, a $48 pair of slacks, a $15.50 belt.

For Problems 38–40, find the x intercepts and the vertex for each parabola.

38. $f(x) = 3x^2 + 6x - 24$

39. $f(x) = x^2 - 6x - 5$

40. $f(x) = 2x^2 - 28x + 101$

41. Find two numbers whose sum is 10, such that the sum of the square of one number plus four times the other number is a minimum.

42. A group of students is arranging a chartered flight to Europe. The charge per person is \$496 if 100 students go on the flight. If more than 100 students go, the charge per student is reduced by an amount equal to \$4 times the number of students above 100. How many students should the airline try to get in order to maximize its revenue?

43. If y varies directly as x and inversely as w, and if $y = 27$ when $x = 18$ and $w = 6$, find the constant of variation.

44. If y varies jointly as x and the square root of w, and if $y = 140$ when $x = 5$ and $w = 16$, find y when $x = 9$ and $w = 49$.

45. The weight of a body above the surface of Earth varies inversely as the square of its distance from the center of Earth. Assuming the radius of Earth to be 4000 miles, determine how much a man would weigh 1000 miles above Earth's surface if he weighs 200 pounds on the surface.

46. The number of hours needed to assemble some furniture varies directly as the number of pieces of furniture and inversely as the number of people working. If it takes 3 people 10 hours to assemble 20 pieces of furniture, how many hours will it take 4 people to assemble 40 pieces of furniture?

1. If $f(x) = -\dfrac{1}{2}x + \dfrac{1}{3}$, find $f(-3)$.

2. If $f(x) = -x^2 - 6x + 3$, find $f(-2)$.

3. If $f(x) = 3x^2 + 2x - 5$, find $\dfrac{f(a + h) - f(a)}{h}$.

4. For the function $f(x) = \dfrac{-3}{2x^2 + 7x - 4}$, determine the domain.

5. For the function $f(x) = \sqrt{5 - 3x}$, determine the domain.

6. If $f(x) = 3x - 1$ and $g(x) = 2x^2 - x - 5$, find $f + g$, $f - g$, and $f \cdot g$.

7. If $f(x) = -3x + 4$ and $g(x) = 7x + 2$, find $(f \circ g)(x)$.

8. If $f(x) = 2x + 5$ and $g(x) = 2x^2 - x + 3$, find $(g \circ f)(x)$.

9. If $f(x) = \dfrac{3}{x - 2}$ and $g(x) = \dfrac{2}{x}$, find $(f \circ g)(x)$.

10. If $f(x) = x^2 - 2x - 3$ and $g(x) = |x - 3|$, find $f(g(-2))$ and $g(f(1))$.

11. Determine the linear function whose graph is a line that has a slope of $-\dfrac{5}{6}$ and contains the point $(4, -8)$.

12. If $f(x) = \dfrac{3}{x}$ and $g(x) = \dfrac{2}{x - 1}$, determine the domain of $\left(\dfrac{f}{g}\right)(x)$.

13. If $f(x) = 2x^2 - x + 1$ and $g(x) = x^2 + 3$, find $(f + g)(-2)$, $(f - g)(4)$, and $(g - f)(-1)$.

14. If $f(x) = x^2 + 5x - 6$ and $g(x) = x - 1$, find $(f \cdot g)(x)$ and $\left(\dfrac{f}{g}\right)(x)$.

15. Find two numbers whose sum is 60, such that the sum of the square of one number plus 12 times the other number is a minimum.

16. If y varies jointly as x and z, and if $y = 18$ when $x = 8$ and $z = 9$, find y when $x = 5$ and $z = 12$.

17. If y varies inversely as x, and if $y = \dfrac{1}{2}$ when $x = -8$, find the constant of variation.

18. The simple interest earned by a certain amount of money varies jointly as the rate of interest and the time (in years) that the money is invested. If \$140 is earned for the money invested at 7% for 5 years, how much is earned if the same amount is invested at 8% for 3 years?

19. A retailer has a number of items that he wants to sell at a profit of 35% of the cost. What linear function can be used to determine selling prices of the items? What price should he charge for a tie that cost him \$13?

20. Find the x intercepts and the vertex of the parabola $f(x) = 4x^2 - 16x - 48$.

For Problems 21–25, graph each function.

21. $f(x) = (x - 2)^3 - 3$

22. $f(x) = -2x^2 - 12x - 14$

23. $f(x) = 3|x - 2| - 1$

24. $f(x) = \sqrt{-x + 2}$

25. $f(x) = -x - 1$

For Problems 1–10, evaluate each expression.

1. $(3^{-2})^{-1}$

2. $\left(\dfrac{7}{9}\right)^{-1}$

3. $\dfrac{1}{\left(\dfrac{1}{2}\right)^{-3}}$

4. $8^{-1} + 2^{-3}$

5. $(3^{-2} + 2^{-3})^{-1}$

6. $-\sqrt{0.16}$

7. $\sqrt[3]{3\dfrac{3}{8}}$

8. $9^{3/2}$

9. $8^{2/3}$

10. $(-27)^{4/3}$

For Problems 11–15, evaluate each algebraic expression for the given values of the variables.

11. $-3(x - 1) + 4(2x + 3) - (3x + 5)$ for $x = -9$

12. $\dfrac{3}{n} - \dfrac{5}{n} + \dfrac{9}{n}$ for $n = -7$

13. $\dfrac{4}{x - 2} + \dfrac{7}{x + 1}$ for $x = 6$

14. $(2x + 5y)(2x - 5y)$ for $x = 5$ and $y = -1$

15. $\dfrac{\dfrac{2}{x} - \dfrac{3}{y}}{\dfrac{1}{x} + \dfrac{4}{y}}$ for $x = -3$ and $y = 11$

For Problems 16–19, simplify each rational expression.

16. $\dfrac{12x^3y^2}{27xy}$

17. $\dfrac{6x^2 + 11x - 7}{8x^2 - 22x + 9}$

18. $\dfrac{8x^3 + 64}{4x^2 - 16}$

19. $\dfrac{xy + 4y - 2x - 8}{x^2 + 4x}$

For Problems 20–24, perform the indicated operations involving rational expressions. Express final answers in simplest form.

20. $\dfrac{3a^2b}{4a^3b^2} \div \dfrac{6a}{27b}$

21. $\dfrac{x^2 - x}{x + 5} \cdot \dfrac{x^2 + 5x + 4}{x^4 - x^2}$

22. $\dfrac{x + 3}{10} + \dfrac{2x + 1}{15} - \dfrac{x - 2}{18}$

23. $\dfrac{7}{12ab} - \dfrac{11}{15a^2}$

24. $\dfrac{8}{x^2 - 4x} + \dfrac{2}{x}$

For Problems 25–27, simplify each complex fraction.

25. $\dfrac{\dfrac{2}{x} - 3}{\dfrac{3}{y} + 4}$

26. $\dfrac{\dfrac{5}{x^2} - \dfrac{3}{x}}{\dfrac{1}{y} + \dfrac{2}{y^2}}$

27. $\dfrac{\dfrac{3a}{2} - 1}{2 - \dfrac{1}{a}}$

For Problems 28–30, perform the indicated operations and simplify. Express final answers using positive exponents only.

28. $(-3x^{-1}y^2)(4x^{-2}y^{-3})$

29. $\dfrac{48x^{-4}y^2}{6xy}$

30. $\left(\dfrac{27a^{-4}b^{-3}}{-3a^{-1}b^{-4}}\right)^{-1}$

For Problems 31–36, express each in simplest radical form. All variables represent positive real numbers.

31. $\sqrt{\dfrac{8}{25}}$

32. $\dfrac{4\sqrt{3}}{7\sqrt{6}}$

33. $\sqrt{48x^3y^7}$

34. $\dfrac{4}{\sqrt{5} - \sqrt{3}}$

35. $\sqrt[3]{48x^4y^5}$

36. $\dfrac{\sqrt[3]{4}}{\sqrt[3]{2}}$

For Problems 37–40, find each of the indicated products or quotients. Express answers in the standard form of a complex number.

37. $(5 - 2i)(6 + 5i)$

38. $(-3 - i)(-2 - 4i)$

39. $\dfrac{5}{4i}$

40. $\dfrac{6 + 2i}{3 - 4i}$

For Problems 41–58, solve each equation.

41. $3(2x - 1) - 2(5x + 1) = 4(3x + 4)$

42. $n + \dfrac{3n - 1}{9} - 4 = \dfrac{3n + 1}{3}$

43. $0.92 + 0.9(x - 0.3) = 2x - 5.95$

44. $|4x - 1| = 11$

45. $|2x - 1| = |-x + 4|$

46. $x^3 = 36x$

47. $(3x - 1)^2 = 45$

48. $(2x + 5)^2 = -32$

49. $2x^2 - 3x + 4 = 0$

50. $(n + 4)(n - 6) = 11$

51. $(2n - 1)(n + 6) = 0$

52. $(x + 5)(3x - 1) = (x + 5)(2x + 7)$

53. $(x - 4)(2x + 9) = (2x - 1)(x + 2)$

54. $(3x - 1)(x + 1) = (2x + 1)(x - 3)$

55. $\sqrt{3x} - x = -6$

56. $\sqrt{x + 19} - \sqrt{x + 28} = -1$

57. $12x^4 - 19x^2 + 5 = 0$

58. $x^3 - 4x^2 - 3x + 12 = 0$

For Problems 59–68, solve each inequality and express the solution set using interval notation.

59. $|5x - 2| > 13$

60. $(x - 2)(x + 4) \le 0$

61. $|6x + 2| \le 8$

62. $x(x + 5) < 24$

63. $-5(y - 1) + 3 > 3y - 4 - 4y$

64. $\dfrac{x - 2}{5} - \dfrac{3x - 1}{4} \le \dfrac{3}{10}$

65. $(2x + 1)(x - 2)(x + 5) > 0$

66. $\dfrac{x - 3}{x - 7} \ge 0$

67. $\dfrac{2x}{x + 3} > 4$

68. $2x^3 + 5x^2 - 3x < 0$

69. On a number line, find the coordinate of the point that is three-fourths of the distance from -6 to 10.

70. In a Cartesian plane, find the coordinates of a point that is two-thirds of the distance from $(-1, 2)$ to $(8, 11)$.

71. Find the slope of the line determined by the equation $-2x + 5y = 7$.

72. Write the equation of the line that contains the two points $(3, -4)$ and $(-2, -1)$.

73. If $f(x) = 3x - 2$ and $g(x) = x^2 + 2x$, find $f(g(3))$ and $g(f(2))$.

74. If $f(x) = 2x - 1$ and $g(x) = \sqrt{x + 2}$, find $f(g(x))$ and $g(f(x))$.

75. Express the domain of the function $f(x) = \sqrt{x^2 + 7x - 30}$.

76. If $f(x) = -x^2 + 6x - 1$, find $\dfrac{f(a + h) - f(a)}{h}$.

For Problems 77–82, graph each function.

77. $f(x) = -|x - 2| + 4$

78. $f(x) = -x^2 - 6x - 10$

79. $f(x) = x - 2$

80. $f(x) = (x - 2)^2$

81. $f(x) = (x - 2)^3$

82. $f(x) = \sqrt{x - 2}$

For Problems 83–97, use an equation or an inequality to help solve each problem.

83. Find three consecutive odd integers whose sum is 57.

84. Eric has a collection of 63 coins consisting of nickels, dimes, and quarters. The number of dimes is 6 more than the number of nickels, and the number of quarters is 1 more than twice the number of nickels. How many coins of each kind are in the collection?

85. One of two supplementary angles is 4° larger than one-third of the other angle. Find the measure of each of the angles.

86. If a ring costs a jeweler $300, at what price should it be sold to make a profit of 50% on the selling price?

87. Beth invested a certain amount of money at 8% interest and $300 more than that amount at 9%. Her total yearly interest was $316. How much did she invest at each rate?

88. Two trains leave the same depot at the same time, one traveling east and the other west. At the end of $4\frac{1}{2}$ hours, the trains are 639 miles apart. If the rate of the train traveling east is 10 miles per hour faster than the rate of the other train, find their rates.

89. A 10-quart radiator contains a 50% solution of antifreeze. How much needs to be drained out and replaced with pure antifreeze to obtain a 70% antifreeze solution?

90. Sam shot rounds of 70, 73, and 76 on the first three days of a golf tournament. What must he shoot on the fourth day of the tournament to average 72 or lower for the four days?

91. The cube of a number equals nine times the same number. Find the number.

92. A strip of uniform width is to be cut off both sides and both ends of a sheet of paper that is 8 inches by 14 inches to reduce the size of the paper to an area of 72 square inches. Find the width of the strip.

93. A sum of $2450 is to be divided between two people in the ratio of 3 to 4. How much does each person receive?

94. Working together, Sue and Dean can complete a task in $1\frac{1}{5}$ hours. Dean can do the task by himself in 2 hours. How long would it take Sue to complete the task by herself?

95. A new diet requires that the number of calories from a serving of starchy vegetables be one-half the number of calories from a serving of meat. Also the number of calories from a serving of fruit must be one-third the number of calories from a serving of meat. For a 770-calorie meal consisting of a serving of meat, starchy vegetables, and fruit, find the allotted number of calories for each type of serving.

96. Marge, the office manager, has a budget of $28,000 to furnish the conference room of a hotel with 24 seating arrangements, each consisting of a table with four chairs. The chairs being considered for purchase cost twenty dollars less than one-half the cost of the table. How much money will remain in the budget after the purchase of the tables and chairs?

97. The sum of the two smallest angles of a triangle is 40° less than the other angle. The sum of the smallest and largest angles is twice the other angle. Find the measures of the three angles of the triangle.

4

Polynomial and Rational Functions

4.1 Dividing Polynomials and Synthetic Division

4.2 Remainder and Factor Theorems

4.3 Polynomial Equations

4.4 Graphing Polynomial Functions

4.5 Graphing Rational Functions

4.6 More on Graphing Rational Functions

The graphs of polynomial functions are smooth curves that can be used to describe the path of objects such as a roller coaster.

© Oba from Poland/Shutterstock.com

Earlier in this text we solved linear and quadratic equations and graphed linear and quadratic functions. In this chapter we will expand our equation-solving processes and graphing techniques to include more general polynomial equations and functions. Then our knowledge of polynomial functions will allow us to work with rational functions. The function concept will again serve as a unifying thread throughout the chapter. To facilitate our study in this chapter, we will first review the concept of dividing polynomials, and we will introduce theorems about division.

| **4.1** | Dividing Polynomials and Synthetic Division |

OBJECTIVES

1 Divide a polynomial by a binomial divisor

2 Use synthetic division to determine the quotient and remainder for division problems

In Chapter 0 we used the properties

$$\frac{a+b}{c} = \frac{a}{c} + \frac{b}{c} \quad \text{and} \quad \frac{a-b}{c} = \frac{a}{c} - \frac{b}{c}$$

as a basis for dividing a polynomial by a monomial. For example,

$$\frac{18x^3 + 24x^2}{6x} = \frac{18x^3}{6x} + \frac{24x^2}{6x} = 3x^2 + 4x$$

and

$$\frac{35x^2y^3 - 55x^3y^4}{5xy^2} = \frac{35x^2y^3}{5xy^2} - \frac{55x^3y^4}{5xy^2} = 7xy - 11x^2y^2$$

You may recall from a previous algebra course that the format used to divide a polynomial by a binomial resembles the long-division format in arithmetic. Let's work through an example step by step.

Step 1 Use the conventional long-division format and arrange both the dividend and the divisor in descending powers of the variable.

$$3x + 1 \overline{)3x^3 - 5x^2 + 10x + 1}$$

Step 2 Find the first term of the quotient by dividing the first term of the dividend by the first term of the divisor.

$$\begin{array}{r} x^2 \\ 3x + 1 \overline{)3x^3 - 5x^2 + 10x + 1} \end{array}$$

Step 3 Multiply the entire divisor by the quotient term in step 2 and place this product in position to be subtracted from the dividend.

$$\begin{array}{r} x^2 \\ 3x + 1 \overline{)3x^3 - 5x^2 + 10x + 1} \\ 3x^3 + x^2 \end{array}$$

Step 4 Subtract.

$$\begin{array}{r} x^2 \\ 3x + 1 \overline{)3x^3 - 5x^2 + 10x + 1} \\ 3x^3 + x^2 \\ \hline -6x^2 + 10x + 1 \end{array}$$

Step 5 Repeat steps 2, 3, and 4, and use $-6x^2 + 10x + 1$ as a new dividend.

$$\begin{array}{r} x^2 - 2x \\ 3x + 1 \overline{)3x^3 - 5x^2 + 10x + 1} \\ 3x^3 + x^2 \\ \hline -6x^2 + 10x + 1 \\ -6x^2 - 2x \\ \hline 12x + 1 \end{array}$$

Step 6 Repeat steps 2, 3, and 4, and use $12x + 1$ as a new dividend.

$$
\begin{array}{r}
x^2 - 2x + 4 \\
3x + 1\overline{)3x^3 - 5x^2 + 10x + 1} \\
\underline{3x^3 + x^2} \\
-6x^2 + 10x + 1 \\
\underline{-6x^2 - 2x} \\
12x + 1 \\
\underline{12x + 4} \\
-3
\end{array}
$$

Therefore $3x^3 - 5x^2 + 10x + 1 = (3x + 1)(x^2 - 2x + 4) + (-3)$, which has the familiar form

Dividend = (Divisor)(Quotient) + Remainder

This result is commonly called the **division algorithm for polynomials,** which can be stated in general terms as follows.

Division Algorithm for Polynomials

If $f(x)$ and $g(x)$ are polynomials and $g(x) \neq 0$, then unique polynomials $q(x)$ and $r(x)$ exist such that

$$f(x) = g(x)q(x) + r(x)$$

Dividend   Divisor   Quotient   Remainder

where $r(x) = 0$ or the degree of $r(x)$ is less than the degree of $g(x)$.

Let's consider one more example to illustrate this division process further.

EXAMPLE 1   Divide $t^2 - 3t + 2t^4 - 1$ by $t^2 + 4t$.

Solution

Don't forget to arrange both the dividend and the divisor in descending powers of the variable.

$$
\begin{array}{r}
2t^2 - 8t + 33 \\
t^2 + 4t\overline{)2t^4 + 0t^3 + t^2 - 3t - 1} \\
\underline{2t^4 + 8t^3} \\
-8t^3 + t^2 - 3t - 1 \\
\underline{-8t^3 - 32t^2} \\
33t^2 - 3t - 1 \\
\underline{33t^2 + 132t} \\
-135t - 1
\end{array}
$$

⟵ Notice the insertion of a t^3 term with a zero coefficient

The division process is completed when the degree of the remainder is less than the degree of the divisor ⟶

Synthetic Division

If the divisor is of the form $x - c$, where c is a constant, then the typical long-division algorithm can be conveniently simplified into a process called **synthetic division**. First, let's consider an example using the usual algorithm. Then, in a step-by-step fashion, we will list some shortcuts to use that will lead us into the synthetic-division procedure. Consider the division problem $(3x^4 + x^3 - 15x^2 + 6x - 8) \div (x - 2)$:

$$
\begin{array}{r}
3x^3 + 7x^2 - x + 4 \\
x - 2 \overline{)3x^4 + x^3 - 15x^2 + 6x - 8} \\
\underline{3x^4 - 6x^3} \\
7x^3 - 15x^2 \\
\underline{7x^3 - 14x^2} \\
-x^2 + 6x \\
\underline{-x^2 + 2x} \\
4x - 8 \\
\underline{4x - 8}
\end{array}
$$

Note that because the dividend $(3x^4 + x^3 - 15x^2 + 6x - 8)$ is written in descending powers of x, the quotient $(3x^3 + 7x^2 - x + 4)$ is also in descending powers of x. In other words, the numerical coefficients are the key, so let's rewrite this problem in terms of its coefficients.

$$
\begin{array}{r}
3 \quad 7 \; -1 \;\; 4 \\
1 - 2 \overline{)3 \quad 1 \; -15 \;\; 6 \; -8} \\
\textcircled{3} \; -6 \\
7 \; \textcircled{-15} \\
\textcircled{7} \; -14 \\
-1 \; \textcircled{6} \\
\textcircled{-1} \; 2 \\
4 \; \textcircled{-8} \\
\textcircled{4} -8
\end{array}
$$

Now observe that the numbers circled are simply repetitions of the numbers directly above them in the format. Thus the circled numbers could be omitted and the format would be as follows. (Disregard the arrows for the moment.)

$$
\begin{array}{r}
3 \; 7 \; -1 \;\; 4 \\
1 - 2 \overline{)3 \; 1 \; -15 \;\; 6 \; -8} \\
-6 \\
7 \\
-14 \\
-1 \\
2 \\
4 \\
-8
\end{array}
$$

Next, move some numbers up as indicated by the arrows, and omit writing 1 as the coefficient of x in the divisor to yield the following more compact form:

$$
\begin{array}{r}
3 \quad 7 \;-1 \quad 4 \\
\hline
-2)\overline{3 \quad 1 \;-15 \quad 6 \;-8} \\
-6 \;-14 \quad 2 \;-8 \\
\hline
7 \;-1 \quad 4
\end{array}
$$

(1)
(2)
(3)
(4)

Note that line (4) reveals all of the coefficients of the quotient in line (1), except for the first coefficient, 3. Thus we can omit line (1), begin line (4) with the first coefficient, and then use the following form:

$$
\begin{array}{r}
-2)\overline{3 \quad 1 \;-15 \quad 6 \;-8} \\
-6 \;-14 \quad 2 \;-8 \\
\hline
3 \quad 7 \;-1 \quad 4 \quad 0
\end{array}
$$

(5)
(6)
(7)

Line (7) contains the coefficients of the quotient; the 0 indicates the remainder. Finally, changing the constant in the divisor to 2 (instead of -2), which will change the signs of the numbers in line (6), allows us to add the corresponding entries in lines (5) and (6) rather than subtract them. Thus the final synthetic-division form for this problem is

$$
\begin{array}{r}
2)\overline{3 \quad 1 \;-15 \quad 6 \;-8} \\
6 \quad 14 \;-2 \quad 8 \\
\hline
3 \quad 7 \;-1 \quad 4 \quad 0
\end{array}
$$

Now we will consider another problem and follow a step-by-step procedure for setting up and carrying out the synthetic division. Suppose that we want to do the following division problem.

$$
x + 4)\overline{2x^3 + 5x^2 - 13x - 2}
$$

1. Write the coefficients of the dividend as follows.

$$
)\overline{2 \quad 5 \;-13 \;-2}
$$

2. In the divisor, use -4 instead of 4 so that later we can add rather than subtract.

$$
-4)\overline{2 \quad 5 \;-13 \;-2}
$$

3. Bring down the first coefficient of the dividend.

$$
\begin{array}{r}
-4)\overline{2 \quad 5 \;-13 \;-2} \\
\hline
2
\end{array}
$$

4. Multiply that first coefficient by the divisor, which yields $2(-4) = -8$. This result is added to the second coefficient of the dividend.

$$
\begin{array}{r}
-4)\overline{2 \quad 5 \;-13 \;-2} \\
-8 \\
\hline
2 \;-3
\end{array}
$$

5. Multiply $(-3)(-4)$, which yields 12; this result is added to the third coefficient of the dividend.

$$
\begin{array}{r|rrrr}
-4 & 2 & 5 & -13 & -2 \\
   &   & -8 & 12 & \\
\hline
   & 2 & -3 & -1 & \\
\end{array}
$$

6. Multiply $(-1)(-4)$, which yields 4; this result is added to the last term of the dividend.

$$
\begin{array}{r|rrrr}
-4 & 2 & 5 & -13 & -2 \\
   &   & -8 & 12 & 4 \\
\hline
   & 2 & -3 & -1 & 2 \\
\end{array}
$$

The last row indicates a quotient of $2x^2 - 3x - 1$ and a remainder of 2.

Let's consider three more examples, showing only the final compact form for synthetic division.

Classroom Example
Find the quotient and remainder for $(3x^3 - 7x^2 + 2x - 8) \div (x - 3)$.

EXAMPLE 2

Find the quotient and remainder for $(2x^3 - 5x^2 + 6x + 4) \div (x - 2)$.

Solution

$$
\begin{array}{r|rrrr}
2 & 2 & -5 & 6 & 4 \\
  &   & 4 & -2 & 8 \\
\hline
  & 2 & -1 & 4 & 12 \\
\end{array}
$$

Therefore the quotient is $2x^2 - x + 4$, and the remainder is 12. ∎

Classroom Example
Find the quotient and remainder for $(2x^4 - 3x^2 + x - 12) \div (x - 2)$.

EXAMPLE 3

Find the quotient and remainder for $(4x^4 - 2x^3 + 6x - 1) \div (x - 1)$.

Solution

$$
\begin{array}{r|rrrrr}
1 & 4 & -2 & 0 & 6 & -1 \\
  &   & 4 & 2 & 2 & 8 \\
\hline
  & 4 & 2 & 2 & 8 & 7 \\
\end{array}
$$

Note that a 0 has been inserted as the coefficient of the missing x^2 term

Thus the quotient is $4x^3 + 2x^2 + 2x + 8$, and the remainder is 7. ∎

Classroom Example
Find the quotient and remainder for $(x^3 - 2x^2 + 2x + 5) \div (x + 1)$.

EXAMPLE 4

Find the quotient and remainder for $(x^3 + 8x^2 + 13x - 6) \div (x + 3)$.

Solution

$$
\begin{array}{r|rrrr}
-3 & 1 & 8 & 13 & -6 \\
   &   & -3 & -15 & 6 \\
\hline
   & 1 & 5 & -2 & 0 \\
\end{array}
$$

Thus the quotient is $x^2 + 5x - 2$, and the remainder is 0. ∎

In Example 4, because the remainder is 0, we can say that $x + 3$ is a factor of $x^3 + 8x^2 + 13x - 6$. We will use this idea a bit later when we solve polynomial equations.

Classroom Example
Find the quotient and remainder
for $(x^3 - 8) \div (x - 2)$

EXAMPLE 5

Find the quotient and the remainder for $(x^4 + 16) \div (x + 2)$.

Solution

$$-2)\overline{\begin{array}{ccccc} 1 & 0 & 0 & 0 & 16 \\ & -2 & 4 & -8 & 16 \\ \hline 1 & -2 & 4 & -8 & 32 \end{array}}$$

Note that zeros have been inserted as coefficients of the missing terms in the dividend

Thus the quotient is $x^3 - 2x^2 + 4x - 8$ and the remainder is 32.   ∎

Concept Quiz 4.1

For Problems 1–3, given $(x^3 + 6x^2 - 5x - 2) \div (x - 1) = x^2 + 7x + 2$, match the mathematical expression with the correct term.

1. $x^2 + 7x + 2$ 2. $x^3 + 6x^2 - 5x - 1$ 3. $x - 1$
A. Dividend   B. Quotient   C. Divisor

For Problems 4–8, answer true or false.

4. For long division of polynomials, the degree of the remainder is always less than the degree of the divisor.
5. The polynomial divisor of $(x + 3)$ would become a divisor of 3 for synthetic division.
6. If a synthetic division problem gave a quotient line of 3 −1 4 7 0, we would know that the remainder is zero.
7. If a synthetic division problem gave a quotient of 2 3 −5 6, we would know that the quotient is $2x^2 + 3x - 5$ with a remainder of 6.
8. If a synthetic division problem gave a quotient line of 4 0 −3 7, we would know that the quotient is $4x - 3$ with a remainder of 7.

Problem Set 4.1

For Problems 1–14, find the quotient and remainder for each division problem. **(Objective 1)**

1. $(12x^2 + 7x - 10) \div (3x - 2)$

2. $(20x^2 - 39x + 18) \div (5x - 6)$

3. $(3t^3 + 7t^2 - 10t - 4) \div (3t + 1)$

4. $(4t^3 - 17t^2 + 7t + 10) \div (4t - 5)$

5. $(6x^2 + 19x + 11) \div (3x + 2)$

6. $(20x^2 + 3x - 1) \div (5x + 2)$

7. $(3x^3 + 2x^2 - 5x - 1) \div (x^2 + 2x)$

8. $(4x^3 - 5x^2 + 2x - 6) \div (x^2 - 3x)$

9. $(5y^3 - 6y^2 - 7y - 2) \div (y^2 - y)$

10. $(8y^3 - y^2 - y + 5) \div (y^2 + y)$

11. $(4a^3 - 2a^2 + 7a - 1) \div (a^2 - 2a + 3)$

12. $(5a^3 + 7a^2 - 2a - 9) \div (a^2 + 3a - 4)$

13. $(3x^2 - 2xy - 8y^2) \div (x - 2y)$

14. $(4a^2 - 8ab + 4b^2) \div (a - b)$

Use synthetic division to determine the quotient and remainder for each problem. **(Objective 2)**

15. $(4x^2 - 5x - 6) \div (x - 2)$

16. $(5x^2 - 9x + 4) \div (x - 1)$

17. $(2x^2 - x - 21) \div (x + 3)$

18. $(3x^2 + 8x + 4) \div (x + 2)$

19. $(3x^2 - 16x + 17) \div (x - 4)$

20. $(6x^2 - 29x - 8) \div (x - 5)$

21. $(4x^2 + 19x - 32) \div (x + 6)$

22. $(7x^2 + 26x - 2) \div (x + 4)$

23. $(x^3 + 2x^2 - 7x + 4) \div (x - 1)$

24. $(2x^3 - 7x^2 + 2x + 3) \div (x - 3)$

25. $(3x^3 + 8x^2 - 8) \div (x + 2)$

26. $(4x^3 + 17x^2 + 75) \div (x + 5)$

27. $(5x^3 - 9x^2 - 3x - 2) \div (x - 2)$

28. $(x^3 - 6x^2 + 5x + 14) \div (x - 4)$

29. $(x^3 + 6x^2 - 8x + 1) \div (x + 7)$

30. $(2x^3 + 11x^2 - 5x + 1) \div (x + 6)$

31. $(-x^3 + 7x^2 - 14x + 6) \div (x - 3)$

32. $(-2x^3 - 3x^2 + 4x + 5) \div (x + 1)$

33. $(-3x^3 + x^2 + 2x + 2) \div (x + 1)$

34. $(-x^3 + 4x^2 + 31x + 2) \div (x - 8)$

35. $(3x^3 - 2x - 5) \div (x - 2)$

36. $(2x^3 - x - 4) \div (x + 3)$

37. $(2x^4 + x^3 + 3x^2 + 2x - 2) \div (x + 1)$

38. $(x^4 - 3x^3 - 6x^2 + 11x - 12) \div (x - 4)$

39. $(x^4 + 4x^3 - 7x - 1) \div (x - 3)$

40. $(3x^4 - x^3 + 2x^2 - 7x - 1) \div (x + 1)$

41. $(x^4 + 5x^3 - x^2 + 25) \div (x + 5)$

42. $(2x^4 + 3x^2 + 3) \div (x + 2)$

43. $(x^4 - 16) \div (x - 2)$

44. $(x^4 - 16) \div (x + 2)$

45. $(x^5 - 1) \div (x + 1)$

46. $(x^5 - 1) \div (x - 1)$

47. $(x^5 + 1) \div (x + 1)$

48. $(x^5 + 1) \div (x - 1)$

49. $(x^5 + 3x^4 - 5x^3 - 3x^2 + 3x - 4) \div (x + 4)$

50. $(2x^5 + 3x^4 - 4x^3 - x^2 + 5x - 2) \div (x + 2)$

51. $(4x^5 - 6x^4 + 2x^3 + 2x^2 - 5x + 2) \div (x - 1)$

52. $(3x^5 - 8x^4 + 5x^3 + 2x^2 - 9x + 4) \div (x - 2)$

53. $(9x^3 - 6x^2 + 3x - 4) \div \left(x - \dfrac{1}{3} \right)$

54. $(2x^3 + 3x^2 - 2x + 3) \div \left(x + \dfrac{1}{2} \right)$

55. $(3x^4 - 2x^3 + 5x^2 - x - 1) \div \left(x + \dfrac{1}{3} \right)$

56. $(4x^4 - 5x^2 + 1) \div \left(x - \dfrac{1}{2} \right)$

Thoughts Into Words

57. How would you describe what is accomplished with synthetic division to someone who had just completed an elementary algebra course?

58. Why is synthetic division restricted to situations in which the divisor is of the form $x - c$?

Answers to the Concept Quiz

1. B   **2.** A   **3.** C   **4.** True   **5.** False   **6.** True   **7.** True   **8.** False

4.2   Remainder and Factor Theorems

OBJECTIVES   **1** Use the remainder theorem to evaluate a function for a given value

2 Determine if an expression is a factor of a given polynomial

3 Find the linear factors of a polynomial

Let's consider the division algorithm (stated in the previous section) when the dividend, $f(x)$, is divided by a linear polynomial of the form $x - c$. Then the division algorithm

$$f(x) = d(x)q(x) + r(x)$$

Dividend   Divisor   Quotient   Remainder

becomes $f(x) = (x - c)q(x) + r(x)$

Because the degree of the remainder, $r(x)$, must be less than the degree of the divisor, $x - c$, the remainder is a constant. Therefore, letting R represent the remainder, we have

$$f(x) = (x - c)q(x) + R$$

If the functional value at c is found, we obtain

$$f(c) = (c - c)q(c) + R$$
$$= 0 \cdot q(c) + R$$
$$= R$$

In other words, if a polynomial is divided by a linear polynomial of the form $x - c$, then the remainder is given by the value of the polynomial at c. Let's state this result more formally as the **remainder theorem**.

> **Property 4.1 Remainder theorem**
>
> If the polynomial $f(x)$ is divided by $x - c$, then the remainder is equal to $f(c)$.

EXAMPLE 1

If $f(x) = x^3 + 2x^2 - 5x - 1$, find $f(2)$ by (a) using synthetic division and the remainder theorem, and (b) evaluating $f(2)$ directly.

Solution

(a)
$$\begin{array}{r|rrrr}
2 & 1 & 2 & -5 & -1 \\
  &   & 2 & 8 & 6 \\
\hline
  & 1 & 4 & 3 & \boxed{5} \quad \longleftarrow \quad R = f(2) = 5
\end{array}$$

(b) $f(2) = 2^3 + 2(2)^2 - 5(2) - 1 = 8 + 8 - 10 - 1 = 5$

EXAMPLE 2

If $f(x) = x^4 + 7x^3 + 8x^2 + 11x + 5$, find $f(-6)$ by (a) using synthetic division and the remainder theorem and (b) evaluating $f(-6)$ directly.

Solution

(a)
$$\begin{array}{r|rrrrr}
-6 & 1 & 7 & 8 & 11 & 5 \\
   &   & -6 & -6 & -12 & 6 \\
\hline
   & 1 & 1 & 2 & -1 & \boxed{11} \quad \longleftarrow \quad R = f(-6) = 11
\end{array}$$

(b) $f(-6) = (-6)^4 + 7(-6)^3 + 8(-6)^2 + 11(-6) + 5$
$$= 1296 - 1512 + 288 - 66 + 5$$
$$= 11$$

In Example 2, note that the computations involved in finding $f(-6)$ by using synthetic division and the remainder theorem are much easier than those required to evaluate $f(-6)$ directly. This is not always the case, but using synthetic division is often easier than evaluating $f(c)$ directly.

EXAMPLE 3

Find the remainder when $x^3 + 3x^2 - 13x - 15$ is divided by $x + 1$.

Solution

Let $f(x) = x^3 + 3x^2 - 13x - 15$, write $x + 1$ as $x - (-1)$, and apply the remainder theorem:
$$f(-1) = (-1)^3 + 3(-1)^2 - 13(-1) - 15 = 0$$

Thus the remainder is 0.

Example 3 illustrates an important aspect of the remainder theorem—the situation in which the remainder is zero. Thus we can say that $x + 1$ is a factor of $x^3 + 3x^2 - 13x - 15$.

Factor Theorem

A general factor theorem can be formulated by considering the equation

$$f(x) = (x - c)q(x) + R$$

If $x - c$ is a factor of $f(x)$, then the remainder R, which is also $f(c)$, must be zero. Conversely, if $R = f(c) = 0$, then $f(x) = (x - c)q(x)$; in other words, $x - c$ is a factor of $f(x)$. The **factor theorem** can be stated as follows:

> ### Property 4.2 Factor Theorem
>
> A polynomial $f(x)$ has a factor $x - c$ if and only if $f(c) = 0$.

Classroom Example
Is $x - 3$ a factor of
$x^3 - 8x^2 + 19x - 12$?

EXAMPLE 4   Is $x - 1$ a factor of $x^3 + 5x^2 + 2x - 8$?

Solution

Let $f(x) = x^3 + 5x^2 + 2x - 8$ and compute $f(1)$ to obtain

$$f(1) = 1^3 + 5(1)^2 + 2(1) - 8 = 0$$

By the factor theorem, therefore, $x - 1$ is a factor of $f(x)$. ∎

Classroom Example
Is $x + 2$ a factor of
$5x^3 + 8x^2 - x + 7$?

EXAMPLE 5   Is $x + 3$ a factor of $2x^3 + 5x^2 - 6x - 7$?

Solution

Use synthetic division to obtain the following:

$$
\begin{array}{r|rrrr}
-3 & 2 & 5 & -6 & -7 \\
   &   & -6 & 3 & 9 \\
\hline
   & 2 & -1 & -3 & 2
\end{array} \quad \longleftarrow R = f(-3) = 2
$$

Because $R \neq 0$, we know that $x + 3$ is not a factor of the given polynomial. ∎

In Examples 4 and 5, we were concerned only with determining whether a linear polynomial of the form $x - c$ was a factor of another polynomial. For such problems, it is reasonable to compute $f(c)$ either directly or by synthetic division, whichever way seems easier for a particular problem. However, if more information is required, such as the complete factorization of the given polynomial, then the use of synthetic division is appropriate, as the next two examples illustrate.

EXAMPLE 6

Show that $x - 1$ is a factor of $x^3 - 2x^2 - 11x + 12$, and find the other linear factors of the polynomial.

Solution

Let's use synthetic division to divide $x^3 - 2x^2 - 11x + 12$ by $x - 1$.

$$\begin{array}{r|rrrr} 1 & 1 & -2 & -11 & 12 \\ & & 1 & -1 & -12 \\ \hline & 1 & -1 & -12 & 0 \end{array}$$

The last line indicates a quotient of $x^2 - x - 12$ and a remainder of 0. The remainder of 0 means that $x - 1$ is a factor. Furthermore, we can write

$$x^3 - 2x^2 - 11x + 12 = (x - 1)(x^2 - x - 12)$$

The quadratic polynomial $x^2 - x - 12$ can be factored as $(x - 4)(x + 3)$ using our conventional factoring techniques. Thus we obtain

$$x^3 - 2x^2 - 11x + 12 = (x - 1)(x - 4)(x + 3)$$ ▪

EXAMPLE 7

Show that $x + 4$ is a factor of $f(x) = x^3 - 5x^2 - 22x + 56$, and complete the factorization of $f(x)$.

Solution

Use synthetic division to divide $x^3 - 5x^2 - 22x + 56$ by $x + 4$.

$$\begin{array}{r|rrrr} -4 & 1 & -5 & -22 & 56 \\ & & -4 & 36 & -56 \\ \hline & 1 & -9 & 14 & 0 \end{array}$$

The last line indicates a quotient of $x^2 - 9x + 14$ and a remainder of 0. The remainder of 0 means that $x + 4$ is a factor. Furthermore, we can write

$$x^3 - 5x^2 - 22x + 56 = (x + 4)(x^2 - 9x + 14)$$

and then complete the factoring to obtain

$$x^3 - 5x^2 - 22x + 56 = (x + 4)(x - 7)(x - 2)$$ ▪

The factor theorem also plays a significant role in determining some general factorization ideas, as the last example of this section demonstrates.

EXAMPLE 8

Verify that $x + 1$ is a factor of $x^n + 1$ for all odd positive integral values of n.

Solution

Let $f(x) = x^n + 1$ and compute $f(-1)$.

$$f(-1) = (-1)^n + 1$$
$$= -1 + 1 \quad \text{Any odd power of } -1 \text{ is } -1$$
$$= 0$$

Because $f(-1) = 0$, we know that $x + 1$ is a factor of $f(x)$.

Concept Quiz 4.2

For Problems 1–6, answer true or false.

1. When a polynomial is divided by a divisor that is a linear factor, the remainder is a constant term.
2. If $f(3) = -12$, then the remainder, when $f(x)$ is divided by $x - 3$, is -12.
3. If $f(-5) = 0$, then $(x - 5)$ is a factor of $f(x)$.
4. If $(x + 3)$ is factor of $f(x)$, then the division of $f(x)$ by $(x + 3)$ has a remainder of 0.
5. For any polynomial of the form $x^n + 1$, where n is an odd positive integer, $(x + 1)$ is a factor.
6. If $f(2) = 8$, then $(x - 2)$ is a factor of $f(x)$.

Problem Set 4.2

For Problems 1–10, find $f(c)$ by (a) evaluating $f(c)$ directly, and (b) using synthetic division and the remainder theorem. (Objective 1)

1. $f(x) = x^2 + 2x - 6$ and $c = 3$
2. $f(x) = x^2 - 7x + 4$ and $c = 2$
3. $f(x) = x^3 - 2x^2 + 3x - 1$ and $c = -1$
4. $f(x) = x^3 + 3x^2 - 4x - 7$ and $c = -2$
5. $f(x) = 2x^4 - x^3 - 3x^2 + 4x - 1$ and $c = 2$
6. $f(x) = 3x^4 - 4x^3 + 5x^2 - 7x + 6$ and $c = 1$
7. $f(n) = 6n^3 - 35n^2 + 8n - 10$ and $c = 6$
8. $f(n) = 8n^3 - 39n^2 - 7n - 1$ and $c = 5$
9. $f(n) = 2n^5 - 1$ and $c = -2$
10. $f(n) = 3n^4 - 2n^3 + 4n - 1$ and $c = 3$

For Problems 11–20, find $f(c)$ either by using synthetic division and the remainder theorem or by evaluating $f(c)$ directly. (Objective 1)

11. $f(x) = 6x^5 - 3x^3 + 2$ and $c = -1$
12. $f(x) = -4x^4 + x^3 - 2x^2 - 5$ and $c = 2$
13. $f(x) = 2x^4 - 15x^3 - 9x^2 - 2x - 3$ and $c = 8$
14. $f(x) = x^4 - 8x^3 + 9x^2 - 15x + 2$ and $c = 7$
15. $f(n) = 4n^7 + 3$ and $c = 3$
16. $f(n) = -3n^6 - 2$ and $c = -3$
17. $f(n) = 3n^5 + 17n^4 - 4n^3 + 10n^2 - 15n + 13$ and $c = -6$
18. $f(n) = -2n^5 - 9n^4 + 7n^3 + 14n^2 + 19n - 38$ and $c = -5$
19. $f(x) = -4x^4 - 6x^2 + 7$ and $c = 4$
20. $f(x) = 3x^5 - 7x^3 - 6$ and $c = 5$

For Problems 21–34, use the factor theorem to help answer some questions about factors. (Objective 2)

21. Is $x - 2$ a factor of $5x^2 - 17x + 14$?

22. Is $x + 1$ a factor of $3x^2 - 5x - 8$?

23. Is $x + 3$ a factor of $6x^2 + 13x - 14$?

24. Is $x - 5$ a factor of $8x^2 - 47x + 32$?

25. Is $x - 1$ a factor of $4x^3 - 13x^2 + 21x - 12$?

26. Is $x - 4$ a factor of $2x^3 - 11x^2 + 10x + 8$?

27. Is $x + 2$ a factor of $x^3 + 7x^2 + x - 18$?

28. Is $x + 3$ a factor of $x^3 + x^2 - 14x - 24$?

29. Is $x - 3$ a factor of $3x^3 - 5x^2 - 17x + 17$?

30. Is $x + 4$ a factor of $2x^3 + 9x^2 - 5x - 39$?

31. Is $x + 2$ a factor of $x^3 + 8$?

32. Is $x - 2$ a factor of $x^3 - 8$?

33. Is $x - 3$ a factor of $x^4 - 81$?

34. Is $x + 3$ a factor of $x^4 - 81$?

For Problems 35–44, use synthetic division to show that $g(x)$ is a factor of $f(x)$, and complete the factorization of $f(x)$. (Objectives 2, 3)

35. $g(x) = x - 2$, $f(x) = x^3 - 6x^2 - 13x + 42$

36. $g(x) = x + 1$, $f(x) = x^3 + 6x^2 - 31x - 36$

37. $g(x) = x + 2$, $f(x) = 12x^3 + 29x^2 + 8x - 4$

38. $g(x) = x - 3$, $f(x) = 6x^3 - 17x^2 - 5x + 6$

39. $g(x) = x + 1$, $f(x) = x^3 - 2x^2 - 7x - 4$

40. $g(x) = x - 5$, $f(x) = 2x^3 + x^2 - 61x + 30$

41. $g(x) = x - 6$, $f(x) = x^5 - 6x^4 - 16x + 96$

42. $g(x) = x + 3$, $f(x) = x^5 + 3x^4 - x - 3$

43. $g(x) = x + 5$, $f(x) = 9x^3 + 21x^2 - 104x + 80$

44. $g(x) = x + 4$, $f(x) = 4x^3 + 4x^2 - 39x + 36$

For Problems 45–48, find the value(s) of k that makes the second polynomial a factor of the first.

45. $k^2x^4 + 3kx^2 - 4; x - 1$

46. $x^3 - kx^2 + 5x + k; x - 2$

47. $kx^3 + 19x^2 + x - 6; x + 3$

48. $x^3 + 4x^2 - 11x + k; x + 2$

49. Argue that $f(x) = 3x^4 + 2x^2 + 5$ has no factor of the form $x - c$, where c is a real number.

50. Show that $x + 2$ is a factor of $x^{12} - 4096$.

51. Verify that $x + 1$ is a factor of $x^n - 1$ for all even positive integral values of n.

52. Verify that $x - 1$ is a factor of $x^n - 1$ for all positive integral values of n.

53. (a) Verify that $x - y$ is a factor of $x^n - y^n$ for all positive integral values of n.

 (b) Verify that $x + y$ is a factor of $x^n - y^n$ for all even positive integral values of n.

 (c) Verify that $x + y$ is a factor of $x^n + y^n$ for all odd positive integral values of n.

Thoughts Into Words

54. State the remainder theorem in your own words.

55. Discuss some of the uses of the factor theorem.

Further Investigations

The remainder and factor theorems are true for any complex value of c. Therefore, for Problems 56–58, find $f(c)$ by (a) using synthetic division and the remainder theorem, and (b) evaluating $f(c)$ directly.

56. $f(x) = x^3 - 5x^2 + 2x + 1$ and $c = i$

57. $f(x) = x^2 + 4x - 2$ and $c = 1 + i$

58. $f(x) = x^3 + 2x^2 + x - 2$ and $c = 2 - 3i$

59. Show that $x - 2i$ is a factor of $f(x) = x^4 + 6x^2 + 8$.

60. Show that $x + 3i$ is a factor of $f(x) = x^4 + 14x^2 + 45$.

61. Consider changing the form of the polynomial $f(x) = x^3 + 4x^2 - 3x + 2$ as follows:

$$f(x) = x^3 + 4x^2 - 3x + 2$$
$$= x(x^2 + 4x - 3) + 2$$
$$= x[x(x + 4) - 3] + 2$$

The final form $f(x) = x[x(x + 4) - 3] + 2$ is called the **nested form** of the polynomial. It is particularly well suited for evaluating functional values of f either by hand or with a calculator. For each of the following, find the indicated functional values using the nested form of the given polynomial.

(a) $f(4)$, $f(-5)$, and $f(7)$ for
$f(x) = x^3 + 5x^2 - 2x + 1$

(b) $f(3)$, $f(6)$, and $f(-7)$ for
$f(x) = 2x^3 - 4x^2 - 3x + 2$

(c) $f(4)$, $f(5)$, and $f(-3)$ for
$f(x) = -2x^3 + 5x^2 - 6x - 7$

(d) $f(5)$, $f(6)$, and $f(-3)$ for
$f(x) = x^4 + 3x^3 - 2x^2 + 5x - 1$

Answers to the Concept Quiz

1. True **2.** True **3.** False **4.** True **5.** True **6.** False

---

4.3   Polynomial Equations

OBJECTIVES

1. Understand the concept of multiplicity of roots

2. Solve polynomial equations using the rational root theorem and the factor theorem

3. Use Descartes' rule of signs

4. Write a polynomial equation given solutions and degree

We have solved a large variety of linear equations of the form $ax + b = 0$ and quadratic equations of the form $ax^2 + bx + c = 0$. Linear and quadratic equations are special cases of a general class of equations we refer to as **polynomial equations**. The equation

$$a_n x^n + a_{n-1} x^{n-1} + \cdots + a_1 x + a_0 = 0$$

where the coefficients $a_0, a_1, \ldots, a_n$ are real numbers and n is a positive integer, is called a **polynomial equation of degree n.** The following are examples of polynomial equations:

$$\sqrt{2}x - 6 = 0 \qquad \text{Degree 1}$$

$$\frac{3}{4}x^2 - \frac{2}{3}x + 5 = 0 \qquad \text{Degree 2}$$

$$4x^3 - 3x^2 - 7x - 9 = 0 \qquad \text{Degree 3}$$

$$5x^4 - x + 6 = 0 \qquad \text{Degree 4}$$

Remark: The most general polynomial equation would allow complex numbers as coefficients. However, for our purposes in this text, we will restrict the coefficients to real numbers. We often refer to such equations as *polynomial equations over the reals.*

In general, solving polynomial equations of degree greater than 2 can be very difficult and often requires mathematics beyond the scope of this text. However, there are some general properties pertaining to the solving of polynomial equations that you should be familiar with; furthermore, there are certain types of polynomial equations that we can solve using the techniques available to us at this time. We can also use a graphical approach to approximate solutions, which, in some cases, is shorter than using an algebraic approach.

Let's begin by listing some polynomial equations and corresponding solution sets that we have already encountered in this text.

Equation	Solution set
$3x + 4 = 7$	$\{1\}$
$x^2 + x - 6 = 0$	$\{-3, 2\}$
$2x^3 - 3x^2 - 2x + 3 = 0$	$\left\{-1, 1, \frac{3}{2}\right\}$
$x^4 - 16 = 0$	$\{-2, 2, -2i, 2i\}$

Note that in each of these examples, the number of solutions corresponds to the degree of the equation. The first-degree equation has one solution, the second-degree equation has two solutions, the third-degree equation has three solutions, and the fourth-degree equation has four solutions. Now consider the equation

$$(x - 4)^2(x + 5)^3 = 0$$

It can be written as

$$(x - 4)(x - 4)(x + 5)(x + 5)(x + 5) = 0$$

which implies that

$$x - 4 = 0 \quad \text{or} \quad x - 4 = 0 \quad \text{or} \quad x + 5 = 0 \quad \text{or}$$
$$x + 5 = 0 \quad \text{or} \quad x + 5 = 0$$

Therefore

$$x = 4 \quad \text{or} \quad x = 4 \quad \text{or} \quad x = -5 \quad \text{or} \quad x = -5 \quad \text{or} \quad x = -5$$

We state that the solution set of the original equation is $\{-5, 4\}$, but we also say that the equation has a solution of 4 with a *multiplicity of two* and a solution of -5 with a *multiplicity of three*. Furthermore, note that the sum of the multiplicities is 5, which agrees with the degree of the equation. The following general property can be stated:

Property 4.3

For $n \geq 1$, a polynomial equation of degree n has n solutions, and any solution of multiplicity p is counted p times.

Finding Rational Solutions

Although solving polynomial equations of degree greater than 2 can, in general, be very difficult, *rational solutions of polynomial equations with integral coefficients* can be found using techniques presented in this chapter. The following property restricts the potential rational solutions of such equations:

Property 4.4 Rational Root Theorem

Consider the polynomial equation

$$a_n x^n + a_{n-1} x^{n-1} + \cdots + a_1 x + a_0 = 0$$

in which the coefficients $a_0, a_1, \ldots, a_n$ are *integers*. If the rational number $\dfrac{c}{d}$, reduced to lowest terms, is a solution of the equation, then c is a factor of the constant term a_0, and d is a factor of the leading coefficient a_n.

The "why" behind the rational root theorem is based on some simple factoring ideas, as indicated by the following outline of a proof for the theorem.

Outline of Proof   If $\dfrac{c}{d}$ is to be a solution, then

$$a_n \left(\frac{c}{d}\right)^n + a_{n-1} \left(\frac{c}{d}\right)^{n-1} + \cdots + a_1 \left(\frac{c}{d}\right) + a_0 = 0$$

Multiply both sides of this equation by d^n and add $-a_0 d^n$ to both sides to yield

$$a_n c^n + a_{n-1} c^{n-1} d + \cdots + a_1 c d^{n-1} = -a_0 d^n$$

Because c is a factor of the left side of this equation, c must also be a factor of $-a_0 d^n$. Furthermore, because $\dfrac{c}{d}$ is in reduced form, c and d have no common factors other than -1 or 1. Thus c is a factor of a_0. In the same way, from the equation

$$a_{n-1} c^{n-1} d + \cdots + a_1 c d^{n-1} + a_0 d^n = -a_n c^n$$

we can conclude that d is a factor of the left side, and therefore d is also a factor of a_n.

The rational root theorem, a graph, synthetic division, the factor theorem, and some previous knowledge pertaining to solving linear and quadratic equations form a basis for finding rational solutions. Let's consider some examples.

Classroom Example
Find all rational solutions of
$2x^3 - 9x^2 - 20x + 12 = 0$.

EXAMPLE 1   Find all rational solutions of $3x^3 + 8x^2 - 15x + 4 = 0$.

Solution

If $\dfrac{c}{d}$ is a rational solution, then c must be a factor of 4, and d must be a factor of 3. Therefore, the possible values for c and d are as follows:

For c	$\pm 1, \pm 2, \pm 4$
For d	$\pm 1, \pm 3$

Thus the possible values for $\dfrac{c}{d}$ are

$$\pm 1, \pm \frac{1}{3}, \pm 2, \pm \frac{2}{3}, \pm 4, \pm \frac{4}{3}$$

Now let's use a graph of $y = 3x^3 + 8x^2 - 15x + 4$ to shorten the list of possible rational solutions (Figure 4.1).

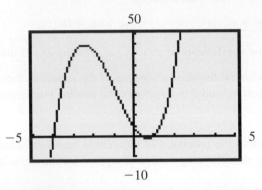

Figure 4.1

The x intercepts appear to be at -4, at 1, and between 0 and 1. Using synthetic division,

$$
\begin{array}{r|rrrr}
1 & 3 & 8 & -15 & 4 \\
  &   & 3 & 11 & -4 \\
\hline
  & 3 & 11 & -4 & 0
\end{array}
$$

we can show that $x - 1$ is a factor of the given polynomial, and therefore 1 is a rational solution of the equation. Furthermore, the result of the synthetic division also indicates that we can factor the given polynomial as follows:

$$3x^3 + 8x^2 - 15x + 4 = 0$$
$$(x - 1)(3x^2 + 11x - 4) = 0$$

The quadratic factor can be factored further using our previous techniques; we can proceed as follows:

$$(x - 1)(3x^2 + 11x - 4) = 0$$
$$(x - 1)(3x - 1)(x + 4) = 0$$
$$x - 1 = 0 \quad \text{or} \quad 3x - 1 = 0 \quad \text{or} \quad x + 4 = 0$$
$$x = 1 \quad \text{or} \quad x = \frac{1}{3} \quad \text{or} \quad x = -4$$

Thus the entire solution set consists of rational numbers, which can be listed as $\left\{ -4, \frac{1}{3}, 1 \right\}$.

■

Remark: The graphs used in this section are done with a graphing utility. In the next section, we will discuss some special situations for which freehand sketches of the graphs are easily obtained.

In Example 1 we used a graph to help shorten the list of possible rational solutions determined by the rational root theorem. Without using a graph, one needs to conduct an organized search of the list of possible rational solutions, as the next example demonstrates.

Classroom Example
Find all rational solutions of
$4x^3 - x^2 - 11x - 6 = 0$.

EXAMPLE 2

Find all rational solutions of $3x^3 + 7x^2 - 22x - 8 = 0$.

Solution

If $\dfrac{c}{d}$ is a rational solution, then c must be a factor of -8, and d must be a factor of 3. Therefore, the possible values for c and d are as follows:

| **For** c | $\pm 1, \pm 2, \pm 4, \pm 8$ |
| **For** d | $\pm 1, \pm 3$ |

Thus the possible values for $\dfrac{c}{d}$ are

$$\pm 1, \pm \frac{1}{3}, \pm 2, \pm \frac{2}{3}, \pm 4, \pm \frac{4}{3}, \pm 8, \pm \frac{8}{3}$$

Let's begin our search for rational solutions; we will try the integers first.

$$\begin{array}{r|rrrr} 1 & 3 & 7 & -22 & -8 \\ & & 3 & 10 & -12 \\ \hline & 3 & 10 & -12 & \boxed{-20} \end{array}$$ ⟵ This remainder indicates that $x - 1$ is not a factor, and thus 1 is not a solution

$$\begin{array}{r|rrrr} -1 & 3 & 7 & -22 & -8 \\ & & -3 & -4 & 26 \\ \hline & 3 & 4 & -26 & \boxed{18} \end{array}$$ ⟵ This remainder indicates that -1 is not a solution

$$\begin{array}{r|rrrr} 2 & 3 & 7 & -22 & -8 \\ & & 6 & 26 & 8 \\ \hline & 3 & 13 & 4 & 0 \end{array}$$ ⟵ This remainder indicates that 2 is a solution

Now we know that $x - 2$ is a factor; we can proceed as follows:

$$3x^3 + 7x^2 - 22x - 8 = 0$$
$$(x - 2)(3x^2 + 13x + 4) = 0$$
$$(x - 2)(3x + 1)(x + 4) = 0$$

$x - 2 = 0$ or $3x + 1 = 0$ or $x + 4 = 0$

$x = 2$ or $3x = -1$ or $x = -4$

$x = 2$ or $x = -\dfrac{1}{3}$ or $x = -4$

The solution set is $\left\{ -4, -\dfrac{1}{3}, 2 \right\}$.   ▄

In Examples 1 and 2, we were solving third-degree equations. Therefore, after finding one linear factor by synthetic division, we were able to factor the remaining quadratic factor in the usual way. However, if the given equation is of degree 4 or more, we may need to find more than one linear factor by synthetic division, as the next example illustrates.

Classroom Example
Solve
$2x^4 - 9x^3 + 4x^2 + 35x - 50 = 0$.

| **EXAMPLE 3** | Solve $x^4 - 6x^3 + 22x^2 - 30x + 13 = 0$. |

Solution

The possible values for $\dfrac{c}{d}$ are as follows:

For $\dfrac{c}{d}$ $\pm 1, \pm 13$

By synthetic division, we find that

$$
\begin{array}{r|rrrr}
1) & 1 & -6 & 22 & -30 & 13 \\
  &   & 1 & -5 & 17 & -13 \\
\hline
  & 1 & -5 & 17 & -13 & 0 \\
\end{array}
$$

which indicates that $x - 1$ is a factor of the given polynomial. The bottom line of the synthetic division indicates that the given polynomial can be factored as follows:

$$x^4 - 6x^3 + 22x^2 - 30x + 13 = 0$$
$$(x - 1)(x^3 - 5x^2 + 17x - 13) = 0$$

Therefore

$$x - 1 = 0 \quad \text{or} \quad x^3 - 5x^2 + 17x - 13 = 0$$

Now we can use the same approach to look for rational solutions of the expression $x^3 - 5x^2 + 17x - 13 = 0$. The possible values for $\dfrac{c}{d}$ are as follows:

For $\dfrac{c}{d}$ $\pm 1, \pm 13$

By synthetic division, we find that

$$
\begin{array}{r|rrr}
1) & 1 & -5 & 17 & -13 \\
  &   & 1 & -4 & 13 \\
\hline
  & 1 & -4 & 13 & 10 \\
\end{array}
$$

which indicates that $x - 1$ is a factor of $x^3 - 5x^2 + 17x - 13$ and that the other factor is $x^2 - 4x + 13$.

Now we can solve the original equation as follows:

$$x^4 - 6x^3 + 22x^2 - 30x + 13 = 0$$
$$(x - 1)(x^3 - 5x^2 + 17x - 13) = 0$$
$$(x - 1)(x - 1)(x^2 - 4x + 13) = 0$$

$$x - 1 = 0 \quad \text{or} \quad x - 1 = 0 \quad \text{or} \quad x^2 - 4x + 13 = 0$$
$$x = 1 \quad \text{or} \quad x = 1 \quad \text{or} \quad x^2 - 4x + 13 = 0$$

Use the quadratic formula on $x^2 - 4x + 13 = 0$:

$$x = \frac{4 \pm \sqrt{16 - 52}}{2} = \frac{4 \pm \sqrt{-36}}{2}$$

$$= \frac{4 \pm 6i}{2} = 2 \pm 3i$$

Thus the original equation has a rational solution of 1 with a multiplicity of two and two complex solutions, $2 + 3i$ and $2 - 3i$. The solution set is listed as $\{1, 2 \pm 3i\}$. ■

Let's graph the equation $y = x^4 - 6x^3 + 22x^2 - 30x + 13$ to give some visual support for our work in Example 3. The graph in Figure 4.2 indicates only an x intercept at 1. This is consistent with the solution set of $\{1, 2 \pm 3i\}$.

Example 3 illustrates two general properties. First, note that the coefficient of x^4 is 1, and thus the possible rational solutions must be integers. In general, the possible rational solutions of $x^n + a_{n-1}x^{n-1} + \cdots + a_1x + a_0 = 0$ are the integral factors of a_0.

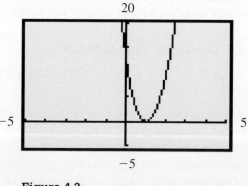

Figure 4.2

Second, note that the complex solutions of Example 3 are conjugates of each other. The following general property can be stated:

Property 4.5

Nonreal complex solutions of polynomial equations with real coefficients, if they exist, must occur in conjugate pairs.

Descartes' Rule of Signs

Each of Properties 4.3, 4.4, and 4.5 yields some information about the solutions of a polynomial equation. Before we state the final property of this section, which will give us some additional information, we need to consider two ideas.

First, in a polynomial that is arranged in descending powers of x, if two successive terms differ in sign, then there is said to be a **variation in sign**. (We disregard terms with zero coefficients when sign variations are counted.) For example, the polynomial

$$3x^3 - 2x^2 + 4x + 7$$

has *two* sign variations, whereas the polynomial

$$x^5 - 4x^3 + x - 5$$

has *three* variations.

Second, the solutions of

$$a_n(-x)^n + a_{n-1}(-x)^{n-1} + \cdots + a_1(-x) + a_0 = 0$$

are the opposites of the solutions of

$$a_n x^n + a_{n-1} x^{n-1} + \cdots + a_1 x + a_0 = 0$$

In other words, if a new equation is formed by replacing x with $-x$ in a given equation, then the solutions of the newly formed equation are the opposites of the solutions of the given equation. For example, the solution set of $x^2 + 7x + 12 = 0$ is $\{-4, -3\}$, and the solution set of $(-x)^2 + 7(-x) + 12 = 0$, which simplifies to $x^2 - 7x + 12 = 0$, is $\{3, 4\}$.

Now we can state a property that can help us to determine the nature of the solutions of a polynomial equation without actually solving the equation.

Property 4.6 Descartes' Rule of Signs

Let $a_n x^n + a_{n-1} x^{n-1} + \cdots + a_1 x + a_0 = 0$ be a polynomial equation with real coefficients.

1. The number of *positive real solutions* of the given equation either is equal to the number of variations in sign of the polynomial or is less than the number of variations by a positive even integer.

2. The number of *negative real solutions* of the given equation either is equal to the number of variations in sign of the polynomial $a_n(-x)^n + a_{n-1}(-x)^{n-1} + \cdots + a_1(-x) + a_0$ or is less than the number of variations by a positive even integer.

Property 4.6 (Descartes' rule of signs), along with Properties 4.3 and 4.5, allow us to acquire some information about the solutions of a polynomial equation without actually solving the equation. Let's consider some equations and see how much we know about their solutions without solving them.

1. $x^3 + 3x^2 + 5x + 4 = 0$
   - **(a)** No variations of sign in $x^3 + 3x^2 + 5x + 4$ means that there are *no positive solutions*.
   - **(b)** Replacing x with $-x$ in the given polynomial produces $(-x)^3 + 3(-x)^2 + 5(-x) + 4$, which simplifies to $-x^3 + 3x^2 - 5x + 4$ and contains three variations of sign; thus there are *three (or one) negative solution(s)*.

   Conclusion   The given equation has three negative real solutions or else one negative real solution and two nonreal complex solutions.

2. $2x^4 + 3x^2 - x - 1 = 0$
   - **(a)** There is one variation of sign; thus the equation has *one positive solution*.
   - **(b)** Replacing x with $-x$ produces $2(-x)^4 + 3(-x)^2 - (-x) - 1$, which simplifies to $2x^4 + 3x^2 + x - 1$ and contains one variation of sign. Thus the equation has *one negative solution*.

   Conclusion   The given equation has one positive, one negative, and two nonreal complex solutions.

3. $3x^4 + 2x^2 + 5 = 0$
   - **(a)** No variations of sign in the given polynomial means that there are *no positive solutions*.
   - **(b)** Replacing x with $-x$ produces $3(-x)^4 + 2(-x)^2 + 5$, which simplifies to $3x^4 + 2x^2 + 5$ and contains no variations of sign. Thus there are *no negative solutions*.

   Conclusion   The given equation contains four nonreal complex solutions. These solutions will appear in conjugate pairs.

4. $2x^5 - 4x^3 + 2x - 5 = 0$
   - **(a)** The fact that there are three variations of sign in the given polynomial implies that there are *three or one positive solutions*.
   - **(b)** Replacing x with $-x$ produces $2(-x)^5 - 4(-x)^3 + 2(-x) - 5$, which simplifies to $-2x^5 + 4x^3 - 2x - 5$ and contains two variations of sign. Thus there are *two (or zero) negative solution(s)*.

   Conclusion   The given equation has either three positive and two negative solutions; three positive and two nonreal complex solutions; one positive, two negative, and two nonreal complex solutions; or one positive and four nonreal complex solution(s).

It should be evident from the previous discussions that sometimes we can truly pinpoint the nature of the solutions of a polynomial equation. However, for some equations (such as in the last example), the best we can do with the properties discussed in this section is to restrict the possibilities for the nature of the solutions. It might be helpful for you to review Examples 1, 2, and 3 of this section and show that the solution sets do satisfy Properties 4.3, 4.5, and 4.6.

EXAMPLE 4

Find a polynomial equation with integral coefficients that has the given numbers as solutions and the indicated degree.

(a) $1, \dfrac{1}{2}, -2$; degree 3   (b) 2 of multiplicity four; degree 4

(c) $1 + i, -3i$; degree 4

Solutions

(a) If $1, \dfrac{1}{2}$, and -2 are solutions, then $(x - 1)$, $\left(x - \dfrac{1}{2}\right)$, and $(x + 2)$ are factors of the polynomial. Thus we can form the following third-degree polynomial equation:

$$(x - 1)\left(x - \frac{1}{2}\right)(x + 2) = 0$$
$$(x - 1)(2x - 1)(x + 2) = 0$$
$$2x^3 + x^2 - 5x + 2 = 0$$

(b) If 2 is to be a solution with multiplicity four, then the equation $(x - 2)^4 = 0$ can be formed. Using the binomial expansion pattern, we can express the equation as follows:

$$(x - 2)^4 = 0$$
$$x^4 - 8x^3 + 24x^2 - 32x + 16 = 0$$

(c) By Property 4.5, if $1 + i$ is a solution, then so is $1 - i$. Likewise, because $-3i$ is a solution, so is $3i$. Therefore we can form the following equation:

$$[x - (1 + i)][x - (1 - i)](x + 3i)(x - 3i) = 0$$
$$[(x - 1) - i][(x - 1) + i](x^2 + 9) = 0$$
$$[(x - 1)^2 - i^2](x^2 + 9) = 0$$
$$(x^2 - 2x + 1 + 1)(x^2 + 9) = 0$$
$$x^4 - 2x^3 + 11x^2 - 18x + 18 = 0$$

Finally, let's consider a situation for which the graphing calculator becomes a very useful tool.

EXAMPLE 5

Find the real number solutions of the equation $x^4 - 2x^3 - 5 = 0$.

Solution

First, let's use a graphing calculator to get a graph of $y = x^4 - 2x^3 - 5$, as shown in Figure 4.3. Obviously, there are two x intercepts, one between -2 and -1 and another between 2 and 3. From the rational root theorem, we know that the only possible rational roots of the given equation are ±1 and ±5. Therefore these x intercepts must be irrational numbers. We can use the ZOOM and TRACE features of the graphing calculator to approximate these values at -1.2 and 2.4, to the nearest tenth. Thus the real number solutions of $x^4 - 2x^3 - 5 = 0$ are approximately -1.2 and 2.4. The other two solutions must be conjugate complex numbers.

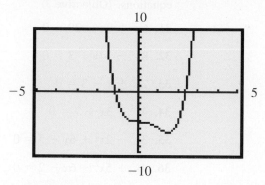

Figure 4.3

Concept Quiz 4.3

For Problems 1–8, answer true or false.

1. For a polynomial equation, the number of solutions is equal to the degree of the polynomial.
2. The equation $(x - 7)^3(x + 1)^2 = 0$ has a solution of 7 with a multiplicity of 3 and a solution of -1 with a multiplicity of 2.
3. Given $2x^4 - 3x^2 + 8 = 0$, the only possible rational solutions are $\pm\dfrac{1}{8}, \pm\dfrac{1}{2}$, and $\pm\dfrac{1}{4}$.
4. According to the rational root theorem, $\dfrac{1}{3}$ is a possible rational solution of the equation $3x^3 - 4x^2 + x + 5 = 0$.
5. The rational root theorem can identify all possible real number roots of a polynomial equation.
6. If $-3 + 5i$ is a solution to a polynomial equation, then $-3 - 5i$ is also a solution of the equation.
7. The equation $2x^3 + 4x^2 + x + 6 = 0$ has no positive solutions.
8. The equation $x^4 + x^2 + 4 = 0$ has no real number solutions.

Problem Set 4.3

For Problems 1–20, use the rational root theorem and the factor theorem to help solve each equation. Be sure that the number of solutions for each equation agrees with Property 4.3, taking into account multiplicity of solutions. (Objectives 1 and 2)

1. $x^3 - 2x^2 - 11x + 12 = 0$

2. $x^3 + x^2 - 4x - 4 = 0$

3. $15x^3 + 14x^2 - 3x - 2 = 0$

4. $3x^3 + 13x^2 - 52x + 28 = 0$

5. $8x^3 - 2x^2 - 41x - 10 = 0$

6. $6x^3 + x^2 - 10x + 3 = 0$

7. $x^3 - x^2 - 8x + 12 = 0$

8. $x^3 - 2x^2 - 7x - 4 = 0$

9. $x^3 - 4x^2 + 8 = 0$

10. $x^3 - 10x - 12 = 0$

11. $x^4 + 4x^3 - x^2 - 16x - 12 = 0$

12. $x^4 - 4x^3 - 7x^2 + 34x - 24 = 0$

13. $x^4 + x^3 - 3x^2 - 17x - 30 = 0$

14. $x^4 - 3x^3 + 2x^2 + 2x - 4 = 0$

15. $x^3 - x^2 + x - 1 = 0$

16. $6x^4 - 13x^3 - 19x^2 + 12x = 0$

17. $2x^4 + 3x^3 - 11x^2 - 9x + 15 = 0$

18. $3x^4 - x^3 - 8x^2 + 2x + 4 = 0$

19. $4x^4 + 12x^3 + x^2 - 12x + 4 = 0$

20. $2x^5 - 5x^4 + x^3 + x^2 - x + 6 = 0$

For Problems 21–26, verify that the equations do not have any rational number solutions. (Objective 2)

21. $x^4 + 3x - 2 = 0$

22. $x^4 - x^3 - 8x^2 - 3x + 1 = 0$

23. $3x^4 - 4x^3 - 10x^2 + 3x - 4 = 0$

24. $2x^4 - 3x^3 + 6x^2 - 24x + 5 = 0$

25. $x^5 + 2x^4 - 2x^3 + 5x^2 - 2x - 3 = 0$

26. $x^5 - 2x^4 + 3x^3 + 4x^2 + 7x - 1 = 0$

For Problems 27–30, solve each equation by first applying the multiplication property of equality to produce an equivalent equation with integral coefficients. (Objective 2)

27. $\frac{1}{10}x^3 + \frac{1}{5}x^2 - \frac{1}{2}x - \frac{3}{5} = 0$

28. $\frac{1}{10}x^3 + \frac{1}{2}x^2 + \frac{1}{5}x - \frac{4}{5} = 0$

29. $x^3 - \frac{5}{6}x^2 - \frac{22}{3}x + \frac{5}{2} = 0$

30. $x^3 + \frac{9}{2}x^2 - x - 12 = 0$

For Problems 31–40, use Descartes' rule of signs (Property 4.6) to help list the possibilities for the nature of the solutions for each equation. *Do not* solve the equations. (Objective 3)

31. $6x^2 + 7x - 20 = 0$

32. $8x^2 - 14x + 3 = 0$

33. $2x^3 + x - 3 = 0$

34. $4x^3 + 3x + 7 = 0$

35. $3x^3 - 2x^2 + 6x + 5 = 0$

36. $4x^3 + 5x^2 - 6x - 2 = 0$

37. $x^5 - 3x^4 + 5x^3 - x^2 + 2x - 1 = 0$

38. $2x^5 + 3x^3 - x + 1 = 0$

39. $x^5 + 32 = 0$

40. $2x^6 + 3x^4 - 2x^2 - 1 = 0$

For Problems 41–50, find a polynomial equation with integral coefficients that has the given numbers as solutions and the indicated degree. (Objective 4)

41. $2, 4, -3;$ degree 3

42. $1, -1, 2, -4;$ degree 4

43. $-2, \frac{1}{2}, \frac{2}{3};$ degree 3

44. $3, -\frac{2}{3}, \frac{3}{4};$ degree 3

45. 1 of multiplicity 5;   degree 5

46. -3 of multiplicity 4;   degree 4

47. $3, 2 + 3i;$ degree 3

48. $-2, 1 - 4i;$ degree 3

49. $1 - i, 2i;$ degree 4

50. $-2 + 3i, -i;$ degree 4

Thoughts Into Words

51. Explain what it means to say that the equation $(x + 3)^2 = 0$ has a solution of -3 with a multiplicity of two.

52. Describe how to use the rational root theorem to show that the equation $x^2 - 3 = 0$ has no rational solutions.

Further Investigations

53. Use the rational root theorem to argue that $\sqrt{2}$ is not a rational number. [*Hint*: The solutions of $x^2 - 2 = 0$ are $\pm\sqrt{2}$.]

54. Use the rational root theorem to argue that $\sqrt{12}$ is not a rational number.

55. Defend this statement: "Every polynomial equation of odd degree with real coefficients has at least one real number solution."

56. The following synthetic division shows that 2 is a solution of $x^4 + x^3 + x^2 - 9x - 10 = 0$:

$$2\overline{)1 \quad 1 \quad 1 \quad -9 \quad -10}$$
$$ 2 \quad 6 \quad 14 \quad 10$$
$$\overline{1 \quad 3 \quad 7 \quad 5 \quad 0} \longleftarrow$$

Note that the new quotient row (indicated by the arrow) consists entirely of nonnegative numbers. This indicates that searching for solutions greater than 2 would be a waste of time because larger divisors would continue to increase each of the numbers (except the one on the far left) in the new quotient row. (Try 3 as a divisor!) Thus we say that 2 is an *upper bound* for the real number solutions of the given equation.

Now consider the following synthetic division, which shows that -1 is also a solution of $x^4 + x^3 + x^2 - 9x - 10 = 0$:

$$-1\overline{)1 \quad 1 \quad 1 \quad -9 \quad -10}$$
$$ -1 \quad 0 \quad -1 \quad 10$$
$$\overline{1 \quad 0 \quad 1 \quad -10 \quad 0} \longleftarrow$$

The new quotient row (indicated by the arrow) shows that there is no need to look for solutions less than -1 because any divisor less than -1 would increase the absolute value of each number (except the one on

the far left) in the new quotient row. (Try -2 as a divisor!) Thus we say that -1 is a *lower bound* for the real number solutions of the given equation.

The following general property can be stated:

If $a_n x^n + a_{n-1} x^{n-1} + \cdots + a_1 x + a_0 = 0$ is a polynomial equation with real coefficients, where $a_n > 0$, and if the polynomial is divided synthetically by $x - c$, then

1. If $c > 0$ and all numbers in the new quotient row of the synthetic division are nonnegative, then c is an upper bound of the solutions of the given equation.

2. If $c < 0$ and the numbers in the new quotient row alternate in sign (with 0 considered either positive or negative, as needed), then c is a lower bound of the solutions of the given equation.

Find the smallest positive integer and the largest negative integer that are upper and lower bounds, respectively, for the real number solutions of each of the following equations. Keep in mind that the integers that serve as bounds do not necessarily have to be solutions of the equation.

(a) $x^3 - 3x^2 + 25x - 75 = 0$

(b) $x^3 + x^2 - 4x - 4 = 0$

(c) $x^4 + 4x^3 - 7x^2 - 22x + 24 = 0$

(d) $3x^3 + 7x^2 - 22x - 8 = 0$

(e) $x^4 - 2x^3 - 9x^2 + 2x + 8 = 0$

Graphing Calculator Activities

57. Solve each of the following equations, using a graphing calculator whenever it seems to be helpful. Express all irrational solutions in lowest radical form.

(a) $x^3 + 2x^2 - 14x - 40 = 0$

(b) $x^3 + x^2 - 7x + 65 = 0$

(c) $x^4 - 6x^3 - 6x^2 + 32x + 24 = 0$

(d) $x^4 + 3x^3 - 39x^2 + 11x + 24 = 0$

(e) $x^3 - 14x^2 + 26x - 24 = 0$

(f) $x^4 + 2x^3 - 3x^2 - 4x + 4 = 0$

58. Find approximations, to the nearest hundredth, of the real number solutions of each of the following equations:

(a) $x^2 - 4x + 1 = 0$

(b) $3x^3 - 2x^2 + 12x - 8 = 0$

(c) $x^4 - 8x^3 + 14x^2 - 8x + 13 = 0$

(d) $x^4 + 6x^3 - 10x^2 - 22x + 161 = 0$

(e) $7x^5 - 5x^4 + 35x^3 - 25x^2 + 28x - 20 = 0$

Answers to the Concept Quiz

1. True   **2.** True   **3.** False   **4.** True   **5.** False   **6.** True   **7.** True   **8.** True

---

4.4   Graphing Polynomial Functions

OBJECTIVES

1 Know the patterns for the graphs of $f(x) = ax^n$

2 Graph polynomial functions

3 Identify the intervals in which a polynomial function is positive or negative

The terms with which we classify functions are analogous to those with which we describe the linear equations, quadratic equations, and polynomial equations. In Chapter 3 we defined a linear function in terms of the equation

$$f(x) = ax + b$$

and a quadratic function in terms of the equation

$$f(x) = ax^2 + bx + c$$

Both are special cases of a general class of functions called polynomial functions. Any function of the form

$$f(x) = a_n x^n + a_{n-1} x^{n-1} + \cdots + a_1 x + a_0$$

is called a **polynomial function of degree** n, where a_n is a nonzero real number, $a_{n-1}, \ldots, a_1, a_0$ are real numbers, and n is a nonnegative integer. The following are examples of polynomial functions:

$$f(x) = 5x^3 - 2x^2 + x - 4 \qquad \text{Degree 3}$$
$$f(x) = -2x^4 - 5x^3 + 3x^2 + 4x - 1 \qquad \text{Degree 4}$$
$$f(x) = 3x^5 + 2x^2 - 3 \qquad \text{Degree 5}$$

Remark: Our previous work with polynomial equations is sometimes presented as "finding zeros of polynomial functions." The *solutions*, or *roots*, of a polynomial equation are also called the **zeros** of the polynomial function. For example, -2 and 2 are solutions of $x^2 - 4 = 0$, and they are zeros of $f(x) = x^2 - 4$. That is, $f(-2) = 0$ and $f(2) = 0$.

For a complete discussion of graphing polynomial functions, we would need some tools from calculus. However, the graphing techniques that we have discussed in this text will allow us to graph certain kinds of polynomial functions. For example, polynomial functions of the form $f(x) = ax^n$ are quite easy to graph. We know from our previous work that if $n = 1$, then functions such as $f(x) = 2x$, $f(x) = -3x$, and $f(x) = \frac{1}{2}x$ are lines through the origin that have slopes of 2, -3, and $\frac{1}{2}$, respectively.

Furthermore, if $n = 2$, we know that the graphs of functions of the form $f(x) = ax^2$ are parabolas that are symmetric with respect to the y axis and have their vertices at the origin.

We have also previously graphed the special case of $f(x) = ax^n$, where $a = 1$ and $n = 3$; namely, the function $f(x) = x^3$. This graph is shown in Figure 4.4.

The graphs of functions of the form $f(x) = ax^3$, where $a \neq 1$, are slight variations of $f(x) = x^3$ and can be determined easily by plotting a few points. The graphs of $f(x) = \frac{1}{2}x^3$ and $f(x) = -x^3$ appear in Figure 4.5(a) and 4.5(b).

Two general patterns emerge from studying functions of the form $f(x) = x^n$. If n is odd and greater than 3, the graphs closely resemble Figure 4.4. The graph of

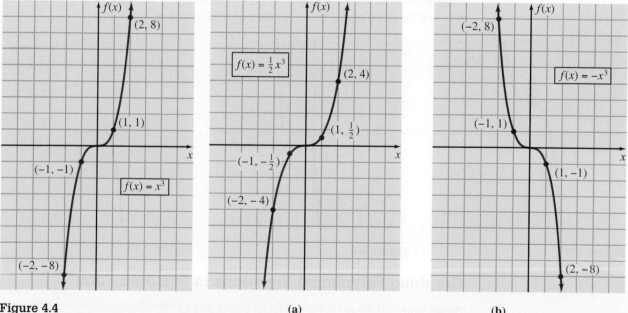

Figure 4.4

(a)

(b)

Figure 4.5

$f(x) = x^5$ is shown in Figure 4.6. Note that the curve "flattens out" a little more around the origin than it does in the graph of $f(x) = x^3$; it increases and decreases more rapidly because of the larger exponent. If n is even and greater than 2, the graphs of $f(x) = x^n$ are not parabolas. They resemble the basic parabola, but they are flatter at the bottom and steeper on the sides. Figure 4.7 shows the graph of $f(x) = x^4$.

Graphs of functions of the form $f(x) = ax^n$, where n is an integer greater than 2 and $a \neq 1$, are variations of those shown in Figures 4.4 and 4.7. If n is odd, the curve is symmetric about the origin. If n is even, the graph is symmetric about the y axis.

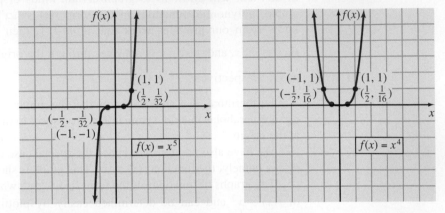

Figure 4.6   Figure 4.7

Remember from our work in Chapter 3 that transformations of basic curves are easy to sketch. For example, in Figure 4.8, we translated the graph of $f(x) = x^3$ upward two units to produce the graph of $f(x) = x^3 + 2$. Figure 4.9 shows the graph of $f(x) = (x - 1)^5$, obtained by translating the graph of $f(x) = x^5$ one unit to the right. In Figure 4.10, we sketched the graph of $f(x) = -x^4$ as the x-axis reflection of $f(x) = x^4$.

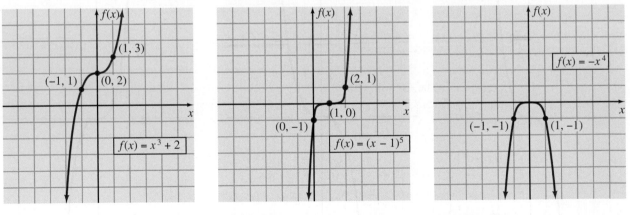

Figure 4.8   Figure 4.9   Figure 4.10

Graphing Polynomial Functions in Factored Form

As the degree of the polynomial increases, the graphs often become more complicated. We do know, however, that polynomial functions produce smooth continuous curves with a number of turning points, as illustrated in Figures 4.11 and 4.12. Some typical graphs of polynomial functions of odd degree are shown in Figure 4.11. As the graphs suggest, every polynomial function of odd degree has at least one *real zero*—that is, at least one real number c such that $f(c) = 0$. Geometrically, the zeros of the function are the x intercepts of the graph. Figure 4.12 illustrates some possible graphs of polynomial functions of even degree.

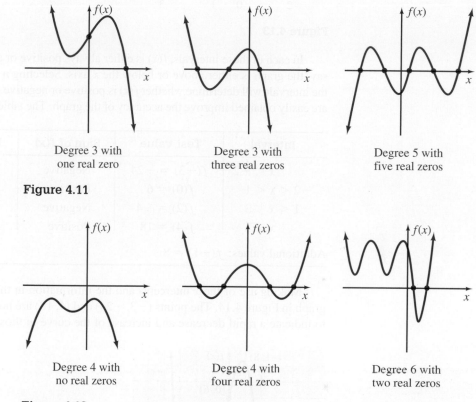

Degree 3 with one real zero

Degree 3 with three real zeros

Degree 5 with five real zeros

Figure 4.11

Degree 4 with no real zeros

Degree 4 with four real zeros

Degree 6 with two real zeros

Figure 4.12

The **turning points** are the places where the function changes either from increasing to decreasing or from decreasing to increasing. Using calculus, we are able to verify that a polynomial function of degree n has at most $n - 1$ turning points. Now let's illustrate how we can use this information, along with some other techniques, to graph polynomial functions that are expressed in factored form.

EXAMPLE 1   Graph $f(x) = (x + 2)(x - 1)(x - 3)$.

Solution

First, let's find the x intercepts (zeros of the function) by setting each factor equal to zero and solving for x:

$$x + 2 = 0 \quad \text{or} \quad x - 1 = 0 \quad \text{or} \quad x - 3 = 0$$
$$x = -2 \qquad\qquad x = 1 \qquad\qquad x = 3$$

Classroom Example
Graph $f(x) = (x + 1) \cdot$
$(x - 4)(x - 2)$.

Thus the points $(-2, 0)$, $(1, 0)$, and $(3, 0)$ are on the graph. Second, the points associated with the x intercepts divide the x axis into four intervals as shown in Figure 4.13.

Figure 4.13

In each of these intervals, $f(x)$ is either always positive or always negative. That is to say, the graph is either above or below the x axis. Selecting a test value for x in each of the intervals will determine whether $f(x)$ is positive or negative. Any additional points that are easily obtained improve the accuracy of the graph. The table summarizes these results.

Interval	Test value	Sign of $f(x)$	Location of graph
$x < -2$	$f(-3) = -24$	Negative	Below x axis
$-2 < x < 1$	$f(0) = 6$	Positive	Above x axis
$1 < x < 3$	$f(2) = -4$	Negative	Below x axis
$x > 3$	$f(4) = 18$	Positive	Above x axis

Additional values: $f(-1) = 8$

Making use of the x intercepts and the information in the table, we can sketch the graph in Figure 4.14. The points $(-3, -24)$ and $(4, 18)$ are not shown, but they are used to indicate a rapid decrease and increase of the curve in those regions.

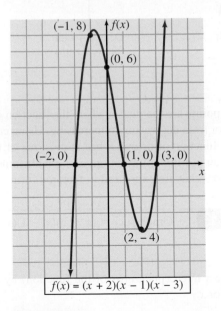

Figure 4.14

Remark: In Figure 4.14, the approximate turning points of the graph are indicated at $(2, -4)$ and $(-1, 8)$. Keep in mind that these are only integral approximations. Using the ZOOM and TRACE features of a graphing calculator, we found that the points $(-0.8, 8.2)$ and $(2.1, -4.1)$ are approximations to the nearest tenth. Again, the tools of calculus are needed to find the exact turning points.

Classroom Example
Graph $f(x) = -x^4 + 2x^3 + 3x^2$.

EXAMPLE 2   Graph $f(x) = -x^4 + 3x^3 - 2x^2$.

Solution

The polynomial can be factored as follows:

$$f(x) = -x^4 + 3x^3 - 2x^2$$
$$= -x^2(x^2 - 3x + 2)$$
$$= -x^2(x - 1)(x - 2)$$

Now we can find the x intercepts.

$$-x^2 = 0 \quad \text{or} \quad x - 1 = 0 \quad \text{or} \quad x - 2 = 0$$
$$x = 0 \quad \text{or} \quad x = 1 \quad \text{or} \quad x = 2$$

The points $(0, 0)$, $(1, 0)$, and $(2, 0)$ are on the graph and divide the x axis into four intervals as shown in Figure 4.15.

Figure 4.15

In the following table, we determine some points and summarize the sign behavior of $f(x)$.

Interval	Test value	Sign of $f(x)$	Location of graph
$x < 0$	$f(-1) = -6$	Negative	Below x axis
$0 < x < 1$	$f\left(\dfrac{1}{2}\right) = -\dfrac{3}{16}$	Negative	Below x axis
$1 < x < 2$	$f\left(\dfrac{3}{2}\right) = \dfrac{9}{16}$	Positive	Above x axis
$x > 2$	$f(3) = -18$	Negative	Below x axis

Making use of the table and the x intercepts, we can draw the graph, as illustrated in Figure 4.16.

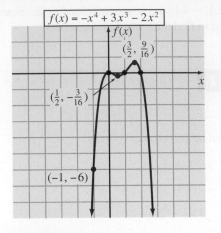

Figure 4.16

EXAMPLE 3   Graph $f(x) = x^3 + 3x^2 - 4$.

Solution

Use the rational root theorem, synthetic division, and the factor theorem to factor the given polynomial as follows.

$$f(x) = x^3 + 3x^2 - 4$$
$$= (x - 1)(x^2 + 4x + 4)$$
$$= (x - 1)(x + 2)^2$$

Now we can find the x intercepts.

$$x - 1 = 0 \qquad \text{or} \qquad (x + 2)^2 = 0$$
$$x = 1 \qquad \text{or} \qquad x = -2$$

The points $(-2, 0)$ and $(1, 0)$ are on the graph and divide the x axis into three intervals as shown in Figure 4.17.

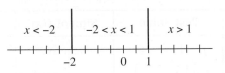

Figure 4.17

In the following table, we determine some points and summarize the sign behavior of $f(x)$.

Interval	Test value	Sign of $f(x)$	Location of graph
$x < -2$	$f(-3) = -4$	Negative	Below x axis
$-2 < x < 1$	$f(0) = -4$	Negative	Below x axis
$x > 1$	$f(2) = 16$	Positive	Above x axis

Additional values: $f(-1) = -2$
$$f(-4) = -20$$

As a result of the table and the x intercepts, we can sketch the graph as shown in Figure 4.18.

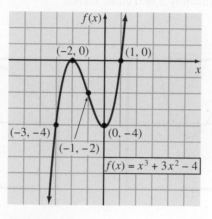

Figure 4.18

Finally, let's use a graphical approach to solve a problem involving a polynomial function.

EXAMPLE 4

Suppose that we have a rectangular piece of cardboard that measures 20 inches by 14 inches. From each corner, a square piece is cut out, and then the flaps are turned up to form an open box (see Figure 4.19). Determine the length of a side of the square pieces to be cut out so that the volume of the box is as large as possible.

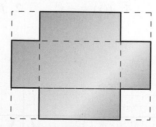

Figure 4.19

Solution

Let x represent the length of a side of the squares to be cut from each corner. Then $20 - 2x$ represents the length of the open box, and $14 - 2x$ represents the width. The volume of a rectangular box is given by the formula $V = lwh$, so the volume of this box can be represented by $V = x(20 - 2x)(14 - 2x)$. Now let $y = V$, and graph the function $y = x(20 - 2x)(14 - 2x)$ as shown in Figure 4.20. For this problem, we are interested only in the part of the graph between $x = 0$ and $x = 7$ because the length of a side of the squares has to be less than 7 inches for a box to be formed. Figure 4.21 gives us a view of that part of the graph. Now we can use the ZOOM and TRACE features to determine that when x equals approximately 2.7, the value of y is a maximum of approximately 339.0. Thus square pieces of length approximately 2.7 inches on a side should be cut from each corner of the rectangular piece of cardboard. The open box formed will have a volume of approximately 339.0 cubic inches.

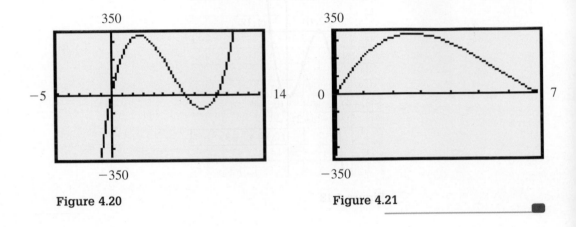

Figure 4.20   Figure 4.21

Concept Quiz 4.4

For Problems 1–4, match the function with its graph.

1. $f(x) = -x^4$ **2.** $f(x) = 2x^3$ **3.** $f(x) = (x + 2)^3$ **4.** $f(x) = x^3 + 2$

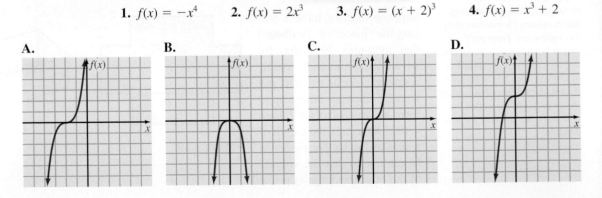

A.   B.   C.   D.

For Problems 5–8, answer true or false.

5. The solutions of a polynomial equation are called the zeros of the polynomial function.

6. The graphs of $f(x) = x^4$ and $f(x) = x^6$ are parabolas.

7. Every polynomial function of odd degree has at least one real number zero.

8. Turning points of polynomial functions are where the function crosses the x axis.

Problem Set 4.4

For Problems 1–22, graph each of the polynomial functions. **(Objective 2)**

1. $f(x) = -(x - 3)^3$

2. $f(x) = (x - 2)^3 + 1$

3. $f(x) = (x + 1)^3$

4. $f(x) = x^3 - 3$

5. $f(x) = (x + 3)^4$

6. $f(x) = x^4 - 2$

7. $f(x) = -(x - 2)^4$

8. $f(x) = (x - 1)^5 + 2$

9. $f(x) = (x + 1)^4 + 3$

10. $f(x) = -x^5$

11. $f(x) = (x - 2)(x + 1)(x + 3)$

12. $f(x) = (x - 1)(x + 1)(x - 3)$

13. $f(x) = x(x + 2)(2 - x)$

14. $f(x) = (x + 4)(x + 1)(1 - x)$

15. $f(x) = -x^2(x - 1)(x + 1)$

16. $f(x) = -x(x + 3)(x - 2)$

17. $f(x) = (2x - 1)(x - 2)(x - 3)$

18. $f(x) = x(x - 2)^2(x - 1)$

19. $f(x) = (x - 2)(x - 1)(x + 1)(x + 2)$

20. $f(x) = (x - 1)^2(x + 2)$

21. $f(x) = x(x - 2)^2(x + 1)$

22. $f(x) = (x + 1)^2(x - 1)^2$

For Problems 23–34, graph each polynomial function by first factoring the given polynomial. You may need to use some factoring techniques from Chapter 0 as well as the rational root theorem and the factor theorem. **(Objective 2)**

23. $f(x) = -x^3 - x^2 + 6x$

24. $f(x) = x^3 + x^2 - 2x$

25. $f(x) = x^4 - 5x^3 + 6x^2$

26. $f(x) = -x^4 - 3x^3 - 2x^2$

27. $f(x) = x^3 + 2x^2 - x - 2$

28. $f(x) = x^3 - x^2 - 4x + 4$

29. $f(x) = x^3 - 8x^2 + 19x - 12$

30. $f(x) = x^3 + 6x^2 + 11x + 6$

31. $f(x) = 2x^3 - 3x^2 - 3x + 2$

32. $f(x) = x^3 + 2x^2 - x - 2$

33. $f(x) = x^4 - 5x^2 + 4$

34. $f(x) = -x^4 + 5x^2 - 4$

For Problems 35–42, (a) find the y intercepts, (b) find the x intercepts, and (c) find the intervals of x where $f(x) > 0$ and those where $f(x) < 0$. *Do not* sketch the graphs. **(Objective 3)**

35. $f(x) = (x + 3)(x - 6)(8 - x)$

36. $f(x) = (x - 5)(x + 4)(x - 3)$

37. $f(x) = (x + 3)^4(x - 1)^3$

38. $f(x) = (x - 4)^2(x + 3)^3$

39. $f(x) = x(x - 6)^2(x + 4)$

40. $f(x) = (x + 2)^2(x - 1)^3(x - 2)$

41. $f(x) = x^2(2 - x)(x + 3)$

42. $f(x) = (x + 2)^5(x - 4)^2$

43. A rectangular piece of cardboard is 13 inches long and 9 inches wide. From each corner, a square piece is cut out, and then the flaps are turned up to form an open box. Use a graphing utility to determine the length (to the nearest tenth) of a side of one of the square pieces so that the volume of the box is as large as possible.

44. A company determines that its weekly profit from manufacturing and selling x units of a certain item is given by $P(x) = -x^3 + 3x^2 + 2880x - 500$. Use a graphing utility to find the weekly production rate that will maximize the profit.

Thoughts Into Words

45. How would you defend the statement that the equation $2x^4 + 3x^3 + x^2 + 5 = 0$ has no positive solutions? Does it have any negative solutions? Defend your answer.

46. How do you know by inspection that the graph of $f(x) = (x + 1)^2(x - 2)^2$ in Figure 4.22 is incorrect?

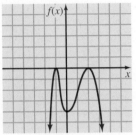

Figure 4.22

Further Investigations

47. A polynomial function with real coefficients is continuous everywhere; that is, its graph has no holes or breaks. This is the basis for the following property: If $f(x)$ is a polynomial with real coefficients, and if $f(a)$ and $f(b)$ are of opposite sign, then there is at least one real zero between a and b. This property, along with our knowledge of polynomial functions, provides the basis for locating and approximating irrational solutions of a polynomial equation.

Consider the equation $x^3 + 2x - 4 = 0$. Applying Descartes' rule of signs, we can determine that this equation has one positive real solution and two nonreal complex solutions. (You may want to confirm this!) The rational root theorem indicates that the only possible rational solutions are 1, 2, and 4. Using a little more compact format for synthetic division, we obtain the following results when testing for 1 and 2 as possible solutions:

	1	0	2	−4
1	1	1	3	−1
2	1	2	6	8

Because $f(1) = -1$ and $f(2) = 8$, there must be an irrational solution between 1 and 2. Furthermore, -1 is closer to 0 than is 8, so our guess is that the solution is closer to 1 than to 2. Let's start looking at 1.0, 1.1, 1.2, and so on, until we can place the solution between two numbers.

	1	0	2	−4	
1.0	1	1	3	−1	A calculator is very
1.1	1	1.1	3.21	−0.469	helpful at this time
1.2	1	1.2	3.44	0.128	

Because $f(1.1) = -0.469$ and $f(1.2) = 0.128$, the irrational solution must be between 1.1 and 1.2. Furthermore, because 0.128 is closer to 0 than is -0.469, our guess is that the solution is closer to

1.2 than to 1.1. Let's start looking at 1.15, 1.16, and so on.

	1	0	2	−4
1.15	1	1.15	3.3225	−0.179
1.16	1	1.16	3.3456	−0.119
1.17	1	1.17	3.3689	−0.058
1.18	1	1.18	3.3924	0.003

Because $f(1.17) = -0.058$ and $f(1.18) = 0.003$, the irrational solution must be between 1.17 and 1.18. Therefore we can use 1.2 as a rational approximation to the nearest tenth.

For each of the following equations, (a) verify that the equation has exactly one irrational solution, and (b) find an approximation, to the nearest tenth, of that solution.

(a) $x^3 + x - 6 = 0$

(b) $x^3 - 6x - 6 = 0$

(c) $x^3 - 27x - 60 = 0$

(d) $x^3 - x^2 - x - 1 = 0$

(e) $x^3 - 2x - 10 = 0$

(f) $x^3 - 5x^2 - 1 = 0$

Graphing Calculator Activities

48. Graph $f(x) = x^3$. Now predict the graphs for $f(x) = x^3 + 2$, $f(x) = -x^3 + 2$, and $f(x) = -x^3 - 2$. Graph these three functions on the same set of axes with the graph of $f(x) = x^3$.

49. Draw a rough sketch of the graphs of the functions $f(x) = x^3 - x^2$, $f(x) = -x^3 + x^2$, and $f(x) = -x^3 - x^2$. Now graph these three functions to check your sketches.

50. Graph $f(x) = x^4 + x^3 + x^2$. What should the graphs of $f(x) = x^4 - x^3 + x^2$ and $f(x) = -x^4 - x^3 - x^2$ look like? Graph them to see if you were right.

51. How should the graphs of $f(x) = x^3$, $f(x) = x^5$, and $f(x) = x^7$ compare? Graph these three functions on the same set of axes.

52. How should the graphs of $f(x) = x^2$, $f(x) = x^4$, and $f(x) = x^6$ compare? Graph these three functions on the same set of axes.

53. For each of the following functions, find the x intercepts, and find the intervals of x where $f(x) > 0$ and those where $f(x) < 0$.

(a) $f(x) = x^3 - 3x^2 - 6x + 8$

(b) $f(x) = x^3 - 8x^2 - x + 8$

(c) $f(x) = x^3 - 7x^2 + 16x - 12$

(d) $f(x) = x^3 - 19x^2 + 90x - 72$

(e) $f(x) = x^4 + 3x^3 - 3x^2 - 11x - 6$

(f) $f(x) = x^4 + 12x^2 - 64$

54. Find the coordinates of the turning points of each of the following graphs. Express x and y values to the nearest integer.

(a) $f(x) = 2x^3 - 3x^2 - 12x + 40$

(b) $f(x) = 2x^3 - 33x^2 + 60x + 1050$

(c) $f(x) = -2x^3 - 9x^2 + 24x + 100$

(d) $f(x) = x^4 - 4x^3 - 2x^2 + 12x + 3$

(e) $f(x) = x^3 - 30x^2 + 288x - 900$

(f) $f(x) = x^5 - 2x^4 - 3x^3 - 2x^2 + x - 1$

55. For each of the following functions, find the x intercepts and find the turning points. Express your answers to the nearest tenth.

(a) $f(x) = x^3 + 2x^2 - 3x + 4$

(b) $f(x) = 42x^3 - x^2 - 246x - 35$

(c) $f(x) = x^4 - 4x^2 - 4$

Answers to the Concept Quiz

1. B **2.** C **3.** A **4.** D **5.** True **6.** False **7.** True **8.** False

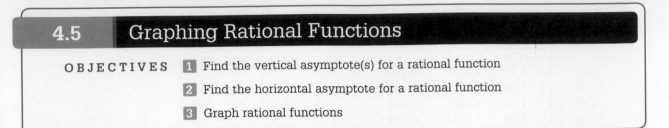

4.5 Graphing Rational Functions

OBJECTIVES

1 Find the vertical asymptote(s) for a rational function

2 Find the horizontal asymptote for a rational function

3 Graph rational functions

Let's begin this section by using a graphing calculator to graph the function $f(x) = \dfrac{x^2}{x^2 - x - 2}$ twice using different boundaries, as indicated in Figures 4.23 and 4.24. It should be evident from the two figures that we really cannot tell what the graph of the function looks like. This happens frequently in graphing rational functions with a graphing calculator. Thus we need to do a careful analysis of rational functions, emphasizing the use of hand-drawn graphs. (By the way, if you are interested in seeing the complete graph of this function, turn to the first example of the next section.)

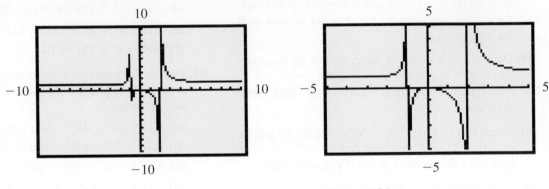

Figure 4.23

Figure 4.24

A function of the form

$$f(x) = \frac{p(x)}{q(x)}, \quad q(x) \neq 0$$

where $p(x)$ and $q(x)$ are polynomials, is called a **rational function**.

The following are examples of rational functions:

$$f(x) = \frac{2}{x - 1} \qquad f(x) = \frac{x}{x - 2}$$

$$f(x) = \frac{x^2}{x^2 - x - 6} \qquad f(x) = \frac{x^3 - 8}{x + 4}$$

In each of these examples, the domain of the rational function is the set of all real numbers except those that make the denominator zero. For example, the domain of $f(x) = \dfrac{2}{x - 1}$ is the set of all real numbers except 1. As we will soon see, these exclusions from the domain are important numbers from a graphing standpoint; they represent breaks in an otherwise continuous curve.

Let's set the stage for graphing rational functions by considering in detail the function $f(x) = \dfrac{1}{x}$. First, note that at $x = 0$ the function is undefined. Second, let's consider a rather extensive table of values to find some number trends and to build a basis for defining the concept of an asymptote.

x	$f(x) = \dfrac{1}{x}$	
1	1	
2	0.5	
10	0.1	These values indicate that the value of $f(x)$ is positive and approaches zero from above as x gets larger and larger
100	0.01	
1000	0.001	
0.5	2	
0.1	10	
0.01	100	These values indicate that $f(x)$ is positive and is getting larger and larger as x approaches zero from the right
0.001	1000	
0.0001	10,000	
-0.5	-2	
-0.1	-10	
-0.01	-100	These values indicate that $f(x)$ is negative and is getting smaller and smaller as x approaches zero from the left
-0.001	-1000	
-0.0001	$-10,000$	
-1	-1	
-2	-0.5	
-10	-0.1	These values indicate that $f(x)$ is negative and approaches zero from below as x gets smaller and smaller without bound
-100	-0.01	
-1000	-0.001	

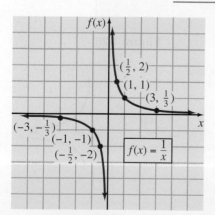

Figure 4.25 shows a sketch of $f(x) = \dfrac{1}{x}$, which is drawn using a few points from this table and the patterns discussed. Note that the graph approaches but does not touch either axis. We say that the y axis (or the $f(x)$ axis) is a **vertical asymptote** and that the x axis is a **horizontal asymptote**.

Remark: We know that the equation $f(x) = \dfrac{1}{x}$ exhibits origin symmetry because $f(-x) = -f(x)$. Thus the graph in Figure 4.25 could have been drawn by first determining the part of the curve in the first quadrant and then reflecting that curve through the origin.

Figure 4.25

Now let's define the concepts of vertical and horizontal asymptotes.

Vertical Asymptote

A line $x = a$ is a vertical asymptote for the graph
of a function f if:

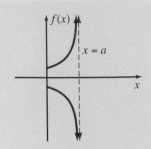

1. $f(x)$ either increases or decreases without
bound as x approaches a from the left, as
in Figure 4.26,

Figure 4.26

or

2. $f(x)$ either increases or decreases without
bound as x approaches a from the right,
as in Figure 4.27.

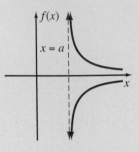

Figure 4.27

Horizontal Asymptote

A line $y = b$ (or $f(x) = b$) is a horizontal asymptote
for the graph of a function f if:

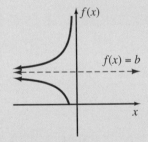

1. $f(x)$ approaches b from above or below as x
gets infinitely small, as in Figure 4.28,

Figure 4.28

or

2. $f(x)$ approaches b from above or below as x
gets infinitely large, as in Figure 4.29.

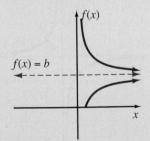

Figure 4.29

Following are some suggestions for graphing rational functions of the type we are considering in this section.

1. Check for y-axis and origin symmetry.
2. For a function in lowest terms, find any vertical asymptote by setting the denominator equal to zero and solving for x.
3. Find any horizontal asymptote by studying the behavior of $f(x)$ as x gets infinitely large or as x gets infinitely small.
4. Study the behavior of the graph when it is close to the asymptotes.
5. Plot as many points as necessary to determine the shape of the graph. The number needed may be affected by whether or not the graph has any kind of symmetry.

Keep these suggestions in mind as you study the following examples.

Classroom Example
Graph $f(x) = \dfrac{3}{x-2}$.

EXAMPLE 1   Graph $f(x) = \dfrac{-2}{x-1}$.

Solution

Because $x = 1$ makes the denominator zero, the line $x = 1$ is a vertical asymptote. We have indicated this with a dashed line in Figure 4.30. Now let's look for a horizontal asymptote by checking some large and some small values of x.

x	$f(x)$
10	$-\dfrac{2}{9}$
100	$-\dfrac{2}{99}$
1000	$-\dfrac{2}{999}$

This table shows that as x gets very large,
the value of $f(x)$ approaches zero from below

x	$f(x)$
-10	$\dfrac{2}{11}$
-100	$\dfrac{2}{101}$
-1000	$\dfrac{2}{1001}$

This table shows that as x gets very small,
the value of $f(x)$ approaches zero from above

Therefore the x axis is a horizontal asymptote.

Finally, let's check the behavior of the graph near the vertical asymptote.

x	f(x)
2	−2
1.5	−4
1.1	−20
1.01	−200
1.001	−2000

x	f(x)
0	2
0.5	4
0.9	20
0.99	200
0.999	2000

As x approaches 1 from the right side, the value of f(x) gets smaller and smaller

As x approaches 1 from the left side, the value of f(x) gets larger and larger

The graph of $f(x) = \dfrac{-2}{x - 1}$ is shown in Figure 4.30.

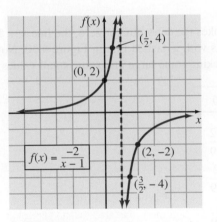

$f(x) = \dfrac{-2}{x - 1}$

$(\frac{1}{2}, 4)$

$(0, 2)$

$(2, -2)$

$(\frac{3}{2}, -4)$

Figure 4.30

Classroom Example

Graph $f(x) = \dfrac{x}{x + 4}$.

EXAMPLE 2   Graph $f(x) = \dfrac{x}{x + 2}$.

Solution

Because $x = -2$ makes the denominator zero, the line $x = -2$ is a vertical asymptote. To study the behavior of $f(x)$ as x gets very large or very small, let's change the form of the rational expression by dividing numerator and denominator by x:

$$f(x) = \frac{x}{x + 2} = \frac{\dfrac{x}{x}}{\dfrac{x + 2}{x}} = \frac{1}{\dfrac{x}{x} + \dfrac{2}{x}} = \frac{1}{1 + \dfrac{2}{x}}$$

Now we can see that as x gets larger and larger, the value of $f(x)$ approaches 1 from below; as x gets smaller and smaller, the value of $f(x)$ approaches 1 from above. (Perhaps you should check these claims by plugging in some values for x.) Thus the line $f(x) = 1$ is a horizontal asymptote. Drawing the asymptotes (dashed lines) and plotting a few points, we complete the graph in Figure 4.31.

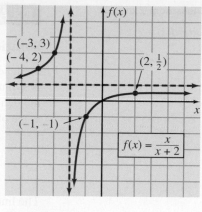

Figure 4.31

In the next two examples, pay special attention to the role of symmetry. It will allow us to direct our efforts toward quadrants I and IV and then to reflect those portions of the curve across the vertical axis to complete the graph.

EXAMPLE 3

Graph $f(x) = \dfrac{2x^2}{x^2 + 4}$.

Solution

First, note that $f(-x) = f(x)$; therefore this graph is symmetric with respect to the vertical axis. Second, the denominator $x^2 + 4$ cannot equal zero for any real number value of x; thus there is no vertical asymptote. Third, dividing both numerator and denominator of the rational expression by x^2 produces

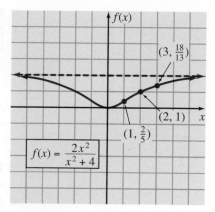

Figure 4.32

$$f(x) = \frac{2x^2}{x^2 + 4} = \frac{\dfrac{2x^2}{x^2}}{\dfrac{x^2 + 4}{x^2}} = \frac{2}{\dfrac{x^2}{x^2} + \dfrac{4}{x^2}} = \frac{2}{1 + \dfrac{4}{x^2}}$$

Now we can see that as x gets larger and larger, the value of $f(x)$ approaches 2 from below. Therefore the line $f(x) = 2$ is a horizontal asymptote. We can plot a few points using positive values for x, sketch this part of the curve, and then reflect across the $f(x)$ axis to obtain the complete graph, as shown in Figure 4.32.

Classroom Example

Graph $f(x) = \dfrac{-2}{x^2 - 16}$.

EXAMPLE 4   Graph $f(x) = \dfrac{3}{x^2 - 4}$.

Solution

First, note that $f(-x) = f(x)$; therefore this graph is symmetric about the y axis. Thus, by setting the denominator equal to zero and solving for x, we obtain

$$x^2 - 4 = 0$$
$$x^2 = 4$$
$$x = \pm 2$$

The lines $x = 2$ and $x = -2$ are vertical asymptotes. Next, we can see that $\dfrac{3}{x^2 - 4}$ approaches zero from above as x gets larger and larger. Finally, we can plot a few points using positive values for x (other than 2), sketch this part of the curve, and then reflect it across the $f(x)$ axis to obtain the complete graph shown in Figure 4.33.

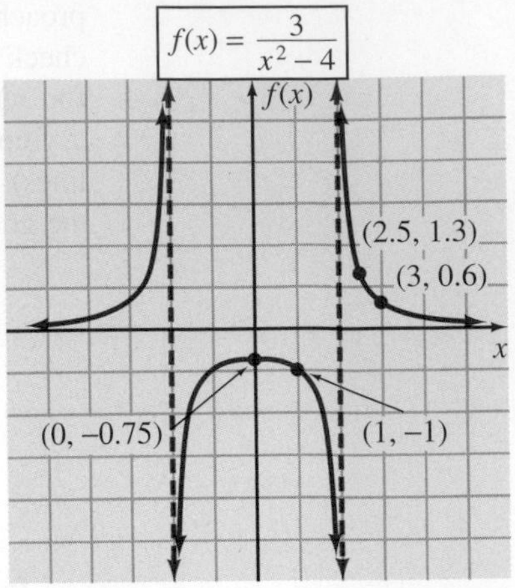

Figure 4.33

Now suppose that we are going to use a graphing utility to obtain a graph of the function $f(x) = \dfrac{4x^2}{x^4 - 16}$. Before we enter this function into a graphing utility, let's analyze what we know about the graph.

1. Because $f(0) = 0$, the origin is a point on the graph.
2. Because $f(-x) = f(x)$, the graph is symmetric with respect to the y axis.
3. By setting the denominator equal to zero and solving for x, we can determine the vertical asymptotes.

$$x^4 - 16 = 0$$
$$(x^2 + 4)(x^2 - 4) = 0$$
$$x^2 + 4 = 0 \quad \text{or} \quad x^2 - 4 = 0$$
$$x^2 = -4 \qquad\qquad x^2 = 4$$
$$x = \pm 2i \qquad\qquad x = \pm 2$$

Remember that we are working with ordered pairs of real numbers. Thus the lines $x = -2$ and $x = 2$ are vertical asymptotes.

4. Divide both the numerator and the denominator of the rational expression by x^4 to produce

$$\frac{4x^2}{x^4 - 16} = \frac{\dfrac{4x^2}{x^4}}{\dfrac{x^4 - 16}{x^4}} = \frac{\dfrac{4}{x^2}}{1 - \dfrac{16}{x^4}}$$

From the last expression, we see that as $|x|$ gets larger and larger, the value of $f(x)$ approaches zero from above. Therefore the x axis is a horizontal asymptote.

Now let's enter the function into a graphing calculator and set the boundaries so that we show the behavior of the function close to the asymptotes. Note that the graph shown in Figure 4.34 is consistent with all of the information that we determined before using the graphing calculator. In other words, our knowledge of graphing techniques enhances our use of a graphing utility.

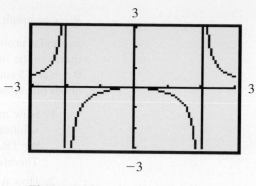

Figure 4.34

Back in Section 1.4 we solved problems of the following type: How much pure alcohol should be added to 6 liters of a 40% alcohol solution to raise it to a 60% alcohol solution? The answer of 3 liters can be found by solving the following equation, in which x represents the amount of pure alcohol to be added:

Now let's consider this problem in a more general setting by writing a function in which x represents the amount of pure alcohol to be added, and y represents the concentration of pure alcohol in the final solution.

$$0.40(6) + x = y(6 + x)$$
$$2.4 + x = y(6 + x)$$
$$\frac{2.4 + x}{6 + x} = y$$

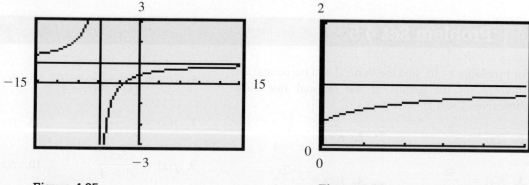

Figure 4.35

Figure 4.36

We can graph the rational function $y = \dfrac{2.4 + x}{6 + x}$ as shown in Figure 4.35. For this particular problem, x is nonnegative, so we are interested only in the part of the graph that is in the first quadrant. We change the boundaries of the viewing rectangle so that $0 \leq x \leq 15$ and $0 \leq y \leq 2$ to obtain Figure 4.36. Now we are ready to answer questions about this situation.

1. How much pure alcohol needs to be added to raise the 40% solution to a 60% solution? [*Hint*: We are looking for the value of x when y is 0.60.] *Answer*: Using the TRACE feature of the graphing utility, we find that when $y = 0.60$, $x = 3$. Therefore 3 liters of pure alcohol need to be added.

2. How much pure alcohol needs to be added to raise the 40% solution to a 70% solution? *Answer*: Using the TRACE feature of the graphing utility, we find that when $y = 0.70$, $x = 6$. Therefore 6 liters of pure alcohol need to be added.

3. What concentration in percent of alcohol do we obtain if we add 9 liters of pure alcohol to 6 liters of a 40% solution? *Answer*: Using the TRACE feature of the graphing utility, we find that when $x = 9$, $y = 0.76$. Therefore adding 9 liters of pure alcohol will give us a 76% alcohol solution.

Concept Quiz 4.5

For Problems 1–5, answer true or false.

1. The domain of $f(x) = \dfrac{x - 4}{2x + 1}$ is all real numbers except 4 and $-\dfrac{1}{2}$.

2. If the graph of a rational function has an asymptote at $x = -3$, then -3 is not in the domain of the function.

3. Horizontal asymptotes can be found by setting the numerator of the function equal to 0.

4. If the numerator of a rational function is a constant, then the horizontal asymptote of the graph of the function is always the line $f(x) = 0$.

5. The graph of a rational function always has a vertical asymptote.

Problem Set 4.5

For Problems 1–10, find the vertical and horizontal asymptotes for the graphs of the rational functions. (Objectives 1 and 2)

1. $f(x) = \dfrac{1}{x + 3}$

2. $f(x) = \dfrac{1}{x - 4}$

3. $f(x) = \dfrac{4x}{x - 1}$

4. $f(x) = \dfrac{-2x}{x + 5}$

5. $f(x) = \dfrac{2}{(x + 3)(x - 4)}$

6. $f(x) = \dfrac{6}{x(x - 1)}$

7. $f(x) = \dfrac{x}{x^2 - 9}$

8. $f(x) = \dfrac{3x}{x^2 - x + 2}$

9. $f(x) = \dfrac{5x^2}{x^2 + 4}$

10. $f(x) = \dfrac{-2x^2}{x^2 + 1}$

For Problems 11–32, graph each of the rational functions. (Objective 3)

11. $f(x) = \dfrac{1}{x^2}$

12. $f(x) = \dfrac{-1}{x}$

13. $f(x) = \dfrac{-1}{x - 3}$

14. $f(x) = \dfrac{3}{x + 1}$

15. $f(x) = \dfrac{-3}{(x + 2)^2}$

16. $f(x) = \dfrac{2}{(x - 1)^2}$

17. $f(x) = \dfrac{2x}{x - 1}$

18. $f(x) = \dfrac{x}{x - 3}$

19. $f(x) = \dfrac{-x}{x + 1}$

20. $f(x) = \dfrac{-3x}{x + 2}$

21. $f(x) = \dfrac{-2}{x^2 - 4}$

22. $f(x) = \dfrac{1}{x^2 - 1}$

23. $f(x) = \dfrac{3}{(x + 2)(x - 4)}$

24. $f(x) = \dfrac{-2}{(x + 1)(x - 2)}$

25. $f(x) = \dfrac{-1}{x^2 + x - 6}$

26. $f(x) = \dfrac{2}{x^2 + x - 2}$

27. $f(x) = \dfrac{2x - 1}{x}$

28. $f(x) = \dfrac{x + 2}{x}$

29. $f(x) = \dfrac{4x^2}{x^2 + 1}$

30. $f(x) = \dfrac{4}{x^2 + 2}$

31. $f(x) = \dfrac{x^2 - 4}{x^2}$

32. $f(x) = \dfrac{2x^4}{x^4 + 1}$

Thoughts Into Words

33. How would you explain the concept of an asymptote to an elementary algebra student?

34. Give a step-by-step description of how you would go about graphing $f(x) = \dfrac{-2}{x^2 - 9}$.

Further Investigations

35. The rational function $f(x) = \dfrac{(x - 2)(x + 3)}{x - 2}$ has a domain of all real numbers except 2 and can be simplified to $f(x) = x + 3$. Thus its graph is a straight line with a hole at (2, 5). Graph each of the following functions.

(a) $f(x) = \dfrac{(x + 4)(x - 1)}{x + 4}$

(b) $f(x) = \dfrac{x^2 - 5x + 6}{x - 2}$

(c) $f(x) = \dfrac{x - 1}{x^2 - 1}$

(d) $f(x) = \dfrac{x + 2}{x^2 + 6x + 8}$

36. Graph the function $f(x) = x + 2 + \dfrac{3}{x - 2}$. It may be necessary to plot a rather large number of points. Also, defend the statement that $f(x) = x + 2$ is an **oblique asymptote**.

Graphing Calculator Activities

37. Use a graphing calculator to check your graphs for Problem 35. What feature of the graphs does not show up on the calculator?

38. Each of the following graphs is a transformation of $f(x) = \dfrac{1}{x}$. First predict the general shape and location of the graph, and then check your prediction with a graphing calculator.

(a) $f(x) = \dfrac{1}{x} - 2$ **(b)** $f(x) = \dfrac{1}{x + 3}$

(c) $f(x) = -\dfrac{1}{x}$ **(d)** $f(x) = \dfrac{1}{x - 2} + 3$

(e) $f(x) = \dfrac{2x + 1}{x}$

39. Graph $f(x) = \dfrac{1}{x^2}$. How should the graph of

$f(x) = \dfrac{1}{(x - 4)^2}$, $f(x) = \dfrac{1 + 3x^2}{x^2}$, and

$f(x) = -\dfrac{1}{x^2}$ compare to the graph of $f(x) = \dfrac{1}{x^2}$?

Graph the three functions on the same set of axes with the graph of $f(x) = \dfrac{1}{x^2}$.

40. Graph $f(x) = \dfrac{1}{x^3}$. How should the graphs of

$f(x) = \dfrac{2x^3 + 1}{x^3}$, $f(x) = \dfrac{1}{(x + 2)^3}$, and $f(x) = \dfrac{-1}{x^3}$

compare to the graph of $f(x) = \dfrac{1}{x^3}$? Graph the

three functions on the same set of axes with the

graph of $f(x) = \dfrac{1}{x^3}$.

41. Use a graphing calculator to check your graphs for Problems 29–32.

42. Suppose that x ounces of pure acid have been added to 14 ounces of a 15% acid solution.
   (a) Set up the rational expression that represents the concentration of pure acid in the final solution.
   (b) Graph the rational function that displays the concentration.
   (c) How many ounces of pure acid need to be added to the 14 ounces of a 15% solution to raise it to a 40.5% solution? Check your answer.
   (d) How many ounces of pure acid need to be added to the 14 ounces of a 15% solution to raise it to a 50% solution? Check your answer.
   (e) What concentration of acid do we obtain if we add 12 ounces of pure acid to the 14 ounces of a 15% solution? Check your answer.

43. Solve the following problem both algebraically and graphically: One solution contains 50% alcohol, and another solution contains 80% alcohol. How many liters of each solution should be mixed to produce 10.5 liters of a 70% alcohol solution? Check your answer.

44. Graph each of the following functions. Be sure that you get a complete graph for each one. Sketch each graph on a sheet of paper, and keep them all handy as you study the next section.

(a) $f(x) = \dfrac{x^2}{x^2 - x - 2}$ **(b)** $f(x) = \dfrac{x}{x^2 - 4}$

(c) $f(x) = \dfrac{3x}{x^2 + 1}$ **(d)** $f(x) = \dfrac{x^2 - 1}{x - 2}$

Answers to the Concept Quiz

1. False   **2.** True   **3.** False   **4.** True   **5.** False

4.6   More on Graphing Rational Functions

OBJECTIVES

1. Find the equation for an oblique asymptote of a rational function

2. Graph rational functions with vertical, horizontal, or oblique asymptotes

The rational functions that we studied in the previous section were pretty straightforward. In fact, once we established the vertical and horizontal asymptotes, a little bit of point plotting usually determined the graph fairly easily. Such is not always the case with rational functions. In this section, we want to investigate some rational functions that behave a little differently.

For rational functions, vertical asymptotes occur at values of x when the denominator is zero, so no points of a graph can be on a vertical asymptote. However, recall that horizontal asymptotes are created by the behavior of $f(x)$ as x gets infinitely large or infinitely small. This does not restrict the possibility that for some values of x, points of the graph will be on the horizontal asymptote. Let's consider some examples.

Classroom Example

Graph $f(x) = \dfrac{-x^2}{x^2 + x - 6}$.

EXAMPLE 1   Graph $f(x) = \dfrac{x^2}{x^2 - x - 2}$.

Solution

First, let's identify the vertical asymptotes by setting the denominator equal to zero and solving for x:

$$x^2 - x - 2 = 0$$
$$(x - 2)(x + 1) = 0$$
$$x - 2 = 0 \quad \text{or} \quad x + 1 = 0$$
$$x = 2 \quad \text{or} \quad x = -1$$

Thus the lines $x = 2$ and $x = -1$ are vertical asymptotes. Next, we can divide both the numerator and the denominator of the rational expression by x^2.

$$f(x) = \frac{x^2}{x^2 - x - 2} = \frac{\dfrac{x^2}{x^2}}{\dfrac{x^2 - x - 2}{x^2}} = \frac{1}{1 - \dfrac{1}{x} - \dfrac{2}{x^2}}$$

Now we can see that as x gets larger and larger, the value of $f(x)$ approaches 1 from above. Thus the line $f(x) = 1$ is a horizontal asymptote. To determine whether any points of the graph are *on* the horizontal asymptote, we can see whether the equation

$$\frac{x^2}{x^2 - x - 2} = 1$$

has any solutions.

$$\frac{x^2}{x^2 - x - 2} = 1$$

$$x^2 = x^2 - x - 2$$

$$0 = -x - 2$$

$$x = -2$$

Therefore the point $(-2, 1)$ is on the graph. Now, by drawing the asymptotes, plotting a few points (including $(-2, 1)$), and studying the behavior of the function close to the asymptotes, we can sketch the curve shown in Figure 4.37.

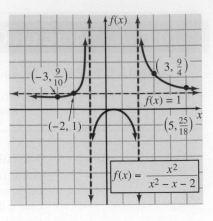

Figure 4.37

Classroom Example
Graph $f(x) = \dfrac{3x}{x^2 - 9}$.

EXAMPLE 2   Graph $f(x) = \dfrac{x}{x^2 - 4}$.

Solution

First, note that $f(-x) = -f(x)$; therefore this graph is symmetric with respect to the origin. Second, let's identify the vertical asymptotes:

$$x^2 - 4 = 0$$

$$x^2 = 4$$

$$x = \pm 2$$

Thus the lines $x = -2$ and $x = 2$ are vertical asymptotes. Next, by dividing the numerator and the denominator of the rational expression by x^2, we obtain

$$f(x) = \frac{x}{x^2 - 4} = \frac{\dfrac{x}{x^2}}{\dfrac{x^2 - 4}{x^2}} = \frac{\dfrac{1}{x}}{1 - \dfrac{4}{x^2}}$$

From this form, we can see that as x gets larger and larger, the value of $f(x)$ approaches zero from above. Therefore the x axis is a horizontal asymptote. Because $f(0) = 0$, we know that the origin is a point of the graph. Finally, by concentrating our point plotting on positive values of x, we can sketch the portion of the curve to the right of the vertical axis, and then use the fact that the graph is symmetric with respect to the origin to complete the graph. Figure 4.38 shows the completed graph.

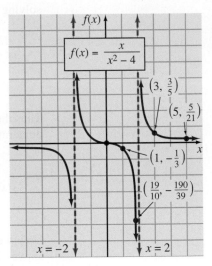

Figure 4.38

Classroom Example
Graph $f(x) = \dfrac{-3x}{x^2 + 1}$.

EXAMPLE 3   Graph $f(x) = \dfrac{3x}{x^2 + 1}$.

Solution

First, observe that $f(-x) = -f(x)$; therefore this graph is symmetric with respect to the origin. Second, because $x^2 + 1$ is a positive number for all real number values of x, there are no vertical asymptotes for this graph. Next, by dividing the numerator and the denominator of the rational expression by x^2, we obtain

$$f(x) = \frac{3x}{x^2 + 1} = \frac{\dfrac{3x}{x^2}}{\dfrac{x^2 + 1}{x^2}} = \frac{\dfrac{3}{x}}{1 + \dfrac{1}{x^2}}$$

From this form, we see that as x gets larger and larger, the value of $f(x)$ approaches zero from above. Thus the x axis is a horizontal asymptote. Because $f(0) = 0$, the origin is a point of the graph. Finally, by concentrating our point plotting on positive values of x, we can sketch the portion of the curve to the right of the vertical axis, and then use origin symmetry to complete the graph, as shown in Figure 4.39.

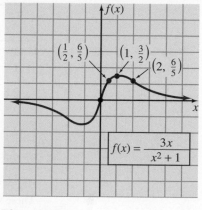

Figure 4.39

Oblique Asymptotes

Thus far we have restricted our study of rational functions to those in which the degree of the numerator is less than or equal to the degree of the denominator. As our final examples of graphing rational functions, we will consider functions in which the degree of the numerator is one greater than the degree of the denominator.

Classroom Example
Graph $f(x) = \dfrac{x^2 + 3}{x + 1}$.

EXAMPLE 4   Graph $f(x) = \dfrac{x^2 - 1}{x - 2}$.

Solution

First, let's observe that $x = 2$ is a vertical asymptote. Second, because the degree of the numerator is greater than the degree of the denominator, we can change the form of the rational expression by division. We use synthetic division.

$$\begin{array}{r} 2)\overline{1 \quad 0 \quad -1} \\ \underline{2 \quad 4} \\ 1 \quad 2 \quad 3 \end{array}$$

Therefore the original function can be rewritten as

$$f(x) = \frac{x^2 - 1}{x - 2} = x + 2 + \frac{3}{x - 2}$$

Now, for very large values of $|x|$, the fraction $\dfrac{3}{x-2}$ is close to zero. Therefore, as $|x|$ gets larger and larger, the graph of $f(x) = x + 2 + \dfrac{3}{x-2}$ gets closer and closer to the line $f(x) = x + 2$. We call this line an **oblique asymptote** and indicate it with a dashed line in Figure 4.40. Finally, because this is a new situation, it may be necessary to plot a large number of points on both sides of the vertical asymptote, so let's make an extensive table of values. The graph of the function is shown in Figure 4.40.

x	$f(x) = \dfrac{x^2 - 1}{x - 2}$
4	7.5
3	8
2.8	8.55
2.5	10.5
2.3	14.3
2.2	19.2
2.1	34.1

x	$f(x) = \dfrac{x^2 - 1}{x - 2}$
-2	-0.75
0	0.5
1	0
1.5	-2.5
1.7	-6.3
1.8	-11.6
1.9	-26.1

These values indicate the behavior of $f(x)$ to the right of the vertical asymptote $x = 2$

These values indicate the behavior of $f(x)$ to the left of the vertical asymptote $x = 2$

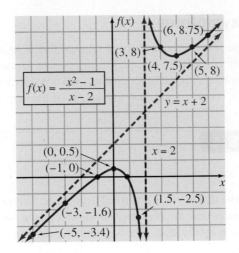

Figure 4.40

If the degree of the numerator of a rational function is *exactly one more* than the degree of its denominator, then the graph of the function has an oblique asymptote. (If the graph is a line, as is the case with $f(x) = \dfrac{(x - 2)(x + 1)}{x - 2}$, then we consider it to be its own asymptote.) As in Example 4, we find the equation of the oblique asymptote by changing the form of the function using long division. Let's consider another example.

Classroom Example
Graph $f(x) = \dfrac{x^2 + 5x - 6}{x + 2}$.

EXAMPLE 5

Graph $f(x) = \dfrac{x^2 - x - 2}{x - 1}$.

Solution

From the given form of the function, we see that $x = 1$ is a vertical asymptote. Then, by factoring the numerator, we can change the form to

$$f(x) = \frac{(x - 2)(x + 1)}{x - 1}$$

which indicates x intercepts of 2 and -1. Then, by long division, we can change the original form of the function to

$$f(x) = x - \frac{2}{x - 1}$$

which indicates an oblique asymptote $f(x) = x$. Finally, by plotting a few additional points, we can determine the graph as shown in Figure 4.41.

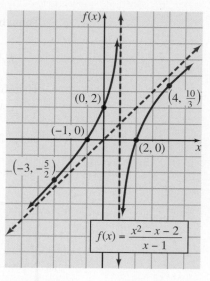

Figure 4.41

Finally, let's combine our knowledge of rational functions with the use of a graphing utility to obtain the graph of a fairly complex rational function.

Classroom Example
Graph
$f(x) = \dfrac{2x^3 - 11x^2 + 12x + 9}{x^2 - 4}$.

EXAMPLE 6

Graph the rational function $f(x) = \dfrac{x^3 - 2x^2 - x - 1}{x^2 - 36}$ using a graphing utility.

Solution

Before entering this function into a graphing utility, let's analyze what we know about the graph.

1. Because $f(0) = \dfrac{1}{36}$, the point $\left(0, \dfrac{1}{36}\right)$ is on the graph.

2. Because $f(-x) \neq f(x)$ and $f(-x) \neq -f(x)$, there is no symmetry with respect to the origin or the y axis.

3. The denominator is zero at $x = \pm 6$. Thus the lines $x = 6$ and $x = -6$ are vertical asymptotes.

4. Let's change the form of the rational expression by division.

$$\begin{array}{r} x - 2 \\ x^2 - 36\overline{)x^3 - 2x^2 - x - 1} \\ \underline{x^3 - 36x} \\ -2x^2 + 35x - 1 \\ \underline{-2x^2 + 72} \\ 35x - 73 \end{array}$$

Thus the original function can be rewritten as

$$f(x) = x - 2 + \frac{35x - 73}{x^2 - 36}$$

Therefore, the line $y = x - 2$ is an oblique asymptote. Now let $Y_1 = x - 2$ and $Y_2 = \dfrac{x^3 - 2x^2 - x - 1}{x^2 - 36}$, and let's use a viewing rectangle in which $-15 \le x \le 15$ and $-30 \le y \le 30$ (Figure 4.42).

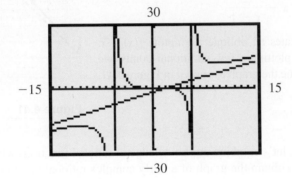

Figure 4.42

Note that the graph in Figure 4.42 is consistent with the information we had before we used the graphing calculator. Keep in mind that the oblique line and the two vertical lines are asymptotes and not part of the graph. Furthermore, the graph may appear to be symmetric about the origin, but remember that the test for origin symmetry failed. For example, the point $\left(0, \dfrac{1}{36}\right)$ is on the graph, but the point $\left(0, -\dfrac{1}{36}\right)$ is not on the graph. Also note that the curve does intersect the oblique asymptote. We can use the ZOOM and TRACE features of the graphing calculator to approximate this point of intersection, or we can use an algebraic approach as follows: Because $y = \dfrac{x^3 - 2x^2 - x - 1}{x^2 - 36}$ and $y = x - 2$, we can equate the two expressions for y and solve the resulting equation for x.

$$\frac{x^3 - 2x^2 - x - 1}{x^2 - 36} = x - 2$$

$$x^3 - 2x^2 - x - 1 = (x - 2)(x^2 - 36)$$

$$x^3 - 2x^2 - x - 1 = x^3 - 2x^2 - 36x + 72$$

$$35x = 73$$

$$x = \frac{73}{35}$$

If $x = \dfrac{73}{35}$, then $y = x - 2 = \dfrac{73}{35} - 2 = \dfrac{3}{35}$. The point of intersection of the curve and

the oblique asymptote is $\left(\dfrac{73}{35}, \dfrac{3}{35}\right)$.

Concept Quiz 4.6

For Problems 1–6, answer true or false.

1. Every graph of a rational function has a horizontal asymptote.
2. For rational functions in which the degree of the numerator is one more than the degree of the denominator, the graph of the function will have an oblique asymptote.
3. The graph of a rational function can cross a horizontal asymptote.
4. The graph of rational function can cross a vertical asymptote.
5. If the graph of a rational function is symmetric with respect to the origin, then the line $f(x) = 0$ is a vertical asymptote.
6. For rational functions in which the degree of the numerator is less than or equal to the degree of the denominator, the graph of the function will have a horizontal asymptote.

Problem Set 4.6

For Problems 1–6, write the equation for the oblique asymptote for the graphs of the following rational functions. (Objective 1)

1. $f(x) = \dfrac{x^2 + 4}{x + 1}$

2. $f(x) = \dfrac{x^2 + 5}{x - 3}$

3. $f(x) = \dfrac{x^2 + 4x - 6}{x + 2}$

4. $f(x) = \dfrac{x^2 - x + 5}{x - 3}$

5. $f(x) = \dfrac{3x^2 + x + 2}{x + 2}$

6. $f(x) = \dfrac{x^2 + 4x - 1}{x}$

For Problems 7–26, graph each rational function. Check first for symmetry, and identify the asymptotes. (Objective 2)

7. $f(x) = \dfrac{x^2}{x^2 + x - 2}$

8. $f(x) = \dfrac{x^2}{x^2 + 2x - 3}$

9. $f(x) = \dfrac{2x^2}{x^2 - 2x - 8}$

10. $f(x) = \dfrac{-x^2}{x^2 + 3x - 4}$

11. $f(x) = \dfrac{-x}{x^2 - 1}$

12. $f(x) = \dfrac{2x}{x^2 - 9}$

13. $f(x) = \dfrac{x}{x^2 + x - 6}$

14. $f(x) = \dfrac{-x}{x^2 - 2x - 8}$

15. $f(x) = \dfrac{x^2}{x^2 - 4x + 3}$

16. $f(x) = \dfrac{1}{x^3 + x^2 - 6x}$

17. $f(x) = \dfrac{x}{x^2 + 2}$

18. $f(x) = \dfrac{6x}{x^2 + 1}$

19. $f(x) = \dfrac{-4x}{x^2 + 1}$

20. $f(x) = \dfrac{-5x}{x^2 + 2}$

21. $f(x) = \dfrac{x^2 + 2}{x - 1}$

22. $f(x) = \dfrac{x^2 - 3}{x + 1}$

23. $f(x) = \dfrac{x^2 - x - 6}{x + 1}$

24. $f(x) = \dfrac{x^2 + 4}{x + 2}$

25. $f(x) = \dfrac{x^2 + 1}{1 - x}$

26. $f(x) = \dfrac{x^3 + 8}{x^2}$

Thoughts Into Words

27. Explain the concept of an oblique asymptote.

28. Explain why it is possible for curves to intersect horizontal and oblique asymptotes but not to intersect vertical asymptotes.

29. Give a step-by-step description of how you would go about graphing $f(x) = \dfrac{x^2 - x - 12}{x - 2}$.

30. Your friend is having difficulty finding the point of intersection of a curve and the oblique asymptote. How can you help?

Graphing Calculator Activities

31. First check for symmetry and identify the asymptotes for the graphs of the following rational functions. Then use your graphing utility to graph each function.

(a) $f(x) = \dfrac{4x^2}{x^2 + x - 2}$

(b) $f(x) = \dfrac{-2x}{x^2 - 5x - 6}$

(c) $f(x) = \dfrac{x^2}{x^2 - 9}$

(d) $f(x) = \dfrac{x^2 - 4}{x^2 - 9}$

(e) $f(x) = \dfrac{x^2 - 9}{x^2 - 4}$

(f) $f(x) = \dfrac{x^2 + 2x + 1}{x^2 - 5x + 6}$

(c) $f(x) = \dfrac{2x^2 + x + 1}{x + 1}$

(d) $f(x) = \dfrac{x^2 + 4}{x - 3}$

(e) $f(x) = \dfrac{3x^2 - x - 2}{x - 2}$

(f) $f(x) = \dfrac{4x^2 + x + 1}{x + 1}$

(g) $f(x) = \dfrac{x^3 + x^2 - x - 1}{x^2 + 2x + 3}$

(h) $f(x) = \dfrac{x^3 + 2x^2 + x - 3}{x^2 - 4}$

32. For each of the following rational functions, first determine and graph any oblique asymptotes. Then, on the same set of axes, graph the function.

(a) $f(x) = \dfrac{x^2 - 1}{x - 2}$

(b) $f(x) = \dfrac{x^2 + 1}{x + 2}$

Answers to the Concept Quiz

1. False **2.** True **3.** True **4.** False **5.** False **6.** True

OBJECTIVE	SUMMARY	EXAMPLE
Division algorithm for polynomials (Section 4.1/Objective 1)	The division algorithm for polynomials states that if $f(x)$ and $g(x)$ are polynomials and $g(x) \neq 0$, then there exist unique polynomials $q(x)$ and $r(x)$ such that $f(x) = g(x)q(x) + r(x)$, where $r(x) = 0$ or the degree of $r(x)$ is less than the degree of $g(x)$.	Given $f(x) = 6x^2 + 5x - 4$ and $g(x) = 2x + 1$, find the unique quotient and remainder polynomials. Solution Performing long division of polynomials yields a quotient of $3x + 1$ and a remainder of -5. Hence $$6x^2 + 5x - 4 = (2x + 1)(3x + 1) - 5$$
Use synthetic division to determine the quotient and remainder for division problems. (Section 4.1/Objective 2)	If the divisor is of the form $x - c$, where c is a constant, then the typical long division format for dividing polynomials can be simplified to a process called synthetic division.	Use synthetic division to find the quotient and remainder for $$(2x^3 - 3x - 6) \div (x - 2)$$ Solution In the division form use a placeholder for the missing x^2 term. $$2\overline{)\begin{array}{rrrr} 2 & 0 & -3 & -6 \\ & 4 & 8 & 10 \\ \hline 2 & 4 & 5 & 4 \end{array}}$$ Thus the quotient is $2x^2 + 4x + 5$ and the remainder is 4.
Use the remainder theorem to evaluate a function for a given value. (Section 4.2/Objective 1)	The remainder theorem states that if a polynomial $f(x)$ is divided by $x - c$, then the remainder is equal to $f(c)$. Thus a polynomial can be evaluated for a given number by either direct substitution or by using synthetic division.	If $f(x) = 2x^3 + x^2 - 3x - 7$, find $f(-3)$ by using synthetic division and the remainder theorem. Solution $$-3\overline{)\begin{array}{rrrr} 2 & 1 & -3 & -7 \\ & -6 & 15 & -36 \\ \hline 2 & -5 & 12 & -43 \end{array}}$$ The remainder is -43, thus $$f(-3) = -43.$$

(continued)

OBJECTIVE	SUMMARY	EXAMPLE
Determine if an expression is a factor of a given polynomial. (Section 4.2/Objective 2)	The factor theorem states that a polynomial $f(x)$ has a factor $x - c$ if and only if $f(c) = 0$.	Is $x + 1$ a factor of $x^3 + 3x^2 - 2x + 1$? **Solution** Use synthetic division to determine the remainder. $$\begin{array}{r} -1)\overline{1 \quad 3 \quad -2 \quad 1} \\ -1 \quad -2 \quad 4 \\ \hline 1 \quad 2 \quad -4 \quad 5 \end{array}$$ Because the remainder does not equal 0, $x + 1$ is not a factor.
Understand the concept of the multiplicity of roots. (Section 4.3/Objective 1)	A polynomial equation of degree n has n solutions, where any solutions of multiplicity p is counted p times.	State the solution set for the polynomial equation $$\begin{aligned} f(x) &= x^4 + 6x^3 + 8x^2 - 6x - 9 \\ &= (x + 1)(x - 1)(x + 3)(x + 3) \end{aligned}$$ **Solution** The polynomial is fourth degree, so there are four solutions. The solutions are -1, 1, -3, and -3. So we would say the equation has solutions of -1 and 1 and a solution of -3 with a multiplicity of 2.
Use Descartes' rule of signs to determine the nature of the solutions of a polynomial equation. (Section 4.3/Objective 3)	Descartes' rule of signs: Let $a_n x^n + a_{n-1}x^{n-1} + \cdots + a_1 x + a_0 = 0$ be a polynomial with real coefficients. **(a)** The number of *positive real solutions* is either equal to the number of sign variations or is less then the number of sign variations by a positive even integer. **(b)** The number of *negative real solutions* either is equal to the number of sign variations in $a_n(-x)^n + a_{n-1}(-x)^{n-1} + \cdots + a_1(-x) + a_0$ or is less than the number of sign variations by a positive even integer.	Use Descartes' rule of signs to determine the possibilities for the nature of the solutions of $2x^4 + 3x^3 - 6x^2 + 1 = 0$. **Solution** The fact that there are two variations in sign implies that there are two or zero positive solutions. Replacing x with $-x$ produces $2x^4 - 3x^3 - 6x^2 + 1 = 0$, which has two variations in sign. Thus there are two or zero negative solutions. **Conclusion:** The given equation has either two positive and two negative solutions, two positive and two nonreal complex solutions, two negative and two nonreal complex solutions, or four nonreal complex solutions.

OBJECTIVE	SUMMARY	EXAMPLE
Solve polynomial equations using the rational root theorem and the factor theorem. **(Section 4.3/Objective 2)**	The following concepts and properties provide a basis for solving polynomial equations. **1.** Synthetic division. **2.** The factor theorem. **3.** Using the degree of the polynomial to determine the number of roots. **4.** The rational root theorem: Consider the polynomial equation $a_n x^n + a_{n-1} x^{n-1} + \cdots + a_1 x + a_0 = 0$ where the coefficients are *integers*. If the rational number $\dfrac{c}{d}$, reduced to lowest terms, is a solution of the equation, then c is a factor of the constant term a_0, and d is a factor of the leading coefficient a_n. **5.** Nonreal complex solutions of polynomial equations with real coefficients, if they exist, must occur in conjugate pairs. **6.** Descartes' rule of signs.	Solve $x^3 + 3x^2 - 2x - 8 = 0$. **Solution** The degree of the polynomial is 3, hence there are 3 roots. By the rational root theorem the potential rational number solutions are ± 1, ± 2, ± 4, or ± 8. Using synthetic division it can be determined that -2 is a root. $$-2\overline{)\begin{array}{rrrr} 1 & 3 & -2 & -8 \\ & -2 & -2 & 8 \\ \hline 1 & 1 & -4 & 0 \end{array}}$$ Thus the equation factors to $(x + 2)(x^2 + x - 4) = 0$. Now apply the quadratic formula to solve $x^2 + x - 4 = 0$ which yields the solutions $\dfrac{-1 + \sqrt{17}}{2}$ and $\dfrac{-1 - \sqrt{17}}{2}$. Thus the solution set is $$\left\{ -2, \frac{-1 + \sqrt{17}}{2}, \frac{-1 - \sqrt{17}}{2} \right\}$$
Know the patterns for the graphs of $f(x) = ax^n$. **(Section 4.4/Objective 1)**	The graph of $f(x) = ax^1$ is a straight line through the origin with a slope of a. The graph of $f(x) = ax^2$ is a parabola symmetric with respect to the y axis. The graph of $f(x) = ax^3$ for $a = 1$ is shown on page 393. The graph of $f(x) = ax^4$ is not a parabola but resembles the basic parabola, except that it is flatter at the bottom and steeper on the sides. There are two general patterns (1) for odd values of n greater than 1 and (2) for even values of n.	Graph $f(x) = -\dfrac{1}{2}x^3$. **Solution** The graph has the basic pattern of $f(x) = ax^3$. Because $a = -\dfrac{1}{2}$, the basic graph is reflected across the x axis and is not as steep.

(continued)

OBJECTIVE	SUMMARY	EXAMPLE
Graph polynomial functions. (Section 4.4/Objective 2)	The following steps may be used to graph a polynomial function that is expressed in factored form: 1. Find the x intercepts, which are also called the zeros of the polynomial function. 2. Use a test value in each interval determined by the x intercepts to find out if the function is positive or negative over that interval. 3. Plot any additional points that are needed to determine the graph.	Graph $f(x) = x^4 + x^3 - x^2 - x$. **Solution** The factored form is $f(x) = x(x + 1)^2(x - 1)$. The zeros are -1, 0, and 1. For the intervals $(-\infty, -1)$, $(-1, 0)$, and $(1, \infty)$, the function is positive. For the interval $(0, 1)$ the function is negative.
Find the vertical asymptote(s) for a rational function. (Section 4.5/Objective 1)	To find any vertical asymptote, set the denominator equal to zero and solve for x. See page 405 for the definition of a vertical asymptote.	Find the vertical asymptote(s) for the graph of $f(x) = \dfrac{3x^2}{x^2 - x - 6}$. **Solution** Set the denominator equal to zero and solve. $x^2 - x - 6 = 0$ $(x - 3)(x + 2) = 0$ $x = 3 \quad$ or $\quad x = -2$ The lines $x = 3$ and $x = -2$ are vertical asymptotes.
Find the horizontal asymptote for a rational function. (Section 4.5/Objective 2)	Find any horizontal asymptotes by studying the behavior of $f(x)$ as x gets very large or very small. This may require changing the form of the original rational expression.	Find the horizontal asymptote for the graph of $f(x) = \dfrac{3x^2}{x^2 - x - 6}$. **Solution** Change the form of the expression by dividing the numerator and denominator by x^2. $$f(x) = \dfrac{\dfrac{3x^2}{x^2}}{\dfrac{x^2}{x^2} - \dfrac{x}{x^2} - \dfrac{6}{x^2}} = \dfrac{3}{1 - \dfrac{1}{x} - \dfrac{6}{x^2}}$$ As x gets larger and larger, the value of $f(x)$ approaches 3 from above. Therefore the line $y = 3$ is a horizontal asymptote.

OBJECTIVE	SUMMARY	EXAMPLE
Find the equation for an oblique asymptote of a rational function. (Section 4.6/Objective 1)	An oblique asymptote occurs when graphing rational functions in which the degree of the numerator is one more than the degree of the denominator. To find the equation of the oblique asymptote, change the form of the rational expression by dividing the denominator into the numerator.	Write the equation for the oblique asymptote for the graph of $$f(x) = \frac{2x^2 - 5x + 8}{x - 3}.$$ **Solution** Use synthetic division to divide $(2x^2 - 5x + 8)$ by $(x - 3)$ to change the form of the original function. $$f(x) = \frac{2x^2 - 5x + 8}{x - 3} = 2x + 1 + \frac{11}{x - 3}$$ As the $\lvert x \rvert$ gets larger and larger, the graph approaches the line $y = 2x + 1$. Hence the line $y = 2x + 1$ is an oblique asymptote.
Graph rational functions with vertical, horizontal, or oblique asymptotes. (Section 4.6/Objective 2)	To graph a rational function, the following steps are useful: 1. Check for symmetry with respect to the vertical axis and with respect to the origin. 2. Find any vertical asymptotes by setting the denominator equal to zero. 3. Find any horizontal asymptotes by studying the behavior of $f(x)$ as x gets very large or very small. 4. If the degree of the numerator is one greater than the degree of the denominator, determine the equation of the oblique asymptote. 5. Study the behavior of the graph when it is close to the asymptotic lines. 6. Plot as many points as necessary to determine the graph.	Graph $f(x) = \dfrac{x^2 + 2}{x + 1}$. **Solution** The graph is not symmetric with respect to the y axis or the origin. The vertical asymptote is $x = -1$. The graph has an oblique asymptote with the equation of $y = x - 1$. Determining some points leads us to the following graph. 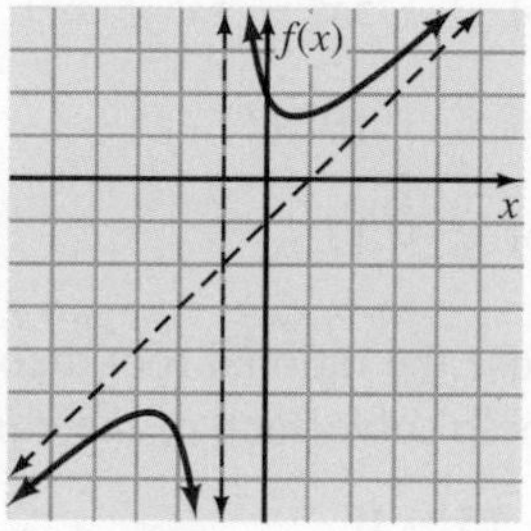

Chapter 4   Review Problem Set

For Problems 1–4, use synthetic division to determine the quotient and the remainder.

1. $(3x^3 - 4x^2 + 6x - 2) \div (x - 1)$

2. $(5x^3 + 7x^2 - 9x + 10) \div (x + 2)$

3. $(-2x^4 + x^3 - 2x^2 - x - 1) \div (x + 4)$

4. $(-3x^4 - 5x^2 + 9) \div (x - 3)$

For Problems 5–8, find $f(c)$ either by using synthetic division and the remainder theorem or by evaluating $f(c)$ directly.

5. $f(x) = 4x^5 - 3x^3 + x^2 - 1$ and $c = 1$

6. $f(x) = 4x^3 - 7x^2 + 6x - 8$ and $c = -3$

7. $f(x) = -x^4 + 9x^2 - x - 2$ and $c = -2$

8. $f(x) = x^4 - 9x^3 + 9x^2 - 10x + 16$ and $c = 8$

For Problems 9–12, use the factor theorem to help answer some questions about factors.

9. Is $x + 2$ a factor of $2x^3 + x^2 - 7x - 2$?

10. Is $x - 3$ a factor of $x^4 + 5x^3 - 7x^2 - x + 3$?

11. Is $x - 4$ a factor of $x^5 - 1024$?

12. Is $x + 1$ a factor of $x^5 + 1$?

For Problems 13–16, use the rational root theorem and the factor theorem to help solve each of the equations.

13. $x^3 - 3x^2 - 13x + 15 = 0$

14. $8x^3 + 26x^2 - 17x - 35 = 0$

15. $x^4 - 5x^3 + 34x^2 - 82x + 52 = 0$

16. $x^3 - 4x^2 - 10x + 4 = 0$

For Problems 17 and 18, use Descartes' rule of signs (Property 4.6) to help list the possibilities for the nature of the solutions. *Do not solve the equations.*

17. $4x^4 - 3x^3 + 2x^2 + x + 4 = 0$

18. $x^5 + 3x^3 + x + 7 = 0$

For Problems 19–22, graph each of the polynomial functions.

19. $f(x) = -(x - 2)^3 + 3$

20. $f(x) = (x + 3)(x - 1)(3 - x)$

21. $f(x) = x^4 - 4x^2$

22. $f(x) = x^3 - 4x^2 + x + 6$

For Problems 23–26, graph each of the rational functions. Be sure to identify the asymptotes.

23. $f(x) = \dfrac{2x}{x - 3}$

24. $f(x) = \dfrac{-3}{x^2 + 1}$

25. $f(x) = \dfrac{-x^2}{x^2 - x - 6}$

26. $f(x) = \dfrac{x^2 + 3}{x + 1}$

Chapter 4   Test

1. Divide $3x^3 + 5x^2 - 14x - 6$ by $x + 3$, and find the quotient and remainder.

2. Find the quotient and remainder when $4x^4 - 7x^2 - x + 4$ is divided by $x - 2$.

3. If $f(x) = x^5 - 8x^4 + 9x^3 - 13x^2 - 9x - 10$, find $f(7)$.

4. If $f(x) = 3x^4 + 20x^3 - 6x^2 + 9x + 19$, find $f(-7)$.

5. If $f(x) = x^5 - 35x^3 - 32x + 15$, find $f(6)$.

6. Is $x - 5$ a factor of $3x^3 - 11x^2 - 22x - 20$?

7. Is $x + 2$ a factor of $5x^3 + 9x^2 - 9x - 17$?

8. Is $x + 3$ a factor of $x^4 - 16x^2 - 17x + 12$?

9. Is $x - 6$ a factor of $x^4 - 2x^2 + 3x - 12$?

For Problems 10–14, solve each equation.

10. $x^3 - 13x + 12 = 0$

11. $2x^3 + 5x^2 - 13x - 4 = 0$

12. $x^4 - 4x^3 - 5x^2 + 38x - 30 = 0$

13. $2x^3 + 3x^2 - 17x + 12 = 0$

14. $3x^3 - 7x^2 - 8x + 20 = 0$

15. Use Descartes' rule of signs to determine the nature of the roots of $5x^4 + 3x^3 - x^2 - 9 = 0$.

16. Find the x intercepts of the graph of the function $f(x) = 3x^3 + 19x^2 - 14x$.

17. Find the equation of the vertical asymptote for the graph of the function $f(x) = \dfrac{5x}{x + 3}$.

18. Find the equation of the horizontal asymptote for the graph of the function $f(x) = \dfrac{5x^2}{x^2 - 4}$.

19. What type of symmetry does the graph of the equation $f(x) = \dfrac{x^2}{x^2 + 2}$ exhibit?

20. What type of symmetry does the graph of the equation $f(x) = \dfrac{-3x}{x^2 + 1}$ exhibit?

For Problems 21–25, graph each of the functions.

21. $f(x) = (2 - x)(x - 1)(x + 1)$

22. $f(x) = -x(x - 3)(x + 2)$

23. $f(x) = \dfrac{-x}{x - 3}$

24. $f(x) = \dfrac{-2}{x^2 - 4}$

25. $f(x) = \dfrac{4x^2 + x + 1}{x + 1}$

For Problems 1–10, evaluate each numerical expression.

1. $\left(\dfrac{3}{4}\right)^{-3}$

2. $\sqrt[3]{-\dfrac{8}{27}}$

3. -5^{-2}

4. $8^{4/3}$

5. $9^{-(3/2)}$

6. $\dfrac{1}{\left(\dfrac{2}{3}\right)^{-3}}$

7. $\left(\dfrac{8}{27}\right)^{-2/3}$

8. -6^{-2}

9. $(-64)^{2/3}$

10. $\sqrt[3]{-\dfrac{64}{27}}$

For Problems 11–33, solve each problem.

11. Express the domain of the function $f(x) = \sqrt{2x^2 + 11x - 6}$ using interval notation.

12. If $f(x) = 3x - 1$ and $g(x) = x^2 - x + 3$, find $(f \circ g)(-2)$ and $(g \circ f)(3)$.

13. If $f(x) = -\dfrac{2}{x}$ and $g(x) = \dfrac{1}{x - 4}$, find $(f \circ g)(x)$ and $(g \circ f)(x)$. Also indicate the domain of each composite function.

14. If $f(x) = x^2 - 4x$ and $g(x) = 2x - 1$, find $(f \circ g)(x)$ and $(g \circ f)(x)$. Also indicate the domain of each composite function.

15. If $f(x) = x^2 + 7x - 2$, find $\dfrac{f(a + h) - f(a)}{h}$.

16. If $f(x) = 2x^4 - 17x^3 - 10x^2 + 11x + 15$, find $f(9)$.

17. Find the quotient for $(3x^5 - 25x^3 - 7x^2 + x + 6) \div (x - 3)$.

18. Is $x + 2$ a factor of $2x^4 + 3x^3 + x^2 + 2x - 16$?

19. Find the remainder when $x^4 + 2x^3 - x^2 + 3x - 4$ is divided by $x - 2$.

20. Find the center and the length of a radius of the circle $x^2 + y^2 + 6x - 4y + 4 = 0$.

21. Write the equation of the line that contains the points $(-4, 2)$ and $(5, -1)$.

22. Write the equation of the perpendicular bisector of the line segment determined by $(-2, -4)$ and $(6, 2)$.

23. Find the length of the major axis of the ellipse $16x^2 + y^2 = 64$.

24. Find the equations of the asymptotes of the hyperbola $x^2 - 9y^2 = 18$.

25. If y varies directly as x and if $y = 3$ when $x = 4$, find y when $x = 16$.

26. If y varies inversely as the square root of x and if $y = \dfrac{2}{5}$ when $x = 25$, find y when $x = 49$.

27. Suppose the number of days it takes to complete a construction job varies inversely as the number of people assigned to the job. If it takes 8 people 10 days to do the job, how long will it take 12 people to complete the job?

28. Find the equation of the oblique asymptote for the graph of the function $f(x) = \dfrac{x^2 + 2x - 1}{x - 1}$.

29. Sandy has a collection of 57 coins worth $10. They consist of nickels, dimes, and quarters, and the number of quarters is 2 more than three times the number of nickels. How many coins of each kind does she have?

30. A retailer bought a dress for $75 and wants to sell it at a profit of 40% of the selling price. What price should she ask for the dress?

31. A container has 8 quarts of a 30% alcohol solution. How much pure alcohol should be added to raise it to a 40% solution?

32. Claire rode her bicycle out into the country at a speed of 15 miles per hour and returned along the same route at 10 miles per hour. If the entire trip took $7\frac{1}{2}$ hours, how far out did she ride?

33. Adam can do a job in 2 hours less time than it takes Carl to do the same job. Working together, they can do the job in 2 hours and 24 minutes. How long would it take Adam to do the job by himself?

For Problems 34–45, solve each equation.

34. $(2x - 5)(6x + 1) = (3x + 2)(4x - 7)$

35. $(2x + 1)(x - 2) = (3x - 2)(x + 4)$

36. $4x^3 + 20x^2 - 56x = 0$

37. $6x^3 + 17x^2 + x - 10 = 0$

38. $|4x - 3| = 7$

39. $\dfrac{2x - 1}{3} - \dfrac{3x + 2}{4} = -\dfrac{5}{6}$

40. $(3x - 2)(3x + 4) = 0$

41. $\sqrt{3x + 1} + 2 = 4$

42. $\sqrt{n - 2} - 6 = -3$

43. $x^4 + 3x^2 - 54 = 0$

44. $(2x - 1)(x + 3) = 49$

45. $x^4 - 2x^3 + 2x^2 - 7x + 6 = 0$

For Problems 46–53, solve each inequality and express the solution set using interval notation.

46. $3(x - 1) - 5(x + 2) > 3(x + 4)$

47. $\dfrac{x - 1}{2} + \dfrac{2x + 1}{5} \geq \dfrac{x - 2}{3}$

48. $x^2 - 3x < 18$

49. $(x - 1)(x + 3)(2 - x) \leq 0$

50. $|2x - 1| > 6$

51. $|3x + 2| \leq 8$

52. $\dfrac{4x - 3}{x - 2} \geq 0$

53. $\dfrac{x + 3}{x - 4} < 3$

For Problems 54–64, graph each function.

54. $f(x) = -2x + 4$

55. $f(x) = 2x^2 - 3$

56. $f(x) = 2x^2 + 4x$

57. $f(x) = 2\sqrt{x + 2} - 1$

58. $f(x) = \dfrac{2x}{x + 1}$

59. $f(x) = -|x - 2| + 1$

60. $f(x) = 2\sqrt{x} + 1$

61. $f(x) = 3x^2 + 12x + 9$

62. $f(x) = -(x - 3)^3 + 1$

63. $f(x) = (x + 1)(x - 2)(x - 4)$

64. $f(x) = x^4 - x^2$

5

Exponential and Logarithmic Functions

5.1 Exponents and
    Exponential Functions

5.2 Applications of
    Exponential Functions

5.3 Inverse Functions

5.4 Logarithms

5.5 Logarithmic Functions

5.6 Exponential Equations,
    Logarithmic Equations,
    and Problem Solving

*Compound interest is a good
illustration of exponential
growth.*

© John Foxx/Jupiter Images

How long will it take $100 to triple if it is invested at 5% interest
compounded continuously? We can use the formula $A = Pe^{rt}$ to generate the
equation $300 = 100e^{0.05t}$, which can be solved for t using logarithms. It will
take approximately 22.0 years for the money to triple.

　　In this chapter, we will (1) extend our understanding of exponents,
(2) work with some exponential functions, (3) consider the concept of a
logarithm, (4) work with some logarithmic functions, and (5) use the concepts
of exponents and logarithms to expand our problem-solving skills. Your
calculator will be a valuable tool throughout this chapter.

5.1	Exponents and Exponential Functions

OBJECTIVES

1 Solve exponential equations

2 Graph exponential functions

In Chapter 0 the expression "b^n" was defined to mean n factors of b, when n is any positive integer and b is any real number. For example,

$$2^3 = 2 \cdot 2 \cdot 2 = 8 \qquad \left(\frac{1}{3}\right)^4 = \left(\frac{1}{3}\right)\left(\frac{1}{3}\right)\left(\frac{1}{3}\right)\left(\frac{1}{3}\right) = \frac{1}{81}$$

$$(-4)^2 = (-4)(-4) = 16 \qquad -(0.5)^3 = -[(0.5)(0.5)(0.5)] = -0.125$$

Then in Chapter 0, by defining "$b^0 = 1$ and $b^{-n} = \dfrac{1}{b^n}$," when n is any positive integer and b is any nonzero real number, we extended the concept of an exponent to include all integers. Examples include

$$(0.76)^0 = 1 \qquad 2^{-3} = \frac{1}{2^3} = \frac{1}{8}$$

$$\left(\frac{2}{3}\right)^{-2} = \frac{1}{\left(\frac{2}{3}\right)^2} = \frac{1}{\frac{4}{9}} = \frac{9}{4} \qquad (0.4)^{-1} = \frac{1}{(0.4)^1} = \frac{1}{0.4} = 2.5$$

In Chapter 0 we also provided for the use of all rational numbers as exponents by defining

$$b^{m/n} = \sqrt[n]{b^m} = \left(\sqrt[n]{b}\right)^m$$

where n is a positive integer greater than 1, and b is a real number such that $\sqrt[n]{b}$ exists. Some examples are

$$27^{2/3} = \left(\sqrt[3]{27}\right)^2 = 9 \qquad 16^{1/4} = \sqrt[4]{16^1} = 2$$

$$\left(\frac{1}{9}\right)^{1/2} = \sqrt{\frac{1}{9}} = \frac{1}{3} \qquad 32^{-1/5} = \frac{1}{32^{1/5}} = \frac{1}{\sqrt[5]{32}} = \frac{1}{2}$$

Formally extending the concept of an exponent to include the use of irrational numbers requires some ideas from calculus and is therefore beyond the scope of this text. However, we can take a brief glimpse at the general idea involved. Consider the number $2^{\sqrt{3}}$. By using the nonterminating and nonrepeating decimal representation $1.73205\ldots$ for $\sqrt{3}$, we can form the sequence of numbers 2^1, $2^{1.7}$, $2^{1.73}$, $2^{1.732}$, $2^{1.7320}$, $2^{1.73205}$, $\ldots\ldots$. It seems reasonable that each successive power gets closer to $2^{\sqrt{3}}$. This is precisely what happens if b^n, when n is irrational, is properly defined using the concept of a limit. Furthermore, this will ensure that an expression such as 2^x will yield exactly one value for each value of x.

From now on, then, we can use any real number as an exponent, and we can extend the basic properties stated in Chapter 0 to include all real numbers as exponents. Let's restate those properties with the restriction that the bases a and

b must be positive numbers so that we avoid expressions such as $(-4)^{1/2}$, which do not represent real numbers.

Property 5.1

If a and b are positive real numbers, and m and n are any real numbers, then

1. $b^n \cdot b^m = b^{n+m}$ Product of two powers

2. $(b^n)^m = b^{mn}$ Power of a power

3. $(ab)^n = a^n b^n$ Power of a product

4. $\left(\dfrac{a}{b}\right)^n = \dfrac{a^n}{b^n}$ Power of a quotient

5. $\dfrac{b^n}{b^m} = b^{n-m}$ Quotient of two powers

Another property that we can use to solve certain types of equations that involve exponents can be stated as follows:

Property 5.2

If $b > 0$, $b \neq 1$, and m and n are real numbers, then $b^n = b^m$ if and only if $n = m$.

The following examples illustrate the use of Property 5.2. To use the property to solve equations, we will want both sides of the equation to have the same base number.

Classroom Example
Solve $5^x = 125$.

EXAMPLE 1   Solve $2^x = 32$.

Solution

$$2^x = 32$$
$$2^x = 2^5 \qquad\qquad 32 = 2^5$$
$$x = 5 \qquad\qquad \text{Property 5.2}$$

The solution set is $\{5\}$.

Classroom Example
Solve $5^{2x} = \dfrac{1}{25}$.

EXAMPLE 2   Solve $3^{2x} = \dfrac{1}{9}$.

Solution

$$3^{2x} = \frac{1}{9} = \frac{1}{3^2}$$
$$3^{2x} = 3^{-2}$$
$$2x = -2 \qquad\qquad \text{Property 5.2}$$
$$x = -1$$

The solution set is $\{-1\}$.

EXAMPLE 3   Solve $\left(\frac{1}{5}\right)^{x-4} = \frac{1}{125}$.

Solution

$$\left(\frac{1}{5}\right)^{x-4} = \frac{1}{125}$$

$$\left(\frac{1}{5}\right)^{x-4} = \left(\frac{1}{5}\right)^{3}$$

$$x - 4 = 3 \qquad \text{Property 5.2}$$

$$x = 7$$

The solution set is $\{7\}$.

EXAMPLE 4   Solve $8^x = 32$.

Solution

$$8^x = 32$$

$$(2^3)^x = 2^5 \qquad 8 = 2^3$$

$$2^{3x} = 2^5$$

$$3x = 5 \qquad \text{Property 5.2}$$

$$x = \frac{5}{3}$$

The solution set is $\left\{\frac{5}{3}\right\}$.

EXAMPLE 5   Solve $(3^{x+1})(9^{x-2}) = 27$.

Solution

$$(3^{x+1})(9^{x-2}) = 27$$

$$(3^{x+1})(3^2)^{x-2} = 3^3$$

$$(3^{x+1})(3^{2x-4}) = 3^3$$

$$3^{3x-3} = 3^3$$

$$3x - 3 = 3 \qquad \text{Property 5.2}$$

$$3x = 6$$

$$x = 2$$

The solution set is $\{2\}$.

Exponential Functions

If b is any positive number, then the expression b^x designates exactly one real number for every real value of x. Therefore the equation $f(x) = b^x$ defines a function in which the domain is the set of real numbers. Furthermore, if we include the additional restriction $b \neq 1$, then any equation of the form $f(x) = b^x$ describes what we will call later a one-to-one function and is known as an **exponential function**. This leads to the following definition:

> ### Definition 5.1
>
> If $b > 0$ and $b \neq 1$, then the function f defined by
>
> $$f(x) = b^x$$
>
> when x is any real number, is called the **exponential function with base b**.

Now let's consider graphing some exponential functions.

Classroom Example
Graph the function $f(x) = 5^x$.

EXAMPLE 6   Graph the function $f(x) = 2^x$.

Solution

Let's set up a table of values; keep in mind that the domain is the set of real numbers and that the equation $f(x) = 2^x$ exhibits no symmetry. Plot these points and connect them with a smooth curve to produce Figure 5.1.

x	2^x
-2	$\dfrac{1}{4}$
-1	$\dfrac{1}{2}$
0	1
1	2
2	4
3	8

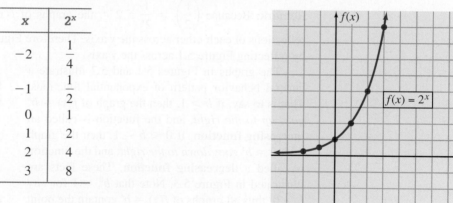

Figure 5.1

In the table for Example 6, we chose integral values for x to keep the computation simple. However, with the use of a calculator, we could easily acquire functional values by using nonintegral exponents. Consider the following additional values for $f(x) = 2^x$:

$$f(0.5) \approx 1.41 \qquad f(1.7) \approx 3.25$$
$$f(-0.5) \approx 0.71 \qquad f(-2.6) \approx 0.16$$

Use your calculator to check these results. Also note that the points generated by these values do fit the graph in Figure 5.1.

 **EXAMPLE 7** Graph $f(x) = \left(\frac{1}{2}\right)^x$.

Solution

Again, let's set up a table of values, plot the points, and connect them with a smooth curve. The graph is shown in Figure 5.2.

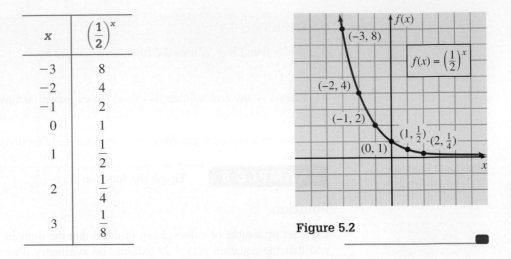

x	$\left(\frac{1}{2}\right)^x$
-3	8
-2	4
-1	2
0	1
1	$\dfrac{1}{2}$
2	$\dfrac{1}{4}$
3	$\dfrac{1}{8}$

Figure 5.2

Remark: Because $\left(\frac{1}{2}\right)^x = \frac{1}{2^x} = 2^{-x}$, the graphs of $f(x) = 2^x$ and $f(x) = \left(\frac{1}{2}\right)^x$ are reflections of each other across the y axis. Therefore Figure 5.2 could have been drawn by reflecting Figure 5.1 across the y axis.

The graphs in Figures 5.1 and 5.2 illustrate a general behavior pattern of exponential functions. That is to say, if $b > 1$, then the graph of $f(x) = b^x$ *goes up to the right*, and the function is called an **increasing function**. If $0 < b < 1$, then the graph of $f(x) = b^x$ *goes down to the right*, and the function is called a **decreasing function**. These facts are illustrated in Figure 5.3. Note that $b^0 = 1$ for any $b > 0$; thus all graphs of $f(x) = b^x$ contain the point $(0, 1)$.

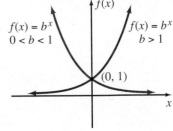

Figure 5.3

As you graph exponential functions, don't forget your previous graphing experiences.

1. The graph of $f(x) = 2^x - 4$ is the graph of $f(x) = 2^x$ *moved down four units*.

2. The graph of $f(x) = 2^{x+3}$ is the graph of $f(x) = 2^x$ *moved three units to the left*.

3. The graph of $f(x) = -2^x$ is the graph of $f(x) = 2^x$ *reflected across the x axis*.

We used a graphing calculator to graph these four functions on the same set of axes, as shown in Figure 5.4.

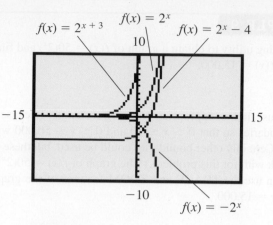

$f(x) = 2^{x+3}$

$f(x) = 2^x$

$f(x) = 2^x - 4$

$f(x) = -2^x$

Figure 5.4

If you are faced with an exponential function that is not of the basic form $f(x) = b^x$ or a variation thereof, don't forget the graphing suggestions offered in earlier chapters. Let's consider one such example.

EXAMPLE 8   Graph $f(x) = 2^{-x^2}$.

Solution

Because $f(-x) = 2^{-(-x)^2} = 2^{-x^2} = f(x)$, we know that this curve is symmetric with respect to the y axis. Therefore let's set up a table of values using nonnegative values for x. Plot these points, connect them with a smooth curve, and reflect this portion of the curve across the y axis to produce the graph in Figure 5.5.

x	2^{-x^2}
0	1
$\dfrac{1}{2}$	0.84
1	0.5
$\dfrac{3}{2}$	0.21
2	0.06

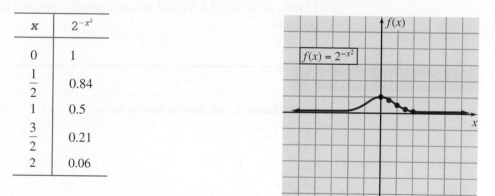

Figure 5.5

Finally, let's consider a problem in which a graphing utility gives us an approximate solution.

EXAMPLE 9

Use a graphing utility to obtain a graph of $f(x) = 50(2^x)$ and find an approximate value for x when $f(x) = 15{,}000$.

Solution

First, we must find an appropriate viewing rectangle. Because $50(2^{10}) = 51{,}200$, let's set the boundaries so that $0 \le x \le 10$ and $0 \le y \le 50{,}000$ with a scale of $10{,}000$ on the y axis. (Certainly other boundaries could be used, but these will give us a graph that we can work with for this problem.) The graph of $f(x) = 50(2^x)$ is shown in Figure 5.6. Now we can use the TRACE and ZOOM features of the graphing utility to find that $x \approx 8.2$ at $y = 15{,}000$.

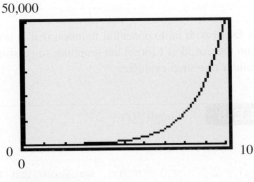

Figure 5.6

Remark: In Example 9 we used a graphical approach to solve the equation $50(2^x) = 15{,}000$. In Section 5.6 we will use an algebraic approach for solving that same kind of equation.

Concept Quiz 5.1

For Problems 1–10, answer true or false.

1. $2^2 \cdot 2^3 = 4^5$
2. $2^2 \cdot 2^3 = 2^6$
3. $2^{-3} = -8$
4. $-2^{-3} = 8$
5. $5^{\frac{3}{4}} = \sqrt[4]{5^3}$
6. The function $f(x) = 1^x$ is an exponential function.
7. The base, b, of an exponential function, $f(x) = b^x$, can be any number.
8. The exponential function $f(x) = b^x$, where $b > 1$ and $b \ne 1$, is an increasing function.
9. All exponential functions are increasing functions.
10. All graphs of $f(x) = b^x$ when $b > 0$ and $b \ne 1$ contain the point $(0, 1)$.

Problem Set 5.1

For Problems 1–26, solve each of the equations.
(Objective 1)

1. $2^x = 64$

2. $3^x = 81$

3. $3^{2x} = 27$

4. $2^{2x} = 16$

5. $\left(\dfrac{1}{2}\right)^x = \dfrac{1}{128}$

6. $\left(\dfrac{1}{4}\right)^x = \dfrac{1}{256}$

7. $3^{-x} = \dfrac{1}{243}$

8. $3^{x+1} = 9$

9. $6^{3x-1} = 36$

10. $2^{2x+3} = 32$

11. $\left(\dfrac{3}{4}\right)^n = \dfrac{64}{27}$

12. $\left(\dfrac{2}{3}\right)^n = \dfrac{9}{4}$

13. $16^x = 64$

14. $4^x = 8$

15. $27^{4x} = 9^{x+1}$

16. $32^x = 16^{1-x}$

17. $9^{4x-2} = \dfrac{1}{81}$

18. $8^{3x+2} = \dfrac{1}{16}$

19. $10^x = 0.1$

20. $10^x = 0.0001$

21. $(2^{x+1})(2^x) = 64$

22. $(2^{2x-1})(2^{x+2}) = 32$

23. $(27)(3^x) = 9^x$

24. $(3^x)(3^{5x}) = 81$

25. $(4^x)(16^{3x-1}) = 8$

26. $(8^{2x})(4^{2x-1}) = 16$

For Problems 27–46, graph each of the exponential functions. (Objective 2)

27. $f(x) = 3^x$

28. $f(x) = 4^x$

29. $f(x) = \left(\dfrac{1}{3}\right)^x$

30. $f(x) = \left(\dfrac{1}{4}\right)^x$

31. $f(x) = \left(\dfrac{3}{2}\right)^x$

32. $f(x) = \left(\dfrac{2}{3}\right)^x$

33. $f(x) = 2^x - 3$

34. $f(x) = 2^x + 1$

35. $f(x) = 2^{x+2}$

36. $f(x) = 2^{x-1}$

37. $f(x) = -2^x$

38. $f(x) = -3^x$

39. $f(x) = 2^{-x-2}$

40. $f(x) = 2^{-x+1}$

41. $f(x) = 2^{x^2}$

42. $f(x) = 2^x + 2^{-x}$

43. $f(x) = 2^{|x|}$

44. $f(x) = 3^{1-x^2}$

45. $f(x) = 2^x - 2^{-x}$

46. $f(x) = 2^{-|x|}$

Thoughts Into Words

47. Explain how you would solve the equation $(2^{x+1})(8^{2x-3}) = 64$.

48. Why is the base of an exponential function restricted to positive numbers not including 1?

49. Explain how you would graph the function $f(x) = -\left(\dfrac{1}{3}\right)^x$.

Graphing Calculator Activities

50. Use a graphing calculator to check your graphs for Problems 27–46.

51. Graph $f(x) = 2^x$. Where should the graphs of $f(x) = 2^{x-5}$, $f(x) = 2^{x-7}$, and $f(x) = 2^{x+5}$ be located? Graph all three functions on the same set of axes with $f(x) = 2^x$.

52. Graph $f(x) = 3^x$. Where should the graphs of $f(x) = 3^x + 2$, $f(x) = 3^x - 3$, and $f(x) = 3^x - 7$ be located? Graph all three functions on the same set of axes with $f(x) = 3^x$.

53. Graph $f(x) = \left(\dfrac{1}{2}\right)^x$. Where should the graphs of

$f(x) = -\left(\dfrac{1}{2}\right)^x$, $f(x) = \left(\dfrac{1}{2}\right)^{-x}$, and $f(x) = -\left(\dfrac{1}{2}\right)^{-x}$

be located? Graph all three functions on the same set of axes with $f(x) = \left(\dfrac{1}{2}\right)^x$.

54. Graph $f(x) = (1.5)^x$, $f(x) = (5.5)^x$, $f(x) = (0.3)^x$, and $f(x) = (0.7)^x$ on the same set of axes. Are these graphs consistent with Figure 5.3?

55. What is the solution for $3^x = 5$? Do you agree that it is between 1 and 2 because $3^1 = 3$ and $3^2 = 9$?

Now graph $f(x) = 3^x - 5$ and use the ZOOM and TRACE features of your graphing calculator to find an approximation, to the nearest hundredth, for the x intercept. You should get an answer of 1.46. Do you see that this is an approximation for the solution of $3^x = 5$? Try it; raise 3 to the 1.46 power.

Find an approximate solution, to the nearest hundredth, for each of the following equations by graphing the appropriate function and finding the x intercept.

(a) $2^x = 19$ **(b)** $3^x = 50$ **(c)** $4^x = 47$

(d) $5^x = 120$ **(e)** $2^x = 1500$ **(f)** $3^{x-1} = 34$

Answers to the Concept Quiz

1. False **2.** False **3.** False **4.** False **5.** True **6.** False **7.** False **8.** True **9.** False **10.** True

---

5.2 Applications of Exponential Functions

OBJECTIVES

1 Solve exponential growth and decay problems

2 Solve compound interest problems

3 Solve half-life problems

4 Solve growth problems involving the number e

5 Graph exponential functions involving a base of e

We can represent many real-world situations that involve growth or decay with equations that describe exponential functions. For example, suppose an economist predicts an annual inflation rate of 5% per year for the next 10 years. This means that an item that presently costs \$8 will cost $8(105\%) = 8(1.05) = \$8.40$ a year from now. The same item will cost $[8(105\%)](105\%) = 8(1.05)^2 = \$8.82$ in 2 years. In general, the equation

$$P = P_0(1.05)^t$$

yields the predicted price P of an item in t years if the present cost is P_0 and the annual inflation rate is 5%. Using this equation, we can look at some future prices based on the prediction of a 5% inflation rate.

A \$1.29 jar of mustard will cost $\$1.29(1.05)^3 = \$1.49$ in 3 years.

A \$3.29 bag of potato chips will cost $\$3.29(1.05)^5 = \$4.20$ in 5 years.

A \$7.69 can of coffee will cost $\$7.69(1.05)^7 = \$10.82$ in 7 years.

Compound Interest

Compound interest provides another illustration of exponential growth. Suppose that $500, called the **principal**, is invested at an interest rate of 4% compounded annually. The interest earned the first year is $500(0.04) = $20, and this amount is added to the original $500 to form a new principal of $520 for the second year. The interest earned during the second year is $520(0.04) = $20.80, and this amount is added to $520 to form a new principal of $540.80 for the third year. Each year a new principal is formed by reinvesting the interest earned during that year.

In general, suppose that a sum of money P (the principal) is invested at an interest rate of r percent compounded annually. The interest earned the first year is Pr, and the new principal for the second year is $P + Pr$, or $P(1 + r)$. Note that the new principal for the second year can be found by multiplying the original principal P by $(1 + r)$. In like fashion, the new principal for the third year can be found by multiplying the previous principal $P(1 + r)$ by $1 + r$, thus obtaining $P(1 + r)^2$. If this process is continued, after t years the total amount of money accumulated, (A), is given by

$$A = P(1 + r)^t$$

Consider the following examples of investments made at a certain rate of interest compounded annually:

1. $750 invested for 5 years at 4% compounded annually produces
   $$A = \$750(1.04)^5 = \$912.49$$

2. $1000 invested for 10 years at 7% compounded annually produces
   $$A = \$1000(1.07)^{10} = \$1967.15$$

3. $5000 invested for 20 years at 6% compounded annually produces
   $$A = \$5000(1.06)^{20} = \$16,035.68$$

We can use the compound interest formula to determine what rate of interest is needed to accumulate a certain amount of money based on a given initial investment. The next example illustrates this idea.

Classroom Example
What rate of interest is needed for an investment of $2500 to yield $7500 in 20 years if the interest is compounded annually?

EXAMPLE 1

What rate of interest is needed for an investment of $1000 to yield $2000 in 10 years if the interest is compounded annually?

Solution

Let's substitute $1000 for P, $2000 for A, and 10 years for t in the compound interest formula and solve for r.

$$A = P(1 + r)^t$$
$$2000 = 1000(1 + r)^{10}$$
$$2 = (1 + r)^{10}$$

$$2^{0.1} = [(1 + r)^{10}]^{0.1} \quad \text{Raise both sides to the 0.1 power}$$

$$1.071773 \approx 1 + r$$

$$0.071773 \approx r$$

$$r = 7.2\% \quad \text{to the nearest tenth of a percent}$$

Therefore a rate of interest of approximately 7.2% is needed. (Perhaps you should check this answer.)

If money invested at a certain rate of interest is compounded more than once a year, then the basic formula $A = P(1 + r)^t$ can be adjusted according to the number of compounding periods in a year. For example, for *semiannual compounding*, the formula becomes $A = P\left(1 + \dfrac{r}{2}\right)^{2t}$; for *quarterly compounding*, the formula becomes $A = P\left(1 + \dfrac{r}{4}\right)^{4t}$. In general, if n represents the number of compounding periods in a year, the formula becomes

$$A = P\left(1 + \frac{r}{n}\right)^{nt}$$

The following examples illustrate the use of the formula:

1. $750 invested for 5 years at 4% compounded semiannually produces

$$A = \$750\left(1 + \frac{0.04}{2}\right)^{2(5)} = \$750(1.02)^{10} = \$914.25$$

2. $1000 invested for 10 years at 7% compounded quarterly produces

$$A = \$1000\left(1 + \frac{0.07}{4}\right)^{4(10)} = \$1000(1.0175)^{40} = \$2001.60$$

3. $5000 invested for 20 years at 6% compounded monthly produces

$$A = \$5000\left(1 + \frac{0.06}{12}\right)^{12(20)} = \$5000(1.005)^{240} = \$16,551.02$$

You may find it interesting to compare these results with those we obtained earlier for annual compounding.

Exponential Decay

Suppose that the value of a car depreciates 15% per year for the first 5 years. Therefore a car that costs $19,500 will be worth $19,500(100% − 15%) = $19,500(85%) = $19,500(0.85) = $16,575 in 1 year. In 2 years the value of the car will have depreciated $19,500(0.85)^2 = $14,088 (to the nearest dollar). The equation

$$V = V_0(0.85)^t$$

yields the value V of a car in t years if the initial cost is V_0, and the value depreciates 15% per year. Therefore we can estimate some car values to the nearest dollar as follows:

A $13,000 car will be worth $13,000(0.85)^3 = 7984 in 3 years.

A $17,000 car will be worth $17,000(0.85)^5 = 7543 in 5 years.

A $25,000 car will be worth $25,000(0.85)^4 = $13,050$ in 4 years.

Another example of exponential decay is associated with radioactive substances. The rate of decay can be described exponentially and is based on the half-life of a substance. The **half-life** of a radioactive substance is the amount of time that it takes for one-half of an initial amount of the substance to disappear as the result of decay. For example, suppose that we have 200 grams of a certain substance that has a half-life of 5 days. After 5 days, $200\left(\dfrac{1}{2}\right) = 100$ grams remain. After 10 days, $200\left(\dfrac{1}{2}\right)^2 = 50$ grams remain. After 15 days, $200\left(\dfrac{1}{2}\right)^3 = 25$ grams remain. In general, after t days, $200\left(\dfrac{1}{2}\right)^{\frac{t}{5}}$ grams remain.

The previous discussion leads to the following half-life formula. Suppose there is an initial amount (Q_0) of a radioactive substance with a half-life of h. The amount of substance remaining (Q) after a time period of t is given by the formula

$$Q = Q_0\left(\frac{1}{2}\right)^{\frac{t}{h}}$$

The units of measure for t and h must be the same.

Classroom Example
A radioactive substance has a half-life of 4 years. If there are 600 milligrams of the substance initially, how many milligrams remain after 1 year? After 20 years?

EXAMPLE 2

Barium-140 has a half-life of 13 days. If there are 500 milligrams of barium initially, how many milligrams remain after 26 days? After 100 days?

Solution

When we use $Q_0 = 500$ and $h = 13$, the half-life formula becomes

$$Q = 500\left(\frac{1}{2}\right)^{\frac{t}{13}}$$

If $t = 26$, then

$$Q = 500\left(\frac{1}{2}\right)^{\frac{26}{13}}$$

$$= 500\left(\frac{1}{2}\right)^2$$

$$= 500\left(\frac{1}{4}\right)$$

$$= 125$$

Thus 125 milligrams remain after 26 days. If $t = 100$, then

$$Q = 500\left(\frac{1}{2}\right)^{\frac{100}{13}}$$

$$= 500(0.5)^{\frac{100}{13}}$$

$$= 2.4 \quad \text{to the nearest tenth of a milligram}$$

Approximately 2.4 milligrams remain after 100 days.

Remark: Example 2 clearly illustrates that a calculator is useful at times but unnecessary at other times. We solved the first part of the problem very easily without a calculator, but it certainly was helpful for the second part of the problem.

Number *e*

An interesting situation occurs if we consider the compound interest formula for $P = \$1$, $r = 100\%$, and $t = 1$ year. The formula becomes $A = 1\left(1 + \dfrac{1}{n}\right)^n$. The following table shows some values, rounded to eight decimal places, of $\left(1 + \dfrac{1}{n}\right)^n$ for different values of *n*.

n	$\left(1 + \dfrac{1}{n}\right)^n$
1	2.00000000
10	2.59374246
100	2.70481383
1000	2.71692393
10,000	2.71814593
100,000	2.71826824
1,000,000	2.71828047
10,000,000	2.71828169
100,000,000	2.71828181
1,000,000,000	2.71828183

The table suggests that as *n* increases, the value of $\left(1 + \dfrac{1}{n}\right)^n$ gets closer and closer to some fixed number. This does happen, and the fixed number is called *e*. To five decimal places, $e = 2.71828$.

The function defined by the equation $f(x) = e^x$ is the **natural exponential function**. It has a great many real-world applications, some of which we will look at in a moment. First, however, let's get a picture of the natural exponential function. Because $2 < e < 3$, the graph of $f(x) = e^x$ must fall between the graphs of $f(x) = 2^x$ and $f(x) = 3^x$. To be more specific, let's use our calculator to determine a table of values. Use the $\boxed{e^x}$ key, and round the results to the nearest tenth to obtain the following table. Plot the points determined by this table, and connect them with a smooth curve to produce Figure 5.7.

x	$f(x) = e^x$
0	1.0
1	2.7
2	7.4
-1	0.4
-2	0.1

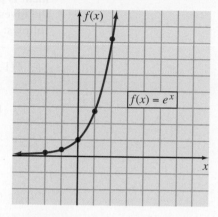

Figure 5.7

Back to Compound Interest

Let's return to the concept of compound interest. If the number of compounding periods in a year is increased indefinitely, we arrive at the concept of **compounding continuously**. Mathematically, we can accomplish this by applying the limit concept to the expression $P\left(1 + \dfrac{r}{n}\right)^{nt}$. We will not show the details here, but the following result is obtained. The formula

$$A = Pe^{rt}$$

yields the accumulated value (A) of a sum of money (P) that has been invested for t years at a rate of r percent compounded continuously. The following examples illustrate the use of the formula.

1. $750 invested for 5 years at 4% compounded continuously produces

$$A = \$750e^{(0.04)(5)} = 750e^{0.20} = \$916.05$$

2. $1000 invested for 10 years at 7% compounded continuously produces

$$A = \$1000e^{(0.07)(10)} = 1000e^{0.7} = \$2013.75$$

3. $5000 invested for 20 years at 6% compounded continuously produces

$$A = \$5000e^{(0.06)(20)} = 5000e^{1.2} = \$16,600.58$$

Again, you may find it interesting to compare these results with those you obtained earlier when you were using a different number of compounding periods.

Is it better to invest at 6% compounded quarterly or at 5.75% compounded continuously? To answer such a question, we can use the concept of *effective yield* (sometimes called effective annual rate of interest). The **effective yield** of an investment is the simple interest rate that would yield the same amount in 1 year. Thus for the investment at 6% compounded quarterly, we can calculate the effective yield as follows:

$$P(1 + r) = P\left(1 + \frac{0.06}{4}\right)^4$$

$$1 + r = \left(1 + \frac{0.06}{4}\right)^4 \qquad \text{Multiply both sides by } \frac{1}{P}$$

$$1 + r = (1.015)^4$$

$$r = (1.015)^4 - 1$$

$$r \approx 0.0613635506$$

$$r = 6.14\% \quad \text{to the nearest hundredth of a percent}$$

Likewise, for the investment at 5.75% compounded continuously, we can calculate the effective yield as follows:

$$P(1 + r) = Pe^{0.0575}$$

$$1 + r = e^{0.0575}$$

$$r = e^{0.0575} - 1$$

$$r \approx 0.0591852707$$

$$r = 5.92\% \quad \text{to the nearest hundredth of a percent}$$

Therefore, comparing the two effective yields, we see that it is better to invest at 6% compounded quarterly than to invest at 5.75% compounded continuously.

Law of Exponential Growth

The ideas behind "compounded continuously" carry over to other growth situations. We use the law of exponential growth,

$$Q(t) = Q_0 e^{kt}$$

as a mathematical model for numerous growth-and-decay applications. In this equation, $Q(t)$ represents the quantity of a given substance at any time t, Q_0 is the initial amount of the substance (when $t = 0$), and k is a constant that depends on the particular application. If $k < 0$, then $Q(t)$ decreases as t increases, and we refer to the model as the **law of decay**.

Let's consider some growth-and-decay applications.

EXAMPLE 3

Suppose that in a certain culture, the equation $Q(t) = 15,000e^{0.3t}$ expresses the number of bacteria present as a function of the time t, where t is expressed in hours. Find (a) the initial number of bacteria and (b) the number of bacteria after 3 hours.

Solution

(a) The initial number of bacteria is produced when $t = 0$.

$$Q(0) = 15,000e^{0.3(0)}$$
$$= 15,000e^{0}$$
$$= 15,000 \quad e^{0} = 1$$

(b) $Q(3) = 15,000e^{0.3(3)}$
$$= 15,000e^{0.9}$$
$$= 36,894 \quad \text{to the nearest whole number}$$

Therefore approximately 36,894 bacteria should be present after 3 hours.

EXAMPLE 4

Suppose the number of bacteria present in a certain culture after t minutes is given by the equation $Q(t) = Q_0e^{0.05t}$, where Q_0 represents the initial number of bacteria. If 5000 bacteria are present after 20 minutes, how many bacteria were present initially?

Solution

If 5000 bacteria are present after 20 minutes, then $Q(20) = 5000$.

$$5000 = Q_0e^{0.05(20)}$$
$$5000 = Q_0e^{1}$$
$$\frac{5000}{e} = Q_0$$
$$1839 = Q_0 \quad \text{to the nearest whole number}$$

Therefore, approximately 1839 bacteria were present initially.

EXAMPLE 5

The number of grams of a certain radioactive substance present after t seconds is given by the equation $Q(t) = 200e^{-0.3t}$. How many grams remain after 7 seconds?

Solution

Use $Q(t) = 200e^{-0.3t}$ to obtain

$$Q(7) = 200e^{(-0.3)(7)}$$
$$= 200e^{-2.1}$$
$$= 24.5 \quad \text{to the nearest tenth}$$

Thus approximately 24.5 grams remain after 7 seconds.

Finally, let's consider two examples where we use a graphing utility to produce the graph.

EXAMPLE 6

Suppose that $1000 was invested at 6.5% interest compounded continuously. How long would it take for the money to double?

Solution

Substitute $1000 for P and 0.065 for r in the formula $A = Pe^{rt}$ to produce $A = 1000e^{0.065t}$. If we let $y = A$ and $x = t$, we can graph the equation $y = 1000e^{0.065x}$. By letting $x = 20$, we obtain $y = 1000e^{0.065(20)} = 1000e^{1.3} \approx 3670$. Therefore let's set the boundaries of the viewing rectangle so that $0 \le x \le 20$ and $0 \le y \le 3700$ with a y scale of 1000. Then we obtain the graph in Figure 5.8. Now we want to find the value of x so that $y = 2000$. (The money is to double.) Using the ZOOM and TRACE features of the graphing utility, we can determine that an x value of approximately 10.7 will produce a y value of 2000. Thus it will take approximately 10.7 years for the $1000 investment to double.

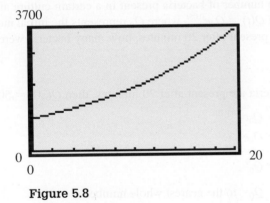

Figure 5.8

EXAMPLE 7

Graph the function $y = \dfrac{1}{\sqrt{2\pi}} e^{-x^2/2}$ and find its maximum value.

Solution

If $x = 0$, then $y = \dfrac{1}{\sqrt{2\pi}} e^0 = \dfrac{1}{\sqrt{2\pi}} \approx 0.4$, so let's set the boundaries of the viewing rectangle so that $-5 \le x \le 5$ and $0 \le y \le 1$ with a y scale of 0.1; the graph of the function is shown in Figure 5.9. From the graph, we see that the maximum value of the function occurs at $x = 0$, which we have already determined to be approximately 0.4.

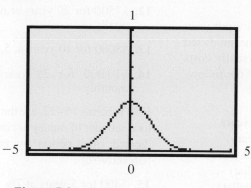

Figure 5.9

Remark: The curve in Figure 5.9 is called a **normal distribution curve**. You may want to ask your instructor to explain what it means to assign grades on the basis of the normal distribution curve.

Concept Quiz 5.2

For Problems 1–5, match each type of problem with its formula.

1. Compound continuously
2. Exponential growth or decay
3. Interest compounded annually
4. Compound interest
5. Half-life

A. $A = P\left(1 + \dfrac{r}{n}\right)^{nt}$ **B.** $Q = Q_0\left(\dfrac{1}{2}\right)^{\frac{t}{h}}$ **C.** $A = P(1 + r)^t$

D. $Q(t) = Q_0 e^{kt}$ **E.** $A = Pe^{rt}$

For Problems 6–10, answer true or false.

6. $500 invested for 2 years at 7% compounded semiannually produces $573.76.
7. $500 invested for 2 years at 7% compounded continuously produces $571.14.
8. The graph of $f(x) = e^{x-5}$ is the graph of $f(x) = e^x$ shifted 5 units to the right.
9. The graph of $f(x) = e^x - 5$ is the graph of $f(x) = e^x$ shifted 5 units downward.
10. The graph of $f(x) = -e^x$ is the graph of $f(x) = e^x$ reflected across the x axis.

Problem Set 5.2

For Problems 1–2, solve the exponential growth or decay problems. (Objective 1)

1. Assuming that the rate of inflation is 4% per year, the equation $P = P_0(1.04)^t$ yields the predicted price (P) of an item in t years that presently costs P_0. Find the predicted price of each of the following items for the indicated years ahead:
   (a) $1.38 can of soup in 3 years
   (b) $3.43 container of cocoa mix in 5 years
   (c) $1.99 jar of coffee creamer in 4 years
   (d) $1.54 can of beans and bacon in 10 years
   (e) $18,000 car in 5 years (nearest dollar)
   (f) $180,000 house in 8 years (nearest dollar)
   (g) $500 TV set in 7 years (nearest dollar)

2. Suppose it is estimated that the value of a car depreciates 30% per year for the first 5 years. The equation $A = P_0(0.7)^t$ yields the value (A) of a car after t years if the original price is P_0. Find the value (to the nearest dollar) of each of the following cars after the indicated time:
   (a) $16,500 car after 4 years
   (b) $22,000 car after 2 years
   (c) $27,000 car after 5 years
   (d) $40,000 car after 3 years

For Problems 3–14, use the formula $A = P\left(1 + \dfrac{r}{n}\right)^{nt}$ to find the total amount of money accumulated at the end of the indicated time period for each of the following investments: (Objective 2)

3. $200 for 6 years at 6% compounded annually

4. $250 for 5 years at 7% compounded annually

5. $500 for 7 years at 4% compounded semiannually

6. $750 for 8 years at 4% compounded semiannually

7. $800 for 9 years at 5% compounded quarterly

8. $1200 for 10 years at 4% compounded quarterly

9. $1500 for 5 years at 8% compounded monthly

10. $2000 for 10 years at 3% compounded monthly

11. $5000 for 15 years at 4.5% compounded annually

12. $7500 for 20 years at 6.5% compounded semiannually

13. $8000 for 10 years at 5.5% compounded quarterly

14. $10,000 for 25 years at 4.25% compounded monthly

For Problems 15–22, use the formula $A = Pe^{rt}$ to find the total amount of money accumulated at the end of the indicated time period by compounding continuously. (Objective 4)

15. $400 for 5 years at 7%

16. $500 for 7 years at 6%

17. $750 for 8 years at 8%

18. $1000 for 10 years at 5%

19. $2000 for 15 years at 7%

20. $5000 for 20 years at 8%

21. $7500 for 10 years at 6.5%

22. $10,000 for 25 years at 4.25%

For Problems 23–33, solve the problem.

23. Rueben has a finance plan with the furniture store where the $4830 he spent accrues finance charges at an annual interest rate of 10.9% compounded monthly for 3 years before he starts to make payments. What will be the balance on the account at the end of those three years?

24. In a certain balloon mortgage loan, the borrower pays the lender all of the principal and interest for the loan at the end of the five years. What will be the payoff amount for a loan of $185,000 at 6% annual interest rate where the interest is compounded monthly?

25. Jody took out a $3200 student loan her freshman year of college. The loan was at a 2.5% annual interest rate and accrued interest quarterly. Jody is obligated to begin repaying the loan back in five years. At that time what will be the amount she needs to repay?

26. To pay the tuition for medical school Melissa borrowed $8400 in student loans her first year. The loan is for seven years at an annual interest rate of 3.4%, and interest is compounded semiannually. What will be the amount of principal and interest in seven years?

27. Mark became overextended in his gambling debt and could not pay $500 he owed. The loan person said he could have three weeks to pay off the $500 at 10% interest per week compounded continuously. How much will Mark have to pay at the end of the three weeks?

28. What rate of interest, to the nearest tenth of a percent, compounded annually is needed for an investment of $200 to grow to $350 in 5 years?

29. What rate of interest, to the nearest tenth of a percent, compounded quarterly is needed for an investment of $1500 to grow to $2700 in 10 years?

30. Find the effective yield, to the nearest tenth of a percent, of an investment at 7.5% compounded monthly.

31. Find the effective yield, to the nearest hundredth of a percent, of an investment at 7.75% compounded continuously.

32. What investment yields the greater return: 7% compounded monthly or 6.85% compounded continuously?

33. What investment yields the greater return: 8.25% compounded quarterly or 8.3% compounded semiannually?

For Problems 34–36, solve the half-life problems. (Objective 3)

34. Suppose that a certain radioactive substance has a half-life of 20 years. If there are presently 2500 milligrams of the substance, how much, to the nearest milligram, will remain after 40 years? After 50 years?

35. Strontium-90 has a half-life of 29 years. If there are 400 grams of strontium-90 initially, how much, to the nearest gram, will remain after 87 years? After 100 years?

36. The half-life of radium is approximately 1600 years. If the present amount of radium in a certain location is 500 grams, how much will remain after 800 years? Express your answer to the nearest gram.

For Problems 37–42, solve the exponential growth problems. (Objective 4)

37. Suppose that in a certain culture, the equation $Q(t) = 1000e^{0.4t}$ expresses the number of bacteria present as a function of the time t, where t is expressed in hours. How many bacteria are present at the end of 2 hours? 3 hours? 5 hours?

38. The number of bacteria present at a given time under certain conditions is given by the equation $Q(t) = 5000e^{0.05t}$, where t is expressed in minutes. How many bacteria are present at the end of 10 minutes? 30 minutes? 1 hour?

39. The number of bacteria present in a certain culture after t hours is given by the equation $Q(t) = Q_0e^{0.3t}$, where Q_0 represents the initial number of bacteria. If 6640 bacteria are present after 4 hours, how many bacteria were present initially?

40. The number of grams Q of a certain radioactive substance present after t seconds is given by the equation $Q(t) = 1500e^{-0.4t}$. How many grams remain after 5 seconds? 10 seconds? 20 seconds?

41. The atmospheric pressure, measured in pounds per square inch, is a function of the altitude above sea level. The equation $P(a) = 14.7e^{-0.21a}$, where a is the altitude measured in miles, can be used to approximate atmospheric pressure. Find the atmospheric pressure at each of the following locations:

(a) Mount McKinley in Alaska: altitude of 3.85 miles

(b) Denver, Colorado: the "mile-high" city

(c) Asheville, North Carolina: altitude of 1985 feet

(d) Phoenix, Arizona: altitude of 1090 feet

42. Suppose that the present population of a city is 75,000. Using the equation $P(t) = 75,000e^{0.01t}$ to estimate future growth, estimate the population (a) 10 years from now, (b) 15 years from now, and (c) 25 years from now.

For Problems 43–48, graph each of the exponential functions. (Objective 5)

43. $f(x) = e^x + 1$ **44.** $f(x) = e^x - 2$

45. $f(x) = 2e^x$ **46.** $f(x) = -e^x$

47. $f(x) = e^{2x}$ **48.** $f(x) = e^{-x}$

Thoughts Into Words

49. Explain the difference between simple interest and compound interest.

50. Would it be better to invest $5000 at 6.25% interest compounded annually for 5 years or to invest $5000 at 6.25% interest compounded continuously for 5 years? Explain your answer.

51. How would you explain the concept of effective yield to someone who missed class when it was discussed?

52. How would you explain the half-life formula to someone who missed class when it was discussed?

Further Investigations

53. Complete the following chart, which illustrates what happens to $1000 invested at various rates of interest for different lengths of time but always compounded continuously. Round your answers to the nearest dollar.

$1000 Compounded continuously

	4%	5%	6%	7%
5 years				
10 years				
15 years				
20 years				
25 years				

54. Complete the following chart, which illustrates what happens to $1000 invested at 6% for different lengths of time and different numbers of compounding periods. Round all of your answers to the nearest dollar.

$1000 at 6%

	1 year	5 years	10 years	20 years
Compounded annually				
Compounded semiannually				
Compounded quarterly				
Compounded monthly				
Compounded continuously				

55. Complete the following chart, which illustrates what happens to $1000 in 10 years based on different rates of interest and different numbers of compounding periods. Round your answers to the nearest dollar.

$1000 for 10 years

	4%	5%	6%	7%
Compounded annually				
Compounded semiannually				
Compounded quarterly				
Compounded monthly				
Compounded continuously				

For Problems 56–60, graph each of the functions.

56. $f(x) = x(2^x)$

57. $f(x) = \dfrac{e^x + e^{-x}}{2}$

58. $f(x) = \dfrac{2}{e^x + e^{-x}}$

59. $f(x) = \dfrac{e^x - e^{-x}}{2}$

60. $f(x) = \dfrac{2}{e^x - e^{-x}}$

Graphing Calculator Activities

61. Use a graphing calculator to check your graphs for Problems 52–56.

62. Graph $f(x) = 2^x$, $f(x) = e^x$, and $f(x) = 3^x$ on the same set of axes. Are these graphs consistent with the discussion prior to Figure 5.7?

63. Graph $f(x) = e^x$. Where should the graphs of $f(x) = e^{x-4}$, $f(x) = e^{x-6}$, and $f(x) = e^{x+5}$ be located? Graph all three functions on the same set of axes with $f(x) = e^x$.

64. Graph $f(x) = e^x$. Now predict the graphs for $f(x) = -e^x$, $f(x) = e^{-x}$, and $f(x) = -e^{-x}$. Graph all three functions on the same set of axes with $f(x) = e^x$.

65. How do you think the graphs of $f(x) = e^x$, $f(x) = e^{2x}$, and $f(x) = 2e^x$ will compare? Graph them on the same set of axes to see if you were correct.

66. Find an approximate solution, to the nearest hundredth, for each of the following equations by graphing the appropriate function and finding the x intercept.

   (a) $e^x = 7$ **(b)** $e^x = 21$ **(c)** $e^x = 53$

   (d) $2e^x = 60$ **(e)** $e^{x+1} = 150$ **(f)** $e^{x\,2} = 300$

67. Use a graphing approach to argue that it is better to invest money at 6% compounded quarterly than at 5.75% compounded continuously.

68. How long will it take $500 to be worth $1500 if it is invested at 7.5% interest compounded semiannually?

69. How long will it take $5000 to triple if it is invested at 6.75% interest compounded quarterly?

Answers to the Concept Quiz

1. E   **2.** D   **3.** C   **4.** A   **5.** B   **6.** True   **7.** False   **8.** True   **9.** True   **10.** True

5.3   Inverse Functions

OBJECTIVES

1   Determine if a function is a one-to-one function

2   Verify if two functions are inverses of each other

3   Find the inverse function in terms of ordered pairs

4   Find the inverse of a function

5   Graph a function and its inverse

6   Determine the intervals for which a function is increasing (or decreasing)

Recall the vertical-line test: If each vertical line intersects a graph in no more than one point, then the graph represents a function. There is also a useful distinction between two basic types of functions. Consider the graphs of the two functions in Figure 5.10: $f(x) = 2x - 1$ and $g(x) = x^2$. In Figure 5.10(a), any *horizontal line* will intersect the graph in no more than one point. Therefore every value of $f(x)$ has only one value of x associated with it. Any function that has this property of having exactly one value of x

associated with each value of $f(x)$ is called a **one-to-one function**. Thus $g(x) = x^2$ is not a one-to-one function because the horizontal line in Figure 5.10(b) intersects the parabola in two points.

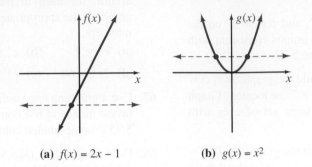

(a) $f(x) = 2x - 1$ **(b)** $g(x) = x^2$

Figure 5.10

The statement that for a function f to be a one-to-one function, every value of $f(x)$ has only one value of x associated with it can be equivalently stated: If $f(x_1) = f(x_2)$ for x_1 and x_2 in the domain of f, then $x_1 = x_2$. Let's use this last if-then statement to verify that $f(x) = 2x - 1$ is a one-to-one function. We start with the assumption that $f(x_1) = f(x_2)$:

$$2x_1 - 1 = 2x_2 - 1$$
$$2x_1 = 2x_2$$
$$x_1 = x_2$$

Thus $f(x) = 2x - 1$ is a one-to-one function.

To show that $g(x) = x^2$ is not a one-to-one function, we simply need to find two distinct real numbers in the domain of f that produce the same functional value. For example, $g(-2) = (-2)^2 = 4$ and $g(2) = 2^2 = 4$. Thus $g(x) = x^2$ is not a one-to-one function.

Now let's consider a one-to-one function f that assigns to each x in its domain D the value $f(x)$ in its range R (Figure 5.11(a)). We can define a new function g that goes from R to D; it assigns $f(x)$ in R back to x in D, as indicated in Figure 5.11(b). The functions f and g are called *inverse functions* of each other. The following definition precisely states this concept.

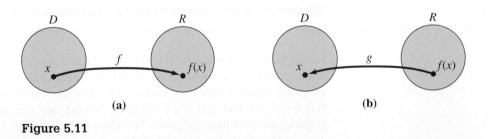

(a)   **(b)**

Figure 5.11

Definition 5.2

Let f be a one-to-one function with a domain of X and a range of Y. A function g with a domain of Y and a range of X is called the **inverse function** of f if

$$(f \circ g)(x) = x \quad \text{for every } x \text{ in } Y$$

and

$$(g \circ f)(x) = x \quad \text{for every } x \text{ in } X$$

In Definition 5.2, note that for f and g to be inverses of each other, the domain of f must equal the range of g, and the range of f must equal the domain of g. Furthermore, g must reverse the correspondences given by f, and f must reverse the correspondences given by g. In other words, inverse functions *undo* each other. Let's use Definition 5.2 to verify that two specific functions are inverses of each other.

Classroom Example
Verify that $f(x) = 7x + 1$ and $g(x) = \dfrac{x - 1}{7}$ are inverse functions.

EXAMPLE 1

Verify that $f(x) = 4x - 5$ and $g(x) = \dfrac{x + 5}{4}$ are inverse functions.

Solution

Because the set of real numbers is the domain and range of both functions, we know that the domain of f equals the range of g and that the range of f equals the domain of g. Furthermore,

$$(f \circ g)(x) = f(g(x))$$

$$= f\left(\frac{x + 5}{4}\right)$$

$$= 4\left(\frac{x + 5}{4}\right) - 5 = x$$

and

$$(g \circ f)(x) = g(f(x))$$

$$= g(4x - 5)$$

$$= \frac{4x - 5 + 5}{4} = x$$

Therefore f and g are inverses of each other.

EXAMPLE 2

Verify that $f(x) = x^2 + 1$ for $x \geq 0$ and $g(x) = \sqrt{x - 1}$ for $x \geq 1$ are inverse functions.

Solution

First, note that the domain of f equals the range of g; namely, the set of nonnegative real numbers. Also, the range of f equals the domain of g; namely, the set of real numbers greater than or equal to 1. Furthermore,

$$(f \circ g)(x) = f(g(x))$$
$$= f(\sqrt{x - 1})$$
$$= (\sqrt{x - 1})^2 + 1$$
$$= x - 1 + 1 = x$$

and

$$(g \circ f)(x) = g(f(x))$$
$$= g(x^2 + 1)$$
$$= \sqrt{x^2 + 1 - 1} = \sqrt{x^2} = x \quad \sqrt{x^2} = x \text{ because } x \geq 1$$

Therefore f and g are inverses of each other.

The inverse of a function f is commonly denoted by f^{-1} (read "f inverse" or "the inverse of f"). Do not confuse the -1 in f^{-1} with a negative exponent. The symbol f^{-1} does *not* mean $1/f^1$ but rather refers to the inverse function of function f.

Remember that a function can also be thought of as a set of ordered pairs no two of which have the same first element. Along those lines, a one-to-one function further requires that no two of the ordered pairs have the same second element. Then, if the components of each ordered pair of a given one-to-one function are interchanged, the resulting function and the given function are inverses of each other. Thus if

$$f = \{(1, 4), (2, 7), (5, 9)\}$$

then

$$f^{-1} = \{(4, 1), (7, 2), (9, 5)\}$$

Graphically, two functions that are inverses of each other are *mirror images with reference to the line $y = x$*. This is because ordered pairs (a, b) and (b, a) are reflections of each other with respect to the line $y = x$, as illustrated in Figure 5.12. (You will

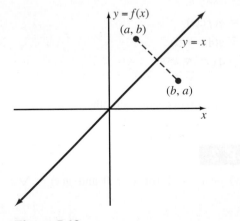

Figure 5.12

verify this in the next set of exercises.) Therefore, if the graph of a function f is known, as in Figure 5.13(a), then the graph of f^{-1} can be determined by reflecting f across the line $y = x$, as in Figure 5.13(b).

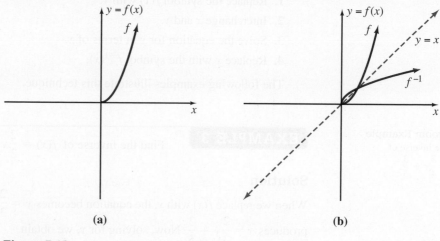

(a)   (b)

Figure 5.13

Finding Inverse Functions

The idea of inverse functions *undoing each other* provides the basis for an informal approach to finding the inverse of a function. Consider the function

$$f(x) = 2x + 1$$

To each x, this function assigns twice x plus 1. To undo this function, we can subtract 1 and divide by 2. Hence the inverse is

$$f^{-1}(x) = \frac{x - 1}{2}$$

Now let's verify that f and f^{-1} are indeed inverses of each other:

$$(f \circ f^{-1})(x) = f(f^{-1}(x)) \qquad (f^{-1} \circ f)(x) = f^{-1}(f(x))$$

$$= f\left(\frac{x - 1}{2}\right) \qquad\qquad = f^{-1}(2x + 1)$$

$$= 2\left(\frac{x - 1}{2}\right) + 1 \qquad\qquad = \frac{2x + 1 - 1}{2}$$

$$= x - 1 + 1 \qquad\qquad\qquad = \frac{2x}{2}$$

$$= x \qquad\qquad\qquad\qquad = x$$

Thus the inverse of $f(x) = 2x + 1$ is $f^{-1}(x) = \dfrac{x - 1}{2}$.

This informal approach may not work very well with more complex functions, but it does emphasize how inverse functions are related to each other. A more formal and systematic technique for finding the inverse of a function can be described as follows:

1. Replace the symbol $f(x)$ with y.
2. Interchange x and y.
3. Solve the equation for y in terms of x.
4. Replace y with the symbol $f^{-1}(x)$.

The following examples illustrate this technique.

Classroom Example
Find the inverse of
$f(x) = \dfrac{3}{4}x + \dfrac{3}{5}$.

EXAMPLE 3   Find the inverse of $f(x) = \dfrac{2}{3}x + \dfrac{3}{5}$.

Solution

When we replace $f(x)$ with y, the equation becomes $y = \dfrac{2}{3}x + \dfrac{3}{5}$. Interchanging x and y produces $x = \dfrac{2}{3}y + \dfrac{3}{5}$. Now, solving for y, we obtain

$$x = \frac{2}{3}y + \frac{3}{5}$$

$$15(x) = 15\left(\frac{2}{3}y + \frac{3}{5}\right)$$

$$15x = 10y + 9$$

$$15x - 9 = 10y$$

$$\frac{15x - 9}{10} = y$$

Finally, by replacing y with $f^{-1}(x)$, we can express the inverse function as

$$f^{-1}(x) = \frac{15x - 9}{10}$$

The domain of f is equal to the range of f^{-1} (both are the set of real numbers), and the range of f equals the domain of f^{-1} (both are the set of real numbers). Furthermore, we could show that $(f \circ f^{-1})(x) = x$ and $(f^{-1} \circ f)(x) = x$. We leave this for you to complete.

_____

Does the function $f(x) = x^2 - 2$ have an inverse? Sometimes a graph of the function helps answer such a question. In Figure 5.14(a), it should be evident that f is not a one-to-one function and therefore cannot have an inverse. However, it should also be apparent from the graph that if we restrict the domain of f to the nonnegative real numbers, Figure 5.14(b), then it is a one-to-one function and should have an inverse function. The next example illustrates how to find the inverse function.

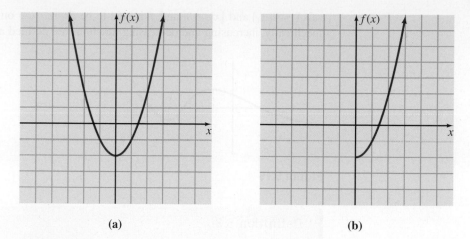

(a)   (b)

Figure 5.14

Classroom Example
Find the inverse of
$f(x) = x^2 + 6$, where $x \geq 0$.

EXAMPLE 4   Find the inverse of $f(x) = x^2 - 2$, where $x \geq 0$.

Solution

When we replace $f(x)$ with y, the equation becomes

$$y = x^2 - 2, \quad x \geq 0$$

Interchanging x and y produces

$$x = y^2 - 2, \quad y \geq 0$$

Now let's solve for y; keep in mind that y is to be nonnegative.

$$x = y^2 - 2$$
$$x + 2 = y^2$$
$$\sqrt{x + 2} = y, \quad x \geq -2$$

Finally, by replacing y with $f^{-1}(x)$, we can express the inverse function as

$$f^{-1}(x) = \sqrt{x + 2}, \quad x \geq -2$$

The domain of f equals the range of f^{-1} (both are the nonnegative real numbers), and the range of f equals the domain of f^{-1} (both are the real numbers greater than or equal to -2). It can also be shown that $(f \circ f^{-1})(x) = x$ and $(f^{-1} \circ f)(x) = x$. Again, we leave this for you to complete.

Increasing and Decreasing Functions

In Section 5.1, we used exponential functions as examples of increasing and decreasing functions. In reality, one function can be both increasing and decreasing over certain intervals. For example, in Figure 5.15, the function f is said to be *increasing* on the intervals $(-\infty, x_1]$ and $[x_2, \infty)$, and f is said to be *decreasing* on the interval $[x_1, x_2]$. More specifically, increasing and decreasing functions are defined as follows:

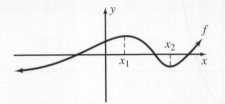

Figure 5.15

> **Definition 5.3**
>
> Let f be a function, with the interval I a subset of the domain of f. Let x_1 and x_2 be in I. Then:
>
> **1.** f is *increasing* on I if $f(x_1) < f(x_2)$ whenever $x_1 < x_2$.
> **2.** f is *decreasing* on I if $f(x_1) > f(x_2)$ whenever $x_1 < x_2$.
> **3.** f is *constant* on I if $f(x_1) = f(x_2)$ for every x_1 and x_2.

Apply Definition 5.3, and you will see that the quadratic function $f(x) = x^2$ shown in Figure 5.16 is decreasing on $(-\infty, 0]$ and increasing on $[0, \infty)$. Likewise, the linear function $f(x) = 2x$ in Figure 5.17 is increasing throughout its domain of real numbers, so we say that it is increasing on $(-\infty, \infty)$. The function $f(x) = -2x$ in Figure 5.18 is decreasing on $(-\infty, \infty)$. For our purposes in this text, we will rely on our knowledge of the graphs of the functions to determine when functions are increasing and decreasing. More formal techniques for determining when functions increase and decrease will be developed in calculus.

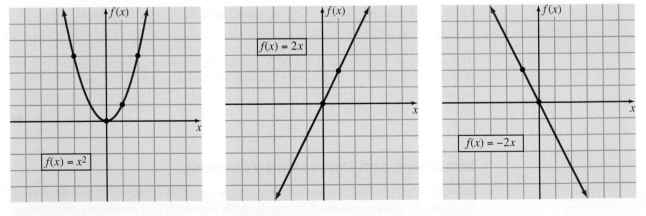

Figure 5.16   **Figure 5.17**   **Figure 5.18**

A function that is always increasing (or is always decreasing) over its entire domain is a one-to-one function and so has an inverse function. Furthermore, as illustrated by Example 4, even if a function is not one-to-one over its entire domain, it may be so over some subset of the domain. It then has an inverse function over this restricted domain. As functions become more complex, a graphing utility can be used to help with problems like those we have discussed in this section. For example, suppose that we want to know whether the function $f(x) = \dfrac{3x + 1}{x - 4}$ is a one-to-one function and therefore has an inverse function. Using a graphing utility, we can quickly get a sketch of the graph (Figure 5.19). Then, by applying the horizontal-line test to the graph, we can be fairly certain that the function is one-to-one.

A graphing utility can also be used to help determine the intervals on which a function is increasing or decreasing. For example, to determine such intervals for the function $f(x) = \sqrt{x^2 + 4}$, let's use a graphing utility to get a sketch of the curve (Figure 5.20). From this graph, we see that the function is decreasing on the interval $(-\infty, 0]$ and is increasing on the interval $[0, \infty)$.

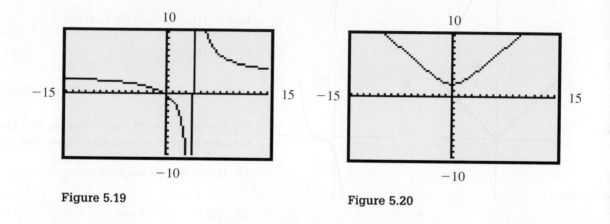

Figure 5.19   Figure 5.20

Concept Quiz 5.3

For Problems 1–10, answer true or false.

1. Over the domain of all real numbers, a quadratic function is never a one-to-one function.
2. The notation f^{-1} refers to the inverse of the function f.
3. If f and g are inverse functions, then the range of f is the domain of g.
4. If a horizontal line intersects the graph of a function in more than one point, then the function is one-to-one.
5. If $f(1) = 4$ and $f(-3) = 4$, then f is not a one-to-one function.
6. The only condition for f and g to be inverse functions is that g must reverse the correspondence given by f.
7. Given that f has an inverse function and $f(2) = -8$, then $f^{-1}(-8) = 2$.

8. The graphs of two functions that are inverses of each other are mirror images with reference to the line $y = -x$.

9. The quadratic function $f(x) = (x - 3)^2$ is decreasing on the interval $(-\infty, 0]$.

10. Any function that is increasing over its entire domain is a one-to-one function.

Problem Set 5.3

For Problems 1–6, determine whether the graph represents a one-to-one function. (Objective 1)

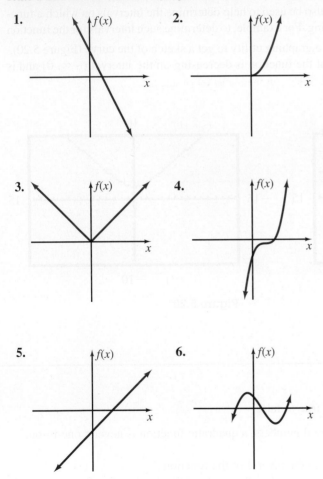

1.

2.

3.

4.

5.

6.

For Problems 7–14, determine whether the function f is one-to-one. (Objective 1)

7. $f(x) = 5x + 4$

8. $f(x) = -3x + 4$

9. $f(x) = x^3$

10. $f(x) = x^5 + 1$

11. $f(x) = |x| + 1$

12. $f(x) = -|x| - 2$

13. $f(x) = -x^4$

14. $f(x) = x^4 + 1$

For Problems 15–18, (a) list the domain and range of the function, (b) form the inverse function f^{-1}, and (c) list the domain and range of f^{-1}. (Objective 3)

15. $f = \{(1, 5), (2, 9), (5, 21)\}$

16. $f = \{(1, 1), (4, 2), (9, 3), (16, 4)\}$

17. $f = \{(0, 0), (2, 8), (-1, -1), (-2, -8)\}$

18. $f = \{(-1, 1), (-2, 4), (-3, 9), (-4, 16)\}$

For Problems 19–26, verify that the two given functions are inverses of each other. (Objective 2)

19. $f(x) = 5x - 9$ and $g(x) = \dfrac{x + 9}{5}$

20. $f(x) = -3x + 4$ and $g(x) = \dfrac{4 - x}{3}$

21. $f(x) = -\dfrac{1}{2}x + \dfrac{5}{6}$ and $g(x) = -2x + \dfrac{5}{3}$

22. $f(x) = x^3 + 1$ and $g(x) = \sqrt[3]{x - 1}$

23. $f(x) = \dfrac{1}{x - 1}$ for $x > 1$, and

   $g(x) = \dfrac{x + 1}{x}$ for $x > 0$

24. $f(x) = x^2 + 2$ for $x \geq 0$, and

   $g(x) = \sqrt{x - 2}$ for $x \geq 2$

25. $f(x) = \sqrt{2x - 4}$ for $x \geq 2$, and

   $g(x) = \dfrac{x^2 + 4}{2}$ for $x \geq 0$

26. $f(x) = x^2 - 4$ for $x \geq 0$, and

$g(x) = \sqrt{x + 4}$ for $x \geq -4$

For Problems 27–36, determine whether f and g are inverse functions. **(Objective 2)**

27. $f(x) = 3x$ and $g(x) = -\dfrac{1}{3}x$

28. $f(x) = \dfrac{3}{4}x - 2$ and $g(x) = \dfrac{4}{3}x + \dfrac{8}{3}$

29. $f(x) = x^3$ and $g(x) = \sqrt[3]{x}$

30. $f(x) = \dfrac{1}{x + 1}$ and $g(x) = \dfrac{1 - x}{x}$

31. $f(x) = x$ and $g(x) = \dfrac{1}{x}$

32. $f(x) = \dfrac{3}{5}x + \dfrac{1}{3}$ and $g(x) = \dfrac{5}{3}x - 3$

33. $f(x) = x^2 - 3$ for $x \geq 0$ and
$g(x) = \sqrt{x + 3}$ for $x \geq -3$

34. $f(x) = |x - 1|$ for $x \geq 1$ and
$g(x) = |x + 1|$ for $x \geq 0$

35. $f(x) = \sqrt{x + 1}$ for $x \geq -1$ and
$g(x) = x^2 - 1$ for $x \geq 0$

36. $f(x) = \sqrt{2x - 2}$ for $x \geq 1$ and
$g(x) = \dfrac{1}{2}x^2 + 1$ for $x \geq 0$

For Problems 37–54, (a) find f^{-1} and (b) verify that $(f \circ f^{-1})(x) = x$ and $(f^{-1} \circ f)(x) = x$. **(Objective 4)**

37. $f(x) = x - 4$ **38.** $f(x) = 2x - 1$

39. $f(x) = -3x - 4$ **40.** $f(x) = -5x + 6$

41. $f(x) = \dfrac{3}{4}x - \dfrac{5}{6}$ **42.** $f(x) = \dfrac{2}{3}x - \dfrac{1}{4}$

43. $f(x) = -\dfrac{2}{3}x$ **44.** $f(x) = \dfrac{4}{3}x$

45. $f(x) = \sqrt{x}$ for $x \geq 0$

46. $f(x) = \sqrt{x} - 2$ for $x \geq 0$

47. $f(x) = \sqrt{x + 4}$ for $x \geq -4$

48. $f(x) = 3\sqrt{x}$ for $x \geq 0$

49. $f(x) = \dfrac{1}{x - 3}$ for $x \neq 3$

50. $f(x) = \dfrac{1}{x}$ for $x \neq 0$

51. $f(x) = x^2 + 4$ for $x \geq 0$

52. $f(x) = x^2 + 1$ for $x \leq 0$

53. $f(x) = 1 + \dfrac{1}{x}$ for $x > 0$

54. $f(x) = \dfrac{x}{x + 1}$ for $x > -1$

For Problems 55–60, (a) find f^{-1} and (b) graph f and f^{-1} on the same set of axes. **(Objective 5)**

55. $f(x) = 3x$

56. $f(x) = -x$

57. $f(x) = 2x + 1$

58. $f(x) = -3x - 3$

59. $f(x) = x^2 - 4$ for $x \geq 0$

60. $f(x) = \sqrt{x - 3}$ for $x \geq 3$

For Problems 61–68, find the intervals on which the given function is increasing and the intervals on which it is decreasing. **(Objective 6)**

61. $f(x) = x^2 + 1$

62. $f(x) = x^3$

63. $f(x) = -3x + 1$

64. $f(x) = (x - 3)^2 + 1$

65. $f(x) = -(x + 2)^2 - 1$

66. $f(x) = x^2 - 2x + 6$

67. $f(x) = -2x^2 - 16x - 35$

68. $f(x) = x^2 + 3x - 1$

Thoughts Into Words

69. Does the function $f(x) = 4$ have an inverse? Explain your answer.

70. Explain why every nonconstant linear function has an inverse.

71. Are the functions $f(x) = x^4$ and $g(x) = \sqrt[4]{x}$ inverses of each other? Explain your answer.

72. What does it mean to say that 2 and -2 are additive inverses of each other? What does it mean to say that 2 and $\dfrac{1}{2}$ are multiplicative inverses of each other? What does it mean to say that the functions $f(x) = x - 2$ and $f(x) = x + 2$ are inverses of each other? Do you think that the concept of "inverse" is being used in a consistent manner? Explain your answer.

Further Investigations

73. The function notation and the operation of composition can be used to find inverses as follows: To find the inverse of $f(x) = 5x + 3$, we know that $f(f^{-1}(x))$ must produce x. Therefore

$$f(f^{-1}(x)) = 5[f^{-1}(x)] + 3 = x$$
$$5[f^{-1}(x)] = x - 3$$
$$f^{-1}(x) = \frac{x - 3}{5}$$

Use this approach to find the inverse of each of the following functions.

(a) $f(x) = 3x - 9$ **(b)** $f(x) = -2x + 6$

(c) $f(x) = -x + 1$ **(d)** $f(x) = 2x$

(e) $f(x) = -5x$ **(f)** $f(x) = x^2 + 6$ for $x \geq 0$

74. If $f(x) = 2x + 3$ and $g(x) = 3x - 5$, find
(a) $(f \circ g)^{-1}(x)$ **(b)** $(f^{-1} \circ g^{-1})(x)$
(c) $(g^{-1} \circ f^{-1})(x)$

Graphing Calculator Activities

75. For Problems 37–44, graph the given function, the inverse function that you found, and $f(x) = x$ on the same set of axes. In each case, the given function and its inverse should produce graphs that are reflections of each other through the line $f(x) = x$.

76. There is another way we can use the graphing calculator to help show that two functions are inverses of each other. Suppose we want to show that $f(x) = x^2 - 2$ for $x \geq 0$ and $g(x) = \sqrt{x + 2}$ for $x \geq -2$ are inverses of each other. Let's make the following assignments for our graphing calculator.

$$f: \ Y_1 = x^2 - 2$$
$$g: \ Y_2 = \sqrt{x + 2}$$
$$f \circ g: \ Y_3 = (Y_2)^2 - 2$$
$$g \circ f: \ Y_4 = \sqrt{Y_1 + 2}$$

Now we can proceed as follows:

a. Graph $Y_1 = x^2 - 2$, and note that for $x > 0$, the range is greater than or equal to -2.

b. Graph $Y_2 = \sqrt{x + 2}$, and note that for $x \geq -2$, the range is greater than or equal to 0.

c. Graph $Y_3 = (Y_2)^2 - 2$ for $x \geq -2$, and observe the line $y = x$ for $x \geq -2$.

d. Graph $Y_4 = \sqrt{Y_1 + 2}$ for $x \geq 0$, and observe the line $y = x$ for $x \geq 0$.

Use this approach to check your answers for Problems 45–54.

77. Use the technique demonstrated in Problem 76 to show that

$$f(x) = \frac{x}{\sqrt{x^2 + 1}}$$

and

$$g(x) = \frac{x}{\sqrt{1 - x^2}} \quad \text{for } -1 < x < 1$$

are inverses of each other.

5.4   Logarithms

OBJECTIVES

1. Change equations between exponential and logarithmic form
2. Evaluate a logarithmic expression
3. Apply the properties of logarithms
4. Solve logarithmic equations

In Sections 5.1 and 5.2 we discussed exponential expressions of the form b^n, where b is any positive real number and n is any real number; we used exponential expressions of the form b^n to define exponential functions; and we used exponential functions to help solve problems. In the next three sections, we will follow the same basic pattern with respect to a new concept: logarithms. Let's begin with the following definition:

> **Definition 5.4**
>
> If r is any positive real number, then the unique exponent t such that $b^t = r$ is called the **logarithm of r with base b** and is denoted by $\log_b r$.

According to Definition 5.4, the logarithm of 16 base 2 is the exponent t such that $2^t = 16$; thus we can write $\log_2 16 = 4$. Likewise, we can write $\log_{10} 1000 = 3$ because $10^3 = 1000$. In general, we can remember Definition 5.4 by the statement

$$\log_b r = t \quad \text{is equivalent to } b^t = r$$

Therefore we can easily switch back and forth between exponential and logarithmic forms of equations, as the next examples illustrate.

$$\log_2 8 = 3 \quad \text{is equivalent to } 2^3 = 8$$
$$\log_{10} 100 = 2 \quad \text{is equivalent to } 10^2 = 100$$
$$\log_3 81 = 4 \quad \text{is equivalent to } 3^4 = 81$$
$$\log_{10} 0.001 = -3 \quad \text{is equivalent to } 10^{-3} = 0.001$$
$$\log_m n = p \quad \text{is equivalent to } m^p = n$$

$$2^7 = 128 \quad \text{is equivalent to } \log_2 128 = 7$$
$$5^3 = 125 \quad \text{is equivalent to } \log_5 125 = 3$$
$$\left(\frac{1}{2}\right)^4 = \frac{1}{16} \quad \text{is equivalent to } \log_{1/2}\left(\frac{1}{16}\right) = 4$$
$$10^{-2} = 0.01 \quad \text{is equivalent to } \log_{10} 0.01 = -2$$
$$a^b = c \quad \text{is equivalent to } \log_a c = b$$

Some logarithms can be determined by changing to exponential form and using the properties of exponents, as the next two examples illustrate.

Classroom Example
Evaluate $\log_{10} 0.01$.

EXAMPLE 1   Evaluate $\log_{10} 0.0001$.

Solution

Let $\log_{10} 0.0001 = x$. Then, by changing to exponential form, we have $10^x = 0.0001$, which can be solved as follows:

$$10^x = 0.0001$$
$$10^x = 10^{-4} \qquad 0.0001 = \frac{1}{10{,}000} = \frac{1}{10^4} = 10^{-4}$$
$$x = -4$$

Thus we have $\log_{10} 0.0001 = -4$.

Classroom Example
Evaluate $\log_3 \sqrt[3]{27}$.

EXAMPLE 2   Evaluate $\log_7 \sqrt[3]{49}$.

Solution

Let $\log_7 \sqrt[3]{49} = x$. Then, by changing to exponential form, we have $7^x = \sqrt[3]{49}$, which can be solved as follows:

$$7^x = \sqrt[3]{49}$$
$$7^x = (49)^{\frac{1}{3}}$$
$$7^x = (7^2)^{\frac{1}{3}}$$
$$7^x = 7^{\frac{2}{3}}$$
$$x = \frac{2}{3}$$

Therefore we have $\log_7 \sqrt[3]{49} = \frac{2}{3}$.

Some equations that involve logarithms can also be solved by changing to exponential form and using our knowledge of exponents.

Classroom Example
Solve $\log_{25} x = \dfrac{3}{2}$.

EXAMPLE 3   Solve $\log_8 x = \dfrac{2}{3}$.

Solution

Changing $\log_8 x = \dfrac{2}{3}$ to exponential form, we obtain

$$8^{2/3} = x$$

Therefore

$$x = \left(\sqrt[3]{8}\right)^2$$
$$= 2^2$$
$$= 4$$

The solution set is $\{4\}$.

Classroom Example
Solve $\log_b \dfrac{36}{121} = 2$.

EXAMPLE 4   Solve $\log_b\left(\dfrac{27}{64}\right) = 3$.

Solution

Change $\log_b\left(\dfrac{27}{64}\right) = 3$ to exponential form to obtain

$$b^3 = \frac{27}{64}$$

Therefore

$$b = \sqrt[3]{\frac{27}{64}}$$
$$= \frac{3}{4}$$

The solution set is $\left\{\dfrac{3}{4}\right\}$.

Properties of Logarithms

There are some properties of logarithms that are a direct consequence of Definition 5.2 and the properties of exponents. For example, the following property is obtained by writing the exponential equations $b^1 = b$ and $b^0 = 1$ in logarithmic form.

> ## Property 5.3
>
> For $b > 0$ and $b \neq 1$,
>
> $$\log_b b = 1 \quad \text{and} \quad \log_b 1 = 0$$

Therefore according to Property 5.3, we can write

$$\log_{10} 10 = 1 \qquad \log_4 4 = 1$$
$$\log_{10} 1 = 0 \qquad \log_5 1 = 0$$

Also, from Definition 5.2, we know that $\log_b r$ is the exponent t such that $b^t = r$. Therefore, raising b to the $\log_b r$ power must produce r. This fact is stated in Property 5.4.

> ## Property 5.4
>
> For $b > 0$, $b \neq 1$, and $r > 0$,
>
> $$b^{\log_b r} = r$$

Therefore according to Property 5.4, we can write

$$10^{\log_{10} 72} = 72 \qquad 3^{\log_3 85} = 85 \qquad e^{\log_e 7} = 7$$

Because a logarithm is by definition an exponent, it seems reasonable to predict that some properties of logarithms correspond to the basic exponential properties. This is an accurate prediction; these properties provide a basis for computational work with logarithms. Let's state the first of these properties and show how we can use our knowledge of exponents to verify it.

> ## Property 5.5
>
> For positive numbers b, r, and s, where $b \neq 1$,
>
> $$\log_b rs = \log_b r + \log_b s$$

To verify Property 5.5, we can proceed as follows. Let $m = \log_b r$ and $n = \log_b s$. Change each of these equations to exponential form:

$$m = \log_b r \quad \text{becomes} \quad r = b^m$$
$$n = \log_b s \quad \text{becomes} \quad s = b^n$$

Thus the product rs becomes

$$rs = b^m \cdot b^n = b^{m+n}$$

Now, by changing $rs = b^{m+n}$ back to logarithmic form, we obtain

$$\log_b rs = m + n$$

Replace m with $\log_b r$ and replace n with $\log_b s$ to yield

$$\log_b rs = \log_b r + \log_b s$$

The following two examples illustrate the use of Property 5.5.

EXAMPLE 5   If $\log_2 5 = 2.3219$ and $\log_2 3 = 1.5850$, evaluate $\log_2 15$.

Solution

Because $15 = 5 \cdot 3$, we can apply Property 5.5 as follows:

$$\begin{aligned}
\log_2 15 &= \log_2(5 \cdot 3) \\
&= \log_2 5 + \log_2 3 \\
&= 2.3219 + 1.5850 \\
&= 3.9069
\end{aligned}$$

EXAMPLE 6

Given that $\log_{10} 178 = 2.2504$ and $\log_{10} 89 = 1.9494$, evaluate $\log_{10}(178 \cdot 89)$.

Solution

$$\begin{aligned}
\log_{10}(178 \cdot 89) &= \log_{10} 178 + \log_{10} 89 \\
&= 2.2504 + 1.9494 \\
&= 4.1998
\end{aligned}$$

Because $\dfrac{b^m}{b^n} = b^{m-n}$, we would expect a corresponding property that pertains to logarithms. Property 5.6 is that property. We can verify it by using an approach similar to the one we used to verify Property 5.5. This verification is left for you to do as an exercise in the next problem set.

Property 5.6

For positive numbers b, r, and s, where $b \neq 1$,

$$\log_b\left(\frac{r}{s}\right) = \log_b r - \log_b s$$

We can use Property 5.6 to change a division problem into an equivalent subtraction problem, as the next two examples illustrate.

Classroom Example
If $\log_5 39 = 2.2763$ and
$\log_5 13 = 1.5937$, evaluate
$\log_5 3$.

EXAMPLE 7   If $\log_5 36 = 2.2266$ and $\log_5 4 = 0.8614$, evaluate $\log_5 9$.

Solution

Because $9 = \dfrac{36}{4}$, we can use Property 5.6 as follows:

$$\log_5 9 = \log_5\left(\frac{36}{4}\right)$$

$$= \log_5 36 - \log_5 4$$

$$= 2.2266 - 0.8614$$

$$= 1.3652$$

Classroom Example
Evaluate $\log_{10}\left(\dfrac{416}{57}\right)$ given that
$\log_{10} 416 = 2.6191$ and
$\log_{10} 57 = 1.7559$.

EXAMPLE 8

Evaluate $\log_{10}\left(\dfrac{379}{86}\right)$ given that $\log_{10} 379 = 2.5786$ and $\log_{10} 86 = 1.9345$.

Solution

$$\log_{10}\left(\frac{379}{86}\right) = \log_{10} 379 - \log_{10} 86$$

$$= 2.5786 - 1.9345$$

$$= 0.6441$$

Another property of exponents states that $(b^n)^m = b^{mn}$. The corresponding property of logarithms is stated in Property 5.7. Again, we will leave the verification of this property as an exercise for you to do in the next set of problems.

> **Property 5.7**
>
> If r is a positive real number, b is a positive real number other than 1, and p is any real number, then
>
> $$\log_b r^p = p(\log_b r)$$

We will use Property 5.7 in the next two examples.

Classroom Example
Evaluate $\log_3 34^{\frac{1}{4}}$ given
that $\log_3 34 = 3.2098$.

EXAMPLE 9   Evaluate $\log_2 22^{1/3}$ given that $\log_2 22 = 4.4598$.

Solution

$$\log_2 22^{1/3} = \frac{1}{3}\log_2 22 \quad\quad \text{Property 5.7}$$

$$= \frac{1}{3}(4.4598)$$

$$= 1.4866$$

Classroom Example
Evaluate $\log_{10}(2057)^{\frac{5}{6}}$ given that $\log_{10}2057 = 3.3132$.

EXAMPLE 10 Evaluate $\log_{10}(8540)^{3/5}$ given that $\log_{10}8540 = 3.9315$.

Solution

$$\log_{10}(8540)^{3/5} = \frac{3}{5}\log_{10}8540$$

$$= \frac{3}{5}(3.9315)$$

$$= 2.3589$$

Used together, the properties of logarithms allow us to change the forms of various logarithmic expressions. For example, we can rewrite an expression such as $\log_b\sqrt{\dfrac{xy}{z}}$ in terms of sums and differences of simpler logarithmic quantities as follows:

$$\log_b\sqrt{\frac{xy}{z}} = \log_b\left(\frac{xy}{z}\right)^{1/2} = \frac{1}{2}\log_b\left(\frac{xy}{z}\right) \qquad \text{Property 5.7}$$

$$= \frac{1}{2}(\log_b xy - \log_b z) \qquad \text{Property 5.6}$$

$$= \frac{1}{2}(\log_b x + \log_b y - \log_b z) \qquad \text{Property 5.5}$$

Classroom Example
Write each expression as the sum or difference of simpler logarithmic quantities. Assume that all variables represent positive real numbers:
(a) $\log_b m^2\sqrt{n}$
(b) $\log_b\dfrac{\sqrt[5]{x}}{y^3}$
(c) $\log_b\dfrac{x^5}{yz^2}$

EXAMPLE 11

Write each expression as the sum or difference of simpler logarithmic quantities. Assume that all variables represent positive real numbers:

(a) $\log_b xy^2$ **(b)** $\log_b\dfrac{\sqrt{x}}{y}$ **(c)** $\log_b\dfrac{x^3}{yz}$

Solution

(a) $\log_b xy^2 = \log_b x + \log_b y^2 = \log_b x + 2\log_b y$

(b) $\log_b\dfrac{\sqrt{x}}{y} = \log_b\sqrt{x} - \log_b y = \dfrac{1}{2}\log_b x - \log_b y$

(c) $\log_b\dfrac{x^3}{yz} = \log_b x^3 - \log_b yz = 3\log_b x - (\log_b y + \log_b z)$

$$= 3\log_b x - \log_b y - \log_b z$$

Sometimes we need to change from an indicated sum or difference of logarithmic quantities to an indicated product or quotient. This is especially helpful when solving certain kinds of equations that involve logarithms. Note in these next two examples how we can use the properties, along with the process of changing from logarithmic form to exponential form, to solve some equations.

EXAMPLE 12 Solve $\log_{10} x + \log_{10}(x + 9) = 1$.

Solution

$$\log_{10} x + \log_{10}(x + 9) = 1$$

$$\log_{10}[x(x + 9)] = 1 \qquad \text{Property 5.5}$$

$$10^1 = x(x + 9) \qquad \text{Change to exponential form}$$

$$10 = x^2 + 9x$$

$$0 = x^2 + 9x - 10$$

$$0 = (x + 10)(x - 1)$$

$$x + 10 = 0 \qquad \text{or} \quad x - 1 = 0$$

$$x = -10 \quad \text{or} \qquad x = 1$$

Logarithms are defined only for positive numbers, so x and $x + 9$ have to be positive. Therefore the solution of -10 must be discarded. The solution set is $\{1\}$.

EXAMPLE 13 Solve $\log_5(x + 4) - \log_5 x = 2$.

Solution

$$\log_5(x + 4) - \log_5 x = 2$$

$$\log_5\left(\frac{x + 4}{x}\right) = 2 \qquad \text{Property 5.6}$$

$$5^2 = \frac{x + 4}{x} \qquad \text{Change to exponential form}$$

$$25 = \frac{x + 4}{x}$$

$$25x = x + 4$$

$$24x = 4$$

$$x = \frac{4}{24} = \frac{1}{6}$$

The solution set is $\left\{\frac{1}{6}\right\}$.

Because logarithms are defined only for positive numbers, we should realize that some logarithmic equations may not have any solutions. (In those cases, the solution set is the null set.) It is also possible for a logarithmic equation to have a negative solution, as the next example illustrates.

Classroom Example
Solve $\log_4 6 + \log_4(x + 7) = 2$.

EXAMPLE 14   Solve $\log_2 3 + \log_2(x + 4) = 3$.

Solution

$$\log_2 3 + \log_2(x + 4) = 3$$
$$\log_2 3(x + 4) = 3 \qquad \text{Property 5.5}$$
$$3(x + 4) = 2^3 \qquad \text{Change to exponential form}$$
$$3x + 12 = 8$$
$$3x = -4$$
$$x = -\frac{4}{3}$$

The only restriction is that $x + 4 > 0$ or $x > -4$. Therefore, the solution set is $\left\{-\dfrac{4}{3}\right\}$. Perhaps you should check this answer.

Concept Quiz 5.4

For Problems 1–7, answer true or false.

1. For $m > 0$, the $\log_m n = q$ is equivalent to $m^q = n$.
2. The $\log_7 7$ is equal to zero.
3. A logarithm by definition is an exponent.
4. The $\log_5 9^2$ is equivalent to $2 \log_5 9$.
5. The expression $\log_2 x - \log_2 y + \log_2 z$ is equivalent to $\log_2 xyz$.
6. $\log_4 4 + \log_4 1 = 1$.
7. For the equation $\log_2(x + 3) + \log_2(x + 5) = 1$, the solutions are restricted to values of x that are greater than -3.

For Problems 8–10, match each expression with its equivalent form.

8. $\log_3(2x)$

A. $\log_3 \dfrac{1}{2} + \log_3 x$

9. $\log_3\left(\dfrac{1}{2}x\right)$

B. $\dfrac{1}{2}\log_3 x$

10. $\log_3 \sqrt{x}$

C. $\log_3 2 + \log_3 x$

Problem Set 5.4

For Problems 1–10, write each exponential statement in logarithmic form. For example, $2^5 = 32$ becomes $\log_2 32 = 5$ in logarithmic form. (Objective 1)

1. $2^7 = 128$

2. $3^3 = 27$

3. $5^3 = 125$

4. $2^6 = 64$

5. $10^3 = 1000$

6. $10^1 = 10$

7. $2^{-2} = \dfrac{1}{4}$

8. $3^{-4} = \dfrac{1}{81}$

9. $10^{-1} = 0.1$

10. $10^{-2} = 0.01$

For Problems 11–20, write each logarithmic statement in exponential form. For example, $\log_2 8 = 3$ becomes $2^3 = 8$ in exponential form. **(Objective 1)**

11. $\log_3 81 = 4$

12. $\log_2 256 = 8$

13. $\log_4 64 = 3$

14. $\log_5 25 = 2$

15. $\log_{10} 10,000 = 4$

16. $\log_{10} 100,000 = 5$

17. $\log_2\left(\dfrac{1}{16}\right) = -4$

18. $\log_5\left(\dfrac{1}{125}\right) = -3$

19. $\log_{10} 0.001 = -3$

20. $\log_{10} 0.000001 = -6$

For Problems 21–44, evaluate each logarithmic expression. **(Objective 2)**

21. $\log_2 16$

22. $\log_3 9$

23. $\log_3 81$

24. $\log_2 512$

25. $\log_6 216$

26. $\log_4 256$

27. $\log_7 \sqrt{7}$

28. $\log_2 \sqrt[3]{2}$

29. $\log_{10} 1$

30. $\log_{10} 10$

31. $\log_3 \sqrt{27}$

32. $\log_{\frac{1}{2}}\left(\dfrac{1}{32}\right)$

33. $\log_{\frac{1}{4}} 64$

34. $\log_2 \sqrt[3]{16}$

35. $\log_{10} 0.1$

36. $\log_{10} 0.0001$

37. $10^{\log_{10} 5}$

38. $10^{\log_{10} 14}$

39. $\log_2\left(\dfrac{1}{32}\right)$

40. $\log_5\left(\dfrac{1}{25}\right)$

41. $\log_5(\log_2 32)$

42. $\log_2(\log_4 16)$

43. $\log_{10}(\log_7 7)$

44. $\log_2(\log_5 5)$

For Problems 45–56, solve each equation. **(Objective 4)**

45. $\log_7 x = 2$

46. $\log_2 x = 5$

47. $\log_8 x = \dfrac{4}{3}$

48. $\log_{16} x = \dfrac{3}{2}$

49. $\log_9 x = -1$

50. $\log_8 x = -2$

51. $\log_4 x = -\dfrac{3}{2}$

52. $\log_9 x = -\dfrac{5}{2}$

53. $\log_{\frac{1}{2}} x = 3$

54. $\log_{\frac{2}{3}} x = 2$

55. $\log_x 2 = \dfrac{1}{2}$

56. $\log_x 3 = \dfrac{1}{2}$

For Problems 57–65, given that $\log_2 5 = 2.3219$ and $\log_2 7 = 2.8074$, evaluate each expression by using Properties 5.5–5.7. **(Objective 3)**

57. $\log_2 35$

58. $\log_2\left(\dfrac{7}{5}\right)$

59. $\log_2 125$

60. $\log_2 49$

61. $\log_2 \sqrt{7}$

62. $\log_2 \sqrt[3]{5}$

63. $\log_2 175$

64. $\log_2 56$

65. $\log_2 80$

For Problems 66–74, given that $\log_8 5 = 0.7740$ and $\log_8 11 = 1.1531$, evaluate each expression using Properties 5.5–5.7. **(Objective 3)**

66. $\log_8 55$

67. $\log_8\left(\dfrac{5}{11}\right)$

68. $\log_8 25$

69. $\log_8 \sqrt{11}$

70. $\log_8 (5)^{2/3}$

71. $\log_8 88$

72. $\log_8 320$

73. $\log_8\left(\dfrac{25}{11}\right)$

74. $\log_8\left(\dfrac{121}{25}\right)$

For Problems 75–86, express each of the following as the sum or difference of simpler logarithmic quantities. Assume that all variables represent positive real numbers. **(Objective 3)** For example,

$$\log_b \frac{x^3}{y^2} = \log_b x^3 - \log_b y^2$$
$$= 3\log_b x - 2\log_b y$$

75. $\log_b xyz$

76. $\log_b 5x$

77. $\log_b\left(\dfrac{y}{z}\right)$

78. $\log_b\left(\dfrac{x^2}{yz}\right)$

79. $\log_b y^3 z^4$

80. $\log_b x^2 y^3$

81. $\log_b\left(\dfrac{x^{1/2}}{y^{1/3}z^4}\right)$

82. $\log_b x^{2/3} y^{3/4}$

83. $\log_b \sqrt[3]{x^2 z}$

84. $\log_b \sqrt{xy}$

85. $\log_b\left(x\sqrt{\dfrac{x}{y}}\right)$

86. $\log_b \sqrt{\dfrac{x}{y}}$

For Problems 87–94, express each of the following as a single logarithm. (Assume that all variables represent positive real numbers.) (Objective 3) For example,

$$3\log_b x + 5\log_b y = \log_b x^3 y^5$$

87. $2\log_b x - 4\log_b y$

88. $\log_b x + \log_b y - \log_b z$

89. $\log_b x - (\log_b y - \log_b z)$

90. $(\log_b x - \log_b y) - \log_b z$

91. $2\log_b x + 4\log_b y - 3\log_b z$

92. $\log_b x + \dfrac{1}{2}\log_b y$

93. $\dfrac{1}{2}\log_b x - \log_b x + 4\log_b y$

94. $2\log_b x + \dfrac{1}{2}\log_b(x - 1) - 4\log_b(2x + 5)$

For Problems 95–112, solve each equation. (Objective 4)

95. $\log_3 x + \log_3 4 = 2$

96. $\log_7 5 + \log_7 x = 1$

97. $\log_{10} x + \log_{10}(x - 21) = 2$

98. $\log_{10} x + \log_{10}(x - 3) = 1$

99. $\log_2 x + \log_2(x - 3) = 2$

100. $\log_3 x + \log_3(x - 2) = 1$

101. $\log_3(x + 3) + \log_3(x + 5) = 1$

102. $\log_2(x + 2) = 1 - \log_2(x + 3)$

103. $\log_2 3 + \log_2(x + 4) = 3$

104. $\log_4 7 + \log_4(x + 3) = 2$

105. $\log_{10}(2x - 1) - \log_{10}(x - 2) = 1$

106. $\log_{10}(9x - 2) = 1 + \log_{10}(x - 4)$

107. $\log_5(3x - 2) = 1 + \log_5(x - 4)$

108. $\log_6 x + \log_6(x + 5) = 2$

109. $\log_2(x - 1) - \log_2(x + 3) = 2$

110. $\log_5 x = \log_5(x + 2) + 1$

111. $\log_8(x + 7) + \log_8 x = 1$

112. $\log_6(x + 1) + \log_6(x - 4) = 2$

113. Verify Property 5.6.

114. Verify Property 5.7.

Thoughts Into Words

115. Explain, without using Property 5.4, why $4^{\log_4 9}$ equals 9.

116. How would you explain the concept of a logarithm to someone who had just completed an elementary algebra course?

117. In the next section, we will show that the logarithmic function $f(x) = \log_2 x$ is the inverse of the exponential function $f(x) = 2^x$. From that information, how could you sketch a graph of $f(x) = \log_2 x$?

Answers to the Concept Quiz

1. True **2.** False **3.** True **4.** True **5.** False **6.** True **7.** True **8.** C **9.** A **10.** B

5.5   Logarithmic Functions

OBJECTIVES

1 Graph logarithmic functions

2 Evaluate common logarithms and natural logarithms

3 Solve equations for common logarithms and natural logarithms

We can now use the concept of a logarithm to define a logarithmic function as follows:

> **Definition 5.5**
>
> If $b > 0$ and $b \neq 1$, then the function defined by
>
> $$f(x) = \log_b x$$
>
> where x is any positive real number, is called the **logarithmic function with base b**.

We can obtain the graph of a specific logarithmic function in various ways. For example, the equation $y = \log_2 x$ can be changed to the exponential equation $2^y = x$, where we can determine a table of values. In the next set of exercises you will be asked to use this approach to graph some logarithmic functions. We can also set up a table of values directly from the logarithmic equation and sketch the graph from the table. Example 1 illustrates this approach.

Classroom Example
Graph $f(x) = \log_3 x$.

EXAMPLE 1   Graph $f(x) = \log_2 x$.

Solution

Let's choose some values for x in which we can easily determine the corresponding values for $\log_2 x$. (Remember that logarithms are defined only for the positive real numbers.)

x	$f(x)$
$\dfrac{1}{8}$	-3
$\dfrac{1}{4}$	-2
$\dfrac{1}{2}$	-1
1	0
2	1
4	2
8	3

$\log_2 \dfrac{1}{8} = -3$ because $2^{-3} = \dfrac{1}{2^3} = \dfrac{1}{8}$

$\log_2 1 = 0$ because $2^0 = 1$

Plot these points and connect them with a smooth curve to produce Figure 5.21.

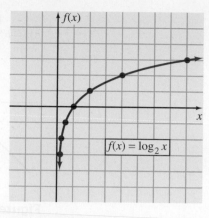

Figure 5.21

Now suppose that we consider two functions f and g as follows:

$f(x) = b^x$ Domain: all real numbers
                      Range: positive real numbers

$g(x) = \log_b x$ Domain: positive real numbers
                      Range: all real numbers

Furthermore, suppose that we consider the composition of f and g and the composition of g and f.

$$(f \circ g)(x) = f(g(x)) = f(\log_b x) = b^{\log_b x} = x$$
$$(g \circ f)(x) = g(f(x)) = g(b^x) = \log_b b^x = x \log_b b = x(1) = x$$

Because the domain of f is the range of g, the range of f is the domain of g, $f(g(x)) = x$, and $g(f(x)) = x$, the two functions f and g are *inverses* of each other.

Remember that the graph of a function and the graph of its inverse are reflections of each other through the line $y = x$. Thus we can determine the graph of a logarithmic function by reflecting the graph of its inverse exponential function through the line $y = x$. We demonstrate this idea in Figure 5.22, in which the graph of $y = 2^x$ has been reflected across the line $y = x$ to produce the graph of $y = \log_2 x$.

The general behavior patterns of exponential functions were illustrated back in Figure 5.3. We can now reflect each of these graphs through the line $y = x$ and observe the general behavior patterns of logarithmic functions shown in Figure 5.23.

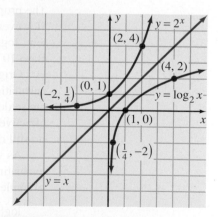

Figure 5.22

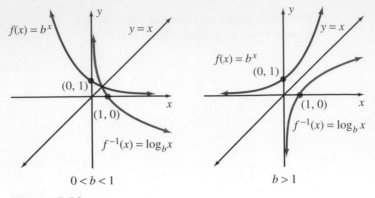

Figure 5.23

As you graph logarithmic functions, don't forget about transformations of basic curves.

1. The graph of $f(x) = 3 + \log_2 x$ is the graph of $f(x) = \log_2 x$ moved up three units. (Because $\log_2 x + 3$ is apt to be confused with $\log_2(x + 3)$, we commonly write $3 + \log_2 x$.)

2. The graph of $f(x) = \log_2(x - 4)$ is the graph of $f(x) = \log_2 x$ moved four units to the right.

3. The graph of $f(x) = -\log_2 x$ is the graph of $f(x) = \log_2 x$ reflected across the x axis.

Common Logarithms—Base 10

The properties of logarithms we discussed in Section 5.4 are true for any valid base. However, because the Hindu-Arabic numeration system that we use is a base-10 system, logarithms to base 10 have historically been used for computational purposes. Base-10 logarithms are called **common logarithms**.

Originally, common logarithms were developed to aid in complicated numerical calculations that involve products, quotients, and powers of real numbers. Today they are seldom used for that purpose because the calculator and computer can much more effectively handle the messy computational problems. However, common logarithms do still occur in applications, so they deserve our attention.

As we know from earlier work, the definition of a logarithm provides the basis for evaluating $\log_{10} x$ for values of x that are integral powers of 10. Consider the following examples:

$$\log_{10} 1000 = 3 \quad \text{because } 10^3 = 1000$$

$$\log_{10} 100 = 2 \quad \text{because } 10^2 = 100$$

$$\log_{10} 10 = 1 \quad \text{because } 10^1 = 10$$

$$\log_{10} 1 = 0 \quad \text{because } 10^0 = 1$$

$$\log_{10} 0.1 = -1 \quad \text{because } 10^{-1} = \frac{1}{10} = 0.1$$

$$\log_{10} 0.01 = -2 \quad \text{because} \quad 10^{-2} = \frac{1}{10^2} = 0.01$$

$$\log_{10} 0.001 = -3 \quad \text{because} \quad 10^{-3} = \frac{1}{10^3} = 0.001$$

When working exclusively with base-10 logarithms, it is customary to omit writing the numeral 10 to designate the base. Thus the expression $\log_{10} x$ is written as $\log x$, and a statement such as $\log_{10} 1000 = 3$ becomes $\log 1000 = 3$. We will follow this practice from now on in this chapter, but don't forget that the base is understood to be 10.

$$\log_{10} x = \log x$$

To find the common logarithm of a positive number that is not an integral power of 10, we can use an appropriately equipped calculator. A calculator that has a common logarithm function (ordinarily, a key labeled $\boxed{\log}$ is used) gives us the following results rounded to four decimal places:

$\log 1.75 = 0.2430$

$\log 23.8 = 1.3766$ Be sure that you can use a calculator and obtain these results

$\log 134 = 2.1271$

$\log 0.192 = -0.7167$

$\log 0.0246 = -1.6091$

In order to use logarithms to solve problems, we sometimes need to be able to determine a number when the logarithm of the number is known. That is to say, we may need to determine x if $\log x$ is known. Let's consider an example.

Classroom Example
Find x if $\log x = 0.6805$.

EXAMPLE 2   Find x if $\log x = 0.2430$.

Solution

If $\log x = 0.2430$, then by changing to exponential form we have $10^{0.2430} = x$. Use the $\boxed{10^x}$ key to find x:

$$x = 10^{0.2430} \approx 1.749846689$$

Therefore $x = 1.7498$ rounded to five significant digits.

Be sure that you can use your calculator and obtain the following results. We rounded the values for x to five significant digits.

If $\log x = 0.7629$, then $x = 10^{0.7629} = 5.7930$.

If $\log x = 1.4825$, then $x = 10^{1.4825} = 30.374$.

If $\log x = 4.0214$, then $x = 10^{4.0214} = 10,505$.

If $\log x = -1.5162$, then $x = 10^{-1.5162} = 0.030465$.

If $\log x = -3.8921$, then $x = 10^{-3.8921} = 0.00012820$.

The **common logarithmic function** is defined by the equation $f(x) = \log x$. It should now be a simple matter to set up a table of values and sketch the function. You will do this in the next set of exercises. Remember that $f(x) = 10^x$ and $g(x) = \log x$ are inverses of each other. Therefore we could also get the graph of $g(x) = \log x$ by reflecting the exponential curve $f(x) = 10^x$ across the line $y = x$.

Natural Logarithms—Base e

In many practical applications of logarithms, the number e (remember that $e \approx 2.71828$) is used as a base. Logarithms with a base of e are called **natural logarithms**, and the symbol $\ln x$ is commonly used instead of $\log_e x$.

$$\log_e x = \ln x$$

Natural logarithms can be found with an appropriately equipped calculator. A calculator that has a natural logarithm function (ordinarily, a key labeled $\boxed{\ln}$) gives us the following results rounded to four decimal places:

$\ln 3.21 = 1.1663$

$\ln 47.28 = 3.8561$

$\ln 842 = 6.7358$

$\ln 0.21 = -1.5606$

$\ln 0.0046 = -5.3817$

$\ln 10 = 2.3026$

Be sure that you can use your calculator to obtain these results. Keep in mind the significance of a statement such as $\ln 3.21 = 1.1663$. By changing to exponential form, we are claiming that e raised to the 1.1663 power is approximately 3.21. Using a calculator, we obtain $e^{1.1663} = 3.210093293$.

Let's do a few more problems to find x when given $\ln x$. Be sure that you agree with these results.

If $\ln x = 2.4156$, then $x = e^{2.4156} = 11.196$.

If $\ln x = 0.9847$, then $x = e^{0.9847} = 2.6770$.

If $\ln x = 4.1482$, then $x = e^{4.1482} = 63.320$.

If $\ln x = -1.7654$, then $x = e^{-1.7654} = 0.17112$.

The **natural logarithmic function** is defined by the equation $f(x) = \ln x$. It is the inverse of the natural exponential function $f(x) = e^x$. Thus one way to graph $f(x) = \ln x$ is to reflect the graph of $f(x) = e^x$ across the line $y = x$. You will be asked to do this in the next set of problems.

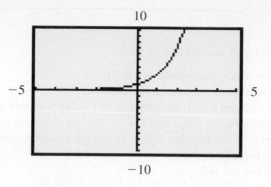

Figure 5.24

In Figure 5.24 we used a graphing utility to sketch the graph of $f(x) = e^x$. Now, on the basis of our previous work with transformations, we should be able to make the following statements:

1. The graph of $f(x) = -e^x$ is the graph of $f(x) = e^x$ reflected through the x axis.

2. The graph of $f(x) = e^{-x}$ is the graph of $f(x) = e^x$ reflected through the y axis.

3. The graph of $f(x) = e^x + 4$ is the graph of $f(x) = e^x$ shifted upward four units.

4. The graph of $f(x) = e^{x+2}$ is the graph of $f(x) = e^x$ shifted two units to the left.

These statements are verified in Figure 5.25, which shows the result of graphing these four functions on the same set of axes by using a graphing utility.

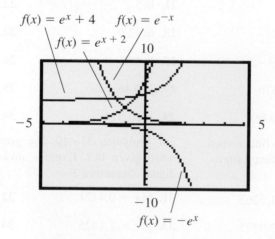

Figure 5.25

Remark: So far, we have used a graphing utility to graph only common logarithmic and natural logarithmic functions. In the next section, we will see how logarithms with bases other than 10 or e are related to common and natural logarithms. This will provide a way of using a graphing utility to graph a logarithmic function with any valid base.

Concept Quiz 5.5

For Problems 1–10, answer true or false.

1. For $f(x) = \log_b x$, the domain of f is $[0, \infty)$.
2. The x axis is an asymptote for the graph of $f(x) = \log_b x$.
3. For all $b > 0$ and $b \neq 1$, the graph of $f(x) = \log_b x$ passes through the point $(1, 0)$.
4. The function $f(x) = \log_2 x$ and $f(x) = \log_{1/2} x^{-1}$ are inverse functions.
5. The inverse of the function $f(x) = \ln x$ is the function $f(x) = e^x$.
6. The base for $\log x$ is 10.
7. The base for $\ln x$ is 2.
8. If $\ln x = 1$, then $x = e$.
9. The graph of $f(x) = \ln(x + 2)$ is the graph of $f(x) = \ln x$ shifted up two units.
10. The graph of $f(x) = \log_4 x$ is the reflection with reference to the line $y = x$ of the graph of $f(x) = 4^x$.

Problem Set 5.5

For Problems 1–10, use a calculator to find each common logarithm. Express answers to four decimal places. **(Objective 2)**

1. $\log 7.24$
2. $\log 2.05$
3. $\log 52.23$
4. $\log 825.8$
5. $\log 3214.1$
6. $\log 14189$
7. $\log 0.729$
8. $\log 0.04376$
9. $\log 0.00034$
10. $\log 0.000069$

For Problems 11–20, use your calculator to find x when given $\log x$. Express answers to five significant digits. **(Objective 3)**

11. $\log x = 2.6143$
12. $\log x = 1.5263$
13. $\log x = 4.9547$
14. $\log x = 3.9335$
15. $\log x = 1.9006$
16. $\log x = 0.5517$
17. $\log x = -1.3148$
18. $\log x = -0.1452$
19. $\log x = -2.1928$
20. $\log x = -2.6542$

For Problems 21–30, use your calculator to find each natural logarithm. Express answers to four decimal places. **(Objective 2)**

21. $\ln 5$
22. $\ln 18$
23. $\ln 32.6$
24. $\ln 79.5$
25. $\ln 430$
26. $\ln 371.8$
27. $\ln 0.46$
28. $\ln 0.524$
29. $\ln 0.0314$
30. $\ln 0.008142$

For Problems 31–40, use your calculator to find x when given $\ln x$. Express answers to five significant digits. **(Objective 3)**

31. $\ln x = 0.4721$
32. $\ln x = 0.9413$
33. $\ln x = 1.1425$
34. $\ln x = 2.7619$
35. $\ln x = 4.6873$
36. $\ln x = 3.0259$
37. $\ln x = -0.7284$
38. $\ln x = -1.6246$
39. $\ln x = -3.3244$
40. $\ln x = -2.3745$

41. (a) Complete the following table, and then graph $f(x) = \log x$. Express the values for $\log x$ to the nearest tenth.

x	0.1	0.5	1	2	4	8	10
log x							

(b) Complete the following table, expressing values for 10^x to the nearest tenth.

x	−1	−0.3	0	0.3	0.6	0.9	1
10ˣ							

Then graph $f(x) = 10^x$, and reflect it across the line $y = x$ to produce the graph for $f(x) = \log x$.

42. (a) Complete the following table, and then graph $f(x) = \ln x$. Express the values for $\ln x$ to the nearest tenth.

x	0.1	0.5	1	2	4	8	10
ln x							

(b) Complete the following table, expressing values for e^x to the nearest tenth.

x	−2.3	−0.7	0	0.7	1.4	2.1	2.3
eˣ							

Then graph $f(x) = e^x$, and reflect it across the line $y = x$ to produce the graph for $f(x) = \ln x$.

43. Graph $y = \log_{\frac{1}{2}} x$ by graphing $\left(\dfrac{1}{2}\right)^y = x$.

44. Graph $y = \log_2 x$ by graphing $2^y = x$.

45. Graph $f(x) = \log_3 x$ by reflecting the graph of $g(x) = 3^x$ across the line $y = x$.

46. Graph $f(x) = \log_4 x$ by reflecting the graph of $g(x) = 4^x$ across the line $y = x$.

For Problems 47–53, graph each of the functions. Remember that the graph of $f(x) = \log_2 x$ is given in Figure 5.21. **(Objective 1)**

47. $f(x) = 3 + \log_2 x$

48. $f(x) = -2 + \log_2 x$

49. $f(x) = \log_2(x + 3)$

50. $f(x) = \log_2(x - 2)$

51. $f(x) = \log_2 2x$

52. $f(x) = -\log_2 x$

53. $f(x) = 2 \log_2 x$

For Problems 54–61, perform the following calculations and express answers to the nearest hundredth. (These calculations are in preparation for our work in the next section.)

54. $\dfrac{\log 7}{\log 3}$

55. $\dfrac{\ln 2}{\ln 7}$

56. $\dfrac{2 \ln 3}{\ln 8}$

57. $\dfrac{\ln 5}{2 \ln 3}$

58. $\dfrac{\ln 3}{0.04}$

59. $\dfrac{\ln 2}{0.03}$

60. $\dfrac{\log 2}{5 \log 1.02}$

61. $\dfrac{\log 5}{3 \log 1.07}$

Thoughts Into Words

62. Why is the number 1 excluded from being a base of a logarithm?

63. How do we know that $\log_2 6$ is between 2 and 3?

Graphing Calculator Activities

64. Graph $f(x) = x$, $f(x) = e^x$, and $f(x) = \ln x$ on the same set of axes.

65. Graph $f(x) = x$, $f(x) = 10^x$, and $f(x) = \log x$ on the same set of axes.

66. Graph $f(x) = \ln x$. How should the graphs of $f(x) = 2\ln x$, $f(x) = 4\ln x$, and $f(x) = 6\ln x$ compare to the graph of $f(x) = \ln x$? Graph the three functions on the same set of axes with $f(x) = \ln x$.

67. Graph $f(x) = \log x$. Now predict the graphs for $f(x) = 2 + \log x$, $f(x) = -2 + \log x$, and $f(x) = -6 + \log x$. Graph the three functions on the same set of axes with $f(x) = \log x$.

68. Graph $\ln x$. Now predict the graphs for $f(x) = \ln(x - 2)$, $f(x) = \ln(x - 6)$, and $f(x) = \ln(x + 4)$. Graph the three functions on the same set of axes with $f(x) = \ln x$.

69. For each of the following, (a) predict the general shape and location of the graph, and (b) use your graphing calculator to graph the function to check your prediction.

    (a) $f(x) = \log x + \ln x$ **(b)** $f(x) = \log x - \ln x$

    (c) $f(x) = \ln x - \log x$ **(d)** $f(x) = \ln x^2$

Answers to the Concept Quiz

1. False   **2.** False   **3.** True   **4.** False   **5.** True   **6.** True   **7.** False   **8.** True   **9.** False   **10.** True

5.6   Exponential Equations, Logarithmic Equations, and Problem Solving

OBJECTIVES

  1   Solve exponential equations

  2   Solve logarithmic equations

  3   Use logarithms to solve problems

  4   Solve problems involving Richter numbers

  5   Evaluate logarithms using the change-of-base formula

In Section 5.1 we solved exponential equations such as $3^x = 81$ by expressing both sides of the equation as a power of 3 and then applying the property: If $b^n = b^m$, then $n = m$. However, if we try this same approach with an equation such as $3^x = 5$, we face the difficulty of expressing 5 as a power of 3. We can solve this type of problem by using the properties of logarithms and the following property of equality:

Property 5.8

If $x > 0$, $y > 0$, $b > 0$, and $b \neq 1$, then $x = y$ if and only if $\log_b x = \log_b y$.

Property 5.8 is stated in terms of any valid base b; however, for most applications, we use either common logarithms or natural logarithms. Let's consider some examples.

Classroom Example
Solve $5^x = 12$ to the nearest hundredth.

EXAMPLE 1   Solve $3^x = 5$ to the nearest hundredth.

Solution

By using common logarithms, we can proceed as follows:

$$3^x = 5$$
$$\log 3^x = \log 5 \qquad \text{Property 5.8}$$
$$x \log 3 = \log 5 \qquad \log r^p = p \log r$$
$$x = \frac{\log 5}{\log 3}$$
$$x = 1.46 \quad \text{to the nearest hundredth}$$

✔ Check

Because $3^{1.46} \approx 4.972754647$, we say that, to the nearest hundredth, the solution set for $3^x = 5$ is $\{1.46\}$.

Classroom Example
Solve $e^{x-3} = 6$ to the nearest hundredth.

EXAMPLE 2   Solve $e^{x+1} = 5$ to the nearest hundredth.

Solution

Because base e is used in the exponential expression, let's use natural logarithms to help solve this equation.

$$e^{x+1} = 5$$
$$\ln e^{x+1} = \ln 5 \qquad \text{Property 5.8}$$
$$(x + 1)\ln e = \ln 5 \qquad \ln r^p = p \ln r$$
$$(x + 1)(1) = \ln 5 \qquad \ln e = 1$$
$$x = \ln 5 - 1$$
$$x = 0.61 \quad \text{to the nearest hundredth}$$

The solution set is $\{0.61\}$. Check it!

Classroom Example
Solve $3^{4x+3} = 4^{5x-1}$ to the nearest hundredth.

EXAMPLE 3   Solve $2^{3x-2} = 3^{2x+1}$ to the nearest hundredth.

Solution

$$2^{3x-2} = 3^{2x+1}$$
$$\log 2^{3x-2} = \log 3^{2x+1}$$
$$(3x - 2)\log 2 = (2x + 1)\log 3$$
$$3x \log 2 - 2 \log 2 = 2x \log 3 + \log 3$$
$$3x \log 2 - 2x \log 3 = \log 3 + 2 \log 2$$
$$x(3 \log 2 - 2 \log 3) = \log 3 + 2 \log 2$$

$$x = \frac{\log 3 + 2\log 2}{3\log 2 - 2\log 3}$$

$$x = -21.10 \quad \text{to the nearest hundredth}$$

The solution set is $\{-21.10\}$. Check it! ▬

Logarithmic Equations

In Example 12 of Section 5.4, we solved the logarithmic equation

$$\log_{10} x + \log_{10}(x + 9) = 1$$

by simplifying the left side of the equation to $\log_{10}[x(x + 9)]$ and then changing the equation to exponential form to complete the solution. Now, using Property 5.8, we can solve such a logarithmic equation another way and also expand our equation-solving capabilities. Let's consider some examples.

EXAMPLE 4   Solve $\log x + \log(x - 15) = 2$.

Solution

Because $\log 100 = 2$, the given equation becomes

$$\log x + \log(x - 15) = \log 100$$

Now simplify the left side, apply Property 5.8, and proceed as follows.

$$\log(x)(x - 15) = \log 100$$
$$x(x - 15) = 100$$
$$x^2 - 15x - 100 = 0$$
$$(x - 20)(x + 5) = 0$$
$$x - 20 = 0 \quad \text{or} \quad x + 5 = 0$$
$$x = 20 \quad \text{or} \quad x = -5$$

The domain of a logarithmic function must contain only positive numbers, so x and $x - 15$ must be positive in this problem. Therefore, we discard the solution -5; the solution set is $\{20\}$. ▬

EXAMPLE 5   Solve $\ln(x + 2) = \ln(x - 4) + \ln 3$.

Solution

$$\ln(x + 2) = \ln(x - 4) + \ln 3$$
$$\ln(x + 2) = \ln[3(x - 4)]$$
$$x + 2 = 3(x - 4)$$
$$x + 2 = 3x - 12$$
$$14 = 2x$$
$$7 = x$$

The solution set is $\{7\}$. ▬

Classroom Example
Solve $\log_b(x - 1) +$
$\log_b(5x + 2) = \log_b x$.

EXAMPLE 6   Solve $\log_b(x + 2) + \log_b(2x - 1) = \log_b x$.

Solution

$$\log_b(x + 2) + \log_b(2x - 1) = \log_b x$$
$$\log_b[(x + 2)(2x - 1)] = \log_b x$$
$$(x + 2)(2x - 1) = x$$
$$2x^2 + 3x - 2 = x$$
$$2x^2 + 2x - 2 = 0$$
$$x^2 + x - 1 = 0$$

Using the quadratic formula, we obtain

$$x = \frac{-1 \pm \sqrt{1 + 4}}{2}$$
$$= \frac{-1 \pm \sqrt{5}}{2}$$

Because $x + 2$, $2x - 1$, and x have to be positive, we must discard the solution $\dfrac{-1 - \sqrt{5}}{2}$; the solution set is $\left\{\dfrac{-1 + \sqrt{5}}{2}\right\}$.

Using Logarithms to Solve Problems

In Section 5.2 we used the compound interest formula

$$A = P\left(1 + \frac{r}{n}\right)^{nt}$$

to determine the amount of money (A) accumulated at the end of t years if P dollars is invested at rate of interest r compounded n times per year. Now let's use this formula to solve other types of problems that deal with compound interest.

Classroom Example
How long will it take $6000 to
double if it is invested at 3%
interest compounded monthly?

EXAMPLE 7

How long will it take for $500 to double if it is invested at 4% interest compounded quarterly?

Solution

"To double" means that the $500 must grow into $1000. Thus

$$1000 = 500\left(1 + \frac{0.04}{4}\right)^{4t}$$
$$= 500(1 + 0.01)^{4t}$$
$$= 500(1.01)^{4t}$$

Multiplying both sides of $1000 = 500(1.01)^{4t}$ by $\dfrac{1}{500}$ yields

$$2 = (1.01)^{4t}$$

Therefore

$$\log 2 = \log(1.01)^{4t}$$

Property 5.8

$$= 4t \log 1.01$$

$\log r^p = p \log r$

Now let's solve for t.

$$4t \log 1.01 = \log 2$$

$$t = \frac{\log 2}{4 \log 1.01}$$

$$t = 17.4 \quad \text{to the nearest tenth}$$

Therefore we are claiming that $500 invested at 4% interest compounded quarterly will double in approximately 17.4 years.

✔ Check

$500 invested at 4% interest compounded quarterly for 17.4 years will produce

$$A = \$500\left(1 + \frac{0.04}{4}\right)^{4(17.4)}$$

$$= \$500(1.01)^{69.6}$$

$$= \$999.40$$

———————————————— ▪

Classroom Example
For a certain virus, the equation $Q(t) = Q_0 e^{-0.2t}$, when t is the time in hours and Q_0 is the initial number of virus particles, yields the number of virus particles as a function of time. How long will it take 5000 particles to be reduced to 500 particles?

EXAMPLE 8

Suppose that the number of bacteria present in a certain culture after t minutes is given by the equation $Q(t) = Q_0 e^{0.04t}$, where Q_0 represents the initial number of bacteria. How long will it take for the bacteria count to grow from 500 to 2000?

Solution

Substituting into $Q(t) = Q_0 e^{0.04t}$ and solving for t, we obtain the following.

$$2000 = 500 e^{0.04t}$$

$$4 = e^{0.04t}$$

$$\ln 4 = \ln e^{0.04t}$$

$$\ln 4 = 0.04t \ln e$$

$$\ln 4 = 0.04t \qquad \ln e = 1$$

$$\frac{\ln 4}{0.04} = t$$

$$34.7 = t \quad \text{to the nearest tenth}$$

It should take approximately 34.7 minutes.   ▪

Richter Numbers

Seismologists use the Richter scale to measure and report the magnitude of earthquakes. The equation

$$R = \log \frac{I}{I_0} \qquad R \text{ is called a Richter number}$$

compares the intensity I of an earthquake to a minimal or reference intensity I_0. The reference intensity is the smallest earth movement that can be recorded on a seismograph. Suppose that the intensity of an earthquake was determined to be 50,000 times the reference intensity. In this case, $I = 50,000\, I_0$, and the Richter number is calculated as follows:

$$R = \log \frac{50,000\, I_0}{I_0}$$
$$= \log 50,000$$
$$\approx 4.698970004$$

Thus a Richter number of 4.7 would be reported. Let's consider two more examples that involve Richter numbers.

Classroom Example
An earthquake has a Richter number of 7.3. How did its intensity compare to the reference intensity?

EXAMPLE 9

An earthquake in the San Francisco, California, area in 1989 was reported to have a Richter number of 6.9. How did its intensity compare to the reference intensity?

Solution

$$6.9 = \log \frac{I}{I_0}$$
$$10^{6.9} = \frac{I}{I_0}$$
$$I = (10^{6.9})(I_0)$$
$$I \approx 7{,}943{,}282\, I_0$$

Its intensity was a little less than 8 million times the reference intensity.   ■

Classroom Example
Another earthquake has a Richter number of 6.7. Compare the intensity level of this earthquake to an earthquake with a Richter number of 7.3.

EXAMPLE 10

An earthquake in Japan in 2011 had a Richter number of 9.0. Compare the intensity of this earthquake to that of the one in San Francisco referred to in Example 9.

Solution

From Example 9 we have $I = (10^{6.9})(I_0)$ for the earthquake in San Francisco. Then, using a Richter number of 9.0, we obtain $I = (10^{9.0})(I_0)$ for the earthquake in Japan. Therefore, by comparison,

$$\frac{(10^{9.0})(I_0)}{(10^{6.9})(I_0)} = 10^{9.0-6.9} = 10^{2.1} \approx 125.9$$

The earthquake in Japan was about 126 times as intense as the one in San Francisco. ■

Change-of-Base Formula for Logarithms with a Base Other Than 10 or e

The basic approach whereby we apply Property 5.8 and use either common or natural logarithms can also be used to evaluate a logarithm to some base other than 10 or e. Consider the following example.

Classroom Example
Evaluate $\log_7 21$.

EXAMPLE 11   Evaluate $\log_3 41$.

Solution

Let $x = \log_3 41$. Change to exponential form to obtain

$$3^x = 41$$

Now we can apply Property 5.8 and proceed as follows.

$$\log 3^x = \log 41$$
$$x \log 3 = \log 41$$
$$x = \frac{\log 41}{\log 3}$$
$$x = 3.3802 \quad \text{rounded to four decimal places}$$

Therefore we are claiming that 3 raised to the 3.3802 power will produce approximately 41. Check it! ■

The method of Example 11 to evaluate $\log_a r$ produces the following formula, which we often refer to as the **change-of-base formula for logarithms**.

> **Property 5.9**
>
> If a, b, and r are positive numbers, with $a \neq 1$ and $b \neq 1$, then
>
> $$\log_a r = \frac{\log_b r}{\log_b a}$$

By using Property 5.9, we can easily determine a relationship between logarithms of different bases. For example, suppose that in Property 5.9 we let $a = 10$ and $b = e$. Then

$$\log_a r = \frac{\log_b r}{\log_b a}$$

becomes

$$\log_{10} r = \frac{\log_e r}{\log_e 10}$$

$$\log_e r = (\log_e 10)(\log_{10} r)$$

$$\log_e r = (2.3026)(\log_{10} r)$$

Thus the natural logarithm of any positive number is approximately equal to the common logarithm of the number times 2.3026.

Now we can use a graphing utility to graph logarithmic functions such as $f(x) = \log_2 x$. Using the change-of-base formula, we can express this function as $f(x) = \dfrac{\log x}{\log 2}$ or as $f(x) = \dfrac{\ln x}{\ln 2}$. The graph of $f(x) = \log_2 x$ is shown in Figure 5.26.

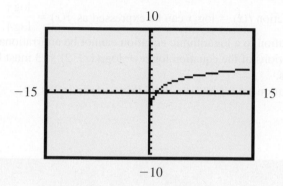

Figure 5.26

Finally, let's use a graphical approach to solve an equation that is cumbersome to solve with an algebraic approach.

EXAMPLE 12   Solve the equation $(5^x - 5^{-x})/2 = 3$.

Solution

First, we need to recognize that the solutions for the equation $(5^x - 5^{-x})/2 = 3$ are the x intercepts of the graph of the equation $y = (5^x - 5^{-x})/2 - 3$. We can use a graphing utility to obtain the graph of this equation as shown in Figure 5.27. Use the ZOOM and TRACE features to determine that the graph crosses the x axis at approximately 1.13. Thus the solution set of the original expression is {1.13}.

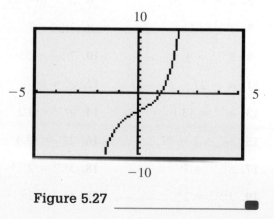

Figure 5.27

Concept Quiz 5.6

For Problems 1–10, answer true or false.

1. For $x > 0$ and $y > 0$, if $\log_2 x = \log_2 y$, then $x = y$.
2. For $x > 0$ and $y > 0$, if $x = y$, then $\ln x = \log y$.
3. The formula $Q = Q_0 e^{at}$ represents the exponential decay of a substance if $0 < a < 1$.
4. The formula $Q = Q_0 e^{at}$ represents the exponential growth of a substance if $a > 0$.
5. An earthquake with a Richter number of 7.0 is 10 times more intense than an earthquake with a Richter number of 6.0.
6. $\log_3 7 = \dfrac{\ln 7}{\ln 3}$
7. The function $f(x) = \log_4 x$ can be expressed as $f(x) = \dfrac{\log x}{\log 4}$.
8. The solution to a logarithmic equation cannot be an irrational number.
9. All solutions of the equation $\log_b x + \log_b(x + 2) = 3$ must be positive numbers.
10. The solution set for $\ln(3x - 4) - \ln(x + 1) = \ln 2$ is $\{8\}$.

Problem Set 5.6

For Problems 1–20, solve each exponential equation and express approximate solutions to the nearest hundredth. (Objective 1)

1. $3^x = 13$
2. $2^x = 21$
3. $4^n = 35$
4. $5^n = 75$
5. $2^x + 7 = 50$
6. $3^x - 6 = 25$
7. $3^{x-2} = 11$
8. $2^{x+1} = 7$
9. $5^{3t+1} = 9$
10. $7^{2t-1} = 35$
11. $e^x = 27$
12. $e^x = 86$
13. $e^{x-2} = 13.1$
14. $e^{x-1} = 8.2$
15. $3e^x - 1 = 17$
16. $2e^x = 12.4$
17. $5^{2x+1} = 7^{x+3}$
18. $3^{x-1} = 2^{x+3}$
19. $3^{2x+1} = 2^{3x+2}$
20. $5^{x-1} = 2^{2x+1}$

For Problems 21–32, solve each logarithmic equation and express irrational solutions in simplest radical form. (Objective 2)

21. $\log x + \log(x + 21) = 2$
22. $\log x + \log(x + 3) = 1$
23. $\log(3x - 1) = 1 + \log(5x - 2)$
24. $\log(2x - 1) - \log(x - 3) = 1$
25. $\log_3 x + \log_3(x + 4) = 2$
26. $\log_2(2x) + \log_2(x - 3) = 3$
27. $\log_2(x + 5) + \log_2(x - 1) = 4$
28. $\log_3(x + 1) + \log_3(x - 1) = 1$
29. $\log(x + 1) = \log 3 - \log(2x - 1)$
30. $\log(x - 2) = 1 - \log(x + 3)$

31. $\log(x + 2) - \log(2x + 1) = \log x$

32. $\log(x + 1) - \log(x + 2) = \log \dfrac{1}{x}$

33. $\ln(2t + 5) = \ln 3 + \ln(t - 1)$

34. $\ln(3t - 4) - \ln(t + 1) = \ln 2$

35. $\log \sqrt{x} = \sqrt{\log x}$

36. $\log x^2 = (\log x)^2$

For Problems 37– 46, approximate each logarithm to three decimal places. (Example 11 and/or Property 5.9 should be of some help.) **(Objective 5)**

37. $\log_2 40$ **38.** $\log_2 93$

39. $\log_3 16$ **40.** $\log_3 37$

41. $\log_4 1.6$ **42.** $\log_4 3.2$

43. $\log_5 0.26$ **44.** $\log_5 0.047$

45. $\log_7 500$ **46.** $\log_8 750$

For Problems 47–55, solve each problem and express answers to the nearest tenth unless stated otherwise. **(Objectives 3, 4)**

47. How long will it take $750 to be worth $1000 if it is invested at 6% interest compounded quarterly?

48. How long will it take $1000 to double if it is invested at 6% interest compounded semiannually?

49. How long will it take $2000 to double if it is invested at 4% interest compounded continuously?

50. How long will it take $500 to triple if it is invested at 5% interest compounded continuously?

51. What rate of interest compounded continuously is needed for an investment of $500 to grow to $900 in 10 years?

52. What rate of interest compounded continuously is needed for an investment of $2500 to grow to $10,000 in 20 years?

53. For a certain strain of bacteria, the number of bacteria present after t hours is given by the equation $Q(t) = Q_0 e^{0.34t}$, where Q_0 represents the initial number of bacteria. How long will it take 400 bacteria to increase to 4000 bacteria?

54. A piece of machinery valued at $30,000 depreciates at a rate of 10% yearly. How long will it take for it to reach a value of $15,000?

55. The equation $P(a) = 14.7e^{-0.21a}$, in which a is the altitude above sea level measured in miles, yields the atmospheric pressure in pounds per square inch. If the atmospheric pressure at Cheyenne, Wyoming, is approximately 11.53 pounds per square inch, find that city's altitude above sea level. Express your answer to the nearest hundred feet.

56. The number of grams of a certain radioactive substance present after t hours is given by the equation $Q(t) = Q_0 e^{-0.45t}$, where Q_0 represents the initial number of grams. How long will it take 2500 grams to be reduced to 1250 grams?

57. For a certain culture, the equation $Q(t) = Q_0 e^{0.4t}$, in which Q_0 is an initial number of bacteria, and t is the time measured in hours, yields the number of bacteria as a function of time. How long will it take 500 bacteria to increase to 2000?

58. Suppose that the equation $P(t) = P_0 e^{0.02t}$, in which P_0 represents an initial population, and t is the time in years, is used to predict population growth. How long will it take a city of 50,000 to double its population?

59. An earthquake in Los Angeles in 1971 had an intensity of approximately 5 million times the reference intensity. What was the Richter number associated with that earthquake?

60. An earthquake in San Francisco in 1906 was reported to have a Richter number of 8.3. How did its intensity compare to the reference intensity?

61. Calculate how many times more intense an earthquake with a Richter number of 7.3 is than an earthquake with a Richter number of 6.4.

62. Calculate how many times more intense an earthquake is with a Richter number of 8.9 than is an earthquake with a Richter number of 6.2.

Thoughts Into Words

63. Explain how to determine $\log_4 76$ without using Property 5.9.

64. Explain the concept of a Richter number.

65. Explain how you would solve the equation $2^x = 64$ and also how you would solve the equation $2^x = 53$.

66. How do logarithms with a base of 9 compare to logarithms with a base of 3? Explain how you reached this conclusion.

Further Investigations

67. Use the approach of Example 11 to develop Property 5.9.

68. Let $r = b$ in Property 5.9, and verify that $\log_a b = \dfrac{1}{\log_b a}$.

69. Solve the equation $\dfrac{5^x - 5^{-x}}{2} = 3$. Express your answer to the nearest hundredth.

70. Solve the equation $y = \dfrac{10^x + 10^{-x}}{2}$ for x in terms of y.

71. Solve the equation $y = \dfrac{e^x - e^{-x}}{2}$ for x in terms of y.

Graphing Calculator Activities

72. Check your answers for Problems 17–20 by graphing the appropriate function and finding the x intercept.

73. Graph $f(x) = x, f(x) = 2^x$, and $f(x) = \log_2 x$ on the same set of axes.

74. Graph $f(x) = x, f(x) = (0.5)^x$, and $f(x) = \log_{0.5} x$ on the same set of axes.

75. Graph $f(x) = \log_2 x$. Now predict the graphs for $f(x) = \log_3 x, f(x) = \log_4 x$, and $f(x) = \log_8 x$. Graph these three functions on the same set of axes with $f(x) = \log_2 x$.

76. Graph $f(x) = \log_5 x$. Now predict the graphs for $f(x) = 2\log_5 x$, $f(x) = -4\log_5 x$, and $f(x) = \log_5(x + 4)$. Graph these three functions on the same set of axes with $f(x) = \log_5 x$.

77. Use both a graphical and an algebraic approach to solve the equation $\dfrac{2^x - 2^{-x}}{3} = 4$.

Answers to the Concept Quiz

1. True   **2.** False   **3.** False   **4.** True   **5.** True   **6.** True   **7.** True   **8.** False   **9.** True   **10.** False

Chapter 5 SUMMARY

OBJECTIVE	SUMMARY	EXAMPLE
Solve exponential equations **(Section 5.1/Objective 1)**	Some exponential equations can be solved by applying Property 5.2: If $b > 0$, $b \neq 1$, and m and n are real numbers, then $b^n = b^m$ if and only if $n = m$. This property can only be applied for equations that can be written in the form where the bases are equal.	Solve $4^{3x} = 32$. **Solution** Rewrite each side of the equation as a power of 2. Then apply Property 5.2 to solve the equation. $4^{3x} = 32$ $(2^2)^{3x} = 2^5$ $2^{6x} = 2^5$ $6x = 5$ $x = \dfrac{5}{6}$ The solution set is $\left\{ \dfrac{5}{6} \right\}$.
Graph exponential functions **(Section 5.1/Objective 2)**	A function defined by an equation of the form $f(x) = b^x$, for $b > 0$ and $b \neq 0$, is called an exponential function with base b.	Graph $f(x) = 4^x$. **Solution** Set up a table of values. $$\begin{array}{c\|c\|c\|c\|c\|c} x & -2 & -1 & 0 & 1 & 2 \\ \hline f(x) & \dfrac{1}{16} & \dfrac{1}{4} & 1 & 4 & 16 \end{array}$$
Solve exponential growth and decay problems **(Section 5.2/Objective 1)**	In general, the equation $P = P_0(1.06)^t$ yields the predicted price P of an item in t years at the annual inflation rate of 6%, where that item presently costs P_0.	Assuming that the rate of inflation is 3% per year, find the price of a $20.00 haircut in 5 years. **Solution** Use the formula $P = P_0(1.03)^t$ and substitute $20.00 for P_0 and 5 for t. $P = 20.00(1.03)^5 \approx 23.19$ The haircut would cost $23.19.

(continued)

OBJECTIVE	SUMMARY	EXAMPLE
Solve compound interest problems (Section 5.2/Objective 2)	A general formula for any principal, P, invested for any number of years (t) at a rate of r percent compounded n times per year is $A = P\left(1 + \dfrac{r}{n}\right)^{nt}$; where A represents the total amount of money accumulated at the end of t years.	Find the total amount of money accumulated at the end of 8 years when \$4000 is invested at 6% compounded quarterly. **Solution** $A = 4000\left(1 + \dfrac{0.06}{4}\right)^{4(8)}$ $A = 4000(1.015)^{32}$ $A = 6441.30$
Solve half-life problems (Section 5.2/Objective 3)	For radioactive substances, the rate of decay is exponential and can be described based on the half-life of a substance. The *half-life* of a radioactive substance is the amount of time that it takes for one-half of an initial amount of the substance to disappear as the result of decay. Suppose there is an initial amount, Q_0, of a radioactive substance with a half-life of h. The amount of substance remaining, Q, after a time period of t, is given by the formula $Q = Q_0\left(\dfrac{1}{2}\right)^{\frac{t}{h}}$. The units of measure for t and h must be the same.	Molybdenum-99 has a half-life of 66 hours. If there are 200 milligrams of molybdenum-99 initially, how many milligrams remain after 16 hours? **Solution** $Q = 200\left(\dfrac{1}{2}\right)^{\frac{16}{66}}$ $Q = 169.1$ to the nearest tenth of a milligram Thus approximately 169.1 milligrams remain after 16 hours.

OBJECTIVE	SUMMARY	EXAMPLE
Solve growth problems involving the number e (Section 5.2/Objective 4)	The law of exponential growth $Q(t) = Q_0 e^{kt}$ is used as a mathematical model for growth-and-decay problems. In this equation, $Q(t)$ represents the quantity of a given substance at any time t; Q_0 is the initial amount of the substance (when $t = 0$); and k is a constant that depends on the particular application. If $k < 0$, then $Q(t)$ decreases as t increases, and we refer to the model as the **law of decay**.	The number of bacteria present in a certain culture after t hours is given by the equation $Q(t) = Q_0 e^{0.42t}$, where Q_0 represents the initial number of bacteria. How long will it take 100 bacteria to increase to 500 bacteria? **Solution** Substitute 100 for Q_0 and 500 for $Q(t)$ into $Q(t) = Q_0 e^{0.42t}$. $$500 = 100 e^{0.42t}$$ $$5 = e^{0.42t}$$ $$\ln 5 = \ln e^{0.42t}$$ $$\ln 5 = 0.42t \ln e$$ $$\ln 5 = 0.42t \quad \ln e = 1$$ $$t = \frac{\ln 5}{0.42} = 3.83 \text{ to the nearest hundredth}$$ It will take approximately 3.83 hours for 100 bacteria to increase to 500 bacteria.
Solve compound continuously problems (Section 5.2/Objective 4)	The value of $\left(1 + \dfrac{1}{n}\right)^n$ as n gets infinitely large, approaches the number e, where $e = 2.71828$ to five decimal places. The formula $A = Pe^{rt}$ yields the accumulated value, A, of a sum of money, P, that has been invested for t years at a rate of r percent **compounded continuously**.	If \$8300 is invested at 6.5% interest compounded continuously, how much will accumulate in 10 years? **Solution** $$A = 8300 e^{0.065(10)}$$ $$= 8300 e^{0.65}$$ $$= 15898.99$$ The accumulated amount will be \$15,898.99.

(continued)

OBJECTIVE	SUMMARY	EXAMPLE
Determine if a function is a one-to-one function (Section 5.3/Objective 1)	A function f is said to be one-to-one if every value of $f(x)$ has only one value of x associated with it. In terms of ordered pairs, a one-to-one function is a function such that no two ordered pairs have the same second component. In terms of a graph, the horizontal-line test is used to determine if a graph is the graph of a one-to-one function. If the function is a one-to-one function, then a horizontal line will intersect the graph of the function in only one point.	Identify the graph as the graph of a one-to-one function or the graph of a function that is not one-to-one. **Solution** The graph is the graph of a one-to-one function because a horizontal line intersects the graph in only one point.
Verify if two functions are inverses of each other (Section 5.3/Objective 2)	Let f be a one-to-one function with a domain of X and a range of Y. A function g, with a domain of Y and a range of X, is called the inverse function of f if $(f \circ g)(x) = x$ for every x in Y and $(g \circ f)(x) = x$ for every x in X.	Verify that the two given functions are inverses of each other. $$f(x) = \frac{2}{3}x - \frac{5}{6}$$ and $$g(x) = \frac{3}{2}x + \frac{5}{4}$$ **Solution** $(f \circ g)(x) = f(g(x))$ $$= f\left(\frac{3}{2}x + \frac{5}{4}\right)$$ $$= \frac{2}{3}\left(\frac{3}{2}x + \frac{5}{4}\right) - \frac{5}{6}$$ $$= x + \frac{5}{6} - \frac{5}{6}$$ $$= x$$ $(g \circ f)(x) = g(f(x))$ $$= g\left(\frac{2}{3}x - \frac{5}{6}\right)$$ $$= \frac{3}{2}\left(\frac{2}{3}x - \frac{5}{6}\right) + \frac{5}{4}$$ $$= x - \frac{5}{4} + \frac{5}{4}$$ $$= x$$ Therefore the inverse of $f(x)$ is $g(x)$.

OBJECTIVE	SUMMARY	EXAMPLE
Find the inverse function in terms of ordered pairs (Section 5.3/Objective 3)	If the components of each ordered pair of a given one-to-one function are interchanged, the resulting function and the given function are **inverses** of each other. The inverse of a function f is denoted by f^{-1}.	Given $f = \{(2,4), (3,5), (7,7), (8,9)\}$, find the inverse function. **Solution** To find the inverse function, interchange the components of the ordered pairs. $f^{-1} = \{(4,2), (5,3), (7,7), (9,8)\}$
Find the inverse of a function (Section 5.3/Objective 4)	A technique for finding the inverse of a function is as follows: **1.** Let $y = f(x)$. **2.** Interchange x and y. **3.** Solve the equation for y in terms of x. **4.** $f^{-1}(x)$ is determined by the final equation. Graphically, two functions that are inverses of each other are mirror images with reference to the line $y = x$. Don't forget the requirement that the domain of f must equal the range of f^{-1}, and the domain f^{-1} must equal the range of f for f and f^{-1} to be inverse functions.	Find the inverse of the function $f(x) = \dfrac{2}{5}x - 7$. **Solution** **1.** Let $y = \dfrac{2}{5}x - 7$. **2.** Interchange x and y. $x = \dfrac{2}{5}y - 7$ **3.** Solve for y. $x = \dfrac{2}{5}y - 7$ $5x = 2y - 35$ Multiply both sides by 5 $5x + 35 = 2y$ $y = \dfrac{5x + 35}{2}$ **4.** $f^{-1}(x) = \dfrac{5x + 35}{2}$ The domain and range of f and f^{-1} is all real numbers.
Determine the intervals for which a function is increasing (or decreasing). (Section 5.3/Objective 6)	Let f be a function, with the interval I a subset of the domain of f. Let x_1 and x_2 be in I. **1.** f is increasing on I if $f(x_1) < f(x_2)$ whenever $x_1 < x_2$. **2.** f is decreasing on I if $f(x_1) > f(x_2)$ whenever $x_1 < x_2$. **3.** f is constant on I if $f(x_1) = f(x_2)$ for every x_1 and x_2.	Find the intervals on which $f(x) = -(x - 2)^2 + 1$ is increasing and the intervals on which it is decreasing. **Solution** $f(x)$ is increasing on the interval $(-\infty, 2]$ and decreasing on the interval $[2, \infty)$.

(continued)

OBJECTIVE	SUMMARY	EXAMPLE
Change equations between exponential and logarithmic form. (Section 5.4/Objective 1)	Definition 5.4 states that the $\log_b r$ is the unique exponent t such that $b^t = r$. Hence $\log_b r = t$ is equivalent to $b^t = r$. Changing forms is an essential skill and the key to solving many problems and equations.	Rewrite $\log_2 32 = 5$ in exponential form. **Solution** By Definition 5.4, $\log_2 32 = 5$ is equivalent to $2^5 = 32$.
Evaluate a logarithmic expression (Section 5.4/Objective 2)	Some logarithmic expressions can be evaluated by switching to exponential form and then applying Property 5.2.	Evaluate $\log_2\left(\dfrac{1}{8}\right)$. **Solution** Let $\log_2\left(\dfrac{1}{8}\right) = x$. Switching to exponential form gives $2^x = \dfrac{1}{8}$. $$2^x = \frac{1}{8}$$ $$2^x = 2^{-3}$$ $$x = -3$$ Therefore $\log_2\left(\dfrac{1}{8}\right) = -3$.
Evaluate a common logarithm (Section 5.5/Objective 2)	Base-10 logarithms are called common logarithms. When working with base-10 logarithms, it is customary to omit writing the numeral 10 to designate the base. Hence $\log_{10} x$ is written as $\log x$. A calculator with a logarithm function key, typically labeled $\boxed{\log}$ is used to evaluate a common logarithm.	Use a calculator to find $\log 245$. Express the answer to four decimal places. **Solution** Follow the instructions for your calculator. $\log 245 = 2.3892$
Evaluate a natural logarithm (Section 5.5/Objective 2)	In many practical applications of logarithms, the number e (remember that $e \approx 2.71828$) is used as a base. Logarithms with a base of e are called **natural logarithms**, and are written as $\ln x$.	Use a calculator to find $\ln 486$. Express the answer to four decimal places. **Solution** Follow the instructions for your calculator. $\ln 486 = 6.1862$

OBJECTIVE	SUMMARY	EXAMPLE
Evaluate logarithms using the change-of-base formula (Section 5.6/Objective 5)	To evaluate logarithms other than base-10 or base-e, a change-of-base formula, $$\log_a r = \frac{\log_b r}{\log_b a},$$ is used. When applying the formula, you can choose base-10 or base-e for b.	Find $\log_8 724$. Round the answer to the nearest hundredth. **Solution** $$\log_8 724 = \frac{\log 724}{\log 8} = 3.17$$
Graph logarithmic functions (Section 5.5/Objective 1)	A function defined by an equation of the form $f(x) = \log_b x$, $b > 0$ and $b \neq 1$ is called a **logarithmic function**. The equation $y = \log_b x$ is equivalent to $x = b^y$. The two functions $f(x) = b^x$ and $g(x) = \log_b x$ are inverses of each other.	Graph $f(x) = \log_4 x$. **Solution** Change $y = \log_4 x$ to $4^y = x$ and determine a table of values.
Apply the properties of logarithms (Section 5.4/Objective 3)	The following properties of logarithms are derived from the definition of a logarithm and the properties of exponents. For positive real numbers b, r, and s, where $b \neq 1$, 1. $\log_b b = 1$ 2. $\log_b 1 = 0$ 3. $b^{\log_b r} = r$ 4. $\log_b rs = \log_b r + \log_b s$ 5. $\log_b\left(\dfrac{r}{s}\right) = \log_b r - \log_b s$ 6. $\log_b r^p = p\log_b r$ p is any real number	Express $\log_b \dfrac{\sqrt{x}}{y^2 z}$ as the sum or difference of simpler logarithmic quantities. **Solution** $$\log_b \frac{\sqrt{x}}{y^2 z} = \log_b \sqrt{x} - \log_b(y^2 z)$$ $$= \frac{1}{2}\log_b x - [\log_b y^2 + \log_b z]$$ $$= \frac{1}{2}\log_b x - [2\log_b y + \log_b z]$$ $$= \frac{1}{2}\log_b x - 2\log_b y - \log_b z$$

For the graph example table of values:

x	$\dfrac{1}{16}$	$\dfrac{1}{4}$	1	4	16
y	-2	-1	0	1	2

(continued)

OBJECTIVE	SUMMARY	EXAMPLE
Solve logarithmic and exponential equations	The properties of equality and the properties of exponents and logarithms combine to help us solve a variety of logarithmic and exponential equations. The techniques for the various types of equations are given as follows. Note the difference in the technique depending on the form of the equation.	
Solve logarithmic equations by switching to exponential form (Section 5.4/Objective 4; Section 5.5/Objective 3; Section 5.6/Objective 2)	This technique is used when a single logarithmic expression is equal to a constant, such as $\log_4(3x + 5) = 2$. You may have to apply properties of logarithms to rewrite a sum or difference of logarithms as a single logarithm.	Solve $\log_3 x + \log_3(x + 8) = 2$. **Solution** Rewrite the left-hand side of the equation as a single logarithm. $\log_3 x(x + 8) = 2$ Switch to exponential form and solve the equation. $$x(x + 8) = 3^2$$ $$x^2 + 8x = 9$$ $$x^2 + 8x - 9 = 0$$ $$(x + 9)(x - 1) = 0$$ $$x = -9 \quad \text{or} \quad x = 1$$ **Always check your answer.** Because -9 would make the expression $\log_3 x$ undefined; the solution set is $\{1\}$.
Solve logarithmic equations of the form $\log_b x = \log_b y$ (Section 5.6/Objective 2)	The following property of equality is used for solving some logarithmic equations. If $x > 0$, and $y > 0$, and $b \neq 1$, then $x = y$ if and only if $\log_b x = \log_b y$. One application of this property is for equations in which a single logarithm equals another single logarithm.	Solve $\ln(9x + 1) - \ln(x + 4) = \ln 4$. **Solution** Write the left-hand side of the equation as a single logarithm. $\ln \dfrac{9x + 1}{x + 4} = \ln 4$ Now apply the property of equality, if $\log_b x = \log_b y$, then $x = y$. $$\dfrac{9x + 1}{x + 4} = 4$$ $$9x + 1 = 4(x + 4)$$ $$9x + 1 = 4x + 16$$ $$5x = 15$$ $$x = 3$$ The answer does check so the solution set is $\{3\}$.

OBJECTIVE	SUMMARY	EXAMPLE
Solve exponential equations by taking the logarithm of each side (Section 5.6/Objectives 1 and 3)	Some exponential equations can be solved by applying the property of equality in the form "If $x = y$, then $\log_b x = \log_b y$ when $x > 0$, and $y > 0$, and $b \neq 1$." If the base of the exponential equation is e, then use natural logarithms and if the base is 10, then use common logarithms. Otherwise, either base can be used when taking the logarithm of both sides of the equation.	Solve $6^{3x-2} = 45$. Express the solution to the nearest hundredth. **Solution** Take the logarithm of both sides of the equation. $$\log 6^{3x-2} = \log 45$$ $$(3x - 2)\log 6 = \log 45$$ $$3x(\log 6) - 2\log 6 = \log 45$$ $$3x(\log 6) = \log 45 + 2\log 6$$ $$x = \frac{\log 45 + 2\log 6}{3\log 6}$$ $$x = 1.37$$ The solution set is $\{1.37\}$.
Solve problems involving Richter numbers (Section 5.6/Objective 4)	Seismologists use the Richter scale to measure and report the magnitude of earthquakes. The equation $R = \log \dfrac{I}{I_0}$ compares the intensity I of an earthquake to a minimum or reference intensity I_0.	An earthquake on the Sandwich Island (in the South Atlantic) in 2006 had an intensity about 5,011,872 times the reference intensity. Find the Richter number for that earthquake. **Solution** $$R = \log\frac{I}{I_0}$$ $$R = \log\frac{I}{I_0} = \log\frac{5,011,872\, I_0}{I_0} = 6.7$$ The Richter number for the earthquake is 6.7.

Chapter 5   Review Problem Set

For Problems 1–10, evaluate each of the following:

1. $8^{5/3}$

2. $-25^{3/2}$

3. $(-27)^{4/3}$

4. $\log_6 216$

5. $\log_7\left(\dfrac{1}{49}\right)$

6. $\log_2 \sqrt[3]{2}$

7. $\log_2\left(\dfrac{\sqrt[4]{32}}{2}\right)$

8. $\log_{10} 0.00001$

9. $\ln e$

10. $7^{\log_7 12}$

For Problems 11–24, solve each equation. Express approximate solutions to the nearest hundredth.

11. $\log_{10} 2 + \log_{10} x = 1$ **12.** $\log_3 x = -2$

13. $4^x = 128$ **14.** $3^t = 42$

15. $\log_2 x = 3$ **16.** $\left(\dfrac{1}{27}\right)^{3x} = 3^{2x-1}$

17. $2e^x = 14$

18. $2^{2x+1} = 3^{x+1}$

19. $\ln(x + 4) - \ln(x + 2) = \ln x$

20. $\log x + \log(x - 15) = 2$

21. $\log(\log x) = 2$

22. $\log(7x - 4) - \log(x - 1) = 1$

23. $\ln(2t - 1) = \ln 4 + \ln(t - 3)$

24. $64^{2t+1} = 8^{-t+2}$

For Problems 25–28, if $\log 3 = 0.4771$ and $\log 7 = 0.8451$, evaluate each of the following:

25. $\log\left(\dfrac{7}{3}\right)$ **26.** $\log 21$

27. $\log 27$ **28.** $\log 7^{2/3}$

29. Express each of the following as the sum or difference of simpler logarithmic quantities. Assume that all variables represent positive real numbers.

(a) $\log_b\left(\dfrac{x}{y^2}\right)$ (b) $\log_b \sqrt[4]{xy^2}$

(c) $\log_b\left(\dfrac{\sqrt{x}}{y^3}\right)$

30. Express each of the following as a single logarithm. Assume that all variables represent positive real numbers.

(a) $3\log_b x + 2\log_b y$

(b) $\dfrac{1}{2}\log_b y - 4\log_b x$

(c) $\dfrac{1}{2}(\log_b x + \log_b y) - 2\log_b z$

For Problems 31–34, approximate each of the logarithms to three decimal places.

31. $\log_2 3$ **32.** $\log_3 2$

33. $\log_4 191$ **34.** $\log_2 0.23$

For Problems 35–42, graph each of the functions.

35. (a) $f(x) = \left(\dfrac{3}{4}\right)^x$

(b) $f(x) = \left(\dfrac{3}{4}\right)^x + 2$

(c) $f(x) = \left(\dfrac{3}{4}\right)^{-x}$

36. (a) $f(x) = 2^x$ (b) $f(x) = 2^{x+2}$

(c) $f(x) = -2^x$

37. (a) $f(x) = e^{x-1}$ (b) $f(x) = e^x - 1$

(c) $f(x) = e^{-x+1}$

38. (a) $f(x) = -1 + \log x$

(b) $f(x) = \log(x - 1)$

(c) $f(x) = -1 - \log x$

39. $f(x) = 3^x - 3^{-x}$ **40.** $f(x) = e^{-x^2/2}$

41. $f(x) = \log_2(x - 3)$ **42.** $f(x) = 3\log_3 x$

For Problems 43–45, use the compound interest formula $A = P\left(1 + \dfrac{r}{n}\right)^{nt}$ to find the total amount of money accumulated at the end of the indicated time period for each of the investments.

43. \$7500 for 10 years at 4% compounded quarterly

44. \$1250 for 15 years at 5% compounded monthly

45. \$2500 for 20 years at 6.5% compounded semiannually

For Problems 46–49, determine whether f and g are inverse functions.

46. $f(x) = 7x - 1$ and $g(x) = \dfrac{x + 1}{7}$

47. $f(x) = -\dfrac{2}{3}x$ and $g(x) = \dfrac{3}{2}x$

48. $f(x) = x^2 - 6$ for $x \geq 0$ and $g(x) = \sqrt{x + 6}$ for $x \geq -6$

49. $f(x) = 2 - x^2$ for $x \geq 0$ and $g(x) = \sqrt{2 - x}$ for $x \leq 2$

For Problems 50–53, (a) find f^{-1}, and (b) verify that $(f \circ f^{-1})(x) = x$ and $(f^{-1} \circ f)(x) = x$.

50. $f(x) = 4x + 5$ **51.** $f(x) = -3x - 7$

52. $f(x) = \dfrac{5}{6}x - \dfrac{1}{3}$

53. $f(x) = -2 - x^2$ for $x \geq 0$

For Problems 54 and 55, find the intervals on which the function is increasing and the intervals on which it is decreasing.

54. $f(x) = -2x^2 + 16x - 35$

55. $f(x) = 2\sqrt{x - 3}$

56. How long will it take $1000 to double if it is invested at 7% interest compounded annually?

57. How long will it take $1000 to be worth $3500 if it is invested at 4.5% interest compounded quarterly?

58. What rate of interest (to the nearest tenth of a percent) compounded continuously is needed for an investment of $500 to grow to $1000 in 8 years?

59. Suppose that the present population of a city is 50,000. Use the equation $P(t) = P_0 e^{0.02t}$ (in which P_0 represents an initial population) to estimate future populations, and estimate the population of that city in 10 years, 15 years, and 20 years.

60. The number of bacteria present in a certain culture after t hours is given by the equation $Q(t) = Q_0 e^{0.29t}$, in which Q_0 represents the initial number of bacteria. How long will it take 500 bacteria to increase to 2000 bacteria?

61. Suppose that a certain radioactive substance has a half-life of 40 days. If there are presently 750 grams of the substance, how much, to the nearest gram, will remain after 100 days?

62. An earthquake occurred in Mexico City, Mexico, in 1985 that had an intensity level about 125,000,000 times the reference intensity. Find the Richter number for that earthquake.

Chapter 5 Test

For Problems 1–4, evaluate each expression.

1. $\log_3 \sqrt{3}$

2. $\log_2(\log_2 4)$

3. $-2 + \ln e^3$

4. $\log_2(0.5)$

For Problems 5–10, solve each equation.

5. $4^x = \dfrac{1}{64}$

6. $9^x = \dfrac{1}{27}$

7. $2^{3x-1} = 128$

8. $\log_9 x = \dfrac{5}{2}$

9. $\log x + \log(x + 48) = 2$

10. $\ln x = \ln 2 + \ln(3x - 1)$

For Problems 11–13, given that $\log_3 4 = 1.2619$ and $\log_3 5 = 1.4650$, evaluate each of the following.

11. $\log_3 100$

12. $\log_3 \dfrac{5}{4}$

13. $\log_3 \sqrt{5}$

14. Find the inverse of the function $f(x) = -3x - 6$.

15. Solve $e^x = 176$ to the nearest hundredth.

16. Solve $2^{x-2} = 314$ to the nearest hundredth.

17. Determine $\log_5 632$ to four decimal places.

18. Find the inverse of the function $f(x) = \dfrac{2}{3}x - \dfrac{3}{5}$.

19. If \$3500 is invested at 7.5% interest compounded quarterly, how much money has accumulated at the end of 8 years?

20. How long will it take \$5000 to be worth \$12,500 if it is invested at 7% compounded annually? Express your answer to the nearest tenth of a year.

21. The number of bacteria present in a certain culture after t hours is given by $Q(t) = Q_0 e^{0.23t}$, in which Q_0 represents the initial number of bacteria. How long will it take 400 bacteria to increase to 2400 bacteria? Express your answer to the nearest tenth of an hour.

22. Suppose that a certain radioactive substance has a half-life of 50 years. If there are presently 7500 grams of the substance, how much will remain after 32 years? Express your answer to the nearest gram.

For Problems 23–25, graph each of the functions.

23. $f(x) = e^x - 2$

24. $f(x) = -3^{-x}$

25. $f(x) = \log_2(x - 2)$

For Problems 1–5, evaluate each algebraic expression for the given values of the variables.

1. $-5(x - 1) - 3(2x + 4) + 3(3x - 1)$ for $x = -2$

2. $\dfrac{14a^3b^2}{7a^2b}$ for $a = -1$ and $b = 4$

3. $\dfrac{2}{n} - \dfrac{3}{2n} + \dfrac{5}{3n}$ for $n = 4$

4. $4\sqrt{2x - y} + 5\sqrt{3x + y}$ for $x = 16$ and $y = 16$

5. $\dfrac{3}{x - 2} - \dfrac{5}{x + 3}$ for $x = 3$

For Problems 6–15, perform the indicated operations and express answers in simplified form.

6. $(-5\sqrt{6})(3\sqrt{12})$

7. $(2\sqrt{x} - 3)(\sqrt{x} + 4)$

8. $(3\sqrt{2} - \sqrt{6})(\sqrt{2} + 4\sqrt{6})$

9. $(2x - 1)(x^2 + 6x - 4)$

10. $\dfrac{x^2 - x}{x + 5} \cdot \dfrac{x^2 + 5x + 4}{x^4 - x^2}$

11. $\dfrac{16x^2y}{24xy^3} \div \dfrac{9xy}{8x^2y^2}$

12. $\dfrac{x + 3}{10} + \dfrac{2x + 1}{15} - \dfrac{x - 2}{18}$

13. $\dfrac{7}{12ab} - \dfrac{11}{15a^2}$

14. $\dfrac{8}{x^2 - 4x} + \dfrac{2}{x}$

15. $(8x^3 - 6x^2 - 15x + 4) \div (4x - 1)$

For Problems 16–19, simplify each of the complex fractions.

16. $\dfrac{\dfrac{5}{x^2} - \dfrac{3}{x}}{\dfrac{1}{y} + \dfrac{2}{y^2}}$

17. $\dfrac{\dfrac{2}{x} - 3}{\dfrac{3}{y} + 4}$

18. $\dfrac{2 - \dfrac{1}{n - 2}}{3 + \dfrac{4}{n + 3}}$

19. $\dfrac{\dfrac{3a}{2} - 1}{2 - \dfrac{1}{a}}$

For Problems 20–25, factor each of the algebraic expressions completely.

20. $20x^2 + 7x - 6$

21. $16x^3 + 54$

22. $4x^4 - 25x^2 + 36$

23. $12x^3 - 52x^2 - 40x$

24. $xy - 6x + 3y - 18$

25. $10 + 9x - 9x^2$

For Problems 26–35, evaluate each of the numerical expressions.

26. $\left(\dfrac{2}{3}\right)^{-4}$

27. $\dfrac{3}{\left(\dfrac{4}{3}\right)^{-1}}$

28. $\sqrt[3]{-\dfrac{27}{64}}$

29. $-\sqrt{0.09}$

30. $(27)^{-4/3}$

31. $4^0 + 4^{-1} + 4^{-2}$

32. $\left(\dfrac{3^{-1}}{2^{-3}}\right)^{-2}$

33. $(2^{-3} - 3^{-2})^{-1}$

34. $\log_2 64$

35. $\log_3\left(\dfrac{1}{9}\right)$

For Problems 36–38, find the indicated products and quotients; express final answers with positive integral exponents only.

36. $(-3x^{-1}y^2)(4x^{-2}y^{-3})$

37. $\dfrac{48x^{-4}y^2}{6xy}$

38. $\left(\dfrac{27a^{-4}b^{-3}}{-3a^{-1}b^{-4}}\right)^{-1}$

For Problems 39–46, express each radical expression in simplest radical form.

39. $\sqrt{80}$

40. $-2\sqrt{54}$

41. $\sqrt{\dfrac{75}{81}}$

42. $\dfrac{4\sqrt{6}}{3\sqrt{8}}$

43. $\sqrt[3]{56}$

44. $\dfrac{\sqrt[3]{3}}{\sqrt[3]{4}}$

45. $4\sqrt{52x^3y^2}$

46. $\sqrt{\dfrac{2x}{3y}}$

For Problems 47–49, use the distributive property to help simplify each of the following:

47. $-3\sqrt{24} + 6\sqrt{54} - \sqrt{6}$

48. $\dfrac{\sqrt{8}}{3} - \dfrac{3\sqrt{18}}{4} - \dfrac{5\sqrt{50}}{2}$

49. $8\sqrt[3]{3} - 6\sqrt[3]{24} - 4\sqrt[3]{81}$

For Problems 50 and 51, rationalize the denominator and simplify.

50. $\dfrac{\sqrt{3}}{\sqrt{6} - 2\sqrt{2}}$

51. $\dfrac{3\sqrt{5} - \sqrt{3}}{2\sqrt{3} + \sqrt{7}}$

For Problems 52–54, use scientific notation to help perform the indicated operations.

52. $\dfrac{(0.00016)(300)(0.028)}{0.064}$

53. $\dfrac{0.00072}{0.0000024}$

54. $\sqrt{0.00000009}$

For Problems 55–58, find each of the indicated products or quotients, and express your answers in standard form.

55. $(5 - 2i)(4 + 6i)$

56. $(-3 - i)(5 - 2i)$

57. $\dfrac{5}{4i}$

58. $\dfrac{-1 + 6i}{7 - 2i}$

59. Find the slope of the line determined by the points $(2, -3)$ and $(-1, 7)$.

60. Find the slope of the line determined by the equation $4x - 7y = 9$.

61. Find the length of the line segment with endpoints at $(4, 5)$ and $(-2, 1)$.

62. Write the equation of the line that contains the points $(3, -1)$ and $(7, 4)$.

63. Write the equation of the line that is perpendicular to the line $3x - 4y = 6$ and contains the point $(-3, -2)$.

64. Write the equation of a line that is perpendicular to the line segment between $(2, 4)$ and $(6, 10)$ and contains the midpoint of the given line segment.

65. Write the equation of a line that is parallel to the line $y = -\dfrac{3}{4}x + 1$ and contains the point $(-4, 0)$.

66. Write the equation of the line parallel to the line $x = 3$ and contains the point $(-2, 7)$.

For Problems 67–76, graph each of the functions.

67. $f(x) = -2x - 4$

68. $f(x) = -2x^2 - 2$

69. $f(x) = x^2 - 2x - 2$

70. $f(x) = \sqrt{x + 1} + 2$

71. $f(x) = 2x^2 + 8x + 9$

72. $f(x) = -|x - 2| + 1$

73. $f(x) = 2^x + 2$

74. $f(x) = \log_2(x - 2)$

75. $f(x) = -x(x + 1)(x - 2)$

76. $f(x) = \dfrac{-x}{x + 2}$

77. If $f(x) = x - 3$ and $g(x) = 2x^2 - x - 1$, find $(g \circ f)(x)$ and $(f \circ g)(x)$.

78. Find the inverse (f^{-1}) of $f(x) = 3x - 7$.

79. Find the inverse of $f(x) = -\dfrac{1}{2}x + \dfrac{2}{3}$.

80. Find the constant of variation if y varies directly as x, and $y = 2$ when $x = -\dfrac{2}{3}$.

81. If y is inversely proportional to the square of x, and $y = 4$ when $x = 3$, find y when $x = 6$.

82. The volume of gas at a constant temperature varies inversely as the pressure. What is the volume of a gas under a pressure of 25 pounds if the gas occupies 15 cubic centimeters under a pressure of 20 pounds?

For Problems 83–110, solve each equation.

83. $3(2x - 1) - 2(5x + 1) = 4(3x + 4)$

84. $n + \dfrac{3n - 1}{9} - 4 = \dfrac{3n + 1}{3}$

85. $0.92 + 0.9(x - 0.3) = 2x - 5.95$

86. $|4x - 1| = 11$

87. $3x^2 = 7x$

88. $x^3 - 36x = 0$

89. $30x^2 + 13x - 10 = 0$

90. $8x^3 + 12x^2 - 36x = 0$

91. $x^4 + 8x^2 - 9 = 0$

92. $(n + 4)(n - 6) = 11$

93. $2 - \dfrac{3x}{x - 4} = \dfrac{14}{x + 7}$

94.
$$\dfrac{2n}{6n^2 + 7n - 3} - \dfrac{n - 3}{3n^2 + 11n - 4} = \dfrac{5}{2n^2 + 11n + 12}$$

95. $\sqrt{3y} - y = -6$

96. $\sqrt{x + 19} - \sqrt{x + 28} = -1$

97. $(3x - 1)^2 = 45$

98. $(2x + 5)^2 = -32$

99. $2x^2 - 3x + 4 = 0$

100. $3n^2 - 6n + 2 = 0$

101. $\dfrac{5}{n - 3} - \dfrac{3}{n + 3} = 1$

102. $12x^4 - 19x^2 + 5 = 0$

103. $2x^2 + 5x + 5 = 0$

104. $x^3 - 4x^2 - 25x + 28 = 0$

105. $6x^3 - 19x^2 + 9x + 10 = 0$

106. $16^x = 64$

107. $\log_3 x = 4$

108. $\log_{10} x + \log_{10} 25 = 2$

109. $\ln(3x - 4) - \ln(x + 1) = \ln 2$

110. $27^{4x} = 9^{x+1}$

For Problems 111–120, solve each inequality.

111. $-5(y - 1) + 3 > 3y - 4 - 4y$

112. $0.06x + 0.08(250 - x) \geq 19$

113. $|5x - 2| > 13$ **114.** $|6x + 2| < 8$

115. $\dfrac{x - 2}{5} - \dfrac{3x - 1}{4} \leq \dfrac{3}{10}$

116. $(x - 2)(x + 4) \leq 0$

117. $(3x - 1)(x - 4) > 0$ **118.** $x(x + 5) < 24$

119. $\dfrac{x - 3}{x - 7} \geq 0$ **120.** $\dfrac{2x}{x + 3} > 4$

For Problems 121–132, set up an equation or an inequality to help solve each problem.

121. Find three consecutive odd integers whose sum is 57.

122. Eric has a collection of 63 coins consisting of nickels, dimes, and quarters. The number of dimes is 6 more than the number of nickels, and the number of quarters is 1 more than twice the number of nickels. How many coins of each kind are in the collection?

123. One of two supplementary angles is 4° more than one-third of the other angle. Find the measure of each of the angles.

124. If a ring costs a jeweler $300, at what price should it be sold to make a profit of 50% on the selling price?

125. Beth invested a certain amount of money at 8% and $300 more than that amount at 9%. Her total yearly interest was $316. How much did she invest at each rate?

126. Two trains leave the same depot at the same time, one traveling east and the other traveling west. At the end of $4\frac{1}{2}$ hours, they are 639 miles apart. If the rate of the train traveling east is 10 miles per hour faster than the other train, find their rates.

127. A 10-quart radiator contains a 50% solution of antifreeze. How much needs to be drained out and replaced with pure antifreeze to obtain a 70% antifreeze solution?

128. Sam shot rounds of 70, 73, and 76 on the first 3 days of a golf tournament. What must he shoot on the fourth day of the tournament to average 72 or less for the 4 days?

129. The cube of a number equals nine times the same number. Find the number.

130. A strip of uniform width is to be cut off both sides and both ends of a sheet of paper that is 8 inches by 14 inches to reduce the size of the paper to an area of 72 square inches. Find the width of the strip.

131. A sum of $2450 is to be divided between two people in the ratio of 3 to 4. How much does each person receive?

132. Working together, Sue and Dean can complete a task in $1\frac{1}{5}$ hours. Dean can do the task by himself in 2 hours. How long would it take Sue to complete the task by herself?

6

Systems of Equations

6.1 Systems of Two Linear Equations in Two Variables

6.2 Systems of Three Linear Equations in Three Variables

6.3 Matrix Approach to Solving Linear Systems

6.4 Determinants

6.5 Cramer's Rule

6.6 Partial Fractions (Optional)

When mixing different solutions, a chemist could use a system of equations to determine how much of each solution is needed to produce a specific concentration.

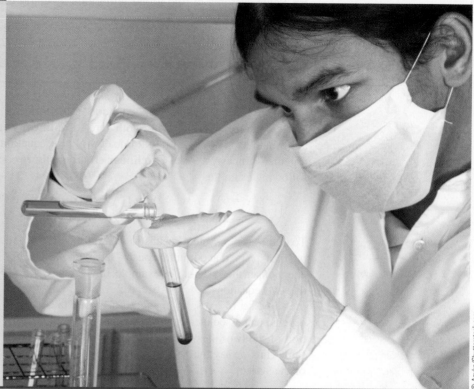

© Anyka/Shutterstock.com

A 10% salt solution is to be mixed with a 20% salt solution to produce 20 gallons of a 17.5% salt solution. How many gallons of the 10% solution and how many gallons of the 20% solution should be mixed? The two equations $x + y = 20$ and $0.10x + 0.20y = 0.175(20)$ algebraically represent the conditions of the problem; x represents the number of gallons of the 10% solution, and y represents the number of gallons of the 20% solution. The two equations considered together form a system of linear equations, and the problem can be solved by solving the system of equations.

Throughout most of this chapter, we consider systems of linear equations and their applications. We will discuss various techniques for solving systems of linear equations.

6.1   Systems of Two Linear Equations in Two Variables

OBJECTIVES

1 Solve systems of two linear equations by graphing

2 Solve systems of two linear equations by using the substitution method

3 Solve systems of two linear equations by using the elimination-by-addition method

4 Solve application problems using a system of equations

In Chapter 2 we stated that any equation of the form $Ax + By = C$, when A, B, and C are real numbers (A and B not both zero), is a **linear equation** in the two variables x and y, and its graph is a straight line. Two linear equations in two variables considered together form a **system of two linear equations in two variables**, as illustrated by the following examples:

$$\begin{pmatrix} x + y = 6 \\ x - y = 2 \end{pmatrix} \quad \begin{pmatrix} 3x + 2y = 1 \\ 5x - 2y = 23 \end{pmatrix} \quad \begin{pmatrix} 4x - 5y = 21 \\ -3x + y = -7 \end{pmatrix}$$

To *solve* such a system means to find all of the ordered pairs that simultaneously satisfy both equations in the system. For example, if we graph the two equations $x + y = 6$ and $x - y = 2$ on the same set of axes, as in Figure 6.1, then the ordered pair associated with the point of intersection of the two lines is the **solution of the system**. Thus we say that $\{(4, 2)\}$ is the solution set of the system

$$\begin{pmatrix} x + y = 6 \\ x - y = 2 \end{pmatrix}$$

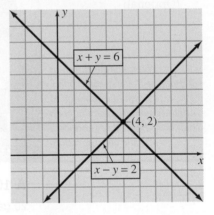

To check the solution, we substitute 4 for x and 2 for y in the two equations.

Figure 6.1

$x + y = 6$ becomes $4 + 2 = 6$, a true statement

$x - y = 2$ becomes $4 - 2 = 2$, a true statement

Because the graph of a linear equation in two variables is a straight line, three possible situations can occur when we are solving a system of two linear equations in two variables. These situations are shown in Figure 6.2.

Case 1   The graphs of the two equations are two lines intersecting in one point. There is exactly one solution, and the system is called a **consistent system**.

Case 2   The graphs of the two equations are parallel lines. There is *no solution*, and the system is called an **inconsistent system**.

Case 3   The graphs of the two equations are the same line, and there are *infinitely many solutions* of the system. Any pair of real numbers that satisfies one of the equations also satisfies the other equation, and we say that the equations are dependent.

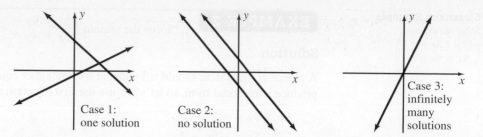

Figure 6.2

Thus as we solve a system of two linear equations in two variables, we can expect one of three outcomes: The system will have *no* solutions, *one* ordered pair as a solution, or *infinitely many* ordered pairs as solutions.

The Substitution Method

Solving specific systems of equations by graphing requires accurate graphs. However, unless the solutions are integers, it is difficult to obtain exact solutions from a graph. Therefore we will consider some other techniques for solving systems of equations.

The **substitution method**, which works especially well with systems of two equations in two unknowns, can be described as follows.

Step 1 Solve one of the equations for one variable in terms of the other. (If possible, make a choice that will avoid fractions.)

Step 2 Substitute the expression obtained in step 1 into the other equation, producing an equation in one variable.

Step 3 Solve the equation obtained in step 2.

Step 4 Use the solution obtained in step 3, along with the expression obtained in step 1, to determine the solution of the system.

Classroom Example
Solve the system
$\begin{pmatrix} 5x + y = 5 \\ 3x - 2y = 16 \end{pmatrix}$.

EXAMPLE 1   Solve the system $\begin{pmatrix} x - 3y = -25 \\ 4x + 5y = 19 \end{pmatrix}$.

Solution

Solve the first equation for x in terms of y to produce

$$x = 3y - 25$$

Substitute $3y - 25$ for x in the second equation and solve for y.

$$4x + 5y = 19$$
$$4(3y - 25) + 5y = 19$$
$$12y - 100 + 5y = 19$$
$$17y = 119$$
$$y = 7$$

Next, substitute 7 for y in the equation $x = 3y - 25$ to obtain

$$x = 3(7) - 25 = -4$$

The solution set of the given system is $\{(-4, 7)\}$. (You should check this solution in both of the original equations.)

Classroom Example
Solve the system:
$$\begin{pmatrix} 12x - 3y = -7 \\ 8x + 9y = -1 \end{pmatrix}$$

EXAMPLE 2   Solve the system $\begin{pmatrix} 5x + 9y = -2 \\ 2x + 4y = -1 \end{pmatrix}$.

Solution

A glance at the system should tell you that solving either equation for either variable will produce a fractional form, so let's just use the first equation and solve for x in terms of y.

$$5x + 9y = -2$$
$$5x = -9y - 2$$
$$x = \frac{-9y - 2}{5}$$

Now we can substitute this value for x into the second equation and solve for y.

$$2x + 4y = -1$$
$$2\left(\frac{-9y - 2}{5}\right) + 4y = -1$$
$$2(-9y - 2) + 20y = -5 \quad \text{Multiplied both sides by 5}$$
$$-18y - 4 + 20y = -5$$
$$2y - 4 = -5$$
$$2y = -1$$
$$y = -\frac{1}{2}$$

Now we can substitute $-\dfrac{1}{2}$ for y in $x = \dfrac{-9y - 2}{5}$.

$$x = \frac{-9\left(-\dfrac{1}{2}\right) - 2}{5} = \frac{\dfrac{9}{2} - 2}{5} = \frac{1}{2}$$

The solution set is $\left\{\left(\dfrac{1}{2}, -\dfrac{1}{2}\right)\right\}$.

Classroom Example
Solve the system:
$$\begin{pmatrix} 4x + 6y = 8 \\ y = -\dfrac{2}{3}x + \dfrac{4}{3} \end{pmatrix}$$

EXAMPLE 3   Solve the system $\begin{pmatrix} 6x - 4y = 18 \\ y = \dfrac{3}{2}x - \dfrac{9}{2} \end{pmatrix}$.

Solution

The second equation is given in appropriate form for us to begin the substitution process. Substitute $\dfrac{3}{2}x - \dfrac{9}{2}$ for y in the first equation to yield

$$6x - 4y = 18$$
$$6x - 4\left(\frac{3}{2}x - \frac{9}{2}\right) = 18$$
$$6x - 6x + 18 = 18$$
$$18 = 18$$

Our obtaining a true numerical statement ($18 = 18$) indicates that the system has infinitely many solutions. Any ordered pair that satisfies one of the equations will also satisfy the other equation. Thus in the second equation of the original system, if we let $x = k$, then $y = \dfrac{3}{2}k - \dfrac{9}{2}$. Therefore the solution set can be expressed as $\left\{ \left(k, \dfrac{3}{2}k - \dfrac{9}{2} \right) \,\middle|\, k \text{ is a real number} \right\}$. If some specific solutions are needed, they can be generated by the ordered pair $\left(k, \dfrac{3}{2}k - \dfrac{9}{2} \right)$. For example, if we let $k = 1$, then we get $\dfrac{3}{2}(1) - \dfrac{9}{2} = -\dfrac{6}{2} = -3$. Thus the ordered pair $(1, -3)$ is a member of the solution set of the given system.

The Elimination-by-Addition Method

Now let's consider the **elimination-by-addition method** for solving a system of equations. This is a very important method because it is the basis for developing other techniques for solving systems that contain many equations and variables. The method involves replacing systems of equations with *simpler equivalent systems* until we obtain a system in which the solutions are obvious. **Equivalent systems** of equations are systems that have exactly the same solution set. The following operations or transformations can be applied to a system of equations to produce an equivalent system:

1. Any two equations of the system can be interchanged.

2. Both sides of any equation of the system can be multiplied by any nonzero real number.

3. Any equation of the system can be replaced by the sum of that equation and a nonzero multiple of another equation.

Classroom Example
Solve the system
$\begin{pmatrix} 2x - 7y = 22 \\ 3x + 5y = 2 \end{pmatrix}$.

EXAMPLE 4   Solve the system $\begin{pmatrix} 3x + 5y = -9 \\ 2x - 3y = 13 \end{pmatrix}$. $\qquad$ (1)(2)

Solution

We can replace the given system with an equivalent system by multiplying equation (2) by -3.

$$\begin{pmatrix} 3x + 5y = -9 \\ -6x + 9y = -39 \end{pmatrix} \qquad \begin{matrix}(3)\\(4)\end{matrix}$$

Now let's replace equation (4) with an equation formed by multiplying equation (3) by 2 and adding this result to equation (4).

$$\begin{pmatrix} 3x + 5y = -9 \\ 19y = -57 \end{pmatrix} \qquad \begin{matrix}(5)\\(6)\end{matrix}$$

From equation (6), we can easily determine that $y = -3$. Then, substituting -3 for y in equation (5) produces

$$3x + 5(-3) = -9$$
$$3x - 15 = -9$$

$$3x = 6$$
$$x = 2$$

The solution set for the given system is $\{(2, -3)\}$.

Remark: We are using a format for the elimination-by-addition method that highlights the use of equivalent systems. In Section 6.3 this format will lead naturally to an approach using matrices. Thus it is beneficial to stress the use of equivalent systems at this time.

Classroom Example
Solve the system:
$$\left(\begin{array}{l} \frac{5}{9}x - \frac{3}{5}y = 14 \\ \frac{1}{3}x + \frac{2}{3}y = -7 \end{array} \right)$$

EXAMPLE 5

Solve the system $\left(\begin{array}{l} \frac{1}{2}x + \frac{2}{3}y = -4 \\ \frac{1}{4}x - \frac{3}{2}y = 20 \end{array} \right)$.

$$(7)$$
$$(8)$$

Solution

The given system can be replaced with an equivalent system by multiplying equation (7) by 6 and equation (8) by 4.

$$\left(\begin{array}{l} 3x + 4y = -24 \\ x - 6y = 80 \end{array} \right)$$

$$(9)$$
$$(10)$$

Now let's exchange equations (9) and (10).

$$\left(\begin{array}{l} x - 6y = 80 \\ 3x + 4y = -24 \end{array} \right)$$

$$(11)$$
$$(12)$$

We can replace equation (12) with an equation formed by multiplying equation (11) by -3 and adding this result to equation (12).

$$\left(\begin{array}{l} x - 6y = 80 \\ 22y = -264 \end{array} \right)$$

$$(13)$$
$$(14)$$

From equation (14) we can determine that $y = -12$. Then, substituting -12 for y in equation (13) produces

$$x - 6(-12) = 80$$
$$x + 72 = 80$$
$$x = 8$$

The solution set of the given system is $\{(8, -12)\}$. (Check this!)

Classroom Example
Solve the system $\left(\begin{array}{l} 8x - y = 5 \\ 8x - y = 9 \end{array} \right)$.

EXAMPLE 6

Solve the system $\left(\begin{array}{l} x - 4y = 9 \\ x - 4y = 3 \end{array} \right)$.

$$(15)$$
$$(16)$$

Solution

We can replace equation (16) with an equation formed by multiplying equation (15) by -1 and adding this result to equation (16).

$$\left(\begin{array}{l} x - 4y = 9 \\ 0 = -6 \end{array} \right)$$

$$(17)$$
$$(18)$$

The statement $0 = -6$ is a contradiction, and therefore the original system is *inconsistent*; it has no solution. The solution set is $\varnothing$.

_____ ■

Both the elimination-by-addition and the substitution methods can be used to obtain exact solutions for any system of two linear equations in two unknowns. Sometimes it is a matter of deciding which method to use on a particular system. Some systems lend themselves to one or the other of the methods by virtue of the original format of the equations. We will illustrate this idea in a moment when we solve some word problems.

Using Systems to Solve Problems

Many word problems that we solved earlier in this text with one variable and one equation can also be solved by using a system of two linear equations in two variables. In fact, in many of these problems, you may find it more natural to use two variables and two equations.

Classroom Example
A boat moving at a constant speed traveled to a destination 35 miles away, upriver. The boat was going against the current, and the trip took $2\frac{1}{3}$ hours. The return trip, going with the current, only took $1\frac{2}{3}$ hours. Find the speed of the boat and the speed of the current in miles per hour.

EXAMPLE 7

John Paul always runs his pontoon boat at full throttle, which results in the boat traveling at a constant speed. Going up the river against the current the boat traveled 72 miles in 4.5 hours. The return trip down the river with the help of the current only took three hours. Find the speed of the boat and the speed of the current.

Solution

Let x represent the speed of the boat and let y represent the speed of the current. Going up the river the rate of the boat against the current is $\dfrac{72 \text{ miles}}{4.5 \text{ hours}} = 16$ miles per hour.

Going down the river the rate of the boat with the current is $\dfrac{72 \text{ miles}}{3 \text{ hours}} = 24$ miles per hour. The problem translates into the following system of equations.

$$\begin{pmatrix} x + y = 24 \\ x - y = 16 \end{pmatrix}$$

Let's use the elimination-by-addition method to solve the system. The second equation can be replaced by an equation formed by adding the two equations.

$$\begin{pmatrix} x + y = 24 \\ 2x = 40 \end{pmatrix}$$

Solving the second equation we can determine that $x = 20$. Now substituting 20 for x in the first equation produces

$$20 + y = 24$$
$$y = 4$$

Therefore, the speed of the boat is 20 miles per hour, and the speed of the current is 4 miles per hour.

_____ ■

EXAMPLE 8

Lucinda invested $9500, part of it at 2% interest and the remainder at 4%. Her total yearly income from the two investments was $330.00. How much did she invest at each rate?

Solution

Let x represent the amount invested at 2% and y the amount invested at 4%. The problem translates into the following system:

$$\begin{pmatrix} x + y = 9500 \\ 0.02x + 0.04y = 330.00 \end{pmatrix}$$

⟵——— The two investments total $9500

⟵——— The yearly interest from the two investments totals $330.00

Multiply the second equation by 100 to produce an equivalent system.

$$\begin{pmatrix} x + y = 9500 \\ 2x + 4y = 33000 \end{pmatrix}$$

Because neither equation is solved for one variable in terms of the other, let's use the elimination-by-addition method to solve the system. The second equation can be replaced by an equation formed by multiplying the first equation by -2 and adding this result to the second equation.

$$\begin{pmatrix} x + y = 950 \\ 2y = 14000 \end{pmatrix}$$

Solving the second equation for y we determine that $y = 7000$. Now we substitute 7000 for y in the equation $x + y = 9500$.

$$x + 7000 = 9500$$
$$x = 2500$$

Therefore Lucinda must have invested $2500 at 2% and $7000 at 4%. ∎

In our final example of this section, we will use a graphing utility to help solve a system of equations.

EXAMPLE 9

Solve the system $\begin{pmatrix} 1.14x + 2.35y = -7.12 \\ 3.26x - 5.05y = 26.72 \end{pmatrix}$.

Solution

We began this section with graphing the equations in a system to find the solution. For this problem let's use a graphing utility to help find the solution of the system of equations. First, we need to solve each equation for y in terms of x. Thus the system becomes

$$\begin{pmatrix} y = \dfrac{-7.12 - 1.14x}{2.35} \\ y = \dfrac{3.26x - 26.72}{5.05} \end{pmatrix}$$

Now we can enter both of these equations into a graphing utility and obtain Figure 6.3. From this figure it appears that the point of intersection is at approximately $x = 2$ and $y = -4$. By direct substitution into the given equations, we can verify that the point of intersection is exactly $(2, -4)$.

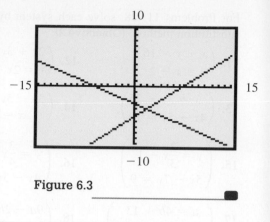

Figure 6.3

Concept Quiz 6.1

For Problems 1–8, answer true or false.

1. To *solve a system of equations* means to find all the ordered pairs that satisfy every equation in the system.
2. A consistent system of linear equations will have more than one solution.
3. If the graph of a system of two distinct linear equations results in two distinct parallel lines, then the system has no solution.
4. If the graphs of the two equations in a system are the same line, then the equations in the system are dependent.
5. Every system of equations has a solution.
6. For the system $\begin{pmatrix} 2x + y = 4 \\ x + 5y = 10 \end{pmatrix}$, the ordered pair $(1, 2)$ is a solution.
7. Graphing a system of equations is the most accurate method for finding the solution of the system.
8. The only possibilities for the solution set of a system of two linear equations are no solutions, one solution, or two solutions.

Problem Set 6.1

For Problems 1–10, use the graphing approach to determine whether the system is consistent, the system is inconsistent, or the equations are dependent. If the system is consistent, find the solution set from the graph and check it. (**Objective 1**)

1. $\begin{pmatrix} x - y = 1 \\ 2x + y = 8 \end{pmatrix}$

2. $\begin{pmatrix} 3x + y = 0 \\ x \quad 2y = -7 \end{pmatrix}$

3. $\begin{pmatrix} 4x + 3y = -5 \\ 2x - 3y = -7 \end{pmatrix}$

4. $\begin{pmatrix} 2x - y = 9 \\ 4x - 2y = 11 \end{pmatrix}$

5. $\begin{pmatrix} \dfrac{1}{2}x + \dfrac{1}{4}y = 9 \\ 4x + 2y - 72 \end{pmatrix}$

6. $\begin{pmatrix} 5x + 2y = -9 \\ 4x - 3y = 2 \end{pmatrix}$

7. $\begin{pmatrix} \dfrac{1}{2}x - \dfrac{1}{3}y = 3 \\ x + 4y - -8 \end{pmatrix}$

8. $\begin{pmatrix} 4x - 9y = -60 \\ \dfrac{1}{3}x - \dfrac{3}{4}y = -5 \end{pmatrix}$

9. $\begin{pmatrix} x - \dfrac{y}{2} = -4 \\ 8x - 4y = -1 \end{pmatrix}$

10. $\begin{pmatrix} 3x - 2y = 7 \\ 6x + 5y = -4 \end{pmatrix}$

For Problems 11–28, solve each system by using the substitution method. **(Objective 2)**

11. $\begin{pmatrix} x + y = 16 \\ y = x + 2 \end{pmatrix}$

12. $\begin{pmatrix} 2x + 3y = -5 \\ y = 2x + 9 \end{pmatrix}$

13. $\begin{pmatrix} x = 3y - 25 \\ 4x + 5y = 19 \end{pmatrix}$

14. $\begin{pmatrix} 3x - 5y = 25 \\ x = y + 7 \end{pmatrix}$

15. $\begin{pmatrix} y = \dfrac{2}{3}x - 1 \\ 5x - 7y = 9 \end{pmatrix}$

16. $\begin{pmatrix} y = \dfrac{3}{4}x + 5 \\ 4x - 3y = -1 \end{pmatrix}$

17. $\begin{pmatrix} a = 4b + 13 \\ 3a + 6b = -33 \end{pmatrix}$

18. $\begin{pmatrix} 9a - 2b = 28 \\ b = -3a + 1 \end{pmatrix}$

19. $\begin{pmatrix} 2x - 3y = 4 \\ y = \dfrac{2}{3}x - \dfrac{4}{3} \end{pmatrix}$

20. $\begin{pmatrix} t + u = 11 \\ t = u + 7 \end{pmatrix}$

21. $\begin{pmatrix} u = t - 2 \\ t + u = 12 \end{pmatrix}$

22. $\begin{pmatrix} y = 5x - 9 \\ 5x - y = 9 \end{pmatrix}$

23. $\begin{pmatrix} 4x + 3y = -7 \\ 3x - 2y = 16 \end{pmatrix}$

24. $\begin{pmatrix} 5x - 3y = -34 \\ 2x + 7y = -30 \end{pmatrix}$

25. $\begin{pmatrix} 5x - y = 4 \\ y = 5x + 9 \end{pmatrix}$

26. $\begin{pmatrix} 2x + 3y = 3 \\ 4x - 9y = -4 \end{pmatrix}$

27. $\begin{pmatrix} 4x - 5y = 3 \\ 8x + 15y = -24 \end{pmatrix}$

28. $\begin{pmatrix} 4x + y = 9 \\ y = 15 - 4x \end{pmatrix}$

For Problems 29–44, solve each system by using the elimination-by-addition method. **(Objective 3)**

29. $\begin{pmatrix} 3x + 2y = 1 \\ 5x - 2y = 23 \end{pmatrix}$

30. $\begin{pmatrix} 4x + 3y = -22 \\ 4x - 5y = 26 \end{pmatrix}$

31. $\begin{pmatrix} x - 3y = -22 \\ 2x + 7y = 60 \end{pmatrix}$

32. $\begin{pmatrix} 6x - y = 3 \\ 5x + 3y = -9 \end{pmatrix}$

33. $\begin{pmatrix} 4x - 5y = 21 \\ 3x + 7y = -38 \end{pmatrix}$

34. $\begin{pmatrix} 5x - 3y = -34 \\ 2x + 7y = -30 \end{pmatrix}$

35. $\begin{pmatrix} 5x - 2y = 19 \\ 5x - 2y = 7 \end{pmatrix}$

36. $\begin{pmatrix} 4a + 2b = -4 \\ 6a - 5b = 18 \end{pmatrix}$

37. $\begin{pmatrix} 5a + 6b = 8 \\ 2a - 15b = 9 \end{pmatrix}$

38. $\begin{pmatrix} 7x + 2y = 11 \\ 7x + 2y = -4 \end{pmatrix}$

39. $\begin{pmatrix} \dfrac{2}{3}s + \dfrac{1}{4}t = -1 \\ \dfrac{1}{2}s - \dfrac{1}{3}t = -7 \end{pmatrix}$

40. $\begin{pmatrix} \dfrac{1}{4}s - \dfrac{2}{3}t = -3 \\ \dfrac{1}{3}s + \dfrac{1}{3}t = 7 \end{pmatrix}$

41. $\begin{pmatrix} \dfrac{x}{2} - \dfrac{2y}{5} = \dfrac{-23}{60} \\ \dfrac{2x}{3} + \dfrac{y}{4} = \dfrac{-1}{4} \end{pmatrix}$

42. $\begin{pmatrix} \dfrac{2x}{3} - \dfrac{y}{2} = \dfrac{3}{5} \\ \dfrac{x}{4} + \dfrac{y}{2} = \dfrac{7}{80} \end{pmatrix}$

43. $\begin{pmatrix} \dfrac{2}{3}x + \dfrac{1}{2}y = \dfrac{1}{6} \\ 4x + 6y = -1 \end{pmatrix}$

44. $\begin{pmatrix} \dfrac{1}{2}x + \dfrac{2}{3}y = -\dfrac{3}{10} \\ 5x + 4y = -1 \end{pmatrix}$

For Problems 45–60, solve each system by using either the substitution method or the elimination-by-addition method, whichever seems more appropriate.

45. $\begin{pmatrix} 5x - y = -22 \\ 2x + 3y = -2 \end{pmatrix}$

46. $\begin{pmatrix} 4x + 5y = -41 \\ 3x - 2y = 21 \end{pmatrix}$

47. $\begin{pmatrix} x = 3y - 10 \\ x = -2y + 15 \end{pmatrix}$

48. $\begin{pmatrix} y = 4x - 24 \\ 7x + y = 42 \end{pmatrix}$

49. $\begin{pmatrix} 3x - 5y = 9 \\ 6x - 10y = -1 \end{pmatrix}$

50. $\begin{pmatrix} y = \dfrac{2}{5}x - 3 \\ 4x - 7y = 33 \end{pmatrix}$

51. $\begin{pmatrix} \dfrac{1}{2}x - \dfrac{2}{3}y = 22 \\ \dfrac{1}{2}x + \dfrac{1}{4}y = 0 \end{pmatrix}$

52. $\begin{pmatrix} \dfrac{2}{5}x - \dfrac{1}{3}y = -9 \\ \dfrac{3}{4}x + \dfrac{1}{3}y = -14 \end{pmatrix}$

53. $\begin{pmatrix} t = 2u + 2 \\ 9u - 9t = -45 \end{pmatrix}$

54. $\begin{pmatrix} 9u - 9t = 36 \\ u = 2t + 1 \end{pmatrix}$

55. $\begin{pmatrix} x + y = 1000 \\ 0.12x + 0.14y = 136 \end{pmatrix}$

56. $\begin{pmatrix} x + y = 10 \\ 0.3x + 0.7y = 4 \end{pmatrix}$

57. $\begin{pmatrix} y = 2x \\ 0.09x + 0.12y = 132 \end{pmatrix}$

58. $\begin{pmatrix} y = 3x \\ 0.1x + 0.11y = 64.5 \end{pmatrix}$

59. $\begin{pmatrix} x + y = 10.5 \\ 0.5x + 0.8y = 7.35 \end{pmatrix}$ **60.** $\begin{pmatrix} 2x + y = 7.75 \\ 3x + 2y = 12.5 \end{pmatrix}$

For Problems 61–80, solve each problem by using a system of equations. **(Objective 4)**

61. The sum of two numbers is 53, and their difference is 19. Find the numbers.

62. The sum of two numbers is −3, and their difference is 25. Find the numbers.

63. The measure of the larger of two complementary angles is 15° more than four times the measure of the smaller angle. Find the measures of both angles.

64. Assume that a plane is flying at a constant speed under unvarying wind conditions. Traveling against a head wind, the plane takes 4 hours to travel 1540 miles. Traveling with a tail wind, the plane flies 1365 miles in 3 hours. Find the speed of the plane and the speed of the wind.

65. The tens digit of a two-digit number is 1 more than three times the units digit. If the sum of the digits is 9, find the number.

66. The units digit of a two-digit number is 1 less than twice the tens digit. The sum of the digits is 8. Find the number.

67. A car rental agency rents sedans at $45 a day and convertibles at $65 a day. If 32 cars were rented one day for a total of $1680, how many convertibles were rented?

68. A video store rents new release movies for $5 and favorites for $2.75. One day the number of new release movies rented was twice the number of favorites. If the total income from those rentals was $956.25, how many movies of each kind were rented?

69. A motel rents double rooms at $100 per day and single rooms at $75 per day. If 23 rooms were rented one day for a total of $2100, how many rooms of each kind were rented?

70. An apartment complex rents one-bedroom apartments for $825 per month and two-bedroom apartments for $1075 per month. One month the number of one-bedroom apartments rented was twice the number of two-bedroom apartments. If the total income for that month was $32,700, how many apartments of each kind were rented?

71. The income from a student production was $32,500. The price of a student ticket was $10, and nonstudent tickets were sold at $15 each. Three thousand tickets were sold. How many tickets of each kind were sold?

72. Michelle can enter a small business as a full partner and receive a salary of $10,000 a year and 15% of the year's profit, or she can be sales manager for a salary of $25,000 plus 5% of the year's profit. What must the year's profit be for her total earnings to be the same whether she is a full partner or a sales manager?

73. Melinda invested three times as much money at 6% yearly interest as she did at 4%. Her total yearly interest from the two investments was $110. How much did she invest at each rate?

74. Sam invested $1950, part of it at 6% and the rest at 8% yearly interest. The yearly income on the 8% investment was $6 more than twice the income from the 6% investment. How much did he invest at each rate?

75. One day last summer, Jim went kayaking on the Little Susitna River in Alaska. Paddling upstream against the current, he traveled 20 miles in 4 hours. Then he turned around and paddled twice as fast downstream and, with the help of the current, traveled 19 miles in 1 hour. Find the rate of the current.

76. One solution contains 30% alcohol and a second solution contains 70% alcohol. How many liters of each solution should be mixed to make 10 liters containing 40% alcohol?

77. Santo bought 4 gallons of green latex paint and 2 gallons of primer for a total of $116. Not having enough paint to finish the project, Santo returned to the same store and bought 3 gallons of green latex paint and 1 gallon of primer for a total of $80. What is the price of a gallon of green latex paint?

78. Four bottles of water and 2 bagels cost $10.54. At the same prices, 3 bottles of water and 5 bagels cost $11.02. Find the price per bottle of water and the price per bagel.

79. A cash drawer contains only five- and ten-dollar bills. There are 12 more five-dollar bills than ten-dollar bills. If the drawer contains $330, find the number of each kind of bill.

80. Brad has a collection of dimes and quarters totaling $47.50. The number of quarters is 10 more than twice the number of dimes. How many coins of each kind does he have?

Thoughts Into Words

81. Give a general description of how to use the substitution method to solve a system of two linear equations in two variables.

82. Give a general description of how to use the elimination-by-addition method to solve a system of two linear equations in two variables.

83. Which method would you use to solve the system $\begin{pmatrix} 9x + 4y = 7 \\ 3x + 2y = 6 \end{pmatrix}$? Why?

84. Which method would you use to solve the system $\begin{pmatrix} 5x + 3y = 12 \\ 3x - y = 10 \end{pmatrix}$? Why?

Further Investigations

A system such as

$$\begin{pmatrix} \dfrac{2}{x} + \dfrac{3}{y} = \dfrac{19}{15} \\ -\dfrac{2}{x} + \dfrac{1}{y} = -\dfrac{7}{15} \end{pmatrix}$$

is not a linear system, but it can be solved using the elimination-by-addition method as follows. Add the first equation to the second to produce the equivalent system

$$\begin{pmatrix} \dfrac{2}{x} + \dfrac{3}{y} = \dfrac{19}{15} \\ \dfrac{4}{y} = \dfrac{12}{15} \end{pmatrix}$$

Now solve $\dfrac{4}{y} = \dfrac{12}{15}$ to produce $y = 5$.

Substitute 5 for y in the first equation and solve for x to produce

$$\dfrac{2}{x} + \dfrac{3}{5} = \dfrac{19}{15}$$

$$\dfrac{2}{x} = \dfrac{10}{15}$$

$$10x = 30$$

$$x = 3$$

The solution set of the original system is $\{(3, 5)\}$.

For Problems 85–90, solve each system.

85. $\begin{pmatrix} \dfrac{1}{x} + \dfrac{2}{y} = \dfrac{7}{12} \\ \dfrac{3}{x} - \dfrac{2}{y} = \dfrac{5}{12} \end{pmatrix}$

86. $\left(\begin{array}{l} \dfrac{3}{x} + \dfrac{2}{y} = 2 \\[2mm] \dfrac{2}{x} - \dfrac{3}{y} = \dfrac{1}{4} \end{array} \right)$

87. $\left(\begin{array}{l} \dfrac{3}{x} - \dfrac{2}{y} = \dfrac{13}{6} \\[2mm] \dfrac{2}{x} + \dfrac{3}{y} = 0 \end{array} \right)$

88. $\left(\begin{array}{l} \dfrac{4}{x} + \dfrac{1}{y} = 11 \\[2mm] \dfrac{3}{x} - \dfrac{5}{y} = -9 \end{array} \right)$

89. $\left(\begin{array}{l} \dfrac{5}{x} - \dfrac{2}{y} = 23 \\[2mm] \dfrac{4}{x} + \dfrac{3}{y} = \dfrac{23}{2} \end{array} \right)$

90. $\left(\begin{array}{l} \dfrac{2}{x} - \dfrac{7}{y} = \dfrac{9}{10} \\[2mm] \dfrac{5}{x} + \dfrac{4}{y} = -\dfrac{41}{20} \end{array} \right)$

91. Consider the linear system $\left(\begin{array}{l} a_1x + b_1y = c_1 \\ a_2x + b_2y = c_2 \end{array} \right)$.

(a) Prove that this system has exactly one solution if and only if $\dfrac{a_1}{a_2} \neq \dfrac{b_1}{b_2}$.

(b) Prove that this system has no solution if and only if $\dfrac{a_1}{a_2} = \dfrac{b_1}{b_2} \neq \dfrac{c_1}{c_2}$.

(c) Prove that this system has infinitely many solutions if and only if $\dfrac{a_1}{a_2} = \dfrac{b_1}{b_2} = \dfrac{c_1}{c_2}$.

92. For each of the following systems, use the results from Problem 91 to determine whether the system is consistent or inconsistent or whether the equations are dependent.

(a) $\left(\begin{array}{l} 5x + y = 9 \\ x - 5y = 4 \end{array} \right)$

(b) $\left(\begin{array}{l} 3x - 2y = 14 \\ 2x + 3y = 9 \end{array} \right)$

(c) $\left(\begin{array}{l} x - 7y = 4 \\ x - 7y = 9 \end{array} \right)$

(d) $\left(\begin{array}{l} 3x - 5y = 10 \\ 6x - 10y = 1 \end{array} \right)$

(e) $\left(\begin{array}{l} 3x + 6y = 2 \\ \dfrac{3}{5}x + \dfrac{6}{5}y = \dfrac{2}{5} \end{array} \right)$

(f) $\left(\begin{array}{l} \dfrac{2}{3}x - \dfrac{3}{4}y = 2 \\[2mm] \dfrac{1}{2}x + \dfrac{2}{5}y = 9 \end{array} \right)$

(g) $\left(\begin{array}{l} 7x + 9y = 14 \\ 8x - 3y = 12 \end{array} \right)$

(h) $\left(\begin{array}{l} 4x - 5y = 3 \\ 12x - 15y = 9 \end{array} \right)$

Graphing Calculator Activities

93. For each of the systems of equations in Problem 92, use your graphing calculator to help determine whether the system is consistent or inconsistent or whether the equations are dependent.

94. Use your graphing calculator to help determine the solution set for each of the following systems. Be sure to check your answers.

(a) $\left(\begin{array}{l} y = 3x - 1 \\ y = 9 - 2x \end{array} \right)$

(b) $\left(\begin{array}{l} 5x + y = -9 \\ 3x - 2y = 5 \end{array} \right)$

(c) $\left(\begin{array}{l} 4x - 3y = 18 \\ 5x + 6y = 3 \end{array} \right)$

(d) $\left(\begin{array}{l} 2x - y = 20 \\ 7x + y = 79 \end{array} \right)$

(e) $\left(\begin{array}{l} 13x - 12y = 37 \\ 15x + 13y = -11 \end{array} \right)$

(f) $\left(\begin{array}{l} 1.98x + 2.49y = 13.92 \\ 1.19x + 3.45y = 16.18 \end{array} \right)$

Answers to the Concept Quiz

1. True **2.** False **3.** True **4.** True **5.** False **6.** False **7.** False **8.** False

Systems of Three Linear Equations in Three Variables

OBJECTIVES

1 Solve systems of three linear equations

2 Solve application problems using a system of three linear equations

Consider a linear equation in three variables x, y, and z, such as $3x - 2y + z = 7$. Any **ordered triple** (x, y, z) that makes the equation a true numerical statement is said to be a *solution* of the equation. For example, the ordered triple $(2, 1, 3)$ is a solution because $3(2) - 2(1) + 3 = 7$. However, the ordered triple $(5, 2, 4)$ is not a solution because $3(5) - 2(2) + 4 \neq 7$. There are infinitely many solutions in the solution set.

Remark: The idea of a linear equation is generalized to include equations of more than two variables. Thus an equation such as $5x - 2y + 9z = 8$ is called a linear equation in three variables; the equation $5x - 7y + 2z - 11w = 1$ is called a linear equation in four variables, and so on.

To *solve* a system of three linear equations in three variables, such as

$$\begin{pmatrix} 3x - y + 2z = 13 \\ 4x + 2y + 5z = 30 \\ 5x - 3y - z = 3 \end{pmatrix}$$

means to find all of the ordered triples that satisfy all three equations. In other words, the solution set of the system is the intersection of the solution sets of all three equations in the system.

The graph of a linear equation in three variables is a *plane*, not a line. In fact, graphing equations in three variables requires the use of a three-dimensional coordinate system. Thus using a graphing approach to solve systems of three linear equations in three variables is not at all practical. However, a simple graphical analysis does provide us with some indication of what we can expect as we begin solving such systems.

In general, because each linear equation in three variables produces a plane, a system of three such equations produces three planes. There are various ways in which three planes can be related. For example, they may be mutually parallel; or two of the planes may be parallel, with the third intersecting the other two. (You may want to analyze all of the other possibilities for the three planes!) However, for our purposes at this time, we need to realize that from a solution set viewpoint, a system of three linear equations in three variables produces one of the following possibilities:

1. There is *one ordered triple* that satisfies all three equations. The three planes have a common *point* of intersection, as indicated in Figure 6.4.

2. There are *infinitely many ordered triples* in the solution set, all of which are co-ordinates of points on a *line* common to the three planes. This can happen if the three planes have a common line of intersection as in Figure 6.5(a), or if two of the planes coincide and the third plane intersects them as in Figure 6.5(b).

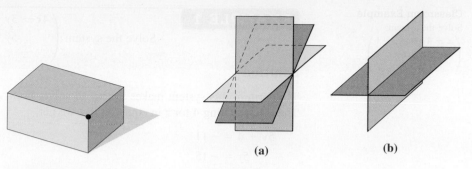

(a)　　　　　　　　　　**(b)**

Figure 6.4　　　　　　**Figure 6.5**

Figure 6.6

3. There are *infinitely many ordered triples* in the solution set, all of which are coordinates of points on a *plane*. This can happen if the three planes coincide, as illustrated in Figure 6.6.

4. The solution set is *empty*; thus we write $\varnothing$. This can happen in various ways, as illustrated in Figure 6.7. Note that in each situation there are no points common to all three planes.

(a) Three parallel planes

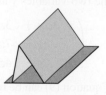

(b) Two planes coincide and the third one is parallel to the coinciding planes.

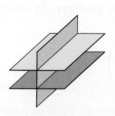

(c) Two planes are parallel and the third intersects them in parallel lines.

(d) No two planes are parallel, but two of them intersect in a line that is parallel to the third plane.

Figure 6.7

Now that we know what possibilities exist, let's consider finding the solution sets for some systems. Our approach will be the elimination-by-addition method, in which systems are replaced with equivalent systems until a system is obtained that allows us to easily determine the solution set. The details of this approach will become apparent as we work a few examples.

EXAMPLE 1

Solve the system $\begin{pmatrix} 4x - 3y - 2z = 5 & \quad (1) \\ 5y + z = -11 & \quad (2) \\ 3z = 12 & \quad (3) \end{pmatrix}$.

Solution

The form of this system makes it easy to solve. From equation (3), we obtain $z = 4$. Then, substituting 4 for z in equation (2), we get

$$5y + 4 = -11$$
$$5y = -15$$
$$y = -3$$

Finally, substituting 4 for z and -3 for y in equation (1) yields

$$4x - 3(-3) - 2(4) = 5$$
$$4x + 1 = 5$$
$$4x = 4$$
$$x = 1$$

Thus the solution set of the given system is $\{(1, -3, 4)\}$. ■

EXAMPLE 2

Solve the system $\begin{pmatrix} x - 2y + 3z = 22 & \quad (4) \\ 2x - 3y - z = 5 & \quad (5) \\ 3x + y - 5z = -32 & \quad (6) \end{pmatrix}$.

Solution

Equation (5) can be replaced with the equation formed by multiplying equation (4) by -2 and adding this result to equation (5). Equation (6) can be replaced with the equation formed by multiplying equation (4) by -3 and adding this result to equation (6). The following equivalent system is produced, in which equations (8) and (9) contain only the two variables y and z:

$$\begin{pmatrix} x - 2y + 3z = 22 & \quad (7) \\ y - 7z = -39 & \quad (8) \\ 7y - 14z = -98 & \quad (9) \end{pmatrix}$$

Equation (9) can be replaced with the equation formed by multiplying equation (8) by -7 and adding this result to equation (9). This produces the following equivalent system:

$$\begin{pmatrix} x - 2y + 3z = 22 & \quad (10) \\ y - 7z = -39 & \quad (11) \\ 35z = 175 & \quad (12) \end{pmatrix}$$

From equation (12), we obtain $z = 5$. Then, substituting 5 for z in equation (11), we obtain

$$y - 7(5) = -39$$
$$y - 35 = -39$$
$$y = -4$$

Finally, substituting -4 for y and 5 for z in equation (10) produces

$$x - 2(-4) + 3(5) = 22$$
$$x + 8 + 15 = 22$$
$$x + 23 = 22$$
$$x = -1$$

The solution set of the original system is $\{(-1, -4, 5)\}$. (Perhaps you should check this ordered triple in all three of the original equations.)

EXAMPLE 3

Solve the system $\begin{pmatrix} 3x - y + 2z = 13 \\ 5x - 3y - z = 3 \\ 4x + 2y + 5z = 30 \end{pmatrix}$.

                                                                  (13)
(14)
(15)

Solution

Equation (14) can be replaced with the equation formed by multiplying equation (13) by -3 and adding this result to equation (14). Equation (15) can be replaced with the equation formed by multiplying equation (13) by 2 and adding this result to equation (15). Thus we produce the following equivalent system, in which equations (17) and (18) contain only the two variables x and z:

$$\begin{pmatrix} 3x - y + 2z = 13 \\ -4x - 7z = -36 \\ 10x + 9z = 56 \end{pmatrix}$$

  (16)
  (17)
  (18)

Now, if we multiply equation (17) by 5 and equation (18) by 2, we get the following equivalent system:

$$\begin{pmatrix} 3x - y + 2z = 13 \\ -20x - 35z = -180 \\ 20x + 18z = 112 \end{pmatrix}$$

  (19)
  (20)
  (21)

Equation (21) can be replaced with the equation formed by adding equation (20) to equation (21).

$$\begin{pmatrix} 3x - y + 2z = 13 \\ -20x - 35z = -180 \\ -17z = -68 \end{pmatrix}$$

  (22)
  (23)
  (24)

From equation (24), we obtain $z = 4$. Then we can substitute 4 for z in equation (23).

$$-20x - 35(4) = -180$$
$$-20x - 140 = -180$$
$$-20x = -40$$
$$x = 2$$

Now we can substitute 2 for x and 4 for z in equation (22).

$$3(2) - y + 2(4) = 13$$
$$6 - y + 8 = 13$$

$$-y + 14 = 13$$
$$-y = -1$$
$$y = 1$$

The solution set of the original system is $\{(2, 1, 4)\}$. ∎

EXAMPLE 4

Solve the system $\begin{pmatrix} 2x + 3y + z = 14 \\ 3x - 4y - 2z = -30 \\ 5x + 7y + 3z = 32 \end{pmatrix}$. (25) (26) (27)

Solution

Equation (26) can be replaced with the equation formed by multiplying equation (25) by 2 and adding this result to equation (26). Equation (27) can be replaced with the equation formed by multiplying equation (25) by -3 and adding this result to equation (27). The following equivalent system is produced, in which equations (29) and (30) contain only the two variables x and y:

$$\begin{pmatrix} 2x + 3y + z = 14 \\ 7x + 2y = -2 \\ -x - 2y = -10 \end{pmatrix}$$ (28) (29) (30)

Now, equation (30) can be replaced with the equation formed by adding equation (29) to equation (30).

$$\begin{pmatrix} 2x + 3y + z = 14 \\ 7x + 2y = -2 \\ 6x = -12 \end{pmatrix}$$ (31) (32) (33)

From equation (33), we obtain $x = -2$. Then, substituting -2 for x in equation (32), we obtain

$$7(-2) + 2y = -2$$
$$2y = 12$$
$$y = 6$$

Finally, substituting 6 for y and -2 for x in equation (31) yields

$$2(-2) + 3(6) + z = 14$$
$$14 + z = 14$$
$$z = 0$$

The solution set of the original system is $\{(-2, 6, 0)\}$. ∎

The ability to solve systems of three linear equations in three unknowns enhances our problem-solving capabilities. Let's conclude this section with a problem that we can solve using such a system.

Classroom Example
A small company that manufactures decorative candles produces three different styles of candles. Each style of candle requires the services of three departments, as indicated by the following table:

	Style A	Style B	Style C
Dipping	0.4 hr	0.6 hr	0.9 hr
Cutting	0.4 hr	0.4 hr	0.7 hr
Packaging	0.1 hr	0.1 hr	0.2 hr

The dipping, cutting, and packaging departments have a maximum of 539, 409, and 107 hours available per week, respectively. How many of each style of candle should be produced each week so that the company is operating at full capacity?

EXAMPLE 5

A small company that manufactures sporting equipment produces three different styles of golf shirts. Each style of shirt requires the services of three departments, as indicated by the following table:

	Style A	Style B	Style C
Cutting department	0.1 hour	0.1 hour	0.3 hour
Sewing department	0.3 hour	0.2 hour	0.4 hour
Packaging department	0.1 hour	0.2 hour	0.1 hour

The cutting, sewing, and packaging departments have available a maximum of 340, 580, and 255 work hours per week, respectively. How many of each style of golf shirt should be produced each week so that the company is operating at full capacity?

Solution

Let a represent the number of shirts of style A produced per week, b the number of style B per week, and c the number of style C per week. Then the problem translates into the following system of equations:

$$\begin{pmatrix} 0.1a + 0.1b + 0.3c = 340 \\ 0.3a + 0.2b + 0.4c = 580 \\ 0.1a + 0.2b + 0.1c = 255 \end{pmatrix} \begin{array}{l} \longleftarrow \text{ Cutting department} \\ \longleftarrow \text{ Sewing department} \\ \longleftarrow \text{ Packaging department} \end{array}$$

Solving this system (we will leave the details for you to carry out) produces $a = 500$, $b = 650$, and $c = 750$. Thus the company should produce 500 golf shirts of style A, 650 of style B, and 750 of style C per week.

◼

Concept Quiz 6.2

For Problems 1–8, answer true or false.

1. For a system of three linear equations, any ordered triple that satisfies one of the equations is a solution of the system.
2. The solution set of a system of equations is the intersection of the solution sets of all the equations in the system.
3. The graph of a linear equation in three variables is a plane.
4. For a system of three linear equations, the only way for the solution set to be the empty set is if the equations represent three planes that are parallel.
5. The ordered triple $(0, 0, 0)$ could not be a solution for a system of three linear equations.
6. The solution set for a system of three linear equations could be two ordered triples.
7. It is not possible for the solution set of a system of three linear equations to have an infinite number of solutions.
8. Graphing is a practical way to solve a system of three linear equations.

Problem Set 6.2

For Problems 1–20, solve each system. (Objective 1)

1. $\begin{pmatrix} 2x - 3y + 4z = 10 \\ 5y - 2z = -16 \\ 3z = 9 \end{pmatrix}$

2. $\begin{pmatrix} -3x + 2y + z = -9 \\ 4x - 3z = 18 \\ 4z = -8 \end{pmatrix}$

3. $\begin{pmatrix} x + 2y - 3z = 2 \\ 3y - z = 13 \\ 3y + 5z = 25 \end{pmatrix}$

4. $\begin{pmatrix} 2x + 3y - 4z = -10 \\ 2y + 3z = 16 \\ 2y - 5z = -16 \end{pmatrix}$

5. $\begin{pmatrix} 3x + 2y - 2z = 14 \\ x - 6z = 16 \\ 2x + 5z = -2 \end{pmatrix}$

6. $\begin{pmatrix} 3x + 2y - z = -11 \\ 2x - 3y = -1 \\ 4x + 5y = -13 \end{pmatrix}$

7. $\begin{pmatrix} x - 2y + 3z = 7 \\ 2x + y + 5z = 17 \\ 3x - 4y - 2z = 1 \end{pmatrix}$

8. $\begin{pmatrix} x - 2y + z = -4 \\ 2x + 4y - 3z = -1 \\ -3x - 6y + 7z = 4 \end{pmatrix}$

9. $\begin{pmatrix} 2x - y + z = 0 \\ 3x - 2y + 4z = 11 \\ 5x + y - 6z = -32 \end{pmatrix}$

10. $\begin{pmatrix} 2x - y + 3z = -14 \\ 4x + 2y - z = 12 \\ 6x - 3y + 4z = -22 \end{pmatrix}$

11. $\begin{pmatrix} 3x + 2y - z = -11 \\ 2x - 3y + 4z = 11 \\ 5x + y - 2z = -17 \end{pmatrix}$

12. $\begin{pmatrix} 9x + 4y - z = 0 \\ 3x - 2y + 4z = 6 \\ 6x - 8y - 3z = 3 \end{pmatrix}$

13. $\begin{pmatrix} 2x + 3y - 4z = -10 \\ 4x - 5y + 3z = 2 \\ 2y + z = 8 \end{pmatrix}$

14. $\begin{pmatrix} x + 2y - 3z = 2 \\ 3x - z = -8 \\ 2x - 3y + 5z = -9 \end{pmatrix}$

15. $\begin{pmatrix} 3x + 2y - 2z = 14 \\ 2x - 5y + 3z = 7 \\ 4x - 3y + 7z = 5 \end{pmatrix}$

16. $\begin{pmatrix} 4x + 3y - 2z = -11 \\ 3x - 7y + 3z = 10 \\ 9x - 8y + 5z = 9 \end{pmatrix}$

17. $\begin{pmatrix} 2x - 3y + 4z = -12 \\ 4x + 2y - 3z = -13 \\ 6x - 5y + 7z = -31 \end{pmatrix}$

18. $\begin{pmatrix} 3x + 5y - 2z = -27 \\ 5x - 2y + 4z = 27 \\ 7x + 3y - 6z = -55 \end{pmatrix}$

19. $\begin{pmatrix} 5x - 3y - 6z = 22 \\ x - y + z = -3 \\ -3x + 7y - 5z = 23 \end{pmatrix}$

20. $\begin{pmatrix} 4x + 3y - 5z = -29 \\ 3x - 7y - z = -19 \\ 2x + 5y + 2z = -10 \end{pmatrix}$

For Problems 21–30, solve each problem by setting up and solving a system of three linear equations in three variables. (Objective 2)

21. A gift store is making a mixture of almonds, pecans, and peanuts, which sell for $6.50 per pound, $8.00 per pound, and $4.00 per pound, respectively. The storekeeper wants to make 20 pounds of the mix to sell at $5.30 per pound. The number of pounds of peanuts is to be three times the number of pounds of pecans. Find the number of pounds of each to be used in the mixture.

22. The organizer for a church picnic ordered coleslaw, potato salad, and beans amounting to 50 pounds. There was to be three times as much potato salad as coleslaw. The number of pounds of beans was to be

6 less than the number of pounds of potato salad. Find the number of pounds of each.

23. A box contains $7.15 in nickels, dimes, and quarters. There are 42 coins in all, and the sum of the numbers of nickels and dimes is 2 less than the number of quarters. How many coins of each kind are there?

24. A handful of 65 coins consists of pennies, nickels, and dimes. The number of nickels is 4 less than twice the number of pennies, and there are 13 more dimes than nickels. How many coins of each kind are there?

25. The measure of the largest angle of a triangle is twice the measure of the smallest angle. The sum of the smallest angle and the largest angle is twice the other angle. Find the measure of each angle.

26. The perimeter of a triangle is 45 centimeters. The longest side is 4 centimeters less than twice the shortest side. The sum of the lengths of the shortest and longest sides is 7 centimeters less than three times the length of the remaining side. Find the lengths of all three sides of the triangle.

27. Part of $3000 is invested at 4%, another part at 5%, and the remainder at 6% yearly interest. The total yearly income from the three investments is $160. The sum of the amounts invested at 4% and 5% equals the amount invested at 6%. How much is invested at each rate?

28. Different amounts are invested at 6%, 7%, and 8% yearly interest. The amount invested at 7% is $300 more than what is invested at 6%, and the total yearly income from all three investments is $208. A total of $2900 is invested. Find the amount invested at each rate.

29. A small company makes three different types of bird houses. Each type requires the services of three different departments, as indicated by the following table.

	Type A	Type B	Type C
Cutting department	0.1 hour	0.2 hour	0.1 hour
Finishing department	0.4 hour	0.4 hour	0.3 hour
Assembly department	0.2 hour	0.1 hour	0.3 hour

The cutting, finishing, and assembly departments have available a maximum of 35, 95, and 62.5 work hours per week, respectively. How many bird houses of each type should be made per week so that the company is operating at full capacity?

30. A certain diet consists of dishes A, B, and C. Each serving of A has 1 gram of fat, 2 grams of carbohydrate, and 4 grams of protein. Each serving of B has 2 grams of fat, 1 gram of carbohydrate, and 3 grams of protein. Each serving of C has 2 grams of fat, 4 grams of carbohydrate, and 3 grams of protein. The diet allows 15 grams of fat, 24 grams of carbohydrate, and 30 grams of protein. How many servings of each dish can be eaten?

Thoughts Into Words

31. Give a general description of how to solve a system of three linear equations in three variables.

32. Give a step-by-step description of how to solve the system

$$\begin{pmatrix} x - 2y + 3z = -23 \\ 5y - 2z = 32 \\ 4z = -24 \end{pmatrix}$$

33. Give a step-by-step description of how to solve the system

$$\begin{pmatrix} 3x - 2y + 7z = 9 \\ x \quad\quad - 3z = 4 \\ 2x \quad\quad + z = 9 \end{pmatrix}$$

Answers to the Concept Quiz

1. False   **2.** True   **3.** True   **4.** False   **5.** False   **6.** False   **7.** False   **8.** False

6.3   Matrix Approach to Solving Linear Systems

OBJECTIVE   **1** Use a matrix approach to solve a system of equations

In the first two sections of this chapter, we found that the substitution and elimination-by-addition techniques worked effectively with two equations and two unknowns, but they started to get a bit cumbersome with three equations and three unknowns. Therefore we will now begin to analyze some techniques that lend themselves to use with larger systems of equations. Some of these techniques form the basis for using a computer to solve systems. Even though these techniques are primarily designed for large systems of equations, we will study them in the context of small systems so that we won't get bogged down with the computational aspects of the techniques.

Matrices

A **matrix** is an array of numbers arranged in horizontal rows and vertical columns and enclosed in brackets. For example, the matrix

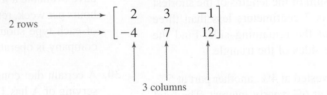

has 2 rows and 3 columns and is called a 2×3 (read "a two by three") matrix. Each number in a matrix is called an **element** of the matrix. Some additional examples of matrices (*matrices* is the plural of *matrix*) follow:

$$
\overset{3 \times 2}{\begin{bmatrix} 2 & 1 \\ 1 & -4 \\ \dfrac{1}{2} & \dfrac{2}{3} \end{bmatrix}} \qquad
\overset{2 \times 2}{\begin{bmatrix} 17 & 18 \\ -14 & 16 \end{bmatrix}} \qquad
\overset{1 \times 2}{\begin{bmatrix} 7 & 14 \end{bmatrix}} \qquad
\overset{4 \times 1}{\begin{bmatrix} 3 \\ -2 \\ 1 \\ 19 \end{bmatrix}}
$$

In general, a matrix of m rows and n columns is called a matrix of **dimension $m \times n$** or **order $m \times n$**.

With every system of linear equations, we can associate a matrix that consists of the coefficients and constant terms. For example, with the system

$$
\begin{pmatrix}
a_1 x + b_1 y + c_1 z = d_1 \\
a_2 x + b_2 y + c_2 z = d_2 \\
a_3 x + b_3 y + c_3 z = d_3
\end{pmatrix}
$$

we can associate the matrix

$$
\begin{bmatrix}
a_1 & b_1 & c_1 & \vdots & d_1 \\
a_2 & b_2 & c_2 & \vdots & d_2 \\
a_3 & b_3 & c_3 & \vdots & d_3
\end{bmatrix}
$$

which is commonly called the **augmented matrix** of the system of equations. The dashed line simply separates the coefficients from the constant terms and reminds us that we are working with an augmented matrix.

In Section 6.1 we listed the operations or transformations that can be applied to a system of equations to produce an equivalent system. Because augmented matrices are essentially abbreviated forms of systems of linear equations, there are analogous transformations that can be applied to augmented matrices. These transformations are usually referred to as **elementary row operations** and can be stated as follows:

> For any augmented matrix of a system of linear equations, the following elementary row operations will produce a matrix of an equivalent system:
>
> **1.** Any two rows of the matrix can be interchanged.
>
> **2.** Any row of the matrix can be multiplied by a nonzero real number.
>
> **3.** Any row of the matrix can be replaced by the sum of a nonzero multiple of another row plus that row.

Let's illustrate the use of augmented matrices and elementary row operations to solve a system of two linear equations in two variables.

Classroom Example
Solve the system:
$$\begin{pmatrix} 4x - y = -10 \\ 3x + 8y = -25 \end{pmatrix}$$

EXAMPLE 1   Solve the system $\begin{pmatrix} x - 3y = -17 \\ 2x + 7y = 31 \end{pmatrix}$.

Solution

The augmented matrix of the system is

$$\begin{bmatrix} 1 & -3 & \vdots & -17 \\ 2 & 7 & \vdots & 31 \end{bmatrix}$$

We would like to change this matrix to one of the form

$$\begin{bmatrix} 1 & 0 & \vdots & a \\ 0 & 1 & \vdots & b \end{bmatrix}$$

where we can easily determine that the solution is $x = a$ and $y = b$. Let's begin by adding -2 times row 1 to row 2 to produce a new row 2.

$$\begin{bmatrix} 1 & -3 & \vdots & -17 \\ 0 & 13 & \vdots & 65 \end{bmatrix}$$

Now we can multiply row 2 by $\dfrac{1}{13}$.

$$\begin{bmatrix} 1 & -3 & \vdots & -17 \\ 0 & 1 & \vdots & 5 \end{bmatrix}$$

Finally, we can add 3 times row 2 to row 1 to produce a new row 1.

$$\begin{bmatrix} 1 & 0 & \vdots & -2 \\ 0 & 1 & \vdots & 5 \end{bmatrix}$$

From this last matrix, we see that $x = -2$ and $y = 5$. In other words, the solution set of the original system is $\{(-2, 5)\}$.

It may seem that the matrix approach does not provide us with much extra power for solving systems of two linear equations in two unknowns. However, as the systems get larger, the compactness of the matrix approach becomes more convenient. Let's consider a system of three equations in three variables.

Classroom Example
Solve the system:
$$\left(\begin{array}{l} x - 3y + 2z = 21 \\ 5x + 2y - 3z = -27 \\ -3x + 4y + 5z = -17 \end{array} \right)$$

EXAMPLE 2

Solve the system $\left(\begin{array}{l} x + 2y - 3z = 15 \\ -2x - 3y + z = -15 \\ 4x + 9y - 4z = 49 \end{array} \right)$.

Solution

The augmented matrix of this system is

$$\begin{bmatrix} 1 & 2 & -3 & \vdots & 15 \\ -2 & -3 & 1 & \vdots & -15 \\ 4 & 9 & -4 & \vdots & 49 \end{bmatrix}$$

If the system has a unique solution, then we will be able to change the augmented matrix to the form

$$\begin{bmatrix} 1 & 0 & 0 & \vdots & a \\ 0 & 1 & 0 & \vdots & b \\ 0 & 0 & 1 & \vdots & c \end{bmatrix}$$

where we will be able to read the solution $x = a$, $y = b$, and $z = c$.
Add 2 times row 1 to row 2 to produce a new row 2. Likewise, add -4 times row 1 to row 3 to produce a new row 3.

$$\begin{bmatrix} 1 & 2 & -3 & \vdots & 15 \\ 0 & 1 & -5 & \vdots & 15 \\ 0 & 1 & 8 & \vdots & -11 \end{bmatrix}$$

Now add -2 times row 2 to row 1 to produce a new row 1. Also, add -1 times row 2 to row 3 to produce a new row 3.

$$\begin{bmatrix} 1 & 0 & 7 & \vdots & -15 \\ 0 & 1 & -5 & \vdots & 15 \\ 0 & 0 & 13 & \vdots & -26 \end{bmatrix}$$

Now let's multiply row 3 by $\dfrac{1}{13}$.

$$\begin{bmatrix} 1 & 0 & 7 & \vdots & -15 \\ 0 & 1 & -5 & \vdots & 15 \\ 0 & 0 & 1 & \vdots & -2 \end{bmatrix}$$

Finally, we can add -7 times row 3 to row 1 to produce a new row 1, and we can add 5 times row 3 to row 2 for a new row 2.

$$\begin{bmatrix} 1 & 0 & 0 & \vdots & -1 \\ 0 & 1 & 0 & \vdots & 5 \\ 0 & 0 & 1 & \vdots & -2 \end{bmatrix}$$

From this last matrix, we can see that the solution set of the original system is $\{(-1, 5, -2)\}$.

The final matrices of Examples 1 and 2,

$$\begin{bmatrix} 1 & 0 & \vdots & -2 \\ 0 & 1 & \vdots & 5 \end{bmatrix} \quad \text{and} \quad \begin{bmatrix} 1 & 0 & 0 & \vdots & -1 \\ 0 & 1 & 0 & \vdots & 5 \\ 0 & 0 & 1 & \vdots & -2 \end{bmatrix}$$

are said to be in *reduced echelon form.* In general, a matrix is in **reduced echelon form** if the following conditions are satisfied:

1. As we read from left to right, the first nonzero entry of each row is 1.

2. In the column containing the leftmost 1 of a row, all the other entries are zeros.

3. The leftmost 1 of any row is to the right of the leftmost 1 of the preceding row.

4. Rows containing only zeros are below all the rows containing nonzero entries.

Like the final matrices of Examples 1 and 2, the following are in reduced echelon form:

$$\begin{bmatrix} 1 & 2 & \vdots & -3 \\ 0 & 0 & \vdots & 0 \end{bmatrix} \quad \begin{bmatrix} 1 & 0 & -2 & \vdots & 5 \\ 0 & 1 & 4 & \vdots & 7 \\ 0 & 0 & 0 & \vdots & 0 \end{bmatrix} \quad \begin{bmatrix} 1 & 0 & 0 & 0 & \vdots & 8 \\ 0 & 1 & 0 & 0 & \vdots & -9 \\ 0 & 0 & 1 & 0 & \vdots & -2 \\ 0 & 0 & 0 & 1 & \vdots & 12 \end{bmatrix}$$

In contrast, the following matrices are *not* in reduced echelon form for the reason indicated below each matrix:

$$\begin{bmatrix} 1 & 0 & 0 & \vdots & 11 \\ 0 & 3 & 0 & \vdots & -1 \\ 0 & 0 & 1 & \vdots & -2 \end{bmatrix} \quad \begin{bmatrix} 1 & 2 & -3 & \vdots & 5 \\ 0 & 1 & 7 & \vdots & 9 \\ 0 & 0 & 1 & \vdots & -6 \end{bmatrix}$$

Violates condition 1   Violates condition 2

$$\begin{bmatrix} 1 & 0 & 0 & \vdots & 7 \\ 0 & 0 & 1 & \vdots & -8 \\ 0 & 1 & 0 & \vdots & 14 \end{bmatrix} \quad \begin{bmatrix} 1 & 0 & 0 & 0 & \vdots & -1 \\ 0 & 0 & 0 & 0 & \vdots & 0 \\ 0 & 0 & 1 & 0 & \vdots & 7 \\ 0 & 0 & 0 & 0 & \vdots & 0 \end{bmatrix}$$

Violates condition 3   Violates condition 4

Once we have an augmented matrix in reduced echelon form, it is easy to determine the solution set of the system. Furthermore, the procedure for changing a given augmented matrix to reduced echelon form can be described in a very systematic way. For example, if an augmented matrix of a system of three linear equations in three unknowns has a unique solution, then it can be changed to reduced echelon form as follows:

1. Write the augmented matrix

$$\begin{bmatrix} * & * & * & * \\ * & * & * & * \\ * & * & * & * \end{bmatrix}$$

2. Get a 1 in upper left-hand corner.

$$\begin{bmatrix} 1 & * & * & * \\ * & * & * & * \\ * & * & * & * \end{bmatrix}$$

3. Get zeros in first column beneath the 1.

$$\begin{bmatrix} 1 & * & * & * \\ 0 & * & * & * \\ 0 & * & * & * \end{bmatrix}$$

4. Get a 1 in the second row/ second column position.

$$\begin{bmatrix} 1 & * & * & * \\ 0 & 1 & * & * \\ 0 & * & * & * \end{bmatrix}$$

5. Get zeros above and below the 1 in the second column.

$$\begin{bmatrix} 1 & 0 & * & * \\ 0 & 1 & * & * \\ 0 & 0 & * & * \end{bmatrix}$$

6. Get a 1 in the third row/ third column position.

$$\begin{bmatrix} 1 & 0 & * & * \\ 0 & 1 & * & * \\ 0 & 0 & 1 & * \end{bmatrix}$$

7. Get zeros above the 1 in the third column.

$$\begin{bmatrix} 1 & 0 & 0 & * \\ 0 & 1 & 0 & * \\ 0 & 0 & 1 & * \end{bmatrix}$$

We can identify inconsistent and dependent systems while we are changing a matrix to reduced echelon form. We will show some examples of such cases in a moment, but first let's consider another example of a system of three linear equations in three unknowns for which there is a unique solution.

Classroom Example
Solve the system:
$$\begin{pmatrix} 4x - 6y + 3z = -19 \\ 3x - y + 5z = -3 \\ -x + 4y + 7z = 7 \end{pmatrix}$$

EXAMPLE 3

Solve the system $\begin{pmatrix} 2x + 4y - 5z = 37 \\ x + 3y - 4z = 29 \\ 5x - y + 3z = -20 \end{pmatrix}$.

Solution

The augmented matrix

$$\begin{bmatrix} 2 & 4 & -5 & \vdots & 37 \\ 1 & 3 & -4 & \vdots & 29 \\ 5 & -1 & 3 & \vdots & -20 \end{bmatrix}$$

does not have a 1 in the upper left-hand corner, but this can be remedied by exchanging rows 1 and 2.

$$\left[\begin{array}{ccc|c} 1 & 3 & -4 & 29 \\ 2 & 4 & -5 & 37 \\ 5 & -1 & 3 & -20 \end{array}\right]$$

Now we can get zeros in the first column beneath the 1 by adding -2 times row 1 to row 2 and by adding -5 times row 1 to row 3.

$$\left[\begin{array}{ccc|c} 1 & 3 & -4 & 29 \\ 0 & -2 & 3 & -21 \\ 0 & -16 & 23 & -165 \end{array}\right]$$

Next, we can get a 1 for the first nonzero entry of the second row by multiplying the second row by $-\dfrac{1}{2}$.

$$\left[\begin{array}{ccc|c} 1 & 3 & -4 & 29 \\ 0 & 1 & -\dfrac{3}{2} & \dfrac{21}{2} \\ 0 & -16 & 23 & -165 \end{array}\right]$$

Now we can get zeros above and below the 1 in the second column by adding -3 times row 2 to row 1 and by adding 16 times row 2 to row 3.

$$\left[\begin{array}{ccc|c} 1 & 0 & \dfrac{1}{2} & -\dfrac{5}{2} \\ 0 & 1 & -\dfrac{3}{2} & \dfrac{21}{2} \\ 0 & 0 & -1 & 3 \end{array}\right]$$

Next, we can get a 1 in the first nonzero entry of the third row by multiplying the third row by -1.

$$\left[\begin{array}{ccc|c} 1 & 0 & \dfrac{1}{2} & -\dfrac{5}{2} \\ 0 & 1 & -\dfrac{3}{2} & \dfrac{21}{2} \\ 0 & 0 & 1 & -3 \end{array}\right]$$

Finally, we can get zeros above the 1 in the third column by adding $-\dfrac{1}{2}$ times row 3 to row 1 and by adding $\dfrac{3}{2}$ times row 3 to row 2.

$$\left[\begin{array}{ccc|c} 1 & 0 & 0 & -1 \\ 0 & 1 & 0 & 6 \\ 0 & 0 & 1 & -3 \end{array}\right]$$

From this last matrix, we see that the solution set of the original system is $\{(-1, 6, -3)\}$.

Example 3 illustrates that even though the process of changing to reduced echelon form can be systematically described, it can involve some rather messy calculations. However, with the aid of a computer, such calculations are not troublesome. For our purposes in this text, the examples and problems involve systems that minimize messy calculations. This will allow us to concentrate on the procedures.

We want to call your attention to another issue in the solution of Example 3. Consider the matrix

$$\begin{bmatrix} 1 & 3 & -4 & \vdots & 29 \\ 0 & 1 & -\dfrac{3}{2} & \vdots & \dfrac{21}{2} \\ 0 & -16 & 23 & \vdots & -165 \end{bmatrix}$$

which is obtained about halfway through the solution. At this step, it seems evident that the calculations are getting a little messy. Therefore, instead of continuing toward the reduced echelon form, let's add 16 times row 2 to row 3 to produce a new row 3.

$$\begin{bmatrix} 1 & 3 & -4 & \vdots & 29 \\ 0 & 1 & -\dfrac{3}{2} & \vdots & \dfrac{21}{2} \\ 0 & 0 & -1 & \vdots & 3 \end{bmatrix}$$

The system represented by this matrix is

$$\begin{pmatrix} x + 3y - 4z = 29 \\ y - \dfrac{3}{2}z = \dfrac{21}{2} \\ -z = 3 \end{pmatrix}$$

and it is said to be in **triangular form**. The last equation determines the value for z; then we can use the process of back-substitution to determine the values for y and x.

Finally, let's consider two examples to illustrate what happens when we use the matrix approach on inconsistent and dependent systems.

Classroom Example
Solve the system:
$$\begin{pmatrix} 3x - y + 2z = 3 \\ 4x + 5y - 2z = 20 \\ 6x - 2y + 4z = 5 \end{pmatrix}$$

EXAMPLE 4

Solve the system $\begin{pmatrix} x - 2y + 3z = 3 \\ 5x - 9y + 4z = 2 \\ 2x - 4y + 6z = -1 \end{pmatrix}$.

Solution

The augmented matrix of the system is

$$\begin{bmatrix} 1 & -2 & 3 & \vdots & 3 \\ 5 & -9 & 4 & \vdots & 2 \\ 2 & -4 & 6 & \vdots & -1 \end{bmatrix}$$

We can get zeros below the 1 in the first column by adding -5 times row 1 to row 2 and by adding -2 times row 1 to row 3.

$$\left[\begin{array}{ccc|c} 1 & -2 & 3 & 3 \\ 0 & 1 & -11 & -13 \\ 0 & 0 & 0 & -7 \end{array}\right]$$

At this step, we can stop because the bottom row of the matrix represents the statement $0(x) + 0(y) + 0(z) = -7$, which is obviously false for all values of x, y, and z. Thus the original system is inconsistent; its solution set is $\varnothing$.

■

Classroom Example
Solve the system:
$$\left(\begin{array}{r} -5x + 2y + 3z = 13 \\ 3x - 4y - z = -25 \\ 10x - 4y - 6z = -26 \end{array}\right)$$

EXAMPLE 5

Solve the system $\left(\begin{array}{r} x + 2y + 2z = 9 \\ x + 3y - 4z = 5 \\ 2x + 5y - 2z = 14 \end{array}\right)$.

Solution

The augmented matrix of the system is

$$\left[\begin{array}{ccc|c} 1 & 2 & 2 & 9 \\ 1 & 3 & -4 & 5 \\ 2 & 5 & -2 & 14 \end{array}\right]$$

We can get zeros in the first column below the 1 in the upper left-hand corner by adding -1 times row 1 to row 2 and adding -2 times row 1 to row 3.

$$\left[\begin{array}{ccc|c} 1 & 2 & 2 & 9 \\ 0 & 1 & -6 & -4 \\ 0 & 1 & -6 & -4 \end{array}\right]$$

Now we can get zeros in the second column above and below the 1 in the second row by adding -2 times row 2 to row 1 and adding -1 times row 2 to row 3.

$$\left[\begin{array}{ccc|c} 1 & 0 & 14 & 17 \\ 0 & 1 & -6 & -4 \\ 0 & 0 & 0 & 0 \end{array}\right]$$

The bottom row of zeros represents the statement $0(x) + 0(y) + 0(z) = 0$, which is true for all values of x, y, and z. The second row represents the statement $y - 6z = -4$, which can be rewritten $y = 6z - 4$. The top row represents the statement $x + 14z = 17$, which can be rewritten $x = -14z + 17$. Therefore, if we let $z = k$, when k is any real number, the solution set of infinitely many ordered triples can be represented by $\{(-14k + 17, 6k - 4, k) | k$ is a real number$\}$. Specific solutions can be generated by letting k take on a value. For example, if $k = 2$, then $6k - 4$ becomes $6(2) - 4 = 8$ and $-14k + 17$ becomes $-14(2) + 17 = -11$. Thus the ordered triple $(-11, 8, 2)$ is a member of the solution set.

■

Concept Quiz 6.3

For Problems 1–8, answer true or false.

1. A matrix with dimension $m \times n$ has m rows and n columns.
2. The augmented matrix of a system of equations consists of just the coefficients of the variables.
3. If two columns of a matrix are interchanged, the result is an equivalent matrix.
4. The matrix $\begin{bmatrix} a_1 & b_1 & c_1 \\ a_2 & b_2 & c_2 \\ a_3 & b_3 & c_3 \end{bmatrix}$ is equivalent to the matrix $\begin{bmatrix} a_1 & b_1 & c_1 \\ da_2 & db_2 & dc_2 \\ a_3 & b_3 & c_3 \end{bmatrix}$, $d \neq 0$.
5. The matrix $\begin{bmatrix} 1 & 0 & 0 & -4 \\ 0 & 1 & 0 & 8 \\ 1 & 0 & 0 & 2 \end{bmatrix}$ is in reduced echelon form.
6. If the augmented matrix for a system of equations is $\begin{bmatrix} 1 & 0 & 0 & -1 \\ 0 & 1 & 0 & 5 \\ 0 & 0 & 1 & 2 \end{bmatrix}$, then the solution of the system of equations is $(-1, 5, 2)$.
7. The system of equations $\begin{pmatrix} 2x + y - z = 25 \\ 3y - 4z = 10 \\ z = 3 \end{pmatrix}$ is said to be in triangular form.
8. If the solution set of a system of equations is represented by $\{(2k + 3, k) | k \text{ is a real number}\}$, then $(11, 4)$ is a specific solution of the system of equations.

Problem Set 6.3

For Problems 1–10, indicate whether each matrix is in reduced echelon form.

1. $\begin{bmatrix} 1 & 0 & -4 \\ 0 & 1 & 14 \end{bmatrix}$

2. $\begin{bmatrix} 1 & 2 & 8 \\ 0 & 0 & 0 \end{bmatrix}$

3. $\begin{bmatrix} 1 & 0 & 2 & 5 \\ 0 & 1 & 3 & 7 \\ 0 & 0 & 0 & 0 \end{bmatrix}$

4. $\begin{bmatrix} 1 & 0 & 0 & 5 \\ 0 & 3 & 0 & 8 \\ 0 & 0 & 1 & -11 \end{bmatrix}$

5. $\begin{bmatrix} 1 & 0 & 0 & 17 \\ 0 & 0 & 0 & 0 \\ 0 & 1 & 0 & -14 \end{bmatrix}$

6. $\begin{bmatrix} 1 & 0 & 0 & -7 \\ 0 & 1 & 0 & 0 \\ 0 & 0 & 1 & 9 \end{bmatrix}$

7. $\begin{bmatrix} 1 & 1 & 0 & -3 \\ 0 & 1 & 2 & 5 \\ 0 & 0 & 1 & 7 \end{bmatrix}$

8. $\begin{bmatrix} 1 & 0 & 3 & 8 \\ 0 & 1 & 2 & -6 \\ 0 & 0 & 0 & 0 \end{bmatrix}$

9. $\begin{bmatrix} 1 & 0 & 0 & 3 & 4 \\ 0 & 1 & 0 & 5 & -3 \\ 0 & 0 & 1 & -1 & 7 \\ 0 & 0 & 0 & 0 & 0 \end{bmatrix}$

10. $\begin{bmatrix} 1 & 0 & 0 & 0 & \vdots & 2 \\ 0 & 0 & 1 & 0 & \vdots & 4 \\ 0 & 1 & 0 & 0 & \vdots & -3 \\ 0 & 0 & 0 & 1 & \vdots & 9 \end{bmatrix}$

For Problems 11–30, use a matrix approach to solve each system. **(Objective 1)**

11. $\begin{pmatrix} x - 3y = 14 \\ 3x + 2y = -13 \end{pmatrix}$ **12.** $\begin{pmatrix} x + 5y = -18 \\ -2x + 3y = -16 \end{pmatrix}$

13. $\begin{pmatrix} 3x - 4y = 33 \\ x + 7y = -39 \end{pmatrix}$ **14.** $\begin{pmatrix} 2x + 7y = -55 \\ x - 4y = 25 \end{pmatrix}$

15. $\begin{pmatrix} x - 6y = -2 \\ 2x - 12y = 5 \end{pmatrix}$ **16.** $\begin{pmatrix} 2x - 3y = -12 \\ 3x + 2y = 8 \end{pmatrix}$

17. $\begin{pmatrix} 3x - 5y = 39 \\ 2x + 7y = -67 \end{pmatrix}$ **18.** $\begin{pmatrix} 3x + 9y = -1 \\ x + 3y = 10 \end{pmatrix}$

19. $\begin{pmatrix} x - 2y - 3z = -6 \\ 3x - 5y - z = 4 \\ 2x + y + 2z = 2 \end{pmatrix}$

20. $\begin{pmatrix} x + 3y - 4z = 13 \\ 2x + 7y - 3z = 11 \\ -2x - y + 2z = -8 \end{pmatrix}$

21. $\begin{pmatrix} -2x - 5y + 3z = 11 \\ x + 3y - 3z = -12 \\ 3x - 2y + 5z = 31 \end{pmatrix}$

22. $\begin{pmatrix} -3x + 2y + z = 17 \\ x - y + 5z = -2 \\ 4x - 5y - 3z = -36 \end{pmatrix}$

23. $\begin{pmatrix} x - 3y - z = 2 \\ 3x + y - 4z = -18 \\ -2x + 5y + 3z = 2 \end{pmatrix}$

24. $\begin{pmatrix} x - 4y + 3z = 16 \\ 2x + 3y - 4z = -22 \\ -3x + 11y - z = -36 \end{pmatrix}$

25. $\begin{pmatrix} x - y + 2z = 1 \\ -3x + 4y - z = 4 \\ -x + 2y + 3z = 6 \end{pmatrix}$

26. $\begin{pmatrix} x + 2y - 5z = -1 \\ 2x + 3y - 2z = 2 \\ 3x + 5y - 7z = 4 \end{pmatrix}$

27. $\begin{pmatrix} -2x + y + 5z = -5 \\ 3x + 8y - z = -34 \\ x + 2y + z = -12 \end{pmatrix}$

28. $\begin{pmatrix} 4x - 10y + 3z = -19 \\ 2x + 5y - z = -7 \\ 2x - 13y - 2z = -2 \end{pmatrix}$

29. $\begin{pmatrix} 2x + 3y - z = 7 \\ 3x + 4y + 5z = -2 \\ 5x + y + 3z = 13 \end{pmatrix}$

30. $\begin{pmatrix} 4x + 3y - z = 0 \\ 3x + 2y + 5z = 6 \\ 5x - y - 3z = 3 \end{pmatrix}$

Subscript notation is frequently used for working with larger systems of equations. For Problems 31–34, use a matrix approach to solve each system. Express the solutions as 4-tuples of the form (x_1, x_2, x_3, x_4). **(Objective 1)**

31. $\begin{pmatrix} x_1 - 3x_2 - 2x_3 + x_4 = -3 \\ -2x_1 + 7x_2 + x_3 - 2x_4 = -1 \\ 3x_1 - 7x_2 - 3x_3 + 3x_4 = -5 \\ 5x_1 + x_2 + 4x_3 - 2x_4 = 18 \end{pmatrix}$

32. $\begin{pmatrix} x_1 - 2x_2 + 2x_3 - x_4 = -2 \\ -3x_1 + 5x_2 - x_3 - 3x_4 = 2 \\ 2x_1 + 3x_2 + 3x_3 + 5x_4 = -9 \\ 4x_1 - x_2 - x_3 - 2x_4 = 8 \end{pmatrix}$

33. $\begin{pmatrix} x_1 + 3x_2 - x_3 + 2x_4 = -2 \\ 2x_1 + 7x_2 + 2x_3 - x_4 = 19 \\ -3x_1 - 8x_2 + 3x_3 + x_4 = -7 \\ 4x_1 + 11x_2 - 2x_3 - 3x_4 = 19 \end{pmatrix}$

34. $\begin{pmatrix} x_1 + 2x_2 - 3x_3 + x_4 = -2 \\ -2x_1 - 3x_2 + x_3 - x_4 = 5 \\ 4x_1 + 9x_2 - 2x_3 - 2x_4 = -28 \\ -5x_1 - 9x_2 + 2x_3 - 3x_4 = 14 \end{pmatrix}$

In Problems 35–42, each matrix is the reduced echelon matrix for a system with variables x_1, x_2, x_3, and x_4. Find the solution set of each system. (Objective 1)

35.
$$\left[\begin{array}{cccc|c} 1 & 0 & 0 & 0 & -2 \\ 0 & 1 & 0 & 0 & 4 \\ 0 & 0 & 1 & 0 & -3 \\ 0 & 0 & 0 & 1 & 0 \end{array}\right]$$

36.
$$\left[\begin{array}{cccc|c} 1 & 0 & 0 & 0 & 0 \\ 0 & 1 & 0 & 0 & -5 \\ 0 & 0 & 1 & 0 & 0 \\ 0 & 0 & 0 & 1 & 4 \end{array}\right]$$

37.
$$\left[\begin{array}{cccc|c} 1 & 0 & 0 & 0 & -8 \\ 0 & 1 & 0 & 0 & 5 \\ 0 & 0 & 1 & 0 & -2 \\ 0 & 0 & 0 & 0 & 1 \end{array}\right]$$

38.
$$\left[\begin{array}{cccc|c} 1 & 0 & 0 & 0 & 2 \\ 0 & 1 & 0 & 2 & -3 \\ 0 & 0 & 1 & 3 & 4 \\ 0 & 0 & 0 & 0 & 0 \end{array}\right]$$

39.
$$\left[\begin{array}{cccc|c} 1 & 0 & 0 & 3 & 5 \\ 0 & 1 & 0 & 0 & -1 \\ 0 & 0 & 1 & 4 & 2 \\ 0 & 0 & 0 & 0 & 0 \end{array}\right]$$

40.
$$\left[\begin{array}{cccc|c} 1 & 3 & 0 & 2 & 0 \\ 0 & 0 & 1 & 0 & 0 \\ 0 & 0 & 0 & 0 & 1 \\ 0 & 0 & 0 & 0 & 0 \end{array}\right]$$

41.
$$\left[\begin{array}{cccc|c} 1 & 3 & 0 & 0 & 9 \\ 0 & 0 & 1 & 0 & 2 \\ 0 & 0 & 0 & 1 & -3 \\ 0 & 0 & 0 & 0 & 0 \end{array}\right]$$

42.
$$\left[\begin{array}{cccc|c} 1 & 0 & 0 & 0 & 7 \\ 0 & 1 & 0 & 0 & -3 \\ 0 & 0 & 1 & -2 & 5 \\ 0 & 0 & 0 & 0 & 0 \end{array}\right]$$

Thoughts Into Words

43. What is a matrix? What is an augmented matrix of a system of linear equations?

44. Describe how to use matrices to solve the system $\begin{pmatrix} x - 2y = 5 \\ 2x + 7y = 9 \end{pmatrix}$.

Further Investigations

For Problems 45–50, change each augmented matrix of the system to reduced echelon form and then indicate the solutions of the system.

45. $\begin{pmatrix} x - 2y + 3z = 4 \\ 3x - 5y - z = 7 \end{pmatrix}$

46. $\begin{pmatrix} x + 3y - 2z = -1 \\ 2x - 5y + 7z = 4 \end{pmatrix}$

47. $\begin{pmatrix} 2x - 4y + 3z = 8 \\ 3x + 5y - z = 7 \end{pmatrix}$

48. $\begin{pmatrix} 3x + 6y - z = 9 \\ 2x - 3y + 4z = 1 \end{pmatrix}$

49. $\begin{pmatrix} x - 2y + 4z = 9 \\ 2x - 4y + 8z = 3 \end{pmatrix}$

50. $\begin{pmatrix} x + y - 2z = -1 \\ 3x + 3y - 6z = -3 \end{pmatrix}$

Graphing Calculator Activities

51. If your graphing calculator has the capability of manipulating matrices, this is a good time to become familiar with those operations. Also if your calculator has a Catalog, look for a [rref] key under the Catalog. The [rref] stands for reduced-row-echelon form. The [rref] key transforms an augmented matrix into reduced echelon form. You may need to refer to your user's manual for the key-punching instructions. To begin the familiarization process, load your calculator with the three augmented matrices in Examples 1, 2, and 3. Then, for each one, carry out the row operations as described in the text.

Answers to the Concept Quiz

1. True **2.** False **3.** False **4.** True **5.** False **6.** True **7.** True **8.** True

---

6.4 Determinants

OBJECTIVES
  1. Evaluate determinants
  2. Apply the properties of determinants to find the determinant

Before we introduce the concept of a determinant, let's agree on some convenient new notation. A **general $m \times n$ matrix** can be represented by

$$A = \begin{bmatrix} a_{11} & a_{12} & a_{13} & \cdots & a_{1n} \\ a_{21} & a_{22} & a_{23} & \cdots & a_{2n} \\ \cdot & \cdot & \cdot & & \cdot \\ \cdot & \cdot & \cdot & & \cdot \\ \cdot & \cdot & \cdot & & \cdot \\ a_{m1} & a_{m2} & a_{m3} & \cdots & a_{mn} \end{bmatrix}$$

The double subscripts are used to identify the number of the row and the number of the column, in that order. For example, a_{23} is the entry at the intersection of the second row and the third column. In general, the entry at the intersection of row i and column j is denoted by a_{ij}.

A **square matrix** is one that has the same number of rows as columns. Each square matrix A with real number entries can be associated with a real number called the **determinant** of the matrix, denoted by $|A|$. We will first define $|A|$ for a 2×2 matrix.

Definition 6.1

If $A = \begin{bmatrix} a_{11} & a_{12} \\ a_{21} & a_{22} \end{bmatrix}$, then

$$|A| = \begin{vmatrix} a_{11} & a_{12} \\ a_{21} & a_{22} \end{vmatrix} = a_{11}a_{22} - a_{12}a_{21}$$

EXAMPLE 1

If $A = \begin{bmatrix} 3 & -2 \\ 5 & 8 \end{bmatrix}$, find $|A|$.

Solution

Use Definition 6.1 to obtain

$$|A| = \begin{vmatrix} 3 & -2 \\ 5 & 8 \end{vmatrix} = 3(8) - (-2)(5)$$
$$= 24 + 10$$
$$= 34$$

Finding the determinant of a square matrix is commonly called **evaluating the determinant**, and the matrix notation is often omitted.

EXAMPLE 2

Evaluate $\begin{vmatrix} -3 & 6 \\ 2 & 8 \end{vmatrix}$.

Solution

$$\begin{vmatrix} -3 & 6 \\ 2 & 8 \end{vmatrix} = (-3)(8) - (6)(2)$$
$$= -24 - 12$$
$$= -36$$

To find the determinants of 3×3 and larger square matrices, it is convenient to introduce some additional terminology.

> **Definition 6.2**
>
> If A is a 3×3 matrix, then the **minor** (denoted by M_{ij}) of the a_{ij} element is the determinant of the 2×2 matrix obtained by deleting row i and column j of A.

EXAMPLE 3

If $A = \begin{bmatrix} 2 & 1 & 4 \\ -6 & 3 & -2 \\ 4 & 2 & 5 \end{bmatrix}$, find (a) M_{11} and (b) M_{23}.

Solution

(a) To find M_{11}, we first delete row 1 and column 1 of matrix A.

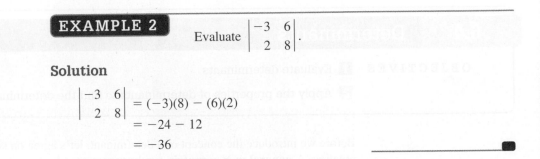

Thus

$$M_{11} = \begin{vmatrix} 3 & -2 \\ 2 & 5 \end{vmatrix} = 3(5) - (-2)(2) = 19$$

(b) To find M_{23}, we first delete row 2 and column 3 of matrix A.

$$\begin{bmatrix} 2 & 1 & 4 \\ -6 & -3 & -2 \\ 4 & 2 & 5 \end{bmatrix}$$

Thus

$$M_{23} = \begin{vmatrix} 2 & 1 \\ 4 & 2 \end{vmatrix} = 2(2) - (1)(4) = 0$$

The following definition will also be used.

Definition 6.3

If A is a 3×3 matrix, then the **cofactor** (denoted by C_{ij}) of the element a_{ij} is defined by

$$C_{ij} = (-1)^{i+j} M_{ij}$$

According to Definition 6.3, to find the cofactor of any element a_{ij} of a square matrix A, we find the minor of a_{ij} and multiply it by 1 if $i + j$ is even, or multiply it by -1 if $i + j$ is odd.

Classroom Example

If $A = \begin{bmatrix} 2 & -1 & 3 \\ 1 & 4 & -2 \\ 3 & -2 & 3 \end{bmatrix}$,

find C_{13}.

EXAMPLE 4

If $A = \begin{bmatrix} 3 & 2 & -4 \\ 1 & 5 & 4 \\ 2 & -3 & 1 \end{bmatrix}$, find C_{32}.

Solution

First, let's find M_{32} by deleting row 3 and column 2 of matrix A.

$$\begin{bmatrix} 3 & 2 & -4 \\ 1 & 5 & 4 \\ 2 & 3 & 1 \end{bmatrix}$$

Thus

$$M_{32} = \begin{vmatrix} 3 & -4 \\ 1 & 4 \end{vmatrix} = 3(4) - (-4)(1) = 16$$

Therefore

$$C_{32} = (-1)^{3+2} M_{32} = (-1)^5(16) = -16$$

The concept of a cofactor can be used to define the determinant of a 3×3 matrix as follows:

> **Definition 6.4**
>
> If $A = \begin{bmatrix} a_{11} & a_{12} & a_{13} \\ a_{21} & a_{22} & a_{23} \\ a_{31} & a_{32} & a_{33} \end{bmatrix}$, then $|A| = a_{11}C_{11} + a_{21}C_{21} + a_{31}C_{31}$.

Definition 6.4 simply states that the determinant of a 3×3 matrix can be found by multiplying each element of the first column by its corresponding cofactor and then adding the three results. Let's illustrate this procedure.

Classroom Example
Find $|A|$ if
$$A = \begin{bmatrix} 1 & 2 & -5 \\ 1 & 4 & 6 \\ -3 & 0 & 5 \end{bmatrix}.$$

EXAMPLE 5

Find $|A|$ if $A = \begin{bmatrix} -2 & 1 & 4 \\ 3 & 0 & 5 \\ 1 & -4 & -6 \end{bmatrix}$.

Solution

$$|A| = a_{11}C_{11} + a_{21}C_{21} + a_{31}C_{31}$$

$$= (-2)(-1)^{1+1}\begin{vmatrix} 0 & 5 \\ -4 & -6 \end{vmatrix} + (3)(-1)^{2+1}\begin{vmatrix} 1 & 4 \\ -4 & -6 \end{vmatrix} + (1)(-1)^{3+1}\begin{vmatrix} 1 & 4 \\ 0 & 5 \end{vmatrix}$$

$$= (-2)(1)(20) + (3)(-1)(10) + (1)(1)(5)$$

$$= -40 - 30 + 5$$

$$= -65$$

When we use Definition 6.4, we often say that "the determinant is being expanded about the first column." It can also be shown that **any row or column can be used to expand a determinant**. For example, for matrix A in Example 5, the expansion of the determinant about the *second row* is as follows:

$$\begin{vmatrix} -2 & 1 & 4 \\ 3 & 0 & 5 \\ 1 & -4 & -6 \end{vmatrix} = (3)(-1)^{2+1}\begin{vmatrix} 1 & 4 \\ -4 & -6 \end{vmatrix} + (0)(-1)^{2+2}\begin{vmatrix} -2 & 4 \\ 1 & -6 \end{vmatrix} + (5)(-1)^{2+3}\begin{vmatrix} -2 & 1 \\ 1 & -4 \end{vmatrix}$$

$$= (3)(-1)(10) + (0)(1)(8) + (5)(-1)(7)$$

$$= -30 + 0 - 35$$

$$= -65$$

Note that when we expanded about the second row, the computation was simplified by the presence of a zero. In general, it is helpful to expand about the row or column that contains the most zeros.

The concepts of minor and cofactor have been defined in terms of 3×3 matrices. Analogous definitions can be given for any square matrix (that is, any $n \times n$ matrix with $n \geq 2$), and the determinant can then be expanded about any row or column. Certainly as the matrices become larger than 3×3, the computations get more tedious. We will concentrate most of our efforts in this text on 2×2 and 3×3 matrices.

$$A = \begin{bmatrix} 1 & 2 & 4 \\ 2 & 4 & 7 \\ -1 & 3 & 5 \end{bmatrix}$$

Now let's form B by replacing row 2 with the result of adding -2 times row 1 to row 2.

$$B = \begin{bmatrix} 1 & 2 & 4 \\ 0 & 0 & -1 \\ -1 & 3 & 5 \end{bmatrix}$$

Next, let's evaluate $|A|$ and $|B|$ by expanding about the second row in each case.

$$|A| = \begin{vmatrix} 1 & 2 & 4 \\ 2 & 4 & 7 \\ -1 & 3 & 5 \end{vmatrix} = (2)(-1)^{2+1}\begin{vmatrix} 2 & 4 \\ 3 & 5 \end{vmatrix} + (4)(-1)^{2+2}\begin{vmatrix} 1 & 4 \\ -1 & 5 \end{vmatrix} + (7)(-1)^{2+3}\begin{vmatrix} 1 & 2 \\ -1 & 3 \end{vmatrix}$$

$$= 2(-1)(-2) + (4)(1)(9) + (7)(-1)(5)$$
$$= 5$$

$$|B| = \begin{vmatrix} 1 & 2 & 4 \\ 0 & 0 & -1 \\ -1 & 3 & 5 \end{vmatrix} = (0)(-1)^{2+1}\begin{vmatrix} 2 & 4 \\ 3 & 5 \end{vmatrix} + (0)(-1)^{2+2}\begin{vmatrix} 1 & 4 \\ -1 & 5 \end{vmatrix} + (-1)(-1)^{2+3}\begin{vmatrix} 1 & 2 \\ -1 & 3 \end{vmatrix}$$

$$= 0 + 0 + (-1)(-1)(5)$$
$$= 5$$

Note that $|B| = |A|$. Furthermore, note that because of the zeros in the second row, evaluating $|B|$ is much easier than evaluating $|A|$. Property 6.4 can often be used to obtain some zeros before we evaluate a determinant.

A word of caution is in order at this time. Be careful not to confuse Properties 6.2, 6.3, and 6.4 with the three elementary row transformations of augmented matrices that were used in Section 6.3. The statements of the two sets of properties do resemble each other, but the properties pertain to *two different concepts*, so be sure you understand the distinction between them.

One final property of determinants should be mentioned.

Property 6.5

If two rows (or columns) of a square matrix A are identical, then $|A| = 0$.

Property 6.5 is a direct consequence of Property 6.2. Suppose that A is a square matrix (any size) with two identical rows. Square matrix B can be formed from A by interchanging the two identical rows. Because identical rows were interchanged, $|B| = |A|$. *But* by Property 6.2, $|B| = -|A|$. For both of these statements to hold, $|A| = 0$.

Let's conclude this section by evaluating a 4×4 determinant, using Properties 6.3 and 6.4 to facilitate the computation.

EXAMPLE 6

Evaluate $\begin{vmatrix} 6 & 2 & 1 & -2 \\ 9 & -1 & 4 & 1 \\ 12 & -2 & 3 & -1 \\ 0 & 0 & 9 & 3 \end{vmatrix}.$

Solution

First, let's add -3 times the fourth column to the third column.

$$\begin{vmatrix} 6 & 2 & 7 & -2 \\ 9 & -1 & 1 & 1 \\ 12 & -2 & 6 & -1 \\ 0 & 0 & 0 & 3 \end{vmatrix}$$

Now, if we expand about the fourth row, we get only one nonzero product.

$$(3)(-1)^{4+4} \begin{vmatrix} 6 & 2 & 7 \\ 9 & -1 & 1 \\ 12 & -2 & 6 \end{vmatrix}$$

Factoring a 3 out of the first column of the 3×3 determinant yields

$$(3)(-1)^8(3) \begin{vmatrix} 2 & 2 & 7 \\ 3 & -1 & 1 \\ 4 & -2 & 6 \end{vmatrix}$$

Next, working with the 3×3 determinant, we can first add column 3 to column 2 and then add -3 times column 3 to column 1.

$$(3)(-1)^8(3) \begin{vmatrix} -19 & 9 & 7 \\ 0 & 0 & 1 \\ -14 & 4 & 6 \end{vmatrix}$$

Finally, by expanding this 3×3 determinant about the second row, we obtain

$$(3)(-1)^8(3)(1)(-1)^{2+3} \begin{vmatrix} -19 & 9 \\ -14 & 4 \end{vmatrix}$$

Our final result is

$$(3)(-1)^8(3)(1)(-1)^5(50) = -450$$

Concept Quiz 6.4

For Problems 1–8, answer true or false.

1. The element of a matrix a_{15} is located at the intersection of the first row and fifth column.

2. If $A = \begin{vmatrix} a_{11} & a_{12} \\ a_{12} & a_{22} \end{vmatrix}$, then $|A| = a_{11}a_{12} - a_{21}a_{22}$.

3. The determinant of a matrix is never a negative value.

4. If $A = \begin{vmatrix} 2 & -1 & 4 \\ 7 & 0 & 0 \\ 8 & -3 & 9 \end{vmatrix}$, the easiest way to find the determinant would be to expand about the second row.

5. The only way for a determinant to be equal to zero is if a row (or column) contains all zeros.

6. If $A = \begin{vmatrix} 3 & -4 \\ 2 & 6 \end{vmatrix}$ and $B = \begin{vmatrix} 2 & 6 \\ 3 & -4 \end{vmatrix}$, then $-|A| = |B|$.

7. Multiplying a row of a matrix by 3 affects the determinant by a factor of $\dfrac{1}{3}$.

8. Interchanging two columns of a matrix has no effect on the determinant.

Problem Set 6.4

For Problems 1–12, evaluate each 2×2 determinant by using Definition 6.1. (Objective 1)

1. $\begin{vmatrix} 4 & 3 \\ 2 & 7 \end{vmatrix}$

2. $\begin{vmatrix} 3 & 5 \\ 6 & 4 \end{vmatrix}$

3. $\begin{vmatrix} -3 & 2 \\ 7 & 5 \end{vmatrix}$

4. $\begin{vmatrix} 5 & 3 \\ 6 & -1 \end{vmatrix}$

5. $\begin{vmatrix} 2 & -3 \\ 8 & -2 \end{vmatrix}$

6. $\begin{vmatrix} -5 & 5 \\ -6 & 2 \end{vmatrix}$

7. $\begin{vmatrix} -2 & -3 \\ -1 & -4 \end{vmatrix}$

8. $\begin{vmatrix} -4 & -3 \\ -5 & -7 \end{vmatrix}$

9. $\begin{vmatrix} 1 & 1 \\ 2 & 3 \\ -3 & -6 \end{vmatrix}$

10. $\begin{vmatrix} 2 & 3 \\ 3 & 4 \\ 8 & 6 \end{vmatrix}$

11. $\begin{vmatrix} \dfrac{1}{2} & \dfrac{2}{3} \\ \dfrac{3}{4} & -\dfrac{1}{3} \end{vmatrix}$

12. $\begin{vmatrix} \dfrac{2}{3} & \dfrac{1}{5} \\ -\dfrac{1}{4} & \dfrac{3}{2} \end{vmatrix}$

For Problems 13–28, evaluate each 3×3 determinant. Use the properties of determinants to your advantage. (Objective 2)

13. $\begin{vmatrix} 1 & 2 & -1 \\ 3 & 1 & 2 \\ 2 & 4 & 3 \end{vmatrix}$

14. $\begin{vmatrix} 1 & -2 & 1 \\ 2 & 1 & -1 \\ 3 & 2 & 4 \end{vmatrix}$

15. $\begin{vmatrix} 1 & -4 & 1 \\ 2 & 5 & -1 \\ 3 & 3 & 4 \end{vmatrix}$

16. $\begin{vmatrix} 3 & -2 & 1 \\ 2 & 1 & 4 \\ -1 & 3 & 5 \end{vmatrix}$

17. $\begin{vmatrix} 6 & 12 & 3 \\ -1 & 5 & 1 \\ -3 & 6 & 2 \end{vmatrix}$

18. $\begin{vmatrix} 2 & 35 & 5 \\ 1 & -5 & 1 \\ -4 & 15 & 2 \end{vmatrix}$

19. $\begin{vmatrix} 2 & -1 & 3 \\ 0 & 3 & 1 \\ 1 & -2 & -1 \end{vmatrix}$

20. $\begin{vmatrix} 2 & -17 & 3 \\ 0 & 5 & 1 \\ 1 & -3 & -1 \end{vmatrix}$

21. $\begin{vmatrix} -3 & -2 & 1 \\ 5 & 0 & 6 \\ 2 & 1 & -4 \end{vmatrix}$

22. $\begin{vmatrix} -5 & 1 & -1 \\ 3 & 4 & 2 \\ 0 & 2 & -3 \end{vmatrix}$

23. $\begin{vmatrix} 3 & -4 & -2 \\ 5 & -2 & 1 \\ 1 & 0 & 0 \end{vmatrix}$

24. $\begin{vmatrix} -6 & 5 & 3 \\ 2 & 0 & -1 \\ 4 & 0 & 7 \end{vmatrix}$

25. $\begin{vmatrix} 24 & -1 & 4 \\ 40 & 2 & 0 \\ -16 & 6 & 0 \end{vmatrix}$

26. $\begin{vmatrix} 2 & -1 & 3 \\ 0 & 3 & 1 \\ 4 & -8 & -4 \end{vmatrix}$

27. $\begin{vmatrix} 2 & 3 & -4 \\ 4 & 6 & -1 \\ -6 & 1 & -2 \end{vmatrix}$

28. $\begin{vmatrix} 1 & 2 & -3 \\ -3 & -1 & 1 \\ 4 & 5 & 4 \end{vmatrix}$

For Problems 29–32, evaluate each 4×4 determinant. Use the properties of determinants to your advantage. (Objective 2)

29. $\begin{vmatrix} 1 & -2 & 3 & 2 \\ 2 & -1 & 0 & 4 \\ -3 & 4 & 0 & -2 \\ -1 & 1 & 1 & 5 \end{vmatrix}$

30. $\begin{vmatrix} 1 & 2 & 5 & 7 \\ -6 & 3 & 0 & 9 \\ -3 & 5 & 2 & 7 \\ 2 & 1 & 4 & 3 \end{vmatrix}$

31. $\begin{vmatrix} 3 & -1 & 2 & 3 \\ 1 & 0 & 2 & 1 \\ 2 & 3 & 0 & 1 \\ 5 & 2 & 4 & -5 \end{vmatrix}$

32. $\begin{vmatrix} 1 & 2 & 0 & 0 \\ 3 & -1 & 4 & 5 \\ -2 & 4 & 1 & 6 \\ 2 & -1 & -2 & -3 \end{vmatrix}$

For Problems 33–42, use the appropriate property of determinants from this section to justify each true statement. *Do not* evaluate the determinants.

33. $(-4)\begin{vmatrix} 2 & 1 & -1 \\ 3 & 2 & 1 \\ 2 & 1 & 3 \end{vmatrix} = \begin{vmatrix} 2 & -4 & -1 \\ 3 & -8 & 1 \\ 2 & -4 & 3 \end{vmatrix}$

34. $\begin{vmatrix} 1 & -2 & 3 \\ 4 & -6 & -8 \\ 0 & 2 & 7 \end{vmatrix} = (-2)\begin{vmatrix} 1 & -2 & 3 \\ -2 & 3 & 4 \\ 0 & 2 & 7 \end{vmatrix}$

35. $\begin{vmatrix} 4 & 7 & 9 \\ 6 & -8 & 2 \\ 4 & 3 & -1 \end{vmatrix} = -\begin{vmatrix} 4 & 9 & 7 \\ 6 & 2 & -8 \\ 4 & -1 & 3 \end{vmatrix}$

36. $\begin{vmatrix} 3 & -1 & 4 \\ 5 & 2 & 7 \\ 3 & -1 & 4 \end{vmatrix} = 0$

37. $\begin{vmatrix} 1 & 3 & 4 \\ -2 & 5 & 7 \\ -3 & -1 & 2 \end{vmatrix} = \begin{vmatrix} 1 & 3 & 4 \\ -2 & 5 & 7 \\ 0 & 8 & 14 \end{vmatrix}$

38. $\begin{vmatrix} 3 & 2 & 0 \\ 1 & 4 & 1 \\ -4 & 9 & 2 \end{vmatrix} = \begin{vmatrix} 3 & 2 & -3 \\ 1 & 4 & 0 \\ -4 & 9 & 6 \end{vmatrix}$

39. $\begin{vmatrix} 6 & 2 & 2 \\ 3 & -1 & 4 \\ 9 & -3 & 6 \end{vmatrix} = 6\begin{vmatrix} 2 & 2 & 1 \\ 1 & -1 & 2 \\ 3 & -3 & 3 \end{vmatrix} = 18\begin{vmatrix} 2 & 2 & 1 \\ 1 & -1 & 2 \\ 1 & -1 & 1 \end{vmatrix}$

40. $\begin{vmatrix} 2 & 1 & -3 \\ 0 & 2 & -4 \\ -5 & 1 & 3 \end{vmatrix} = -\begin{vmatrix} 2 & 1 & -3 \\ -5 & 1 & 3 \\ 0 & 2 & -4 \end{vmatrix}$

41. $\begin{vmatrix} 2 & -3 & 2 \\ 1 & -4 & 1 \\ 7 & 8 & 7 \end{vmatrix} = 0$

42. $\begin{vmatrix} 3 & 1 & 2 \\ -4 & 5 & -1 \\ 2 & -2 & -4 \end{vmatrix} = \begin{vmatrix} 3 & 1 & 0 \\ -4 & 5 & -11 \\ 2 & -2 & 0 \end{vmatrix}$

Thoughts Into Words

43. Explain the difference between a matrix and a determinant.

44. Explain the concept of a cofactor and how it is used to help expand a determinant.

45. What does it mean to say that any row or column can be used to expand a determinant?

46. Give a step-by-step explanation of how to evaluate the determinant

$$\begin{vmatrix} 3 & 0 & 2 \\ 1 & -2 & 5 \\ 6 & 0 & 9 \end{vmatrix}$$

Further Investigations

For Problems 47–50, use

$$A = \begin{bmatrix} a_{11} & a_{12} & a_{13} \\ a_{21} & a_{22} & a_{23} \\ a_{31} & a_{32} & a_{33} \end{bmatrix}$$

as a general representation for any 3×3 matrix.

47. Verify Property 6.2 for 3×3 matrices.

48. Verify Property 6.3 for 3×3 matrices.

49. Verify Property 6.4 for 3×3 matrices.

50. Show that $|A| = a_{11}a_{22}a_{33}a_{44}$ if

$$A = \begin{bmatrix} a_{11} & a_{12} & a_{13} & a_{14} \\ 0 & a_{22} & a_{23} & a_{24} \\ 0 & 0 & a_{33} & a_{34} \\ 0 & 0 & 0 & a_{44} \end{bmatrix}$$

Graphing Calculator Activities

51. Use a calculator to check your answers for Problems 29–32.

52. Consider the following matrix:

$$A = \begin{bmatrix} 2 & 5 & 7 & 9 \\ -4 & 6 & 2 & 4 \\ 6 & 9 & 12 & 3 \\ 5 & 4 & -2 & 8 \end{bmatrix}$$

Form matrix B by interchanging rows 1 and 3 of matrix A. Now use your calculator to show that $|B| = -|A|$.

53. Consider the following matrix:

$$A = \begin{bmatrix} 2 & 1 & 7 & 6 & 8 \\ 3 & -2 & 4 & 5 & -1 \\ 6 & 7 & 9 & 12 & 13 \\ -4 & -7 & 6 & 2 & 1 \\ 9 & 8 & 12 & 14 & 17 \end{bmatrix}$$

Form matrix B by multiplying each element of the second row of matrix A by 3. Now use your calculator to show that $|B| = 3|A|$.

54. Consider the following matrix:

$$A = \begin{bmatrix} 4 & 3 & 2 & 1 & 5 & -3 \\ 5 & 2 & 7 & 8 & 6 & 3 \\ 0 & 9 & 1 & 4 & 7 & 2 \\ 4 & 3 & 2 & 1 & 5 & -3 \\ -4 & -6 & 7 & 12 & 11 & 9 \\ 5 & 8 & 6 & -3 & 2 & -1 \end{bmatrix}$$

Use your calculator to show that $|A| = 0$.

Answers to the Concept Quiz

1. True **2.** False **3.** False **4.** True **5.** False **6.** True **7.** False **8.** False

6.5   Cramer's Rule

OBJECTIVE   1 Use Cramer's Rule to solve 2 × 2 and 3 × 3 systems of equations

Determinants provide the basis for another method of solving linear systems. Consider the following linear system of two equations and two unknowns:

$$\begin{pmatrix} a_1x + b_1y = c_1 \\ a_2x + b_2y = c_2 \end{pmatrix}$$

The augmented matrix of this system is

$$\left[\begin{array}{cc|c} a_1 & b_1 & c_1 \\ a_2 & b_2 & c_2 \end{array} \right]$$

Using the elementary row transformation of augmented matrices, we can change this matrix to the following reduced echelon form. (The details are left for you to do as an exercise.)

$$\left[\begin{array}{cc|c} 1 & 0 & \dfrac{c_1b_2 - c_2b_1}{a_1b_2 - a_2b_1} \\ 0 & 1 & \dfrac{a_1c_2 - a_2c_1}{a_1b_2 - a_2b_1} \end{array} \right], \quad a_1b_2 - a_2b_1 \neq 0$$

The solution for x and y can be expressed in determinant form as follows:

$$x = \frac{c_1b_2 - c_2b_1}{a_1b_2 - a_2b_1} = \frac{\begin{vmatrix} c_1 & b_1 \\ c_2 & b_2 \end{vmatrix}}{\begin{vmatrix} a_1 & b_1 \\ a_2 & b_2 \end{vmatrix}} \qquad y = \frac{a_1c_2 - a_2c_1}{a_1b_2 - a_2b_1} = \frac{\begin{vmatrix} a_1 & c_1 \\ a_2 & c_2 \end{vmatrix}}{\begin{vmatrix} a_1 & b_1 \\ a_2 & b_2 \end{vmatrix}}$$

This method of using determinants to solve a system of two linear equations in two variables is called **Cramer's rule** and can be stated as follows:

Cramer's Rule (2 × 2 case)

Given the system

$$\begin{pmatrix} a_1x + b_1y = c_1 \\ a_2x + b_2y = c_2 \end{pmatrix}$$

with

$$D = \begin{vmatrix} a_1 & b_1 \\ a_2 & b_2 \end{vmatrix} \neq 0 \qquad D_x = \begin{vmatrix} c_1 & b_1 \\ c_2 & b_2 \end{vmatrix} \qquad \text{and} \qquad D_y = \begin{vmatrix} a_1 & c_1 \\ a_2 & c_2 \end{vmatrix}$$

then the solution for this system is given by

$$x = \frac{D_x}{D} \qquad \text{and} \qquad y = \frac{D_y}{D}$$

Note that the elements of D are the coefficients of the variables in the given system. In D_x, the coefficients of x are replaced by the corresponding constants, and in D_y, the coefficients of y are replaced by the corresponding constants. Let's illustrate the use of Cramer's rule to solve some systems.

Classroom Example
Solve the system:
$$\begin{pmatrix} 5x - 2y = -12 \\ 3x + 7y = 1 \end{pmatrix}$$

EXAMPLE 1

Solve the system $\begin{pmatrix} 6x + 3y = 2 \\ 3x + 2y = -4 \end{pmatrix}$.

Solution

The system is in the proper form for us to apply Cramer's rule, so let's determine D, D_x, and D_y.

$$D = \begin{vmatrix} 6 & 3 \\ 3 & 2 \end{vmatrix} = 12 - 9 = 3$$

$$D_x = \begin{vmatrix} 2 & 3 \\ -4 & 2 \end{vmatrix} = 4 + 12 = 16$$

$$D_y = \begin{vmatrix} 6 & 2 \\ 3 & -4 \end{vmatrix} = -24 - 6 = -30$$

Therefore

$$x = \frac{D_x}{D} = \frac{16}{3}$$

and

$$y = \frac{D_y}{D} = \frac{-30}{3} = -10$$

The solution set is $\left\{ \left(\dfrac{16}{3}, -10 \right) \right\}$.

Classroom Example
Solve the system:
$$\begin{pmatrix} y = -8x - 4 \\ 4x + 7y = 11 \end{pmatrix}$$

EXAMPLE 2

Solve the system $\begin{pmatrix} y = -2x - 2 \\ 4x - 5y = 17 \end{pmatrix}$.

Solution

To begin, we must change the form of the first equation so that the system fits the form given in Cramer's rule. The equation $y = -2x - 2$ can be rewritten $2x + y = -2$. The system now becomes

$$\begin{pmatrix} 2x + y = -2 \\ 4x - 5y = 17 \end{pmatrix}$$

and we can proceed to determine D, D_x, and D_y.

$$D = \begin{vmatrix} 2 & 1 \\ 4 & -5 \end{vmatrix} = -10 - 4 = -14$$

$$D_x = \begin{vmatrix} -2 & 1 \\ 17 & -5 \end{vmatrix} = 10 - 17 = -7$$

$$D_y = \begin{vmatrix} 2 & -2 \\ 4 & 17 \end{vmatrix} = 34 - (-8) = 42$$

Thus

$$x = \frac{D_x}{D} = \frac{-7}{-14} = \frac{1}{2} \quad \text{and} \quad y = \frac{D_y}{D} = \frac{42}{-14} = -3$$

The solution set is $\left\{ \left(\frac{1}{2}, -3 \right) \right\}$, which can be verified, as always, by substituting back into the original equations.

Classroom Example
Solve the system:
$$\begin{pmatrix} \frac{3}{4}x - \frac{1}{2}y = -17 \\ \frac{5}{6}x + \frac{7}{8}y = 4 \end{pmatrix}$$

EXAMPLE 3

Solve the system $\begin{pmatrix} \frac{1}{2}x + \frac{2}{3}y = -4 \\ \frac{1}{4}x - \frac{3}{2}y = 20 \end{pmatrix}$.

Solution

With such a system, either we can first produce an equivalent system with integral coefficients and then apply Cramer's rule, or we can apply the rule immediately. Let's avoid some work with fractions by multiplying the first equation by 6 and the second equation by 4 to produce the following equivalent system:

$$\begin{pmatrix} 3x + 4y = -24 \\ x - 6y = 80 \end{pmatrix}$$

Now we can proceed as before.

$$D = \begin{vmatrix} 3 & 4 \\ 1 & -6 \end{vmatrix} = -18 - 4 = -22$$

$$D_x = \begin{vmatrix} -24 & 4 \\ 80 & -6 \end{vmatrix} = 144 - 320 = -176$$

$$D_y = \begin{vmatrix} 3 & -24 \\ 1 & 80 \end{vmatrix} = 240 - (-24) = 264$$

Therefore

$$x = \frac{D_x}{D} = \frac{-176}{-22} = 8 \quad \text{and} \quad y = \frac{D_y}{D} = \frac{264}{-22} = -12$$

The solution set is $\{(8, -12)\}$.

In the statement of Cramer's rule, the condition that $D \neq 0$ was imposed. If $D = 0$ and either D_x or D_y (or both) is nonzero, then the system is inconsistent and has no solution. If $D = 0$, $D_x = 0$, and $D_y = 0$, then the equations are dependent and there are infinitely many solutions.

Cramer's Rule Extended

Without showing the details, we will simply state that Cramer's rule also applies to solving systems of three linear equations in three variables. It can be stated as follows:

Cramer's Rule (3 × 3 case)

Given the system

$$\begin{pmatrix} a_1x + b_1y + c_1z = d_1 \\ a_2x + b_2y + c_2z = d_2 \\ a_3x + b_3y + c_3z = d_3 \end{pmatrix}$$

with

$$D = \begin{vmatrix} a_1 & b_1 & c_1 \\ a_2 & b_2 & c_2 \\ a_3 & b_3 & c_3 \end{vmatrix} \neq 0 \qquad D_x = \begin{vmatrix} d_1 & b_1 & c_1 \\ d_2 & b_2 & c_2 \\ d_3 & b_3 & c_3 \end{vmatrix}$$

$$D_y = \begin{vmatrix} a_1 & d_1 & c_1 \\ a_2 & d_2 & c_2 \\ a_3 & d_3 & c_3 \end{vmatrix} \qquad D_z = \begin{vmatrix} a_1 & b_1 & d_1 \\ a_2 & b_2 & d_2 \\ a_3 & b_3 & d_3 \end{vmatrix}$$

then $x = \dfrac{D_x}{D}$, $y = \dfrac{D_y}{D}$, and $z = \dfrac{D_z}{D}$.

Again, note the restriction that $D \neq 0$. If $D = 0$ and at least one of D_x, D_y, and D_z is not zero, then the system is inconsistent. If D, D_x, D_y, and D_z are all zero, then the equations are dependent, and there are infinitely many solutions.

Classroom Example
Solve the system:
$$\begin{pmatrix} 2x - y + 3z = 1 \\ x + 4y - 2z = 3 \\ 3x - 2y + 3z = 5 \end{pmatrix}$$

EXAMPLE 4

Solve the system $\begin{pmatrix} x - 2y + z = -4 \\ 2x + y - z = 5 \\ 3x + 2y + 4z = 3 \end{pmatrix}$.

Solution

We will simply indicate the values of D, D_x, D_y, and D_z and leave the computations for you to check.

$$D = \begin{vmatrix} 1 & -2 & 1 \\ 2 & 1 & -1 \\ 3 & 2 & 4 \end{vmatrix} = 29 \qquad D_x - \begin{vmatrix} -4 & -2 & 1 \\ 5 & 1 & -1 \\ 3 & 2 & 4 \end{vmatrix} = 29$$

$$D_y = \begin{vmatrix} 1 & -4 & 1 \\ 2 & 5 & -1 \\ 3 & 3 & 4 \end{vmatrix} = 58 \qquad D_z = \begin{vmatrix} 1 & -2 & -4 \\ 2 & 1 & 5 \\ 3 & 2 & 3 \end{vmatrix} = -29$$

Therefore

$$x = \frac{D_x}{D} = \frac{29}{29} = 1$$

$$y = \frac{D_y}{D} = \frac{58}{29} = 2$$

$$z = \frac{D_z}{D} = \frac{-29}{29} = -1$$

The solution set is $\{(1, 2, -1)\}$. (Be sure to check it!)

Classroom Example
Solve the system:
$$\begin{pmatrix} 4x - 10y + 6z = 10 \\ 7x + 3y - 2z = 10 \\ 2x - 5y + 3z = 6 \end{pmatrix}$$

EXAMPLE 5

Solve the system $\begin{pmatrix} x + 3y - z = 4 \\ 3x - 2y + z = 7 \\ 2x + 6y - 2z = 1 \end{pmatrix}$.

Solution

$$D = \begin{vmatrix} 1 & 3 & -1 \\ 3 & -2 & 1 \\ 2 & 6 & -2 \end{vmatrix} = 2\begin{vmatrix} 1 & 3 & -1 \\ 3 & -2 & 1 \\ 1 & 3 & -1 \end{vmatrix} = 2(0) = 0$$

$$D_x = \begin{vmatrix} 4 & 3 & -1 \\ 7 & -2 & 1 \\ 1 & 6 & -2 \end{vmatrix} = -7$$

Therefore because $D = 0$ and at least one of D_x, D_y, and D_z is not zero, the system is inconsistent. The solution set is $\varnothing$.

Example 5 illustrates why D should be determined first. Once we found that $D = 0$ and $D_x \neq 0$, we knew that the system was inconsistent, and there was no need to find D_y and D_z.

Finally, it should be noted that Cramer's rule can be extended to systems of n linear equations in n variables; however, that method is not considered to be a very efficient way of solving a large system of linear equations.

Concept Quiz 6.5

For Problems 1–8, answer true or false.

1. When using Cramer's rule the elements of D are the coefficients of the variables in the given system.

2. The system $\begin{pmatrix} 2x - y + 3z = 9 \\ -x + z - 4y = 2 \\ 5x + 2y - z = 8 \end{pmatrix}$ is in the proper form to apply Cramer's rule.

3. When using Cramer's rule for D_y the coefficients of y are replaced by the corresponding constants from the system of equations.

4. Applying Cramer's rule to the system $\left(\begin{array}{l} \dfrac{1}{4}x + \dfrac{5}{12}y = -1 \\ \dfrac{1}{3}x - \dfrac{2}{3}y = 7 \end{array} \right)$ produces the same

solution set as applying Cramer's rule to the system $\left(\begin{array}{l} 3x + 5y = -12 \\ x - 2y = 21 \end{array} \right)$.

5. When using Cramer's rule, if $D = 0$, then the system either has no solution or an infinite number of solutions.

6. When using Cramer's rule, if $D = 0$ and $D_y = 4$, then the system is inconsistent.

7. When using Cramer's rule, if $D_x \neq 0$, then the system of equations always has a solution.

8. Cramer's rule can be extended to solve systems of n linear equations in n variables.

Problem Set 6.5

For Problems 1–32, use Cramer's rule to find the solution set for each system. If the equations are dependent, simply indicate that there are infinitely many solutions. (Objective 1)

1. $\left(\begin{array}{l} 2x - y = -2 \\ 3x + 2y = 11 \end{array} \right)$

2. $\left(\begin{array}{l} 3x + y = -9 \\ 4x - 3y = 1 \end{array} \right)$

3. $\left(\begin{array}{l} 5x + 2y = 5 \\ 3x - 4y = 29 \end{array} \right)$

4. $\left(\begin{array}{l} 4x - 7y = -23 \\ 2x + 5y = -3 \end{array} \right)$

5. $\left(\begin{array}{l} 5x - 4y = 14 \\ -x + 2y = -4 \end{array} \right)$

6. $\left(\begin{array}{l} -x + 2y = 10 \\ 3x - y = -10 \end{array} \right)$

7. $\left(\begin{array}{l} y = 2x - 4 \\ 6x - 3y = 1 \end{array} \right)$

8. $\left(\begin{array}{l} -3x - 4y = 14 \\ -2x + 3y = -19 \end{array} \right)$

9. $\left(\begin{array}{l} -4x + 3y = 3 \\ 4x - 6y = -5 \end{array} \right)$

10. $\left(\begin{array}{l} x = 4y - 1 \\ 2x - 8y = -2 \end{array} \right)$

11. $\left(\begin{array}{l} 9x - y = -2 \\ 8x + y = 4 \end{array} \right)$

12. $\left(\begin{array}{l} 6x - 5y = 1 \\ 4x - 7y = 2 \end{array} \right)$

13. $\left(\begin{array}{l} -\dfrac{2}{3}x + \dfrac{1}{2}y = -7 \\ \dfrac{1}{3}x - \dfrac{3}{2}y = 6 \end{array} \right)$

14. $\left(\begin{array}{l} \dfrac{1}{2}x + \dfrac{2}{3}y = -6 \\ \dfrac{1}{4}x - \dfrac{1}{3}y = -1 \end{array} \right)$

15. $\left(\begin{array}{l} 2x + 7y = -1 \\ x = 2 \end{array} \right)$

16. $\left(\begin{array}{l} 5x - 3y = 2 \\ y = 4 \end{array} \right)$

17. $\left(\begin{array}{l} x - y + 2z = -8 \\ 2x + 3y - 4z = 18 \\ -x + 2y - z = 7 \end{array} \right)$

18. $\left(\begin{array}{l} x - 2y + z = 3 \\ 3x + 2y + z = -3 \\ 2x - 3y - 3z = -5 \end{array} \right)$

19. $\left(\begin{array}{l} 2x - 3y + z = -7 \\ -3x + y - z = -7 \\ x - 2y - 5z = -45 \end{array} \right)$

20. $\left(\begin{array}{l} 3x - y - z = 18 \\ 4x + 3y - 2z = 10 \\ -5x - 2y + 3z = -22 \end{array} \right)$

21. $\left(\begin{array}{l} 4x + 5y - 2z = -14 \\ 7x - y + 2z = 42 \\ 3x + y + 4z = 28 \end{array} \right)$

22. $\left(\begin{array}{l} -5x + 6y + 4z = -4 \\ -7x - 8y + 2z = -2 \\ 2x + 9y - z = 1 \end{array} \right)$

23. $\begin{pmatrix} 2x - y + 3z = -17 \\ 3y + z = 5 \\ x - 2y - z = -3 \end{pmatrix}$

24. $\begin{pmatrix} 2x - y + 3z = -5 \\ 3x + 4y - 2z = -25 \\ -x + z = 6 \end{pmatrix}$

25. $\begin{pmatrix} x + 3y - 4z = -1 \\ 2x - y + z = 2 \\ 4x + 5y - 7z = 0 \end{pmatrix}$

26. $\begin{pmatrix} x - 2y + z = 1 \\ 3x + y - z = 2 \\ 2x - 4y + 2z = -1 \end{pmatrix}$

27. $\begin{pmatrix} 3x - 2y - 3z = -5 \\ x + 2y + 3z = -3 \\ -x + 4y - 6z = 8 \end{pmatrix}$

28. $\begin{pmatrix} 3x - 2y + z = 11 \\ 5x + 3y = 17 \\ x + y - 2z = 6 \end{pmatrix}$

29. $\begin{pmatrix} x - 2y + 3z = 1 \\ -2x + 4y - 3z = -3 \\ 5x - 6y + 6z = 10 \end{pmatrix}$

30. $\begin{pmatrix} 2x - y + 2z = -1 \\ 4x + 3y - 4z = 2 \\ x + 5y - z = 9 \end{pmatrix}$

31. $\begin{pmatrix} -x - y + 3z = -2 \\ -2x + y + 7z = 14 \\ 3x + 4y - 5z = 12 \end{pmatrix}$

32. $\begin{pmatrix} -2x + y - 3z = -4 \\ x + 5y - 4z = 13 \\ 7x - 2y - z = 37 \end{pmatrix}$

Thoughts Into Words

33. Give a step-by-step description of how you would solve the system

$$\begin{pmatrix} 2x - y + 3z = 31 \\ x - 2y - z = 8 \\ 3x + 5y + 8z = 35 \end{pmatrix}$$

34. Give a step-by-step description of how you would find the value of x in the solution for the system

$$\begin{pmatrix} x + 5y - z = -9 \\ 2x - y + z = 11 \\ -3x - 2y + 4z = 20 \end{pmatrix}$$

Further Investigations

35. A linear system in which the constant terms are all zero is called a **homogeneous system**.

   (a) Verify that for a 3×3 homogeneous system, if $D \neq 0$, then $(0, 0, 0)$ is the only solution for the system.

   (b) Verify that for a 3×3 homogeneous system, if $D = 0$, then the equations are dependent.

For Problems 36–39, solve each of the homogeneous systems (see the text above). If the equations are dependent, indicate that the system has infinitely many solutions.

36. $\begin{pmatrix} x - 2y + 5z = 0 \\ 3x + y - 2z = 0 \\ 4x - y + 3z = 0 \end{pmatrix}$

37. $\begin{pmatrix} 2x - y + z = 0 \\ 3x + 2y + 5z = 0 \\ 4x - 7y + z = 0 \end{pmatrix}$

38. $\begin{pmatrix} 3x + y - z = 0 \\ x - y + 2z = 0 \\ 4x - 5y - 2z = 0 \end{pmatrix}$

39. $\begin{pmatrix} 2x - y + 2z = 0 \\ x + 2y + z = 0 \\ x - 3y + z = 0 \end{pmatrix}$

Graphing Calculator Activities

40. Use determinants and your calculator to solve each of the following systems:

(a) $\begin{pmatrix} 4x - 3y + z = 10 \\ 8x + 5y - 2z = -6 \\ -12x - 2y + 3z = -2 \end{pmatrix}$

(b) $\begin{pmatrix} 2x + y - z + w = -4 \\ x + 2y + 2z - 3w = 6 \\ 3x - y - z + 2w = 0 \\ 2x + 3y + z + 4w = -5 \end{pmatrix}$

(c) $\begin{pmatrix} x - 2y + z - 3w = 4 \\ 2x + 3y - z - 2w = -4 \\ 3x - 4y + 2z - 4w = 12 \\ 2x - y - 3z + 2w = -2 \end{pmatrix}$

(d) $\begin{pmatrix} 1.98x + 2.49y + 3.45z = 80.10 \\ 2.15x + 3.20y + 4.19z = 97.16 \\ 1.49x + 4.49y + 2.79z = 83.92 \end{pmatrix}$

6.6   Partial Fractions (Optional)

OBJECTIVE   **1** Find partial fraction decompositions for rational expressions

In Chapter 0, we reviewed the process of adding rational expressions. For example,

$$\frac{3}{x-2} + \frac{2}{x+3} = \frac{3(x+3) + 2(x-2)}{(x-2)(x+3)} = \frac{3x+9+2x-4}{(x-2)(x+3)} = \frac{5x+5}{(x-2)(x+3)}$$

Now suppose that we want to reverse the process. That is, suppose we are given the rational expression

$$\frac{5x+5}{(x-2)(x+3)}$$

and we want to express it as the sum of two simpler rational expressions called **partial fractions**. This process, called **partial fraction decomposition**, has several applications in calculus and differential equations. The following property provides the basis for partial fraction decomposition.

Property 6.6

Let $f(x)$ and $g(x)$ be polynomials with real coefficients, such that the degree of $f(x)$ is less than the degree of $g(x)$. The indicated quotient $f(x)/g(x)$ can be decomposed into partial fractions as follows.

1. If $g(x)$ has a linear factor of the form $ax + b$, then the partial fraction decomposition will contain a term of the form

$$\frac{A}{ax + b} \quad \text{where } A \text{ is a constant}$$

2. If $g(x)$ has a linear factor of the form $ax + b$ raised to the kth power, then the partial fraction decomposition will contain terms of the form

$$\frac{A_1}{ax + b} + \frac{A_2}{(ax + b)^2} + \cdots + \frac{A_k}{(ax + b)^k}$$

where $A_1, A_2, \ldots, A_k$ are constants.

3. If $g(x)$ has a quadratic factor of the form $ax^2 + bx + c$, where $b^2 - 4ac < 0$, then the partial fraction decomposition will contain a term of the form

$$\frac{Ax + B}{ax^2 + bx + c} \quad \text{where } A \text{ and } B \text{ are constants.}$$

4. If $g(x)$ has a quadratic factor of the form $ax^2 + bx + c$ raised to the kth power, where $b^2 - 4ac < 0$, then the partial fraction decomposition will contain terms of the form

$$\frac{A_1 x + B_1}{ax^2 + bx + c} + \frac{A_2 x + B_2}{(ax^2 + bx + c)^2} + \cdots + \frac{A_k x + B_k x}{(ax^2 + bx + c)^k}$$

where $A_1, A_2, \ldots, A_k$, and $B_1, B_2, \ldots, B_k$ are constants.

Note that Property 6.6 applies only to **proper fractions**—that is, fractions in which the degree of the numerator is less than the degree of the denominator. If the numerator is not of lower degree, we can divide and then apply Property 6.6 to the remainder, which will be a proper fraction. For example,

$$\frac{x^3 - 3x^2 - 3x - 5}{x^2 - 4} = x - 3 + \frac{x - 17}{x^2 - 4}$$

and the proper fraction $\dfrac{x - 17}{x^2 - 4}$ can be decomposed into partial fractions by applying Property 6.6. Now let's consider some examples to illustrate the four cases in Property 6.6.

EXAMPLE 1   Find the partial fraction decomposition of $\dfrac{11x + 2}{2x^2 + x - 1}$.

Solution

The denominator can be expressed as $(x + 1)(2x - 1)$. Therefore, according to part 1 of Property 6.6, each of the linear factors produces a partial fraction of the form *constant over linear factor*. In other words, we can write

$$\frac{11x + 2}{(x + 1)(2x - 1)} = \frac{A}{x + 1} + \frac{B}{2x - 1} \tag{1}$$

for some constants A and B. To find A and B, we multiply both sides of equation (1) by the least common denominator $(x + 1)(2x - 1)$:

$$11x + 2 = A(2x - 1) + B(x + 1) \tag{2}$$

Equation (2) is an **identity**: *It is true for all values of x.* Therefore, let's choose some convenient values for x that will determine the values for A and B. If we let $x = -1$, then equation (2) becomes an equation in only A.

$$11(-1) + 2 = A[2(-1) - 1] + B(-1 + 1)$$
$$-9 = -3A$$
$$3 = A$$

If we let $x = \dfrac{1}{2}$, then equation (2) becomes an equation only in B.

$$11\left(\frac{1}{2}\right) + 2 = A\left[2\left(\frac{1}{2}\right) - 1\right] + B\left(\frac{1}{2} + 1\right)$$
$$\frac{15}{2} = \frac{3}{2}B$$
$$5 = B$$

Therefore the given rational expression can now be written

$$\frac{11x + 2}{2x^2 + x - 1} = \frac{3}{x + 1} + \frac{5}{2x - 1}$$

The key idea in Example 1 is the statement that equation (2) is true for all values of x. If we had chosen *any* two values for x, we still would have been able to determine the values for A and B. For example, letting $x = 1$ and then $x = 2$ produces the equations $13 = A + 2B$ and $24 = 3A + 3B$. Solving this system of two equations in two unknowns produces $A = 3$ and $B = 5$. In Example 1, our choices of letting $x = -1$ and then $x = \dfrac{1}{2}$ simply eliminated the need for solving a system of equations to find A and B.

EXAMPLE 2   Find the partial fraction decomposition of $\dfrac{-2x^2 + 7x + 2}{x(x - 1)^2}$.

Solution

Apply part 1 of Property 6.6 to determine that there is a partial fraction of the form A/x corresponding to the factor of x. Next, applying part 2 of Property 6.6 and the squared factor $(x - 1)^2$ gives rise to a sum of partial fractions of the form

$$\frac{B}{x - 1} + \frac{C}{(x - 1)^2}$$

Therefore, the complete partial fraction decomposition is of the form

$$\frac{-2x^2 + 7x + 2}{x(x - 1)^2} = \frac{A}{x} + \frac{B}{x - 1} + \frac{C}{(x - 1)^2} \tag{1}$$

Multiply both sides of equation (1) by $x(x - 1)^2$ to produce

$$-2x^2 + 7x + 2 = A(x - 1)^2 + Bx(x - 1) + Cx \tag{2}$$

which is true for all values of x. If we let $x = 1$, then equation (2) becomes an equation in only C.

$$-2(1)^2 + 7(1) + 2 = A(1 - 1)^2 + B(1)(1 - 1) + C(1)$$
$$7 = C$$

If we let $x = 0$, then equation (2) becomes an equation in just A.

$$-2(0)^2 + 7(0) + 2 = A(0 - 1)^2 + B(0)(0 - 1) + C(0)$$
$$2 = A$$

If we let $x = 2$, then equation (2) becomes an equation in A, B, and C.

$$-2(2)^2 + 7(2) + 2 = A(2 - 1)^2 + B(2)(2 - 1) + C(2)$$
$$8 = A + 2B + 2C$$

But we already know that $A = 2$ and $C = 7$, so we can easily determine B.

$$8 = 2 + 2B + 14$$
$$-8 = 2B$$
$$-4 = B$$

Therefore, the original rational expression can be written

$$\frac{-2x^2 + 7x + 2}{x(x - 1)^2} = \frac{2}{x} - \frac{4}{x - 1} + \frac{7}{(x - 1)^2}$$

■

EXAMPLE 3

Find the partial fraction decomposition of $\dfrac{4x^2 + 6x - 10}{(x + 3)(x^2 + x + 2)}$.

Solution

Apply part 1 of Property 6.6 to determine that there is a partial fraction of the form $A/(x + 3)$ that corresponds to the factor $x + 3$. Apply part 3 of Property 6.6 to determine that there is also a partial fraction of the form

$$\frac{Bx + C}{x^2 + x + 2}$$

Thus the complete partial fraction decomposition is of the form

$$\frac{4x^2 + 6x - 10}{(x + 3)(x^2 + x + 2)} = \frac{A}{x + 3} + \frac{Bx + C}{x^2 + x + 2} \tag{1}$$

Multiply both sides of equation (1) by $(x + 3)(x^2 + x + 2)$ to produce

$$4x^2 + 6x - 10 = A(x^2 + x + 2) + (Bx + C)(x + 3) \tag{2}$$

which is true for all values of x. If we let $x = -3$, then equation (2) becomes an equation in A alone.

$$4(-3)^2 + 6(-3) - 10 = A[(-3)^2 + (-3) + 2] + [B(-3) + C][(-3) + 3]$$
$$8 = 8A$$
$$1 = A$$

If we let $x = 0$, then equation (2) becomes an equation in A and C.

$$4(0)^2 + 6(0) - 10 = A(0^2 + 0 + 2) + [B(0) + C](0 + 3)$$
$$-10 = 2A + 3C$$

Because $A = 1$, we obtain the value of C.

$$-10 = 2 + 3C$$
$$-12 = 3C$$
$$-4 = C$$

If we let $x = 1$, then equation (2) becomes an equation in A, B, and C.

$$4(1)^2 + 6(1) - 10 = A(1^2 + 1 + 2) + [B(1) + C](1 + 3)$$
$$0 = 4A + 4B + 4C$$
$$0 = A + B + C$$

But because $A = 1$ and $C = -4$, we obtain the value of B.

$$0 = A + B + C$$
$$0 = 1 + B + (-4)$$
$$3 = B$$

Therefore the original rational expression can now be written

$$\frac{4x^2 + 6x - 10}{(x + 3)(x^2 + x + 2)} = \frac{1}{x + 3} + \frac{3x - 4}{x^2 + x + 2}$$

Classroom Example
Find the partial fraction decomposition

of $\dfrac{x^3 + 2x^2 + 3x + 9}{(x^2 + 3)^2}$.

EXAMPLE 4   Find the partial fraction decomposition of $\dfrac{x^3 + x^2 + x + 3}{(x^2 + 1)^2}$.

Solution

Apply part 4 of Property 6.6 to determine that the partial fraction decomposition of this fraction is of the form

$$\frac{x^3 + x^2 + x + 3}{(x^2 + 1)^2} = \frac{Ax + B}{x^2 + 1} + \frac{Cx + D}{(x^2 + 1)^2} \qquad (1)$$

Multiply both sides of equation (1) by $(x^2 + 1)^2$ to produce

$$x^3 + x^2 + x + 3 = (Ax + B)(x^2 + 1) + Cx + D \qquad (2)$$

which is true for all values of x. Equation (2) is an identity, so we know that the coefficients of similar terms on both sides of the equation must be equal. Therefore, let's collect similar terms on the right side of equation (2).

$$x^3 + x^2 + x + 3 = Ax^3 + Ax + Bx^2 + B + Cx + D$$
$$= Ax^3 + Bx^2 + (A + C)x + B + D$$

Now we can equate coefficients from both sides:

$$1 = A \qquad 1 = B \qquad 1 = A + C \qquad \text{and} \qquad 3 = B + D$$

From these equations, we can determine that $A = 1$, $B = 1$, $C = 0$, and $D = 2$. Therefore the original rational expression can be written

$$\frac{x^3 + x^2 + x + 3}{(x^2 + 1)^2} = \frac{x + 1}{x^2 + 1} + \frac{2}{(x^2 + 1)^2}$$

_____ ■

Concept Quiz 6.6

For Problems 1–8, answer true or false.

1. The process of partial fraction decomposition expresses a rational expression as the sum of two or more simpler rational expressions.
2. A rational expression is considered a proper fraction if the degree of the numerator is equal to or less than the degree of the denominator.
3. The process of partial fraction decomposition applies only to proper fractions.
4. To apply partial fraction decomposition to a rational expression that is not a proper fraction, use long division to obtain a remainder that is a proper fraction.
5. If an equation is an identity, any value of x substituted into the equation produces an equivalent equation.
6. A quadratic expression such as $ax^2 + bx + c$ is not factorable over the real numbers if $b^2 - 4ac < 0$.
7. Given that $5x + 3 = A(x - 4) + B(x + 7)$ is an identity, the value of A can be determined by substituting any value of x into the identity.
8. Given that $3x - 1 = A(x - 2) + B(x + 5)$ is an identity, the value of B can be determined by substituting -5 for x into the identity.

Problem Set 6.6

For Problems 1–22, find the partial fraction decomposition for each rational expression. **(Objective 1)**

1. $\dfrac{11x - 10}{(x - 2)(x + 1)}$

2. $\dfrac{11x - 2}{(x + 3)(x - 4)}$

3. $\dfrac{-2x - 8}{x^2 - 1}$

4. $\dfrac{-2x + 32}{x^2 - 4}$

5. $\dfrac{20x - 3}{6x^2 + 7x - 3}$

6. $\dfrac{-2x - 8}{10x^2 - x - 2}$

7. $\dfrac{x^2 - 18x + 5}{(x - 1)(x + 2)(x - 3)}$

8. $\dfrac{-9x^2 + 7x - 4}{x^3 - 3x^2 - 4x}$

9. $\dfrac{-6x^2 + 7x + 1}{x(2x - 1)(4x + 1)}$

10. $\dfrac{15x^2 + 20x + 30}{(x + 3)(3x + 2)(2x + 3)}$

11. $\dfrac{2x + 1}{(x - 2)^2}$

12. $\dfrac{-3x + 1}{(x + 1)^2}$

13. $\dfrac{-6x^2 + 19x + 21}{x^2(x + 3)}$

14. $\dfrac{10x^2 - 73x + 144}{x(x - 4)^2}$

15. $\dfrac{-2x^2 - 3x + 10}{(x^2 + 1)(x - 4)}$

16. $\dfrac{8x^2 + 15x + 12}{(x^2 + 4)(3x - 4)}$

17. $\dfrac{3x^2 + 10x + 9}{(x + 2)^3}$

18. $\dfrac{2x^3 + 8x^2 + 2x + 4}{(x + 1)^2(x^2 + 3)}$

19. $\dfrac{5x^2 + 3x + 6}{x(x^2 - x + 3)}$

20. $\dfrac{x^3 + x^2 + 2}{(x^2 + 2)^2}$

21. $\dfrac{2x^3 + x + 3}{(x^2 + 1)^2}$

22. $\dfrac{4x^2 + 3x + 14}{x^3 - 8}$

Thoughts Into Words

23. Give a general description of partial fraction decomposition for someone who missed class the day it was discussed.

24. Give a step-by-step explanation of how to find the partial fraction decomposition of $\dfrac{11x + 5}{2x^2 + 5x - 3}$.

Answers to the Concept Quiz

1. True **2.** False **3.** True **4.** True **5.** True **6.** True **7.** False **8.** False

OBJECTIVE	SUMMARY	EXAMPLE
Solve systems of two linear equations by graphing. (Section 6.1/Objective 1)	Graphing a **system of two linear equations in two variables** produces one of the following results. 1. The graphs of the two equations are two intersecting lines, which indicates that there is *one unique solution* of the system. Such a system is called a *consistent system*. 2. The graphs of the two equations are two parallel lines, which indicates that there is *no solution* for the system. It is called an *inconsistent system*. 3. The graphs of the two equations are the same line, which indicates *infinitely many solutions* for the system. The equations are called *dependent* equations.	Solve $\begin{pmatrix} x - 3y = 6 \\ 2x + 3y = 3 \end{pmatrix}$ by graphing. **Solution** Graph the lines by determining the x and y intercepts and a check point. $x - 3y = 6$ $\qquad$ $2x + 3y = 3$ <table><tr><th>x</th><th>y</th></tr><tr><td>0</td><td>−2</td></tr><tr><td>6</td><td>0</td></tr><tr><td>−3</td><td>−3</td></tr></table> <table><tr><th>x</th><th>y</th></tr><tr><td>0</td><td>1</td></tr><tr><td>$\frac{3}{2}$</td><td>0</td></tr><tr><td>−1</td><td>$\frac{5}{3}$</td></tr></table> It appears that $(3, -1)$ is the solution. Checking these values in the equations, we can determine that the solution set is $\{(3, -1)\}$.

OBJECTIVE	SUMMARY	EXAMPLE
Solve systems of two linear equations by using the substitution method. (Section 6.1/Objective 2)	We can describe the **substitution method** of solving a system of equations as follows: **Step 1** Solve one of the equations for one variable in terms of the other variable if neither equation is in such a form. (If possible, make a choice that will avoid fractions.) **Step 2** Substitute the expression obtained in step 1 into the other equation to produce an equation with one variable. **Step 3** Solve the equation obtained in step 2. **Step 4** Use the solution obtained in step 3, along with the expression obtained in step 1, to determine the solution of the system.	Solve the system $\begin{pmatrix} 3x + y = -9 \\ 2x + 3y = 8 \end{pmatrix}$. **Solution** Solving the first equation for y gives the equation $y = -3x - 9$. In the second equation, substitute $-3x - 9$ for y and solve. $2x + 3(-3x - 9) = 8$ $2x - 9x - 27 = 8$ $-7x = 35$ $x = -5$ Now to find the value of y, substitute -5 for x in the equation $y = -3x - 9$. $y = -3(-5) - 9 = 6$ The solution set of the system is $\{(-5, 6)\}$.
Solve systems of two linear equations by using the elimination-by-addition method. (Section 6.1/Objective 3)	The **elimination-by-addition method** involves the replacement of a system of equations with equivalent systems until a system is obtained whereby the solutions can be easily determined. The following operations or transformations can be performed on a system to produce an equivalent system. **1.** Any two equations of the system can be interchanged. **2.** Both sides of any equation of the system can be multiplied by any nonzero real number. **3.** Any equation of the system can be replaced by the *sum* of that equation and a nonzero multiple of another equation.	Solve the system $\begin{pmatrix} 2x - 5y = 31 \\ 4x + 3y = 23 \end{pmatrix}$. **Solution** Let's multiply the first equation by -2 and add the result to the second equation to eliminate the x variable. Then the equivalent system is $\begin{pmatrix} 2x - 5y = 31 \\ 13y = -39 \end{pmatrix}$. Now solving the second equation for y, we obtain $y = -3$. Substitute -3 for y in either of the original equations and solve for x. $2x - 5(-3) = 31$ $2x + 15 = 31$ $2x = 16$ $x = 8$ The solution set of the system is $\{(8, -3)\}$.

(continued)

OBJECTIVE	SUMMARY	EXAMPLE
Solve application problems using a system of equations. (Section 6.1/Objective 4)	Many problems that were solved earlier using only one variable may seem easier to solve by using two variables and a system of equations.	A car dealership has 220 vehicles on the lot. The number of cars on the lot is five less than twice the number of trucks. Find the number of cars and the number of trucks on the lot. **Solution** Letting x represent the number of cars and y represent the number of trucks, we obtain the following system: $$\left(\begin{array}{l} x + y = 220 \\ x = 2y - 5 \end{array} \right)$$ Solving the system we can determine that the dealership has 145 cars and 75 trucks on the lot.
Solve systems of three linear equations. (Section 6.2/Objective 1)	Solving **a system of three linear equations in three variables** produces one of the following results. 1. There is *one ordered triple* that satisfies all three equations. 2. There are *infinitely many ordered triples* in the solution set, all of which are coordinates of points on a line common to the planes. 3. There are *infinitely many ordered triples* in the solution set, all of which are coordinates of points on a plane. 4. The solution set is empty; it is ∅.	Solve $\left(\begin{array}{rcl} 4x + 3y - 2z & = & -5 \\ 2y + 3z & = & -7 \\ y - 3z & = & -8 \end{array} \right)$. **Solution** Replacing the third equation with the sum of the second equation and the third equation yields $3y = -15$. Therefore we can determine that $y = -5$. Substituting -5 for y in the third equation gives $-5 - 3z = -8$. Solving this equation yields $z = 1$. Substituting -5 for y and 1 for z in the first equation gives $4x + 3(-5) - 2(1) = -5$. Solving this equation gives $x = 3$. The solution set for the system is $\{(3, -5, 1)\}$.

OBJECTIVE	SUMMARY	EXAMPLE
Solve application problems using a system of three linear equations. (Section 6.2/Objective 2)	Many word problems involving three variables can be solved using a system of three linear equations.	The sum of the measures of the angles in a triangle is 180°. The largest angle is eight times the smallest angle. The sum of the smallest and the largest angle is three times the other angle. Find the measure of each angle. **Solution** Let x represent the measure of the largest angle, let y represent the measure of the middle angle, and let z represent the measure of the smallest angle. From the information in the problem we can write the following system of equations: $$\begin{pmatrix} x + y + z = 180 \\ x = 8z \\ x + z = 3y \end{pmatrix}$$ By solving this system, we can determine that the measure of the angles of the triangle are 15°, 45°, and 120°.
Use a matrix approach to solve a system of equations. (Section 6.3/Objective 1)	The following elementary row operations provide the basis for transforming matrices. 1. Any two rows of an augmented matrix can be interchanged. 2. Any row can be multiplied by a nonzero constant. 3. Any row can be replaced by adding a nonzero multiple of another row to that row. Transforming an augmented matrix to triangular form and then using back-substitution provides a systematic technique for solving systems of linear equations.	Solve $\begin{pmatrix} x + 3y = 1 \\ 3x + 4y = 8 \end{pmatrix}$. **Solution** The augmented matrix is $\begin{bmatrix} 1 & 3 & 1 \\ 3 & 4 & 8 \end{bmatrix}$. Multiply row 1 by -3 and add this result to row 2 to produce a new row 2. $\begin{bmatrix} 1 & 3 & 1 \\ 0 & -5 & 5 \end{bmatrix}$. This matrix represents the system $\begin{pmatrix} x + 3y = 1 \\ -5y = 5 \end{pmatrix}$. From the last equation we can determine that $y = -1$. Now substitute -1 for y in the equation $x + 3y = 1$ to determine that $x = 4$. The solution set is $\{(4, -1)\}$.

(continued)

OBJECTIVE	SUMMARY	EXAMPLE
Evaluate the determinant of a 2 × 2 matrix. (Section 6.4/Objective 1)	A rectangular array of numbers is called a matrix. A square matrix has the same number of rows as columns. For a 2 × 2 matrix $\begin{bmatrix} a_1 & b_1 \\ a_2 & b_2 \end{bmatrix}$ the determinant of the matrix is written as $\begin{vmatrix} a_1 & b_1 \\ a_2 & b_2 \end{vmatrix}$ and defined by $$\begin{vmatrix} a_1 & b_1 \\ a_2 & b_2 \end{vmatrix} = a_1 b_2 - a_2 b_1$$	Find the determinant of the matrix $$\begin{bmatrix} 8 & -3 \\ 5 & 2 \end{bmatrix}$$ **Solution** $$\begin{vmatrix} 8 & -3 \\ 5 & 2 \end{vmatrix}$$ $$= 8(2) - (5)(-3) = 16 + 15 = 31$$
Evaluate the determinant for a 3 × 3 matrix by expansion. (Section 6.4/Objective 2)	A 3 × 3 determinant is defined by $$\begin{vmatrix} a_1 & b_1 & c_1 \\ a_2 & b_2 & c_2 \\ a_3 & b_3 & c_3 \end{vmatrix} = a_1 \begin{vmatrix} b_2 & c_2 \\ b_3 & c_3 \end{vmatrix}$$ $$- a_2 \begin{vmatrix} b_1 & c_1 \\ b_3 & c_3 \end{vmatrix} + a_3 \begin{vmatrix} b_1 & c_1 \\ b_2 & c_2 \end{vmatrix}$$ and this is called the expansion of the determinant by minors about the first column.	Evaluate $\begin{vmatrix} 2 & -1 & 3 \\ 0 & 5 & 4 \\ -3 & 6 & 1 \end{vmatrix}$ by expanding about the first column. **Solution** $$\begin{vmatrix} 2 & -1 & 3 \\ 0 & 5 & 4 \\ -3 & 6 & 1 \end{vmatrix}$$ $$= 2 \begin{vmatrix} 5 & 4 \\ 6 & 1 \end{vmatrix} - 0 \begin{vmatrix} -1 & 3 \\ 6 & 1 \end{vmatrix}$$ $$+ (-3) \begin{vmatrix} -1 & 3 \\ 5 & 4 \end{vmatrix}$$ $$= 2(-19) - 0 - 3(-19)$$ $$= 19$$

OBJECTIVE	SUMMARY	EXAMPLE
Use Cramer's Rule to solve a 2×2 system of equations. (Section 6.5/Objective 1)	Cramer's rule for solving a system of two linear equations in two variables is stated as follows: Given the system $\begin{pmatrix} a_1x + b_1y = c_1 \\ a_2x + b_2y = c_2 \end{pmatrix}$ with $D = \begin{vmatrix} a_1 & b_1 \\ a_2 & b_2 \end{vmatrix} \neq 0$ $$D_x = \begin{vmatrix} c_1 & b_1 \\ c_2 & b_2 \end{vmatrix}$$ $$D_y = \begin{vmatrix} a_1 & c_1 \\ a_2 & c_2 \end{vmatrix}$$ then $x = \dfrac{D_x}{D}$, and $y = \dfrac{D_y}{D}$.	Use Cramer's rule to solve $$\begin{pmatrix} 2x + 3y = -10 \\ x + 4y = -5 \end{pmatrix}$$ **Solution** $$D = \begin{vmatrix} 2 & 3 \\ 1 & 4 \end{vmatrix} = 2(4) - 1(3) = 5$$ $$D_x = \begin{vmatrix} -10 & 3 \\ -5 & 4 \end{vmatrix} = -10(4) - (-5)(3)$$ $$= -25$$ $$D_y = \begin{vmatrix} 2 & -10 \\ 1 & -5 \end{vmatrix} = 2(-5) - 1(-10) = 0$$ $$x = \frac{D_x}{D} = \frac{-25}{5} = -5$$ and $$y = \frac{D_y}{D} = \frac{0}{5} = 0$$ The solution set is $\{(-5, 0)\}$.
Use Cramer's Rule to solve a 3×3 system of equations. (Section 6.5/Objective 1)	Cramer's rule for solving a system of three linear equations in two variables is stated as follows: Given the system $$\begin{pmatrix} a_1x + b_1y + c_1z = d_1 \\ a_2x + b_2y + c_2z = d_2 \\ a_3x + b_3y + c_3z = d_3 \end{pmatrix} \text{ with}$$ $$D = \begin{vmatrix} a_1 & b_1 & c_1 \\ a_2 & b_2 & c_2 \\ a_3 & b_3 & c_3 \end{vmatrix} \neq 0$$ $$D_x = \begin{vmatrix} d_1 & b_1 & c_1 \\ d_2 & b_2 & c_2 \\ d_3 & b_3 & c_3 \end{vmatrix} \quad D_y = \begin{vmatrix} a_1 & d_1 & c_1 \\ a_2 & d_2 & c_2 \\ a_3 & d_3 & c_3 \end{vmatrix}$$ $$D_z = \begin{vmatrix} a_1 & b_1 & d_1 \\ a_2 & b_2 & d_2 \\ a_3 & b_3 & d_3 \end{vmatrix}$$ then $x = \dfrac{D_x}{D}, y = \dfrac{D_y}{D}$, and $z = \dfrac{D_z}{D}$.	Use Cramer's rule to solve $$\begin{pmatrix} 2x - y + z = 8 \\ x - 2y - 3z = -5 \\ 3x + y - 2z = -1 \end{pmatrix}$$ **Solution** Setting up and expanding the appropriate determinants we can determine that $D = 28, D_x = 56, D_y = -28$, and $D_z = 84$. Therefore, $$x = \frac{D_x}{D} = \frac{56}{28} = 2$$ $$y = \frac{D_y}{D} = \frac{-28}{28} = -1 \quad \text{and}$$ $$z = \frac{D_z}{D} = \frac{84}{28} = 3$$ The solution set is $\{(2, -1, 3)\}$.

Chapter 6   Review Problem Set

For Problems 1–4, solve each system by using the *substitution* method.

1. $\begin{pmatrix} 3x - y = 16 \\ 5x + 7y = -34 \end{pmatrix}$

2. $\begin{pmatrix} 6x + 5y = -21 \\ x - 4y = 11 \end{pmatrix}$

3. $\begin{pmatrix} 2x - 3y = 12 \\ 3x + 5y = -20 \end{pmatrix}$

4. $\begin{pmatrix} 5x + 8y = 1 \\ 4x + 7y = -2 \end{pmatrix}$

For Problems 5–8, solve each system by using the *elimination-by-addition* method.

5. $\begin{pmatrix} 4x - 3y = 34 \\ 3x + 2y = 0 \end{pmatrix}$

6. $\begin{pmatrix} \dfrac{1}{2}x - \dfrac{2}{3}y = 1 \\ \dfrac{3}{4}x + \dfrac{1}{6}y = -1 \end{pmatrix}$

7. $\begin{pmatrix} 2x - y + 3z = -19 \\ 3x + 2y - 4z = 21 \\ 5x - 4y - z = -8 \end{pmatrix}$

8. $\begin{pmatrix} 3x + 2y - 4z = 4 \\ 5x + 3y - z = 2 \\ 4x - 2y + 3z = 11 \end{pmatrix}$

For Problems 9–12, solve each system by *changing the augmented matrix to reduced echelon form.*

9. $\begin{pmatrix} x - 3y = 17 \\ -3x + 2y = -23 \end{pmatrix}$

10. $\begin{pmatrix} 2x + 3y = 25 \\ 3x - 5y = -29 \end{pmatrix}$

11. $\begin{pmatrix} x - 2y + z = -7 \\ 2x - 3y + 4z = -14 \\ -3x + y - 2z = 10 \end{pmatrix}$

12. $\begin{pmatrix} -2x - 7y + z = 9 \\ x + 3y - 4z = -11 \\ 4x + 5y - 3z = -11 \end{pmatrix}$

For Problems 13–16, solve each system by using *Cramer's rule.*

13. $\begin{pmatrix} 5x + 3y = -18 \\ 4x - 9y = -3 \end{pmatrix}$

14. $\begin{pmatrix} 0.2x + 0.3y = 2.6 \\ 0.5x - 0.1y = 1.4 \end{pmatrix}$

15. $\begin{pmatrix} 2x - 3y - 3z = 25 \\ 3x + y + 2z = -5 \\ 5x - 2y - 4z = 32 \end{pmatrix}$

16. $\begin{pmatrix} 3x - y + z = -10 \\ 6x - 2y + 5z = -35 \\ 7x + 3y - 4z = 19 \end{pmatrix}$

For Problems 17–24, solve each system by using the method you think is most appropriate.

17. $\begin{pmatrix} 4x + 7y = -15 \\ 3x - 2y = 25 \end{pmatrix}$

18. $\begin{pmatrix} \dfrac{3}{4}x - \dfrac{1}{2}y = -15 \\ \dfrac{2}{3}x + \dfrac{1}{4}y = -5 \end{pmatrix}$

19. $\begin{pmatrix} x + 4y = 3 \\ 3x - 2y = 1 \end{pmatrix}$

20. $\begin{pmatrix} 7x - 3y = -49 \\ y = \dfrac{3}{5}x - 1 \end{pmatrix}$

21. $\begin{pmatrix} x - y - z = 4 \\ -3x + 2y + 5z = -21 \\ 5x - 3y - 7z = 30 \end{pmatrix}$

22. $\begin{pmatrix} 2x - y + z = -7 \\ -5x + 2y - 3z = 17 \\ 3x + y + 7z = -5 \end{pmatrix}$

23. $\begin{pmatrix} 3x - 2y - 5z = 2 \\ -4x + 3y + 11z = 3 \\ 2x - y + z = -1 \end{pmatrix}$

24. $\begin{pmatrix} 7x - y + z = -4 \\ -2x + 9y - 3z = -50 \\ x - 5y + 4z = 42 \end{pmatrix}$

For Problems 25–30, evaluate each determinant.

25. $\begin{vmatrix} -2 & 6 \\ 3 & 8 \end{vmatrix}$

26. $\begin{vmatrix} 5 & -4 \\ 7 & -3 \end{vmatrix}$

27. $\begin{vmatrix} 2 & 3 & -1 \\ 3 & 4 & -5 \\ 6 & 4 & 2 \end{vmatrix}$

28. $\begin{vmatrix} 3 & -2 & 4 \\ 1 & 0 & 6 \\ 3 & -3 & 5 \end{vmatrix}$

29. $\begin{vmatrix} 5 & 4 & 3 \\ 2 & -7 & 0 \\ 3 & -2 & 0 \end{vmatrix}$

30. $\begin{vmatrix} 5 & -4 & 2 & 1 \\ 3 & 7 & 6 & -2 \\ 2 & 1 & -5 & 0 \\ 3 & -2 & 4 & 0 \end{vmatrix}$

For Problems 31–34, solve each problem by setting up and solving a system of linear equations.

31. How many quarts of 1% milk must be mixed with 4% milk to obtain 10 quarts of 2% milk?

32. The perimeter of a rectangle is 56 centimeters. The length of the rectangle is three times the width. Find the dimensions of the rectangle.

33. Antonio had a total of $4200 debt on two credit cards. One of the cards charged 1% interest per month, and the other card charged 1.5% interest per month. Find the amount of debt on each card if he paid $57 in interest charges for the month.

34. After working her shift as a waitress, Kelly had collected 30 bills consisting of one-dollar bills and five-dollar bills. If her tips amounted to $50, how many bills of each type did she have?

35. In an ideal textbook, every problem set had a fixed number of review problems and a fixed number of problems on the new material. Professor Kelly always assigned 80% of the review problems and 40% of the problems on the new material, which amounted to 56 problems. Professor Edward always assigned 100% of the review problems and 60% of the problems on the new material, which amounted to 78 problems. How many problems of each type are in the problem sets?

36. Sara invested $2500, part of it at 4% and the rest at 6% yearly interest. The yearly income on the 6% investment was $60 more than the income on the 4% investment. How much money did she invest at each rate?

37. A box contains $17.70 in nickels, dimes, and quarters. The number of dimes is 8 less than twice the number of nickels. The number of quarters is 2 more than the sum of the numbers of nickels and dimes. How many coins of each kind are there in the box?

38. After an evening of selling flowers, a vendor had collected 64 bills consisting of five-dollar bills, ten-dollar bills, and twenty-dollar bills, which amounted to $620. The number of ten-dollar bills was three times the number of twenty-dollar bills. Find the number of each type of bill.

39. The measure of the largest angle of a triangle is twice the measure of the smallest angle of the triangle. The sum of the measures of the largest angle and the smallest angle of a triangle is twice the measure of the remaining angle of the triangle. Find the measure of each angle of the triangle.

40. The measure of the largest angle of a triangle is 10° more than four times the smallest angle. The sum of the smallest and largest angles is three times the measure of the other angle. Find the measure of each angle of the triangle.

41. Kenisha has a Bank of US credit card that charges 1% interest per month, a Community Bank credit card that charges 1.5% interest per month, and a First National credit card that charges 2% interest per month. In total she has $6400 charged between the three credit cards. The total interest for the month for all three cards is $99. The amount charged on the Community Bank card is $500 less than the amount charged on the Bank of US card. Find the amount charged on each card.

42. The perimeter of a triangle is 33 inches. The longest side is 3 inches more than twice the shortest side. The sum of the lengths of the shortest side and the longest side is 9 more than the remaining side. Find the length of each side of the triangle.

For Problems 1–4, refer to the following systems of equations:

I. $\begin{pmatrix} 3x - 2y = 4 \\ 9x - 6y = 12 \end{pmatrix}$ II. $\begin{pmatrix} 5x - y = 4 \\ 3x + 7y = 9 \end{pmatrix}$

III. $\begin{pmatrix} 2x - y = 4 \\ 2x - y = -6 \end{pmatrix}$

1. For which system are the graphs parallel lines?

2. For which system are the equations dependent?

3. For which system is the solution set $\varnothing$?

4. Which system is consistent?

For Problems 5–8, evaluate each determinant.

5. $\begin{vmatrix} -2 & 4 \\ -5 & 6 \end{vmatrix}$

6. $\begin{vmatrix} \dfrac{1}{2} & \dfrac{1}{3} \\ \dfrac{3}{4} & -\dfrac{2}{3} \end{vmatrix}$

7. $\begin{vmatrix} -1 & 2 & 1 \\ 3 & 1 & -2 \\ 2 & -1 & 1 \end{vmatrix}$

8. $\begin{vmatrix} 2 & 4 & -5 \\ -4 & 3 & 0 \\ -2 & 6 & 1 \end{vmatrix}$

9. How many ordered pairs of real numbers are in the solution set for the system $\begin{pmatrix} y = 3x - 4 \\ 9x - 3y = 12 \end{pmatrix}$?

10. Solve the system $\begin{pmatrix} 3x - 2y = -14 \\ 7x + 2y = -6 \end{pmatrix}$

11. Solve the system $\begin{pmatrix} 4x - 5y = 17 \\ y = -3x + 8 \end{pmatrix}$

12. Find the value of x in the solution for the system
$$\begin{pmatrix} \dfrac{3}{4}x - \dfrac{1}{2}y = -21 \\ \dfrac{2}{3}x + \dfrac{1}{6}y = -4 \end{pmatrix}$$

13. Find the value of y in the solution for the system
$$\begin{pmatrix} 4x - y = 7 \\ 3x + 2y = 2 \end{pmatrix}$$

14. Suppose that the augmented matrix of a system of three linear equations in the three variables x, y, and z can be changed to the matrix
$$\begin{bmatrix} 1 & 1 & -4 & \vline & 3 \\ 0 & 1 & 4 & \vline & 5 \\ 0 & 0 & 3 & \vline & 6 \end{bmatrix}$$

Find the value of x in the solution for the system.

15. Suppose that the augmented matrix of a system of three linear equations in the three variables x, y, and z can be changed to the matrix
$$\begin{bmatrix} 1 & 2 & -3 & \vline & 4 \\ 0 & 1 & 2 & \vline & 5 \\ 0 & 0 & 2 & \vline & -8 \end{bmatrix}$$

Find the value of y in the solution for the system.

16. How many ordered triples are there in the solution set for the following system?
$$\begin{pmatrix} x + 3y - z = 5 \\ 2x - y - z = 7 \\ 5x + 8y - 4z = 22 \end{pmatrix}$$

17. How many ordered triples are there in the solution set for the following system?
$$\begin{pmatrix} 3x - y - 2z = 1 \\ 4x + 2y + z = 5 \\ 6x - 2y - 4z = 9 \end{pmatrix}$$

18. Solve the following system:
$$\begin{pmatrix} 5x - 3y - 2z = -1 \\ 4y + 7z = 3 \\ 4z = -12 \end{pmatrix}$$

19. Solve the following system:
$$\begin{pmatrix} x - 2y + z = 0 \\ y - 3z = -1 \\ 2y + 5z = -2 \end{pmatrix}$$

20. Find the value of x in the solution for the system

$$\begin{pmatrix} x - 4y + z = 12 \\ -2x + 3y - z = -11 \\ 5x - 3y + 2z = 17 \end{pmatrix}$$

21. Find the value of y in the solution for the system

$$\begin{pmatrix} x - 3y + z = -13 \\ 3x + 5y - z = 17 \\ 5x - 2y + 2z = -13 \end{pmatrix}$$

22. One solution is 30% alcohol and another solution is 70% alcohol. Some of each of the two solutions is mixed to produce 8 liters of a 40% solution. How many liters of the 70% solution should be used?

23. A car wash charges $5.00 for an express wash and $15.00 for a full wash. On a recent day there were 75 car washes of these two types, which brought in $825.00. Find the number of express washes.

24. A catering company makes batches of three different types of pastries to serve at brunches. Each batch requires the services of three different operations, as indicated by the following table:

	Cream puffs	Eclairs	Danish rolls
Dough	0.2 hour	0.5 hour	0.4 hour
Baking	0.3 hour	0.1 hour	0.2 hour
Frosting	0.1 hour	0.5 hour	0.3 hour

The dough, baking, and frosting operations have available a maximum of 7.0, 3.9, and 5.5 hours, respectively. How many batches of each type should be made so that the company is operating at full capacity?

25. The measure of the largest angle of a triangle is 20° more than the sum of the measures of the other two angles. The difference in the measures of the largest and smallest angles is 65°. Find the measure of each angle.

For Problems 1–10, evaluate each expression.

1. $(3^{-2} + 2^{-1})^{-2}$

2. $\left(\dfrac{4^{-2}}{2^{-3}}\right)^{-1}$

3. $\ln e^5$

4. $\log 0.001$

5. $\sqrt{2\dfrac{1}{4}}$

6. $(-27)^{4/3}$

7. $\log_2 64$

8. $\log_4 64$

9. $\left(\dfrac{3}{2}\right)^{-3}$

10. $\sqrt[3]{-0.008}$

For Problems 11–14, evaluate each algebraic expression for the given values of the variables.

11. $5(2x - 1) - 3(x + 4) - 2(3x + 11)$
for $x = -13$

12. $\dfrac{14x^3y^2}{28x^2y^3}$ for $x = 7$ and $y = -6$

13. $\dfrac{7}{n} - \dfrac{9}{2n} + \dfrac{5}{3n}$ for $n = 15$

14. $\dfrac{6x^2 + 7x - 20}{3x^2 - 25x + 28}$ for $x = 8$

For Problems 15–18, perform the indicated operations involving rational expressions and express final answers in simplest form.

15. $\dfrac{3a^2b}{7a} \div \dfrac{9ab^3}{14b^2}$

16. $\dfrac{3}{x^2 - 4} - \dfrac{2}{x^2 + 2x}$

17. $\dfrac{x^3 + 1}{x^2 + 5x + 6} \cdot \dfrac{x^2 - 9}{x^2 - 2x - 3}$

18. $\dfrac{2x - 1}{4} - \dfrac{x + 2}{6} + \dfrac{3x - 1}{8}$

For Problems 19–21, perform the indicated operations and simplify. Express final answers using positive exponents only.

19. $\dfrac{36x^{-2}y^{-4}}{24xy^{-2}}$

20. $\left(\dfrac{28a^2b^{-4}}{7a^{-1}b^3}\right)^{-1}$

21. $(-5x^{-1}y^2)(6x^{-2}y^{-5})$

For Problems 22–24, express each in simplest radical form. All variables represent positive real numbers.

22. $8\sqrt{72}$

23. $\sqrt[3]{54x^3y^5}$

24. $\dfrac{3\sqrt{6}}{4\sqrt{27}}$

25. Write the equation of the line that is perpendicular to the line $2x - y = 4$ and contains the point $(6, 2)$.

26. Determine the linear function whose graph is a line that contains the points $(-2, -3)$ and $(4, 8)$.

27. If $f(x) = -x^2 - 2x - 4$ and $g(x) = -4x + 5$, find $f(g(-2))$ and $g(f(3))$.

28. If $f(x) = x + 7$ and $g(x) = 2x^2 + x - 3$, find $f(g(x))$ and $g(f(x))$.

29. Find the indicated product $(4 - 3i)(-2 + 6i)$ and express the answer in the standard form of a complex number.

30. If $f(x) = -3x + 10$, find the inverse of f.

31. Find the length of the minor axis of the ellipse $3x^2 + y^2 = 27$.

32. Find the remainder when $3x^3 - 2x^2 + x - 4$ is divided by $x - 2$.

33. Find the remainder when $2x^3 + 11x^2 - 2x - 21$ is divided by $2x + 3$.

34. Find the quotient and the remainder when $3x^3 + 22x^2 + 4x - 1$ is divided by $3x + 1$.

35. Find the quotient and the remainder when $2x^4 - 3x^3 + 2x^2 - x + 6$ is divided by $x + 1$.

36. Is $x + 3$ a factor of $x^3 + 9x^2 + 23x + 15$?

37. Is $x - 1$ a factor of $x^6 + 1$?

38. Is $x + 1$ a factor of $x^7 + 1$?

39. Find the equations of the asymptotes of the hyperbola $y^2 - 9x^2 = 16$.

40. If y varies directly as x, and if $y = -2$ when $x = 3$, find y when $x = 9$.

41. If y is inversely proportional to x, and $y = 2$ when $x = -2$, find y when $x = 4$.

42. Evaluate $\log_2 101$ to the nearest hundredth.

43. Find the equations of the vertical and horizontal asymptotes for the graph of the function

$$f(x) = \frac{2x}{x - 1}.$$

44. What type of symmetry does the graph of

$$f(x) = \frac{x^2}{x^2 - 3} \text{ possess?}$$

45. Find the equation of the oblique asymptote for the graph of the function $f(x) = \dfrac{2x^2 + 3}{x + 1}$.

For Problems 46–58, solve each equation or system of equations.

46. $\dfrac{3}{2}(x - 1) - \dfrac{2}{3}(x + 2) = \dfrac{3}{4}(2x - 5)$

47. $\dfrac{2x - 1}{6} + \dfrac{x + 3}{8} = -2$

48. $|2x + 5| = 6$

49. $\begin{pmatrix} 3x - 2y = -11 \\ 4x + 5y = 16 \end{pmatrix}$

50. $14x^3 + 45x^2 - 14x = 0$

51. $2x^3 + x^2 - 3x + 6 = 0$

52. $12x^2 - 14x - 10 = 0$

53. $(x + 1)(3x - 2) = (4x + 5)(x + 1)$

54. $\begin{pmatrix} x - y + z = -4 \\ 2x + y + 3z = -5 \\ -3x - 2y - z = -4 \end{pmatrix}$

55. $9^{x-2} = 27^{x+3}$

56. $4^{x+1} = 16^{2x-1}$

57. $2^{x+3} = 7^{x-1}$ (to the nearest hundredth)

58. $\log(x + 3) + \log(x - 1) = 1$

For Problems 59–66, solve each inequality and express the solution set using interval notation.

59. $\dfrac{x - 1}{4} - \dfrac{x + 2}{12} \geq 1$

60. $|2x - 1| < 4$ **61.** $|3x + 2| > 6$

62. $-3 \leq 2(x - 1) - (x + 4)$

63. $(x - 2)(x + 4)(x - 7) \geq 0$

64. $(x - 1)(x + 5) < (x - 1)(2x + 3)$

65. $\dfrac{x + 1}{x - 4} - 2 > 0$ **66.** $x^2 + 5x \leq 24$

For Problems 67–74, graph each function.

67. $f(x) = 2|x + 3| + 1$ **68.** $f(x) = \log_3(x - 1)$

69. $f(x) = -x^2 + 4x - 5$

70. $f(x) = 2\sqrt{x + 1} + 2$

71. $f(x) = 2^{x-2}$

72. $f(x) = (x - 1)(x + 1)(x - 4)$

73. $f(x) = \dfrac{-1}{x^2 - 9}$ **74.** $f(x) = \dfrac{x^2 + x + 1}{x - 1}$

For Problems 75–83, use an equation, a system of equations, or an inequality to help solve each problem.

75. The ratio of female students to male students at a certain university is 5 to 6. If there are 13,200 students at the university, find the number of female students and the number of male students.

76. A retailer of sporting goods bought a driver for $170. He wants to sell the driver to make a 15% profit based on the selling price. What price should he mark on the driver?

77. In Problem 76, suppose the retailer wanted a profit of 15% based on the cost of the driver. What price should he mark on the driver?

78. The perimeter of a rectangle is 38 centimeters, and the area is 84 square centimeters. Find the length and width of the rectangle.

79. Maria can do a certain task in 30 minutes. Dana can accomplish that same task in 20 minutes. One day Maria started the task, then after 10 minutes she was joined by Dana and they finished the task together. How long did it take them to finish the task once they started working together?

80. How many liters of a 50% acid solution must be added to 5 liters of a 10% acid solution to produce a 30% acid solution?

81. A car can be rented from agency A at $30 per day plus $0.15 a mile or from agency B at $20 per day plus $0.20 a mile. If the car is driven m miles in one day, for what values of m does it cost less to rent from agency A?

82. The cost of labor varies jointly as the number of workers and the number of days they work. If it costs $12,500 to have 25 people work for 5 days, how much will it cost to have 30 people work for 6 days?

83. How long will it take for $500 to grow to $1000 if it is invested at 6% interest compounded semiannually?

9 Sequences and Mathematical Induction

9.1 Arithmetic Sequences

9.2 Geometric Sequences

9.3 Another Look at Problem Solving

9.4 Mathematical Induction

When objects are arranged in a sequence, the total number of objects is the sum of the terms of the sequence.

© David Durochik/Corbis

Suppose that an auditorium has 35 seats in the first row, 40 seats in the second row, 45 seats in the third row, and so on, for ten rows. The numbers 35, 40, 45, 50, . . . , 80 represent the number of seats per row from row 1 through row 10. This list of numbers has a constant difference of 5 between any two successive numbers in the list; such a list is called an *arithmetic sequence*. (Used in this sense, the word arithmetic is pronounced with the accent on the syllable *met*.)

Suppose that a fungus culture growing under controlled conditions doubles in size each day. If today the size of the culture is 6 units, then the numbers 12, 24, 48, 96, 192 represent the size of the culture for the next 5 days. In this list of numbers, each number after the first is twice the previous number; such a list is called a *geometric sequence*. Arithmetic sequences and geometric sequences will be the center of our attention in this chapter.

681

9.1 Arithmetic Sequences

OBJECTIVES

1. Write the terms of a sequence
2. Find the general term for an arithmetic sequence
3. Find a specific term for an arithmetic sequence
4. Find the sum of the terms of an arithmetic sequence
5. Determine the sum indicated by summation notation

An **infinite sequence** is a function with a domain that is the set of positive integers. For example, consider the function defined by the equation

$$f(n) = 5n + 1$$

in which the domain is the set of positive integers. If we substitute the numbers of the domain in order, starting with 1, we can list the resulting ordered pairs:

$$(1, 6) \quad (2, 11) \quad (3, 16) \quad (4, 21) \quad (5, 26)$$

and so on. However, because we know we are using the domain of positive integers in order, starting with 1, there is no need to use ordered pairs. We can simply express the infinite sequence as

$$6, 11, 16, 21, 26, \ldots$$

Often the letter a is used to represent sequential functions, and the functional value of a at n is written a_n (this is read "a sub n") instead of $a(n)$. The sequence is then expressed as

$$a_1, a_2, a_3, a_4, \ldots$$

where a_1 is the *first term*, a_2 is the *second term*, a_3 is the *third term*, and so on. The expression a_n, which defines the sequence, is called the *general term* of the sequence. Knowing the general term of a sequence enables us to find as many terms of the sequence as needed and also to find any specific terms. Consider the following example.

Classroom Example
Find the first five terms of the sequence in which $a_n = 3n^3 + 1$, and then find the 10th term.

EXAMPLE 1

Find the first five terms of the sequence when $a_n = 2n^2 - 3$; find the 20th term.

Solution

The first five terms are generated by replacing n with 1, 2, 3, 4, and 5:

$$a_1 = 2(1)^2 - 3 = -1 \qquad a_2 = 2(2)^2 - 3 = 5$$
$$a_3 = 2(3)^2 - 3 = 15 \qquad a_4 = 2(4)^2 - 3 = 29$$
$$a_5 = 2(5)^2 - 3 = 47$$

The first five terms are thus $-1, 5, 15, 29,$ and 47. The 20th term is

$$a_{20} = 2(20)^2 - 3 = 797$$

Arithmetic Sequences

An **arithmetic sequence** (also called an **arithmetic progression**) is a sequence that has a common difference between successive terms. The following are examples of arithmetic sequences:

$$1, 8, 15, 22, 29, \ldots$$
$$4, 7, 10, 13, 16, \ldots$$
$$4, 1, -2, -5, -8, \ldots$$
$$-1, -6, -11, -16, -21, \ldots$$

The common difference in the first sequence is 7. That is, $8 - 1 = 7$, $15 - 8 = 7$, $22 - 15 = 7$, $29 - 22 = 7$, and so on. The common differences for the next three sequences are 3, -3, and -5, respectively.

In a more general setting, we say that the sequence

$$a_1, a_2, a_3, a_4, \ldots, a_n, \ldots$$

is an arithmetic sequence if and only if there is a real number d such that

$$a_{k+1} - a_k = d$$

for every positive integer k. The number d is called the **common difference**.

From the definition, we see that $a_{k+1} = a_k + d$. In other words, we can generate an arithmetic sequence that has a common difference of d by starting with a first term a_1 and then simply adding d to each successive term.

First term:	a_1
Second term:	$a_1 + d$
Third term:	$a_1 + 2d$ $(a_1 + d) + d = a_1 + 2d$
Fourth term:	$a_1 + 3d$
.	
.	
.	
nth term:	$a_1 + (n - 1)d$

Thus the **general term** of an arithmetic sequence is given by

$$a_n = a_1 + (n - 1)d$$

where a_1 is the first term, and d is the common difference. This formula for the general term can be used to solve a variety of problems involving arithmetic sequences.

Classroom Example
Find the general term of the arithmetic sequence $-4, 3, 10, 17, \ldots$.

EXAMPLE 2

Find the general term of the arithmetic sequence $6, 2, -2, -6, \ldots$.

Solution

The common difference, d, is $2 - 6 = -4$, and the first term, a_1, is 6. Substitute these values into $a_n = a_1 + (n - 1)d$ and simplify to obtain

$$a_n = a_1 + (n - 1)d$$
$$= 6 + (n - 1)(-4)$$
$$= 6 - 4n + 4$$
$$= -4n + 10$$

EXAMPLE 3

Find the 40th term of the arithmetic sequence $1, 5, 9, 13, \ldots$.

Solution

Using $a_n = a_1 + (n - 1)d$, we obtain
$$a_{40} = 1 + (40 - 1)4$$
$$= 1 + (39)(4)$$
$$= 157$$

EXAMPLE 4

Find the first term of the arithmetic sequence if the fourth term is 26 and the ninth term is 61.

Solution

Using $a_n = a_1 + (n - 1)d$ with $a_4 = 26$ (the fourth term is 26) and $a_9 = 61$ (the ninth term is 61), we have

$$26 = a_1 + (4 - 1)d = a_1 + 3d$$
$$61 = a_1 + (9 - 1)d = a_1 + 8d$$

Solving the system of equations

$$\begin{pmatrix} a_1 + 3d = 26 \\ a_1 + 8d = 61 \end{pmatrix}$$

yields $a_1 = 5$ and $d = 7$. Thus the first term is 5.

Sums of Arithmetic Sequences

We often use sequences to solve problems, so we need to be able to find the sum of a certain number of terms of the sequence. Before we develop a general-sum formula for arithmetic sequences, let's consider an approach to a specific problem that we can then use in a general setting.

EXAMPLE 5   Find the sum of the first 100 positive integers.

Solution

We are being asked to find the sum of $1 + 2 + 3 + 4 + \cdots + 100$. Rather than adding in the usual way, we will find the sum in the following manner: Let's simply write the indicated sum forward and backward, and then add in columns:

$$1 + 2 + 3 + 4 + \cdots + 100$$
$$\underline{100 + 99 + 98 + 97 + \cdots + 1}$$
$$101 + 101 + 101 + 101 + \cdots + 101$$

We have produced 100 sums of 101. However, this result is double the amount we want because we wrote the sum twice. To find the sum of just the numbers 1 to 100, we need to multiply 100 by 101 and then divide by 2:

$$\frac{100(101)}{2} = \frac{\overset{50}{\cancel{100}}(101)}{\cancel{2}} = 5050$$

Thus the sum of the first 100 positive integers is 5050.

The *forward–backward* approach we used in Example 5 can be used to develop a formula for finding the sum of the first n terms of any arithmetic sequence. Consider an arithmetic sequence $a_1, a_2, a_3, a_4, \ldots, a_n$ with a common difference of d. Use S_n to represent the sum of the first n terms, and proceed as follows:

$$S_n = a_1 + (a_1 + d) + (a_1 + 2d) + \cdots + (a_n - 2d) + (a_n - d) + a_n$$

Now write this sum in reverse:

$$S_n = a_n + (a_n - d) + (a_n - 2d) + \cdots + (a_1 + 2d) + (a_1 + d) + a_1$$

Add the two equations to produce

$$2S_n = (a_1 + a_n) + (a_1 + a_n) + (a_1 + a_n) + \cdots + (a_1 + a_n) + (a_1 + a_n) + (a_1 + a_n)$$

That is, we have n sums $a_1 + a_n$, so

$$2S_n = n(a_1 + a_n)$$

from which we obtain a **sum formula**:

$$S_n = \frac{n(a_1 + a_n)}{2}$$

Using the nth-term formula and/or the sum formula, we can solve a variety of problems involving arithmetic sequences.

Classroom Example
Find the sum of the first 20 terms of the arithmetic sequence 2, 7, 12, 17, ...

EXAMPLE 6

Find the sum of the first 30 terms of the arithmetic sequence 3, 7, 11, 15, ...

Solution

To use the formula $S_n = \dfrac{n(a_1 + a_n)}{2}$, we need to know the number of terms (n), the first term (a_1), and the last term (a_n). We are given the number of terms and the first term, so we need to find the last term. Using $a_n = a_1 + (n - 1)d$, we can find the 30th term.

$$a_{30} = 3 + (30 - 1)4 = 3 + 29(4) = 119$$

Now we can use the sum formula.

$$S_{30} = \frac{30(3 + 119)}{2} = 1830$$

_____ ■

EXAMPLE 7   Find the sum $7 + 10 + 13 + \cdots + 157$.

Solution

To use the sum formula, we need to know the number of terms. Applying the nth-term formula will give us that information:

$$a_n = a_1 + (n - 1)d$$
$$157 = 7 + (n - 1)3$$
$$157 = 7 + 3n - 3$$
$$157 = 3n + 4$$
$$153 = 3n$$
$$51 = n$$

Now we can use the sum formula:

$$S_{51} = \frac{51(7 + 157)}{2} = 4182$$

_____ ■

Keep in mind that we developed the sum formula for an arithmetic sequence by using the forward–backward technique, which we had previously used on a specific problem. Now that we have the sum formula, we have two choices when solving problems. We can either memorize the formula and use it or simply use the forward–backward technique. If you choose to use the formula and some day you forget it, don't panic. Just use the forward–backward technique. In other words, understanding the development of a formula often enables you to do problems even when you forget the formula itself.

Summation Notation

Sometimes a special notation is used to indicate the sum of a certain number of terms of a sequence. The capital Greek letter *sigma,* Σ, is used as a **summation symbol**. For example,

$$\sum_{i=1}^{5} a_i$$

represents the sum $a_1 + a_2 + a_3 + a_4 + a_5$. The letter i is frequently used as the **index of summation**; the letter i takes on all integer values from the lower limit to the upper limit, inclusive. Thus

$$\sum_{i=1}^{4} b_i = b_1 + b_2 + b_3 + b_4$$

$$\sum_{i=3}^{7} a_i = a_3 + a_4 + a_5 + a_6 + a_7$$

$$\sum_{i=1}^{15} i^2 = 1^2 + 2^2 + 3^2 + \cdots + 15^2$$

$$\sum_{i=1}^{n} a_i = a_1 + a_2 + a_3 + \cdots + a_n$$

If $a_1, a_2, a_3, \ldots$ represents an arithmetic sequence, we can now write the sum formula

$$\sum_{i=1}^{n} a_i = \frac{n}{2}(a_1 + a_n)$$

Classroom Example
Find the sum $\displaystyle\sum_{i=1}^{28}(5i - 3)$.

EXAMPLE 8

Find the sum $\displaystyle\sum_{i=1}^{50}(3i + 4)$.

Solution

This indicated sum means

$$\sum_{i=1}^{50}(3i + 4) = [3(1) + 4] + [3(2) + 4] + [3(3) + 4] + \cdot \ \cdot \ \cdot \ + [3(50) + 4]$$

$$= 7 + 10 + 13 + \cdots + 154$$

Because this is an indicated sum of an arithmetic sequence, we can use our sum formula:

$$S_{50} = \frac{50}{2}(7 + 154) = 4025$$

Classroom Example
Find the sum $\displaystyle\sum_{i=4}^{9} 3i^2$.

EXAMPLE 9

Find the sum $\displaystyle\sum_{i=2}^{7} 2i^2$.

Solution

This indicated sum means

$$\sum_{i=2}^{7} 2i^2 = 2(2)^2 + 2(3)^2 + 2(4)^2 + 2(5)^2 + 2(6)^2 + 2(7)^2$$

$$= 8 + 18 + 32 + 50 + 72 + 98$$

This is not the indicated sum of an *arithmetic* sequence; therefore let's simply add the numbers in the usual way. The sum is 278.

Example 9 suggests a word of caution. Be sure to analyze the sequence of numbers that is represented by the summation symbol. You may or may not be able to use a formula for adding the numbers.

Concept Quiz 9.1

For Problems 1–8, answer true or false.

1. An infinite sequence is a function whose domain is the set of all real numbers.
2. An arithmetic sequence is a sequence that has a common difference between successive terms.
3. The sequence 2, 4, 8, 16, . . . is an arithmetic sequence.
4. The odd whole numbers form an arithmetic sequence.
5. The terms of an arithmetic sequence are always positive.
6. The 6th term of an arithmetic sequence is equal to the first term plus 6 times the common difference.
7. The sum formula for n terms of an arithmetic sequence is n times the average of the first and last terms.
8. The indicated sum $\sum_{i=1}^{4} (2i - 7)^2$ is the sum of the first four terms of an arithmetic sequence.

Problem Set 9.1

For Problems 1–10, write the first five terms of the sequence that has the indicated general term. (Objective 1)

1. $a_n = 3n - 7$

2. $a_n = 5n - 2$

3. $a_n = -2n + 4$

4. $a_n = -4n + 7$

5. $a_n = 3n^2 - 1$

6. $a_n = 2n^2 - 6$

7. $a_n = n(n - 1)$

8. $a_n = (n + 1)(n + 2)$

9. $a_n = 2^{n+1}$

10. $a_n = 3^{n-1}$

11. Find the 15th and 30th terms of the sequence when $a_n = -5n - 4$.

12. Find the 20th and 50th terms of the sequence when $a_n = -n - 3$.

13. Find the 25th and 50th terms of the sequence when $a_n = (-1)^{n+1}$.

14. Find the 10th and 15th terms of the sequence when $a_n = -n^2 - 10$.

For Problems 15–24, find the general term (the nth term) for each arithmetic sequence. (Objective 2)

15. 11, 13, 15, 17, 19, . . .

16. 7, 10, 13, 16, 19, . . .

17. 2, −1, −4, −7, −10, . . .

18. 4, 2, 0, −2, −4, . . .

19. $\dfrac{3}{2}, 2, \dfrac{5}{2}, 3, \dfrac{7}{2}, \ldots$

20. $0, \dfrac{1}{2}, 1, \dfrac{3}{2}, 2, \ldots$

21. 2, 6, 10, 14, 18, . . .

22. 2, 7, 12, 17, 22, . . .

23. −3, −6, −9, −12, −15, . . .

24. −4, −8, −12, −16, −20, . . .

For Problems 25–30, find the required term for each arithmetic sequence. (Objective 3)

25. The 15th term of 3, 8, 13, 18, . . .

26. The 20th term of 4, 11, 18, 25, . . .

27. The 30th term of 15, 26, 37, 48, . . .

28. The 35th term of 9, 17, 25, 33, . . .

29. The 52nd term of $1, \dfrac{5}{3}, \dfrac{7}{3}, 3, \ldots$

30. The 47th term of $\frac{1}{2}, \frac{5}{4}, 2, \frac{11}{4}, \dots$

For Problems 31–42, solve each problem.

31. If the 6th term of an arithmetic sequence is 12 and the 10th term is 16, find the first term.

32. If the 5th term of an arithmetic sequence is 14 and the 12th term is 42, find the first term.

33. If the 3rd term of an arithmetic sequence is 20 and the 7th term is 32, find the 25th term.

34. If the 5th term of an arithmetic sequence is -5 and the 15th term is -25, find the 50th term.

35. Find the sum of the first 50 terms of the arithmetic sequence $5, 7, 9, 11, 13, \dots$.

36. Find the sum of the first 30 terms of the arithmetic sequence $0, 2, 4, 6, 8, \dots$.

37. Find the sum of the first 40 terms of the arithmetic sequence $2, 6, 10, 14, 18, \dots$.

38. Find the sum of the first 60 terms of the arithmetic sequence $-2, 3, 8, 13, 18, \dots$.

39. Find the sum of the first 75 terms of the arithmetic sequence $5, 2, -1, -4, -7, \dots$.

40. Find the sum of the first 80 terms of the arithmetic sequence $7, 3, -1, -5, -9, \dots$.

41. Find the sum of the first 50 terms of the arithmetic sequence $\frac{1}{2}, 1, \frac{3}{2}, 2, \frac{5}{2}, \dots$.

42. Find the sum of the first 100 terms of the arithmetic sequence $-\frac{1}{3}, \frac{1}{3}, 1, \frac{5}{3}, \frac{7}{3}, \dots$.

For Problems 43–50, find the indicated sum. (Objective 4)

43. $1 + 5 + 9 + 13 + \cdots + 197$

44. $3 + 8 + 13 + 18 + \cdots + 398$

45. $2 + 8 + 14 + 20 + \cdots + 146$

46. $6 + 9 + 12 + 15 + \cdots + 93$

47. $(-7) + (-10) + (-13) + (-16) + \cdots + (-109)$

48. $(-5) + (-9) + (-13) + (-17) + \cdots + (-169)$

49. $(-5) + (-3) + (-1) + 1 + \cdots + 119$

50. $(-7) + (-4) + (-1) + 2 + \cdots + 131$

For Problems 51–58, solve each problem.

51. Find the sum of the first 200 odd whole numbers.

52. Find the sum of the first 175 positive even whole numbers.

53. Find the sum of all even numbers between 18 and 482, inclusive.

54. Find the sum of all odd numbers between 17 and 379, inclusive.

55. Find the sum of the first 30 terms of the arithmetic sequence with the general term $a_n = 5n - 4$.

56. Find the sum of the first 40 terms of the arithmetic sequence with the general term $a_n = 4n - 7$.

57. Find the sum of the first 25 terms of the arithmetic sequence with the general term $a_n = -4n - 1$.

58. Find the sum of the first 35 terms of the arithmetic sequence with the general term $a_n = -5n - 3$.

For Problems 59–70, find each sum. (Objective 5)

59. $\displaystyle\sum_{i=1}^{45} (5i + 2)$

60. $\displaystyle\sum_{i=1}^{38} (3i + 6)$

61. $\displaystyle\sum_{i=1}^{30} (-2i + 4)$

62. $\displaystyle\sum_{i=1}^{40} (-3i + 3)$

63. $\displaystyle\sum_{i=4}^{32} (3i - 10)$

64. $\displaystyle\sum_{i=6}^{47} (4i - 9)$

65. $\displaystyle\sum_{i=10}^{20} 4i$

66. $\displaystyle\sum_{i=15}^{30} (-5i)$

67. $\displaystyle\sum_{i=1}^{5} i^2$

68. $\displaystyle\sum_{i=1}^{6} (i^2 + 1)$

69. $\displaystyle\sum_{i=3}^{8} (2i^2 + i)$

70. $\displaystyle\sum_{i=4}^{7} (3i^2 - 2)$

Thoughts Into Words

71. Before developing the formula $a_n = a_1 + (n-1)d$, we stated the equation $a_{k+1} - a_k = d$. In your own words, explain what this equation says.

72. Explain how to find the sum $1 + 2 + 3 + 4 + \cdots + 175$ without using the sum formula.

73. Explain in words how to find the sum of the first n terms of an arithmetic sequence.

74. Explain how one can tell that a particular sequence is an arithmetic sequence.

Further Investigations

The general term of a sequence can consist of one expression for certain values of n and another expression (or expressions) for other values of n. That is, a *multiple description* of the sequence can be given. For example,

$$a_n = \begin{cases} 2n + 3 & \text{for } n \text{ odd} \\ 3n - 2 & \text{for } n \text{ even} \end{cases}$$

means that we use $a_n = 2n + 3$ for $n = 1, 3, 5, 7, \ldots$, and we use $a_n = 3n - 2$ for $n = 2, 4, 6, 8, \ldots$. The first six terms of this sequence are 5, 4, 9, 10, 13, and 16.

For Problems 75–78, write the first six terms of each sequence.

75. $a_n = \begin{cases} 2n + 1 & \text{for } n \text{ odd} \\ 2n - 1 & \text{for } n \text{ even} \end{cases}$

76. $a_n = \begin{cases} \dfrac{1}{n} & \text{for } n \text{ odd} \\ n^2 & \text{for } n \text{ even} \end{cases}$

77. $a_n = \begin{cases} 3n + 1 & \text{for } n \le 3 \\ 4n - 3 & \text{for } n > 3 \end{cases}$

78. $a_n = \begin{cases} 5n - 1 & \text{for } n \text{ a multiple of 3} \\ 2n & \text{otherwise} \end{cases}$

The multiple-description approach can also be used to give a *recursive description* for a sequence. A sequence is said to be *described recursively* if the first n terms are stated, and then each succeeding term is defined as a function of one or more of the preceding terms. For example,

$$\begin{cases} a_1 = 2 \\ a_n = 2a_{n-1} & \text{for } n \ge 2 \end{cases}$$

means that the first term, a_1, is 2 and each succeeding term is 2 times the previous term. Thus the first six terms are 2, 4, 8, 16, 32, and 64.

For Problems 79–84, write the first six terms of each sequence.

79. $\begin{cases} a_1 = 4 \\ a_n = 3a_{n-1} & \text{for } n \ge 2 \end{cases}$

80. $\begin{cases} a_1 = 3 \\ a_n = a_{n-1} + 2 & \text{for } n \ge 2 \end{cases}$

81. $\begin{cases} a_1 = 1 \\ a_2 = 1 \\ a_n = a_{n-2} + a_{n-1} & \text{for } n \ge 3 \end{cases}$

82. $\begin{cases} a_1 = 2 \\ a_2 = 3 \\ a_n = 2a_{n-2} + 3a_{n-1} & \text{for } n \ge 3 \end{cases}$

83. $\begin{cases} a_1 = 3 \\ a_2 = 1 \\ a_n = (a_{n-1} - a_{n-2})^2 & \text{for } n \ge 3 \end{cases}$

84. $\begin{cases} a_1 = 1 \\ a_2 = 2 \\ a_3 = 3 \\ a_n = a_{n-1} + a_{n-2} + a_{n-3} & \text{for } n \ge 4 \end{cases}$

Answers to the Concept Quiz

1. False **2.** True **3.** False **4.** True **5.** False **6.** False **7.** True **8.** False

9.2 Geometric Sequences

OBJECTIVES

1. Find the general term for a geometric sequence
2. Find a specific term for a geometric sequence
3. Determine the sum of the terms of a geometric sequence
4. Determine the sum of an infinite geometric sequence
5. Change a repeating decimal into $\dfrac{a}{b}$ form

A **geometric sequence** (or **geometric progression**) is a sequence in which we obtain each term after the first by multiplying the preceding term by a common multiplier, which is called the *common ratio* of the sequence. We can find the **common ratio** of a geometric sequence by dividing any term (other than the first) by the preceding term. The following geometric sequences have common ratios of 3, 2, $\dfrac{1}{2}$, and -4, respectively:

$1, 3, 9, 27, 81, \ldots$

$3, 6, 12, 24, 48, \ldots$

$16, 8, 4, 2, 1, \ldots$

$-1, 4, -16, 64, -256, \ldots$

In a more general setting, we say that the sequence $a_1, a_2, a_3, \ldots, a_n, \ldots$ is a geometric sequence if and only if there is a nonzero real number r such that

$$a_{k+1} = ra_k$$

for every positive integer k. The nonzero real number r is called the common ratio of the sequence.

The previous equation can be used to generate a general geometric sequence that has a_1 as a first term and r as a common ratio. We can proceed as follows:

First term:	a_1
Second term:	a_1r
Third term:	a_1r^2 $\quad(a_1r)(r) = a_1r^2$
Fourth term:	a_1r^3
.	
.	
.	
nth term:	a_1r^{n-1}

Thus the **general term** of a geometric sequence is given by

$$a_n = a_1r^{n-1}$$

where a_1 is the first term and r is the common ratio.

EXAMPLE 1

Find the general term for the geometric sequence 8, 16, 32, 64, ...

Solution

The common ratio (r) is $\dfrac{16}{8} = 2$, and the first term (a_1) is 8. Substitute these values into $a_n = a_1 r^{n-1}$ and simplify to obtain

$$a_n = 8(2)^{n-1} = (2^3)(2)^{n-1} = 2^{n+2}$$

EXAMPLE 2

Find the ninth term of the geometric sequence $27, 9, 3, 1, \ldots$.

Solution

The common ratio (r) is $\dfrac{9}{27} = \dfrac{1}{3}$, and the first term (a_1) is 27. Using $a_n = a_1 r^{n-1}$, we obtain

$$a_9 = 27\left(\frac{1}{3}\right)^{9-1} = 27\left(\frac{1}{3}\right)^8$$

$$= \frac{3^3}{3^8}$$

$$= \frac{1}{3^5}$$

$$= \frac{1}{243}$$

Sums of Geometric Sequences

As with arithmetic sequences, we often need to find the sum of a certain number of terms of a geometric sequence. Before we develop a general-sum formula for geometric sequences, let's consider an approach to a specific problem that we can then use in a general setting.

EXAMPLE 3   Find the sum of $1 + 3 + 9 + 27 + \cdots + 6561$.

Solution

Let S represent the sum and proceed as follows:

$$S = 1 + 3 + 9 + 27 + \cdots + 6561 \tag{1}$$

$$3S = \quad 3 + 9 + 27 + \cdots + 6561 + 19{,}683 \tag{2}$$

Equation (2) is the result of multiplying equation (1) by the common ratio 3. Subtracting equation (1) from equation (2) produces

$$2S = 19,683 - 1 = 19,682$$
$$S = 9841$$

Now let's consider a general geometric sequence $a_1, a_1r, a_1r^2, \ldots, a_1r^{n-1}$. By applying a procedure similar to the one we used in Example 3, we can develop a formula for finding the sum of the first n terms of any geometric sequence. We let S_n represent the sum of the first n terms.

$$S_n = a_1 + a_1r + a_1r^2 + \cdots + a_1r^{n-1} \tag{3}$$

Next, we multiply both sides of equation (3) by the common ratio r.

$$rS_n = a_1r + a_1r^2 + a_1r^3 + \cdots + a_1r^n \tag{4}$$

We then subtract equation (3) from equation (4).

$$rS_n - S_n = a_1r^n - a_1$$

When we apply the distributive property to the left side and then solve for S_n, we obtain

$$S_n(r - 1) = a_1r^n - a_1$$
$$S_n = \frac{a_1r^n - a_1}{r - 1}, \qquad r \neq 1$$

Therefore the sum of the first n terms of a geometric sequence with a first term a_1 and a common ratio r is given by

$$S_n = \frac{a_1r^n - a_1}{r - 1}, \qquad r \neq 1$$

Classroom Example
Find the sum of the first ten terms of the geometric sequence $1, 3, 9, 27, \ldots$.

EXAMPLE 4

Find the sum of the first eight terms of the geometric sequence $1, 2, 4, 8, \ldots$.

Solution

To use the sum formula $S_n = \dfrac{a_1r^n - a_1}{r - 1}$, we need to know the number of terms (n), the first term (a_1), and the common ratio (r). We are given the number of terms and the first term, and we can determine that $r = \dfrac{2}{1} = 2$. Using the sum formula, we obtain

$$S_8 = \frac{1(2)^8 - 1}{2 - 1} = \frac{2^8 - 1}{1} = 255$$

If the common ratio of a geometric sequence is less than 1, it may be more convenient to change the form of the sum formula. That is, the fraction

$$\frac{a_1r^n - a_1}{r - 1}$$

can be changed to

$$\frac{a_1 - a_1 r^n}{1 - r}$$

by multiplying both the numerator and the denominator by -1. Thus by using

$$S_n = \frac{a_1 - a_1 r^n}{1 - r}$$

we can sometimes avoid unnecessary work with negative numbers when $r < 1$, as the next example illustrates.

Classroom Example
Find the sum
$$1 + \frac{1}{3} + \frac{1}{9} + \cdots + \frac{1}{729}.$$

EXAMPLE 5   Find the sum $1 + \frac{1}{2} + \frac{1}{4} + \cdots + \frac{1}{256}$.

Solution A

To use the sum formula, we need to know the number of terms, which can be found by counting them or by applying the nth-term formula, as follows:

$$a_n = a_1 r^{n-1}$$

$$\frac{1}{256} = 1\left(\frac{1}{2}\right)^{n-1}$$

$$\left(\frac{1}{2}\right)^8 = \left(\frac{1}{2}\right)^{n-1}$$

$$8 = n - 1 \qquad \text{If } b^n = b^m, \text{ then } n = m$$

$$9 = n$$

Now we use $n = 9$, $a_1 = 1$, and $r = \frac{1}{2}$ in the sum formula of the form

$$S_n = \frac{a_1 - a_1 r^n}{1 - r}$$

$$S_9 = \frac{1 - 1\left(\frac{1}{2}\right)^9}{1 - \frac{1}{2}} = \frac{1 - \frac{1}{512}}{\frac{1}{2}} = \frac{\frac{511}{512}}{\frac{1}{2}} = 1\frac{255}{256}$$

We can also do a problem like Example 5 without finding the number of terms; we use the general approach illustrated in Example 3. Solution B demonstrates this idea.

Solution B

Let S represent the desired sum.

$$S = 1 + \frac{1}{2} + \frac{1}{4} + \cdots + \frac{1}{256}$$

Multiply both sides by the common ratio $\frac{1}{2}$.

$$\frac{1}{2}S = \frac{1}{2} + \frac{1}{4} + \frac{1}{8} + \cdots + \frac{1}{256} + \frac{1}{512}$$

Subtract the second equation from the first, and solve for S.

$$\frac{1}{2}S = 1 - \frac{1}{512} = \frac{511}{512}$$

$$S = \frac{511}{256} = 1\frac{255}{256}$$

Summation notation can also be used to indicate the sum of a certain number of terms of a geometric sequence.

Classroom Example

Find the sum $\sum_{i=1}^{8} 3^i$.

EXAMPLE 6

Find the sum $\sum_{i=1}^{10} 2^i$.

Solution

This indicated sum means

$$\sum_{i=1}^{10} 2^i = 2^1 + 2^2 + 2^3 + \cdots + 2^{10}$$

$$= 2 + 4 + 8 + \cdots + 1024$$

This is the indicated sum of a geometric sequence, so we can use the sum formula with $a_1 = 2$, $r = 2$, and $n = 10$.

$$S_{10} = \frac{2(2)^{10} - 2}{2 - 1} = \frac{2(2^{10} - 1)}{1} = 2046$$

The Sum of an Infinite Geometric Sequence

Let's take the formula

$$S_n = \frac{a_1 - a_1 r^n}{1 - r}$$

and rewrite the right-hand side by applying the property

$$\frac{a - b}{c} = \frac{a}{c} - \frac{b}{c}$$

Thus we obtain

$$S_n = \frac{a_1}{1 - r} - \frac{a_1 r^n}{1 - r}$$

Now let's examine the behavior of r^n for $|r| < 1$, that is, for $-1 < r < 1$. For example, suppose that $r = \dfrac{1}{2}$. Then

$$r^2 = \left(\frac{1}{2}\right)^2 = \frac{1}{4} \qquad\qquad r^3 = \left(\frac{1}{2}\right)^3 = \frac{1}{8}$$

$$r^4 = \left(\frac{1}{2}\right)^4 = \frac{1}{16} \qquad\qquad r^5 = \left(\frac{1}{2}\right)^5 = \frac{1}{32}$$

and so on. We can make $\left(\dfrac{1}{2}\right)^n$ as close to zero as we please by choosing sufficiently large values for n. In general, for values of r such that $|r| < 1$, the expression r^n approaches zero as n gets larger and larger. Therefore the fraction $a_1 r^n / (1 - r)$ in equation (1) approaches zero as n increases. We say that the **sum of the infinite geometric sequence** is given by

$$S_\infty = \frac{a_1}{1 - r}, \qquad |r| < 1$$

Classroom Example
Find the sum of the infinite geometric sequence:
$1, \dfrac{1}{4}, \dfrac{1}{16}, \dfrac{1}{64}, \cdots$

EXAMPLE 7

Find the sum of the infinite geometric sequence $1, \dfrac{1}{2}, \dfrac{1}{4}, \dfrac{1}{8}, \ldots$.

Solution

Because $a_1 = 1$ and $r = \dfrac{1}{2}$, we obtain

$$S_\infty = \frac{1}{1 - \dfrac{1}{2}} = \frac{1}{\dfrac{1}{2}} = 2$$

When we state that $S_\infty = 2$ in Example 7, we mean that as we add more and more terms, the sum approaches 2. Observe what happens when we calculate the sum up to five terms.

First term:	1
Sum of first two terms:	$1 + \dfrac{1}{2} = 1\dfrac{1}{2}$
Sum of first three terms:	$1 + \dfrac{1}{2} + \dfrac{1}{4} = 1\dfrac{3}{4}$
Sum of first four terms:	$1 + \dfrac{1}{2} + \dfrac{1}{4} + \dfrac{1}{8} = 1\dfrac{7}{8}$
Sum of first five terms:	$1 + \dfrac{1}{2} + \dfrac{1}{4} + \dfrac{1}{8} + \dfrac{1}{16} = 1\dfrac{15}{16}$

If $|r| > 1$, the absolute value of r^n increases without bound as n increases. In the next table, note the unbounded growth of the absolute value of r^n.

Let $r = 3$	Let $r = -2$	
$r^2 = 3^2 = 9$	$r^2 = (-2)^2 = 4$	
$r^3 = 3^3 = 27$	$r^3 = (-2)^3 = -8$	$\lvert -8 \rvert = 8$
$r^4 = 3^4 = 81$	$r^4 = (-2)^4 = 16$	
$r^5 = 3^5 = 243$	$r^5 = (-2)^5 = -32$	$\lvert -32 \rvert = 32$

If $r = 1$, then $S_n = na_1$, and as n increases without bound, $\lvert S_n \rvert$ also increases without bound. If $r = -1$, then S_n will be either a_1 or 0. Therefore we say that the sum of any infinite geometric sequence where $|r| \geq 1$ *does not exist*.

Repeating Decimals as Sums of Infinite Geometric Sequences

In Section 0.1, we defined rational numbers to be numbers that have either a terminating or a repeating decimal representation. For example,

$$2.23 \quad 0.147 \quad 0.\overline{3} \quad 0.\overline{14} \quad \text{and} \quad 0.5\overline{6}$$

are rational numbers. (Remember that $0.\overline{3}$ means 0.3333 . . . .) Place value provides the basis for changing terminating decimals such as 2.23 and 0.147 to a/b form, where a and b are integers and $b \neq 0$.

$$2.23 = \frac{223}{100} \quad \text{and} \quad 0.147 = \frac{147}{1000}$$

However, changing repeating decimals to a/b form requires a different technique, and our work with sums of infinite geometric sequences provides the basis for one such approach. Consider the following examples.

EXAMPLE 8

Change $0.\overline{14}$ to a/b form, where a and b are integers and $b \neq 0$.

Solution

The repeating decimal $0.\overline{14}$ can be written as the indicated sum of an infinite geometric sequence with first term 0.14 and common ratio 0.01.

$$0.14 + 0.0014 + 0.000014 + \cdots$$

Using $S_\infty = a_1/(1 - r)$, we obtain

$$S_\infty = \frac{0.14}{1 - 0.01} = \frac{0.14}{0.99} = \frac{14}{99}$$

Thus $0.\overline{14} = \dfrac{14}{99}$.

If the repeating block of digits does not begin immediately after the decimal point, as in $0.5\overline{6}$, we can make an adjustment in the technique we used in Example 8.

EXAMPLE 9

Change $0.5\overline{6}$ to a/b form, where a and b are integers and $b \neq 0$.

Solution

The repeating decimal $0.5\overline{6}$ can be written

$$(0.5) + (0.06 + 0.006 + 0.0006 + \cdots)$$

where

$$0.06 + 0.006 + 0.0006 + \cdots$$

is the indicated sum of the infinite geometric sequence with $a_1 = 0.06$ and $r = 0.1$. Therefore

$$S_\infty = \frac{0.06}{1 - 0.1} = \frac{0.06}{0.9} = \frac{6}{90} = \frac{1}{15}$$

Now we can add 0.5 and $\dfrac{1}{15}$.

$$0.5\overline{6} = 0.5 + \frac{1}{15} = \frac{1}{2} + \frac{1}{15} = \frac{15}{30} + \frac{2}{30} = \frac{17}{30}$$

Concept Quiz 9.2

For Problems 1–8, answer true or false.

1. The common ratio for a geometric sequence is found by dividing any term by the next successive term.
2. The 5th term of a geometric sequence is equal to the first term multiplied by the common ratio raised to the fourth power.
3. The common ratio of a geometric sequence could be zero.
4. The common ratio of a geometric sequence can be negative.
5. S_∞ denotes the sum of an infinite geometric sequence.
6. If the common ratio of an infinite geometric sequence is greater than 1, then the sum of the sequence does not exist.
7. For the sequence, $2, -2, 2, -2, 2, \ldots, S_9 = 2$.
8. Every repeating decimal can be changed into $\dfrac{a}{b}$ form in which a and b are integers, and $b \neq 0$.

Problem Set 9.2

For Problems 1–12, find the general term (the nth term) for each geometric sequence. **(Objective 1)**

1. $3, 6, 12, 24, \ldots$

2. $2, 6, 18, 54, \ldots$

3. $3, 9, 27, 81, \ldots$

4. $2, 6, 18, 54, \ldots$

5. $\dfrac{1}{4}, \dfrac{1}{8}, \dfrac{1}{16}, \dfrac{1}{32}, \ldots$

6. $8, 4, 2, 1, \ldots$

7. $4, 16, 64, 256, \ldots$

8. $6, 2, \dfrac{2}{3}, \dfrac{2}{9}, \ldots$

9. $1, 0.3, 0.09, 0.027, \ldots$

10. $0.2, 0.04, 0.008, 0.0016, \ldots$

11. $1, -2, 4, -8, \ldots$

12. $-3, 9, -27, 81, \ldots$

For Problems 13–20, find the required term for each geometric sequence. **(Objective 2)**

13. The 8th term of $\dfrac{1}{2}, 1, 2, 4, \ldots$

14. The 7th term of $2, 6, 18, 54, \ldots$

15. The 9th term of $729, 243, 81, 27, \ldots$

16. The 11th term of $768, 384, 192, 96, \ldots$

17. The 10th term of $1, -2, 4, -8, \ldots$

18. The 8th term of $-1, -\dfrac{3}{2}, -\dfrac{9}{4}, -\dfrac{27}{8}, \ldots$

19. The 8th term of $\dfrac{1}{2}, \dfrac{1}{6}, \dfrac{1}{18}, \dfrac{1}{54}, \ldots$

20. The 9th term of $\dfrac{16}{81}, \dfrac{8}{27}, \dfrac{4}{9}, \dfrac{2}{3}, \ldots$

For Problems 21–32, solve each problem.

21. Find the first term of the geometric sequence with 5th term $\dfrac{32}{3}$ and common ratio 2.

22. Find the first term of the geometric sequence with 4th term $\dfrac{27}{128}$ and common ratio $\dfrac{3}{4}$.

23. Find the common ratio of the geometric sequence with 3rd term 12 and 6th term 96.

24. Find the common ratio of the geometric sequence with 2nd term $\dfrac{8}{3}$ and 5th term $\dfrac{64}{81}$.

25. Find the sum of the first ten terms of the geometric sequence $1, 2, 4, 8, \ldots$.

26. Find the sum of the first seven terms of the geometric sequence $3, 9, 27, 81, \ldots$.

27. Find the sum of the first nine terms of the geometric sequence $2, 6, 18, 54, \ldots$.

28. Find the sum of the first ten terms of the geometric sequence $5, 10, 20, 40, \ldots$.

29. Find the sum of the first eight terms of the geometric sequence $8, 12, 18, 27, \ldots$.

30. Find the sum of the first eight terms of the geometric sequence $9, 12, 16, \dfrac{64}{3}, \ldots$.

31. Find the sum of the first ten terms of the geometric sequence $-4, 8, -16, 32, \ldots$.

32. Find the sum of the first nine terms of the geometric sequence $-2, 6, -18, 54, \ldots$.

For Problems 33–38, find each indicated sum. **(Objective 3)**

33. $9 + 27 + 81 + \cdots + 729$

34. $2 + 8 + 32 + \cdots + 8192$

35. $4 + 2 + 1 + \cdots + \dfrac{1}{512}$

36. $1 + (-2) + 4 + \cdots + 256$

37. $(-1) + 3 + (-9) + \cdots + (-729)$

38. $16 + 8 + 4 + \cdots + \dfrac{1}{32}$

For Problems 39–44, find each indicated sum.
(Objective 3)

39. $\displaystyle\sum_{i=1}^{9} 2^{i-3}$ **40.** $\displaystyle\sum_{i=1}^{6} 3^{i}$

41. $\displaystyle\sum_{i=2}^{5} (-3)^{i+1}$ **42.** $\displaystyle\sum_{i=3}^{8} (-2)^{i-1}$

43. $\displaystyle\sum_{i=1}^{6} 3\left(\frac{1}{2}\right)^{i}$ **44.** $\displaystyle\sum_{i=1}^{5} 2\left(\frac{1}{3}\right)^{i}$

For Problems 45–56, find the sum of each infinite geometric sequence. If the sequence has no sum, so state.
(Objective 4)

45. $2, 1, \dfrac{1}{2}, \dfrac{1}{4}, \ldots$ **46.** $9, 3, 1, \dfrac{1}{3}, \ldots$

47. $1, \dfrac{2}{3}, \dfrac{4}{9}, \dfrac{8}{27}, \ldots$ **48.** $5, 3, \dfrac{9}{5}, \dfrac{27}{25}, \ldots$

49. $4, 8, 16, 32, \ldots$ **50.** $32, 16, 8, 4, \ldots$

51. $9, -3, 1, -\dfrac{1}{3}, \ldots$ **52.** $2, -6, 18, -54, \ldots$

53. $\dfrac{1}{2}, \dfrac{3}{8}, \dfrac{9}{32}, \dfrac{27}{128}, \ldots$ **54.** $4, -\dfrac{4}{3}, \dfrac{4}{9}, -\dfrac{4}{27}, \ldots$

55. $8, -4, 2, -1, \ldots$ **56.** $7, \dfrac{14}{5}, \dfrac{28}{25}, \dfrac{56}{125}, \ldots$

For Problems 57–68, change each repeating decimal to a/b form, in which a and b are integers and $b \neq 0$. Express a/b in reduced form. (Objective 5)

57. $0.\overline{3}$ **58.** $0.\overline{4}$ **59.** $0.\overline{26}$

60. $0.\overline{18}$ **61.** $0.\overline{123}$ **62.** $0.\overline{273}$

63. $0.2\overline{6}$ **64.** $0.4\overline{3}$ **65.** $0.21\overline{4}$

66. $0.37\overline{1}$ **67.** $2.\overline{3}$ **68.** $3.\overline{7}$

Thoughts Into Words

69. Explain the difference between an arithmetic sequence and a geometric sequence.

70. What does it mean to say that the sum of the infinite geometric sequence $1, \dfrac{1}{2}, \dfrac{1}{4}, \dfrac{1}{8}, \ldots$ is 2?

71. What do we mean when we say that the infinite geometric sequence $1, 2, 4, 8, \ldots$ has no sum?

72. Why don't we discuss the sum of an infinite arithmetic sequence?

Answers to the Concept Quiz

1. False **2.** True **3.** False **4.** True **5.** True **6.** True **7.** True **8.** True

9.3   Another Look at Problem Solving

OBJECTIVES **1** Solve application problems involving arithmetic sequences

2 Solve application problems involving geometric sequences

In the previous two sections, many of the exercises fell into one of the following four categories:

1. Find the nth term of an arithmetic sequence:

$$a_n = a_1 + (n-1)d$$

2. Find the sum of the first n terms of an arithmetic sequence:

$$S_n = \frac{n(a_1 + a_n)}{2}$$

3. Find the nth term of a geometric sequence:

$$a_n = a_1 r^{n-1}$$

4. Find the sum of the first n terms of a geometric sequence:

$$S_n = \frac{a_1 r^n - a_1}{r - 1}$$

In this section we want to use this knowledge of arithmetic sequences and geometric sequences to expand our problem-solving capabilities. Let's begin by restating some old problem-solving suggestions that continue to apply here; we will also consider some other suggestions that are directly related to problems that involve sequences of numbers. (We will indicate the new suggestions with an asterisk.)

Suggestions for Solving Word Problems

1. Read the problem carefully and make certain that you understand the meanings of all the words. Be especially alert for any technical terms used in the statement of the problem.

2. Read the problem a second time (perhaps even a third time) to get an overview of the situation being described and to determine the known facts, as well as what you are to find.

3. Sketch a figure, diagram, or chart that might be helpful in analyzing the problem.

*4. Write down the first few terms of the sequence to describe what is taking place in the problem. Be sure that you understand, term by term, what the sequence represents in the problem.

*5. Determine whether the sequence is arithmetic or geometric.

*6. Determine whether the problem is asking for a specific term of the sequence or for the sum of a certain number of terms.

7. Carry out the necessary calculations and check your answer for reasonableness.

As we work out some examples, these suggestions will become more meaningful.

Classroom Example
Don started to work in 2000 at an annual salary of $43,600. He received a $1744 raise each year. What was his annual salary in 2009?

EXAMPLE 1

Domenica started to work in 2003 at an annual salary of $32,500. She received a $1200 raise each year. What was her annual salary in 2012?

Solution

The following sequence represents her annual salary beginning in 2003:

32,500,   33,700,   34,900,   36,100,   . . .

This is an arithmetic sequence, with $a_1 = 32{,}500$ and $d = 1200$. Her salary in 2003 is the first term of the sequence, and her salary in 2012 is the tenth term of the sequence. So, using $a_n = a_1 + (n - 1)d$, we obtain the tenth term of the arithmetic sequence:

$$a_{10} = 32{,}500 + (10 - 1)1200 = 32{,}500 + 9(1200) = 43{,}300$$

Her annual salary in 2012 was $43,300.

Classroom Example
An auditorium has 10 seats in the front row, 15 seats in the second row, 20 seats in the third row, and so on, for 18 rows. How many seats are there in the auditorium?

EXAMPLE 2

An auditorium has 20 seats in the front row, 24 seats in the second row, 28 seats in the third row, and so on, for 15 rows. How many seats are there in the auditorium?

Solution

The following sequence represents the number of seats per row, starting with the first row:

$$20, 24, 28, 32, \ldots$$

This is an arithmetic sequence, with $a_1 = 20$ and $d = 4$. Therefore the 15th term, which represents the number of seats in the 15th row, is given by

$$a_{15} = 20 + (15 - 1)4 = 20 + 14(4) = 76$$

The total number of seats in the auditorium is represented by

$$20 + 24 + 28 + \cdots + 76$$

Use the sum formula for an arithmetic sequence to obtain

$$S_{15} = \frac{15}{2}(20 + 76) = 720$$

There are 720 seats in the auditorium.

Classroom Example
Suppose you are given 10 cents the first day of a week, 30 cents the second day, and 90 cents the third day, and then that amount triples each day. How much will you be given on the seventh day? What will the total amount be for the week?

EXAMPLE 3

Suppose that you save 25 cents the first day of a week, 50 cents the second day, and one dollar the third day, and then you continue to double your savings each day. How much will you save on the seventh day? What will be your total savings for the week?

Solution

The following sequence represents your savings per day, expressed in cents:

$$25, 50, 100, \ldots$$

This is a geometric sequence, with $a_1 = 25$ and $r = 2$. Your savings on the seventh day is the seventh term of this sequence. Therefore, using $a_n = a_1 r^{n-1}$, we obtain

$$a_7 = 25(2)^6 = 1600$$

You will save $16 on the seventh day. Your total savings for the seven days is given by

$$25 + 50 + 100 + \cdots + 1600$$

Use the sum formula for a geometric sequence to obtain

$$S_7 = \frac{25(2)^7 - 25}{2 - 1} = \frac{25(2^7 - 1)}{1} = 3175$$

Thus you will save a total of $31.75 for the week.

EXAMPLE 4

A pump is attached to a container for the purpose of creating a vacuum. For each stroke of the pump, $\frac{1}{4}$ of the air that remains in the container is removed. To the nearest tenth of a percent, how much of the air remains in the container after six strokes?

Solution

Let's draw a chart to help with the analysis of this problem.

First stroke:	$\frac{1}{4}$ of the air is removed	$1 - \frac{1}{4} = \frac{3}{4}$ of the air remains
Second stroke:	$\frac{1}{4}\left(\frac{3}{4}\right) = \frac{3}{16}$ of the air is removed	$\frac{3}{4} - \frac{3}{16} = \frac{9}{16}$ of the air remains
Third stroke:	$\frac{1}{4}\left(\frac{9}{16}\right) = \frac{9}{64}$ of the air is removed	$\frac{9}{16} - \frac{9}{64} = \frac{27}{64}$ of the air remains

The diagram suggests two approaches to the problem.

Approach A   The sequence $\frac{1}{4}, \frac{3}{16}, \frac{9}{64}, \ldots$ represents, term by term, the fractional amount of air that is removed with each successive stroke. Therefore, we can find the total amount removed and subtract it from 100%. The sequence is geometric with

$a_1 = \frac{1}{4}$ and $r = \dfrac{\frac{3}{16}}{\frac{1}{4}} = \frac{3}{16} \cdot \frac{4}{1} = \frac{3}{4}$. Using the sum formula $S_n = \dfrac{a_1 - a_1 r^n}{1 - r}$, we obtain

$$S_6 = \frac{\frac{1}{4} - \frac{1}{4}\left(\frac{3}{4}\right)^6}{1 - \frac{3}{4}} = \frac{\frac{1}{4}\left[1 - \left(\frac{3}{4}\right)^6\right]}{\frac{1}{4}}$$

$$= 1 - \frac{729}{4096} = \frac{3367}{4096} = 82.2\%$$

Therefore $100\% - 82.2\% = 17.8\%$ of the air remains after six strokes.

Approach B The sequence

$$\frac{3}{4}, \frac{9}{16}, \frac{27}{64}, \dots$$

represents, term by term, the amount of air that remains in the container after each stroke. Therefore when we find the sixth term of this geometric sequence, we will have the answer to the problem. Because $a_1 = \dfrac{3}{4}$ and $r = \dfrac{3}{4}$, we obtain

$$a_6 = \frac{3}{4}\left(\frac{3}{4}\right)^5 = \left(\frac{3}{4}\right)^6 = \frac{729}{4096} = 17.8\%$$

Therefore 17.8% of the air remains after six strokes. _____ ▪

It will be helpful for you to take another look at the two approaches we used to solve Example 4. Note that in Approach B, finding the sixth term of the sequence produced the answer to the problem without any further calculations. In Approach A, we had to find the sum of six terms of the sequence and then subtract that amount from 100%. As we solve problems that involve sequences, we must understand what each particular sequence represents on a term-by-term basis.

Problem Set 9.3

Use your knowledge of arithmetic sequences and geometric sequences to help solve Problems 1–28. (Objectives 1 and 2)

1. A man started to work in 1992 at an annual salary of $19,500. He received a $1700 raise each year. How much was his annual salary in 2012?

2. A woman started to work in 1997 at an annual salary of $23,400. She received a $1200 raise each year. How much was her annual salary in 2012?

3. State University had an enrollment of 15,600 students in 1995. Each year the enrollment increased by 1050 students. What was the enrollment in 2010?

4. Math University had an enrollment of 12,800 students in 2005. Each year the enrollment decreased by 75 students. What was the enrollment in 2012?

5. The enrollment at Online University is predicted to increase at the rate of 10% per year. If the enrollment

for 2008 was 5000 students, find the predicted enrollment for 2012. Express your answer to the nearest whole number.

6. If you pay $22,000 for a car and it depreciates 20% per year, how much will it be worth in 5 years? Express your answer to the nearest dollar.

7. A tank contains 16,000 liters of water. Each day one-half of the water in the tank is removed and not replaced. How much water remains in the tank at the end of 7 days?

8. If the price of a pound of coffee is $6.20, and the projected rate of inflation is 5% per year, how much per pound will coffee cost in 5 years? Express your answer to the nearest cent.

9. A tank contains 5832 gallons of water. Each day one-third of the water in the tank is removed and not replaced. How much water remains in the tank at the end of 6 days?

10. A fungus culture growing under controlled conditions doubles in size each day. How many units will the culture contain after 7 days if it originally contains 4 units?

11. Sue is saving quarters. She saves 1 quarter the first day, 2 quarters the second day, 3 quarters the third day, and so on for 30 days. How much money will she have saved in 30 days?

12. Suppose you save a penny the first day of a month, 2 cents the second day, 3 cents the third day, and so on for 31 days. What will be your total savings for the 31 days?

13. Suppose you save a penny the first day of a month, 2 cents the second day, 4 cents the third day, and continue to double your savings each day. How much will you save on the 15th day of the month? How much will your total savings be for the 15 days?

14. Eric saved a nickel the first day of a month, a dime the second day, and 20 cents the third day and then continued to double his daily savings each day for 14 days. What were his daily savings on the 14th day? What were his total savings for the 14 days?

15. An object falling from rest in a vacuum falls approximately 16 feet the first second, 48 feet the second second, 80 feet the third second, 112 feet the fourth second, and so on. How far will it fall in 11 seconds?

16. A raffle is organized so that the amount paid for each ticket is determined by the number on the ticket. The tickets are numbered with the consecutive odd whole numbers 1, 3, 5, 7, ... Each contestant pays as many cents as the number on the ticket drawn. How much money will the raffle take in if 1000 tickets are sold?

17. Suppose an element has a half-life of 4 hours. This means that if n grams of it exist at a specific time, then only $\frac{1}{2}n$ grams remain 4 hours later. If at a

particular moment we have 60 grams of the element, how many grams of it will remain 24 hours later?

18. Suppose an element has a half-life of 3 hours. (See Problem 17 for a definition of half-life.) If at a particular moment we have 768 grams of the element, how many grams of it will remain 24 hours later?

19. A rubber ball is dropped from a height of 1458 feet, and at each bounce it rebounds one-third of the height from which it last fell. How far has the ball traveled by the time it strikes the ground for the sixth time?

20. A rubber ball is dropped from a height of 100 feet, and at each bounce it rebounds one-half of the height from which it last fell. What distance has the ball traveled up to the instant it hits the ground for the eighth time?

21. A pile of logs has 25 logs in the bottom layer, 24 logs in the next layer, 23 logs in the next layer, and so on, until the top layer has 1 log. How many logs are in the pile?

22. A well driller charges $9.00 per foot for the first 10 feet, $9.10 per foot for the next 10 feet, $9.20 per foot for the next 10 feet, and so on, at a price increase of $0.10 per foot for succeeding intervals of 10 feet. How much does it cost to drill a well to a depth of 150 feet?

23. A pump is attached to a container for the purpose of creating a vacuum. For each stroke of the pump, one-third of the air remaining in the container is removed. To the nearest tenth of a percent, how much of the air remains in the container after seven strokes?

24. Suppose that in Problem 23, each stroke of the pump removes one-half of the air remaining in the container. What fractional part of the air has been removed after six strokes?

25. A tank contains 20 gallons of water. One-half of the water is removed and replaced with antifreeze. Then one-half of this mixture is removed and replaced with antifreeze. This process is continued eight times. How much water remains in the tank after the eighth replacement process?

26. The radiator of a truck contains 10 gallons of water. Suppose we remove 1 gallon of water and replace it with antifreeze. Then we remove 1 gallon of this mixture and replace it with antifreeze. This process is carried out seven times. To the nearest tenth of a gallon, how much antifreeze is in the final mixture?

Thoughts Into Words

27. Your friend solves Problem 6 as follows: If the car depreciates 20% per year, then at the end of 5 years it will have depreciated 100% and be worth zero dollars. How would you convince him that his reasoning is incorrect?

28. A contractor wants you to clear some land for a housing project. He anticipates that it will take 20 working days to do the job. He offers to pay you one of two ways: (1) a fixed amount of $3000 or (2) a penny the first day, 2 cents the second day, 4 cents the third day, and so on, doubling your daily wages each day for the 20 days. Which offer should you take and why?

9.4 Mathematical Induction

> **OBJECTIVE** **1** Use mathematical induction to prove mathematical statements

Is $2^n > n$ for all positive integer values of n? In an attempt to answer this question, we might proceed as follows:

If $n = 1$, then $2^n > n$ becomes $2^1 > 1$, a true statement.

If $n = 2$, then $2^n > n$ becomes $2^2 > 2$, a true statement.

If $n = 3$, then $2^n > n$ becomes $2^3 > 3$, a true statement.

We can continue in this way as long as we want, but obviously we can never show in this manner that $2^n > n$ for *every* positive integer n. However, we do have a form of proof, called **proof by mathematical induction**, that can be used to verify the truth of many mathematical statements involving positive integers. This form of proof is based on the following principle.

> ### Principle of Mathematical Induction
>
> Let P_n be a statement in terms of n, where n is a positive integer. If
>
> 1. P_1 is true, and
> 2. the truth of P_k implies the truth of P_{k+1} for every positive integer k,
>
> then P_n is true for every positive integer n.

The principle of mathematical induction, a proof that some statement is true for all positive integers, consists of two parts. First, we must show that the statement is true for the positive integer 1. Second, we must show that if the statement is true for some positive integer, then it follows that it is also true for the next positive integer. Let's illustrate what this means.

Classroom Example
Prove that $3^n > n$ for all positive values of n.

EXAMPLE 1   Prove that $2^n > n$ for all positive integer values of n.

Proof

Part 1   If $n = 1$, then $2^n > n$ becomes $2^1 > 1$, which is a true statement.

Part 2   We must prove that if $2^k > k$, then $2^{k+1} > k + 1$ for all positive integer values of k. In other words, we should be able to start with $2^k > k$ and from that deduce $2^{k+1} > k + 1$. This can be done as follows:

$$2^k > k$$
$$2(2^k) > 2(k) \qquad \text{Multiply both sides by 2}$$
$$2^{k+1} > 2k$$

We know that $k \geq 1$ because we are working with positive integers. Therefore

$$k + k \geq k + 1 \qquad \text{Add } k \text{ to both sides}$$
$$2k \geq k + 1$$

Because $2^{k+1} > 2k$ and $2k \geq k + 1$, by the transitive property we conclude that

$$2^{k+1} > k + 1$$

Therefore, using parts 1 and 2, we proved that $2^n > n$ for *all* positive integers.   ■

It will be helpful for you to look back over the proof in Example 1. Note that in part 1, we established that $2^n > n$ is true for $n = 1$. Then, in part 2, we established that if $2^n > n$ is true for any positive integer, then it must be true for the next consecutive positive integer. Therefore, because $2^n > n$ is true for $n = 1$, it must be true for $n = 2$. Likewise, if $2^n > n$ is true for $n = 2$, then it must be true for $n = 3$, and so on, for *all* positive integers.

We can depict proof by mathematical induction with dominoes. Suppose that in Figure 9.1, we have infinitely many dominoes lined up. If we can push the first domino over (part 1 of a mathematical induction proof), and if the dominoes are spaced so that each time one falls over, it causes the next one to fall over (part 2 of a mathematical induction proof), then by pushing the first one over we will cause a chain reaction that will topple all of the dominoes (Figure 9.2).

....

....

Figure 9.1

Figure 9.2

Recall that in the first three sections of this chapter, we used a_n to represent the nth term of a sequence and S_n to represent the sum of the first n terms of a sequence. For example, if $a_n = 2n$, then the first three terms of the sequence are $a_1 = 2(1) = 2$, $a_2 = 2(2) = 4$, and $a_3 = 2(3) = 6$. Furthermore, the kth term is $a_k = 2(k) = 2k$, and the $(k + 1)$ term is $a_{k+1} = 2(k + 1) = 2k + 2$. Relative to this same sequence, we can state that $S_1 = 2$, $S_2 = 2 + 4 = 6$, and $S_3 = 2 + 4 + 6 = 12$.

There are numerous sum formulas for sequences that can be verified by mathematical induction. For such proofs, the following property of sequences is used:

$$S_{k+1} = S_k + a_{k+1}$$

This property states that *the sum of the first $k + 1$ terms is equal to the sum of the first k terms plus the $(k + 1)$ term.* Let's see how this can be used in a specific example.

Classroom Example
Prove $S_n = 2n(n + 1)$ for the sequence $a_n = 4n$, if n is any positive integer.

EXAMPLE 2

Prove that $S_n = n(n + 1)$ for the sequence $a_n = 2n$, when n is any positive integer.

Proof

Part 1 If $n = 1$, then $S_1 = 1(1 + 1) = 2$, and 2 is the first term of the sequence $a_n = 2n$, so $S_1 = a_1 = 2$.

Part 2 Now we need to prove that if $S_k = k(k + 1)$, then $S_{k+1} = (k + 1)(k + 2)$. Using the property $S_{k+1} = S_k + a_{k+1}$, we can proceed as follows:

$$S_{k+1} = S_k + a_{k+1}$$
$$= k(k + 1) + 2(k + 1)$$
$$= (k + 1)(k + 2)$$

Therefore, using parts 1 and 2, we proved that $S_n = n(n + 1)$ will yield the correct sum for any number of terms of the sequence $a_n = 2n$. ∎

Classroom Example
Prove that $S_n = \dfrac{n(3n + 5)}{2}$ for the sequence $a_n = 3n + 1$, if n is any positive integer.

EXAMPLE 3

Prove that $S_n = 5n(n + 1)/2$ for the sequence $a_n = 5n$, when n is any positive integer.

Proof

Part 1 Because $S_1 = 5(1)(1 + 1)/2 = 5$, and 5 is the first term of the sequence $a_n = 5n$, we have $S_1 = a_1 = 5$.

Part 2 We need to prove that if $S_k = 5k(k + 1)/2$, then $S_{k+1} = \dfrac{5(k + 1)(k + 2)}{2}$.

$$S_{k+1} = S_k + a_{k+1}$$
$$= \frac{5k(k + 1)}{2} + 5(k + 1)$$
$$= \frac{5k(k + 1)}{2} + 5k + 5$$
$$= \frac{5k(k + 1) + 2(5k + 5)}{2}$$

$$= \frac{5k^2 + 5k + 10k + 10}{2}$$

$$= \frac{5k^2 + 15k + 10}{2}$$

$$= \frac{5(k^2 + 3k + 2)}{2}$$

$$= \frac{5(k + 1)(k + 2)}{2}$$

Therefore, using parts 1 and 2, we proved that $S_n = 5n(n + 1)/2$ yields the correct sum for any number of terms of the sequence $a_n = 5n$.

Classroom Example

Prove that $S_n = \dfrac{3^n - 1}{2}$ for the sequence $a_n = 3^{n-1}$, if n is any positive integer.

EXAMPLE 4

Prove that $S_n = (4^n - 1)/3$ for the sequence $a_n = 4^{n-1}$, where n is any positive integer.

Proof

Part 1 Because $S_1 = (4^1 - 1)/3 = 1$, and 1 is the first term of the sequence $a_n = 4^{n-1}$, we have $S_1 = a_1 = 1$.

Part 2 We need to prove that if $S_k = (4^k - 1)/3$, then $S_{k+1} = (4^{k+1} - 1)/3$:

$$S_{k+1} = S_k + a_{k+1}$$

$$= \frac{4^k - 1}{3} + 4^k$$

$$= \frac{4^k - 1 + 3(4^k)}{3}$$

$$= \frac{4^k + 3(4^k) - 1}{3}$$

$$= \frac{4^k(1 + 3) - 1}{3}$$

$$= \frac{4^k(4) - 1}{3}$$

$$= \frac{4^{k+1} - 1}{3}$$

Therefore, using parts 1 and 2, we proved that $S_n = (4^n - 1)/3$ yields the correct sum for any number of terms of the sequence $a_n = 4^{n-1}$.

As our final example of this section, let's consider a proof by mathematical induction involving the concept of divisibility.

EXAMPLE 5

Prove that for all positive integers n, the number $3^{2n} - 1$ is divisible by 8.

Proof

Part 1   If $n = 1$, then $3^{2n} - 1$ becomes $3^{2(1)} - 1 = 3^2 - 1 = 8$, and of course 8 is divisible by 8.

Part 2   We need to prove that if $3^{2k} - 1$ is divisible by 8, then $3^{2k+2} - 1$ is divisible by 8 for all integer values of k. This can be verified as follows. If $3^{2k} - 1$ is divisible by 8, then for some integer x, we have $3^{2k} - 1 = 8x$. Therefore

$$3^{2k} - 1 = 8x$$
$$3^{2k} = 1 + 8x$$
$$3^2(3^{2k}) = 3^2(1 + 8x) \qquad \text{Multiply both sides by } 3^2$$
$$3^{2k+2} = 9(1 + 8x)$$
$$3^{2k+2} = 9 + 9(8x)$$
$$3^{2k+2} = 1 + 8 + 9(8x) \qquad 9 = 1 + 8$$
$$3^{2k+2} = 1 + 8(1 + 9x) \qquad \text{Apply distributive property to } 8 + 9(8x)$$
$$3^{2k+2} - 1 = 8(1 + 9x)$$

Therefore $3^{2k+2} - 1$ is divisible by 8.

Thus using parts 1 and 2, we proved that $3^{2n} - 1$ is divisible by 8 for all positive integers n.

We conclude this section with a few final comments about proof by mathematical induction. Every mathematical induction proof is a two-part proof, and both parts are absolutely necessary. There can be mathematical statements that hold for one or the other of the two parts but not for both. For example, $(a + b)^n = a^n + b^n$ is true for $n = 1$, but it is false for every positive integer greater than 1. Therefore, if we were to attempt a mathematical induction proof for $(a + b)^n = a^n + b^n$, we could establish part 1 but not part 2. Another example of this type is the statement that $n^2 - n + 41$ produces a prime number for all positive integer values of n. This statement is true for $n = 1, 2, 3, 4, \ldots, 40$, but it is false when $n = 41$ (because $41^2 - 41 + 41 = 41^2$, which is not a prime number).

It is also possible that part 2 of a mathematical induction proof can be established but not part 1. For example, consider the sequence $a_n = n$ and the sum formula $S_n = (n + 3)(n - 2)/2$. If $n = 1$, then $a_1 = 1$ but $S_1 = (4)(-1)/2 = -2$, so part 1 does not hold. However, it is possible to show that $S_k = (k + 3)(k - 2)/2$ implies $S_{k+1} = (k + 4)(k - 1)/2$. We will leave the details of this for you to do.

Finally, it is important to realize that some mathematical statements are true for all positive integers greater than some fixed positive integer other than 1. (In Figure 9.1, this implies that we cannot knock down the first four dominoes; however, we can knock down the fifth domino and every one thereafter.) For example, we can prove by mathematical induction that $2^n > n^2$ for all positive integers $n > 4$. It requires a slight variation in the statement of the principle of mathematical induction. We will not concern ourselves with such problems in this text, but we want you to be aware of their existence.

Concept Quiz 9.4

For Problems 1–4, answer true or false.

1. Mathematical induction is used to prove mathematical statements involving positive integers.
2. A proof by mathematical induction consists of two parts.
3. Because $(a + b)^n = a^n + b^n$ is true for $n = 1$, it is true for all positive integer values of n.
4. To prove a mathematical statement involving positive integers by mathematical induction, the statement must be true for $n = 1$.

Problem Set 9.4

For Problems 1–10, use mathematical induction to prove each of the sum formulas for the indicated sequences. They are to hold for all positive integers n. (Objective 1)

1. $S_n = \dfrac{n(n + 1)}{2}$ for $a_n = n$

2. $S_n = n^2$ for $a_n = 2n - 1$

3. $S_n = \dfrac{n(3n + 1)}{2}$ for $a_n = 3n - 1$

4. $S_n = \dfrac{n(5n + 9)}{2}$ for $a_n = 5n + 2$

5. $S_n = 2(2^n - 1)$ for $a_n = 2^n$

6. $S_n = \dfrac{3(3^n - 1)}{2}$ for $a_n = 3^n$

7. $S_n = \dfrac{n(n + 1)(2n + 1)}{6}$ for $a_n = n^2$

8. $S_n = \dfrac{n^2(n + 1)^2}{4}$ for $a_n = n^3$

9. $S_n = \dfrac{n}{n + 1}$ for $a_n = \dfrac{1}{n(n + 1)}$

10. $S_n = \dfrac{n(n + 1)(n + 2)}{3}$ for $a_n = n(n + 1)$

In Problems 11–20, use mathematical induction to prove that each statement is true for all positive integers n.

11. $3^n \geq 2n + 1$
12. $4^n \geq 4n$
13. $n^2 \geq n$
14. $2^n \geq n + 1$
15. $4^n - 1$ is divisible by 3
16. $5^n - 1$ is divisible by 4
17. $6^n - 1$ is divisible by 5
18. $9^n - 1$ is divisible by 4
19. $n^2 + n$ is divisible by 2
20. $n^2 - n$ is divisible by 2

Thoughts Into Words

21. How would you describe proof by mathematical induction?

22. Compare inductive reasoning to prove by mathematical induction.

Answers to the Concept Quiz

1. True   2. True   3. False   4. False

OBJECTIVE	SUMMARY	EXAMPLE
Write the terms of a sequence. (Section 9.1/Objective 1)	An infinite sequence is a function with a domain that is the set of positive integers. When the letter a represents the function, the functional value of a at n is written as a_n. The expression a_n, which defines the function, is called the general term.	Find the first four terms of the sequence when $a_n = 2n + 7$. **Solution** $a_1 = 2(1) + 7 = 9$ $a_2 = 2(2) + 7 = 11$ $a_3 = 2(3) + 7 = 13$ $a_4 = 2(4) + 7 = 15$ The first four terms are 9, 11, 13, and 15.
Find the general term for an arithmetic sequence. (Section 9.1/Objective 2)	An arithmetic sequence is a sequence that has a common difference between successive terms. The general term of an arithmetic sequence is given by the formula $a_n = a_1 + (n - 1)d$ in which a_1 is the first term, n is the number of terms, and d is the common difference.	Find the general term of the arithmetic sequence 8, 11, 14, 17, ... **Solution** The common difference is $11 - 8 = 3$ and the first term is 8. Substitute these values into $a_n = a_1 + (n - 1)d$ and simplify: $a_n = 8 + (n - 1)(3)$ $\quad = 8 + 3n - 3$ $\quad = 3n + 5$
Find a specific term for an arithmetic sequence. (Section 9.1/Objective 3)	The formula $a_n = a_1 + (n - 1)d$ can be used to find specific terms of an arithmetic sequence.	Find the 13th term of the arithmetic sequence 56, 52, 48, 44, ... **Solution** The common difference is $52 - 56 = -4$, the first term is 56 and $n = 13$. Substitute these values into $a_n = a_1 + (n - 1)d$ and simplify: $a_{13} = 56 + (13 - 1)(-4)$ $\quad = 8$
Find the sum of the terms of an arithmetic sequence. (Section 9.1/Objective 4)	The sum of the first n terms of an arithmetic sequence is given by the formula $S_n = \dfrac{n(a_1 + a_n)}{2}$. The formula can be interpreted as the average of the first and last terms times the number of terms.	Find the sum of the first 60 terms of the sequence when $a_n = 3n - 2$. **Solution** To use the sum formula we need to know the value of the first term, the last term, and the number of terms. The number of terms is 60, $a_1 = 1$, and $a_n = 178$. $S_{60} = \dfrac{60(1 + 178)}{2} = 5370$

OBJECTIVE	SUMMARY	EXAMPLE
Determine the sum indicated by summation notation. (Section 9.1/Objective 5)	The capital Greek letter sigma, $\sum$, is used as a summation symbol. The letter i is usually used as the index of summation; the letter i takes on all integer values from the lower limit to the upper limit, inclusively.	Find the sum $\sum_{i=3}^{7} i^2$. **Solution** The indicated sum means $$\sum_{i=3}^{7} i^2 = 3^2 + 4^2 + 5^2 + 6^2 + 7^2 = 135$$
Find the general term for a geometric sequence. (Section 9.2/Objective 1)	A geometric sequence has a common ratio between successive terms *after the first term*. The common ratio can be found by dividing any term (other than the first term) by the preceding term. The general term of a geometric sequence is given by the formula $a_n = a_1 r^{n-1}$ where a_1 is the first term, n is the number of terms, and r is the common ratio.	Find the general term for the geometric sequence $-2, 4, -8, 16, \ldots$. **Solution** The common ratio, r, is $\frac{4}{-2} = -2$, and the first term, a_1, is -2. Substituting these values into $a_n = a_1 r^{n-1}$, we obtain $a_n = -2(-2)^{n-1} = (-2)^n$.
Find a specific term for a geometric sequence. (Section 9.2/Objective 2)	The formula $a_n = a_1 r^{n-1}$ can be used to find specific terms of a geometric sequence.	Find the sixth term of the geometric sequence $24, 36, 54, 81, \ldots$. **Solution** The common ratio is $\frac{36}{24} = \frac{3}{2}$. Using $a_n = a_1 r^{n-1}$, we obtain $$a_6 = 24\left(\frac{3}{2}\right)^{6-1}$$ $$= 24\left(\frac{3}{2}\right)^5$$ $$= 182\frac{1}{4}$$ $$= \frac{729}{4}$$

(continued)

OBJECTIVE	SUMMARY	EXAMPLE
Determine the sum of the terms of a geometric sequence. (Section 9.2/Objective 3)	The sum of the first n terms of a geometric sequence with a first term a_1 and a common ratio of r is given by $$S_n = \frac{a_1 r^n - a_1}{r - 1}, r \neq 1$$	Find the sum of the first ten terms of the geometric sequence $-10, 30, -90, 270, \ldots$. **Solution** From the given we can determine that $n = 10$, $r = -3$, and $a_1 = -10$. Substituting these values into the sum formula yields $$S_{10} = \frac{(-10)(-3)^{10} - (-10)}{(-3) - 1} = 147{,}620$$
Determine the sum of an infinite geometric sequence. (Section 9.2/Objective 4)	For values of r such that $-1 < r < 1$, the sum of an infinite geometric sequence can be determined.	Find the sum of the infinite geometric sequence $-9, 6, -4, \frac{8}{3}, -\frac{16}{9}, \ldots$. **Solution** $$a_1 = -9 \text{ and } r = \frac{6}{-9} = -\frac{2}{3}$$ $$S_\infty = \frac{a_1}{1 - r}$$ $$= \frac{-9}{1 - \left(-\frac{2}{3}\right)}$$ $$= \frac{-9}{\frac{5}{3}} = -\frac{27}{5}$$
Change a repeating decimal into $\frac{a}{b}$ form. (Section 9.2/Objective 5)	Repeating decimals (such as $0.\overline{4}$) can be changed to $\frac{a}{b}$ form, where a and b are integers and $b \neq 0$, by treating them as the sum of an infinite geometric sequence. For example, the repeating decimal $0.\overline{4}$ can be written $0.4 + 0.04 + 0.004 + 0.0004 + \cdots$	Change $0.\overline{09}$ to reduced $\frac{a}{b}$ form, in which a and b are integers and $b \neq 0$. **Solution** Write $0.\overline{09}$ as the indicated sum of an infinite geometric sequence: $0.09 + 0.0009 + 0.000009 + \cdots$ Using $$S_\infty = \frac{a_1}{1 - r} = \frac{0.09}{1 - 0.01} = \frac{0.09}{0.99} = \frac{1}{11}$$

OBJECTIVE	SUMMARY	EXAMPLE
Solve application problems involving sequences. (Section 9.3/Objectives 1 and 2)	Many of the problem-solving suggestions offered earlier in this text are still appropriate when we are solving problems that deal with sequences. However, there are also some special suggestions pertaining to sequence problems. 1. Write down the first few terms of the sequence to describe what is taking place in the problem. Drawing a picture or diagram may help with this step. 2. Be sure that you understand, term by term, what the sequence represents in the problem. 3. Determine whether the sequence is arithmetic or geometric. 4. Determine whether the problem is asking for a specific term or for the sum of a certain number of terms.	Mary Ann received an email message about a computer virus requesting her to forward the email to three people. Assuming Mary Ann and all the recipients did forward the message, how many emails in total were sent if the emails were forwarded ten times? **Solution** This problem can be represented by the sequence 3, 9, 27, 81, . . . where $a_1 = 3$ and $r = 3$. The sequence is a geometric sequence. Use the formula $S_n = \dfrac{a_1 r^n - a_1}{r - 1}$ to find the sum of the first ten terms: $$S_{10} = \frac{3(3)^{10} - 3}{3 - 1} = \frac{177,144}{2} = 88,572$$ A total of 88,572 emails were sent.
Use mathematical induction to prove mathematical statements. (Section 9.4/Objective 1)	Proof by mathematical induction relies on the following principle of induction: Let P_n be a statement in terms of n, where n is a positive integer. If 1. P_1 is true, and 2. the truth of P_k implies the truth of P_{k+1} for every positive integer k, then P_n is true for every positive integer n.	See Section 9.4 for examples of proof by induction.

Chapter 9   Review Problem Set

For Problems 1–10, find the general term (the nth term) for each sequence. These problems include both arithmetic sequences and geometric sequences.

1. $3, 9, 15, 21, \ldots$

2. $\dfrac{1}{3}, 1, 3, 9, \ldots$

3. $10, 20, 40, 80, \ldots$

4. $5, 2, -1, -4, \ldots$

5. $-5, -3, -1, 1, \ldots$

6. $9, 3, 1, \dfrac{1}{3}, \ldots$

7. $-1, 2, -4, 8, \ldots$

8. $12, 15, 18, 21, \ldots$

9. $\dfrac{2}{3}, 1, \dfrac{4}{3}, \dfrac{5}{3}, \ldots$

10. $1, 4, 16, 64, \ldots$

For Problems 11–16, find the required term of each of the sequences.

11. The 19th term of $1, 5, 9, 13, \ldots$

12. The 28th term of $-2, 2, 6, 10, \ldots$

13. The 9th term of $8, 4, 2, 1, \ldots$

14. The 8th term of $\dfrac{243}{32}, \dfrac{81}{16}, \dfrac{27}{8}, \dfrac{9}{4}, \ldots$

15. The 34th term of $7, 4, 1, -2, \ldots$

16. The 10th term of $-32, 16, -8, 4, \ldots$

For Problems 17–29, solve each problem.

17. If the 5th term of an arithmetic sequence is -19 and the 8th term is -34, find the common difference of the sequence.

18. If the 8th term of an arithmetic sequence is 37 and the 13th term is 57, find the 20th term.

19. Find the first term of a geometric sequence if the third term is 5 and the sixth term is 135.

20. Find the common ratio of a geometric sequence if the second term is $\dfrac{1}{2}$ and the sixth term is 8.

21. Find the sum of the first nine terms of the sequence $81, 27, 9, 3, \ldots$

22. Find the sum of the first 70 terms of the sequence $-3, 0, 3, 6, \ldots$

23. Find the sum of the first 75 terms of the sequence $5, 1, -3, -7, \ldots$

24. Find the sum of the first ten terms of the sequence if $a_n = 2^{5-n}$.

25. Find the sum of the first 95 terms of the sequence if $a_n = 7n + 1$.

26. Find the sum $5 + 7 + 9 + \cdots + 137$.

27. Find the sum $64 + 16 + 4 + \cdots + \dfrac{1}{64}$.

28. Find the sum of all even numbers between 8 and 384, inclusive.

29. Find the sum of all multiples of 3 between 27 and 276, inclusive.

For Problems 30–33, find each indicated sum.

30. $\displaystyle\sum_{i=1}^{45}(-2i + 5)$

31. $\displaystyle\sum_{i=1}^{5} i^3$

32. $\displaystyle\sum_{i=1}^{8} 2^{8-i}$

33. $\displaystyle\sum_{i=4}^{75}(3i - 4)$

For Problems 34–36, solve each problem.

34. Find the sum of the infinite geometric sequence $64, 16, 4, 1, \ldots$

35. Change $0.\overline{36}$ to reduced a/b form, when a and b are integers and $b \neq 0$.

36. Change $0.4\overline{5}$ to reduced a/b form, when a and b are integers and $b \neq 0$.

Solve each of Problems 37–40 by using your knowledge of arithmetic sequences and geometric sequences.

37. Suppose that your savings account contains \$3750 at the beginning of a year. If you withdraw \$250 per month from the account, how much will it contain at the end of the year?

38. Sonya decides to start saving dimes. She plans to save one dime the first day of April, two dimes the second day, three dimes the third day, four dimes the fourth day, and so on for the 30 days of April. How much money will she save in April?

39. Nancy decides to start saving dimes. She plans to save one dime the first day of April, two dimes the second day, four dimes the third day, eight dimes the fourth day, and so on for the first 15 days of April. How much will she save in 15 days?

40. A tank contains 61,440 gallons of water. Each day one-fourth of the water is drained out. How much water remains in the tank at the end of 6 days?

For Problems 41–43, show a mathematical induction proof.

41. Prove that $5^n > 5n - 1$ for all positive integer values of n.

42. Prove that $n^3 - n + 3$ is divisible by 3 for all positive integer values of n.

43. Prove that
$$S_n = \frac{n(n + 3)}{4(n + 1)(n + 2)}$$

is the sum formula for the sequence
$$a_n = \frac{1}{n(n + 1)(n + 2)}$$

where n is any positive integer.

1. Find the 15th term of the sequence for which $a_n = -n^2 - 1$.

2. Find the fifth term of the sequence for which $a_n = 3(2)^{n-1}$.

3. Find the general term of the sequence $-3, -8, -13, -18, \ldots$.

4. Find the general term of the sequence
$5, \dfrac{5}{2}, \dfrac{5}{4}, \dfrac{5}{8}, \ldots$.

5. Find the general term of the sequence $10, 16, 22, 28, \ldots$.

6. Find the seventh term of the sequence $8, 12, 18, 27, \ldots$.

7. Find the 75th term of the sequence $1, 4, 7, 10, \ldots$.

8. Find the number of terms in the sequence $7, 11, 15, \ldots, 243$.

9. Find the sum of the first 40 terms of the sequence $1, 4, 7, 10, \ldots$.

10. Find the sum of the first eight terms of the sequence $3, 6, 12, 24, \ldots$.

11. Find the sum of the first 45 terms of the sequence for which $a_n = 7n - 2$.

12. Find the sum of the first ten terms of the sequence for which $a_n = 3(2)^n$.

13. Find the sum of the first 150 positive even whole numbers.

14. Find the sum of the odd whole numbers between 11 and 193, inclusive.

15. Find the indicated sum $\displaystyle\sum_{i=1}^{50} (3i + 5)$.

16. Find the indicated sum $\displaystyle\sum_{i=1}^{10} (-2)^{i-1}$.

17. Find the sum of the infinite geometric sequence
$3, \dfrac{3}{2}, \dfrac{3}{4}, \dfrac{3}{8}, \ldots$.

18. Find the sum of the infinite geometric sequence for which $a_n = 2\left(\dfrac{1}{3}\right)^{n+1}$.

19. Change $0.\overline{18}$ to reduced a/b form, if a and b are integers and $b \neq 0$.

20. Change $0.2\overline{6}$ to reduced a/b form, if a and b are integers and $b \neq 0$.

For Problems 21–23, solve each problem.

21. A tank contains 49,152 liters of gasoline. Each day, three-fourths of the gasoline remaining in the tank is pumped out and not replaced. How much gasoline remains in the tank at the end of 7 days?

22. Suppose that you save a dime the first day of a month, $0.20 the second day, and $0.40 the third day and that you continue to double your savings each day for 14 days. Find the total amount that you will save at the end of 14 days.

23. A woman invests $350 at 6% simple interest at the beginning of each year for a period of 10 years. Find the total accumulated value of all the investments at the end of the 10-year period.

For Problems 24 and 25, show a mathematical induction proof.

24. $S_n = \dfrac{n(3n - 1)}{2}$ for $a_n = 3n - 2$

25. $9^n - 1$ is divisible by 8 for all positive integer values for n.

APPENDIX

A   Binomial Theorem

In Chapter 0, when multiplying polynomials, we developed patterns for squaring and cubing binomials. Now we want to develop a general pattern that can be used to raise a binomial to any positive integral power. Let's begin by looking at some specific expansions that can be verified by direct multiplication. (Note that the patterns for squaring and cubing a binomial are a part of this list.)

$$(x + y)^0 = 1$$
$$(x + y)^1 = x + y$$
$$(x + y)^2 = x^2 + 2xy + y^2$$
$$(x + y)^3 = x^3 + 3x^2y + 3xy^2 + y^3$$
$$(x + y)^4 = x^4 + 4x^3y + 6x^2y^2 + 4xy^3 + y^4$$
$$(x + y)^5 = x^5 + 5x^4y + 10x^3y^2 + 10x^2y^3 + 5xy^4 + y^5$$

First, note the pattern of the exponents for x and y on a term-by-term basis. The exponents of x begin with the exponent of the binomial and decrease by 1, term by term, until the last term has x^0, which is 1. The exponents of y begin with zero ($y^0 = 1$) and increase by 1, term by term, until the last term contains y to the power of the binomial. In other words, the variables in the expansion of $(x + y)^n$ have the following pattern.

$$x^n, x^{n-1}y, x^{n-2}y^2, x^{n-3}y^3, \ldots, xy^{n-1}, y^n$$

Note that for each term, the sum of the exponents of x and y is n.

Now let's look for a pattern for the coefficients by examining specifically the expansion of $(x + y)^5$.

$$(x + y)^5 = x^5 + 5x^4y^1 + 10x^3y^2 + 10x^2y^3 + 5x^1y^4 + 1y^5$$

$$\uparrow \qquad \uparrow \qquad \uparrow \qquad \uparrow \qquad \uparrow$$
$$C(5, 1) \quad C(5, 2) \quad C(5, 3) \quad C(5, 4) \quad C(5, 5)$$

As indicated by the arrows, the coefficients are numbers that arise as different-sized combinations of five things. To see why this happens, consider the coefficient for the term containing x^3y^2. The two y's (for y^2) come from two of the factors of $(x + y)$, and therefore the three x's (for x^3) must come from the other three factors of $(x + y)$. In other words, the coefficient is $C(5, 2)$.

We can now state a general expansion formula for $(x + y)^n$; this formula is often called the **binomial theorem.** But before stating it, let's make a small switch in notation. Instead of $C(n, r)$, we shall write $\binom{n}{r}$, which will prove to be a little more convenient at this time. The symbol $\binom{n}{r}$, still refers to the number of combinations of n things taken r at a time, but in this context, it is called a **binomial coefficient.**

719

> ## Binomial Theorem
>
> For any binomial $(x + y)$ and any natural number n,
>
> $$(x + y)^n = x^n + \binom{n}{1}x^{n-1}y + \binom{n}{2}x^{n-2}y^2 + \cdots + \binom{n}{n}y^n$$

The binomial theorem can be proved by mathematical induction, but we will not do that in this text. Instead, we'll consider a few examples that put the binomial theorem to work.

EXAMPLE 1   Expand $(x + y)^7$.

Solution

$$(x + y)^7 = x^7 + \binom{7}{1}x^6y + \binom{7}{2}x^5y^2 + \binom{7}{3}x^4y^3 + \binom{7}{4}x^3y^4$$

$$+ \binom{7}{5}x^2y^5 + \binom{7}{6}xy^6 + \binom{7}{7}y^7$$

$$= x^7 + 7x^6y + 21x^5y^2 + 35x^4y^3 + 35x^3y^4 + 21x^2y^5 + 7xy^6 + y^7$$

EXAMPLE 2   Expand $(x - y)^5$.

Solution

We shall treat $(x - y)^5$ as $[x + (-y)]^5$:

$$[x + (-y)]^5 = x^5 + \binom{5}{1}x^4(-y) + \binom{5}{2}x^3(-y)^2 + \binom{5}{3}x^2(-y)^3$$

$$+ \binom{5}{4}x(-y)^4 + \binom{5}{5}(-y)^5$$

$$= x^5 - 5x^4y + 10x^3y^2 - 10x^2y^3 + 5xy^4 - y^5$$

EXAMPLE 3   Expand $(2a + 3b)^4$.

Solution

Let $x = 2a$ and $y = 3b$ in the binomial theorem:

$$(2a + 3b)^4 = (2a)^4 + \binom{4}{1}(2a)^3(3b) + \binom{4}{2}(2a)^2(3b)^2$$

$$+ \binom{4}{3}(2a)(3b)^3 + \binom{4}{4}(3b)^4$$

$$= 16a^4 + 96a^3b + 216a^2b^2 + 216ab^3 + 81b^4 \quad \blacksquare$$

EXAMPLE 4   Expand $\left(a + \dfrac{1}{n}\right)^5$.

Solution

$$\left(a + \frac{1}{n}\right)^5 = a^5 + \binom{5}{1}a^4\left(\frac{1}{n}\right) + \binom{5}{2}a^3\left(\frac{1}{n}\right)^2 + \binom{5}{3}a^2\left(\frac{1}{n}\right)^3 + \binom{5}{4}a\left(\frac{1}{n}\right)^4 + \binom{5}{5}\left(\frac{1}{n}\right)^5$$

$$= a^5 + \frac{5a^4}{n} + \frac{10a^3}{n^2} + \frac{10a^2}{n^3} + \frac{5a}{n^4} + \frac{1}{n^5} \quad \blacksquare$$

EXAMPLE 5   Expand $(x^2 - 2y^3)^6$.

Solution

$$[x^2 + (-2y^3)]^6 = (x^2)^6 + \binom{6}{1}(x^2)^5(-2y^3) + \binom{6}{2}(x^2)^4(-2y^3)^2$$

$$+ \binom{6}{3}(x^2)^3(-2y^3)^3 + \binom{6}{4}(x^2)^2(-2y^3)^4$$

$$+ \binom{6}{5}(x^2)(-2y^3)^5 + \binom{6}{6}(-2y^3)^6$$

$$= x^{12} - 12x^{10}y^3 + 60x^8y^6 - 160x^6y^9 + 240x^4y^{12} - 192x^2y^{15} + 64y^{18} \quad \blacksquare$$

Finding Specific Terms

Sometimes it is convenient to be able to write down the specific term of a binomial expansion without writing out the entire expansion. For example, suppose that we want the sixth term of the expansion $(x + y)^{12}$. We can proceed as follows: The sixth term will contain y^5. (Note in the binomial theorem that the *exponent of y is always one less than the number of the term.*) Because the sum of the exponents for x and y must be 12 (the exponent of the binomial), the sixth term will also contain x^7. The coefficient is $\binom{12}{5}$, and the 5 agrees with the exponent of y^5. Therefore the sixth term of $(x + y)^{12}$ is

$$\binom{12}{5}x^7y^5 = 792x^7y^5$$

EXAMPLE 6   Find the fourth term of $(3a + 2b)^7$.

Solution

The fourth term will contain $(2b)^3$, and therefore it will also contain $(3a)^4$. The coefficient is $\binom{7}{3}$. Thus the fourth term is

$$\binom{7}{3}(3a)^4(2b)^3 = (35)(81a^4)(8b^3) = 22{,}680a^4b^3$$

EXAMPLE 7   Find the sixth term of $(4x - y)^9$.

Solution

The sixth term will contain $(-y)^5$, and therefore it will also contain $(4x)^4$. The coefficient is $\binom{9}{5}$. Thus the sixth term is

$$\binom{9}{5}(4x)^4(-y)^5 = (126)(256x^4)(-y^5) = -32{,}256x^4y^5$$

Practice Exercises

For Problems 1–26, expand and simplify each binomial.

1. $(x + y)^8$

2. $(x + y)^9$

3. $(x - y)^6$

4. $(x - y)^4$

5. $(a + 2b)^4$

6. $(3a + b)^4$

7. $(x - 3y)^5$

8. $(2x - y)^6$

9. $(2a - 3b)^4$

10. $(3a - 2b)^5$

11. $(x^2 + y)^5$

12. $(x + y^3)^6$

13. $(2x^2 - y^2)^4$

14. $(3x^2 - 2y^2)^5$

15. $(x + 3)^6$

16. $(x + 2)^7$

17. $(x - 1)^9$

18. $(x - 3)^4$

19. $\left(1 + \dfrac{1}{n}\right)^4$

20. $\left(2 + \dfrac{1}{n}\right)^5$

21. $\left(a - \dfrac{1}{n}\right)^6$

22. $\left(2a - \dfrac{1}{n}\right)^5$

23. $\left(1 + \sqrt{2}\right)^4$

24. $\left(2 + \sqrt{3}\right)^3$

25. $\left(3 - \sqrt{2}\right)^5$

26. $\left(1 - \sqrt{3}\right)^4$

For Problems 27–36, write the first four terms of each expansion.

27. $(x + y)^{12}$

28. $(x + y)^{15}$

29. $(x - y)^{20}$

30. $(a - 2b)^{13}$

31. $(x^2 - 2y^3)^{14}$

32. $(x^3 - 3y^2)^{11}$

33. $\left(a + \dfrac{1}{n}\right)^9$

34. $\left(2 - \dfrac{1}{n}\right)^6$

35. $(-x + 2y)^{10}$

36. $(-a - b)^{14}$

For Problems 37–46, find the specified term for each binomial expansion.

37. The fourth term of $(x + y)^8$

38. The seventh term of $(x + y)^{11}$

39. The fifth term of $(x - y)^9$

40. The fourth term of $(x - 2y)^6$

41. The sixth term of $(3a + b)^7$

42. The third term of $(2x - 5y)^5$

43. The eighth term of $(x^2 + y^3)^{10}$

44. The ninth term of $(a + b^3)^{12}$

45. The seventh term of $\left(1 - \dfrac{1}{n}\right)^{15}$

46. The eighth term of $\left(1 - \dfrac{1}{n}\right)^{13}$

Chapter 0

Problem Set 0.1 (page 16)

1. True   **3.** False   **5.** False   **7.** True
9. False   **11.** $\{46\}$ **13.** $\{0, -14, 46\}$
15. $\{\sqrt{5}, -\sqrt{2}, -\pi\}$ **17.** $\{0, -14\}$ **19.** $\subseteq$
21. $\subseteq$ **23.** $\not\subseteq$ **25.** $\subseteq$ **27.** $\not\subseteq$
29. $\subseteq$ **31.** $\not\subseteq$ **33.** $\{1\}$ **35.** $\{0, 1, 2, 3\}$
37. $\{\ldots, -2, -1, 0, 1\}$ **39.** $\varnothing$ **41.** $\{0, 1, 2\}$
43. a. 18   **c.** 39   **e.** 35
45. Commutative property of multiplication
47. Identity property of multiplication
49. Multiplication property of negative one
51. Distributive property
53. Commutative property of multiplication
55. Distributive property
57. Associative property of multiplication
59. -22 **61.** 100   **63.** -21 **65.** 8
67. 19   **69.** 66   **71.** -75 **73.** 34
75. 1   **77.** 11   **79.** 4
81.

83.

85.

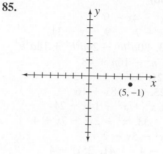

87. Quadrant IV   **89.** Quadrant III   **91.** Quadrant I

Problem Set 0.2 (page 28)

1. $\dfrac{1}{8}$ **3.** $-\dfrac{1}{1000}$ **5.** 27   **7.** 4

9. $-\dfrac{27}{8}$ **11.** 1   **13.** $\dfrac{16}{25}$ **15.** 4

17. $\dfrac{1}{100}$ or 0.01   **19.** $\dfrac{1}{100,000}$ or 0.00001   **21.** 81

23. $\dfrac{1}{16}$ **25.** $\dfrac{3}{4}$ **27.** $\dfrac{256}{25}$ **29.** $\dfrac{16}{25}$

31. $\dfrac{64}{81}$ **33.** 64   **35.** $\dfrac{1}{100,000}$ or 0.00001

37. $\dfrac{17}{72}$ **39.** $\dfrac{1}{6}$ **41.** $\dfrac{48}{19}$ **43.** $\dfrac{1}{x^4}$

45. $\dfrac{1}{a^2}$ **47.** $\dfrac{1}{a^6}$ **49.** $\dfrac{y^4}{x^3}$ **51.** $\dfrac{c^3}{a^3 b^6}$

53. $\dfrac{y^2}{4x^4}$ **55.** $\dfrac{x^4}{y^6}$ **57.** $\dfrac{9a^2}{4b^4}$ **59.** $\dfrac{1}{x^3}$

61. $\dfrac{a^3}{b}$ **63.** $-20x^4 y^5$ **65.** $-27x^3 y^9$

67. $\dfrac{8x^6}{27y^9}$ **69.** $-8x^6$ **71.** $\dfrac{6}{x^3 y}$ **73.** $\dfrac{6}{a^2 y^3}$

75. $\dfrac{4x^3}{y^5}$ **77.** $-\dfrac{5}{a^2 b}$ **79.** $\dfrac{1}{4x^2 y^4}$ **81.** $\dfrac{x+1}{x^2}$

83. $\dfrac{y - x^2}{x^2 y}$ **85.** $\dfrac{3b^3 + 2a^2}{a^2 b^3}$ **87.** $\dfrac{y^2 - x^2}{xy}$

89. $12x^{3a+1}$ **91.** 1 **93.** x^{2a} **95.** $-4y^{6b+2}$

97. x^b **99.** $(6.2)(10)^7$ **101.** $(4.12)(10)^{-4}$

103. 180,000 **105.** 0.0000023 **107.** 0.04

109. 30,000 **111.** 0.03

117. a. $(4.385)(10^{14})$ **c.** $(2.322)(10^{17})$ **e.** $(3.052)(10^{12})$

Problem Set 0.3 (page 38)

1. $14x^2 + x - 6$ **3.** $-x^2 - 4x - 9$

5. $6x - 11$ **7.** $6x^2 - 5x - 7$ **9.** $-x - 34$

11. $12x^3 y^2 + 15x^2 y^3$ **13.** $30a^4 b^3 - 24a^5 b^3 + 18a^4 b^4$

15. $x^2 + 20x + 96$ **17.** $n^2 - 16n + 48$

19. $sx + sy - tx - ty$ **21.** $6x^2 + 7x - 3$

23. $12x^2 - 37x + 21$ **25.** $x^2 + 8x + 16$

27. $4n^2 + 12n + 9$ **29.** $x^3 + x^2 - 14x - 24$

31. $6x^3 - x^2 - 11x + 6$ **33.** $x^3 + 2x^2 - 7x + 4$

35. $t^3 - 1$ **37.** $6x^3 + x^2 - 5x - 2$

39. $x^4 + 8x^3 + 15x^2 + 2x - 4$ **41.** $25x^2 - 4$

43. $x^4 - 10x^3 + 21x^2 + 20x + 4$ **45.** $4x^2 - 9y^2$

47. $x^3 + 15x^2 + 75x + 125$ **49.** $8x^3 + 12x^2 + 6x + 1$

51. $64x^3 - 144x^2 + 108x - 27$

53. $125x^3 - 150x^2 y + 60xy^2 - 8y^3$

55. $a^7 + 7a^6 b + 21a^5 b^2 + 35a^4 b^3 + 35a^3 b^4 + 21a^2 b^5 + 7ab^6 + b^7$

57. $x^5 - 5x^4 y + 10x^3 y^2 - 10x^2 y^3 + 5xy^4 - y^5$

59. $x^4 + 8x^3 y + 24x^2 y^2 + 32xy^3 + 16y^4$

61. $64a^6 - 192a^5 b + 240a^4 b^2 - 160a^3 b^3 + 60a^2 b^4 - 12ab^5 + b^6$

63. $x^{14} + 7x^{12} y + 21x^{10} y^2 + 35x^8 y^3 + 35x^6 y^4 + 21x^4 y^5 + 7x^2 y^6 + y^7$

65. $32a^5 - 240a^4 b + 720a^3 b^2 - 1080a^2 b^3 + 810ab^4 - 243b^5$ **67.** $3x^2 - 5x$ **69.** $-5a^4 + 4a^2 - 9a$

71. $5ab + 11a^2 b^4$ **73.** $x^{2a} - y^{2b}$

75. $x^{2b} - 3x^b - 28$ **77.** $6x^{2b} + x^b - 2$

79. $x^{4a} - 2x^{2a} + 1$ **81.** $x^{3a} - 6x^{2a} + 12x^a - 8$

Problem Set 0.4 (page 49)

1. $2xy(3 - 4y)$ **3.** $6x^2 y^3 z^2(2z^2 - x^2 z + 1)$

5. $(z + 3)(x + y)$ **7.** $(x + y)(3 + a)$

9. $(x - y)(a - b)$ **11.** $(x + 5)(x - 5)$

13. $(1 + 9n)(1 - 9n)$ **15.** $(x + 4 + y)(x + 4 - y)$

17. $(3s + 2t - 1)(3s - 2t + 1)$ **19.** $(x - 7)(x + 2)$

21. $(5 + x)(3 - x)$ **23.** Not factorable

25. $(3x - 5)(x - 2)$ **27.** $(10x + 7)(x + 1)$

29. $(5x - 3)(2x + 9)$ **31.** $(6a - 1)^2$

33. $(4x - y)(2x + y)$ **35.** Not factorable

37. $(x - 2)(x^2 + 2x + 4)$

39. $(4x + 3y)(16x^2 - 12xy + 9y^2)$

41. $4(x^2 + 4)$ **43.** $x(x + 3)(x - 3)$

45. $(3a - 7)^2$ **47.** $2n(n^2 + 3n + 5)$

49. $2n(n^2 + 7n - 10)$ **51.** $4(x + 2)(x^2 - 2x + 4)$

53. $(x + 3)(x - 3)(x^2 + 5)$

55. $2y(x + 4)(x - 4)(x^2 + 3)$

57. $(a + b + c + d)(a + b - c - d)$

59. $(x + 4 + y)(x + 4 - y)$

61. $(x + y + 5)(x - y - 5)$ **63.** $(10x + 3)(6x - 5)$

65. $3x(7x - 4)(4x + 5)$ **67.** $(x^a + 4)(x^a - 4)$

69. $(x^n - y^n)(x^{2n} + x^n y^n + y^{2n})$

71. $(x^a + 4)(x^a - 7)$ **73.** $(2x^n - 5)(x^n + 6)$

75. $(x^{2n} + y^{2n})(x^n + y^n)(x^n - y^n)$

77. a. $(x + 32)(x + 3)$ **c.** $(x - 21)(x - 24)$

  e. $(x + 28)(x + 32)$

Problem Set 0.5 (page 61)

1. $\dfrac{2x}{3}$ **3.** $\dfrac{7y^3}{9x}$ **5.** $\dfrac{8x^4 y^4}{9}$ **7.** $\dfrac{a + 4}{a - 9}$

9. $\dfrac{x(2x + 7)}{y(x + 9)}$ **11.** $\dfrac{x^2 + xy + y^2}{x + 2y}$ **13.** $-\dfrac{2}{x + 1}$

15. $\dfrac{2x + y}{x - y}$ **17.** $\dfrac{9x^2 - 6xy + 4y^2}{x - 5}$ **19.** $\dfrac{x}{2y^3}$

21. $-\dfrac{8x^3 y^3}{15}$ **23.** $\dfrac{14}{27a}$ **25.** $5y$

27. $\dfrac{5(a + 3)}{a(a - 2)}$ **29.** $\dfrac{(x + 6y)^2(2x + 3y)}{y^3(x + 4y)}$

31. $\dfrac{3xy}{4(x + 6)}$ **33.** $\dfrac{x - 9}{42x^2}$ **35.** $\dfrac{8x + 5}{12}$

37. $\dfrac{7x}{24}$ **39.** $\dfrac{35b + 12a^3}{80a^2 b^2}$ **41.** $\dfrac{12 + 9n - 10n^2}{12n^2}$

43. $\dfrac{9y + 8x - 12xy}{12xy}$ **45.** $\dfrac{13x + 14}{(2x + 1)(3x + 4)}$

47. $\dfrac{7x + 21}{x(x + 7)}$ **49.** $\dfrac{1}{a - 2}$ **51.** $\dfrac{5}{2(x - 1)}$

53. $\dfrac{2n + 10}{3(n + 1)(n - 1)}$ **55.** $\dfrac{1}{x + 1}$

57. $\dfrac{9x + 73}{(x + 3)(x + 7)(x + 9)}$

59. $\dfrac{3x^2 + 30x - 78}{(x + 1)(x - 1)(x + 8)(x - 2)}$ **61.** $\dfrac{x + 6}{(x - 3)^2}$

63. $\dfrac{-x^2 - x + 1}{(x + 1)(x - 1)}$ **65.** $\dfrac{-8}{(n^2 + 4)(n + 2)(n - 2)}$

67. $\dfrac{5x^2 + 16x + 5}{(x + 1)(x - 4)(x + 7)}$

69. a. $\dfrac{5}{x - 1}$ **c.** $\dfrac{5}{a - 3}$ **e.** $x + 3$ **71.** $\dfrac{5y^2 - 3xy^2}{x^2 y + 2x^2}$

73. $\dfrac{x + 1}{x - 1}$ **75.** $\dfrac{n - 1}{n + 1}$ **77.** $\dfrac{-6x - 4}{3x + 9}$

79. $\dfrac{x^2 + x + 1}{x + 1}$ **81.** $\dfrac{a^2 + 4a + 1}{4a + 1}$ **83.** $-\dfrac{2x + h}{x^2(x + h)^2}$

85. $-\dfrac{1}{(x + 1)(x + h + 1)}$ **87.** $-\dfrac{4}{(2x - 1)(2x + 2h - 1)}$

89. $\dfrac{y + 2x}{x^2 y - xy^2}$ **91.** $\dfrac{x^2 y^2 + 2}{4y^2 - 3x}$

Problem Set 0.6 (page 73)

1. 9   **3.** 5   **5.** $\dfrac{6}{7}$ **7.** $-\dfrac{3}{2}$ **9.** $2\sqrt{6}$

11. $4\sqrt{7}$ **13.** $-6\sqrt{11}$ **15.** $\dfrac{3\sqrt{5}}{2}$

17. $2x\sqrt{3}$ **19.** $8x^2 y^3 \sqrt{y}$ **21.** $\dfrac{9y^3 \sqrt{5x}}{7}$

23. $4\sqrt[3]{2}$ **25.** $2x\sqrt[3]{2x}$ **27.** $2x\sqrt[4]{3x}$

29. $\dfrac{2\sqrt{3}}{5}$ **31.** $\dfrac{\sqrt{14}}{4}$ **33.** $\dfrac{4\sqrt{15}}{5}$

35. $\dfrac{3\sqrt{2}}{7}$ **37.** $\dfrac{\sqrt{15}}{6x^2}$ **39.** $\dfrac{2\sqrt{15a}}{5ab}$

41. $\dfrac{3\sqrt[3]{2}}{2}$ **43.** $\dfrac{\sqrt[3]{18x^2 y}}{3x}$ **45.** $12\sqrt{3}$ **47.** $3\sqrt{7}$

49. $\dfrac{11\sqrt{3}}{6}$ **51.** $-\dfrac{89\sqrt{2}}{30}$ **53.** $48\sqrt{6}$

55. $10\sqrt{6} + 8\sqrt{30}$ **57.** $3x\sqrt{6y} - 6\sqrt{2xy}$

59. $13 + 7\sqrt{3}$ **61.** $30 + 11\sqrt{6}$ **63.** 16

65. $x + 2\sqrt{xy} + y$ **67.** $a - b$ **69.** $3\sqrt{5} - 6$

71. $\sqrt{7} + \sqrt{3}$ **73.** $\dfrac{-2\sqrt{10} + 3\sqrt{14}}{43}$

75. $\dfrac{x + \sqrt{x}}{x - 1}$ **77.** $\dfrac{x - \sqrt{xy}}{x - y}$ **79.** $\dfrac{6x + 7\sqrt{xy} + 2y}{9x - 4y}$

81. $\dfrac{2}{\sqrt{2x + 2h} + \sqrt{2x}}$ **83.** $\dfrac{1}{\sqrt{x + h - 3} + \sqrt{x - 3}}$

91. $4x^2$ **93.** $y^2 \sqrt{3y}$ **95.** $2m^4 \sqrt{7}$
97. $3d^3 \sqrt{2d}$ **99.** $4n^{10}\sqrt{5}$

Problem Set 0.7 (page 79)

1. 7   **3.** 8   **5.** -4 **7.** 2   **9.** 64

11. 0.001   **13.** $\dfrac{1}{32}$ **15.** 2   **17.** $15x^{7/12}$

19. $y^{5/12}$ **21.** $64x^{3/4} y^{3/2}$ **23.** $4x^{4/15}$

25. $\dfrac{7}{a^{1/12}}$ **27.** $\dfrac{16x^{4/3}}{81y}$ **29.** $\dfrac{y^{3/2}}{x}$ **31.** $8a^{9/2} x^2$

33. $\sqrt[4]{8}$ **35.** $\sqrt[12]{x^7}$ **37.** $xy\sqrt[4]{xy^3}$ **39.** $a\sqrt[12]{a^5 b^{11}}$

41. $4\sqrt[6]{2}$ **43.** $\sqrt[6]{2}$ **45.** $\sqrt{2}$ **47.** $x\sqrt[12]{x^7}$

49. $\dfrac{5\sqrt[3]{x^2}}{x}$ **51.** $\dfrac{\sqrt[6]{x^3 y^4}}{y}$ **53.** $\dfrac{\sqrt[20]{x^{15} y^8}}{y}$

55. $\dfrac{5\sqrt[12]{x^9 y^8}}{4x}$ **57. a.** $\sqrt[6]{2}$ **c.** $\sqrt{x}$

61. $\dfrac{2x - 2}{(2x - 1)^{3/2}}$ **63.** $\dfrac{x}{(x^2 + 2x)^{3/2}}$ **65.** $\dfrac{4x}{(2x)^{4/3}}$

69. a. 13.391   **c.** 2.702   **e.** 4.304

Problem Set 0.8 (page 88)

1. $13 + 8i$ **3.** $3 + 4i$ **5.** $-11 + i$ **7.** $-1 - 2i$

9. $-\dfrac{3}{20} + \dfrac{5}{12}i$ **11.** $\dfrac{7}{10} - \dfrac{11}{12}i$ **13.** $4 + 0i$

15. $3i$ **17.** $i\sqrt{19}$ **19.** $\dfrac{2}{3}i$ **21.** $2i\sqrt{2}$

23. $3i\sqrt{3}$ **25.** $3i\sqrt{6}$ **27.** $18i$ **29.** $12i\sqrt{2}$

31. $-2 - i\sqrt{3}$ **33.** $-1 - i\sqrt{2}$ **35.** $\dfrac{4 + i\sqrt{5}}{2}$

37. -8 **39.** $-\sqrt{6}$ **41.** $-2\sqrt{5}$ **43.** $-2\sqrt{15}$
45. $-2\sqrt{14}$ **47.** 3   **49.** $\sqrt{6}$ **51.** $-21 + 0i$
53. $8 + 12i$ **55.** $0 + 26i$ **57.** $53 - 26i$
59. $10 - 24i$ **61.** $-14 - 8i$ **63.** $-7 + 24i$
65. $-3 + 4i$ **67.** $113 + 0i$ **69.** $13 + 0i$

71. $-\dfrac{8}{13} + \dfrac{12}{13}i$ **73.** $1 - \dfrac{2}{3}i$ **75.** $0 - \dfrac{3}{2}i$

77. $\dfrac{22}{41} - \dfrac{7}{41}i$ **79.** $-1 + 2i$ **81.** $-\dfrac{17}{10} + \dfrac{1}{10}i$

83. $\dfrac{5}{13} - \dfrac{1}{13}i$ **89. a.** $2 + 11i$ **c.** $-11 + 2i$ **e.** $-7 - 24i$
                    b. $-2 - 2i$ **d.** $-4 + 0i$ **f.** $4 - 4i$

Chapter 0 Review Problem Set (page 100)

1. $\dfrac{1}{125}$ **2.** $-\dfrac{1}{81}$ **3.** $\dfrac{16}{9}$ **4.** $\dfrac{1}{9}$ **5.** -8 **6.** $\dfrac{3}{2}$

7. $-\dfrac{1}{2}$ **8.** $\dfrac{1}{6}$ **9.** 4   **10.** -8 **11.** $12x^2 y$

12. $-30x^{7/6}$ **13.** $\dfrac{48}{a^{1/6}}$ **14.** $\dfrac{27y^{3/5}}{x^2}$ **15.** $\dfrac{4y^5}{x^5}$

16. $\dfrac{8y}{x^{7/12}}$ **17.** $\dfrac{16x^6}{y^6}$ **18.** $-\dfrac{a^3 b^1}{3}$ **19.** $4x - 1$

20. $-3x + 8$ **21.** $12a - 19$ **22.** $20x^2 - 11x - 42$
23. $-12x^2 + 17x - 6$ **24.** $-35x^2 + 22x - 3$
25. $x^3 + x^2 - 19x - 28$ **26.** $6x^3 - x^2 + 10x + 6$
27. $25x^2 - 30x + 9$ **28.** $9x^2 + 42x + 49$
29. $8x^3 - 12x^2 + 6x - 1$
30. $27x^3 + 135x^2 + 225x + 125$

31. $x^4 + 2x^3 - 6x^2 - 22x - 15$
32. $2x^4 + 11x^3 - 16x^2 - 8x + 8$ **33.** $-4x^2y^3 + 8xy^2$
34. $-7y + 9xy^2$ **35.** $(3x + 2y)(3x - 2y)$
36. $3x(x + 5)(x - 8)$ **37.** $(2x + 5)^2$
38. $(x - y + 3)(x - y - 3)$ **39.** $(x - 2)(x - y)$
40. $(4x - 3y)(16x^2 + 12xy + 9y^2)$
41. $(3x - 4)(5x + 2)$ **42.** $3(x^3 + 12)$
43. Not factorable   **44.** $3(x + 2)(x^2 - 2x + 4)$
45. $(x + 3)(x - 3)(x + 2)(x - 2)$
46. $(2x - 1 - y)(2x - 1 + y)$ **47.** $\dfrac{2}{3y}$ **48.** $\dfrac{-5a^2}{3}$

49. $\dfrac{3x + 5}{x}$ **50.** $\dfrac{2(3x - 1)}{x^2 + 4}$ **51.** $\dfrac{29x - 10}{12}$

52. $\dfrac{x - 38}{15}$ **53.** $\dfrac{-6n + 15}{5n^2}$ **54.** $\dfrac{-3x - 16}{x(x + 7)}$

55. $\dfrac{3x^2 - 8x - 40}{(x + 4)(x - 4)(x - 10)}$ **56.** $\dfrac{8x - 4}{x(x + 2)(x - 2)}$

57. $\dfrac{3xy - 2x^2}{5y + 7x^2}$ **58.** $\dfrac{3x - 2}{4x + 3}$ **59.** $-\dfrac{6x + 3h}{x^2(x + h)^2}$

60. $\dfrac{12}{(x^2 + 2)^{3/2}}$ **61.** $20\sqrt{3}$ **62.** $6x\sqrt{6x}$

63. $2xy\sqrt[3]{4xy^2}$ **64.** $\sqrt{3}$ **65.** $\dfrac{\sqrt{10x}}{2y}$

66. $\dfrac{15 - 3\sqrt{2}}{23}$ **67.** $\dfrac{24 - 4\sqrt{6}}{15}$ **68.** $\dfrac{3x + 6\sqrt{xy}}{x - 4y}$

69. $\sqrt[6]{5^5}$ **70.** $\sqrt[12]{x^{11}}$ **71.** $x^2\sqrt[6]{x^5}$

72. $x\sqrt[10]{xy^9}$ **73.** $\sqrt[6]{5}$ **74.** $\dfrac{\sqrt[12]{x^{11}}}{x}$ **75.** $-11 - 6i$

76. $-1 - 2i$ **77.** $1 - 2i$ **78.** $21 + 0i$
79. $26 - 7i$ **80.** $-25 + 15i$ **81.** $-14 - 12i$
82. $29 + 0i$ **83.** $0 - \dfrac{5}{3}i$ **84.** $-\dfrac{6}{25} + \dfrac{17}{25}i$

85. $0 + i$ **86.** $-\dfrac{12}{29} - \dfrac{30}{29}i$ **87.** $10i$

88. $2i\sqrt{10}$ **89.** $16i\sqrt{5}$ **90.** -12

91. $-4\sqrt{3}$ **92.** $2\sqrt{2}$

93. 600,000,000   **94.** 800,000

Chapter 0 Test (page 102)

1. a. $-\dfrac{1}{49}$ **b.** $\dfrac{8}{27}$ **c.** $\dfrac{8}{27}$ **d.** $\dfrac{3}{4}$ **2.** $-\dfrac{15}{x^4y^2}$

3. $-12x - 8$ **4.** $-30x^2 + 32x - 8$
5. $3x^3 + 4x^2 - 11x - 14$ **6.** $64x^3 - 48x^2 + 12x - 1$
7. $9x^3y + 12x^4y^2$ **8.** $3x(2x + 1)(3x - 4)$
9. $(5x + 2)(6x - 5)$ **10.** $8(x + 2)(x^2 - 2x + 4)$

11. $(x - 2)(x + y)$ **12.** $\dfrac{21x^5}{20}$ **13.** $\dfrac{x + 3}{x^2 + 2x + 4}$

14. $\dfrac{n - 8}{12}$ **15.** $\dfrac{23x + 6}{6x(x - 3)(x + 2)}$ **16.** $\dfrac{8 - 13n}{2n^2}$

17. $\dfrac{2y^2 - 5xy}{3y^2 + 4x}$ **18.** $12x^2\sqrt{7x}$ **19.** $\dfrac{5\sqrt{2}}{6}$

20. $\dfrac{4\sqrt{3} + 3\sqrt{2}}{5}$ **21.** $2xy\sqrt[3]{6xy^2}$ **22.** $-4 - 3i$

23. $34 - 18i$ **24.** $85 + 0i$ **25.** $\dfrac{1}{10} + \dfrac{7}{10}i$

Chapter 1

Problem Set 1.1 (page 112)

1. $\{-2\}$ **3.** $\left\{-\dfrac{1}{2}\right\}$ **5.** $\{7\}$ **7.** $\left\{-\dfrac{3}{2}\right\}$ **9.** $\left\{-\dfrac{10}{3}\right\}$

11. $\{-10\}$ **13.** $\{23\}$ **15.** $\left\{-\dfrac{21}{16}\right\}$ **17.** $\left\{\dfrac{3}{5}\right\}$

19. $\{-14\}$ **21.** $\{9\}$ **23.** $\left\{\dfrac{10}{7}\right\}$ **25.** $\{-10\}$

27. $\{1\}$ **29.** $\{-12\}$ **31.** $\{27\}$ **33.** $\left\{\dfrac{159}{5}\right\}$

35. $\{3\}$ **37.** $\{0\}$ **39.** $\left\{-\dfrac{2}{3}\right\}$ **41.** $\left\{\dfrac{1}{2}\right\}$

43. Chicken sandwich 30 grams, pasta salad 70 grams

45. 14, 16, and 18   **47.** 18 and 19
49. 10, 11, 12, and 13   **51.** 110°, 40°, and 30°
53. $12 per hour
55. 48 pennies, 21 nickels, and 11 dimes
57. 17 females and 26 males   **59.** 13 years old
61. Brad is 29 and Pedro is 23.

Problem Set 1.2 (page 124)

1. $\{1\}$ **3.** $\{9\}$ **5.** $\left\{\dfrac{10}{3}\right\}$ **7.** $\{4\}$ **9.** $\{14\}$

11. $\{9\}$ **13.** $\left\{\dfrac{1}{2}\right\}$ **15.** $\left\{\dfrac{1}{4}\right\}$ **17.** $\left\{\dfrac{2}{3}\right\}$

19. $\{-8\}$ **21.** $\varnothing$ **23.** $\{12\}$

25. $\{300\}$ **27.** $\{275\}$

29. $\left\{-\dfrac{66}{37}\right\}$ **31.** $\{6\}$ **33.** $w = \dfrac{P - 2l}{2}$

35. $h = \dfrac{A - 2lw}{2w + 2l}$ **37.** $h = \dfrac{A - 2\pi r^2}{2\pi r}$

39. $F = \dfrac{9C + 160}{5}$ or $F = \dfrac{9}{5}C + 32$

41. $T = \dfrac{NC - NV}{C}$ **43.** $T = \dfrac{I + klt}{kl}$

45. $R_n = \dfrac{R_1 R_2}{R_1 + R_2}$ **47.** \$1050   **49.** \$900 and \$1350

51. 168 two-wheel drive, 21 four-wheel drive   **53.** \$65

55. \$1540 per month   **57.** \$49.00   **59.** \$75

61. \$30   **63.** 14 nickels and 29 dimes

65. 15 dimes, 45 quarters, and 10 half-dollars

67. \$2000 at 4% and \$3500 at 6%   **69.** \$4000

71. 6 centimeters by 10 centimeters   **73.** 14 centimeters

83. a. \$1.00   **b.** \$11.33   **c.** \$83.33   **d.** \$400

e. \$21,176.47

Problem Set 1.3 (page 138)

1. $\{-4, 7\}$ **3.** $\left\{-3, \dfrac{4}{3}\right\}$ **5.** $\left\{0, \dfrac{3}{2}\right\}$ **7.** $\left\{\pm\dfrac{2\sqrt{3}}{3}\right\}$

9. $\left\{\dfrac{-1 \pm 2\sqrt{5}}{2}\right\}$ **11.** $\left\{-\dfrac{5}{3}, \dfrac{2}{5}\right\}$ **13.** $\{2 \pm 2i\}$

15. $\left\{-\dfrac{7}{2}, \dfrac{1}{5}\right\}$ **17.** $\{-3 \pm i\sqrt{5}\}$ **19.** $\{4, 6\}$

21. $\{-5 \pm 3\sqrt{3}\}$ **23.** $\left\{\dfrac{3 \pm \sqrt{5}}{2}\right\}$

25. $\{-2 \pm i\sqrt{2}\}$ **27.** $\left\{\dfrac{-6 \pm \sqrt{46}}{2}\right\}$

29. $\{-16, 18\}$ **31.** $\left\{\dfrac{-5 \pm \sqrt{37}}{6}\right\}$

33. $\{-6, 9\}$ **35.** $\left\{-5, -\dfrac{1}{3}\right\}$ **37.** $\{1 \pm \sqrt{5}\}$

39. $\left\{\dfrac{3 \pm \sqrt{7}}{2}\right\}$ **41.** $\left\{\dfrac{3 \pm i\sqrt{19}}{2}\right\}$

43. $\{4 \pm 2\sqrt{3}\}$ **45.** $\left\{\dfrac{1}{2}\right\}$ **47.** $\left\{-\dfrac{3}{2}, \dfrac{1}{4}\right\}$

49. $\{-14, 12\}$ **51.** $\left\{\dfrac{3 \pm i\sqrt{47}}{4}\right\}$ **53.** $\left\{-1, \dfrac{5}{3}\right\}$

55. $\left\{\dfrac{-1 \pm \sqrt{2}}{2}\right\}$ **57.** $\{8 \pm 5\sqrt{2}\}$

59. $\{-10 \pm 5\sqrt{5}\}$ **61.** $\left\{\dfrac{1 \pm \sqrt{6}}{5}\right\}$

63. a. Two equal real solutions
 b. Two complex but nonreal solutions
 c. Two equal real solutions
 d. Two unequal real solutions
 e. Two complex but nonreal solutions
 f. Two equal real solutions
 g. Two unequal real solutions
 h. Two unequal real solutions
65. 11 and 12   **67.** 12 feet

69. 10 meters and 24 meters   **71.** 8 inches by 14 inches

73. 7 meters wide and 18 meters long   **75.** 1 meter

77. 7 inches by 11 inches   **79.** 8 units

85. a. $r = \dfrac{\sqrt{A\pi}}{\pi}$ **c.** $t = \dfrac{\sqrt{2gs}}{g}$

 e. $y = \dfrac{b\sqrt{x^2 - a^2}}{a}$

87. $k = \pm 4$

89. a. $\{-1.359, 7.359\}$ **c.** $\{-10.280, 4.280\}$
 e. $\{-0.258, -7.742\}$ **g.** $\{0.191, 1.309\}$
 i. $\{-0.422, 5.922\}$

Problem Set 1.4 (page 152)

1. $\{-12\}$ **3.** $\left\{\dfrac{37}{15}\right\}$ **5.** $\{-2\}$ **7.** $\{-8, 1\}$

9. $\left\{\dfrac{6}{29}\right\}$ **11.** $\left\{n \mid n \neq \dfrac{3}{2} \text{ and } n \neq 3\right\}$

13. $\left\{-4, \dfrac{4}{3}\right\}$ **15.** $\left\{-\dfrac{1}{4}\right\}$ **17.** $\varnothing$ **19.** $\{3\}$

21. 9 rows and 14 trees per row   **23.** $4\dfrac{1}{2}$ hours

25. 50 miles

27. 50 mph for the freight and 70 mph for the express

29. 3 liters

31. 3.5 liters of the 50% solution and 7 liters of the 80% solution

33. 5 quarts   **35.** $2\dfrac{2}{5}$ hours   **37.** 60 minutes

39. 9 hours   **41.** 8 hours   **43.** 7 candy bars

45. 60 hours

Problem Set 1.5 (page 162)

1. $\{-2, 1 \pm i\sqrt{3}\}$ **3.** $\left\{1, \dfrac{-1 \pm i\sqrt{3}}{2}\right\}$

5. $\{-2, -1, 2\}$ **7.** $\left\{\pm i, \dfrac{3}{2}\right\}$ **9.** $\left\{-\dfrac{5}{4}, 0, \pm\dfrac{\sqrt{2}}{2}\right\}$

11. $\{0, 16\}$ **13.** $\{1\}$ **15.** $\{6\}$ **17.** $\{3\}$

19. $\varnothing$ **21.** $\{-1\}$ **23.** $\left\{\dfrac{13}{2}\right\}$ **25.** $\{-15\}$

27. $\{9\}$ **29.** $\left\{\dfrac{2}{3}, 1\right\}$ **31.** $\{5\}$ **33.** $\{7\}$

35. $\{-2, -1\}$ **37.** $\{0\}$ **39.** $\{6\}$

41. $\{0, 4\}$ **43.** $\{\pm 1, \pm 2\}$

45. $\left\{\pm\dfrac{\sqrt{2}}{2}, \pm 2\right\}$ **47.** $\{\pm i\sqrt{5}, \pm\sqrt{7}\}$

49. $\{\pm\sqrt{2+\sqrt{3}}, \pm\sqrt{2-\sqrt{3}}\}$ **51.** $\{-125, 8\}$

53. $\left\{-\dfrac{8}{27}, \dfrac{27}{8}\right\}$ **55.** $\left\{-\dfrac{1}{6}, \dfrac{1}{2}\right\}$ **57.** $\{25, 36\}$

59. $\{4\}$ **61.** $\left\{\pm\dfrac{1}{2}, \pm2\right\}$ **63.** $\left\{\pm\dfrac{1}{8}, \pm1\right\}$

65. $\left\{-\dfrac{2}{3}, 5\right\}$ **67.** 12 inches   **69.** 320 feet

75. a. $\{\pm1.62, \pm0.62\}$ **c.** $\{\pm1.78, \pm0.56\}$
    e. $\{\pm8.00, \pm6.00\}$

Problem Set 1.6 (page 172)

1. $(-\infty, -2]$

3. $(1, 4)$

5. $(0, 2)$

7. $[-2, -1]$

9. $(-\infty, 1) \cup (3, \infty)$

11. $(-2, \infty)$

13. $(-\infty, \infty)$

15. $(4, \infty)$

17. $[-3, 2)$

19. $[-5, 4]$ **21.** $\left(-1, \dfrac{3}{2}\right)$ **23.** $(-11, 13)$

25. $(-1, 5)$ **27.** $(-\infty, -2)$ **29.** $\left[-\dfrac{5}{3}, \infty\right)$

31. $[7, \infty)$ **33.** $\left(-\infty, \dfrac{17}{5}\right]$ **35.** $\left(-\infty, \dfrac{7}{3}\right)$

37. $[-20, \infty)$ **39.** $(300, \infty)$ **41.** $\left(\dfrac{1}{5}, \dfrac{7}{5}\right)$

43. $[1, 5]$ **45.** Greater than 6%   **47.** 98 or higher
49. Between 5°C and 15°C, inclusive
51. Between 8.8 and 15.4, inclusive
53. Greater than 11.7

Problem Set 1.7 (page 178)

1. $(-4, 1)$ **3.** $(-\infty, -3) \cup (5, \infty)$

5. $[-1, 2]$ **7.** $(-\infty, -4) \cup \left(\dfrac{1}{3}, \infty\right)$ **9.** $\left[\dfrac{2}{5}, \dfrac{4}{3}\right]$

11. $\left(-\infty, \dfrac{1}{2}\right) \cup \left(\dfrac{1}{2}, \infty\right)$ **13.** $(-\infty, -2) \cup (2, \infty)$

15. $(-6, 6)$ **17.** $(-\infty, \infty)$ **19.** $(-\infty, 0] \cup [2, \infty)$

21. $(-4, 0) \cup (0, \infty)$ **23.** $(-2, -1)$ **25.** $\left(-\infty, \dfrac{22}{3}\right]$

27. $(-4, 1) \cup (2, \infty)$ **29.** $(-\infty, -2] \cup \left[\dfrac{1}{2}, 5\right]$

31. $[-4, 0] \cup [6, \infty)$ **33.** $(-3, 2) \cup (2, \infty)$

35. $(-\infty, -1) \cup (5, \infty)$ **37.** $\left(-2, \dfrac{1}{2}\right)$ **39.** $\left(\dfrac{1}{3}, 3\right]$

41. $[-3, -2)$ **43.** $(-\infty, -5) \cup (-2, \infty)$
45. $(-\infty, -5)$ **47.** $(-3, 2)$

Problem Set 1.8 (page 186)

1. $\{-4, 8\}$ **3.** $\left\{-\dfrac{13}{20}, \dfrac{3}{20}\right\}$ **5.** $\{-3, 4\}$

7. $\left\{-3, \dfrac{1}{3}\right\}$ **9.** $\varnothing$ **11.** $\left\{-\dfrac{10}{3}, 2\right\}$

13. $\{-3, 9\}$ **15.** $\left\{-\dfrac{1}{5}\right\}$ **17.** $\{-4, 1\}$

19. $\left\{\dfrac{1}{4}, \dfrac{7}{4}\right\}$ **21.** $\{-2, 5\}$ **23.** $\{1, 7\}$

25. $\left\{-\dfrac{5}{3}, 1\right\}$ **27.** $\left\{-\dfrac{2}{5}, 4\right\}$ **29.** $\{-2, 0\}$

31. $\{-1\}$ **33.** $(-6, 6)$ **35.** $(-\infty, -8) \cup (8, \infty)$

37. $(-\infty, \infty)$ **39.** $(-\infty, -2) \cup (8, \infty)$ **41.** $[-3, 4]$

43. $\left(-\infty, -\dfrac{11}{3}\right) \cup \left(\dfrac{7}{3}, \infty\right)$ **45.** $\varnothing$ **47.** $\left(-\dfrac{1}{2}, \dfrac{7}{2}\right)$

49. $(-\infty, \infty)$ **51.** $(-\infty, -9] \cup [7, \infty)$ **53.** $(-6, 0)$

55. $(-\infty, -6) \cup (-2, \infty)$ **57.** $(-\infty, 0] \cup [4, \infty)$

59. $(-6, 4)$ **61.** $(-\infty, -1] \cup \left[\dfrac{5}{3}, \infty\right)$ **63.** $\varnothing$

65. $\left(-\infty, \dfrac{5}{4}\right) \cup \left(\dfrac{7}{2}, \infty\right)$ **67.** $(-\infty, -3) \cup (-3, -1)$

69. $\left[-\dfrac{2}{5}, 0\right) \cup \left(0, \dfrac{2}{3}\right]$ **71.** $\left(-\infty, \dfrac{2}{5}\right] \cup \left[\dfrac{2}{3}, \infty\right)$

Chapter 1 Review Problem Set (page 199)

1. $\{-14\}$ **2.** $\{-19\}$ **3.** $\left\{\dfrac{10}{7}\right\}$ **4.** $\{200\}$

5. $\left\{-1, \dfrac{5}{3}\right\}$ **6.** $\left\{\dfrac{5}{4}, 6\right\}$ **7.** $\{3 \pm i\}$

8. $\{-22, 18\}$ **9.** $\left\{-\dfrac{2}{5}, 0, \dfrac{1}{3}\right\}$ **10.** $\{-5\}$

11. $\left\{\dfrac{1}{2}, 6\right\}$ **12.** $\{\pm3i, \pm\sqrt{5}\}$

13. $\left\{\pm\dfrac{\sqrt{5}}{5}, \pm\sqrt{2}\right\}$ **14.** $\left\{-1, 2, \dfrac{-5 \pm \sqrt{33}}{2}\right\}$

15. $\{2\}$ **16.** $\left\{-1, \dfrac{1}{2}\right\}$ **17.** $\{0\}$

18. $\left\{-\dfrac{6}{5}, \dfrac{8}{5}\right\}$ **19.** $\left\{\dfrac{2}{5}, 12\right\}$ **20.** $\left\{\dfrac{1}{4}, \dfrac{7}{4}\right\}$

21. $\{-\sqrt{2}, -1, \sqrt{2}\}$ **22.** $\left\{-64, \dfrac{27}{8}\right\}$

23. $(-8, \infty)$ **24.** $\left[-\dfrac{65}{4}, \infty\right)$ **25.** $\left(-\infty, -\dfrac{9}{2}\right)$

26. $(-\infty, 400]$ **27.** $[-2, 1]$ **28.** $\left(-\dfrac{2}{3}, 2\right)$

29. $(-3, 6)$ **30.** $(-\infty, -2] \cup [7, \infty)$

31. $(-\infty, -2) \cup (1, 4)$ **32.** $\left[-4, \dfrac{3}{2}\right)$

33. $\left(-\infty, \dfrac{1}{5}\right) \cup (2, \infty)$ **34.** $[-7, -3]$

35. $(-\infty, 4)$ **36.** $\left(-\infty, -\dfrac{1}{2}\right) \cup (2, \infty)$

37. $\left[-\dfrac{19}{3}, 3\right]$ **38.** $\left(-\dfrac{9}{2}, \dfrac{3}{2}\right)$

39. $(-1, 0) \cup \left(0, \dfrac{1}{3}\right)$ **40.** $\left(-\dfrac{3}{2}, \infty\right)$

41. 21, 23, and 25 **42.** 49 men
43. 7 centimeters by 12 centimeters
44. 13 nickels, 39 dimes, and 36 quarters
45. \$20 **46.** 20 gallons
47. Rosie is 14 years old, and her mother is 33 years old.
48. \$3500 at 4% and \$4500 at 6.5% **49.** 95 or higher
50. Amy 4.5 hours, Angie 9 hours

51. $26\dfrac{2}{3}$ minutes **52.** \$7600 at 5% and \$3600 at 3%

53. 54 mph for Mike and 52 mph for Larry
54. Cindy 4 hours and Bill 6 hours
55. 15 centimeters and 20 centimeters
56. 5 inches by 7 inches

Chapter 1 Test (page 201)

1. $\{2\}$ **2.** $\left\{-\dfrac{3}{2}, \dfrac{1}{5}\right\}$ **3.** $\left\{-\dfrac{7}{5}, \dfrac{3}{5}\right\}$

4. $\{-1\}$ **5.** $\left\{\dfrac{1 \pm i\sqrt{31}}{4}\right\}$ **6.** $\{-4, -1\}$

7. $\{600\}$ **8.** $\left\{-1, \dfrac{11}{3}\right\}$ **9.** $\left\{\dfrac{1 \pm \sqrt{7}}{3}\right\}$

10. $\{-9, 0, 2\}$ **11.** $\left\{-\dfrac{6}{7}, 3\right\}$ **12.** $\{8\}$

13. $\varnothing$ **14.** $\left\{-\dfrac{1}{4}, \dfrac{2}{3}\right\}$ **15.** $(-\infty, -35]$

16. $(3, \infty)$ **17.** $\left(-1, \dfrac{7}{3}\right)$

18. $\left(-\infty, -\dfrac{11}{4}\right] \cup \left[\dfrac{1}{4}, \infty\right)$ **19.** $\left[-\dfrac{1}{2}, 5\right]$

20. $(-\infty, -2) \cup \left(\dfrac{1}{3}, \infty\right)$ **21.** $[-10, -6)$

22. $\dfrac{2}{3}$ cup **23.** 15 mph

24. \$8000 at 4.5% and \$10,000 at 5%
25. 9 centimeters by 14 centimeters

Chapter 2

Problem Set 2.1 (page 212)

1. 10 **3.** -5 **5.** 5 units **7.** 9 units **9.** 7

11. $\dfrac{1}{3}$ **13.** -7 **15.** 5 units **17.** $2\sqrt{13}$ units

19. 10 units **21.** $\left(2, -\dfrac{5}{2}\right)$ **23.** $\left(\dfrac{15}{2}, -\dfrac{11}{2}\right)$

25. $\left(\dfrac{1}{12}, \dfrac{11}{12}\right)$ **27.** $(3, 5)$ **29.** $(2, 5)$

31. $\left(\dfrac{17}{8}, -7\right)$ **33.** $(-2, -3)$

35. $\left(3, \dfrac{13}{2}\right)$ **37.** $\left(4, \dfrac{25}{4}\right)$

43. $15 + 9\sqrt{5}$ **47.** 3 or -7 **49.** $(3, 8)$

51. Both midpoints are at $\left(\dfrac{7}{2}, \dfrac{5}{2}\right)$.

Problem Set 2.2 (page 223)

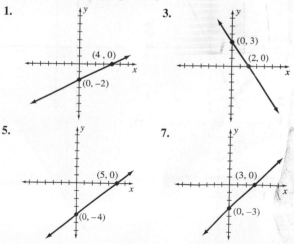

1. (4, 0), (0, −2)

3. (0, 3), (2, 0)

5. (5, 0), (0, −4)

7. (3, 0), (0, −3)

9.

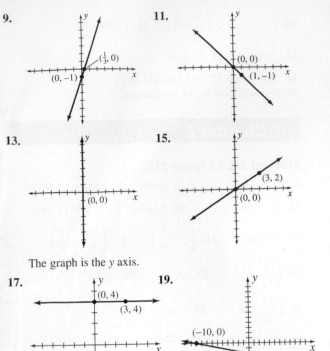

11.

13.

15.

The graph is the y axis.

17.

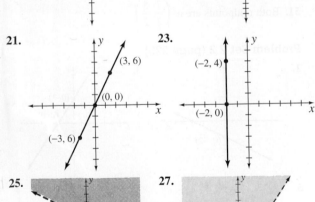

19.

21.

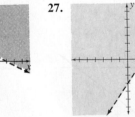

23.

25.

27.

29.

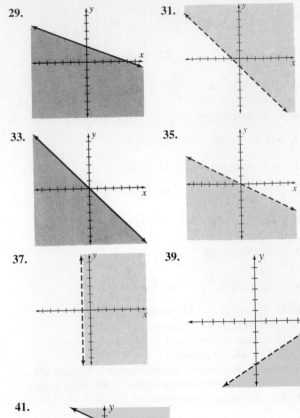

31.

33.

35.

37.

39.

41.

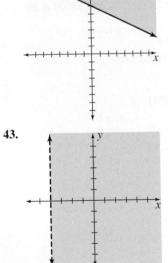

43.

45.

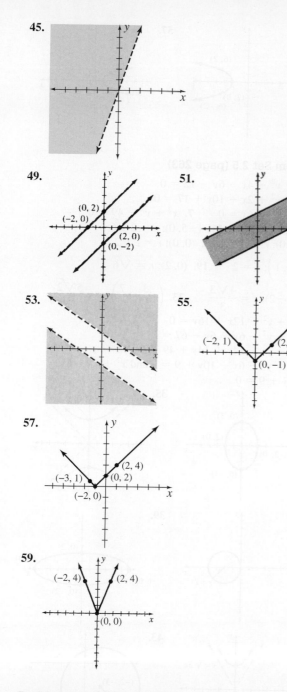

49.

51.

53.

55.

57.

59.

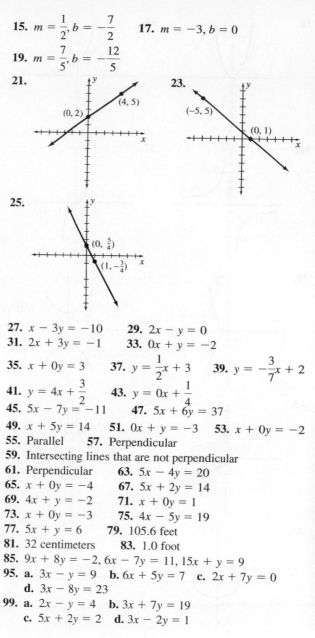

15. $m = \dfrac{1}{2}, b = -\dfrac{7}{2}$ **17.** $m = -3, b = 0$

19. $m = \dfrac{7}{5}, b = -\dfrac{12}{5}$

21.

23.

25.

27. $x - 3y = -10$ **29.** $2x - y = 0$
31. $2x + 3y = -1$ **33.** $0x + y = -2$

35. $x + 0y = 3$ **37.** $y = \dfrac{1}{2}x + 3$ **39.** $y = -\dfrac{3}{7}x + 2$

41. $y = 4x + \dfrac{3}{2}$ **43.** $y = 0x + \dfrac{1}{4}$

45. $5x - 7y = -11$ **47.** $5x + 6y = 37$

49. $x + 5y = 14$ **51.** $0x + y = -3$ **53.** $x + 0y = -2$

55. Parallel   **57.** Perpendicular

59. Intersecting lines that are not perpendicular

61. Perpendicular   **63.** $5x - 4y = 20$

65. $x + 0y = -4$ **67.** $5x + 2y = 14$

69. $4x + y = -2$ **71.** $x + 0y = 1$

73. $x + 0y = -3$ **75.** $4x - 5y = 19$

77. $5x + y = 6$ **79.** 105.6 feet

81. 32 centimeters   **83.** 1.0 foot

85. $9x + 8y = -2, 6x - 7y = 11, 15x + y = 9$

95. a. $3x - y = 9$ **b.** $6x + 5y = 7$ **c.** $2x + 7y = 0$
   d. $3x - 8y = 23$

99. a. $2x - y = 4$ **b.** $3x + 7y = 19$
   c. $5x + 2y = 2$ **d.** $3x - 2y = 1$

Problem Set 2.4 (page 250)

1. $(4, -3); (-4, 3); (-4, -3)$ **3.** $(-6, 1); (6, -1); (6, 1)$

5. $(0, -4); (0, 4); (0, -4)$ **7.** y axis   **9.** x axis

11. x axis, y axis, and origin   **13.** None **15.** Origin

17. None   **19.** y axis   **21.** Origin   **23.** x axis

25. x axis, y axis, and origin   **27.** None   **29.** Origin

Problem Set 2.3 (page 238)

1. $\dfrac{3}{4}$ **3.** -5 **5.** 0 **7.** $-\dfrac{b}{a}$ **9.** $x = \dfrac{23}{2}$

11. $x = -\dfrac{22}{9}$ **13.** $m = \dfrac{2}{3}, b = -\dfrac{4}{3}$

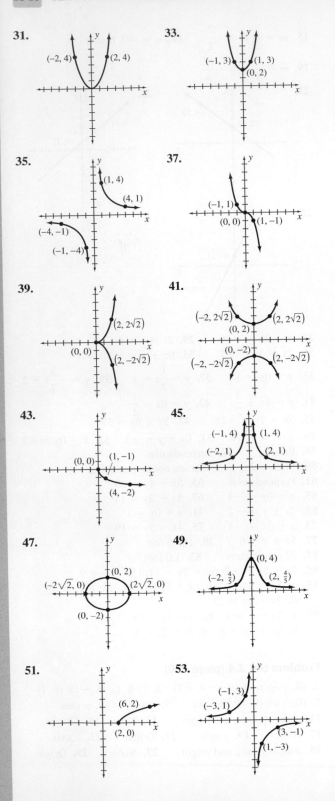

31. with points $(-2, 4)$ $(2, 4)$

33. with points $(-1, 3)$ $(1, 3)$ $(0, 2)$

35. with points $(1, 4)$ $(4, 1)$ $(-4, -1)$ $(-1, -4)$

37. with points $(-1, 1)$ $(0, 0)$ $(1, -1)$

39. with points $(2, 2\sqrt{2})$ $(0, 0)$ $(2, -2\sqrt{2})$

41. with points $(-2, 2\sqrt{2})$ $(2, 2\sqrt{2})$ $(0, 2)$ $(0, -2)$ $(-2, -2\sqrt{2})$ $(2, -2\sqrt{2})$

43. with points $(0, 0)$ $(1, -1)$ $(4, -2)$

45. with points $(-1, 4)$ $(1, 4)$ $(-2, 1)$ $(2, 1)$

47. with points $(0, 2)$ $(-2\sqrt{2}, 0)$ $(2\sqrt{2}, 0)$ $(0, -2)$

49. with points $(0, 4)$ $\left(-2, \frac{4}{5}\right)$ $\left(2, \frac{4}{5}\right)$

51. with points $(6, 2)$ $(2, 0)$

53. with points $(-1, 3)$ $(-3, 1)$ $(3, -1)$ $(1, -3)$

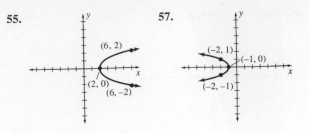

55. with points $(6, 2)$ $(2, 0)$ $(6, -2)$

57. with points $(-2, 1)$ $(-1, 0)$ $(-2, -1)$

Problem Set 2.5 (page 263)

1. $x^2 + y^2 - 4x - 6y - 12 = 0$
3. $x^2 + y^2 + 2x + 10y + 17 = 0$
5. $x^2 + y^2 - 6x = 0$ 7. $x^2 + y^2 - 49 = 0$
9. $(3, 5)$; $r = 2$ 11. $(-5, 0)$; $r = 2\sqrt{6}$
13. $(5, 0)$; $r = 5$ 15. $(0, 0)$; $r = 2\sqrt{2}$
17. $\left(\frac{1}{2}, 1\right)$; $r = 2$ 19. $(0, 2)$; $r = \sqrt{6}$
21. $(1, -2)$; $r = \dfrac{4\sqrt{3}}{3}$ 23. $\left(-\dfrac{3}{2}, -\dfrac{7}{2}\right)$; $r = \dfrac{5\sqrt{2}}{2}$
25. $x^2 + y^2 - 12x + 16y = 0$
27. $x^2 + y^2 - 6x - 6y - 67 = 0$
29. $x^2 + y^2 - 14x + 14y + 49 = 0$
31. $x^2 + y^2 + 6x - 10y + 9 = 0$ and $x^2 + y^2 + 6x + 10y + 9 = 0$

33. with points $(0, 3)$ $(2, 0)$ $(-2, 0)$ $(0, -3)$

35. with $y = -x$, $(0, 3)$, $y = x$, $(0, -3)$

37. with $r = 2$

39. with points $(0, 2)$ $(6, 0)$ $(-6, 0)$ $(0, -2)$

41. with $y = \sqrt{3}x$, $y = -\sqrt{3}x$

43. with point $(-2, -3)$, $r = 5$

Unless otherwise noted, all art on this page is © Cengage Learning.

45.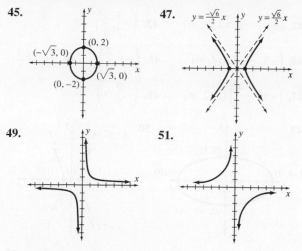

47.

$y = \frac{-\sqrt{6}}{2}x$ $y = \frac{\sqrt{6}}{2}x$

49.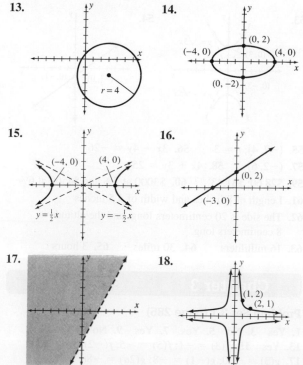

51.

55. a. $(1, 4); r = 3$ **c.** $(-6, -4); r = 8$
e. $(0, 6); r = 9$

Chapter 2 Review Problem Set (page 273)

1. 5   **2.** -5 **3.** $\left(9, \frac{1}{3}\right)$ **4.** $(-2, 6)$

7. x axis   **8.** None   **9.** x axis, y axis, and origin
10. y axis   **11.** Origin   **12.** y axis

13.   **14.**

(0, 2)

(−4, 0)   (4, 0)

(0, −2)

$r = 4$

15.   **16.**

(−4, 0)   (4, 0)

(0, 2)

(−3, 0)

$y = \frac{1}{2}x$ $y = -\frac{1}{2}x$

17.   **18.**

(1, 2)
(2, 1)

19.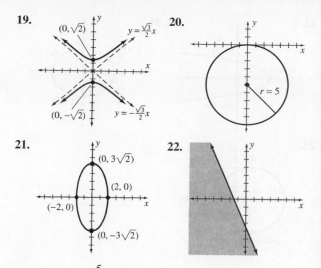

$y = \frac{\sqrt{3}}{2}x$

(0, $\sqrt{2}$)

(0, $-\sqrt{2}$) $y = -\frac{\sqrt{3}}{2}x$

20.

$r = 5$

21.

(0, $3\sqrt{2}$)

(2, 0)

(−2, 0)

(0, $-3\sqrt{2}$)

22.

23. -5 **24.** $\frac{5}{7}$ **25.** $3x + 4y = 29$
26. $2x - y = -4$ **27.** $4x + 3y = -4$
28. $x + 2y = 3$ **29.** $x^2 + y^2 - 10x + 12y + 60 = 0$
30. $x^2 + y^2 - 4x - 6y - 4 = 0$
31. $x^2 + y^2 + 10x - 24y = 0$
32. $x^2 + y^2 + 8x + 8y + 16 = 0$

Chapter 2 Test (page 274)

1. 8   **2.** $(-4, 6)$ **3.** $(6, -4)$ **4.** $-\frac{4}{9}$
5. $\frac{2}{7}$ **6.** $3x + 4y = -12$ **7.** $11x - 3y = 23$
8. $x - 5y = -21$ **9.** $7x - 4y = 1$
10. $x + 0y = -2$
11. $x^2 + y^2 + 6x + 12y + 29 = 0$
12. $x^2 + y^2 - 4x - 8y + 10 = 0$
13. $x^2 + y^2 - 8x + 6y = 0$
14. Center at $(-8, 5)$ and radius of length three units
15. 5, $\sqrt{37}$, and $2\sqrt{5}$ units   **16.** 1 and 5
17. $\pm\sqrt{3}$ **18.** Six units   **19.** $y = \pm\frac{3}{4}x$
20. a. x axis **b.** Origin **c.** y axis
    d. x axis, y axis, and origin

21.   **22.**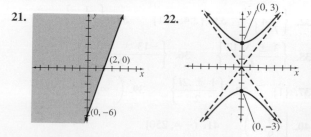

(2, 0)

(0, −6)

(0, 3)

(0, −3)

23.

24.

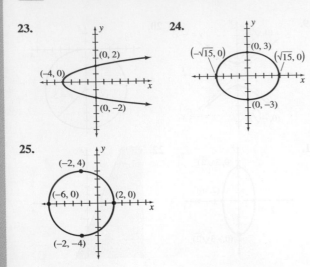

25.

Chapters 0–2 Cumulative Review Problem Set (page 275)

1. $\dfrac{1}{27}$ **2.** $-\dfrac{1}{16}$ **3.** $\dfrac{9}{4}$ **4.** $-\dfrac{2}{3}$ **5.** 9 **6.** $\dfrac{9}{16}$

7. $\dfrac{20}{x^2y^3}$ **8.** $-\dfrac{56a}{b}$ **9.** $4x^4y^2$ **10.** $\dfrac{5y^2}{x^4}$

11. $\dfrac{x^{1/3}}{17y^{7/4}}$ **12.** $\dfrac{4a^8}{b^{14}}$ **13.** $-30\sqrt{2}$ **14.** $6xy\sqrt{3x}$

15. $2xy^2\sqrt[3]{7xy}$ **16.** $\dfrac{3\sqrt{6}}{10}$ **17.** $\dfrac{\sqrt{21xy}}{7y}$

18. $-\dfrac{5(\sqrt{2}+3)}{7}$ **19.** $\dfrac{6\sqrt{14}+3\sqrt{42}}{2}$

20. $\dfrac{4x-12\sqrt{xy}}{x-9y}$ **21.** $\dfrac{3x^3y^2}{8}$ **22.** $-\dfrac{3b^3}{8a^3}$

23. $\dfrac{5x+1}{x}$ **24.** $\dfrac{21x+5}{24}$ **25.** $\dfrac{10-3n}{6n^2}$

26. $\dfrac{5x^2+18x+27}{(x+9)(x-3)(x+3)}$ **27.** $\left\{-\dfrac{23}{4}\right\}$ **28.** $\{3\}$

29. $\left\{\dfrac{3}{7}\right\}$ **30.** $\left\{\pm\dfrac{2}{3}\right\}$ **31.** $\{-4, 0, 2\}$

32. $\left\{\dfrac{3}{7}, 4\right\}$ **33.** $\{\pm 4i, \pm 1\}$ **34.** $\left\{-\dfrac{1}{5}, 1\right\}$

35. $\left\{\dfrac{3\pm\sqrt{17}}{4}\right\}$ **36.** $\left\{\dfrac{-13\pm\sqrt{205}}{2}\right\}$

37. $\{1\}$ **38.** $\left\{\dfrac{1\pm 2i}{2}\right\}$ **39.** $\left(-\infty, \dfrac{1}{8}\right)$

40. $\left[-\dfrac{5}{9}, \infty\right)$ **41.** $(-\infty, 250]$

42. $(-\infty, -8)\cup(3, \infty)$ **43.** $\left(-\dfrac{3}{2}, \dfrac{1}{3}\right)$

44. $\left(-3, \dfrac{1}{2}\right)\cup(4, \infty)$ **45.** $\left(-1, \dfrac{2}{3}\right]$ **46.** $(1, 7]$

47. $\left(-\infty, -\dfrac{4}{3}\right)\cup(2, \infty)$ **48.** $\left(-\dfrac{9}{5}, 3\right)$

49. **50.**

51. **52.**

53. **54.**

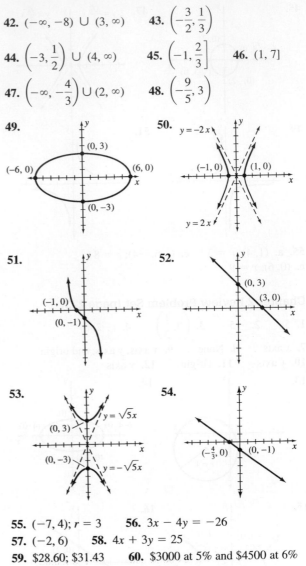

55. $(-7, 4); r = 3$ **56.** $3x - 4y = -26$
57. $(-2, 6)$ **58.** $4x + 3y = 25$
59. \$28.60; \$31.43 **60.** \$3000 at 5% and \$4500 at 6%
61. Length of 8 inches and width of 4.5 inches
62. The side is 20 centimeters long, and the altitude is 8 centimeters long.
63. 16 milliliters **64.** 30 miles **65.** 3 hours

Chapter 3

Problem Set 3.1 (page 285)

1. Yes **3.** No **5.** Yes **7.** Yes **9.** No **11.** Yes
13. Yes **15.** $f(3) = -1; f(5) = -5; f(-2) = 9$
17. $g(3) = -20; g(-1) = -8; g(2a) = -8a^2 + 2a - 5$

19. $h(3) = \dfrac{5}{4}$; $h(4) = \dfrac{23}{12}$; $h\left(-\dfrac{1}{2}\right) = -\dfrac{13}{12}$

21. $f(5) = 3$; $f\left(\dfrac{1}{2}\right) = 0$; $f(23) = 3\sqrt{5}$

23. $-2a + 7$, $-2a + 3$, $-2a - 2h + 7$

25. $a^2 + 4a + 10$, $a^2 - 12a + 42$,
$a^2 + 2ah + h^2 - 4a - 4h + 10$

27. $x^2 - 3x + 5$; $9x^2 + 9x + 5$; $x^2 - 5x + 9$

29. $f(4) = 4$; $f(10) = 10$; $f(-3) = 9$; $f(-5) = 25$

31. $f(3) = 6$; $f(5) = 10$; $f(-3) = 6$; $f(-5) = 10$

33. $f(2) = 1$; $f(0) = 0$; $f\left(-\dfrac{1}{2}\right) = 0$; $f(-4) = -1$

35. $D = \left\{x \mid x \ge \dfrac{4}{3}\right\}$; $R = \{f(x) \mid f(x) \ge 0\}$

37. $D = \{x \mid x$ is any real number$\}$; $R = \{f(x) \mid f(x) \ge -2\}$

39. $D = \{x \mid x$ is any real number$\}$;
$R = \{f(x) \mid f(x)$ is any nonnegative real number$\}$

41. $D = \{x \mid x$ is any nonnegative real number$\}$;
$R = \{f(x) \mid f(x)$ is any nonpositive real number$\}$

43. $D = \{x \mid x$ is any real number$\}$; $R = \{f(x) \mid f(x) = 6\}$

45. $D = \{x \mid x \ge -4\}$; $R = \{f(x) \mid f(x) \ge -2\}$

47. $D = \{x \mid x$ is any real number$\}$; $R = \{f(x) \mid f(x) \le -6\}$

49. $D = \{x \mid x \ne -2\}$

51. $D = \left\{x \mid x \ne \dfrac{1}{2} \text{ and } x \ne -4\right\}$

53. $D = \{x \mid x \ne 2 \text{ and } x \ne -2\}$

55. $D = \{x \mid x \ne -3 \text{ and } x \ne 4\}$

57. $D = \left\{x \mid x \ne -\dfrac{5}{2} \text{ and } x \ne \dfrac{1}{3}\right\}$

59. $D = \{x \mid x$ is any real number$\}$ **61.** $D = \left\{x \mid x \le \dfrac{3}{4}\right\}$

63. $(-\infty, -4] \cup [4, \infty)$ **65.** $(-\infty, \infty)$

67. $(-\infty, -5] \cup [8, \infty)$ **69.** $\left(-\infty, -\dfrac{5}{2}\right] \cup \left[\dfrac{7}{4}, \infty\right)$

71. $[-1, 1]$ **73.** Even   **75.** Even   **77.** Neither

79. Odd   **81.** Odd   **83.** $30.40

85. 12.57; 28.27; 452.39; 907.92   **87.** 48; 64; 48; 0

89. $55; $60; $67.50; $75   **91.** 125.66; 301.59; 804.25

Problem Set 3.2 (page 295)

1.   **3.**

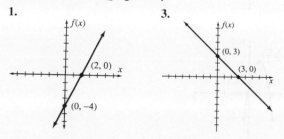

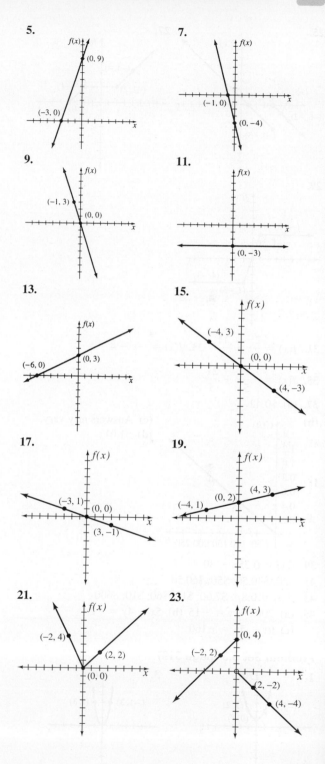

25.

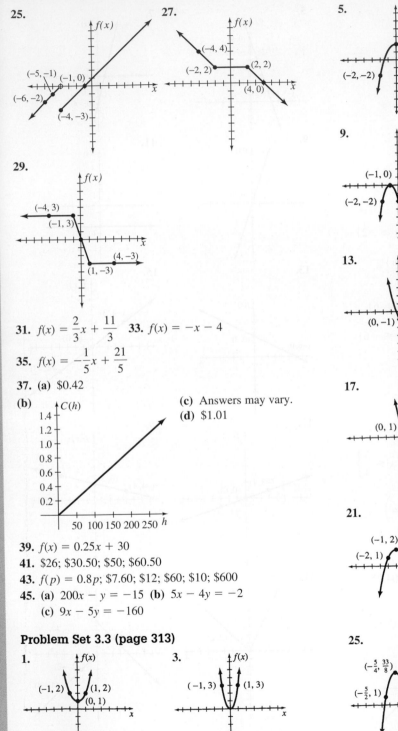

27.

29.

31. $f(x) = \dfrac{2}{3}x + \dfrac{11}{3}$ **33.** $f(x) = -x - 4$

35. $f(x) = -\dfrac{1}{5}x + \dfrac{21}{5}$

37. **(a)** $0.42

(b)

(c) Answers may vary.
(d) $1.01

39. $f(x) = 0.25x + 30$

41. $26; $30.50; $50; $60.50

43. $f(p) = 0.8p$; $7.60; $12; $60; $10; $600

45. **(a)** $200x - y = -15$ **(b)** $5x - 4y = -2$
(c) $9x - 5y = -160$

Problem Set 3.3 (page 313)

1.

3.

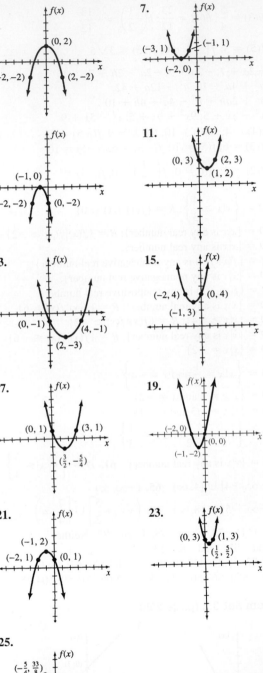

5.

7.

9.

11.

13.

15.

17.

19.

21.

23.

25.

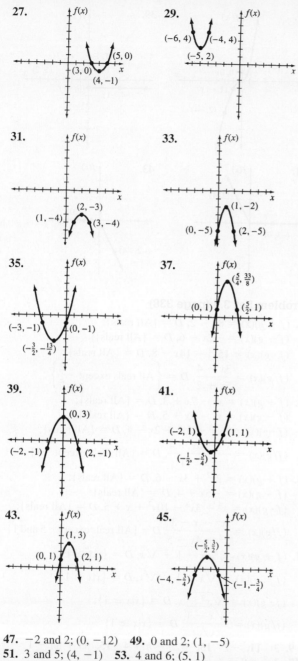

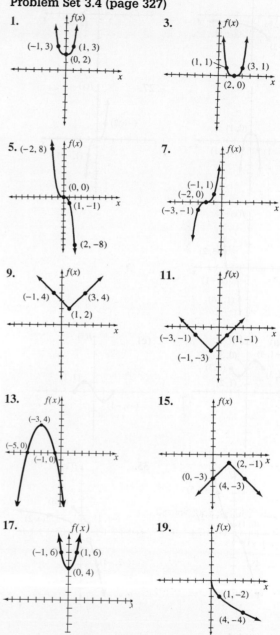

27.

29. (−6, 4) (−4, 4) (−5, 2)

71. 60 meters by 60 meters
73. 1100 subscribers at $13.75 per month

Problem Set 3.4 (page 327)

1. (−1, 3) (1, 3) (0, 2)

3. (1, 1) (3, 1) (2, 0)

31. (1, −4) (2, −3) (3, −4)

33. (0, −5) (1, −2) (2, −5)

5. (−2, 8) (0, 0) (1, −1) (2, −8)

7. (−1, 1) (−2, 0) (−3, −1)

35. (−3, −1) (0, −1) $(-\frac{3}{2}, -\frac{13}{4})$

37. $(\frac{5}{4}, \frac{33}{8})$ (0, 1) $(\frac{5}{2}, 1)$

9. (−1, 4) (3, 4) (1, 2)

11. (−3, −1) (1, −1) (−1, −3)

39. (0, 3) (−2, −1) (2, −1)

41. (−2, 1) (1, 1) $(-\frac{1}{2}, -\frac{5}{4})$

13. (−3, 4) (−5, 0) (−1, 0)

15. (2, −1) (0, −3) (4, −3)

43. (1, 3) (0, 1) (2, 1)

45. $(-\frac{5}{2}, \frac{3}{2})$ $(-4, -\frac{3}{4})$ $(-1, -\frac{3}{4})$

17. (−1, 6) (1, 6) (0, 4)

19. (1, −2) (4, −4)

47. −2 and 2; (0, −12)   **49.** 0 and 2; (1, −5)
51. 3 and 5; (4, −1)   **53.** 4 and 6; (5, 1)
55. No x intercepts; $\left(\frac{9}{2}, -\frac{3}{4}\right)$
57. $\dfrac{1 + \sqrt{5}}{2}$ and $\dfrac{1 - \sqrt{5}}{2}$; $\left(\frac{1}{2}, 5\right)$ **59.** −11 and 8
61. 3 and 9   **63.** $2 - i\sqrt{7}$ and $2 + i\sqrt{7}$
65. 70   **67.** 144 feet   **69.** 25 and 25

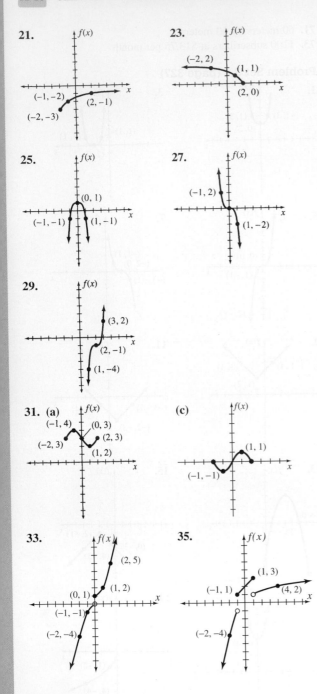

21.

23.

25.

27.

29.

31. (a) **(c)**

33. **35.**

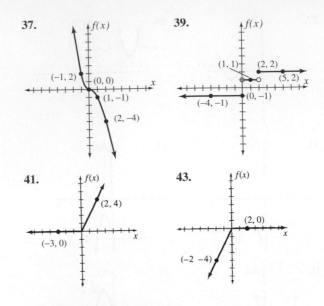

37. **39.**

41. **43.**

Problem Set 3.5 (page 338)

1. $(f + g)(x) = 8x - 2, D = \{\text{All reals}\}$;
$(f - g)(x) = -2x - 6, D = \{\text{All reals}\}$;
$(f \cdot g)(x) = 15x^2 - 14x - 8, D = \{\text{All reals}\}$;
$(f/g)(x) = \dfrac{3x - 4}{5x + 2}, D = \left\{\text{All reals except } -\dfrac{2}{5}\right\}$

3. $(f + g)(x) = x^2 - 7x + 3, D = \{\text{All reals}\}$;
$(f - g)(x) = x^2 - 5x + 5, D = \{\text{All reals}\}$;
$(f \cdot g)(x) = -x^3 + 5x^2 + 2x - 4, D = \{\text{All reals}\}$;
$(f/g)(x) = \dfrac{x^2 - 6x + 4}{-x - 1}, D = \{\text{All reals except } -1\}$

5. $(f + g)(x) = 2x^2 + 3x - 6, D = \{\text{All reals}\}$;
$(f - g)(x) = -5x + 4, D = \{\text{All reals}\}$;
$(f \cdot g)(x) = x^4 + 3x^3 - 10x^2 + x + 5, D = \{\text{All reals}\}$;
$(f/g)(x) = \dfrac{x^2 - x - 1}{x^2 + 4x - 5}, D = \{\text{All reals except } -5 \text{ and } 1\}$

7. $(f + g)(x) = \sqrt{x - 1} + \sqrt{x}, D = \{x | x \geq 1\}$;
$(f - g)(x) = \sqrt{x - 1} - \sqrt{x}, D = \{x | x \geq 1\}$;
$(f \cdot g)(x) = \sqrt{x^2 - x}, D = \{x | x \geq 1\}$;
$(f/g)(x) = \dfrac{\sqrt{x - 1}}{\sqrt{x}}, D = \{x | x \geq 1\}$

9. 3 **11.** −7 **13.** −2a − h + 4 **15.** 6a + 3h − 1

17. $3a^2 + 3ah + h^2 - 2a - h + 2$

19. $-\dfrac{2}{(a - 1)(a + h - 1)}$ **21.** $-\dfrac{2a + h}{a^2(a + h)^2}$

23. $(f \circ g)(x) = 6x - 2, D = \{\text{All reals}\}$;
$(g \circ f)(x) = 6x - 1, D = \{\text{All reals}\}$

25. $(f \circ g)(x) = 10x + 2, D = \{\text{All reals}\}$;
$(g \circ f)(x) = 10x - 5, D = \{\text{All reals}\}$

27. $(f \circ g)(x) = 3x^2 + 7, D = \{\text{All reals}\};$
$(g \circ f)(x) = 9x^2 + 24x + 17, D = \{\text{All reals}\}$

29. $(f \circ g)(x) = 3x^2 + 9x - 16, D = \{\text{All reals}\};$
$(g \circ f)(x) = 9x^2 - 15x, D = \{\text{All reals}\}$

31. $(f \circ g)(x) = \dfrac{1}{2x + 7}, D = \left\{x \middle| x \neq -\dfrac{7}{2}\right\};$

$(g \circ f)(x) = \dfrac{7x + 2}{x}, D = \{x|x \neq 0\}$

33. $(f \circ g)(x) = \sqrt{3x - 3}, D = \{x|x \geq 1\};$
$(g \circ f)(x) = 3\sqrt{x - 2} - 1, D = \{x|x \geq 2\}$

35. $(f \circ g)(x) = \dfrac{x}{2 - x}, D = \{x|x \neq 0 \text{ and } x \neq 2\};$
$(g \circ f)(x) = 2x - 2, D = \{x|x \neq 1\}$

37. $(f \circ g)(x) = 2\sqrt{x - 1} + 1, D = \{x|x \geq 1\};$
$(g \circ f)(x) = \sqrt{2x}, D = \{x|x \geq 0\}$

39. $(f \circ g)(x) = x, D = \{x|x \neq 0\};$
$(g \circ f)(x) = x, D = \{x|x \neq 1\}$

41. 4; 50   **43.** 9; 0   **45.** $\sqrt{11}$; 5

Problem Set 3.6 (page 346)

1. $y = kx^3$ **3.** $A = klw$ **5.** $V = \dfrac{k}{P}$ **7.** $V = khr^2$

9. 24   **11.** $\dfrac{22}{7}$ **13.** $\dfrac{1}{2}$ **15.** 7   **17.** 6   **19.** 8   **21.** 96

23. 5 hours   **25.** 2 seconds   **27.** 24 days   **29.** 28

31. \$2400   **37.** 2.8 seconds   **39.** 1.4

Chapter 3 Review Problem Set (page 358)

1. 7; 4; 32   **2. (a)** -5 **(b)** $4a + 2h - 1$
(c) $-6a - 3h + 2$

3. $D = \{x | x \text{ is any real number}\}; R = \{f(x)|f(x) \geq 5\}$

4. $D = \left\{x \middle| x \neq \dfrac{1}{2}, x \neq -4\right\}$

5. $(-\infty, 2] \cup [5, \infty)$

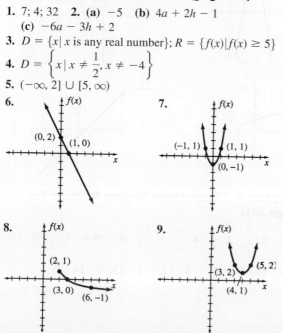

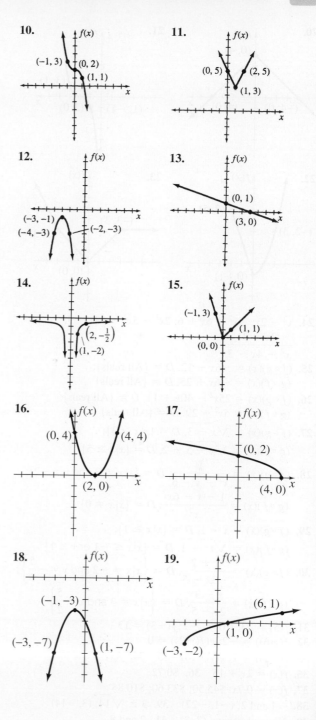

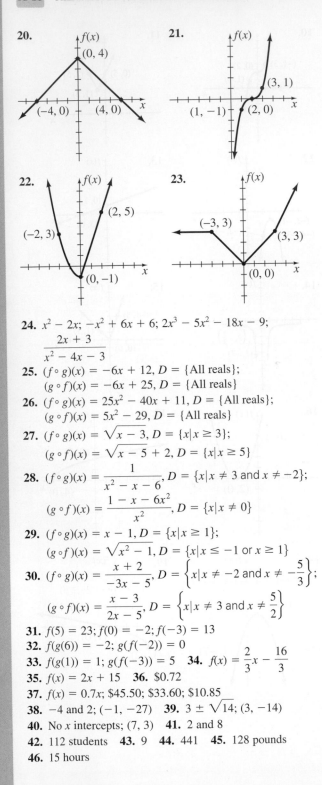

20.

f(x)
(0, 4)
(−4, 0)   (4, 0)   x

21.

f(x)
(3, 1)
(1, −1)   (2, 0)   x

22.

f(x)
(2, 5)
(−2, 3)
(0, −1)   x

23.

f(x)
(−3, 3)
(3, 3)
(0, 0)   x

24. $x^2 - 2x$; $-x^2 + 6x + 6$; $2x^3 - 5x^2 - 18x - 9$;

$$\frac{2x + 3}{x^2 - 4x - 3}$$

25. $(f \circ g)(x) = -6x + 12$, $D = \{\text{All reals}\}$;
$(g \circ f)(x) = -6x + 25$, $D = \{\text{All reals}\}$

26. $(f \circ g)(x) = 25x^2 - 40x + 11$, $D = \{\text{All reals}\}$;
$(g \circ f)(x) = 5x^2 - 29$, $D = \{\text{All reals}\}$

27. $(f \circ g)(x) = \sqrt{x - 3}$, $D = \{x | x \geq 3\}$;
$(g \circ f)(x) = \sqrt{x - 5} + 2$, $D = \{x | x \geq 5\}$

28. $(f \circ g)(x) = \dfrac{1}{x^2 - x - 6}$, $D = \{x | x \neq 3 \text{ and } x \neq -2\}$;

$(g \circ f)(x) = \dfrac{1 - x - 6x^2}{x^2}$, $D = \{x | x \neq 0\}$

29. $(f \circ g)(x) = x - 1$, $D = \{x | x \geq 1\}$;
$(g \circ f)(x) = \sqrt{x^2 - 1}$, $D = \{x | x \leq -1 \text{ or } x \geq 1\}$

30. $(f \circ g)(x) = \dfrac{x + 2}{-3x - 5}$, $D = \left\{x | x \neq -2 \text{ and } x \neq -\dfrac{5}{3}\right\}$;

$(g \circ f)(x) = \dfrac{x - 3}{2x - 5}$, $D = \left\{x | x \neq 3 \text{ and } x \neq \dfrac{5}{2}\right\}$

31. $f(5) = 23$; $f(0) = -2$; $f(-3) = 13$

32. $f(g(6)) = -2$; $g(f(-2)) = 0$

33. $f(g(1)) = 1$; $g(f(-3)) = 5$ **34.** $f(x) = \dfrac{2}{3}x - \dfrac{16}{3}$

35. $f(x) = 2x + 15$ **36.** \$0.72

37. $f(x) = 0.7x$; \$45.50; \$33.60; \$10.85

38. -4 and 2; $(-1, -27)$ **39.** $3 \pm \sqrt{14}$; $(3, -14)$

40. No x intercepts; $(7, 3)$ **41.** 2 and 8

42. 112 students   **43.** 9   **44.** 441   **45.** 128 pounds

46. 15 hours

Chapter 3 Test (page 360)

1. $\dfrac{11}{6}$ **2.** 11   **3.** $6a + 3h + 2$

4. $\left\{x | x \neq -4 \text{ and } x \neq \dfrac{1}{2}\right\}$ **5.** $\left\{x | x \leq \dfrac{5}{3}\right\}$

6. $(f + g)(x) = 2x^2 + 2x - 6$; $(f - g)(x) = -2x^2 + 4x + 4$;
$(f \cdot g)(x) = 6x^3 - 5x^2 - 14x + 5$

7. $(f \circ g)(x) = -21x - 2$ **8.** $(g \circ f)(x) = 8x^2 + 38x + 48$

9. $(f \circ g)(x) = \dfrac{3x}{2 - 2x}$ **10.** 12; 7   **11.** $f(x) = -\dfrac{5}{6}x - \dfrac{14}{3}$

12. $\{x | x \neq 0 \text{ and } x \neq 1\}$ **13.** 18; 10; 0

14. $(f \cdot g)(x) = x^3 + 4x^2 - 11x + 6$; $\left(\dfrac{f}{g}\right)(x) = x + 6$

15. 6 and 54   **16.** 15   **17.** -4 **18.** \$96

19. $s(c) = 1.35c$; \$17.55   **20.** -2 and 6; $(2, -64)$

21.

f(x)
(3, −2)
(2, −3)
(1, −4)   x

22.

(−3, 4)   f(x)
(−5, −4)
(−1, −4)   x

23.

f(x)
(1, 2)
(3, 2)
(2, −1)   x

24.

f(x)
(0, √2)
(2, 0)   x

25.

f(x)
(−1, 0)   (0, −1)   x

Chapters 0–3 Cumulative Review Problem Set (page 361)

1. 9   **2.** $\dfrac{9}{7}$ **3.** $\dfrac{1}{8}$ **4.** $\dfrac{1}{4}$ **5.** $\dfrac{72}{17}$ **6.** -0.4 **7.** $\dfrac{3}{2}$ **8.** 27

9. 4   **10.** 81   **11.** -8 **12.** -1 **13.** 2   **14.** 75

15. -31 **16.** $\dfrac{4x^2y}{9}$ **17.** $\dfrac{3x+7}{4x-9}$ **18.** $\dfrac{2(x^2-2x+4)}{x-2}$

19. $\dfrac{y-2}{x}$ **20.** $\dfrac{27}{8a^2}$ **21.** $\dfrac{x+4}{x(x+5)}$ **22.** $\dfrac{16x+43}{90}$

23. $\dfrac{35a-44b}{60a^2b}$ **24.** $\dfrac{2}{x-4}$ **25.** $\dfrac{2y-3xy}{3x+4xy}$

26. $\dfrac{5y^2-3xy^2}{x^2y+2x^2}$ **27.** $\dfrac{3a^2-2a+1}{2a-1}$ **28.** $-\dfrac{12}{x^3y}$ **29.** $\dfrac{8y}{x^5}$

30. $-\dfrac{a^3}{9b}$ **31.** $\dfrac{2\sqrt{2}}{5}$ **32.** $\dfrac{2\sqrt{2}}{7}$ **33.** $4xy^3\sqrt{3xy}$

34. $2(\sqrt{5}+\sqrt{3})$ **35.** $2xy\sqrt[3]{6xy^2}$ **36.** $\sqrt[3]{2}$

37. $40+13i$ **38.** $2+14i$ **39.** $0-\dfrac{5}{4}i$ **40.** $\dfrac{2}{5}+\dfrac{6}{5}i$

41. $\left\{-\dfrac{21}{16}\right\}$ **42.** $\left\{\dfrac{40}{3}\right\}$ **43.** $\{6\}$ **44.** $\left\{-\dfrac{5}{2},3\right\}$

45. $\left\{-3,\dfrac{5}{3}\right\}$ **46.** $\{-6,0,6\}$ **47.** $\left\{\dfrac{1\pm3\sqrt{5}}{3}\right\}$

48. $\left\{\dfrac{-5\pm4i\sqrt{2}}{2}\right\}$ **49.** $\left\{\dfrac{3\pm i\sqrt{23}}{4}\right\}$ **50.** $\{-5,7\}$

51. $\left\{-6,\dfrac{1}{2}\right\}$ **52.** $\{-5,8\}$ **53.** $\{-17\}$

54. $\left\{\dfrac{-7\pm\sqrt{41}}{2}\right\}$ **55.** $\{12\}$ **56.** $\{-3\}$

57. $\left\{\pm\dfrac{\sqrt{5}}{2},\pm\dfrac{\sqrt{3}}{3}\right\}$ **58.** $\{\pm\sqrt{3},4\}$

59. $\left(-\infty,-\dfrac{11}{5}\right)\cup(3,\infty)$ **60.** $[-4,2]$ **61.** $\left[-\dfrac{5}{3},1\right]$

62. $(-8,3)$ **63.** $(-\infty,3)$ **64.** $\left[-\dfrac{9}{11},\infty\right)$

65. $\left(-5,-\dfrac{1}{2}\right)\cup(2,\infty)$ **66.** $(-\infty,3]\cup(7,\infty)$

67. $(-6,-3)$ **68.** $(-\infty,-3)\cup\left(0,\dfrac{1}{2}\right)$ **69.** 6

70. $(5,8)$ **71.** $\dfrac{2}{5}$ **72.** $3x+5y=-11$ **73.** 43; 24

74. $2\sqrt{x+2}-1;\ \sqrt{2x+1}$

75. $(-\infty,-10]\cup[3,\infty)$ **76.** $-2a+6-h$

77.

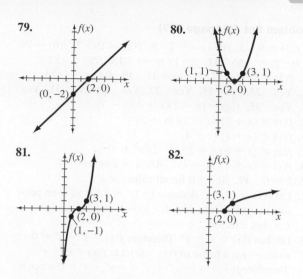

79. ... **80.** ... **81.** ... **82.** ...

83. 17, 19, and 21   **84.** 14 nickels, 20 dimes, and 29 quarters   **85.** 48° and 132°   **86.** $600
87. $1700 at 8% and $2000 at 9%
88. 66 mph and 76 mph   **89.** 4 quarts
90. 69 or less   **91.** -3, 0, or 3   **92.** 1 inch
93. $1050 and $1400   **94.** 3 hours
95. Meat 420 calories; vegetable 210 calories; fruit 140 calories   **96.** $40   **97.** 10°, 60°, and 110°

Chapter 4

Problem Set 4.1 (page 371)

1. $Q: 4x+5;\ R: 0$ **3.** $Q: t^2+2t-4;\ R: 0$
5. $Q: 2x+5;\ R: 1$ **7.** $Q: 3x-4;\ R: 3x-1$
9. $Q: 5y-1;\ R: -8y-2$ **11.** $Q: 4a+6;\ R: 7a-19$
13. $Q: 3x+4y;\ R: 0$ **15.** $Q: 4x+3;\ R: 0$
17. $Q: 2x-7;\ R: 0$ **19.** $Q: 3x-4;\ R: 1$
21. $Q: 4x-5;\ R: -2$ **23.** $Q: x^2+3x-4;\ R: 0$
25. $Q: 3x^2+2x-4;\ R: 0$ **27.** $Q: 5x^2+x-1;\ R: -4$
29. $Q: x^2-x-1;\ R: 8$ **31.** $Q: -x^2+4x-2;\ R: 0$
33. $Q: -3x^2+4x-2;\ R: 4$ **35.** $Q: 3x^2+6x+10;\ R: 15$
37. $Q: 2x^3-x^2+4x-2;\ R: 0$
39. $Q: x^3+7x^2+21x+56;\ R: 167$
41. $Q: x^3-x+5;\ R: 0$ **43.** $Q: x^3+2x^2+4x+8;\ R: 0$
45. $Q: x^4-x^3+x^2-x+1;\ R: -2$
47. $Q: x^4-x^3+x^2-x+1;\ R: 0$
49. $Q: x^4-x^3-x^2+x-1;\ R: 0$
51. $Q: 4x^4-2x^3+2x-3;\ R: -1$
53. $Q: 9x^2-3x+2;\ R: -\dfrac{10}{3}$
55. $Q: 3x^3-3x^2+6x-3;\ R: 0$

Problem Set 4.2 (page 377)

1. $f(3) = 9$ **3.** $f(-1) = -7$ **5.** $f(2) = 19$ **7.** $f(6) = 74$
9. $f(-2) = -65$ **11.** $f(-1) = -1$ **13.** $f(8) = -83$
15. $f(3) = 8751$ **17.** $f(-6) = 31$ **19.** $f(4) = -1113$
21. Yes **23.** No **25.** Yes **27.** Yes **29.** No **31.** Yes
33. Yes **35.** $f(x) = (x - 2)(x + 3)(x - 7)$
37. $f(x) = (x + 2)(4x - 1)(3x + 2)$
39. $f(x) = (x + 1)^2(x - 4)$
41. $f(x) = (x - 6)(x + 2)(x - 2)(x^2 + 4)$
43. $f(x) = (x + 5)(3x - 4)^2$ **45.** $k = 1$ or $k = -4$
47. $k = 6$ **49.** $f(c) > 0$ for all values of c
51. Let $f(x) = x^n - 1$. Because $(-1)^n = 1$ for all even positive integral values of n, $f(-1) = 0$ and $x - (-1) = x + 1$ is a factor.
53. (a) Let $f(x) = x^n - y^n$. Therefore $f(y) = y^n - y^n = 0$ and $x - y$ is a factor of $f(x)$. (c) Let $f(x) = x^n + y^n$. Therefore $f(-y) = (-y)^n + y^n = -y^n + y^n = 0$ when n is odd, and $x - (-y) = x + y$ is a factor of $f(x)$.
57. $f(1 + i) = 2 + 6i$
61. (a) $f(4) = 137; f(-5) = 11; f(7) = 575$
   (c) $f(4) = -79; f(5) = -162; f(-3) = 110$

Problem Set 4.3 (page 389)

1. $\{-3, 1, 4\}$ **3.** $\left\{-1, -\frac{1}{3}, \frac{2}{5}\right\}$ **5.** $\left\{-2, -\frac{1}{4}, \frac{5}{2}\right\}$

7. $\{-3, 2\}$ **9.** $\{2, 1 \pm \sqrt{5}\}$ **11.** $\{-3, -2, -1, 2\}$

13. $\{-2, 3, -1 \pm 2i\}$ **15.** $\{1, \pm i\}$

17. $\left\{-\frac{5}{2}, 1, \pm\sqrt{3}\right\}$ **19.** $\left\{-2, \frac{1}{2}\right\}$

27. $\{-3, -1, 2\}$ **29.** $\left\{-\frac{5}{2}, \frac{1}{3}, 3\right\}$

31. 1 positive and 1 negative solution
33. 1 positive and 2 nonreal complex solutions
35. 1 negative and 2 positive solutions *or* 1 negative and 2 nonreal complex solutions
37. 5 positive solutions *or* 3 positive and 2 nonreal complex solutions *or* 1 positive solution and 4 nonreal complex solutions
39. 1 negative and 4 nonreal complex solutions
41. $x^3 - 3x^2 - 10x + 24 = 0$
43. $6x^3 + 5x^2 - 12x + 4 = 0$
45. $x^5 - 5x^4 + 10x^3 - 10x^2 + 5x - 1 = 0$
47. $x^3 - 7x^2 + 25x - 39 = 0$
49. $x^4 - 2x^3 + 6x^2 - 8x + 8 = 0$
57. (a) $\{4, -3 \pm i\}$ (c) $\{-2, 6, 1 \pm \sqrt{3}\}$
   (e) $\{12, 1 \pm i\}$

Problem Set 4.4 (page 401)

1.
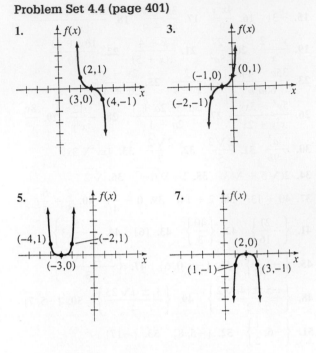

3.

5.
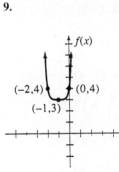

7.

9.
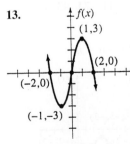

11.
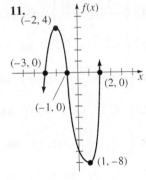

13.

15.
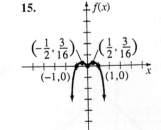

17.
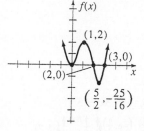

19.
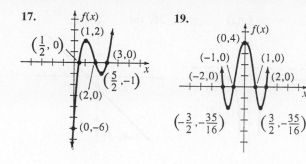

33.
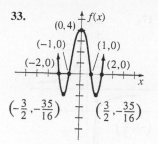

21.
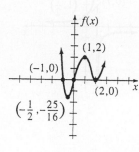

23.
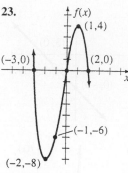

25.
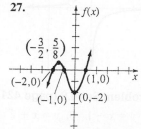

27.

29.

31.
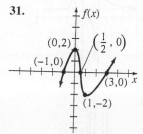

35. (a) -144 (b) $-3, 6$, and 8
(c) $f(x) > 0$ for $\{x | x < -3$ or $6 < x < 8\}$; $f(x) < 0$ for $\{x | -3 < x < 6$ or $x > 8\}$
37. (a) -81 (b) -3 and 1 (c) $f(x) > 0$ for $\{x | x > 1\}$; $f(x) < 0$ for $\{x | x < -3$ or $-3 < x < 1\}$
39. (a) 0 (b) $-4, 0$, and 6
(c) $f(x) > 0$ for $\{x | x < -4$ or $0 < x < 6$ or $x > 6\}$; $f(x) < 0$ for $\{x | -4 < x < 0\}$
41. (a) 0 (b) $-3, 0$, and 2
(c) $f(x) > 0$ for $\{x | -3 < x < 0$ or $0 < x < 2\}$; $f(x) < 0$ for $\{x | x < -3$ or $x > 2\}$
43. 1.7 inches
47. (a) 1.6 (c) 6.1 (e) 2.5
53. (a) $-2, 1$, and 4; $f(x) > 0$ for $(-2, 1) \cup (4, \infty)$; $f(x) < 0$ for $(-\infty, -2) \cup (1, 4)$
(c) 2 and 3; $f(x) > 0$ for $(3, \infty)$; $f(x) < 0$ for $(2, 3) \cup (-\infty, -2)$ (e) $-3, -1$, and 2; $f(x) > 0$ for $(-\infty, -3) \cup (2, \infty)$; $f(x) < 0$ for $(-3, -1) \cup (-1, 2)$
55. (a) -3.3; $(0.5, 3.1), (-1.9, 10.1)$
(c) $-2.2, 2.2$; $(-1.4, -8.0), (0, -4.0), (1.4, -8.0)$

Problem Set 4.5 (page 412)

1. V.A. $x = -3$; H.A. $y = 0$
3. V.A. $x = 1$; H.A. $y = 4$
5. V.A. $x = -3, x = -4$; H.A. $y = 0$
7. V.A. $x = -3, x = 3$; H.A. $y = 0$
9. V.A. none; H.A. $y = 5$
11.
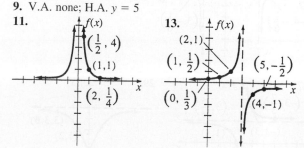

13.

15.

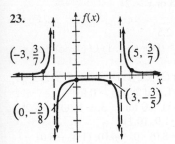

17.

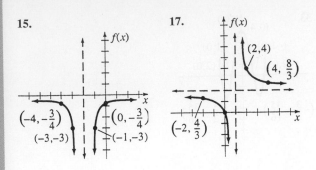

(2,4)

$\left(4, \frac{8}{3}\right)$

$\left(-2, \frac{4}{3}\right)$

19.

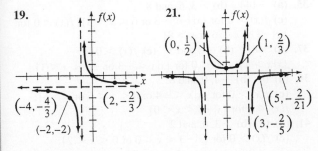

$\left(-4, -\frac{4}{3}\right)$ $\left(2, -\frac{2}{3}\right)$

$(-2, -2)$

21.

$\left(0, \frac{1}{2}\right)$ $\left(1, \frac{2}{3}\right)$

$\left(5, -\frac{2}{21}\right)$

$\left(3, -\frac{2}{5}\right)$

23.

$\left(-3, \frac{3}{7}\right)$ $\left(5, \frac{3}{7}\right)$

$\left(3, -\frac{3}{5}\right)$

$\left(0, -\frac{3}{8}\right)$

25.

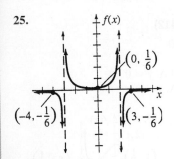

$\left(0, \frac{1}{6}\right)$

$\left(-4, -\frac{1}{6}\right)$ $\left(3, -\frac{1}{6}\right)$

27.

$\left(-3, \frac{7}{3}\right)$ $\left(3, \frac{5}{3}\right)$

$(-1, 3)$ $(1, 1)$

$\left(\frac{1}{2}, 0\right)$

29.

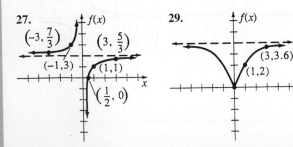

(3, 3.6)

(1, 2)

31.

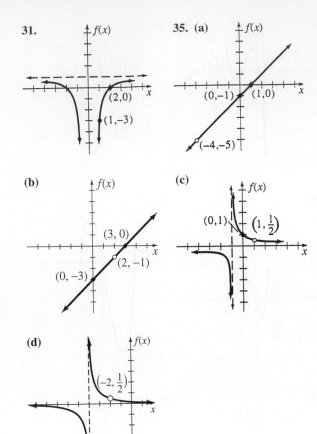

(2, 0)

(1, −3)

35. (a)

(0, −1)   (1, 0)

(−4, −5)

(b)

(3, 0)

(2, −1)

(0, −3)

(c)

(0, 1) $\left(1, \frac{1}{2}\right)$

(d)

$\left(-2, \frac{1}{2}\right)$

Problem Set 4.6 (page 421)

1. $y = x - 1$ **3.** $y = x + 2$ **5.** $y = 3x - 5$

7.

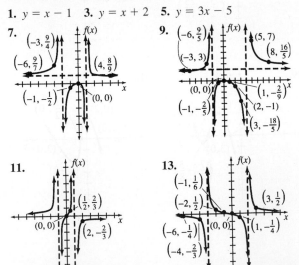

$\left(-3, \frac{9}{4}\right)$

$\left(-6, \frac{9}{7}\right)$ $\left(4, \frac{8}{9}\right)$

$\left(-1, -\frac{1}{2}\right)$ (0, 0)

9.

$\left(-6, \frac{9}{5}\right)$ (5, 7)

$(-3, 3)$ $\left(8, \frac{16}{5}\right)$

(0, 0) $\left(1, -\frac{2}{9}\right)$

$\left(-1, -\frac{2}{5}\right)$ (2, −1)

$\left(3, -\frac{18}{5}\right)$

11.

(0, 0) $\left(\frac{1}{2}, \frac{2}{3}\right)$

$\left(2, -\frac{2}{3}\right)$

13.

$\left(-1, \frac{1}{6}\right)$

$\left(-2, \frac{1}{2}\right)$ $\left(3, \frac{1}{2}\right)$

$\left(-6, -\frac{1}{4}\right)$ (0, 0) $\left(1, -\frac{1}{4}\right)$

$\left(-4, -\frac{2}{3}\right)$

15. 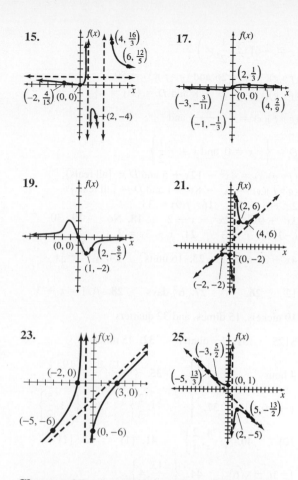 **17.** **19.** 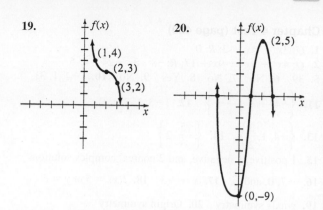 **20.**

19. **21.**

23. **25.**

Chapter 4 Review Problem Set (page 428)

1. $Q: 3x^2 - x + 5; R: 3$ **2.** $Q: 5x^2 - 3x - 3; R: 16$

3. $Q: -2x^3 + 9x^2 - 38x + 151; R: -605$

4. $Q: -3x^3 - 9x^2 - 32x - 96; R: -279$ **5.** $f(1) = 1$

6. $f(-3) = -197$ **7.** $f(-2) = 20$ **8.** $f(8) = 0$

9. Yes **10.** No **11.** Yes **12.** Yes **13.** $\{-3, 1, 5\}$

14. $\left\{-\dfrac{7}{2}, -1, \dfrac{5}{4}\right\}$ **15.** $\{1, 2, 1 \pm 5i\}$

16. $\{-2, 3 \pm \sqrt{7}\}$

17. 2 positive and 2 negative solutions *or* 2 positive and
2 nonreal complex solutions *or* 2 negative and 2 nonreal
complex solutions *or* 4 nonreal complex solutions

18. 1 negative and 4 nonreal complex solutions

21.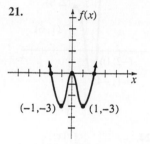

22.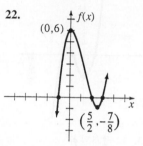

23.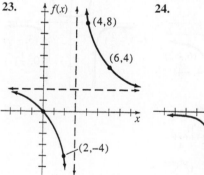

24.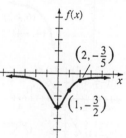

25.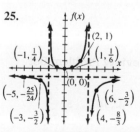

26.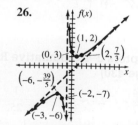

Chapter 4 Test (page 429)

1. $Q: 3x^2 - 4x - 2$; $R: 0$

2. $Q: 4x^3 + 8x^2 + 9x + 17$; $R: 38$ **3.** -24 **4.** 5

5. 39   **6.** No   **7.** No   **8.** Yes   **9.** No   **10.** $\{-4, 1, 3\}$

11. $\left\{-4, \dfrac{3 \pm \sqrt{17}}{4}\right\}$ **12.** $\{-3, 1, 3 \pm i\}$

13. $\left\{-4, 1, \dfrac{3}{2}\right\}$ **14.** $\left\{-\dfrac{5}{3}, 2\right\}$

15. 1 positive, 1 negative, and 2 nonreal complex solutions

16. $-7, 0,$ and $\dfrac{2}{3}$ **17.** $x = -3$ **18.** $f(x) = 5$ or $y = 5$

19. y-axis symmetry   **20.** Origin symmetry

21.

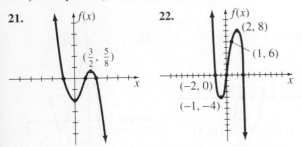

22.

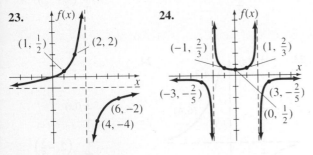

23.

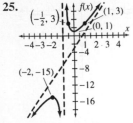

24.

25.

Chapters 0–4 Cumulative Review Problem Set (page 430)

1. $\dfrac{64}{27}$ **2.** $-\dfrac{2}{3}$ **3.** $-\dfrac{1}{25}$ **4.** 16   **5.** $\dfrac{1}{27}$

6. $\dfrac{8}{27}$ **7.** $\dfrac{9}{4}$ **8.** $-\dfrac{1}{36}$ **9.** 16   **10.** $-\dfrac{4}{3}$

11. $(-\infty, -6] \cup \left[\dfrac{1}{2}, \infty\right)$

12. $(f \circ g)(-2) = 26$ and $(g \circ f)(3) = 59$

13. $(f \circ g)(x) = -2x + 8$ and $D = \{x | x \neq 4\}$

$(g \circ f)(x) = -\dfrac{x}{4x + 2}$ and

$D = \left\{x | x \neq 0 \text{ and } x \neq -\dfrac{1}{2}\right\}$

14. $(f \circ g)(x) = 4x^2 - 12x + 5$ and $D = \{\text{all reals}\}$;
$(g \circ f)(x) = 2x^2 - 8x - 1$ and $D = \{\text{all reals}\}$

15. $2a + h + 7$ **16.** $f(9) = 33$

17. $3x^4 + 9x^3 + 2x^2 - x - 2$ **18.** No   **19.** 30

20. $(-3, 2)$; $r = 3$ **21.** $x + 3y = 2$

22. $4x + 3y = 5$ **23.** 16 units   **24.** $y = \pm\dfrac{1}{3}x$

25. 12   **26.** $\dfrac{2}{7}$ **27.** $6\frac{2}{3}$ days   **28.** $f(x) = x + 3$

29. 10 nickels, 15 dimes, and 32 quarters

30. $125   **31.** $1\dfrac{1}{3}$ quarts   **32.** 45 miles

33. 4 hours   **34.** $\left\{\dfrac{3}{5}\right\}$ **35.** $\left\{\dfrac{-13 \pm \sqrt{193}}{2}\right\}$

36. $\{-7, 0, 2\}$ **37.** $\left\{-\dfrac{5}{2}, -1, \dfrac{2}{3}\right\}$ **38.** $\left\{-1, \dfrac{5}{2}\right\}$

39. $\{0\}$ **40.** $\left\{-\dfrac{4}{3}, \dfrac{2}{3}\right\}$ **41.** $\{1\}$ **42.** $\{11\}$

43. $\{\pm 3i, \pm\sqrt{6}\}$ **44.** $\left\{-\dfrac{13}{2}, 4\right\}$

45. $\left\{1, 2, \dfrac{-1 \pm i\sqrt{11}}{2}\right\}$ **46.** $(-\infty, -5)$

47. $\left[-\dfrac{11}{17}, \infty\right)$ **48.** $(-3, 6)$

49. $[-3, 1] \cup [2, \infty)$ **50.** $\left(-\infty, -\dfrac{5}{2}\right) \cup \left(\dfrac{7}{2}, \infty\right)$

51. $\left[-\dfrac{10}{3}, 2\right]$ **52.** $\left(-\infty, \dfrac{3}{4}\right] \cup (2, \infty)$

53. $(-\infty, 4) \cup \left(\dfrac{15}{2}, \infty\right)$

54.

55.

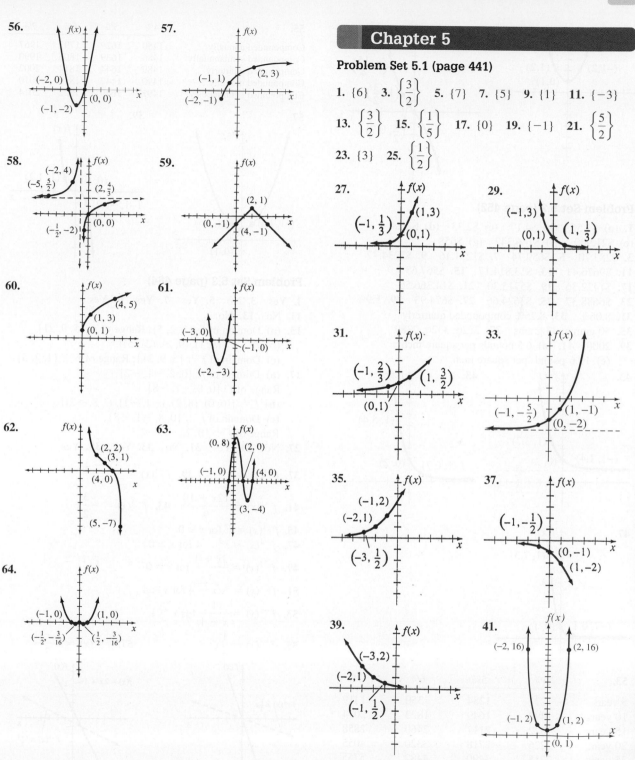

Chapter 5

Problem Set 5.1 (page 441)

1. $\{6\}$ 3. $\left\{\dfrac{3}{2}\right\}$ 5. $\{7\}$ 7. $\{5\}$ 9. $\{1\}$ 11. $\{-3\}$

13. $\left\{\dfrac{3}{2}\right\}$ 15. $\left\{\dfrac{1}{5}\right\}$ 17. $\{0\}$ 19. $\{-1\}$ 21. $\left\{\dfrac{5}{2}\right\}$

23. $\{3\}$ 25. $\left\{\dfrac{1}{2}\right\}$

43.

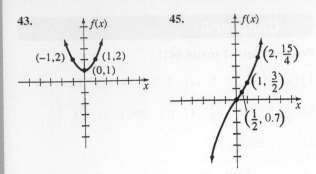

45.

f(x) graph with points $(2, \frac{15}{4})$, $(1, \frac{3}{2})$, $(\frac{1}{2}, 0.7)$

55.

	4%	5%	6%	7%
Compounded annually	1480	1629	1791	1967
Compounded semiannually	1486	1639	1806	1990
Compounded quarterly	1489	1644	1814	2002
Compounded monthly	1490	1647	1819	2010
Compounded continuously	1492	1649	1822	2014

57.

f(x) graph with points $(-1, 1.5)$, $(1, 1.5)$, $(0, 1)$

59.

f(x) graph with points $(0, 0)$, $(1, 1.2)$, $(-1, -1.2)$

Problem Set 5.2 (page 452)

1. (a) $1.55 **(b)** $4.17 **(c)** $2.33 **(d)** $2.28
(e) $21,900 **(f)** $246,342 **(g)** $658
3. $283.70 **5.** $659.74 **7.** $1251.16 **9.** $2234.77
11. $9676.41 **13.** $13,814.17 **15.** $567.63
17. $1422.36 **19.** $5715.30 **21.** $14,366.56
23. $6688.37 **25.** $3624.66 **27.** $674.93 **29.** 5.9%
31. 8.06% **33.** 8.25% compounded quarterly
35. 50 grams; 37 grams **37.** 2226; 3320; 7389
39. 2000 **41. (a)** 6.5 pounds per square inch
(c) 13.6 pounds per square inch

43.

f(x) graph with points $(-1, 1.4)$, $(0, 2)$, $(1, 3.7)$

45.

f(x) graph with points $(-1, 0.7)$, $(0, 2)$, $(1, 5.4)$

47.

f(x) graph with points $(-1, 0.1)$, $(0, 1)$, $(1, 7.3)$

53.

	4%	5%	6%	7%
5 years	1221	1284	1350	1419
10 years	1492	1649	1822	2014
15 years	1822	2117	2460	2858
20 years	2226	2718	3320	4055
25 years	2718	3490	4482	5755

Problem Set 5.3 (page 464)

1. Yes **3.** No **5.** Yes **7.** Yes **9.** Yes
11. No **13.** No
15. (a) Domain of f: $\{1, 2, 5\}$; Range of f: $\{5, 9, 21\}$
   (b) $f^{-1} = \{(5, 1), (9, 2), (21, 5)\}$
   (c) Domain of f^{-1}: $\{5, 9, 21\}$; Range of f^{-1}: $\{1, 2, 5\}$
17. (a) Domain of f: $\{0, 2, -1, -2\}$;
   Range of f: $\{0, 8, -1, -8\}$
   (b) f^{-1}: $\{(0, 0), (8, 2), (-1, -1), (-8, -2)\}$
   (c) Domain of f^{-1}: $\{0, 8, -1, -8\}$;
   Range of f^{-1}: $\{0, 2, -1, -2\}$
27. No **29.** Yes **31.** No **33.** Yes **35.** Yes

37. $f^{-1}(x) = x + 4$ **39.** $f^{-1}(x) = \dfrac{-x - 4}{3}$

41. $f^{-1}(x) = \dfrac{12x + 10}{9}$ **43.** $f^{-1}(x) = -\dfrac{3}{2}x$

45. $f^{-1}(x) = x^2$ for $x \geq 0$
47. $f^{-1}(x) = x^2 - 4$ for $x \geq 0$

49. $f^{-1}(x) = \dfrac{3x + 1}{x}$ for $x \neq 0$

51. $f^{-1}(x) = \sqrt{x - 4}$ for $x \geq 4$

53. $f^{-1}(x) = \dfrac{1}{x - 1}$ for $x > 1$

55. $f^{-1}(x) = \dfrac{1}{3}x$ **57.** $f^{-1}(x) = \dfrac{x - 1}{2}$

Graph for 55: $f(x) = 3x$, $f^{-1}(x) = \frac{1}{3}x$

Graph for 57: $f(x) = 2x + 1$, $f^{-1}(x) = \frac{x-1}{2}$

59. $f^{-1}(x) = \sqrt{x + 4}$ for $x \geq -4$

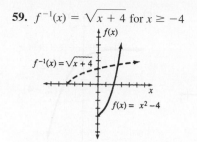

61. Increasing on $[0, \infty)$ and decreasing on $(-\infty, 0]$
63. Decreasing on $(-\infty, \infty)$
65. Increasing on $(-\infty, -2]$ and decreasing on $[-2, \infty)$
67. Increasing on $(-\infty, -4]$ and decreasing on $[-4, \infty)$

73. **(a)** $f^{-1}(x) = \dfrac{x + 9}{3}$ **(c)** $f^{-1}(x) = -x + 1$

(e) $f^{-1}(x) = -\dfrac{1}{5}x$

Problem Set 5.4 (page 475)

1. $\log_2 128 = 7$ **3.** $\log_5 125 = 3$ **5.** $\log_{10} 1000 = 3$

7. $\log_2\left(\dfrac{1}{4}\right) = -2$ **9.** $\log_{10} 0.1 = -1$ **11.** $3^4 = 81$

13. $4^3 = 64$ **15.** $10^4 = 10,000$ **17.** $2^{-4} = \dfrac{1}{16}$

19. $10^{-3} = 0.001$ **21.** 4 **23.** 4 **25.** 3 **27.** $\dfrac{1}{2}$ **29.** 0

31. $\dfrac{3}{2}$ **33.** -3 **35.** -1 **37.** 5 **39.** -5 **41.** 1

43. 0 **45.** $\{49\}$ **47.** $\{16\}$ **49.** $\left\{\dfrac{1}{9}\right\}$ **51.** $\left\{\dfrac{1}{8}\right\}$

53. $\left\{\dfrac{1}{8}\right\}$ **55.** $\{4\}$ **57.** 5.1293 **59.** 6.9657

61. 1.4037 **63.** 7.4512 **65.** 6.3219 **67.** -0.3791
69. 0.5766 **71.** 2.1531 **73.** 0.3949

75. $\log_b x + \log_b y + \log_b z$ **77.** $\log_b y - \log_b z$

79. $3 \log_b y + 4 \log_b z$ **81.** $\dfrac{1}{2}\log_b x - \dfrac{1}{3}\log_b y - 4\log_b z$

83. $\dfrac{2}{3}\log_b x + \dfrac{1}{3}\log_b z$ **85.** $\dfrac{3}{2}\log_b x - \dfrac{1}{2}\log_b y$

87. $\log_b\left(\dfrac{x^2}{y^4}\right)$ **89.** $\log_b\left(\dfrac{xz}{y}\right)$ **91.** $\log_b\left(\dfrac{x^2 z^4}{z^3}\right)$

93. $\log_b\left(\dfrac{y^4\sqrt{x}}{x}\right)$ **95.** $\left\{\dfrac{9}{4}\right\}$ **97.** $\{25\}$ **99.** $\{4\}$

101. $\{-2\}$ **103.** $\left\{-\dfrac{4}{3}\right\}$ **105.** $\left\{\dfrac{19}{8}\right\}$ **107.** $\{9\}$

109. $\varnothing$ **111.** $\{1\}$

Problem Set 5.5 (page 484)

1. 0.8597 **3.** 1.7179 **5.** 3.5071 **7.** -0.1373
9. -3.4685 **11.** 411.43 **13.** 90,095 **15.** 79.543

17. 0.048440 **19.** 0.0064150 **21.** 1.6094 **23.** 3.4843
25. 6.0638 **27.** -0.7765 **29.** -3.4609 **31.** 1.6034
33. 3.1346 **35.** 108.56 **37.** 0.48268 **39.** 0.035994

41. **43.**

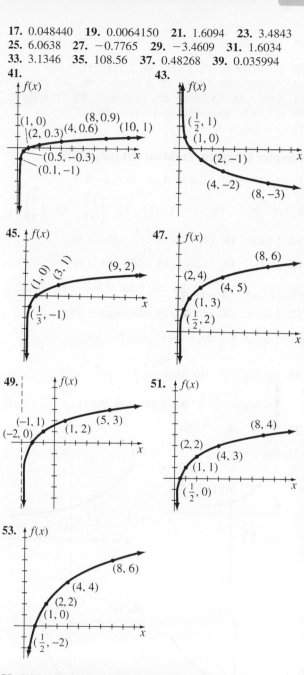

55. 0.36 **57.** 0.73 **59.** 23.10 **61.** 7.93

Problem Set 5.6 (page 494)

1. $\{2.33\}$ **3.** $\{2.56\}$ **5.** $\{5.43\}$ **7.** $\{4.18\}$ **9.** $\{0.12\}$
11. $\{3.30\}$ **13.** $\{4.57\}$ **15.** $\{1.79\}$ **17.** $\{3.32\}$

19. $\{2.44\}$ **21.** $\{4\}$ **23.** $\left\{\dfrac{19}{47}\right\}$ **25.** $\{-2 + \sqrt{13}\}$

27. {3}   **29.** $\left\{\dfrac{-1 + \sqrt{33}}{4}\right\}$ **31.** {1}   **33.** {8}

35. {1, 10,000}   **37.** 5.322   **39.** 2.524   **41.** 0.339
43. -0.837 **45.** 3.194   **47.** 4.8 years   **49.** 17.3 years
51. 5.9%   **53.** 6.8 hours   **55.** 6100 feet   **57.** 3.5 hours
59. 6.7   **61.** Approximately 8 times   **69.** {1.13}
71. $x = \ln(y + \sqrt{y^2 + 1})$

Chapter 5 Review Problem Set (page 505)

1. 32   **2.** -125 **3.** 81   **4.** 3   **5.** -2 **6.** $\dfrac{1}{3}$ **7.** $\dfrac{1}{4}$

8. -5 **9.** 1   **10.** 12   **11.** {5}   **12.** $\left\{\dfrac{1}{9}\right\}$ **13.** $\left\{\dfrac{7}{2}\right\}$

14. {3.40}   **15.** {8}   **16.** $\left\{\dfrac{1}{11}\right\}$ **17.** {1.95}

18. {1.41}   **19.** {1.56}   **20.** {20}   **21.** $\{10^{100}\}$

22. {2}   **23.** $\left\{\dfrac{11}{2}\right\}$ **24.** {0}   **25.** 0.3680   **26.** 1.3222

27. 1.4313   **28.** 0.5634   **29. (a)** $\log_b x - 2\log_b y$

(b) $\dfrac{1}{4}\log_b x + \dfrac{1}{2}\log_b y$ **(c)** $\dfrac{1}{2}\log_b x - 3\log_b y$

30. (a) $\log_b x^3 y^2$ **(b)** $\log_b\left(\dfrac{\sqrt{y}}{x^4}\right)$

(c) $\log_b\left(\dfrac{\sqrt{xy}}{z^2}\right)$ **31.** 1.585   **32.** 0.631

33. 3.789   **34.** -2.120

35. (a)   **(b)**
(c)   **36. (a)**

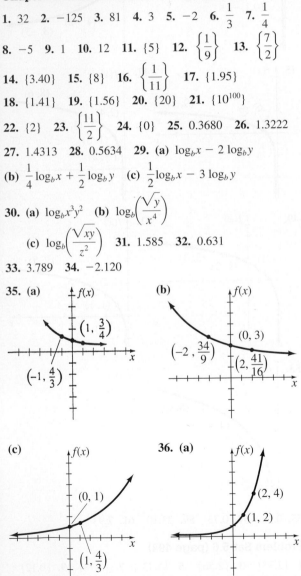

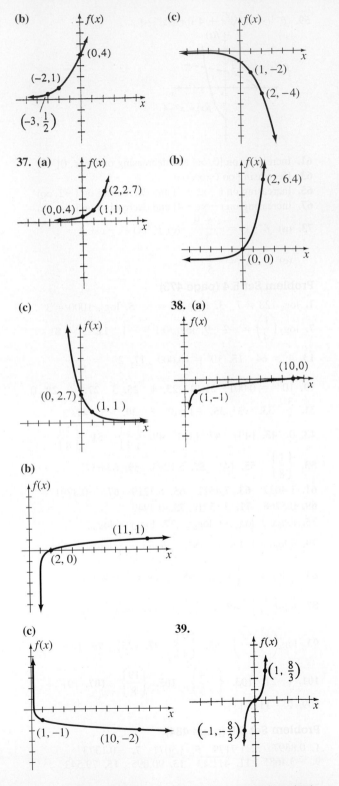

(b)   **(c)**
37. (a)   **(b)**
38. (a)   **(b)**
(c)   **39.**

40.

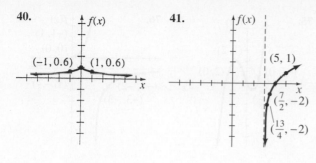

41.

42.

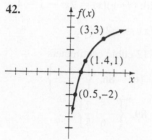

23.

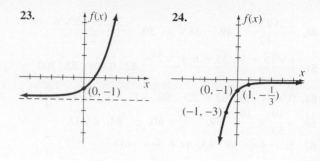

24.

25.

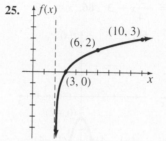

43. \$11,166.48   **44.** \$2642.13   **45.** \$8985.50   **46.** Yes

47. No   **48.** Yes   **49.** Yes   **50.** $f^{-1}(x) = \dfrac{x-5}{4}$

51. $f^{-1}(x) = \dfrac{-x-7}{3}$ **52.** $f^{-1}(x) = \dfrac{6x+2}{5}$

53. $f^{-1}(x) = \sqrt{-2-x}$

54. Increasing on $(-\infty, 4]$ and decreasing on $[4, \infty)$

55. Increasing on $[3, \infty)$ **56.** Approximately 10.2 years

57. Approximately 28 years   **58.** Approximately 8.7%

59. 61,070; 67,493; 74,591   **60.** Approximately 4.8 hours

61. 133 grams   **62.** 8.1

Chapter 5 Test (page 508)

1. $\dfrac{1}{2}$ **2.** 1   **3.** 1   **4.** -1 **5.** $\{-3\}$ **6.** $\left\{-\dfrac{3}{2}\right\}$

7. $\left\{\dfrac{8}{3}\right\}$ **8.** $\{243\}$ **9.** $\{2\}$ **10.** $\left\{\dfrac{2}{5}\right\}$ **11.** 4.1919

12. 0.2031   **13.** 0.7325   **14.** $f^{-1}(x) = \dfrac{-6-x}{3}$

15. $\{5.17\}$ **16.** $\{10.29\}$ **17.** 4.0069

18. $f^{-1}(x) = \dfrac{3}{2}x + \dfrac{9}{10}$ **19.** \$6342.08   **20.** 13.5 years

21. 7.8 hours   **22.** 4813 grams

Chapters 0–5 Cumulative Review Problem Set (page 509)

1. -6 **2.** -8 **3.** $\dfrac{13}{24}$ **4.** 56   **5.** $\dfrac{13}{6}$ **6.** $-90\sqrt{2}$

7. $2x + 5\sqrt{x} - 12$ **8.** $-18 + 22\sqrt{3}$

9. $2x^3 + 11x^2 - 14x + 4$ **10.** $\dfrac{x+4}{x(x+5)}$ **11.** $\dfrac{16x^2}{27y}$

12. $\dfrac{16x+43}{90}$ **13.** $\dfrac{35a-44b}{60a^2b}$ **14.** $\dfrac{2}{x-4}$

15. $2x^2 - x - 4$ **16.** $\dfrac{5y^2 - 3xy^2}{x^2y + 2x^2}$ **17.** $\dfrac{2y-3xy}{3x+4xy}$

18. $\dfrac{(2n-5)(n+3)}{(n-2)(3n+13)}$ **19.** $\dfrac{3a^2 - 2a + 1}{2a - 1}$

20. $(5x-2)(4x+3)$ **21.** $2(2x+3)(4x^2 - 6x + 9)$

22. $(2x+3)(2x-3)(x+2)(x-2)$

23. $4x(3x+2)(x-5)$ **24.** $(y-6)(x+3)$

25. $(5-3x)(2+3x)$ **26.** $\dfrac{81}{16}$ **27.** 4   **28.** $-\dfrac{3}{4}$

29. -0.3 **30.** $\dfrac{1}{81}$ **31.** $\dfrac{21}{16}$ **32.** $\dfrac{9}{64}$ **33.** 72   **34.** 6

35. -2 **36.** $\dfrac{-12}{x^3y}$ **37.** $\dfrac{8y}{x^5}$ **38.** $-\dfrac{a^3}{9b}$ **39.** $4\sqrt{5}$

40. $-6\sqrt{6}$ **41.** $\dfrac{5\sqrt{3}}{9}$ **42.** $\dfrac{2\sqrt{3}}{3}$ **43.** $2\sqrt[3]{7}$

44. $\dfrac{\sqrt[3]{6}}{2}$ **45.** $8xy\sqrt{13x}$ **46.** $\dfrac{\sqrt{6xy}}{3y}$ **47.** $11\sqrt{6}$

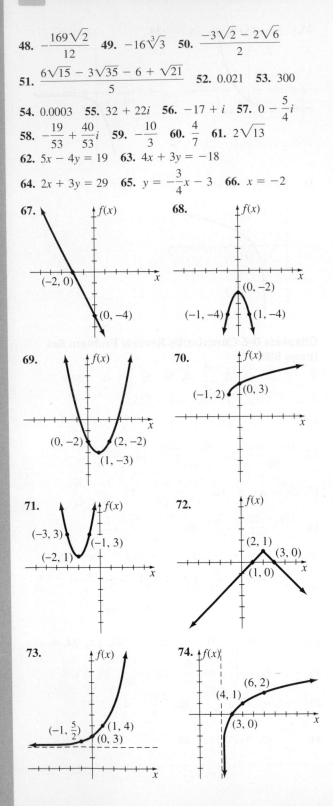

48. $-\dfrac{169\sqrt{2}}{12}$ **49.** $-16\sqrt[3]{3}$ **50.** $\dfrac{-3\sqrt{2}-2\sqrt{6}}{2}$

51. $\dfrac{6\sqrt{15}-3\sqrt{35}-6+\sqrt{21}}{5}$ **52.** 0.021 **53.** 300

54. 0.0003 **55.** $32+22i$ **56.** $-17+i$ **57.** $0-\dfrac{5}{4}i$

58. $-\dfrac{19}{53}+\dfrac{40}{53}i$ **59.** $-\dfrac{10}{3}$ **60.** $\dfrac{4}{7}$ **61.** $2\sqrt{13}$

62. $5x-4y=19$ **63.** $4x+3y=-18$

64. $2x+3y=29$ **65.** $y=-\dfrac{3}{4}x-3$ **66.** $x=-2$

77. $(g\circ f)(x)=2x^2-13x+20;\ (f\circ g)(x)=2x^2-x-4$

78. $f^{-1}(x)=\dfrac{x+7}{3}$ **79.** $f^{-1}(x)=-2x+\dfrac{4}{3}$

80. $k=-3$ **81.** $y=1$ **82.** 12 cubic centimeters

83. $\left\{-\dfrac{21}{16}\right\}$ **84.** $\left\{\dfrac{40}{3}\right\}$ **85.** $\{6\}$ **86.** $\left\{-\dfrac{5}{2},3\right\}$

87. $\left\{0,\dfrac{7}{3}\right\}$ **88.** $\{-6,0,6\}$ **89.** $\left\{-\dfrac{5}{6},\dfrac{2}{5}\right\}$

90. $\left\{-3,0,\dfrac{3}{2}\right\}$ **91.** $\{\pm1,\pm3i\}$ **92.** $\{-5,7\}$

93. $\{-29,0\}$ **94.** $\left\{\dfrac{7}{2}\right\}$ **95.** $\{12\}$ **96.** $\{-3\}$

97. $\left\{\dfrac{1\pm3\sqrt{5}}{3}\right\}$ **98.** $\left\{\dfrac{-5\pm4i\sqrt{2}}{2}\right\}$

99. $\left\{\dfrac{3\pm i\sqrt{23}}{4}\right\}$ **100.** $\left\{\dfrac{3\pm\sqrt{3}}{3}\right\}$ **101.** $\{1\pm\sqrt{34}\}$

102. $\left\{\pm\dfrac{\sqrt{5}}{2},\pm\dfrac{\sqrt{3}}{3}\right\}$ **103.** $\left\{\dfrac{-5\pm i\sqrt{15}}{4}\right\}$

104. $\{-4,1,7\}$ **105.** $\left\{-\dfrac{1}{2},\dfrac{5}{3},2\right\}$ **106.** $\left\{\dfrac{3}{2}\right\}$

107. $\{81\}$ **108.** $\{4\}$ **109.** $\{6\}$ **110.** $\left\{\dfrac{1}{5}\right\}$

111. $(-\infty,3)$ **112.** $(-\infty,50]$

113. $\left(-\infty,-\dfrac{11}{5}\right)\cup(3,\infty)$ **114.** $\left(-\dfrac{5}{3},1\right)$

115. $\left[-\dfrac{9}{11},\infty\right)$ **116.** $[-4,2]$

117. $\left(-\infty,\dfrac{1}{3}\right)\cup(4,\infty)$ **118.** $(-8,3)$

119. $(-\infty,3]\cup(7,\infty)$ **120.** $(-6,-3)$
121. 17, 19, and 21   **122.** 14 nickels, 20 dimes, and
29 quarters   **123.** $48°$ and $132°$ **124.** $600
125. $1700 at 8% and $2000 at 9%
126. 66 miles per hour and 76 miles per hour
127. 4 quarts   **128.** 69 or less   **129.** -3, 0, or 3
130. 1-inch strip   **131.** $1050 and $1400   **132.** 3 hours

Chapter 6

Problem Set 6.1 (page 521)

1. $\{(3, 2)\}$ 3. $\{(-2, 1)\}$ 5. Dependent   7. $\{(4, -3)\}$
9. Inconsistent   11. $\{(7, 9)\}$ 13. $\{(-4, 7)\}$ 15. $\{(6, 3)\}$
17. $a = -3$ and $b = -4$

19. $\left\{\left(k, \frac{2}{3}k - \frac{4}{3}\right)\right\}$, a dependent system

21. $u = 5$ and $t = 7$ 23. $\{(2, -5)\}$

25. $\varnothing$, an inconsistent system   27. $\left\{\left(-\frac{3}{4}, -\frac{6}{5}\right)\right\}$

29. $\{(3, -4)\}$ 31. $\{(2, 8)\}$ 33. $\{(-1, -5)\}$
35. $\varnothing$, an inconsistent system   37. $a = 2$ and $b = -\frac{1}{3}$

39. $s = -6$ and $t = 12$ 41. $\left\{\left(-\frac{1}{2}, \frac{1}{3}\right)\right\}$

43. $\left\{\left(\frac{3}{4}, -\frac{2}{3}\right)\right\}$ 45. $\{(-4, 2)\}$ 47. $\{(5, 5)\}$

49. $\varnothing$, an inconsistent system   51. $\{(12, -24)\}$
53. $t = 8$ and $u = 3$ 55. $\{(200, 800)\}$ 57. $\{(400, 800)\}$
59. $\{(3.5, 7)\}$ 61. 17 and 36   63. $15°, 75°$ 65. 72
67. 12   69. 8 single rooms and 15 double rooms
71. 2500 student tickets and 500 nonstudent tickets
73. \$500 at 4% and \$1500 at 6%
75. 3 miles per hour   77. \$22.00
79. 30 five-dollar bills and 18 ten-dollar bills

85. $\{(4, 6)\}$ 87. $\{(2, -3)\}$ 89. $\left\{\left(\frac{1}{4}, -\frac{2}{3}\right)\right\}$

Problem Set 6.2 (page 532)

1. $\{(-4, -2, 3)\}$ 3. $\{(-2, 5, 2)\}$ 5. $\{(4, -1, -2)\}$
7. $\{(3, 1, 2)\}$ 9. $\{(-1, 3, 5)\}$ 11. $\{(-2, -1, 3)\}$
13. $\{(0, 2, 4)\}$ 15. $\{(4, -1, -2)\}$ 17. $\{(-4, 0, -1)\}$
19. $\{(2, 2, -3)\}$
21. 4 pounds of pecans, 4 pounds of almonds, and
    12 pounds of peanuts
23. 7 nickels, 13 dimes, and 22 quarters
25. $40°, 60°$, and $80°$
27. \$500 at 4%, \$1000 at 5%, and \$1500 at 6%
29. 50 of type A, 75 of type B, and 150 of type C

Problem Set 6.3 (page 542)

1. Yes   3. Yes   5. No   7. No   9. Yes   11. $\{(-1, -5)\}$
13. $\{(3, -6)\}$ 15. $\varnothing$ 17. $\{(-2, -9)\}$ 19. $\{(-1, -2, 3)\}$
21. $\{(3, -1, 4)\}$ 23. $\{(0, -2, 4)\}$
25. $\{(-7k + 8, -5k + 7, k)\}$ 27. $\{(-4, -3, -2)\}$
29. $\{(4, -1, -2)\}$ 31. $\{(1, -1, 2, -3)\}$
33. $\{(2, 1, 3, -2)\}$ 35. $\{(-2, 4, -3, 0)\}$
37. $\varnothing$ 39. $\{(-3k + 5, -1, -4k + 2, k)\}$
41. $\{(-3k + 9, k, 2, -3)\}$ 45. $\{(17k - 6, 10k - 5, k)\}$

47. $\left\{\left(-\frac{1}{2}k + \frac{34}{11}, \frac{1}{2}k - \frac{5}{11}, k\right)\right\}$ 49. $\varnothing$

Problem Set 6.4 (page 553)

1. 22   3. -29 5. 20   7. 5   9. -2 11. $-\frac{2}{3}$

13. -25 15. 58   17. 39   19. -12 21. -41
23. -8 25. 1088   27. -140 29. 81   31. 146
33. Property 6.3   35. Property 6.2   37. Property 6.4
39. Property 6.3   41. Property 6.5

Problem Set 6.5 (page 561)

1. $\{(1, 4)\}$ 3. $\{(3, -5)\}$ 5. $\{(2, -1)\}$ 7. $\varnothing$

9. $\left\{\left(-\frac{1}{4}, \frac{2}{3}\right)\right\}$ 11. $\left\{\left(\frac{2}{17}, \frac{52}{17}\right)\right\}$ 13. $\{(9, -2)\}$

15. $\left\{\left(2, -\frac{5}{7}\right)\right\}$ 17. $\{(0, 2, -3)\}$ 19. $\{(2, 6, 7)\}$

21. $\{(4, -4, 5)\}$ 23. $\{(-1, 3, -4)\}$

25. Infinitely many solutions   27. $\left\{\left(-2, \frac{1}{2}, -\frac{2}{3}\right)\right\}$

29. $\left\{\left(3, \frac{1}{2}, -\frac{1}{3}\right)\right\}$ 31. $(-4, 6, 0)$ 37. $(0, 0, 0)$

39. Infinitely many solutions

Problem Set 6.6 (page 569)

1. $\dfrac{4}{x - 2} + \dfrac{7}{x + 1}$ 3. $\dfrac{3}{x + 1} - \dfrac{5}{x - 1}$

5. $\dfrac{1}{3x - 1} + \dfrac{6}{2x + 3}$ 7. $\dfrac{2}{x - 1} + \dfrac{3}{x + 2} - \dfrac{4}{x - 3}$

9. $\dfrac{-1}{x} + \dfrac{2}{2x - 1} - \dfrac{3}{4x + 1}$ 11. $\dfrac{2}{x - 2} + \dfrac{5}{(x - 2)^2}$

13. $\dfrac{4}{x} + \dfrac{7}{x^2} - \dfrac{10}{x + 3}$ 15. $\dfrac{-3}{x^2 + 1} - \dfrac{2}{x - 4}$

17. $\dfrac{3}{x + 2} - \dfrac{2}{(x + 2)^2} + \dfrac{1}{(x + 2)^3}$

19. $\dfrac{2}{x} + \dfrac{3x + 5}{x^2 - x + 3}$ 21. $\dfrac{2x}{x^2 + 1} + \dfrac{3 - x}{(x^2 + 1)^2}$

Chapter 6 Review Problem Set (page 576)

1. $\{(3, -7)\}$ 2. $\{(-1, -3)\}$ 3. $\{(0, -4)\}$

4. $\left\{\left(\frac{23}{3}, -\frac{14}{3}\right)\right\}$ 5. $\{(4, -6)\}$ 6. $\left\{\left(-\frac{6}{7}, -\frac{15}{7}\right)\right\}$

7. $\{(-1, 2, -5)\}$ 8. $\{(2, -3, -1)\}$ 9. $\{(5, -4)\}$
10. $\{(2, 7)\}$ 11. $\{(-2, 2, -1)\}$ 12. $\{(0, -1, 2)\}$
13. $\{(-3, -1)\}$ 14. $\{(4, 6)\}$ 15. $\{(2, -3, -4)\}$
16. $\{(-1, 2, -5)\}$ 17. $\{(5, -5)\}$ 18. $\{(-12, 12)\}$

19. $\left\{\left(\frac{5}{7}, \frac{4}{7}\right)\right\}$ 20. $\{(-10, -7)\}$ 21. $\{(1, 1, -4)\}$

22. $\{(-4, 0, 1)\}$ 23. $\varnothing$ 24. $\{(-2, -4, 6)\}$ 25. -34
26. 13   27. -40 28. 16   29. 51   30. 125

31. $6\frac{2}{3}$ quarts of the 1% milk and $3\frac{1}{3}$ quarts of the 4% milk

32. 7 centimeters by 21 centimeters

33. $1200 at 1% and $3000 at 1.5%

34. 5 five-dollar bills and 25 one-dollar bills

35. 30 review problems and 80 new material problems

36. $900 at 4% and $1600 at 6%

37. 20 nickels, 32 dimes, and 54 quarters

38. 24 five-dollar bills, 30 ten-dollar bills, 10 twenty-dollar bills

39. $40°, 60°, 80°$ **40.** $25°, 45°,$ and $110°$

41. $2100 on Bank of US; $1600 on Community Bank; and $2700 on First National

42. 6 inches, 12 inches, 15 inches

Chapter 6 Test (page 578)

1. III **2.** I **3.** III **4.** II **5.** 8 **6.** $-\dfrac{7}{12}$ **7.** -18

8. 112 **9.** Infinitely many **10.** $\{(-2, 4)\}$ **11.** $\{(3, -1)\}$

12. $x = -12$ **13.** $y = -\dfrac{13}{11}$ **14.** $x = 14$ **15.** $y = 13$

16. Infinitely many **17.** None **18.** $\left\{\left(\dfrac{11}{5}, 6, -3\right)\right\}$

19. $\{(-2, -1, 0)\}$ **20.** $x = 1$ **21.** $y = 4$ **22.** 2 liters

23. 30 express washes **24.** 5 batches of cream puffs, 4 batches of eclairs, and 10 batches of Danish rolls

25. $100°, 45°,$ and $35°$

Chapters 0–6 Cumulative Review Problem Set (page 580)

1. $\dfrac{324}{121}$ **2.** 2 **3.** 5 **4.** -3 **5.** $\dfrac{3}{2}$ **6.** 81 **7.** 6 **8.** 3

9. $\dfrac{8}{27}$ **10.** -0.2 **11.** -52 **12.** $-\dfrac{7}{12}$ **13.** $\dfrac{5}{18}$ **14.** 21

15. $\dfrac{2}{3}$ **16.** $\dfrac{x + 4}{x(x + 2)(x - 2)}$ **17.** $\dfrac{x^2 - x + 1}{x + 2}$

18. $\dfrac{17x - 17}{24}$ **19.** $\dfrac{3}{2x^3 y^2}$ **20.** $\dfrac{b^7}{4a^3}$ **21.** $-\dfrac{30}{x^3 y^3}$

22. $48\sqrt{2}$ **23.** $3xy\sqrt[3]{2y^2}$ **24.** $\dfrac{\sqrt{2}}{4}$

25. $x + 2y = 10$ **26.** $f(x) = \dfrac{11}{6}x + \dfrac{2}{3}$

27. $f(g(-2)) = -199$ and $g(f(3)) = 81$

28. $f(g(x)) = 2x^2 + x + 4$ and $g(f(x)) = 2x^2 + 29x + 102$

29. $10 + 30i$ **30.** $f^{-1}(x) = -\dfrac{1}{3}x + \dfrac{10}{3}$ **31.** 6 units

32. 14 **33.** 0 **34.** $Q: x^2 + 7x - 1;\ R: 0$

35. $Q: 2x^3 - 5x^2 + 7x - 8;\ R: 14$ **36.** Yes

37. No **38.** Yes **39.** $y = \pm 3x$ **40.** -6

41. -1 **42.** 6.66 **43.** $x = 1$ and $f(x) = 2$

44. y axis **45.** $f(x) = 2x - 2$ **46.** $\left\{\dfrac{11}{8}\right\}$

47. $\left\{-\dfrac{53}{11}\right\}$ **48.** $\left\{-\dfrac{11}{2}, \dfrac{1}{2}\right\}$ **49.** $\{(-1, 4)\}$

50. $\left\{-\dfrac{7}{2}, 0, \dfrac{2}{7}\right\}$ **51.** $\left\{-2, \dfrac{3 \pm i\sqrt{15}}{4}\right\}$

52. $\left\{-\dfrac{1}{2}, \dfrac{5}{3}\right\}$ **53.** $\{-7, -1\}$ **54.** $\{(1, 2, -3)\}$

55. $\{-13\}$ **56.** $\{1\}$ **57.** $\{3.21\}$ **58.** $\{-1 + \sqrt{14}\}$

59. $\left[\dfrac{17}{2}, \infty\right)$ **60.** $\left(-\dfrac{3}{2}, \dfrac{5}{2}\right)$ **61.** $\left(-\infty, -\dfrac{8}{3}\right) \cup \left(\dfrac{4}{3}, \infty\right)$

62. $[3, \infty)$ **63.** $[-4, 2] \cup [7, \infty)$

64. $(-\infty, 1) \cup (2, \infty)$ **65.** $(4, 9)$ **66.** $[-8, 3]$

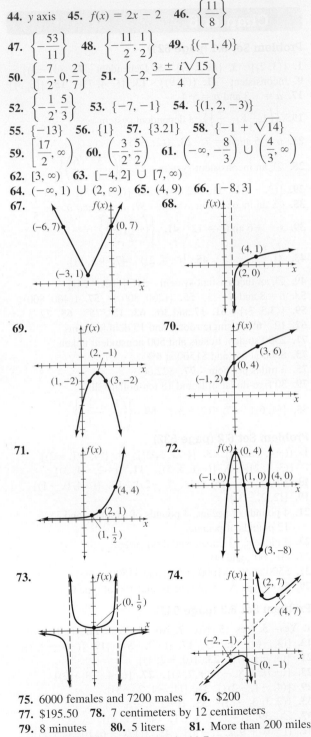

75. 6000 females and 7200 males **76.** $200

77. $195.50 **78.** 7 centimeters by 12 centimeters

79. 8 minutes **80.** 5 liters **81.** More than 200 miles

82. $18,000 **83.** Approximately 11.7 years

Chapter 7

Problem Set 7.1 (page 589)

1. $\begin{bmatrix} 3 & -5 \\ 8 & 3 \end{bmatrix}$ **3.** $\begin{bmatrix} -2 & 21 \\ -7 & 2 \end{bmatrix}$ **5.** $\begin{bmatrix} -2 & 1 \\ -3 & 19 \end{bmatrix}$

7. $\begin{bmatrix} -1 & -5 \\ 2 & 3 \end{bmatrix}$ **9.** $\begin{bmatrix} -12 & -14 \\ -18 & -20 \end{bmatrix}$ **11.** $\begin{bmatrix} 2 & -11 \\ -7 & 0 \end{bmatrix}$

13. $AB = \begin{bmatrix} 4 & -6 \\ 8 & -12 \end{bmatrix}, BA = \begin{bmatrix} -5 & 5 \\ 3 & -3 \end{bmatrix}$

15. $AB = \begin{bmatrix} -5 & -18 \\ -4 & 42 \end{bmatrix}, BA = \begin{bmatrix} 19 & -39 \\ -16 & 18 \end{bmatrix}$

17. $AB = \begin{bmatrix} 14 & -28 \\ 7 & -14 \end{bmatrix}, BA = \begin{bmatrix} 0 & 0 \\ 0 & 0 \end{bmatrix}$

19. $AB = \begin{bmatrix} -14 & -7 \\ -12 & -1 \end{bmatrix}, BA = \begin{bmatrix} -2 & -3 \\ -32 & -13 \end{bmatrix}$

21. $AB = \begin{bmatrix} 1 & 0 \\ 0 & 1 \end{bmatrix}, BA = \begin{bmatrix} 1 & 0 \\ 0 & 1 \end{bmatrix}$

23. $AB = \begin{bmatrix} 0 & -\dfrac{5}{3} \\ \dfrac{17}{6} & -3 \end{bmatrix}, BA = \begin{bmatrix} 0 & -\dfrac{17}{6} \\ \dfrac{5}{3} & -3 \end{bmatrix}$

25. $AB = \begin{bmatrix} 1 & 0 \\ 0 & 1 \end{bmatrix}, BA = \begin{bmatrix} 1 & 0 \\ 0 & 1 \end{bmatrix}$

27. $AB = \begin{bmatrix} 3 & -2 \\ 4 & 5 \end{bmatrix}, BA = \begin{bmatrix} 5 & 4 \\ -2 & 3 \end{bmatrix}$

29. $AD = \begin{bmatrix} 1 & 1 \\ 9 & 9 \end{bmatrix}, DA = \begin{bmatrix} 3 & 7 \\ 3 & 7 \end{bmatrix}$

49. $A^2 = \begin{bmatrix} -1 & -4 \\ 8 & 7 \end{bmatrix}, A^3 = \begin{bmatrix} -9 & -11 \\ 22 & 13 \end{bmatrix}$

Problem Set 7.2 (page 596)

1. $\begin{bmatrix} 3 & -7 \\ -2 & 5 \end{bmatrix}$ **3.** $\begin{bmatrix} -5 & 8 \\ 2 & -3 \end{bmatrix}$ **5.** $\begin{bmatrix} -\dfrac{2}{5} & \dfrac{1}{5} \\ \dfrac{3}{10} & \dfrac{1}{10} \end{bmatrix}$

7. Does not exist **9.** $\begin{bmatrix} -\dfrac{5}{7} & \dfrac{2}{7} \\ -\dfrac{4}{7} & \dfrac{3}{7} \end{bmatrix}$ **11.** $\begin{bmatrix} -\dfrac{3}{5} & \dfrac{1}{5} \\ 1 & 0 \end{bmatrix}$

13. $\begin{bmatrix} -\dfrac{4}{5} & \dfrac{3}{5} \\ \dfrac{1}{5} & -\dfrac{2}{5} \end{bmatrix}$ **15.** $\begin{bmatrix} 2 & -\dfrac{5}{3} \\ 1 & -\dfrac{2}{3} \end{bmatrix}$ **17.** $\begin{bmatrix} \dfrac{1}{2} & \dfrac{1}{2} \\ \dfrac{1}{2} & -\dfrac{1}{2} \end{bmatrix}$

19. $\begin{bmatrix} 30 \\ 36 \end{bmatrix}$ **21.** $\begin{bmatrix} 0 \\ 5 \end{bmatrix}$ **23.** $\begin{bmatrix} -4 \\ 13 \end{bmatrix}$ **25.** $\begin{bmatrix} -4 \\ -13 \end{bmatrix}$

27. $\{(2, 3)\}$ **29.** $\{(-2, 5)\}$ **31.** $\{(0, -1)\}$

33. $\{(-1, -1)\}$ **35.** $\{(4, 7)\}$ **37.** $\left\{\left(-\dfrac{1}{3}, \dfrac{1}{2}\right)\right\}$

39. $\{(-9, 20)\}$

Problem Set 7.3 (page 604)

1. $\begin{bmatrix} 1 & 3 & -3 \\ 3 & -6 & 7 \end{bmatrix}; \begin{bmatrix} 3 & -5 & 11 \\ -7 & 6 & 3 \end{bmatrix}; \begin{bmatrix} 1 & 10 & -13 \\ 11 & -18 & 16 \end{bmatrix};$
$\begin{bmatrix} 10 & -12 & 30 \\ -18 & 12 & 16 \end{bmatrix}$

3. $[-1 \quad -7 \quad 13 \quad 7]; [5 \quad 5 \quad -5 \quad 17];$
$[-5 \quad -20 \quad 35 \quad 9]; [14 \quad 8 \quad -2 \quad 58]$

5. $\begin{bmatrix} 8 & -3 & -2 \\ 9 & 2 & -3 \\ 7 & 5 & 21 \end{bmatrix}; \begin{bmatrix} -2 & -1 & 4 \\ -11 & 6 & -11 \\ -7 & 5 & -3 \end{bmatrix}; \begin{bmatrix} 21 & -7 & -7 \\ 28 & 2 & -2 \\ 21 & 10 & 54 \end{bmatrix};$
$\begin{bmatrix} 2 & -6 & 10 \\ -24 & 20 & -36 \\ -14 & 20 & 12 \end{bmatrix}$

7. $\begin{bmatrix} 0 & 2 \\ -1 & 10 \\ 1 & -9 \\ 2 & 9 \end{bmatrix}; \begin{bmatrix} -2 & -2 \\ 5 & -4 \\ -11 & 1 \\ -16 & 13 \end{bmatrix}; \begin{bmatrix} 1 & 6 \\ -5 & 27 \\ 8 & -23 \\ 13 & 16 \end{bmatrix}; \begin{bmatrix} -6 & -4 \\ 14 & -2 \\ -32 & -6 \\ -46 & 48 \end{bmatrix}$

9. $AB = \begin{bmatrix} 11 & -8 & 14 \\ 4 & -16 & 8 \\ -28 & 22 & -36 \end{bmatrix}; BA = \begin{bmatrix} -20 & 21 \\ 8 & -21 \end{bmatrix}$

11. $AB = \begin{bmatrix} 22 & -8 & 1 & 3 \\ -42 & 36 & -26 & -20 \end{bmatrix}; BA$ does not exist.

13. $AB = \begin{bmatrix} -12 & 5 & -5 \\ 14 & -2 & 4 \\ -10 & 13 & -5 \end{bmatrix}; BA = \begin{bmatrix} -1 & 0 & -6 \\ 10 & -2 & 16 \\ -8 & 5 & -16 \end{bmatrix}$

15. $AB = [-9]; BA = \begin{bmatrix} -2 & 1 & -3 & -4 \\ -6 & 3 & -9 & -12 \\ 4 & -2 & 6 & 8 \\ -8 & 4 & -12 & -16 \end{bmatrix}$

17. AB does not exist; $BA = \begin{bmatrix} 20 \\ 2 \\ -30 \end{bmatrix}$

19. $AB = \begin{bmatrix} 9 & -12 \\ -12 & 16 \\ 6 & -8 \end{bmatrix}; BA$ does not exist.

21. $\begin{bmatrix} -\dfrac{1}{5} & \dfrac{3}{10} \\ \dfrac{2}{5} & -\dfrac{1}{10} \end{bmatrix}$ **23.** $\begin{bmatrix} 4 & -1 \\ -7 & 2 \end{bmatrix}$ **25.** $\begin{bmatrix} -\dfrac{4}{5} & -\dfrac{1}{5} \\ -\dfrac{3}{5} & -\dfrac{2}{5} \end{bmatrix}$

27. $\begin{bmatrix} \dfrac{7}{2} & -3 & \dfrac{1}{2} \\ -\dfrac{1}{2} & 0 & \dfrac{1}{2} \\ -\dfrac{1}{2} & 1 & -\dfrac{1}{2} \end{bmatrix}$ **29.** $\begin{bmatrix} -50 & -9 & 11 \\ -23 & -4 & 5 \\ 5 & 1 & -1 \end{bmatrix}$

31. Does not exist **33.** $\begin{bmatrix} \dfrac{4}{7} & -1 & -\dfrac{9}{7} \\ -\dfrac{3}{14} & \dfrac{1}{2} & \dfrac{6}{7} \\ \dfrac{2}{7} & 0 & -\dfrac{1}{7} \end{bmatrix}$

35. $\begin{bmatrix} \dfrac{1}{2} & 0 & 0 \\ 0 & \dfrac{1}{4} & 0 \\ 0 & 0 & \dfrac{1}{10} \end{bmatrix}$ **37.** $\{(-3, 2)\}$ **39.** $\{(2, 5)\}$

41. $\{(-1, -2, 1)\}$ **43.** $\{(-2, 3, 5)\}$ **45.** $\{(-4, 3, 0)\}$
47. (a) $\{(-1, 2, 3)\}$ **(c)** $\{(-5, 0, -2)\}$ **(e)** $\{(1, -1, -1)\}$

Problem Set 7.4 (page 614)

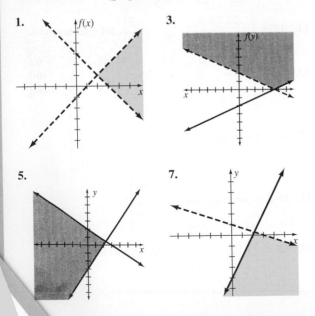

9.

11.

13.

15.

17. $\varnothing$

19.

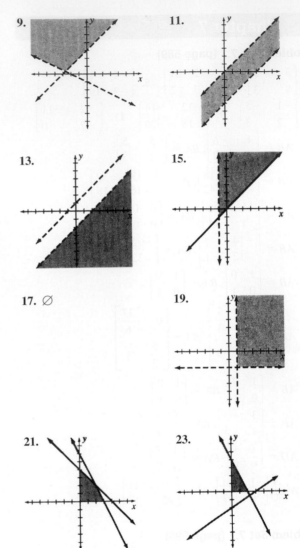

21.

23.

25. Minimum of 8 and maximum of 52
27. Minimum of 0 and maximum of 28
29. 63 **31.** 340 **33.** 2 **35.** 98
37. $5000 at 9% and $5000 at 12%
39. 300 of type A and 200 of type B
41. 12 units of A and 16 units of B

Chapter 7 Review Problem Set (page 622)

1. $\begin{bmatrix} 7 & -5 \\ -3 & 10 \end{bmatrix}$ **2.** $\begin{bmatrix} 3 & 3 \\ 3 & -6 \end{bmatrix}$ **3.** $\begin{bmatrix} 2 & 1 \\ -6 & 8 \\ -2 & 2 \end{bmatrix}$

4. $\begin{bmatrix} 19 & -11 \\ -6 & 22 \end{bmatrix}$ **5.** $\begin{bmatrix} 7 & 1 \\ -14 & 20 \\ 1 & -2 \end{bmatrix}$

6. $\begin{bmatrix} -11 & -3 & 15 \\ 24 & 2 & -20 \\ -40 & -5 & 38 \end{bmatrix}$ **7.** $\begin{bmatrix} 16 & -26 \\ 0 & 13 \end{bmatrix}$

8. $\begin{bmatrix} 26 & -36 \\ -15 & 32 \end{bmatrix}$ **9.** $\begin{bmatrix} -27 \\ 26 \end{bmatrix}$

10. Does not exist. **14.** $\begin{bmatrix} 4 & -5 \\ -7 & 9 \end{bmatrix}$ **15.** $\begin{bmatrix} -3 & 4 \\ 7 & -9 \end{bmatrix}$

16. $\begin{bmatrix} -\dfrac{3}{8} & \dfrac{1}{8} \\ \dfrac{1}{4} & \dfrac{1}{4} \end{bmatrix}$ **17.** Does not exist. **18.** $\begin{bmatrix} \dfrac{5}{7} & -\dfrac{3}{7} \\ -\dfrac{4}{7} & \dfrac{1}{7} \end{bmatrix}$

19. $\begin{bmatrix} \dfrac{2}{7} & \dfrac{1}{7} \\ -\dfrac{1}{3} & 0 \end{bmatrix}$ **20.** $\begin{bmatrix} \dfrac{39}{8} & -\dfrac{17}{8} & -\dfrac{1}{8} \\ 2 & -1 & 0 \\ \dfrac{1}{8} & \dfrac{1}{8} & \dfrac{1}{8} \end{bmatrix}$

21. $\begin{bmatrix} 8 & -8 & 5 \\ -3 & 2 & -1 \\ -1 & -1 & 1 \end{bmatrix}$ **22.** Does not exist.

23. $\begin{bmatrix} -\dfrac{20}{3} & -\dfrac{7}{3} & \dfrac{1}{3} \\ -\dfrac{1}{3} & -\dfrac{2}{3} & -\dfrac{1}{3} \\ -\dfrac{5}{3} & \dfrac{1}{3} & \dfrac{1}{3} \end{bmatrix}$ **24.** $\{(-2, 6)\}$ **25.** $\{(4, -1)\}$

26. $\{(2, -3, -1)\}$ **27.** $\{(-3, 2, 5)\}$ **28.** $\{(-4, 3, 4)\}$

29.

30.

31.

32.

33. 37 **34.** 56 **35.** 57 **36.** 1700
37. 75 one-gallon and 175 two-gallon freezers

Chapter 7 Test (page 624)

1. $\begin{bmatrix} 9 & -1 \\ 4 & -6 \end{bmatrix}$ **2.** $\begin{bmatrix} -11 & 13 \\ -8 & 14 \end{bmatrix}$ **3.** $\begin{bmatrix} -1 & -3 & 11 \\ -4 & -5 & 18 \\ 37 & -1 & 9 \end{bmatrix}$

4. Does not exist. **5.** $\begin{bmatrix} -35 \\ 8 \end{bmatrix}$ **6.** $\begin{bmatrix} -5 & 8 \\ 4 & -3 \end{bmatrix}$

7. $\begin{bmatrix} 4 & 9 \\ 13 & -16 \\ 24 & 23 \end{bmatrix}$ **8.** $\begin{bmatrix} -3 & -5 \\ -20 & 8 \end{bmatrix}$ **9.** $\begin{bmatrix} 8 & 33 \\ -12 & 13 \end{bmatrix}$

10. $\begin{bmatrix} 1 & -34 \\ 16 & -19 \end{bmatrix}$ **11.** $\begin{bmatrix} -3 & 2 \\ -5 & 3 \end{bmatrix}$ **12.** $\begin{bmatrix} 7 & 5 \\ 3 & 2 \end{bmatrix}$

13. $\begin{bmatrix} 4 & \dfrac{3}{2} \\ 1 & \dfrac{1}{2} \end{bmatrix}$ **14.** $\begin{bmatrix} \dfrac{4}{7} & -\dfrac{5}{7} \\ -\dfrac{1}{7} & \dfrac{3}{7} \end{bmatrix}$

15. $\begin{bmatrix} -\dfrac{4}{3} & -\dfrac{5}{3} & 1 \\ -\dfrac{4}{3} & -\dfrac{8}{3} & 1 \\ \dfrac{1}{3} & \dfrac{2}{3} & 0 \end{bmatrix}$ **16.** $\begin{bmatrix} 1 & 2 & -10 \\ 0 & 1 & -3 \\ 0 & 0 & 1 \end{bmatrix}$

17. $\{(8, -12)\}$ **18.** $\{(-6, -14)\}$ **19.** $\{(9, 13)\}$

20. $\left\{ \left(\dfrac{7}{3}, -\dfrac{1}{3}, \dfrac{13}{3} \right) \right\}$ **21.** $\{(-1, 2, 1)\}$

22.

23.

24.

25. 4050

Chapters 0–7 Cumulative Review Problem Set
(page 625)

1. Multiplicative Inverse Property
2. Associative Property of Multiplication
3. Commutative Property of Addition
4. Identity Property of Addition

5. 35 6. $-\dfrac{16}{3}$ 7. -1 8. $-\dfrac{43}{72}$ 9. $-\dfrac{3}{2}$ 10. -11

11. 1 12. $\dfrac{3}{2}$ 13. $\begin{bmatrix} -4 & -4 \\ 5 & -2 \end{bmatrix}$ 14. $\begin{bmatrix} -8 & 13 \\ -8 & -7 \end{bmatrix}$

15. $\begin{bmatrix} 18 & 31 \\ -18 & 4 \end{bmatrix}$ 16. $\begin{bmatrix} 7 & 21 \\ -25 & 15 \end{bmatrix}$ 17. -23

18. -139 19. $9x + 7y = -3$ 20. $2x + 3y = 2$

21. $5x + 2y = 17$ 22. $x - y = -3$

23. $\dfrac{9}{64a}$ 24. $\dfrac{4n^6}{9m^{10}}$ 25. $2\sqrt{17}$ 26. $3\sqrt[3]{3}$

27. $\dfrac{4\sqrt{5}}{5}$ 28. $\dfrac{\sqrt{14a}}{6a^2}$ 29. $\dfrac{3x}{2}\sqrt{3y}$ 30. $2a\sqrt{2b}$

31. $\dfrac{\sqrt[3]{6}}{2}$ 32. $4cd^2\sqrt[3]{2c^2d}$ 33. $\dfrac{3(\sqrt{5} + 1)}{2}$

34. $\dfrac{12\sqrt{6} - 16\sqrt{2}}{11}$ 35. $x = 2 + 3y$ 36. $x = \dfrac{4y - 13}{9}$

37. $x = \dfrac{by}{c - d - ay}$ 38. $x = \dfrac{6c - 3a}{8}$

39. $\dfrac{c^2 + 2c - 2}{c - 1}$ 40. $-\dfrac{(4a + 3)(a - 2)}{(3a - 2)(a + 1)}$

41. $f(-1) = -14$ 42. $f(-2) = 7$

43. $f(0) = -9, f(-1) = -12, f(a) = -2a^2 + a - 9$

44. $f(0) = 0, f(3) = 6, f(-1) = -1, f(-3) = -9$

45. -2 46. $6a + 3h - 1$

47. D: $\left\{ x \,\middle|\, x \neq -1 \text{ and } x \neq \dfrac{2}{3} \right\}$

48. D: $\{x \,|\, x \neq 1 \text{ and } x \neq -1\}$

49. D: $\left\{ x \,\middle|\, x \geq -\dfrac{2}{3} \right\}$; R: $\{f(x) \,|\, f(x) \geq 0\}$

50. D: $\{x \,|\, x \text{ is real}\}$; R: $\{f(x) \,|\, f(x) \geq 0\}$

51. D: $\{x \,|\, x \text{ is real}\}$; R: $\{f(x) \,|\, f(x) \leq -1\}$

52. D: $(-\infty, -5] \cup [5, \infty)$ 53. D: $(-\infty, \infty)$

54. D: $\left(-\infty, -\dfrac{1}{4} \right] \cup [3, \infty)$

55. $(f \circ g)(x) = 3x^2 + 9x - 13$, D: $\{x \,|\, x \text{ is real}\}$;
$(g \circ f)(x) = 9x^2 + 3x - 6$, D: $\{x \,|\, x \text{ is real}\}$

56. $(f \circ g)(x) = 2x - 2$, D: $\{x \,|\, x \neq 1\}$;

$(g \circ f)(x) = \dfrac{x}{2 - x}$, D: $\{x \,|\, x \neq 0 \text{ and } x \neq 2\}$

57. $\left\{ -\dfrac{5}{12} \right\}$ 58. $\left\{ -\dfrac{21}{13} \right\}$ 59. $\left\{ -4, \dfrac{20}{3} \right\}$

60. $\left\{ -\dfrac{1}{2} \right\}$ 61. $\left\{ -\dfrac{7}{2}, 1 \right\}$ 62. $\left\{ -\dfrac{3}{2}, 0, \dfrac{3}{2} \right\}$

63. $\left\{ -\dfrac{9}{4}, \dfrac{7}{3} \right\}$ 64. $\left\{ -\dfrac{4}{3}, 5 \right\}$ 65. $\left\{ \dfrac{7}{3}, 3 \right\}$ 66. $\{25\}$

67. $\varnothing$ 68. $\{-4, 4\}$ 69. $\{8\}$ 70. $\{25\}$ 71. $\left\{ 0, \dfrac{7}{3} \right\}$

72. $\left\{ -\dfrac{\sqrt{5}}{2}, \dfrac{\sqrt{5}}{2} \right\}$ 73. $\left\{ \dfrac{-11 - 5\sqrt{5}}{2}, \dfrac{-11 + 5\sqrt{5}}{2} \right\}$

74. $\left\{ \dfrac{-1 - i\sqrt{55}}{4}, \dfrac{-1 + i\sqrt{55}}{4} \right\}$

75. $\{-\sqrt{3}, \sqrt{3}, -3i\sqrt{2}, 3i\sqrt{2}\}$

76. $\left\{ \dfrac{6 - \sqrt{30}}{2}, \dfrac{6 + \sqrt{30}}{2} \right\}$ 77. $\{-5, 2, 3\}$

78. $\{-1, 3, 2 - i, 2 + i\}$ 79. $\left\{ \dfrac{3}{2} \right\}$ 80. $\left\{ \dfrac{1}{3} \right\}$

81. $\left\{ \dfrac{1}{20} \right\}$ 82. $\{7\}$ 83. $\{-2\}$ 84. $\left\{ -\dfrac{3}{2} \right\}$

85. $\{1.37\}$ 86. $\{4.61\}$ 87. $\{-1.75\}$ 88. $\{1.75\}$

89. $\left(-\infty, -\dfrac{1}{2} \right)$ 90. $[6, 12]$ 91. $\left(-6, \dfrac{22}{3} \right)$

92. $\left(-\infty, \dfrac{8}{3} \right) \cup \left(\dfrac{8}{3}, \infty \right)$

93. $\left(-\infty, -\dfrac{7}{2} \right] \cup [0, \infty)$ 94. $(-1, 3)$ 95. $\{(2, 5)\}$

96. $\{(-27, -5)\}$ 97. $\{(-1, 0, 3)\}$

98.   99.

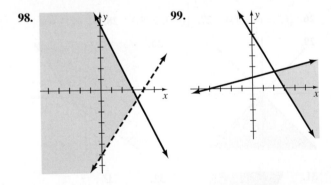

100.

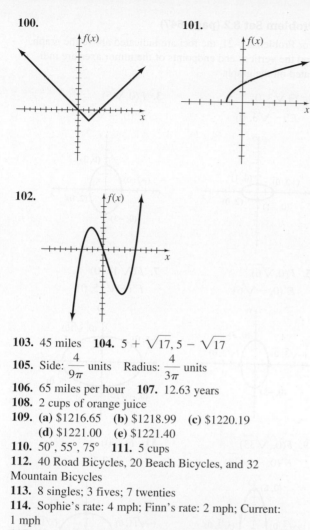

101.

102.

103. 45 miles **104.** $5 + \sqrt{17}, 5 - \sqrt{17}$

105. Side: $\dfrac{4}{9\pi}$ units Radius: $\dfrac{4}{3\pi}$ units

106. 65 miles per hour **107.** 12.63 years

108. 2 cups of orange juice

109. (a) $1216.65 (b) $1218.99 (c) $1220.19
(d) $1221.00 (e) $1221.40

110. 50°, 55°, 75° **111.** 5 cups

112. 40 Road Bicycles, 20 Beach Bicycles, and 32 Mountain Bicycles

113. 8 singles; 3 fives; 7 twenties

114. Sophie's rate: 4 mph; Finn's rate: 2 mph; Current: 1 mph

115. 32 "cricket" figures; 18 "beetle" figures

Chapter 8

Problem Set 8.1 (page 637)

1. $V(0, 0)$, $F(2, 0)$,
$x = -2$

3. $V(0, 0)$, $F(0, -3)$,
$y = 3$

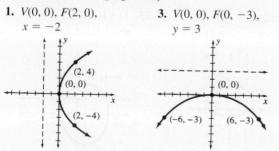

5. $V(0, 0)$, $F\left(-\dfrac{1}{2}, 0\right)$,
$x = \dfrac{1}{2}$

7. $V(0, 0)$, $F\left(0, \dfrac{3}{2}\right)$,
$y = -\dfrac{3}{2}$

9. $V(0, -1)$, $F(0, 2)$,
$y = -4$

11. $V(3, 0)$, $F(1, 0)$,
$x = 5$

13. $V(0, 2)$, $F(0, 3)$,
$y = 1$

15. $V(0, -2)$,
$F(0, -4)$,
$y = 0$

17. $V(2, 0)$, $F(5, 0)$,
$x = -1$

19. $V(2, -2)$, $F(2, -3)$,
$y = -1$

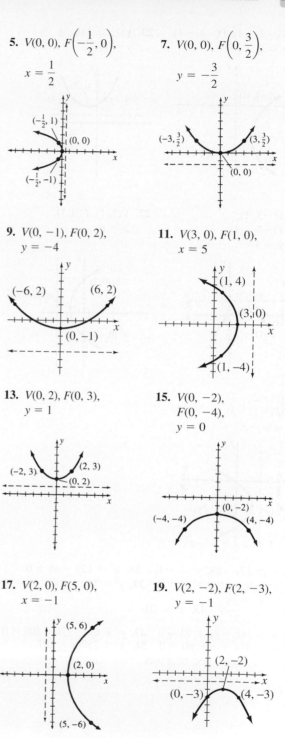

21. $V(-2, -4)$, $F(-4, -4)$, $x = 0$

23. $V(1, 2)$, $F(1, 3)$, $y = 1$

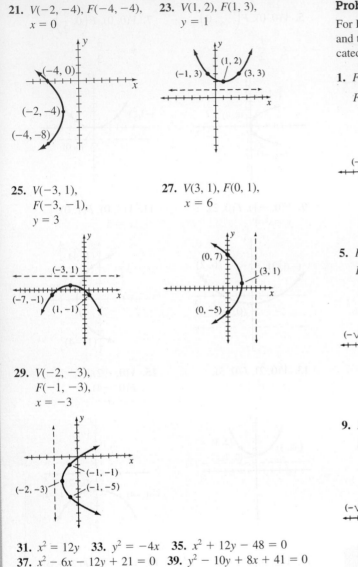

25. $V(-3, 1)$, $F(-3, -1)$, $y = 3$

27. $V(3, 1)$, $F(0, 1)$, $x = 6$

29. $V(-2, -3)$, $F(-1, -3)$, $x = -3$

31. $x^2 = 12y$ **33.** $y^2 = -4x$ **35.** $x^2 + 12y - 48 = 0$
37. $x^2 - 6x - 12y + 21 = 0$ **39.** $y^2 - 10y + 8x + 41 = 0$
41. $y^2 = \dfrac{-25}{3}x$ **43.** $y^2 = 10x$
45. $x^2 - 14x - 8y + 73 = 0$ **47.** $y^2 + 6y - 12x + 105 = 0$
49. $x^2 + 18x + y + 80 = 0$ **51.** $x^2 = 750(y - 10)$
53. $10\sqrt{2}$ feet   **55.** 62.5 feet

Problem Set 8.2 (page 647)

For Problems 1–21, the foci are indicated above the graph, and the vertices and endpoints of the minor axes are indicated on the graph.

1. $F(\sqrt{3}, 0)$, $F'(-\sqrt{3}, 0)$

3. $F(0, \sqrt{5})$, $F'(0, -\sqrt{5})$

5. $F(0, \sqrt{6})$, $F'(0, -\sqrt{6})$

7. $F(\sqrt{15}, 0)$, $F'(-\sqrt{15}, 0)$

9. $F(0, \sqrt{33})$, $F'(0, -\sqrt{33})$

11. $F(2, 0)$, $F'(-2, 0)$

13. $F(2 + \sqrt{5}, 1)$, $F'(2 - \sqrt{5}, 1)$

15. $F(-1, -2 + \sqrt{7})$, $F'(-1, -2 - \sqrt{7})$

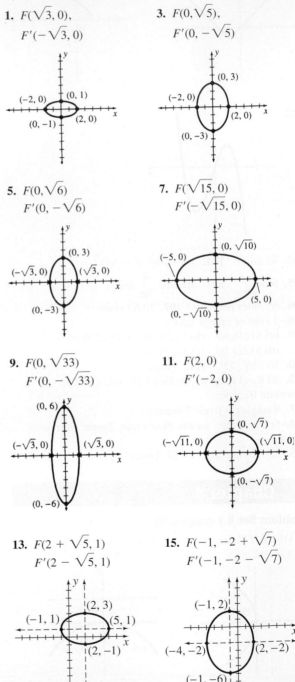

17. $F(1 + \sqrt{5}, 2)$
$F'(1 - \sqrt{5}, 2)$

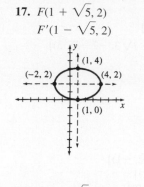

19. $F(-2, -1 + 2\sqrt{3})$
$F'(-2, -1 - 2\sqrt{3})$

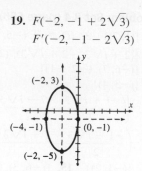

21. $F(3 + \sqrt{3}, 0)$
$F'(3 - \sqrt{3}, 0)$

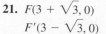
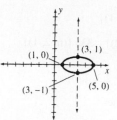

23. $F(4, -1 + \sqrt{7})$
$F'(4, -1 - \sqrt{7})$

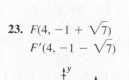
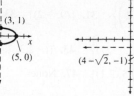

25. $F(0, 4)$, $F'(-6, 4)$

27. $16x^2 + 25y^2 = 400$ **29.** $36x^2 + 11y^2 = 396$
31. $x^2 + 9y^2 = 9$ **33.** $100x^2 + 36y^2 = 225$
35. $7x^2 + 3y^2 = 75$ **37.** $3x^2 - 6x + 4y^2 - 8y - 41 = 0$
39. $9x^2 + 25y^2 - 50y - 200 = 0$ **41.** $3x^2 + 4y^2 = 48$

43. $\dfrac{10\sqrt{5}}{3}$ feet

Problem Set 8.3 (page 657)

For Problems 1–25, the foci and equations of the asymptotes are indicated above the graphs. The vertices are given on the graphs.

1. $F(\sqrt{13}, 0)$,
$F'(-\sqrt{13}, 0)$
$y = \pm\dfrac{2}{3}x$

3. $F(0, \sqrt{13})$,
$F'(0, -\sqrt{13})$
$y = \pm\dfrac{2}{3}x$

5. $F(0, 5)$,
$F(0, -5)$
$y = \pm\dfrac{4}{3}x$

7. $F(3\sqrt{2}, 0)$
$F(-3\sqrt{2}, 0)$
$y = \pm x$

9. $F(0, \sqrt{30})$,
$F(0, -\sqrt{30})$
$y = \pm\dfrac{\sqrt{5}}{5}x$

11. $F(\sqrt{10}, 0)$,
$F'(-\sqrt{10}, 0)$
$y = \pm 3x$

13. $F(1 + \sqrt{13}, -1)$,
$F'(1 - \sqrt{13}, -1)$
$2x - 3y = 5$ and
$2x + 3y = -1$

15. $F(1, 7)$,
$F'(1, -3)$
$3x - 4y = -5$ and
$3x + 4y = 11$

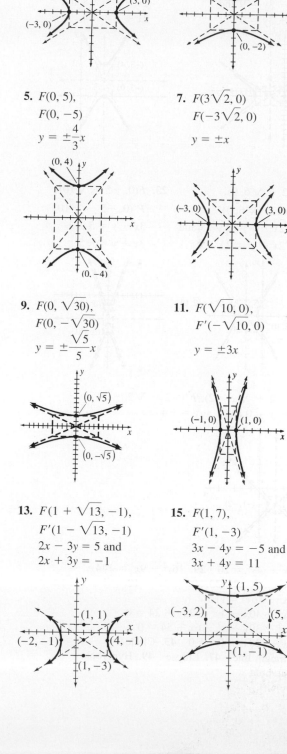

17. $F(13 + \sqrt{13}, -1)$,
$F'(3 - \sqrt{13}, -1)$
$2x - 3y = 9$ and
$2x + 3y = 3$

19. $F(-3, 2 + \sqrt{5})$,
$F'(-3, 2 - \sqrt{5})$
$2x - y = -8$ and
$2x + y = -4$

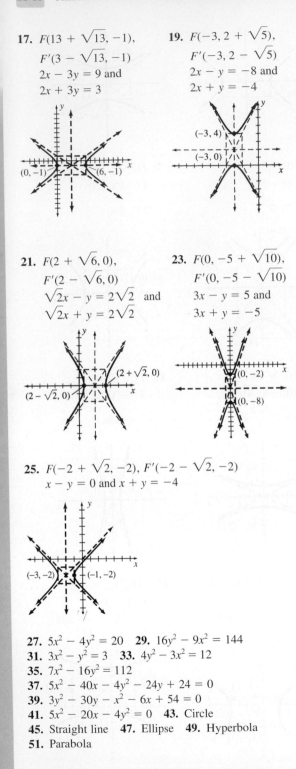

21. $F(2 + \sqrt{6}, 0)$,
$F'(2 - \sqrt{6}, 0)$
$\sqrt{2}x - y = 2\sqrt{2}$ and
$\sqrt{2}x + y = 2\sqrt{2}$

23. $F(0, -5 + \sqrt{10})$,
$F'(0, -5 - \sqrt{10})$
$3x - y = 5$ and
$3x + y = -5$

25. $F(-2 + \sqrt{2}, -2)$, $F'(-2 - \sqrt{2}, -2)$
$x - y = 0$ and $x + y = -4$

27. $5x^2 - 4y^2 = 20$ **29.** $16y^2 - 9x^2 = 144$
31. $3x^2 - y^2 = 3$ **33.** $4y^2 - 3x^2 = 12$
35. $7x^2 - 16y^2 = 112$
37. $5x^2 - 40x - 4y^2 - 24y + 24 = 0$
39. $3y^2 - 30y - x^2 - 6x + 54 = 0$
41. $5x^2 - 20x - 4y^2 = 0$ **43.** Circle
45. Straight line   **47.** Ellipse   **49.** Hyperbola
51. Parabola

Problem Set 8.4 (page 665)

1. $\{(1, 2)\}$ **3.** $\{(1, -5), (-5, 1)\}$
5. $\{(2 + i\sqrt{3}, -2 + i\sqrt{3}), (2 - i\sqrt{3}, -2 - i\sqrt{3})\}$
7. $\{(-6, 7), (-2, -1)\}$
9. $\{(-3, 4)\}$
11. $\left\{\left(\dfrac{-1 + i\sqrt{3}}{2}, \dfrac{-7 - i\sqrt{3}}{2}\right),\right.$
$\left.\left(\dfrac{-1 - i\sqrt{3}}{2}, \dfrac{-7 + i\sqrt{3}}{2}\right)\right\}$
13. $\{(-1, 2)\}$ **15.** $\{(-6, 3), (-2, -1)\}$
17. $\{(5, 3)\}$ **19.** $\{(1, 2,), (-1, 2)\}$
21. $\{(-3, 2)\}$ **23.** $\{(2, 0), (-2, 0)\}$
25. $\{(\sqrt{2}, \sqrt{3}), (\sqrt{2}, -\sqrt{3}), (-\sqrt{2}, \sqrt{3}),$
$(-\sqrt{2}, -\sqrt{3})\}$
27. $\{(1, 1), (1, -1), (-1, 1), (-1, -1)\}$
29. $\left\{\left(2, \dfrac{3}{2}\right), \left(\dfrac{3}{2}, 2\right)\right\}$ **31.** $\{(9, -2)\}$ **33.** $\{(\ln 2, 1)\}$
35. $\left\{\left(\dfrac{1}{2}, \dfrac{1}{8}\right), (-3, -27)\right\}$ **43.** $\{(-2.3, 7.4)\}$
45. $\{(6.7, 1.7), (9.5, 2.1)\}$ **47.** None

Chapter 8 Review Problem Set (page 673)

1. $F(4, 0), F'(-4, 0)$

2. $F(-3, 0)$

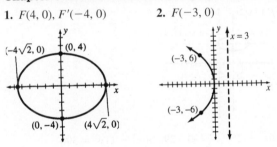

3. $F(0, 2\sqrt{3})$,
$F'(0, -2\sqrt{3})$
$y = \pm\dfrac{\sqrt{3}}{3}x$

4. $F(\sqrt{15}, 0)$,
$F'(-\sqrt{15}, 0)$
$y = \pm\dfrac{\sqrt{6}}{3}x$

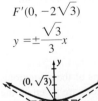

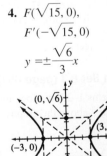

5. $F(0, \sqrt{6})$,
$F'(0, -\sqrt{6})$

6. $F\left(0, \dfrac{1}{2}\right)$

11. $F(-5 + 2\sqrt{3}, 2)$, $F'(-5 - 2\sqrt{3}, 2)$

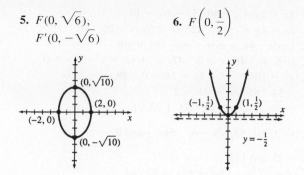

7. $F(4 + \sqrt{6}, 1)$, $F'(4 - \sqrt{6}, 1)$
$\sqrt{2}x - 2y = 4\sqrt{2} - 2$ and $\sqrt{2}x + 2y = 4\sqrt{2} + 2$

8. $F(3, -2 + \sqrt{7})$, $F'(3, -2 - \sqrt{7})$

9. $F(-3, 1)$, $x = -1$

10. $F(-1, -5)$, $y = -1$

12. $F(-2, -2 + \sqrt{10})$, $F'(-2, -2 - \sqrt{10})$
$\sqrt{6}x - 3y = 6 - 2\sqrt{6}$ and
$\sqrt{6}x + 3y = -6 - 2\sqrt{6}$

13. $y^2 = -20x$ **14.** $16x^2 + y^2 = 16$
15. $25x^2 - 2y^2 = 50$ **16.** $4x^2 + 3y^2 = 16$

17. $x^2 = \dfrac{2}{3}y$ **18.** $9y^2 - x^2 = 9$

19. $9x^2 - 108x + y^2 - 8y + 331 = 0$
20. $y^2 + 4y - 8x + 36 = 0$
21. $3y^2 + 24y - x^2 - 10x + 20 = 0$
22. $x^2 + 12x - y + 33 = 0$ **23.** $4x^2 + 40x + 25y^2 = 0$
24. $4x^2 - 32x - y^2 + 48 = 0$ **25.** $\{(-1, 4)\}$
26. $\{(3, 1)\}$ **27.** $\{(-1, -2), (-2, -3)\}$
28. $\left\{\left(\dfrac{4\sqrt{2}}{3}, \dfrac{4}{3}i\right), \left(\dfrac{4\sqrt{2}}{3}, -\dfrac{4}{3}i\right), \left(-\dfrac{4\sqrt{2}}{3}, \dfrac{4}{3}i\right),\right.$
$\left.\left(-\dfrac{4\sqrt{2}}{3}, -\dfrac{4}{3}i\right)\right\}$ **29.** $\{(0, 2), (0, -2)\}$
30. $\left\{\left(\dfrac{\sqrt{15}}{5}, \dfrac{2\sqrt{10}}{5}\right), \left(\dfrac{\sqrt{15}}{5}, -\dfrac{2\sqrt{10}}{5}\right),\right.$
$\left.\left(-\dfrac{\sqrt{15}}{5}, \dfrac{2\sqrt{10}}{5}\right), \left(-\dfrac{\sqrt{15}}{5}, -\dfrac{2\sqrt{10}}{5}\right)\right\}$

Chapter 8 Test (page 675)

1. $(0, -5)$ **2.** $(-3, 2)$ **3.** $x = -3$ **4.** $(6, 0)$
5. $(-2, -1)$ **6.** $y = 4$ **7.** $y^2 + 8x = 0$
8. $x^2 - 6x + 12y - 39 = 0$
9. $(0, 6)$ and $(0, -6)$ **10.** 6 units

11. $(-7, 1)$ and $(-3, 1)$ **12.** $(-2\sqrt{3}, 0)$ and $(2\sqrt{3}, 0)$

13. $(-5, 8)$ **14.** $25x^2 + 9y^2 = 900$

15. $x^2 - 12x + 4y^2 + 16y + 36 = 0$ **16.** $y = \pm\dfrac{3}{2}x$

17. $(-1, 6)$ and $(-1, 0)$ **18.** $(\pm 3, 0)$ **19.** $x^2 - 3y^2 = 36$

20. $8x^2 + 16x - y^2 + 8y - 16 = 0$ **21.** 2

22. $\left\{ (3, 2), (-3, -2), \left(4, \dfrac{3}{2}\right), \left(-4, -\dfrac{3}{2}\right) \right\}$

23. **24.**

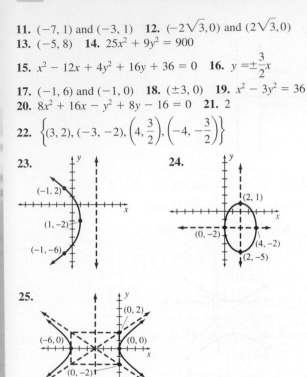

25.

Chapters 0–8 Cumulative Review Problem Set (page 676)

1. $\dfrac{9}{4}$ **2.** $\dfrac{4}{3}$ **3.** $\dfrac{1}{2}$ **4.** $\dfrac{18}{7}$ **5.** 64

6. 243   **7.** 3   **8.** 2   **9.** 5   **10.** 15

11. $x - 6$ **12.** $-6 - 11x - 4x^2$

13. $3x^3 - 17x^2 + 11x - 5$

14. $2x^4 + x^3 - 2x^2 - 10x - 21$

15. $8x^3 - 36x^2 + 54x - 27$ **16.** $-6x^2y + 9xy^3$

17. $x^2 - 4x + 6$ **18.** $3x^3 + 4x^2 - 5x - 3$

19. $(-3 + 2x)(4 - 3x)$ **20.** $(x + 2y)(x - 3)$

21. $2x(x + 6)(x - 3)$ **22.** Not factorable

23. $(2x + 3)(4x^2 - 6x + 9)$

24. $(x + 1)(x - 1)(2x + 1)(2x - 1)$ **25.** -48

26. $\dfrac{1}{28}$ **27.** $\dfrac{1}{24}$ **28.** $26 - 7i$

29. $-12 + 9i$ **30.** $\dfrac{2}{25} - \dfrac{11}{25}i$ **31.** $4\sqrt{3} - 4\sqrt{6}$

32. -33 **33.** $\dfrac{5\sqrt{3}}{9}$ **34.** $\sqrt[6]{5}$ **35.** $\dfrac{3}{8}$

36. $(0, 3)$ **37.** $(1, 3)$ **38.** 160 feet

39. $3x + 2y = 2$ **40.** $5x - 6y = 18$

41. $2x - 3y = -14$ **42.** $7x + 5y = -26$

43. x axis   **44.** x axis, y axis, and origin

45. $(-6, 4)$ **46.** $r = 4$ **47.** $x^2 + 6x + y^2 - 8y = 0$

48. $x^2 - 10x + y^2 - 2y + 16 = 0$ **49.** $y = \pm 3x$

50. -34 **51.** $8a + 4h - 2$

52. $(-\infty, 2) \cup (2, \infty)$ **53.** $[-3, 2]$

54. $(-2, 7)$ **55.** $(8, -6)$ **56.** $\dfrac{1}{2}$ and 9

57. -23 and 113

58. $f(g(x)) = -12x^2 + 62x - 72$ and $g(f(x)) = 6x^2 + 2x - 11$

59. $f^{-1}(x) = -\dfrac{3}{2}x + \dfrac{3}{2}$ **60.** -90 **61.** 64

62. 52.1 milligrams   **63.** $21,870

64. 13.6 grams   **65.** Yes   **66.** Yes   **67.** No

68. $-2, 1$, and 3   **69.** $y = x + 3$

70. $\dfrac{-3}{2x - 1} + \dfrac{2}{x - 4}$ **71.** $\begin{bmatrix} -14 & 4 \\ 9 & -7 \end{bmatrix}$

72. $AB = \begin{bmatrix} -7 & -2 \\ -17 & -8 \end{bmatrix}$; $BA = \begin{bmatrix} -15 & 22 \\ -1 & 0 \end{bmatrix}$

73. $\begin{bmatrix} 2 & -3 \\ -1 & 2 \end{bmatrix}$

74. a. Ellipse **b.** Parabola **c.** Parabola **d.** Circle **e.** Hyperbola

75. **76.**

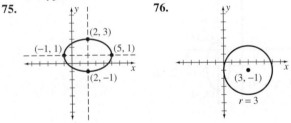

77. **78.**

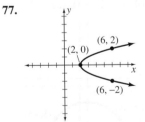 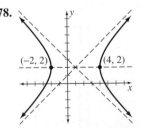

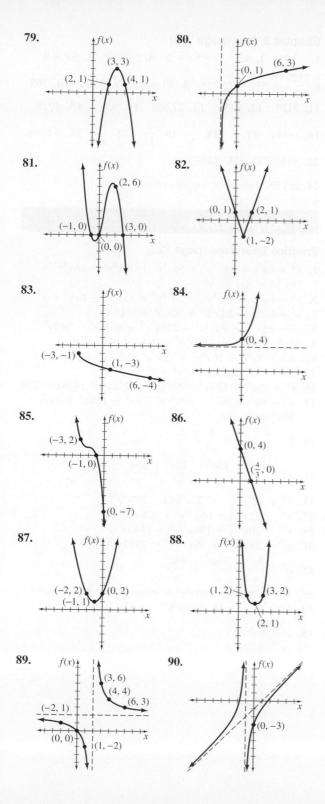

79. (graph with points (3, 3), (2, 1), (4, 1))

80. (graph with points (6, 3), (0, 1))

81. (graph with points (2, 6), (−1, 0), (3, 0), (0, 0))

82. (graph with points (0, 1), (2, 1), (1, −2))

83. (graph with points (−3, −1), (1, −3), (6, −4))

84. (graph with point (0, 4))

85. (graph with points (−3, 2), (−1, 0), (0, −7))

86. (graph with points (0, 4), $\left(\frac{4}{3}, 0\right)$)

87. (graph with points (−2, 2), (0, 2), (−1, 1))

88. (graph with points (1, 2), (3, 2), (2, 1))

89. (graph with points (3, 6), (4, 4), (6, 3), (−2, 1), (0, 0), (1, −2))

90. (graph with point (0, −3))

91. $\left\{-\dfrac{7}{3}, 3\right\}$ **92.** $\left\{-\dfrac{1}{2}, \dfrac{2}{3}\right\}$ **93.** {2}

94. $[-9, 3]$ **95.** $\left\{\dfrac{2 \pm 3\sqrt{2}}{5}\right\}$

96. $\left\{\dfrac{-1 \pm i\sqrt{39}}{4}\right\}$ **97.** $\left\{\left(\dfrac{34}{19}, \dfrac{13}{19}\right)\right\}$

98. $\left\{-\dfrac{19}{5}, 2\right\}$ **99.** $(-6, -2) \cup (1, \infty)$

100. $\{-6, -2, 1\}$ **101.** $\{(0, -1, 4)\}$ **102.** $\{-5\}$

103. $\left\{\dfrac{-3 \pm 4i}{4}\right\}$ **104.** $\left\{\dfrac{1 \pm \sqrt{37}}{6}\right\}$

105. $(-8, 6)$ **106.** $\left\{\left(\dfrac{11}{17}, -\dfrac{35}{17}\right)\right\}$

107. $\{-16, 18\}$ **108.** $\left(-\infty, -\dfrac{10}{7}\right) \cup (2, \infty)$

109. {4}   **110.** {3.79}   **111.** $\left\{\dfrac{-3 + \sqrt{33}}{2}\right\}$

112. $\left\{\dfrac{1 \pm 3\sqrt{5}}{6}\right\}$ **113.** $(-\infty, -2) \cup \left[-\dfrac{1}{2}, \infty\right)$

114. $\{-1, 64\}$

115. $0.75 per can of soda and $1.29 per bag of potato chips

116. 6 cups   **117.** 20 nickels, 25 dimes, and 42 quarters

118. Tina is 21 and Sherry is 17.   **119.** 14 and 86

120. $40   **121.** 15 gallons   **122.** 50 miles

123. Higher than 12%   **124.** 25 weeks

125. Approximately 34.7 minutes

Chapter 9

Problem Set 9.1 (page 688)

1. $-4, -1, 2, 5, 8$ **3.** $2, 0, -2, -4, -6$

5. $2, 11, 26, 47, 74$ **7.** $0, 2, 6, 12, 20$ **9.** $4, 8, 16, 32, 64$

11. $a_{15} = -79; a_{30} = -154$ **13.** $a_{25} = 1; a_{50} = -1$

15. $2n + 9$ **17.** $-3n + 5$ **19.** $\dfrac{n + 2}{2}$ **21.** $4n - 2$

23. $-3n$ **25.** 73   **27.** 334   **29.** 35   **31.** 7   **33.** 86

35. 2700   **37.** 3200   **39.** -7950 **41.** 637.5   **43.** 4950

45. 1850   **47.** -2030 **49.** 3591   **51.** 40,000

53. 58,250   **55.** 2205   **57.** -1325 **59.** 5265

61. -810 **63.** 1276   **65.** 660   **67.** 55   **69.** 431

75. $3, 3, 7, 7, 11, 11$ **77.** $4, 7, 10, 13, 17, 21$

79. $4, 12, 36, 108, 324, 972$ **81.** $1, 1, 2, 3, 5, 8$

83. $3, 1, 4, 9, 25, 256$

Problem Set 9.2 (page 699)

1. $3(2)^{n-1}$ **3.** 3^n **5.** $\left(\dfrac{1}{2}\right)^{n+1}$ **7.** 4^n **9.** $(0.3)^{n-1}$

11. $(-2)^{n-1}$ **13.** 64   **15.** $\dfrac{1}{9}$ **17.** -512 **19.** $\dfrac{1}{4374}$

21. $\dfrac{2}{3}$ **23.** 2   **25.** 1023   **27.** 19,682   **29.** $394\dfrac{1}{16}$

31. 1364   **33.** 1089   **35.** $7\dfrac{511}{512}$ **37.** -547 **39.** $127\dfrac{3}{4}$

41. 540   **43.** $2\dfrac{61}{64}$ **45.** 4   **47.** 3   **49.** No sum   **51.** $\dfrac{27}{4}$

53. 2   **55.** $\dfrac{16}{3}$ **57.** $\dfrac{1}{3}$ **59.** $\dfrac{26}{99}$ **61.** $\dfrac{41}{333}$ **63.** $\dfrac{4}{15}$

65. $\dfrac{106}{495}$ **67.** $\dfrac{7}{3}$

Problem Set 9.3 (page 704)

1. $53,500   **3.** 31,550 students   **5.** 7321   **7.** 125 liters
9. 512 gallons   **11.** $116.25   **13.** $163.84; $327.67

15. 1936 feet   **17.** $\dfrac{15}{16}$ gram   **19.** 2910 feet

21. 325 logs   **23.** 5.9%   **25.** $\dfrac{5}{64}$ gallon

Problem Set 9.4 (page 711)

These problems call for proof by mathematical induction
and require class discussion.

Chapter 9 Review Problem Set (page 716)

1. $6n - 3$ **2.** 3^{n-2} **3.** $5(2^n)$ **4.** $-3n + 8$ **5.** $2n - 7$

6. 3^{3-n} **7.** $-(-2)^{n-1}$ **8.** $3n + 9$ **9.** $\dfrac{n+1}{3}$ **10.** 4^{n-1}

11. 73   **12.** 106   **13.** $\dfrac{1}{32}$ **14.** $\dfrac{4}{9}$ **15.** -92 **16.** $\dfrac{1}{16}$

17. -5 **18.** 85   **19.** $\dfrac{5}{9}$ **20.** 2 or -2 **21.** $121\dfrac{40}{81}$

22. 7035   **23.** $-10,725$ **24.** $31\dfrac{31}{32}$ **25.** 32,015

26. 4757   **27.** $85\dfrac{21}{64}$ **28.** 37,044   **29.** 12,726

30. -1845 **31.** 225   **32.** 255   **33.** 8244   **34.** $85\dfrac{1}{3}$

35. $\dfrac{4}{11}$ **36.** $\dfrac{41}{90}$ **37.** $750   **38.** $46.50

39. $3276.70   **40.** 10,935 gallons

Chapter 9 Test (page 718)

1. -226 **2.** 48   **3.** $-5n + 2$ **4.** $5(2)^{1-n}$ **5.** $6n + 4$

6. $\dfrac{729}{8}$ or $91\dfrac{1}{8}$ **7.** 223   **8.** 60 terms   **9.** 2380   **10.** 765

11. 7155   **12.** 6138   **13.** 22,650   **14.** 9384   **15.** 4075

16. -341 **17.** 6   **18.** $\dfrac{1}{3}$ **19.** $\dfrac{2}{11}$ **20.** $\dfrac{4}{15}$ **21.** 3 liters

22. $1638.30   **23.** $4655

24. and **25.** Instructor supplies proof.

Appendix A

Practice Exercises (page 722)

1. $x^8 + 8x^7y + 28x^6y^2 + 56x^5y^3 + 70x^4y^4 + 56x^3y^5 + 28x^2y^6 + 8xy^7 + y^8$

3. $x^6 - 6x^5y + 15x^4y^2 - 20x^3y^3 + 15x^2y^4 - 6xy^5 + y^6$

5. $a^4 + 8a^3b + 24a^2b^2 + 32ab^3 + 16b^4$

7. $x^5 - 15x^4y + 90x^3y^2 - 270x^2y^3 + 405xy^4 - 243y^5$

9. $16a^4 - 96a^3b + 216a^2b^2 - 216ab^3 + 81b^4$

11. $x^{10} + 5x^8y + 10x^6y^2 + 10x^4y^3 + 5x^2y^4 + y^5$

13. $16x^8 - 32x^6y^2 + 24x^4y^4 - 8x^2y^6 + y^8$

15. $x^6 + 18x^5 + 135x^4 + 540x^3 + 1215x^2 + 1458x + 729$

17. $x^9 - 9x^8 + 36x^7 - 84x^6 + 126x^5 - 126x^4 + 84x^3 - 36x^2 + 9x - 1$

19. $1 + \dfrac{4}{n} + \dfrac{6}{n^2} + \dfrac{4}{n^3} + \dfrac{1}{n^4}$

21. $a^6 - \dfrac{6a^5}{n} + \dfrac{15a^4}{n^2} - \dfrac{20a^3}{n^3} + \dfrac{15a^2}{n^4} - \dfrac{6a}{n^5} + \dfrac{1}{n^6}$

23. $17 + 12\sqrt{2}$ **25.** $843 - 589\sqrt{2}$

27. $x^{12} + 12x^{11}y + 66x^{10}y^2 + 220x^9y^3$

29. $x^{20} - 20x^{19}y + 190x^{18}y^2 - 1140x^{17}y^3$

31. $x^{28} - 28x^{26}y^3 + 364x^{24}y^6 - 2912x^{22}y^9$

33. $a^9 + \dfrac{9a^8}{n} + \dfrac{36a^7}{n^2} + \dfrac{84a^6}{n^3}$

35. $x^{10} - 20x^9y + 180x^8y^2 - 960x^7y^3$ **37.** $56x^5y^3$

39. $126x^5y^4$ **41.** $189a^2b^5$ **43.** $120x^6y^{21}$

45. $\dfrac{5005}{n^6}$

INDEX

Abscissa, 13

Absolute value, 7, 8, 180

Absolute value equations and inequalities, 180–185, 198

Addition
matrices, 584–585
polynomial, 32
rational expressions, 54–58

Addition property
equality, 105
inequality, 165

Additive identity element, 585

Additive inverse, 10, 585, 599

Algebra of matrices, 583–624. *See also* Matrix
addition of matrices, 584–585, 618
end-of-chapter summary, 618–621
linear programming, 610–613, 620, 621
$m \times n$ matrices, 598–603
minimum/maximum values, 610–613, 620, 621
multiplication of matrices, 587–588, 594, 618
multiplicative inverse, 591–594, 619
scalar multiplication, 585–586, 618
solving systems of equations, 594–595, 603, 619
subtraction of matrices, 585, 618
systems of linear inequalities, 608–610, 620

Algebraic expression, 2, 10–11

Algebraic fraction, 51

Algebraic inequalities, 165

Analytic geometry, 14, 203. *See also* Coordinate geometry and graphing techniques

Application problems. *See* Problem solving; word problems

Arithmetic progression, 683

Arithmetic sequence, 682–687
defined, 683
end-of-chapter summary, 713
general term, 683, 712
specific term, 684, 712
sum, 684–685, 712
summation notation, 686–687, 713

Associative operations, 9

Associative property, 8

Asymptote
horizontal, 406–407, 415–417, 426
hyperbola, 259, 651
oblique, 417–421, 427
vertical, 406, 415–417, 426

Augmented matrix, 535

Axis of symmetry, 630

Base, 19

Binomial, 31

Binomial coefficient, 719

Binomial expansion pattern, 36

Binomial theorem, 719–721

Bounded, 611

Branches (hyperbola), 649

Calculator, 14–16
MODE key, 28
number of digits displayed, 27
scientific notation, 27
TRACE, 388, 666
ZOOM, 388, 666

Cartesian coordinate system, 12–14

Center
circle, 253
ellipse, 641
hyperbola, 650

Change-of-base formula, 492–493, 502

Circle, 252–256, 629
defined, 253
end-of-chapter summary, 271, 272, 667
graphs, 272
standard form, 252, 253, 256

Closure property, 8, 9

Cofactor, 547

Combined linear equality and inequality statements, 219

Combining function, 329–331

Comet, 657

Common difference, 683

Common logarithm, 480–481, 502

Common logarithmic function, 482

Commutative operations, 9

Commutative property, 8

Completely factored form, 41

Completing the square, 130–132, 133

Complex fraction, 58

Complex numbers, 82–87
addition/subtraction, 83–84
defined, 82
end-of-chapter summary, 99
multiplication/division, 84–87
standard form, 82
terminology, 82

Composite function, 331–335, 356

Composition of functions, 331–335, 356

Compound continuously problems, 447–448, 499

Compound interest problems, 443–444, 498

Compound statement, 168

Concrete bridge, 646

Conditional equation, 104

Conic sections, 629–675
　circle. *See* Circle
　defined, 629
　ellipse. *See* Ellipse
　end-of-chapter summary,
　　667–673
　hyperbola. *See* Hyperbola
　parabola. *See* Parabola
　systems of nonlinear equations,
　　659–664, 672, 673
Conjugate, 86
Conjugate axis, 651
Conjunction, 168
Consistent system, 514
Constant function, 291
Constant of proportionality, 340
Constant of variation, 340
Constraints, 612
Consumer problems, 122, 123
Coordinate, 6, 13, 204–205
Coordinate axes, 12
Coordinate geometry, 14
Coordinate geometry and graphing
　　techniques, 203–276
　circle, 256–258, 271, 272
　coordinate, 204–205
　distance between two points,
　　206–209, 266
　ellipse, 256–258, 272
　end-of-chapter summary,
　　266–272
　equations of lines, 229–234,
　　269
　general graphing techniques,
　　242, 247
　graphing exponential functions,
　　437–439, 497
　graphing linear equations,
　　216–219, 266
　graphing linear inequalities,
　　219–222, 268
　graphing nonlinear equations,
　　247–250, 271
　graphing polynomial functions,
　　392–400, 425, 426
　graphing rational functions,
　　407–412, 415–421, 427

hyperbola, 258–261, 272
intercepts, 216, 267
kinds of problems, 203–204
parallel and perpendicular lines,
　　234–237, 269
point-slope form, 232
points of division of line segment,
　　209–212
rectangular coordinate system,
　　206
restricting a variable, 246
slope, 225–229, 268
slope-intercept form, 233–234
symmetry, 243–246, 270
Counting numbers, 3
Cramer's rule, 556–560, 575
Critical number, 175
Cross-multiplication property of
　　proportions, 117
Cube root, 65
Cubed, 19, 65
Cubing-of-a-binomial patterns, 35

Declaring the variable, 109
Decreasing function, 438, 461–462,
　　501
Degree
　monomial, 31
　polynomial, 31
Dependent variable, 284
Descartes, René, 14, 204
Descartes' rules of signs, 386, 424
Determinant, 545–552, 574
Difference, 2
Difference of two squares, 35, 43
Difference quotient, 335–337, 357
Dimension $m \times n$ (matrix), 534
Direct variation, 340–342,
　　343–344
Directed distance, 204
Directrix, 630
Discriminant, 135
Disjunction, 168
Distance between two points,
　　206–209, 266
Distance-rate-time formula, 118,
　　145

Distributive property, 9
Division
　polynomial, 37–38, 366
　rational expressions, 53–54
　synthetic, 368
Division algorithm for polynomials,
　　367
Domain, 278, 282

e, 446
Earthquake, 491–492
Element
　matrix, 534
　set, 3
Elementary row operations, 535
Elimination-by-addition method
　linear equations, 517–519, 571
　nonlinear equations, 659–660,
　　673
Ellipse, 256–258, 639–646
　defined, 639
　end-of-chapter summary, 272,
　　667, 670
　graphs, 272
　hyperbola, compared, 649
　practical uses, 645–646
　standard equations, 641, 643
　standard form, 640
Elliptical gears, 646
Empty set, 3
End-of-chapter summary
　algebra of matrices, 618–621
　conic sections, 667–673
　coordinate geometry and graph-
　　ing, 266–272
　equations, inequalities and prob-
　　lem solving, 188–198
　exponential and logarithmic func-
　　tions, 497–505
　functions, 349–357
　mathematical induction, 715
　polynomial and rational func-
　　tions, 423–427
　review chapter, 91–99
　sequences, 712–714
　systems of equations, 570–575
Enter-the-exponent key, 27

Equality, properties, 105
Equation. *See also* Systems of
  equations
  absolute value, 180–185, 198
  conditional, 104
  ellipse, 641, 643
  equivalent, 104
  linear. *See* Linear equations
  logarithmic, 488
  nonlinear, 659–664, 672, 673
  parabola, 632, 634
  polynomial, 379
  quadratic. *See* Quadratic equation
  quadratic form, 160–161, 195
  radical, 157–159, 195
Equations of lines, 229–232, 269
Equivalent equation, 104
Equivalent system, 517
Evaluating an algebraic expression,
  11
Evaluating the determinant, 546
Even function, 283
Exponent, 19–31
  defined, 19
  negative integers, 21–24
  properties, 20–23
  roots, and, 75–80, 98–99
  scientific notation, 26–27
  terminology, 19
  zero, 21, 22
Exponential and logarithmic func-
    tions, 433–508. *See also*
    Logarithm
  change-of-base formula for loga-
    rithms, 492–493, 502
  common logarithm, 480–481, 502
  compound continuously prob-
    lems, 447–448, 499
  compound interest problems,
    443–444, 498
  decreasing function, 438,
    461–462, 501
  end-of-chapter summary, 497–505
  evaluate logarithmic expressions,
    467–475, 502
  exponential decay problems,
    444–446, 498

exponential growth problems,
    442, 498
  graphing exponential functions,
    437–439, 497
  graphing logarithmic functions,
    478–480
  growth-and-decay problems,
    442–446, 448–450, 498, 499
  half-life problems, 445–446, 498
  increasing function, 438,
    461–462, 501
  inverse function, 456–461, 463,
    500, 501
  logarithmic equation, 488–489
  natural logarithm, 482, 502
  number *e*, 446–447, 499
  one-to-one function, 455–456,
    463, 500
  Richter number, 491–492
  solving exponential equations,
    434–436, 486–488, 497
Exponential decay problems,
    444–446, 498
Exponential function, 437
Exponential growth problems, 442,
    498
Extraneous solution, 159

Factor, 41
Factor theorem, 375–377, 424
Factoring, 41–51
  applying more than one tech-
    nique, 48–49
  completely factored form, 41
  defined, 41
  difference of two squares, 42–43
  distributive property, 42
  end-of-chapter summary, 94–95
  grouping, 42
  polynomial equations, 155–156,
    194
  quadratic equation, 128–129
  sum/difference of two cubes, 48
  trinomials, 44–45
Factoring by grouping, 42
Factoring out the highest common
    monomial factor, 42

Focal chord, 631
Focus
  ellipse, 639
  hyperbola, 649
  parabola, 630
Forward-backward approach (sum
    of arithmetic sequence),
    684–685
Fraction
  algebraic, 51
  complex, 58
  partial, 563–568
  proper, 564
Fractional equation, 142–143
Fractional expression, 51
Function, 277–364
  combining, 329–331
  common logarithmic, 482
  composite, 331–332
  constant, 291
  correspondence, 278
  decreasing, 438, 461–462, 501
  defined, 278
  difference quotient, 335–337, 357
  domain, 278, 282
  end-of-chapter summary, 349–357
  even, 283
  exponential, 437
  graph, 279
  graphing suggestions, 317
  horizontal translation, 320
  identity, 291
  increasing, 438, 461–462, 501
  inverse, 456–461, 500
  linear, 288–290, 292–294
  logarithmic, 478
  maximum/minimum value, 310
  natural exponential, 446
  natural logarithmic, 482
  objective, 612
  odd, 283
  one-to-one, 455–456, 500
  parabola (*x*-intercept/vertex),
    308–310
  piecewise-defined, 280–281, 326,
    355
  polynomial, 392

Function *(continued)*
  product, 329
  quadratic, 298–308
  quotient, 329
  range, 278, 282
  rational, 404
  real number zeros, 310
  reflections, 321–322
  successive transformations,
      323–324, 355
  sum, 329
  variation situations, 340–346,
      357
  vertical-line test, 280
  vertical stretching and shrinking,
      323
  vertical translation, 320

General term
  arithmetic sequence, 683, 712
  geometric sequence, 691, 692,
      713
Geometric progression, 691
Geometric sequence, 691
  common ratio, 691
  end-of-chapter summary, 713,
      714
  general term, 691, 692, 713
  infinite, 695–697, 714
  specific term, 692, 713
  sum, 692–695, 714
  summation notation, 695
Graphing. *See* Coordinate geometry
    and graphing techniques
Graphing calculator, 14–16. *See also*
    Calculator
Graphing utility, 14
Growth-and-decay problems,
    442–446, 448–450, 498, 499

Half-life, 445
Half-life problems, 445–446, 498
Highway construction, 229
Homogeneous system, 562
Horizontal asymptote, 405,
    406–407, 415–417, 426
Horizontal axis, 12

Horizontal translation, 302, 320
How to Solve It (Polya), 119
Hyperbola, 258–261, 649–657
  asymptotes, 259, 651
  defined, 649
  ellipse, compared, 649
  end-of-chapter summary, 272,
      668, 671, 672
  graphs, 272
  standard equations, 650, 653
Hyperbolic paraboloid, 656, 657

Identity, 104, 565
Identity element
  addition (matrices), 585, 599
  addition (real numbers), 9
  multiplication (matrices), 591, 600
  multiplication (real numbers), 9
Identity function, 291
Identity property, 9
Image, 278
Imaginary number, 83
Imaginary part, 82
Imaginary unit, 82
Inconsistent system, 514
Increasing function, 438, 461–462,
    501
Independent variable, 284
Index, 66
Index of summation, 686
Inequality
  absolute value, 180–185, 198
  addition property, 165
  algebraic, 165
  application problems, 171, 197
  compound, 168–170, 196
  graphing, 219–222, 268
  multiplication property, 165
  quadratic, 174–176, 197
  quotients, 176–178, 198
  solution, 165
  solving, 164–166, 196, 608–610,
      620
  statements of, 164
Infinite geometric sequence,
    695–698
Infinite sequence, 682

Integer, 3
Intercept, 216, 267
Intercept form, 241
Intersection, 169
Interval notation, 167–168, 170
Inverse function, 456–461, 463,
    500, 501
Inverse property, 9
Inverse variation, 342–344
Investment problems, 123–124
Irrational number, 4
Isosceles triangle, 209

Joint variation, 344

Kepler, Johannes, 646
Kidney stones, 645

Law of decay, 446
Law of exponential growth, 446
LCD. *See* Least common
    denominator
Least common denominator (LCD),
    55, 56
Least common multiple, 55
Like terms, 10
Linear equations
  decimals, 117–118
  defined, 105, 216
  denominator of zero, 115–116
  graphing, 216–219, 266
  solving, 105–108
  straight line graph, 216
Linear function, 288–290, 292–294
Linear function in two variables, 610
Linear programming, 610–613, 620,
    621
Literal factors, 10
Lithotriptor, 645
Logarithm
  change-of-base formula, 492–493,
      502
  common, 480–481, 502
  defined, 467
  exponential *vs.* logarithmic form,
      467–468
  natural, 482, 502

properties, 469–472
word problems, and, 489–500
Logarithmic equation, 488–489
Logarithmic function, 478
Look back (problem solving), 120
LORAN, 656

Major axis, 257, 641
Margin of profit, 123
Markon, 123
Markup, 123
Mathematical induction, 706–711
Matrix addition, 584–585, 618. *See also* Algebra of matrices
    augmented, 535
    cofactor, 547
    defined, 534
    determinant, 545
    double transcripts, 545
    elementary row operations, 535
    equal, 584
    reduced echelon form, 537
    square, 545
    terminology, 534
    triangular form, 540
    zero, 585
Matrix approach to solving linear systems, 534–541, 573
Matrix multiplication, 587–588, 618
Matrix subtraction, 585, 618
Maximum/minimum value
    algebra of matrices, 610–613, 620, 621
    function, 310
Median (triangle), 214
Member (set), 3
Midpoint formula, 211, 212
Minor, 546
Minor axis, 257, 641
Mirror image, 321
Mixture problems, 148, 194
Monomial, 31
Multiple description (sequence), 690
Multiplication
    binomial (special patterns), 35
    matrices, 587–588, 594, 618
    polynomial, 32–35

radicals, 67–68
rational expressions, 53–54
Multiplication property
    equality, 105
    inequality, 165
Multiplicative identity element, 591
Multiplicative inverse, 10, 591–594, 619
Multiplicity of roots, 380–381, 424

Natural exponential function, 446
Natural logarithm, 482, 502
Natural logarithmic function, 482
Natural numbers, 3
Negative integers, 3
Nonnegative integers, 3
Nonpositive integers, 3
Nonrepeating decimals, 4
Normal distribution curve, 451
Notation
    interval, 167–168, 170
    scientific, 26–27
    set-builder, 3
    summation, 686–687, 695
Null set, 3
Number
    complex. *See* Complex numbers
    counting, 3
    critical, 175
    irrational, 4
    natural, 3
    rational, 3
    real. *See* Real number
    whole, 3
Number *e*, 446–447, 499
Numerical coefficient, 10
Numerical expression, 2
Numerical statement, 104
Numerical statements of inequality, 164

Objective function, 612
Oblique asymptote, 417–421, 418, 427
Odd function, 283
One-to-one function, 455–456, 463, 500

Open sentence, 104, 165
Opposite, 10
Order $m \times n$ (matrix), 534
Order of operations, 12
Ordered pairs, 13
Ordered triple, 526
Ordinate, 14
Origin, 12
Origin symmetry, 245

Parabola, 298–310, 630–636
    defined, 630
    end-of-chapter summary, 667, 669
    graphing rules, 302, 303
    practical uses, 636
    standard equations, 632, 634
    standard form, 631
    usefulness, 308
    x intercept/vertex, 308–310
Parallel lines, 234–237, 269
Partial fraction, 563–568
Partial fraction decomposition, 563
Pascal, Blaise, 37
Pascal's triangle, 37
Perfect-square trinomial, 35, 130, 131
Perpendicular lines, 234–237, 269
Piecewise-defined function, 280–281, 326, 355
Point-slope form, 232
Points of division of line segment, 209–212
Polya's problem-solving plan, 119–120
Polynomial, 31–40
    addition/subtraction, 32
    defined, 31
    division, 37–38, 366
    division algorithm, 367
    end-of-chapter summary, 93–94
    factoring. *See* Factoring
    multiplication, 32–35
Polynomial and rational functions, 365–432
    Descartes' rules of signs, 386, 424

Polynomial and rational functions
    (continued)
    division algorithm for polynomials, 367, 423
    end-of-chapter summary, 423–427
    factor theorem, 375–377, 424
    graph polynomial functions, 392–400, 425, 426
    graph rational functions, 407–412, 415–421, 427
    horizontal asymptote, 406–407, 415–417, 426
    multiplicity of roots, 380–381, 424
    oblique asymptote, 417–421, 427
    rational root theorem, 381
    rational solutions, 381–386
    remainder theorem, 373–375, 423
    solving polynomial equations, 379, 380, 425
    synthetic division, 368–371, 423
    vertical asymptote, 406, 415–417, 426
Polynomial equations, 379–389
    Descartes' rule of signs, 386, 424
    rational root theorem, 381
    solve, factoring, 155–156, 194
    solve, general principles, 425
    terminology, 379, 380
Polynomial function, 392
Positive integers, 3
Power of a power, 23
Primary focal chord, 631
Principal, 443
Principal square root, 65
Principle of mathematical induction, 706
Problem solving. *See also* Word problems
    changing forms of formulas, 118–119
    declaring the variable, 109
    end-of-chapter summary, 190
    inequalities, 171, 197
    Polya's four-phase plan, 119–120
    sketching, 146

slope, 228–229
step-by-step process, 143–144, 190, 701
Product, 2
Profit, 123
Proof by mathematical induction, 706
Proper fraction, 564
Properties
    absolute value, 8
    determinants, 549–551
    equality, 105
    exponents, 20–23
    logarithms, 469–472
    proportion, 117
    real numbers, 8–10
Proportion, 116, 117
Pure imaginary number, 82, 83
Pythagorean theorem, 137, 207

Quadrant, 12
Quadratic equation, 128–140
    completing the square, 130–132
    defined, 128
    discriminant, 135–136
    end-of-chapter summary, 190–192
    factoring, 128–129
    quadratic formula, 133–135
    standard form, 128
    which method to use?, 136, 137
Quadratic formula, 133–135
Quadratic function, 298–308
Quadratic inequality, 174–176, 197
Quarterly compounding, 444
Quotient, 2

Radar antenna, 636
Radical, 64–75
    defined, 65
    end-of-chapter summary, 97–98
    exponents, and, 75–80, 98–99
    multiplication, 67–68
    rationalizing radical expressions, 69–71
    simplest radical form, 66–67, 68–69

terminology, 65, 66
variables, and, 71–72
Radical equation, 157–159, 195
Radical sign, 65
Radicand, 65
Radioactive substance, 445–446, 498
Radius, 253
Range, 278, 282
Rate-time problems, 149–152, 193
Ratio, 116
Rational expressions, 51–64
    addition/subtraction, 54–58
    defined, 51
    end-of-chapter summary, 95–97
    multiplication/division, 53–54
    simplifying complex fractions, 58–60
Rational function, 404
Rational number, 3
Rational root theorem, 381
Rational solutions, 381–386
Rationalizing the denominator, 69
Rationalizing the numerator, 71
Real number, 3–10
    number line, 6
    properties, 8–10
    set, 4
    tree diagram, 5
Real number line, 6
Real number zeros, 310
Real part, 82
Reciprocal, 10
Rectangular coordinate system, 14, 206
Rectangular hyperbola, 264
Recursive description (sequence), 690
Reduced echelon form, 537
Reference intensity, 491
Reflection
    x-axis, 321
    y-axis, 322
Reflexive property, 105
Relation, 279
Remainder theorem, 373–375, 423
Repeating decimals, 4

Repeating decimals (*a*/*b* form), 697–698, 714
Restricting a variable, 246
Richter number, 491–492
Rigid transformation, 322
Roof, 228
Root (equation), 104
Roots of numbers. *See* Radical
Rotunda (Capitol Building), 645
Row-by-column multiplication, 587

Scalar, 585
Scalar multiplication, 585–586, 618
Scalar product, 599
Scientific form, 26
Scientific notation, 26–27
Searchlight, 636
Semiannual compounding, 444
Sequence
    arithmetic. *See* Arithmetic sequence
    geometric. *See* Geometric sequence
    infinite, 682
    infinite geometric, 695–698
    multiple description, 690
    recursive description, 690
Sequence problems, 700–704, 715
Set
    defined, 3
    elements, 3
    equal, 3
    intersection, 169
    null, 3
    union, 169
Set-builder notation, 3
Set of feasible solutions, 612
Shrinking (graph of function), 323
Sigma (Σ), 686
Similar terms, 10
Simplest radical form, 66–67, 68–69
Simplifying complex fractions, 58–60
Slope, 225–229, 268
Slope-intercept form, 233–234
Solution
    equation, 104
    equation in two variables, 215

extraneous, 159
inequality, 165
rational, 381–386
system, 514
Solution set, 104
Solving problems. *See* Problem solving
Special patterns (multiplying binomials), 35
Specific term
    arithmetic sequence, 684, 712
    binomial expansion, 721–723
    geometric sequence, 692, 713
Square matrix, 545
Square root, 64–65
Squared, 19, 64
Stairs, 228
Standard form
    circle, 252, 253, 256
    complex number, 82
    ellipse, 640
    parabola, 631
    quadratic equation, 128
    straight line, 237
Statements of inequality, 164
Stretching (graph of function), 323
Subset, 5
Substitution method
    linear equations, 515–517, 571
    nonlinear equations, 659–660, 672
Substitution of functions, 331
Substitution property, 105
Subtraction
    matrices, 585
    polynomial, 32
    rational expressions, 54–58
Sum, 2
    arithmetic sequence, 684–685, 712
    geometric sequence, 692–695, 714
    infinite geometric sequence, 695, 697, 714
Sum formula
    arithmetic sequence, 685
    geometric sequence, 693

Summary. *See* End-of-chapter summary
Summation notation, 686–687, 713
Summation symbol, 686
Symmetric property, 105
Symmetry, 243–246, 270
    origin, 245
    x axis, 244
    y axis, 243
Synthesis (plan), 120
Synthetic division, 368–371, 423
Systems of equations, 513–5279
    Cramer's rule, 556–560, 575
    determinant, 545–552, 574
    elimination-by-addition method, 517–519, 571
    end-of-chapter summary, 570–575
    equivalent system, 517
    matrix approach, 534–541, 573
    nonlinear equations, 659–664, 672, 673
    ordered triple, 526
    partial fraction, 563–568
    substitution method, 515–517, 571
    three linear equations, 526–530, 572, 603, 619
    two linear equations, 514–515, 570, 594–595
    word problems, 519–521, 531, 572, 573

Telescope, 636
Term
    algebraic expression, 10, 31
    general. *See* General term
    sequence, 682, 712
    similar, 10
    specific. *See* Specific term
Terminating decimals, 4
Transitive property, 105
Translation
    horizontal, 302, 320
    vertical, 299, 320
Transverse axis, 650
Triangular form, 540

Trinomial, 31
Turning points, 395
TWA Flight Center (Kennedy
    Airport), 656
Two-point form, 241

Unbounded, 611
Uniform-motion problems,
    145–148, 193
Union, 169

Variable, 2
Variation in sign, 386
Variation situations, 340–346, 357
    direct variation, 340–342,
        343–344
    general principles, 344
    inverse variation, 342–344
    joint variation, 344
Vertex
    ellipse, 641
    hyperbola, 650
    parabola, 308–310, 630
Vertical asymptote, 405, 406,
    415–417, 426

Vertical axis, 12
Vertical-line test, 280, 455
Vertical stretching and shrinking,
    323
Vertical translation, 299, 320

Whispering galleries, 645
Whole numbers, 3
Word problems. *See also* Problem
    solving
    compound continuously prob-
        lems, 447–448, 499
    compound interest problems,
        443–444, 498
    consumer problems, 122, 123
    exponential decay problems,
        444–446, 498
    exponential growth problems,
        442, 498
    growth-and-decay problems,
        442–446, 448–450, 498, 499
    half-life problems, 445–446, 498
    investment problems, 123–124
    linear function, 292–294
    mixture problems, 148, 194

rate-time problems, 149–152, 193
sequence problems, 700–704, 715
systems of equations, 519–521,
    531, 572, 573
uniform-motion problems,
    145–148, 193
work problems, 149–152, 193
Work problems, 149–152, 193

x-axis, 14
x-axis reflection, 321
x-axis symmetry, 244
x intercept, 108, 216

y-axis, 14
y-axis reflection, 322
y-axis symmetry, 243
y intercept, 216

Zero
    exponent, as, 21, 22
    real numbers, 9
Zero matrix, 585
Zeros (of polynomial function), 393

Properties of Absolute Value

$|a| \geq 0$

$|a| = |-a|$

$|a - b| = |b - a|$

$|a^2| = |a|^2 = a^2$

Multiplication Patterns

$(a + b)^2 = a^2 + 2ab + b^2$

$(a - b)^2 = a^2 - 2ab + b^2$

$(a + b)(a - b) = a^2 - b^2$

$(a + b)^3 = a^3 + 3a^2b + 3ab^2 + b^3$

$(a - b)^3 = a^3 - 3a^2b + 3ab^2 - b^3$

Properties of Exponents

$b^n \cdot b^m = b^{n+m}$ $\dfrac{b^n}{b^m} = b^{n-m}$

$(b^n)^m = b^{mn}$

$(ab)^n = a^nb^n$

$\left(\dfrac{a}{b}\right)^n = \dfrac{a^n}{b^n}$

Equations Determining Functions

Linear function: $f(x) = ax + b$

Quadratic function: $f(x) = ax^2 + bx + c$

Polynomial function: $f(x) = a_nx^n + a_{n-1}x^{n-1} + \cdots + a_1x + a_0$

Rational function: $f(x) = \dfrac{g(x)}{h(x)}$,   where g and h are polynomials; $h(x) \neq 0$

Exponential function: $f(x) = b^x$,   where $b > 0$ and $b \neq 1$

Logarithmic function: $f(x) = \log_b x$,   where $b > 0$ and $b \neq 1$

Interval Notation   Set Notation

Interval Notation	Set Notation
(a, ∞)	$\{x \mid x > a\}$
$(-\infty, b)$	$\{x \mid x < b\}$
(a, b)	$\{x \mid a < x < b\}$
$[a, \infty)$	$\{x \mid x \geq a\}$
$(-\infty, b]$	$\{x \mid x \leq b\}$
$(a, b]$	$\{x \mid a < x \leq b\}$
$[a, b)$	$\{x \mid a \leq x < b\}$
$[a, b]$	$\{x \mid a \leq x \leq b\}$

Properties of Logarithms

$\log_b b = 1$

$\log_b 1 = 0$

$\log_b rs = \log_b r + \log_b s$

$\log_b\left(\dfrac{r}{s}\right) = \log_b r - \log_b s$

$\log_b r^p = p(\log_b r)$

Factoring Patterns

$a^2 - b^2 = (a + b)(a - b)$

$a^3 - b^3 = (a - b)(a^2 + ab + b^2)$

$a^3 + b^3 = (a + b)(a^2 - ab + b^2)$

Formulas

Quadratic formula:
The roots of $ax^2 + bx + c = 0$, where $a \neq 0$, are
$$\frac{-b \pm \sqrt{b^2 - 4ac}}{2a}$$

Distance formula for 2-space:
$$d = \sqrt{(x_2 - x_1)^2 + (y_2 - y_1)^2}$$

Slope of a line:
$$m = \frac{y_2 - y_1}{x_2 - x_1}$$

Midpoint of a line segment:
$$\left(\frac{x_1 + x_2}{2}, \frac{y_1 + y_2}{2} \right)$$

Simple interest:
$$i = Prt \qquad \text{and} \qquad A = P + Prt$$

Compound interest:
$$A = P\left(i + \frac{r}{n} \right)^{nt} \qquad \text{and} \qquad A = Pe^{rt}$$

nth term of an arithmetic sequence:
$$a_n = a_1 + (n - 1)d$$

Sum of n terms of an arithmetic sequence:
$$S_n = \frac{n(a_1 + a_n)}{2}$$

nth term of a geometric sequence:
$$a_n = a_1 r^{n-1}$$

Sum of n terms of a geometric sequence:
$$S_n = \frac{a_1 r^n - a_1}{r - 1}$$

Sum of infinite geometric sequence:
$$S = \frac{a_1}{1 - r}$$

Temperature:
$$F = \frac{9}{5}C + 32 \quad \text{and} \quad C = \frac{5}{9}(F - 32)$$

Counting Techniques, Probability, and the Binomial Theorem

15.1 Fundamental Principle of Counting

15.2 Permutations and Combinations

15.3 Probability

15.4 Some Properties of Probability: Expected Values

15.5 Conditional Probability: Dependent and Independent Events

15.6 Binomial Theorem

© AP/Wide World

Probability theory can determine the probability of winning a game of chance such as a lottery.

In a group of 30 people, there is approximately a 70% chance that at least 2 of them will have the same birthday (same month and same day of the month). In a group of 60 people, there is approximately a 99% chance that at least 2 of them will have the same birthday.

With an ordinary deck of 52 playing cards, there is 1 chance out of 54,145 that you will be dealt four aces in a five-card hand. The radio is predicting a 40% chance of locally severe thunderstorms by late afternoon. The odds in favor of the Cubs winning the pennant are 2 to 3. Suppose that in a box containing 50 light bulbs, 45 are good ones, and 5 are burned out. If 2 bulbs are chosen at random, the probability of getting at least 1 good bulb is $\frac{243}{245}$. Historically, many basic probability concepts have been developed as a result of studying various games of chance. However, in recent years, applications of probability have been surfacing at a phenomenal rate in a large variety of fields, such as physics, biology, psychology, economics, insurance, military science, manufacturing, and politics. It is our purpose in this chapter first to introduce some counting techniques and then to use those techniques to explore some basic concepts of probability. The last section of the chapter will be devoted to the binomial theorem.

15.1 Fundamental Principle of Counting

One very useful counting principle is referred to as the **fundamental principle of counting**. We will offer some examples, state the property, and then use it to solve a variety of counting problems. Let's consider two problems to lead up to the statement of the property.

PROBLEM 1

A woman has four skirts and five blouses. Assuming that each blouse can be worn with each skirt, how many different skirt–blouse outfits does she have?

Solution

For *each* of the four skirts, she has a choice of five blouses. Therefore she has $4(5) = 20$ different skirt–blouse outfits from which to choose. ■

PROBLEM 2

Eric is shopping for a new bicycle and has two different models (5-speed or 10-speed) and four different colors (red, white, blue, or silver) from which to choose. How many different choices does he have?

Solution

His different choices can be counted with the help of a **tree diagram**.

Models	Colors	Choices
5-speed	red	5-speed red
	white	5-speed white
	blue	5-speed blue
	silver	5-speed silver
10-speed	red	10-speed red
	white	10-speed white
	blue	10-speed blue
	silver	10-speed silver

For each of the two model choices, there are four choices of color. Altogether, then, Eric has $2(4) = 8$ choices.   ■

These two problems exemplify the following general principle:

Fundamental Principle of Counting

If one task can be accomplished in x different ways and, following this task, a second task can be accomplished in y different ways, then the first task followed by the second task can be accomplished in $x \cdot y$ different ways. (This counting principle can be extended to any finite number of tasks.)

As you apply the fundamental principle of counting, it is often helpful to analyze a problem systematically in terms of the tasks to be accomplished. Let's consider some examples.

P R O B L E M   3   How many numbers of three different digits each can be formed by choosing from the digits 1, 2, 3, 4, 5 and 6?

Solution

Let's analyze this problem in terms of three tasks.

Task 1   Choose the hundreds digit, for which there are six choices.

Task 2   Now choose the tens digit, for which there are only five choices because one digit was used in the hundreds place.

Task 3   Now choose the units digit, for which there are only four choices because two digits have been used for the other places.

Therefore task 1 followed by task 2 followed by task 3 can be accomplished in $(6)(5)(4) = 120$ ways. In other words, there are 120 numbers of three different digits that can be formed by choosing from the six given digits.   ■

Now look back over the solution for Problem 3 and think about each of the following questions:

1. Can we solve the problem by choosing the units digit first, then the tens digit, and finally the hundreds digit?

2. How many three-digit numbers can be formed from 1, 2, 3, 4, 5, and 6 if we do not require each number to have three *different* digits? (Your answer should be 216.)

3. Suppose that the digits from which to choose are 0, 1, 2, 3, 4, and 5. Now how many numbers of three different digits each can be formed, assuming that we do not want zero in the hundreds place? (Your answer should be 100.)

4. Suppose that we want to know the number of *even* numbers with three different digits each that can be formed by choosing from 1, 2, 3, 4, 5, and 6. How many are there? (Your answer should be 60.)

PROBLEM 4

Employee ID numbers at a certain factory consist of one capital letter followed by a three-digit number that contains no repeat digits. For example, A-014 is an ID number. How many such ID numbers can be formed? How many can be formed if repeated digits *are* allowed?

Solution

Again, let's analyze the problem in terms of tasks to be completed.

Task 1 Choose the letter part of the ID number: there are 26 choices.

Task 2 Choose the first digit of the three-digit number: there are ten choices.

Task 3 Choose the second digit: there are nine choices.

Task 4 Choose the third digit: there are eight choices.

Therefore, applying the fundamental principle, we obtain $(26)(10)(9)(8) = 18{,}720$ possible ID numbers.

If repeat digits were allowed, then there would be $(26)(10)(10)(10) = 26{,}000$ possible ID numbers. ∎

PROBLEM 5

In how many ways can Al, Barb, Chad, Dan, and Edna be seated in a row of five seats so that Al and Barb are seated side by side?

Solution

This problem can be analyzed in terms of three tasks.

Task 1 Choose the two adjacent seats to be occupied by Al and Barb. An illustration such as Figure 15.1 helps us to see that there are four choices for the two adjacent seats.

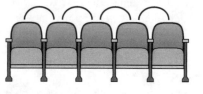

Figure 15.1

Task 2 Determine the number of ways in which Al and Barb can be seated. Because Al can be seated on the left and Barb on the right, or vice versa, there are two ways to seat Al and Barb for each pair of adjacent seats.

Task 3 The remaining three people must be seated in the remaining three seats. This can be done in $(3)(2)(1) = 6$ different ways.

Therefore, by the fundamental principle, task 1 followed by task 2 followed by task 3 can be done in $(4)(2)(6) = 48$ ways.   ■

Suppose that in Problem 5, we wanted instead the number of ways in which the five people can sit so that Al and Barb are *not* side by side. We can determine this number by using either of two basically different techniques: (1) analyze and count the number of nonadjacent positions for Al and Barb, or (2) subtract the number of seating arrangements determined in Problem 5 from the total number of ways in which five people can be seated in five seats. Try doing this problem both ways, and see whether you agree with the answer of 72 ways.

As you apply the fundamental principle of counting, you may find that for certain problems, simply thinking about an appropriate tree diagram is helpful, even though the size of the problem may make it inappropriate to write out the diagram in detail. Consider the following problem.

PROBLEM 6

Suppose that the undergraduate students in three departments — geography, history, and psychology — are to be classified according to sex and year in school. How many categories are needed?

Solution

Let's represent the various classifications symbolically as follows:

M:	Male	1.	Freshman	G:	Geography
F:	Female	2.	Sophomore	H:	History
		3.	Junior	P:	Psychology
		4.	Senior		

We can mentally picture a tree diagram such that each of the two sex classifications branches into four school-year classifications, which in turn branch into three department classifications. Thus we have $(2)(4)(3) = 24$ different categories.   ■

Another technique that works on certain problems involves what some people call the *back door* approach. For example, suppose we know that the classroom contains 50 seats. On some days, it may be easier to determine the number of students present by counting the number of empty seats and subtracting from 50 than by counting the number of students in attendance. (We suggested this back door approach as one way to count the nonadjacent seating arrangements in the discussion following Problem 5.) The next example further illustrates this approach.

PROBLEM 7

When rolling a pair of dice, in how many ways can we obtain a sum greater than 4?

Solution

For clarification purposes, let's use a red die and a white die. (It is not necessary to use different-colored dice, but it does help us analyze the different possible outcomes.) With a moment of thought, you will see that there are more ways to get a sum greater than 4 than there are ways to get a sum of 4 or less. Therefore let's determine the number of possibilities for getting a sum of 4 or less; then we'll subtract that number from the total number of possible outcomes when rolling a pair of dice. First, we can simply list and count the ways of getting a sum of 4 or less.

Red die	White die
1	1
1	2
1	3
2	1
2	2
3	1

There are six ways of getting a sum of 4 or less.

Second, because there are six possible outcomes on the red die and six possible outcomes on the white die, there is a total of $(6)(6) = 36$ possible outcomes when rolling a pair of dice.

Therefore, subtracting the number of ways of getting 4 or less from the total number of possible outcomes, we obtain $36 - 6 = 30$ ways of getting a sum greater than 4. ■

Problem Set 15.1

Solve Problems 1–37.

1. If a woman has two skirts and ten blouses, how many different skirt–blouse combinations does she have?

2. If a man has eight shirts, five pairs of slacks, and three pairs of shoes, how many different shirt–slacks–shoe combinations does he have?

3. In how many ways can four people be seated in a row of four seats?

4. How many numbers of two different digits can be formed by choosing from the digits 1, 2, 3, 4, 5, 6, and 7?

5. How many *even* numbers of three different digits can be formed by choosing from the digits 2, 3, 4, 5, 6, 7, 8, and 9?

6. How many *odd* numbers of four different digits can be formed by choosing from the digits 1, 2, 3, 4, 5, 6, 7, and 8?

7. Suppose that the students at a certain university are to be classified according to their college (College of Applied Science, College of Arts and Sciences, College of Business, College of Education, College of Fine Arts, College of Health and Physical Education), sex (female, male), and year in school (1, 2, 3, 4). How many categories are possible?

8. A medical researcher classifies subjects according to sex (female, male), smoking habits (smoker, nonsmoker), and weight (below average, average, above average). How many different combined classifications are used?

9. A pollster classifies voters according to sex (female, male), party affiliation (Democrat, Republican, Independent), and family income (below $10,000, $10,000–$19,999, $20,000–$29,999, $30,000–$39,999, $40,000–$49,999, $50,000 and above). How many combined classifications does the pollster use?

10. A couple is planning to have four children. How many ways can this happen in terms of boy–girl classification? (For example, *BBBG* indicates that the first three children are boys and the last is a girl.)

11. In how many ways can three officers — president, secretary, and treasurer — be selected from a club that has 20 members?

12. In how many ways can three officers — president, secretary, and treasurer — be selected from a club with 15 female and 10 male members so that the president is female and the secretary and treasurer are male?

13. A disc jockey wants to play six songs once each in a half-hour program. How many different ways can he order these songs?

14. A state has agreed to have its automobile license plates consist of two letters followed by four digits. State officials do not want to repeat any letters or digits in any license numbers. How many different license plates will be available?

15. In how many ways can six people be seated in a row of six seats?

16. In how many ways can Al, Bob, Carlos, Don, Ed, and Fern be seated in a row of six seats if Al and Bob want to sit side by side?

17. In how many ways can Amy, Bob, Cindy, Dan, and Elmer be seated in a row of five seats so that neither Amy nor Bob occupies an end seat?

18. In how many ways can Al, Bob, Carlos, Don, Ed, and Fern be seated in a row of six seats if Al and Bob are not to be seated side by side? [*Hint*: Either Al and Bob will be seated side by side or they will not be seated side by side.]

19. In how many ways can Al, Bob, Carol, Dawn, and Ed be seated in a row of five chairs if Al is to be seated in the middle chair?

20. In how many ways can three letters be dropped in five mailboxes?

21. In how many ways can five letters be dropped in three mailboxes?

22. In how many ways can four letters be dropped in six mailboxes so that no two letters go in the same box?

23. In how many ways can six letters be dropped in four mailboxes so that no two letters go in the same box?

24. If five coins are tossed, in how many ways can they fall?

25. If three dice are tossed, in how many ways can they fall?

26. In how many ways can a sum less than ten be obtained when tossing a pair of dice?

27. In how many ways can a sum greater than five be obtained when tossing a pair of dice?

28. In how many ways can a sum greater than four be obtained when tossing three dice?

29. If no number contains repeated digits, how many numbers greater than 400 can be formed by choosing from the digits 2, 3, 4, and 5? [*Hint*: Consider both three-digit and four-digit numbers.]

30. If no number contains repeated digits, how many numbers greater than 5000 can be formed by choosing from the digits 1, 2, 3, 4, 5, and 6?

31. In how many ways can four boys and three girls be seated in a row of seven seats so that boys and girls occupy alternating seats?

32. In how many ways can three different mathematics books and four different history books be exhibited on a shelf so that all of the books in a subject area are side by side?

33. In how many ways can a true–false test of ten questions be answered?

34. If no number contains repeated digits, how many even numbers greater than 3000 can be formed by choosing from the digits 1, 2, 3, and 4?

35. If no number contains repeated digits, how many odd numbers greater than 40,000 can be formed by choosing from the digits 1, 2, 3, 4, and 5?

36. In how many ways can Al, Bob, Carol, Don, Ed, Faye, and George be seated in a row of seven seats so that Al, Bob, and Carol occupy consecutive seats in some order?

37. The license plates for a certain state consist of two letters followed by a four-digit number such that the first digit of the number is not zero. An example is PK-2446.
    (a) How many different license plates can be produced?
    (b) How many different plates do not have a repeated letter?
    (c) How many plates do not have any repeated digits in the number part of the plate?
    (d) How many plates do not have a repeated letter and also do not have any repeated digits?

■ ■ ■ **THOUGHTS INTO WORDS**

38. How would you explain the fundamental principle of counting to a friend who missed class the day it was discussed?

39. Give two or three simple illustrations of the fundamental principle of counting.

40. Explain how you solved Problem 29.

15.2   Permutations and Combinations

As we develop the material in this section, **factorial notation** becomes very useful. The notation $n!$ (which is read "n factorial") is used with positive integers as follows:

$$1! = 1$$
$$2! = 2 \cdot 1 = 2$$
$$3! = 3 \cdot 2 \cdot 1 = 6$$
$$4! = 4 \cdot 3 \cdot 2 \cdot 1 = 24$$

Note that the factorial notation refers to an *indicated product*. In general, we write

$$n! = n(n-1)(n-2) \cdots 3 \cdot 2 \cdot 1$$

We also define $0! = 1$ so that certain formulas will be true for all nonnegative integers.

Now, as an introduction to the first concept of this section, let's consider a counting problem that closely resembles problems from the previous section.

PROBLEM 1   In how many ways can the three letters A, B, and C be arranged in a row?

Solution A

Certainly one approach to the problem is simply to list and count the arrangements.

ABC   ACB   BAC   BCA   CAB   CBA

There are six arrangements of the three letters.

Solution B

Another approach, one that can be generalized for more difficult problems, uses the fundamental principle of counting. Because there are three choices for the first letter of an arrangement, two choices for the second letter, and one choice for the third letter, there are $(3)(2)(1) = 6$ arrangements. ■

■ Permutations

Ordered arrangements are called **permutations**. In general, a permutation of a set of n elements is an ordered arrangement of the n elements; we will use the symbol $P(n, n)$ to denote the number of such permutations. For example, from Problem 1, we know that $P(3, 3) = 6$. Furthermore, by using the same basic approach as in Solution B of Problem 1, we can obtain

$$P(1, 1) = 1 = 1!$$

$$P(2, 2) = 2 \cdot 1 = 2!$$

$$P(4, 4) = 4 \cdot 3 \cdot 2 \cdot 1 = 4!$$

$$P(5, 5) = 5 \cdot 4 \cdot 3 \cdot 2 \cdot 1 = 5!$$

In general, the following formula becomes evident:

$$P(n, n) = n!$$

Now suppose that we are interested in the number of two-letter permutations that can be formed by choosing from the four letters A, B, C, and D. (Some examples of such permutations are AB, BA, AC, BC, and CB.) In other words, we want to find the number of two-element permutations that can be formed from a set of four elements. We denote this number by $P(4, 2)$. To find $P(4, 2)$, we can reason as follows. First, we can choose any one of the four letters to occupy the first position in the permutation, and then we can choose any one of the three remaining letters for the second position. Therefore, by the fundamental principle of counting, we have $(4)(3) = 12$ different two-letter permutations; that is, $P(4, 2) = 12$. By using a similar line of reasoning, we can determine the following numbers. (Make sure that you agree with each of these.)

$$P(4, 3) = 4 \cdot 3 \cdot 2 = 24$$

$$P(5, 2) = 5 \cdot 4 = 20$$

$$P(6, 4) = 6 \cdot 5 \cdot 4 \cdot 3 = 360$$

$$P(7, 3) = 7 \cdot 6 \cdot 5 = 210$$

In general, we say that the **number of r-element permutations** that can be formed from a set of n elements is given by

$$P(n, r) = \underbrace{n(n - 1)(n - 2) \cdots}_{r \text{ factors}}$$

Note that the indicated product for $P(n, r)$ begins with n. Thereafter, each factor is 1 less than the previous one, and there is a total of r factors. For example,

$$P(6, 2) = 6 \cdot 5 = 30$$

$$P(8, 3) = 8 \cdot 7 \cdot 6 = 336$$

$$P(9, 4) = 9 \cdot 8 \cdot 7 \cdot 6 = 3024$$

Let's consider two problems that illustrate the use of $P(n, n)$ and $P(n, r)$.

P R O B L E M   2

In how many ways can five students be seated in a row of five seats?

Solution

The problem is asking for the number of five-element permutations that can be formed from a set of five elements. Thus we can apply $P(n, n) = n!$.

$$P(5, 5) = 5! = 5 \cdot 4 \cdot 3 \cdot 2 \cdot 1 = 120$$ ■

P R O B L E M   3

Suppose that seven people enter a swimming race. In how many ways can first, second, and third prizes be awarded?

Solution

This problem is asking for the number of three-element permutations that can be formed from a set of seven elements. Therefore, using the formula for $P(n, r)$, we obtain

$$P(7, 3) = 7 \cdot 6 \cdot 5 = 210$$ ■

It should be evident that both Problem 2 and Problem 3 could have been solved by applying the fundamental principle of counting. In fact, the formulas for $P(n, n)$ and $P(n, r)$ do not really give us much additional problem-solving power. However, as we will see in a moment, they do provide the basis for developing a formula that is very useful as a problem-solving tool.

■ Permutations Involving Nondistinguishable Objects

Suppose we have two identical H's and one T in an arrangement such as HTH. If we switch the two identical H's, the newly formed arrangement, HTH, will not be distinguishable from the original. In other words, there are fewer distinguishable permutations of n elements when some of those elements are identical than when the n elements are distinctly different.

To see the effect of identical elements on the number of distinguishable permutations, let's look at some specific examples:

2 identical H's   1 permutation (HH)

2 different letters   2! permutations (HT, TH)

Therefore, having two different letters affects the number of permutations by a *factor of* 2!.

> 3 identical H's   1 permutation (HHH)
>
> 3 different letters   3! permutations

Therefore, having three different letters affects the number of permutations by a *factor of* 3!.

> 4 identical H's   1 permutation (HHHH)
>
> 4 different letters   4! permutations

Therefore, having four different letters affects the number of permutations by a *factor of* 4!.

Now let's solve a specific problem.

P R O B L E M   4

How many distinguishable permutations can be formed from three identical H's and two identical T's?

Solution

If we had five distinctly different letters, we could form 5! permutations. But the three identical H's affect the number of distinguishable permutations by a factor of 3!, and the two identical T's affect the number of permutations by a factor of 2!. Therefore we must divide 5! by 3! and 2!. We obtain

$$\frac{5!}{(3!)(2!)} = \frac{5 \cdot \overset{2}{4} \cdot 3 \cdot 2 \cdot 1}{3 \cdot 2 \cdot 1 \cdot 2 \cdot 1} = 10$$

distinguishable permutations of three H's and two T's. ∎

The type of reasoning used in Problem 4 leads us to the following general counting technique. If there are n elements to be arranged, where there are r_1 of one kind, r_2 of another kind, r_3 of another kind, . . . , r_k of a kth kind, then the total number of distinguishable permutations is given by the expression

$$\frac{n!}{(r_1!)(r_2!)(r_3!) \cdots (r_k!)}$$

P R O B L E M   5

How many different 11-letter permutations can be formed from the 11 letters of the word MISSISSIPPI?

Solution

Because there are 4 I's, 4 S's, and 2 P's, we can form

$$\frac{11!}{(4!)(4!)(2!)} = \frac{11 \cdot 10 \cdot 9 \cdot 8 \cdot 7 \cdot 6 \cdot 5 \cdot 4 \cdot 3 \cdot 2 \cdot 1}{4 \cdot 3 \cdot 2 \cdot 1 \cdot 4 \cdot 3 \cdot 2 \cdot 1 \cdot 2 \cdot 1} = 34,650$$

distinguishable permutations. ∎

■ Combinations (Subsets)

Permutations are *ordered* arrangements; however, *order* is often not a consideration. For example, suppose that we want to determine the number of three-person committees that can be formed from the five people Al, Barb, Carol, Dawn, and Eric. Certainly the committee consisting of Al, Barb, and Eric is the same as the committee consisting of Barb, Eric, and Al. In other words, the order in which we choose or list the members is not important. Therefore we are really dealing with subsets; that is, we are looking for the number of three-element subsets that can be formed from a set of five elements. Traditionally in this context, subsets have been called **combinations**. Stated another way, then, we are looking for the number of combinations of five things taken three at a time. In general, *r*-element subsets taken from a set of *n* elements are called **combinations of *n* things taken *r* at a time**. The symbol $C(n, r)$ denotes the number of these combinations.

Now let's restate that committee problem and show a detailed solution that can be generalized to handle a variety of problems dealing with combinations.

PROBLEM 6

How many three-person committees can be formed from the five people Al, Barb, Carol, Dawn, and Eric?

Solution

Let's use the set {A, B, C, D, E} to represent the five people. Consider one possible three-person committee (subset), such as {A, B, C}; there are 3! permutations of these three letters. Now take another committee, such as {A, B, D}; there are also 3! permutations of these three letters. If we were to continue this process with all of the three-letter subsets that can be formed from the five letters, we would be counting all possible three-letter permutations of the five letters. That is, we would obtain $P(5, 3)$. Therefore, if we let $C(5, 3)$ represent the number of three-element subsets, then

$$(3!) \cdot C(5, 3) = P(5, 3)$$

Solving this equation for $C(5, 3)$ yields

$$C(5, 3) = \frac{P(5, 3)}{3!} = \frac{5 \cdot 4 \cdot 3}{3 \cdot 2 \cdot 1} = 10$$

Thus ten three-person committees can be formed from the five people. ■

In general, $C(n, r)$ times $r!$ yields $P(n, r)$. Thus

$$(r!) \cdot C(n, r) = P(n, r)$$

and solving this equation for $C(n, r)$ produces

$$C(n, r) = \frac{P(n, r)}{r!}$$

In other words, we can find the number of *combinations* of n things taken r at a time by dividing by $r!$, the number of permutations of n things taken r at a time. The following examples illustrate this idea:

$$C(7, 3) = \frac{P(7, 3)}{3!} = \frac{7 \cdot 6 \cdot 5}{3 \cdot 2 \cdot 1} = 35$$

$$C(9, 2) = \frac{P(9, 2)}{2!} = \frac{9 \cdot 8}{2 \cdot 1} = 36$$

$$C(10, 4) = \frac{P(10, 4)}{4!} = \frac{10 \cdot 9 \cdot 8 \cdot 7}{4 \cdot 3 \cdot 2 \cdot 1} = 210$$

P R O B L E M   7

How many different five-card hands can be dealt from a deck of 52 playing cards?

Solution

Because the order in which the cards are dealt is not an issue, we are working with a combination (subset) problem. Thus, using the formula for $C(n, r)$, we obtain

$$C(52, 5) = \frac{P(52, 5)}{5!} = \frac{52 \cdot 51 \cdot 50 \cdot 49 \cdot 48}{5 \cdot 4 \cdot 3 \cdot 2 \cdot 1} = 2{,}598{,}960$$

There are 2,598,960 different five-card hands that can be dealt from a deck of 52 playing cards.   ■

Some counting problems, such as Problem 8, can be solved by using the fundamental principle of counting along with the combination formula.

P R O B L E M   8

How many committees that consist of three women and two men can be formed from a group of five women and four men?

Solution

Let's think of this problem in terms of two tasks.

Task 1   Choose a subset of three women from the five women. This can be done in

$$C(5, 3) = \frac{P(5, 3)}{3!} = \frac{5 \cdot 4 \cdot 3}{3 \cdot 2 \cdot 1} = 10 \text{ ways}$$

Task 2   Choose a subset of two men from the four men. This can be done in

$$C(4, 2) = \frac{P(4, 2)}{2!} = \frac{4 \cdot 3}{2 \cdot 1} = 6 \text{ ways}$$

Task 1 followed by task 2 can be done in $(10)(6) = 60$ ways. Therefore there are 60 committees consisting of three women and two men that can be formed.   ■

Sometimes it takes a little thought to decide whether permutations or combinations should be used. Remember that **if order is to be considered, permutations should be used, but if order does not matter, then use combinations**. It is helpful to think of combinations as subsets.

PROBLEM 9

A small accounting firm has 12 computer programmers. Three of these people are to be promoted to systems analysts. In how many ways can the firm select the three people to be promoted?

Solution

Let's call the people A, B, C, D, E, F, G, H, I, J, K, and L. Suppose A, B, and C are chosen for promotion. Is this any different from choosing B, C, and A? Obviously not, so order does not matter, and we are being asked a question about combinations. More specifically, we need to find the number of combinations of 12 people taken three at a time. Thus there are

$$C(12, 3) = \frac{P(12, 3)}{3!} = \frac{12 \cdot 11 \cdot 10}{3 \cdot 2 \cdot 1} = 220$$

different ways to choose the three people to be promoted. ■

PROBLEM 10

A club is to elect three officers — president, secretary, and treasurer — from a group of six people, all of whom are willing to serve in any office. How many different ways can the officers be chosen?

Solution

Let's call the candidates A, B, C, D, E, and F. Is electing A as president, B as secretary, and C as treasurer different from electing B as president, C as secretary, and A as treasurer? Obviously it is, so we are working with permutations. Thus there are

$$P(6, 3) = 6 \cdot 5 \cdot 4 = 120$$

different ways of filling the offices. ■

Problem Set 15.2

In Problems 1–12, evaluate each.

1. $P(5, 3)$

2. $P(8, 2)$

3. $P(6, 4)$

4. $P(9, 3)$

5. $C(7, 2)$

6. $C(8, 5)$

7. $C(10, 5)$

8. $C(12, 4)$

9. $C(15, 2)$

10. $P(5, 5)$

11. $C(5, 5)$

12. $C(11, 1)$

For Problems 13–44, solve each problem.

13. How many permutations of the four letters A, B, C, and D can be formed by using all the letters in each permutation?

14. In how many ways can six students be seated in a row of six seats?

15. How many three-person committees can be formed from a group of nine people?

16. How many two-card hands can be dealt from a deck of 52 playing cards?

17. How many three-letter permutations can be formed from the first eight letters of the alphabet (a) if repetitions are not allowed? (b) if repetitions are allowed?

18. In a seven-team baseball league, in how many ways can the top three positions in the final standings be filled?

19. In how many ways can the manager of a baseball team arrange his batting order of nine starters if he wants his best hitters in the top four positions?

20. In a baseball league of nine teams, how many games are needed to complete the schedule if each team plays 12 games with each other team?

21. How many committees consisting of four women and four men can be chosen from a group of seven women and eight men?

22. How many three-element subsets containing one vowel and two consonants can be formed from the set {a, b, c, d, e, f, g, h, i}?

23. Five associate professors are being considered for promotion to the rank of full professor, but only three will be promoted. How many different combinations of three could be promoted?

24. How many numbers of four different digits can be formed from the digits 1, 2, 3, 4, 5, 6, 7, 8, and 9 if each number must consist of two odd and two even digits?

25. How many three-element subsets containing the letter A can be formed from the set {A, B, C, D, E, F}?

26. How many four-person committees can be chosen from five women and three men if each committee must contain at least one man?

27. How many different seven-letter permutations can be formed from four identical H's and three identical T's?

28. How many different eight-letter permutations can be formed from six identical H's and two identical T's?

29. How many different nine-letter permutations can be formed from three identical A's, four identical B's, and two identical C's?

30. How many different ten-letter permutations can be formed from five identical A's, four identical B's, and one C?

31. How many different seven-letter permutations can be formed from the seven letters of the word ALGEBRA?

32. How many different 11-letter permutations can be formed from the 11 letters of the word MATHEMATICS?

33. In how many ways can x^4y^2 be written without using exponents? [*Hint*: One way is *xxxxyy*.]

34. In how many ways can $x^3y^4z^3$ be written without using exponents?

35. Ten basketball players are going to be divided into two teams of five players each for a game. In how many ways can this be done?

36. Ten basketball players are going to be divided into two teams of five in such a way that the two best players are on opposite teams. In how many ways can this be done?

37. A box contains nine good light bulbs and four defective bulbs. How many samples of three bulbs contain one defective bulb? How many samples of three bulbs contain *at least* one defective bulb?

38. How many five-person committees consisting of two juniors and three seniors can be formed from a group of six juniors and eight seniors?

39. In how many ways can six people be divided into two groups so that there are four in one group and two in the other? In how many ways can six people be divided into two groups of three each?

40. How many five-element subsets containing A and B can be formed from the set {A, B, C, D, E, F, G, H}?

41. How many four-element subsets containing A or B but not both A and B can be formed from the set {A, B, C, D, E, F, G}?

42. How many different five-person committees can be selected from nine people if two of those people refuse to serve together on a committee?

43. How many different line segments are determined by five points? By six points? By seven points? By *n* points?

44. (a) How many five-card hands consisting of two kings and three aces can be dealt from a deck of 52 playing cards?

(b) How many five-card hands consisting of three kings and two aces can be dealt from a deck of 52 playing cards?

(c) How many five-card hands consisting of three cards of one face value and two cards of another face value can be dealt from a deck of 52 playing cards?

■ ■ ■ THOUGHTS INTO WORDS

45. Explain the difference between a permutation and a combination. Give an example of each one to illustrate your explanation.

46. Your friend is having difficulty distinguishing between permutations and combinations in problem-solving situations. What might you do to help her?

■ ■ ■ FURTHER INVESTIGATIONS

47. In how many ways can six people be seated at a circular table? [*Hint*: Moving each person one place to the right (or left) does not create a new seating.]

48. The quantity $P(8, 3)$ can be expressed completely in factorial notation as follows:

$$P(8, 3) = \frac{P(8, 3) \cdot 5!}{5!} = \frac{(8 \cdot 7 \cdot 6)(5 \cdot 4 \cdot 3 \cdot 2 \cdot 1)}{5!} = \frac{8!}{5!}$$

Express each of the following in terms of factorial notation.
(a) $P(7, 3)$
(b) $P(9, 2)$
(c) $P(10, 7)$
(d) $P(n, r)$, $r \leq n$ and $0!$ is defined to be 1

49. Sometimes the formula

$$C(n, r) = \frac{n!}{r!(n - r)!}$$

is used to find the number of combinations of n things taken r at a time. Use the result from part (d) of Problem 48 and develop this formula.

50. Compute $C(7, 3)$ and $C(7, 4)$. Compute $C(8, 2)$ and $C(8, 6)$. Compute $C(9, 8)$ and $C(9, 1)$. Now argue that $C(n, r) = C(n, n - r)$ for $r \leq n$.

▨ GRAPHING CALCULATOR ACTIVITIES

Before doing Problems 51–56, be sure that you can use your calculator to compute the number of permutations and combinations. Your calculator may possess a special sequence of keys for such computations. You may need to refer to your user's manual for this information.

51. Use your calculator to check your answers for Problems 1–12.

52. How many different five-card hands can be dealt from a deck of 52 playing cards?

53. How many different seven-card hands can be dealt from a deck of 52 playing cards?

54. How many different five-person committees can be formed from a group of 50 people?

55. How many different juries consisting of 11 people can be chosen from a group of 30 people?

56. How many seven-person committees consisting of three juniors and four seniors can be formed from 45 juniors and 53 seniors?

15.3   Probability

In order to introduce some terminology and notation, let's consider a simple experiment of tossing a regular six-sided die. There are six possible outcomes to this experiment: The 1, the 2, the 3, the 4, the 5, or the 6 will land up. This set of possible outcomes is called a "sample space," and the individual elements of the sample space are called "sample points." We will use S (sometimes with subscripts for identification purposes) to refer to a particular sample space of an experiment; then we will denote the number of sample points by $n(S)$. Thus for the experiment of tossing a die, $S = \{1, 2, 3, 4, 5, 6\}$ and $n(S) = 6$.

In general, the set of all possible outcomes of a given experiment is called the **sample space**, and the individual elements of the sample space are called **sample points**. (In this text, we will be working only with sample spaces that are finite.)

Now suppose we are interested in some of the various possible outcomes in the die-tossing experiment. For example, we might be interested in the event, *an even number comes up*. In this case we are satisfied if a 2, 4, or 6 appears on the top face of the die, and therefore the event, *an even number comes up*, is the subset $E = \{2, 4, 6\}$, where $n(E) = 3$. Perhaps, instead, we might be interested in the event, *a multiple of 3 comes up*. This event determines the subset $F = \{3, 6\}$, where $n(F) = 2$.

In general, any subset of a sample space is called an **event** or an **event space**. If the event consists of exactly one element of the sample space, then it is called a **simple event**. Any nonempty event that is not simple is called a **compound event**. A compound event can be represented as the union of simple events.

It is now possible to give a very simple definition for *probability* as we want to use the term in this text.

Definition 15.1

In an experiment where all possible outcomes in the sample space S are equally likely to occur, the **probability** of an event E is defined by

$$P(E) = \frac{n(E)}{n(S)}$$

where $n(E)$ denotes the number of elements in the event E, and $n(S)$ denotes the number of elements in the sample space S.

Many probability problems can be solved by applying Definition 15.1. Such an approach requires that we be able to determine the number of elements in the sample space and the number of elements in the event space. For example, in the die-tossing experiment, the probability of getting an even number with one toss of the die is given by

$$P(E) = \frac{n(E)}{n(S)} = \frac{3}{6} = \frac{1}{2}$$

Let's consider two examples where the number of elements in both the sample space and the event space are easy to determine.

PROBLEM 1

A coin is tossed. Find the probability that a head turns up.

Solution

Let the sample space be $S = \{H, T\}$; then $n(S) = 2$. The event of a head turning up is the subset $E = \{H\}$, so $n(E) = 1$. Therefore the probability of getting a head with one flip of a coin is given by

$$P(E) = \frac{n(E)}{n(S)} = \frac{1}{2}$$

■

PROBLEM 2

Two coins are tossed. What is the probability that *at least* one head will turn up?

Solution

For clarification purposes, let the coins be a penny and a nickel. The possible outcomes of this experiment are (1) a head on both coins, (2) a head on the penny and a tail on the nickel, (3) a tail on the penny and a head on the nickel, and (4) a tail on both coins. Using ordered-pair notation, where the first entry of a pair represents the penny and the second entry the nickel, we can write the sample space as

$$S = \{(H, H), (H, T), (T, H), (T, T)\}$$

and $n(S) = 4$.

Let E be the event of getting at least one head. Thus $E = \{(H, H), (H, T), (T, H)\}$ and $n(E) = 3$. Therefore the probability of getting at least one head with one toss of two coins is

$$P(E) = \frac{n(E)}{n(S)} = \frac{3}{4}$$

■

As you might expect, the counting techniques discussed in the first two sections of this chapter can frequently be used to solve probability problems.

PROBLEM 3

Four coins are tossed. Find the probability of getting three heads and one tail.

Solution

The sample space consists of the possible outcomes for tossing four coins. Because there are two things that can happen on each coin, by the fundamental principle of counting there are $2 \cdot 2 \cdot 2 \cdot 2 = 16$ possible outcomes for tossing four coins. Thus we know that $n(S) = 16$ without taking the time to list all of the elements. The event of getting three heads and one tail is the subset $E = \{(H, H, H, T), (H, H, T, H), (H, T, H, H), (T, H, H, H)\}$, where $n(E) = 4$. Therefore the requested probability is

$$P(E) = \frac{n(E)}{n(S)} = \frac{4}{16} = \frac{1}{4}$$

■

PROBLEM 4

Al, Bob, Chad, Dorcas, Eve, and Françoise are randomly seated in a row of six chairs. What is the probability that Al and Bob are seated in the end seats?

Solution

The sample space consists of all possible ways of seating six people in six chairs or, in other words, the permutations of six things taken six at a time. Thus $n(S) = P(6, 6) = 6! = 6 \cdot 5 \cdot 4 \cdot 3 \cdot 2 \cdot 1 = 720$.

The event space consists of all possible ways of seating the six people so that Al and Bob both occupy end seats. The number of these possibilities can be determined as follows:

Task 1   Put Al and Bob in the end seats. This can be done in two ways because Al can be on the left end and Bob on the right end, or vice versa.

Task 2   Put the other four people in the remaining four seats. This can be done in $4! = 4 \cdot 3 \cdot 2 \cdot 1 = 24$ different ways.

Therefore task 1 followed by task 2 can be done in $(2)(24) = 48$ different ways, so $n(E) = 48$. Thus the requested probability is

$$P(E) = \frac{n(E)}{n(S)} = \frac{48}{720} = \frac{1}{15}$$ ∎

Note that in Problem 3, by using the fundamental principle of counting to determine the number of elements in the sample space, we did not actually have to list all of the elements. For the event space, we listed the elements and counted them in the usual way. In Problem 4, we used the permutation formula $P(n, n) = n!$ to determine the number of elements in the sample space, and then we used the fundamental principle to determine the number of elements in the event space. There are no definite rules about when to list the elements and when to apply some sort of counting technique. In general, we suggest that if you do not immediately see a counting pattern for a particular problem, you should begin the listing process. If a counting pattern then emerges as you are listing the elements, use the pattern at that time.

The combination (subset) formula we developed in Section 15.2, $C(n, r) = P(n, r)/r!$, is also a very useful tool for solving certain kinds of probability problems. The next three examples illustrate some problems of this type.

PROBLEM 5

A committee of three people is randomly selected from Alice, Bjorn, Chad, Dee, and Eric. What is the probability that Alice is on the committee?

Solution

The sample space, S, consists of all possible three-person committees that can be formed from the five people. Therefore

$$n(S) = C(5, 3) = \frac{P(5, 3)}{3!} = \frac{5 \cdot 4 \cdot 3}{3 \cdot 2 \cdot 1} = 10$$

The event space, E, consists of all the three-person committees that have Alice as a member. Each of those committees contains Alice and two other people chosen from the four remaining people. Thus the number of such committees is $C(4, 2)$, so we obtain

$$n(E) = C(4, 2) = \frac{P(4, 2)}{2!} = \frac{4 \cdot 3}{2 \cdot 1} = 6$$

The requested probability is

$$P(E) = \frac{n(E)}{n(S)} = \frac{6}{10} = \frac{3}{5}$$

■

PROBLEM 6

A committee of four is chosen at random from a group of five seniors and four juniors. Find the probability that the committee will contain two seniors and two juniors.

Solution

The sample space, S, consists of all possible four-person committees that can be formed from the nine people. Thus

$$n(S) = C(9, 4) = \frac{P(9, 4)}{4!} = \frac{9 \cdot 8 \cdot 7 \cdot 6}{4 \cdot 3 \cdot 2 \cdot 1} = 126$$

The event space, E, consists of all four-person committees that contain two seniors and two juniors. They can be counted as follows.

Task 1 Choose two seniors from the five available seniors in $C(5, 2) = 10$ ways.

Task 2 Choose two juniors from the four available juniors in $C(4, 2) = 6$ ways.

Therefore there are $10 \cdot 6 = 60$ committees consisting of two seniors and two juniors. The requested probability is

$$P(E) = \frac{n(E)}{n(S)} = \frac{60}{126} = \frac{10}{21}$$

■

PROBLEM 7

Eight coins are tossed. Find the probability of getting two heads and six tails.

Solution

Because either of two things can happen on each coin, the total number of possible outcomes, $n(S)$, is $2^8 = 256$.

We can select two coins, which are to fall heads, in $C(8, 2) = 28$ ways. For each of these ways, there is only one way to select the other six coins that are to fall tails. Therefore there are $28 \cdot 1 = 28$ ways of getting two heads and six tails, so $n(E) = 28$. The requested probability is

$$P(E) = \frac{n(E)}{n(S)} = \frac{28}{256} = \frac{7}{64}$$

■

Problem Set 15.3

For Problems 1–4, *two* coins are tossed. Find the probability of tossing each of the following events:

1. One head and one tail

2. Two tails

3. At least one tail

4. No tails

For Problems 5–8, *three* coins are tossed. Find the probability of tossing each of the following events:

5. Three heads

6. Two heads and a tail

7. At least one head

8. Exactly one tail

For Problems 9–12, *four* coins are tossed. Find the probability of tossing each of the following events:

9. Four heads

10. Three heads and a tail

11. Two heads and two tails

12. At least one head

For Problems 13–16, *one* die is tossed. Find the probability of rolling each of the following events:

13. A multiple of 3

14. A prime number

15. An even number

16. A multiple of 7

For Problems 17–22, *two* dice are tossed. Find the probability of rolling each of the following events:

17. A sum of 6

18. A sum of 11

19. A sum less than 5

20. A 5 on exactly one die

21. A 4 on at least one die

22. A sum greater than 4

For Problems 23–26, *one* card is drawn from a standard deck of 52 playing cards. Find the probability of each of the following events:

23. A heart is drawn.

24. A king is drawn.

25. A spade or a diamond is drawn.

26. A red jack is drawn.

For Problems 27–30, suppose that 25 slips of paper numbered 1 to 25, inclusive, are put in a hat, and then one is drawn out at random. Find the probability of each of the following events:

27. The slip with the 5 on it is drawn.

28. A slip with an even number on it is drawn.

29. A slip with a prime number on it is drawn.

30. A slip with a multiple of 6 on it is drawn.

For Problems 31–34, suppose that a committee of two boys is to be chosen at random from the five boys Al, Bill, Carl, Dan, and Eli. Find the probability of each of the following events:

31. Dan is on the committee.

32. Dan and Eli are both on the committee.

33. Bill and Carl are not both on the committee.

34. Dan or Eli, but not both of them, is on the committee.

For Problems 35–38, suppose that a five-person committee is selected at random from the eight people Al, Barb, Chad, Dominique, Eric, Fern, George, and Harriet. Find the probability of each of the following events:

35. Al and Barb are both on the committee.

36. George is not on the committee.

37. Either Chad or Dominique, but not both, is on the committee.

38. Neither Al nor Barb is on the committee.

For Problems 39–41, suppose that a box of ten items from a manufacturing company is known to contain two defective and eight nondefective items. A sample of three items is selected at random. Find the probability of each of the following events:

39. The sample contains all nondefective items.

40. The sample contains one defective and two nondefective items.

41. The sample contains two defective and one nondefective item.

For Problems 42–60, solve each problem.

42. A building has five doors. Find the probability that two people, entering the building at random, will choose the same door.

43. Bill, Carol, and Alice are to be seated at random in a row of three seats. Find the probability that Bill and Carol will be seated side by side.

44. April, Bill, Carl, and Denise are to be seated at random in a row of four chairs. What is the probability that April and Bill will occupy the end seats?

45. A committee of four girls is to be chosen at random from the five girls Alice, Becky, Candy, Dee, and Elaine. Find the probability that Elaine is not on the committee.

46. Three boys and two girls are to be seated at random in a row of five seats. What is the probability that the boys and girls will be in alternating seats?

47. Four different mathematics books and five different history books are randomly placed on a shelf. What is the probability that all of the books on a subject are side by side?

48. Each of three letters is to be mailed in any one of five different mailboxes. What is the probability that all will be mailed in the same mailbox?

49. Randomly form a four-digit number by using the digits 2, 3, 4, and 6 once each. What is the probability that the number formed is greater than 4000?

50. Randomly select one of the 120 permutations of the letters a, b, c, d, and e. Find the probability that in the chosen permutation, the letter a precedes the b (the a is to the left of the b).

51. A committee of four is chosen at random from a group of six women and five men. Find the probability that the committee contains two women and two men.

52. A committee of three is chosen at random from a group of four women and five men. Find the probability that the committee contains at least one man.

53. Ahmed, Bob, Carl, Dan, Ed, Frank, Gino, Harry, Julio, and Mike are randomly divided into two five-man teams for a basketball game. What is the probability that Ahmed, Bob, and Carl are on the same team?

54. Seven coins are tossed. Find the probability of getting four heads and three tails.

55. Nine coins are tossed. Find the probability of getting three heads and six tails.

56. Six coins are tossed. Find the probability of getting at least four heads.

57. Five coins are tossed. Find the probability of getting no more than three heads.

58. Each arrangement of the 11 letters of the word MISSISSIPPI is put on a slip of paper and placed in a hat. One slip is drawn at random from the hat. Find the probability that the slip contains an arrangement of the letters with the four S's at the beginning.

59. Each arrangement of the seven letters of the word OSMOSIS is put on a slip of paper and placed in a hat. One slip is drawn at random from the hat. Find the probability that the slip contains an arrangement of the letters with an O at the beginning and an O at the end.

60. Consider all possible arrangements of three identical H's and three identical T's. Suppose that one of these arrangements is selected at random. What is the probability that the selected arrangement has the three H's in consecutive positions?

■ ■ ■ **THOUGHTS INTO WORDS**

61. Explain the concepts of sample space and event space.

62. Why must probability answers fall between 0 and 1, inclusive? Give an example of a situation for which the probability is 0. Also give an example for which the probability is 1.

■ ■ ■ **FURTHER INVESTIGATIONS**

In Problem 7 of Section 15.2, we found that there are 2,598,960 different five-card hands that can be dealt from a deck of 52 playing cards. Therefore, probabilities for certain kinds of five-card poker hands can be calculated by using 2,598,960 as the number of elements in the sample space. For Problems 63–71, determine the number of different five-card poker hands of the indicated type that can be obtained.

63. A straight flush (five cards in sequence and of the same suit; aces are both low and high, so A2345 and 10JQKA are both acceptable)

64. Four of a kind (four of the same face value, such as four kings)

65. A full house (three cards of one face value and two cards of another face value)

66. A flush (five cards of the same suit but not in sequence)

67. A straight (five cards in sequence but not all of the same suit)

68. Three of a kind (three cards of one face value and two cards of two different face values)

69. Two pairs

70. Exactly one pair

71. No pairs

15.4   Some Properties of Probability; Expected Values

There are several basic properties that are useful in the study of probability from both a theoretical and a computational viewpoint. We will discuss two of these properties at this time and some additional ones in the next section. The first property may seem to state the obvious, but it still needs to be mentioned.

Property 15.1

For all events E,

$$0 \leq P(E) \leq 1$$

Property 15.1 simply states that probabilities must fall in the range from 0 to 1, inclusive. This seems reasonable because $P(E) = n(E)/n(S)$, and E is a subset of S. The next two examples illustrate circumstances where $P(E) = 0$ and $P(E) = 1$.

PROBLEM 1   Toss a regular six-sided die. What is the probability of getting a 7?

Solution

The sample space is $S = \{1, 2, 3, 4, 5, 6\}$, thus $n(S) = 6$. The event space is $E = \emptyset$, so $n(E) = 0$. Therefore the probability of getting a 7 is

$$P(E) = \frac{n(E)}{n(S)} = \frac{0}{6} = 0$$

∎

PROBLEM 2   What is the probability of getting a head or a tail with one flip of a coin?

Solution

The sample space is $S = \{H, T\}$, and the event space is $E = \{H, T\}$. Therefore $n(S) = n(E) = 2$, and

$$P(E) = \frac{n(E)}{n(S)} = \frac{2}{2} = 1$$

∎

An event that has a probability of 1 is sometimes called **certain success**, and an event with a probability of 0 is called **certain failure**.

It should also be mentioned that Property 15.1 serves as a check for reasonableness of answers. In other words, when computing probabilities, we know that our answer must fall between 0 and 1, inclusive. Any other probability answer is simply not reasonable.

■ Complementary Events

Complementary events are complementary sets such that S, the sample space, serves as the universal set. The following examples illustrate this idea.

Sample space	Event space	Complement of event space
$S = \{1, 2, 3, 4, 5, 6\}$	$E = \{1, 2\}$	$E' = \{3, 4, 5, 6\}$
$S = \{H, T\}$	$E = \{T\}$	$E' = \{H\}$
$S = \{2, 3, 4, \ldots, 12\}$	$E = \{2, 3, 4\}$	$E' = \{5, 6, 7, \ldots, 12\}$
$S = \{1, 2, 3, \ldots, 25\}$	$E = \{3, 4, 5, \ldots, 25\}$	$E' = \{1, 2\}$

In each case, note that E' (the complement of E) consists of all elements of S that are *not* in E. Thus E and E' are called *complementary events*. Also note that for each example, $P(E) + P(E') = 1$. We can state the following general property:

Property 15.2

If E is any event of a sample space S, and E' is the complementary event, then

$$P(E) + P(E') = 1$$

From a computational viewpoint, Property 15.2 provides us with a double-barreled attack on some probability problems. That is, once we compute either $P(E)$ or $P(E')$, we can determine the other one simply by subtracting from 1. For example, suppose that for a particular problem we can determine that $P(E) = \frac{3}{13}$. Then we immediately know that $P(E') = 1 - P(E) = 1 - \frac{3}{13} = \frac{10}{13}$. The following examples further illustrate the usefulness of Property 15.2.

PROBLEM 3

Two dice are tossed. Find the probability of getting a sum greater than 3.

Solution

Let S be the familiar sample space of ordered pairs for this problem, where $n(S) = 36$. Let E be the event of obtaining a sum greater than 3. Then E' is the event of obtaining a sum less than or equal to 3; that is, $E' = \{(1, 1), (1, 2), (2, 1)\}$. Thus

$$P(E') = \frac{n(E')}{n(S)} = \frac{3}{36} = \frac{1}{12}$$

From this, we conclude that

$$P(E) = 1 - P(E') = 1 - \frac{1}{12} = \frac{11}{12}$$ ∎

PROBLEM 4

Toss three coins and find the probability of getting at least one head.

Solution

The sample space, S, consists of all possible outcomes for tossing three coins. Using the fundamental principle of counting, we know that there are $(2)(2)(2) = 8$ outcomes, so $n(S) = 8$. Let E be the event of getting at least one head. Then E' is the complementary event of not getting any heads. The set E' is easy to list: $E' = \{(T, T, T)\}$. Thus $n(E') = 1$ and $P(E') = \frac{1}{8}$. From this, $P(E)$ can be determined to be

$$P(E) = 1 - P(E') = 1 - \frac{1}{8} = \frac{7}{8}$$ ∎

PROBLEM 5

A three-person committee is chosen at random from a group of five women and four men. Find the probability that the committee contains at least one woman.

Solution

Let the sample space, S, be the set of all possible three-person committees that can be formed from nine people. There are $C(9, 3) = 84$ such committees; therefore $n(S) = 84$.

Let E be the event, *the committee contains at least one woman*. Then E' is the complementary event, *the committee contains all men*. Thus E' consists of all three-man committees that can be formed from four men. There are $C(4, 3) = 4$ such committees; thus $n(E') = 4$. We have

$$P(E') = \frac{n(E')}{n(S)} = \frac{4}{84} = \frac{1}{21}$$

which determines $P(E)$ to be

$$P(E) = 1 - P(E') = 1 - \frac{1}{21} = \frac{20}{21}$$ ∎

The concepts of **set intersection** and **set union** play an important role in the study of probability. If E and F are two events in a sample space S, then $E \cap F$ is the event consisting of all sample points of S that are in both E and F as indicated in Figure 15.2. Likewise, $E \cup F$ is the event consisting of all sample points of S that are in E or F, or both, as shown in Figure 15.3.

In Figure 15.4, there are 47 sample points in E, 38 sample points in F, and 15 sample points in $E \cap F$. How many sample points are there in $E \cup F$? Simply adding the number of points in E and F would result in counting the 15 points in

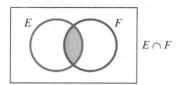

Figure 15.2

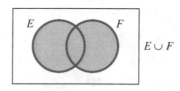

Figure 15.3

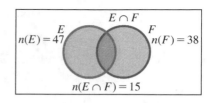

Figure 15.4

$E \cap F$ twice. Therefore, 15 must be subtracted from the total number of points in E and F, yielding $47 + 38 - 15 = 70$ points in $E \cup F$. We can state the following general counting property:

$$n(E \cup F) = n(E) + n(F) - n(E \cap F)$$

If we divide both sides of this equation by $n(S)$, we obtain the following probability property:

Property 15.3

For events E and F of a sample space S,

$$P(E \cup F) = P(E) + P(F) - P(E \cap F)$$

P R O B L E M   6

What is the probability of getting an odd number or a prime number with one toss of a die?

Solution

Let $S = \{1, 2, 3, 4, 5, 6\}$ be the sample space, $E = \{1, 3, 5\}$ the event of getting an odd number, and $F = \{2, 3, 5\}$ the event of getting a prime number. Then $E \cap F = \{3, 5\}$, and using Property 15.3, we obtain

$$P(E \cup F) = \frac{3}{6} + \frac{3}{6} - \frac{2}{6} = \frac{4}{6} = \frac{2}{3}$$

∎

P R O B L E M   7

Toss three coins. What is the probability of getting at least two heads or exactly one tail?

Solution

Using the fundamental principle of counting, we know that there are $2 \cdot 2 \cdot 2 = 8$ possible outcomes of tossing three coins; thus $n(S) = 8$. Let

$$E = \{(H, H, H), (H, H, T), (H, T, H), (T, H, H)\}$$

be the event of getting at least two heads, and let

$$F = \{(H, H, T), (H, T, H), (T, H, H)\}$$

be the event of getting exactly one tail. Then

$$E \cap F = \{(H, H, T), (H, T, H), (T, H, H)\}$$

and we can compute $P(E \cup F)$ as follows.

$$P(E \cup F) = P(E) + P(F) - P(E \cap F)$$

$$= \frac{4}{8} + \frac{3}{8} - \frac{3}{8}$$

$$= \frac{4}{8} = \frac{1}{2}$$

∎

In Property 15.3, if $E \cap F = \varnothing$, then the events E and F are said to be **mutually exclusive**. In other words, mutually exclusive events are events that cannot occur at the same time. For example, when we roll a die, the event of getting a 4 and the event of getting a 5 are mutually exclusive; they cannot both happen on the same roll. If $E \cap F = \varnothing$, then $P(E \cap F) = 0$, and Property 15.3 becomes $P(E \cup F) = P(E) + P(F)$ **for mutually exclusive events**.

P R O B L E M   8

Suppose we have a jar that contains five white, seven green, and nine red marbles. If one marble is drawn at random from the jar, find the probability that it is white or green.

Solution

The events of drawing a white marble and drawing a green marble are mutually exclusive. Therefore the probability of drawing a white or a green marble is

$$\frac{5}{21} + \frac{7}{21} = \frac{12}{21} = \frac{4}{7}$$

∎

Note that in the solution for Problem 8, we did not explicitly name and list the elements of the sample space or event spaces. It was obvious that the sample space contained 21 elements (21 marbles in the jar) and that the event spaces contained five elements (five white marbles) and seven elements (seven green marbles). Thus it was not necessary to name and list the sample space and event spaces.

P R O B L E M   9

Suppose that the data in the following table represent the results of a survey of 1000 drivers after a holiday weekend.

	Rain (R)	No rain (R')	Total
Accident (A)	35	10	45
No accident (A')	450	505	955
Total	485	515	1000

If a person is selected at random, what is the probability that the person was in an accident or that it rained?

Solution

First, let's form a **probability table** by dividing each entry by 1000, the total number surveyed.

	Rain (*R*)	No rain (*R'*)	Total
Accident (*A*)	0.035	0.010	0.045
No accident (*A'*)	0.450	0.505	0.955
Total	0.485	0.515	1.000

Now we can use Property 15.3 and compute $P(A \cup R)$.

$$P(A \cup R) = P(A) + P(R) - P(A \cap R)$$
$$= 0.045 + 0.485 - 0.035$$
$$= 0.495$$
∎

■ Expected Value

Suppose we toss a coin 500 times. We would expect to get approximately 250 heads. In other words, because the probability of getting a head with one toss of a coin is $\frac{1}{2}$, in 500 tosses we should get approximately $500\left(\frac{1}{2}\right) = 250$ heads. The word "approximately" conveys a key idea. As we know from experience, it is possible to toss a coin several times and get all heads. However, with a large number of tosses, things should average out so that we get about equal numbers of heads and tails.

As another example, consider the fact that the probability of getting a sum of 6 with one toss of a pair of dice is $\frac{5}{36}$. Therefore, if a pair of dice is tossed 360 times, we should expect to get a sum of 6 approximately $360\left(\frac{5}{36}\right) = 50$ times.

Let us now define the concept of *expected value.*

Definition 15.2

If the k possible outcomes of an experiment are assigned the values x_1, x_2, $x_3, \ldots , x_k$, and if they occur with probabilities of $p_1, p_2, p_3, \ldots , p_k$, respectively, then the **expected value** of the experiment (E_v) is given by

$$E_v = x_1 p_1 + x_2 p_2 + x_3 p_3 + \cdots + x_k p_k$$

The concept of expected value (also called **mathematical expectation**) is used in a variety of probability situations that deal with such things as fairness of games and decision making in business ventures. Let's consider some examples.

PROBLEM 10

Suppose that you buy one ticket in a lottery where 1000 tickets are sold. Furthermore, suppose that three prizes are awarded: one of $500, one of $300, and one of $100. What is your mathematical expectation?

Solution

Because you bought one ticket, the probability of you winning $500 is $\dfrac{1}{1000}$; the probability of you winning $300 is $\dfrac{1}{1000}$; and the probability of you winning $100 is $\dfrac{1}{1000}$. Multiplying each of these probabilities by the corresponding prize money and then adding the results yields your mathematical expectation.

$$E_v = \$500\left(\frac{1}{100}\right) + \$300\left(\frac{1}{1000}\right) + \$100\left(\frac{1}{100}\right)$$

$$= \$0.50 + \$0.30 + \$0.10$$

$$= \$0.90 \qquad \blacksquare$$

In Problem 10, if you pay more than $0.90 for a ticket, then it is not a **fair game** from your standpoint. If the price of the game is included in the calculation of the expected value, then a fair game is defined to be one where the expected value is zero.

PROBLEM 11

A player pays $5 to play a game where the probability of winning is $\dfrac{1}{5}$ and the probability of losing is $\dfrac{4}{5}$. If the player wins the game, he receives $25. Is this a fair game for the player?

Solution

From Definition 15.2, let $x_1 = \$20$, which represents the $25 won minus the $5 paid to play, and let $x_2 = -\$5$, the amount paid to play the game. We are also given that $p_1 = \dfrac{1}{5}$ and $p_2 = \dfrac{4}{5}$. Thus the expected value is

$$E_v = \$20\left(\frac{1}{5}\right) + (-\$5)\left(\frac{4}{5}\right)$$

$$= \$4 - \$4$$

$$= 0$$

Because the expected value is zero, it is a fair game. $\blacksquare$

PROBLEM 12

Suppose you are interested in insuring a diamond ring for $2000 against theft. An insurance company charges a premium of $25 per year, claiming that there is a probability of 0.01 that the ring will be stolen during the year. What is your expected gain or loss if you take out the insurance?

Solution

From Definition 15.2, let $x_1 = \$1975$, which represents the $2000 minus the cost of the premium, $25, and let $x_2 = -\$25$. We also are given that $p_1 = 0.01$, so $p_2 = 1 - 0.01 = 0.99$. Thus the expected value is

$$E_v = \$1975(0.01) + (-\$25)(0.99)$$

$$= \$19.75 - \$24.75$$

$$= -\$5.00$$

This means that if you insure with this company over many years, and the circumstances remain the same, you will have an average net loss of $5 per year.   ■

Problem Set 15.4

For Problems 1–4, *two* dice are tossed. Find the probability of rolling each of the following events:

1. A sum of 6

2. A sum greater than 2

3. A sum less than 8

4. A sum greater than 1

For Problems 5–8, *three* dice are tossed. Find the probability of rolling each of the following events:

5. A sum of 3

6. A sum greater than 4

7. A sum less than 17

8. A sum greater than 18

For Problems 9–12, *four* coins are tossed. Find the probability of getting each of the following events:

9. Four heads

10. Three heads and a tail

11. At least one tail

12. At least one head

For Problems 13–16, *five* coins are tossed. Find the probability of getting each of the following events:

13. Five tails

14. Four heads and a tail

15. At least one tail

16. At least two heads

For Problems 17–23, solve each problem.

17. Toss a pair of dice. What is the probability of not getting a double?

18. The probability that a certain horse will win the Kentucky Derby is $\frac{1}{20}$. What is the probability that it will lose the race?

19. One card is randomly drawn from a deck of 52 playing cards. What is the probability that it is not an ace?

20. Six coins are tossed. Find the probability of getting at least two heads.

21. A subset of two letters is chosen at random from the set {a, b, c, d, e, f, g, h, i}. Find the probability that the subset contains at least one vowel.

22. A two-person committee is chosen at random from a group of four men and three women. Find the probability that the committee contains at least one man.

23. A three-person committee is chosen at random from a group of seven women and five men. Find the probability that the committee contains at least one man.

For Problems 24–27, one die is tossed. Find the probability of rolling each of the following events:

24. A 3 or an odd number

25. A 2 or an odd number

26. An even number or a prime number

27. An odd number or a multiple of 3

For Problems 28–31, two dice are tossed. Find the probability of rolling each of the following events:

28. A double or a sum of 6

29. A sum of 10 or a sum greater than 8

30. A sum of 5 or a sum greater than 10

31. A double or a sum of 7

For Problems 32–56, solve each problem.

32. Two coins are tossed. Find the probability of getting exactly one head or at least one tail.

33. Three coins are tossed. Find the probability of getting at least two heads or exactly one tail.

34. A jar contains seven white, six blue, and ten red marbles. If one marble is drawn at random from the jar, find the probability that (a) the marble is white or blue; (b) the marble is white or red; (c) the marble is blue or red.

35. A coin and a die are tossed. Find the probability of getting a head on the coin or a 2 on the die.

36. A card is randomly drawn from a deck of 52 playing cards. Find the probability that it is a red card or a face card. (Jacks, queens, and kings are the face cards.)

37. The data in the following table represent the results of a survey of 1000 drivers after a holiday weekend.

	Rain (R)	No rain (R')	Total
Accident (A)	45	15	60
No accident (A')	350	590	940
Total	395	605	1000

If a person is selected at random from those surveyed, find the probability of each of the following events. (Express the probabilities in decimal form.)
(a) The person was in an accident or it rained.
(b) The person was not in an accident or it rained.
(c) The person was not in an accident or it did not rain.

38. One hundred people were surveyed, and one question pertained to their educational background. The results of this question are given in the following table.

	Female (F)	Male (F')	Total
College degree (D)	30	20	50
No college degree (D')	15	35	50
Total	45	55	100

If a person is selected at random from those surveyed, find the probability of each of the following events. Express the probabilities in decimal form.
(a) The person is female or has a college degree.
(b) The person is male or does not have a college degree.
(c) The person is female or does not have a college degree.

39. In a recent election there were 1000 eligible voters. They were asked to vote on two issues, A and B. The results were as follows: 300 people voted for A, 400 people voted for B, and 175 voted for both A and B. If one person is chosen at random from the 1000 eligible voters, find the probability that the person voted for A or B.

40. A company has 500 employees among whom 200 are females, 15 are high-level executives, and 7 of the high-level executives are females. If one of the 500 employees is chosen at random, find the probability that the person chosen is female or is a high-level executive.

41. A die is tossed 360 times. How many times would you expect to get a 6?

42. Two dice are tossed 360 times. How many times would you expect to get a sum of 5?

43. Two dice are tossed 720 times. How many times would you expect to get a sum greater than 9?

44. Four coins are tossed 80 times. How many times would you expect to get one head and three tails?

45. Four coins are tossed 144 times. How many times would you expect to get four tails?

46. Two dice are tossed 300 times. How many times would you expect to get a double?

47. Three coins are tossed 448 times. How many times would you expect to get three heads?

48. Suppose 5000 tickets are sold in a lottery. There are three prizes: The first is $1000, the second is $500, and the third is $100. What is the mathematical expectation of winning?

49. Your friend challenges you with the following game: You are to roll a pair of dice, and he will give you $5 if you roll a sum of 2 or 12, $2 if you roll a sum of 3 or 11, $1 if you roll a sum of 4 or 10. Otherwise you are to pay him $1. Should you play the game?

50. A contractor bids on a building project. There is a probability of 0.8 that he can show a profit of $30,000 and a probability of 0.2 that he will have to absorb a loss of $10,000. What is his mathematical expectation?

51. Suppose a person tosses two coins and receives $5 if 2 heads come up, receives $2 if 1 head and 1 tail come up, and has to pay $2 if 2 tails come up. Is it a fair game for him?

52. A "wheel of fortune" is divided into four colors: red, white, blue, and yellow. The probability of the spinner landing on each of the colors and the money received is given by the following chart. The price to spin the wheel is $1.50. Is it a fair game?

Color	Probability of landing on the color	Money received for landing on the color
Red	$\frac{4}{10}$	$.50
White	$\frac{3}{10}$	1.00
Blue	$\frac{2}{10}$	2.00
Yellow	$\frac{1}{10}$	5.00

53. A contractor estimates a probability of 0.7 of making $20,000 on a building project and a probability of 0.3 of losing $10,000 on the project. What is his mathematical expectation?

54. A farmer estimates his corn crop at 30,000 bushels. On the basis of past experience, he also estimates a probability of $\frac{3}{5}$ that he will make a profit of $0.50 per bushel and a probability of $\frac{1}{5}$ of losing $0.30 per bushel. What is his expected income from the corn crop?

55. Bill finds that the annual premium for insuring a stereo system for $2500 against theft is $75. If the probability that the set will be stolen during the year is 0.02, what is Bill's expected gain or loss by taking out the insurance?

56. Sandra finds that the annual premium for a $2000 insurance policy against the theft of a painting is $100. If the probability that the painting will be stolen during the year is 0.01, what is Sandra's expected gain or loss in taking out the insurance?

■ ■ ■ **THOUGHTS INTO WORDS**

57. If the probability of some event happening is 0.4, what is the probability of the event not happening? Explain your answer.

58. Explain each of the following concepts to a friend who missed class the day this section was discussed: using complementary events to determine probabilities, using union and intersection of sets to determine probabilities, and using expected value to determine the fairness of a game.

■ ■ ■ **FURTHER INVESTIGATIONS**

The term **odds** is sometimes used to express a probability statement. For example, we might say, "the odds in favor of the Cubs winning the pennant are 5 to 1," or "the odds against the Mets winning the pennant are 50 to 1." *Odds in* *favor* and *odds against* for equally likely outcomes can be defined as follows:

$$\text{Odds in favor} = \frac{\text{Number of favorable outcomes}}{\text{Number of unfavorable outcomes}}$$

$$\text{Odds against} = \frac{\text{Number of unfavorable outcomes}}{\text{Number of favorable outcomes}}$$

We have used the fractional form to define odds; however, in practice, the *to* vocabulary is commonly used. Thus the odds in favor of rolling a 4 with one roll of a die are usually stated as *1 to 5* instead of $\frac{1}{5}$. The odds against rolling a 4 are stated as *5 to 1*.

The *odds in favor of* statement about the Cubs means that there are 5 favorable outcomes compared to 1 unfavorable, or a total of 6 possible outcomes, so the *5 to 1 in favor of* statement also means that the probability of the Cubs winning the pennant is $\frac{5}{6}$. Likewise, the *50 to 1 against* statement about the Mets means that the probability that the Mets will not win the pennant is $\frac{50}{51}$.

Odds are usually stated in reduced form. For example, odds of 6 to 4 are usually stated as 3 to 2. Likewise, a fraction representing probability is reduced before being changed to a statement about odds.

59. What are the odds in favor of getting three heads with a toss of three coins?

60. What are the odds against getting four tails with a toss of four coins?

61. What are the odds against getting three heads and two tails with a toss of five coins?

62. What are the odds in favor of getting four heads and two tails with a toss of six coins?

63. What are the odds in favor of getting a sum of 5 with one toss of a pair of dice?

64. What are the odds against getting a sum greater than 5 with one toss of a pair of dice?

65. Suppose that one card is drawn at random from a deck of 52 playing cards. Find the odds against drawing a red card.

66. Suppose that one card is drawn at random from a deck of 52 playing cards. Find the odds in favor of drawing an ace or a king.

67. If $P(E) = \frac{4}{7}$ for some event E, find the odds in favor of E happening.

68. If $P(E) = \frac{5}{9}$ for some event E, find the odds against E happening.

69. Suppose that there is a predicted 40% chance of freezing rain. State the prediction in terms of the odds against getting freezing rain.

70. Suppose that there is a predicted 20% chance of thunderstorms. State the prediction in terms of the odds in favor of getting thunderstorms.

71. If the odds against an event happening are 5 to 2, find the probability that the event will occur.

72. The odds against Belly Dancer winning the fifth race are 20 to 9. What is the probability of Belly Dancer winning the fifth race?

73. The odds in favor of the Mets winning the pennant are stated as 7 to 5. What is the probability of the Mets winning the pennant?

74. The following chart contains some poker-hand probabilities. Complete the last column, "Odds Against Being Dealt This Hand." Note that fractions are reduced before being changed to odds.

5-Card hand	Probability of being dealt this hand	Odds against being dealt this hand
Straight flush	$\frac{40}{2,598,960} = \frac{1}{64,974}$	64,973 to 1
Four of a kind	$\frac{624}{2,598,960} =$	
Full house	$\frac{3744}{2,598,960} =$	
Flush	$\frac{5108}{2,598,960} =$	
Straight	$\frac{10,200}{2,598,960} =$	
Three of a kind	$\frac{54,912}{2,598,960} =$	
Two pairs	$\frac{123,552}{2,598,960} =$	
One pair	$\frac{1,098,240}{2,598,960} =$	
No pairs	$\frac{1,302,540}{2,598,960} =$	

15.5 Conditional Probability: Dependent and Independent Events

Two events are often related in such a way that the probability of one of them may vary depending on whether the other event has occurred. For example, the probability of rain may change drastically if additional information is obtained indicating a front moving through the area. Mathematically, the additional information about the front changes the sample space for the probability of rain.

In general, the probability of the occurrence of an event E, given the occurrence of another event F, is called a **conditional probability** and is denoted $P(E|F)$. Let's look at a simple example and use it to motivate a definition for conditional probability.

What is the probability of rolling a prime number in one roll of a die? Let $S = \{1, 2, 3, 4, 5, 6\}$, so $n(S) = 6$; and let $E = \{2, 3, 5\}$, so $n(E) = 3$. Therefore

$$P(E) = \frac{n(E)}{n(S)} = \frac{3}{6} = \frac{1}{2}$$

Next, what is the probability of rolling a prime number in one roll of a die, *given that an odd number has turned up*? Let $F = \{1, 3, 5\}$ be the new sample space of odd numbers. Then $n(F) = 3$. We are now interested in only that part of E (rolling a prime number) that is also in F—in other words, $E \cap F$. Therefore, because $E \cap F = \{3, 5\}$, the probability of E given F is

$$P(E|F) = \frac{n(E \cap F)}{n(F)} = \frac{2}{3}$$

When we divide both the numerator and the denominator of $n(E \cap F)/n(F)$ by $n(S)$, we obtain

$$\frac{\dfrac{n(E \cap F)}{n(S)}}{\dfrac{n(F)}{n(S)}} = \frac{P(E \cap F)}{P(F)}$$

Therefore we can state the following general definition of the conditional probability of E given F for arbitrary events E and F:

Definition 15.3

$$P(E|F) = \frac{P(E \cap F)}{P(F)}, \qquad P(F) \neq 0$$

In a problem in the previous section, the following probability table was formed relative to car accidents and weather conditions on a holiday weekend.

	Rain (R)	No rain (R')	Total
Accident (A)	0.035	0.010	0.045
No accident (A')	0.450	0.505	0.955
Total	0.485	0.515	1.000

Some conditional probabilities that can be calculated from the table follow:

$$P(A|R) = \frac{P(A \cap R)}{P(R)} = \frac{0.035}{0.485} = \frac{35}{485} = \frac{7}{97}$$

$$P(A'|R) = \frac{P(A' \cap R)}{P(R)} = \frac{0.450}{0.485} = \frac{450}{485} = \frac{90}{97}$$

$$P(A|R') = \frac{P(A \cap R')}{P(R')} = \frac{0.010}{0.515} = \frac{10}{515} = \frac{2}{103}$$

Note that the probability of an accident given that it was raining, $P(A|R)$, is greater than the probability of an accident given that it was not raining, $P(A|R')$. This seems reasonable.

PROBLEM 1

A die is tossed. Find the probability that a 4 came up if it is known that an even number turned up.

Solution

Let E be the event of rolling a 4, and let F be the event of rolling an even number. Therefore $E = \{4\}$ and $F = \{2, 4, 6\}$, from which we obtain $E \cap F = \{4\}$. Using Definition 15.3, we obtain

$$P(E|F) = \frac{P(E \cap F)}{P(F)} = \frac{\dfrac{1}{6}}{\dfrac{3}{6}} = \frac{1}{3}$$

■

PROBLEM 2

Suppose the probability that a student will enroll in a mathematics course is 0.45, the probability that he or she will enroll in a science course is 0.38, and the probability that he or she will enroll in both courses is 0.26. Find the probability that a student will enroll in a mathematics course, given that he or she is also enrolled in a science course. Also, find the probability that a student will enroll in a science course, given that he or she is enrolled in mathematics.

Solution

Let M be the event, *will enroll in mathematics*, and let S be the event, *will enroll in science*. Therefore, using Definition 10.3, we obtain

$$P(M|S) = \frac{P(M \cap S)}{P(S)} = \frac{0.26}{0.38} = \frac{26}{38} = \frac{13}{19}$$

and

$$P(S|M) = \frac{P(S \cap M)}{P(M)} = \frac{0.26}{0.45} = \frac{26}{45}$$

■

■ Independent and Dependent Events

Suppose that, when computing a conditional probability, we find that

$$P(E|F) = P(E)$$

This means that the probability of E is not affected by the occurrence or nonoccurrence of F. In such a situation, we say that event E is *independent* of event F. It can be shown that if event E is independent of event F, then F is also independent of E; thus E and F are referred to as **independent events**. Furthermore, from the equations

$$P(E|F) = \frac{P(E \cap F)}{P(F)} \qquad \text{and} \qquad P(E|F) = P(E)$$

we see that

$$\frac{P(E \cap F)}{P(F)} = P(E)$$

which can be written

$$P(E \cap F) = P(E)P(F)$$

Therefore we state the following general definition:

Definition 15.4

> Two events E and F are said to be **independent** if and only if
>
> $$P(E \cap F) = P(E)P(F)$$
>
> Two events that are not independent are called **dependent events**.

In the probability table preceding Problem 1, we see that $P(A) = 0.045$, $P(R) = 0.485$, and $P(A \cap R) = 0.035$. Because

$$P(A)P(R) = (0.045)(0.485) = 0.021825$$

and this does not equal $P(A \cap R)$, the events A (have a car accident) and R (rainy conditions) are not independent. This is not too surprising; we would certainly expect rainy conditions and automobile accidents to be related.

PROBLEM 3

Suppose we roll a white die and a red die. If we let E be the event, *we roll a 4 on the white die*, and if we let F be the event, *we roll a 6 on the red die*. Are E and F independent events?

Solution

The sample space for rolling a pair of dice has $(6)(6) = 36$ elements. Using ordered-pair notation, where the first entry represents the white die and the second entry the red die, we can list events E and F as follows:

$$E = \{(4, 1), (4, 2), (4, 3), (4, 4), (4, 5), (4, 6)\}$$
$$F = \{(1, 6), (2, 6), (3, 6), (4, 6), (5, 6), (6, 6)\}$$

Therefore $E \cap F = \{(4, 6)\}$. Because $P(F) = \dfrac{1}{6}$, $P(E) = \dfrac{1}{6}$, and $P(E \cap F) = \dfrac{1}{36}$, we see that $P(E \cap F) = P(E)P(F)$, and the events E and F are independent. ∎

PROBLEM 4

Two coins are tossed. Let E be the event, *toss not more than one head*, and let F be the event, *toss at least one of each face*. Are these events independent?

Solution

The sample space has $(2)(2) = 4$ elements. The events E and F can be listed as follows:

$$E = \{(H, T), (T, H), (T, T)\}$$
$$F = \{(H, T), (T, H)\}$$

Therefore $E \cap F = \{(H, T), (T, H)\}$. Because $P(E) = \dfrac{3}{4}$, $P(F) = \dfrac{1}{2}$, and $P(E \cap F) = \dfrac{1}{2}$, we see that $P(E \cap F) \neq P(E)P(F)$, so the events E and F are dependent. ∎

Sometimes the independence issue can be decided by the physical nature of the events in the problem. For instance, in Problem 3, it should seem evident that rolling a 4 on the white die is not affected by rolling a 6 on the red die. However, as in Problem 4, the description of the events may not clearly indicate whether the events are dependent.

From a problem-solving viewpoint, the following two statements are very helpful.

1. If E and F are independent events, then

$$P(E \cap F) = P(E)P(F)$$

(This property generalizes to any finite number of independent events.)

2. If E and F are dependent events, then

$$P(E \cap F) = P(E)P(F|E)$$

Let's analyze some problems using these ideas.

PROBLEM 5

A die is rolled three times. (This is equivalent to rolling three dice once each.) What is the probability of getting a 6 all three times?

Solution

The events of a 6 on the first roll, a 6 on the second roll, and a 6 on the third roll are independent events. Therefore the probability of getting three 6's is

$$\left(\frac{1}{6}\right)\left(\frac{1}{6}\right)\left(\frac{1}{6}\right) = \frac{1}{216}$$ ∎

PROBLEM 6

A jar contains five white, seven green, and nine red marbles. If two marbles are drawn in succession *without replacement*, find the probability that both marbles are white.

Solution

Let E be the event of drawing a white marble on the first draw, and let F be the event of drawing a white marble on the second draw. Because the marble drawn first is not to be replaced before the second marble is drawn, we have dependent events. Therefore

$$P(E \cap F) = P(E)P(F|E)$$

$$= \left(\frac{5}{21}\right)\left(\frac{4}{20}\right) = \frac{20}{420} = \frac{1}{21}$$

$P(F|E)$ means the probability of drawing a white marble on the second draw, given that a white marble was obtained on the first draw.   ∎

The concept of *mutually exclusive events* may also enter the picture when we are working with independent or dependent events. Our final problems of this section illustrate this idea.

PROBLEM 7

A coin is tossed three times. Find the probability of getting two heads and one tail.

Solution

Two heads and one tail can be obtained in three different ways: (1) HHT (head on first toss, head on second toss, and tail on third toss), (2) HTH, and (3) THH. Thus we have three *mutually exclusive* events, each of which can be broken into *independent* events: first toss, second toss, and third toss. Therefore the probability can be computed as follows:

$$\left(\frac{1}{2}\right)\left(\frac{1}{2}\right)\left(\frac{1}{2}\right) + \left(\frac{1}{2}\right)\left(\frac{1}{2}\right)\left(\frac{1}{2}\right) + \left(\frac{1}{2}\right)\left(\frac{1}{2}\right)\left(\frac{1}{2}\right) = \frac{3}{8}$$ ∎

PROBLEM 8

A jar contains five white, seven green, and nine red marbles. If two marbles are drawn in succession *without replacement*, find the probability that one of them is white and the other is green.

Solution

The drawing of a white marble and a green marble can occur in two different ways: (1) by drawing a white marble first and then a green, and (2) by drawing a green marble first and then a white. Thus we have two mutually exclusive events, each of which is broken into two *dependent* events: first draw and second draw. Therefore the probability can be computed as follows:

$$\left(\frac{5}{21}\right)\left(\frac{7}{20}\right) \quad + \quad \left(\frac{7}{21}\right)\left(\frac{5}{20}\right) = \frac{70}{420} = \frac{1}{6}$$

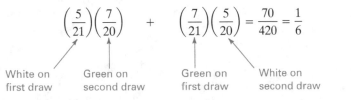

White on first draw   Green on second draw   Green on first draw   White on second draw ∎

PROBLEM 9

Two cards are drawn in succession *with replacement* from a deck of 52 playing cards. Find the probability of drawing a jack and a queen.

Solution

Drawing a jack and a queen can occur in two different ways: (1) a jack on the first draw and a queen on the second and (2) a queen on the first draw and a jack on the second. Thus we have two mutually exclusive events, and each one is broken into the *independent* events of first draw and second draw with replacement. Therefore the probability can be computed as follows:

$$\left(\frac{4}{52}\right)\left(\frac{4}{52}\right) \quad + \quad \left(\frac{4}{52}\right)\left(\frac{4}{52}\right) = \frac{32}{2704} = \frac{2}{169}$$

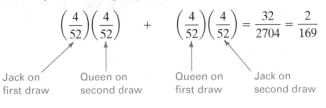

Jack on first draw   Queen on second draw   Queen on first draw   Jack on second draw ∎

Problem Set 15.5

For Problems 1–22, solve each problem.

1. A die is tossed. Find the probability that a 5 came up if it is known that an odd number came up.

2. A die is tossed. Find the probability that a prime number was obtained, given that an even number came up.

Also find the probability that an even number came up, given that a prime number was obtained.

3. Two dice are rolled and someone indicates that the two numbers that come up are different. Find the probability that the sum of the two numbers is 6.

4. Two dice are rolled, and someone indicates that the two numbers that come up are identical. Find the probability that the sum of the two numbers is 8.

5. One card is randomly drawn from a deck of 52 playing cards. Find the probability that it is a jack, given that the card is a face card. (We are considering jacks, queens, and kings as face cards.)

6. One card is randomly drawn from a deck of 52 playing cards. Find the probability that it is a spade, given the fact that it is a black card.

7. A coin and a die are tossed. Find the probability of getting a 5 on the die, given that a head comes up on the coin.

8. A family has three children. Assume that each child is as likely to be a boy as it is to be a girl. Find the probability that the family has three girls if it is known that the family has at least one girl.

9. The probability that a student will enroll in a mathematics course is 0.7, the probability that he or she will enroll in a history course is 0.3, and the probability that he or she will enroll in both mathematics and history is 0.2. Find the probability that a student will enroll in mathematics, given that he or she is also enrolled in history. Also find the probability that a student will enroll in history, given that he or she is also enrolled in mathematics.

10. The following probability table contains data relative to car accidents and weather conditions on a holiday weekend.

	Rain (R)	No rain (R')	Total
Accident (A)	0.025	0.015	0.040
No accident (A')	0.400	0.560	0.960
Total	0.425	0.575	1.000

Find the probability that a person chosen at random from the survey was in an accident, given that it was raining. Also find the probability that a person was not in an accident, given that it was not raining.

11. One hundred people were surveyed, and one question pertained to their educational background. The responses to this question are given in the following table.

	Female (F)	Male (F')	Total
College degree (D)	30	20	50
No college degree (D')	15	35	50
Total	45	55	100

Find the probability that a person chosen at random from the survey has a college degree, given that the person is female. Also find the probability that a person chosen is male, given that the person has a college degree.

12. In a recent election there were 1000 eligible voters. They were asked to vote on two issues, A and B. The results were as follows: 200 people voted for A, 400 people voted for B, and 50 people voted for both A and B. If one person is chosen at random from the 100 eligible voters, find the probability that the person voted for A, given that he or she voted for B. Also find the probability that the person voted for B, given that he or she voted for A.

13. A small company has 100 employees; among them 75 are males, 7 are administrators, and 5 of the administrators are males. If a person is chosen at random from the employees, find the probability that the person is an administrator, given that he is male. Also find the probability that the person chosen is female, given that she is an administrator.

14. A survey claims that 80% of the households in a certain town have a high-definition TV, 10% have a microwave oven, and 2% have both a high-definition TV and a microwave oven. Find the probability that a randomly selected household will have a microwave oven, given that it has a high-definition TV.

15. Consider a family of three children. Let E be the event, *the first child is a boy*, and let F be the event, *the family has exactly one boy*. Are events E and F dependent or independent?

16. Roll a white die and a green die. Let E be the event, *roll a 2 on the white die*, and let F be the event, *roll a 4 on the green die*. Are E and F dependent or independent events?

17. Toss three coins. Let E be the event, *toss not more than one head*, and let F be the event, *toss at least one of each face*. Are E and F dependent or independent events?

18. A card is drawn at random from a standard deck of 52 playing cards. Let E be the event, *the card is a 2*, and let F be the event, *the card is a 2 or a 3*. Are the events E and F dependent or independent?

19. A coin is tossed four times. Find the probability of getting three heads and one tail.

20. A coin is tossed five times. Find the probability of getting four heads and one tail.

21. Toss a pair of dice three times. Find the probability that a double is obtained on all three tosses.

22. Toss a pair of dice three times. Find the probability that each toss will produce a sum of 4.

For Problems 23–26, suppose that two cards are drawn in succession *without replacement* from a deck of 52 playing cards. Find the probability of each of the following events:

23. Both cards are 4's.

24. One card is an ace and one card is a king.

25. One card is a spade and one card is a diamond.

26. Both cards are black.

For Problems 27–30, suppose that two cards are drawn in succession *with replacement* from a deck of 52 playing cards. Find the probability of each of the following events:

27. Both cards are spades.

28. One card is an ace and one card is a king.

29. One card is the ace of spades and one card is the king of spades.

30. Both cards are red.

For Problems 31 and 32, solve each problem.

31. A person holds three kings from a deck of 52 playing cards. If the person draws two cards without replacement from the 49 cards remaining in the deck, find the probability of drawing the fourth king.

32. A person removes two aces and a king from a deck of 52 playing cards and draws, without replacement, two more cards from the deck. Find the probability that the person will draw two aces, or two kings, or an ace and a king.

For Problems 33–36, a bag contains five red and four white marbles. Two marbles are drawn in succession *with*

replacement. Find the probability of each of the following events:

33. Both marbles drawn are red.

34. Both marbles drawn are white.

35. The first marble is red and the second marble is white.

36. At least one marble is red.

For Problems 37–40, a bag contains five white, four red, and four blue marbles. Two marbles are drawn in succession *with replacement*. Find the probability of each of the following events:

37. Both marbles drawn are white.

38. Both marbles drawn are red.

39. One red and one blue marble are drawn.

40. One white and one blue marble are drawn.

For Problems 41–44, a bag contains one red and two white marbles. Two marbles are drawn in succession *without replacement*. Find the probability of each of the following events:

41. One marble drawn is red, and one marble drawn is white.

42. The first marble drawn is red and the second is white.

43. Both marbles drawn are white.

44. Both marbles drawn are red.

For Problems 45–48, a bag contains five red and 12 white marbles. Two marbles are drawn in succession *without replacement*. Find the probability of each of the following events:

45. Both marbles drawn are red.

46. Both marbles drawn are white.

47. One red and one white marble are drawn.

48. At least one marble drawn is red.

For Problems 49–52, a bag contains two red, three white, and four blue marbles. Two marbles are drawn in succession *without replacement*. Find the probability of each of the following events:

49. Both marbles drawn are white.

50. One marble drawn is white, and one is blue.

51. Both marbles drawn are blue.

52. At least one red marble is drawn.

For Problems 53–56, a bag contains five white, one blue, and three red marbles. Three marbles are drawn in succession *with replacement*. Find the probability of each of the following events:

53. All three marbles drawn are blue.

54. One marble of each color is drawn.

55. One white and two red marbles are drawn.

56. One blue and two white marbles are drawn.

For Problems 57–60, a bag contains four white, one red, and two blue marbles. Three marbles are drawn in succession *without replacement*. Find the probability of each of the following events:

57. All three marbles drawn are white.

58. One red and two blue marbles are drawn.

59. One marble of each color is drawn.

60. One white and two red marbles are drawn.

For Problems 61 and 62, solve each problem.

61. Two boxes with red and white marbles are shown here. A marble is drawn at random from Box 1, and then a second marble is drawn from Box 2. Find the probability that both marbles drawn are white. Find the probability that both marbles drawn are red. Find the probability that one red and one white marble are drawn.

3 red	2 red
4 white	1 white
Box 1	Box 2

62. Three boxes containing red and white marbles are shown here. Randomly draw a marble from Box 1 and put it in Box 2. Then draw a marble from Box 2 and put it in Box 3. Then draw a marble from Box 3. What is the probability that the last marble drawn, from Box 3, is red? What is the probability that it is white?

2 red	3 red	
2 white	1 white	3 white
Box 1	Box 2	Box 3

■ ■ ■ THOUGHTS INTO WORDS

63. How would you explain the concept of conditional probability to a classmate who missed the discussion of this section?

64. How would you give a nontechnical description of conditional probability to an elementary algebra student?

65. Explain in your own words the concept of independent events.

66. Suppose that a bag contains two red and three white marbles. Furthermore, suppose that two marbles are drawn from the bag in succession *with replacement*. Explain how the following tree diagram can be used to determine that the probability of drawing two white marbles is $\dfrac{9}{25}$.

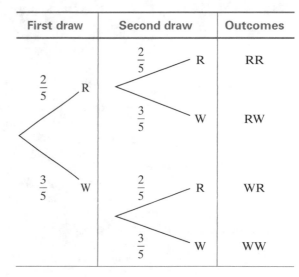

First draw	Second draw	Outcomes
$\frac{2}{5}$ R	$\frac{2}{5}$ R	RR
	$\frac{3}{5}$ W	RW
$\frac{3}{5}$ W	$\frac{2}{5}$ R	WR
	$\frac{3}{5}$ W	WW

67. Explain how a tree diagram can be used to determine the probabilities for Problems 41–44.

15.6   Binomial Theorem

In Chapter 4, when multiplying polynomials, we developed patterns for squaring and cubing binomials. Now we want to develop a general pattern that can be used to raise a binomial to any positive integral power. Let's begin by looking at some specific expansions that can be verified by direct multiplication. (Note that the patterns for squaring and cubing a binomial are a part of this list.)

$$(x + y)^0 = 1$$
$$(x + y)^1 = x + y$$
$$(x + y)^2 = x^2 + 2xy + y^2$$
$$(x + y)^3 = x^3 + 3x^2y + 3xy^2 + y^3$$
$$(x + y)^4 = x^4 + 4x^3y + 6x^2y^2 + 4xy^3 + y^4$$
$$(x + y)^5 = x^5 + 5x^4y + 10x^3y^2 + 10x^2y^3 + 5xy^4 + y^5$$

First, note the pattern of the exponents for x and y on a term-by-term basis. The exponents of x begin with the exponent of the binomial and decrease by 1, term by term, until the last term has x^0, which is 1. The exponents of y begin with zero ($y^0 = 1$) and increase by 1, term by term, until the last term contains y to the power of the binomial. In other words, the variables in the expansion of $(x + y)^n$ have the following pattern.

$$x^n, \quad x^{n-1}y, \quad x^{n-2}y^2, \quad x^{n-3}y^3, \quad \ldots, \quad xy^{n-1}, \quad y^n$$

Note that for each term, the sum of the exponents of x and y is n.

Now let's look for a pattern for the coefficients by examining specifically the expansion of $(x + y)^5$.

$$(x + y)^5 = x^5 + 5x^4y^1 + 10x^3y^2 + 10x^2y^3 + 5x^1y^4 + 1y^5$$

$$ C(5, 1) \quad C(5, 2) \quad C(5, 3) \quad C(5, 4) \quad C(5, 5)$$

As indicated by the arrows, the coefficients are numbers that arise as different-sized combinations of five things. To see why this happens, consider the coefficient for the term containing x^3y^2. The two y's (for y^2) come from two of the factors of $(x + y)$, and therefore the three x's (for x^3) must come from the other three factors of $(x + y)$. In other words, the coefficient is $C(5, 2)$.

We can now state a general expansion formula for $(x + y)^n$; this formula is often called the **binomial theorem**. But before stating it, let's make a small switch in notation. Instead of $C(n, r)$, we shall write $\binom{n}{r}$, which will prove to be a little more convenient at this time. The symbol $\binom{n}{r}$, still refers to the number of combinations of n things taken r at a time, but in this context it is often called a **binomial coefficient**.

Binomial Theorem

For any binomial $(x + y)$ and any natural number n,

$$(x + y)^n = x^n + \binom{n}{1}x^{n-1}y + \binom{n}{2}x^{n-2}y^2 + \cdots + \binom{n}{n}y^n$$

The binomial theorem can be proved by mathematical induction, but we will not do that in this text. Instead, we'll consider a few examples that put the binomial theorem to work.

EXAMPLE 1

Expand $(x + y)^7$.

Solution

$$(x + y)^7 = x^7 + \binom{7}{1}x^6y + \binom{7}{2}x^5y^2 + \binom{7}{3}x^4y^3 + \binom{7}{4}x^3y^4$$

$$+ \binom{7}{5}x^2y^5 + \binom{7}{6}xy^6 + \binom{7}{7}y^7$$

$$= x^7 + 7x^6y + 21x^5y^2 + 35x^4y^3 + 35x^3y^4 + 21x^2y^5 + 7xy^6 + y^7 \quad \blacksquare$$

EXAMPLE 2

Expand $(x - y)^5$.

Solution

We shall treat $(x - y)^5$ as $[x + (-y)]^5$.

$$[x + (-y)]^5 = x^5 + \binom{5}{1}x^4(-y) + \binom{5}{2}x^3(-y)^2 + \binom{5}{3}x^2(-y)^3$$

$$+ \binom{5}{4}x(-y)^4 + \binom{5}{5}(-y)^5$$

$$= x^5 - 5x^4y + 10x^3y^2 - 10x^2y^3 + 5xy^4 - y^5 \quad \blacksquare$$

EXAMPLE 3

Expand $(2a + 3b)^4$.

Solution

Let $x = 2a$ and $y = 3b$ in the binomial theorem.

$$(2a + 3b)^4 = (2a)^4 + \binom{4}{1}(2a)^3(3b) + \binom{4}{2}(2a)^2(3b)^2$$

$$+ \binom{4}{3}(2a)(3b)^3 + \binom{4}{4}(3b)^4$$

$$= 16a^4 + 96a^3b + 216a^2b^2 + 216ab^3 + 81b^4 \quad \blacksquare$$

EXAMPLE 4

Expand $\left(a + \dfrac{1}{n} \right)^5$.

Solution

$$\left(a + \frac{1}{n} \right)^5 = a^5 + \binom{5}{1}a^4\left(\frac{1}{n}\right) + \binom{5}{2}a^3\left(\frac{1}{n}\right)^2 + \binom{5}{3}a^2\left(\frac{1}{n}\right)^3 + \binom{5}{4}a\left(\frac{1}{n}\right)^4 + \binom{5}{5}\left(\frac{1}{n}\right)^5$$

$$= a^5 + \frac{5a^4}{n} + \frac{10a^3}{n^2} + \frac{10a^2}{n^3} + \frac{5a}{n^4} + \frac{1}{n^5}$$ ■

EXAMPLE 5

Expand $(x^2 - 2y^3)^6$.

Solution

$$[x^2 + (-2y^3)]^6 = (x^2)^6 + \binom{6}{1}(x^2)^5(-2y^3) + \binom{6}{2}(x^2)^4(-2y^3)^2$$

$$+ \binom{6}{3}(x^2)^3(-2y^3)^3 + \binom{6}{4}(x^2)^2(-2y^3)^4$$

$$+ \binom{6}{5}(x^2)(-2y^3)^5 + \binom{6}{6}(-2y^3)^6$$

$$= x^{12} - 12x^{10}y^3 + 60x^8y^6 - 160x^6y^9 + 240x^4y^{12} - 192x^2y^{15}$$
$$+ 64y^{18}$$ ■

■ Finding Specific Terms

Sometimes it is convenient to be able to write down the specific term of a binomial expansion without writing out the entire expansion. For example, suppose that we want the sixth term of the expansion $(x + y)^{12}$. We can proceed as follows: The sixth term will contain y^5. (Note in the binomial theorem that the **exponent of y is always one less than the number of the term**.) Because the sum of the exponents for x and y must be 12 (the exponent of the binomial), the sixth term will also contain x^7. The coefficient is $\binom{12}{5}$, where the 5 agrees with the exponent of y^5. Therefore the sixth term of $(x + y)^{12}$ is

$$\binom{12}{5}x^7y^5 = 792x^7y^5$$

EXAMPLE 6

Find the fourth term of $(3a + 2b)^7$.

Solution

The fourth term will contain $(2b)^3$, and therefore it will also contain $(3a)^4$. The coefficient is $\binom{7}{3}$. Thus the fourth term is

$$\binom{7}{3}(3a)^4(2b)^3 = (35)(81a^4)(8b^3) = 22{,}680a^4b^3$$ ■

EXAMPLE 7   Find the sixth term of $(4x - y)^9$.

Solution

The sixth term will contain $(-y)^5$, and therefore it will also contain $(4x)^4$. The coefficient is $\binom{9}{5}$. Thus the sixth term is

$$\binom{9}{5}(4x)^4(-y)^5 = (126)(256x^4)(-y^5) = -32,256x^4y^5$$

■

Problem Set 15.6

For Problems 1–26, expand and simplify each binomial.

1. $(x + y)^8$

2. $(x + y)^9$

3. $(x - y)^6$

4. $(x - y)^4$

5. $(a + 2b)^4$

6. $(3a + b)^4$

7. $(x - 3y)^5$

8. $(2x - y)^6$

9. $(2a - 3b)^4$

10. $(3a - 2b)^5$

11. $(x^2 + y)^5$

12. $(x + y^3)^6$

13. $(2x^2 - y^2)^4$

14. $(3x^2 - 2y^2)^5$

15. $(x + 3)^6$

16. $(x + 2)^7$

17. $(x - 1)^9$

18. $(x - 3)^4$

19. $\left(1 + \dfrac{1}{n}\right)^4$

20. $\left(2 + \dfrac{1}{n}\right)^5$

21. $\left(a - \dfrac{1}{n}\right)^6$

22. $\left(2a - \dfrac{1}{n}\right)^5$

23. $(1 + \sqrt{2})^4$

24. $(2 + \sqrt{3})^3$

25. $(3 - \sqrt{2})^5$

26. $(1 - \sqrt{3})^4$

For Problems 27–36, write the first four terms of each expansion.

27. $(x + y)^{12}$

28. $(x + y)^{15}$

29. $(x - y)^{20}$

30. $(a - 2b)^{13}$

31. $(x^2 - 2y^3)^{14}$

32. $(x^3 - 3y^2)^{11}$

33. $\left(a + \dfrac{1}{n}\right)^9$

34. $\left(2 - \dfrac{1}{n}\right)^6$

35. $(-x + 2y)^{10}$

36. $(-a - b)^{14}$

For Problems 37–46, find the specified term for each binomial expansion.

37. The fourth term of $(x + y)^8$

38. The seventh term of $(x + y)^{11}$

39. The fifth term of $(x - y)^9$

40. The fourth term of $(x - 2y)^6$

41. The sixth term of $(3a + b)^7$

42. The third term of $(2x - 5y)^5$

43. The eighth term of $(x^2 + y^3)^{10}$

44. The ninth term of $(a + b^3)^{12}$

45. The seventh term of $\left(1 - \dfrac{1}{n}\right)^{15}$

46. The eighth term of $\left(1 - \dfrac{1}{n}\right)^{13}$

■ ■ ■ **THOUGHTS INTO WORDS**

47. How would you explain binomial expansions to an elementary algebra student?

48. Explain how to find the fifth term of the expansion of $(2x + 3y)^9$ without writing out the entire expansion.

49. Is the tenth term of the expansion $(1 - 2)^{15}$ positive or negative? Explain how you determined the answer to this question.

■ ■ ■ **FURTHER INVESTIGATIONS**

For Problems 50–53, expand and simplify each complex number.

50. $(1 + 2i)^5$

51. $(2 + i)^6$

52. $(2 - i)^6$

53. $(3 - 2i)^5$

Chapter 15   Summary

We can summarize this chapter with three main topics: counting techniques, probability, and the binomial theorem.

(15.1) Counting Techniques

The **fundamental principle of counting** states that if a first task can be accomplished in x ways and, following this task, a second task can be accomplished in y ways, then task 1 followed by task 2 can be accomplished in $x \cdot y$ ways. The principle extends to any finite number of tasks. As you solve problems involving the fundamental principle of counting, it is often helpful to analyze the problem in terms of the tasks to be completed.

(15.2) Ordered arrangements are called **permutations**. The number of permutations of n things taken n at a time is given by

$$P(n, n) = n!$$

The number of r-element permutations that can be formed from a set of n elements is given by

$$\underbrace{P(n, r) = n(n - 1)(n - 2) \cdots}_{r \text{ factors}}$$

If there are n elements to be arranged, where there are r_1 of one kind, r_2 of another kind, r_3 of another kind, ..., r_k of a kth kind, then the number of distinguishable permutations is given by

$$\frac{n!}{(r_1!)(r_2!)(r_3!) \ldots (r_k!)}$$

Combinations are subsets; the order in which the elements appear does not make a difference. The number of r-element combinations (subsets) that can be formed from a set of n elements is given by

$$C(n, r) = \frac{P(n, r)}{r!}$$

Does the order in which the elements appear make any difference? This is a key question to consider when trying to decide whether a particular problem involves permutations or combinations. If the answer to the question is yes, then it is a permutation problem; if the answer is no, then it is a combination problem. Don't forget that combinations are subsets.

(15.3–15.5) Probability

In an experiment where all possible outcomes in the sample space S are equally likely to occur, the **probability** of an event E is defined by

$$P(E) = \frac{n(E)}{n(S)}$$

where $n(E)$ denotes the number of elements in the event E, and $n(S)$ denotes the number of elements in the sample space S. The numbers $n(E)$ and $n(S)$ can often be determined by using one or more of the previously listed counting techniques. For all events E, it is always true that $0 \leq P(E) \leq 1$. That is, all probabilities fall in the range from 0 to 1, inclusive.

If E and E' are **complementary events**, then $P(E) + P(E') = 1$. Therefore, if we can calculate either $P(E)$ or $P(E')$, then we can find the other one by subtracting from 1.

For two events E and F, the probability of E or F is given by

$$P(E \cup F) = P(E) + P(F) - P(E \cap F)$$

If $E \cap F = \varnothing$, then E and F are **mutually exclusive events**.

The probability that an event E occurs, given that another event F has already occurred, is called **conditional probability**. It is given by the equation

$$P(E|F) = \frac{P(E \cap F)}{P(F)}$$

Two events E and F are said to be **independent** if and only if

$$P(E \cap F) = P(E)P(F)$$

Two events that are not independent are called **dependent events**, and the probability of two dependent events is given by

$$P(E \cap F) = P(E)P(F|E)$$

(15.6) The Binomial Theorem

For any binomial $(x + y)$ and any natural number n,

$$(x + y)^n = x^n + \binom{n}{1}x^{n-1}y + \binom{n}{2}x^{n-2}y^2$$

$$+ \cdots + \binom{n}{n}y^n$$

Note the following patterns in a binomial expansion:

1. In each term, the sum of the exponents of x and y is n.

2. The exponents of x begin with the exponent of the binomial and decrease by 1, term by term, until the last

term has x^0, which is 1. The exponents of y begin with zero ($y^0 = 1$) and increase by 1, term by term, until the last term contains y to the power of the binomial.

3. The coefficient of any term is given by $\binom{n}{r}$, where the value of r agrees with the exponent of y for that term. For example, if the term contains y^3, then the coefficient of that term is $\binom{n}{3}$.

4. The expansion of $(x + y)^n$ contains $n + 1$ terms.

Chapter 15   Review Problem Set

Problems 1–14 are counting type problems.

1. How many different arrangements of the letters A, B, C, D, E, and F can be made?

2. How many different nine-letter arrangements can be formed from the nine letters of the word APPARATUS?

3. How many odd numbers of three different digits each can be formed by choosing from the digits 1, 2, 3, 5, 7, 8, and 9?

4. In how many ways can Arlene, Brent, Carlos, Dave, Ernie, Frank, and Gladys be seated in a row of seven seats so that Arlene and Carlos are side by side?

5. In how many ways can a committee of three people be chosen from six people?

6. How many committees consisting of three men and two women can be formed from seven men and six women?

7. How many different five-card hands consisting of all hearts can be formed from a deck of 52 playing cards?

8. If no number contains repeated digits, how many numbers greater than 500 can be formed by choosing from the digits 2, 3, 4, 5, and 6?

9. How many three-person committees can be formed from four men and five women so that each committee contains at least one man?

10. How many different four-person committees can be formed from eight people if two particular people refuse to serve together on a committee?

11. How many four-element subsets containing A or B but not both A and B can be formed from the set {A, B, C, D, E, F, G, H}?

12. How many different six-letter permutations can be formed from four identical H's and two identical T's?

13. How many four-person committees consisting of two seniors, one sophomore, and one junior can be formed from three seniors, four juniors, and five sophomores?

14. In a baseball league of six teams, how many games are needed to complete a schedule if each team plays eight games with each other team?

Problems 15–35 pose some probability questions.

15. If three coins are tossed, find the probability of getting two heads and one tail.

16. If five coins are tossed, find the probability of getting three heads and two tails.

17. What is the probability of getting a sum of 8 with one roll of a pair of dice?

18. What is the probability of getting a sum greater than 5 with one roll of a pair of dice?

19. Aimée, Brenda, Chuck, Dave, and Eli are randomly seated in a row of five seats. Find the probability that Aimée and Chuck are not seated side by side.

20. Four girls and three boys are to be randomly seated in a row of seven seats. Find the probability that the girls and boys will be seated in alternating seats.

21. Six coins are tossed. Find the probability of getting at least two heads.

22. Two cards are randomly chosen from a deck of 52 playing cards. What is the probability that two jacks are drawn?

23. Each arrangement of the six letters of the word CYCLIC is put on a slip of paper and placed in a hat. One slip is drawn at random. Find the probability that the slip contains an arrangement with the Y at the beginning.

24. A committee of three is randomly chosen from one man and six women. What is the probability that the man is not on the committee?

25. A four-person committee is selected at random from the eight people Alice, Bob, Carl, Dee, Enrique, Fred, Gina, and Hilda. Find the probability that Alice or Bob, but not both, is on the committee.

26. A committee of three is chosen at random from a group of five men and four women. Find the probability that the committee contains two men and one woman.

27. A committee of four is chosen at random from a group of six men and seven women. Find the probability that the committee contains at least one woman.

28. A bag contains five red and eight white marbles. Two marbles are drawn in succession *with replacement*. What is the probability that at least one red marble is drawn?

29. A bag contains four red, five white, and three blue marbles. Two marbles are drawn in succession *with replacement*. Find the probability that one red and one blue marble are drawn.

30. A bag contains four red and seven blue marbles. Two marbles are drawn in succession *without replacement*. Find the probability of drawing one red and one blue marble.

31. A bag contains three red, two white, and two blue marbles. Two marbles are drawn in succession *without*

replacement. Find the probability of drawing at least one red marble.

32. Each of three letters is to be mailed in any one of four different mailboxes. What is the probability that all three letters will be mailed in the same mailbox?

33. The probability that a customer in a department store will buy a blouse is 0.15, the probability that she will buy a pair of shoes is 0.10, and the probability that she will buy both a blouse and a pair of shoes is 0.05. Find the probability that the customer will buy a blouse, given that she has already purchased a pair of shoes. Also find the probability that she will buy a pair of shoes, given that she has already purchased a blouse.

34. A survey of 500 employees of a company produced the following information.

Employment level	College degree	No college degree
Managerial	45	5
Nonmanagerial	50	400

Find the probability that an employee chosen at random (a) is working in a managerial position, given that he or she has a college degree; and (b) has a college degree, given that he or she is working in a managerial position.

35. From a survey of 1000 college students, it was found that 450 of them owned cars, 700 of them owned sound systems, and 200 of them owned both a car and a sound system. If a student is chosen at random from the 1000 students, find the probability that the student (a) owns a car, given the fact that he or she owns a sound system, and (b) owns a sound system, given the fact that he or she owns a car.

For Problems 36–41, expand each binomial and simplify.

36. $(x + 2y)^5$ 37. $(x - y)^8$ 38. $(a^2 - 3b^3)^4$

39. $\left(x + \dfrac{1}{n}\right)^6$ 40. $(1 - \sqrt{2})^5$ 41. $(-a + b)^3$

42. Find the fourth term of the expansion of $(x - 2y)^{12}$.

43. Find the tenth term of the expansion of $(3a + b^2)^{13}$.

Chapter 15 Test

For Problems 1–21, solve each problem.

1. In how many ways can Abdul, Barb, Corazon, and Doug be seated in a row of four seats so that Abdul occupies an end seat?

2. How many even numbers of four different digits each can be formed by choosing from the digits 1, 2, 3, 5, 7, 8, and 9?

3. In how many ways can three letters be mailed in six mailboxes?

4. In a baseball league of ten teams, how many games are needed to complete the schedule if each team plays six games against each other team?

5. In how many ways can a sum greater than 5 be obtained when tossing a pair of dice?

6. In how many ways can six different mathematics books and three different biology books be placed on a shelf so that all of the books in a subject area are side by side?

7. How many four-element subsets containing A or B, but not both A and B, can be formed from the set {A, B, C, D, E, F, G}?

8. How many five-card hands consisting of two aces, two kings, and one queen can be dealt from a deck of 52 playing cards?

9. How many different nine-letter arrangements can be formed from the nine letters of the word SASSAFRAS?

10. How many committees consisting of four men and three women can be formed from a group of seven men and five women?

11. What is the probability of rolling a sum less than 9 with a pair of dice?

12. Six coins are tossed. Find the probability of getting three heads and three tails.

13. All possible numbers of three different digits each are formed from the digits 1, 2, 3, 4, 5, and 6. If one number is then chosen at random, find the probability that it is greater than 200.

14. A four-person committee is selected at random from Anwar, Barb, Chad, Dick, Edna, Fern, and Giraldo. What is the probability that neither Anwar nor Barb is on the committee?

15. From a group of three men and five women, a three-person committee is selected at random. Find the probability that the committee contains at least one man.

16. A box of 12 items is known to contain one defective and 11 nondefective items. If a sample of three items is selected at random, what is the probability that all three items are nondefective?

17. Five coins are tossed 80 times. How many times should you expect to get three heads and two tails?

18. Suppose 3000 tickets are sold in a lottery. There are three prizes: The first prize is $500, the second is $300, and the third is $100. What is the mathematical expectation of winning?

19. A bag contains seven white and 12 green marbles. Two marbles are drawn in succession, *with replacement*. Find the probability that one marble of each color is drawn.

20. A bag contains three white, five green, and seven blue marbles. Two marbles are drawn *without replacement*. Find the probability that two green marbles are drawn.

21. In an election there were 2000 eligible voters. They were asked to vote on two issues, A and B. The results were as follows: 500 people voted for A, 800 people voted for B, and 250 people voted for both A and B. If one person is chosen at random from the 2000 eligible voters, find the probability that this person voted for A, given that he or she voted for B.

22. Expand and simplify $\left(2 - \dfrac{1}{n}\right)^6$.

23. Expand and simplify $(3x + 2y)^5$.

24. Find the ninth term of the expansion of $\left(x - \dfrac{1}{2}\right)^{12}$.

25. Find the fifth term of the expansion of $(x + 3y)^7$.

5 Probability Distributions (Discrete Variables)

Image copyright Michael Shake, 2012. Used under license from Shutterstock.com

5.1 Random Variables
*A **numerical value** assigned to each outcome*

5.2 Probability Distributions of a Discrete Random Variable
*The probability for each value of the random variable is listed in a **probability distribution**.*

5.3 The Binomial Probability Distribution
*Binomial situations occur when each trial has **two possible outcomes**.*

5.1 Random Variables

USA and Its Automobiles

Americans are very much in love with the automobile, and many have more than one available to them. The national average is 2.28 vehicles per household, with nearly 34% being single-vehicle and 31% being two-vehicle households. However, nearly 35% of all households have three or more vehicles.

Vehicles, x	1	2	3	4	5	6	7	8
$P(x)$	0.34	0.31	0.22	0.06	0.03	0.02	0.01	0.01

By pairing the number of vehicles per household as the variable x with the probability for each value of x, a probability distribution is created. This is much like the relative frequency distribution that we studied in Chapter 2.

If each outcome of a probability **experiment** is assigned a numerical value, then as we observe the results of the experiment, we are observing the values of a random variable. This numerical value is the *random variable value*.

> **Random variable** A variable that assumes a unique numerical value for each of the outcomes in the sample space of a probability experiment.

In other words, a random variable is used to denote the outcomes of a probability experiment. The random variable can take on any numerical value that belongs to the set of all possible outcomes of the experiment. (It is called "random" because the value it assumes is the result of a chance, or random, event.) Each event in a probability experiment must also be defined in such a way that only one value of the random variable is assigned to it **(mutually exclusive events)**, and every event must have a value assigned to it **(all-inclusive events)**.

The following example demonstrates random variables.

EXAMPLE 5.1

RANDOM VARIABLES

a. We toss five coins and observe the "number of heads" visible. The random variable x is the number of heads observed and may take on integer values from 0 to 5.

b. Let the "number of phone calls received" per day by a company be the random variable. Integer values ranging from zero to some very large number are possible values.

c. Let the "length of the cord" on an electrical appliance be a random variable. The random variable is a numerical value between 12 and 72 inches for most appliances.

d. Let the "qualifying speed" for race cars trying to qualify for the Indianapolis 500 be a random variable. Depending on how fast the driver can go, the speeds are approximately 220 and faster and are measured in miles per hour (to the nearest thousandth).

Numerical random variables can be subdivided into two classifications: *discrete random variables* and *continuous random variables*.

FYI Discrete and continuous variables were defined on page 8.

Discrete random variable A quantitative random variable that can assume a countable number of values.

Continuous random variable A quantitative random variable that can assume an uncountable number of values.

The random variables "number of heads" and "number of phone calls received" in Example 5.1 parts a and b are discrete. They each represent a count, and therefore there is a countable number of possible values. The random variables "length of the cord" and "qualifying speed" in Example 5.1 parts c and d are continuous. They each represent measurements that can assume any value along an interval, and therefore there is an infinite number of possible values.

◉ SECTION 5.1 EXERCISES

5.1 Refer to the chart accompanying "USA and Its Automobiles" on page 230.

a. What percentage of households have three vehicles?

b. What number of vehicles per household has the highest likelihood?

c. What variable could be used to describe all eight of the events shown on the chart?

d. Are the events mutually exclusive? Explain.

5.2 Based on the information depicted in "USA and Its Automobiles" on page 230,

a. what statistical graph could be used to picture or display this information? Draw it.

b. what other statistical methods could be used to describe this information?

5.3 Survey your classmates about the number of siblings they have and the length of the last conversation they had with their mother. Identify the two random variables of interest and list their possible values.

5.4 a. Explain why the variable "number of saved telephone numbers on a person's cell phone" is discrete.

b. Explain why the variable "weight of a statistics textbook" is continuous.

5.5 a. The variables in Exercise 5.3 are either discrete or continuous. Which are they and why?

b. Explain why the variable "number of dinner guests for Thanksgiving dinner" is discrete.

c. Explain why the variable "number of miles to your grandmother's house" is continuous.

5.6 A social worker is involved in a study about family structure. She obtains information regarding the number of children per family in a certain community from the census data. Identify the random variable of interest, determine whether it is discrete or continuous, and list its possible values.

5.7 *FORTUNE* Magazine released its annual list of The 100 Best Companies to Work For® on February 8, 2010. Many of the companies on the list plan to hire during 2010. Those adding the most employees include:

Company	New Jobs
51. Ernst + Young	2800
5. Wegmans	2000
2. Edward Jones	1040

Source: http://money.cnn.com

a. What is the random variable involved in this study?

b. Is the random variable discrete or continuous? Explain.

5.8 Above-average hot weather extended over the northwest on August 3, 2009. The day's forecasted high temperatures in four cities in the affected area were:

City	Temperature
Boise, ID	100°
Spokane, WA	95°
Portland, OR	91°
Helena, MT	91°

a. What is the random variable involved in this study?

b. Is the random variable discrete or continuous? Explain.

5.9 An archer shoots arrows at the bull's-eye of a target and measures the distance from the center of the target to the arrow. Identify the random variable of interest, determine whether it is discrete or continuous, and list its possible values.

5.10 A *USA Today* Snapshot titled "What women 'splurge' on" (July 21, 2009) reported that 34% of women said "shoes"; 22% said "handbags"; 15% said "work clothing"; 12% said "formal wear"; and 10% said "jewelry."

a. What is the variable involved, and what are the possible values?

b. Why is this variable not a random variable?

5.11 A March 11, 2009, *USA Today* article titled "College freshmen study booze more than books" presents the following chart depicting average hours per week spent on various activities by college freshmen. The study's sponsor, Outside the Classroom, surveyed more than 30,000 first-year students on 76 campuses.

Activity	Average Amount of Time/Week
Partying	10.2 hours
Studying	8.4 hours
Exercising	5.0 hours
Online social networking or playing video games	4.1 hours
Social networking	2.5 hours
Working for pay	2.2 hours

a. What is the random variable involved in this study?

b. Is the random variable discrete or continuous? Explain.

5.12 [EX05-012] If you could stop time and live forever in good health, what age would you pick? Answers to this question were reported in a *USA Today* Snapshot. The average ideal age for each age group is listed in the following table; the average ideal age for all adults was found to be 41. Interestingly, those younger than 30 years want to be older, whereas those older than 30 years want to be younger.

Age Group	18–24	25–29	30–39	40–49	50–64	65+
Ideal Age	27	31	37	40	44	59

Age is used as a variable twice in this application.

a. The age of the person being interviewed is not the random variable in this situation. Explain why and describe how "age" is used with regard to age group.

b. What is the random variable involved in this study? Describe its role in this situation.

c. Is the random variable discrete or continuous? Explain.

5.2 Probability Distributions of a Discrete Random Variable

Consider a coin-tossing experiment where two coins are tossed and no heads, one head, or two heads are observed. If we define the random variable x to be the number of heads observed when two coins are tossed, x can take on the value 0, 1, or 2. The probability of each of these three events can be calculated using techniques from Chapter 4:

$$P(x = 0) = P(0H) = P(TT) = \frac{1}{2} \cdot \frac{1}{2} = \frac{1}{4} = 0.25$$

$$P(x = 1) = P(1H) = P(HT \text{ or } TH) = \frac{1}{2} \cdot \frac{1}{2} + \frac{1}{2} \cdot \frac{1}{2} = \frac{1}{2} = 0.50$$

$$P(x = 2) = P(2H) = P(HH) = \frac{1}{2} \cdot \frac{1}{2} = \frac{1}{4} = 0.25$$

These probabilities can be listed in any number of ways. One of the most convenient is a table format known as a *probability distribution* (see Table 5.1).

TABLE 5.1
Probability Distribution: Tossing Two Coins

x	P(x)
0	0.25
1	0.50
2	0.25

> **Probability distribution** A distribution of the probabilities associated with each of the values of a random variable. The probability distribution is a theoretical distribution; it is used to represent populations.

In an experiment in which a single die is rolled and the number of dots on the top surface is observed, the random variable is the number observed. The probability distribution for this random variable is shown in Table 5.2.

FYI Can you see why the name "probability distribution" is used?

TABLE 5.2
Probability Distribution: Rolling a Die

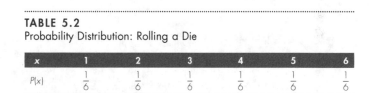

x	1	2	3	4	5	6
P(x)	$\frac{1}{6}$	$\frac{1}{6}$	$\frac{1}{6}$	$\frac{1}{6}$	$\frac{1}{6}$	$\frac{1}{6}$

Sometimes it is convenient to write a rule that algebraically expresses the probability of an event in terms of the value of the random variable. This expression is typically written in formula form and is called a *probability function*.

> **Probability function** A rule that assigns probabilities to the values of the random variables.

A probability function can be as simple as a list that pairs the values of a random variable with their probabilities. Tables 5.1 and 5.2 show two such listings. However, a probability function is most often expressed in formula form.

Consider a die that has been modified so that it has one face with one dot, two faces with two dots, and three faces with three dots. Let x be the number of dots observed when this die is rolled. The probability distribution for this experiment is presented in Table 5.3.

TABLE 5.3
Probability Distribution: Rolling
the Modified Die

x	P(x)
1	$\frac{1}{6}$
2	$\frac{2}{6}$
3	$\frac{3}{6}$

FYI These properties
were presented in
Chapter 4.

Each of the probabilities can be represented by the value of x divided by 6; that is, each $P(x)$ is equal to the value of x divided by 6, where $x = 1, 2,$ or 3. Thus,

$$P(x) = \frac{x}{6} \quad \text{for} \quad x = 1, 2, 3$$

is the formula for the probability function of this experiment.

The probability function for the experiment of rolling one ordinary die is

$$P(x) = \frac{1}{6} \quad \text{for} \quad x = 1, 2, 3, 4, 5, 6$$

This particular function is called a **constant function** because the value of $P(x)$ does not change as x changes.

Every probability function must display the two basic properties of probability (see p. 179). These two properties are (1) the probability assigned to each value of the random variable must be between zero and one, inclusive, and (2) the sum of the probabilities assigned to all the values of the random variable must equal one—that is,

Property 1 $0 \leq$ each $P(x) \leq 1$

Property 2 $\sum_{\text{all } x} P(x) = 1$

E X A M P L E   5 . 2

DETERMINING A PROBABILITY FUNCTION

Is $P(x) = \frac{x}{10}$ for $x = 1, 2, 3, 4$ a probability function?

TABLE 5.4
Probability Distribution for
$P(x) = \frac{x}{10}$ for $x = 1, 2, 3, 4$

x	P(x)
1	$\frac{1}{10} = 0.1$ ✓
2	$\frac{2}{10} = 0.2$ ✓
3	$\frac{3}{10} = 0.3$ ✓
4	$\frac{4}{10} = 0.4$ ✓
	$\frac{10}{10} = 1.0$ Ⓒⓚ

Solution

To answer this question we need only test the function in terms of the two basic properties. The probability distribution is shown in Table 5.4.

Property 1 is satisfied because 0.1, 0.2, 0.3, and 0.4 are all numerical values between zero and one. (See the ✓ indicating each value was checked.) Property 2 is also satisfied because the sum of all four probabilities is exactly one. (See the Ⓒⓚ indicating the sum was checked.) Since both properties are satisfied, we can conclude that $P(x) = \frac{x}{10}$ for $x = 1, 2, 3, 4$ is a probability function.

What about $P(x = 5)$ (or any value other than $x = 1, 2, 3,$ or 4) for the function $P(x) = \frac{x}{10}$ for $x = 1, 2, 3, 4$? $P(x = 5)$ is considered to be zero. That is, the probability function provides a probability of zero for all values of x other than the values specified as part of the domain.

Probability distributions can be presented graphically. Regardless of the specific graphic representation used, the values of the random variable are plotted on the horizontal scale, and the probability associated with each value of the random variable is plotted on the vertical scale. The probability distribution of a discrete random variable could be presented by a set of line segments drawn at the values of x with lengths that represent the probability of each x. Figure 5.1 shows the probability distribution of $P(x) = \frac{x}{10}$ for $x = 1, 2, 3, 4$.

A regular histogram is used more frequently to present probability distributions. Figure 5.2 shows the probability distribution of Figure 5.1 as a

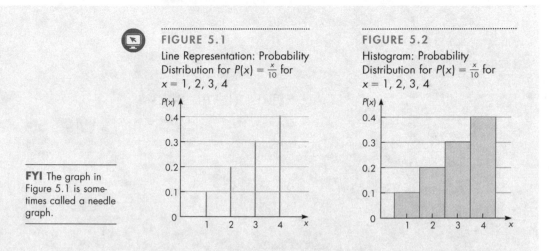

FIGURE 5.1
Line Representation: Probability Distribution for $P(x) = \frac{x}{10}$ for $x = 1, 2, 3, 4$

FIGURE 5.2
Histogram: Probability Distribution for $P(x) = \frac{x}{10}$ for $x = 1, 2, 3, 4$

FYI The graph in Figure 5.1 is sometimes called a needle graph.

probability histogram. The histogram of a probability distribution uses the physical area of each bar to represent its assigned probability. The bar for $x = 2$ is 1 unit wide (from 1.5 to 2.5) and 0.2 unit high. Therefore, its area (length × width) is $(0.2)(1) = 0.2$, the probability assigned to $x = 2$. The areas of the other bars can be determined in similar fashion. This area representation will be an important concept in Chapter 6 when we begin to work with continuous random variables.

TECHNOLOGY INSTRUCTIONS: GENERATE RANDOM DATA

MINITAB	Input the possible values of the random variable into C1 and the corresponding probabilities into C2; then continue with:

Choose: **Calc > Random Data > Discrete**
Enter: Number of rows of data to generate: **25** (number wanted)
                 Store in column(s): **C3**
                 Values (of x) in: **C1**
                 Probabilities in: **C2 > OK**

Excel	Input the possible values of the random variable into column A and the corresponding probabilities into column B; then continue with:

Choose: **Data > Data Analysis > Random Number Generation > OK**
Enter: Number of Variables: **1**
                 Number of Random Numbers: **25** (# wanted)
                 Distribution: **Discrete**
                 Value & Prob. Input Range: (**A2:B5 select data cells, not labels**)
Select: **Output Range**
Enter: (**C1 or select cell**)

APPLIED EXAMPLE 5.3

APPLYING FOR ADMISSION

Students hedge their bets

Most students apply to more than one school, making it difficult for colleges to predict how many will actually enroll. Last fall's freshman class was asked:

To how many colleges, other than the one where you enrolled, did you apply for admission this year?

None	19.6%
One	13.1%
Two	16.2%
Three	16.8%
Four	12.1%
Five	8.2%
Six	5.4%
Seven to 10	7.2%
11 or more	1.4%

Source: The American Freshman: National Norms for Fall 2001, survey of 281,064 freshmen entering 421 four-year colleges and universities.

Data from Julie Snider, © 2002 USA Today.

COLLEGES STRIVE TO FILL DORMS

By Mary Beth Marklein, *USA Today*

Colleges and universities will mail their last batch of admission offers in the next few days, but the process is far from over.

Now, students have until May 1 to decide where they'll go this fall. And with lingering concerns about the economy and residual fears about travel and security since Sept. 11, many admissions officials are less able this year to predict how students will respond.

Note the distribution depicted on the bar graph. It has the makings of a discrete probability distribution. The random variable, "number of colleges applied to," is a discrete random variable with values from zero to 11 or more. Each of the values has a corresponding probability, and the sum of the probabilities is equal to 1.

Mean and Variance of a Discrete Probability Distribution

Recall that in Chapter 2 we calculated several numerical sample statistics (mean, variance, standard deviation, and others) to describe empirical sets of data. Probability distributions may be used to represent theoretical populations, the counterpart to samples. We use **population parameters** (mean, variance, and standard deviation) to describe these probability distributions just as we use **sample statistics** to describe samples.

Notes:

1. $\bar{x}$ is the mean of the sample.
2. s^2 and s are the variance and standard deviation of the sample, respectively.
3. $\bar{x}, s^2$, and s are called *sample statistics*.
4. μ (lowercase Greek letter mu) is the mean of the population.
5. σ^2 (sigma squared) is the variance of the population.
6. σ (lowercase Greek letter sigma) is the standard deviation of the population.
7. μ, σ^2, and σ are called *population parameters*. (A parameter is a constant; μ, σ^2, and σ are typically unknown values in real statistics problems. About the only time they are known is in a textbook problem setting for the purposes of learning and understanding.)

The *mean of the probability distribution* of a discrete random variable, or the *mean of a discrete random variable*, is found in a manner that takes full advantage of the table format of a discrete probability distribution. The mean of a discrete random variable is often referred to as its *expected value*.

> **Mean of a discrete random variable (expected value)** The mean, μ, of a discrete random variable x is found by multiplying each possible value of x by its own probability and then adding all the products together:
>
> mean of x: $mu = sum\ of\ (each\ x\ multiplied\ by\ its\ own\ probability)$
>
> $$\mu = \Sigma[xP(x)] \tag{5.1}$$

The variance of a discrete random variable is defined in much the same way as the variance of sample data, the mean of the squared deviations from the mean.

> **Variance of a discrete random variable** The variance, σ^2, of a discrete random variable x is found by multiplying each possible value of the squared deviation from the mean, $(x - \mu)^2$, by its own probability and then adding all the products together:
>
> variance: $sigma\ squared = sum\ of\ (squared\ deviation\ times\ probability)$
>
> $$\sigma^2 = \Sigma[(x - \mu)^2 P(x)] \tag{5.2}$$

Formula (5.2) is often inconvenient to use; it can be reworked into the following form(s):

variance: $sigma\ squared = sum\ of\ (x^2\ times\ probability)$
$$- [sum\ of\ (x\ times\ probability)]^2$$
$$\sigma^2 = \Sigma[x^2 P(x)] - \{\Sigma[xP(x)]\}^2 \tag{5.3a}$$

or

$$\sigma^2 = \Sigma[x^2 P(x)] - \mu^2 \tag{5.3b}$$

Likewise, standard deviation of a random variable is calculated in the same manner as is the standard deviation of sample data.

> **Standard deviation of a discrete random variable** The positive square root of variance.
>
> $$standard\ deviation:\ \sigma = \sqrt{\sigma^2} \tag{5.4}$$

E X A M P L E   5 . 4

STATISTICS FOR A PROBABILITY FUNCTION (DISTRIBUTION)

Find the mean, variance, and standard deviation of the probability function

$$P(x) = \frac{x}{10} \text{ for } x = 1, 2, 3, 4$$

Solution

We will find the mean using formula (5.1), the variance using formula (5.3a), and the standard deviation using formula (5.4). The most convenient way to organize the products and find the totals we need is to expand the probability distribution into an extensions table (see Table 5.5).

TABLE 5.5

Extensions Table: Probability Distribution, $P(x) = \dfrac{x}{10}$ for $x = 1, 2, 3, 4$

x	$P(x)$	$xP(x)$	x^2	$x^2P(x)$
1	$\dfrac{1}{10} = 0.1$ ✓	0.1	1	0.1
2	$\dfrac{2}{10} = 0.2$ ✓	0.4	4	0.8
3	$\dfrac{3}{10} = 0.3$ ✓	0.9	9	2.7
4	$\dfrac{4}{10} = 0.4$ ✓	1.6	16	6.4
	$\dfrac{10}{10} = 1.0$ (ck)	$\Sigma[xP(x)] = 3.0$		$\Sigma[x^2P(x)] = 10.0$

Find the mean of x: The $xP(x)$ column contains each value of x multiplied by its corresponding probability, and the sum at the bottom is the value needed in formula (5.1):

$$\mu = \Sigma[xP(x)] = \mathbf{3.0}$$

Find the variance of x: The totals at the bottom of the $xP(x)$ and $x^2P(x)$ columns are substituted into formula (5.3a):

$$\sigma^2 = \Sigma[x^2P(x)] - \{\Sigma[xP(x)]\}^2$$
$$= 10.0 - \{3.0\}^2 = \mathbf{1.0}$$

Find the standard deviation of x: Use formula (5.4):

$$\sigma = \sqrt{\sigma^2} = \sqrt{1.0} = \mathbf{1.0}$$

Notes:

1. The purpose of the extensions table is to organize the process of finding the three column totals: $\Sigma[P(x)]$, $\Sigma[xP(x)]$, and $\Sigma[x^2P(x)]$.
2. The other columns, x and x^2, should not be totaled; they are not used.
3. $\Sigma[P(x)]$ will always be 1.0; use this only as a check.
4. $\Sigma[xP(x)]$ and $\Sigma[x^2P(x)]$ are used to find the mean and variance of x.

EXAMPLE 5.5

MEAN, VARIANCE, AND STANDARD DEVIATION OF A DISCRETE RANDOM VARIABLE

A coin is tossed three times. Let the "number of heads" that occur in those three tosses be the random variable, x. Find the mean, variance, and standard deviation of x.

 Video tutorial available—logon and learn more at cengagebrain.com

Solution

There are eight possible outcomes (all equally likely) to this experiment: {HHH, HHT, HTH, HTT, THH, THT, TTH, TTT}. One outcome results in $x = 0$, three in $x = 1$, three in $x = 2$, and one in $x = 3$. Therefore, the probabilities for this random variable are $\frac{1}{8}$, $\frac{3}{8}$, $\frac{3}{8}$, and $\frac{1}{8}$. The probability distribution associated with this experiment is shown in Figure 5.3 and in Table 5.6. The necessary extensions and summations for the calculation of the mean, variance, and standard deviation are also shown in Table 5.6.

FIGURE 5.3

Probability Distribution: Number of Heads in Three Tosses of Coin

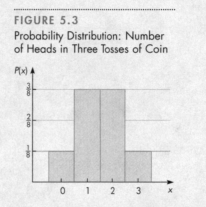

TABLE 5.6 Extensions Table of Probability Distribution of Number of Heads in Three Coin Tosses

x	$P(x)$	$xP(x)$	x^2	$x^2P(x)$
0	$\frac{1}{8}$ ✓	$\frac{0}{8}$	0	$\frac{0}{8}$
1	$\frac{3}{8}$ ✓	$\frac{3}{8}$	1	$\frac{3}{8}$
2	$\frac{3}{8}$ ✓	$\frac{6}{8}$	4	$\frac{12}{8}$
3	$\frac{1}{8}$ ✓	$\frac{3}{8}$	9	$\frac{9}{8}$

$$\Sigma[P(x)] = \frac{8}{8} = 1.0 \text{ ⓒⓀ} \quad \Sigma[xP(x)] = \frac{12}{8} = 1.5 \qquad \Sigma[x^2P(x)] = \frac{24}{8} = 3.0$$

The mean is found using formula (5.1):

$$\mu = \Sigma[xP(x)] = \mathbf{1.5}$$

This result, 1.5, is the mean of the theoretical distribution for the random variable "number of heads" observed per set of three coin tosses. It is expected that the mean for many observed values of the random variable will also be approximately equal to this value.

The variance is found using formula (5.3a):

$$\sigma^2 = \Sigma[x^2P(x)] - \{\Sigma[xP(x)]\}^2$$
$$= 3.0 - (1.5)^2 = 3.0 - 2.25 = \mathbf{0.75}$$

The standard deviation is found using formula (5.4):

$$\sigma = \sqrt{\sigma^2} = \sqrt{0.75} = 0.866 = \mathbf{0.87}$$

That is, 0.87 is the standard deviation of the theoretical distribution for the random variable "number of heads" observed per set of three coin tosses. It is expected that the standard deviation for many observed values of the random variable will also be approximately equal to this value.

⌨ SECTION 5.2 EXERCISES

5.13 Express the tossing of one coin as a probability distribution of x, the number of heads occurring (that is, $x = 1$ if a head occurs and $x = 0$ if a tail occurs).

5.14 a. Express $P(x) = \frac{1}{6}$, for $x = 1, 2, 3, 4, 5, 6$, in distribution form.

b. Construct a histogram of the probability distribution $P(x) = \frac{1}{6}$, for $x = 1, 2, 3, 4, 5, 6$.

c. Describe the shape of the histogram in part b.

5.15 a. Explain how the various values of x in a probability distribution form a set of mutually exclusive events.

b. Explain how the various values of x in a probability distribution form a set of "all-inclusive" events.

5.16 Test the following function to determine whether it is a probability function. If it is not, try to make it into a probability function.

$$R(x) = 0.2, \text{ for } x = 0, 1, 2, 3, 4$$

a. List the distribution of probabilities.

b. Sketch a histogram.

5.17 Test the following function to determine whether it is a probability function.

$$P(x) = \frac{x^2 + 5}{50}, \text{ for } x = 1, 2, 3, 4$$

a. List the probability distribution.

b. Sketch a histogram.

5.18 Test the following function to determine whether it is a probability function. If it is not, try to make it into a probability function.

$$S(x) = \frac{6 - |x - 7|}{36}, \text{ for } x = 2, 3, 4, 5, 6, 7, \ldots, 11, 12$$

a. List the distribution of probabilities and sketch a histogram.

b. Do you recognize $S(x)$? If so, identify it.

5.19 Census data are often used to obtain probability distributions for various random variables. Census data for families in a particular state with a combined income of $50,000 or more show that 20% of these families have no children, 30% have one child, 40% have two children, and 10% have three children. From this information, construct the probability distribution for x, where x represents the number of children per family for this income group.

5.20 In a *USA Today* Snapshot (June 1, 2009), the following statistics were reported on the number of hours of sleep that adults get.

Number of Hours	Percentage
5 or less	12%
6	29%
7	37%
8 or more	24%

Source: StrategyOne survey for Tempur-Pedic of 1004 adults in April

a. Are there any other values that the number of hours can attain?

b. Explain why the total of the percentages is not 100%.

c. Is this a discrete probability distribution? Is it a probability distribution? Explain.

5.21 Verify that formulas (5.3a) and (5.3b) are equivalent to formula (5.2).

5.22 a. Form the probability distribution table for $P(x) = \frac{x}{6}$, for $x = 1, 2, 3$.

b. Find the extensions $xP(x)$ and $x^2P(x)$ for each x.

c. Find $\Sigma[xP(x)]$ and $\Sigma[x^2P(x)]$.

d. Find the mean for $P(x) = \frac{x}{6}$, for $x = 1, 2, 3$.

e. Find the variance for $P(x) = \frac{x}{6}$, for $x = 1, 2, 3$.

f. Find the standard deviation for $P(x) = \frac{x}{6}$, for $x = 1, 2, 3$.

5.23 If you find the sum of the x and the x^2 columns on the extensions table, exactly what have you found?

5.24 Given the probability function $P(x) = \frac{5-x}{10}$, for $x = 1, 2, 3, 4$, find the mean and standard deviation.

5.25 Given the probability function $R(x) = 0.2$, for $x = 0, 1, 2, 3, 4$, find the mean and standard deviation.

5.26 The number of ships to arrive at a harbor on any given day is a random variable represented by x. The probability distribution for x is as follows:

x	10	11	12	13	14
$P(x)$	0.4	0.2	0.2	0.1	0.1

Find the mean and standard deviation of the number of ships that arrive at a harbor on a given day.

5.27 The College Board website provides much information for students, parents, and professionals with respect to the many aspects involved in Advanced Placement (AP) courses and exams. One particular annual report provides the percent of students who obtain each of the possible AP grades (1 through 5). The 2008 grade distribution for all subjects was as follows:

AP Grade	Percent
1	20.9
2	21.3
3	24.1
4	19.4
5	14.3

a. Express this distribution as a discrete probability distribution.

b. Find the mean and standard deviation of the AP exam scores for 2008.

5.28 The number of children per household, x, in the United States in 2008 is expressed as a probability distribution here.

x	0	1	2	3	4	5+
$P(x)$	0.209	0.384	0.249	0.106	0.032	0.020

Source: U.S. Census Bureau

a. Is this a discrete probability distribution? Explain.

b. Draw a histogram for the distribution of x, the number of children per household.

c. Replacing "5+" with exactly "5," find the mean and standard deviation.

5.29 Is a dog "man's best friend"? One would think so, with 60 million pet dogs nationwide. But how many friends are needed? In the American Pet Products Association's 2007–2008 National Pet Owners Survey, the following statistics were reported.

Number of Pet Dogs	Percentage
One	63
Two	25
Three or more	12

Source: APPMA 2007–2008 National Pet Owners Survey

a. Is this a discrete probability distribution? Explain.

b. Draw a relative frequency histogram to depict the results shown in the table.

c. Replacing the category "Three or more" with exactly "Three," find the mean and standard deviation of the number of pet dogs per household.

d. How do you interpret the mean?

e. Explain the effect that replacing the category "Three or more" with "Three" has on the mean and standard deviation.

5.30 As reported in the chapter opener "USA and Its Automobiles," Americans are in love with the automobile—the majority have more than one vehicle per household. In fact, the national average is 2.28 vehicles per household. The number of vehicles per household in the United States can be described as follows:

Vehicles, x	$P(x)$
1	0.34
2	0.31
3	0.22
4	0.06
5	0.03
6	0.02
7	0.01
8 or more	0.01

a. Replacing the category "8 or more" with exactly "8," find the mean and standard deviation of the number of vehicles per household in the United States.

b. How does the mean calculated in part a correspond to the national average of 2.28?

(continue on page 242)

c. Explain the effect that replacing the category "8 or more" with "8" has on the mean and standard deviation.

5.31 The random variable A has the following probability distribution:

A	1	2	3	4	5
$P(A)$	0.6	0.1	0.1	0.1	0.1

a. Find the mean and standard deviation of A.

b. How much of the probability distribution is within 2 standard deviations of the mean?

c. What is the probability that A is between $\mu - 2\sigma$ and $\mu + 2\sigma$?

5.32 The random variable $\bar{x}$ has the following probability distribution:

$\bar{x}$	1	2	3	4	5
$P(\bar{x})$	0.6	0.1	0.1	0.1	0.1

a. Find the mean and standard deviation of $(\bar{x})$.

b. What is the probability that $\bar{x}$ is between $\mu - \sigma$ and $\mu + \sigma$?

5.33 a. Draw a histogram of the probability distribution for the single-digit random numbers 0, 1, 2, ..., 9.

b. Calculate the mean and standard deviation associated with the population of single-digit random numbers.

c. Represent (1) the location of the mean on the histogram with a vertical line and (2) the magnitude of the standard deviation with a line segment.

d. How much of this probability distribution is within 2 standard deviations of the mean?

5.34 Skillbuilder Applet Exercise simulates playing a game where a player has a 0.2 probability of winning $3 and a 0.8 probability of losing $1. Repeat the simulations for several sets of 100 plays using the "Play 25 times" button.

a. What would you estimate for your expected value (average gain or loss) from the results?

b. Using the following probability distribution, calculate the mean.

x	$P(x)$
$3	0.2
−$1	0.8

c. How do your answers to parts a and b compare? Would you consider this a fair game? Why?

5.35 A *USA Today* Snapshot (March 4, 2009) presented a pie chart depicting how workers damage their laptops. Statistics were derived from a survey conducted by Ponemon Institute for Dell of 714 IT managers. Is this a probability distribution? Explain.

Reason for Damage to Laptop	Percentage (%)
Spilled food or liquids	34
Dropping them	28
Not protecting during travel	25
Worker anger	13

5.36 a. Use a computer (or random number table) to generate a random sample of 25 observations drawn from the following discrete probability distribution.

x	1	2	3	4	5
$P(x)$	0.2	0.3	0.3	0.1	0.1

Compare the resulting data to your expectations.

b. Form a relative frequency distribution of the random data.

c. Construct a probability histogram of the given distribution and a relative frequency histogram of the observed data using class midpoints of 1, 2, 3, 4, and 5.

d. Compare the observed data with the theoretical distribution. Describe your conclusions.

e. Repeat parts a through d several times with $n = 25$. Describe the variability you observe between samples.

f. Repeat parts a through d several times with $n = 250$. Describe the variability you see between samples of this much larger size.

MINITAB

a. Input the x values of the random variable into C1 and their corresponding probabilities, $P(x)$, into C2; then continue with the generating random data MINITAB commands on page 235.

b. To obtain the frequency distribution, continue with:

Choose:　Stat > Tables > Cross Tabulation
Enter:　Categorical variables: For rows: C3
Select:　Display: Total percents > OK

c. To construct the histogram of the generated data in C3, continue with the histogram MINITAB commands on page 53, selecting scale > Y-Scale Type > Percent. (Use Binning followed by midpoint and midpoint positions 1:5/1 if necessary.)

To construct a bar graph of the given distribution:

Choose:	**Graph > Bar Chart > Bars represent: Values from a table >** One Column of values: **Simple > OK**
Enter:	Graph variables: **C2** Categorical variables: **C1**
Select:	**Labels > Data Labels** > Label Type: **Use y-value labels > OK**
Select:	**Data View** > Data Display: **Bars > OK > OK**

Excel

a. Input the x values of the random variable in column A and their corresponding probabilities, P(x), in column B; then continue with the generating random data Excel commands on page 235 for n = 25.

b. & c. The frequency distribution is given with the histogram of the generated data. Use the histogram Excel commands on page 53 using the data in column C and the bin range in column A.

To construct a histogram of the given distribution, activate A1:B6 or select cells and continue with:

Choose:	**Insert > Column > 1st** picture(usually) **Chart Layouts > Layout 9**
Choose:	**Select Data > Series 1 > Remove > OK**
Enter:	**Chart and axes titles** (Edit as needed)

5.37 a. Use a computer (or random number table) and generate a random sample of 100 observations drawn from the discrete probability population $P(x) = \frac{5-x}{10}$, for $x = 1, 2, 3, 4$. List the resulting sample. (Use the computer commands in Exercise 5.36; just change the arguments.)

b. Form a relative frequency distribution of the random data.

c. Form a probability distribution of the expected probability distribution. Compare the resulting data with your expectations.

d. Construct a probability histogram of the given distribution and a relative frequency histogram of the observed data using class midpoints of 1, 2, 3, and 4.

e. Compare the observed data with the theoretical distribution. Describe your conclusions.

f. Repeat parts a–d several times with $n = 100$. Describe the variability you observe between samples.

5.38 Every Tuesday, Jason's Video has "roll-the-dice" day. A customer may roll two fair dice and rent a second movie for an amount (in cents) determined by the numbers showing on the dice, the larger number first. For example, if the customer rolls a one and a five, a second movie may be rented for $0.51. Let x represent the amount paid for a second movie on roll-the-dice Tuesday.

a. Use the sample space for the rolling of a pair of dice and express the rental cost of the second movie, x, as a probability distribution.

b. What is the expected mean rental cost (mean of x) of the second movie on roll-the-dice Tuesday?

c. What is the standard deviation of x?

d. Using a computer and the probability distribution found in part a, generate a random sample of 30 values for x and determine the total cost of renting the second movie for 30 rentals.

e. Using a computer, obtain an estimate for the probability that the total amount paid for 30 second movies will exceed $15.00 by repeating part d 500 times and using the 500 results.

5.3 The Binomial Probability Distribution

Consider the following probability experiment. Your instructor gives the class a surprise four-question multiple-choice quiz. You have not studied the material, and therefore you decide to answer the four questions by randomly guessing the answers without reading the questions or the answers.

Answer Page to Quiz

Directions: Circle the best answer to each question.

1. a   b   c
2. a   b   c
3. a   b   c
4. a   b   c

FYI That's right, guess!

Circle your answers before continuing.

Before we look at the correct answers to the quiz and find out how you did, let's think about some of the things that might happen if you answered a quiz this way.

1.   How many of the four questions are you likely to have answered correctly?
2.   How likely are you to have more than half of the answers correct?
3.   What is the probability that you selected the correct answers to all four questions?
4.   What is the probability that you selected wrong answers for all four questions?
5.   If an entire class answers the quiz by guessing, what do you think the class "average" number of correct answers will be?

To find the answers to these questions, let's start with a tree diagram of the sample space, showing all 16 possible ways to answer the four-question quiz. Each of the four questions is answered with the correct answer (C) or with a wrong answer (W). See Figure 5.4.

FIGURE 5.4

Tree Diagram: Possible Answers to a Four-Question Quiz

FYI WWWW? represents wrong on 1 and wrong on 2 and wrong on 3 and wrong on 4; therefore, its probability is found using the multiplication rule, formula (4.7).

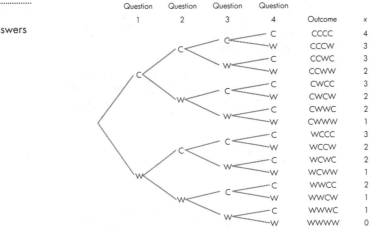

We can convert the information on the tree diagram into a probability distribution. Let x be the "number of correct answers" on one person's quiz when the quiz was taken by randomly guessing. The random variable x may take on any one of the values 0, 1, 2, 3, or 4 for each quiz. Figure 5.4 shows 16 branches representing five different values of x. Notice that the event $x = 4$, "four correct answers," is represented by the top branch of the tree diagram, and the event

$x = 0$, "zero correct answers," is shown on the bottom branch. The other events, "one correct answer," "two correct answers," and "three correct answers," are each represented by several branches of the tree. We find that the event $x = 1$ occurs on four different branches, event $x = 2$ occurs on six branches, and event $x = 3$ occurs on four branches.

Each individual question has only one correct answer among the three possible answers, so the probability of selecting the correct answer to an individual question is $\frac{1}{3}$. The probability that a wrong answer is selected on an individual question is $\frac{2}{3}$. The probability of each value of x can be found by calculating the probabilities of all the branches and then combining the probabilities for branches that have the same x values. The calculations follow, and the resulting probability distribution appears in Table 5.7.

$P(x = 0)$ is the probability that the correct answers are given for zero questions and the wrong answers are given for four questions (there is only one branch on Figure 5.4 where all four are wrong—WWWW):

$$P(x = 0) = \frac{2}{3} \times \frac{2}{3} \times \frac{2}{3} \times \frac{2}{3} = \left(\frac{2}{3}\right)^4 = \frac{16}{81} = \mathbf{0.198}$$

Note: Answering each individual question is a separate and independent event, thereby allowing us to use formula (4.7), which states that we should multiply the probabilities.

$P(x = 1)$ is the probability that the correct answer is given for exactly one question and wrong answers are given for the other three (there are four branches on Figure 5.4 where this occurs—namely, CWWW, WCWW, WWCW, WWWC—and each has the same probability):

$$P(x = 1) = (4) \times \frac{1}{3} \times \frac{2}{3} \times \frac{2}{3} \times \frac{2}{3} = (4)\left(\frac{1}{3}\right)^1\left(\frac{2}{3}\right)^3 = \mathbf{0.395}$$

$P(x = 2)$ is the probability that correct answers are given for exactly two questions and wrong answers are given for the other two (there are six branches on Figure 5.4 where this occurs—CCWW, CWCW, CWWC, WCCW, WCWC, WWCC—and each has the same probability):

$$P(x = 2) = (6) \times \frac{1}{3} \times \frac{1}{3} \times \frac{2}{3} \times \frac{2}{3} = (6)\left(\frac{1}{3}\right)^2\left(\frac{2}{3}\right)^2 = \mathbf{0.296}$$

$P(x = 3)$ is the probability that correct answers are given for exactly three questions and a wrong answer is given for the other question (there are four branches on Figure 5.4 where this occurs—CCCW, CCWC, CWCC, WCCC—and each has the same probability):

$$P(x = 3) = (4) \times \frac{1}{3} \times \frac{1}{3} \times \frac{1}{3} \times \frac{2}{3} = (4)\left(\frac{1}{3}\right)^3\left(\frac{2}{3}\right)^1 = \mathbf{0.099}$$

$P(x = 4)$ is the probability that correct answers are given for all four questions (there is only one branch on Figure 5.4 where all four are correct—CCCC):

$$P(x = 4) = \frac{1}{3} \times \frac{1}{3} \times \frac{1}{3} \times \frac{1}{3} = \left(\frac{1}{3}\right)^4 = \frac{1}{81} = \mathbf{0.012}$$

Now we can answer the five questions that were asked about the four-question quiz (p. 244).

Answer 1: The most likely occurrence would be to get one answer correct; it has a probability of 0.395. Zero, one, or two correct answers are expected to result approximately 89% of the time (0.198 + 0.395 + 0.296 = 0.889).

TABLE 5.7
Probability Distribution for the Four-Question Quiz

x	P(x)
0	0.198
1	0.395
2	0.296
3	0.099
4	0.012
	1.000 (ck)

Answer 2: Having more than half correct is represented by $x = 3$ or 4; their total probability is $0.099 + 0.012 = 0.111$. (You will pass this quiz only 11% of the time by random guessing.)

Answer 3: $P(\text{all four correct}) = P(x = 4) = 0.012$. (All correct occurs only 1% of the time.)

Answer 4: $P(\text{all four wrong}) = P(x = 0) = 0.198$. (That's almost 20% of the time.)

Answer 5: The class average is expected to be $\frac{1}{3}$ of 4, or 1.33 correct answers.

The correct answers to the quiz are b, c, b, a. How many correct answers did you have? Which branch of the tree in Figure 5.4 represents your quiz results? You might ask several people to answer this same quiz by guessing the answers. Then construct an observed relative frequency distribution and compare it with the distribution shown in Table 5.7.

Many experiments are composed of repeated trials whose outcomes can be classified into one of two categories: **success** or **failure**. Examples of such experiments are coin tosses, right/wrong quiz answers, and other, more practical experiments such as determining whether a product did or did not do its prescribed job and whether a candidate gets elected or not. There are experiments in which the trials have many outcomes that, under the right conditions, may fit this general description of being classified in one of two categories. For example, when we roll a single die, we usually consider six possible outcomes. However, if we are interested only in knowing whether a "one" shows or not, there are really only two outcomes: the "one" shows or "something else" shows. The experiments just described are called *binomial probability experiments*.

Binomial probability experiment An experiment that is made up of repeated trials that possess the following properties:
1. There are n repeated identical independent trials.
2. Each trial has two possible outcomes (success or failure).
3. $P(\text{success}) = p$, $P(\text{failure}) = q$, and $p + q = 1$.
4. The **binomial random variable** x is the count of the number of successful trials that occur; x may take on any integer value from zero to n.

Notes:
1. Properties 1 and 2 describe the two basic characteristics of any binomial experiment.
2. **Independent trials** mean that the result of one trial does not affect the probability of success on any other trial in the experiment. In other words, the probability of success remains constant throughout the entire experiment.
3. Property 3 gives the algebraic notation for each trial.
4. Property 4 concerns the algebraic notation for the complete experiment.
5. It is of utmost importance that both x and p be associated with "success."

The four-question quiz qualifies as a binomial experiment made up of four trials when all four of the answers are obtained by random guessing.

Property 1: A **trial** is the **answering of one question**, and it is repeated $n = 4$ times. The trials are **independent** because the probability of a correct answer on any one question is not affected by the answers on other questions.

Property 2: The two possible outcomes on each trial are **success = C**, correct answer, and **failure = W**, wrong answer.

Property 3: For each trial (each question): $p = P(correct) = \frac{1}{3}$ and $q = P(incorrect) = \frac{2}{3}$. $[p + q = 1 \text{ ck}]$

Property 4: For the total experiment (the quiz): $x =$ **number of correct answers** and can be any integer value from zero to $n = 4$.

EXAMPLE 5.6

DEMONSTRATING THE PROPERTIES OF A BINOMIAL PROBABILITY EXPERIMENT

Consider the experiment of rolling a die 12 times and observing a "one" or "something else." At the end of all 12 rolls, the number of "ones" is reported. The random variable x is the number of times that a "one" is observed in the $n = 12$ trials. Since "one" is the outcome of concern, it is considered "success"; therefore, $p = P(\text{one}) = \frac{1}{6}$ and $q = P(\text{not one}) = \frac{5}{6}$. This experiment is binomial.

EXAMPLE 5.7

DEMONSTRATING THE PROPERTIES OF A BINOMIAL PROBABILITY EXPERIMENT

If you were an inspector on a production line in a plant where television sets are manufactured, you would be concerned with identifying the number of defective television sets. You probably would define "success" as the occurrence of a defective television. This is not what we normally think of as success, but if we count "defective" sets in a binomial experiment, we must define "success" as a "defective." The random variable x indicates the number of defective sets found per lot of n sets; $p = P(\text{television is defective})$ and $q = P(\text{television is good})$.

The key to working with any probability experiment is its probability distribution. All binomial probability experiments have the same properties, and therefore the same organization scheme can be used to represent all of them. The *binomial probability function* allows us to find the probability for each possible value of x.

Binomial probability function For a binomial experiment, let p represent the probability of a "success" and q represent the probability of a "failure" on a single trial. Then $P(x)$, the probability that there will be exactly x successes in n trials, is

$$P(x) = \binom{n}{x}(p^x)(q^{n-x}) \quad \text{for } x = 0, 1, 2, \ldots, n \qquad (5.5)$$

When you look at the probability function, you notice that it is the product of three basic factors:

1. The number of ways that exactly x successes can occur in n trials, $\binom{n}{x}$
2. The probability of exactly x successes, p^x
3. The probability that failure will occur on the remaining $(n - x)$ trials, q^{n-x}

The number of ways that exactly x successes can occur in a set of n trials is represented by the symbol $\binom{n}{x}$, which must always be a positive integer. This term is called the **binomial coefficient** and is found by using the formula

$$\binom{n}{x} = \frac{n!}{x!(n - x)!} \qquad (5.6)$$

Notes:
1. $n!$ ("*n factorial*") is an abbreviation for the product of the sequence of integers starting with n and ending with one. For example, $3! = 3 \cdot 2 \cdot 1 = 6$ and $5! = 5 \cdot 4 \cdot 3 \cdot 2 \cdot 1 = 120$. There is one special case, $0!$, that is defined to be 1. For more information about **factorial notation**, see the *Student Solutions Manual*.
2. The values for $n!$ and $\binom{n}{x}$ can be readily found using most scientific calculators.
3. The binomial coefficient $\binom{n}{x}$ is equivalent to the number of combinations $_nC_x$, the symbol most likely on your calculator.
4. See the *Student Solutions Manual* for general information on the binomial coefficient.

Let's reconsider Example 5.5 (pp. 238–240): A coin is tossed three times and we observe the number of heads that occur in the three tosses. This is a binomial experiment because it displays all the properties of a binomial experiment:

1. There are $n = 3$ repeated **independent** trials (each coin toss is a separate trial, and the outcome of any one trial has no effect on the probability of another trial).
2. Each trial (each toss of the coin) results in one of two possible outcomes: success = **heads** (what we are counting) or failuare = **tails**.
3. The probability of success is $p = P(\text{H}) = \textbf{0.5}$, and the probability of failure is $q = P(\text{T}) = \textbf{0.5}$. $[p + q = 0.5 + 0.5 = 1 \text{ⓒⓚ}]$
4. The random variable x is the **number of heads** that occur in the three trials. x will assume exactly one of the values **0, 1, 2, or 3** when the experiment is complete.

The binomial probability function for the tossing of three coins is

$$P(x) = \binom{n}{x}(p^x) \ (q^{n-x}) = \binom{3}{x}(0.5)^x(0.5)^{3-x} \quad \text{for} \quad x = 0, 1, 2, 3$$

FYI In Table 5.6 (p. 239), $P(1) = \frac{3}{8}$. Here, $P(1) = 0.375$ and $\frac{3}{8} = 0.375$.

Let's find the probability of $x = 1$ using the preceding binomial probability function:

$$P(x = 1) = \binom{3}{1}(0.5)^1(0.5)^2 = 3(0.5)(0.25) = \textbf{0.375}$$

Note that this is the same value found in Example 5.5 (p. 238).

EXAMPLE 5.8

DETERMINING A BINOMIAL EXPERIMENT AND ITS PROBABILITIES

Consider an experiment that calls for drawing five cards, one at a time with replacement, from a well-shuffled deck of playing cards. The drawn card is identified as a spade or not a spade, it is returned to the deck, the deck is reshuffled, and so on. The random variable x is the number of spades observed in the set of five drawings. Is this a binomial experiment? Let's identify the four properties.

1. There are **five repeated drawings**; **$n = 5$**. These individual trials are **independent** because the drawn card is returned to the deck and the deck is reshuffled before the next drawing.

2. Each drawing is a trial, and each drawing has two outcomes: **spade** or **not spade**.

3. $p = P(\text{spade}) = \frac{13}{52}$ and $q = P(\text{not spade}) = \frac{39}{52}$

4. x is the **number of spades** recorded upon completion of the five trials; the possible values are **0, 1, 2, . . . , 5**.

The binomial probability function is

$$P(x) = \binom{5}{x}\left(\frac{13}{52}\right)^x\left(\frac{39}{52}\right)^{5-x} = \binom{5}{x}\left(\frac{1}{4}\right)^x\left(\frac{3}{4}\right)^{5-x} = \binom{5}{x}(0.25)^x(0.75)^{5-x}$$

$$\text{for } x = 0,\ 1, \ldots,\ 5$$

$$P(0) = \binom{5}{0}(0.25)^0(0.75)^5 = (1)(1)(0.2373) = \mathbf{0.2373}$$

$$P(1) = \binom{5}{1}(0.25)^1(0.75)^4 = (5)(0.25)(0.3164) = \mathbf{0.3955}$$

$$P(2) = \binom{5}{2}(0.25)^2(0.75)^3 = (10)(0.0625)(0.421875) = \mathbf{0.2637}$$

$$P(3) = \binom{5}{3}(0.25)^3(0.75)^2 = (10)(0.15625)(0.5625) = \mathbf{0.0879}$$

The two remaining probabilities are left for you to compute in Exercise 5.52.

FYI Answer: five

The preceding distribution of probabilities indicates that the single most likely value of x is one, the event of observing exactly one spade in a hand of five cards. What is the least likely number of spades that would be observed?

EXAMPLE 5.9

BINOMIAL PROBABILITY OF "BAD EGGS"

The manager of Steve's Food Market guarantees that none of his cartons of a dozen eggs will contain more than one bad egg. If a carton contains more than one bad egg, he will replace the whole dozen and allow the customer to keep the original eggs. If the probability that an individual egg is bad is 0.05, what is the probability that the manager will have to replace a given carton of eggs?

 Video tutorial available—logon and learn more at cengagebrain.com

Solution

At first glance, the manager's situation appears to fit the properties of a binomial experiment if we let x be the number of bad eggs found in a carton of a dozen eggs, let $p = P(bad) = 0.05$, and let the inspection of each egg be a trial that results in finding a "bad" or "not bad" egg. There will be $n = 12$ trials to account for the 12 eggs in a carton. However, trials of a binomial experiment must be independent; therefore, we will assume that the quality of one egg in a carton is independent of the quality of any of the other eggs. (This may be a big assumption! But with this assumption, we will be able to use the binomial probability distribution as our model.) Now, based on this assumption, we will be able to find/estimate the probability that the manager will have to make good on his guarantee. The probability function associated with this experiment will be:

$$P(x) = \binom{12}{x}(0.05)^x(0.95)^{12-x} \qquad \text{for } x = 0, 1, 2, \ldots, 12$$

The probability that the manager will replace a dozen eggs is the probability that $x = 2, 3, 4, \ldots, 12$. Recall that $\Sigma P(x) = 1$; that is,

$$P(0) + P(1) + P(2) + \cdots + P(12) = 1$$

$$P(\text{replacement}) = P(2) + P(3) + \cdots + P(12) = 1 - [P(0) + P(1)]$$

It is easier to find the probability of replacement by finding $P(x = 0)$ and $P(x = 1)$ and subtracting their total from 1 than by finding all of the other probabilities. We have

$$P(x) = \binom{12}{x}(0.05)^x(0.95)^{12-x}$$

$$P(0) = \binom{12}{0}(0.05)^0(0.95)^{12} = \mathbf{0.540}$$

$$P(1) = \binom{12}{1}(0.05)^1(0.95)^{11} = \mathbf{0.341}$$

$$P(\text{replacement}) = 1 - (0.540 + 0.341) = \mathbf{0.119}$$

If $p = 0.05$ is correct, then the manager will be busy replacing cartons of eggs. If he replaces 11.9% of all the cartons of eggs he sells, he certainly will be giving away a substantial proportion of his eggs. This suggests that he should adjust his guarantee (or market better eggs). For example, if he were to replace a carton of eggs only when four or more were found to be bad, he would expect to replace only 3 out of 1000 cartons $[1.0 - (0.540 + 0.341 + 0.099 + 0.017)]$, or 0.3% of the cartons sold. Notice that the manager will be able to control his "risk" (probability of replacement) if he adjusts the value of the random variable stated in his guarantee.

Note: The value of many binomial probabilities for values of $n \leq 15$ and common values of p are found in Table 2 of Appendix B. In this example, we have $n = 12$ and $p = 0.05$, and we want the probabilities for $x = 0$ and 1. We need to locate the section of Table 2 where $n = 12$, find the column headed $p = 0.05$, and read the numbers across from $x = 0$ and $x = 1$. We find .540 and .341, as shown in Table 5.8. (Look up these values in Table 2 in Appendix B.)

TABLE 5.8
Excerpt of Table 2 in Appendix B, Binomial Probabilities

								p							
n	x	0.01	0.05	0.10	0.20	0.30	0.40	0.50	0.60	0.70	0.80	0.90	0.95	0.99	x
⋮															
12	0	.886	.540	.282	.069	.014	.002	0+	0+	0+	0+	0+	0+	0+	0
	1	.107	.341	.377	.206	.071	.017	.003	0+	0+	0+	0+	0+	0+	1
	2	.006	.099	.230	.283	.168	.064	.016	.002	0+	0+	0+	0+	0+	2
	3	0+	.017	.085	.236	.240	.142	.054	.012	.001	0+	0+	0+	0+	3
	4	0+	.002	.021	.133	.231	.213	.121	.042	.008	.001	0+	0+	0+	4
⋮															

Note: A convenient notation to identify the binomial probability distribution for a binomial experiment with $n = 12$ and $p = 0.05$ is $B(12, 0.05)$. $B(12, 0.05)$, read *"binomial distribution for $n = 12$ and $p = 0.05$,"* represents the entire distribution or "block" of probabilities shown in purple in Table 5.8. When used in combination with the $P(x)$ notation, $P(x = 1 | B(12, 0.05))$ indicates the probability of $x = 1$ from this distribution, or 0.341, as shown on Table 5.8.

TECHNOLOGY INSTRUCTIONS: BINOMIAL AND CUMULATIVE BINOMIAL PROBABILITIES

MINITAB

For binomial probabilities, input x values into C1; then continue with:

Choose: **Calc > Probability Distributions > Binomial**
Select: **Probability***
Enter: Number of trials: **n**
          Event probability: **p**
Select: **Input column**
Enter: **C1**
          Optional Storage: **C2 (not necessary) > OK**

Or
Select: **Input constant**
Enter: **One single x value > OK**

*For cumulative binomial probabilities, repeat the preceding commands but replace the probability selection with:
Select: **Cumulative Probability**

Excel

For binomial probabilities, input x values into column A and activate the column B cell across from the first x value; then continue with:

Choose: **Insert function, f_x > Statistical > BINOMDIST > OK**
Enter: Number_s: **(A1:A4 or select "x value" cells)**
          Trials: **n**
          Probability_s: **p**
          Cumulative: **false* (gives individual probabilities) > OK**

Drag: **Bottom-right corner of probability value cell in column B down to give other probabilities**

*For cumulative binomial probabilities, repeat the preceding commands but replace the false cumulative with:
Cumulative: **true (gives cumulative probabilities) > OK**

TI-83/84 Plus

To obtain a complete list of probabilities for a particular n and p, continue with:

Choose: **2nd > DISTR > 0:binompdf(**
Enter: **n, p)**

Use the right arrow key to scroll through the probabilities.
To scroll through a vertical list in L1:

Choose: **STO → > L1 > ENTER**
                STAT > EDIT > 1:Edit

To obtain individual probabilities for a particular n, p, and x, continue with:

Choose: **2nd > DISTR > 0:binompdf(**
Enter: **n, p, x)**

To obtain cumulative probabilities for $x = 0$ to $x = n$ for a particular n and p, continue with:

Choose: **2nd > DISTR > A:binomcdf(**
Enter: **n, p)*** (see previous for scrolling through probabilities)

*To obtain individual cumulative probabilities for a particular n, p, and x, repeat the preceding commands but replace the enter with:
Enter: **n, p, x)**

A P P L I E D   E X A M P L E   5 . 1 0

LIVING WITH THE LAW

WHAT IS AN AFFIRMATIVE ACTION PROGRAM (AAP)?

As a condition of doing business with the federal government, federal contractors meeting certain contract and employee population levels agree to prepare, in accordance with federal regulations at 41 CFR 60-1, 60-2, etc., an Affirmative Action Program (AAP). A contractor's AAP is a combination of numerical reports, commitments of action and description of policies. A quick overview of an AAP based on the federal regulations (41 CFR 60-2.10), is as follows:

AAPs must be developed for
- Minorities and women (41 CFR 60-1 and 60-2)
- Special disabled veterans, Vietnam era veterans, and other covered veterans (41 CFR 60-250)
- Individuals with disabilities (41 CFR 60-741)

Source: http://eeosource.peopleclick.com/aap/

The AAP regulations do not endorse the use of a specific test for determining whether the percentage of minorities or women is less than would be reasonably expected. However, several tests are commonly used. One of the tests is called the *exact binomial test* as defined here.

EXACT BINOMIAL TEST

The variables used are:

T = The total number of employees in the job group

M = The number of females or minorities in the job group

A = The availability percentage of females or minorities for the job group

This test involves the calculation of a probability, denoted as P, and the comparison of that probability to 0.05. If P is less than or equal to 0.05, the percentage of minorities or women is considered to be "less than would be reasonably expected." The formula for calculating P is as follows:

1. Calculate probability, Q, the cumulative binomial probability for the binomial probability distribution with n = T, x = M, and p = A/100.
2. If Q is less than or equal to 0.5, then $P = 2Q$; otherwise, $P = Q$.

For example, if T = 50 employees and M = 2 females, A = 6% female availability.

Using a computer, the value Q is found: $Q = 0.41625$. Since Q is less than 0.5, $P = 2Q = 0.8325$. P, 0.8325, is greater than 0.05, so the percentage of women is found to be "**not** less than would be reasonably expected."

Mean and Standard Deviation of the Binomial Distribution

The mean and standard deviation of a theoretical binomial probability distribution can be found by using these two formulas:

Mean of Binomial Distribution

$$\mu = np \tag{5.7}$$

and

Standard Deviation of Binomial Distribution

$$\sigma = \sqrt{npq} \tag{5.8}$$

The formula for the mean, μ, seems appropriate: the number of trials multiplied by the probability of "success." [Recall that the mean number of correct answers on the binomial quiz (Answer 5, p. 246) was expected to be $\frac{1}{3}$ of 4, $4(\frac{1}{3})$, or np.] The formula for the standard deviation, σ, is not as easily understood. Thus, at this point it is appropriate to look at an example that demonstrates that formulas (5.7) and (5.8) yield the same results as formulas (5.1), (5.3a), and (5.4).

In Example 5.5 (pp. 236–238), x is the number of heads in three coin tosses, $n = 3$, and $p = \frac{1}{2} = 0.5$. Using formula (5.7), we find the mean of x to be

$$\mu = np = (3)(0.5) = 1.5$$

(Continued)
be used at Scotland Yard in 1901, and was soon used throughout the world as an identifier in criminal investigations.

Using formula (5.8), we find the standard deviation of x to be

$$\sigma = \sqrt{npq} = \sqrt{(3)(0.5)(0.5)} = \sqrt{0.75} = 0.866 = 0.87$$

Now look back at the solution for Example 5.5 (p. 237). Note that the results are the same, regardless of which formula you use. However, formulas (5.7) and (5.8) are much easier to use when x is a binomial random variable.

E X A M P L E   5 . 1 1

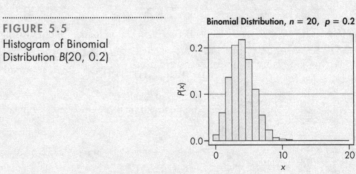

CALCULATING THE MEAN AND STANDARD DEVIATION OF A BINOMIAL DISTRIBUTION

Find the mean and standard deviation of the binomial distribution when $n = 20$ and $p = \frac{1}{5}$ (or 0.2, in decimal form). Recall that the "binomial distribution where $n = 20$ and $p = 0.2$" has the probability function

$$P(x) = \binom{20}{x}(0.2)^x(0.8)^{20-x} \quad \text{for} \quad x = 0, 1, 2, \ldots, 20$$

and a corresponding distribution with 21 x values and 21 probabilities, as shown in the distribution chart, Table 5.9, and on the histogram in Figure 5.5.

TABLE 5.9
Binomial Distribution: $n = 20$, $p = 0.2$

x	P(x)
0	0.012
1	0.058
2	0.137
3	0.205
4	0.218
5	0.175
6	0.109
7	0.055
8	0.022
9	0.007
10	0.002
11	0+
12	0+
13	0+
⋮	⋮
20	0+

FIGURE 5.5

Histogram of Binomial Distribution $B(20, 0.2)$

Binomial Distribution, $n = 20$, $p = 0.2$

Let's find the mean and the standard deviation of this distribution of x using formulas (5.7) and (5.8):

$$\mu = np = (20)(0.2) = \mathbf{4.0}$$
$$\sigma = \sqrt{npq} = \sqrt{(20)(0.2)(0.8)} = \sqrt{3.2} = \mathbf{1.79}$$

FIGURE 5.6

Histogram of Binomial Distribution $B(20, 0.2)$

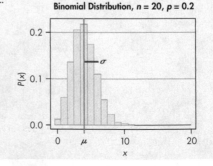

Binomial Distribution, $n = 20$, $p = 0.2$

Video tutorial available—logon and learn more at cengagebrain.com

Figure 5.6 shows the mean, $\mu = 4$ (shown by the location of the vertical blue line along the x-axis), relative to the variable x. This 4.0 is the mean value expected for x, the number of successes in each random sample of size 20 drawn from a population with $p = 0.2$. Figure 5.6 also shows the size of the standard deviation, $\sigma = 1.79$ (as shown by the length of the horizontal red line segment). It is the expected standard deviation for the values of the random variable x that occur in samples of size 20 drawn from this same population.

▣ SECTION 5.3 EXERCISES

5.39 Consider the four-question multiple-choice quiz presented at the beginning of this section (pp. 244–246).

a. Explain why the four questions represent four independent trials.

b. Explain why the number 4 is multiplied into the $P(x = 1)$.

c. In Answer 5 on page 246, where did $\frac{1}{3}$ and 4 come from? Why multiply them to find an expected average?

5.40 Identify the properties that make flipping a coin 50 times and keeping track of heads a binomial experiment.

5.41 State a very practical reason why the defective item in an industrial situation might be defined to be the "success" in a binomial experiment.

5.42 What does it mean for the trials to be independent in a binomial experiment?

5.43 Evaluate each of the following.

a. $4!$ b. $7!$ c. $0!$ d. $\dfrac{6!}{2!}$

e. $\dfrac{5!}{2!3!}$ f. $\dfrac{6!}{4!(6-4)!}$ g. $(0.3)^4$ h. $\dbinom{7}{3}$

i. $\dbinom{5}{2}$ j. $\dbinom{3}{0}$ k. $\dbinom{4}{1}(0.2)^1(0.8)^3$

l. $\dbinom{5}{0}(0.3)^0(0.7)^5$

5.44 Show that each of the following is true for any values of n and k. Use two specific sets of values for n and k to show that each is true.

a. $\dbinom{n}{0} = 1$ and $\dbinom{n}{n} = 1$

b. $\dbinom{n}{1} = n$ and $\dbinom{n}{n-1} = n$ c. $\dbinom{n}{k} = \dbinom{n}{n-k}$

5.45 A carton containing 100 T-shirts is inspected. Each T-shirt is rated "first quality" or "irregular." After all 100 T-shirts have been inspected, the number of irregulars is reported as a random variable. Explain why x is a binomial random variable.

5.46 A die is rolled 20 times, and the number of "fives" that occur is reported as being the random variable. Explain why x is a binomial random variable.

5.47 Four cards are selected, one at a time, from a standard deck of 52 playing cards. Let x represent the number of aces drawn in the set of four cards.

a. If this experiment is completed without replacement, explain why x is not a binomial random variable.

b. If this experiment is completed with replacement, explain why x is a binomial random variable.

5.48 The employees at a General Motors assembly plant are polled as they leave work. Each is asked, "What brand of automobile are you riding home in?" The random variable to be reported is the number of each brand mentioned. Is x a binomial random variable? Justify your answer.

5.49 Consider a binomial experiment made up of three trials with outcomes of success, S, and failure, F, where $P(S) = p$ and $P(F) = q$.

a. Complete the accompanying tree diagram. Label all branches completely.

b. In column (b) of the tree diagram, express the probability of each outcome represented by the branches as a product of powers of p and q.

(continue on page 256)

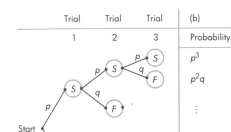

Trial	Trial	Trial	(b)	(c)
1	2	3	Probability	x

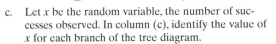

p^3 3

p^2q 2

⋮   ⋮

c. Let x be the random variable, the number of successes observed. In column (c), identify the value of x for each branch of the tree diagram.

d. Notice that all the products in column (b) are made up of three factors and that the value of the random variable is the same as the exponent for the number p. Write the equation for the binomial probability function for this situation.

5.50 Draw a tree diagram picturing a binomial experiment of four trials.

5.51 Use the probability function for three coin tosses as demonstrated on page 239 and verify the probabilities for $x = 0, 2,$ and 3.

5.52 a. Calculate $P(4)$ and $P(5)$ for Example 5.8 on page 249.

     b. Verify that the six probabilities $P(0), P(1),$ $P(2), \ldots, P(5)$ form a probability distribution.

5.53 Skillbuilder Applet Exercise demonstrates calculating a binomial probability along with a visual interpretation. Suppose that you buy 20 plants from a nursery and the nursery claims that 95% of its plants survive when planted. Inputting $n = 20$ and $p = 0.95$, compute the following:

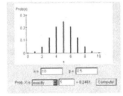

a. The probability that all 20 will survive

b. The probability that at most 16 survive

c. The probability that at least 18 survive

5.54 Skillbuilder Applet Exercise demonstrates calculating a binomial probability along with a visual interpretation. Suppose that you are in a class of 30 students and it is assumed that approximately

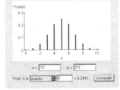

11% of the population is left-handed. Inputting $n = 30$ and $p = 0.11$, compute the following:

a. The probability that exactly five students are left-handed

b. The probability that at most four students are left-handed

c. The probability that at least six students are left-handed

5.55 If x is a binomial random variable, calculate the probability of x for each case.

a. $n = 4, x = 1, p = 0.3$ b. $n = 3, x = 2, p = 0.8$

c. $n = 2, x = 0, p = \dfrac{1}{4}$ d. $n = 5, x = 2, p = \dfrac{1}{3}$

e. $n = 4, x = 2, p = 0.5$ f. $n = 3, x = 3, p = \dfrac{1}{6}$

5.56 If x is a binomial random variable, use Table 2 in Appendix B to determine the probability of x for each of the following:

a. $n = 10, x = 8, p = 0.3$ b. $n = 8, x = 7, p = 0.95$

c. $n = 15, x = 3, p = 0.05$ d. $n = 12, x = 12, p = 0.99$

e. $n = 9, x = 0, p = 0.5$ f. $n = 6, x = 1, p = 0.01$

g. Explain the meaning of the symbol $0+$ that appears in Table 2.

5.57 Test the following function to determine whether or not it is a binomial probability function. List the distribution of probabilities and sketch a histogram.

$$T(x) = \binom{5}{x}\left(\frac{1}{2}\right)^{x}\left(\frac{1}{2}\right)^{5-x} \quad \text{for} \quad x = 0, 1, 2, 3, 4, 5$$

5.58 Let x be a random variable with the following probability distribution:

x	0	1	2	3
P(x)	0.4	0.3	0.2	0.1

Does x have a binomial distribution? Justify your answer.

5.59 According to a December 2008 *Self* magazine online poll, 66% responded "Yes" to "Do you want to relive your college days?" What is the probability that exactly half of the next 10 randomly selected poll participants also respond "Yes" to this question?

5.60 According to a National Safety Council report, up to 78% of automobile collisions are a result of distractions such as text messaging, phoning a pal, or fumbling with the stereo. Consider a randomly selected group of 18 reported collisions.

Source: *Self* magazine, December 2008, "Cruise Control"

a.   What is the probability that all of the collisions will be due to the distractions mentioned?

b.   What is the probability that 15 of the collisions will be due to the distractions mentioned?

5.61 According to the article "Season's Cleaning," the U.S. Department of Energy reports that 25% of people with two-car garages don't have room to park any cars inside.

Source: January 1, 2009, Rochester D&C

Assuming this to be true, what is the probability of the following?

a.   Exactly 3 two-car-garage households of a random sample of 5 two-car-garage households do not have room to park any cars inside.

b.   Exactly 7 two-car-garage households of a random sample of 15 two-car-garage households do not have room to park any cars inside.

c.   Exactly 20 two-car-garage households of a random sample of 30 two-car-garage households do not have room to park any cars inside.

5.62 Can playing video games as a child and teenager lead to a gambling or substance addiction? According to the April 11, 2009, *USA Today* article "Kids show addiction symptoms," research published in the Journal *Psychological Science* found that 8.5% of video-game-playing children and teens displayed behavioral signs that may indicate addiction. Suppose a randomly selected group of 30 video-gaming eighth-grade students is selected.

a.   What is the probability that exactly 2 will display addiction symptoms?

b.   If the study also indicated that 12% of video-gaming boys display addiction symptoms, what is the probability that exactly 2 out of the 17 boys in the group will display addiction symptoms?

c.   If the study also indicated that 3% of video-gaming girls display addiction symptoms, what is the probability that exactly 2 out of the 13 girls in the group will display addiction symptoms?

5.63 Of the parts produced by a particular machine, 0.5% are defective. If a random sample of 10 parts produced by this machine contains 2 or more defective parts, the machine is shut down for repairs. Find the probability that the machine will be shut down for repairs based on this sampling plan.

5.64 As a quality-control inspector of toy trucks, you have observed that 3% of the time, the wooden wheels are bored off-center. If six wooden wheels are used on each toy truck, what is the probability that a randomly selected toy truck has no off-center wheels?

5.65 The survival rate during a risky operation for patients with no other hope of survival is 80%. What is the probability that exactly four of the next five patients survive this operation?

5.66 Of all the trees planted by a landscaping firm, 90% survive. What is the probability that 8 or more of the 10 trees they just planted will survive? (Find the answer by using a table.)

5.67 In the biathlon event of the Olympic Games, a participant skis cross-country and on four intermittent occasions stops at a rifle range and shoots a set of five shots. If the center of the target is hit, no penalty points are assessed. If a particular man has a history of hitting the center of the target with 90% of his shots, what is the probability of the following?

a.   He will hit the center of the target with all five of his next set of five shots.

b.   He will hit the center of the target with at least four of his next set of five shots. (Assume independence.)

5.68 The May 26, 2009, *USA Today* Snapshot "Overcoming identity theft" reported the results from a poll of identity-theft victims. According to the source, Affinion Security Center, 20% of the victims stated that it took "one week to one month" to recover from identity theft. A group of 14 identity-theft victims are randomly selected in your hometown.

a.   What is the probability that none of them was able to recover from the theft in one week to one month?

b.   What is the probability that exactly 3 were able to recover from the theft in one week to one month?

c.   What is the probability that at least 5 were able to recover from the theft in one week to one month?

d.   What is the probability that no more than 4 were able to recover from the theft in one week to one month?

5.69 A January 2005 survey of bikers, commissioned by the Progressive Group of Insurance Companies, showed that 40% of bikers have body art, such as tattoos and piercings. A group of 10 bikers are in the process of buying motorcycle insurance.

Source: http://www.syracuse.com/

a.   What is the probability that none of the 10 has any body art?

b.   What is the probability that exactly 3 have some body art?

c.   What is the probability that at least 4 have some body art?

(continue on page 258)

d. What is the probability that no more than 2 have some body art?

5.70 Consider the manager of Steve's Food Market as illustrated in Example 5.9. What would be the manager's "risk" if he bought "better" eggs, say with $P(\text{bad}) = 0.01$ using the "more than one" guarantee?

5.71 If boys and girls are equally likely to be born, what is the probability that in a randomly selected family of six children, there will be at least one boy? (Find the answer using a formula.)

5.72 One-fourth of a certain breed of rabbits are born with long hair. What is the probability that in a litter of six rabbits, exactly three will have long hair? (Find the answer by using a formula.)

5.73 Find the mean and standard deviation for the binomial random variable x with $n = 30$ and $p = 0.6$, using formulas (5.7) and (5.8).

5.74 Consider the binomial distribution where $n = 11$ and $p = 0.05$.

a. Find the mean and standard deviation using formulas (5.7) and (5.8).

b. Using Table 2 in Appendix B, list the probability distribution and draw a histogram.

c. Locate μ and σ on the histogram.

5.75 Consider the binomial distribution where $n = 11$ and $p = 0.05$ (see Exercise 5.74).

a. Use the distribution [Exercise 5.74(b) or Table 2] and find the mean and standard deviation using formulas (5.1), (5.3a), and (5.4).

b. Compare the results of part a with the answers found in Exercise 5.74(a).

5.76 Given the binomial probability function
$$P(x) = \binom{5}{x} \cdot \left(\tfrac{1}{2}\right)^x \cdot \left(\tfrac{1}{2}\right)^{5-x} \quad \text{for} \quad x = 0, 1, 2, 3, 4, 5$$

a. Calculate the mean and standard deviation of the random variable by using formulas (5.1), (5.3a), and (5.4).

b. Calculate the mean and standard deviation using formulas (5.7) and (5.8).

c. Compare the results of parts a and b.

5.77 Find the mean and standard deviation of x for each of the following binomial random variables:

a. The number of tails seen in 50 tosses of a quarter

b. The number of left-handed students in a classroom of 40 students (Assume that 11% of the population is left-handed.)

c. The number of cars found to have unsafe tires among the 400 cars stopped at a roadblock for inspection (Assume that 6% of all cars have one or more unsafe tires.)

d. The number of melon seeds that germinate when a package of 50 seeds is planted (The package states that the probability of germination is 0.88.)

5.78 Find the mean and standard deviation for each of the following binomial random variables in parts a–c:

a. The number of sixes seen in 50 rolls of a die

b. The number of defective televisions in a shipment of 125 (The manufacturer claimed that 98% of the sets were operative.)

c. The number of operative televisions in a shipment of 125 (The manufacturer claimed that 98% of the sets were operative.)

d. How are parts b and c related? Explain.

5.79 According to United Mileage Plus Visa (November 22, 2004), 41% of passengers say they "put on the earphones" to avoid being bothered by their seatmates during flights. To show how important, or not important, the earphones are to people, consider the variable x to be the number of people in a sample of 12 who say they "put on the earphones" to avoid their seatmates. Assume the 41% is true for the whole population of airline travelers and that a random sample is selected.

a. Is x a binomial random variable? Justify your answer.

b. Find the probability that $x = 4$ or 5.

c. Find the mean and standard deviation of x.

d. Draw a histogram of the distribution of x: label it completely, highlight the area representing $x = 4$ and $x = 5$, draw a vertical line at the value of the mean, and mark the location of x that is 1 standard deviation larger than the mean.

5.80 According to the *USA Today* Snapshot "Knowing drug addicts," 45% of Americans know somebody who became addicted to a drug other than alcohol. Assuming this to be true, what is the probability of the following?

a. Exactly 3 people of a random sample of 5 know someone who became addicted. Calculate the value.

b. Exactly 7 people of a random sample of 15 know someone who became addicted. Estimate using Table 2 in Appendix B.

c. At least 7 people of a random sample of 15 know someone who became addicted. Estimate using Table 2.

d. No more than 7 people of a random sample of 15 know someone who became addicted. Estimate using Table 2.

5.81 a. Use a calculator or computer to find the probability that $x = 3$ in a binomial experiment where $n = 12$ and $p = 0.30$: $P(x = 3 | B(12, 0.30))$. (See Note about this notation on p. 251.)

b. Use Table 5.8 to verify the answer in part a.

5.82 If the binomial $(q + p)$ is squared, the result is $(q + p)^2 = q^2 + 2qp + p^2$. For the binomial experiment with $n = 2$, the probability of no successes in two trials is q^2 (the first term in the expansion), the probability of one success in two trials is $2qp$ (the second term in the expansion), and the probability of two successes in two trials is p^2 (the third term in the expansion). Find $(q + p)^3$ and compare its terms to the binomial probabilities for $n = 3$ trials.

5.83 Use a computer to find the probabilities for all possible x values for a binomial experiment where $n = 30$ and $p = 0.35$.

MINITAB
Choose: **Calc > Make Patterned Data > Simple Set of Numbers**
Enter: **Store patterned data in: C1**
            From first value: 0
            To last value: 30
            In steps of: 1 > OK

Continue with the binomial probability MINITAB commands on page 251, using $n = 30$, $p = 0.35$, and C2 for optional storage.

Excel
Enter: **0,1,2, . . . , 30 into column A**

Continue with the binomial probability Excel commands on page 251–252, using $n = 30$ and $p = 0.35$.

TI-83/84 Plus
Use the binomial probability TI-83 commands on page 252, using $n = 30$ and $p = 0.35$.

5.84. Use a computer to find the cumulative probabilities for all possible x values for a binomial experiment where $n = 45$ and $p = 0.125$.

a. Explain why there are so many 1.000s listed.

b. Explain what is represented by each number listed.

MINITAB
Choose: **Calc > Make Patterned Data > Simple Set of Numbers . . .**
Enter: **Store patterned data in: C1**
            From first value: 0
            To last value: 45
            In steps of: 1 > OK

Continue with the **cumulative** binomial probability MINITAB commands on page 251, using $n = 45$, $p = 0.125$, and C2 as optional storage.

Excel
Enter: **0,1,2, . . . , 45 into column A**

Continue with the **cumulative** binomial probability Excel commands on pages 251–252, using $n = 45$ and $p = 0.125$.

TI-83/84 Plus
Use the **cumulative** binomial probability TI-83 commands on page 252, using $n = 45$ and $p = 0.125$.

5.85 Where does all that Halloween candy go? The October 2004 issue of *Readers' Digest* quoted that "90% of parents admit taking Halloween candy from their children's trick-or-treat bags." The source of information was the National Confectioners Association. Suppose that 25 parents are interviewed. What is the probability that 20 or more took Halloween candy from their children's trick-or-treat bags?

5.86 Harris Interactive conducted a survey for Tylenol PM asking U.S. drivers what they do if they are driving while drowsy. The results were reported in a *USA Today* Snapshot on January 18, 2005, with 40% of the respondents saying they "open the windows" to fight off sleep. Suppose that 35 U.S. drivers are interviewed. What is the probability that between 10 and 20 of the drivers will say they "open the windows" to fight off sleep?

5.87 Of all mortgage foreclosures in the United States, 48% are caused by disability. People who are injured or ill cannot work—they then lose their jobs and thus their incomes. With no income, they cannot make their mortgage payments and the bank forecloses.

Source: http://www.ricedelman.com

Given that 20 mortgage foreclosures are audited by a large lending institution, find the probability of the following:

a. Five or fewer of the foreclosures are due to a disability.

b. At least three foreclosures are due to a disability.

5.88 The increase in Internet usage over the past few years has been phenomenal, as demonstrated by the February 2004 report from the Pew Internet & American Life Project. The survey of Americans 65 or older (about 8 million adults) reported that 22% have access to the Internet. By contrast, 58% of 50 to 64-year-olds, 75% of 30- to 49-year-olds, and 77% of 18- to 29-year-olds currently go online.

Source: http://www.suddenlysenior.com/

Suppose that 50 adults in each age group are to be interviewed.

a. What is the probability that "have Internet access" is the response of 10 to 20 adults in the 65 or older group?

b. What is the probability that "have Internet access" is the response of 30 to 40 adults in the 50- to 64-year-old group?

c. What is the probability that "have Internet access" is the response of 30 to 40 adults in the 30- to 49-year-old group?

d. What is the probability that "have Internet access" is the response of 30 to 40 adults in the 18- to 29-year-old group?

e. Why are the answers for parts a and d nearly the same? Explain.

f. What effect did the various values of p have on the probabilities? Explain.

5.89 A binomial random variable has a mean equal to 200 and a standard deviation of 10. Find the values of n and p.

5.90 The probability of success on a single trial of a binomial experiment is known to be $\frac{1}{4}$. The random variable x, number of successes, has a mean value of 80. Find the number of trials involved in this experiment and the standard deviation of x.

5.91 A binomial random variable x is based on 15 trials with the probability of success equal to 0.4. Find the probability that this variable will take on a value more than 2 standard deviations above the mean.

5.92 A binomial random variable x is based on 15 trials with the probability of success equal to 0.2. Find the probability that this variable will take on a value more than 2 standard deviations from the mean.

5.93 a. When using the exact binomial test (Applied Example 5.10, pp. 252–253), what is the interpretation of the situation when the calculated value of P is less than or equal to 0.05?

b. When using the exact binomial test, what is the interpretation of the situation when the calculated value of P is larger than 0.05?

c. An employer has 15 employees in a very specialized job group, of which 2 are minorities. Based on 2000 census information, the proportion of minorities available for this type of work is 5%. Using the binomial test, is the percentage of minorities what would be reasonably expected?

d. For this same employer and the same job group, there are three female employees. The percentage of female availability for this position is 50%. Does it appear that the percentage of females is what would be reasonably expected?

5.94 Extended to overtime in game 7 on the road in the 2002 NBA play-offs, the two-time defending champion Los Angeles Lakers did what they do best—thrived when the pressure was at its highest. Both of the Lakers' star players had their chance at the foul line late in overtime.

a. With 1:27 minutes left in overtime and the game tied at 106–106, Shaquille (Shaq) O'Neal was at the line for two free-throw attempts. He has a history of making 0.555 of his free-throw attempts, and during this game, prior to these two shots, he had made 9 of his 13 attempts. Justify the statement "The law of averages was working against him."

b. With 0:06 seconds left in overtime and the game score standing at 110–106, Kobe Bryant was at the line for two free-throw shots. He has a history of making 0.829 of his free throws, and during this game, prior to these two shots, he had made 6 of his 8 attempts. Justify the statement "The law of averages was working for him."

Both players made both shots, and the series with the Sacramento Kings was over.

5.95 Imprints Galore buys T-shirts (to be imprinted with an item of the customer's choice) from a manufacturer who guarantees that the shirts have been inspected and that no more than 1% are imperfect in any way. The shirts arrive in boxes of 12. Let x be the number of imperfect shirts found in any one box.

a. List the probability distribution and draw the histogram of x.

b. What is the probability that any one box has no imperfect shirts?

c. What is the probability that any one box has no more than one imperfect shirt?

d. Find the mean and standard deviation of x.

e. What proportion of the distribution is between $\mu - \sigma$ and $\mu + \sigma$?

f. What proportion of the distribution is between $\mu - 2\sigma$ and $\mu + 2\sigma$?

g. How does this information relate to the empirical rule and Chebyshev's theorem? Explain.

h. Use a computer to simulate Imprints Galore's buying 200 boxes of shirts and observing x, the number of imperfect shirts per box of 12. Describe how the information from the simulation compares to what was expected (answers to parts a–g describe the expected results).

i. Repeat part h several times. Describe how these results compare with those of parts a–g and with part h.

MINITAB

a.

Choose:	**Calc > Make Patterned Data > Simple Set of Numbers . . .**
Enter:	Store patterned data in: **C1**
	From first value: **−1** (see note)
	To last value: **12**
	In steps of: **1 > OK**

c. Continue with the binomial probability MINITAB commands on page 251, using $n = 12$, $p = 0.01$, and C2 for optional storage.

Choose:	**Graph > Scatterplot > Simple > OK**
Enter:	Y variables: **C2** X variables: **C1**
Select:	Data view: Data Display: **Area > OK**

The graph is not a histogram, but can be converted to a histogram by double clicking on "area" of graph.

Select:	**Options** Select: **Step > OK > OK**

h. Continue with the **cumulative** binomial probability MINITAB commands on page 251, using $n = 12$, $p = 0.01$, and C3 for optional storage.

Choose:	**Calc > Random Data > Binomial**
Enter:	Number of rows of data to generate:
	200 rows of data
	Store in column **C4**
	Number of trials: **12**
	Probability: **.01 > OK**
Choose:	**Stat > Tables > Cross Tabulation**
Enter:	Categorical variables: For rows: **C4**
Select:	Display: **Total percents > OK**
Choose:	**Calc > Column Statistics**
Select:	Statistic: **Mean**
Enter:	Input variable: **C4 > OK**
Choose:	**Calc > Column Statistics**
Select:	Statistic: **Standard deviation**
Enter:	Input variable: **C4 > OK**

Continue with the histogram MINITAB commands on page 53, using the data in C4 and selecting the options: percent and midpoint with intervals 0:12/1.

Note: The binomial variable x cannot take on the value −1. The use of −1 (the next would-be class midpoint to left of 0) allows MINITAB to draw the histogram of a probability distribution. Without −1, PLOT will draw only half of the bar representing $x = 0$.

Excel

a.

Enter:	**0, 1, 2, . . . , 12 into column A**

Continue with the binomial probability Excel commands on pages 251–252, using $n = 12$ and $p = 0.01$. Activate columns A and B; then continue with:

Choose:	**Insert > Column > 1st picture**(usually)
Choose:	**Select Data > Series 1 > Remove > OK**

If necessary:

Click on:	**Anywhere clear on the chart**
	—use handles to size so x values fall under corresponding bars

Continue with the **cumulative** binomial probability Excel commands on pages 251–252, using $n = 12$, $p = 0.01$, and column C for the activated cell.

h.

Choose:	**Data > Data analysis > Random Number Generation > OK**
Enter:	Number of Variables: **1**
	Number of Random Numbers: **200**
	Distribution: **Binomial**
	p Value = **0.01**
	Number of Trials = **12**
Select:	Output Options: **Output Range**
Enter	(D1 or select cell) **> OK**
	Activate the E1 cell, then:
Choose:	**Insert function, f_x > Statistical > AVERAGE > OK**
Enter:	Number 1: **D1:D200 > OK**
	Activate the E2 cell, then:
Choose:	**Insert function, f_x > Statistical > STDEV > OK**
Enter:	Number 1: **D1:D200 > OK**

Continue with the histogram Excel commands on pages 53–54, using the data in column D and the bin range in column A.

TI-83/84 Plus

a.

Choose:	**STAT > EDIT > 1:Edit**
Enter:	**L1: 0,1,2,3,4,5,6,7,8,9,10,11,12**
Choose:	**2nd QUIT > 2nd DISTR > 0:binompdf(**
Enter:	**12, 0.01) > ENTER**
Choose:	**STO→ > L2 > ENTER**
Choose:	**2nd > STAT PLOT > 1:Plot1**
Choose:	**WINDOW**
Enter:	**0, 13, 1, − .1, .9, .1, 1**
Choose:	**TRACE > > >**

c.

Choose:	**2nd > DISTR > A:binomcdf(**
Enter:	**12, 0.01)**
Choose:	**STO→ > L3 > ENTER**
	STAT > EDIT > 1:Edit

h.

Choose:	**MATH > PRB > 7:randBin(**
Enter:	**12, .01, 200)** (takes a while to process)
Choose:	**STO→ > L4 > ENTER**

(continue on page 262)

Choose: 2nd LIST > Math > 3:mean(
Enter: L4
Choose: 2nd LIST > Math > 7:StdDev(
Enter: L4

Continue with the histogram TI-83/84 commands on page 54, using the data in column L4 and adjusting the window after the initial look using ZoomStat.

5.96 Did you ever buy an incandescent light bulb that failed (either burned out or did not work) the first time you turned the light switch on? When you put a new bulb into a light fixture, you expect it to light, and most of the time it does. Consider 8-packs of 60-watt bulbs and let x be the number of bulbs in a pack that "fail" the first time they are used. If 0.02 of all bulbs of this type fail on their first use and each 8-pack is considered a random sample,

a. List the probability distribution and draw the histogram of x.

b. What is the probability that any one 8-pack has no bulbs that fail on first use?

c. What is the probability that any one 8-pack has no more than one bulb that fails on first use?

d. Find the mean and standard deviation of x.

e. What proportion of the distribution is between $\mu - \sigma$ and $\mu + \sigma$?

f. What proportion of the distribution is between $\mu - 2\sigma$ and $\mu + 2\sigma$?

g. How does this information relate to the empirical rule and Chebyshev's theorem? Explain.

h. Use a computer to simulate testing 100 8-packs of bulbs and observing x, the number of failures per 8-pack. Describe how the information from the simulation compares with what was expected (answers to parts a–g describe the expected results).

i. Repeat part h several times. Describe how these results compare with those of parts a–g and with part h.

Chapter Review

In Retrospect

In this chapter we combined concepts of probability with some of the ideas presented in Chapter 2. We now are able to deal with distributions of probability values and find means, standard deviations, and other statistics.

In Chapter 4 we explored the concepts of mutually exclusive events and independent events. We used the addition and multiplication rules on several occasions in this chapter, but very little was said about mutual exclusiveness or independence. Recall that every time we add probabilities, as we did in each of the probability distributions, we need to know that the associated events are mutually exclusive. If you look back over the chapter, you will notice that the random variable actually requires events to be mutually exclusive; therefore, no real emphasis was placed on this concept. The same basic comment can be made in reference to the multiplication of probabilities and the concept of independent events. Throughout this chapter, probabilities were multiplied, and occasion-

ally independence was mentioned. Independence, of course, is necessary to be able to multiply probabilities.

Now, after completing Chapter 5, if we were to take a close look at some of the sets of data in Chapter 2, we would see that several problems could be reorganized to form probability distributions. Here are some examples: (1) Let x be the number of credit hours for which a student is registered this semester, paired with the percentage of the entire student body reported for each value of x. (2) Let x be the number of correct passageways through which an experimental laboratory animal passes before going down a wrong one, paired with the probability of each x value. (3) Let x be the number of college applications made other than to the college where you enrolled (Applied Example 5.3), paired with the probability of each x value. The list of examples is endless.

We are now ready to extend these concepts to continuous random variables in Chapter 6.

CourseMate The **Statistics CourseMate** site for this text brings chapter topics to life with interactive learning, study, and exam preparation tools, including quizzes and flashcards for the Vocabulary and Key Concepts that follow. The site also provides an **eBook** version of the text with highlighting and note taking capabilities. Throughout chapters, the CourseMate icon 🖥 flags concepts and examples that have corresponding interactive resources such as **video** and **animated tutorials** that demonstrate, step by step, how to solve problems; **datasets** for exercises and examples; **Skillbuilder Applets** to help you better understand concepts; **technology manuals**; and software to download including **Data Analysis Plus** (a suite of statistical macros for Excel) and **TI-83/84 Plus** programs—logon at **www.cengagebrain.com**.

Vocabulary List and Key Concepts

all-inclusive events (p. 230)
binomial coefficient (p. 248)
binomial probability experiment (p. 246)
binomial probability function (p. 247)
binomial random variable (p. 246)
constant function (p. 234)
continuous random variable (p. 231)

discrete random variable (p. 231)
experiment (p. 230)
factorial notation (p. 248)
failure (p. 246)
independent trials (p. 246)
mean of discrete random variable (p. 237)
mutually exclusive events (p. 230)
population parameter (p. 236)
probability distribution (p. 233)

probability function (p. 233)
probability histogram (p. 235)
random variable (p. 230)
sample statistic (p. 236)
standard deviation of discrete random variable (p. 237)
success (p. 246)
trial (p. 246)
variance of discrete random variable (p. 237)

Learning Outcomes

- Understand that a random variable is a numerical quantity whose value depends on the conditions and probabilities associated with an experiment. — pp. 230–231, EXP. 5.1

- Understand the difference between a discrete and a continuous random variable. — Ex. 5.4, 5.5, 5.9

- Be able to construct a discrete probability distribution based on an experiment or given function. — pp. 233–234, Ex. 5.13, 5.19

- Understand the terms *mutually exclusive* and *all-inclusive* as they apply to the variables for probability distributions. — p. 231, Ex. 5.15

- Understand the similarities and differences between frequency distributions and probability distributions. — p. 231, Ex. 5.98

- Understand and be able to utilize the two main properties of probability distributions to verify compliance. — p. 234, EXP. 5.2, Ex. 5.17, 5.97, 5.99

- Understand that a probability distribution is a theoretical probability distribution and that the mean and standard deviation (μ and σ, respectively) are parameters. — pp. 236–238, Ex. 5.98

- Compute, describe, and interpret the mean and standard deviation of a probability distribution. — EXP. 5.5, Ex. 5.26, 5.27

- Understand the key elements of a binomial experiment and be able to define x, n, p, and q. — p. 246, EXP. 5.6, 5.7

- Know and be able to calculate binomial probabilities using the binomial probability function. — EXP. 5.8, Ex. 5.55, 5.61

- Understand and be able to use Table 2 in Appendix B, Binomial Probabilities, to determine binomial probabilities. — p. 251, Ex. 5.56, 5.111

- Compute, describe, and interpret the mean and standard deviation of a binomial probability distribution. — EXP. 5.11, Ex. 5.77, 5.79

Chapter Exercises

5.97 What are the two basic properties of every probability distribution?

5.98 a. Explain the difference and the relationship between a probability distribution and a probability function.

b. Explain the difference and the relationship between a probability distribution and a frequency distribution, and explain how they relate to a population and a sample.

5.99 Verify whether or not each of the following is a probability function. State your conclusion and explain.

a. $f(x) = \dfrac{\frac{3}{4}}{x!(3-x)!}$, for $x = 0, 1, 2, 3$

b. $f(x) = 0.25$, for $x = 9, 10, 11, 12$

c. $f(x) = (3 - x)/2$, for $x = 1, 2, 3, 4$

d. $f(x) = (x^2 + x + 1)/25$, for $x = 0, 1, 2, 3$

5.100 Verify whether or not each of the following is a probability function. State your conclusion and explain.

a. $f(x) = \dfrac{3x}{8x!}$, for $x = 1, 2, 3, 4$

b. $f(x) = 0.125$, for $x = 0, 1, 2, 3$, and $f(x) = 0.25$, for $x = 4, 5$

c. $f(x) = (7 - x)/28$, for $x = 0, 1, 2, 3, 4, 5, 6, 7$

d. $f(x) = (x^2 + 1)/60$, for $x = 0, 1, 2, 3, 4, 5$

5.101 The number of ships to arrive at a harbor on any given day is a random variable represented by x. The probability distribution for x is as follows:

x	10	11	12	13	14
P(x)	0.4	0.2	0.2	0.1	0.1

Find the probability of the following for any a given day:

a. Exactly 14 ships arrive.

b. At least 12 ships arrive.

c. At most 11 ships arrive.

5.102 "How many TVs are there in your household?" was one of the questions on a questionnaire sent to 5000 people in Japan. The collected data resulted in the following distribution:

Number of TVs/Household	0	1	2	3	4	5 or more
Percentage	1.9	31.4	23.0	24.4	13.0	6.3

Source: http://www.japan-guide.com/

a. What percentage of the households have at least one television?

b. What percentage of the households have at most three televisions?

c. What percentage of the households have three or more televisions?

d. Is this a binomial probability experiment? Justify your answer.

e. Let x be the number of televisions per household. Is this a probability distribution? Explain.

f. Assign $x = 5$ for "5 or more" and find the mean and standard deviation of x.

5.103 Patients who have hip-replacement surgery experience pain the first day after surgery. Typically, the pain is measured on a subjective scale using values of 1 to 5. Let x represent the random variable, the pain score as determined by a patient. The probability distribution for x is believed to be:

x	1	2	3	4	5
P(x)	0.10	0.15	0.25	0.35	0.15

a. Find the mean of x.

b. Find the standard deviation of x.

5.104 The coffee consumption per capita in the United States is approximately 1.9 cups per day for men and 1.4 cups for women. The number of cups consumed per day, x, by women coffee drinkers is expressed as the accompanying distribution.

x	1	2	3	4	5	6	7
P(x)	0.20	0.33	0.28	0.10	0.05	0.02	0.02

a. Is this a discrete probability distribution? Explain.

b. Draw a histogram of the distribution.

c. Find the mean and standard deviation of x.

5.105 Imagine that you are in the midst of purchasing a lottery ticket and the person behind the counter prints too many tickets with your numbers. What would you do? The results of an online survey were as follows:

Let them keep the tickets.	30.77%
Trust the person to delete them.	15.38%
Buy the extra ones and hope they win.	30.77%
Other	23.08%

Is this a probability distribution? Explain.

5.106 "Sustainability" is quite the buzzword for environmentalists. When they think about sustainability, the word that typically comes to mind for most Americans is "recycling." A May 2008 Harris Poll of 2602 U.S. adults surveyed online asked the question: "Have you heard the phrase 'environmental sustainability' used?" The percentage of adults who answered "Yes" for each age group was reported as follows:

Age Group	18–31	32–43	44–62	63+
Percent	46%	47%	42%	30%

Is this a probability distribution? Explain.

5.107 A doctor knows from experience that 10% of the patients to whom she gives a certain drug will have undesirable side effects. Find the probabilities that among the 10 patients to whom she gives the drug:

a. At most two will have undesirable side effects.

b. At least two will have undesirable side effects.

5.108 In a recent survey of women, 90% admitted that they had never looked at a copy of *Vogue* magazine. Assuming that this is accurate information, what is the probability that a random sample of three women will show that fewer than two have read the magazine?

5.109 Of those seeking a driver's license, 70% admitted that they would not report someone if he or she copied some answers during the written exam. You have just entered the room and see 10 people waiting to take the written exam. What is the probability that if copying took place, 5 of the 10 would not report what they saw?

5.110 The engines on an airliner operate independently. The probability that an individual engine operates for a given trip is 0.95. A plane will be able to complete a trip successfully if at least one-half of its engines operate for the entire trip. Determine whether a four-engine or a two-engine plane has the higher probability of a successful trip.

5.111 The Pew Internet & American Life Project found that nearly 70% of "wired" senior citizens go online

every day. In a randomly selected group of 15 "wired" senior citizens:

a. What is the probability that more than four will say they go online every day?

b. What is the probability that exactly 10 will say that they go online every day?

c. What is the probability that fewer than 10 will say that they go online every day?

5.112 There are 750 players on the active rosters of the 30 Major League Baseball teams. A random sample of 15 players is to be selected and tested for use of illegal drugs.

a. If 5% of all the players are using illegal drugs at the time of the test, what is the probability that 1 or more players test positive and fail the test?

b. If 10% of all the players are using illegal drugs at the time of the test, what is the probability that 1 or more players test positive and fail the test?

c. If 20% of all the players are using illegal drugs at the time of the test, what is the probability that 1 or more players test positive and fail the test?

5.113 A box contains 10 items, of which 3 are defective and 7 are nondefective. Two items are selected without replacement, and x is the number of defective items in the sample of two. Explain why x is not a binomial random variable.

5.114 A box contains 10 items, of which 3 are defective and 7 are nondefective. Two items are randomly selected, one at a time, with replacement, and x is the number of defectives in the sample of two. Explain why x is a binomial random variable.

5.115 A large shipment of radios is accepted upon delivery if an inspection of 10 randomly selected radios yields no more than 1 defective radio.

a. Find the probability that this shipment is accepted if 5% of the total shipment is defective.

b. Find the probability that this shipment is not accepted if 20% of this shipment is defective.

c. The binomial probability distribution is often used in situations similar to this one, namely, large populations sampled without replacement. Explain why the binomial yields a good estimate.

5.116 The town council has nine members. A proposal to establish a new industry in this town has been tabled, and all proposals must have at least two-thirds of the votes to be accepted. If we know that two members of the town council are opposed and that the others randomly vote "in favor" and "against," what is the probability that the proposal will be accepted?

5.117 The state bridge design engineer has devised a plan to repair North Carolina's 4706 bridges that are currently listed as being in either poor or fair condition. The state has a total of 13,268 bridges. Before the governor will include the cost of this plan in his budget, he has decided to personally visit and inspect five bridges, which are to be randomly selected. What is the probability that in the sample of five bridges, the governor will visit the following?

a. No bridges rated as poor or fair

b. One or two bridges rated as poor or fair

c. Five bridges rated as poor or fair

5.118 A discrete random variable has a standard deviation equal to 10 and a mean equal to 50. Find $\Sigma x^2 P(x)$.

5.119 A binomial random variable is based on $n = 20$ and $p = 0.4$. Find $\Sigma x^2 P(x)$.

5.120 [EX05-120] In a germination trial, 50 seeds were planted in each of 40 rows. The number of seeds germinating in each row was recorded as listed in the following table.

Number Germinated	Number of Rows	Number Germinated	Number of Rows
39	1	45	8
40	2	46	4
41	3	47	3
42	4	48	1
43	6	49	1
44	7		

a. Use the preceding frequency distribution table to determine the observed rate of germination for these seeds.

b. The binomial probability experiment with its corresponding probability distribution can be used with the variable "number of seeds germinating per row" when 50 seeds are planted in every row. Identify the specific binomial function and list its distribution using the germination rate found in part a. Justify your answer.

c. Suppose you are planning to repeat this experiment by planting 40 rows of these seeds, with 50 seeds in each row. Use your probability model from part b to find the frequency distribution for x that you would expect to result from your planned experiment.

d. Compare your answer in part c with the results that were given in the preceding table. Describe any similarities and differences.

5.121 In another germination experiment involving old seed, 50 rows of seeds were planted. The number of seeds germinating in each row were recorded in the following table (each row contained the same number of seeds).

Number Germinating	Number of Rows	Number Germinating	Number of Rows
0	17	3	2
1	20	4	1
2	10	5 or more	0

a. What probability distribution (or function) would be helpful in modeling the variable "number of seeds germinating per row"? Justify your choice.

b. What information is needed in order to apply the probability distribution you chose in part a?

c. Based on the information you do have, what is the highest or lowest rate of germination that you can estimate for these seeds? Explain.

5.122 A business firm is considering two investments. It will choose the one that promises the greater payoff. Which of the investments should it accept? (Let the mean profit measure the payoff.)

Invest in Tool Shop		Invest in Book Store	
Profit	Probability	Profit	Probability
$100,000	0.10	$400,000	0.20
50,000	0.30	90,000	0.10
20,000	0.30	−20,000	0.40
−80,000	0.30	−250,000	0.30
	Total 1.00		Total 1.00

5.123 Bill has completed a 10-question multiple-choice test on which he answered 7 questions correctly. Each question had one correct answer to be chosen from five alternatives. Bill says that he answered the test by randomly guessing the answers without reading the questions or answers.

a. Define the random variable x to be the number of correct answers on this test, and construct the probability distribution if the answers were obtained by random guessing.

b. What is the probability that Bill guessed 7 of the 10 answers correctly?

c. What is the probability that anybody can guess six or more answers correctly?

d. Do you believe that Bill actually randomly guessed as he claims? Explain.

Chapter Practice Test

PART I: Knowing the Definitions

Answer "True" if the statement is always true. If the statement is not always true, replace the words shown in bold with words that make the statement always true.

5.1 The number of hours you waited in line to register this semester is an example of a **discrete** random variable.

5.2 The number of automobile accidents you were involved in as a driver last year is an example of a **discrete** random variable.

5.3 The sum of all the probabilities in any probability distribution is always exactly **two**.

5.4 The various values of a random variable form a list of **mutually exclusive events**.

5.5 A binomial experiment always has **three or more** possible outcomes to each trial.

5.6 The formula $\mu = np$ may be used to compute the mean of a **discrete** population.

5.7 The binomial parameter p is the probability of **one success occurring in n** trials when a binomial experiment is performed.

5.8 A parameter is a statistical measure of some aspect of a **sample**.

5.9 **Sample statistics** are represented by letters from the Greek alphabet.

5.10 The probability of event A or B is equal to the sum of the probability of event A and the probability of event B when A and B are **mutually exclusive events**.

PART II: Applying the Concepts

5.11 a. Show that the following is a probability distribution:

x	1	3	4	5
$P(x)$	0.2	0.3	0.4	0.1

b. Find $P(x = 1)$.

c. Find $P(x = 2)$.

d. Find $P(x > 2)$.

e. Find the mean of x.

f. Find the standard deviation of x.

5.124 A random variable that can assume any one of the integer values $1, 2, \ldots, n$ with equal probabilities of $\frac{1}{n}$ is said to have a uniform distribution. The probability function is written $P(x) = \frac{1}{n}$, for $x = 1, 2, 3, \ldots, n$. Show that $\mu = \frac{n+1}{2}$.

(*Hint:* $1 + 2 + 3 + \cdots + n = [n(n + 1)]/2$.)

5.12 A T-shirt manufacturing company advertises that the probability of an individual T-shirt being irregular is 0.1. A box of 12 such T-shirts is randomly selected and inspected.

a. What is the probability that exactly 2 of these 12 T-shirts are irregular?

b. What is the probability that exactly 9 of these 12 T-shirts are not irregular?

Let x be the number of T-shirts that are irregular in all such boxes of 12 T-shirts.

c. Find the mean of x.

d. Find the standard deviation of x.

PART III: Understanding the Concepts

5.13 What properties must an experiment possess in order for it to be a binomial probability experiment?

5.14 Student A uses a relative frequency distribution for a set of sample data and calculates the mean and standard deviation using formulas from Chapter 5. Student A justifies her choice of formulas by saying that since relative frequencies are empirical probabilities, her sample is represented by a probability distribution and therefore her choice of formulas was correct. Student B argues that since the distribution represents a sample, the mean and standard deviation involved are known as $\bar{x}$ and s and must be calculated using the corresponding frequency distribution and formulas from Chapter 2. Who is correct, A or B? Justify your choice.

5.15 Student A and Student B were discussing one entry in a probability distribution chart:

x	$P(x)$
-2	0.1

Student B thought this entry was okay because $P(x)$ is a value between 0.0 and 1.0. Student A argued that this entry was impossible for a probability distribution because x is -2 and negatives are not possible. Who is correct, A or B? Justify your choice.